# The Columbia Anthology of Gay Literature

BETWEEN MEN ~ BETWEEN WOMEN

*Lesbian and Gay Studies*

Lillian Faderman and Larry Gross, Editors

**Columbia University Press**

*New York*

# The Columbia Anthology of Gay Literature

## Readings from Western Antiquity to the Present Day

EDITED BY BYRNE R. S. FONE

**Columbia University Press**

Publisher Since 1893

New York     Chichester, West Sussex

Copyright © 1998 by Byrne R. S. Fone

All rights reserved

Library of Congress Cataloging-in-Publication Data

The Columbia anthology of gay literature  :  readings from Western
   antiquity to the present day / edited by Byrne R. S. Fone.
      p.  cm.
   Includes bibliographical references.
   ISBN 0–231–09670–4 (cloth  :  alk. paper)
   1. Gay men — Literary collections.  2. Homosexuality — Literary
collections.   I. Fone, Byrne R. S.
   PN6071.H724C65   1998
   808.8 ' 0353 — dc21                                         97 — 39727


∞

Casebound editions of Columbia University Press books
are printed on permanent and durable acid-free paper.
Printed in the United States of America

c 10 9 8 7 6 5 4 3 2 1

For Alain…
and in memory: sweet Sophie,
and my Tucker, always with me

# Contents

## Part Nine: Out There    727

American Literature from 1969

### 29. BECOMING GAY    729

**Out There: Gay American Literature**    729
*Questions*    732

*Answers*    733

# Preface

This anthology offers a chronological survey of writing that represents, interprets, and constructs the experience of love, friendship, intimacy, desire, and sex between men over time—that is, what most readers would call gay male literature. The selections include poetry, fiction, essays, and autobiography drawn from the traditional periods and cultural locations of Western literary history, beginning with texts translated from the Sumerian, from classical Greek and Latin, continuing from there through European, English, Latin American, and American literary periods, and concluding with a selection of texts from modern gay writing. I have tried to find texts and translations of the literature of classical antiquity, of medieval Latin and vernacular texts, and of modern European languages concerned with the subject of this book. When possible I have commissioned new translations of texts not adequately translated in the past, and of some works never before translated into English. It is my hope that this book will reflect the cultural diversity, the historical range, and the rich variety of writing that deals with male homosexuality.

When constructing an anthology, an editor faces several options and must be sensitive to a number of issues. Does the anthology try at least to represent, though of course not reprint, everything concerned with the subject of the book? Does it try to provide texts that are relatively unknown or not easily accessible, and trust that the more familiar texts will be sought elsewhere by a curious reader? Should a historical anthology try to be timely by reprinting contemporary selections even though these may be in print elsewhere?

My practice in this book has been to offer a broad range of material that at the time of its writing made a significant contribution to the history of homosexuality. Certain familiar texts—like some of the poetry of Martial, or Whitman's poems, or Forster's *Maurice*, or Halloran's *Dancer from the Dance* (to name a broad and disparate group of writings)—are because of their familiarity almost canonical, and no anthology concerned with trying to represent homoeroticisms in texts and charting the varying images of homosexuality constructed over time can afford to be without them. If one purpose of this book is to reveal a hidden heritage of lost or unfamiliar writing, another purpose of such a historically structured anthology is surely to present a broad selection of the essential materials of the history it intends to chronicle.

This having been said, however, limits must be set, not least those answering the limits set upon length by a patient publisher. In my original compilation I had collected enough material for three anthologies the length of the present volume (and even that was the result of editing and selection). I have chosen, therefore, in all sections of the book except the last, which deals with post-Stonewall American gay literature, to end my selections of twentieth-century non-American texts at a time more or less contemporaneous with Stonewall—the June 1969 resistance at a New York City gay bar (the Stonewall)that marks the beginning of gay modern times and inspired the literary manifestations in America that led to a renaissance of gay culture. Stonewall, of course, was only one of many liberationist movements manifest in both Europe and America in the late 1960s. However, a case can be made that post-Stonewall American gay literature had a catalytic, seminal, and invigorating effect on European, Latin American, and other developing national gay literatures. To try to include here what Stonewall inspired outside the United States would require another anthology as large as this one.

To suggest the nature and vibrancy of the American gay literary renaissance, I bring the "story," as it were, of American gay writing up to the beginning of the last decade of the twentieth century, a point in time that may signal a new direction in the development of gay culture, life, and texts. The products of this new direction—a response to what can be called a postmodern queer, rather than gay, interpretation of the place of lesbians and gay men in society—would require an equally sizable anthology to adequately represent them, and consequently I do not do so here.

One problem less easily solved, however, was whether to include works from modern gay theater. Gay theater itself has a long and spectacular history: homosexual characters have been seen on the American stage since at least the 1930s, and no one needs to be told that since 1968 (the premier of Mart Crowley's landmark *Boys in the Band*) gay theater has been the site of one of the most energetic and explosively creative movements in mainstream as well as gay culture. Yet this very exuberance and rich variety defeats any attempt to choose representative or even singular examples of gay theater. Therefore, despite its popularity (and despite the fact that gay theater has probably done more than any other genre to confront nongay people with wide-ranging visions of gay life—though television and motion pictures seem to be catching up fast), I have, reluctantly, included no examples of gay drama: there is so much from which to choose that to try to represent this creative ferment by selecting a single work would be unjust as well as unrepresentative. Works such as Lanford Wilson's *The Madness of Lady Bright* (1964) and Robert Patrick's *The Haunted Host* (1964) or his *T-Shirts* (1978), and works by Charles Ludlam, Ronald Tavel, John Vacarro, Richard Hall, and others come to mind as seminal plays that made room for a gay presence on the American stage, allowing Broadway to produce Harvey Fierstein's breakthrough *Torch Song Trilogy* (1978–79), Tony Kushner's dazzling two-part *Angels in America* (1992–93), and Terrence McNally's 1994 comedy-drama *Love! Valour! Compassion!* (all Tony-award winners for Best Play during their respective seasons). Moreover, drama does not abbreviate well, and space in an already extensive book does not allow the reprinting of a full-length three-act play. The bare minimum alternative—to include a single one-act play—would, again, scarcely hint at the extent, richness, and variety of available material.

Since this anthology does not intend to be (nor can it be) *both* a historical collection *and* an anthology of the latest gay literature, I have tried to be mindful of what can readily be found elsewhere, being content to let readers supplement this book by constructing their own anthologies or reading list of modern texts from the remarkable number of collections of modern gay literature available today. They can then add their own modern choices to the material in this book, which never-theless offers a scope and selection of texts unlike any other anthology of gay liter-ature.

In ordering the texts, I employ the historical periodization familiar to most read-ers, but I deviate from this practice in a few areas. In the arrangement of nine-teenth-century English literature I employ a generic arrangement of poetry, fiction, and autobiography, since most of the pertinent material was written within a fairly brief compass. To suggest his symbolic importance in the chronology of homosex-ual history, I have given Oscar Wilde a special place of his own, as I have also done for Walt Whitman in the selection of American writing. In the arrangement of twentieth-century European and Latin American texts, writers are ordered by nationality. Finally, I place American literature pertinent to the subject of this book—readings from 1840 to 1990—at the end of the book, concluding with a selection of modern gay literature.

Each section is provided with its own general introduction and, when necessary, headnotes identify and sometimes comment upon writers or individual texts. These commentaries address some of the concerns of the study of gay history and literature, pointing out themes and images that recur in texts over time, and indi-cating crises in gay texts that led to new conceptions of homosexual identity or to new forms of resistance. These headnotes also chart the presence and growth of homophobia and interpret the nature of the response of homosexual writers to it. Footnote annotation has been kept to a minimum, save in a few instances where I have written notes for (or reprinted a translator's notes to) an especially thorny text. A general bibliographical note at the beginning of the book and shorter ones at the end of the introduction to each section suggest further reading.

The title of the book, *The Columbia Anthology of Gay Literature*, will no doubt (even at this late date in the history of debates about nomenclature) move many readers—mostly academic ones—to anxious or irritated objection or to satisfied agreement. Though the book employs "gay" in its title, it should be obvious that this is, historically, an anachronistic choice. In my selections and in my commen-taries I intend neither summary of nor enticement to debates about essentialist or constructionist interpretations of gay history. These debates inquire whether "we" have always existed in history as identifiable social and sexual entities unchanged over time, or are instead a constantly changing and constantly redefined and redefining group of people whose persistent self-identification or lack of it responds to the always shifting forces of social change and the manifestations of social power. These debates ask, in short, if there is a "we" at all.

It is a tenet of modern gay theory that homosexuals can only have come into being—as Foucault so famously notes—after the coinage in 1869 of that word and after the creation of all the medicalized concepts of difference it represents. Much evidence has been amassed and scholarship published to assert that gay people as now constructed and imagined are a product of a very recent past. Indeed, *gay* and *homosexual* are not interchangeable, nor does *queer* now mean what *gay* meant in

1969 (nor does *gay* for that matter). Certainly to call Greek or Renaissance men who loved men either homosexual or gay is a historical inaccuracy; nor indeed is it precise to call anyone gay who lived before the 1920s, when *gay* began to make a tentative appearance in the vernacular in our modern sense. Few of the writers anthologized here were gay in our sense of the term, and many may not have been homosexual in our restrictive and exclusive meaning.

For some in the academy especially, this title may not reflect the more recent conflation of homo- (and all) eroticisms within a poststructuralist and postmodern concern with identifying difference under the rubric of "queer" rather than the more gender- and identity-linked "gay." "Queers" now march under a banner that proclaims difference to be a matter no longer merely of activist liberation or identity politics. Instead the identification of difference has become a social, scholarly, and activist task for those who want to subvert social oppression and negative interpretations of difference and transform old notions of gay and lesbian identities into newer constructions.

An attempt at reinterpretation has taken place, a move away from post-Stonewall liberation politics and from the identity politics of the late seventies and pre-AIDS eighties to the queer consciousness and AIDS-inspired activism of the nineties. This is a move that amounts to a political and social redefinition of *gay*, perhaps even of an end to the use of that term, at least in some quarters of the activist and academic community. This anthology does not, by design, reflect the queer activist and literary activity of this period. I conclude this book at the beginning of this discourse, which marks an era still too new (at this writing) to assess or place in perspective.

By "gay literature," then, I intend no transhistorical interpretation, nor do I mean to imply or even support the notion of a universally unchanging "gay sensibility." However, names for men who loved men over time range from *ganymede* and *catamite* to *sodomite*, from *invert* to *pervert* to *homosexual*; and names given to themselves by homosexual writers range from *Uranian* and *similisexual* and *intersexual* to *gay* and *queer* in our immediately contemporary sense. They have also included other less scientific or legal appellations—*monsters, mollies, effeminates, counterjumpers, patapoufs, queers, fairies, fruits, pansies,* and *fags.* Current scholarship prefers constructions like "same-sex desire" or "male-male desire." But these terms are also bound by chronology and by culture. Many—perhaps most—readers of this book will define themselves as gay, and for that reason if no other I have decided simply to employ the most popular and recognizable name that we have given ourselves—the one most potent in modern times. This anthology collects a literary heritage, until even recent times a hidden heritage, to which gay people—lesbians and gay men and all variety of queers—are indubitably heirs and of which they are the legitimate interpreters. In the sense that this book is a modern recovery, re-possession, and re-reading of the past, it is an anthology of gay literature.

What I hope this anthology *will* demonstrate is that the literature in these pages has helped to shape who we are. From the texts selected from two millennia of writing, gay readers today may find if not a common at least a not unfamiliar language, and recognize that what they feel now, desire now, and write now, resonates against a past rich in prophecies of the present.

A word about the all-male content of the book, and about the topics of gender, race, and class. The history of lesbian texts, like the social, sexual, and political history of lesbians, is in a thousand radical ways very different from the literary, social, sexual, and political history of gay men. Lesbian texts deserve books of their own. In Lillian Faderman's anthology *Chloe Plus Olivia*, and in a host of other lesbian theoretical texts and anthologies that far outstrip in variety what gay men have thus far produced, they have found them.

The present volume is also color blind, including material by people of color chosen because these texts are signal contributions to the literatures this book chronicles. If some readers find the book too inclusive of writers to whom the now pejorative catchword *elite* might be applied, it should be recalled that many of these writers were themselves victims of the homophobia inflicted by those who employed "normality" to define their own privileged status. Many of these writers were among those whose reputations were sometimes shattered beyond recall, whose books went unpublished or could only appear under the mask of pseudo-nymity, whose careers were sometimes ruined by exposure, whose sanity was threatened or whose very lives were blighted by, as one nineteenth-century writer put it, a "consciousness of pariahdom."

The anthologist's task is to select from the riches spread across time and to strive for comprehensiveness where such a goal is often impossible. It is fashionable among some scholars to eschew and even denigrate anthologies as mere collections of incomplete selections that, by being excerpted, compromise the integrity of longer works. For the time-short and economy-minded student or general reader, longer works may be difficult to come by or expensive to procure. This anthology allows the reader who is unwilling to search through all of Proust or Whitman, or unable to track down rare Uranian poetry, or to translate non-English texts, to discover quickly what in some cases only long investigation and patience have been able to obtain. I have tried to include enough to reveal a writers's self-identification and the nature of a writer's positioning of himself with regard to a hostile society. If some of what I have selected seems familiar to the scholar, I will only say that I can testify from my years of teaching gay studies and living among gay people that much of what I include is not familiar either to the student or to the nonacademic reader.

The texts I have chosen reflect in what way writers imagined themselves to be either an unhampered part of, or distant from, the mainstream of their society. The selections show a spectrum that runs from friendship to devotion and sometimes proceeds through physical desire to sex and love. In collecting selections I have not been overly concerned with constructing any immutable or privileged canon of texts. If I do not intend to create a canon — there are materials for a dozen canons in texts I include or have not been able to include — I *do* intend to enlarge the concept of gay literature now held by most nongay readers (and perhaps by many gay readers as well). If most conventional nongay readers tend to imagine that gay books are only pornographic and by definition inferior achievements, many gay readers suppose that gay literature can only mean love stories or sex stories, prose or poetic fictions or plays that reflect only the modern predicament or celebration of contemporary gay life.

This ought not to be a surprise, since even with the advent of gay studies, gay texts and gay writers are rarely identified as such in school. Even gay students—unless they take a gay studies course (which many still fear to do)—remain unaware that they are heirs to a substantial literature and a long history. The insulated heart of academe, involved in controversies about gay textualities and theory, might momentarily skip a beat if it heard the surprised comments of many literate and worldly gay women and men when confronted with the notion of a lesbian or gay literary or historical tradition. More often than those of us in the ivory closet might care to recognize, even after Stonewall many still ask, "Gay history, what gay history?"

For most lesbians and gay people, writing has indeed been our history. What we wrote defined who we were and who we hoped to be. Our literature is therefore at once archive and the historical event, the place where we have described and invented ourselves.

Unlike mainstream nongay literature, which rarely if ever needs to mount a defense of its basic premise of "normality," gay writing has always been shadowed by the condemnation of homophobia. Consequently, gay literature may reflect gay life, but just as often it fantasizes about it, offering propositions or speculations about what gay life might be or ought to be if the world were different or better. Gay texts are therefore often prescriptions for change as much as they are mirrors of reality. Because gay writing writes against homophobia as well as for homosexuality, I have also included a few selections that might be called the shadow texts of gay literature, those that implement or construct homophobia.

The *Columbia Anthology of Gay Literature* is an extensive collection of writings that covers a broad spectrum of materials useful for the study of gay social, sexual, political, and literary history. Perhaps readers of this book may discover in the nearly two thousand years of texts here represented a shared tradition and a common language, traditions and tongues which may seem somehow familiar to gay men everywhere. Or it may reveal instead that men who loved and desired other men in other times nevertheless inhabited alien worlds wherein indeed we might well have found ourselves strangers despite seemingly similar promptings of desire. Whatever interpretations of the past that may be constructed from these texts, they will, I hope, at least enable readers to answer in their own way the question that Whitman asked when he wondered if there were "men in other lands yearning and thoughtful" to whom "I should become attached . . . as I do to men in my own land." His answer was: "Oh I know we should be brethren and lovers."

# Acknowledgments

No book is ever done alone, and this one especially benefits from the help and advice of friends and professional colleagues. Professor Louis Crompton and an old friend, the poet Perry Brass, were both kind enough to read and make extensive and useful comments on the manuscript. This help has been invaluable and their comments illuminating. Without my editor, Ann Miller, I would have fallen into error far more often than perhaps I have.

For new translations from Greek and Latin done specifically for this book I want to thank Eugene O'Connor, who was generous not only with his words but with astute advice and direction. American poet and translator Daryl Hine, to whose name no mention here can add more luster than it already possesses, also very generously contributed new translations from the *Greek Anthology* as did another poet, Alfred Corn. Professors Richard E. Prior and Joseph Salemi took on the intricate task of making new translations of the thorny epigrams of Martial. I want to thank Professor Samuel N. Rosenberg for bringing to my attention—and providing his translation of—the Old French story of Lancelot and Galehut. Professor Eugenio Guisti has done work beyond thanks for advising me about important Italian Renaissance writers and for providing translated texts. Not least I am indebted to him for introducing me to Jill Claretta Robbins, who has also contributed a number of lively translations of these texts. Much advice was given and accordingly much thanks goes to an old friend and colleague, Professor James M. Saslow, whose definitive translations of Michelangelo grace these pages. To Jerrod Hayes, whose remarkable knowledge of French literature was freely shared, I owe special mention since he not only made immensely useful suggestions but introduced me to Gina Fisch-Freedman, whose translation of a difficult French text allows it to appear here in English.

For students of gay studies and German literature, the name of Hubert Kennedy, author of the definitive biography of Karl Heinrich Ulrichs, the pioneering homosexual theorist, needs little annotation, nor can praise from me add to his reputation. His insight and immense kindness helped move this book rapidly along as did his translations of a number of German writers. Of great value were the suggestions and translations of Michael A. Lombardi-Nash, whose diligent reclamation of early German homosexual rights texts has been a major contribution to gay studies. One of the great pleasures in this project has been sharing the insightful observations and the enthusiasm of Carl Skoggaard, who provides original translations of German texts never before translated into English. His work and eager discovery of materials have made my work easier and delightful.

For his very generous help I want to thank Professor Simon Karlinsky, whose authoritative study of homosexuality in Russian literature and history guided me and whose translations appear here. So too Professor Michael Green, whose translations of Kuzmin are definitive, was not only a source of entertaining correspondence but of scholarly insight. Equally delightful to write to and equally scholarly is Professor John McRae, who gave me many leads, translated Sandro Penna, and let me have a copy of his superb edition of and introduction to *Teleny*, the best essay on that text. Professor David William Foster, whose book on gay and lesbian themes in Latin American writing guided me in some of my choices, also provided other texts here included and further obtained the services of Jeff Bingham, Juan Antonio Servin, Fanny Arango-Ramos, and William Keeth, who offer fine new translations of this material. In addition, for this anthology Professor Foster generously provides a number of new translations of Federico García Lorca's *Sonetos de amor oscura*.

Professor Daniel Eisenberg, whose work in charting the history of Spanish homosexuality may well be definitive, offered much valuable advice, indicating avenues to explore and texts to examine.

For Gabriel de la Portilla no thanks will ever suffice, since he has been the person more than any other with whom I have shared the making of this book, testing its contents out on him and sharing the sometimes exhausting process of its devising.

No writer in gay studies can be anything but indebted to Louis Crompton, whose writings have helped to shape an entire discipline. So too the work—it can only be called monumental—of Professor Wayne Dynes touches this text as it illuminates so many of his own. I want to thank especially Andrew Holleran, Felice Picano, and Edmund White for special generosity. Michael Rumaker has been supportive, unfailingly available, and always perceptive. Carl Morse gave of his time, his knowledge, his vast fund of information, his library, his list of names, and his experience in editing his own superb anthology, *Gay and Lesbian Poetry in Our Time*. He was there from the start of the project and has stayed till the end. There from the start as well has been Alain Pioton. Every day he left me at my desk and usually came home at night to find me still there in front of the flickering screen, on the floor piles of books. He would tiptoe out and never complain. What can I say of Tucker, who was with me all the time?

# Bibliographical Note

Over the seminal decades of the 1970s, 1980s, and 1990s, lesbian and gay studies have produced an impressive library of critical texts, research tools, and theoretical discussions of which the following—specifically devoted to examining homosexuality in given cultural periods—are only a small and recent sampling.

Useful for the study of homosexuality in Greek literature and history are K. J. Dover, *Greek Homosexuality* (Cambridge: Harvard University Press, 1978); David M. Halperin, *One Hundred Years of Homosexuality and Other Essays on Greek Love* (New York and London: Routledge and Kegan Paul, 1990); David M. Halperin, John J. Winkler, Froma I. Zeitlin, *Before Sexuality: The Construction of Erotic Experience in the Ancient World* (Princeton: Princeton University Press, 1990); Bernard Sargent, *Homosexuality in Greek Myth* (Boston: Beacon Press, 1984).

For Latin literature and the European Middle Ages see John Boswell, *Christianity, Social Tolerance, and Homosexuality: Gay People in Western Europe from the Beginnings of the Christian Era to the Fourteenth Century* (Chicago and London: University of Chicago Press, 1980); Derrick Bailey, *Homosexuality and the Western Christian Tradition* (New York: Archon Books, 1975); John Boswell, *Same-Sex Unions in Pre-Modern Europe* (New York: Villard Books, 1994).

In Renaissance studies see Alan Bray, *Homosexuality in Renaissance England* (London: Gay Men's Press, 1982); Gregory W. Bredbeck, *Sodomy and Interpretation: Marlowe to Milton* (Ithaca, N.Y., and London: Cornell University Press, 1991); Jonathan Goldberg, ed., *Queering the Renaissance* (Durham, N.C., and London: Duke University Press, 1994); Jonathan Goldberg, *Sodometries: Renaissance Texts, Modern Sexualities* (Stanford, Calif.: Stanford University Press, 1992); James M. Saslow, *Ganymede in the Renaissance: Homosexuality in Art and Society* (New Haven and London: Yale University Press, 1986); James M. Saslow, *The Poetry of Michelangelo: An Annotated Translation* (New Haven: Yale University Press, 1991); Bruce R. Smith, *Homosexual Desire in Shakespeare's England* (Chicago and London: University of Chicago Press, 1991).

For the study of eighteenth-, nineteenth-, and early twentieth-century texts, the following should be consulted by any reader: Louis Crompton, *Byron and Greek Love: Homophobia in Nineteenth-Century England* (Berkeley: University of California Press, 1985); Richard Dellamora, *Masculine Desire: The Sexual Politics of Victorian Aestheticism* (Chapel Hill: University of North Carolina Press, 1990); Byrne R. S. Fone, *A Road To Stonewall: Homosexuality and Homophobia in English and American Literature, 1750–1969* (New York: Macmillan/Twayne, 1995); David William Foster, *Gay and Lesbian Themes in Latin American Writing* (Austin: University of Texas Press, 1991); Kent Gerard and Gert Hekma, eds., *The Pursuit of Sodomy: Male Homosexuality in Renaissance and Enlightenment Europe* (New York: Harrington Park Press, 1989), especially for articles by Randolph

Trumbach and Michel Rey; Winston Leyland, ed., *Gay Roots I* and *Gay Roots II* (San Francisco: Gay Sunshine Press, 1991, 1993), for essays by Leyland, E. A. Lacey et al.; Robert P. Maccubbin, ed., *Unauthorized Sexual Behavior During the Enlightenment*, in a Special Issue of *Eighteenth-Century Life* 9, n.s. 3, (May 1985), especially essays by Randolph Trumbach, George Rousseau, Arend H. Huussen, and Michel Rey; Harry Oosterhuis and Hubert Kennedy, eds., *Homosexuality and Male Bonding in Pre-Nazi Germany: Original Transcripts from "Der Eigene," the First Gay Journal in the World* (New York and London: Haworth Press, 1991); Brian Reade, *Sexual Heretics: Male Homosexuality in English Literature from 1850 to 1900* (New York: Howard McCann, 1970); Timothy d'Arch Smith, *Love in Earnest: Some Notes on the Lives and Writings of English Uranian Poets from 1889 to 1930* (London: Routledge and Kegan Paul, 1970); George Stambolian and Elaine Marks, eds., *Homosexualities and French Literature* (Ithaca, N.Y.: Cornell University Press, 1979); and Jeffrey Weeks, *Coming Out: Homosexual Politics in Britain from the Nineteenth Century to the Present* (London: Quartet Books, 1977).

For American studies I direct the reader's attention to the following texts. Jonathan Ned Katz's two groundbreaking books—*Gay American History* (New York: Thomas Y. Crowell, 1976) and *Gay/Lesbian Almanac* (New York: Harper and Row, 1983)—provide access to rare homosexual texts and the homophobic countertexts from our American past. Another seminal and wise book is Roger Austen's *Playing the Game: The Homosexual Novel in America* (New York: Bobbs-Merrill, 1977). This is complemented by James Levin, *The Gay Novel in America* (New York: Garland, 1991). Robert K. Martin's *The Homosexual Tradition in American Poetry* (Austin and London: University of Texas Press, 1979) was the first important study of homoeroticism in American poetry; other useful studies are Gregory Woods, *Articulate Flesh: Male Homoeroticism in Modern Poetry* (New Haven and London: Yale University Press, 1987); Thomas Yingling, *Hart Crane and the Homosexual Text* (Chicago and London: University of Chicago Press, 1990); Michael Moon, *Disseminating Whitman: Revision and Corporeality in "Leaves of Grass"* (Cambridge and London: Harvard University Press, 1991); David Bergman, *Gaiety Transfigured: Gay Self-Representation in American Literature* (Madison: University of Wisconsin Press, 1991); and Byrne R. S. Fone, *Masculine Landscapes: Walt Whitman and the Homoerotic Text* (Carbondale: Southern Illinois University Press, 1992).

For theoretical discusssions (e.g., social construction versus essentialism; gay and queer theory), I direct the reader to Edward Stein, *Forms of Desire: Sexual Orientation and the Social Construction Controversy* (New York and London: Routledge, 1990), a collection of essays that pursues the debate as to whether gay people—in terms of style and social substance—have existed throughout history in much the same way we imagine ourselves now to be, or if homosexuality and homosexual style is rather, instead of being a constant and "essential" element of human nature, a "social construction," an invention of recent times. David Greenberg, *The Construction of Homosexuality* (Chicago: University of Chicago Press, 1988), also addresses the topic. Jonathan Ned Katz, *The Invention of Heterosexuality* (New York: Dutton, 1995), and Frank Browning, *The Culture of Desire: Paradox and Perversity in Gay Lives Today* (New York: Crown, 1993), each considers significant social questions. For literary discussions see Jonathan Dollimore, *Sexual Dissidence: Augustine to Wilde, Freud to Foucault* (Oxford: Clarendon Press, 1991).

Collections of essays valuable for looking at the range of gay and queer studies are Stuart Kellog, ed., *Literary Visions of Homosexuality* (New York: Haworth Press, 1983); Salvatore Licata and Robert Petersen, eds., *The Gay Past: A Collection of Historical Essays* (New York: Harrington Park Press, 1985); Martin Duberman, *About Time: Exploring the Gay Past* (New York: Gay Presses of New York, 1986); Martin Duberman, Martha Vicinus, and George Chauncey, Jr., eds., *Hidden from History: Reclaiming the Gay and Lesbian Past* (New York: New American Library, 1989); Ronald Butters, John M. Clum, Michael Moon, eds., *Displacing Homophobia: Gay Male Perspectives in Literature and Culture* (Durham, N.C., and London: Duke University Press, 1989); John D'Emilio, *Making Trouble: Essays on Gay History, Politics, and the University* (New York: Routledge and Kegan Paul, 1992); David Bergman, ed., *Camp Grounds: Style and Homosexuality* (Amherst: University of Massachusetts Press, 1993); Lee Edelman, *Homographesis: Essays in Gay Literary and Cultural Theory* (New York: Routledge, 1994); Moe Meyer, ed., *The Politics and Poetics of Camp* (London and New York: Routledge, 1994); and Eve Kosofsky Sedgwick, *Tendencies* (Durham, N.C.: Duke University Press, 1994).

Founding texts in gay and queer theory are Eve Kosofsky Sedgwick, *Between Men: English Literature and Male Homosocial Desire* (New York: Columbia University Press, 1985), and Sedgwick's *Epistemology of the Closet* (Berkeley: University of California Press, 1990). In addition, Joseph A. Boone and Michael Cadden, *Engendering Men: The Question of Male Feminist Criticism* (New York and London: Routledge and Kegan Paul, 1990), and Diana Fuss, *Inside/Out: Lesbian and Gay Theories* (New York and London: Routledge and Kegan Paul, 1991), address questions of theory.

The history of Stonewall has been definitively addressed in Martin Duberman, *Stonewall* (New York: Dutton, 1993), and the history of the gay civil rights movement in Adam Barry, *The Rise of a Gay and Lesbian Movement* (Boston: Twayne, 1987). A special study is George Chauncey, *Gay New York: Gender, Urban Culture, and the Making of the Gay Male World, 1890–1940* (New York: Basic Books, 1994).

Indispensable for research are Wayne Dynes, *Homosexuality: A Research Guide* (New York: Garland, 1987); Wayne R. Dynes et. al., eds., *The Encyclopedia of Homosexuality* (New York: Garland, 1990); Sharon Malinowski, ed., *Gay and Lesbian Literature* (Detroit and London: St. James Press, 1994); and Claude J. Summers, ed., *The Gay and Lesbian Literary Heritage* (New York: Henry Holt, 1995).

*The Columbia Anthology of Gay Literature*

# Part One
Inventing Eros

*Literature of the Ancient World from the Earliest Texts to the Beginning of Premodern Times*

# 1. The Earliest Texts

The Mesopotamian *Epic of Gilgamesh*, predating Homer by nearly fifteen hundred years, is a tale of adventure, tragedy, and male comradeship that details the meeting and exploits of the two heroes Gilgamesh and Enkidu, and the eventual death of Enkidu, which leaves Gilgamesh inconsolable. In the eighth century B.C.E., the *Iliad* told the story of the Trojan War and portrayed Achilles and Patroclus as inseparable comrades. Like Gilgamesh, Achilles loses his comrade to death, and like the *Gilgamesh*, an important element of the *Iliad* is the grief of Achilles over this loss. The story of David and Jonathan, written around the fifth century B.C.E. in the Hebrew Bible, also describes the intimate companionship of two men, and also includes an account of one lost to death and David's subsequent profound grief. These early texts in general do not specifically imply any sexual connection between their male couples. However, love and intimate friendship is clearly celebrated as an emotion appropriate to relations between men. These stories are the earliest known in literature to reflect such emotions, and they foretell a tradition that would be central to Greek texts and that would be retold in all literary constructions of erotic male relationships.

## Mesopotamia

### From the *Epic of Gilgamesh* (3rd millennium B.C.E.)

*English version by N. K. Sandars*

The *Epic of Gilgamesh* is the earliest known text in world literature to celebrate intimate friendship between men. The text has been found in versions in Hittite, Akkadian, and Sumerian. The friendship of Gilgamesh and Enkidu is both intense and suggestively passionate. Inseparable friends in life, in death the survivor is inconsolable. To calm the rampaging Gilgamesh, whose sexual appetites are destroying the people, Enkidu is created for him by the goddess of creation. After Gilgamesh defeats Enkidu at wrestling, the two become bound together as one and engage in numerous adventures, one of which results in Enkidu's death by decree of the gods. Gilgamesh, devastated, sings a moving lament for Enkidu, after which he goes on a journey to seek the secret of eternal life, but he cannot forget the loss of his friend.

[THE COMING OF ENKIDU]

Gilgamesh went abroad in the world, but he met with none who could withstand his arms till he came to Uruk. . . . But the men of Uruk muttered in their houses, "Gilgamesh sounds the tocsin for his amusement, his arrogance has no bounds by day or night. No son is left with his father, for Gilgamesh takes them all, even the children; yet the king should be a shepherd to his people. His lust leaves no virgin to her lover, neither the warrior's daughter nor the wife of the noble; yet this is the shepherd of the city, wise, comely, and resolute." . . .

When Anu had heard their lamentation the gods cried to Aruru, the goddess of creation, "You made him, O Aruru, now create his equal; let it be as like him as his own reflection, his second self, stormy heart for stormy heart. Let them contend together and leave Uruk in quiet."

So the goddess conceived an image in her mind, and it was of the stuff of Anu of the firmament. She dipped her hands in water and pinched off clay, she let it fall in the wilderness, and noble Enkidu was created. There was virtue in him of the god of war, of Ninurta himself. His body was rough, he had long hair like a woman's; it waved like the hair of Nisaba, the goddess of corn. His body was covered with matted hair like Samuqan's, the god of cattle. He was innocent of mankind; he knew nothing of the cultivated land.

[Gilgamesh hears of Enkidu and sends a harlot to seduce him.]

She was not ashamed to take him, she made herself naked and welcomed his eagerness; as he lay on her murmuring love she taught him the woman's art. For six days and seven nights they lay together, for Enkidu had forgotten his home in the hills; but when he was satisfied he went back to the wild beasts. Then, when the gazelle saw him, they bolted away; when the wild creatures saw him they fled. Enkidu would have followed, but his body was bound as though with a cord, his knees gave way when he started to run, his swiftness was gone. And now the wild creatures had all fled away; Enkidu was grown weak, for wisdom was in him, and the thoughts of a man were in his heart. So he returned and sat down at the woman's feet, and listened intently to what she said. "You are wise, Enkidu, and now you have become like a god. Why do you want to run wild with the beasts in the hills? Come with me. I will take you to strong-walled Uruk, to the blessed temple of Ishtar and of Anu, of love and of heaven: there Gilgamesh lives, who is very strong, and like a wild bull he lords it over men."

When she had spoken Enkidu was pleased; he longed for a comrade, for one who would understand his heart. "Come, woman, and take me to that holy temple, to the house of Anu and of Ishtar, and to the place where Gilgamesh lords it over the people. I will challenge him boldly, I will cry out aloud in Uruk, 'I am the strongest here, I have come to change the old order, I am he who was born in the hills, I am he who is strongest of all.'"

She said, "Let us go, and let him see your face. I know very well where Gilgamesh is in great Uruk. . . . O Enkidu, you who love life, I will show you Gilgamesh, a man of many moods; you shall look at him well in his radiant manhood. His body is perfect in strength and maturity; he never rests by night or day. He is stronger than you, so leave your boasting. Shamash the glorious sun has given favors to Gilgamesh, and Anu of the heavens, and Enlil, and Ea the wise has given him deep understanding. I tell you, even before you have left the wilderness, Gilgamesh will know in his dreams that you are coming."

Now Gilgamesh got up to tell his dream to his mother, Ninsun, one of the wise gods. "Mother, last night I had a dream. I was full of joy, the young heroes were round me, and I walked through the night under the stars of the firmament, and one, a meteor of the stuff of Anu, fell down from heaven. I tried to lift it but it proved too heavy. All the people of Uruk came round to see it, the common people jostled and the nobles thronged to kiss its feet; and to me its attraction was like the love of woman. They helped me, I braced my forehead and I raised it with thongs and brought it to you, and you yourself pronounced it my brother."

Then Ninsun, who is well-beloved and wise, said to Gilgamesh, "This star of heaven which descended like a meteor from the sky; which you tried to lift, but found too heavy, when you tried to move it would not budge, and so you brought it to my feet; I made it for you, a goad and spur, and you were drawn as though to a woman. This is the strong comrade, the one who brings help to his friend in his need. He is the strongest of wild creatures, the stuff of Anu; born in the grasslands and the wild hills reared him; when you see him you will be glad; you will love him as a woman and he will never forsake you. This is the meaning of the dream."

Gilgamesh said, "Mother, I dreamed a second dream. In the streets of strong-walled Uruk there lay an axe; the shape of it was strange and the people thronged round. I saw it and was glad. I bent down, deeply drawn towards it; I loved it like a woman and wore it at my side." Ninsun answered, "That axe, which you saw, which drew you so powerfully like love of a woman, that is the comrade whom I give you, and he will come in his strength like one of the host of heaven. He is the brave companion who rescues his friend in necessity." Gilgamesh said to his mother, "A friend, a counselor has come to me from Enlil, and now I shall befriend and counsel him." . . .

[Enkidu] was merry living with the shepherds, till one day lifting his eyes he saw a man approaching. He said to the harlot, "Woman, fetch that man here. Why has he come? I wish to know his name." She went and called the man, saying, "Sir, where are you going on this weary journey?" The man answered, saying to Enkidu, "Gilgamesh has gone into the marriage-house and shut out the people. He does strange things in Uruk, the city of great streets. At the roll of the drum work begins for the men, and work for the women. Gilgamesh the king is about to celebrate marriage with the Queen of Love, and he still demands to be first with the bride, the king to be first and the husband to follow, for that was ordained by the gods from his birth, from the time the umbilical cord was cut. But now the drums roll for the choice of the bride and the city groans." At these words Enkidu turned white in the face. "I will go to the place where Gilgamesh lords it over the people, I will challenge him boldly, and I will cry aloud in Uruk, 'I have come to change the old order, for I am the strongest here.'"

Now Enkidu strode in front and the woman followed behind. He entered Uruk, that great market, and all the folk thronged round him where he stood in the street in strong-walled Uruk. The people jostled; speaking of him they said, "He is the spit[ting image] of Gilgamesh." "He is shorter." "He is bigger of bone." "This is the one who was reared on the milk of wild beasts. His is the greatest strength." The men rejoiced: "Now Gilgamesh has met his match. This great one, this hero whose beauty is like a god, he is a match even for Gilgamesh."

In Uruk the bridal bed was made, fit for the goddess of love. The bride waited for the bridegroom, but in the night Gilgamesh got up and came to the house.

Then Enkidu stepped out, he stood in the street and blocked the way. Mighty Gilgamesh came on and Enkidu met him at the gate. He put out his foot and prevented Gilgamesh from entering the house, so they grappled, holding each other like bulls. They broke the doorposts and the walls shook, they snorted like bulls locked together. They shattered the doorposts and the walls shook. Gilgamesh bent his knee with his foot planted on the ground and . . . Enkidu was thrown. Then immediately his fury died. When Enkidu was thrown he said to Gilgamesh, "There is not another like you in the world. Ninsun, who is as strong as a wild ox in the byre, she was the mother who bore you, and now you are raised above all men, and Enlil has given you the kingship, for your strength surpasses the strength of men." So Enkidu and Gilgamesh embraced and their friendship was sealed.

[Gilgamesh and Enkidu further cement their friendship by seeking out and killing the demon Humbaba. They present the head to the god Enlil, but the gods are enraged by this blasphemy. Gilgamesh then confronts the goddess Ishtar who attempts to seduce him, but he refuses to become her lover. Gilgamesh and Enkidu slay the Bull of Heaven, brought by Ishtar to punish Gilgamesh for his rejection, and Ishtar curses them. The council of the gods decrees that one of the pair must die, and the choice falls on Enkidu.]

[THE DEATH OF ENKIDU]

When the daylight came Enkidu got up and cried to Gilgamesh, "O my brother, such a dream I had last night. Anu, Enlil, Ea, and heavenly Shamash took counsel together, and Anu said to Enlil, 'Because they have killed the Bull of Heaven, and because they have killed Humbaba who guarded the Cedar Mountain, one of the two must die.' Then glorious Shamash answered the hero Enlil, 'It was by your command they killed the Bull of Heaven, and killed Humbaba, and must Enkidu die although innocent?' Enlil flung round in rage at glorious Shamash, 'You dare to say this, you who went about with them every day like one of themselves!'"

So Enkidu lay stretched out before Gilgamesh; his tears ran down in streams and he said to Gilgamesh, "O my brother, so dear as you are to me, brother, yet they will take me from you." Again he said, "I must sit down on the threshold of the dead and never again will I see my dear brother with my eyes."

. . . . As Enkidu slept alone in his sickness, in bitterness of spirit he poured out his heart to his friend. "It was I who cut down the cedar, I who leveled the forest, I who slew Humbaba, and now see what has become of me. Listen, my friend, this is the dream I dreamed last night. The heavens roared, and the earth rumbled back an answer; between them stood I before an awful being, the somber-faced man-bird; he had directed on me his purpose. His was a vampire face, his foot was a lion's foot, his hand was an eagle's talon. He fell on me and his claws were in my hair, he held me fast and I smothered; then he transformed me so that my arms became wings covered with feathers. He turned his stare towards me, and he led me away to the palace of Irkalla, the Queen of Darkness, to the house from which none who enters ever returns, down the road from which there is no coming back.

. . . Then I awoke like a man drained of blood who wanders alone in a waste of rushes; like one whom the bailiff has seized and his heart pounds with terror."

Gilgamesh had peeled off his clothes, he listened to his words and wept quick tears, Gilgamesh listened and his tears flowed. He opened his mouth and spoke to Enkidu: "Who is there in strong-walled Uruk who has wisdom like this? Strange things have been spoken, why does your heart speak strangely? The dream was marvelous but the terror was great; we must treasure the dream whatever the terror; for the dream has shown that misery comes at last to the healthy man, the end of life is sorrow." And Gilgamesh lamented, "Now I will pray to the great gods, for my friend had an ominous dream."

This day on which Enkidu dreamed came to an end and he lay stricken with sickness. One whole day he lay on his bed and his suffering increased. He said to Gilgamesh, the friend on whose account he had left the wilderness, "Once I ran for you, for the water of life, and I now have nothing." A second day he lay on his bed and Gilgamesh watched over him, but the sickness increased. A third day he lay on his bed, he called out to Gilgamesh, rousing him up. Now he was weak and his eyes were blind with weeping. Ten days he lay and his suffering increased, eleven and twelve days he lay on his bed of pain. Then he called to Gilgamesh, "My friend, the great goddess cursed me and I must die in shame. I shall not die like a man fallen in battle; I feared to fall, but happy is the man who falls in the battle, for I must die in shame." And Gilgamesh wept over Enkidu. With the first light of dawn he raised his voice and said to the counselors of Uruk:

[The Lament of Gilgamesh for Enkidu]

"Hear me, great ones of Uruk,
I weep for Enkidu, my friend,
Bitterly moaning like a woman moaning
I weep for my brother.
O Enkidu, my brother,
You were the axe at my side,
My hand's strength, the sword in my belt,
The shield before me,
A glorious robe, my fairest ornament;
An evil Fate has robbed me.
The wild ass and the gazelle
That were father and mother,
All long-tailed creatures that nourished you
Weep for you,
All the wild things of the plain and pastures;
The paths that you loved in the forest of cedars
Night and day murmur.
Let the great ones of strong-walled Uruk
Weep for you;
Let the finger of blessing

Be stretched out in mourning;
Enkidu, young brother. Hark,
There is an echo through all the country
Like a mother mourning.
Weep all the paths where we walked together;
And the beasts we hunted, the bear and hyena,
Tiger and panther, leopard and lion,
The stag and the ibex, the bull and the doe.
The river along whose banks we used to walk,
Weeps for you,
Ula of Elam and dear Euphrates
Where once we drew water for the water-skins.
The mountain we climbed where we slew the Watchman,
Weeps for you.
The warriors of strong-walled Uruk
Where the Bull of Heaven was killed,
Weep for you.
All the people of Eridu
Weep for you Enkidu.
Those who brought grain for your eating
Mourn for you now;
Who rubbed oil on your back
Mourn for you now;
Who poured beer for your drinking
Mourn for you now.
The harlot who anointed you with fragrant ointment
Laments for you now;
The women of the palace, who brought you a wife,
A chosen ring of good advice,
Lament for you now.
And the young men your brothers
As though they were women
Go long-haired in mourning.
What is this sleep which holds you now?
You are lost in the dark and cannot hear me."

He touched his heart but it did not beat, nor did he lift his eyes again. When Gilgamesh touched his heart it did not beat. So Gilgamesh laid a veil, as one veils the bride, over his friend. He began to rage like a lion, like a lioness robbed of her whelps. This way and that he paced round the bed, he tore out his hair and strewed it around. He dragged off his splendid robes and flung them down as though they were abominations.

In the first light of dawn Gilgamesh cried out, "I made you rest on a royal bed, you reclined on a couch at my right hand, the princes of the earth kissed your feet. I will cause all the people of Uruk to weep over you and raise the dirge of the dead.

The joyful people will stoop with sorrow; and when you have gone to the earth I will let my hair grow long for your sake, I will wander through the wilderness in the skin of a lion." The next day also, in the first light, Gilgamesh lamented; seven days and seven nights he wept for Enkidu, until the worm fastened on him. Only then he gave him up to the earth, for the Anunnaki, the judges, had seized him.

Then Gilgamesh issued a proclamation through the land, he summoned them all, the coppersmiths, the goldsmiths, the stone-workers, and commanded them, "Make a statue of my friend." The statue was fashioned with a great weight of lapis lazuli for the breast and of gold for the body. A table of hard-wood was set out, and on it a bowl of camelian filled with honey, and a bowl of lapis lazuli filled with butter. These he exposed and offered to the Sun; and weeping he went away.

# The Old Testament

## The Friendship of David and Jonathan

The friendship of Jonathan, son of King Saul, and the shepherd David (c. 1012–872 B.C.E.) is one of the few texts in the Old Testament to provide an approved example of intimate friendship between men. The story has served as a subject for numerous literary texts celebrating male-male love, such as Peter Abelard's medieval interpretation of the story in the "Lament for Jonathan," Abraham Cowley's epic *Davideis* (1656), John Addington Symonds's poem *The Meeting of David and Jonathan* (1878), and Wallace Hamilton's novel *David at Olivet* (1979).

1 SAMUEL 17:55–58 AND 18:1–4

*Authorized (King James) Version*

And when Saul saw David go forth against the Philistine [Goliath], he said unto Abner, the captain of the host, Abner, whose son is this youth? And Abner said, As thy soul liveth, O King, I cannot tell.

And the King said, Inquire thou whose son the stripling is.

And as David returned from the slaughter of the Philistine, Abner took him, and brought him before Saul, with the head of the Philistine in his hand.

And Saul said to him, Whose son art thou, young man? And David answered, I am the son of thy servant Jesse the Beth-lehemite.

And it came to pass, when he had made an end of speaking unto Saul, that the soul of Jonathan was knit with the soul of David, and Jonathan loved him as his own soul.

And Saul took him that day, and would let him go no more home to his father's house.

Then Jonathan and David made a covenant, because he loved him as his own soul.

And Jonathan stripped himself of the robe that was upon him, and gave it to David, and his garments, even to his sword, and to his bow, and to his girdle.

## David's Lament for Jonathan

2 SAMUEL 1:17–27

*Authorized (King James) Version*

And David lamented with this lamentation over Saul and over Jonathan his son:
. . . . The beauty of Israel is slain upon thy high places: how are the mighty fallen!

Tell it not in Gath, publish it not in the streets of Askelon; lest the daughters of the Philistines rejoice, lest the daughters of the uncircumcised triumph.

Ye mountains of Gilboa, let there be no dew, neither let there be rain, upon you, nor fields of offerings: for there the shield of the mighty is vilely cast away, the shield of Saul, as though he had not been anointed with oil.

From the blood of the slain, from the fat of the mighty, the bow of Jonathan turned not back, and the sword of Saul returned not empty.

Saul and Jonathan were lovely and pleasant in their lives, and in their death they were not divided: they were swifter than eagles, they were stronger than lions.

Ye daughters of Israel, weep over Saul, who clothed you in scarlet, with other delights, who put on ornaments of gold upon your apparel.

How are the mighty fallen in the midst of the battle! O Jonathan, thou wast slain in thine high places.

I am distressed for thee, my brother Jonathan: very pleasant hast thou been unto me: thy love to me was wonderful, passing the love of women.

How are the mighty fallen, and the weapons of war perished!

# 2. Eros in Arcadia: Greek Literature

## "Homosexuality" in Greek Literature

Near the end of the second century of the common era in the *Deipnosophistai* (The Banquet of the Learned) by Athenaeus of Naucratis, the guests at the banquet enter into discussions of a wide variety of topics. Book 13 turns to love among the gods and men. Athenaeus mentions such a large number of texts dealing with erotic relations between men—many now lost—that it is soon clear that the extent of the material discussed and the matter-of-fact tone of the discussion reflect not only the significant place of such literature in classical civilization but the general lack of a negative attitude toward such texts and the relationships they mirrored. That desire between men and the sexual consummation of that desire was a fact of life in Greece is indeed confirmed by a substantial library of texts and a large iconography drawn from the visual arts. In poems, drama, and prose romance, in philosophy and the law, in sculpture and in painting, in graffiti written on rocks and on shards of pottery, the evidence is extensive that relations between men, as encompassed in friendship, desire, love, and sex, played an important and even a central role in Greek life and culture. The following selections are drawn from literature written in Greek between the seventh century B.C.E. and the fourth century of the common era—that is, from Archaic to late Hellenistic times. These selections represent some of the essential texts in Greek that illuminate the mythology, history, and theory of same-sex desire.

## "Homosexuality" in Greece

To describe the Greeks as "homosexual," let alone "gay" or "queer," is to anachronistically import to ancient times a modern idea of sexual acts and our cultural reading of sexualities. Any interpretation of Greek homosexual practice—and indeed of any specific homoerotic situations and of the texts involved—is of necessity profoundly influenced by the cultural meanings associated with attitudes toward same-sex physical activity that have been constructed over time. It need hardly be said that a lexicon of cultural meaning has been constructed from a tapestry of prohibition and proscription derived from the Judeo-Christian interpretation of same-sex relationships. The Judeo-Christian tradition asserts that sexuality and its exercise is to be judged by dogmatic proscriptions and social prohibitions of a specific code of moral conduct rather than as an erotic response to the biological prompting of erogenous and genital areas of the body. To assume that Greek "homosexuality" and our homosexuality is one and the same thing is fraught, therefore, with danger. We generally tend to think of homosexuality as irreducibly opposed to heterosexuality, as a largely exclusive preoccupation with same-sex desire, and as a largely exclusive dedication to same-sex practice, all this coupled with a sense that in some way this desire and this practice not only define the self but encode that desire in areas far broader than sex alone, and in so encoding it render those areas—of society, of the intellect, of spirituality, of creativity—somehow dependent on that desire for their interpretation and definition. To apply such a concept to the Greeks may cloud rather than clarify what the Greeks did in practice and what they achieved when enacting and interpreting that practice in texts.

That a person or a personality could be judged and interpreted by exclusive reference to the object of sexual desire would have been considered by the Greeks a curious, even perplexing, proposition. Nor would the Greeks have assumed that anyone was one thing *or* the other. Indeed, with regard to sexuality, the notion of *being* something—a "homosexual," a "heterosexual"—in connection with a sex act was meaningless; *doing* something was the key to the interpretation and judgment of sexual acts. Thus men could do all things, one thing and the other, at different times in life, and indeed were expected to do so, as numerous epigrams in the *Greek Anthology* make clear. Sex for the Greeks was interpreted within the parameters of age, social rank, and the nature of sexual activity—that is, within the bounds of active or passive sexuality. Males were thus defined not as homosexual or heterosexual—indeed they could not be so defined since the Greeks did not possess these words nor indeed any word cognate or equivalent to them—but as active or passive, and that activity or passivity was governed and judged by their age, by their sex (i.e., by their status as adult males), by their social relationship to their sexual partner or partners, and all of this by their own place in society. Boys and women were passive (and expected to be so) and were legitimate objects of desire. Adult males were expected to take the active—that is, penetrative—role in sex not only as a result of their adult and masculine nature but by virtue of their superior status in society. As Jeffrey Henderson in *The Maculate Muse: Obscene Language in Attic Comedy* (New Haven and London: Yale University Press, 1975) observes, "The Greeks showed a pronounced tendency to attach the greatest importance to (indeed, to glorify) the sexual instinct itself rather than the particular object" (205).

The notion that the fulfillment of sexual desire, or the desire itself, was a matter to be regulated by religious teaching, by a presumed universal moral law delivered and interpreted dogmatically by a priestly caste, would have been unthinkable to most Greeks of that period. Neither would Greek law have commented on the legality or illegality of same-sex relationships or desire, save in certain specifically prohibited areas such as rape, congress between slaves and freeborn boys, or between adults and underaged boys. Though there are a number of Greek texts that satirize effeminate males, and others— both literary and legal—that suggest it is unmanly behavior to accept a passive role in sexual intercourse after passing a certain age, there is little evidence to suggest that the Greeks found homosexual desire or its practice to be a matter for religious or even for much legal or social regulation. The net effect of these cautionary remarks, and the sum of the argument that labels "homosexuality" as a socially constructed invention of modern times rather than as an essential, transhistorical possession of all cultures in all ages, might seem to suggest that, strictly speaking, the Greeks were not homosexual and that there was no homosexuality in Greece. It is surely true that the binary paradigm heterosexual/homosexual would have been foreign to the Greeks, just as would the contemporary ongoing debate over the morality of homosexual behavior. What remains is that Greek males desired other males and built a literary, artistic, philosophical, and legal discourse on the accomplishment and fulfillment of that desire.

## HOMOEROTICISM IN GREEK LITERATURE

Greek literature tells stories of the loves of the gods for youths, of men for boys, of comrades for comrades. Greek literature offers tales of love and fidelity between two men as well as tragic accounts of the loss of love, of the pain of parting, of separation by death.

Poems that celebrate male beauty and erotic conquest detail not only the manners and customs associated with desire but often reveal also the specific mechanics of sexual consummation. In romances as convoluted as any modern soap opera, characters whom we could now describe as gay or straight pursue their various forms of desire side by side without blame, condemnation, or even surprise. Always present, the sharp prick of satire deflates the obsessiveness of lust and the vain imaginings of love, ridicules effeminacy, and turns a bright spotlight on greedy boys who seek reward for sex and on sexually obsessed men who too willingly submit in adulthood to acts in which only boys ought to engage. Theoretical discussions probe the origins and nature of male-male desire, anatomize its nature, and propound rules of right conduct for the *erastes* (lover) and the *eromenos* (beloved), employing allegory and philosophy to theorize desire.

## EROTIC IDEALS

The ideal erotic object pictured in these texts is a male between the ages of fourteen and eighteen, a youth most desirable before the growth of his beard. Greek visual arts provide much information concerning the ideal youth. Black and red figures on painted vases, many of which include graffito praising the beauty of one boy or another, show that youthful beauty was identified with specific physical characteristics: a well-formed body (including broad shoulders and large chest, slim waist, muscular thighs, and well-formed muscular buttocks), a masculine body strengthened by the vigorous life of the palaestra and gymnasium and combined with a confident and manly though modest demeanor. In later evidence the erotic ideal begins to change: late classical period imagery suggests interest in boys whose masculinity is tempered by a certain androgyny, and by the Hellenistic period in the fourth century C.E. seductive and effeminate youths make an initial appearance as objects of desire. Such youths were expected, ideally, to be unresponsive to adult desire. The adult male alone, ideally, took pleasure in or achieved orgasm from sex. The general presumption of many texts was that passive homosexuality was by definition unenjoyable and that manhood was defined by active not passive sexual activity. However, despite the ideal, many Greek texts—from as early as Theognis in the sixth century B.C.E. to later Hellenistic texts—complain about the seductive manner and promiscuity of youths.

## SEX

Sex is not absent from Greek texts or art. Vase paintings show adult males fondling the genitals of youths, and copulating intercrurally (between the thighs), often modestly hiding—though not always completely—the copulation beneath a cloak. While penetration of all kinds is also part of the iconography of sexual activity, in paintings anal penetration seems to be limited to activity between males of the same age, these usually satyrs. Similarly, fellatio and masturbation seem to be the province of satyrs in visual arts. Of course there were no satyrs save in myth, and it may be naive to imagine that what license the Greeks gave to the satyr they forbade to themselves. Certainly several texts refer to both fellatio and anal intercourse between males, and drama constantly exploits the comic possibilities of mutual masturbation and anal penetration.

The Greeks were much interested, both in literature and in visual art, in the shape and size of the penis. Admired youths are shown in paintings with penises thin, short, and (because of the foreskin) pointed. Nor are adults generally shown with a penis of larger size. Only satyrs are pictured with a very large, often clublike penis, almost always erect, associated perhaps with sexual license and unbridled promiscuity. The size of the penis, therefore, was not the object of admiration so much as what that size implies: namely, that the admired figure is still a boy in the bloom of youth, modest and submissive. Handsome men, heroes, and gods are all generally pictured with such idealized, that is youthful, attributes.

## PHILOSOPHY

Greek texts present a considerable, even conflicting, spectrum of opinion about the manner in which same-sex relations ought to be conducted: all men are capable of homosexual behavior and under the right conditions no blame attaches to it; some men seem to engage in it exclusively; the love of boys is superior to love of women, though the socially approved arrangement is that between a younger beloved and an older lover (yet some men remain lovers into mutual adulthood). Greek homosexuality was often defined within the philosophical ideal of *paiderastia*, a word derived from the combination of *pais* (boy) and the verb *eran* (to love), from which was derived *eros* (desire). The Greeks took some pains to define the difference between legitimate *eros* and the *eros* that referred only to sexual desire and act. "Legitimate" eros prescribed conduct and attitude. In a relationship between an adult and a younger male, *paiderastia* carried with it not only the expectation (indeed perhaps the obligation) of sex between them but also, in its ideal form, implied a relationship between the two that combined the role of lover and beloved with that of teacher and student. Greek provided specific terms for each role. In most literary contexts the beloved or desired boy is called *pais*, which can also mean girl, child, slave, daughter, and son. He is also sometimes nominated as *paidika* in the sense of "the one [boy] who is beloved." In other dialects and in various texts he is called (again from *eran*) the *eromenos*, "one who one loves or desires," or *aitas*, "the listener, receiver, or the [intellectually] receptive," and *kleinos*, "the famous" or perhaps "the admired." The lover is called the *erastes* (again from the verb *eran*), or in other dialects *eispnelos*, the "inspirer" who inspires the *aitas*, or a *philetor*, the "befriender," who befriends the one who is *kleinos*. The erastes was presumed not only to woo and seduce the eromenos but also to instruct him in the arts of the hunt and of war, in right conduct in life and in proper conduct as a citizen. It was presumed that the erastes would also eventually marry—which did not necessarily mean that he would abandon homosexual experience—and that the eromenos in his turn would become an erastes to other youth.

There is evidence that same-sex relationships may have existed between men of relatively similar ages, and these for long or even lifelong duration. Plato suggests in the myth he gives to Aristophanes in the *Symposium* that, when a same-sex couple discovers one another, they might spend their whole lives together. There is other evidence that Greek homosexual relationships were in fact not always solely modeled upon or governed by the cultural ideal. Pausanias and Agathon, speakers in the *Symposium*, appear to be lovers of long duration, while Theocritus hopes in one of his idylls (no. 29) that his lover and he will be lifelong partners, and Hellenistic prose romances sometimes describe long-lasting homosexual relationships in terms not unlike those applied to heterosexual marriages.

Aeschines' oration *Against Timarkhos* (*The Prosecution of Timarkhos*, 346 B.C.E.) is the most complete text in Greek literature that gives us, as K. J. Dover says in *Greek Homosexuality*, "access to the sentiments which it was prudent to profess in public on the subject of homosexuality in Athens during the classical period" (12). Plutarch, in the *Erotic Discourses*, presents a debate between an advocate of male-male love and an advocate of love between men and women. The pederast declares that the only true love is the love of boys while his opponent declares that it is unnatural. In most texts opinion seems fairly unanimous, however, that blame does attach to men who continue to be passive recipients of sexual favors into adulthood, and that effeminacy, by which is meant not only effeminacy in our sense but cowardice on the battlefield, is to be ridiculed and is a proper subject of satire. Some texts imply that male-male desire may be a function of the special "nature" of certain men, as Aristotle seems to suggest in the *Nichomachean Ethics* (1148b) and as Xenophon implies in his *Symposium*. That such men have special roles to play in the structure of society Plato has Socrates argue in the *Symposium*. Later Plato in the *Laws* seems to argue that pederasty is "against nature" and should be repressed by law. But even that argument is not framed within an absolute definition of the unnaturalness of homosexual *desire* but instead within a framework in which *any* sexual desire excessively indulged in—or for that matter any excessive indulgence at all—is in that sense against nature.

## THE "IDEA OF GREECE" AND HOMOEROTIC TEXTS

Few readers can fail to recognize how the arts and literature of ancient Greece have become woven into the texture of Western cultures. Over time the idea of "Greece" has been so rich a source that nearly every age has created a Greece of the imagination. Rome employed the materials of Grecian glory to enhance Roman grandeur. Greece was a dim and nostalgic recollection of a distant past in some medieval literature and a demonized site of paganism in other early Christian texts. It became the source of an aesthetic and a poetics in the Italian Renaissance (as well as the English), and a model upon which to found systems of education, ethics, and government for the inventors of nineteenth-century national images and imperial dreams. "Greece"—and the homoeroticism of its texts—has been incorporated into the cultural poetics of nearly every age since Roman times. Whether the Greeks are kin to us, sharing a sensibility and a sexuality that we recognize and that truly speaks to us over time, or are an alien nation practicing customs and a morality we only dimly comprehend and only partially understand (or that we have perhaps totally misread), may be only the stuff of dry debate. If, as we read, we reach back to those texts and try to understand, we may quite possibly find in them voices as modern as our own.

## Further Reading

K. J. Dover, *Greek Homosexuality* (Cambridge: Harvard University Press, 1978); David M. Halperin, *One Hundred Years of Homosexuality and Other Essays on Greek Love* (New York and London: Routledge and Kegan Paul, 1990); David M. Halperin, John J. Winkler, Froma I. Zeitlin, *Before Sexuality: The Construction of Erotic Experience in the Ancient World* (Princeton: Princeton University Press, 1990); Hans Licht, *Sexual Life in Ancient Greece* (London: Routledge and Kegan Paul, 1932); Bernard Sargent, *Homosexuality in Greek Myth* (Boston: Beacon Press, 1984).

# Legendary Lovers

Greek myth contains numerous stories attesting to homosexual involvements between gods, between men and gods, and between men. Some indicate individuals who were believed to be the first to love one of their own sex, inventors of pederasty. Myths such as those of Zeus and Ganymede, Laius and Khrysippus, Hercules and Hylas could be described as founding myths of Greek homosexuality. Zeus is often credited with being the first to engage in homosexual love when he kidnapped Ganymede, while other legends point to Laius, father of Oedipus, who fell in love with Khrysippus, son of Pelops.

## Zeus and Ganymede

*Homer*

From the *Iliad*, Book 20:215–35 (8th cent. B.C.E.)

*Translated by E. V. Rieu*

Ganymede makes his first appearance in Greek literature in the *Iliad*. He was generally agreed to be the most handsome of mortals. Zeus found him so attractive that he abducted him, descending to the earth disguised as an eagle, and carried him back to Olympus where he became the god's cupbearer. Some readers insist that Homer could not have intended a pederastic reading of the Ganymede story, arguing that such homosexual eros was unknown to the Homeric age. Others assert that the focus on Ganymede's beauty indicates that homoerotic desire is present, arguing that the absence of a specific reference to same-sex desire in the text does not necessarily mean that such a desire did not exist in society outside the text.

No matter what the truth may be about the homosexual status of the myth at the time of Homer's writing, there can be no doubt that later readers generally interpreted the story to be a founding myth of male love and named Zeus as the inventor of pederasty. From its first appearance in the few lines of Homer, the Ganymede legend became increasingly homosexualized in Greek texts until, by the time of Theognis and Euripides, Ganymede was presumed unquestionably to have been the bedfellow of Zeus just as Patroclus was by then presumed to have been the lover of Achilles. By the fifth century B.C.E., Plato invokes Zeus and Ganymede as a precedent and parallel for Socrates' affairs with boys, and in Hellenistic and Latin texts the very name Ganymede comes to mean a passive youth available for sex.

Dardanus . . . was son of Zeus the Lord of the clouds. Dardanus founded Dardania at a time when the sacred city of Ilium had not been built to shelter people on the plain and they still habited the watered slopes of Ida. Dardanus had a son, Erichthonius, who was the richest man on earth. . . . Erichthonius had a son called Tros, who was King of the Trojans; and Tros himself had three excellent sons, Ilus, Assaracus, and the godlike Ganymedes, who grew up to be the most beautiful youth in the world and because of his good looks was kidnapped by the gods to be cupbearer to Zeus and foregather with the immortals.

## Achilles and Patroclus

*Homer*

From the *Iliad*, Books 18 and 23

*Translated by E. V. Rieu*

Because of a quarrel with Agamemnon, Achilles refuses to fight in the battle to capture Troy. His comrade Patroclus, son of Menoetius, is fearful that the war may be lost, and he urges Achilles to allow him to wear Achilles' armor and go into battle in his place so that the Trojans will think that Achilles has returned to the field. He does so, but the dreadful consequence is that he is slain in battle by Hector, Priam's son and Achilles' great enemy. Antilochus, son of King Nestor, is sent to bring the terrible news to Achilles. When he hears it, Achilles vows revenge against Hector and calls upon his mother, the sea goddess Thetis. When Patroclus' body is returned, Achilles laments and Patroclus appears to him in a dream asking that their ashes be buried together in the same funeral urn.

As in the Ganymede story, Homer nowhere says that Achilles and Patroclus engaged in a sexual relationship. Yet many argue the sheer intensity of Achilles' grief and the ferocity of his response to the death of Patroclus reflects a relationship that goes beyond simple comradeship and creates an ambiance—whether sexual or not is immaterial—that suggests passion if not desire. That Patroclus takes Achilles' armor and thus assumes his likeness and that Patroclus appears to Achilles in a dream suggests a special psychic intimacy. Patroclus' request that their bones should be interred together effects in death the union— even the marriage—that life perhaps did not afford. Finally, Achilles' decision to remain and avenge Patroclus, a decision he knows will lead to his own death, makes clear that Achilles has no desire to live without Patroclus. The nearly universal opinion of later commentators was that they were in fact lovers. Aeschylus' (525–456 B.C.E.) lost play the *Myrmidons* (part of his lost trilogy *Achilleis*) presents Achilles as being in love with Patroclus—that is, as being Patroclus' *erastes*—and Aeschylus has Achilles say to the dead Patroclus in a surviving fragment: "And you felt no compunction for (*sc.*my?) pure reverence of (*sc.*your?) thighs—O what an ill return you have made for so many kisses!" (Dover, *Greek Homosexuality*, 197). Phaedrus in Plato's *Symposium* insists that Patroclus was in love with Achilles, not the other way around, making Achilles younger than Patroclus (as Homer does) and hence his *eromenos*. Lucian (c. 120–180 C.E.) insisted about Achilles and Patroclus that the "driving power of this friendship was also lust."

Achilles and Patroclus stand as exemplars of ideal male love, of a fidelity and a loyalty such that both are willing to die for the other; they are invoked as such by most Greek writers, and their passion came to be seen as the central and most dramatic element of the story and indeed as the founding text against which all subsequent tales of love between men were measured.

## From Book 18 [Achilles' Lament and the Funeral of Patroclus]

So the fight went on, like an inextinguishable fire. Meanwhile Antilochus ran hotfoot to Achilles with his news and found him in front of his beaked ships. Achilles had had a presentiment of what had happened, and was communing, in his anguish, with that great heart of his. "Why," he asked himself with a groan, "are the long-haired Achaeans bolting once more across the plain and flocking to the ships? Heaven forfend that I should have to suffer what my heart forebodes—my Mother's prophecy. She told me once that while I was still alive the best of the Myrmidons would fall to the Trojans and leave the light of day. And now I am sure that Menoetius' gallant son is dead. Foolhardy man! Did I not order him to come back here when he had saved the ships from fire, and not to fight it out with Hector?"

While these thoughts were chasing through his mind, King Nestor's son halted before him with the hot tears pouring down his cheeks and gave him the lamentable news: "Alas, my royal lord Achilles! I have a dreadful thing to tell you—I would to God it were not true. Patroclus has been killed. They are fighting round his naked corpse and Hector of the flashing helmet has your arms."

When Achilles heard this he sank into the black depths of despair. He picked up the dark dust in both his hands and poured it on his head. He soiled his comely face with it, and filthy ashes settled on his scented tunic. He cast himself down on the earth and lay there like a fallen giant, fouling his hair and tearing it out with his own hands. The maidservants whom he and Patroclus had captured caught the alarm and all ran screaming out of doors. They beat their breasts with their hands and sank to the ground beside their royal master. On the other side, Antilochus shedding tears of misery held the hands of Achilles as he sobbed out his noble heart, for fear that he might take a knife and cut his throat.

Suddenly Achilles gave a loud and dreadful cry, and his lady Mother heard him where she sat in the depths of the sea beside her ancient Father. Then she herself took up the cry of grief, and there gathered round her every goddess, every Nereid that was in the deep salt sea. . . . "Unhappy mother of the best of men, I brought into the world a flawless child to be a mighty hero and eclipse his peers. I nursed him as one tends a little plant in a garden bed, and he shot up like a sapling. I sent him to Ilium with his beaked ships to fight against the Trojans; and never again now shall I welcome him to Peleus' house. And yet he has to suffer, every day he lives and sees the sun; and I can do no good by going to his side. But I will go, nonetheless, to see my darling child and hear what grief has come to him, although he has abstained from fighting."

With that she left the cave. The rest went with her, weeping, and on either side of them the surging sea fell back. When they reached the deep-soiled land of Troy, they came up one by one onto the beach, where the Myrmidon ships were clustered round the swift Achilles. His lady Mother went up to him as he lay groaning there, and with a piercing cry took her son's head in her hands and spoke to him in her compassion-passion. "My child," she asked him, "why these tears? What is it that has grieved you? Tell me and do not keep your sorrow to yourself. Some part, at any rate, of what you prayed for when you lifted up your hands to Zeus has been fulfilled by him. The Achaeans have been penned in at the ships for want of you, and have suffered horribly."

Achilles of the nimble feet gave a great sigh. "Mother," he said, "it is true that the Olympian has done that much in my behalf. But what satisfaction can I get from that, now that my dearest friend is dead, Patroclus, who was more to me than any other of my men, whom I loved as much as my own life? I have lost Patroclus. And Hector, who killed him, has stripped him of my splendid armor, the huge and wonderful arms that the gods gave Peleus as a wedding-present on the day when they married you off to a mortal man. Ah, how I wish that you had stayed there with the deathless salt-sea Nymphs and that Peleus had taken home a mortal wife! But you became my mother; and now, to multiply your sorrows too, you are going to lose your son and never welcome him at home again. For I have no wish to live and linger in the world of men, unless, before all else, Hector is felled by my spear and dies, paying the price for slaughtering Menoetius' son."

Thetis wept. She said: "If that is so, my child, you surely have not long to live; for after Hector's death you are doomed forthwith to die."

"Then let me die forthwith," Achilles said with passion, since I have failed to save my friend from death. He has fallen, far from his motherland, wanting my help in his extremity. So now, since I shall never see my home again, since I have proved a broken reed to Patroclus and all my other comrades whom Prince Hector killed, and have sat here by my ships, an idle burden on the earth, I, the best man in all the Achaean force, the best in battle, defeated only in the war of words . . . Ah, how I wish that discord could be banished from the world of gods and men, and with it anger, insidious as trickling honey, anger that makes the wisest man flare up and spreads like smoke through his whole being, anger such as King Agamemnon roused in me that day! However, what is done is better left alone, though we resent it still, and we must curb our hearts perforce. I will go now and seek out Hector, the destroyer of my dearest friend. As for my death, when Zeus and the other deathless gods appoint it, let it come. Even the mighty Heracles did not escape his doom, dear as he was to Zeus the Royal Son of Cronos, but was laid low by Fate and Hera's bitter enmity. And I too shall lie low when I am dead, if the same lot awaits me. But for the moment, glory is my aim. I will make these Trojan women and deep-bosomed daughters of Dardanus wipe the tears from their tender cheeks with both their hands as they raise the dirge, to teach them just how long I have been absent from the war. And you, Mother, as you love me, do not try to keep me from the field. You will never hold me now."

"Indeed, my child," said Thetis of the Silver Feet, "it could not be an evil thing for you to rescue your exhausted comrades from destruction. But your beautiful burnished armor is in Trojan hands. Hector of the flashing helmet is swaggering about in it himself—not that he will enjoy it long, for he is very near to death. So do not think of throwing yourself into the fight before you see me here again. I will come back at sunrise tomorrow with a splendid set of armor from the Lord Hephaestus."

With that, she turned away from her son and spoke to her sister Nereids. She told them to withdraw into the broad bosom of the deep and make their way to the Old Man of the Sea, returning to her Father's house. "Tell him everything," she said. "I myself am going to high Olympus to ask the Master-smith Hephaestus whether he would like to give my son a splendid set of glittering arms."

The Nymphs now disappeared from view into the heaving waters of the sea, and the divine Thetis of the Silver Feet set out for Olympus to procure a glorious set of armor for her son.

While she was on her journey to Olympus, the Achaean men-at-arms, fleeing with cries of terror from man-killing Hector, reached the ships and the Hellespont. It was more than they could do to drag the body of Achilles' squire Patroclus out of range. Once more it was overtaken by the Trojan infantry and horse, and Hector son of Priam, raging like a fire. Three times illustrious Hector, coming up behind and shouting for his men's support, seized its feet and tried to drag it back; and thrice the two Aiantes flung him from the corpse, fighting like men possessed. But Hector's resolution was unshaken. When he was not hurling himself into the press, he stood his ground, calling aloud to his men, and he never once fell back. The bronze-clad Aiantes could no more scare Prince Hector from the corpse than the shepherds in the fields can chase a famished lion off his kill. In fact Hector would have hauled it away and covered himself with glory, if Iris of the Whirlwind Feet had not come down in hot haste from Olympus to tell Achilles to prepare for battle. (She was sent by Hera; Zeus and the other gods were not consulted.) Presenting herself to Achilles she delivered her message. "Up, my lord Achilles, most redoubtable of men. Rise and defend Patroclus, for whom they are fighting tooth and nail and men are killing men beside the ships, the Achaeans in their efforts to protect his corpse, and the Trojans in the hope of hauling it away to windy Ilium. Prince Hector above all has set his heart on dragging off Patroclus. He wants to cut his head off from his tender neck and stick it on the palisade. So up with you, and lie no longer idle. The very thought that Patroclus may become a plaything for the dogs of Ilium should appall you. It is you who will be put to shame if the body comes into your hands defiled."

[The body of Patroclus is retrieved and preparations are made for the funeral.]

. . . . All night long the Achaeans wept and wailed for Patroclus. The son of Peleus was their leader in the melancholy dirge. He laid his man-killing hands on his comrade's breast and uttered piteous groans, like a bearded lion when a huntsman has stolen his cubs from a thicket and he comes back too late, discovers his loss, and follows the man's trail through glade after glade, hoping in his misery to track him down. Thus Achilles groaned among his Myrmidons. He thought with a pang of the idle words he had let fall one day at home in his attempts to reassure Patroclus' noble father. "I told Menoetius," he said, "that I would bring him back his son to Opus from the sack of Ilium, covered with glory and laden with his share of plunder. But Zeus makes havoc of the schemes of men; and now the pair of us are doomed to redden with our blood one patch of earth, here in the land of Troy. For I shall never see my home again, nor be welcomed there by Peleus the old charioteer and my Mother Thetis, but shall be swallowed by the earth I stand on. So then, Patroclus, since I too am going below, but after you, I shall not hold your funeral till I have brought back here the armor and the head of Hector, who slaughtered you, my noble-hearted friend. And at your pyre I will cut the throats of a dozen of the highborn youths of Troy, to vent my wrath on them for killing you. Till then, you shall lie as you are by my beaked ships, wailed and wept for days and night by the Trojan women and the deep-bosomed daughters of Dardanus whom we captured after much toil, with our own hands and our long spears, when we sacked rich cities full of men."

Prince Achilles then told his followers to put a big three-legged cauldron on the fire and make haste to wash the clotted gore from Patroclus' body. They put a large cauldron on the glowing fire, filled it with water, and brought faggots, which they kindled beneath it. The flames began to lick the belly of the cauldron and the water grew warm. When it came to the boil in the burnished copper, they washed the corpse, anointed it with olive oil, and filled the wounds with an unguent nine years old. Then they laid it on a bier and covered it from head to foot with a soft sheet, over which they spread a white cloak. And for the rest of the night the Myrmidons with the great runner Achilles wept and wailed for Patroclus.

## From Book 23 [Achilles' Dream]

While the city of Troy gave itself up to lamentation, the Achaeans withdrew to the Hellespont, and when they reached the ships, dispersed to their several vessels.

Only the battle-loving Myrmidons were not dismissed. Achilles kept his followers with him and addressed them. "Myrmidons," he said, "lovers of the fast horse, my trusty band; we will not unyoke our horses from their chariots yet, but mounted as we are, will drive them past Patroclus and mourn for him as a dead man should be mourned. Then, when we have wept and found some solace in our tears, we will unharness them and all have supper here."

The Myrmidons with one accord broke into lamentation. Achilles led the way, and the mourning company drove their long-maned horses three times round the dead, while Thetis stirred them all to weep without restraint. The sands were moistened and their warlike panoply was bedewed with tears, fit tribute to so great a panic-maker. And now the son of Peleus, laying his man-killing hands on his comrade's breast, led them in the melancholy dirge: "Rejoice, Patroclus, even in the Halls of Hades. I am keeping all the promises I made you. I have dragged Hector's body here, for the dogs to eat it raw; and at your pyre I am going to cut the throats of a dozen of the highborn youths of Troy, to vent my anger at your death.

Achilles, when he had finished, thought of one more indignity to which he could subject Prince Hector. He flung him down on his face in the dust by the bier of Menoetius' son. His soldiers then took off their burnished bronze equipment, unyoked their neighing horses, and sat down in their hundreds by the ship of the swift son of Peleus, who had provided for them a delicious funeral feast. Many a white ox fell with his last gasp to the iron knife, many a sheep and bleating goat was slaughtered, and many a fine fat hog was stretched across the flames to have his bristles singed. Cupfuls of blood were poured all round the corpse.

Meanwhile Prince Achilles, the swift son of Peleus, was taken by the Achaean kings to dine with the lord Agamemnon, though they had hard work to make him come, still grieving for his comrade as he was. When they reached Agamemnon's hut they told the clear-voiced heralds to put a big three-legged cauldron on the fire in the hope of inducing Achilles to wash the clotted gore from his body. But he would not hear of such a thing. He even took a vow and said: "By Zeus, who is the best and greatest of the gods, it shall be sacrilege for any water to come near my head till I have burnt Patroclus, made him a mound, and shorn my hair, for I shall never suffer again as I am suffering now, however long I live. But for the moment, though I hate the thought of food, we must yield to necessity and dine. And at dawn, perhaps your majesty King Agamemnon will order wood to be collected and everything to be provided that a dead man ought to have with him when he travels into the western gloom, so that Patroclus may be consumed by fire as soon as possible and the men return to their duties when he is gone."

They readily agreed and set to with a will on the preparation of their supper, in which they all had equal shares. They ate with zest, and when they had satisfied their thirst and hunger they retired for the night to their several huts. But the son of Peleus groaning wearily lay down on the shore of the sounding sea, among his many Myrmidons, but in an open space, where the waves were splashing on the beach. His splendid limbs were exhausted by his chase of Hector to the very walls of windy Ilium; but he had no sooner fallen into a sleep that soothed and enfolded him, resolving all his cares, than he was visited by the ghost of poor Patroclus, looking and talking exactly like the man himself, with the same stature, the same lovely eyes, and the same clothes as those he used to wear.

It halted by his head and said to him: "You are asleep: you have forgotten me, Achilles. You neglect me now that I am dead; you never did so when I was alive. Bury me instantly and let me pass the Gates of Hades. I am kept out by the disembodied spirits of the dead, who have not let me cross the River and join them, but have left me to pace up and down forlorn on this side of the Gaping Gates. And give me that hand, I beseech you; for once you have passed me through the flames I shall never come back again from Hades. Never again on earth will you and I sit down together, out of earshot of our men, to lay our plans. For I have been engulfed by the dreadful fate that must have been my lot at birth; and it is your destiny too, most worshipful Achilles, to perish under the walls of the rich town of Troy. And now, one more request. Do not let them bury my bones apart from yours Achilles. Let them lie together, just as you and I grew up together in your house, after Menoetius brought me there from Opus as a child because I had had the misfortune to commit homicide and kill Amphidamas' boy by accident in a childish quarrel over a game of knuckle-bones. The knightly Peleus welcomed me to his palace and brought me up with loving care. And he appointed me your squire. So let one urn, the golden vase your lady Mother gave you, hold our bones." "Dear heart," said the swift Achilles, "what need was there for you to come and ask me to attend to all these things? Of course I will see to everything and do exactly as you wish. But now come nearer to me, so that we may hold each other in our arms, if only for a moment, and draw cold comfort from our tears."

With that, Achilles held out his arms to clasp the spirit, but in vain. It vanished like a wisp of smoke and went gibbering underground. Achilles leapt up in amazement. He beat his hands together and in his desolation cried: "Ah then, it is true that something of us does survive even in the Halls of Hades, but with no intellect at all, only the ghost and semblance of a man; for all night long the ghost of poor Patroclus (and it looked exactly like him) has been standing at my side, weeping and wailing, and telling me of all the things I ought to do." Achilles' outcry woke the Myrmidons to further lamentation, and Dawn, when she stole up to them on crimson toes, found them wailing round the pitiable dead.

## Harmodius and Aristogeiton

*Thucydides (471–400 C.E.)*

[THE HISTORY OF HARMODIUS AND ARISTOGEITON]

*Translated by Benjamin Jowett*

The lovers Harmodius and Aristogeiton killed Hipparchus, the brother of the tyrant Hippias, in 514 B.C.E. Legend claims that their action resulted in the overthrow of the tyrant and the two were consequently celebrated as having freed Athens from tyranny and that in later times lovers pledged fidelity before their shrine. They were commonly cited in Greek texts and, indeed, in homosexual literature well into the nineteenth century, as an illustration of two men whose devotion to one another and to the cause of freedom was more important to them than life itself.

Now the attempt of Aristogeiton and Harmodius arose out of a love affair, which I will narrate at length. . . . . Pisistratus died at an advanced age in possession of the tyranny, and then, not as is the common opinion Hipparchus, but Hippias (who was the eldest of his sons) succeeded to his power.

Harmodius was in the flower of his youth, and Aristogeiton, a citizen of the middle class, became his lover. Hipparchus made an attempt to gain the affections of Harmodius, but he would not listen to him, and told Aristogeiton. The latter was naturally tormented at the idea, and fearing that Hipparchus, who was powerful, would resort to violence, at once formed such a plot as a man in his station might for the overthrow of the tyranny. Meanwhile, Hipparchus made another attempt; he had no better success, and thereupon he determined, not indeed to take any violent step, but to insult Harmodius in some underhanded manner, so that his motive could not be suspected. . . .

When Hipparchus found his advances repelled by Harmodius he carried out his intention of insulting him. There was a young sister of his whom Hipparchus and his friends first invited to come and carry a sacred basket in a procession, and then rejected her, declaring that she had never been invited by them at all because she was unworthy. At this Harmodius was very angry, and Aristogeiton for his sake more angry still.

They and the other conspirators had already laid their preparations, but were waiting for the festival of the great Panathenaea, when the citizens who took part in the procession assembled in arms; for to wear arms on any other day would have aroused suspicion. Harmodius and Aristogeiton were to begin the attack, and the rest were immediately to join in, and engage with the guards. The plot had been communicated to a few only, the better to avoid detection; but they hoped that, however few struck the blow, the crowd who would be armed, although not in on the secret, would at once rise and assist in the recovery of their own liberties.

The day of the festival arrived, and Hippias went out of the city to the place called the Ceramicus, where he was occupied with his guards in marshaling the procession. Harmodius and Aristogeiton, who were ready with their daggers, stepped forward to do the deed. But seeing one of the conspirators in familiar conversation with Hippias, who was readily accessible to all, they took alarm and imagined that they had been betrayed, and were on the point of being seized. Whereupon they determined to take their revenge first on the man who had outraged them and was the cause of their desperate attempt. So they rushed, just as they were, within the gates. They found Hipparchus near the Leocorium, as it was called, and then and there falling upon him with all the blind fury, one of an injured lover, the other of a man smarting under an insult, they smote and slew him. The crowd ran together, and so Aristogeiton for the present escaped the guards; but he was afterwards taken, and not very gently handled (i.e., tortured). Harmodius perished on the spot.

## Orestes and Pylades

*Lucian (c. 120–80 C.E.)*

From *Amores* 47

*Translated by W. J. Baylis*

Phocis preserves from early times the memory of the union between Orestes and

Pylades, who taking a god as witness of the passion between them, sailed through life together as though in one boat. Both together put to death Klytemnestra, as though both were sons of Agamemnon; and Aegisthus was slain by both. Pylades suffered more than his friend by the punishment which pursued Orestes. He stood by him when condemned, nor did they limit their tender friendship by the bounds of Greece, but sailed to the furthest boundaries of the Scythians — the one sick, the other ministering to him. When they had come into the Tauric land straightway they were met by the matricidal fury; and while the barbarians were standing round in a circle Orestes fell down and lay on the ground, seized by his usual mania, while Pylades "wiped away the foam, tended his body, and covered him with his well-woven cloak" — acting not only like a lover but like a father.

When it was determined that one should remain to be put to death, and the other should go to Mycenae to convey a letter, each wished to remain for the sake of the other, thinking that if he saved the life of his friend he saved his own life. Orestes refused to take the letter, saying that Pylades was more worthy to carry it, acting more like the lover than the beloved. "For," he said, "the slaying of this man would be a great grief to me, as I am the cause of these misfortunes." And he added, "Give the tablet to him for (turning to Pylades) I will send thee to Argos, in order that it may be well with thee; as for me, let any one kill me who desires it."

Such love is always like that; for when from boyhood a serious love has grown up and it becomes adult at the age of reason, the long-loved object returns reciprocal affection, and it is hard to determine which is the lover of which, for as from a mirror the affection of the lover is reflected from the beloved.

## The Sacred Band of Thebes

*Plutarch (46–120 C.E.)*

From *The Life of Pelopidas*

*Translated by Edward Carpenter*

In Plutarch's *Lives*, which contains biographies of notable Greeks, several examples of male lovers are offered, including a description of the Sacred Band of Thebes, whose devotion to one another and to liberty made them the most powerful fighting force in Greece for fifty years after their formation about 378 B.C.E. The Band consisted of three hundred men, sworn lovers, chosen for their courage and fidelity to one another and to the state. The Sacred Band remained undefeated until the battle of Chaeronea against Philip II, king of Macedonia (and father of Alexander the Great), in 338 B.C.E. when the entire band perished. By the second century B.C.E. most writers assumed that the comradeship of such men was cemented not only by valor but by desire and by love.

Gorgidas, according to some, first formed the Sacred Band of three hundred chosen men, to whom as being a guard for the citadel the State allowed provision, and all things necessary for exercise; and hence they were called the city band, as citadels of old were usually called cities. Others say that it was composed of young men attached to each other by personal affection, and a pleasant saying of Pammenes is current, that Homer's Nestor was not well skilled in ordering an army, when he advised the Greeks to rank tribe and tribe, and family and family, together, so that "tribe might tribe, and kinsmen and kinsmen aid," but that he should have joined lovers and their beloved. For men of the same tribe or family little value one another when dangers press; but a band cemented together by friendship grounded upon love is never to be broken, and invincible; since the lovers, ashamed to be base in sight of their beloved, and the beloved before their lovers, willingly rush into danger for the relief of one another. Nor can that be wondered at since they have more regard for their absent lovers than for others present; as in the instance of the man who, when his enemy was going to kill him, earnestly requested him to run him through the breast, that his lover might not blush to see him wounded in the back. It is a tradition likewise that Iolaus, who assisted Hercules in his labors and fought at his side, was beloved of him; and Aristotle observes that even in his time lovers plighted their faith at Iolaus' tomb. It is likely, therefore, that this band was called sacred on this account; as Plato calls a lover a divine friend. It is stated that it was never beaten till the battle at Chaeronea; and when Philip after the fight took a view of the slain, and came to the place where the three-hundred that fought his phalanx lay dead together, he wondered, and understanding that it was the band of lovers, he shed tears and said, "Perish any man who suspects that these men either did or suffered anything that was base."

It was not the disaster of Laius, as the poets imagine, that first gave rise to this form of attachment among the Thebans, but their lawgivers, designing to soften whilst they were young their natural fickleness, brought great encouragement to those friendships in the Palaestra, to temper the manner and character of the youth. With a view to this, they did well again to make Harmony, the daughter of Mars and Venus, their tutelary deity; since where force and courage is joined with grace-fulness and winning behavior, a harmony ensues that combines all the elements of society in perfect consonance and order. Gorgidas distributed this sacred Band all through the front ranks of the infantry, and thus made their gallantry less conspic-uous; not being united in one body, but mingled with many others of inferior res-olution, they had no fair opportunity of showing what they could do. But Pelopidas, having sufficiently tried their bravery at Tegyrae, where they had fought alone, and around his own person, never afterwards divided them, but keeping them entire, and as one man, gave them the first duty in the greatest battles. For as two horses run brisker in a chariot than single, not that their joint force divides the air with greater ease, but because being matched one against another circulation kindles and inflames their courage; thus, he thought, brave men, provoking one another to noble actions, would prove most serviceable and most resolute where all were united together.

## Theorizing Desire: Inventing Paiderastia

*Plato (427–347 B.C.E.)*

From *Symposium* (c. 385 B.C.E.)

*Translated by Walter Hamilton*

In a series of speeches on the subject of love given by participants in a symposium—a ban-quet during which topics of erotic interest were discussed and which internal evidence dates as occurring in 416 B.C.E. — Plato offers differing and sometimes conflicting views on homosexual desire. The subject is *paiderastia*—the Greek term that signified the erotic relationship between an adult male and a youth—and it is addressed in commentary ranging from Aristophanes' story about the origins of homosexual desire, through Phaedrus' and Pausanias' dialogues that both site *paiderastia* as a social and moral force valuable to the state and the individual.

Aristophanes says there were three kinds of living creatures, men, women, and hermaphrodites. When, because of their pride, the gods divided these original humans in half, each half of each creature perpetually sought union with its missing other half, men with men, women with women, and in the case of the hermaphrodite, women with men. Interpretations of the myth vary. Some readers assert that it is to be taken as a serious attempt to explain the existence of different sexual orientations and that it therefore postulates "homosexuality" as a category of desire and "homosexuals" as a species of individual recognizable to the Greeks. Others insist that the tale is meant to be humorous, given to the satirist Aristophanes as a sly and ironic account of human sexuality meant to stand in contrast to the more serious and quite different discussion of the nature of love in Socrates' later dialogue with Diotima.

In Socrates' account of his dialogue with the wise woman Diotima, he defines homosexual desire not only as a sexual but, more importantly, as a philosophical basis for relations between males and as the starting point for the spiritual revelation of the ideal of the good and the beautiful. Plato addresses the subject of homosexual desire in several other dialogues, including the *Lysis* and the *Phaedrus* in which male-male love is approvingly supported. In later works, however, including the *Laws* and the *Republic*, he seems to reverse his earlier position, and it is there that he declares pederasty to be "against nature," a formula that would be as enthusiastically adopted by later antihomosexual commentators in order to condemn homosexuality as Plato's earlier positions were employed by homosexual apologists to celebrate it. Plato's text may have reflected the views of only a small and aristocratic elite of fifth century B.C.E. Athens, but it expresses a view of homosexual behavior that will be appropriated by later writers—especially during the Renaissance and perhaps most potently in the nineteenth century—to justify homosexual love, a justification that will be employed in the face of a social and religious disapprobation unknown to Plato or any Greek.

## [THE SPEECH OF PHAEDRUS]

Now, as Love is the oldest of the gods, so also he confers upon us the greatest benefits, for I would maintain that there can be no greater benefit for a boy than to have a worthy lover from his earliest youth, nor for a lover than to have a worthy object for his affection. The principle which ought to guide the whole life of those who intend to live nobly cannot be implanted either by family or by position or by wealth or by anything else so effectively as by love. "What principle?" you ask. I mean the principle that inspires shame at what is disgraceful and ambition for what is noble; without these feelings neither a state nor an individual can accomplish anything great or fine. Suppose a lover to be detected in the performance of some dishonorable action or in failing through cowardice to defend himself when dishonor is inflicted upon him by another; I assert that there is no one, neither his father nor his friends nor anyone else, whose observation would cause him so much pain in such circumstances as his beloved's. And conversely we see with regard to the beloved that he is peculiarly sensitive to dishonor in the presence of his lovers. If then one could contrive that a state or an army should entirely consist of lovers and loved, it would be impossible for it to have a better organization than that which it would then enjoy through their avoidance of all dishonor and their mutual emulation; moreover, a handful of such men, fighting side by side, would defeat practically the whole world. A lover would rather be seen by all his comrades leaving his post or throwing away his arms than by his beloved; rather than that, he would prefer a thousand times to die. And if it were a question of deserting his beloved or not standing by him in danger, no one is so base as not to be inspired on such an occasion by Love himself with a spirit that would make him the equal of men with the best natural endowment of courage. In short, when Homer spoke of God "breathing might" into some of the heroes, he described exactly the effect that Love, of his very nature, produces in men who are in love.

Moreover, only lovers will sacrifice their lives for another. . . . They honored Achilles the son of Thetis and dispatched him to the Islands of the Blessed, because he, when he learned from his mother that he would die if he killed Hector, but that if he did not kill him he would reach home and die at a good old age, made the heroic choice to go to the rescue of his beloved Patroclus and to avenge him though this involved dying after him as well as for him. He thus earned the extreme admiration of the gods, who treated him with special distinction for showing in his way how highly he valued his lover.

Aeschylus, by the way, is quite wrong when he says that Achilles was the lover of Patroclus. Achilles was the more beautiful of the two—indeed he was the most beautiful of all the heroes—and he was still beardless and, according to Homer, much younger than Patroclus. The truth is that, while the gods greatly honor the courage of a lover, they admire even more and reward more richly affection shown towards a lover by the beloved, because a lover is possessed and thus comes nearer than the beloved to being divine. . . .

I maintain then that Love is not only the oldest and most honorable of the gods but also the most powerful to assist men in the acquisition of merit and happiness, both here and hereafter.

## [THE SPEECH OF PAUSANIAS]

I cannot agree, Phaedrus, with the condition laid down for our speeches, that they should be a simple and unqualified panegyric of Love. If Love had a single nature, it would be all very well, but not as it is, since Love is not single; and that being so the better course would be to declare in advance which Love it is that we have to praise. I will try to put the matter right by determining first of all which Love ought to be our subject, before going on to praise him in such terms as he deserves. We all know that Aphrodite is inseparably linked with Love. If there were a single Aphrodite there would be a single Love, but as there are two Aphrodites, it follows that there must be two Loves as well. Now what are the two Aphrodites? One is the elder and is the daughter of Uranus and had no mother; her we call Heavenly Aphrodite. The other is younger, the child of Zeus and Dione, and is called

Common Aphrodite. It follows that the Love that is the partner of the latter should be called Common Love and the other Heavenly Love. Of course, I am not denying that we ought to praise all the gods, but our present business is to discover what are the respective characters of these two Loves. Now the truth about every activity is that in itself it is neither good nor bad. Take the activities in which we are at present engaged, drinking and singing and conversation; none of these is good in itself; they derive their character from the way in which they are used. If it is well and rightly used, an activity becomes good, if wrongly, bad. So with the activity of love and Love himself. It is not Love absolutely that is good or praiseworthy, but only that Love which impels men to love aright.

There can be no doubt of the common nature of the Love which goes with Common Aphrodite; it is quite random in the effects which it produces, and it is this love that the baser sort of men feel. Its marks are, first, that it is directed towards women quite as much as young men; second, that in either case it is physical rather than spiritual; third, that it prefers that its objects should be as unintelligent as possible, because its only aim is the satisfaction of its desires, and it takes no account of the manner in which this is achieved. That is why its effect is purely a matter of chance, and quite as often bad as good. In all this it partakes of the nature of its corresponding goddess, who is far younger than her heavenly counterpart, and who owes her birth to the conjunction of male and female. But the Heavenly Aphrodite to whom the other Love belongs for one thing has no female strain in her, but springs entirely from the male, and for another is older and consequently free from wantonness. Hence those who are inspired by this Love are attracted towards the male sex, and value it as being naturally the stronger and more intelligent. Besides, even among the lovers of their own sex one can distinguish those whose motives are entirely dictated by this second Love; they do not fall in love with mere boys, but wait until they reach the age at which they begin to show some intelligence, that is to say, until they are near growing a beard. By choosing that moment in the life of their favorite to fall in love they show, if I am not mistaken, that their intention is to form a lasting attachment and a partnership for life; they are not the kind who take advantage of the ignorance of a boy to deceive him, and then are off with a jeer in pursuit of some fresh darling. If men were forbidden by law, as they should be, to form connections with young boys, they would be saved from laying out immense pains for a quite uncertain return; nothing is more unpredictable than whether a young boy will turn out spiritually and physically perfect or the reverse. As things are, good men impose this rule voluntarily on themselves, and it would be a good thing if a similar restriction were laid upon the common sort of lovers; it would be a correlative of the attempt that we already make to forbid them to form connections with freeborn women. It is men like these who bring love into disrepute, and encourage some people to say that it is disgraceful to yield to a lover; it is their lack of discretion and self-control that gives rise to such strictures, for there is no action whatever that deserves to be reprobated if it is performed in a decent and regular way.

If we go on to consider what men's code of behavior prescribes in the matter of love, we shall find that, whereas in other cities principles are laid down in black and white and are thus easily comprehensible, ours are more complicated. In Elis and Boeotia and Sparta and wherever men are unready of speech, the code states quite simply that it is good to gratify a lover, and no one, young or old, would say that it is disgraceful. The fact is, I imagine, that being poor speakers they wish to save themselves the trouble of having to win young men's favors by persuasive speeches. In many parts of Ionia, on the other hand, and elsewhere under Persian rule, the state of affairs is quite the reverse. The reason why such love, together with love of intellectual and physical achievement, is condemned by the Persians is to be found in the absolute nature of their empire; it does not suit the interest of the government that a generous spirit and strong friendships and attachments should spring up among their subjects, and these are effects which love has an especial tendency to produce. The truth of this was actually experienced by our tyrants at Athens; it was the love of Aristogeiton and the strong affection of Harmodius that destroyed their power. We may conclude then that where such love has been condemned it is the poor character of the people, greed for power in the rulers and cowardice in the subjects, which lies behind such a condemnation, but that where it has been thought to be unreservedly good this is due to mental indolence in the legislators.

Our institutions are far nobler than these, but, as I said, are not easily comprehensible. On the one hand, a love that courts no concealment is reckoned among us nobler than a love that shuns observation, and the love of those who are most eminent by birth or merit, even though they may be inferior in looks, is held in highest esteem. Besides this, the universal encouragement that a lover receives is evidence that no stigma attaches to him; success in a love affair is glorious, and it is only failure that is disgraceful, and we do not merely tolerate, we even praise the most extraordinary behavior in a lover in pursuit of his beloved, behavior that would meet with the severest condemnation if it were practiced for any other end. If a man, for example, with the object of obtaining a present of money or a public post or some other position of power, brought himself to behave as a lover behaves toward his favorite, begging and praying for the fulfillment of his requests, making solemn promises, camping on doorsteps, and voluntarily submitting to a slavery such as no slave ever knew, he would be restrained from such conduct by enemies and friends alike; the former would abuse him for his servility and lack of spirit, and the latter would give him good advice and blush for him. But in a lover such actions as these constitute an added charm, and no disgrace attends their performance by our standards because we recognize that the business which he is about is supremely noble. What is strangest of all is the popular conviction that a lover, and none but a lover, can forswear himself with impunity—a lover's vow, they say, is no vow at all. So we see that according to our way of thinking a lover is allowed the utmost license by both God and man, and the natural conclusion would be that in this country it is a very fine thing both to be in love and to show complaisance toward one's lovers. But when we reflect that the boys who inspire this passion are placed by their fathers in the charge of tutors, with injunctions not to allow them to hold any communication with their lovers, and that a boy who is involved in such communication is teased by his contemporaries and friends, and that their elders make no attempt to stop this teasing and do not condemn it, we are led to the opposite conclusion and infer that such love is reckoned among us to be highly disgraceful.

The truth of the matter I believe to be this. There is, as I stated at first, no absolute right and wrong in love, but everything depends upon the circumstances;

to yield to a bad man in a bad way is wrong, but to yield to a worthy man in a right way is right. The bad man is the common or vulgar lover, who is in love with the body rather than the soul; he is not constant because what he loves is not constant; as soon as the flower of physical beauty, which is what he loves, begins to fade, he is gone "even as a dream," and all his professions and promises are as nothing. But the lover of a noble nature remains its lover for life, because the thing to which he cleaves is constant. The object of our custom then is to subject lovers to a thorough test; it encourages the lover to pursue and the beloved to flee, in order that the right kind of lover may in the end be gratified and the wrong kind eluded; it sets up a kind of competition to determine to which kind lover and beloved respectively belong. This is the motive which lies behind our general feeling that two things are discreditable, first, to give in quickly to a lover—time, which is the best test of most things, must be allowed to elapse—and second, to give in on account of his wealth or power, either because one is frightened and cannot hold out under the hardships that he inflicts, or because one cannot resist the material and political advantages that he confers; none of these things is stable or constant, quite apart from the fact that no noble friendship can be founded upon them.

According to our principles there is only one way in which a lover can honorably enjoy the possession of his beloved. We hold that, just as a lover may submit to any form of servitude to his beloved without shameful servility, so there is one, and only one, other form of voluntary servitude which brings with it no dishonor, and that is servitude which has for its object the acquisition of excellence. If a person likes to place himself at the disposal of another because he believes that in this way he can improve himself in some department of knowledge, or in some other excellent quality, such a voluntary submission involves by our standards no taint of disgrace or servility. If the connection between a lover and his beloved is to be honorable, both the principles which I have enunciated must be found in combination, that which deals with the behavior of a lover of boys, and that which is concerned with the desire for knowledge or other forms of excellence. When a lover and his favorite come together, each in conformity with the principle that is appropriate to him, which is for the former that he is justified in performing any service whatever in return for the favors of his beloved, and for the latter that he is justified in any act of compliance to one who can make him wise and good, and when the lover is able to contribute toward wisdom and excellence, and the beloved is anxious to improve his education and knowledge in general, then and then only, when these two principles coincide, and in no other circumstances, is it honorable for a boy to yield to his lover. In these instances too there is no disgrace in being deceived, whereas in all others a boy is disgraced whether he is deceived or not. Suppose that a boy grants favors to a lover, believing him to be rich, and is then disappointed of his hope of gain by the lover's turning out to be poor; the boy is disgraced nonetheless, because he has shown himself to be the sort of person who would do any service to anybody for money. But by the same reasoning if a boy grants favors to a lover, believing that he is a good man and that he himself will be improved by association with him, and is disappointed because the lover turns out to be bad and devoid of merit, it does him credit to have been so deceived; he also has revealed his true nature, which is to be willing to do anything for anybody in order to attain excellence and improve himself, and nothing can be more honorable than that. So we conclude that it is in all cases honorable to comply with a lover to attain excellence. This is the Heavenly Love which is associated with the Heavenly Goddess, and which is valuable both to states and to individuals because it entails upon both lover and beloved self-discipline for the attainment of excellence.

[THE SPEECH OF ARISTOPHANES]

First of all, you must learn the constitution of man and the modifications which it has undergone, for originally it was different from what it is now. In the first place there were three sexes, not, as with us, two, male and female; the third partook of the nature of both the others and has vanished, though its name survives. The hermaphrodite was a distinct sex in form as well as in name, with the characteristics of both male and female, but now the name alone remains, and that solely as a term of abuse. Second, each human being was a rounded whole, with double back and flanks forming a complete circle; it had four hands and an equal number of legs, and two identically similar faces upon a circular neck, with one head common to both the faces, which were turned in opposite directions. It had four ears and two organs of generation and everything else to correspond. These people could walk upright like us in either direction, backwards or forwards, but when they wanted to run quickly they used all their eight limbs, and turned rapidly over and over in a circle, like tumblers who perform a cartwheel and return to an upright position. The reason for the existence of three sexes and for their being of such a nature is that originally the male sprang from the sun and the female from the earth, while the sex which was both male and female came from the moon, which partakes of the nature of both sun and earth. . . . Their strength and vigor made them very formidable, and their pride was overweening; they attacked the gods. . . .

So Zeus and the other gods debated what was to be done with them. For a long time they were at a loss, unable to bring themselves either to kill them by lightning, as they had the giants, and extinguish the race, thus depriving themselves forever of the honors and sacrifice due from humanity—or to let them go on in their insolence. At last, after much painful thought, Zeus had an idea. "I think," he said, "that I have found a way by which we can allow the human race to continue to exist and also put an end to their wickedness by making them weaker. I will cut each of them in two; in this way they will be weaker, and at the same time more profitable to us by being more numerous. They shall walk upright upon two legs. If there is any sign of wantonness in them after that, and they will not keep quiet, I will bisect them again, and they shall hop on one leg." With these words he cut the members of the human race in half, just like fruit which is to be dried and preserved, or like eggs which are cut with a hair. As he bisected each, he bade Apollo turn round the face and the half-neck attached to it towards the cut side, so that the victim, having the evidence of bisection before his eyes, might behave better in future. . . .

Man's original body having been thus cut in two, each half yearned for the half from which it had been severed. When they met they threw their arms around one another and embraced, in their longing to grow together again, and they perished

of hunger and general neglect of their concerns, because they would not do anything apart. When one member of a pair died and the other was left, the latter
sought after and embraced another partner, which might be the half either of a
female whole (what is now called a woman) or a male. So they went on perishing
till Zeus took pity on them, and hit upon a second plan. He moved their repro-
ductive organs to the front: hitherto they had been placed on the outer side of their
bodies, and the processes of begetting and birth had been carried on not by the
physical union of the sexes, but by emission onto the ground, as is the case with
grasshoppers. By moving their genitals to the front, as they are now, Zeus made it
possible for reproduction to take place by the intercourse of the male with the
female. His object in making this change was twofold; if male coupled with female,
children might be begotten and the race thus continued, but if male coupled with
male, at any rate the desire for intercourse would be satisfied, and men set free from
it to turn to other activities and to attend to the rest of the business of life. It is from
this distant epoch, then, that we may date the innate love which human beings feel
for one another, the love which restores us to our ancient state by attempting to
weld two beings into one and to heal the wounds which humanity suffered.

Each of us then is the mere broken tally of a man, the result of a bisection which
has reduced us to a condition like that of flat fish, and each of us is perpetually in
search of his corresponding tally. Those men who are halves of a being of the common sex, which was called, as I told you, hermaphrodite, are lovers of women, and
most adulterers come from this class, as also do women who are mad about men
and sexually promiscuous. Women who are halves of a female whole direct their
affections towards women and pay little attention to men; Lesbians belong to this
category. But those who are halves of a male whole pursue males, and being slices,
so to speak, of the male, love men throughout their boyhood, and take pleasure in
physical contact with men. Such boys and lads are the best of their generation,
because they are the most manly. Some people say that they are shameless, but they
are wrong. It is not shamelessness which inspires their behavior, but high spirit and
manliness and virility which lead them to welcome the society of their own kind.
A striking proof of this is that such boys alone, when they reach maturity, engage in
public life. When they grow to be men, they become lovers of boys, and it requires
the compulsion of convention to overcome their natural disinclination to marriage
and procreation; they are quite content to live with one another unwed. In a word,
such persons are devoted to lovers in boyhood and themselves lovers of boys in
manhood, because they always cleave to what is akin to themselves.

Whenever the lover of boys—or any other person for that matter—has the good
fortune to encounter his own actual other half, affection and kinship and love combined inspire in him an emotion which is quite overwhelming, and such a pair
practically refuses ever to be separated even for a moment. It is people like these
who form lifelong partnerships, although they would find it difficult to say what
they hope to gain from one another's society. No one can suppose that it is mere
physical enjoyment which causes the one to take such intense delight in the company of the other. It is clear that the soul of each has some other longing which it
cannot express, but can only surmise and obscurely hint at. Suppose Hephaestus
with his tools were to visit them as they lie together, and stand over them and ask:

"What is it, mortals, that you hope to gain from one another?" Suppose too that when they could not answer he repeated his question in these terms: "Is the object of your desire to be always together as much as possible, and never to be separated from one another day or night? If that is what you want, I am ready to melt and weld you together, so that, instead of two, you shall be one flesh; as long as you live you shall live a common life, and when you die, you shall suffer a common death, and be still one, not two, even in the next world. Would such a fate as this content you, and satisfy your longings?" We know what their answer would be; no one would refuse the offer; it would be plain that this is what everybody wants, and everybody would regard it as the precise expression of the desire which he had long felt but had been unable to formulate, that he should melt into his beloved, and that henceforth they should be one being instead of two. The reason is that this was our primitive condition when we were wholes, and love is simply the name for the desire and pursuit of the whole. Originally as I say, we were whole beings, before our wickedness caused us to be split by Zeus, as the Arcadians have been split apart by the Spartans. We have reason to fear that if we do not behave ourselves in the sight of heaven, we may be split in two again, like dice which are bisected for tallies, and go about like the people represented in profile on tombstones, sawn in two vertically down the line of our noses. That is why we ought to exhort everyone to conduct himself reverently towards the gods; we shall thus escape a worse fate, and even win the blessings which Love has in his power to bestow, if we take him for our guide and captain. Let no man set himself in opposition to Love, which is the same thing as incurring the hatred of the gods—for if we are his friends and make our peace with him, we shall succeed, as few at present succeed, in finding the person to love who in the strictest sense belongs to us. I know that Eryximachus is anxious to make fun of my speech, but he is not to suppose that in saying this I am pointing at Pausanias and Agathon. They may, no doubt, belong to this class, for they are both unquestionably halves of male wholes, but I am speaking of men and women in general when I say that the way to happiness for our race lies in fulfilling the behests of Love, and in each finding himself the mate who properly belongs to him; in a word, returning to our original condition. If that condition was the best, it follows that it is best for us to come as near to it as our present circumstances allow; and the way to do that is to find a sympathetic and congenial object for our affections.

If we are to praise the god who confers this benefit upon us, it is to Love that our praises should be addressed. It is Love who is the author of our well-being in this present life, by leading us towards what is akin to us, and it is Love who gives us a sure hope that, if we conduct ourselves well in the sight of heaven, he will hereafter make us blessed and happy by restoring us to our former state and healing our wounds.

[THE DIALOGUE OF SOCRATES AND DIOTIMA]

"There is indeed a theory," she continued, "that lovers are people who are in search of the other half of themselves, but according to my view of the matter, my friend, love is not desire either of the half or of the whole, unless that half or whole happens to be good. Men are quite willing to have their feet or their hands amputated if they believe those parts of themselves to be diseased. The truth is, I think, that people are not attached to what particularly belongs to them, except insofar as they can identify what is good with what is their own, and what is bad with what is not their own. The only object of men's love is what is good. . . . But we must add, mustn't we, that the aim of their love is the possession of the good for themselves?" "Yes." "And not only its possession but its perpetual possession?" "Certainly." "To sum up, then, love is desire for the perpetual possession of the good." "Very true."

"Now that we have established what love invariably is, we must ask in what way and by what type of action men must show their intense desire if it is to deserve the name of love. What will this function be? Can you tell me?" "If I could, Diotima, I should not be feeling such admiration for your wisdom, or putting myself to school with you to learn precisely this." "Well," she said, "I will tell you. The function is that of procreation in what is beautiful, and such procreation can be either physical or spiritual." "What you say needs an interpreter. I don't understand." "I will put it more plainly. All men, Socrates, have a procreative impulse, both spiritual and physical, and when they come to maturity they feel a natural desire to beget children, but they can do so only in beauty and never in ugliness. There is something divine about the whole matter; in procreation and bringing to birth the mortal creature is endowed with a touch of immortality. But the process cannot take place in disharmony, and ugliness is out of harmony with everything divine, whereas beauty is in harmony with it. That is why Beauty is the goddess who presides over birth, and why, when a person in a state of desire comes into contact with beauty, he has a feeling of serenity and happy relaxation which makes procreation possible. But, when ugliness is near, the effect is just the opposite; he frowns and withdraws gloomily into himself and recoils and contracts and cannot unite with it, but has painfully to retain what is teeming within him. So a person in whom desire is already active is violently attracted towards beauty, because beauty can deliver its possessor from the severity of his pangs. The object of love, Socrates, is not, as you think, beauty." "What is it then?" "Its object is to procreate and bring forth in beauty." "Really?" "It is so, I assure you. Now, why is procreation the object of love? Because procreation is the nearest thing to perpetuity and immortality that a mortal being can attain. If, as we agreed, the aim of love is the perpetual possession of the good, it necessarily follows that it must desire immortality together with the good, and the argument leads us to the inevitable conclusion that love is love of immortality as well as of the good."

 . . . . "The love of fame and the desire to win a glory that shall never die have the strongest effects upon people. For this even more than for their children they are ready to run risks, spend their substance, endure every kind of hardship and even sacrifice their lives. Do you suppose that Alcestis would have died to save Admetus, or Achilles to avenge Patroclus, or your Codrus to preserve his kingdom for his sons, if they had not believed that their courage would live forever in men's memory, as it does in ours? On the contrary: it is desire for immortal renown and glorious reputation such as theirs that is the incentive of all actions, and the better a man is, the stronger the incentive: he is in love with immortality. Those whose creative instinct is physical have recourse to women, and show their love in this way, believing that by begetting children they can secure for themselves an immortal and blessed memory hereafter forever, but there are some whose creative desire is of the soul, and who long to beget spiritually, not physically, the progeny that it is the nature of the soul to create and bring to birth. And if you ask what that progeny is, it is wisdom and virtue in general; of this all poets and such craftsmen as have found out some new thing may be said to be begetters; but far the greatest and fairest branch of wisdom is that which is concerned with the due ordering of states and families, whose name is moderation and justice. When by divine inspiration a man finds himself from his youth up spiritually fraught with these qualities, as soon as he comes of due age he desires to procreate and to have children and goes in search of a beautiful object in which to satisfy his desire; for he can never bring his children to birth in ugliness. In this condition physical beauty is more pleasing to him than ugliness, and if in a beautiful body he finds also a beautiful and noble and gracious soul, he welcomes the combination warmly, and finds much to say to such a one about virtue and the qualities and actions which mark a good man, and takes his education in hand. By intimate association with beauty embodied in his friend, and by keeping him always before his mind, he succeeds in bringing to birth the children he has long desired to have, and once they are born he shares their upbringing with his friend; the partnership between them will be far closer and the bond of affection far stronger than between ordinary parents, because the children that they share surpass human children by being immortal as well as more beautiful. Everyone would prefer children such as these to children after the flesh.

"The man who would pursue the right way to his goal must begin, when he is young, by applying himself to the contemplation of physical beauty, and, if he is properly directed by his guide, he will first fall in love with one particular beautiful person and beget noble sentiments in partnership with him. Later he will observe that physical beauty in any person is closely akin to physical beauty in any other, and that, if he is to make beauty of outward form the object of his quest, it is great folly not to acknowledge that the beauty exhibited in all bodies is one and the same; when he has reached this conclusion he will become a lover of all physical beauty, and will relax the intensity of his passion for one particular person, because he will realize that such a passion is beneath him and of small account. The next stage is for him to reckon the beauty of soul more valuable than beauty of body; the result will be that, when he encounters a virtuous soul in a body that has little of the bloom of beauty, he will be content to love and cherish it and to bring forth such notions as may serve to make young people better; in this way he will be compelled to contemplate beauty as it exists in activities and institutions, and to recognize that here too all beauty is akin, so that he will be led to consider physical beauty taken as a whole a poor thing in comparison. From morals he must be directed to the sciences and contemplate their beauty also, so that, having his eyes fixed upon beauty in the widest sense, he may no longer be the slave of a base and mean-spirited devotion to an individual example of beauty, whether the object of his love be a boy or a man or an activity, but, by gazing upon the vast ocean of beauty to which his attention is now turned, may bring forth in the abundance of his love of wisdom many beautiful and magnificent sentiments and ideas, until at last, strengthened and increased in stature by this experience, he catches sight of one unique science whose object is the beauty of which I am about to speak. And here I must ask you to pay the closest possible attention.

"The man who has been guided thus far in the mysteries of love, and who has directed his thoughts towards examples of beauty in due and orderly succession, will suddenly have revealed to him as he approaches the end of his initiation a beauty whose nature is marvelous indeed, the final goal, Socrates, of all his previous efforts. This beauty is first of all eternal; it neither comes into being nor passes away, neither waxes nor wanes; next, it is not beautiful in part and ugly in part, nor beautiful at one time and ugly at another, nor beautiful in this relation and ugly in that, nor beautiful here and ugly there, as varying according to its beholders; nor again will this beauty appear to him like the beauty of a face or hands or anything else corporeal, or like the beauty of a thought or a science, or like beauty which has its seat in something other than itself, be it a living thing or the earth or the sky or anything else whatever; he will see it as absolute, existing alone with itself, unique, eternal, and all other beautiful things as partaking of it, yet in such a manner that, while they come into being and pass away, it neither undergoes any increase or diminution nor suffers any change.

"When a man, starting from this sensible world and making his way upward by a right use of his feeling of love for boys, begins to catch sight of that beauty, he is very near his goal. This is the right way of approaching or being initiated into the mysteries of love — to begin with examples of beauty in this world and use them as steps to ascend continually with that absolute beauty as one's aim, and from one instance of physical beauty to two and from two to all, then from physical beauty to moral beauty, and from moral beauty to the beauty of knowledge, until from knowledge of various kinds one arrives at the supreme knowledge whose sole object is that absolute beauty, and knows at last what absolute beauty is."

"This above all others, my dear Socrates," the woman from Mantinea continued, "is the region where a man's life should be spent, in the contemplation of absolute beauty. Once you have seen that, you will not value it in terms of gold or rich clothing or of the beauty of boys and young men, the sight of whom at present throws you and many people like you into such an ecstasy that, provided that you could always enjoy the sight and company of your darlings, you would be content to go without food and drink, if that were possible, and to pass your whole time with them in the contemplation of their beauty. What may we suppose to be the felicity of the man who sees absolute beauty in its essence, pure and unalloyed, who, instead of a beauty tainted by human flesh and color and a mass of perishable rubbish, is able to apprehend divine beauty where it exists apart and alone? Do you think that it will be a poor life that a man leads who has his gaze fixed in that direction, who contemplates absolute beauty with the appropriate faculty and is in constant union with it? Do you not see that in that region alone where he sees beauty with the faculty capable of seeing it, will he be able to bring forth not mere reflected images of goodness but true goodness, because he will be in contact not with a reflection but with the truth? And having brought forth and nurtured true goodness, he will have the privilege of being beloved of God, and becoming, if ever a man can, immortal himself."

# *Musa Paidika:* Greek Homoerotic Poetry

A fragment of a poem by Solon (638–558 B.C.E.), who promulgated laws regulating ped-erasty, indicates his opinion that the love of boys was a supreme pleasure: "when in the delicious flower of youth he falls in love with a boy, yearning for thighs and sweet mouth" (Dover, *Greek Homosexuality*, 195). Both Anacreon of Teos (570–485 B.C.E.) and Theognis of Megara (570–490 B.C.E.) have left substantial numbers of poems, the larger number being those of Theognis (the last 164 poems of "Book 2" of his work), which deal with homosexual desire and with pederastic love. Both Anacreon and Theognis devote many of their lyrics to specifically named boys. Smerdis, Cleobulus, and Bathyllus held special fascination for Anacreon, while Theognis devoted a large number of the poems not only to boys generally but to Cyrnus especially. So passionate and so caring are these poems that they could have been used—and perhaps were—as a primer for proper conduct between male lovers. Theognis offers advice to Cyrnus, chastises him when he is fickle or cruel, suggests modes of right conduct, and asks for favors in return for generosity or gifts. His poems can be direct ("Happy the lover who can sleep all day with a handsome boy") or sexually allusive ("I grabbed a fawn from a deer . . . O I scaled the tops of the walls . . . I did it, but didn't do it"). Pindar (518–438 B.C.E.), one of the most celebrated of all the Greek poets, left more than forty odes,, including one to the First Olympian, which employs pederastic themes as he sings the praises of athletic youths. In addition, Pindar's devotion to Theoxenos is itself legendary and is celebrated in a fragmentary encomium for Theoxenos that is far less elevated though far more passionate than his formal odes. In poetry of the Hellenistic period (c. 350–90 B.C.E.), eight of the idylls of Theocritus (308–240 B.C.E.) are devoted to homosexual love, as are several of the poems in the col-lection known as the *Greek Anthology.*

*Solon (c. 638–558 B.C.E.)*

[THE LOVE OF BOYS]

*Translated by John Addington Symonds*

In the flower-time of youth
Thou shalt love boys,
Yearning for their honied mouths.

*Anacreon of Teos (570–485 B.C.E.)*

FRAGMENT 17

*Translated by Eugene O'Connor*

May the youths love me for my words and songs;
I sing beautifully, and know what charming words to say.

ELEGY 2

*Translated by Peter Bing and Rip Cohen*

I don't kiss the guy who guzzles wine beside the brimming bowl
   and talks battles and tearful war,

but the one who mingles dazzling gifts of the Muses and Aphrodite
    singing of lusty play.

### FRAGMENT 360

*Translated by Alfred Corn*

Boy, yes, you with the teasing glances:
I dog your steps, but you never notice —
Still unaware you hold the reins
To the old battlecar of my soul.

*Theognis (570–490 B.C.E.)*

### FROM THE "SECOND BOOK" OF THEOGNIS

*Translated by Peter Bing and Rip Cohen*

[lines 1255–56]

The man who doesn't love boys and single-foot horses
    and dogs, his heart will never know pleasure.

[lines 1267–70]

Boy and horse, a similar brain: the horse
    doesn't cry when its rider lies in the dust;
no, it takes on the next man, once it's sated with seed.
    Same with a boy: whoever's there he loves.

[lines 1345–50]

It's a thrill to love a boy: even Kronos' son,
    king of immortals, once longed for Ganymede,
snatched him, brought him to Olympos and made him
    a god with the lovely bloom of boyhood.
So Simonides, don't be amazed if I too
    am revealed, tamed by love for a gorgeous boy.

*Pindar (518–438 B.C.E.)*

### [TO THEOXENOS]

*Translated by John Addington Symonds*

O soul, 'tis thine in season meet
    To pluck of love the blossom sweet
When hearts are young;
    But he who sees the blazing beams,
    The light that from that forehead streams,
        And is not stung,

Who is not storm-tossed with desire,
Lo! he, I ween, with frozen fire
    Of adamant or stubborn steel
Is forged, in his cold heart that cannot feel.

Disowned, dishonored and denied
By Aphrodite glittering-eyed,
    He either toils
All day for gold, a sordid gain,
Or, bent beneath a woman's reign,
    In petty broils
Endures her insolence, a drudge
Compelled the common path to trudge.

But I, immune to that disease,
    Wasting away like wax of holy bees
Which the sun's splendor wounds, do pine
    Whenever I see the young-limbed bloom divine
Of boys. Lo! look you well;
      For here in Tenedos
Grace and Persuasion dwell
      In young Theoxenos.

*Euripides (480–406 B.C.E.)*

FRAGMENT 652

*Translated by John Addington Symonds*

O what a magic comfort are boys to
men!

*Theocritus (308–250 B.C.E.)*

IDYLL 29

*Translated by W. Douglas P. Hill*

"Truth in the cups" men say, dear youth;
So we who drink must speak the truth,
And I my inmost thoughts impart;
Thou lov'st me not with all thy heart.
I know it; half my life is mine,
The rest is vain; the fault is thine,
Who art so lovely. Dost comply?
The Blessed no more blest than I.
Dost thou deny me? Dark the day
As darkest night. Thus to betray

A loving heart were deadly wrong!
Boy, I am old and thou art young;
Heed then my counsel; so shalt thou
Thank me hereafter; profit now.
Build thou upon one tree one nest;
So shall no creeping thing molest
Thy quiet home; each day to perch
On different boughs and ever search
New branches—these were fickle ways!
Doth one scarce met behold and praise
Thy beauty? He's a friend long known;
The love that loved thee first, outgrown.
Heed me, and honored shalt thou be;
Love will deal tenderly with thee,
Love, tamer of men's souls, whose art
Has robbed of steel my powerless heart.
By thy soft lips I pray thee, bear
In mind, the passage of one year
Cheats thee of one year's youth; apace
Comes ruthless age, the wrinkled face.
Youth past returns not; youth wears wings
Upon his shoulders; flying things
Are hard to capture, so be kind,
Kinder for this thou hast in mind.
Guileless return my guileless love.
When bearded cheeks thy manhood prove,
We may swear friendship, as of yore
Patroclus and Achilles swore.
Now would I seek, thy whim to please,
The apples of Hesperides;
Now ravish from Hell's portal dread
Cerberus, guardian of the dead;
But if thou bid the heedless wind
Bear off my words, with thoughts unkind,
Then, should'st thou call me at the door,
All passion spent, I'd come no more!

## From the *Greek Anthology* (1st cent. B.C.E.—4th cent. C.E.)

*Translated by Daryl Hine, with additional versions by Byrne Fone*

Book 12 of the *Greek Anthology* (compiled in the tenth century C.E. by Constantine Cephalas) is a collection of over 250 epigrams devoted to pederastic sentiment. It includes not only one of the earliest anthologies of homoerotic verse, the *Garland of Meleager* (100 B.C.E.), but also an anthology of poems by Strato (120 C.E.) known as the *Musa Paidika* (The muse of boy love). In addition, poetry by a wide selection of Greek writers celebrates love, desire, and sex between adult males and youths, often with great specificity. The selections below have been translated especially for this anthology and have been rearranged in a sequence to suggest some of the themes in the *Anthology*.

## [Prelude]

*Strato 12, 1*

"Begin with Zeus," Aratus said; but, Muse
    I do not think I'll trouble you today.
If hanging out with boys is what I choose
    To do, does that concern you anyway?

## [Boys]

*Meleager 12, 95*

[To DIODORUS, DOROTHEUS, CALLICRATES ET AL.]

Philodes, if Desire, sweet Blandishment,
And Graces, beauty's botanists, consent,
Embracing Diodorus may you see
Sweet Dorotheus singing vis-à-vis
While holding Callicrates on your knee;
May Dion's little fingers hotly grip
Your horny prick, which Uliades will strip;
May you share Philo's kiss and Thero's talk
And feel Eudemus up beneath his smock.
If, blessed man, god granted you such joys,
You'd have arranged a smorgasbord of boys.

*Meleager 12, 122*

[To ARISTOGORAS]

Staring Aristogoras in the face,
The Graces clasped him in a fond embrace,
His beauty blazes now, his talk is sweet,
When mute his smiling eyes are indiscreet.
I wish he'd go away! But what's the use?
He throws his thunderbolts as far as Zeus.

*Rhianos 12, 93*

[To THEODORUS ET AL.]

Boys are an inextricable maze;
Like glue they hold the transitory gaze.

Here Theodorus' carnal charms attract
You, limbs so round and firm and fully packed;
Here golden-skinned Philodes, who is all
Heavenly grace, although not very tall.
If on Leptinus' form your eyes you cast,
You cannot budge, your feet will be stuck fast
As adamant; that youngster's looks are so
Ardent they'll kindle you from top to toe.
Hail, lovely boys! May you attain your prime,
And live until your hair turns white with time.

*Strato 12, 192*

Long hair, and curls woven not by Nature but by Art,
In the list of charms for me can play no part.
Give me a boy covered with dust and grime,
Body oiled, fresh from the field, anytime.
It's women's work when false art mars Beauty's form.
Love is best when unadorned.

[Youth and Aging]

*Strato 12, 10*

Despite the ruddy down upon your cheek
    And lovelocks that have recently appeared,
I'll not leave my beloved, whose physique
    Enthralls me, even though he grows a beard.

*Diodes 12, 35*

Somebody said when snubbed, "Is Damon so
Beautiful he doesn't say hello?
Time will exact revenge when, bye and bye,
Grown hairy, he greets men who won't reply."

*Strato 12, 4*

A twelve-year-old looks fetching in his prime,
Thirteen's an even more beguiling time.
That lusty bloom blows sweeter at fourteen;
Sexier yet a boy just turned fifteen.
The sixteenth year seems perfectly divine,
And seventeen is Jove's tidbit, not mine.
But if you fall for older fellows, that,
Suggests child's play no more but tit-for-tat.

[Choices]

*Anonymous 5, 65*

Zeus as an eagle came to Ganymede
    The godlike, as a swan to Helen's mother.
The two things are incomparable; I need
    Both, though one likes one and one the other.

*Anonymous 12, 17*

The love of women leaves me cold; desire
For men, though, scorches me with coals of fire.
As women are the weaker sex, my yen
Is stronger, warmer, more intense for men.

[Desire]

*Scythinus 12, 22*

Calamity and conflagration! Strife!
Elissus has attained the time of life,
Sixteen, that's made for love, and he has all
The adolescent graces great and small:
A honeyed voice, a mouth that's sweet to kiss,
And an accommodating orifice.
But, "Look, don't touch!" he tells me.
What a fate! I'll lie awake all night and— meditate.

*Anonymous 12, 145*

Unhappy pedophiles, cease your inane
Exertions! All our hopes are mad. As vain
As dredging up sea-water on dry land
Or numbering the grains of desert sand
Is a yen for boys, whose indiscreet
Charms are to mortals and immortals sweet.
Just look at me! My efforts heretofore
Have all been emptied on the arid shore.

[Seduction]

*Strato 12, 200*

I loathe a boy who won't be hugged and kissed,
Raises his voice and hits me with his fist,
Nor do I wish the wanton willingness
Of one who in my arms at once says,

Yes. I like one in between who seems to know
The secret of saying at once Yes and No.

*Strato 12, 206*

A. To start with, grapple your opponent 'round
The waist, bestride and pin him to the ground.
B. You're mad! For that I'm hardly competent,
Wrestling with boys is something different.
Withstand my onslaught, Cyris, hold your own!
Let's practice together what you do alone.

*Addaeus 10, 20*

When you meet a young boy, be direct,
Do not prate of fraternal respect.
Speak frankly and grope
His balls, or all hope
Of achieving your ends will be wrecked.

*Glaucus 12, 44*

Where once you could win over grasping boys
With birds and balls and jacks, all that beguiles
Them now is sweets or cash; old-fashioned toys
Don't work. Find something new, you pedophiles!

[Sex]

*Strato 12, 3*

Boys' members, Diodorus, come in three
Conditions: learn their nicknames properly.
A *dink* before you take the thing in hand
Is called a *dick* when it begins to stand.
A *tool's* what you manipulate till ready
To—but I think you know that term already?

*Antipater of Thessalonika 11, 224*

Priapus, seeing Cimon's rigid rod,
Cried, "Beaten by a man! and me a god!"

*Strato 11, 21 [12, 242]*

Your rosy-fingered prick that used to charm
Us, Alcimus, is now a rosy arm.

*Strato 12, 207*

Yesterday in the bath Diodes' penis
Rose from the water like *The Birth of Venus.*
On Ida, if he'd sprung this same surprise,
Paris would have given it the prize.


*Strato 11, 225*

In the bed are two, submissive,
And another two, in action.
2 x 2 by any reckoning
Makes four, you're thinking.
But no, there's three, no more.
But, you say, "How so?"
Its done this way. You know
The middle lad? Well, he
Does the job of two, you see,
By providing sport in either port.
    (Translated by Byrne Fone)


[Conclusion]

*Strato 12, 258*

In years to come, I ask, be kind
As you read these little poems of mine.
You should know that though
I wrote them, the complaints of love
Were not all my own,
But were for that one or another
Who loved both boys and men.
I tried to scribble with a truthful pen,
For from the gods came this gift of art
To sound the depths of a lover's heart.
    (Translated by Byrne Fone)


# Affairs of the Heart: Romance and Debate

A substantial number of homoerotic texts were written during the late Hellenistic period, including most of the poems collected in the *Greek Anthology*, the love letters to boys in the *Epistles* of Philostratus, and prose romances like those of Achilles Tatius' *Clitophon and Leucippe*, Xenophon's *Ephesiaca*, and (pseudo) Lucian's *Affairs of the Heart*. Though such texts often reflect cultural attitudes toward homosexual relationships that would have been familiar to Greeks of the fifth century B.C.E., they were, nevertheless, produced in a world far different from that of Plato—a cosmopolitan world now influenced by the cross-fertilization occasioned by the expansion of the Roman Empire, and by the cultural and religious encroachment of eastern Mediterranean thought regarding various sexual questions, including ideas about sexual morality just being formulated by early Christians. In prose romances of the Hellenistic period homosexual relationships are routinely presented, and debates about the superiority of the love of men versus the love of women form a staple of these texts. In the *Dionysiaca*, an epic romance by Nonnus of Panopolis (c. 450 C.E.) devoted to the life and exploits of Dionysus, Nonnus retells homoerotic myths associated with Dionysus and with other gods and heroes. Nearly two books are devoted to a description of the passion of Dionysus and Ampelos, the handsome youth who is eventually killed by a raging bull and whom the gods, to console Dionysus, turn into a grapevine. Dionysus makes wine from the grapes (the first ever to do so) and by this invention memorializes Ampelos forever. As further consolation, Eros tells Dionysus the story of Carpos and Calamos. Carpos is drowned and Calamos is turned into a reed whose rustling in the wind recalls his beloved Carpos. Millennia later Calamos—now Calamus—is again recalled in the name that Whitman chose for the "Calamus" sequence in his *Leaves of Grass*. Prose romances like the *Ephesiaca* of Xenophon of Ephesus (third century C.E.) or *Clitophon and Leucippe* of Achilles Tatius (c. 300 C.E.) assume that homosexuality is natural to the general conduct of life. These romances seem to envision men who desire other men as indeed a separate species. In *Clitophon and Leucippe*, for example, certain of the characters are decidedly what we would call heterosexual, while others seem to be solely devoted to the love of males. In *Affairs of the Heart* a debate between a lover of boys and a lover of women could well be mistaken for a modern debate between a present-day "homosexual" and his "heterosexual" counterpart.

## Philostratus (2nd–3rd cent. C.E.)

### From the *Epistles*

*Translated by Allen Rogers Benner and Francis Forbes*

Probably not addressed to actual people, these letters were literary exercises intended to illustrate a form or a style or simply to amuse.

### LETTER 19: TO A BOY WHO IS A PROSTITUTE

You offer yourself for sale; yes, mercenary soldiers do the like. You belong to anyone who pays your price; yes, so do pilots. We drink of you as of the streams; we feel of you as of the roses. Your lovers like you because you too stand naked and offer yourself for examination—something that is a peculiar right of beauty alone—beauty fortunate in its freedom of action. Pray, do not be ashamed of your complaisance, but be proud of your readiness; for water too is public property, and fire belongs to no individual, and the stars belong to all, and the sun is a common god. Your house is a citadel of beauty; those who enter are priests, those who are garlanded are sacred envoys, their silver is tribute money. Rule graciously over your subjects, and receive what they offer, and, furthermore, accept their adoration.

### LETTER 57: TO A BOY

You are persuaded, I fancy, but you hesitate for fear the deed might bring disgrace. Are you, then, shirking an act that makes a friend? Was it not because of this that the poems of Homer were filled with beautiful lads when he brought Nireus and Achilles to Troy? Was it not because of this that all Harmodiuses and Aristogeitons were friends even to the point of death by the sword? And was it not because of this that Apollo fell into subjection to Admetus and to Branchus? And did not Zeus carry off Ganymede, in whom he delights even more than in his nectar? For you handsome lads, and you alone, inhabit even heaven as your city. I do not begrudge you a lover who cannot indeed give you immortality but can give you his own life. If you do believe me, I am ready to die, if that is your command, at this very moment. If I plait the noose inhuman boy, will you not take it from me?

## Xenophon of Ephesus (3rd cent. C.E.)

From the *Ephesiaca*

*Translated by Moses Hadas*

Xenophon's *Ephesiaca* is a complicated novel of romance and adventure in which homosexual and heterosexual love exist side by side. Habrocomes is a prodigy of beauty unrivaled in Ionia, and Anthia is the most beautiful woman of Ephesus. Habrocomes is smitten by Anthia and wastes away, sick with love. Anthia does likewise. They seek out the Oracle of Apollo, who warns them that dire adventures lie in store for them, though ultimately there will be a happy ending. Taking heart, they marry and their parents send them away on a honeymoon to the island of Rhodes where the are captured by pirates, and where Habrocomes hears the sad tale of the doomed love of Hippothoos for Hyperanthes.

### [HIPPOTHOOS AND HYPERANTHES]

Now Habrocomes proceeded on his road to Cilicia. Not far from the cave of the brigands (he had wandered from the straight road) he encountered Hippothoos, who was fully armed. When the latter saw him he ran to meet him and greeted him in friendly wise and invited him to share the road with him. "Whoever you may be, my boy," said he, "I see that you are handsome to look at and have a manly bearing. Your wandering about indicates that you have somehow been wronged. Let us leave Cilicia behind, then, and go to Cappadocia and to Pontus; those that live there, they say, are happy." Habrocomes said nothing of his search for Anthia, but he agreed to the proposal of Hippothoos, who was insistent, and they swore to render one another cooperation and assistance. It was Habrocomes' hope that in the course of much wandering he might find Anthia. For that day, then, they returned to the cave, to spend as much of it as was left in refreshing themselves and their horses. For Hippothoos, too, had a horse, which he kept concealed in the forest.

It chanced as they were feasting that Hippothoos fetched a deep sigh and began to weep. Habrocomes inquired what the cause of his tears might be. "Mine is a long history," said Hippothoos, "and one rich in tragedy." Habrocomes begged him to speak, and promised that he would recount his own history in turn. They happened to be alone, and so Hippothoos, beginning his tale at the beginning, related the following narrative of his life:

"By birth I belong to the city of Perinthos, which lies near Thrace, and my family is among the most distinguished in that place. You have surely heard tell how celebrated a city Perinthos is, and how happy its inhabitants are. In Perinthos, when I was still young, I fell in love with a lad; he was a native boy, and his name was Hyperanthes. My love first began when I saw him wrestling in the gymnasium, and I could not contain myself. When a local festival that included all-night vigils was being celebrated, I approached Hyperanthes and implored him to take pity on me; and when the lad heard all my story he promised to show me compassion. The first stages of love were kisses and fondlings and (on my part) abundant tears. Finally we seized an opportunity to be alone together; our equal age obviated suspicion.

"For a long time we were together and loved one another passionately, until some deity begrudged us. There came from Byzantium (Byzantium is near Perinthos) a certain man who held great influence there; he was proud and rich, and he was called Aristomachos. As soon as this man set foot in Perinthos—as if some deity had specifically sent him to my bane—he caught sight of Hyperanthes and was straightway smitten; he admired the lad's beauty—which was indeed enough to allure anyone. And, having fallen in love, he could not keep his passion within moderation, but immediately sent proposals to the boy. When this proved futile (for Hyperanthes would admit no one because of his affection for me) he persuaded the lad's father, who was a vile creature with a weakness for money. The father delivered Hyperanthes over to the man on the pretext of education, for he was an accomplished rhetorician. So the man took him, and at first kept him shut up fast, and afterwards went off to Byzantium with him. I abandoned all my own concerns and followed, and on every possible occasion I was in the lad's company; but the occasions were few indeed; a rare kiss fell to my lot, a snatch of difficult conversation—there were too many people to keep watch.

"Finally, when I could endure it no longer, I roused myself to action; I returned to Perinthos, sold everything I possessed, and with the moneys I collected I went to Byzantium. I took a dagger (this had been agreed to by Hyperanthes), entered Aristomachos' house at night, and found him lying beside the boy; filled with fury, I struck Aristomachos a fatal blow. It was quiet and everyone was asleep, and I departed as secretly as I had come, taking Hyperanthes with me. All that night we made our way to Perinthos, and at once, none being privy, we went aboard ship and sailed for Asia. Up to a point our voyage prospered well, but presently, when we were near Lesbos, a mighty gale struck us and overturned our vessel. I swam along with Hyperanthes, supporting him and making his swimming lighter; but when night came the boy could no longer sustain the effort and gave over swimming and so died. I did what I could to get the body safe to land and bury it. Much did I weep and groan, and I collected the remains; and when I succeeded in securing a suitable stone I set up a marker on the grave, and as a memorial of the unfortunate lad I inscribed upon it an epitaph which I composed on the spur of the moment:

This monument hath Hippothoos fashioned for famous Hyperanthes,
Not worthy of a sacred citizen deceased,
A famous flower, whom on a time from land to the deep a deity
Ravished in the sea, when a stiff gale blew.

"Thereafter I determined not to return to Perinthos, and directed my footsteps through Asia to great Phrygia and Pamphylia. There, for want of livelihood and in discouragement at my lot, I devoted myself to brigandage. At first I became an underling in a robber band, but eventually I myself set up such a band in Gilicia. I achieved a great reputation, until, shortly before I caught sight of you, the men of my company were taken prisoner. Such then is the narrative of my fortunes."

[Complicated adventures befall them. Habrocomes finds Anthia, but she is kidnapped by robbers; Habrocomes becomes the victim of an unscrupulous woman and is thrown into prison on a false charge. Kept apart by fate, Habrocomes and Anthia are buffeted from country to country and from one peril to the next. Hippothoos carries on his voyages of conquest and robbery but in Sicily encounters the handsome young Clisthenes. Finally they are all united once again in Ephesus. Anthia and Habrocomes and Hippothoos and Clisthenes all live together as a happy family.]

And when they had offered sacrifice during that day and had well feasted, many and varied were the tales each had to tell, so much had each suffered, so much had each done, and they protracted the banquet on and on, for it was after a weary time that they were now reunited. And when night was fallen they all went to their rest as fortune decreed: Leucon with Rhode; Hippothoos and the young man from Sicily who had followed him when he went to Italy, the handsome Clisthenes; and Anthia went to rest with Habrocomes. . . .

When day broke they embarked upon their ship, upon which they had laden their possessions, and all the multitude of the Rhodians came to escort them and wish them good speed. Hippothoos, too, departed with them, taking his goods and Clisthenes. And in a few days they completed their voyage and landed at Ephesus. All the city had learned of their deliverance in advance; and when they disembarked, immediately and just as they were they proceeded to the temple of Artemis and offered many prayers and performed various sacrifices, but in particular they dedicated to the goddess an inscription which recounted all that they had suffered and all that they had done. And when they had accomplished this they ascended to the city and raised large tombs for their parents (who, as it happened, had died by reason of old age and despair), and the remainder of their lives they passed with one another, keeping, as it were, continuous festival. And Leucon and Rhode shared all the good things that their comrades had; and Hippothoos, too, resolved to pass the remainder of his days in Ephesus. For Hyperanthes he had raised a great tomb when he was in Lesbos, and now Hippothoos adopted Clisthenes as his son and lived in Ephesus with Habrocomes and Anthia.

*(Pseudo) Lucian (Early 4th cent. C.E.)*

From *Affairs of the Heart*

*Translated by M. D. McLeod*

The debate over the relative merits of the love of women versus the love of youths that appears in this selection from the Hellenistic romance *Affairs of the Heart* is only one example of a popular literary genre common to the period — and which would reappear in the late Middle Ages. The narrator is Lycinus, who on a voyage to Italy has encountered Callicratidas (who argues for the love of males) and Charicles (who favors the love of women). The two enter into a debate and Lycinus, acting as moderator, is called upon at the end to render a verdict. The following selection excerpts Callicratidas' remarks. Though it is ascribed to Lucian, some details in the dialogue suggest a later date.

[THE TWO TYPES OF LOVE]

"Let no one expect love of males in early times. For intercourse with women was necessary so that our race might not utterly perish for lack of seed. But the manifold branches of wisdom and men's desire for this virtue that loves beauty were only with difficulty to be brought to light by time which leaves nothing unexplored, so that divine philosophy and with it love of boys might come to maturity. Do not then, Charicles, again censure this discovery as worthless because it wasn't made earlier, nor, because intercourse with women can be credited with greater antiquity than love of boys, must you think love of boys inferior. No, we must consider the pursuits that are old to be necessary, but assess as superior the later additions invented by human life when it had leisure for thought.

36. For I came very close to laughing just now when Charicles was praising irrational beasts and the lonely life of Scythians. Indeed his excessive enthusiasm for the argument almost made him regret his Greek birth. For he did not hide his words in restrained tones like a man contradicting the thesis that he maintained, but with raised voice from the full depth of his throat says, 'Lions, bears, boars do not love others of their own sort but are ruled by their urge only for the female.' And what's surprising in that? For the things which one would rightly choose as a result of thought, it is not possible for those that cannot reason to have because of their lack of intellect. For, if Prometheus or else some god had endowed each animal with a human mind, they would not be satisfied with a lonely life among the mountains, nor would they find their food in each other, but just like us they would have built themselves temples and, though each making his hearth the center of his private life, they would live as fellow-citizens governed by common laws. Is it any wonder that, since animals have been condemned by nature not to receive from the bounty of Providence any of the gifts afforded by intellect, they have with all else also been deprived of desire for males? Lions do not have such a love, because they are not philosophers either. Bears have no such love, because they are ignorant of the beauty that comes from friendship. But for men wisdom coupled with knowledge has after frequent experiments chosen what is best, and has formed the opinion that love between males is the most stable of loves.

37. Do not, therefore, Charicles, heap together courtesans' tales of wanton living and insult our dignity with unvarnished language nor count Heavenly Love as an infant, but learn better about such things though it's late in your life, and now at any rate, since you've never done so before, reflect in spite of all that Love is a twofold god who does not walk in but a single track or exert but a single influence to excite our souls; but the one love (because, I imagine, his mentality is completely childish and no reason can guide his thoughts) musters with great force in the souls of the foolish and concerns himself mainly with yearnings for women. This love is the companion of the violence that lasts but a day, and he leads men with unreasoning precipitation to their desires. But the other Love is the ancestor

of the Ogygian age, a sight venerable to behold and hedged around with sanctity, and is a dispenser of temperate passions who sends his kindly breath into the minds of all. If we find this god propitious to us, we meet with a welcome pleasure that is blended with virtue. For in truth, as the tragic poet says, Love blows in two different ways, and the one name is shared by differing passions. . . .

38. Charicles may ask if I therefore think marriage worthless and banish women from this life, and if so, how we humans are to survive. Indeed, as the wise Euripides says, it would be greatly to be desired if we had no intercourse with women but, in order to provide ourselves with heirs, we went to shrines and temples and bought children for gold and silver. For we are constrained by necessity that puts a heavy yoke on our shoulders and bides us obey her. Though therefore we should by use of reason choose what is beautiful, let our need yield to necessity. Let women be ciphers and be retained merely for childbearing; but in all else away with them, and may I be rid of them. For what man of sense could endure from dawn onwards women who beautify themselves with artificial devices, women whose true form is unshapely, but who have extraneous adornments to beguile the unsightliness of nature?

[Here follows a diatribe directed against the use of makeup by women and against what Callicratidas conceives of as their social and sexual immodesty and opportunism.]

We ought therefore to contrast with the evils associated with women the manly life of a boy. He rises at dawn from his unwed couch, washes away with pure water such sleep as still remains in his eyes, and after securing his shirt and his mantle with pins at the shoulder 'he leaves his father's hearth with eyes bent down' and without facing the gaze of anyone he meets. He is followed by an orderly company of attendants and tutors, who grip in their hands the revered instruments of virtue, not the points of a toothed comb that can caress the hair nor mirrors that without artists' aid reproduce the shapes confronting them, but behind him come many-leaved writing tablets or books that preserve the merit of ancient deeds, along with a tuneful lyre, should he have to go to a music master.

45. But, after he has toiled zealously through all the lessons that teach the soul philosophy, and his intellect has had its fill of these benefits of a standard education, he perfects his body with noble exercises. For he interests himself in Thessalian horses. Soon, after he has broken in his youth as one does a colt, he practices in peace the pursuits of war, throwing javelins and hurling spears with unerring aim. Next come the glistening wrestling-schools, where beneath the heat of the midday sun his developing body is covered in dust; then comes the sweat, that pours forth from his toils in the contest, and next a quick bath and a sober meal suited to the activities that soon follow. For again he has his schoolmasters and records of deeds of old with hints for the study of such questions as what hero was brave, who is cited for his wisdom, or what men cherished justice and temperance. Such are the virtues that he uses to irrigate his soul while still tender, and, when evening brings an end to his activities, he metes out the tribute due to the necessities of his stomach, and then sleeps the sweeter, enjoying a rest that none could grudge after his exertions during the day.

46. Who would not fall in love with such a youth? Whose eyesight could be so blind, whose mental processes so stunted? How could one fail to love him who is a Hermes in the wrestling-school, an Apollo with the lyre, a horseman to rival Castor, and one who strives after the virtues of the gods with a mortal body? For my part, ye gods of heaven, I pray that it may forever be my lot in life to sit opposite my dear one and hear close to me his sweet voice, to go out when he goes out and share every activity with him. And so a lover might well pray that his cherished one should journey to old age—without any sorrow through a life free from stumbling or swerving, without having experienced at all any malicious spite of Fortune. But, if in accordance with the law governing the human body, illness should lay its hand on him, I shall ail with him when he is weak, and, when he puts out to sea through stormy waves, I shall sail with him. And, should a violent tyrant bind him in chains, I shall put the same fetters around myself. All who hate him will be my enemies and those well disposed to him shall I hold dear. Should I see bandits or foemen rushing upon him, I would arm myself even beyond my strength, and if he dies, I shall not bear to live. I shall give final instructions to those I love next best after him to pile up a common tomb for both of us, to unite my bones with his and not to keep even our dumb ashes apart from each other. . . .

For, when the honorable love inbred in us from childhood matures to the manly age that is now capable of reason, the object of our long-standing affection gives love in return and it's difficult to detect which is the lover of which, since the image of the lover's tenderness has been reflected from the loved one as though from a mirror. Why then do you censure this as being an exotic indulgence of our times, though it is an ordinance enacted by divine laws and a heritage that has come down to us? We have been glad to receive it, and we tend its shrine with a pure heart. For that man is truly blessed according to the verdict of the wise,

'Whoso hath youthful lads and whole-hooved steeds;
And that old man doth age with greatest ease
Whom youths do love.'

The teaching of Socrates and his famous tribunal of virtue were honored by the Delphic tripod, for the Pythian god uttered an oracle of truth,

'Of all men Socrates the wisest is.'

For along with the other discoveries with which he benefited human life, did he not also welcome love of boys as the greatest of boons?

49. One should love youths as Alcibiades was loved by Socrates who slept like a father with him under the same cloak. And for my part I would most gladly add to the end of my discourse the words of Callimachus as a message to all:

'May you who cast your longing eyes on youths
So love the young as Erchius bid you do,
That in its men your city may be blessed.'

Knowing this, young men, be temperate when you approach virtuous boys. Do not for the sake of a brief pleasure squander lasting affection, nor till you've reached manhood put on show counterfeit feelings of affection, but worship Heavenly Love and keep your emotions constant from boyhood to old age. For those who love thus, having nothing disgraceful on their conscience, find their lifetime sweetest and after their death their glorious report goes out to all men. If it's right to believe the children of philosophy, the heavens await men with these ideals after their stay on earth. By entering a better life at death they have immortality as the reward for their virtue."

50. After Callicratidas had delivered this very spirited sermon, Charicles tried to speak for a second time but I stopped him; for it was now time to return to the ship. They pressed me to pronounce my opinion, but, after weighing up for a short time the speeches of both, I said: "Your words, my friends, do not seem to me to be hurried, thoughtless improvisations, but give clear proof of continued and, by heaven, concentrated thought. For of all the possible arguments there's hardly one you've left for another to use. And, though your experience of the world is great, it is surpassed by your eloquence, so that I for one could wish, if it were possible . . . that you could both be victorious and walk off on equal terms. However, since I do not think you'll let the matter be, and I myself am resolved not to be exercised on the same topic during the voyage, I shall give the verdict that has struck me as the fairest.

51. "Marriage is a boon and a blessing to men when it meets with good fortune, while the love of boys, that pays court to the hallowed dues of friendship, I consider to be the privilege only of philosophy. Therefore all men should marry, but let only the wise be permitted to love boys."

*Nonnus (c. 450 C.E.)*

From *Dionysiaca*

*Translated by W. H. D. Rouse*

Dionysus (Gr., Dionysos), the god of wine and of sexual and emotional abandon, is in love with the youth Ampelos. After a wrestling match with strong sexual overtones, their affair is tragically ended when Ampelos is killed, gored by a bull. Dionysus laments for his dead lover, and Eros comforts him with the story of Carpos and Calamos. (*Note:* Dionysos is also called Bacchos, Iobacchos, Lyaios, Bromios, and Euios.)

[DIONYSOS AND AMPELOS]

From Book 10:175–372

Once while hunting in the shady lurking wood he [Dionysos] was delighted by the rosy form of a young comrade. For Ampelos was a merry boy who had grown up already on the Phrygian hills, a new sprout of the Loves. No dainty bloom was yet on a reddening chin, no down yet marked the snowy circles of his cheeks, the golden flower of youth: curling clusters of hair ran loose behind over his silver-glistering shoulders and floated in the whispering wind that lifted them with its breath. As the hair blew aside the neck showed above rising bare in the middle.

Unshadowed light flashed from him, like the shining moon when she pierces a damp cloud and shows within it. From his rosy lips escaped a voice breathing honey. Spring itself shone from his limbs; where his silvery foot stept the meadow blushed with roses; if he turned his eyes, the gleam of the bright eyeballs as soft as a cow's eye was like the light of the full moon.

Dionysos took him as a playmate in his dainty sports. Then in admiration of his beauty he spoke to him as a man, artfully concealing his divine nature, and asked him:

"What father begat you? What immortal womb brought you forth? Which of the Graces gave you birth? What handsome Apollo made you? Tell me, my friend, do not hide your kin. If you come another Eros, unwinged, without arrows, without quiver, which of the Blessed slept with Aphrodite and bred you? But indeed I tremble to name Cypris as your mother, for I would not call Hephaistos or Ares your father. Or if you are the one they call Hermes come from the sky, show me your light wings, and the lively soles of your shoes. How is it you wear the hair uncut falling along your neck? Can you be Phoibos himself come to me without harp, without bow, Phoibos shaking the locks of his unshorn hair unbound! If Cronides begat me, and you are from a mortal stock, if you have the short-living blood of the horned Satyrs, be king at my side, a mortal with a god; for your looks will not disgrace the heavenly blood of Lyaios. But why do I call you one of the creatures of a day? I recognize your blood even if you wish to hide it; Selene slept with Helios and brought you to birth wholly like the gracious Narcissos; for you have a like heavenly beauty, the image of horned Selene."

So he spoke, and the youth was delighted with his words, and proud that he surpassed the beauty of his young age-mates by a more brilliant display. And in the mountain coppice if the boy made melody Bacchos listened with pleasure; no smile was on his face if the boy stayed away. If at his caper-loving board a Satyr beat the drums with his hands and struck out his rattling tune, while the boy was away on stag-hunting quest, Bacchos refused the doubled sound so long as he was not there. If ever Ile lingered by the flowery stream of Pactolos, that he might bring himself sweeter water for the supper of his king, Bacchos was lashed with trouble so long as the boy stayed away.

If he took up the bold hoboy [oboe], the instrument of Libyan Echo, and blew a light breath with swollen cheek, Bacchos thought he heard the Mygdonian flotist [flutist] whom divine Hyagnis begat, who to his cost challenged Phoibos as he pressed the fingerholes on Athena's double pipe. If he sat with the young man at one table, when the boy spoke he lent delighted ear, when he ceased, melancholy spread over his cheeks. If Ampelos, carried away by wild passion for high capers, twirled with dancing paces and joined hands with a sporting Satyr in the round, stepping across foot over foot, Bacchos looked on shaken with envious feeling. If he ever conversed with the Satyrs, if he joined with a yearsmate hunter to follow chase, Dionysos jealous held him back, lest another be struck like himself with a heart-bewitching shaft, and now enslaved by love should seduce the fickle boy's fancy and estrange the lovely youth from Lyaios, as a fresh-blooming boy might well charm a comrade of his own age.

When Bacchos lifted his thyrsus against a maddened bear, or cast his stout fennel javelin-like at a lion, he looked aside watchfully towards the west; for fear the death-bringing breath of Zephyros might blow again, as it did once before when the bitter blast killed a young man while it turned the hurtling quoit against Hyacinthos. He feared Cronides might suddenly appear over Tmolos as a love-bird on amorous wing unapproachable, carrying off the boy with harmless talons into the air, as once he did the Trojan boy to serve his cups. He feared also the love-stricken ruler of the sea, that as once he took up Tantalides in his golden car, so now he might drive a winged wagon coursing through the air and ravish Ampelos—the Earthshaker mad with love!

He had a sweet dream on his dream-breeding bed, beheld the shadowy phantom of a counterfeit shape and whispered loving words to the mocking vision of the boy. If his passionate gaze saw any blemish, this appeared lovely to lovesick Dionysos, even more dear than the whole young body; if the end of the tail which grew on him hung slack by his loins, this was sweeter than honey to Bacchos. Matted hair on an unkempt head even so gave more pleasure to his impassioned gaze. By day he was charmed to be with him; when night came he was troubled to part from him, when he no longer heard the familiar voice enchanting his ears, as he slept in the grotto of Rheia mother of mighty sons.

A Satyr saw the boy, and enchanted with his divine beauty he whispered, concealing his words—

"All friendly Persuasion, manager of the human heart! Grant only that this lovely boy be gracious to me! If I can have him to play with me like Bacchos, I wish not to be translated into the sky, I would not be a god—not Phaethon the light of mankind, I covet not the nectar, I want no ambrosia! I care nothing, if Ampelos loves me, even if Cronion hates me!"

So much he said to himself in envious tone, hugging the love-poison in his heart, drunk with the magic potion of adoration. But Euios himself, pierced by the sting of the young man's sweetness, smiled as he cried out to Cronides his father, another unhappy lover:

"Grant one grace to me the lover, O Phrygian Zeus! When I was a little one, Rheia who is still my nurse told me that you gave lightning to Zagreus, the first Dionysos, before he could speak plain—gave him your fiery lance and rattling thunder and showers of rain out of the sky, and he was another Rainy Zeus while yet a babbling baby! But I do not ask the heavenly fire of your lightning, nor the cloud, nor the thunderclap. If it please you, give fiery Hephaistos the spark of your thunderbolt; let Ares have a corselet of your clouds to cover his chest with; give the pouring rainshower of Zeus as largess to Hermaon; let Apollo, if you will, wield his father's lightning. My ambition is not so high, dear father! I am springheel Dionysos! A fine thing it would be for me to wield Semele's minikin lightning! The sparks of thunderbolt that killed my mother are no pleasure to me. Maionia is my dwelling-place; what is the sky to Dionysos? My Satyr's beauty is dearer to me than Olympos. Tell me, father, do not hide it, swear by your own young friend—when you were an Eagle, when you picked up the boy on the slopes of Teucrian Ida with greedy gentle claw, and brought him to heaven, had the clown such beauty as this, when you made him one of the heavenly table still smelling of the byre? Forgive me, Father Longwing! Don't talk to me of your Trojan winepourer, the servant of your cups. Lovely Ampelos outshines Ganymedes, he has a brilliancy in his countenance more radiant—the Tmolian beats the Idaian! There are plenty more beautiful lads in troops—court them all if you like, and leave one boy to Lyaios!"

So he spoke, shaken by the sting of desire. Not Apollo in the thick Magnesian woods, when he was herdsman to Admetos and tended his cattle, was pierced by the sweet sting of love for a winsome boy, as Bacchos rejoiced in heart sporting with the youth. Both played in the woods together, now throwing the thyrsus to travel through the air, now on some unshaded flat, or again they tramped the rocks hunting the hillbred lion's cubs. Sometimes alone on a deserted bank, they played on the sands of a pebbly river and had a wrestling-bout in friendly sport; no tripod was their prize, no flower-graven cauldron lay ready for the victory, no horses from the grass, but a double pipe of love with clearsounding notes. It was a delightsome strife for both, for mad Love stood between them, a winged Hermes in the Ring, wreathing a love-garland of daffodil and iris.

Both stood forward as love's athletes. They joined their palms garlandwise over each other's back, packed at the waist with a knot of the hands, squeezed the ribs tight with the muscles of their two forearms, lifted each other from the ground alternately. Bacchos was in heaven amid this honeysweet wrestling, and love gave him a double joy, lifting and lifted. . . . Ampelos enclosed the wrist of Bromios in his palm, then joining hands and tightening that intruding grip interlaced his fingers and brought them together in a double knot, squeezing the right hand of willing Dionysos. Next Bacchos ran his two hands round the young man's waist, squeezing his body with a loving grip, and lifted Ampelos high; but the other kicked Bromios neatly behind the knee; and Euios laughing merrily at the blow from his young comrade's tender foot, let himself fall on his back in the dust. Thus while Bacchos lay willingly on the ground the boy sat across his naked belly, and Bacchos in delight lay stretched at full length on the ground sustaining the sweet burden on his paunch. Now raising one of his legs he set the sole of the foot firmly upon the sand and raised his overturned back; but he showed mercy in his strength, as with a rival movement of a reluctant hand he dislodged the beloved burden. The young man, no novice at the game, turned sideways and rested his elbow on the ground, then jumped across on his adversary's back, then over his flanks with a foot behind one knee and another set on the other ankle he encircled the waist with a double bond and squeezed the ribs and pressed flat and straight out the lifted leg under his knee. Both rolled in the dust, and the sweat poured out to tell that they were tired.

[Carpos and Calamos]

From Book 11

[After Ampelos is killed by the bull, Bacchos is devastated with grief. Eros comes to comfort him, and tells him the story of another lover who lost his love.]

[lines 351–400]

Eros came near in the horned shape of a shaggy Silenos, holding a thyrsus, with a dappled skin draped upon him, as he supported his frame on a fennel stalk, and he spoke comfortable words to groaning Bacchos:

"Let loose on another love the sparks of this love of yours; turn the sting upon another youth in exchange, and forget the dead. For new love is ever the physic for older love, since old time knows not how to destroy love even if he has learnt to hide all things. If you need a painhealing medicine for your trouble, court a better boy: fancy can wither fancy. A young Laconian shook Zephyros; but he died, and the amorous Wind found young Cyparissos a consolation for Amyclaian Hyacinthos. Ask the gardener, if you like; when a countryman sees a flower on the ground lying in the dust, he plants another new one to comfort him for the dead one.

"Listen while I tell you a story of the men of old. There was a dainty boy, superior to all his yearsmates, who lived beside the stream of Maiandros, that many-branching river. Tall and delicate he was, swift of foot, with long straight hair, no down on his chin; on both cheeks was a natural grace playing over his face with its modest eyes; a farshooting radiance ever flowed from his eyelids and his arrows of beauty. He had skin like milk, but over the white the rose showed upon the surface, two glowing colours together. His own father called him Calamos: his father Maiandros, lurking in the secret places with his water in the lap of earth—who rolls deep through the earth and drags his crooked stream towards the light crawling unseen and traveling slantwise underground, until he leaps up quickly and lifts his neck above the ground.

"Such was lovely Calamos, the quick one. The rosy-armed youth was fond of a charming playfellow Carpos, who had such beauty for his lot as mortal man never had. For if this youth had lived in the older generations, he would have been bride-groom of Eos Fairtress; since he shone lovelier than Cephalos, was handsomer of face than Orion, he alone outdid them with his rosy skin. Deo would not have embraced Iasion as bridegroom with her fruitful arm, nor Selene Endymion. No—this youth with his nobler beauty would soon have espoused both goddesses, one husband for two—he would have taken on the couch of Goldilocks Deo rich in harvests, he would have had beside him also the jealous Mene. Such was the charming friend of Calamos, the flower of love, a real beauty: both comrades of one age were playfellows on the bank of that river of many windings hard by."

[Carpos and Calamos lead an idyllic life, but Carpos suddenly dies and Calamos laments for him.]


[lines 460–482]

" 'Where Carpos wandered and died, I will fall headlong, I will quench my burning love with a draught of water from Acheron.'

"So he spoke, with streams bubbling from his eyes. To honour the dead he cut with sorrowful steel a dark lock of his hair, long cherished and kept, and holding out this mourning tress to Maiandros his father, he said these last words:

" 'Accept this hair, and then my body; for I cannot see the light for one later dawn without Carpos. Carpos and Calamos had one life, and both felt a like ardour of love on the earth: let there be one watery death for both together in the same stream. Build on the river bank, ye Naiads, one empty barrow for both and on the tombstone let this verse be engraved in letters of mourning: I am the grave of Carpos and Calamos, a pair of lovers, whom the pitiless water slew in days of yore.

Cut off just one small tress of your hair for Calamos too, your own dying brother so unhappy in love, and for Carpos cut all the hair of your heads.'

"With these words, he threw himself into the river and sank as he swallowed the Sonslaying water of an unwilling father. Then Calamos gave his form to the reeds which took his name and like substance; and Carpos grew up as the fruit of the earth."

## From Book 12

[Dionysos still laments, but is comforted by the gods, who promise to turn Ampelos, like Calamos, into a living plant—in this case, the grapevine, and thus Ampelos becomes wine.]

[lines 117–251]

But Dionysos had no healing physic for his comrade fallen, of dancing he thought no more. Shaken to the heart by his loving passion, he sounded bitter laments; he left to uncaring silence the bronze back of the timbrel unbeaten, and had no joy in the cithern. Before the unsmiling countenance of Dionysos, full of love and piteous pining, the reedy Lydian Hermos held up his course, and his fast-rolling waves which poured on with weatherbeaten throb—he cared no more to flow; Pactolos yellow as saffron with the wealth deep under his flood, stayed his water in mourning, like the image of a sorrowful man; Sangarios the Phrygian stream, in honour of the dead, checked back the course of his banked fountains; the unbreathing image of Tantalos's daughter, the unhappy mother drowned in sighs wept double tears for mourning Dionysos. The fir whispered softly, moaning to its young friend the pine; even the tree of unshorn Phoibos himself, the laurel, shook her foliage to the sorrowful winds; the glossy olive never felled shed her leaves on the ground, for all that she was Athena's tree.

Since then Dionysos, who never wept, lamented thus in his love, the awful threads of Fate were unloosened and turned back; and Atropos Neverturnback, whose word stands fast, uttered a voice divine to console Dionysos in sorrow:

"He lives, I declare, Dionysos; your boy lives, and shall not pass the bitter water of Acheron. Your lamentation has found out how to undo the inflexible threads of unturning Fate, it has turned back the irrevocable. Ampelos is not dead, even if he died; for I will change your boy to a lovely drink, a delicious nectar. He shall be worshiped with dancing beat of trippling fingers, when the double-sounding pipe shall strike up harmony over the feast, be it in Phrygian rhythm or Dorian tune; or on the boards a musical man shall sing him, pouring out the voice of Aonian reeds for Ismenians or the burghers of Marathon. The Muses shall cry triumph for Ampelos the lovely with Lyaios of the Vine. You shall throw off the twisting coronal of snakes from your head, and entwine your hair with tendrils of the vine; you shall make Phoibos jealous, that he holds out his melancholy iris with its leafy dirge. You too dispense a drink, the earthly image of heavenly nectar, the comfort of the human race, and your young friend shall eclipse the flowery glory of the Amyclaian boy: if his country produces the bronze of battle, your boy's country too increases the shining torrent of red juice like a river—she is all proud of her gold, and she likes not steel. If one boasts of a roaring river, Pactolos has better water than Eurotas! Ampelos, you have brought mourning to Dionysos who never mourns— yes, that when your honeydropping wine shall grow, you may bring its delight to all the four quarters of the world, a libation for the Blessed, and for Dionysos a heart of merry cheer. Lord Bacchos has wept tears, that he may wipe away man's tears!"

Having spoken thus, the divinity departed with her sisters.

Then a great miracle was shown to sorrowful Bacchos witnessing. For Ampelos the lovely dead rose of himself and took the form of a creeping snake, and became the healtrouble flower. As the body changed, his belly was a long stalk, his fingers grew into top tendrils, his feet took root, his curl clusters were grape clusters, his very fawnskin changed into the many-coloured bloom of the growing fruit, his long neck became a bunch of grapes, his elbow gave place to a bending twig swollen with berries, his head changed until the horns took the shape of twisted clumps of drupes. There grew rows of plants without end; there self-made was an orchard of vines, twining green twigs round the neighbouring trees with garlands of the unknown wineblushing fruit.

And a new miracle was then seen! Since young Cissos in his play, climbing with legs across the branches high in a leafy tree, changed his form and took the air as another plant: he became the twining ivy plant which bears his name, and encircled the new grown orchard of tame vines with slanting knots.

Then Dionysos triumphant covered his temples with the friendly shady foliage, and made his tresses drunken with the toper's leaves. Now the boy grown plant was quickly ripening, and he plucked a fruit of the vintage. The god untaught, without winepress and without treading, squeezed the grapes firmly with hand against wrist, interlacing his fingers until he pressed out the inebriating issue, and disclosed the new-flowing load of the purple fruitage, and discovered the sweet potation: Dionysos Tapster found his white fingers drenched in red! For goblet he held a curved oxhorn. Then Bacchos tasted the sweet sap with sipping lips, tasted also the fruit and both so delighted his heart, that he broke out into speech with proud throat: "O Ampelos! this is the nectar and ambrosia of my Zeus which you have made! Apollo wears two favourite plants, but he never ate laurel fruit or drank of the iris! Corn brings forth no sweet potation, by your leave, Deo! I will provide not only drink but food for mortal men! Your fate also is enviable, O Ampelos! Verily even Moira's threads have been turned womanish for you and your beauty; for you Hades himself has become merciful, for you Persephone herself has changed her hard temper, and saved you alive in death for brother Bacchos. You did not die as Atymnios is dead; you saw not the water of Styx, the fire of Tisiphone, the eye of Megaira! You are still alive, my boy, even if you died. The water of Lethe did not cover you, nor the tomb which is common to all, but the earth herself shrank from covering your form. No, my father made you a plant in honour of his son; Lord Cronion changed your body into sweet nectar. Nature has not graven Alas upon your tearless leaves, as on the inscribed clusters of Therapne. You keep your colour, my boy, even on your shoots. Your end proclaims the radiance of your limbs; your blushing body has not left you yet. But I will never cease avenging your death; I will pour your wine in libation to your murderous destroyer, the wine of his victim!

Your lovely petals put the Hamadryads to shame; the juice of your fragrant bunches brings round me a breath of your love. Can I ever mix the applefruit in the bowl? Can I drop figjuice in the cup of nectar? Fig and apple have their grace as far as the teeth; but no other plant can rival your grapes — not the rose, not the tinted daffodil, not anemone, not lily, not iris is equal to the plant of Bacchos! For with the newfound streams of your crushed fruitage your drink will contain all flowers: that one drink will be a mixture of all, it will combine in one the scent of all the flowers that blow, your flowers will embellish all the spring-time herbs and grass of the meadow!

"Give me best, Lord of Archery, because you wreathed your unmourning hair with your mourning chaplet of dolorous petals! Alas alas is graven on those leaves of yours; and if the Lord of Archery wears his wreath in the garden, I ladle my sweet wine, I put on a lovely wreath, I absorb all Ampelos to be at home in my heart by that delicious draught."

# 3. Rome: Love Poems and Satire

## Latin Literature from the First Century B.C.E. to the Second Century C.E.

### Introduction: Roman Homosexuality and Latin Literature

#### ROMAN LAW AND CUSTOM

Though Latin literature devotes much space to satirizing certain types of homosexual activity, homosexual desire itself was generally accepted and tolerated in the Republic and early Empire. No Roman legal precedent has been discovered that categorically prohibits homosexual acts or that indicates any history of such prohibition. References to the Lex Scantinia, a law that may have regulated homosexual activity between men and freeborn boys, are as obscure as the law itself since no text of the law exists and no prosecution under it has been satisfactorily documented. Certainly no law prohibited relations with male slaves, who were more numerous. In Augustan Rome homosexual prostitution, far from being illegal, was taxed by the government, and male prostitutes were granted their own holiday on April 25. Roman poets regularly indicated their own involvement in homosexual activities, celebrating or lamenting their love for handsome boys. Though most of these were handsome slave boys, some (like Catullus' Juventius) undoubtedly were not. As John Boswell points out in *Christianity, Social Tolerance, and Homosexuality*, no specific regulation of homosexual behavior can be discovered in Roman law until the third century C.E., and it was not until the fourth century C.E. that homosexual acts per se may have been prohibited by Roman law when laws enacted under the emperors Constans and Constantius and under Theodosius II prescribed the death penalty for male homosexual acts, though the scope of these laws remains unclear (see the *Theodosian Code* in part two).

#### SOCIAL ATTITUDES AND LITERATURE

If the Greeks idealized same-sex relationships and ascribed to them an important place in the political life of the nation and the spiritual and ethical life of the individual, the Romans held no such exalted view of sex between males. Few Roman writers, unless consciously imitating Greek models, would maintain that sexual relations between men or between men and freeborn boys would benefit the state or improve the mind and the conduct of the boy. Indeed, if for the Greeks a potential educational advantage for a youth might result from the gift of sexual favors, for the Romans, sex, quite simply, began with desire and ended with gratification. The object of gratification was of less moment than the experience itself. Slave boys were as legitimate as women, and some writers asserted that they were better. In several poems Martial, for example, observes that using both sexes provides far more pleasure than restriction to one.

The only imperative strongly enforced by custom and which was the primary source of satire against homosexual acts in Roman poetry was for an adult male to passively submit to anal penetration or to willingly fellate another male. The former was deemed to be an act tantamount to relinquishing not only manhood but the moral if not the legal right to be a citizen of the Roman state. As Boswell observes, the major cause of the prejudice against passive sexual behavior was the "popular association of sexual passivity with political impotence. Those who most commonly played the passive role in intercourse were women, boys, and slaves — all persons excluded from the power structure" (Boswell, 74). In addition, for an adult male to engage in oral sex was thought to be both reprehensible and impure — reprehensible because it indicated, like passive anal intercourse, a willingness to submit to sexual mastery, and impure because it was imagined that the person and the mouth were defiled by making it a receptacle like the anus or vagina. However, engaging in anal penetration or receiving oral sex was deemed to be an appropriate activity on the part of a free male citizen.

## TERMINOLOGY

In Latin poetry the desired youth — the *puer delicatus* (best translated perhaps as "sweetheart") — might be called an *ephebus* when an elevated tone was desired and sometimes, if he was in a relationship with another male, he might be called *frater* (brother). But in much poetry the delicate boy was a prostitute or *catamitus*. This latter word was derived from a corruption of Ganymede and meant a passive youth sexually available to older lovers. More pejoratively still he might be a *cinaedus*: one whose sexual promiscuity was advertised by gesture and manner of speech, by excessive and uninhibited sexual activity. Our derogative terms "queen" and "fag" perhaps convey something of the style of the cinaedi. When not demanding *pedicare* — active anal penetration — men might seek *irrumation*, a word not easily translated into English but that implies forcible oral intercourse performed on someone who does not want it (i.e., oral rape). Some texts suggest that both fellators and "pathics" (from *pathici*, discussed in the next paragraph) were attracted to another special class, *Drauci*, homosexuals with especially large genitals, who were often prostitutes or slaves. The *exoleti*, also often slaves, and adults rather than boys, were available as active prostitutes to service men and women. *Concubinus* and *amicus* both appear as terms for male concubines. A *spintria*, a male prostitute, whose name was derived from the muscle that contracts the anal opening, might perform any action his client desired, from pathic (i.e., passive) receptivity to active anal penetration.

*Pathici* and *cinaedi* were associated not only with specific sexual acts but with a number of specific identifying gestures and customs. Effeminate men were described as walking with a rolling or seductive walk or being agile with their buttocks. Pathic homosexuals, it was asserted, depilated their eyebrows or beard (or in some cases their entire body), used makeup on the skin and eyes, and often smoothed their skin with pumice stones, reflecting the Latin judgment that effeminate men were *mollis* — soft. Effeminate men who tried to disguise their effeminacy and their desires by wearing beards and assuming a false aspect of virility are as much a target as obvious effeminates: Juvenal devotes the Second Satire to them and Martial targets them in a number of epigrams, suggesting that under their beards stoic philosophers are pathics in disguise.

## ROMANTIC LOVE

Most of the major Roman poets—Catullus, Virgil, Horace, Tibullus, Ovid, Martial, and Juvenal—dealt with homoerotic sentiments in their work. Though the satires of Martial and Juvenal more often come to mind when discussing Latin homoerotic literature, many poets wrote romantic homosexual love poems. Virgil recounts the story of Nisus and Euryalus in the *Aeneid* and that of Corydon and Alexis in the Second Eclogue. Ovid retells Greek legend in *Metamorphoses* and casts these homoerotic myths in the form of Latin romantic homoerotic tales. Martial, whose epigrams can be sexually specific, scurrilous, and very funny, also writes movingly of his passion for certain young men, while Catullus's love for Juventius—no matter how ill the return from this thoughtless though seductive youth—provides if not the pleasure of viewing love triumphant at least the pleasure of hearing it described in the best Latin verse.

## SATIRE

Roman satire harnessed an invective that is often brutal and obscene, directed against men who engaged in something other than what the Romans might have described—had they possessed the term—as "normal homosexuality." Poems by Catullus and Martial that celebrated beautiful boys were matched by others that satirized them, especially if they were mercenary or sexually promiscuous. Men gone mad with love for an unattainable youth, or who lusted excessively or exclusively after boys were satirized. Latin texts derided sexual triangles, especially between a master, a male slave, and a wife. Indulgence in disapproved sexual practices like fellatio was mocked and ridicule directed against those whose manhood was compromised either by effeminate appearance or submissive sexual behavior.

## SATIRE AND THE APPEARANCE OF HOMOPHOBIA

A few Roman writers, like Virgil in the *Aeneid*, idealized love between men and youths in the Greek fashion, but many more employed the voice of satire, the genre that Latin writers had so triumphantly perfected as most suited to their vision of a world obsessed by desire. Latin poets, like their Greek predecessors, mostly presume that all men feel at one time or another homosexual desire. But Latin texts focused more often on men who *exclusively* preferred to do so, and in spotlighting them helped to define them. Roman "homosexuality" is still a term that probably should be considered under the same cautionary rubric about the construction of homosexualities as has been applied to Greek texts. Yet by the third and fourth centuries of the common era both legal and popular perception began to note that some men preferred same-sex love. Such men, it was increasingly believed, could be detected by certain signs, and were stimulated only by their own sex. That such men were seen as a discrete minority and viewed by the majority as almost a separate species (or at least as a distinct sexual culture) may be a subtext that could be read in Latin literature. We may presume that such satire reinforced Christian prejudices based on Old Testament laws. It is surely true that Juvenal's self-righteous moralizing, for example, appealed to later Christian writers, who found there ammunition to support their demonized view of pagan morals.

Further Reading

John Boswell, *Christianity, Social Tolerance, and Homosexuality: Gay People in Western Europe from the Beginnings of the Christian Era to the Fourteenth Century* (Chicago and London: University of Chicago Press, 1980); and Louis Crompton, "Roman Literature," in Claude J. Summers, ed., *The Gay and Lesbian Literary Heritage* (New York: Henry Holt, 1995).

## Catullus (c. 84–54 B.C.E.)

Of the 116 poems of Catullus that survive (most written after 68 B.C.E.), a number deal with homoerotic subjects, and four are love poems to a youth. Catullus's poetry is urbane and cynical, direct and sexually explicit. In some poems he wields his own erect penis like a weapon, threatening to use it on several men who have angered him or who he imagines have betrayed him with some woman or a boy he desires, especially a young man named Juventius. The four poems addressed to Juventius—Nos. 24, 48, 81, and 99—are written in the tradition of poems of the *Greek Anthology*: complaints about Juventius' cruelty, about his affairs with other men, about his rejection of his lover.

### 16 / To Aurelius and Furius

*Translated by Eugene O'Connor*

I'll bugger you and fuck you in the mouth,
Aurelius you faggot, Furius you sodomite
for impugning my morals (and my manhood)
based on your reading of my verses
rather wanton and indecent.

Separate rules apply to poets' lives
(which should be moral, free from taint)
and to their poems, which
aren't considered witty and urbane
unless they're rather wanton and indecent—
I'm not speaking to young impressionable
boys but to grown men whose hairy genitalia
are but slow to move.

You read "thousands of kisses"
and conclude that I'm a trifle *fey*?
I'll bugger you and fuck you in the mouth.

### 21 / To Aurelius

*Translated by Eugene O'Connor*

Aurelius! patron of starvelings
not only those who ever were

but are and ever will be:
you long to bugger my love.
You make no secret of it: as soon
as he arrives, you're joking with him,
cleaving to his side,
attempting every mode of seduction . . .
But it won't work:
even as you lay your trap
I'll be there first and fuck you
in the mouth.

If you took nourishment like any normal person
I'd say nothing.
But what I can't abide is that
you teach my boyfriend starveling ways:
Therefore, desist while you still can
with rectitude intact.
Otherwise pursue your dream, but only when
You've had a mouthful of Catullus.


## 99 / To Juventius

*Translated by Frank O. Copley*

I stole from you, my coy Juventius honey,
a kiss sweeter than ambrosia sweet
but I was punished: longer than an hour
fixed on a cross was I—well I remember
but all my pleas for pardon, all my tears
took not a tittle from your cruel wrath.
Scarce had I kissed you when you splashed your lips
with water and scrubbed and rubbed them with your fists
that no contagion from my mouth remain
like the foul spittle of some filthy tramp.
Then you consigned me to a cursed love
over and over, and tortured me so sore
that from ambrosia changed that kiss became
more bitter than the bitterest gall to me.
Since this is the fine you levy on poor love
never again your kisses will I steal.


## Virgil (70–19 B.C.E.)

The influence of Virgil upon homoerotic literature far outweighs the extent of what he
contributed to it. His *Aeneid* describes the epic founding of Rome, and one of the greatest Latin texts dealing with devoted love between men appears in it: the episode of Nisus
and Euryalus (Books 5 and 9) that celebrates the fidelity and loyalty of two Greek lovers

who died for one another on the plains of Troy (see Books 5 and 9). Perhaps the greatest and most influential homoerotic poem of the ancient world, and equally influential on later homoerotic texts, was the Second Eclogue, which tells the story of Corydon's unrequited love for Alexis, a catamite hardly worthy of the eloquent Corydon. The Eclogue established for Latin texts the special homoerotic ambiance that would attach itself to the pastoral tradition, an ambiance exploited especially by writers of homoerotic texts in the Renaissance and in the nineteenth century. Like Ganymede, the very name Corydon would become a sign for male love.

## Eclogue 2: The Lament of Corydon for His Faithless Alexis

*English Version by Byrne Fone*

The shepherd Corydon burned with fire for fair Alexis,
But Alexis was another's, his master's pet and pride.
Underneath the beech-tree shade Corydon, alone, moaned
For his fruitless love, singing this artless song
in the woodland glade:
Oh Alexis, cruel boy! Why do you ignore my song?
Have you no pity? I, without your love, will surely die.
Now cattle seek the cooling shade,
Now lizards lounge in the dusky glade,
Now reapers, hot from toil and heat
Seek repose, and grateful, eat sweet thyme and garlic
Made by Thestylis into savory feast,
But I, alone, retrace your steps in vain,
Under the sun's cruel ray, and
The burning fields resound
With the cicada's voice and mine
In pointless supplication joined.

Ah, I should have borne Proud Amaryllis' rage and scorn;
Or endured sweet Menalcos' whim (who was once my only care,
Though he was dark, and you: so fair!).
Beware Alexis, love, my lad, trust not pale beauty's eternal grace.
Do not presume that your handsome face will always charm.
White lilies fall, die my dear, are not reborn.
Only dusky hyacinths, I fear, stay, remain and are plucked again.

You scorn me, and thus you do not know
What flocks I have, what treasures to bestow,
What ripe Sicilian pastures rich with pretty lambs I hold.
Nor do you hear my songs, songs as sweet
As Amphion's honeyed lays as he called home his
Flocks from Aracynthus' mount on honeyed summer days.

Nor am I such an ugly sight; indeed, one day as on the beach
I stood, in the mirror of the flood I saw my face.

'Twas handsome! Why even 'gainst Daphnis' manly grace I would
Not fear to vie so long as you would judge.

Come, live with me and be my love in my simple pastoral home.
There, we'll plant the vine, and hunting deer and driving goats
We'll sing our songs, and in glades resounding
With our fluting notes we'll play like Pan, who first
Taught man to sing and then
Fashioned into flutes the reeds, whose stops
Play amorous songs to men.
(For Pan loves flocks and those who keep
Them, the shepherds of the sheep.)

Alexis, my Alex, do not mock the pipes or scorn
Their song. For sweet Amyntas offered kisses
To be the first to learn the tuneful secret of the hemlock horn.
And Damoetas laid in my hand a pipe of seven hemlock lengths and
With his final breath (to Amyntas' rage and envy)
Imparted: "This I leave to thee. Be deserving of its song.
You are its second master. Play it well hereafter."

Oh Alex, my Alexis
Not only song I'll bring but as a prize for you
Two wild goats I have of dappled hue.
I found them in a dark ravine
And Thestylis for them has asked in vain.
But now she'll have them for her use
Since the love—and lover—you refuse.

Ah Alexis, my love, my lad,
Come to my arms, and have the gifts which nymphs prepare:
Lilies sweet in rich abundance; while Naiad, daughter of the sea,
Gives violets pale and poppy flowers to thee.
She cassia blends; narcissus and the fennel flower
and the hyacinth she weaves, and hides the marigold
Amidst the scented leaves.
And I, I will pluck the down-soft peach,
Scatter chestnuts and the purple plum;
For fragrance' sake the laurel and the myrtle too
I'll blend. All this I'll do for you, as once I
Did for Amaryllis too.

O Corydon, Corydon!
(The unhappy shepherd to himself he cried),
Alexis will your gifts despise for he has the wealth of Iollas
(his older friend) at his beck and call.
If I offered all I own then Iollas, who I've dared to name,

Would add another gift, to play the game.
My heart's full measure is, alas, no match for such a splendid treasure.
What hope have I? He was my fondest wish.
I, quite mad, let the winds my flowers crush;
The boars pollute my crystal spring;
While I, at Love's altar, make vain offering.

Oh Alexis, Alexis, who do you flee?
Alexis, Alexis, more fool thee to spurn such woodland glades as these.
The Gods Themselves and Dardan Paris, Troy's bold son,
Have wandered in such leafy meads. Pallas can, in cities She has raised,
Dwell happy till the end of days. But I delight in shadowy woods and trees.
In this Arcadian glade I'll take my ease.

Corydon, like the lioness who the wolf pursues;
Corydon, like the wolf who the tempting kid desires;
Corydon, like the kid who would on clover browse
(Each drawn by ravening appetite),
Corydon, his Alexis seeks, hungry, like these,
To feast on that delight.

But now the sunset tells the parting day;
Ox and ploughman homeward make their way.
But for my love there is no rest; for me
No limit, no sweet surcease.
The fire burns! I wish for sleep.

Ah Corydon (the shepherd sighed), what madness this?
What frenzy has enthralled you?
Though Alexis (handsome lad) has spurned you,
Though Alexis (wicked lad) rejects you,
Life and Need, your daily tasks, are calling!
The grape untended hangs forlorn and spoiling.
Up! Arise! weave the willows, plait the boughs!
Find solace in your toiling.
Then 'tis sure you'll find a fairer youth come dawning,
Or even before the night is fallen.

## Ovid (43 B.C.E.–C.E. 18)

From *Metamorphoses*

*Translated by Rolfe Humphries*

Ovid—Publius Ovidius Naso—was one of the most successful and popular of Roman poets. His collection of ancient myth called *Metamorphoses* reworks mythology to illustrate the mutability of life. Among the myths he included were a number of Greek homoerotic legends, including those of Ganymede, Narcissus, Apollo and Cyparissus, Apollo and Hyacinthus, as well as that of Orpheus. Ovid is neither so serious or dignified as Virgil, nor ever scandalous like Martial or Juvenal. He is humorous and, quite simply, fun to read, gracefully including the loves of men for men among the many marvels of the fantasy worlds he constructs. It may not matter whether Ovid was himself touched by homosexual desire, as Virgil, Horace, Tibullus, Catullus, and Martial all may have been. He does seem to believe, like Chaucer centuries later, who found his tales so useful, that in nature nothing is alien or to be despised.

### [ZEUS AND GANYMEDE] (BOOK 10:155–62)

The king of the gods once loved a Trojan boy
Named Ganymede; for once, there was something found
That Jove would rather have been than what he was.
He made himself an eagle, the only bird
Able to bear his thunderbolts, went flying
On his false wings, and carried off the youngster
Who now, though much against the will of Juno,
Tends to the cups of Jove and serves his nectar.

### [APOLLO AND HYACINTHUS] (BOOK 10:163–219)

There was another boy, who might have had
A place in Heaven, at Apollo's order,
Had Fate seen fit to give him time, and still
He is, in his own fashion, an immortal.
Whenever spring drives winter out, and the Ram
Succeeds the wintry Fish, he springs to blossom
On the green turf. My father loved him dearly,
This Hyacinthus, and left Delphi for him,
Outward from the world's center, on to Sparta,
The town that has no walls, and Eurotas River.
Quiver and lyre were nothing to him there,
No more than his own dignity; he carried
The nets for fellows hunting, and held the dogs
In leash for them, and with them roamed the trails
Of the rough mountain ridges. In their train
He fed the fire with long association.
It was noon one day: Apollo, Hyacinthus,
Stripped, rubbed themselves with oil, and tried their skill
At discus-throwing. Apollo sent the missile
Far through the air, so far it pierced the clouds,
A long time coming down, and when it fell
Proved both his strength and skill, and Hyacinthus,
All eager for his turn, heedless of danger,
Went running to pick it up, before it settled
Fully to earth. It bounded once and struck him

Full in the face, and he grew deadly pale
As the pale god caught up the huddled body,
Trying to warm the dreadful chill that held it,
Trying to staunch the wound, to keep the spirit
With healing herbs, but all the arts were useless,
The wound was past all cure. So, in a garden,
If one breaks off a violet or poppy
Or lilies, bristling with their yellow stamens,
And they droop over, and cannot raise their heads,
But look on earth, so sank the dying features,
The neck, its strength all gone, lolled on the shoulder.
"Fallen before your time, O Hyacinthus,"
Apollo cried, "I see your wound, my crime:
You are my sorrow, my reproach; my hand
Has been your murderer. But how am I
To blame? Where is my guilt, except in playing
With you, in loving you? I cannot die
For you, or with you either; the law of Fate
Keeps us apart: it shall not! You will be
With me forever, and my songs and music
Will tell of you, and you will be reborn
As a new flower whose markings will spell out
My cries of grief, and there will come a time
When a great hero's name will be the same
As this flower's markings." So Apollo spoke,
And it was truth he told, for on the ground
The blood was blood no longer; in its place
A flower grew, brighter than any crimson,
Like lilies with their silver changed to crimson.
That was not all; Apollo kept the promise
About the markings, and inscribed the flower
With his own grieving words: *Ai, Ai*
The petals say, Greek for *Alas!* In Sparta,
Even to this day, they hold their son in honor,
And when the day comes round, they celebrate
The rites for Hyacinthus, as did their fathers.

## Petronius (c. C.E. 66)

Gaius Petronius, the elegant arbiter of Neronian taste, calmly took his own life upon being falsely accused by Nero, the emperor whose cruelty he had refined and whose court he had ornamented. After sending to Nero a sealed list of the imperial debaucheries naming the men and women who had been the emperor's partners, Petronius let his life slip away with the blood that flowed from his severed veins while he discussed with friends some fine points of verse. His death displayed, in the best sense of the term, a model of stoic bravery. He left a reputation for impeccable taste, penetrating wit, easy charm, and impatience with hypocrisy whether in mere men or emperors. He also left one of the most remarkable documents of Roman literature: the *Satyricon*. In Latin *satire* literally meant a collection of mixed subjects written in a variety of styles, and it came to mean the witty castigation of human folly. The *Satyricon* is both of those. But if its name is accurate—and there is some doubt about the proper spelling—then it may be meant to be a tale about Satyrs—that is, a lecherous, lewd, and erotic tale. The *Satyricon* is that also. It is also a mock-epic of a rather loose kind, a collection of erotic tales and of moral exempla with a decidedly comic twist. It caricatures stock literary figures and parodies literary genres. It has been called a prose romance, a novel, a picaresque fiction, an obscene story worthy of the censor, an erotic fantasy of breathtaking invention and originality. It is all of those things. It is entirely devoted to the exploits of Giton, the beautiful boy who is constantly unfaithful to Encolpius, the narrator of the book, who is Giton's devoted but constantly deceived lover. In the story the boys cover much ground—both geographical and erotic—yet they must have covered more in the original, for what is left is reported to be only a fragment of what must have been a vast endeavor. Unlike many Roman satirists, Petronius offers no bitter invective, no rage or indignation. He is precise, funny, deflating. Though everything is seen through the eyes of Encolpius, madly in love with Giton, Petronius no more judges that madness than he judges the promiscuity of Giton. Their story is surely about sex and the variations of desire, but it is also about love, because no matter how often Encolpius vows to free himself from Giton he always goes back to him; no matter how often Giton strays, he always returns to Encolpius. The *Satyricon*, in both a jocular and serious sense, is the first gay novel. It is always dangerous to say such things when dealing with a distant time, but it is worth the risk: in the sprawling over-the-top extravagance of the *Satyricon*, Petronius creates voices surely recognizable to us today, voices whose ironic overtones and meaningful inflections would not be out of place in gay modern times. There are more recent translations of the book, but this one attributed to Oscar Wilde is a happy collaboration of two arbiters of style.

## FROM THE *SATYRICON*

### *Translation Attributed to Oscar Wilde*

The narrator, Encolpius, is listening to an orator declaim on the decline of eloquence when he notices that his friend and occasional sex partner, Ascyltos, has disappeared. Encolpius is suspicious of Ascyltos because Encolpius is currently enamored of Giton, upon whom he has reason to suspect Ascyltos has designs.

[6] Listening attentively to the speaker, I never noticed that Ascyltos had given me the slip; and I was still walking up and down in the gardens full of the burning words I had heard, when a great mob of students rushed into the Portico. Apparently these had just come from hearing an impromptu lecture of some critic or other who had been cutting up Agamemnon's speech. So whilst the lads were making fun of his sentiments and abusing the arrangement of the whole discourse, I seized the opportunity to escape, and started off at a run in pursuit of Ascyltos. But I was heedless about the road I followed, and indeed felt by no means sure of the situation of our inn, the result being that whichever direction I took, I presently found myself back again at my starting point. At last, exhausted with running and dripping with sweat, I came across a little old woman, who was selling herbs.

[7] "Prithee, good mother," say I, "can you tell me where I live?" — Charmed with the quiet absurdity of my question, "Why certainly!" she replied; and getting up, went on before me. I thought she must be a witch; but presently, when we had arrived at a rather shy neighborhood, the obliging old lady drew back the curtain of a doorway, and said, "Here is where you ought to live."

I was just protesting I did not know the house, when I caught sight of mysterious figures prowling between rows of name-boards, and naked harlots. Then when too late, I saw I had been brought into a house of ill fame. So cursing the old woman's falseness, I threw my robe over my head and made a dash right through the brothel to the opposite door, when lo! just on the threshold, whom should I meet but Ascyltos, fagged out and half dead like myself? You would have thought the very same old hag had been his conductress. I made him a mocking bow, and asked him what he was doing in such a disreputable place?

[8] Wiping the sweat from his face with both hands, he replied, "If you only knew what happened to me!"

"Why! what has happened?" said I.

Then in a faint voice he went on, "I was wandering all over the town, without being able to discover where I had left our inn, when a respectable looking man accosted me, and most politely offered to show me the way. Then after traversing some very dark and intricate alleys, he brought me where we are, and producing his affair [wallet], began begging me to grant him my favours. . . . The man laid hold of me; and if I had not proved the stronger, I should have fared very ill indeed [been raped]."

[9] I caught sight of Giton, as it were a fog, standing at the corner of an alley close to the door of our inn, and hurried to join him. I asked my favourite whether he had got anything ready for our dinner, whereupon the lad sat down on the bed and began wiping away the tears with his thumb. Much disturbed at my favourite's distress, I demanded what had happened. For a long time I could not drag a word out of him,—not indeed till I had added threats to prayers. Then he reluctantly told me. "That favourite or comrade of yours came into our lodging just now, and set to work to force me. When I screamed he drew a sword and said, 'If you're a Lucretia, you've found a Tarquin.' "

Hearing this, I exclaimed, shaking my two fists in Ascyltos' face. "What have you to say now, you pathic prostitute, you, whose very breath is abominable?" Ascyltos feigned extreme indignation, and immediately repeated my gesture with greater emphasis, cried in still louder tones, "Will you hold your tongue, you filthy gladiator, who after murdering your host, had luck enough to escape from the criminal's cage at the Amphitheatre. Will you hold your tongue you midnight cut-throat, who never, when at your bravest, durst face an honest woman? Didn't I serve you for a minion in an orchard, just as this lad does now in an inn?"

"Did you or did you not," I interrupted, "sneak off from the master's lecture?"

[10] "What was I to do, fool, when I was dying of hunger? Stop and listen to a string of phrases no better than the tinkling of broken glass or the nonsensical interpretations in dream books? By great Hercules, you are baser than I; to compass a dinner

you have condescended to flatter a Poet!" This ended our unseemly wrangle, and we both burst into a fit of laughter, and proceeded to discuss other matters in a more peaceable tone.

But the recollection of his late violence coming over me afresh, "Ascyltos," I said, "I see we can get on together, so let us divide between us our bits of common funds, and each try to make head against poverty on his own bottom. You are a scholar; so am I. I don't wish to spoil your profits, so I'll take up another line. Else shall we find a thousand causes of quarrel every day, and soon make ourselves the talk of the town."

Ascyltos raised no objections, merely saying, "For to-day, as we have accepted, in our quality of men of letters, an invitation to dine out, don't let us lose our evening; but to-morrow, since you wish it, I will look out for a new lodging and another bedfellow."

"Poor work," said I, "putting off the execution of a good plan." It was really my naughty passions that urged me to so speedy a parting; indeed I had been long wishing to be rid of his jealous observation, in order to renew my old relations with my sweet Giton.

[11] After looking through the whole city [for work], I came back to my little room, and now at length claiming my full tale of kisses, I [held] my darling lad in the tightest of embraces; my utmost hopes of bliss are fulfilled to the envy of all mankind. The rites were not yet complete, when Ascyltos crept up stealthily to the door, and violently bursting in the bolts, caught me at play. . . . His laughter and applause filled the room, and tearing off the mantle that covered us, "Why! what are you after," he cries, "my sainted friend? What! both tucked cosily under one coverlet?" Nor did he stop at words, but detaching the strap from his wallet, he fell to thrashing me with no perfunctory hand, seasoning his blows with insulting remarks, "This is the way you divide stock with a comrade, is it? . . . .

[The boys try to sell the stolen cloak in the marketplace but are themselves made the victim of a confidence game in which they lose the cloak they stole. They return hurriedly to their inn where they are visited by a woman whose rites in the grotto of Priapus they had apparently disturbed in a section of the text now lost. The woman, Quartilla, extracts punishment of sorts for their sacrilege in the form of an orgy in which the boys engage in multiple sexual experiences.]

Finally there entered a catamite, tricked out in a coat of chestnut frieze, and wearing a sash, who would alternately writhe his buttocks and bump against us, and beslaver us with most evil-smelling kisses, until Quartilla, holding a whalebone wand in her hand and with skirts tucked up, ordered him to give the poor fellows quarter. Then we all three swore the most solemn oaths the horrid secret should die with us.

Next a company of [masseurs] appeared, who rubbed us over with the proper gymnastic oil, which was very refreshing. This removed our fatigue, (we resumed the dinner clothes that we had taken off) and we were then conducted into the adjoining room, where the couches were laid and all preparations made for an elegant feast in the most sumptuous style. We were requested to take our places, and the banquet opened with some wonderful hors d'oeuvres, while the Falernian [wine] flowed like water. A number of other courses followed, and we were all but falling asleep, when Quartilla cried, "Come, come! can you think of sleep, when you know this livelong night is owed to the service of Priapus?"

[22] Ascyltos was so worn out with all he had gone through he could not keep his eyes open a moment longer, and the waiting-maid, whom he had scorned and slighted, now proceeded to daub his face all over with streaks of soot, and bepaint his lips and shoulders, as he lay unconscious.

I too, tired with the persecutions I had endured, was just enjoying forty winks, as they say, while all the household, within doors and without, had copied my example. . . . By this time the chief butler had wakened up and put fresh oil into the expiring lamps, while the other slaves, after rubbing their eyes a bit, had resumed their posts, and presently a cymbal-player came in and roused us all up with a clash of her instruments.

[23] So the banquet was resumed, and Quartilla challenged us to start a fresh carouse, the tinkle of the cymbals still further stimulating her reckless gaiety.

The next to appear is a catamite, the silliest of mankind and quite worthy of the house, who beat his hands together, gave a groan, and then spouted the following delightful effusion:

"Who hath a pathic lust,
With Delian vice accurst;
Who loves the pliant thigh,
Quick hand and wanton sigh;
Come hither, come hither, come hither,
Here shall he see
Gross beasts as he,
Lechers of every feather!"

Then, his poetry exhausted, he spat a most stinking kiss in my face; before long he mounted on the couch where I lay and exposed me by force in spite of my resistance. He laboured hard and long to bring up my member, but in vain. Streams of gummy paint and sweat poured from his heated brow, and such a lot of chalk filled the wrinkles of his cheeks, you might have thought his face was an old dilapidated wall with the plaster crumbling away in the rain.

[24] I could no longer restrain my tears, but driven to the last extremity of disgust, "I ask you, lady," I cried, "is this the 'night-cap' you promised me?" At this she clapped her hands daintily, exclaiming. "Oh you clever boy what a pretty wit you have! Of course you didn't know 'night-cap' is another name for a catamite?" Then, that my comrade might not miss his share too, I asked her, "Now, on your conscience, is Ascyltos to be the only guest in the room to keep holiday!" "So?" she cried, "why! let Ascyltos have his 'night-cap' too!" In obedience to her order, the catamite now changed his mount, and transferring his attentions to my friend, set to grinding him under his buttocks and smothering him with lecherous kisses.

All this while Giton had been standing by, laughing as if his sides would split. Now Quartilla, catching sight of him, asked with eager curiosity, whose lad he was. When I told her he was my little favourite, "Why hasn't he kissed me then?" she cried, and calling him to her glued her lips to his. Next minute she slipped her hand under his clothes, and pulling out his unpracticed tool, she observed, "This will be a very pretty whet to-morrow to our naughty appetite. For to-day,—'After such a dainty dish, I will taste no common fish!'"

[The boys fall into bed and spend the night unmolested. The next day they ponder how to escape another orgy with Quartilla, when one of Agamemnon's slaves appears and reminds them that it is the day of a free banquet at Trimalchio's palace.]

. . . . The third day had now arrived. . . . Whilst we were still debating sadly with ourselves how we might best escape the storm, a slave of Agamemnon's broke into our trembling conclave, crying, "What! don't you recollect whose entertainment it is this day? —Trimalchio's, a most elegant personage; he has a time-piece in his dining-room and a trumpeter specially provided for the purpose keeps him constantly informed how much of his lifetime is gone." So, forgetting all our troubles, we proceed to make a careful toilette, and bid Giton, who had always hitherto been very ready to act as servant, to attend us at the bath.

[27] Meantime [at the baths] in our gala dresses, we began to stroll about, or rather to amuse ourselves by approaching the different groups of ballplayers. Amongst these we all of a sudden catch sight of a baldheaded old man in a russet tunic, playing ball amid a troupe of long-haired boys. It was not however so much the boys, though these were worth looking at, which drew us to the spot, as the master himself, who wore sandals and was playing with green balls. He never stooped for a ball that had once touched ground, but an attendant stood by with a sackful, and supplied the players as they required them. We noticed other novelties too. For two eunuchs were stationed at opposite points of the circle, one holding a silver chamberpot, while the other counted the balls,—not those that were in play and flying from hand to hand, but such as fell on the floor.

We were still admiring these refinements of elegance when Menelaus runs up, saying, "See, that's the gentleman you are to dine with; why this is really nothing else than a prelude to the entertainment." He had not finished speaking when Trimalchio snapped his fingers, and at the signal the eunuch held out the chamber-pot for him, without his ever stopping play. After easing his bladder, he called for water, and having dipped his hands momentarily in the bowl, dried them on one of the lads' hair.

[28] There was no time to notice every detail; so we entered the bath, and after stewing in the sweatingroom, passed instantly into the cold chamber. Trimalchio, after being drenched with unguent, was being rubbed down, not however with ordinary towels but with pieces of blanketing of the softest and finest wool. Meanwhile three bagnio doctors were swilling Falernian under his eyes; and seeing how the fellows were brawling over their liquor and spilling most of it, Trimalchio declared it was a libation they were making in his particular honour.

Presently muffled in a wrapper of scarlet frieze, he was placed in a litter, preceded by four running footmen in tinseled liveries, and a wheeled chair, in which his favourite rode, a little old young man, sore-eyed and uglier even than his master. As the latter was borne along, a musician took up his place at his head with a pair of miniature flutes, and played softly to him, as if he were whispering secrets in his ear. Full of wonder we follow the procession and arrive at the same moment as Agamemnon at the outer door. . . . [We had] by this time reached the banquet-hall, at the outer door of which the house steward sat receiving accounts. . . . [As] we were just making for the entrance of the banquet-hall, one of the slaves, stationed there for the purpose, called out, "Right foot first!" Not unnaturally there was a moment's hesitation, for fear one of us should break the rule. But this was not all; for just as we stepped out in line right leg foremost, another slave, stripped of his outer garments, threw himself before our feet, beseeching us to save him from punishment. Not indeed that his fault was a very serious one; in point of fact the Intendant's clothes had been stolen when in his charge at the bath,—a matter of ten sesterces or so at the outside. So facing about, still right foot in front, we approached the Intendant, who was counting gold in the hall, and asked him to forgive the poor man. He looked up haughtily and said, "It's not so much the loss that annoys me as the rascal's carelessness. He has lost my dinner robes, which a client gave me on my birthday,—genuine Tyrian purple, I assure you, though only once dipped. But there! I will pardon the delinquent at your request."

Deeply grateful for so signal a favour, we now returned to the banquet-hall, where we were met by the same slave for whom we had interceded, who to our astonishment overwhelmed us with a perfect storm of kisses, thanking us again and again for our humanity. "Indeed," he cried, "you shall presently know who it is you have obliged; the master's wine is the cupbearer's thank-offering."

Well! at last we take our places, Alexandrian slaveboys pouring snow water over our hands, and others succeeding them to wash our feet and cleanse our toe nails with extreme dexterity. Not even while engaged in this unpleasant office were they silent, but sang away over their work. I had a mind to try whether all the house servants were singers, and accordingly asked for a drink of wine. Instantly an attendant was at my side, pouring out the liquor to the accompaniment of the same sort of shrill recitative. Demand what you would, it was the same; you might have supposed yourself among a troupe of pantomime actors rather than at a respectable citizen's table.

Then the preliminary course was served in very elegant style. For all were now at table except Trimalchio, for whom the first place was reserved,—by a reversal of ordinary usage. Among the other hors d'oeuvres stood a little ass of Corinthian bronze with a packsaddle holding olives, white olives on one side, black on the other. The animal was flanked right and left by silver dishes, on the rim of which Trimalchio's name was engraved and the weight. On arches built up in the form of miniature bridges were dormice seasoned with honey and poppy-seed. There were sausages too smoking hot on a silver grill, and underneath (to imitate coals) Syrian plums and pomegranate seeds.

We were in the middle of these elegant trifles when Trimalchio himself was carried in to the sound of music, and was bolstered up among a host of tiny cushions,—a sight that set one or two indiscreet guests laughing. And no wonder; his bald head poked up out of a scarlet mantle, his neck was closely muffled, and over all was laid a napkin with a broad purple stripe or laticlave, and long fringes hanging down either side. Moreover he wore on the little finger of his left hand a massive ring of silver gilt, and on the last joint of the next finger a smaller ring, apparently of solid gold, but starred superficially with little ornaments of steel. Nay! to show this was not the whole of his magnificence, his left arm was bare, and displayed a gold bracelet and an ivory circlet with a sparkling clasp to put it on.

[The scene of Trimalchio's banquet proceeds over several chapters [29–79], each of which enlarges on the excess and pretension of Trimalchio, each of which produces yet more complex dishes served to the guests, and ends in an orgy of intoxication and display. The boys leave and drunkenly find their way to their inn, where Encolpius goes to bed at last with Giton.]

[79] We had never a torch to guide our wandering steps, while the silent hour of midnight gave small hope of procuring light from chance wayfarers. Added to this was our own intoxication and ignorance of the locality, baffling even by daylight. After dragging our bleeding feet for the best part of an hour over all sorts of stumbling-blocks and fragments of projecting pavingstones, we were finally saved by Giton's ingenuity. For being afraid even by daylight of missing his way, he had taken the precaution the day before to mark every post and pillar on the road with chalk. The strokes he had drawn were visible on the darkest night, their conspicuous whiteness showing wanderers the way. Though truly we were in no less of a fix, even when we did get to our inn. For the old woman had been swilling so long with her customers, you might have set her afire without her knowing anything about it. And we might very likely have passed the night on the doorstep, had not one of Trimalchio's carriers come up, in charge of ten wagons. Accordingly, without stopping to make any more ado, he burst in the door, and let us in by the same road.

Going to my chamber, I went to bed with my dear lad, and burning with amorous ardor as I was after my sumptuous meal, gave myself up heart and soul to all the delights of love.

Oh! what a night was that! how soft
The couch, ye gods! as many a time and oft
Our lips met burning in o'ermastering bliss,
And interchanged our souls in every kiss.
To mortal cares I bid farewell for aye—
So sweet I find it in thine arms to die!

But my self-congratulations were premature. For no sooner had my enfeebled hands relaxed their tipsy hold than Ascyltos, that everlasting contriver of mischief, drew the boy away from me in the dark and carried him off to his own bed; and there rolling about in wanton excess with another man's minion, the latter either not noticing the fraud or pretending not to, he went off to sleep enfolded in an embrace he had no sort of right to, utterly regardless of all human justice. So when I awoke, and feeling the bed over, found it robbed of delight, I declare by all that lovers hold sacred, I had half a mind to run them both through with my sword where they lay, and make their sleep eternal. But presently adopting safer counsels, I thumped Giton awake, and turning a stern countenance on Ascyltos, said severely, "You have broken faith by your dastardly conduct and sinned against our mutual friendship; remove your things as quick as may be, and go seek another place to be the scene of your abominations."

[80] He made no objection to this, but after we had divided our loot with scrupulous exactness, "Come now," said he, "let's divide the boy." I thought this were merely a parting jest. But murderously drawing a sword, "Never," he cried, "shall you enjoy this prey you gloat over so selfishly. I've been slighted, and I must have my share, even if I have to cut it off with this sword." I followed suit on my side, and wrapping my cloak round my arm, took up a fighting posture.

In wretched trepidation at our unhappy fury the boy fell at our knees in tears and begged and besought us not to repeat in a miserable tavern the tragedy of the two Theban brothers, nor pollute with each other's blood the sanctity of so noble a friendship. "But if murder must be done," he declared, "lo! here I lay bare my throat; here strike, here bury your points. 'Tis I should die, who have violated the sacred bond of friendship."

At these entreaties we put up our swords. Then Ascyltos taking the initiative, said, "I will end this difference. Let the lad himself follow whom he will, so that he may be perfectly free to choose his friend and favourite."

For my part, supposing my long, long, intimacy had bound the boy to me in ties as strong as those of blood, I felt not the slightest fear, but gladly and eagerly accepted the proposal to submit the question to this arbitrament. Yet the instant the words were out of my mouth, without a moment's hesitation or one look of uncertainty, he sprang up and declared Ascyltos to be his choice.

Thunderstruck at this decision, I threw myself just as I was and unarmed on my bed, and in my despair would certainly have laid violent hands on myself, had I not grudged such a victory to my adversary. Off goes Ascyltos in triumph with his prize, leaving me forlorn in a strange place—me who so short a while before had been his dearest comrade and the partner in all his escapades.

[Encolpius determines to seek revenge, but instead meets the poet Eumolpus who tells him a story about a youthful adventure.]

[85] "When I went to Asia," he began, "as a paid officer in the Quaestor's suite, I lodged with a family at Pergamus. I found my quarters very pleasant, first on account of the convenience and elegance of the apartments, and still more so because of the beauty of my host's son. I devised the following method to prevent the master of the house entertaining any suspicions of me as a seducer. Whenever the conversation at table turned on the abuse of handsome boys, I showed such extreme indignation and protested with such an air of austerity and offended dignity against the violence done to my ears by filthy talk of the sort, that I came to be regarded, especially by the mother, as one of the greatest of moralists and philosophers. Before long I was allowed to take the lad to the gymnasium; it was I that

directed his studies, I that guided his conduct, and guarded against any possible debaucher of his person being admitted to the house.

"It happened on one occasion that we were sleeping in the dining-hall, — the school having closed early as it was a holiday, and our amusements having rendered us too lazy to retire to our sleeping-chambers. Somewhere about midnight I noticed that the lad was awake; so whispering soft and low, I murmured a timid prayer in these words, 'Lady Venus, if I may kiss this boy, so that he know it not, to-morrow I will present him with a pair of doves.' Hearing the price offered for the gratification, the boy set up a snore. So approaching him, where he lay still making pretense to be asleep, I stole two or three flying kisses. Satisfied with this beginning, I rose betimes next morning, and discharged my vow by bringing the eager lad a choice pair of doves.

[86] "The following night, the same opportunity occurring, I changed my petition, 'If I may pass a naughty hand over this boy, and he not feel it, I will present him for his complaisance with a brace of the best fighting cocks ever seen.' At this promise the child came nestling up to me of his own accord, and was actually afraid, I think, lest I might drop asleep again. I soon quieted his uneasiness on this point, and amply satisfied my longings, short of the supreme bliss, on every part of his beautiful body. Then when daylight came, I made him happy with the gift I had promised him.

"As soon as the third night left me free to try again, I rose as before, and creeping up to the rascal, who was lying awake expecting me, whispered at his ear, 'If only, ye Immortal Gods, I may win of this sleeping darling full and happy satisfaction of my love, for such bliss I will to-morrow present the lad with an Asturian of the Macedonian strain, the best to be had for money, but always on the condition he shall not feel my violence.' Never did the stripling sleep more sound. So first I handled his plump and snowy bosom, then kissed him on the mouth, and finally concentrated all my arduous in one supreme delight. Next morning he sat still in his room, expecting my present as usual. Well! you know as well as I do, it is a much easier matter to buy doves and fighting cocks than an Asturian; besides which, I was afraid so valuable a present might rouse suspicion as to the real motives of my liberality. After walking about for an hour or so, I returned to the house, and gave the boy a kiss — and nothing else. He looked about inquiringly, then threw his arms round my neck, and 'Please, sir!' he said, 'where is my Asturian?'

[87] "Although by this breach of faith I had closed against myself the door of access so carefully contrived, I returned once more to the attack. For, after allowing a few days to elapse, one night when similar circumstances had created just such another opportunity for us as before, I began, the moment I heard the father snoring, to beg and pray the boy to be friends with me again, — that is to let me give him pleasure for pleasure, adding all the arguments my burning concupiscence could suggest. But he was positively angry and refused to say one word beyond, 'Go to sleep, or I will tell my father.' But there is never an obstacle so difficult audacity will not vanquish it. He was still repeating, 'I will wake my father,' when I slipped into his bed and took my pleasure of him in spite of his half-hearted resistance. However, he

found a certain pleasure in my naughty ways, for after a string of complaints about my having cheated and cajoled him and made him the laughing stock of his school-fellows, to whom he had boasted of his rich friend, he whispered, 'Still I won't be so unkind as you; if you like, do it again.' So forgetting all our differences, I was reconciled to the dear lad once more, and after utilizing his kind permission, I slipped off to sleep in his arms. But the stripling was not satisfied with only one repetition, all ripe for love as he was and just at the time of life for passive enjoyment. So he woke me up from my slumbers, and, 'Anything you'd like, eh?' said he. Nor was I, so far, indisposed to accept his offer. So working him the best ever I could, to the accompaniment of much panting and perspiration, I gave him what he wanted, and then dropped asleep again, worn out with pleasure. Less than an hour had passed before he started pinching me and asking, 'Eh! why are we not at work?' Hereupon, sick to death of being so often disturbed, I flew into a regular rage, and retorted his own words upon him; 'Go to sleep,' I cried, 'or I'll tell your father!' "

[At the baths, Encolpius encounters a miserable Giton.]

[91] I catch sight of Giton laden with towels and scrapers, leaning against a wall and wearing a look of melancholy embarrassment on his face. You could easily see he was an unwilling servant; and indeed, to show my eyes had not deceived me, he now turned upon me a countenance beaming with pleasure, saying, "Oh! have pity on me, brother! there are no weapons to fear here, so I can speak freely. Save me, save me, from the murderous ruffian; and then lay upon your judge, now your penitent, any punishment you please, no matter how severe. It will be comfort enough for me in my misery to have perished by your good pleasure."

I bade him hush his complaints, that no one might surprise our plans, and leaving Eumolpus to his own devices,—he was engaged in reciting a poem to his fellow bathers,—I dragged Giton down a dark and dirty passage, and so hurried him away to my lodging. Then after bolting the door, I threw my arms round his neck, pressing my lips convulsively to his tear-stained face. It was long before either of us could find his voice; for my darling's bosom was quivering like my own with quick-coming sobs. "I am ashamed of my criminal weakness," I cried, "but I love you still, though you did forsake me, and the wound that pierced my heart has left not a scar behind. What can you say to excuse your surrender to another? Did I deserve so base a wrong?"

Seeing he was still loved, he put on a less downcast look:

To chide, to love,—how make these two agree?
The task beyond e'en Hercules would be.
Let Love appear, all angry passions cease.

"Yet," I could not help adding, "I never meant to refer the choice of whom you should love to any third person; but there! all is forgiven and forgotten, if only you show yourself sincerely penitent." My words were interspersed with groans and tears; when I had done, the dear boy dried my cheeks with his mantle, saying, "I beg you, Encolpius, let me appeal to your own recollection of the circumstances.

Did I desert you, or did you throw me over? I am ready to confess,—and it is my best excuse,—when I saw you both sword in hand, I fled for safety to the stronger fighter." Kissing the bosom so full of wise prudence, I threw my arms round his neck, and to let him see he was restored to favour and my affection and confidence were as strong as ever, I pressed him closely to my heart.

## Martial (40–104 C.E.)

Martial's fourteen books of epigrams anatomize and pillory nearly every kind of sexual practice, and every variety of sexual desire. While satirizing the passions of others and mercilessly castigating passive and effeminate men, Martial himself reveals much about his own homosexual desire, and some of his epigrams relating his own desire and love for boys are as passionate and tender as any in Latin literature. Capable of a broad range of styles, he sometimes employs the most elevated Latin diction to dissect the most sordid events, and at other times employs rough vernacular and streetwise slang that is at once as difficult to translate as it is obscene (for those who find such unflinching, hilarious, and uncompromising talk of sex obscene). No one is left untouched, and the historian of Roman gossip can find in Martial's pages enough information about the sex lives of the Roman great and famous to fill a dozen weekly scandal sheets. No act is disguised by euphemism, no desire concealed by veiled language. Martial tells what was done, with whom, and when, and though he claims that his life is pure even though his page is lewd, it is sometimes difficult to believe his disclaimer when such precise descriptions of the mechanics of desire follow hard upon even more precise catalogues of the possibilities of lust. Opening Martial's pages at random introduces us to a man whose godly talk and dignified manner do not hide the fact that "yesterday he was a bride," or ironically takes note of another who spends his days in the baths with his eyes fixed on the "luscious members" of young men, or discusses men who raise a hearty cheer when the well-endowed young Maro reveals "that tool that has no peer," or makes lewd reference to Artemidorus, who sold his land to buy a boy from Calliodorus. Both of them, Martial assures us, "now have fresh fields to plow." Yet it is also Martial who so seductively observes that incense from altars and the smell of sweet Falernian wine resemble and perfume "my boy's kisses at early dawn."

Epigrams

I.67

You often say my work is coarse. It's true;
But then it must be so—it deals with you.
  (Translated by J. A. Pott)

III.71

Your slave boy's cock is aching, Naevolus
And so is your asshole
I'm no soothsayer
But I know what you've been up to.
  (Translated by Joseph S. Salemi)

## IV.42

If by chance, Flaccus, someone could offer me for the asking
The kind of boy I'd like, here's what I'd want:
First of all, let him be born on the banks of the Nile,
No land knows better how to raise naughtiness.
Let him be whiter than snow, in swarthy Egypt
That color is made all the more handsome by its rareness.
Let his eyes vie with the stars
And soft locks thrash his neck (I don't like curly hair).
He should have a low forehead and a slightly aquiline nose,
Let his lips rival the red roses of Paestum.
Let him often force me when I'm not in the mood and deny me when I am,
Let him often be freer than his master.
Let him not fear boys, but often shut out girls.
Though a man to others, let him be a boy to me alone.
"Now I know; you're not fooling me. It's true and I agree," you'll say,
"That's the way my Amazonicus was."
  (Translated by Richard E. Prior)


## IX.21

Artemidorus sold his land to buy a boy
From Calliodorus. Both are happy now:
Both have fresh fields to plow.
  (Translated by Richard O'Connell)


## IX.27

Chrestus, your balls are depilated
And your cock is as smooth as a vulture's neck.
Your scalp is slicker than a hooker's butt
And there isn't a bit of stubble on your legs.
Relentless tweezers have plucked your pale lips clean.

Still, you prate on about our hairy ancestors
And all those sturdy old republican virtues
That we read of in history books.
You also sound off in no uncertain terms
About the vices of this age —
You rant against our frivolous theatrics.

But if, in the midst of all this sermonizing,
Some faggot schoolboy comes along
Fresh from his dancing-master, and fancy free,
A prancing gymnast whose swollen schlong

Has been released from its restraining jockstrap,
You'll wink at him, call him over,
And I'm ashamed to say, Chrestus, what you do then
With your virtuous old republican tongue.
   (Translated by Joseph S. Salemi)


## XI.28

Nasica raped the doctor's pretty lad;
But then, they say, the fellow's raving mad.
   Mad? I maintain
   He's very sane.
(Translated by Brian Hill)


## XII.42

Bearded Callistratus wedded rugged Afer
In the way a young woman usually weds a man.
The torches glowed, the veil covered his face
Nor were you, Thalassus, short on words.
There was even a dowry. Well, Rome, is this enough for you?
Or are you waiting for him to give birth too?
   (Translated by Richard E. Prior)


# Juvenal (55–140 C.E.)

Juvenal's satires are the most indignant of those that attack what he saw as the general decay of ancient Roman virtue and the immorality of Roman sexual life. Where Martial is witty if obscene, urbane even when coarse, Juvenal can be vicious, bitter, and cruel. Juvenal had little personal success, and his disillusion with Roman life is revealed in his attacks upon it. He is a dark moralist—beneath the slashing, often violent invective there is much of that same savage indignation that Swift displayed. A misogynist, xenophobic, a conservative in all things, a moralist perhaps even more than satirist, his laments for lost Roman virtue and his castigation of corruption and loose sexual morality derive not so much from a radical urge to reform but instead to restore a morality long dead and values grown obsolete and by most largely ignored. Juvenal's Latin is complex, dignified, lucid and precise, and rarely resorts to obscenity, impressively embodying antique Roman probity while being able to render with chilling accuracy the most sordid aspects, as he saw them, of Roman morality. To read his great Second Satire is not to find any hint of the tolerance accorded to homosexual acts or desire by other Roman writers, even though a poem by Martial hints that Juvenal himself found love or passion in the arms of handsome youths. It is clear that he detested the hypocrisy of men who pretended to virtue while embracing vice, who professed philosophy without its rigor, and who acted one part while living another. In the Second Satire, Juvenal almost seems to prefer obvious and effeminate men—he would have used "queen" if he had had the word—to the seemingly moral and august stoic philosophers who in fact conceal pederastic lust beneath their dignified demeanor. He preferred instead the outright queen to the Roman equivalent of our own present-day right-wing ultra-moralists who are discovered in fact to be devotees of ganymedic passions even while preaching about the so-called loss of "family values." With horror Juvenal sees a wellborn man marry another: male brides will soon want wedding notices published in the paper, he predicts. At a party, men—if he had had *this* phrase he would have said "in drag"—put on makeup and hairnets and women's clothes. What has brought Rome to such a pass? he asks. There is probably no doubt that what Juvenal saw he saw with reasonable if jaundiced accuracy: some men were effeminate, some boys did sell themselves, some husbands were sodomized by the slaves purchased for their wives, money ruled everywhere. Though it is hard to find in his poems much that he admires (save for the long-dead past), yet at one point in the Sixth Satire he warns a young man soon to marry about the tyranny of domestic life and slyly asks: "Isn't it better to sleep with a pretty boy?/Boys don't quarrel all night, or nag you for little presents/While they're on the job, or complain that you don't come/Up to their expectations, or demand more gasping passion."


## FROM SATIRE 2

*Translated by Peter Green*

Northward beyond the Lapps to the world's end, the frozen
Polar ice-cap—there's where I long to escape when I hear
High-flown moral discourse from that clique in Rome who
    affect
Ancestral peasant virtues as a front for their lechery.
An ignorant crowd, too, for all the plaster busts
Of Stoic philosophers on display in their houses:
The nearest they come to doctrine is when they possess
Some original portrait—Aristotle, or one of the Seven Sages—
Hung on the library wall. Appearances are deceptive:
Every back street swarms with solemn-faced humbuggers.
You there—have you the nerve to thunder at vice, who are
The most notorious dyke among all our Socratic fairies?
Your shaggy limbs and the bristling hair on your forearms
Suggest a fierce male virtue; but the surgeon called in
To lance your swollen piles dissolves in laughter
At the sight of that well-smoothed passage. Such creatures talk
In a clipped, laconic style, and crop their hair crew-cut fashion,
As short as their eyebrows. I prefer the perverted
Eunuch priest of the Mother Goddess: at least he's open
And honest about it. Gait, gestures, expression, all
Proclaim his twisted nature. He is sick, a freak of fate,
Not to be blamed. Indeed, his wretched self-exposure,
The very strength of his passion, beg pity and forgiveness.
Far worse is he who attacks such practices with hairy
Masculine fervour, and after much talk of virtue
Proceeds to cock his dish like a perfect lady. "What?

Respect you?" screams the common-or-garden queen,
"When you're in the trade yourself? There's nothing to choose
Between us. It takes a hale man to mock a cripple,
And you can't bait niggers when you're tarred with the same
     brush."
True enough: who would stand for a radical deploring
The latest revolution? Wouldn't you think the world
Had turned upside-down if rapacious provincial governors
Condemned extortion, or gangsters repudiated murder?
Supposing a co-respondent clamped down on adultery,
Or some arch-conspirator flayed his henchmen in treason
With a patriotic lecture, or dictators inveighed
Against purges and proscriptions—wouldn't it turn your wits?
Such was the case, not so long since, when you-know-who
Was busy reviving those stern decrees against
Adultery: even Mars and Venus blushed. But all
The while he himself was flouting the law—and spiced
His crime with a dash of incest, in the proper tragic tradition.
His niece, a fertile creature, had her row of abortions,
And every embryo lump was the living spit of Uncle.
Then isn't it right and proper for even the worst of men
To despise these bogus moralists, cast their censure
Back in their teeth? "Where now are our marriage laws?"
Was the daily complaint of one such sour-faced pussy,
Till a courtesan, maddened, took up the cudgels against him:
"How lucky we are today," says she with a grin, "in having
You to look after our morals! Rome had better behave—
A real old-fashioned killjoy has dropped on us out of the skies.
Do tell me, darling—where did you buy that divine
Perfume I can smell on your bristly neck? Come, come:
Don't be ashamed to tell me the name of the shop!
If we must rake up old laws, surely our list should be headed
By the Sodomy Act. What's more, you should first examine
The conduct of men, not women. Men are the worse by far,
But their numbers protect them. They all back each other up,
And queers stick together like glue. Besides, you will never find
Our sex indulging in such detestable perversions:
All of us know our roles, from famous courtesan
To randy amateur harlot; we would not dream of giving
Tongue to each other's parts. . . ."
After a while you will find yourself taken up
By a very queer fraternity. In the secrecy of their homes
They put on ribboned mitres and three or four necklaces,
Then disembowel a pig and offer up bowls of wine
To placate the great Mother Goddess. Their rituals all
     widdershins;

Here it is women who may not cross the threshold: none
But males can approach this altar. "Away, away, profane
Women!" they cry, "no flute-girls here, no booming conches!"
(Such secret torch-lit orgies were known in Athens once,
When the randy Thracian priests outwore the Goddess herself.)
You'll see one initiate busy with eyebrow-pencil, kohl
And mascara, eyelids aflutter; a second sips wine
From a big glass phallus, his long luxuriant curls
Caught up in a golden hairnet. He'll be wearing fancy checks
With a sky-blue motif, or smooth green gabardine,
And he and his slave will both use women's oaths.
Here's another clutching a mirror—just like that fag of an
    Emperor
Otho, who peeked at himself to see how his armour looked
Before riding into battle. A fine heroic trophy
That was indeed, fit matter for modern annals and histories,
A civil war where mirrors formed part of the fighting kit!
To polish off a rival *and* keep your complexion fresh
Demands consummate generalship; to camp in palatial
    splendour
On the field of battle *and* give yourself a face-pack
Argues true courage. No Eastern warrior-queen,
Not Cleopatra herself aboard that unlucky flagship
Behaved in such a fashion.
            Here you will find no
Restraint of speech, no decent table-manners;
These are the Goddess's minions, here shrill affected voices
Are quite in order, here the white-haired old rogue of a priest
Who conducts the rites is a rare and memorable
Glutton for meat, a teacher worthy of hire.
Yet one thing they omit: the Phrygian devotees
Would by now have slashed away that useless member: why
Draw the line at self-castration? And what about
That noble sprig who went through a "marriage" with some
    common
Horn-player or trumpeter—and brought him a cool half-
    million
As a bridal dowry? The contract was signed, the blessing
Pronounced, and the blushing bride hung round "her" husbands
    neck
At a lavish wedding-breakfast. Shades of our ancestors!
Is it a moral reformer we need, or an augur
Of evil omens? Would *you* be more horrified, or think it
A more ghastly portent, if women calved, or cows
Gave birth to lambs? Here is a man who once
Was a priest of Mars, who walked in the solemn procession

Sweating under the thongs of his nodding sacred shield;
And now he decks himself out in bridal frills, assumes
The train and veil! O Father of our City,
What brought your simple shepherd people to such a pitch
Of blasphemous perversion? Great Lord of War, whence came
This prurient itch upon them? A wealthy, well-born
Man is betrothed in marriage to another man
And you do nothing! Not a shake of the helmet, no pounding
The ground with your spear, not even a complaint
To your father! Away with you then, remove yourself
From the broad Roman acres that bear your name, and suffer
Neglect at your hands! This is the kind of talk
We soon shall hear: "I must go downtown tomorrow
First thing: a special engagement."
        "What's happening?"
     "Need
   you ask?
I'm going to a wedding. Old So-and-so's got his boyfriend
To the altar at last—just a few close friends are invited."
We have only to wait now: soon such things will be done,
And done in public: male brides will yearn for a mention
In the daily gazette. But still they have one big problem
Of a painful kind: they can't keep their marriage solvent
By producing babies. Nature knows best: their desires
Have no physical issue. In vain they sample foreign nostrums
Guaranteed to induce conception, or hold out eager hands
To be struck by the wolf-boys' goatskins. But the very worst
Remains to be told: our male bride took a trident,
Put on the net-thrower's tunic, and dodged about the arena
In a gladiatorial act. Yet this was the man whose blood
Was the truest of blue, whose Republican family tree
Outshone them all—privileged ringside spectators,
Even the noble patron in whose honour the show was staged.
Today not even children—except those small enough
To get a free public bath—believe all that stuff about ghosts,
Or underground kingdoms and rivers, or black frogs croaking
In the waters of Styx, or thousands of dead men ferried
Across by one small skiff. But just for a moment
Imagine it's true—how would our great dead captains
Greet such a new arrival? And what about the flower
Of our youth who died in battle, our slaughtered legionaries,
Those myriad shades of war? If only they had
Sulphur and torches in Hades, and a few damp laurel-twigs
They'd insist on being purified. Yes: even among the dead
Rome stands dishonoured. Though our armies have advanced
To Ireland, though the Orkneys are ours, and northern Britain

With its short clear nights, these conquered tribes abhor
The vices that flourish in their conquerors' capital. Yet
We hear of one Armenian who outstripped our most effeminate
Young Roman pansies: *he* surrendered his person
To the lusts of a *tribune*. A good deal more than the mind
Is broadened by travel: he came to Rome as a hostage,
But Rome turns boys into men. If they stay here long enough
To catch her deadly sickness, there's never a shortage
Of lovers for them. Trousers, sheath-knives, whips
And bridles are cast aside, and so they carry back
Upper-class Roman habits to distant Adaschan.

# Part Two
Inventing Sodom

*The European Middle Ages from the Third to the*
*Thirteenth Century of the Common Era*

# 4. Inventing Sodom: Introduction

## Creating Sodomites—Making Friends

### SCRIPTURE AND THE LAW

Literate citizens of the Roman Empire in the third century of the common era, heirs of classical antiquity and standing at the beginning of premodern times, could read tales of same-sex and opposite-sex romance that appeared side by side in novels like *Clitophon and Leucippe* or in dialogues like *Affairs of the Heart.* They could read poetry in Greek celebrating love between males, or in Latin celebrating or satirizing it. All such writings reflected the sophisticated attitudes toward sexual practice of all kinds in the late empire, attitudes derived from diverse cultural styles and reasonably tolerant pagan attitudes toward morality and desire. However, by the end of the fourth century, when Christianity had established not only a religious but a political presence (most of Europe was by then nominally Christian, and the empire itself was officially Christian), popular and official attitudes toward sexual morality had changed: legal prohibitions against same-sex activity were codified and increasingly enforced, Christian asceticism, though perhaps more the practice of the clergy than the preference of the laity, brought eroticism and sexuality in literary texts under suspicion though perhaps not always under ban. Indeed Christian writers demonized all sexual experience and exalted virginity and celibacy as spiritual ideals. Consequently, as John Boswell in *Christianity, Social Tolerance, and Homosexuality* observes, "passionate, sexual love largely disappeared from Latin *belles lettres*—in which it had been a major subject—throughout the more than half millennium from about 400 to about 1000 of the Christian Era" (Boswell 1980:109). As the civilization of classical antiquity gradually disappeared during the third to the fifth centuries of the common era, and as Christian Europe moved into the High Middle Ages of the twelfth and thirteenth centuries, perceptions of homosexual acts changed from the easy tolerance of the empire to a state-enforced and religiously sanctioned intolerance in most of the new nation states that by the thirteenth century had arisen to take the place of a long-vanished empire. Those who engaged in homosexual acts (and who under the empire might have done so with little notice) became the subject of laws that declared their actions a criminal offense punishable by death. They were beginning to be designated as *sodomites*, and their private sexual activities were associated with all the evils that were believed to trouble society: heresy, sorcery, natural calamity, disease, and civic chaos.

### CHRISTIAN ASCETICISM AND LITERATURE

Though Christian asceticism began to dominate both life and literature, there was also a discernible tradition of romantic male friendship in both devotional Latin literature and in the more belletristic texts. In addition, secular literature—epics and the heroic romance—show strong elements of this same romantic friendship. Some writers, perhaps obscurely stirred by male beauty and by the erotic side of friendship, were willing to hint at that passion in writings in which the spiritual ecstasy of the love of God was described in words normally reserved for a more carnal human desire. Some, such as the twelfth century "Ganymede and Helen" that rejects homosexuality and "Ganymede and Hebe" that champions it, recall classical debates that asked whether the love of boys or women was the more pleasurable. By the late twelfth and early thirteenth century some writers were writing poems of undoubted homoerotic content, and in some poems Ganymede again appears as an image denoting homosexual desire.

## HOMOPHOBIA: THE MEDIEVAL BACKGROUND

Shadowing this literature, however, were secular and religious homophobic writings that condemned sodomites as pernicious and perhaps incorrigible sinners. The Middle Ages saw the creation of the sodomite as a distinct sexual type and excoriated sodomy as an offense almost as heinous as murder itself. By the fourth century, laws against homosexual behavior had been enacted, and the concept of "sodomy"—if not specifically the term— as a species of activity that defined all manner of illicit sexual behavior was also beginning to focus on prohibited same-sex sexual behavior. St. Boniface complained that the people of England "are living foul lives of adultery and lust like the people of Sodom" (Boswell 1980:203). He does not, however, seem to suggest that the sin of Sodom is necessarily only homosexuality. The Latin term *sodomia* does not in fact appear in general use as imply- ing only homosexual acts until near the end of the thirteenth century when Albertus Magnus in his *Summa theologiae* describes *sodomia* as sexual activity between two people of the same gender and describes it as "peccatum contra naturam"—the sin contrary to nature (see Boswell 1980: ch. 11). In a commentary on the Gospel of St. Luke, Albertus asserts that homosexual acts are so dangerous that they overthrow the order of nature and so persistent that "when it afflicts someone it almost never leaves him," and that homo- sexuality, like a contagious disease, "spreads from one person to another" (Boswell 1980:316). In a poem written in the twelfth century the anonymous author cites homosex- ual desire as a matter of choice rather than orientation, arguing that it is "a perverse cus- tom . . . to prefer boys to girls/since this type of love rebels against nature," and asserting that though God "hates all vices/He despises this one in particular," condemning those to hell and punishment by "flames and sulfur" who "wish to have tender youths as spouses" (Boswell 1980:390). By the end of the twelfth century, in "On Sodomy" (*De vitio sodomitico*), Peter Cantor is concerned specifically with associating the sin of Sodom with homosexual acts and marshals an array of scriptural quotation to prove that the sin of Sodom was "males doing evil with males and women with women."

## THE GROWTH OF ROMANTIC FRIENDSHIP

The twelfth century was the most brilliant and intellectually seminal period of the pre- Renaissance Middle Ages. States were becoming established, the cities that had fallen into decay after the demise of the empire were thriving, and an urban culture was being born throughout Europe. The great universities were in especial ferment, and therein rediscovered classical texts (including those that were to contribute to the theorization of courtly love and to a reevaluation of homoerotic love) were at the center of discourse. Indeed love itself was in the process of being reinvented. The proper conduct of roman- tic love between men and women, between husband and wife, and between lovers became the topic not only of treatises on the nature of courtly love but the subject of art, music, and poetry. In this milieu the first homoerotic literature outside of Arab Spain to be found in Europe since the fall of Rome began again to appear.

   If some poetry of the eighth and ninth centuries exhibited a subtle homoeroticism usu- ally portrayed as passionate Christian or romantic friendship, by the eleventh and twelfth centuries some literature appears that hints at homoerotic themes reminiscent of classical literature and that speaks of love between men. Much of the literature emanating from monastic sources must be treated with caution—there is little evidence of actual genital sensuality between the men who so passionately wrote these texts. Similarly, while it has been possible to read in these texts a manifestation of what has been, perhaps incautiously, described as gay literature and a gay sensibility, it should be recalled that the language of friendship in which these texts are couched is one that calls upon classical models without necessarily calling upon classical sexual experience. It can certainly be argued that such intense seemingly eroticized language need imply neither actual sexual experience nor even any sublimation of desire. The conventions of literary expression in the High Middle Ages were well attuned to an exaggerated profession of feeling between friends as well as between lovers. The poetic conventions that are evident in courtly love poetry demanded such eroticized address, and such highly charged language blurs the division between friends and lovers.

By the end of the twelfth century, out of the spiritual traditions of Christian monastic life, there had grown a parallel tradition of literature—what Boswell calls the "monastic love tradition" (1980:244)—that validated powerful emotions between men. Where once such literature had conflated such desire with the Christian ideal of the love of God and had safely spoken about homosexual desire in a language freighted with Christian piety, now texts directly celebrated love between males and increasingly ignored such coded strategies, deploying in texts a more pronounced interest in the homoerotic for its own sake. In addition, vernacular epic and heroic romance also depicted the strong attachment of adult males for one another, appearing not only in some of the early medieval lives of the saints but also in vernacular tales like the Old French *Amis and Amile* and the Old French *Lancelot-Grail*.

It is difficult to know whether these poets did more than idealize their passions. But what they did accomplish was to contribute a distinct homoerotic ambiance to the literature of what has been called the renaissance of the twelfth century. They perhaps possessed no theory that men who loved men were in any way different or to be set apart, nor may they have sensed any need for a declaration of difference, or to announce a program of liberation from what may not have seemed to them (and may not have been) oppression. But what they did seem to believe was that love itself was surely the greatest of all the gospels. As the Benedictine monk and poet Baudri of Bourgueil said: "God made our natures full of love. . . . What we are is a crime, if it is a crime to love,/For the God who made me live made me love" ( quoted in Boswell 1980:247).

## THE THIRTEENTH CENTURY: THE GROWTH OF HOMOPHOBIA

By the end of the thirteenth century the brief renaissance of homoerotic literature began to wane and what there was of a homosexual subculture began to be subject to increasing intolerance and to stringent legal penalties. By 1350 most countries of Europe decreed the death penalty for homosexual acts. And sodomy, as Edward Gibbon later observed, became a capital crime that was imputed when no other crime could be proven. The association of heresy with sodomy in ecclesiastical law, the definition of sodomy as a crime in civil law, and the view of sodomites as a special and dangerous segment of society marked some of the changes of this period. In 1102, during the reign of Henry I, the Council of London enacted what may have been the first English law against "the shameful sin of sodomy," ruling that any layman convicted of this crime should be "deprived of his legal status and dignity in the whole realm of England." In 1290, during the reign of Edward I, sodomy was equated with sorcery and heresy, and the punishment for conviction was death by burning.

In the thirteenth century Thomas Aquinas formulated what remains to the present day the position of the Roman Catholic Church concerning those sex acts believed to be "contra naturum"—against nature. Aquinas lists three kinds of intercourse that he defines as sinful and unnatural: those with the wrong species (i.e., with animals), those with the wrong organ (i.e., oral and anal intercourse), and those with the wrong gender (i.e., homosexuality). These sins, Aquinas claimed, are second only to murder in their seriousness.

By the beginning of the fifteenth century, the social and official intolerance of homosexual acts and of the now recognized and vilified species of sodomite was nearly universal.

## Further Reading

Derrick Bailey, *Homosexuality and the Western Christian Tradition* (New York: Archon Books, 1975); John Boswell, *Christianity, Social Tolerance, and Homosexuality: Gay People in Western Europe from the Beginnings of the Christian Era to the Fourteenth Century* (Chicago and London: University of Chicago Press, 1980); and John Boswell, *Same Sex Unions in Pre-Modern Europe* (New York: Villard Books, 1994).

# 5. Inventing Sodom: Scripture and Law from the Sodom Story to 1290 C.E.

The story of Sodom (Gen. 18–19) was to become the biblical source for prohibitions against homosexuality, and the site from which the most generally employed name for its practitioners was derived. Some scholars assert, however, that the early Church did not universally interpret the story as a warning against the consequences of same-sex desire. As Derrick Bailey (1975) and Boswell (1980) have shown, nothing in the Old Testament story itself or in texts of those interpreting it throughout the first century of the Christian Era conclusively indicates the story to be a warning against such transgression. Instead the Sodom story may be read as a cautionary tale concerning the consequences of the Sodomites' inhospitality toward strangers in their midst, who happened to be, of course, the visiting angels of God. A comparison with a very similar biblical tale—that of the outrage at Gibeah (Judges 19–20), which is pointedly about such inhospitality—renders a certain validity to the persuasive argument that the Sodom story does not in fact prohibit homosexual relationships and indeed is not even concerned with them.

The most specific Old Testament prohibitions against same-sex desire seem to appear in Leviticus 18:22 and Leviticus 20:13. As influential were probably the New Testament strictures in Romans 1:27 and 1 Corinthians 6:9–10. These passages seem to take a proscriptive position against some kind of sexual irregularity, though there is no firm evidence that same-sex love—as opposed to same-sex lust—is necessarily that which is proscribed. Though by the first century C.E. some Christian theorists like Philo had begun to associate the Sodom story with same-sex practice, in law it was not until the Novellae (New Laws) of Justinian in 538 and 544 C.E. that sodomy and Sodom were formally conflated: "certain men . . . practice among themselves . . . disgraceful lusts, and act contrary to nature . . . with the result that cities perish with all their inhabitants." The texts below suggest the development of legal and ecclesiastical definitions of sodomy and sodomites from the story of Sodom in the Hebrew Bible to the codification of England's first antisodomy laws.

## The Old Testament

### The Story of Sodom

Genesis 18–19

*Authorized (King James) Version*

Chapter 18

1 And the Lord appeared unto him in the plains of Mamre: and he sat in the tent door in the heat of the day;

2 And he lift up his eyes and looked, and, lo, three men stood by him: and when he saw them, he ran to meet them from the tent door, and bowed himself toward the ground,

3 And said, My Lord, if now I have found favour in thy sight, pass not away, I pray thee, from thy servant:

4 Let a little water, I pray you, be fetched, and wash your feet, and rest yourselves under the tree:

5 And I will fetch a morsel of bread, and comfort ye your hearts; after that ye shall pass on: for therefore are ye come to your servant. And they said, So do, as thou hast said.

6 And Abraham hastened into the tent unto Sarah, and said, Make ready quickly three measures of fine meal, knead it, and make cakes upon the hearth.

7 And Abraham ran unto the herd, and fetcht a calf tender and good, and gave it unto a young man; and he hasted to dress it.

8 And he took butter, and milk, and the calf which he had dressed, and set it before them; and he stood by them under the tree, and they did eat.

9 And they said unto him, Where is Sarah thy wife? And he said, Behold, in the tent.

10 And he said, I will certainly return unto thee according to the time of life; and, lo, Sarah thy wife shall have a son. And Sarah heard it in the tent door, which was behind him.

11 Now Abraham and Sarah were old and well stricken in age; and it ceased to be with Sarah after the manner of women.

12 Therefore Sarah laughed within herself, saying, After I am waxed old shall I have pleasure, my lord being old also?

13 And the Lord said unto Abraham, Wherefore did Sarah laugh, saying, Shall I of a surety bear a child, which am old?

14 Is any thing too hard for the Lord? At the time appointed I will return unto thee, according to the time of life, and Sarah shall have a son.

15 Then Sarah denied, saying, I laughed not; for she was afraid. And he said, Nay; but thou didst laugh.

16 And the men rose up from thence, and looked toward Sodom: and Abraham went with them to bring them on the way.

17 And the Lord said, Shall I hide from Abraham that thing which I do;;

18 Seeing that Abraham shall surely become a great and mighty nation, and all the nations of the earth shall be blessed in him?

19 For I know him, that he will command his children and his household after him, and they shall keep the way of the Lord, to do justice and judgment; that the Lord may bring upon Abraham that which he hath spoken of him.

20 And the Lord said, Because the cry of Sodom and Gomorrah is great, and because their sin is very grievous;

21 I will go down now, and see whether they have done altogether according to the cry of it, which is come unto me; and if not, I will know.

22 And the men turned their faces from thence, and went toward Sodom: but Abraham stood yet before the Lord.

23 And Abraham drew near, and said, Wilt thou also destroy the righteous with the wicked?

24 Peradventure there be fifty righteous within the city: wilt thou also destroy and not spare the place for the fifty righteous that are therein?

25 That be far from thee to do after this manner, to slay the righteous with the wicked: and that the righteous should be as the wicked, that be far from thee: Shall not the Judge of all the earth do right?

26 And the Lord said, If I find in Sodom fifty righteous within the city, then I will spare all the place for their sakes.

27 And Abraham answered and said, Behold now, I have taken upon me to speak unto the Lord, which am but dust and ashes:

28 Peradventure there shall lack five of the fifty righteous: wilt thou destroy all the city for lack of five? And he said, If I find there forty and five, I will not destroy it.

29 And he spake unto him yet again, and said, Peradventure there shall be forty found there. And he said, I will not do it for forty's sake.

30 And he said unto him, Oh let not the Lord be angry, and I will speak: Peradventure there shall thirty be found there. And he said, I will not do it, if I find thirty there.

31 And he said, Behold now, I have taken upon me to speak unto the Lord: Peradventure there shall be twenty found there. And he said, I will not destroy it for twenty's sake.

32 And he said, Oh let not the Lord be angry, and I will speak yet but this once: Peradventure ten shall be found there. And he said, I will not destroy it for ten's sake.

33 And the Lord went his way, as soon as he had left communing with Abraham: and Abraham returned unto his place.

## Chapter 19

1 And there came two angels to Sodom at even; and Lot sat in the gate of Sodom: and Lot seeing them rose up to meet them; and he bowed himself with his face toward the ground;

2 And he said, Behold now, my lords, turn in, I pray you, into your servant's house, and tarry all night, and wash your feet, and ye shall rise up early, and go on your ways. And they said, Nay; but we will abide in the street all night.

3 And he pressed upon them greatly; and they turned in unto him, and entered into his house; and he made them a feast, and did bake unleavened bread, and they did eat.

4 But before they lay down, the men of the city, even the men of Sodom, compassed the house round, both old and young, all the people from every quarter:

5 And they called unto Lot, and said unto him, Where are the men which came in to thee this night? bring them out unto us, that we may know them.

6 And Lot went out at the door unto them, and shut the door after him,

7 And said, I pray you, brethren, do not so wickedly.

8 Behold now, I have two daughters which have not known man; let me, I pray you, bring them out unto you, and do ye to them as is good in your eyes; only unto these men do nothing; for therefore came they under the shadow of my roof.

9 And they said, Stand back. And they said again, This one fellow came in to sojourn, and he will needs be a judge: now will we deal worse with thee, than with them. And they pressed sore upon the man, even Lot, and came near to break the door.

10 But the men put forth their hand, and pulled Lot into the house to them, and shut to the door.

11 And they smote the men that were at the door of the house with blindness, both small and great: so that they wearied themselves to find the door.

12 And the men said unto Lot, Hast thou any here besides? son in law, and thy sons, and thy daughters, and whatsoever thou hast in the city, bring them out of this place:

13 For we will destroy this place, because the cry of them is waxen great before the face of the Lord; and the Lord hath sent us to destroy it.

14 And Lot went out, and spake unto his sons in law, which married his daughters, and said, Up, get you out of this place; for the Lord will destroy this city. But he seemed as one that mocked unto his sons in law.

15 And when the morning arose, then the angels hastened Lot, saying, Arise, take thy wife, and thy two daughters, which are here; lest thou be consumed in the iniquity of the city.

16 And while he lingered, the men laid hold upon his hand, and upon the hand of his wife, and upon the hand of his two daughters; the Lord being merciful unto him: and they brought him forth, and set him without the city.

17 And it came to pass, when they had brought them forth abroad, that he said, Escape for thy life; look not behind thee, neither stay thou in all the plain; escape to the mountain, lest thou be consumed.

18 And Lot said unto them, Oh, not so, my Lord:

19 Behold now, thy servant hath found grace in thy sight, and thou hast magnified thy mercy, which thou hast shewed unto me in saving my life; and I cannot escape to the mountain, lest some evil take me, and I die:

20 Behold now, this city is near to flee unto, and it is a little one: Oh, let me escape thither, (is it not a little one?) and my soul shall live.

21 And he said unto him, See, I have accepted thee concerning this thing also, that I will not overthrow this city, for the which thou hast spoken.

22 Haste thee, escape thither; for I cannot do any thing till thou be come thither. Therefore the name of the city was called Zoar.

23 The sun was risen upon the earth when Lot entered into Zoar.

24 Then the Lord rained upon Sodom and upon Gomorrah brimstone and fire from the Lord out of heaven;

25 And he overthrew those cities, and all the plain, and all the inhabitants of the cities, and that which grew upon the ground.

26 But his wife looked back from behind him, and she became a pillar of salt.

27 And Abraham gat up early in the morning to the place where he stood before the Lord:

28 And he looked toward Sodom and Gomorrah, and toward all the land of the plain, and beheld, and, lo, the smoke of the country went up as the smoke of a furnace.

29 And it came to pass, when God destroyed the cities of the plain, that God remembered Abraham, and sent Lot out of the midst of the overthrow, when he overthrew the cities in which Lot dwelt.

30 And Lot went up out of Zoar, and dwelt in the mountain, and his two daughters

with him; for he feared to dwell in Zoar: and he dwelt in a cave, he and his two daughters.

31 And the firstborn said unto the younger, Our father is old, and there is not a man in the earth to come in unto us after the manner of all the earth:

32 Come, let us make our father drink wine, and we will lie with him, that we may preserve seed of our father.

33 And they made their father drink wine that night: and the firstborn went in, and lay with her father; and he perceived not when she lay down, nor when she arose.

34 And it came to pass on the morrow, that the firstborn said unto the younger, Behold, I lay yesternight with my father: let us make him drink wine this night also; and go thou in, and lie with him, that we may preserve seed of our father.

35 And they made their father drink wine that night also: and the younger arose, and lay with him; and he perceived not when she lay down, nor when she arose.

36 Thus were both the daughters of Lot with child by their father.

37 And the firstborn bare a son, and called his name Moab: the same is the father of the Moabites unto this day.

38 And the younger, she also bare a son, and called his name Ben-ammi: the same is the father of the children of Ammon unto this day.

## The Holiness Code (7th cent. B.C.E.?)

LEVITICUS 18:22

*Authorized (King James) Version*

Thou shalt not lie with mankind, as with womankind: it is abomination.

LEVITICUS 20:13

*Authorized (King James) Version*

If a man also lie with mankind, as he lieth with a woman, both of them have committed an abomination: they shall surely be put to death; their blood shall be upon them.

# The New Testament

## From the Epistles of St. Paul

ROMANS 1:26–27

*Authorized (King James) Version*

For this cause God gave them up unto vile affections: for even their women did change the natural use into that which is against nature: And likewise also the men, leaving the natural use of the woman, burned in their lust one toward another; men with men working that which is unseemly. . . .

1 CORINTHIANS 6:9 – 10
*Authorized (King James) Version*

. . . . Be not deceived: neither fornicators, nor idolaters, nor adulterers, no effeminate, nor abusers of themselves with mankind . . . shall inherit the kingdom of God.

# Policing Sodomites: Religious Commentary and Civil Law

## Religious Commentary

*Philo Judaeus (c. 13 B.C.E.–C.E. 45)*

From *De Abrahamo* (1st cent. C.E.)

*Translated by F. H. Colson*

The land of the Sodomites . . . was brimful of innumerable iniquities. . . . Not only
in their mad lust for women did they violate the marriages of their neighbours, but
also men mounted males without respect for the sex nature which the active partner shares with the passive. . . . Then, as little by little they accustomed those who
were by nature men to submit to play the part of women, they saddled them with
the formidable curse of a female disease. For not only did they emasculate their
bodies by luxury and voluptuousness, but they worked a further degeneration in
their souls and, so far as in them lay, were corrupting the whole of mankind.

*Clement of Alexandria (c. 150–215 C.E.)*

*Paedagogos* 3.8

The Sodomites had ". . . through much luxury fallen into uncleanness, practicing
adultery shamelessly, and burning with insane love for boys."

## Civil Law

FROM THE *THEODOSIAN CODE* 9.8.3 (342 C.E.)

When a man "marries" and is about to offer himself to men in a womanly fashion
. . . [let] the laws [be] armed with an avenging sword, that those infamous persons
who are now, or who hereafter may be guilty, be subjected to exquisite punishment.

THE CODE OF JUSTINIAN

## NOVELLA 77 (538 C.E.)

. . . since certain men, seized by diabolical incitement, practice among themselves
the most disgraceful lusts, and act contrary to nature: we enjoin them to take to
heart the fear of God and the judgment to come, and to abstain from suchlike diabolical and unlawful lusts, so that they may not be visited by the just wrath of God

on account of these impious acts, with the result that cities perish with all their inhabitants. For we are taught by the Holy Scriptures that because of like impious conduct cities have indeed perished, together with the men in them. For because of such crimes there are famines, earthquakes, and pestilences; wherefore we admonish men to abstain from said unlawful acts, that they may not lose their souls. But if, after this our admonition, any are found persisting in such offenses, first, they render themselves unworthy of the mercy of God, and then they are subjected to the punishment enjoined by the law. For we order the most illustrious prefect of the Capital to arrest those who persist in the aforesaid lawless and impious acts after they have been warned by us, and to inflict on them the extreme punishments, so that the city and the state may not come to harm by reason of such wicked deeds.

## NOVELLA 141 (544 C.E.)

[I]nstructed by the Holy Scriptures, we know that God brought a just judgment upon those who lived in Sodom, on account of this very madness of intercourse, so that to this very day that land burns with inextinguishable fire. By this God teaches us, in order that by means of legislation we may avert such an untoward fate. Again, we know what the blessed Apostle says about such things, and what laws our state enacts. Wherefore it behooves all who desire to fear God to abstain from conduct so base and criminal that we do not find it committed even by brute beasts. Let those who have not taken part in such doings continue to refrain in the future. But as for those who have been consumed by this kind of disease let them not only cease to sin in the future, but let them also do penance, and fall down before God and renounce their plague. . . . Next, we proclaim to all who are conscious that they have committed any such sin, that unless they desist and, renouncing it . . . they will bring upon themselves severer penalties, even though on other counts they are held guilty of no fault. For there will be no relaxation of enquiry and correction so far as this matter is concerned, nor will they be dealt with carelessly who do not submit themselves during the time of the holy season, or who persist in such impious conduct, lest if we are negligent we arouse God's anger against us. If, with eyes as it were blinded, we overlook such impious and forbidden conduct, we may provoke the good God to anger and bring ruin upon all—a fate which would be but deserved.

# England

## Henry I

### COUNCIL OF LONDON (C. 1102)

Conc. London. 28: In this council, those who commit the shameful sin of sodomy, and especially those who of their own free will take pleasure in doing so, were condemned by a weighty anathema, until by penitence and confession they should show themselves worthy of absolution. As for anyone who is found guilty of this crime, it was resolved that if he were an ecclesiastic he should not be promoted to any higher rank, and should be deposed from his present order; while if he were a layman he should be deprived of his legal status and dignity in the whole realm of England. And let none but the bishop presume to give absolution for this offense, save in the case of those who are members of the regular clergy.

## Edward I

### BRITTON 1.10 (C. 1290)

Let enquiry also be made of those who feloniously in time of peace have burnt others' corn or houses, and those who are attainted thereof shall be burnt, so that they may be punished in like manner as they have offended. The same sentence shall be passed upon sorcerers, sorceresses, renegades, sodomists, and heretics publicly convicted.

# 6. God Made Our Natures Full of Love

## Romantic Friendship Between Men in Literature from the Fourth to the Fourteenth Century of the Common Era

### Paulinus of Nola (353–431)

Paulinus, Bishop of Nola, wrote a poem to his former teacher Ausonius (310–395), the best Latin poet of the fourth century and the last "classical" poet of the decaying Roman Empire, that suggests the passion that could be attendant upon friendship between men. Paulinus draws upon the Platonic myth of the souls that seek their other half when he hopes that after death Ausonius will "share my soul." Paulinus, humane student of the last classical poet, reflects the world order that was passing.

[To Ausonius]

*Translated by Jack Lindsay*

Through all the fates of earth, through every spell
    that works on man its spleen,
while I am bolted in the body's cell,
    though worlds should come between,
I hold you mine, entwined in every part—
    not dim, with distant face.
Clasping you close, I see you in my heart,
    here and in every place;
and when, set free, I go another quest
    and pay no more earth's toll,
wherever God, our Father, bids me rest,
    still you shall share my soul.
O there's no end of love, we'll safely find,
    when there's an end of earth.
The mind survives the wreck of flesh, the mind
    from heaven had its birth.
The sense is quick, the emotion prospers yet,
    eternal in the sky.
The soul would die if it could once forget,
    and, friend, it cannot die.

### Hrabanus Maurus (776–856)

Hrabanus Maurus, Abbot of Fuld, wrote poems of eroticized friendship to Grimold, Abbot of St. Gall. His poems center the love of his friend in the love of Christ, yet as in the poem below, he suggests that such love can outlast the earth and heaven itself. The poem, couched in a vocabulary that is distinctly Christian, suggests that their intimacy is blessed by Christ himself.

[TO GRIMOLD, ABBOT OF ST. GALL]

*Translated by Helen Waddell*

Then live, my strength, anchor of weary ships,
    Safe shore and land at last, thou, for my wreck,
My honour, thou, and my abiding rest,
My city safe for a bewildered heart.
What though the plains and mountains and the sea
    Between us are, that which no earth can hold
Still follows thee, and love's own singing follows,
Longing that all things may be well with thee.
Christ who first gave thee for a friend to me,
Christ keep thee well, where'er thou art, for me.
    Earth's self shall go and the swift wheel of heaven
Perish and pass, before our love shall cease.
    Do but remember me, as I do thee,
And God, who brought us on this earth together,
Bring us together in His house of heaven.

## Walafrid Strabo (809–849)

Walafrid Strabo, born in Germany and eventually Abbot of Reichnau, maintained a poetic correspondence with his friend Liutger.

[DEAREST, YOU COME SUDDENLY AND SUDDENLY YOU DEPART]

*Translated by John Boswell*

Dearest, you come suddenly, and suddenly, dearest, you depart:
I hear, I do not see, yet inwardly I see, and inwardly
I embrace you, fleeing in body, but not in love.
For as certain as I have been, I am and shall always be
That I am cherished in your heart, and you in mine.
Nor shall time persuade me, nor you, of anything else . . .

[WHEN THE SPLENDOR OF THE MOON]

*Translated by Helen Waddell*

When the moon's splendour shines in naked heaven,
    Stand thou and gaze beneath the open sky.
See how that radiance from her lamp is riven,
    And in one splendour foldeth gloriously

Two that have loved, and now divided far,
Bound by love's bond, in heart together are.

What though thy lover's eyes in vain desire thee,
    Seek for love's face, and find that face denied?
Let that light be between us for a token;
    Take this poor verse that love and faith inscribe.
Love, art thou true? and fast love's chain about thee?
Then for all time, o love, God give thee joy!

## Marbod of Rennes (1035–1123)

Marbod of Rennes, born in Angers, was master of the Cathedral school and eventually became Bishop of Rennes in 1097. He wrote poetry addressed both to women and to men and praises the beauty of girls and boys equally and often seems rather casually indifferent to the sex of the person he loves, an attitude not dissimilar to that in classical texts.

[THE UNYIELDING YOUTH]

*Translated by John Boswell*

Horace composed an ode about a certain boy
Whose face was so lovely he could easily have been a girl,
Whose hair fell in waves against his ivory neck,
Whose forehead was white as snow and his eyes as black as pitch,
Whose soft cheeks were full of delicious sweetness
When they bloomed in the brightness of a blush of beauty.
His nose was perfect, his lips flame red, lovely his teeth—
An exterior formed in measure to match his mind.

. . . . . . . . . . . . . . . . . . . . . . . . . . . .

This vision of a face, radiant and full of beauty,
Kindled with the torch of love the heart of whoever beheld him.
But this boy, so lovely and appealing,
A torment to all who looked upon him,
Was made by nature so cruel and unyielding
That he would die rather than yield to love.
Harsh and ungrateful, as if born of a tiger,
He only laughed at the soft words of admirers,
Laughed at their vain efforts,
Laughed at the tears of a sighing lover.
He laughed at those whom he himself was causing to perish.
Surely he is wicked, cruel and wicked,
Who by the viciousness of his character denies the beauty of his body.
A fair face should have a wholesome mind,
Patient and not proud but yielding in this or that.
The little flower of age is swift, of surpassing brevity;
Soon it wastes away, vanishes, and cannot be revived.

This flesh so fair, so milky, so flawless,
So healthy, so lovely, so glowing, so soft—
The time will come when it is ugly and rough,
When this youthful skin will become repulsive.
So while you bloom, adopt a more becoming demeanor.

## Baudri of Bourgueil (1046–1130)

Baudri of Bourgueil was a pupil of Marbod's at Angers. He became a Benedictine monk
and eventually Archbishop of Dol in Brittany. He wrote over two hundred poems, most
addressed to men, only fifteen to women. Baudri confesses that "I wrote of certain things
which treat of love/And both sexes are pleased with my songs."

### [YOUR APPEARANCE IS PLEASING]

*Translated by Thomas Stehling*

Your appearance is pleasing because it is proper and handsome;
So too your delicate cheek, your blond hair, and modest mouth.
Your voice, sounding as sweetly as the nightingale's,
Caresses and soothes our ears.
It could be a boy's or a girl's;
You will be another Orpheus, unless age injures it—
Age which distinguishes girls from boys
When young men's cheeks are first clothed with down
And a strong nose enhances their faces and looks.
Your bright, clear eyes touch my breast and heart,
For I believe those crystalline lights truly are a double star.
Your milky flesh and ivory chest match them;
The touch of hands plays over your snowy body.
    (No. 38, ll. 7–19)

## Hilary (c. 1125)

The English poet Hilary wrote a number of poems that passionately praise handsome
young men. Hilary's love poems to boys bring to medieval poetry a new kind of direct
homoeroticism that at once recalls classical conventions and mirrors and forecasts some
of the conventions of the poetry of courtly love: his love for the boy is a sickness that only
the boy can cure, no other mortal is as beautiful as he, the boy's power over him is like
that of the hunter over the hunted, the whims of the boy hold him in thrall.

### [TO AN ENGLISH BOY]

*Translated by John Boswell*

Hail, fair youth, who seeks no bribe,
Who regards being won with a gift as the height of vice,

In whom beauty and honesty have made their home,
Whose comeliness draws to itself the eyes of all who see him.

Golden haired, fair of face, with a small white neck,
Soft-spoken and gentle — but why do I praise these singly?
Everything about you is beautiful and lovely; you have no imperfection,
Except that such fairness has no business devoting itself to chastity.

When nature formed you, she doubted for a moment
Whether to offer you as a girl or a boy,
But while she sets her mind's eye to settling this,
Behold! You come forth born as a vision for all.

Afterward, she does finally extend her hand to you
And is astonished that she could have created anyone like you.
But it is clear that nature erred in only this one thing:
That when she had bestowed on you so much, she made you mortal.

No other mortal can be compared with you,
Whom nature made for herself, as if an only child;
Beauty establishes its home in you,
Whose sweet flesh shines as brightly as the lily.

## Ganymede (12th–13th cent.)

By the later Middle Ages Ganymede's name was invoked not only in texts sympathetic to male-male love but in those that attacked it: an eleventh-century bishop is excoriated as being "ganimedior est Ganimede"—more like Ganymede than Ganymede (quoted in Boswell, *Christianity, Social Tolerance, and Homosexuality* [1980:217]), while Hidebert of Lavardin attacks the "plague of Sodom" and employs "Ganymede" to indicate sodomites ("Numberless ganymedes cultivate countless shrines . . . both man and boy are sullied by this vice . . . and no way of life escapes it"). Hidebert warns that one should not "expect to go to heaven for the sin of ganymede" (Boswell 1980:236–37). Yet Hidebert himself in a poem attributed to him describes Jove's passion for Ganymede and observes, "The god ordained that all things were licit with a boy" (Boswell 1980:401). In *Hebe and Ganymede*, Ganymede is the unapologetic advocate of homosexual love. The poem is an example of an extensive debate literature that argued the merits of desire for boys and of that for women. By the beginning of the thirteenth century, Ganymede—the androgynous and somewhat wanton boy—had become the eponymous symbol for homosexual love. In the following I have deleted the translator's textual notes. For these see John Boswell (1980:392–95).

HEBE AND GANYMEDE

*Translated by John Boswell*

After the abduction by the eagle, after the lovely indiscretion with the boy,
Juno bemoans in her chambers the cup stolen from Hebe.

But she dares not air her grief openly,
So she rouses Hebe to the fight and promises her aid.

She arms her beforehand with rhetorical devices,
Teaches her sharp words to cut the boy to the quick.

From her mistress the servant learns her part:
What words to use, what arts to employ.

The council is convened and begins to consider the arguments.
When Hebe seeks justice in its midst and begins to speak,

Her face reddens, and the hue of her countenance colors her words.
She blushes to speak, and her blush itself says all.

"Immortal race, image of eternal Paris,
Treasure of nature, nature's first source,

You who restrain the unjust by divine law,
I seek justice from the just; I ask that rights be restored to the injured.

I was Jove's cup bearer while grace allowed,
With the . . . [?] of Jove, and with the sanction of your blessing.

But a new arrival has occupied my place: a unique enemy.
Should I keep silent, boy? Why? You know all.

The Phrygian youth and Troy's shame have invaded the heavens
And founded Trojan strongholds in the skies.

Here a hare hunts hare; he breathes his charm
And the scent of game into the heavens.

A new prey, the boy! Preying on what is mine.
Has the abducted come to ravish the rights of goddesses?

But the fates prepare justice, as you, Apollo, urge.
Troy is in ruins, and a woman will render its just deserts.

Already our young man has invaded the marriage rites;
Already the ends of the earth are marked with his name as gifts for him.

O houses and seats of virtue! O mindless lust!
In you sounds the dead flute of Troy.

Here with a movement of his side, of his leg, his foot,
Virtue is cast aside and sits and weeps from afar.

He adorns his face and curls his hair with an iron.
With Ganymede as master, crime spreads everywhere.

With his face he provides reason for a thousand evils;
With such an incentive, let every god beware—

Those thousand deities of land and sea and sky.
A boy—this impure boy—is wed in heaven.

The lord summons the Trojan nephew by day
And importunes him by night.

I pass over what Jove's handmaid is about by day,
But this I say: Who sleeps with her at night?

Already, O gods, Nature blushes, and the kindly mother
Implores you with tears, let the punishment fit the crime.

This Juno asks, and Pallas, and the other goddesses:
Let the judgment of the goddesses be swift."

She had finished. A murmur begins, and a louder tumult,
But the boy rises: his face commands silence.

Night has fled, and the day follows. As the sun outshines the moon,
So the glory of Ganymede surpasses that of Hebe.

Atlas, who bears it, delights in the weight of this star,
And Pallas is moved by him for whom a woman sighed.

Apollo thinks of Hyacinth, Silvanus of Ciparissus;
Venus remembers Adonis: such beauty was his.

Mars, as if embracing him, looks with longing eyes
And sighs, seeing the delicate lips, for tender kisses.

Silently his joys conquer Jove; he imagines
He is more of a god because in this even grace yields to him.

He raises his eyes from the ground, like a Trojan son,
And seems to spread twin suns in the sky.

Such beauty would implore pardon if he sinned:
His face and body intercede for him with the lord.

His mind is shaken by all this, like a boy in a childhood fright,
[But] words of grace flow from his sweet mouth.

"The father of Trojans is here, and his whole posterity;
The people of Teucer are noted among the stars.

What have I done? I did not force my arms into the heavens.
I was shown the way—not ravished—by my loving friend.

'Jove's company,' he said, 'the council of the gods,
The heavens, the fates—all will welcome you to life in the skies.'

So I accepted the offered glory and enjoy it: Is this the charge against me?
Was my mixing the nectar a base offer from a base person?

Or was it better for a vile old woman with the hand of a Moor—
A shrew like this—to be the servant of Jove's table?

As long as Jove is Jove, I will be whatever you want.
Before, a woman reared her haunches; now a man offers his mouth.

Those who assail a particular type of sex—which is approved regardless of type—
Are fools: a thunderbolt will strike the gaping hole.

Would you look at the sky during the day to see if the moon is full?
And do you blush with every wave of the Red Sea?

In a wolf's den the woman sits and spins tales;
Speaking falsehood with deceit, the pen of her tongue paints evil.

Was it my fault that Ida pleased the hunters?
No woman faithless to herself can be expected to keep faith.

She assails and provokes me with the poison of long speaking,
But a rare thing is a chaste whore or a peaceful woman.

Either I rightly enjoy the ruler in heaven, or one must regard as a crime
Something which the providence of fate has made necessary."

## From *The Leiden Manuscript* (12th cent.)

[THE WISE REJOICE WITH GANYMEDE]

*Translated by John Boswell*

The indiscriminate Venus grasps at any remedy,
But the wise one rejoices with the tender Ganymede.

I have heard it said that he plays Venus more than she,
But Venus is happy, since he only stuffs boys.

Nothing is more certain than this, that Venus would
Be devoid of every sweetness if she lacked Ganymede.

For his face smiles, his complexion shines, his legs are soft,
His lap is sweet, his heart gentle and his beauty charming;
His demeanor is open, suppressing shyness, his spirit
Is ready for the boyish sin, and his body prepared
To undergo anything his seducer should ask:
This boy surpasses all treasure; nothing is more blessed than he.

Many you will find for whom the boyish sin is execrable in words
But who do not dislike the deed.
　　The more they detest it with their words—to hide what they love and freely
do—
　　The more they indulge it in their acts.

Venus kindles all fires, but the greatest heat
Is in sex with males; whoever has tried it knows it . . .

## The Story of Lancelot and Galehaut

The Old French *Lancelot-Grail*, in which Lancelot and his friend Galehaut (also, vari-
ously, Galahut, Galehout, Galehut) share knightly quests and manly devotion, reveals the
world of men at arms to be one also of passion and perhaps desire. Lancelot and Galehaut
appear in one of the many Arthurian romances and from the moment of their meeting in
battle are bound together not only by loyalty but by an outspoken and specifically
described passion. Lancelot is the center of Galehaut's life, and though Lancelot loves
Guinevere, as the legend obliges him to do, yet there can be no doubt that the two men
share an intimacy that even Guinevere and King Arthur must recognize and honor.

FROM *LANCELOT-GRAIL* (PART II)

*Translated by Carleton W. Carroll*

[In a battle against King Arthur, the knight Galehaut is amazed by the feats of a mysterious Black Knight. When fighting ceases for the day, Galehaut follows him.]

When night fell, they began to disperse on each side, and he [the Black Knight]
went off as secretly as he could and went up the fields between the hill and the
river. And Galehaut, who was paying close attention to him, saw him go, spurred
his horse in pursuit and followed him at a distance along the path on the hill, until
he caught up with him at the bottom. He drew alongside him as courteously as he
could and said, "God bless you, my lord!"
　　The other looked at him askance and reluctantly returned his greeting.
　　"My lord," said Galehaut, "who are you?"
　　"Good sir, I am a knight, as you can see."

"Indeed," said Galehaut, "a knight you are, the best there is, and the man I would most wish to honor in all the world: I've come to ask you, as a favor, to come stay with me tonight."

And the knight spoke to him as if he did not know him and had never seen him before: "Who are you, my lord, who beg me to stay with you?"

"My lord," he said, "I am Galehaut, son of the Fair Giantess, lord of all these troops against whom you have today defended the kingdom of Logres, which I had made a good start at conquering, and I would have conquered it, had it not been for you."

"What?" exclaimed the knight. "You are an enemy of King Arthur, and you ask me to stay with you? I'll never stay with you, God willing, as things now stand."

"My lord," said Galehaut, "I would do more for you than you believe, and I have already begun. Again I beg you, for God's sake, to stay with me tonight, on condition that I'll do whatever you ask of me."

Then the knight halted, and looked fixedly at Galehaut and said, "Truly, my lord, you are a great maker of promises! But I don't know how good you are at keeping them."

And Galehaut replied, "My lord, I tell you truly that I make the fewest promises of any powerful man in the world. And again I assure you that if you come stay with me I'll grant you what you ask of me, and I'll guarantee this in whatever way you stipulate."

"My lord," said the knight, "you are considered a very worthy knight, and it would not be to your honor to promise something if you didn't intend to keep your word."

"My lord," said Galehaut, "have no doubt of that, for I wouldn't lie to win the whole kingdom of Logres. And I pledge you, on my honor as a loyal knight, that I'll give you what you ask of me, for I'm not a king, and I wish to have your company this night; and if I can have more of it, I'll take it. And if you're not satisfied with my pledge, I'll make whatever additional guarantees you wish."

"My lord," said the knight, "it seems to me that you greatly desire my company, if your intentions are like your words. I'll stay with you tonight, provided you pledge to give me whatever I ask. And I ask you to give me an additional guarantee."

Thus the two of them reached an agreement, and Galehaut pledged that he would honor his side of the compact.

. . . . They kept on riding meanwhile, and when they approached the camp, the knight called to Galehaut and said, "My lord, I'm going with you, but I request, before I enter your camp, that you arrange for me speak to the two gentlemen you most trust in all the world." And he granted that.

Then Galehaut went to two of his men and said, "Follow me, and this very night you'll see the most powerful man in all the world."

And they said to him, "What, my lord, are you not the most powerful man in all the world?"

"No," he said, "but I will be this very night, before I go to sleep."

. . . . With such joy was the knight received and honored. When his armor had been removed, Galehaut had a very costly and beautiful robe brought to him, and after much urging, the knight put it on. When it was time to eat, they ate.

Afterwards, Galehaut had four beds prepared in his chamber: one was very large, both broad and high; the second, beside it, was less large; the other two were much smaller. When the high bed was adorned with all the finery that can be put upon a bed—and this was all for the knight who was to sleep there—and it came time for bed, Galehaut said to him, "My lord, you will sleep in that bed."

"My lord," said the knight, "then who will sleep in the other beds?"

"My lord," said Galehaut, "my servants who will keep you company; I'll sleep in a nearby chamber, with my men, to solace and comfort them; you'll sleep here, where you will be more tranquil and more comfortable."

"My lord," he said, "for God's sake, don't make me lie higher than the other knights who are to keep me company; you mustn't disgrace me so."

"Don't be concerned," said Galehaut; "you'll never be considered base or cowardly because of what you do by my orders."

Then Galehaut departed. The knight began to think about the great honor shown him by Galehaut, and in his heart he esteemed him most highly. Once he was in bed, he very quickly fell asleep, for he was exceedingly tired. When Galehaut was sure the knight was asleep, he lay down beside him as quietly as he could, and two of his knights joined him; there were no others in the room. The knight slept very soundly, but all night long he moaned in his sleep. Galehaut heard him clearly, for he scarcely slept at all, but spent the time thinking of a way to retain the knight.

In the morning the knight rose and heard Mass. Galehaut had already risen quietly, for he did not wish the knight to notice. When they had heard Mass, the knight asked for his armor; Galehaut asked him why, and he replied that he wished to leave. Then Galehaut said to him, "My dear friend, stay yet awhile, and do not think I wish to deceive you, for there's nothing you could request that you would not have, if you will stay. I assure you, you can have the company of a more powerful man than I, but you'll never have that of a man who loves you as much. And since I would do more than anyone else to have your company, then I deserve it more than anyone else."

"My lord," said the knight, "I'll stay, for I could have no better company than yours. Now I'll tell you the gift that will make me stay; if I don't receive it, your talk of staying will be in vain."

"My lord," said Galehaut, "speak confidently, and you'll have it, if it is within my power."

Then the knight called for the two guarantors, and in their presence said, "My lord, I ask you that as soon as you overcome King Arthur, and his forces are totally unable to recover, as soon as I summon you, you are to ask him for mercy and put yourself entirely in his power."

When Galehaut heard this, he was aghast and became very pensive. And the two kings said to him, "My lord, what are you thinking about? There is nothing to be gained from reflection now: you have gone so far that there is no turning back."

"What?" he exclaimed. "Do you suppose I have any regrets? If all the world were mine, I wouldn't hesitate to give it to him. I was thinking of the splendid thing he said, for never did any man say anything finer. My lord," he said, "may God never help me if you don't receive this gift, for I could do nothing for you that would bring me shame, but I beg you not to deprive me of your company, since I would do more to have you with me than any other."

The knight granted him this, and he remained. The meal was prepared, and they went to eat. In Galehaut's camp there was great rejoicing over the knight who was staying, but in King Arthur's camp, where they did not know of the compact, there was bitter mourning.

So they spent that day. The next day Galehaut and his companion rose and went to hear Mass. And Galehaut said, "My lord, today is the day of the battle; do you intend to fight?" The knight replied that he did. "Then I ask you," said Galehaut, "to wear my armor, as a beginning of our companionship."

He answered, "Most willingly. But you must not wear the armor of a foot-soldier."

"No, if you wish it," said Galehaut.

Then they had the armor brought, and they completely armed the knight except for the hauberk and the greaves, which were too large. Then Galehaut's men put on their armor, as did King Arthur's, and all who were there passed onto the field of battle.

[The Black Knight wins in battle, and as agreed Galehaut swears allegiance to King Arthur. Galehaut goes to attend the king but at night returns to his castle and the Black Knight.]

He returned to his companion and asked him how he had been; he replied, "Very well."

Then Galehaut said to him, "My lord, what shall I do? The king has insistently begged me to return to him, but it would grieve me to leave you at this point."

"Ah, my lord," said the knight, "for God's sake, you must do what my lord the king wishes, for be assured that you have never met a more worthy man than he. But I wish to ask a favor of you, which it will be to your benefit and mine for you to grant."

Galehaut replied, "Ask whatever you wish, and I'll never refuse you, for you are dearer to me than worldly honor."

"My lord," he said, "many thanks. You have granted that you will not ask me my name until I have revealed it to you, or someone else has done so for me."

"Then I will keep silent," said Galehaut, "since you wish it so, and yet that would have been the first thing I would have asked, but I don't wish to know it until you wish me to."

[Galehaut returns again to court and upon returning to his own tents the next day learns that the knight has been in despair all the preceding night. The Black Knight—who is, of course Sir Lancelot—reveals to Galehaut that he loves the queen. The queen commands Galehaut to bring the unknown knight to her. They meet and the queen accepts his love and they vow fidelity.]

Then the queen, who was a most wise and worthy lady, began to speak: "Dear friend," she said to the knight, "I'm yours, because you have done so much, and this gives me great joy. Now take care that this be kept secret: this is necessary, for I'm one of the ladies in all the world about whom the greatest good has been said. If my reputation were to suffer because of you, it would be a base and ugly love. And I ask the same of you, Galehaut, who are so wise, for if harm came to me from this, it could only be because of you; but if it brings me benefit or joy, you will have bestowed it."

"My lady," said Galehaut, "he could do you no wrong, but I've merely done what you ordered me to do. Now you must hear a request from me, for I told you yesterday that you could soon do more for me than I for you."

"Speak confidently," she said, "for there's nothing you could request that I wouldn't do."

"Then you have accepted, my lady," he said, "to grant me his companionship."

"Indeed," she replied, "if you didn't have that, then you would have profited little by the great sacrifice you made for him."

Then she took the knight by the right hand and said, "Galehaut, I give you this knight forevermore, except for what I have previously had of him. And you," she said to the knight, "give your solemn word on this." And the knight did so. "Now do you know," she said to Galehaut, "whom I have given you?"

"My lady, I do not."

"I have given you Lancelot of the Lake, the son of King Ban of Benoic."

And in this way she revealed his identity to Galehaut, whose joy was the greatest he had ever known, for he had heard many rumors that this was Lancelot of the Lake and that he was the finest knight in the world, though landless, and he knew well that King Ban had been a very noble man.


## From *Lancelot-Grail* (Part III)

*Translated by Samuel N. Rosenberg*

[Many battles and trials ensue. In one, King Arthur, Sir Gawain, and Galehaut are captured and imprisoned. Lancelot goes to rescue them. Galehaut, however, believes that Lancelot is dead.]

Now, riding away with his companion, Galehaut was both happy and unhappy: happy that he had his companion with him and unhappy that he had become part of King Arthur's household, for he was sure that he would thereby lose him forever. And he had given him his heart with a love greater than loyal companionship alone could make a man feel for someone outside his family. But no proof of this is needed here, for in the end, as our story will go on to show, it was clear that the grief it caused him swept away all joy and brought him death. But his death ought not be spoken of at this point, for the death of such a worthy man as Galehaut is not a thing to bring up before its time. And all the stories that speak of him agree that he was in every way the most valiant of all great princes, after King Arthur, with whom no man living in those years can be compared.

[Galehaut and Lancelot return to Sorelois, Galehaut's castle, where Galehaut hears alarming news.]

[Galehaut] and Lancelot, accompanied by only four squires, rode along down-cast and thoughtful. They were both upset, Galehaut because he feared losing his companion to the king's household to which he now belonged, and Lancelot heavyhearted over the lady he was leaving behind and heavily burdened by the suf-fering he was causing Galehaut. They were so worried about each other that they both lost all appetite for food or drink, and they were so caught up in brooding that their faces paled and their strength was sapped. Each, out of loyal friendship, was so concerned about the other that neither dared to utter a word that might prove hurtful, as if they felt they had wronged each other in some way.

But no sorrow could match Galehaut's, for he had put into his love for Lancelot everything a man could put: heart and body and, most precious of all, his honor. He had so given up his body to him that he would rather have seen himself die than Lancelot; he had so given him his heart that he could have no joy without him. And out of his great love for him he had cried mercy to King Arthur even though he had overcome the king and almost dispossessed him.

They rode along like this until they drew near to the kingdom of Sorelois, and Galehaut was so far along that all he could think of was death. The night before coming to Sorelois, they reached a castle belonging to the king of the Franks that was named the King's Fortress, for the kingdom of the Franks bordered Sorelois on the northwest, which is where the Humber flows. That night Galehaut was very sick, though he put on a better face than his heart would have dictated. Lancelot, who was sorely pained by his sickness, did his best to soothe him, but to no avail; nor did Lancelot dare ask the reason for his suffering, because he remembered how graciously Galehaut had endured his suffering, without asking a thing, when they became companions. On the other hand, Lancelot thought too that he could not go on like this for long but would have to seek the truth from him, for he could not bear the thought that Galehaut might be burdened on his account; and he had lit-tle doubt that the trouble lay indeed with him.

When Galehaut was in bed and thought that Lancelot was asleep, he began to grieve and between groans and tears kept saying, "God! How he betrayed me, that man who was so honorable!"

Galehaut's lament went on right through the night, but while he lay in pain, Lancelot lay at ease, sleeping until day. In the morning they mounted their horses and left the castle, taking the straight road to Sorelois. Galehaut, his hood half-cov-ering his face, was riding behind the others but then, head bowed, spurred his horse forward to the utmost and pulled ahead of Lancelot and the squires. Then they came into a forest named Glorinde, which stood between the land of the Frankish king and Sorelois, over there where the Humber flows.

Galehaut rode along so sad and downcast that he never said a word to Lancelot or anyone else; his palfrey, meanwhile, was covered with sweat. Then he started down a stony path. The knight, tall and heavy and full of sad thoughts as he was, was a great burden for the horse, and the pace of their movement was a further trial. The animal stumbled on one of the stones thickly scattered along the path, falling to its two front knees as the reins flew out of Galehaut's hands and startled him out of his thoughts. Vexed by the horse's fall, he struck the animal so hard with his spurs that blood spurted from both flanks, and the horse reared and rushed forward with all its strength. Galehaut, unable to seize the reins dangling from the horse's neck, lost his grip in the rush forward and went flying out of his saddle in a rough somersault that badly wrenched his neck.

Galehaut, tall as he was, was hurled out of the saddle, and his back hit the stones with such a thud that his heart nearly burst in his chest. When Lancelot saw him fall like that, he feared Galehaut was dead; he jumped down from his horse and ran toward where he was lying. When he saw that not one limb was moving, he cried out in the loudest possible voice, "Holy Mary!" Then he bent down to embrace him, and the stabbing pain he felt in his heart lest Galehaut be dead chilled him through; he fell to the ground in a faint and lay stretched out alongside his companion. In the fall he hit his forehead against the sharp edge of a stone, which cut through skin and flesh above the left eyebrow all the way to the skull.

The four squires were all shocked, thinking that both men were dead. They wrung their hands and pulled out their hair and carried on so that their grief could not have been greater. But it was not long before Galehaut stirred and groaned loudly and, opening his eyes, stared in wonder at the men around him. But at the sight of Lancelot and the blood streaming from his wound, he was deeply pained, even more than by his own injuries. When he saw him come to, he asked him what had happened, and Lancelot told him through his sighs how fearful he had been for Galehaut's life. Galehaut, astonished by all this, turned to treat Lancelot's wound himself; then a squire brought him up a fresh palfrey, as the first had died. He mounted and the two started off again, and so did the squires.

[Lancelot's wounds so frighten Galehaut that he begins talking with Lancelot more than he had done before. Lancelot entreats him to be forthright.]

"Please, my lord," he said, "if I have ever done anything to please you, tell me the truth without holding anything back. You shouldn't keep any secrets from me, because you well know that I love you more than any man who has ever lived; and I am right to do so, since I owe all my success to you."

"No," said Galehaut, "I can't hide my heart from you. I'll tell you what I have never dared tell anyone else. The sadness and anguish that I have been feeling all this while go back to two cruel and frightening dreams that I had not long ago. It seemed to me, as I slept, that I was in my lord King Arthur's court, together with a great company of knights. Out of the queen's room came a serpent, the biggest I had ever heard of, and it was coming straight toward me, and all the fire and flames it was belching forth made me lose half of my limbs. That's what I dreamt the first night. In the second dream I seemed to have two hearts in my chest, so alike that they could hardly be told apart. And when I looked at myself, I lost one of them. And once it was gone from me, it turned into a leopard and threw itself into the midst of a great pack of wild beasts. With that, my heart and my whole body suddenly dried up, and I dreamt that I was dying. Those are the two dreams that made me brood so much, and I'll never rest until I know for certain what they mean, though I do know something about them even now."

"My lord," said Lancelot, "you are too wise a man to believe in dreams! A dream can't reveal any truth. It's as false in the dreaming as in the foretelling, and you have nothing to be afraid of. No man in the world is powerful enough to overcome you; you are the most powerful man alive today!"

"There is no way I can be harmed," said Galehaut, "except by one man; and if he wants to harm me, I am beyond help. But if there is any learning that can teach me what my two dreams mean, I will find out, for I have never had so great a desire to know something as I have now."

[They ride toward Galehaut's castle. As they near it, Lancelot thinks about Galehaut and they discuss their companionship and the question of the queen.]

Thus the two companions rode along talking, and Lancelot was very surprised by what Galehaut had just told him. "God!" he thought to himself, "this man should really hate me, for all these things I've stopped him from doing! I have turned the most vigorous man into the most sluggish. That's what I've done to him!"

Lancelot was deeply pained and wept so hard that the tears fell from his eyes onto his front saddlebow, but he took care not to let Galehaut notice. . . .

[They discuss the question of the queen, and Galehaut becomes more impassioned.]

"My good companion, the forebodings in my heart concern only two possible fears, for you and for myself; and I would greet the misfortune of one of us just as I would the other. Moreover, I have framed my love in such a way that if you died I would pray God to let me not live another day. I am very much afraid I will lose you soon, afraid we will be parted by death or some other separation. I'll tell you, too, that if the queen were as kindhearted toward me as I have been toward her, she wouldn't strip me of your companionship and offer it to someone else, even if I had done no more for her than fulfill her great desire and bring you your great joy. Still, I mustn't blame her if she wants to please her own heart more than another's; she even told me once that you can't be generous with something that you can't give up. And I have realized as much. So I want you to know that when I lose you, the world will lose me."

"Please God, my lord," said Lancelot, "our bond will never be broken! You have done so much for me that I would never dare do anything against your will. And it's only because you wanted it—and my lady, too—that I belong to King Arthur's household, since if my own heart had had its way, I'd have never stayed there."

Thus the two of them went on talking, and Lancelot offered whatever comfort he could, until Galehaut showed more cheer than had long been the case.

[The next day they go to the city of Alantine where Galehaut determines to seek counsel concerning his dream from the King's wise men.]

In the morning he dictated letters to his learned clerks, and he sent word to all the barons who held land from him that, as they prized his love, they should join him before Christmas in his castle at Sorelois, each bringing along the best advisors he could find, whether men of learning or knights. Next, he sent a letter to King Arthur, asking him, as his lord and his friend, to please send him the wisest men in his land, the very ones, in fact, who had interpreted Arthur's own dream; he said he now needed such help more than ever before.

[Galehaut speaks to the learned men that King Arthur has sent.]

"Into my heart . . . a sickness has crept that is destroying me. I have lost all craving for food and drink, and can find no rest in bed. Nor do I know where this sickness has come from, though I think it came over me only lately, when a certain fear overtook me as well. Yet I don't know for sure which came from which, the fear from the sickness or the sickness from the fear; it all happened to me at once.

"This is why I have sent for you. This is the guidance I mentioned that I need so much. Please give it all your thought, for the sake of God, of course, and for love of King Arthur, too, and for the sake of great rewards, but also to bind to yourselves forever a man of my kind."

[The wise men offer various explanations of his illness and foretell his death. Galehaut questions the tenth wise man as Lancelot looks on.]

"My lord," said the learned man, "when you want to treat a man's wound, you don't attend to it as his heart would like but as the treatment requires, since healing comes not from the heart's desire but from good medicine. For that reason you need to follow my instructions; if not, you will be denying my skill. In no way will I have the two of you listen to what I want to say, even though I know that you would not like to hear anything that this knight could not hear as well. But I will not be swayed: no one is to hear our conversation but God and the two of us alone."

He stopped speaking, and Galehaut looked at Lancelot. Lancelot rose at once and went out of the chapel, so anguished and pained that he did not know where to reach for comfort. He flung himself into a small room, closing the door behind him, and there gave vent to his immense grief, for he was quite sure that Galehaut expected his death to come through him.

While Lancelot was grieving, Master Elias said to Galehaut in the chapel, "My lord, I believe you are one of the wisest princes of our time in the whole world and I am sure that, if you have behaved foolishly, it was more out of goodness of heart than lack of intelligence, so I'll give you a very useful little lesson: take care, as far as you can, never to say in front of any man or woman with whom you are in love anything that would trouble his or her heart, for everyone should do his utmost to keep anger and distress away from the one he loves. I say this because of the knight who has just left us. I know that you love him with all the love that can exist between two true companions, and would have wanted him to share in this discussion. But it would have been wrong, as he would have risked hearing words that would have burdened his heart with shame and sorrow, and he would perhaps have been more pained than you will be. Of course, you could never care less for his happiness or his welfare than he could, but you are more sensible and reasonable than he."

"Master," said Galehaut, "it seems you know him well, to judge by what you say."

"I do," he answered; "I think I know him, though not through any personal report save that I have heard that the man who made peace between you and King Arthur is the finest knight alive. He is the leopard that appeared in your dream and in our findings."

[Elias then shows Galehaut the holiest things in the world.]

Master Elias said, "My lord, take this box, which encloses the holiest thing in the whole world, and I'll hold the cross, which is the next most noble. As long as we hold them, we need not fear any untoward event."

Then Master Elias sat down on a stone bench, opened his book, and began to read. He went on at length, until his heart grew very warm and his face became flushed; from his forehead sweat trickled down his cheeks, and he began to weep and could not stop.

. . . . Then, in almost no time at all, such thick darkness settled over the chapel that you could no more see anything there than if it were an abyss. A voice called out, so hideous and shrill that in the whole city of Sorhaut [sic] there was no man or woman who did not hear it. Galehaut, stunned by the voice, put the box down in front of him and flattened himself face down on the ground. . . .

Then the darkness faded away and the light of day came back. Master Elias came out of his faint, heaving sad sighs and looking all around. He asked Galehaut how he was, and he answered that all was well now, thank God. But only a moment later the ground began to quake.

"My lord," said Master Elias, "lean against that seat over there. Your body can't support you by itself through the wonders that you're about to see."

Galehaut leaned against the seat, and his master against a stone pillar; and all along Galehaut held on to the box. Soon it seemed to the two men that the whole chapel was spinning. When it stopped, Galehaut looked up and saw nearby, coming through the tightly shut door, a hand and arm that went back as far as the shoulder. It was wearing a wide sleeve of purple satin that trailed down to the floor; the sleeve came down a little below the elbow, and from that point forward to the wrist the arm was covered with a kind of white silk. The arm was extraordinarily long, and the hand was as red as live coals and held a sword just as red, which was dripping red blood from the hilt to the point.

The sword came right up to Master Elias and looked as if it were about to run him through and kill him. In his terror, he held the cross out in front of him, and the sword began to circle him, still threatening to kill him; he kept moving the cross around to face it down. In a while, he became aware that it was moving away from him and straight toward Galehaut. Galehaut held the box out in front of him, just as he had seen Master Elias do, and went on like that until the sword moved away from him as well. With the arm and hand that gripped it, it went up to the wall where the black circles were drawn and struck so sharply into the stone that half a foot of it came away, removing three of the circles and part of a fourth. Having done this, it turned back to the door it had come through and disappeared.

Galehaut was more astonished than he had ever been in his life. When he could speak, he said, "You have really kept your promise to me, master. You have shown me, as far as I can tell, the greatest wonders that have ever been witnessed, and you have let it be clear to me that I still have three years and more to live. . . .

"Now I'll tell you," said Master Elias, "that I was very worried about your death when I showed you those symbols of it. You might yet live beyond the end indicated, but that depends upon my lady the queen. And if you could somehow have your companion remain with you, you would indeed live beyond it, because your death will only come from his absence."

[The story details many battles and complicated subplots during which Lancelot is wounded, champions Guinevere, breaks with and is reconciled with Arthur, and is imprisoned by Morgan le Fay. Galehaut sets out to find him and, discovering Lancelot's shield, battles successfully, though not without being wounded, to gain possession of it. He eventually hears news that Lancelot has escaped and is alive and seeks him at the castle of Sorelois. In the meantime, Lancelot fights in a tournament and for the first time is defeated. He goes to seek Galehaut.]

Then Lancelot . . . pondered and wondered where he might go; in the end, he made up his mind to go to Galehaut, who had always been so good to him, and he started on his way to Sorelois. If he had known that Galehaut was away looking for him, he would not have gone there. . . . When he reached Sorelois, he was welcomed very warmly, but of Galehaut he found no trace, since he and Lionel had gone off to search for him. Lancelot was so deeply disturbed by that that he almost took leave of his senses, since he did not know whom to turn to for comfort, and all the joyous warmth of his welcome only galled him.

One night, he stole away from Galehaut's people at midnight, taking only his tunic, shirt, and underclothes. His great anguish had made his nose bleed while he was still in bed. and he had lost a whole bowlful of blood. Then he went away. When the blood was found the next morning, he was thought to have been killed, and the mourning for him was endless.

[Galehaut, at court, hears that Lancelot is back in Sorelois; he returns, only to hear the news of Lancelot's apparent death, and dies heartbroken.]

When Galehaut and Lionel left Sorelois, they went first to court and there found Sir Gawain, who gave them news of Lancelot, saying that he was quite sure he had gone to Sorelois, "since I forgot to tell him that you were looking for him."

Then Galehaut went back to Sorelois, but when he heard how Lancelot had disappeared and heard about the blood in his bed, he was sure that he was dead and had even killed himself. From that time on, there was no comfort for Galehaut, who could surely have found some comfort had he not been convinced that Lancelot was dead; but this thought made him lose all hope, so that he spurned all food and drink. Whatever comfort he had came from Lancelot's shield, which he kept at all times before his eyes.

Lancelot's death . . . made him go without eating or drinking for eleven days and nights, to the point where the men of religion who often came to see him claimed that, if he died as a result, his soul would be damned. So they forced him to eat, but it was to no avail, for too much harm had been done by the long fast. Besides, another problem arose, in that the wound that he had received when fighting for the shield, having been poorly treated, festered and made his flesh rot. And then he fell into an illness that made his body and all his limbs turn dry.

Galehaut languished in that way from the Feast of Mary Magdalene to the last week of September. Then he took leave of this world, according to all reports, as the worthiest man of his age during those times. . . .

## The Story of Amis and Amile (13th cent.)

*Translated by Walter Pater*

In the Old French *Li Amitiez de Amis et Amile*—certainly one of the most famous and constantly rewritten legends of the period—Amis and Amile, near twins and eternally devoted, live together and even reject wives and sacrifice children for one another. Like Achilles and Patroclus, they end their days interred together. Walter Pater, whose fascination with the beauty of young men is a constant though often coded theme in his texts, retold the story in *Studies in the History of the Renaissance* in 1873.

It happened that a leprosy fell upon Amis, so that his wife would not approach him, and wrought to strangle him. He departed, therefore, from his home, and at last prayed his servants to carry him to the house of Amile.

His servants, willing to do as he commanded, carried him to the place where Amile was; and they began to sound their rattles before the court of Amile's house, as lepers are accustomed to do. And when Amile heard the noise he commanded one of his servants to carry meat and bread to the sick man, and the cup which was given to him at Rome filled with good wine. And when the servant had done as he was commanded, he returned and said, Sir, if I had not thy cup in my hand, I should believe that the cup which the sick man has was thine, for they are alike, the one to the other, in height and fashion. And Amile said, Go quickly and bring him to me. And when Amis stood before his comrade Amile demanded of him who he was, and how he had gotten that cup. I am of Briquain le Chastel, answered Amis, and the cup was given to me by the Bishop of Rome, who baptized me. And when Amile heard that, he knew that it was his comrade Amis, who had delivered him from death, and won for him the daughter of the king of France to be his wife. And straightway he fell upon him, and began weeping greatly, and kissed him. And when his wife heard that, she ran out with her hair in disarray, weeping and distressed exceedingly, for she remembered that it was he who had slain the false Ardres. And thereupon they placed him in a fair bed, and said to him, Abide with us until God's will be accomplished in thee, for all we have is at thy service. So he and the two servants abode with them.

And it came to pass one night, when Amis and Amile lay in one chamber without other companions, that God sent His angel Raphael to Amis, who said to him, Amis, art thou asleep? And he, supposing that Amile had called him, answered and said, I am not asleep, fair comrade! And the angel said to him, Thou hast answered well, for thou art the comrade of the heavenly citizens. I am Raphael, the angel of our Lord, and am come to tell thee how thou mayest be healed; for thy prayers are heard. Thou shalt bid Amile, thy comrade, that he slay his two children and wash thee in their blood, and so thy body shall be made whole. And Amis said to him, Let not this thing be, that my comrade should become a murderer for my sake. But the angel said, It is convenient that he do this. And thereupon this angel departed.

And Amile also, as if in sleep, heard those words; and he awoke and said, Who is it, my comrade, that hath spoken with thee? And Amis answered, No man; only I have prayed to our Lord, as I am accustomed. And Amile said, Not so! but some one hath spoken with thee. Then he arose and went to the door of the chamber; and finding it shut he said, Tell me, my brother, who it was said those words to thee tonight. And Amis began to weep greatly, and told him that it was Raphael, the angel of the Lord, who had said to him, Amis, our Lord commands thee that thou bid Amile slay his two children, and wash thee in their blood, and so thou shalt be healed of thy leprosy. And Amile was greatly disturbed at those words, and said, I would have given to thee my man-servants and my maidservants and all my goods, and thou feignest that an angel hath spoken to thee that I should slay my two children. And immediately Amis began to weep, and said, I know that I have spoken to thee a terrible thing, but constrained thereto; I pray thee cast me not away from the shelter of thy house. And Amile answered that what he had covenanted with him, that he would perform, unto the hour of his death: But I conjure thee, said he, by the faith which there is between me and thee, and by our comradeship, and by the baptism we received together at Rome, that thou tell me whether it was man or angel said that to thee. And Amis answered again, So truly as an angel hath spoken to me this night, so may God deliver me from my infirmity!

Then Amile began to weep in secret, and thought within himself: if this man was ready to die before the king for me, shall I not for him slay my children? Shall I not keep faith with him who was faithful to me even unto death? And Amile tarried no longer, but departed to the chamber of his wife, and bade her go hear the Sacred Office. And he took a sword, and went to the bed where the children were lying, and found them asleep. And he lay down over them and began to weep bitterly and said, Hath any man yet heard of a father who of his own will slew his children? Alas, my children! I am no longer your father, but your cruel murderer.

And the children awoke at the tears of their father, which fell upon them; and they looked up into his face and began to laugh. And as they were of the age of about three years, he said, Your laughing will be turned into tears, for your innocent blood must now be shed, and therewith he cut off their heads. Then he laid them back in the bed, and put the heads upon the bodies, and covered them as though they slept: and with the blood which he had taken he washed his comrade, and said, Lord Jesus Christ: who hast commanded men to keep faith on earth, and didst heal the leper by Thy word! cleanse now my comrade, for whose love I have shed the blood of my children.

Then Amis was cleansed of his leprosy. And Amile clothed his companion in his best robes; and as they went to the church to give thanks, the bells, by the will of God, rang of their own accord. And when the people of the city heard that, they ran together to see the marvel. And the wife of Amile, when she saw Amis and Amile coming, asked which of the twain was her husband, and said, I know well the vesture of them both, but I know not which of them is Amile. And Amile said to her, I am Amile, and my companion is Amis, who is healed of his sickness. And she was full of wonder, and desired to know in what manner he was healed. Give thanks to our Lord, answered Amile, but trouble not thyself as to the manner of the healing.

Now neither the father nor the mother had yet entered where the children were; but the father sighed heavily, because they were dead, and the mother asked for them, that they might rejoice together; but Amile said, Dame! let the children sleep. And it was already the hour of Tierce. And going in alone to the children to weep over them, he found them at play in the bed; only, in the place of the sword-cuts about their throats was as it were a thread of crimson. And he took them in his arms and carried them to his wife and said, Rejoice greatly, for thy children whom I had slain by the commandment of the angel are alive, and by their blood is Amis healed.

For, as God had united them in their lives in one accord, so they were not divided in their death, falling together side by side, with a host of other brave men, in battle for King Charles at Mortara, so called from that great slaughter. And the bishops gave counsel to the king and queen that they should bury the dead, and build a church in that place; and their counsel pleased the king greatly and there were built two churches, the one by commandment of the king in honour of Saint Oseige, and the other by commandment of the queen in honour of Saint Peter.

And the king caused the two chests of stone to be brought in the which the bodies of Amis and Amile lay; and Amile was carried to the church of Saint Peter, and Amis to the church of Saint Oseige; and the other corpses were buried, some in one place and some in the other. But lo! next morning, the body of Amile in his coffin was found lying in the church of Saint Oseige, beside the coffin of Amis his comrade. Behold then this wondrous amity, which by death could not be dissevered!

This miracle God did, who gave to His disciples power to remove mountains. And by reason of this miracle the king and queen remained in that place for a space of thirty days, and performed the offices of the dead who were slain, and honoured the said churches with great gifts. And the bishop ordained many clerks to serve in the church of Saint Oseige, and commanded them that they should guard duly, with great devotion, the bodies of the two companions, Amis and Amile.

# Part Three
Platonic Dialogues

*European and English Literature from the
Fourteenth to the Seventeenth Century*

# 7. Platonic Dialogues: Introduction

## Friendship, Homoeroticism, and the Renaissance

### UNIQUE FRIENDSHIP

The mid-fifteenth century saw a renewal of interest in intimate masculine friendship and even in homoerotic feelings as a literary subject. Appealing to rediscovered and newly translated classical authorities, especially Plato, what is called Neoplatonism combined an artistic and literary reinterpretation of the classical past and its often powerfully homoerotic imagery with a revivified male friendship tradition to create a homoerotic literature that Giovanni Dall'Orto describes as "so rich that it has no equal in quantity and quality until the twentieth century" (*Encyclopedia of Homosexuality* 2:1104).

Friendship theory called upon three major sources. Plato celebrated male love as a path that friendship took, even if over sexual ground, toward right perceptions of the divine, the true, the good, and the beautiful. Aristotle was somewhat less sure of the nature of friendship, in the *Nichomachean Ethics* (Books 8 and 9) celebrating its idealization but unsure that what was ideal was always reflected in real practice and expressing some doubt about the place of desire in friendship. The other text upon which both the Middle Ages and the Renaissance relied for theorizing friendship, Cicero's *De Amicitia*, describes friendship with little reference to sexuality, finding in its ideal the exercise of both loyalty and virtue, the one supporting the other. If Cicero had a reservation about the possibilities of sex between males, it would have been that same reservation familiar to the Greek and Roman texts: the fear that passivity, not homosexuality, might corrupt manhood. Neither in Plato or Aristotle, nor in Cicero, is there any concept comparable to the complex of prohibitions that Christianity would call "sodomy"; nor did they link "sin" with homosexual activity. Late Roman Christianity and the Middle Ages, however, provided more than enough theory about sodomy and its linkage with sin, and so with these texts as a background the conflation of sodomy with male friendship became a specter haunting literature in the Renaissance.

### ROMANTIC LOVE

The Renaissance also relied on the literature of romantic love—sometimes called "courtly love"—to inform its speculations about friendship. Theorists of courtly love valued "illicit" and romantic and sexual relations between men and women, finding in such involvements a more profound and literarily seminal venue than that provided by marriage. Such a literary fashion could hardly have been without a shadow text of desire between men or an even dimmer image of desire between women. The early church had taught and continued to teach that the proper direction of the emotion of love was toward God alone, hoping indeed to eradicate or at least radically subordinate sexual lust to spiritual love. Renaissance texts, heirs of medieval theorizations of chaste friendship between men as much as of homoerotic classical textuality, stood at the center of a social, sexual, and textual ferment in which romantic love and sexual experiment made at least the covert expression of homosexual emotions and homoerotic imagery possible in texts.

## SODOMY AND FRIENDSHIP

Friendship between men was implicated in a web of fascinated speculation about sodomy and its association with intimate male friendship. Indeed satire often asserted that the association between "philosophy" and friendship was in fact merely a disguise for sodomy. In a celebrated instance, Ariosto, in his *Satires*, warns about the dangers of turning your back when sleeping with philosophers, while some writers almost too urgently insist on the absence of homosexual desires in a text, as did Mario Equicola in his *Libro d'Amore* (1525) when he urged that "not a word of this work is to be understood as the love of boys or sexual acts against nature" (Saslow, *Ganymede in the Renaissance: Homosexuality in Art and Society* [1986:98]). Yet approval of homoeroticized friendship and of homosexual sex itself was not wanting either. In a story by Matteo Bandello, one character asserts that "to divert myself with boys is more natural to me than eating and drinking" (quoted in Saslow 1986:99), and the genially pornographic *L'Alcibiade fanciullo a scola* by Antonio Rocco offers specific descriptions of male-male sex while Poliziano's *Orfeo* seems to approve the decision of Orpheus to choose boys instead of women for love.

Theorization of friendship finds its way in an eroticized form into the specifically homoerotic and romantic contexts of Michelangelo's sonnets to Cavalieri and in sonnets by Cecco Nuccoli and Marino Ceccoli. The subject of friendship was addressed most extensively by Marsilio Ficino (1443–1499) in his influential commentary (1469) on Plato's *Symposium*. Ficino interpreted Platonic ideals of friendship within a Christianized framework and attempted to explain the homoerotic implications of the *Symposium* as allegorical. His commentary revealed the anxious division between sodomy and friendship. It opened a discussion in which those who hoped to exclude desire from definitions of masculine love could spar, as it were, with those who wished to combine the two. Now friendship, hitherto at least theoretically unimplicated in sexuality of any kind, was itself to become suspect. On the one hand friendship, celebrated and approved, could be seen as a form of chaste and manly attachment, on the other as the hidden and suspicious locale of forbidden desire. If read as the latter, this allowed a space for the growth of homophobia—perhaps much as we know it now—since the suspicion that attached to such imagined (or real) private intimacies was soon translated into general and public condemnation and official proscription.

## GANYMEDE

Though letters and diaries and some records of legal prosecutions suggest that friendships and sex between men of a roughly similar age were not uncommon, literature nevertheless largely enshrined the classically derived and sanctioned relationship between an adult male and a youth as the model that homoerotic literature most often addressed and celebrated. Again Ganymede, popular in Greek and Roman literature and appearing in medieval texts, became perhaps the most available and deployed image in Renaissance literature and visual arts with which to express desire for youths by men, and to indicate homosexuality in the broadest sense. Renaissance writers appealed to Ovid's retelling of the Ganymede story in his *Metamorphoses* (10:155–162), which provides indeed the *locus classicus* from which derive most Renaissance versions of the Ganymede story. Virgil's version of the rape of Ganymede in the *Aeneid* (5:250–57) and Statius's in the *Thebiad* (1:548–51) provide supporting sources and models. Renaissance satirists were pleased by Martial's epigrams wherein Ganymede became very specifically a symbol of homosexual relationships between men. From the fourteenth to the mid-sixteenth century, as James

Saslow in *Ganymede in the Renaissance* points out, for Italian readers "Ganymede was the single most appropriate, if not the exclusive, symbol for male-male love as it was then understood" (1986:7–8). Boccaccio in his *Genealogy of the Pagan Gods* retells the story with no attempt at Christianizing or concealment, while references to Ganymede in a homoerotic context are to be found in the writings of Castiglione, Aretino, Cellini, Michelangelo, and Poliziano. In the visual arts especially, as Saslow definitively explains, Ganymede became a primary image for many Renaissance artists including Michelangelo, Correggio, and Cellini.

## RENAISSANCE "HOMOSEXUALITY" AND THE "MODERN HOMOSEXUAL"

Perhaps far more so than we are used to in the literary expression of our own homoeroticism, Renaissance writers advocated—whether in allegiance to theory or because of the threat of law—a conceptual division between desire and act. As Saslow points out, sodomy was "outlawed . . . while passionate male emotional intimacy, modeled on the classical notion of *amicitia*, was held up as the highest earthly happiness" (Saslow 1986:97). Thus, it cannot be, nor should it be assumed, that any Renaissance text that can be read, however seemingly easily, to suggest homoerotic desire also indicates sodomitical practice. However, as Saslow elsewhere cautions, the other approach is equally filled with ambiguity: "The urge to establish on little or no evidence, that an artist's passions were heterosexual and thus orthodox" is as unwise as attempting to prove homosexuality where equally little evidence is available (Saslow 1986:15). Therefore, when discussing Renaissance texts, it may be more productive to speak about homoerotic texts rather than the homosexuality of authors, even though it should also be taken as an axiom that the *known* homosexuality of an author is a significant element in an interpretation of a text, an element that has often been ignored or rejected by critics for whom such information may be personally distasteful.

Many modern theorists profess to see the "modern homosexual" as a discrete product of the late twentieth century, while others, following Foucault, argue for the late nineteenth century as the point when, in Foucault's words, the homosexual became a species. Still others find evidence of the first homosexuals—that is, self-identified homosexual men, exclusively or predominantly lovers of their own sex, aware of societal oppression and consciously willing to act out their difference despite this oppression—as present in the streets of eighteenth-century urban cultures. Renaissance literature, however, tentatively suggests another location for the nascent development of such self-aware manifestations of difference. The Renaissance has been commonly and historically described as that point when modern man first began to explore notions of individual identity, individual creative originality, and of human worth. It has been equally commonly described as the site where the Christian dogmatic exposition of human insignificance in the face of the divine, of a cycle of sin, penance, and punishment, and of a denigration of human sexuality and a virtual denial of the possibility of human freedom in the face of the presumption of a divine plan for the ordering of the universe was confronted by an even older but newly revivified humanistic, relativistic, and more tolerant vision of human will and of the uses of human sexuality. If this is so, then it may be possible, in a broad sense, to suggest that in the Renaissance a path was opened and the way tentatively charted that would lead to the identification of a variety of human identities, identities founded no longer on dogmatic conceptions of the "natural" or the "normal," but derived instead from personal judgments concerning the many possible directions of erotic desire.

Further Reading

Alan Bray, *Homosexuality in Renaissance England* (London: Gay Men's Press, 1982); Gregory W. Bredbeck, *Sodomy and Interpretation: Marlowe to Milton* (Ithaca, N.Y., and London: Cornell University Press, 1991); Wayne R. Dynes et. al., eds., *The Encyclopedia of Homosexuality* (New York: Garland, 1990); Kent Gerard and Gert Hekma, eds., *The Pursuit of Sodomy: Male Homosexuality in Renaissance and Enlightenment Europe* (New York: Harrington Park Press, 1989); Jonathan Goldberg, *Sodometries: Renaissance Texts, Modern Sexualities* (Stanford, Calif.: Stanford University Press, 1992); Jonathan Goldberg, ed., *Queering the Renaissance* (Durham, N.C.: Duke University Press, 1994); Joseph Pequigney, *Such Is My Love: A Study of Shakespeare's Sonnets* (Chicago: University of Chicago Press, 1985); James M. Saslow, *Ganymede in the Renaissance: Homosexuality in Art and Society* (New Haven and London: Yale University Press, 1986); James M. Saslow, *The Poetry of Michelangelo: An Annotated Translation* (New Haven: Yale University Press, 1991); Bruce R. Smith, *Homosexual Desire in Shakespeare's England* (Chicago and London: University of Chicago Press, 1991).

# 8. The Italian Renaissance

## Amor Socraticus

### Marsilio Ficino (1443–1499)

Marsilio Ficino, in his commentary on Plato's *Symposium*, makes little attempt to disguise the homoerotic underpinning of Plato's texts. But he is at pains to disassociate friendship as Plato envisions it from actual sexual relations. Ficino reads Plato as a proponent of a theory of friendship wherein loyalty is allied to that chaste and virtuous love which is properly given to the Christian God. He argues that Plato's assertions of love between two men must be read only as allegories of the spirit, not of the flesh. Such love between two men, each man enhanced and enriched by mutual intellectual connection and strengthened by chaste affection, becomes the means through which God's love could be received and through which the Ideal of the divine could be perceived. Ficino is at pains to desexualize such relations and indeed to de-homosexualize Plato's philosophy itself. Thus Ficino revises the concept of the "Platonic," removing from its definition not only the imputation associated with *paiderastia* but any hint of the physicality of sex. However eager he may have been to establish Plato within the safe precincts of a non- and even anti-sodomitical discussion, he is unable finally to do so with absolute conviction or success. He comments, for example, that there are "some men" who are better suited to "offspring of the soul" than others and observes that these men "naturally love men more than women." This suggests that Ficino may have imagined that such men were "naturally" a distinct even separate species. He thus seems to be saying that despite the ideal of chaste Platonism that he espouses, mere theory might not account for the erotic realities of life or for the intensity of desire. Such intensity, in fact, seems to inform the thoughtful and philosophizing content of impassioned letters that Ficino himself wrote to his "unique friend" Giovanni Cavalcanti (1444–1509), the young man who Ficino cast as the central character of the commentary.

FROM *COMMENTARIUM IN PLATONIS CONVIVIUM* (1469)

[COMMENTARY ON PLATO'S *SYMPOSIUM*]
*Translated by Sears Jayne*

#### Book 6, ch. 14

According to Plato, the soul is as pregnant as the body, and they are both aroused to procreation by the stimuli of love. But some men, either on account of their nature or their training, are better equipped for offspring of the soul than for those of the body. Others, and certainly the majority of them, are the opposite. The former pursue heavenly love, the latter earthly. The former, therefore, naturally love men more than women and those nearly adults rather than children, because the first two are much stronger in mental keenness, and this because of its higher beauty is most essential to knowledge, which they naturally wish to generate. But the others are just the opposite, because of their passion for the physical union of love, and the sensuous effect of bodily generation. But, since that genital force of the soul has no power of cognition, it makes no discrimination between the sexes; but is, naturally, aroused for generation whenever we see any beautiful object, and it consequently happens that those who associate with males have intercourse with them in order to satisfy the urge of their genital parts.

### How Easily We Are Ensnared by Love (Book 7, ch. 5)

. . . . [T]he amatory infection comes into being easily and becomes the most serious disease of all. Certainly that spiritual vapor and blood which is injected by a young man directly into an older has four qualities, as we have said. It is *clear, thin, warm,* and *sweet.* Because it is *clear,* it harmonizes very well with the clarity of the eyes and spirits in the older man; it entices and allures them. Whence it happens that it is eagerly swallowed up by them. Because it is *thin,* it flies into the heart very quickly. from there through the veins and arteries it easily spreads throughout the whole body. Because it is *warm,* it acts and moves vigorously, it infects the blood of the older man very powerfully, and changes it into its own nature. This Lucretius touches on thus: *"Hence first that drop of Venus' honey distilled in your heart, and then came freezing pain."*

Moreover, because it is *sweet,* it comforts the viscera in some way; it feeds, and pleases them. Hence it happens that all the blood of the older man, when it has been converted into the nature of young blood, seeks the body of the youth in order to inhabit its own veins, and also in order that humor of the young blood may flow in equally young and tender veins. It also happens that this sick one is touched by pleasure and pain at the same time. By pleasure on account of the clarity and sweetness of that vapor and blood. Certainly the former attracts and the latter pleases. By pain on account of the *thinness* and warmth of the same. . . .

### On a Certain Strange Effect of Vulgar Love (Book 7, ch. 6)

. . . . The great transformation that occurs in an older man who is inclined toward the likeness of a younger causes him to want to transfer his whole body into the youth, and to draw the whole of the youth into himself, in order that either the young humor may obtain young arteries, or the younger arteries may obtain younger blood. Hence they are driven to do many sinful things together. For since the genital semen flows down from the whole body, they believe that merely by ejaculating or receiving this, they can give or receive the whole body . . . [and] lovers desire to take the whole beloved into themselves. . . .

### How the Lover Becomes Like the Beloved (Book 7, ch. 8)

For this reason none of you should be surprised if you have heard that some lover has taken on in his own body a certain similarity of likeness to his beloved. . . . What wonder if the features are so firmly implanted and embedded in the breast by mere thought that they are imprinted on the spirit, and by the spirit are immediately imprinted on the blood? . . . But since all parts of the body, as they dry out every day, so they revive every day, having taken moisture from food, it follows that from day to day the body of each man which has gradually dried out is little by little restored. But the parts are restored by the blood flowing from the channels of the veins. Therefore will you be surprised if blood imprinted with a certain likeness [of the beloved] has impressed that likeness on the parts of the body, so that eventually [the lover] will seem to have become like [the beloved] in some colors, or features, or feelings, or gestures?

### By Whom Especially Are We Ensnared? (Book 7, ch. 9

Perhaps someone will ask, by whom especially, and in what way, lovers are ensnared, and how they are freed. Women, of course, catch men easily, and even more easily women who display a certain masculine character. Men catch men still more easily, since they are more like men than women are, and they have blood and spirit which is clearer, warmer, and thinner, which is the basis of erotic entrapment. But among males those attract men or women most quickly who are predominantly sanguine *but* partly choleric, and who have large eyes, blue and shining; and especially if they live chastely, and have not, through coitus, exhausting the clear sap of the humors, disfigured their serene faces. For these qualities are required in order for the arrows themselves which wound the heart to be sent out properly. . . .

Hence certainly a reciprocal love is innate in men, the conciliator of their original nature, striving to make one out of two and to heal the nature of men. For each of us is half of a man, just as the little fish that are called . . . goldfish, being sliced, from one become two. But each human half seeks its own half. And so whenever his own half meets someone, of whichever sex he may be desirous, he is most violently aroused, clings to it with burning love, and does not even for a moment permit being separated from it. And so the desire and longing for the whole to be restored receives the name of love. This, for the present time, helps us greatly while it leads each of us to his own formerly lost half, and for the future, inspires the highest hope in us who worship God piously, that by restoring us to our former condition and healing us He will make us most blessed.

### Do You Ask for What the Socratic Love Is Useful? (Book 7, ch. 16)

First, indeed, it avails most to a man for recovering those wings by which to fly back to his fatherland. Second, it avails greatly to his state for living honestly, and happily. Truly, "men, not stones, make up a state." But men, from their youth, like trees, have to be protected from weaker men and trained for the best fruit. Parents and teachers have the care of children, but youths no sooner escape the supervision of parents and teachers than they are debased by wicked association with the mob. Certainly they would follow that higher level of living received from their master, if they were not deflected from it by the intimacy and the companionship of wicked men, especially those who flatter them. . . .

So the true love, like a shepherd, keeps his flock of lambs safe from false lovers as from the ravage of wolves and disease. Since, in fact, equals are easily congregated with equals, he makes himself equal with the young man in purity of life, in simplicity of language, games, jokes, and witticisms. He makes himself a boy instead of an old man in the first place, so that he may at some time make boys into mature men by his personal and pleasing intimacy.

FROM "LETTERS TO GIOVANNI CAVALCANTI WRITTEN BETWEEN 1474 AND 1492"

*Translated by Members of the Language Department of the School of Economics and Science, London*

## LETTER 42

### The truth of God is splendour, beauty, and love

It was the chief work of the divine Plato, as the dialogues of Parmenides and Epinomis show, to reveal the principle of unity in all things, which he called appropriately the One itself. . . . Whoever wishes to profess the study of Plato should therefore honour the one truth, which is the single ray of the one God. This ray passes through angels, souls, the heavens and other bodies. As we discussed in the book on love [the *Symposium*, which Ficino calls the *Convivium*], its splendour shines in every individual thing according to its nature and is called grace and beauty; and where it shines more clearly, it especially attracts the man who is watching, stimulates him who thinks, and catches and possesses him who draws near to it. . . .

This is plain, because the lover is not content with the sight or touch of the beloved and continually exclaims, "I do not know what this man has that sets me on fire, nor do I understand what I desire." The soul, consumed by the divine brilliance which shines in the beauteous man as though in a mirror, is seized unknowingly by that brilliance, and is drawn upward as by a hook, so that the soul becomes God. Then must a man be considered mad as well as miserable, who whilst thus called to the sublime through vision, plunges himself into the mire through touch. Although he could become God instead of man by contemplating the divine through human beauty, from man he returns to beast by preferring the physical shadow of form to true spiritual beauty.

## LETTER 47

### The lawful end of love is union

You ask what chiefly caused me to write letters about love. There are very many men, Giovanni, who in speaking or writing on matters of love stray a long way from its law. But a mistake of this kind is as harmful as lawful love is useful; and love has as many forms as there are lovers. In truth all men love; men, I say, Giovanni, for he who loves no one is not a man. So not only in the book which I have written on love but also in my letters, I have pointed out for those who love the mark to which they should advance. Since the man who oversteps this mark is his own real enemy, he can be no true friend to others. He alone will keep to the right mark in speaking or writing, who first keeps to it in thinking. But he will keep to it in thinking who knows both what true beauty is and what is not true but its imitation. The right end of loving is union, which consists in these three: thinking, seeing, and hearing.

Certainly, love (as all philosophers define it) is the longing for beauty. The beauty of the body lies not in the shadow of matter, but in the light and grace of form; not in dark mass, but in clear proportion; not in sluggish and senseless weight, but in harmonious number and measure. But we come to that light, that grace, proportion, number, and measure only through thinking, seeing, and hearing. It is thus far that the true passion of a true lover extends. However, it is not love when the appetite of the other senses drives us rather towards matter, mass, weight, and the deformity that is the opposite of beauty or love, but a stupid, gross, and ugly *lust*.

But why do I, like Socrates and Plato, consider for so long the populace rather than myself? For perhaps the more I strive to prevent the people from loving basely all the more will these insane and ungrateful people suspect my love is excessive. This is said to have happened also to those heroes, Socrates and Plato, our divine guides. So let that be enough on this subject; indeed it is more than enough for now.

## LETTER 51

### A friendship is lasting which is forged by God

My dear Giovanni, the Platonic philosophers defined true friendship as the permanent union of the lives of two men. But I think that life is one only for those men who work towards one end, as it were treading the same path towards a common goal. I believe their fellowship will only be permanent when the aim which they have set themselves as a common duty is not only single but also permanent and sure.

Now the whole study and business of Man is always to strive for what is thought to be good. Since there seem to be three kinds of good for mortals, which are those of the soul, body, and external objects, man seeks the virtue of the soul, the pleasures of the body, or abundance of riches. The first of these is sure and everlasting. The other two are transitory and mortal. Therefore that permanent union of lives, which is true friendship, can only exist for those who neither seek to accumulate riches nor to satisfy sensual pleasures which change and perish. It is possible only for those who apply themselves with common zeal and determination to acquire and exercise the single and permanent virtue of the soul. . . .

We have now defined friends as those who strive for virtue with equal zeal, and who help one another to cultivate their souls. The cultivation of the soul is established in virtue alone, virtue is wisdom, and wisdom is understanding the divine. Divine light bestows knowledge of this kind upon us. Therefore, to cultivate the soul is to cultivate God himself

And so friendship, as it endeavors through the single aim of two men to cultivate the soul through virtue, is clearly nothing but the supreme harmony of two souls in the cultivation of God. And as God loves those who cultivate Him with devoted minds, there cannot be the two friends on their own, but there must always be three, the two men and God; God, or in other words Jupiter, the patron of hospitality, protector of friendship, and sustainer of human life, worshipped at all times by Plato and honored by Socrates. He is the guide of human life; He unites us as one; He is the unbreakable bond of friendship, and our constant guardian....

And although I have little confidence in being able to follow the footsteps of these men through the heavenly regions, there is one thing I do seem to have acquired in full measure for the study of sacred philosophy, the exercise of virtue and the search for truth; that is, the fitting and joyful company of the best of men. For I hold the friendship of Giovanni Cavalcanti and Marsilio Ficino worthy of being numbered among those I have just mentioned. With God to guide us, who has so fortunately established and quickened this bond, our friendship will serve us well in our necessary tasks, in leading a tranquil life and in discovering the divine.

## Filippo Scarlatti (c. 1442–c. 1487)

*Translated by James J. Wilhelm*

Scarlatti wrote over one hundred poems in many forms, from love songs to burlesques.

*[Lanza 51]*

O beautiful adolescent, O young man,
Cupid has opened my eyes to you,
So that I (though undeserving) appeal only to you
As my master with me your chosen slave,
And I see beneath your outer look
So many good things you offer me,
Kindnesses and favors that indeed
Have carved my very heart out of my breast!
But you needn't look down on my presumptions.
I praise you, my excellent young man,
To please show some compassion toward your servant,
Who comes before you timidly, with head bent down.
Please exercise some discretion with him,
So that he won't wander vagrantly through the world.
            He, poor wretched thing,
Has seized the courage to make a frail proposal,
And he would be overjoyed if you respond.

## Angelo Poliziano (1454–1494)

Poliziano studied with Marsilio Ficino, translated part of Homer, and became tutor to the children of Lorenzo de'Medici. In 1477 he became the Prior of San Paolo and was one of the most prolific writers of his times. His works in which homoeroticism has a place include imitations of Greek and Latin verse and his drama *Orfeo*, in which the hero, Orpheus, renounces women after losing his wife Eurydice.

GREEK EPIGRAMS

*Translated by James J. Wilhelm*

7

*To Giovan Battista Buoninsegni*

As much as pilots are happy when they are traversing the sea
      When they hear the halcyon birds proclaiming a safe passage;
As much as a king delights when he's razed to the ground a hostile city,

As much as a sick man rejoices when he's escaped a grave illness,
As much as a newlywed full of love feels as he enters the virgin's bed—
    This much my heart exults within my breast when I see
Your face and I suddenly hear your words.
    O day that's worthy of a sign of white and incantation!
O day that's worthy to be remembered for many years!
    O friend who is sweeter to me than honey, O lovable face
May you always be happy and may Zeus yield to you all good fortune!
    And please conserve in your breast our mutual love!

## 23

*On the Love of Two Boys*

A double love torments me; I strain because of two boys
    Who are equally resplendent in their eyes and equally appealing.
The one is hard and insolent; the other virginlike in his face;
    Both arouse in me an equally sweet desire.
One of them has dark locks cascading from his head,
    While the other has billowing blond tresses.
The rest of them is not the least bit similar—except for their lack of pity;
    Neither of them overcomes by his graceful charm.
It's not possible, Aphrodite, to hold on to both; so counsel me:
Which of these two flames should I try to hold on to?

## 26

*Love Song for Chrysokomos (Goldenlocks)*

Watch over me from heaven while within my arms I hold my boy,
    And don't envy me, Zeus, because I envy no other.
Be contented, Zeus, be contented with your Ganymede, and leave to me
    My shiny Chrysokomos, who to me is sweeter than honey.
O how happy I am—three and four times! O yes, I have kissed—
    Truly kissed your mouth, you delicious boy-love!
O mouth, O locks, O smile, O light from your eyes!
    O gods, truly you are mine, you delightful boy, yes mine!
I say you are truly mine, my little lover boy! How much I have anguished,
    How much I have suffered and undergone to receive this prize!
My heart, why now are you suffering torment, as you did before? There's no
    Danger now; you shouldn't be trembling, O heart!
Because the thing that once destroyed us and made us fearful—look!
    I now hold him vanquished between my arms.
So take this, my goddess, take this dove to place on your altar,
    And arrange for me that this joy shall be eternal!
And you, rise up! How much more gently you inspire my love
    As you hold my tongue intertwined in your mouth, O my boy!

## FROM *FAVOLA DI ORFEO* (1480)

*Translated by Elizabeth Basset Welles*

The myth of Orpheus, a mythological figure skilled in poetry and music, is told by Ovid in *Metamorphoses*. Ovid recounts how Orpheus goes down to the underworld in order to win back his wife Euridice, who has been taken there after dying from the bite of a poisonous snake. Orpheus is warned not to look at Euridice on the trip back to the world of the living, but unable to resist he does so, and she is lost to him forever. After this Orpheus vows never to consort with women again and instead introduces the love of men to the young men of Thrace, thus becoming, according to one Greek legend, the inventor of pederasty. Eventually, Orpheus is dismembered by a band of women who are identified in different versions of the myth as either the rejected female lovers of the young men of Thrace or as the orgiastic Maenads of the cult of Dionysus. In this selection from an Italian version of the story, Orpheus explains why he chooses young men to love.

[Orpheus, having lost Euridice, vows never to love women again.]

What song will ever be so sorrowful
That it be equal to this pain of loss?
How will I ever weep for long enough
To mourn forever for my mortal wound?
Grieving, disconsolate, shall I lament,
Until the heavens take me while I live.
And since my fortune is so very cruel
I never wish to love another woman.

From now on I shall clip the tender buds
Of this the springtime of the better sex,
When they are all slender and beautiful.
This is a sweeter and a gentler love.
Let no one talk to me of women now,
Since she is dead who once did own my heart.
Whoever wishes to converse with me—
Speak not to me about a woman's love.

How sad is he who for a woman would
Change his will, ever suffer or rejoice;
O he gives up his liberty for her,
He, who believes her glances and her words.
For she is lighter than a leaf in wind,
Wants and unwants a thousand times a day,
Seeks him who flees, yet flees him who seeks her,
And comes and goes like waves upon the shore.

Thus, Jove, enthralled by that delicious knot
Shows faith in what I have to say of love,
For Ganymede he did enjoy in heaven,
While Phoebus had sweet Hyacinth on earth
And to this blessed love did Hercules cede,
Who won the world and was by Hylas won.

To married men, a comfort is divorce,
So each may flee the company of women.


## Cecco Nuccoli (14th cent.)

THREE POEMS

*Translated by Jill Claretta Robbins*

Both Nuccoli and Ceccoli were part of a group of poets who wrote in Perugia in the late thirteenth and early fourteenth centuries.

In love poems, expressions of desire were often directed at a beloved whose name and gender could often be conveniently hidden behind conventional imagery. However, in the poetry of Michelangelo (see below) and of Nuccoli and Ceccoli, the gender of the beloved is not difficult to discover.


### 1

Since I abandoned and tied my soul to your sweet appearance and manners, oh Sir, guide and light of my life, will I ever see you before I die?

I left you and left my heart, thus I must keep on wasting away; and although I shed a river of tears, seemingly I cannot cry enough.

Crying will never make me happy—neither does it give peace to sad souls—until I see you in person Sir.

But this anguish that undoes me, Sir, now reminds you of my servant heart: which. since it is Yours, do not forget it.


### 2

You have the light of my life, in your clear and pleasing face, and don't see me, your subject, that Love, because of you brings toward Death;

since I can't be close enough to embrace you, and I suffer from not speaking with you, oh, don't be harsh in showing me yourself, since it would shine as a ray of health to my heart.

For which I come so often to look: and because you hide it, I become earthly, and always my sad spirit recedes.

I have no shame in coming, nor restraint, although others say bad things about me or point at me: the pain that I sustain is greater.

Before his person may you be placed, my sonnet, substitute for myself.


### 3

Your promises come to me always together with your betrayals, which you have more of than the fox; neither can I shield myself from the mortal blows that Love gives me, because I am choked up with you.

Thus I ask of you, and I remind you of this, that you at least apologize: because I feel my soul leaving my flesh, cold in sorrow, because of which I bite my hands.

However, I ask of you, Sir, that you succour me with your medicine and cure me, since such an illness needs to be purged by you.

If not, I will no longer be part of this world; and already I would go, conquered, to Death, without your face, that I have painted in my heart.

Go at once, sonnet, and bring me back the answer that I desire, before I am rotted by Death.

## Marino Ceccoli (14th cent.)

Two Poems

*Translated by Jill Claretta Robbins*

1

Oh, and yet I see that I will return to you anyway, and throw myself at your feet and cry a lot over my sins, until my crime will be pardoned.

From my eyes tears fall often, which go copiously to the heart, saying: Wicked one, every man should stone you for what you have done!

And I will say: Mercy in the name of God; I am guilty! Don't kill me, although I deserve that neither bone nor flesh of me remain.

Perhaps then my kind Sir, hearing his servant, who apologizes, will disdain me somewhat less.

2

Sir, I have remained so overcome, that I can no longer suffer your attacks; my strength has abandoned me so, that my body is half dead.

In my miserable heart I feel a mortal blow, such that my heart has no hope of finding salvation; your disdain of me has been so cruel, that I am beside myself.

It has been already many years that I have gone crying in your shadow, and now I have reached the point, that, so wounded, brings me to death:

because you have reached me with your arrow, and by now it was not worth my fleeing, to avoid your arrows.

Sonnet, whoever asks your maker, tell him you saw him on the point of death, when you left.

## Pacifico Massimi (15th cent.)

*Translated by James J. Wilhelm*

Almost nothing is known about Massimi, save that he was born in Asoli and lived for a time in Naples. His *Hecateleguim* (One hundred elegies) was written in Latin.

*Advice to Paulinus (Book I, 9)*

That man is pleasing and worthy of praise who shuns vice and always,
    Always follows virtues and beautiful deeds.
He who wants to be a companion of the wicked
    Will eventually pick up the same bad name that they bear. . . .
The only taint on my morals came from the tutor
    That my father and mother unwittingly wished upon me.
He was the king of the pederasts; no prey ever
    Escaped his hands, since he was a master of that art.
O yes, I learned a lot of things I'd have preferred not to.
    I learned a lot about using my mouth—and my asshole.
Now you, my Paulinus—don't you want to avoid all this?
    Don't you see the appearance of that man you associate with?
I'm wondering in fact if you're not being sucked down in the same filth,
    Because, as we know, like is attracted to like.
Already some not very pretty stories are circulating about you.
    A lot of people are ripping you apart with their teeth.
You might as well cut off the long prick of your dog
    Because your old reputation is going to give way to the new.
If you're not careful, if you don't move away from that guy,
    No water of the ocean will ever wash you clean.
That guy could steal an egg from under a sitting hen;
    He could sneak away with a sandal from a woman who's watching.
If a pederast once gets a young kid in his clutches,
    He knows how to drill the recruit in his art.
He will handle you with his hands and his tongue so expertly that he
    Could overcome Hermogenes in thievery and Battus in fraud.
Just recently I happened to be sitting at the theater,
    And that guy slid away a soft cushion from under my butt.
He didn't touch a boy who was there or utter a word to him;
    In fact, he didn't even seem to see him, yet he took down one's breeches.
The boy's grandpa and dad were bamboozled as the kid was buggered,
    And that's the way the kid will end up his life.
Have no doubt! the same punishment will be reserved for you.
    Look and see if a noose isn't already dangling around your neck.
You don't think my words are worth a damn. That's why they say this about you:
"Nobody ever gets back a sheep that's fallen into the mouth of a wolf."


*A Love Song for Marcus (Book II, 10)*

You couldn't find a better time to meet me, Marcus,
    Or a place that was more convenient.
May my soul disappear and my senses fail
    And a blast of cold sweep over my limbs
When I look at you and when I picture

Your honeyed lips bitten by my teeth!
Often I wanted to talk to you, but the words
    Choked in my palate and a chill overcame my tongue.
O how many times my tears and my sighs
    Have offered a sure proof of my passion!
What do they mean—this thinness, pallor, moisture and fasting
    That flees my lips—O, but you don't care!
The devout simplicity of your tender years causes this;
    Your snowy-white virginity makes you rude.
Don't you know the power of Cupid's golden weapons,
    And doesn't your heart tell you what love is?
Nothing is harsher than that, nothing more bitter;
    I would undergo a thousand deaths to have it taken away.
I'd like to know if you want to be totally rid of me
    Or if there is ever some hope for ending my pain.
Either give me some life or remove the time that is left to me;
    Now I've decided to live—yet now to die.
I have no arbiter for either choice; I totally lack a judge.
    No woman or man could tell me anything right.
Let the matter lie between some willows and green pastures.
    Let a shade-tree cover us over with its leaves.
Let a brook lull us to sleep with its dulcet murmurs
    Along with the songs of many a bird from the branches.
Come here and gradually glide down over my bosom,
    O you cause and cure for my desires!
Now I'd like to exhale my breath; now I'd like to die
    Among all these blandishments and pleasures.
No man on earth or in heaven would be happier than I am,
    No one would consider Jove a greater being than I!


*On Happiness (Book V, 8)*

Happy is the day which saw me when I was joined to my boyfriend
    On some grass that supplied us with a delightful bed!
Happy was that place, happy the waving branches and the tree
    That made me feel greater than Jupiter himself
When was there ever anyone happier on earth than I,
    Or who could be considered an equal to me?
I was swimming in joy; I could scarcely hold myself back.
    The earth could scarcely sustain my swift-running feet.
Even if Croesus had given me great riches or wealthy Alcinous
    His gold, I would not have exchanged this for anything—
Not if I were given what the Tagus River carries in its current
    Or what the Pactolus and the Hermus have hidden,
Or what the dusky Indian searches for in the Red Sea
    Or what Danae or Midas once controlled.

Let wealth incline to the happy! Who, if he's sad,
    Is truly rich? Only a happy soul has wealth.
I possess everything; my mind wishes nothing more,
    Except what I hold and will always enjoy;
May that never end, may it never be lacking,
    And may Fortune never envy me my pleasures.
May no day ever separate my sweet lover from me
    And no day ever cut me off from my love.
May high noon always see me happy in its brief shade,
    And may the rising and setting sun see me the same way
May a propitious stone mark that continuous hour
    As only white stones issue out of the divining urn.
As an object of envy, may I seem miserable to no one,
    And may everyone always see me heaped with goods.
May the heavens nod yes to me, or if there is anything greater,
    May that god absorb my prayers with a willing ear!
Shall I speak to anyone? No, I say. Arrogantly
    I move forward with an obdurate face. Pride orders me to do so.
Let the passive crowds give way. I want to march down Broadway.
    Who would dare to touch my nose or finger my hair?
If anyone interrogates me, I'll say: No! Nobody will know
    If my grain or my greens support my great claim.
No one will know this—not as long as the rivers
    Run down to the sea or the fish adore their flowing waters.
I would die before anything fell from my lips that told
    When this all happened and how—that love that blessed me.
That man, that is a sage who reveals his love to no one.
    A man who gabs about his joys in love is a damned fool!

## Michelangelo Buonarroti (1475–1564)

Sometime in 1532, Michelangelo met Tommaso de'Cavalieri, a handsome twenty-three-year-old Roman nobleman. Michelangelo sent him a number of drawings based on subjects from Ovid, including one of the rape of Ganymede. He also began writing passionate poetry to Cavalieri, and the poems soon became a record of Michelangelo's love for the young man, a passion that was accepted but not requited. Sonnets declaring love were not, of course, an unusual form. However, as James Saslow observes in his edition of Michelangelo's poetry (*The Poetry of Michelangelo: An Annotated Translation*, 1991), Michelangelo's sonnets were the "first large body of love poetry written by one man to another in any European vernacular literature" (Saslow 1991:26). As such, Michelangelo created for the Italian Renaissance a body of homoerotic texts that would not be equaled until Shakespeare's sonnets. His letters to Cavalieri suggest more directly than the sometimes oblique poems just how intense was his feeling. Michelangelo has been often quoted as having described himself as "of all men most inclined to love persons," and when he meets someone of great beauty or personal worth he confessed that "I am compelled to fall in love with him" (quoted in Saslow 1991:17). His poems to Cavalieri and others, to Gherardo Perini and to Febo di Poggio, treat of his love in conventional

Neoplatonic terms. He employs also conventional imagery to describe it: he is the slave or prisoner of love, the prisoner indeed of his knight and master—Cavalieri. Love burns him, wounds him with its darts, he is unable to withstand it, he is obsessed by it and loses control of himself because of it.

His fear of loss of control, of course, may have other more complex implications, since loss of control that might lead to homosexual sex could also lead to prosecution and prison, a possibility that makes clear just why there is little evidence of actual homosexual activity in Michelangelo's life, though the sonnets provide more than adequate evidence of homoerotic feelings and some evidence that he tried to resist the power of homosexual desire. Though he couches his desirous monologue in Neoplatonic terms that set chaste divine love against earthly physical love, and attempts always to subjugate the latter to the former, his poems to Cavalieri seems always to be shadowed by a struggle against sensual expression that he felt he could not and perhaps did not want to win. For him love, whether earthly or divine, always is a product of physical beauty. The actual presence of such beauty—in men like Cavalieri—contrasted sharply with the abstraction inherent in ideals of Divine Love. Here, as Saslow suggests, lay Michelangelo's dilemma: "he was both exceptionally loving and passionate toward men and exceptionally endowed with moral scruples" (Saslow 1991:17). Yet in Sonnet 260 he is impelled to say that "a violent burning for prodigious beauty/is not always the source of harsh and deadly sin." The burning he describes in that poem—specifically recorded in his letters and poems to Cavalieri—is for the love "that aspires to heights" that "draws toward heaven." This love for Michelangelo was the love of one man for another. That this love was forbidden by his times made his dilemma even more acute and his accomplishment, in a life filled with unrivaled and unmatched achievement, even more remarkable.

## Early Poems (possibly for Gherardo Perini)

*Translated by James M. Saslow*

### 18 (1522)

The soul tries a thousand remedies in vain;
since I was captured, it's been struggling
in vain to get back on its earlier road.
The sea, and the mountain, and the fire with the sword:
I live in the midst of all of these together.
The one who's deprived me of my mind, and taken
away my reason, won't let me up the mountain.

### 27 (c. 1524)

Flee, lovers, from Love, flee from his fire;
its flame is cruel and its wound is deadly.
For after its first assault, nothing avails—
neither force nor reason nor changing location.
Flee, now that an example is not lacking
of the power of a fierce arm and a sharp arrow:

read in me what your own misfortune will be,
what his merciless, ungodly sport will be.
    Flee at the first glance, and do not linger:
for I thought we could come to terms at any time;
now I feel, and you can see, how much I'm burning.


## 32 (c. 1525)

    I live in sin, and dying to myself I live;
my life no longer belongs to me, but to sin.
My good comes from heaven, my evil from myself,
from my own free will, of which I've been deprived
    My freedom's been made a slave, my godly part
made mortal for me. O unhappy condition!
To what misery, to what a life I was born!


## 36 (c. 1524–1526)

    It was over here that my love, in his mercy,
took my heart from me and, farther on there, my life;
here with his beautiful eyes he promised me solace,
and here, with the same, he turned to take it from me.
    Over here he bound me, there he set me loose;
here I wept for myself, and from this rock,
with infinite pain, I saw him go away,
he who took me from myself and didn't turn back to me.


LETTER TO TOMMASO DE'CAVALIERI

*Translated by John Addington Symonds*

*July 28, 1533*

My dear Lord, — Had I not believed that I had made you certain of the very great,
nay, measureless love I bear you, it would not have seemed strange to me nor have
roused astonishment to observe the great uneasiness you show in your last letter,
lest, through my not having written, I should have forgotten you. Still it is nothing
new or marvelous when so many other things go counter, that this also should be
topsy-turvy. For what your lordship says to me, I could say to yourself: nevertheless,
you do this perhaps to try me, or to light a new and stronger flame, if that indeed
were possible: but be it as it wills: I know well that, at this hour, I could as easily forget your name as the food by which I live; nay, it were easier to forget the food,
which only nourishes my body miserably, than your name, which nourishes both
body and soul, filling the one and the other with such sweetness that neither weariness nor fear of death is felt by me when memory preserves you to my mind. Think,
if the eyes could enjoy their portion, in what condition I should find myself.

POEMS TO TOMMASO DE'CAVALIERI (1532 — C. 1542)

*Translated by James M. Saslow*

## 60

You know that I know, my lord, that you know
that I come closer to take delight in you,
and you know I know you know just who I am:
why then delay our meeting any longer?

If the hope that you give to me is real,
if the great desire I've been granted is real,
let the wall raised between them be broken down,
for troubles left concealed have double strength.

If I love in you, my dear lord, only what
you love most in yourself, do not be angry,
for it's one spirit falling in love with the other.

What I yearn for and learn from your fair face
is poorly understood by mortal minds;
whoever wants to know it must die first.

## 78

From sweet weeping to a painful smile,
from an eternal to a briefer peace
have I fallen; for, where truth keeps silent,
the senses take over whoever's cut off from it.

And I don't know whether my heart or your face
deserves the blame for this pain, which hurts less
the more it grows, or if it's the burning torch
of your eyes, which are stolen from paradise.

Your beauty is not an earthly thing,
but made up in heaven as something divine among us;
thus, though deprived, I'm comforted by burning,

for near to you I cannot be otherwise.
Since heaven has ordained these weapons of my death,
who, if I die, could say you both were wrong?

## 83

I see in your beautiful face, my lord,
what can scarcely be related in this life:
my soul, although still clothed in its flesh,
has already risen often with it to God.

And if the evil, cruel, and stupid rabble
point the finger at others for what they feel themselves,
my intense longing is no less welcome to me,
nor my love, my faith, and my virtuous desire.

To people of good judgment, every beauty
seen here resembles, more than anything else does,
that merciful fountain from which we all derive;
    nor have we another sample or other fruit
of heaven on earth; so he who loves you in faith
rises up to God and holds death sweet.

## 96

Like dry wood in a burning fire
may I burn, if I don't love you from my heart,
and lose my soul, if it feels anything else.
    And if a spirit of love heat and inflame me
with any beauty other than your eyes,
may they be taken from me, who'd die without them.
    If I don't love and adore you, may my boldest
thoughts, along with their hope, become as sad
as they are firm and constant in love of you.

## 98

Why should I still pour out my intense desire
in weeping or in mournful words,
if heaven, which clothes all souls with such a fate,
strips no one of it, either early or late?
    Why does my tired heart still make me long to languish
if others must also die? Therefore let my
final hours be made less wearisome for these eyes,
since all other good is worth less than all my pain.
    Yet at least, if I cannot dodge the blow
I steal and rob from him—if it's ordained—
then who will win out between sweetness and sorrow?
    If, to be happy, I must be conquered and chained,
it is no wonder that, naked and alone,
an armed cavalier's prisoner I remain.

## 260 [ON SPIRITUAL FRIENDSHIP, C. 1546]

A violent burning for prodigious beauty
is not always a source of harsh and deadly sin,
if then the heart is left so melted by it
that a divine dart can penetrate it quickly.
    Far from hindering empty passion from flying higher,
love stirs and wakes us, and feathers our wings;
and from that first step, with which it's not satisfied,
the soul can mount up and rise to its creator.

The love I speak of aspires to the heights;
woman is too different from that, and it's not worthy
of a wise and manly heart to burn for her.
    One love draws toward heaven, the other draws down to earth;
one dwells in the soul, the other in the senses,
and draws its bow at base and vile things.

## Benedetto Varchi (1503–1565)

*Translated by James J. Wilhelm*

What part of my holiest and most beautiful feelings
For the young man Alloro, while I was still young,
Did Love with his chaste torch and golden arrows
Light up and then engrave in a high and noble refuge?
If I walk or sit, if I'm quiet or am talking,
Whatever I see or hear or think or feel or smell
Is nothing except that extraordinary honor
Of that green, pure, noble, happy sapling

With whom (if I live) I hope one day to fly
Above, so that, far from the vulgar crowd,
I'll have no cares about the final assault of death,
But always, seated in a happy place
High up in the third heaven with my handsome Giulio,
I'll extol my Giulio above all the rest.

## Torquato Tasso (1544–1595)

Tasso is best known for his epic *Gerusaleme liberata* (1581), celebrating the First Crusade which took Jerusalem in 1099. Tasso only hints at homoeroticism in some of his portraits of the non-Christian defenders of Jerusalem. However, letters written a few years earlier to one Luca Scalabrino wherein Tasso writes about a young man who intrigues him suggest that Tasso may have been more familiar in life with what he did not feel able to portray in his public writings.

TWO LETTERS TO LUCA SCALABRINO (1576)

*Translated by Jill Claretta Robbins*

*To Luca Scalabrino—Rome*
I saw the letter of my Lord, [he is] beautiful certainly, but? I have never had doubts about his intelligence, and now I am very confident and I have hopes for him of every success. But you admire his [devotion] to eloquence, and I his knightly disposition, because he has learned more in a few months of this art than I have in many years in court. In sum, I am not deceiving myself, and I speak by experience,

not by suspicion or by conjecture; you believe what you want; but if you were here and you found yourself present at one or two of our conversations you would see clearly; because he deals with me in a way that shows that he doesn't care about leaving me satisfied: it is enough for him that I cannot tell others that he offends me. I love him, and I will still love him for some months, because that impression that love made in my soul was too strong, nor can it be removed in a few days, even if the offense may be grave; nevertheless I hope that time will heal my soul of this amorous wound and make it completely healthy, because I certainly would not want to love him, because as much as his wit is lovable, and his manners are generally good, the more a particular behavior toward me seems odious. This behavior, begun a little while ago, comes from some feeling to me unknown, if not perhaps from emulation, or from a desire to satisfy others, which seems more believable to me. I call this my love and not benevolence because, in sum, it is love; neither did I notice it at first and I didn't notice it, because I didn't feel any of those appetites that love usually brings awaken in me, nor in bed, where we were together. But now I realize that I was and am not friend, but very true lover, because I feel immense pain, not only that he hardly reciprocates my love, but also not to be able to speak to him with that freedom that I used to, and his absence afflicts me very heavily. I never wake up at night without his image being the first to appear before me, and, turning over in my soul how much I have loved him and honored him, and how much he has scorned and offended me, and what weighs on me most appearing to me too hardened in the resolution not to love me, afflicts me so much, that two or three times I have cried very bitterly, and if I lie in that, forget me, God. I would hope that if he were certain of my soul, he would be constrained to love me, but how can he be, being certainly aware of his. And if you, to whom no feeling of my soul was ever hidden, and who, after many years, should know how well I know how to pretend, doubt it, it is reasonable that he, who is less well-acquainted with me, doubts it. Enough about him; now I come to us.

*To Luca Scalabrino—Rome*
Your Lordship, in your last letter you ask forgiveness of me for not having revealed your sexual desire for me; and in your other ones that you wrote to me before, you have always shown that you believe that I am scornful of you, because you have not revealed to me this carnal desire of yours, and you express a very good reason for your secrecy and silence used with me. I, who have decided to confirm what I said many years ago, that is that I consider your Lordship not only a dear and cordial friend, but as the dearest and most valuable of all the others, and in sum as part of my soul; I don't want to leave you in this error and this deception any longer, and if however you don't deceive yourself, but want to seem as if you deceive yourself, I don't want to leave you this opportunity, neither can I allow that at least in my matters, and in that which belongs to me, you don't equal my naïveté, silly or philosophical as it is. Know then, that I was not offended because your Lordship didn't tell me of your love because you were not for any reason obliged to do this, but I was offended because you suffered such a large injury that Ariosto told me something about it. Neither only were you offended, but you wrote to him in such a way

that he could understand that you felt yourself offended by him gravely. Then, you wrote a letter to me full of so much scorn, without any further explanation. I confess that you had a reason to complain, that Ariosto had told me this secret, and I know he has difficulty in keeping my own secrets; but certainly there was no reason that, for something of so little importance, words so bitter should be said so openly by you against my reputation both to him and to me. A friend must conceal the defects of his friend; and I, the most loquacious man in the world, have never said anything that could displease you, neither in this nor in other matters; if not that I revealed to your father and to Sir Antenore your illness because of my concern about your health. And may God be my witness, I did not discuss anything else, if not in that way that I knew and I really believed it was in your interest. But let this be the end of my defense. I will remember only the many courtesies and kindnesses that I have received from you; and I will not remember this incident, but I will ascribe the impetuousness of those letters to your nature; so I beg you to attribute to mine the harshness of some letters, in which, urging you to purge yourself, I used words too hard and vehement. We're even, as they say: from now on, not with less love or confidence in you, I will try to avoid provoking your anger. I beg your forgiveness for the past letters; you do not need to ask me as if I were a superior, because I am superior in nothing, and in many things I bow to you. And if, however, you want to use these good manners, use them without offending me, while you want to satisfy me: because not the superiority of the person, but the superiority of the cause makes it worthy to me that you should ask my forgiveness; and I give it to you, and you give it to me, and a toast! And speak no longer of these things. . . . In sum, I am all yours.

## Roman Pasquinades (16th cent.)

*Translated by James J. Wilhelm*

Pasquinades were anonymous and scurrilous poetry attacking political and religious figures. The poems often employed homosexuality as one of the weapons of attack.

## 329

*Advice to a Young Man*

Young man, before time flies further away,
Devote yourself, I tell you, to having a good sexy time,
And if it enters your heart, don't be afraid
To find out where Sodom and Gomorrah are located.
Don't enter into projects where the sperm should run
And then try to hold it back—Because ejaculation is just like pissing.
Wherever you're heading, let it flow and fly!
Don't ever worry about what the nuts will say
If she's your aunt and you're her relative,
Screw on, and get to wherever you're bound to come to.

If you're afraid that you're committing a sin,
Aren't jubilee celebrations held for all the living
And the dead? Two thousand for a single sin.


## 356

*What Really Goes on in the College of Cardinals*

My patron has truly opened up my eyes:
Cardinal Francesco Pisani's ass is always open;
I've seen Innocenzo Cybo, who fucked Cardinal Trani
And then Fernando Ponzetta, plugging it into Ercole Rangone.
I've seen in the College of Cardinals a big question
About who's a buggerer, browning queen or pimp.
I've seen Niccolo Ridolfi hoisting up his robes
Like a kneeling slave waiting for his turn.
I've watched Andrea della Valle get behind Franciotto Orsini,
And seen Brother Egidio Canisio with full hypocrisy
Doing battle with cute Alessandro Cesarini.
I've seen that crazy Archbishop of Siena
Wanting to rub his thighs with Francesco Armellini,
As Cardinal Aracelli does with that heretic De Vio.
Every cardinal quite courteously
Joins in fucking every other one—
Except for old Tough-Drinker, who only rams it down his throat.


## Antonio Rocco (17th cent.)

From *L'ALCIBIADE FANCIULLO A SCOLA* (1652)

[ALCIBIADES IN SCHOOL]

*Translated by Michael Taylor*

Though pederasty was defended in both medieval and Renaissance texts, Rocco's seventeenth-century defense of sodomy, contained within the story of the erotic education of Alcibiades, is one of the first modern texts to openly celebrate sexuality between males. In this section Philotimus welcomes his new pupil, young Alcibiades.

PHILOTIMUS: I shall fill the vessel of thy mind with the seed of doctrines plentiful and pleasant, such doctrines as will seem to thee supernatural. Thou shalt not encounter the stern rigor I am accustomed to use with the other children to gain their respect; nay, our first interviews will brim o'er with pleasure and sweet trust. Indeed, as a gauge of my affection, and to seal the equality of our intercourse, let me bestow this, need I say honorable, kiss on thy young lips.

    At this renewed attack the child, quivering and growing suddenly pale, took a hasty step backwards.

"Fear not, my son," spake the master, "no man's tongue will harm thee, save when its brash impudence offends the bounds of Justice. That eloquence thou wishest to learn from me, which thy first instructors pursued so zealously, my devotion will impart to thee, but thou shalt not possess it truly until thy tongue be joined to mine. For the hand helpeth the hand, the mind assisteth the mind, the tongue aideth the tongue. Come here, come here, my ruby . . ." and folding him against his bosom, he punctuated each word he spake with a lingering kiss.

The child turned away a little, and looked scornful, but it was only one of those coy rebuffs which but kindle lust and add spice to wantonness. Indeed Alcibiades rebelled not and even suffered his master to fondle the shapely, small and velvet globes of his apples. Therefore the latter was feverishly visiting the lad's garden of Eden, and, in the futile transports of unsatisfied desire, nevertheless, upon touching the delicious entry with his finger, he apprehended the surpassing felicity of the blessed. This delightful play continued a short while ere Philotimus was called away upon some pressing affair; but his senses having been moved to such rapture, the merest thought of that bliss he had just quit obliged him to interrupt his business.

Alcibiades questions his teacher: "Pray tell me whether the pleasure is keener with lads or with the wenches, and why."

PHILOTIMUS: There is something offensive in the mingling of juices; 'tis like an untimely and unseasonable downpour which wearies and enfeebles the senses. So vast is the cunt's capacity 'tis frightening. 'Tis a labyrinth inviting one to lose oneself in its passages rather than to tarry and take one's pleasure there. Mark, on the contrary, that pretty declivity leading to the flowered garden of a boy. Doth it not enclose all the delights? Doth not the motion of those two fresh, rounded, velvety little cushions gamboling between thy thighs incline one to the pitch of wantonness? Doth it not surpass all the pleasures, both real and imagined, in a wench? Doth it not seem to thee that Nature, in giving thee these happy, happy cheeks, that plump form and that dainty softness, expressly intended to teach us her purpose, which is to fill the concavity of our body when it presseth against them? 'Tis the opposite with women. In congress the convexity of the two stomachs joining together leaveth a gap between the parts and hindereth the perfect harmony necessary to extreme bliss. Whereas taking one's pleasure of a boy one is neither deprived of the sweetness of his kiss, nor of the delight in breathing in the perfumed breeze that escapeth between his passionate lips. Here too the agreement is complete and the rapture entirely shared, so long as the beloved lieth in such a way that he can turn his visage and bring it close to his lover's; meanwhile, depending on the charming stripling's fancy, the spring onion is planted in his garden or quivereth in his hand. . . . As to know why some youths discharge more frequently and plentifully than others, the reason is that, in them, the parts of their "garden" are connected to their little "finch" with subtler nerves, which improveth the circulation of the spirits; so that the wanton agitation of the "bird" accompanieth and sometimes even precedeth the transports of the "garden." Certain lads find such delight in being mounted that they become mad with desire, begging and praying and even forcing their lovers to do the thing to them. These are keener and quicker than all others because the abundance of lascivious spirits in them maketh their motions nimble and causeth them to be hotter in action; and therefore their body constantly betrayeth the goal to which it tendeth, not to mention the wanton movements of their hips and a certain lascivious to-and-fro which is produced in them by the circulation of the spirits. There are other boys who are tranquil and modest, and have not the same immoderate urge to "chime," but notwithstanding how feebly the amorous inclination common to all creatures in them dwells, they are nevertheless as readily inclined as the others to yield to tender toyings, which they like though they'll ne'er admit to it. . . .

ALCIBIADES: I'll submit to thy urgings. 'Tis the desire to learn above all which decideth me. Look, I am ready to satisfy thee. . . .

Thereupon he lifted his gown and modestly took the posture the circumstances required. The master assisted him with his hand, and ere long the lad's arse displayed its glorious love treasures which put the sky and the stars to shame. The sun himself, vanquished by those more than celestial glories, hastened to veil his visage. What poet could e'er describe the wonders richly scattered through that epitome of the marvels of the universe. The two hemispheres, like unto two celestial spheres, with coursing blood tinted, were starred with sprightly tufts of hyacinths and privet. They quivered at the slightest touch, darkened with a thousand rubies that sparkled on a bed of milk and cinnabar. All was but delightful meadows, flowered gardens, many-hued rainbows, white beams of light and twinkling stars. Their constant, slow, and amorous motions would have roused a statue of marble or bronze; ah, the majestic and beauteous spectacle of that little bud, whose folds were tight and dainty like a rose before it blossoms, a lovely floweret tinted with a thousand mottled tones among which the purest snow disputed with gorgeous purple. . . .

## From L'Alcibiade fanciullo a scola

*Translated by Jill Claretta Robbins*

PHILOTIMUS: But let's come now to the point. In which of our gods do we have faith? In Jupiter, king of the gods and of men. Didn't he kidnap Ganymede? Or if the deeds of the gods are for the example and imitation of men, why are we prohibited from that which they teach with their deeds? Jupiter was allowed to use force, he was a god, his divine will is the measure of justice for our deeds, since we don't have the sovereign ruling power; let prayers be in place of force, let it be that the desires of the deaf bend to uniform consent. Apollo didn't enjoy Cyparissus and Hyacinth? Hercules of Ilus [Hylas]? And is not Cupid, moreover, man and boy in order to show the principal love to be of boys, and for the feminine love there is Venus, who has no weapons nor fire, if she does not borrow them from her son.

Boys then have the first scepter in love, the women have delegated and dependent authority; therefore, so very far it is from the truth that this sovereign delight is abhorred by the gods, that they prepare atrocious punishments, as it is far from right that a servant should be punished for executing the orders and the examples of his master; and to you it will be believable exactly as if you heard it said that the sun at night shuts itself up in a cocoon of the moon.

If God is always God, immutable and very wise in works of justice and clemency, why is it that now he doesn't punish that fault? Is he perhaps different from what he was? Has he changed his opinion? Is he perhaps afraid of us? Or is he destroying the work of the world he has made?

If a watch has motion from wheels and counterweights that its maker has given it, is it the defect of this watch that it tells the hours in this way or in another? Inclinations are counterweights given us by nature and God; whoever follows these doesn't stray from his own origins, he does not go against his maker. . . .

And it is . . . a notable thing that of all the very diligent, famous, and universal writers of our Greeks, there is not even one that made mention of [the punishment of Sodom as described in the Bible]. . . .

"Perhaps," responded Alcibiades, "perhaps being of your view, they didn't, for their self-interest, want to take away this pleasure from men by frightening them."

"It isn't likely, son, that which you propose if they had believed it to be a divine scourge, this pleasure prohibited and punished by God to whose rule everything is subject, [so] as to not fall into his disdain and not be esteemed guilty of a tacit offense. Or at least if they were so obstinate, keeping it only for themselves by frightening the others at the same time, [they] would have had themselves judged as pious and would have put themselves in secure possession of this power, so that they would have filled up volumes, as well as papers and sheets. This is easier to believe because some of them preferred life to the truth, and they had the utmost integrity and were very observant of justice; so that then they did not write of it because there was no foundation of truth upon which they could base their writing.

"In fact, the author of this invention [sanctions against pederasty], [since] it seemed to him that it was too severe to put into action what he had invented by amplification and by terror in his written laws, does not say that through the simple use of young boys the aforementioned cities [Sodom and Gomorrah] were submerged, but because they were impious, cruel, miserly, greedy, violent; and that their final ruin was the violence they directed against the angels. And thus . . . violence, therefore, was punished, not pleasure; cruelty, not love; inhumanity, not embraces. I say this, however, alluding to the tale, not to what happened. . . . [T]here is stated a decree in which one of the very excellent ones, who extolled and was believed to have dealings with God, threatened punishments for the crimes of the people: and when it came to the use of young boys, did not complain of this, but reproached those who left the young boys of their nation for foreigners. . . . If it is a crime to leave them, it is therefore praiseworthy and a virtuous act to take care of them; and owing love in the first place to one's own rather than to foreigners, abandoning those for these is against the laws of nature. So that, by reproaching the mingling with others, he wants us to get together with our own. But if the human laws, made by whoever wants to, become the universals, the infallible ones of nature, you will find the use of young boys ordained rather than prohibited by them. And here I come to the proof.

"I call laws of nature . . . those that by the light of the intellect are in every man, of whatever sect or nation, naturally, without artifice, and approved by universal consensus, by the wisest and by the most just. They are divided into two principal parts: one concerns the honor of God, the other the benevolence and equity of the neighbor. . . .

"To love God above everything; [and one's] neighbor as oneself; or not to offend God or the neighbor. Now these two precepts, if in effect they are different, should not be confused with one another, because if they were contained in one another and confused they would not be distinct, so that there would be only one. And if not offending God or the neighbor were the same, it would be enough to say not offending God: they are then indubitably distinct, neither the one depends nor belongs to the other. Now I ask you: if your neighbor is happy about what you want, has pleasure and is satisfied, and sometimes benefited, could one call him offended? Would the precept be transgressed? Could we call him insulted? Would he summon you to justice?"

"On the contrary," responded Alcibiades, "the precept will have been fulfilled, and will be rewarded; and I consider calling him offended as different as giving would be from robbing."

"You conclude well," answered the teacher, "but if it is so, that a young boy is happy to give of himself to whoever desires him, and he takes delight and use from it, is the neighbor offended here? Who would say this nonsense? And if from free will, the royal gift of God, comes the will and the power to do what pleases him, why can't he do it? If one can lend a house, a horse, a dog, why not his own limbs? Who is a tyrant so wicked that giving liberty to a servant of his, he prohibits him the use? Therefore, did God make us free so that we are slaves of our passions and the reckless excesses of them? He, thus, in the tempering that He gave to our fragility, will see the causes weaken, will take again that which is His? Or perhaps he pities our well-being? Does he envy our pleasure? If one does not give solace with pleasures to human calamity, the inhabitants of the world will be prisoners of Pluto. Man would not be king of the animals, but the epilogue of sorrows and torments. These foolish beliefs should not disturb the gloriousness of your soul."

"Why then is it that the young boys that submit to the pleasures of men are despised and considered infamous under the disgraceful name of *bardassi*? And if what you say is true, perhaps the common way of men has not transformed reality into language. Relieve me of this doubt," said Alcibiades.

"This name of *bardassa*," responded the teacher, "is not suitable nor should be given, and in effect is not given, to boys who through affection and courtesy graciously give themselves to respectable and worthy lovers. As one does not give the title of prostitute to that fair amorous damsel who kindly gives in to her lover to satisfy the laws of love: on the contrary, it is so far from reasonable and just, that in place of these unworthy epithets, by wise and discreet people, they are called *divi* and *dive*, redeemers of human afflictions, restorers of falling and afflicted spirits. And by many great princes altars and temples have been erected to them, priests have been dedicated to them and sacrifices and incense have been offered to them. Of these things the history of the Greeks and of the Roman writers is full. *Bardassa* really means mercenary and venal boy, who only for simple recompense, almost by measurement, sells himself, nor is concerned with other than his servile earnings. An amorous young boy is as different from the mercenary as a venerable priest would be from a vituperous simoniac; each is a priest, each administers the same sacerdotal offices: but the first in the ministry seeks excellent works, the greatness of his office, the spiritual gratification of the people, the due of divine laws; the other, the useful, self-interest and earnings. So that the first is sacrosanct and detestable the second. Things of high value must not be exposed to the baseness of a price: and what thing is more valuable and more worthy than amorous young boys? Glorious and divine boy, who, without a mercenary goal, blesses men on earth; vile infamous mercenary, who sells himself for a price, who from being gardener and treasurer of the joys of love becomes vile butcher of his own flesh."

"Isn't it perhaps reasonable," answered Alcibiades, "that whoever does things for others receives benefits? That he who is ready to serve others is relieved in his needs? Why, therefore, can't a boy, without falling from the glorious into the foul, receive money from whoever receives such sweetness from him?"

"My beautiful boy," responded the teacher, "markets are one thing and courtesies are another. A man is never so rich nor so powerful that at a certain time he doesn't need another man; and whoever gives benefits expects them too. The beloved boy, then, should be remembered and given gifts by his kind lover; he should be to him very liberal and kind, but far from the terms of convention and wages, neither tacit nor expressed.

"Love makes rules in these cases; he develops and works it out honorably and in a worthwhile manner; gifts and kindness and favors are not prohibited, only sordid merchandising."

# 9. Affectionate Shepherds

## English Homoerotic Literature (1500–1685)

SPECIAL FRIENDS

Like Italian writers, English writers employed the conventions of friendship or classical allusion to denote homosexual desire, and such conventions were often strongly eroticized, even sexualized. In a 1611 dictionary a "ganimede" is defined as an "ingle," that is, a passive catamite. In Richard Barnfield's *Affectionate Shephearde*, the youth Daphnis addresses his love poems to the youth he calls "Ganimede." while in Thomas Heywood's *Jupiter and Ganimede* there is no doubt about his availability for sex, since Jupiter importunes Ganymede for kisses.

However, classical allusion is not the only location of homoeroticized relationships in English texts. Other more general categories are emphasized by Bruce R. Smith in *Homosexual Desire in Shakespeare's England* (1991). Relations between equals—the kind of male bonding that obtains in some of Shakespeare's plays (e.g., *Coriolanus*, *Troilus and Cressida*, or *Romeo and Juliet*)—provide possible homoerotic readings. The pastoral—derived largely from Virgil's Second Eclogue and exemplified in Spenser's *The Shepheardes Calender*, Marlowe's "The Passionate Shepherd," or Barnfield's *The Affectionate Shephearde*—suggests an Arcadian realm outside the binding law of the Christian dispensation, one in which men are allowed free play of homoerotic feelings. Androgyny, seen in depictions of Ganymede and in Shakespeare's transvestite characters, and in most of the sexually desirable youths described in Renaissance erotic texts, offers another possibility for the interpretation of homoeroticism. Young men often adopt the dress of the other sex, which provides an obvious source for homoerotic entertainment. Situations in which sexual power is the key to the tension of the text—whether it is the sexual power held by an older man over a younger or exercised by a younger over a desiring elder—provide opportunities both for satire and for more serious explorations of homoerotic relationships, such as that between Barnfield's Daphnis and Ganimede, Spenser's Hobbinol and Colin, Marlowe's Gaveston and Edward, or between Shakespeare's "Will" and a "Mr. W. H."

Homoeroticism is suggested in prose romance as well. Narratives like Sir Philip Sidney's *The Countess of Pembroke's Arcadia* (1593), though ultimately celebrating heterosexual marriage, nevertheless portrays the attachment between Pyrocles and Musidorus in terms that suggest passion as well as friendship, and in Sir Francis Bacon's celebrated essay "Of Friendship," Bacon, in common with Italian writers like Ficino, argues that friendship between men is the most noble of all relationships. However, in most English Renaissance texts (just as in many Italian texts), the possibility of a sexual component in friendship is often implicitly but less often explicitly expressed. Like Italian homoeroticism, English homoeroticism existed in a social milieu which was often intensely homosocial and which celebrated classical homoeroticism in texts and in theory. Yet at the same time, denunciations of sodomy in sermons, in homophobic pamphlets and satirical poems such as John Marston's *Certaine Satyrs* (1598), expressed fear, loathing, and condemnation of the actual practice of homosexual relations. English texts therefore, are heirs to classical approbation that informed and created a decidedly homoerotic literary language. Yet they were written within a social milieu that increasingly condemned sodomy. Nonetheless, the great writers, like Marlowe and Shakespeare, were willing to write about love between men in language that would not only celebrate it but deliberately transgress against anti-sodomitical social and dogmatic orthodoxy.

## Henry VIII

### THE LAW OF 25 (1533)

For as moche as there is not yett sufficient and condigne punyshment appoynted and lymytted by the due course of the Lawes of this Realme for the detestable and abhomynable Vice of Buggery committed with mankynde or beaste; It may therfore please the Kinges Highness with the assent of his Lords spiritual and temporal and the Commons of this present Parliament assembled, that it may be enacted by authority of the same, that the same offence be henceforth adjudged Felonye, and suche order and forme of process therein to be used against the offenders as in cases of Felonye at the common law; and that the offenders being herof convicte by Verdicte, Confession, or Outlawry shall suffer suche peynes of death and losses and penalties of their goods, chattels, debts, lands, tenements and herditaments as Felons be accustomed to do accordynge to the order of the common-lawes of this Realme, and that no person offending in any such offence shall be admitted to his clergie: And that Justice of Peace shall have power and authority within the limits of their commissions and jurisdiccion, to hear and determine the said offence as they do use to do in case of other Felonyes: this acte to endure to the last day of the next Parliamente.

## Edmund Spenser (1552–1599)

Edmund Spenser employs classical references to same-sex romance in Book 4 of *The Faerie Queene*, especially in the description of "thousand of payre of lovers" in the Temple of Venus. Yet in the "Januarye" eclogue of *The Shepheardes Calender*, he resists such a reading. Hobbinol, like Corydon in Virgil's Second Eclogue, loves Colin Clout, but Colin Clout (who is the major figure of the poem) likes the handsome Alexis, spurns him, and indeed makes it clear that Hobbinol is not the object of *his* affection. In his "Glosse" supplied for the text, the anonymous "E. K." rather overanxiously insists that "paederastice" is absolutely not what Spenser implies.

### FROM *THE SHEPHEARDES CALENDAR* (1579)

A Shepheardes boye (no better do him call),
When Winters wastful spight was almost spent
All in a sunneshine day, as did befall,
Led forth his flock that had bene long ypent:
    So faynt they woxe, and feeble in the folde,
    That now unnethes their feete could them uphold.

All as the Sheepe, such was the shepeheards looke,
For pale and wanne he was, (alas the while!)
May seeme he lovd, or els some care he tooke;
Well couth he tune his pipe and frame his stile:
    Tho to a hill his faynting flocke he ledde,
    And thus him playnd, the while his shepe there fedde.

"Ye Gods of love, that pitie lovers payne,
(If any gods the paine of lovers pitie)
Looke from above, where you in joyes remaine,
And bowe your eares unto my dolefull dittie:
    And, Pan, thou shepheards God that once didst love,
    Pitie the paines that thou thy selfe didst prove.

"Thou barrein ground, whome winters wrath hath wasted,
Art made a myrrhour to behold my plight:
Whilome thy fresh spring flowrd, and after hasted
Thy sommer prowrde, with Daffadilies dight;
    And now is come thy wynters stormy state,
    Thy mantle mard, wherein thou maskedst late.

"Such rage as winters reigneth in my heart,
My life-bloud friesing with unkindly cold,
Such stormy stoures do breede my balefull smart,
As if my yeare were wast and woxen old;
    And yet, alas! but now my spring begonne,—
    And yet, alas! yt is already donne.

"You naked trees, whose shady leaves are lost,
Wherein the byrds were wont to build tbeir bowre,
And now are clothd with mosse and hoary frost
Instede of bloosmes, wherewith your buds did flowre;
    I see your teares that from your boughes doe raine,
    Whose drops in drery ysicles remaine.

"All so my lustfull leafe is drye and sere,
My timely buds with wayling all are wasted;
The blossome which my braunch of youth did beare
With breathed sighes is blowne away and blasted
    And from mine eyes the drizling teares descend,
    As on your boughes the ysicles depend.

"Thou feeble flocke, whose fleece is rough and rent,
Whose knees are weake through fast and evil fare,
Mayst witnesse well, by thy ill governement,
Thy maysters mind is overcome with care:
    Thou weake, I wanne; thou leane, I quite' forlorne:
    With mourning pyne I; you with pyning mourne.

"A thousand sithes I curse that carefull howrer
Wherein I longd the neighbour towne to see,
And eke tenne thousand sithes I blesse the stoure
Wherein I sawe so fayre a sight as shee:
    Yet all for naught: such sight hath bred my bane.
    Ah, God! that love should breede both joy and payne!

"It is not Hobbinol wherefore I plaine,
Albee my love he seeke with dayly suit;
His clownish gifts and curtsies I disdaine,
His kiddes, his cracknelles, and his early fruit.
    Ah, foolish Hobbinol! thy gyfts bene vayne;
    Colin them gies to Rosalind againe.

"I love thilke lasse, (alas! why doe I love?)
And am forlorne, (alas! why am I lorne?)
Shee deignes not my good will, but doth reprove,
And of my rurall musicke holdeth scorne.
    Shepheards devise she hateth as the snake,
    And laughes the songs that Colin Clout doth make.

"Wherefore, my pype, albee rude Pan thou please,
Yet for thou pleasest not where most I would:
And thou, unlucky Muse, that wontst to ease
My musing mynd, yet canst not when thou should;
    Both pype and Muse shall sore the while abye."
    So broke his oaten pype, and downe dyd lye.

By that, the welked Phoebus gan availe
His weary waine; and now the frosty Night
Her mantle black through heaven gan overhaile:
Which seene, the pensife boy, halfe in despight,
    Arose, and homeward drove his sonned sheepe
    Whose hanging heads did seeme his careful case to wepe.

## "Glosse" on Hobbinol by E. K.

[Hobbinol] is a fained country name, whereby, it being so commune and usuall, seemeth to be hidden the person of some his very speciall and most familiar freend, whom he entirely and extraordinarily beloved, as peraduenture shall be more largely declared hereafter. In thys place seemeth to be some savour of disorderly love, which the learned call *paederastice*: but it is gathered beside his meaning. For who that hath red Plato his dialogue called Alcybiades, Xenophon and Maximus Tyrius of Socrates opinions, may easily perceive, that such love is muche to be alowed and liked of, specially so meant, as Socrates used it: who sayth, that in deede he loved Alcybiades extremely, yet not Alcybiades person, but hys soule, which is

Alcybiades owne selfe. And so is paederastice much to be praeferred before gyn-
erastice, that is the love whiche enflameth men with lust toward woman kind. But
yet let no man thinke, that herein I stand with Lucian or hys develish disciple
Unico Aretino, in defence of execrable and horrible sinnes of forbidden and unlawful fleshlinesse, Whose abominable errour is fully confuted of Perionius, and others.

## FROM *THE FAERIE QUEENE* (1590–1596)

[Una is brought by fauns and satyrs before Sylvanus, and when he sees her he is reminded
of his love for Cyparissus.]

    By vew of her he ginneth to revive
His ancient love, and dearest *Cyparisse*,
And calles to mind his pourtraiture alive,
How faire he was, and yet not faire to this,
And how he slew with glauncing dart amisse
A gentle Hynd, the which the lovely boy
Did love as life, above all worldly blisse;
For griefe whereof the lad n'ould after joy.
But pynd away in anguish and selfe-wild annoy.
    (1.6.17)

[In the Garden of Adonis, Cupid and Adonis are seen in wanton play. Adonis praises
Cupid.]

    There now he lives in everlasting joy,
With many of the Gods in company,
Which thither haunt, and with the winged boy
Sporting himselfe in safe felicity:
Who when he hath with Spoiles and cruelty
Ransackt the world, and in the wofull harts
Of many wretches set his triumphes hye,
Thither resorts, and laying his sad darts
Aside, with fair *Adonis* playes his wanton parts.
    (3.6.49)

[In Book 3, a Masque is performed and some of the Masquers appear as characters from
classical erotic legends.]

    The first was *Fancy*, like a lovely boy,
Of rare aspect, and beautie without peare;
Matchable either to that ympe of *Troy*,
Whom Joue did love, and chose his cup to beare,
Or that same daintie lad, which waas so deare
To Great *Alcides*, that when as he dyde,

He wailed womanlike with many a teare,
And every wood, and every valley wyde
He fild with *Hylas* name, the Nymphes eke *Hylas* cryde.
    (3.12.7)

[In Canto 9 Spenser debates the virtues of different kinds of love.]

Hard is the doubt, and difficult to deeme,
When all three kinds of love together meet
And doe dispart the hart with powre extreme,
Whether shall weigh the balance down; to weet,
The deare affection unto kindred sweet,
Or raging fire of love to womankind,
Or zeale of friends combynd with vertues meet:
But of them all the band of vertuous mind,
Me seemse, the gentle hart should most assured bind.

For naturall affection soone doth cesse,
And quenched is *Cupids* greater flame:
But faithful friendship doth them both suppresse,
And them with maystring discipline doth tame,
Through thoughts aspyring to eternall fame:
For as the soule doth rule the earthly masse,
No lesse then perfect gold surmounts the meanest brasse.

All which who list by tryall to assay
Shall in this storie find approved plaine;
In which these Squires true friendship more did sway
Than either care of parents could refraine,
Or love of fairest Ladie could constrain;
For though Poeana were faire as morne,
Yet did this trustie squire with proud disdaine
For his friends sake her offred favours scorne,
And she her selfe her syre of whom she was yborn.
    (4.9.1–3)

[In the Temple of Venus, Scudamore sees "thousand of payres of lovers" and among them, "another sort of lover" from classical homoerotic myth. He laments that he cannot be among them.]

But farre away from these, another sort
Of lovers lincked in true harts consent;
Which loved not as these, for like intent,
But on chast virtue grounded their desire,
Farre from all fraud, or fayned blandishments;
Which in their spirits kindling zealous flre,
Brave thoughts and noble deedes did evermore aspire.

"Such were great *Hercules* and *Hylas* deare;
Trew *Jonathon* and *David* trustie tryde;
Stout *Theseus*, and *Pirithous* his feare;
*Pylades* and *Orestes* by his syde;
Myld *Titus* and *Gesippus* without pryde
*Damon* and *Pythias* whom death could not sever;
All these and all that ever had bene tyde
In bands of friendship, there did live for ever,
Whose lives although decay'd, yet loves decayed never.

"Which when as I, that never tasted blis
Nor happie howre, beheld with gazefull eye,
I thought there was none other heaven then this;
And gan their endlesse happinesse envye,
That being free from feare and gealosye
Might frankely there their loves desire possesse;
Whilest I, through paines and perlous jeopardie,
Was forst to seeke my lifes deare patronnesse:
Much dearer be the things which come through hard distresse.
  (4.10.26–28)

## Michael Drayton (1563–1631)

Drayton wrote a number of what he called "historical legends" to patriotically celebrate important moments in English history. One of these was a retelling of the story of Edward and Gaveston. The play deals with the effects of private passion on the fortunes of the state. However, within the political frame Drayton paints the relationship between Edward and Gaveston in sympathetic terms that do not condemn their love. But Drayton's tale is a moral one, and its point is to show the consequences of uncontrolled desire, which even Gaveston describes as the "roote of our woe." Drayton moved in the circle of writers that included Christopher Marlowe, and Drayton's homosexualized story may have influenced Marlowe's version, which appeared the following year.

FROM *PIERS GAVESTON* (1593)

[Gaveston tells the story of his affair with Prince Edward.]

[lines 211–270]

This Edward in the Aprill of his age,
Whil'st yet the Crowne sate on his fathers head,
My *Jove* with me, his *Ganimed*, his page,
Frolick as May, a lustie life we led:
    He might commaund, he was my Soveraigns sonne,
    And what I saide, by him was ever done.

My words as lawes, Autentique he alloude,
Mine yea, by him was never crost with no,
All my conceite as currant he avowde,
And as my shadowe still he served so,
    My hand the racket, he the tennis ball,
    My voyces echo, answering every call.

My youth the glasse where he his youth beheld,
Roses his lipps, my breath sweete *Nectar* showers,
For in my face was natures fayrest field,
Richly adornd with Beauties rarest flowers.
    My breast his pillow, where he laide his head,
    Mine eyes his booke, my bosome was his bed.

My smiles were life, and Heaven unto his sight,
All his delight concluding my desier,
From my sweete sunne, he borrowed all his light,
And as a flie play'd with my beauties fier,
    His love-sick lippes at every kissing qualme,
    Cling to my lippes, to cure their griefe with balme.

Like as the wanton Yvie with his twyne,
Whenas the Oake his rootlesse bodie warmes,
The straightest saplings strictly doth combyne,
Clipping the woodes with his lacivious armes:
    Such our imbraces when our sporte begins,
    Lapt in our armes, like *Ledas* lovely Twins.

Or as Love-nursing *Venus* when she sportes,
With cherry-lipt *Adonis* in the shade,
Figuring her passions in a thousand sortes,
With sighes, and teares, or what else might perswade,
    Her deere, her sweete, her joy, her life, her love
    Kissing his browe, his cheeke, his hand, his glove.

My bewtie was the Load-starre of his thought,
My lookes the Pilot to his wandring eye,
By me his sences all a sleepe were brought,
When with sweete love I sang his lullaby.
    Nature had taught my tongue her perfect time,
    Which in his eare stroake duely as a chyme.

With sweetest speech, thus could I syranize,
Which as strong *Philters* youthes desire could move,
And with such method could I rhetorize,
My musik plaied the measures to his love:

In his faire brest, such was my soules impression,
As to his eyes, my thoughts made intercession.

Thus like an *Eagle* seated in the sunne,
But yet a *Phenix* in my soveraigns eye,
We act with shame, our revels are begunne,
The wise could judge of our Catastrophe:
 But we proceede to play our wanton prize,
 Our mournfull Chorus was a world of eyes.

The table now of all delight is layd,
Serv'd with what banquets bewtie could devise,
The *Sirens* singe, and false *Calypso* playd,
Our feast is grac'd with youthes sweete comoedies,
 Our looks with smiles, are sooth'd of every eye,
 Carrousing love in boules of Ivorie.

[lines 313–324]

And thus like slaves we sell our soules to sinne,
Vertue forgot by worldes deceitfull trust,
Alone by pleasure are we entred in,
Now wandring in the labyrinth of lust,
 For when the soule is drowned once in vice,
 The sweete of sinne, makes hell a paradice.

O Pleasure thou, the very lure of sinne,
The roote of woe, our youthes deceitfull guide,
A shop where all confected poysons been,
The bayte of lust, the instrument of pride,
 Inchanting *Circes*, smoothing cover-guile,
 Aluring *Siren*, flattering Crockodile.

[lines 403–444]

Why doe I quake my down-fall to reporte?
Tell on my ghost, the storie of my woe,
The King commaunds, I must depart the court,
I aske no question, he will have it so:
 The Lyons roring, lesser beastes doe feare,
 The greatest flye, when he approacheth neare.

My Prince is now appointed to his guarde,
As from a traytor he is kept from me,
My banishment already is preparde,
Away I must, there is no remedie:

On paine of death I may no longer stay,
Such is revenge which brooketh no delaye.

The skies with cloudes are all invelloped,
The pitchie fogs eclipse my cheerfull Sunne,
The geatie night hath all her curtaines spred
And all the ayre with vapours overrun:
    Wanting those rayes whose deernes lent me light,
    My sun-shine day is turn'd to black-fac'd night.

Like to the birde of *Ledaes* lemmans die,
Beating his breast against the silver streame,
The fatall prophet of his destinie,
With mourning chants, his death approching theame:
    So now I sing the dirges of my fall,
    The Anthemes of my fatall funerall.

Or as the faithfull Turtle for her make
Whose youth enjoyed her deere virginitie,
Sits shrouded in some melancholie brake
Chirping forth accents of her miserie,
    Thus halfe distracted sitting all alone,
    With speaking sighs, to utter forth my mone.

My bewties' dayning to behold the light
Now weather-beaten with a thousand stormes,
My daintie lims must travaile day and night,
Which oft were lulde in princely *Edwards* armes,
    Those eyes where bewtie sate in all her pride,
    With fearefull objects fild on every side.

The Prince so much astonisht with the blowe,
So that it seem'd as yet he felt no paine,
Untill at length awakned by his woe,
He sawe the wound by which his joyes were slaine,
    His cares fresh bleeding fainting more and more,
    No Cataplasma now to cure the sore.

[Edward laments the loss of Gaveston.]

[lines 469–515]

O breake my hart quoth he, O breake and dye,
Whose infant thoughts were nurst with sweete delight;
But now the Inne of care and miserie,
Whose pleasing hope is murthered with despight:

O end my dayes, for now my joyes are done,
Wanting my *Peirs*, my sweetest *Gaveston*.

Farewell my Love, companion of my youth,
My soules delight, the subject of my mirth,
My second selfe if I reporte the truth,
The rare and onely *Phenix* of the earth,
   Farewell sweete friend, with thee my joyes are gone,
   Farewell my *Peirs*, my lovely *Gaveston*.

What are the rest but painted Imagrie,
Dombe Idols made to fill up idle roomes,
But gaudie anticks, sportes of foolerie,
But fleshly coffins, goodly gilded tombes,
   But puppets which with others words replie,
   Like pratling ecchoes soothing every lie?

O damned world, I scorne thee and thy worth,
The very source of all iniquitie:
An ougly damme that brings such monsters forth,
The maze of death, nurse of impietie,
   A filthie sinke, where lothsomnes doth dwell,
   A labyrinth, a jayle, a very hell.

Deceitfull *Siren* traytor to my youth,
Bane to my blisse, false theefe that stealst my joyes:
Mother of lyes, sworne enemie to truth,
The ship of fooles fraught all with gaudes and toyes,
   A vessell stuft with foule hypocrisie,
   The very temple of Idolatrie.

O earth-pale Saturne most malevolent,
Combustious Planet, tyrant in thy raigne,
The sworde of wrath, the roote of discontent,
In whose ascendant all my joyes are slaine:
   Thou executioner of foule bloodie rage,
   To act the will of lame decrepit age.

My life is but a very mappe of woes,
My joyes the fruite of an untimely birth,
My youth in labour with unkindly throwes,
My pleasures are like plagues that raigne on earth,
   All my delights like streames that swiftly run,
   Or like the dewe exhaled by the Sun.

O Heavens why are you deafe unto my mone?

S'dayne you my prayers? or scorne to heare my misse?
Cease you to move, or is your pittie gone?
Or is it you that rob me of my blisse?
    What are you blinde, or winke and will not see?
    Or doe you sporte at my calamitie?

## Christopher Marlowe (1564–1593)

Like many Renaissance writers, Marlowe looked to classical allusion to indicate homosexuality. In *Edward II* the relationship of Jove and Ganymede is called upon as both precedent and justification for that of Edward and Gaveston. In "Hero and Leander" love between men is wittily mythologized as the apparently heterosexual Leander is taken to be the available Ganymede by Poseidon, who leaves no doubt as to the nature and intention of his desire. *Dido, Queen of Carthage* opens to a scene showing "Jupiter dandling Ganimed upon his knee," and in Marlowe's poem "The Passionate Shepherd to his Love," the invitation "come live with me and be my love" echoes Corydon's plea to Alexis in Virgil's Second Eclogue.

While he employed homosexualized classical allusions in poems, in his picture of France's Henry III in *The Massacre at Paris,* and especially in *Edward II,* Marlowe looked to the sanction of history for stories of male friendship with sexual implications. Edward II's love for Gaveston is set not only within a classical context by Gaveston himself in his opening speech (*Edward II,* 1.1.53–70) but also by the Elder Mortimer (1.4.387–400). Their relationship raises questions about the use of sex as a means of gaining power and the effect of private homosexual passion on the public life of the state.

Interpretations of *Edward II* vary. In one reading Edward and Gaveston are presented as brave men who declare their passion in the face of the overwhelming disdain, homophobia, and political machinations of his queen; in another their ill-conceived passion threatens not only the stability of the Crown and the state but the fabric of hierarchical society itself, since the nobility are as much offended by Gaveston's rank as by his sexual hold upon the king. When Edward is murdered at the end of the play, raped with a red-hot poker that effectively stands, as Gregory Bredbeck in *Sodomy and Interpretation* suggests, for the brand of sodomy, the play again offers a place for a double interpretation. Edward's murder, from one viewpoint, is the just punishment for a sodomite and for a failed king. But it may also be seen as the persecution and unjust punishment that a homophobic society inflicts on those who have dared the consequences of openly declaring a homosexual love, consequences that not even the sanctity and divinity that hedges a king can prevent.

FROM *DIDO, QUEEN OF CARTHAGE* (1593)

[Jupiter woos Ganymede.]

[*Here the Curtaines draw, there is discovered* Jupiter *dandling* Ganimed *upon his knee, and* Mercury *lying asleepe*]
JUPITER: What is't, sweet wag, I should deny thy youth?
Whose face reflects such pleasure to mine eyes,
As I, exhal'd with thy fire-darting beams,

Have oft driven back the horses of the Night,
Whence they would have hal'd thee from my sight.
Sit on my knee, and call for thy content,
Control proud Fate, and cut the thread of Time:
Why, are not all the gods at thy command,
And heaven and earth the bounds of thy delight?
Vulcan shall dance to make thee laughing sport,
And my nine daughters sing when thou art sad;
From Juno's bird I'll pluck her spotted pride,
To make thee fans wherewith to cool thy face;
And Venus' swans shall shed their silver down,
To sweeten out the slumbers of thy bed;
Hermes no more shall show the world his wings,
If that thy fancy in his feathers dwell,
But, as this one, I'll tear them all from him.

[*Plucks feather from Hermes' wings*]

Do thou but say, "their colour pleaseth me."
Hold here, my little love; these linked gems.

[*Gives jewels*]

My Juno ware upon her marriage day,
Put thou about thy neck, my own sweet heart,
And trick thy arms and shoulders with my theft.

GANIMED: I would have a jewel for mine ear,
And a fine brooch to put in my hat,
And then I'll hug with you an hundred times.

JUP: And shalt have, Ganymede, if thou wilt be my love.


FROM *EDWARD II* (1594)

[1.1.1–174] [*Enter Gaveston reading on a letter that was brought him from the King*]

GAVESTON: "My father is deceas'd. Come, Gaveston,
And share the kingdom with thy dearest friend."
Ah, words that make me surfeit with delight!
What greater bliss can hap to Gaveston
Than live and be the favorite of a king?
Sweet prince, I come! These, these thy amorous lines
Might have enforc'd me to have swum from France
And, like Leander, gasp'd upon the sand
So thou would'st smile and take me in thine arms!

The sight of London to my exil'd eyes
Is as Elysium to a new-come soul.
Not that I love the city or the men
—But that it harbors him I hold so dear,
The King—upon whose bosom let me die,
And with the world be still at enmity!
What need the arctic people love starlight,
To whom the sun shines both by day and night?
Farewell base stooping to the lordly peers,
My knee shall bow to none but to the King.
As for the multitude that are but sparks
Rak'd up in embers of their poverty,

TANTI: I'll fawn first on the wind
That glanceth at my lips, and flieth away.

[Gaveston interviews some "poor men" as possible servants but because of their roughness decides against them.]

GAV: Go. These are not men for me.
I must have wanton poets, pleasant wits,
Musicians that with touching of a string
May draw the pliant King which way I please.
Music and poetry is his delight.
Therefore I'll have Italian masques by night,
Sweet speeches, comedies, and pleasing shows;
And in the day when he shall walk abroad,
Like sylvan nymphs my pages shall be clad:
My men, like satyrs grazing on the lawns,
Shall with their goat feet dance an antic hay:
Sometime a lovely boy in Dian's shape,
With hair that gilds the water as it glides,
Crownets of pearl about his naked arms
And in his sportful hands an olive-tree
To hide those parts which men delight to see
Shall bathe him in a spring: and there hard by,
One like Actaeon peeping through the grove,
Shall by the angry goddess be transform'd:
And running in the likeness of an hart
By yelping hounds pull'd down, and seem to die.
Such things as these best please His Majesty,
My lord!—Here comes the King and the nobles
From the parliament.—I'll stand aside.

[*Enter the King, Lancaster, Mortimer Senior, Mortimer Junior, Edmund Earl of Kent, Guy Earl of Warwick, etc.*]
KING EDWARD: Lancaster!

LANCASTER: My lord!

GAV: [aside] (That Earl of Lancaster do I abhor.)

K. EDW: Will you not grant me this? [aside]–(In spite of them
I'll have my will! And these two Mortimers
That cross me thus, shall know I am displeas'd!)

ELDER MORTIMER: If you love us, my lord, hate Gaveston!

GAV: [aside] (That villain Mortimer, I'll be his death!)

YOUNG MORTIMER: Mine uncle here, this earl, and I myself
Were sworn to your father at his death,
That he should ne'er return into the realm.
And know, my lord, ere I will break my oath,
This sword of mine, that should offend your foes,
Shall sleep within the scabbard at thy need,
And underneath thy banners march who will,
For Mortimer will hang his armor up.

GAV: [aside] (Mort Dieu!)

K. EDW: Well, Mortimer, I'll make thee rue these words!
Beseems it thee to contradict thy King?
Frown'st thou thereat, aspiring Lancaster?
The sword shall plane the furrows of thy brows
And hew these knees that now are grown so stiff!
I will have Gaveston—and you shall know
What danger 'tis to stand against your King!

GAV: [aside] (Well done, Ned!)

LAN: My lord, why do you thus incense your peers
That naturally would love and honor you
But for that base and obscure Gaveston?
Four earldoms have I, besides Lancaster—
Derby, Salisbury, Lincoln, Leicester—
These will I sell to give my soldiers pay
Ere Gaveston shall stay within the realm!
Therefore if he be come, expel him straight!

KENT: Barons and earls, your pride hath made me mute,
But now I'll speak, and to the proof, I hope.
I do remember in my father's days
Lord Percy of the north being highly mov'd
Brav'd Mowbray in presence of the King:
For which, had not His Highness lov'd him well,
He should have lost his head: but with his look
Th' undaunted spirit of Percy was appeas'd
And Mowbray and he were reconcil'd.
Yet dare you brave the King unto his face?
Brother, revenge it, and let these their heads
Preach upon poles for trespass of their tongues!

WARWICK: O, our heads!

K. EDW: Ay, yours. And therefore I would wish you grant—

WAR: Bridle thy anger, gentle Mortimer.

Y. MOR: I cannot, nor I will not. I must speak.
Cousin, our hands I hope shall fence our heads
And strike off his that makes you threaten us.
Come, uncle, let us leave the brain-sick King,
And henceforth parle with our naked swords.
E. MOR: Wiltshire hath men enough to save our heads.
WAR: All Warwickshire will love him for my sake.
LAN: And northward Gaveston hath many friends.
Adieu, my lord. And either change your mind,
Or look to see the throne where you should sit
To float in blood and at thy wanton head,
The glozing head of thy base minion thrown!

[*Exeunt Nobles*]

K. EDW: I cannot brook these haughty menaces.
Am I a king, and must be overrul'd?
Brother, display my ensigns in the field!
I'll bandy with the barons and the earls,
And either die — or live with Gaveston.
GAV: I can no longer keep me from my lord.

[*Comes forward*]

K. EDW: What, Gaveston! Welcome! Kiss not my hand —
Embrace me, Gaveston as I do thee.
Why should'st thou kneel? knowest thou not who I am?
— Thy friend, thyself, another Gaveston!
Not Hylas was more mourn'd of Hercules
Than thou hast been of me since thy exile.
GAV: And since I went from hence, no soul in Hell
Hath felt more torment than poor Gaveston.
K. EDW: I know it. Brother, welcome home my friend.
Now let the treacherous Mortimers conspire,
And that high-minded Earl of Lancaster.
I have my wish in that I joy thy sight!
And sooner shall the sea o'erwhelm my land,
Than bear the ship that shall transport thee hence!
I here create thee Lord High Chamberlain,
Chief Secretary to the state and me,
Earl of Cornwall, King and Lord of Man.
GAV: My lord, these titles far exceed my worth.
KENT: Brother, the least of these may well suffice
For one of greater birth than Gaveston.
K. EDW: Cease, brother, for I cannot brook these words.
Thy worth, sweet friend, is far above my gifts.

Therefore, to equal it, receive my heart!
If for these dignities thou be envied
I'll give thee more, for but to honor thee
Is Edward pleas'd with kingly regiment.
Fear'st thou thy person? Thou shalt have a guard.
Want'st thou gold? Go to my treasury.
Would'st thou be lov'd and fear'd? Receive my seal,
Save or condemn, and in our name command
Whatso thy mind affects or fancy likes.
GAV: It shall suffice me to enjoy your love,
Which whiles I have, I think myself as great
As Caesar riding in the Roman street,
With captive kings at his triumphant car.

[1.2.1–84] [*Enter both the Mortimers, Warwick, and Lancaster*]

[They complain about Gaveston's ascendancy at court and plot against him.]

LAN: . . . Ah, wicked King! Accursed Gaveston!
This ground which is corrupted with their steps
Shall be their timeless sepulcher or mine.
Y. MOR: Well, let that peevish Frenchman guard him sure—
Unless his breast be sword-proof he shall die.
E. MOR: How now, why droops the Earl of Lancaster?
Y. MOR: Wherefore is Guy of Warwick discontent?
LAN: That villain Gaveston is made an earl.
E. MOR: An earl!
WAR: Ay, and besides Lord Chamberlain of the realm,
And Secretary too, and Lord of Man.
E. MOR: We may not, nor we will not suffer this!
Y. MOR: Why post we not from hence to levy men?
LAN: "My Lord of Cornwall," now at every word!
And happy is the man whom he vouchsafes,
For vailing of his bonnet, one good look.
Thus, arm in arm, the King and he doth march—
Nay more, the guard upon his lordship waits,
And all the court begins to flatter him.
WAR: Thus leaning on the shoulder of the King,

[*Leans on Lancaster*]

He nods and scorns and smiles at those that pass.
E. MOR: Doth no man take exceptions at the slave?
LAN: All stomach him, but none dare speak a word.
Y. MOR: Ah, that betrays their baseness, Lancaster!
Were all the earls and barons of my mind,

We'll hale him from the bosom of the King
And at the court-gate hang the peasant up:
Who swoln with venom of ambitious pride
Will be the ruin of the realm and us. . . .

[*Enter the Queen*]

Y. MOR: Madam, whither walks Your Majesty so fast!
QUEEN ISABELLA: Unto the forest, gentle Mortimer,
To live in grief and baleful discontent,
For now my lord the King regards me not,
But dotes upon the love of Gaveston—
He claps his cheeks, and hangs about his neck,
Smiles in his face, and whispers in his ears—
And when I come he frowns, as who should say,
"Go whither thou wilt seeing I have Gaveston!"
E. MOR: Is it not strange that he is thus bewitch'd?
Y. MOR: Madam, return unto the court again.
That sly inveigling Frenchman we'll exile,
Or lose our lives. And yet, ere that day come,
The King shall lose his crown, for we have power,
And courage too, to be reveng'd at full.
ARCHBISHOP OF CANTERBURY: But yet lift not your swords against the King.
LAN: No but we'll lift Gaveston from hence.
WAR: And war must be the means, or he'll stay still.
Q. ISAB: Then let him stay. For rather than my lord
Shall be oppress'd by civil mutinies,
I will endure a melancholy life.
—And let him frolic with his minion.
A. OF CANT: My lords, to ease all this, but hear me speak:
We and the rest that are his counsellors
Will meet, and with a general consent
Confirm his banishment with our hands and seals.
LAN: What we confirm the King will frustrate.
Y. MOR: Then may we lawfully revolt from him.
WAR: But say, my lord, where shall this meeting be?
A. OF CANT: At the New Temple.
Y. MOR: Content.
A. OF CANT: And, in the meantime, I'll entreat you all
To cross to Lambeth, and there stay with me.
LAN: Come then, let's away.
Y. MOR: Madam, farewell!
Q. ISAB: Farewell, sweet Mortimer; and for my sake
Forbear to levy arms against the King.
Y. MOR: Ay, if words will serve; if not, I must.

[1.4.1–187] [*Enter nobles (Lancaster with document, Warwick. Pembroke, Elder Mortimer, Younger Mortimer, the Archbishop of Canterbury, and attendants)*]

LAN: Here is the form of Gaveston's exile.
May it please your lordship to subscribe your name.
A. OF CANT: Give me the paper.

  [*Subscribes, as do the rest*]

LAN: Quick, quick, my lord, I long to write my name.
WAR: But I long more to see him banish'd hence.
Y. MOR: The name of Mortimer shall fright the King,
Unless he be declin'd from that base peasant.

[*Enter the King and Gaveston (and Kent. Edward seats Gaveston by him on the throne)*]

K. EDW: What, are you mov'd that Gaveston sits here?
It is our pleasure, we will have it so!
LAN: Your Grace doth well to place him by your side,
For nowhere else the new earl is so safe.
E. MOR: What man of noble birth can brook this sight?
*Quam male conveniunt!*
See what a scornful look the peasant casts!
PEMBROKE: Can kingly lions fawn on creeping ants?
WAR: Ignoble vassal, that like Phaeton
Aspir'st unto the guidance of the sun!
Y. MOR: Their downfall is at hand, their forces down—
We will not thus be fac'd and over-peer'd.
K. EDW: Lay hands on that traitor Mortimer!
E. MOR: Lay hands on that traitor Gaveston!

  [*Attendants hold Gaveston*]

KENT: Is this the duty that you owe your King?
WAR: We know our duties, let him know his peers.
K. EDW: Whither will you bear him? Stay, or ye shall die!
E. MOR: We are no traitors: therefore threaten not.
GAV: No, threaten not, my lord, but pay them home.
Were I a king . . .
Y. MOR: Thou villain, wherefore talk'st thou of a king
That hardly art a gentleman by birth!
K. EDW: Were he a peasant, being my minion,
I'll make the proudest of you stoop to him.
LAN: My lord, you may not thus disparage us!
Away, I say, with hateful Gaveston!

E. MOR: And with the Earl of Kent that favors him.

[*Attendants remove Kent and Gaveston*]

K. EDW: Nay, then, lay violent hands upon your King.
Here, Mortimer, sit thou in Edward's throne.
Warwick and Lancaster, wear you my crown.
Was ever king thus over-rul'd as I?
LAN: Learn then to rule us better, and the realm.
Y. MOR: What we have done our heart blood shall maintain.
WAR: Think you that we can brook this upstart pride?
K. EDW: Anger and wrathful fury stops my speech.
A. OF CANT: Why are you mov'd ? Be patient, my lord,
And see what we your counsellors have done.

[*Gives him document exiling Gaveston*]

Y. MOR: My lords, now let us all be resolute:
And either have our wills, or lose our lives.
K. EDW: Meet you for this, proud over-daring peers?
Ere my sweet Gaveston shall part from me,
This isle shall fleet upon the ocean
And wander to the unfrequented Inde.
A. OF CANT: You know that I am legate to the Pope.
On your allegiance to the see of Rome
Subscribe as we have done to his exile.
Y. MOR: Curse him, if he refuse; and then may we
Depose him and elect another king!
K. EDW: Ay, there it goes! But yet I will not yield.
Curse me, depose me, do the worst you can!
LAN: Then linger not, my lord, but do it straight.
A. OF CANT: Remember how the bishop was abus'd.
Either banish him that was the cause thereof,
Or I will presently discharge these lords
Of duty and allegiance due to thee.
K. EDW: [aside] (It boots me not to threat. I must speak fair.
The legate of the Pope will be obey'd.)
—My lord, [*to Archbishop*] you shall be Chancellor of the realm;
Thou, Lancaster, High Admiral of our fleet;
Young Mortimer and his uncle shall be earls;
And you, Lord Warwick, President of the North;
And thou [*to Pembroke*] of Wales. If this content you not,
Make several kingdoms of this monarchy
And share it equally amongst you all—
So I may have some nook or corner left
To frolic with my dearest Gaveston.

A. OF CANT: Nothing shall alter us. We are resolv'd.
LAN: Come, come, subscribe.
Y. MOR: Why should you love him whom the world hates so
K. EDW: Because he loves me more than all the world!
Ah, none but rude and savage-minded men
Would seek the ruin of my Gaveston!
You that be noble-born should pity him.
WAR: You that are princely-born should shake him off.
For shame subscribe, and let the lown depart.
E. MOR: Urge him, my lord.
A. OF CANT: Are you content to banish him the realm?
K. EDW: I see I must, and therefore am content.
Instead of ink I'll write it with my tears. [*Subscribes*]
Y. MOR: The King is love-sick for his minion.
K. EDW: 'Tis done—and now, accursed hand, fall off!
LAN: Give it me. I'll have it publish'd in the streets.
Y. MOR: I'll see him presently dispatch'd away.
A. OF CANT: Now is my heart at ease.
WAR: And so is mine.
PEMB: This will be good news to the common sort.
E. MOR: Be it or no, he shall not linger here.

  [*Exeunt Nobles*]

K. EDW: How fast they run to banish him I love!
They would not stir, were it to do me good.
Why should a king be subject to a priest?
Proud Rome, that hatchest such imperial grooms,
For these thy superstitious taper-lights,
Wherewith thy antichristian churches blaze,
I'll fire thy crazed buildings and enforce
The papal towers to kiss the lowly ground!
With slaughter'd priests may Tiber's channel swell,
And banks rais'd higher with their sepulchers!
As for the peers that back the clergy thus,
If I be King, not one of them shall live.

  [*Enter Gaveston*]

GAV: My lord, I hear it whisper'd everywhere
that I am banish'd and must fly the land.
K. EDW: 'Tis true, sweet Gaveston.—O! were it false!
The legate of the Pope will have it so—
And thou must hence, or I shall be depos'd.
But I will reign to be reveng'd of them!
And therefore, sweet friend, take it patiently.

Live where thou wilt, I'll send thee gold enough;
And long thou shalt not stay, or if thou dost,
I'll come to thee. My love shall ne'er decline!
GAV: Is all my hope turn'd to this hell of grief?
K. EDW: Rend not my heart with thy too-piercing words—
Thou from this land, I from myself am banish'd.
GAV: To go from hence grieves not poor Gaveston—
But to forsake you, in whose gracious looks
The blessedness of Gaveston remains:
For nowhere else seeks he felicity.
K. EDW: And only this torments my wretched soul
That, whether I will or no, thou must depart.
Be governor of Ireland in my stead,
And there abide till fortune call thee home.
Here, take my picture, and let me wear thine.

[*They exchange pictures and embrace*]

O, might I keep thee here as I do this,
Happy were I, but now most miserable!
GAV: 'Tis something to be pitied of a king.
K. EDW: Thou shalt not hence—I'll hide thee, Gaveston.
GAV: I shall be found, and then 'twill grieve me more.
K. EDW: Kind words and mutual talk makes our grief greater:
Therefore, with dumb embracement, let us part.
Stay, Gaveston, I cannot leave thee thus.
GAV: For every look, my lord drops down a tear.
Seeing I must go, do not renew my sorrow.
K. EDW: The time is little that thou hast to stay,
And, therefore, give me leave to look my fill.
But come, sweet friend, I'll bear thee on thy way.
GAV: The peers will frown.
K. EDW: I pass not for their anger. Come, let's go.
that we might as well return as go!

[*Enter Queen Isabella*]

Q. ISAB: Whither goes my lord?
K. EDW: Fawn not on me, French strumpet! Get thee gone!
Q. ISAB: On whom but on my husband should I fawn?
GAV: On Mortimer, with whom, ungentle Queen—
I say no more. Judge you the rest, my lord.
Q. ISAB: In saying this, thou wrong'st me, Gaveston.
Is't not enough that thou corrupt'st my lord,
And art a bawd to his affections,
But thou must call mine honor thus in question?

GAV: I mean not so. Your Grace must pardon me.
K. EDW: Thou art too familiar with that Mortimer:
And by thy means is Gaveston exil'd.
But I would wish thee reconcile the lords —
Or thou shalt ne'er be reconcil'd to me.
Q. ISAB: Your Highness knows, it lies not in my power.
K. EDW: Away then! touch me not, come, Gaveston.
Q. ISAB: Villain, 'tis thou that robb'st me of my lord!
GAV: Madam, 'tis you that rob me of my lord!
K. EDW: Speak not unto her, let her droop and pine.
Q. ISAB: Wherein, my lord, have I deserv'd these words?
Witness the tears that Isabella sheds;
Witness this heart that sighing for thee breaks,
How dear my lord is to poor Isabel!
K. EDW: And witness Heaven how dear thou art to me!
There weep. For till my Gaveston be repeal'd,
Assure thyself thou com'st not in my sight.

[*Exeunt Edward and Gaveston*]

Q. ISAB: O miserable and distressed Queen!
Would when I left sweet France and was embark'd
That charming Circes walking on the waves
Had chang'd my shape, or at the marriage-day
The cup of Hymen had been full of poison!
Or with those arms that twin'd about my neck
I had been stifled, and not liv'd to see
The King my lord thus to abandon me!
Like frantic Juno will I fill the earth
With ghastly murmur of my sighs and cries,
For never doted Jove on Ganymede
So much as he on cursed Gaveston.
But that will more exasperate his wrath.
I must entreat him, I must speak him fair,
And be a means to call home Gaveston —
And yet he'll ever dote on Gaveston!
And so am I for ever miserable!

[The nobles and the Queen determine to murder Gaveston. Gaveston flees to Ireland.]

[*Enter King Edward mourning (Beaumont, attendants)*]

[1.4.307–37]
K. EDW: He's gone, and for his absence thus I mourn.
Did never sorrow go so near my heart
As doth the want of sweet Gaveston!

And could my crown's revenue bring him back,
I would freely give it to his enemies—
And think I gain'd, having bought so dear a friend!
Q. ISAB: Hark, how he harps upon his minion.
K. EDW: My heart is as an anvil unto sorrow,
Which beats upon it like the Cyclops' hammers
And with the noise turns up my giddy brain
And makes me frantic for my Gaveston!
Ah, had some bloodless fury rose from Hell,
And with my kingly scepter sick me dead
When I was forc'd to leave my Gaveston!
LAN: Diablo, what passions call you these?
Q. ISAB: My gracious lord, I come to bring you news.
K. EDW: —That you have parled with your Mortimer?
Q. ISAB: —That Gaveston, my lord, shall be repeal'd.
K. EDW: Repeal'd! The news is too sweet to be true.
Q. ISAB: But will you love me, if you find it so?
K. EDW: If it be so, what will not Edward do?
Q. ISAB: For Gaveston, but not for Isabel—.
K. EDW: For thee, fair Queen, if thou lov'st Gaveston!
I'll hang a golden tongue about thy neck,
Seeing thou hast pleaded with so good success.
Q. ISAB: No other jewels hang about my neck

[Puts his arms around her]

Than these, my lord! Nor let me have more wealth
Than I may fetch from this rich treasury. [Kisses him]
O how a kiss revives poor Isabel!
K. EDW: Once more receive my hand, and let this be
A second marriage 'twixt thyself and me.

[The king promises the queen and the nobles all they ask if they will return Gaveston to him. But the nobles still plot secretly against Gaveston and the king.]

[1.4.388–426]
E. MOR: Nephew, I must to Scotland. Thou stay'st here.
Leave now to oppose thyself against the King.
Thou seest by nature he is mild and calm.
And seeing his mind so dotes on Gaveston,
Let him without controlment have his will:
The mightiest kings have had their minions—
Great Alexander lov'd Hephestion;
The conquering Hector for Hylas wept;
And for Patroclus stern Achilles droop'd.
And not kings only, but the wisest men—
The Roman Tully lov'd Octavius;

Grave Socrates, wild Alcibiades.
Then let His Grace, whose youth is flexible
And promiseth as much as we can wish,
Freely enjoy that vain, light-headed earl,
For riper years will wean him from such toys.
Y. MOR: Uncle, his wanton humor grieves not me.
But this I scorn, that one so basely
Should by his sovereign's favor grow so pert
And riot it with the treasure of the realm
While soldiers mutiny for want of pay —.
He wears a lord's revenue on his back,
And Midas-like he jets it in the court
With base outlandish cullions at his heels
Whose proud fantastic liveries make such show
As if that Proteus, god of shapes, appear'd!
I have not seen a dapper Jack so brisk:
He wears a short Italian hooded cloak,
Larded with pearl, and in his Tuscan cap
A jewel of more value than the crown.
While others walk below, the King and he
From out a window laugh at such as we,
And flout our train, and jest at our attire —.
Uncle, 'tis this makes me impatient.
E. MOR: But, nephew, now you see the King is chang'd.
Y. MOR: Then so am I, and live to do him service.
But whiles I have a sword, a hand, a heart,
I will not yield to any such upstart!
You know my mind. Come, uncle, let's away.

[Though Gaveston returns, not even the king's love and favor can protect him. The nobles threaten the king with civil war rather than have Gaveston in a position of power so near the king. Edward refuses to reject him, and the queen and the nobles continue their efforts to kill him, which they eventually do. Edward and the nobles are now set against each other, and the king is deposed, imprisoned, and murdered.]

## From *Hero and Leander* (1598)

Amorous Leander, beautiful and young
(Whose tragedy divine Musaeus sung)
Dwelt at Abydos; since him dwelt there none
For whom succeeding times make greater moan.
His dangling tresses that were never shorn,
Had they been cut, and unto Colchos borne,
Would have allured the vent'rous youth of Greece
To hazard more than for the Golden Fleece.
Fair Cynthia wished his arms might be her sphere;
Grief makes her pale because she moves not there.

His body was as straight as Circe's wand;
Jove might have sipped out nectar from his hand.
Even as delicious meat is to the taste,
So was his neck in touching, and surpassed
The white of Pelops' shoulder. I could tell ye
How smooth his breast was, and how white his belly,
And whose immortal fingers did imprint
That heavenly path with many a curious dint
That runs along his back, but my rude pen
Can hardly blazon forth the loves of men,
Much less of powerful gods: let it suffice
That my slack muse sings of Leander's eyes,
Those orient cheeks and lips, exceeding his
That leapt into the water for a kiss
Of his own shadow, and despising many,
Died ere he could enjoy the love of any.
Had wild Hippolytus Leander seen,
Enamoured of his beauty had he been;
His presence made the rudest peasant melt,
That in the vast uplandish country dwelt.
The barbarous Thracian soldier, moved with nought,
Was moved with him, and for his favour sought.
Some swore he was a maid in man's attire,
For in his looks were all that men desire,
A pleasant smiling cheek, a speaking eye,
A brow for love to banquet royally;
And such as knew he was a man would say,
"Leander, thou art made for amorous play:
Why art thou not in love, and loved of all?
Though thou be fair, yet be not thine own thrall."

[Leander swims the Hellespont to Hero's tower and encounters Neptune, who tries to
seduce him.]

The light of hidden fire itself discovers,
And love that is concealed betrays poor lovers.
His secret flame apparently was seen,
Leander's father knew where he had been
And for the same mildly rebuked his son
Thinking to quench the sparkles new begun.
But love resisted once grows passionate,
And nothing more than counsel lovers hate.
For as a hot proud horse highly disdains
To have his head controlled, but breaks the reins,
Spits forth the ringled bit, and with his hooves
Checks the submissive ground: so he that loves,

The more he is restrained, the worse he fares.
What is it now, but mad Leander dares?
"O Hero, Hero!" thus he cried full oft,
And then he got him to a rock aloft,
Where having spied her tower, long stared he on't,
And prayed the narrow toiling Hellespont
To part in twain, that he might come and go,
But still the rising billows answered "No."
With that he stripped him to the ivory skin,
And crying, "Love, I come," leapt lively in.
Whereat the sapphire-visaged god grew proud,
And made his capering Triton sound aloud,
Imagining that Ganymede, displeased,
Had left the heavens; therefore on him he seized.
Leander strived, the waves about him wound,
And pulled him to the bottom, where the ground
Was strewed with pearl, and in low coral groves
Sweet singing mermaids sported with their loves
On heaps of heavy gold, and took great pleasure
To spurn in careless sort the shipwrack treasure.
For here the stately azure palace stood
Where kingly Neptune and his train abode.
The lusty god embraced him, called him love,
And swore he never should return to Jove.
But when he knew it was not Ganymede,
For under water he was almost dead,
He heaved him up, and looking on his face,
Beat down the bold waves with his triple mace,
Which mounted up, intending to have kissed him,
And fell in drops like tears because they missed him.
Leander being up, began to swim,
And, looking back, saw Neptune follow him;
Whereat aghast, the poor soul 'gan to cry,
"O let me visit Hero ere I die."
The god put Helle's bracelet on his arm,
And swore the sea should never do him harm.
He clapped his plump cheeks, with his tresses played,
And smiling wantonly, his love bewrayed.
He watched his arms, and as they opened wide
At every stroke, betwixt them would he slide
And steal a kiss, and then run out and dance,
And as he turned, cast many a lustful glance,
And threw him gaudy toys to please his eye,
And dive into the water, and there pry
Upon his breast, his thighs, and every limb,
And up again, and close beside him swim,

And talk of love. Leander made reply,
"You are deceived, I am no woman, I."
Thereat smiled Neptune, and then told a tale,
How that a shepherd, sitting in a vale,
Played with a boy so fair and kind,
As for his love both earth and heaven pined;
That of the cooling river durst not drink,
Lest water-nymphs should pull him from the brink;
And when he sported in the fragrant lawns,
Goat-footed satyrs and up-staring fauns
Would steal him thence. Ere half this tale was done,
"Aye me," Leander cried, "th' enamoured sun,
That now should shine on Thetis' glassy bower,
Descends upon my radiant Hero's tower.
O that these tardy arms of mine were wings!"
And as he spake, upon the waves he springs.
Neptune was angry that he gave no ear,
And in his heart revenging malice bare:
He flung at him his mace, but as it went,
He called it in, for love made him repent.
The mace returning back, his own hand hit,
As meaning to be venged for darting it.
When this fresh bleeding wound Leander viewed,
His colour went and came, as if he rued
The grief which Neptune felt. In gentle breasts
Relenting thoughts, remorse and pity rests.
And who have hard hearts and obdurate minds,
But vicious, harebrained, and illit'rate hinds?
The god, seeing him with pity to be moved,
Thereon concluded that he was beloved.
(Love is too full of faith, too credulous,
With folly and false hope deluding us.)
Wherefore Leander's fancy to surprise,
To the rich Ocean for gifts he flies.
'Tis wisdom to give much, a gift prevails
When deep persuading oratory fails.

## Richard Barnfield (1574–1627)

Richard Barnfield in *The Affectionate Shephearde* (1594) had little compunction about writing about same-sex relationships, and in some of the most openly homoerotic poems of the period insists that "if it be a sinne to love a lovely lad, O than sinne I." Barnfield's pastoral eclogue tells the conventional story of an older man, Daphnis, infatuated by a younger, Ganymede. In the preface to a second miscellany of poems, *Cynthia, with Certain Sonnets* (1595), he declares his debt to Virgil's "second Eglogue [*sic*] of Alexis" and coyly hopes that his readers will not misunderstand his intentions: "Some there were, that did interpret the Affectionate Shepherd, otherwise . . . than I meant, touching the subject . . . the love of a Shepherd boy; a fault . . . I never made [it being] nothing else but an imitation of Virgil." However, Barnfield's audience, as Bruce Smith points out (*Homosexual Desire in Shakespeare's England*, 1991), may have taken his explanation as disingenuous. The poem is addressed to an audience of learned and sophisticated men, who as Smith notes, were proud of their "classical erudition," their "scorn for conventional morality [and] their sense of themselves as an all-male group" (Smith 1991:104). In this sense then, Barnfield's poems were written for special readers, those for whom the language of classical homoeroticism had a particular historical — and perhaps personal — resonance, but for whom the leap from the homoerotic to the homosexual may still have been best achieved only in texts.

To achieve this homoerotic texture, Barnfield sets up a rivalry for the affections of Ganymede between Daphnis and the "faire Queene Guendolen," and the resulting comparison of the beauty of Ganymede with the voracious sexuality of the woman plays to a general misogynistic theme in Renaissance texts. Barnfield is open about sex. Sexual language and homosexual puns abound: when he sees the "faire boy" who "had my hart intangled" "Cursing the time, the Place, the sense, the sin: I came, I saw, I view'd, I slipped in." The language of the poems is not so complex as to require much explication, nor are they, like Shakespeare's sonnets, profound explorations of homosexual desire; instead they are firmly situated in a homoerotic convention and their purpose is to amuse, to tease, to sexually titillate. Nevertheless, Barnfield's poems leave little doubt that homoeroticism conflated with classical tales of male friendship and love had been converted in some English Renaissance texts into sites where homosexual desire and homosexual sex were, if not equally valorized, at least effectively and often openly represented.

## From *The Affectionate Shephearde* (1594)

*The Teares of an Affectionate Shepheard Sicke for Love;*
*Or, The Complaint of Daphnis for the Love of Ganimede*

### 1

Scarce had the morning starre hid from the light
    Heavens crimson canopie with stars bespangled,
But I began to rue th' unhappy sight
    Of that faire boy that had my hart intangled;
Cursing the time, the place, the sense, the sin;
I came, I saw, I viewed, I slipped in.

### 2

If it be sinne to love a sweet-fac'd boy,
    Whose amber locks trust up in golden tramels
Dangle adowne his lovely cheekes with joy,
    When pearle and flowers his faire haire enamels
If it be sinne to love a lovely lad,
Oh then sinne I, for whom my soul is sad.

3

His ivory-white and alabaster skin
    Is staind throughout with rare vermillion red,
Whose twinckling starrie lights doe never blin
    To shine on lovely Venus, Beauties bed;
But as the lillie and the blushing rose,
So white and red on him in order growes.

16

Oh would to God he would but pitty mee,
    That love him more than any mortall wight!
Then he and I with love would soone agree,
    That now cannot abide his sutors sight.
O would to God, so I might have my fee,
My lips were honey, and thy mouth a bee.

17

Then shouldst thou sucke my sweete and my faire flower,
    That now is ripe and full of honey-berries;
Then would I leade thee to my pleasant bower,
    Fild full of grapes, of mulberries, and cherries:
Then shouldst thou be my waspe or else my bee,
I would thy hive, and thou my honey, bee.

28

If thou wilt come and dwell with me at home,
    My sheepcote shall be strowed with new greene rushes;
Weele haunt the trembling prickets as they rome
    About the fields, along the hauthorne bushes;
I have a pie-bald curre to hunt the hare,
So we will live with daintie forrest fare.

34

But if thou wilt not pittie my complaint,
    My teares, nor vowes, nor oathes, made to thy beautie:
What shall I do but languish, die, or faint,
    Since thou dost scorne my teares, and my soules duetie:
And teares contemned, vowes and oaths must faile,
And where teares cannot, nothing can prevaile.

## 38

When will my May come, that I may embrace thee?
  When will the hower be of my soules joying?
Why dost thou seeke in mirth still to disgrace mee?
  Whose mirth's my health, whose griefe's my hearts annoying:
Thy bane my bale, thy blisse my blessedness,
Thy ill my hell, thy weale my welfare is.

## 39

Thus doo I honour thee that I love thee so,
  And love thee so, that so do honour thee
Much more than anie mortall man doth know,
  Or can discerne by love or jealozie:
But if that thou disdainst my loving ever,
Oh happie I, if I had loved never!

### From *Cynthia, with Certaine Sonnets* (1595)

## 1

Sporting at fancie, setting light by love,
  There came a theefe, and stole away my heart
  (And therefore rob'd me of my chiefest part)
Yet cannot Reason him a felon prove.
For why his beauty (my hearts thiefe) affirmeth,
  Piercing no skin (the bodies fensive wall)
  And having leave, and free consent withall,
Himselfe not guilty, from love guilty tearmeth,
Conscience the Judge, twelve Reasons are the Jurie,
  They finde mine eies the beutie t' have let in,
  And on this verdict given, agreed they bin,
Wherefore, because his beauty did allure yee,
  Your Doome is this; in teares still to be drowned,
When his faire forehead with disdain is frowned.

## 6

Sweet Corrall lips, where Nature's treasure lies,
  The balme of blisse, the soveraigne salve of sorrow,
  The secret touch of loves heart-burning arrow,
Come quench my thirst or els poor *Daphnis* dies.
One night I dream'd (alas twas but a Dreame)
  That I did feele the sweetnes of the same,
  Where-with inspir'd, I young againe became,

And from my heart a spring of blood did streame,
But when I wak't, I found it nothing so,
    Save that my limbs (me thought) did waxe more strong
    And I more lusty far, and far more yong.
This gift on him rich Nature did bestow.
    Then if in dreaming so, I so did speede,
    What should I doe, if I did so indeede?


## 10

Thus was my love, thus was my *Ganymed,*
    (Heavens joy, worlds wonder, natures fairest work,
    In whose aspect Hope and Dispaire doe lurke)
Made of pure blood in whitest snow yshed,
And for sweete Venus only form'd his face,
    And his each member delicately framed,
    And last of all faire *Ganymede* him named,
His limbs (as their Creatrix) her imbrace.
But as for his pure, spotles, vertuous minde,
    Because it sprung of chaste *Dianaes* blood,
    (Goddesse of Maides, directresse of all good,)
Hit wholy is to chastity inclinde.
    And thus it is: as far as I can prove,
    He loves to be beloved, but not to love.


## 11

Sighing, and sadly sitting by my Love,
    He ask't the cause of my hearts sorrowing,
    Conjuring me by heavens eternall King
To tell the cause which me so much did move.
Compell'd: (quoth I) to thee will I confesse,
    Love is the cause; and only love it is
    That doth deprive me of my heavenly blisse.
Love is the paine that doth my heart oppresse.
And what is she (quoth he) whom thou do'st love?
    Looke in this glasse (quoth I) there shalt thou see
    The perfect forme of my faelicitie.
When, thinking that it would strange Magique prove,
    He open'd it: and taking of the cover,
He straight perceav'd himselfe to be my Lover.


## 12

Some talke of *Ganimede* th' *Idalian* Boy,
    And some of faire *Adonis* make their boast

Some talke of him whom lovely Laeda lost
And some of *Ecchoes* love that was so coy.
They speake by heere-say, I of perfect truth,
    They partially commend the persons named
    And for them, sweet Encomions I have framed:
I onely t'him have sacrifized my youth.
As for those wonders of antiquitie,
    And those whom later ages have injoy'd,
    (But ah what hath not cruell death destroide?
Death, that envies this worlds felicitie),
They were (perhaps) lesse faire then Poets write.
    But he is fairer then I can indite.

## William Shakespeare (1564–1616)

In his *Sonnets* (1609) William Shakespeare summons sometimes specific and sometimes coded homoerotic strategies to explore the implications of an amorous relationship between men. Some readings deny the thesis that the sonnets detail homosexual experience or that they are even homoerotic at all. But Joseph Pequigney in *Such Is My Love: A Study of Shakespeare's Sonnets* argues that the sonnets are not only the literary record of desire but of a physical union between Shakespeare and the still unidentified "Mr. W. H." to whom the sonnets were dedicated. This dedication, however, was not made by Shakespeare but by the later editor who first published the sonnets. Of the 154 poems of the sequence, the first 126 are largely concerned with the poet's relationship to an unnamed youth, while the others deal with his involvement with an equally unknown " Dark Lady." The poems written to the young man are certainly exemplars of caring friendship, for the speaker is constantly concerned with the young man's place in society, his career, his reputation, and even with his prospects for marriage. However, they are also far more than simply expressions of friendship or platonic affection. The poet is clearly enamored of the young man, and the sonnets describe the growth, maturity, and decline of a passionate affair and, as Pequigney argues, a physical relationship between the two men.

The first nineteen sonnets might be described as a courtship sequence, in which the poet woos the young man, praises his beauty and personality, and determines to memorialize that beauty in poetry. With Sonnet 20, however, a distinct change takes place in the tone, for it is here that the poet calls the youth his subject as "the master-mistress of my passion" and seems to realize, perhaps to his own surprise and even consternation, that his interest in the young man has been translated from the conventional sentiments of male friendship to language where the possibility of desire and sexual consummation seems now dangerously present. Whether this sexual ambiance is reciprocated by the young man is not entirely clear. However, Sonnet 20 sets up a series of oppositions between concepts of masculine and feminine, between male and female, even between masculine and effeminate personae.

Sonnets 21–126 detail the continuance and conclusion of the affair. Pequigney argues that the sexual consummation is described—perhaps in a coded manner—in sonnets 24–99, with consummation occurring by sonnet 33. No certain particular sonnet can be pointed out that clearly states any such actual sexual union, nor, perhaps, does it matter if one does or does not. What does seem to be clear is that the language of the sonnets after Sonnet 20 is increasingly homoerotic, and obsessive images denoting homosexual desire rather than spiritual or amicable passion dominate, both in the poet's appeal to the young man and in his description of the young man's response to him. Indeed the poet himself seems almost incapable of controlling his desire or his jealousy. In some sonnets the poet expresses his obsessive jealously over the young man's conduct—namely, the latter's possible sexual relations with an unnamed person, and with a woman, and his acquiescence to the blandishments of another man, the so-called rival poet. Finally, the affair begins to languish, and the poet realizes that the young man is "too dear for my possessing." However, the affair has had one vital affect on the poet, and that is to allow him to defend without care of consequence his own actions and the course of his desire. In Sonnet 121, he argues that it is "better to be vile than vile esteem'd." He affirms "I am that I am."

Whether the poet of the sonnets can be equated with William Shakespeare is to the point biographically but perhaps not so relevant here. Shakespeare's sonnets are not as openly homoerotic as Barnfield's *Affectionate Shephearde*, but unlike those poems Shakespeare's poems need no such classical or conventional disguise. They record and explore not only the conventions of Renaissance friendship and the generally homoerotic but as well the specifically homosexual in relationships between men.

## From *Sonnets* (1609)

### 20

A woman's face with Nature's own hand painted
Hast thou, the master-mistress of my passion;
A woman's gentle heart, but not acquainted
With shifting change, as is false women's fashion;
An eye more bright than theirs, less false in rolling,
Gilding the object whereupon it gazeth;
A man in hue, all hues in his controlling,
Which steals men's eyes and women's souls amazeth.
And for a woman wert thou first created;
Till Nature, as she wrought thee, fell a-doting,
And by addition me of thee defeated,
By adding one thing to my purpose nothing.
　　But since she prick'd thee out for women's pleasure,
　　Mine be thy love, and thy love's use their treasure.

### 26

Lord of my love, to whom in vassalage
Thy merit hath my duty strongly knit,
To thee I send this written embassage,
To witness duty, not to show my wit:
Duty so great, which wit so poor as mine
May make seem bare, in wanting words to show it,
But that I hope some good conceit of thine
In thy soul's thought, all naked, will bestow it;
Till whatsoever star that guides my moving

Points on me graciously with fair aspect,
And puts apparel on my tatter'd loving,
To show me worthy of thy sweet respect:
    Then may I dare to boast how I do love thee;
    Till then not show my head where thou mayst prove me.


## 27

Weary with toil, I haste me to my bed,
The dear repose for limbs with travel tir'd,
But then begins a journey in my head,
To work my mind, when body's work's expir'd;
For then my thoughts, from far where I abide,
Intend a zealous pilgrimage to thee,
And keep my drooping eyelids open wide,
Looking on darkness which the blind do see:
Save that my soul's imaginary sight
Presents thy shadow to my sightless view,
Which, like a jewel hung in ghastly night,
Makes black night beauteous and her old face new.
    Lo! thus, by day my limbs, by night my mind,
    For thee and for myself no quiet find.


## 57

Being your slave, what should I do but tend
Upon the hours and times of your desire?
I have no precious time at all to spend,
Nor services to do, till you require.
Nor dare I chide the world-without-end hour
Whilst I, my sovereign, watch the clock for you,
Nor think the bitterness of absence sour
When you have bid your servant once adieu;
Nor dare I question with my jealous thought
Where you may be, or your affairs suppose,
But, like a sad slave, stay and think of nought
Save, where you are how happy you make those.
    So true a fool is love that in your will,
    Though you do any thing, he thinks no ill.


## 61

Is it thy will thy image should keep open
My heavy eyelids to the weary night?
Dost thou desire my slumbers should be broken,
While shadows like to thee do mock my sight?

Is it thy spirit that thou send'st from thee
So far from home into my deeds to pry,
To find out shames and idle hours in me,
The scope and tenour of thy jealousy?
O, no! thy love, though much, is not so great:
It is my love that keeps mine eye awake;
Mine own true love that doth my rest defeat,
To play the watchman ever for thy sake:
    For thee watch I whilst thou dost wake elsewhere,
    From me far off, with others all too near.

## 80

O, how I faint when I of you do write,
Knowing a better spirit doth use your name,
And in the praise thereof spends all his might,
To make me tongue-tied, speaking of your fame!
But since your worth, wide as the ocean is,
The humble as the proudest sail doth bear,
My saucy bark, inferior far to his,
On your broad main doth wilfully appear.
Your shallowest help will hold me up afloat,
Whilst he upon your soundless deep doth ride;
Or, being wrack'd, I am a worthless boat,
He of tall building and of goodly pride.
    Then if he thrive and I be cast away,
    The worst was this,—my love was my decay.

## 87

Farewell! thou art too dear for my possessing,
And like enough thou know'st thy estimate:
The charter of thy worth gives thee releasing;
My bonds in thee are all determinate.
For how do I hold thee but by thy granting?
And for that riches where is my deserving?
The cause of this fair gift in me is wanting,
And so my patent back again is swerving.
Thyself thou gav'st, thy own worth then not knowing,
Or me, to whom thou gav'st it, else mistaking;
So thy great gift, upon misprision growing,
Comes home again, on better judgment making.
    Thus have I had thee, as a dream doth flatter,
    In sleep a king, but waking no such matter.

121

'Tis better to be vile than vile esteem'd,
When not to be receives reproach of being,
And the just pleasure lost which is so deem'd
Not by our feeling but by others' seeing;
For why should others' false adulterate eyes
Give salutation to my sportive blood?
Or on my frailties why are frailer spies,
Which in their wills count bad what I think good?
No, I am that I am, and they that level
At my abuses reckon up their own:
I may be straight, though they themselves be bevel;
By their rank thoughts my deeds must not be shown;
    Unless this general evil they maintain,
    All men are bad, and in their badness reign.

# Part Four

Reinventing Sodomites

*Homophobia and Resistance (1625–1869)*

# 10. Introduction: Satirizing Sodomites

From the Middle Ages through the late seventeenth century, religious and legal opinion conceived of sodomy as any sexual act not aimed at procreation, including bestiality and homosexuality. It was thought of as a single and occasional act which, though judged contrary to nature, anyone could commit. "Sodomy" did not necessarily define sexual sensibility, suggest a preference for one sexual object to the exclusion of the other, indicate any special and ineradicable predisposition, nor identify a special population who were inevitably unmanly or effeminate. However, this did not mean that such identities were not imagined in literature, identified in popular attitudes, or conceived of by sodomites themselves. As early as the twelfth century, a French text, *Eneas*, specifically defined men not attracted to women as sodomites. In both fifteenth-century Venice and in sixteenth- and seventeenth-century Lisbon and Madrid, respectively, what appear to be sodomite subcultures have been identified, while France had self-identified sodomite poets among the libertine writers of the seventeenth century. In England, however, sodomite subcultures and self-identification by sodomites seems to be a product of the late seventeenth and early eighteenth centuries.

## Shifting Perceptions of Sodomy: Identifying Sodomites

By the early eighteenth century in England, sodomites were indeed becoming fearful specters associated with the disruption of society itself, while in 1784 one French writer concerned about the prevalence of sodomitical acts and the presence of "pederasts" in Paris warns that "there is no order of society, from dukes on down to footmen, that is not infected." D'Angerville's choice of "infected" to describe homosexuality is telling, for like a disease it was believed that sodomitical vice infected those touched by it and by infection thus convert a populace. For this reason social control of sodomites was seen as the responsibility of the state. A Parisian document discussing sodomy reports that the "police discover dangerous inclinations in certain souls which may promptly lead them to misdeeds. Such a character already turns to crime; it is time to sequester him from society" (quoted in Rey, 145).

It was believed that such men—for women were rarely mentioned as being so "perverted"—were demarcated by special signs. In 1734, for example, a Dutch publicist, Justus van Effen, described sodomites as "hermaphrodites in their minds" and "effeminate weaklings," while a pamphlet attacking sodomites labeled them as having a "feminine mind in a man's body" (quoted in Boon, 246). What is perhaps most striking about homosexual life in the eighteenth century was that sodomites *as a group* were becoming visible. In London the existence of such subcultures and of special private meeting places is attested to by documented raids on sodomite establishments. These meeting places, called "molly houses" after the "mollies" (male cross-dressing homosexuals who frequented them), were generally private clubs or taverns in which a back room was reserved for the use of special patrons. By the early nineteenth century, "molly" denominated in the public view an effeminate male with a predilection for sexual activity with members of his own sex and a social life that involved participation in social rituals of a homosexual subculture in which transvestism and role reversal was dominant. The molly houses provided safe places where mollies could meet and have sex with one another or with men who may not have necessarily shared their passion for female manners or dress but who did seek homosexual sex. Mollies' effeminate mannerisms imitated or even parodied what was imagined to be the reality of aristocratic manners and included the adoption of pseudo-aristocratic names— My Lady, Princess Seraphina, and so forth. Of course not all homosexual men were mollies, and indeed probably most were not. Many rejected effeminate practices and role-playing as did one man, a painter, who in 1748 "withdrew from these gatherings [of mollies] because they were too scandalous. Several members imitated women and made gestures which showed what they were." The painter admonished them: "Can't you adopt men's mannerisms rather than women's?" (Rey, 188).

## HOMOPHOBIA IN LITERATURE

The presence of same-sex love in eighteenth-century literature is most often found in homophobic contexts, though some writings like the *Love Letters Between a Certain late Nobleman and the Famous Mr Wilson* (1726) and the correspondence of Thomas Gray, the correspondence and diaries of Lord Hervey, the diaries and fiction of William Beckford, and Gothic novels of Matthew Gregory Lewis and Horace Walpole suggest a homoerotic sensibility in texts as well as hint at actual homosexuality in life. Homophobia, however, was a significant anxiety in eighteenth-century materials and was expressed not only through legal prosecution and persecution but as literary satire, biased reportage, and in the form of journalistic or moralistic attacks against sodomites. There are few texts in the period between 1700 and the early nineteenth century that portray sodomites in any light that could be described as sympathetic or positive or that places sodomy in a context that is social rather than exclusively sexual. Literature and polemic made the sodomite both monstrous and contemptible, a creature at once the object of everyone's anxiety and the butt of every man's jest. But when practicing their "infectious" vice they were seen as dangerous monsters whose existence undermined morality and social stability, and whose uncontrolled sexuality threatened to destroy all virtue and corrupt all innocence.

The general horror occasioned by sodomites is suggested by the title of a 1729 pamphlet: *A Hell upon Earth, or, the Town in an Uproar . . . Occasion'd by the late Horrible Scenes of . . . Sodomy.* The level of literary homophobia is reflected in the rhetoric in Edward Gibbon's *Decline and Fall of the Roman Empire* (1776), wherein this urbane historian observes about sodomy: "I touch with reluctance and dispatch with impatience, a more odious vice, of which modesty rejects the name, and nature abominates the idea."

## Further Reading

L. J. Boon, "Those Damned Sodomites: Public Images of Sodomy in the Eighteenth-Century Netherlands," in Kent Gerard and Gert Hekma, eds., *The Pursuit of Sodomy: Male Homosexuality in Renaissance and Enlightenment Europe* (New York and London: Harrington Park Press, 1989); Louis Crompton, *Byron and Greek Love: Homophobia in Nineteenth-Century England* (Berkeley: University of California Press, 1985); Byrne R. S. Fone, *A Road To Stonewall: Homosexuality and Homophobia in English and American Literature, 1750–1969* (New York: Macmillan/Twayne, 1995); Rictor Norton, *Mother Clap's Molly House: The Gay Subculture in England, 1700–1830* (London: Gay Men's Press, 1992); Michel Rey, "Police and Sodomy in Eighteenth-Century Paris: From Sin to

Disorder," in Gerard and Hekma, eds., *The Pursuit of Sodomy*; articles by George S. Rousseau in Claude J. Summers, ed., *The Gay and Lesbian Literary Heritage* (New York: Henry Holt, 1995), 228–36, and by Randolph Trumbach in Wayne Dynes et al., eds., *The Encyclopedia of Homosexuality* 1:358–61 (New York: Garland, 1990).

# English Homophobia (1628–1810)

## Sir Edward Coke

From the Third Part of the *Institutes of the Laws of England* (1628)

### THE LAW OF BUGGERY, OR SODOMY

*Bugeria* is an Italian word, and signifies so much, as is before described, *paederastes* or *paiderestes* is a Greek word, *amator puerorum*, which is a species of buggery, and it was complained of in parliament, that the Lumbards brought into the realm the shameful sin of sodomy, that is not to be named, as there it is said. . . .

Our ancient Authors doe conclude, that it deserveth death, *ultimum supplicium*, though they differ in the manner of the punishment. Britton saith [see part two, sec. 5], that Sodomites and Miscreants shall be burnt, and so were the Sodomites by Almighty God. Fleta saith, *Pecorantes & Sodomitae in terra vivi confodiantur*: and therewith agreeth with the Mirror, *pur le grand abomination*, and in another place he saith, *Sodomie est crime de Majestie, vers le Roy celestre*. But (to say it once for all) the judgment in all cases of Felony is that the person attainted be hanged by the neck, until he or she be dead. But in ancient times in that case, the man was hanged, and the woman was drowned, whereof we have seen examples in the reign of Richard I, and this is the meaning of ancient Franchises granted *de Furca & Fossa*, of the Gallows, and the Pit for the hanging upon the one, and drowning in the other, but *Fossa* is taken away, and *Furca* remains. . . .

The Act of 25 [Henry VIII (1533): see part three, sec. 9] hath adjudged it a felony, and therefore the judgment of felony doth now belong to this offense, viz. to be hanged by the neck till he be dead.

## George Lesly (c. 1650)

### FROM *FIRE AND BRIMSTONE; OR, THE DESTRUCTION OF SODOM* (1675)

George Lesly's anti-sodomitical pamphlet of 1675 conflates sodomy with general sexual promiscuity and excess of all kinds including pride, gluttony, and lust: "Because there's no distinction made of Sex/Nor age, but all promiscuously do go,/Like Goats and Leopards that all they may know/Each other."

[The inhabitants of Sodom are introduced.]

Behold, how Sodom swaggers in its Pride,
And Lust, and Gluttony! none is espied,
That thoughts of Heaven have; or bowe a knee:
But one poor Stranger, who adoreth me.

My servant Lot: Whose holy Soul they vex;
Because there's no distinction made of Sex
Nor age, but all promiscuously do go,
Like Goats and Leopards that all they may know
Each other.

[They demand that Lot give up the Angels.]

*Sodomites:*
Confounded Dog, bring forth thy handsome Guests
Or by our great God Priapus we swear,
That we thy Body will in pieces tear.
*Lot:*
. . . Neighbours be rul'd, this wickedness give o're.
And if your Beastly lust cannot refrain,
But that these strangers you with sin would stain,
See here two Maids of mine who Virgins be,
Use them at pleasure, and let them go free.
*Sodomites:*
Rogue, runagate, slave, think not that thou must,
Make such exchanges to restraine our Lust.
Who made thee a Judge? If we be rul'd by thee,
Then must we bid adieu to Buggary.
But hold, stand back, or we will break the Door.

[God punishes them.]

Oh Heav'ns! I'm choack'd with Smoak, I'm burn'd with fire,
Brimston, Brimston! Where shall we retire?
We dye, we dye, O may this be the last
Of Heav'ns dreadful Sentence on us past!
We're burn'd and damn'd, there is no remedy;
We would not hear Lot, when he bid us fly
From wrath to come. O how our Limbs crack
With fire! Our Conscience is upon the rack
For by-past Crimes; our beastly Lusts Torment
Us, as the pretious time that we have spent.
O wretched Nature, whither hast thou brought
Us fools, and made us sell our Souls for nought?
Luxurious Eyes, why wer ye so unkind
To dote on objects, who have made you blind?
And you Tenacious hands, why did you grasp
The Poyson of the Spider? Why from Wasp
Did you seek Honey? did not Heav'n bestow,
As upon Lot, so also upon you,
The Lawful helps, and remedies for lust?

Was not all this enough? but that you must
In spite of Heav'n, lay hold on all that came,
Although they man his members had or name.
Could not a lawful Wedlock satisfie
Thy burning flame, proud flesh? No, thou must cry
Bring out thy handsome Guests, them we must know,
Not knowing they were not from below:
Whose Just revenge doth make us miserable,
To bear these scorching flames we were not able.
And yet alas! our wo doth but begin,
The vengeance is Eternal that's for sin.
O that Lot's God would grant us a reprieve
But for one hour, that wretched we might live,
To wail our by-past sins; and beg his aid,
Who never yet to humble sinners said,
I scorn your plaints, but always graciously
Prepar'd a bottle for a melting Eye,
And piece-meal Pray'rs made whole with his own merit,
Sa'ing be comforted, 'tis you must inherit
My endless Joy; which sentence now doth pierce
Our Souls so much, that we cannot rehearse
Our woes, though Oh! alas! it is too late,
We must expect nought but Almightie's hate.
See how the Devils laugh, whom we have serv'd:
O cursed Spirits is't this we have deserv'd
From you, for all those things that we have done
At your Command?

## Tobias Smollett (1721–1771)

### From *Roderick Random* (1748)

In no text is there presented such a full-scale picture of the popular conception of the sodomite as in Tobias Smollett's *Roderick Random*. There Lord Strutwell and Captain Whiffle represent not only the effeminacy and evil imagined to be associated with homosexuality but also demonstrate that the entire social spectrum is "infected" by such men. Whiffle, together with Simper his surgeon and Vergette his valet, are full-length portraits of stereotypical homosexuals. Lord Strutwell is portrayed as an urbane sodomitical monster, representing both incarnate evil and dangerous intelligence. He represents a new sodomitical kind: the sodomite apologist and activist who tries to seduce not only by offers of material advantage but by perversion of the intellect as well. He is a spokesman not only for sodomitical acts but for a style of life which he justifies and defines in his favorable discussion of Petronius' *Satyricon*. Strutwell's arguments amount to a defense of sodomy. He asserts that it is the lack of "true . . . deliberation" on the subject of sodomy that is in violation of the principles of reason and thus leads to prejudice. He argues that the severe laws against sodomy are irrational, derived from prejudice rather than from justice, and ineffectual against a natural desire. Strutwell's argument is firmly founded in a view of what the sodomite is, namely a species, not an accident of nature. Strutwell sees sodomy as an "appetite" and an "inclination," appealing to psychology, not the law or morality, and to nature not nurture. Despite his class and his effete and rakish manners, Strutwell could be read as a popular activist homosexual who identifies sodomites as a discrete and self-identified group, and advocates social tolerance and legal reform of the proscriptions levied against them.

## Captain Whiffle

### From chapters 34–35

[O]ur new commander came on board in a ten-oared barge, overshadowed with a vast umbrella . . . being a tall, thin, young man, dressed in this manner: a white hat garnished with a red feather adorned his head, from whence his hair flowed upon his shoulders in ringlets tied behind with a ribbon. His coat, consisting of pink-coloured silk lined with white, by the elegance of the cut retired backward, as it were to discover a white satin waistcoat embroidered with gold, unbuttoned at the upper part to display a brooch set with garnets that glittered in the breast of his shirt, which was of the finest cambric, edged with right Mechlin. The knees of his crimson velvet breeches scarce descended so low as to meet his silk stockings, which rose without spot or wrinkle on his meagre legs from shoes of blue Meroquin studded with diamond buckles that flamed forth rivals to the sun! A steel-hilted sword, inlaid with gold and decked with a knot of ribbon which fell down in a rich tassel, equipped his side, and an amber-headed cane hung dangling from his wrist. But the most remarkable parts of his furniture were a mask on his face and white gloves on his hands, which did not seem to be put on with the intention to be pulled off occasionally, but were fixed with a curious ring on the little finger of each hand. In this garb Captain Whiffle, for that was his name, took possession of the ship, surrounded with a crowd of attendants, all of whom, in their different degrees, seemed to be of their patron's disposition, and the air was so impregnated with perfumes that one may venture to affirm the clime of Arabia Felix was not half so sweet-scented. My fellow-mate, observing no surgeon among his train, thought he had found an occasion too favourable for himself to be neglected, and remembering the old proverb, "Spare to speak, and spare to speed," resolved to solicit the new captain's interest immediately, before any other surgeon could be appointed for the ship.

With this view he repaired to the cabin in his ordinary dress, consisting of a check shirt and trousers, a brown linen waistcoat, and a nightcap of the same (neither of them very clean), which, for his future misfortune, happened to smell strong of tobacco. Entering without any ceremony into this sacred place, he found Captain Whiffle reposing upon a couch with a wrapper of fine chintz about his body and a muslin cap bordered with lace about his head, and after several low congees, began in this manner: "Sir, I hope you will forgive, and excuse, and pardon the presumption of one who has not the honour of being known unto you, but who is, nevertheless, a shentleman porn and pred, and moreover has had misfortunes, Cot help me, in the world." Here he was interrupted by the captain, who, on seeing him, had started up with great amazement at the novelty of the apparition, and having recollected himself, pronounced, with a look and tone signifying disdain, curiosity, and surprise, "Zauns! who art thou?" "I am surgeon's first mate on board of this ship," replied Morgan, "and I most vehemently desire and beseech you, with all submission, to be pleased to condescend, and vouchsafe to inquire into my character, and my pehaviour, and my deserts, which, under Cot, I hope will entitle me to the vacancy of surgeon." As he proceeded in his speech, he continued advancing towards the captain, whose nostrils were no sooner saluted with the aromatic flavour that exhaled from him than he cried, with great emotion, "Heaven preserve me! I am suffocated! Fellow, fellow, away with thee. Curse thee, fellow! get thee gone. I shall be stunk to death!" At the noise of his outcries, his servants ran into his apartment, and he accosted them thus: "Villains! Cut-throats! traitors! I am betrayed! I am sacrificed!—Will you not carry that monster away? Or must I be stifled with the stench of him! oh! oh!" With these interjections he sunk down upon his settee in a fit; his valet de chambre plied him with a smelling bottle, one footman chafed his temples with Hungary water, another sprinkled the floor with spirits of lavender, a third pushed Morgan out of the cabin; who, coming to the place where I was, sat down with a demure countenance, and, according to his custom, when he received any indignity which he durst not revenge, began to sang a Welsh ditty. I guessed he was under some agitation of spirits, and desired to know the cause, but, instead of answering me directly, he asked with great emotion if I thought him a monster and a stinkard? " 'A monster and a stinkard,' said I, with some surprise, "did anybody call you so?" "Cot is my judge," replied he, "Captain Fifle did call me both, aye, and all the water in the Tawy will not wash it out of my remembrance. I do affirm, and vouch, and maintain, with my soul, and my pody, and my plood, look you, that I have no smells about me but such as a Christian ought to have, except the effluvia of tobacco, which is a cephalic, odoriferous, aromatic herb, and he is a son of a mountain goat who says otherwise. As for my being a monster, let that be as it is: I am as Cot was pleased to create me, which peradventure, is more than I shall aver of him who gave me that title, for I will proclaim it before the world that he is disguised, and transfigured and transmogrified with affectation and whimsies. And that he is more like a papoon than one of the human race."

## Chapter 35

He was going on with an eulogium upon the captain, when I received a message to clean myself and go up to the great cabin. This I immediately performed, sweetening myself with rose water from the medicine chest. When I entered the room, I was ordered to stand by the door until Captain Whiffle had reconnoitered me at a distance with a spyglass. He having consulted one sense in this manner, bade me advance gradually, that his nose might have intelligence before it could be much offended. I therefore approached with great caution and success, and he was pleased to say, "Aye, this creature is tolerable." I found him lolling on his couch with a languishing air, his head supported by his valet de chambre, who, from time to time, applied a smelling bottle to his nose. "Vergette," said he, in a squeaking tone "dost thou think this wretch (meaning me) will do me no injury? may I venture to submit my arm to him?" "Pon my vord," replied the valet, "I do tink dat dere be great occasion for your honour losing one small quantity of blodt, and the young man ave quelque chose of de bonne mien." "Well, then," said his master, "I think I must venture." Then, adressing himself to me, "Hast thou ever blooded anybody but brutes. But I need not ask thee, for thou wilt tell me a most damnable lie." "Brutes, sir?" answered I, pulling down his glove in order to feel his pulse, "I never meddle with brutes." "What the devil art thou about?" cried he—"dost thou intend to twist off my hand? God's curse! my arm is benumbed up to the very shoulder! Heaven have mercy upon me! must I perish under the hands of savages? What an unfortunate dog was I, to come on board without my own surgeon, Mr. Simper!" I craved pardon for having handled him so roughly, and, with the utmost care and tenderness, tied up his arm with a fillet of silk. While I was feeling for the vein, he desired to know how much blood I intended to take from him, and when I answered, "Not above twelve ounces," started up with a look full of horror, and bid me be gone, swearing I had a design upon his life. Vergette appeased him with difficulty, and, opening a bureau, took out a pair of scales, in one of which was placed a small cup; and putting them into my hands, told me the captain never lost above an ounce and three drachms at one time. While I prepared for this important evacuation, there came into the cabin a young man gaily dressed, of a very delicate complexion, with a kind of languid smile on his face, which seemed to have been rendered habitual by a long course of affectation. The captain no sooner perceived him than, rising hastily, he flew into his arms, crying, "O! my dear Simper! I am excessively disordered! I have been betrayed, frighted, murdered, by the negligence of my servants, who suffered a beast, a mule, a bear, to surprise me, and stink me into convulsions with the fumes of tobacco." Simper, who by this time I found was obliged to art for the clearness of his complexion, assumed an air of softness and sympathy, and lamented, with many tender expressions of sorrow, the sad accident that had thrown him into that condition; then, feeling his patient's pulse on the outside of his glove, gave it as his opinion that his disorder was entirely nervous, and that some drops of tincture of castor and liquid laudanum would be of more service to him than bleeding, by bridling the inordinate sallies of his spirits and composing the fermentation of his bile. I was therefore sent to prepare this prescription, which was administered in a glass of sack posset, after the captain had been put to bed and orders sent to the officers on the quarter-deck to let nobody walk on that side under which he lay. While the captain enjoyed his repose, the doctor watched over him, and indeed became so necessary that a cabin was made for him contiguous to the state-room where Whiffle slept, that he might be at hand in case of accidents in the night. Next day, our commander, being happily recovered, gave orders that none of the lieutenants should appear upon deck without a wig, sword, and ruffles, nor any midshipman other petty officer be seen with a check shirt or dirty linen. He also prohibited any person whatever, except Simper and his own servants, from coming into the great cabin without first sending in to obtain leave. These singular regulations did not prepossess the ship's company in his favour, but on the contrary gave Scandal an opportunity to be very busy with his character, and accuse him of maintaining a correspondence with the surgeon not fit to be named.

## Lord Strutwell

From chapter 51

[Roderick is introduced to Lord Strutwell.]

I was received with great kindness and familiarity by his lordship, whom I found just risen, in his morning gown and slippers. After breakfast, he entered into a particular conversation with me about my travels, the remarks I had made abroad, and examined me to the full extent of my understanding. My answers seemed to please him very much; he frequently squeezed my hand, and, looking at me with a singular complacency in his countenance, bade me depend upon his good offices with the ministry in my behalf. "Young men of your qualifications," said he, "ought to be cherished by every administration. For my own part, I see so little merit in the world that I have laid it down as a maxim to encourage the least appearance of genius and virtue to the utmost of my power—you have a great deal of both and will not fail of making a figure one day, if I am not mistaken, but you must lay your account with mounting by gradual steps to the summit of your fortune. Rome was not built in a day. As you understand the languages perfectly well, how would you like to cross the sea as secretary to an embassy?" I assured his lordship with great eagerness that nothing could be more agreeable to my inclination. Upon which he bade me make myself easy, my business was done, for he had a place of that kind in his view. This piece of generosity affected me so much that I was unable for some time to express my gratitude, which at length broke out in my own unworthiness and encomiums on his benevolence. I could not even help shedding tears at the goodness of this noble lord, who no sooner perceived them than he caught me in his arms, and hugged and kissed me with a seemingly paternal affection. Confounded at this uncommon instance of fondness for a stranger, I remained a few moments silent and ashamed, then got up and took my leave, after he had assured me that he would speak to the minister in my favour that very day, and desired that I would not for the future give myself the trouble of attending at his levee, but come at the same hour every day when he was at leisure, that is, three times a week.

   Though my hopes were now very sanguine, I determined to conceal my prospect from everybody, even Strap, until I should be more certain of success, and, in the meantime, give my patron no respite from my solicitations. When I renewed my visit, I found the street door open to me as if by enchantment, but in my passage towards the presence room I was met by the valet de chambre, who cast some furious looks at me, the meaning of which I could not comprehend. The earl saluted me at entrance with a tender embrace, and wished me joy of his success with the premier, who, he said, had preferred his recommendation to that of two other noblemen very urgent in behalf of their respective friends, and absolutely promised that I should go to a certain foreign court, in quality of secretary to an ambassador and plenipotentiary, who was to set out in a few weeks on an affair of vast importance to the nation. I was thunder-struck with my good fortune, and could make no other reply than kneel, and attempt to kiss my benefactor's hand, which submission he would not permit, but, raising me up, pressed me to his breast with surprising emotion, and told me he had now taken upon himself the care of making my fortune. What enhanced the value of the benefit still the more was his making light of the favour, and shifting the conversation to another subject. Among other topics of discourse, that of the Belles-Lettres was introduced, upon which his lordship held forth with great taste and erudition and discovered an intimate knowledge of the authors of antiquity. "Here's a book," said he, taking one from his bosom, "written with great elegance and spirit, and though the subject may give offence to some narrow-minded people, the author will always be held in esteem by every person of wit and learning." So saying, he put into my hand Petronius Arbiter and asked my opinion of his wit and manner. I told him that, in my opinion, he wrote with great ease and vivacity, but was withal so lewd and indecent that he ought to find no quarter or protection among people of morals and taste. "I own," replied the earl, "that his taste in love is generally decried, and indeed condemned by our laws, but perhaps it at may be more owing to prejudice and misapprehension than to true reason and deliberation. The best man among the ancients is said to have entertained that passion; one of the wisest of their legislators has permitted the indulgence of it in his commonwealth; the most celebrated poets have not scrupled to avow it. At this day it prevails not only over all the East, but in most parts of Europe; in our own country, it gains ground apace, and in all probability will become in a short time a more fashionable vice than simple fornication. Indeed, there is something to be said in vindication of it, for, notwithstanding the severity of the law against offenders in this way, it must be confessed that the practice of this passion is unattended with that curse and burden upon society which proceeds from a race of miserable and deserted bastards, who are either murdered by their parents, deserted to the utmost want and wretchedness, or bred up to prey upon the commonwealth. And it likewise prevents the debauchery of many a young maiden, and the prostitution of honest men's wives, not to mention the consideration of health, which is much less liable to be impaired in the gratification of this appetite than in the exercise of common venery, which, by ruining the constitutions of our young men, has produced a puny progeny that degenerates from generation to generation. Nay, I have been told that there is another motive, perhaps more powerful than all these, that induces people to cultivate this inclination, namely, the exquisite pleasure attending its success."

From this discourse, I began to be apprehensive that his lordship, finding I had travelled, was afraid I might have been infected with this spurious and sordid desire abroad, and took this method of sounding my sentiments on the subject. Fired at this supposed suspicion, I argued against it with great warmth, as an appetite unnatural, absurd, and of pernicious consequences, and declared my utter detestation and abhorrence of it in these lines of the satirist:

Eternal infamy the wretch confound
Who planted first that vice on British ground!
A vice! that, 'spite of sense and nature, reigns,
And poisons genial love, and manhood stains.

The earl smiled at my indignation, told me he was glad to find my opinion of the matter so conformable to his own, and that what he had advanced was only to provoke me to an answer, with which he professed himself perfectly well pleased.

# John Cleland

FROM *MEMOIRS OF A WOMAN OF PLEASURE* (1748)

In *Memoirs of a Woman of Pleasure* ("Fanny Hill"), among the scenes of heterosexual promiscuity, Cleland includes a depiction of homosexual sex. As well as being a fictional testament to the actuality of sexual practice, it demonstrates how, even in a book devoted to the portrayal and celebration of illicit sexuality, homosexuality is condemned.

Here, whilst I was amusing myself with looking out of the window, a single horse-chaise stopt at the door, out of which lightly leap'd two young gentlemen, for so they seem'd, who came in only as it were to bait and refresh a little, for they gave their horse to be held in readiness against they came out. And presently I heard the door of the next room, where they were let in, and call'd about them briskly; and as soon as they were serv'd, I could just hear that they shut and fastened the door on the inside.

A spirit of curiosity, far from sudden, since I do not know when I was without it, prompted me, without any particular suspicion, or other drift or view, to see what they were, and examine their persons and behaviour. The partition of our rooms was one of those moveable ones that, when taken down, serv'd occasionally to lay them into one, for the conveniency of a large company; and now, my nicest search could not show me the shadow of a peep-hole, a circumstance which probably had not escap'd the review of the parties on the other side, whom much it stood upon not to be deceived in it; but at length I observed a paper patch of the same colour as the wainscot, which I took to conceal some flaw; but then it was so high, that I was obliged to stand upon a chair to reach it, which I did as softly as possibly, and, with a point of a bodkin, soon pierc'd it, and open'd myself espial room-sufficient. And now, applying my eye close, I commanded the room perfectly, and could see my two young sparks romping and pulling one another about, entirely, to my imagination, in frolic and innocent play.

The eldest might be, on my nearest guess, towards nineteen, a tall comely young man, in a white fustian frock, with a green velvet cape, and a cut bob-wig. The youngest could not be above seventeen, fair, ruddy, compleatly well made, and to say the truth, a sweet pretty stripling: he was—I fancy too, a country lad, by his dress, which was a green plush frock, and breeches of the same, white waistcoat and stockings, a jockey cap, with his yellowish hair, long and loose, in natural curls.

But after a look of circumspection, which I saw the eldest cast every way round the room, probably in too much hurry and heat not to overlook the very small opening I was posted at, especially at the height it was, whilst my eye close to it kept the light from shining through and betraying it, he said something to his companion that presently chang'd the face of things.

For now the elder began to embrace, to press and kiss the younger, to put his hands in to his bosom, and give him such manifest signs of an amorous intention, as made me conclude the other to be a girl in disguise: a mistake that nature kept me in countenance for, for she had certainly made one, when she gave him the male stamp.

In the rashness then of their age, and bent as they were to accomplish their project of preposterous pleasure, at the risk of the very worst of consequences, where a discovery was nothing less than improbable, they now proceeded to such lengths as soon satisfied me what they were.

For presently the eldest unbutton'd the other's breeches and removing the linnen barrier, brought out to view a white shaft, middle-sized, and scarce fledg'd, when after handling and playing with it a little, with other dalliance, all receiv'd by the boy without other opposition than certain wayward coyness, ten times more alluring than repulsive, he got him to turn round, with his face from him, to a chair that stood hard by; when knowing, I suppose his office the Ganymede now obsequiously lean'd his head against the back of it, and projecting his body, made a fair mark, still covered with his shirt, as he thus stood in a side view to me, but fronting his companion, who presently unmasking his battery, produc'd an engine very fit to confirm me in my disbelief of the possibility of things being push'd to odious extremities, which I had built on the disproportion of parts; but this disbelief was now to be cured of, as by my consent all young men hould likewise be, that their innocence may not be beetray'd into such snares, for want of knowing the extent of their danger: for nothing is more certain than that ignorance of a vice is by no means a guard against it.

Slipping, then, aside the young lad's shirt, and tucking it up under his cloaths behind, he shewed to the open air Those globular fleshy eminences that compose the Mount Pleasants of Rome, and which now, with all the narrow vale that intersects them, stood displayed and exposed to his attack, nor could I without a shudder behold the dispositions he made for it. First, then moistening well with spittle his instrument, obviously to make it glib, he anointed, he introduced it, as I could plainly discern, not only from its direction and my losing sight of it, but by the writhing, twisting and soft murmur'd complaints of the young sufferer; but at length, the first straights of entrance being pretty well got throught, every thing seem'd to move and go pretty currently on, as on a carpet road, without much rub or resistance; and now, passing his hand round his minion's hips, he got hold of his red-topt ivory toy, that stood perfectly stiff, and shewed, that if he was like his mother behind, he was like his father before; this he diverted himself with, whilst, with the other he wanton'd with his hair, and leaning forward over his back, drew his face, from which the boy shook the loose curls that fell over it, in the posture he stood him in, and brought him towards his, so as to receive a long-breathed kiss; after which, renewing his driving, and thus continuing to harass his rear, the height of the fit came on with its usual symptoms, and dismissed the action.

All this, so criminal a scene, I had the patience to see to an end, purely that I might gather more facts and certainty against them in my design to do their deserts instant justice; accordingly, when they had re-adjusted themselves, and were preparing to go out, burning as I was with rage and indignation, I jump'd down from the chair, in order to raise the house upon them, but with such an unlucky impetuosity, that some nail or ruggedness in the floor caught my foot, and flung me on my face with such violence, that I fell senseless on the ground, and must have lain there some time e'er any one came to my relief: so that they, alarmed, I suppose, by the noise of my fall, had more than the necessary time to make a safe retreat. This they effected, as I learnt with a precipitation nobody could account for, till, when come to myself, and compos'd enough to speak, I acquainted those of the house with the whole transaction I had been evidence to.

When I came home again, and told Mrs. Cole this adventure, she very sensibly observ'd to me, that "there was no doubt of due vengeance one time or other overtaking these miscreants, however they might escape for the present; and that, had I been the temporal instrument of it, I should have been at least put to a great deal more trouble and confusion than I imagined; that, as to the thing itself, the less said of it was the better; but that though she might be suspected of partiality, from its being the common cause of woman-kind, out of whose mouths this practise tended to take something more than bread, yet she protested against any mixture of passion, with a declaration extorted from her by pure regard to truth; which was, "that whatever effect this infamous passion had in other ages and other countries, it seem'd a peculiar blessing on our air and climate, that there was a plague-spot visibly imprinted on all that are tainted with it, in this nation at least; for that among numbers of that stamp whom she had known, or at least were universally under the scandalous suspicion of it, she would not name an exception hardly of one of them, whose character was not, in all other respects, the most worthless and despicable that could be, stript of all the manly virtues of their own sex, and fill'd up with only the worst vices and follies of ours: that, in fine, they were scarce less execrable than ridiculous in their monstrous inconsistence, of loathing and condemning women, and all at the same time apeing their manners, airs, lips, skuttle, and, in general, all their little modes of affectation, which become them at least better, than they do these unsex'd, male-misses."

## Ned Ward

FROM *A COMPLETE AND HUMOROUS ACCOUNT OF ALL THE REMARKABLE CLUBS AND SOCIETIES IN THE CITIES OF LONDON AND WESTMINSTER* .... (1709)

Ward's *Humorous Account* exposed the sexual underworld of London and provided a popular description of homosexual subculture that both ridiculed and demonized it.

### The Mollies

There are a particular Gang of Sodomitical Wretches in this Town, who call themselves the Mollies, and are so far degenerated from all masculine Deportment, or manly Exercises, that they rather fancy themselves Women, imitating all the little Vanities that custom has reconcil'd to the female Sex, affecting to speak, walk, tattle, courtesy, cry, scold, and to mimick all manner of Effeminacy, that ever has fallen within their several Observations; not omitting the Indecencies of lewd Women, that they may tempt one another, by such immodest Freedoms, to commit those odious Bestialities, that ought for ever to be without a Name. At a certain Tavern in the City, whose sign I shall not mention, because I am unwilling to fix an Odium upon the House, where they have settled a constant Meeting every evening in the Week, that they may have the better Opportunity of drawing unwary Youth into the like Corruption. When they are met together, it is their usual Practice to mimick a female Gossiping, and fall into all the impertinent Tittle-Tattle, that a merry Society of good Wives can be subject to, when they have laid aside their Modesty for the delights of the Bottle. Not long since, upon one of their

Festival Nights, they had cushion'd up the Belly of one of their Sodomitical brethren, or rather Sisters, as they commonly called themselves, disguising him in a Woman's Night-Gown, Sarsnet-Hood, and Nightrale, who, when the Company were met, was to mimick the wry Faces of a groaning Woman, to be deliver'd of a joynted Baby they had provided for that Purpose, and to undergo all the formalities of a Lying-in. The wooden Off-Spring to be afterwards christen'd, and the holy Sacrament of Baptism to be impudently profan'd, for the Diversion of the Profligates, who, when their infamous Society were assembled in a Body, put their wicked Contrivance accordingly into practice.

One in a high crown'd Hat, and an old Bedlams Pinner representing a Country Midwife, another busy Ape, dizen'd up in a Hussife's Coif, taking upon himself the Duty of a very officious Nurse, and the rest as Gossips, apply'd themselves to the travelling woman, according to the Midwife's direction, all being as intent upon the Business in Hand, as if they had been Women, the Occasion real, and their Attendance necessary. After Abundance of Bustle and that they had ridiculously counterfeited all the Difficulties that they fancy'd were customary in such Cases, their Buffoonary Maukin was at length disburthen'd of her little jointed Bastard, and then putting their shotten Impostor to bed upon a double Row of Chairs; the Baby was drest by the Midwife; the Father brought to compliment his New-born Son, the Parson sent for; the Gossips appointed; the Child christen'd, and then the Cloth was spread; the Table furnished with cold Tongues and Chickens; the Guests invited to sit down, and much Joy expressed that my Gammar Molly had brought her honest Gaffer a Son and Heir to Town, so very like him, that as soon as born, had the Eyes, Nose, and Mouth of its own credulous Daddy. Now for the further Promotion of their unbecoming Mirth, everyone was to tattle about their Husbands and Children: And to use no other Dialect but what Gossips are wont to do upon such loquacious Occasions. One would up with a story of her little Tommy, to show the promising Genius of so witty a Child, that if he let but a Fizzle, would perfectly cry out, Mammy how I tink. Another would be extolling the Vertues of her Husband, and declare he was a Man of that affable, kind, and easy Temper, and so avers'd to Jealousy, that she believed, were he to see another Man in Bed with her he would be so far from thinking her an ill Woman, that no-body should perswade him they had been naught together. A third would be telling what a forward Baggage her Daughter Nancy was; for though she was but just turn'd of her seventh Year, yet the young Jade had the Confidence to ask her Father "Where Girls carry'd their Maidenheads that they were so apt to loose them?" A fourth would be wishing no Woman to marry a drunken Husband, for her Sake; for all the Satisfaction that she found in Bed with him, was to creep as close to the Wall as she could to avoid his Tobacco breath and unsavory Belches, swearing that his son Roger was just like him, for that the guzling Rogue would drink a Pint of Strong Ale at a Draught before he was three Years old, and would cry Mam, more Ale. A fifth would sit sighing at her ill Fortune, and wishing her Husband would follow the steps of his Journeyman; for that was as careful a young Fellow as ever came into a Family. A sixth would express himself sorrowfully under the Character of a Widow; saying, "Alas, you have all Husbands, and ought to pray heartily that you never know the Miss of them; for though I had but a sorry one, when I was in your

Condition, yet, God help me, I have cause enough to repent my Loss; for I am sure, both Day and Night, I find the Want of him." Thus every one in his turn, would make a Scoff and Banter of the little effeminate Weaknesses which Women are subject to when gossiping o'er their Cups, on purpose to extinguish that natural Affection which is due to the fair Sex, and to turn their juvenile Desires towards preternatural Pollutions. No sooner had they ended their Feast, and run through all the Ceremonies of their theatrical Way of Gossiping, but having wash'd away with Wine, all fear of Shame, as well as the checks of Modesty, then they began to enter upon their beastly Obscenities, and to take those infamous Liberties with one another that no Man who is not sunk into a state of Devilism, can think on without Blushing, or mention without a Christian Abhorrence of all such heathenish Brutalities. Thus, without Detection, they continu'd in their odious Society for some Years, till their sodomitical Practices were happily discover'd by the cunning Management of some of the under Agents to the reforming Society; so that several were brought to open Shame and Punishment; others flying from Justice to escape the Ignominy, that by this Means the Diabolical Society were forc'd to put a Period to their filthy scandalous Revels.

## The Punishment of Sodomites

Public anxiety about the existence and activities of sodomites led to an increase in public fascination with their punishment. The popular press pandered to this desire to participate vicariously in the actual persecution and punishment of homosexuals by daily newspaper accounts of the trials, convictions, and executions of those defendants who were almost always described as "miscreants" or "wretches" or "monsters." Death could be inflicted by burning, drowning, or strangling, though in England hanging was the favored method to usher the convicted sodomite into eternity. Men convicted of solicitation were often confined in the pillory and exposure to the verbal and physical insults of the wrathful mob who, in an orgy of community revenge, would so mistreat the confined sodomite by throwing offal, dung, mud, and rocks that some would not survive the ordeal, or if they did, suffered loss of sight and broken limbs. The London press was not only happy to report these instances but to echo what was probably the general opinion of such offenders: "Some of them cannot survive the punishment; and should it prove their death, they will not only die unpitied, but justly execrated by every moral mind throughout the universe" (quoted in Crompton 1985:167). In 1810, after a raid on a molly house in Vere Street, twenty-three men were arrested, tried, and seven found guilty and sentenced to imprisonment and to stand in the pillory in the Haymarket. A contemporary account describes the scene of their transportation to the pillory.

### From *The Trying and Pillorying of the Vere Street Club* (1810)

The disgust felt by all ranks in Society at the detestable conduct of these wretches occasioned many thousands to become spectators of their punishment. At an early hour the Old Bailey was completely blockaded, and the increase of the mob about l o'clock, put a stop to the business of the Sessions. The shops from Ludgate-Hill to the Haymarket were shut up, and the streets lined with people, waiting to see the offenders pass. . . .

Shortly after twelve, the ammunition waggons from the neighbouring markets appeared in motion. These consisted of a number of carts which were driven by butchers' boys, who had previously taken care to fill them with the offal, dung &c. appertaining to their several slaughter-houses. A number of hucksters were also put in requisition, who carried on their heads baskets of apples, potatoes, turnips, cabbage-stalks and other vegetables, together with the remains of divers dogs and cats. The whole of these were sold to the populace at a high price, who spared no expence to provide themselves with the necessary articles of assault.

A number of fishwomen attended with stinking flounders and the entrails of other fish which had been in preparation for several days. These articles, however, were not to be sold, as their proprietors, hearty in the cause, declared they wanted them "for their own use."

About half-past 12 the Sheriffs and the City Marshals arrived with more than 100 Constables mounted and armed with pistols, and 100 on foot. This force was ordered to rendezvous in the Old Bailey Yard, where a caravan, used occasionally for conveying prisoners from the gaols of London to the Hulks, waited to receive the culprits. The caravan was drawn by two shaft horses, led by two men, armed with a brace of pistols. The gates of the Old Bailey Yard were shut, and all strangers turned out. The miscreants were then brought out, and all placed in the caravan. Amos began a laugh, which induced his vile companions to reprove him, and they all sat upright, apparently in a composed state, but having cast their eyes upwards, the sight of the spectators on the tops of the houses operated strongly on their fears, and they soon appeared to feel terror and dismay. At the instant the church clock went half-past twelve, the gates were thrown open. The mob at the same time attempted to force their way in, but they were repulsed. A grand sortie of the police was then made. About 60 officers, armed and mounted as before described, went forward with the City Marshals. The caravan went next, followed by about 40 officers and the Sheriffs. The first salute received by the offenders was a volley of mud, and a serenade of hisses, hooting and execration, which compelled them to fall flat on their faces in the caravan. The mob, and particularly the women, had piled up balls of mud to afford the objects of their indignation a warm reception. The depots in many places appeared like pyramids of shot in a gun wharf. These were soon exhausted, and when the caravan passed the old house which once belonged to the notorious Jonathan Wild, the prisoners resembled bears dipped in a stagnant pool. The shower of mud continued during their passage to the Haymarket. Before they reached half way to the scene of their exposure, they were not discernible as human beings. If they had had much further to go, the cart would have been absolutely filled over them. The one who sat rather aloof from the rest, was the landlord of the house, a fellow of a stout bulky figure, who could not stow himself away as easily as the others, who were slighter; he was therefore, as well on account of his being known, attacked with double fury. Dead cats and dogs, offal, potatoes, turnips &c. rebounded from him on every side; while his apparently manly appearance drew down peculiar execrations on him, and nothing but the motion of the cart prevented his being killed on the spot. At one o'clock four of them were exalted on a new pillory, made purposely for their accommodation. The remaining two, Cooke and Amos, were honoured by being allowed to enjoy a triumph in the pillory alone.

They were accordingly taken back in the caravan to St. Martin's watch-house. Before any of them reached the place of punishment, their faces were completely disfigured by blows and mud; and before they mounted, their whole persons appeared one heap of filth. Upwards of 50 women were permitted to stand in the ring, who assailed them incessantly with mud, dead cats, rotten eggs, potatoes, and buckets filled with blood, offal, and dung, which were brought by a number of butchers' men from St. James's Market. These criminals were very roughly handled; but as there were four of them, they did not suffer so much as a less number might. When the hour was expired, they were again put in the cart, and conveyed to Cold Bath Fields Prison, through St. Martin's-lane, Compton-street, and Holborn, and in their journey received similar salutes to what they met with in their way from Newgate. When they were taken from the stand, the butchers' men, and the women, who had been so active, were plentifully regaled with gin and beer, procured from a subscription made upon the spot. In a few minutes, the remaining two, Cook, (who had been the landlord) and Amos, alias Fox, were desired to mount. Cook held his hand to his head, and complained of the blows he had already received; and Amos made the same complaint, and shewed a large brickbat, which had struck him in the face. The Under Sheriff told them that the sentence must be executed, and they reluctantly mounted. Cook said nothing; but Amos seeing the preparations that were making, declared in the most solemn manner that he was innocent; but it was vociferated from all quarters that he had been convicted before, and in one minute they appeared a complete heap of mud, and their faces were much more battered than those of the former four. Cook received several hits in his face, and he had a lump raised upon his eye-brow as large as an egg. Amos's two eyes were completely closed up; and when they were untied, Cook appeared almost insensible, and it was necessary to help them both down and into the cart, when they were conveyed to Newgate by the same road they had come, and in their passage they continued to receive the same salutations the spectators had given them in going out. Cook continued to lie upon the seat in the cart, but Amos lay down among the filth, till their entrance into Newgate sheltered the wretches from the further indignation of the most enraged populace we ever saw. As they passed the end of Catherine-street, Strand, on their return, a coachman stood upon his box, and gave Cook five or six cuts with his whip.

It is impossible for language to convey an adequate idea of the universal expressions of execration which accompanied these monsters on their journey; it was fortunate for them that the weather was dry, had it been otherwise they would have been smothered. From the moment the cart was in motion, the fury of the mob began to display itself in showers of mud and filth of every kind. Before the cart reached Temple-bar, the wretches were so thickly covered with filth, that a vestige of the human figure was scarcely discernible. They were chained, and placed in such a manner that they could not lie down in the cart, and could only hide and shelter their heads from the storm by stooping. This, however, could afford but little protection. Some of them were cut in the head with brickbats, and bled profusely. The streets, as they passed, resounded with the universal shouts and execrations of the populace.

# 11. Natural Passions: Resisting Homophobia

## English Literature (1785–1833)

Jeremy Bentham (1748–1832)

From *On Paederasty* (1785–1816)

Perhaps the most significant document advocating reform in social and legal attitudes is the essay "Paederasty" by the utilitarian philosopher and advocate of law reform, Jeremy Bentham. Though written in 1785, with an elaboration of his position in notes written in 1816, the text was not published until the twentieth century. Bentham advocates the decriminalization of sodomy and insists that it poses no threat to marriage or manhood. He theorizes the causes of sodomy and also of homophobia, suggesting that antipathy to and fear of sexual pleasure is the root cause of homophobia. He supports his argument by reference to ancient Greek practice and with an appeal to the principles of utilitarian philosophy, arguing that the "ethical value of an act" is to be tested by whether it "increased pleasure and diminished pain" (precisely the test, by the way, that Strutwell applies to sodomy). But Bentham also expresses fear of the possible consequences to himself of writing about sodomy, thus illustrating the homophobic climate of the times: "On this subject" he says, "if you let it be seen that you have not sat down in a rage you have given judgment against yourself at once." Bentham continues: "I am ashamed to own that I have often hesitated whether for the sake of the interests of humanity I should expose my personal interest so much to hazard as it must be exposed to by the free discussion of a subject of this nature." To write about homosexuality exposes the writer to as much danger as the practice of it for "when a man attempts to search this subject it is with a halter about his neck. On this subject a man may indulge his spleen without control. Cruelty and intolerance . . . screen themselves behind a mask of virtue." The Bentham manuscript was discovered and published by Louis Crompton, whose book *Byron and Greek Love* (1985) remains the definitive discussion of the texts of this period.

To what class of offences shall we refer these irregularities of the venereal appetite which are stiled unnatural? When hidden from the public eye there could be no colour for placing them any where else: could they find a place any where it would be here. I have been tormenting myself for years to find if possible a sufficient ground for treating them with the severity with which they are treated at this time of day by all European nations: but upon the principle of utility I can find none.

   . . .

### Whether they produce any primary mischief

As to any primary mischief, it is evident that it [pederasty] produces no pain in anyone. On the contrary it produces pleasure and that a pleasure which, by their perverted taste, is by this supposition preferred to that pleasure which is in general reputed the greatest. The partners are both willing. If either of them be unwilling, the act is not that which we have here in view: it is an offence totally different in its nature of effects: it is a personal injury; it is a kind of rape.

## What says history?

What says historical experience? The result of this can be measured only upon a large scale or upon a very general survey. . . . [T]hroughout Greece . . . everybody practised it; nobody was ashamed of it. They might be ashamed of what they looked upon as an excess in it, or they might be ashamed of it as a weakness, as a propensity that had a tendency to distract men from more worthy and important occupations, just as a man with us might be ashamed of excess or weakness in his love for women. In itself one may be sure they were not ashamed of it. Agesilaus, upon somebody's taking notice of the care he took to avoid taking any familiarities with a youth who passed for being handsome acknowledges it, indeed, but upon what ground? Not on account of the turpitude but the danger. Xenophon in his retreat of the ten thousand gives an anecdote of himself in which he mentions himself as particularly addicted to this practise without seeming to entertain the least suspicion that any apology was necessary. In his account of Socrates's conversation he introduces that philosopher censuring or rather making merry with a young man for his attachment to the same practise. But in what light does he consider it? As a weakness unbecoming to a philosopher, not as a turpitude or a crime unbecoming to a man. It is not because an object of the one sex more than one of the other is improper game: but on account of the time that must be spent and the humiliation submitted to in the pursuit.

What is remarkable is that there is scarce a striking character in antiquity, nor one that in other respects men . . . cite as virtuous, of whom it does not appear by one circumstance or another, that he was infected with this inconceivable propensity. It makes a conspicuous figure in the very opening of Thucydides's history, and by an odd accident it was to the spirit of two young men kindled and supported by this passion that Athens according to that historian stood indebted on a trying occasion for the recovery of its liberty. The firmness and spirit of the Theban band—the band of lovers as it was called—is famous in history; and the principle by which the union among the members of it was commonly supposed to be cemented is . . . well known. . . . Many moderns, and among others Mr. Voltaire, dispute the fact, but that intelligent philosopher sufficiently intimates the ground of his incredulity—if he does not believe it, it is because he likes not to believe it. What the antients called love in such a case was what we call Platonic, that is, was not love but friendship. But the Greeks knew the difference between love and friendship as well as we—they had distinct terms to signify them by: it seems reasonable therefore to suppose that when they say love they mean love, and that when they say friendship only they mean friendship only. And with regard to Xenophon and his master, Socrates, and his fellow-scholar Plato, it seems more reasonable to believe them to have been addicted to this taste when they or any of them tell us so in express terms than to trust to the interpretations, however ingenious and however well-intended, of any men who write at this time of day, when they tell us it was no such thing. . . .

With regard to the people in general it may be presumed that if the Gods amused themselves in this way—if Apollo loved Hyacinthus, if Hercules could be in a frenzy for the loss of Hylas, and the father of the Gods and men could solace himself with Ganymede, it was neither an odious nor an unfrequent thing for mortal men to do so. The Gods we make, it has been well and often said, we make always after our own image. . . .

### If it were more frequent than the regular connection in what sense could it be termed unnatural?

. . . . I would wish it to be considered what meaning a man would have to annex to the expression, when he bestows on the propensity under consideration the epithet of unnatural. If contrary to all appearance the case really were that if all men were left perfectly free to choose, as many men would make choice of their own sex as of the opposite one, I see not what reason there would be for applying the word natural to the one rather than to the other. All the difference would be that the one was both natural and necessary whereas the other was natural but not necessary. If the mere circumstance of its not being necessary were sufficient to warrant the terming it unnatural it might as well be said that the taste a man has for music is unnatural. . . .

### Causes of this taste

I have already intimated how little reason there seems to be to apprehend that the preference of the improper to the proper object should ever be constant or general. A very extraordinary circumstance it undoubtedly is that it should ever have arrived at the heighth at which we find it to have arrived. . . . Its prevalence, wherever it prevails to a considerable degree, seems always to be owing to some circumstance relative to the education of youth. It is the constraint in which the venereal appetite is kept under the system of manners established in all civilized nations that seems to be the principal cause of its deviating every now and then into these improper channels. When the desire is importunate and no proper object is at hand it will sometimes unavoidably seek relief in an improper way. In the antient as well as the modern plans of education young persons of the male sex are kept as much as possible together: they are kept as much at a distance as possible from the female. They are in a way to use all sorts of familiarities with each other: they are kept as much as possible from using any sorts of familiarities with females. Among the antients they used to be brought together in circumstances favourable to the giving birth to such desires by the custom of exercising themselves naked. . . . On the present plan they are often forced together under circumstances still more favourable to it by the custom of lying naked together in feather beds, implements of indulgence and incentives to the venereal appetite with which the antients were unacquainted. When a propensity of this sort is once accquired it is easier to conceive how it should continue than how it should be at first acquired. It is no such great wonder if the sensation be regarded as if it were naturally connected with the object, whatever it be, by means of which it came to be first experienced. That this practise is the result not of indifference to the proper object but of the difficulty of coming at the proper object, the offspring not of wantoness but of necessity. . . .

### Inducements for punishing it not justified on the ground of mischievousness

When the punishment [is] so severe, while the mischief of the offence is so remote and even so problematical, one cannot but suspect that the inducements which govern are not the same with those which are avowed. . . . [I]n England this offence was punished with death before ever the malicious destruction or fraudulent obtainment or embezzlement of property was punished at all, unless the obligation of making pecuniary amends is to be called a punishment; before even the mutilation of or the perpetual disablement of a man was made punishable otherwise than by simple imprisonment and fine. . . .

### [Is Punishment justified] on the grounds of antipathy[?]

In this case, in short, as in so many other cases the disposition to punish seems to have had no other ground than the antipathy with which persons who had punishment at their disposal regarded the offender. The circumstances from which this antipathy may have taken its rise may be worth enquiring to. 1. One is the physical antipathy to the offence.

This circumstance indeed, were we to think and act consistently, would of itself be nothing to the purpose. The act is to the highest degree odious and disgusting, that is, not to the man who does it, for he does it only because it gives him pleasure, but to one who thinks of it. Be it so, but what is that to him? He has the same reason for doing it that I have for avoiding it. . . . From a man's possessing a thorough aversion to a practice himself, the transition is but too natural to his wishing to see all others punished who give into it. Any pretence, however slight, which promises to warrant him in giving way to this intolerant propensity is eagerly embraced. Look the world over, we shall find that differences in point of taste and opinion are grounds of animosity as frequent and as violent as any opposition in point of interest. To disagree with our taste [and] to oppose our opinions is to wound our sympathetic feelings and to affront our pride. James the Ist of England, a man [more] remarkable for weakness than for cruelty, conceived a violent antipathy against certain persons who were called Anabaptists on account of their differing from him in regard to certain speculative points of religion. As the circumstances of the times were favourable to [the] gratification of antipathy arising from such causes, he found means to give himself the satisfaction of committing one of them to the flames. The same king happened to have an antipathy to the use of tobacco. But as the circumstances of the times did not afford the same pretences nor the same facility for burning tobacco smokers as for burning Anabaptists, he was forced to content himself with writing a flaming book against it. The same king . . . reckons this practise [pederasty] among the few offences which no Sovereign ever ought to pardon. This must needs seem rather extraordinary to those who have a notion that a pardon in this case is what he himself, had he been a subject, might have stood in need of.[1]

. . .

### Religion

We need not consider at any length [the length] to which the rigour of . . . philosophy may be carried when reinforced by notions of religion. Such as we are ourselves, such and in many respects worse it is common for us to make God to be: for fear blackens every object that it looks upon. It is almost as common for men to

---

1. James I was reputed to be homosexual.

conceive of God as a being of worse than human malevolence in their hearts, as to stile him a being of infinite benevolence with their lips. This act is one amongst others which some men . . . have a strong propensity to commit. In some persons it produces . . . a pleasure: there needs no more to prove that it is God's pleasure they should abstain from it. For it is God's pleasure that in the present life we should give up all manner of pleasure, whether it stands in the way of another's happiness or not, which is the sure sign and earnest of the pleasure he will take in bestowing on us all imaginable happiness hereafter; that is, in a life of the futurity of which he has given us no other proofs than these. . . . It may be asked indeed, if pleasure is not a good, what is life good for, and what is the purpose of preserving it? But the most obvious and immediate consequences of a proposition may become invisible when a screen has been set before by the prejudices of false philosophy or the terrors of a false religion. . . .

### How far the antipathy is a just ground [for punishment]

There remain . . . reasons against punishing it. The antipathy in question (and the appetite of malevolence that results from it) as far as it is not warranted by the essential mischieviousness of the offence is grounded only in prejudice. . . .

### Danger of false prosecutions greater in this case than others

A very serious objection, however, to the punishment of this offence is the opening it makes for false and malicious prosecutions. This danger in every case weighs something against the reasons for applying punishment, but in this case it weighs much more considerably than perhaps in any other. Almost every other offence affords some particular tests of guilt, the absence of which constitutes so many criterions of innocence. . . . But when a filthiness of this sort is committed between two persons, both willing, no such circumstances need have been exhibited; no proof therefore of such circumstances will be required. Wherever, therefore, two men are together, a third person may allege himself to have seen them thus employing themselves without fear of having the truth of his story disproved. With regard to a bare proposal of this sort the danger is still greater: one man may charge it upon any other man without the least danger of being detected. For a man to bring a charge of this sort against any other man without the possibility of its being disproved there needs no more than for them to have been alone together for a few moments.

### Used as an instrument of extortion

This mischief is often very severely felt. In England the severity of the punishment and what is supported by it, the moral antipathy to the offence, is frequently made use of as a means of extorting money. It is the most terrible weapon that a robber can take in hand; and a number of robberies that one hears of, which probably are much fewer than the ones which one does not hear of, are committed by this means. If a man has resolution and the incidental circumstances are favourable, he may stand the brunt and meet his accuser in the face of justice; but the danger to his reputation will at any rate be considerable. Men of timid natures have often been almost ruined in their fortunes ere they can summon up resolution to commit their reputations to the hazard of a trial. A man's innocence can never be his security; knowing this it must be an undaunted man to whom it can give confidence; a well-seasoned perjurer will have finally the advantage over him. Whether a man be thought to have actually been guilty of this practise or only to be disposed to it, his reputation suffers equal ruin.

## George Gordon Byron, Lord Byron (1788–1824)

Byron's homosexuality and his views about it in both his life and poetry have been documented by Louis Crompton in *Byron and Greek Love* (1985). Byron's guarded expression of these views is hinted at in the "Thyrza" poems and in later work, such as in lines intended for (though later omitted from) *Childe Harold's Pilgrimage* (1812), where Byron mentions William Beckford, the author of the novel *Vathek*, whose affair with William Courtenay led to his ruin and ostracism. He describes Beckford as smitten with the "unhallowed thirst/Of nameless crime," lamenting that "thy sad day must close/To scorn, and Solitude unsought." His correspondence with several intimate friends suggests that Byron and members of his circle saw homosexual desire and sex as markers of personality and that they seemed to envision themselves if not as a political, certainly as an oppressed, sexual minority. Byron and his friends Charles Skinner Matthews and John Cam Hobhouse, as Crompton shows, were quite possibly a group of homosexual or bisexual friends. Their correspondence suggests that "in a sense these three share what would today be called a gay identity, based on common interests and a sense of alienation from a society they must protect themselves from by a special 'mysterious' style and mutually understood codes" (Crompton 1985:129). It is in one of these letters to Byron in Turkey that Matthews notes that Byron can there, for a small fee, have whatever homosexual experience he wants, but in England "what you get for £5 we must risque our necks for; and we are content to risque them" (Crompton, 161). Byron's early Thyrza poems and "The Cornelian" both celebrate and disguise a passionate love for a schoolmate, John Edleston (spelled "Eddleston" by Byron), while later poems intimate a similar affection for Nicolo Giraud, a young man he met in Greece, where he died in 1824 after joining the Greek revolt against the Turks.

THE CORNELIAN (1807)

No specious splendour of this stone
Endears it to my memory ever;
With lustre only once it shone,
And blushes modest as the giver.

Some, who can sneer at friendship's ties,
Have, for my weakness, oft reproved me;
Yet still the simple gift I prize,
For I am sure the giver loved me.

He offer'd it with downcast look,
As fearful that I might refuse it;
I told him, when the gift I took,
My only fear should be to lose it.

This pledge attentively I view'd,
And sparkling as I held it near,
Methought one drop the stone bedew'd,
And ever since I've loved a tear.

Still, to adorn his humble youth,
Nor wealth nor birth their treasures yield;
But he who seeks the flowers of truth
Must quit the garden for the field.

'Tis not the plant uprear'd in sloth,
Which beauty shows, and sheds perfume;
The flowers which yield the most of both
In Nature's wild luxuriance bloom.

Had Fortune aided Nature's care,
For once forgetting to be blind,
His would have been an ample share,
If well proportion'd to his mind.

But had the goodness clearly seen,
His form had fix'd her fickle breast;
Her countless hoards would his have been
And none remain'd to give the rest.


To Thyrza (1811)

Without a stone to mark the spot,
    And say, what Truth might well have said
By all, save one, perchance forgot,
    Ah! wherefore art thou lowly laid?

By many a shore and many a sea
    Divided, yet beloved in vain;
The past, the future fled to thee
    To bid us meet—no—ne'er again!

Could this have been—a word, a look
    That softly said, "We part in peace,"
Had taught my bosom how to brook
    With fainter sighs, thy soul's release.

And didst thou not, since Death for thee
    Prepared a light and pangless dart,
Once long for him thou ne'er shalt see,
    Who held, and holds thee in his heart?

Oh! who like him had watch'd thee here?
   Or sadly mark'd thy glazing eye,
In that dread hour ere death appear,
   When silent sorrow fears to sigh,

Till all was past? But when no more
   'Twas thine to reck of human woe,
Affection's heart-drops, gushing o'er,
   Had flow'd as fast—as now they flow.

Shall they not flow, when many a day
   In these, to me, deserted towers,
Ere call'd but for a time away,
   Affection's mingling tears were ours?

Ours too the glance none saw beside;
   The smile none else might understand;
The whisper'd thought of hearts allied,
   The pressure of the thrilling hand;

The kiss, so guiltless and refined,
   That Love each warmer wish forbore;
Those eyes proclaim'd so pure a mind,
   Even passion blush'd to plead for more.

The tone, that taught me to rejoice,
   When prone, unlike thee, to repine;
The song, celestial from thy voice,
   But sweet to me from none but thine;

The pledge we wore—I wear it still,
   But where is thine?—Ah! where art thou?
Oft have I borne the weight of ill,
   But never bent beneath till now!

Well hast thou left in life's best bloon
   The cup of woe for me to drain.
If rest alone be in the tomb,
   I would not wish thee here again.

But if in worlds more blest than this
   Thy virtues seek a fitter sphere,
Impart some portion of thy bliss,
   To wean me from mine anguish here.

Teach me—too early taught by thee!
   To bear, forgiving and forgiven:

On earth thy love was such to me;
    It fain would form my hope in heaven!

### One Struggle More, and I am Free (1811–12)

One struggle more and I am free
    From pangs that rend my heart in twain;
One last long sigh to love and thee,
    Then back to busy life again.
It suits me well to mingle now
    With things that never pleased before!
Though every joy is fled below,
    What future grief can touch me more?

Then bring me wine, the banquet bring;
    Man was not form'd to live alone:
I'll be that light, unmeaning thing
    That smiles with all, and weeps with none.
It was not thus in days more dear,
    It never would have been, but thou
Hast fled, and left me lonely here;
Thou'rt nothing—all are nothing now.

In vain my lyre would lightly breathe!
    The smile that sorrow fain would wear
But mocks the woe that lurks beneath,
    Like roses o'er a sepulchre.
Though gay companions o'er the bowl
    Dispel awhile the sense of ill:
Though pleasure fires the maddening soul,
    The heart,—the heart is lonely still!

On many a lone and lovely night
    It sooth'd to gaze upon the sky;
For then I deem'd the heavenly light
    Shone sweetly on thy pensive eye:
And oft I thought at Cynthia's noon,
    When sailing o'er the Aegean wave,
"Now Thyrza gazes on that moon"—
    Alas, it gleam'd upon her grave!

When stretch'd on fever's sleepless bed,
    And sickness shrunk my throbbing veins,
"'Tis comfort still," I faintly said,
    "That Thyrza cannot know my pains":
Like freedom to the time-worn slave,

A boon 'tis idle then to give,
Relenting Nature vainly gave
    My life, when Thyrza ceased to live!

My Thyrza's pledge in better days,
    When love and life alike were new!
How different now thou meet'st my gaze!
    How tinged by time with sorrow's hue!
The heart that gave itself with thee
    Is silent—ah, were mine as still!
Though cold as e'en the dead can be,
    It feels, it sickens with the chill.

Thou bitter pledge! thou mournful token!
    Though painful, welcome to my breast!
Still, still preserve that love unbroken,
    Or break the heart to which thou'rt press'd.
Time tempers love, but not removes,
    More hallow'd when its hope is fled:
Oh! what are thousand living loves
    To that which cannot quit the dead?

## If sometimes in the haunts of men (1812)

If sometimes in the haunts of men
    Thine image from my breast may fade,
The lonely hour presents again
    The semblance of thy gentle shade:
And now that sad and silent hour
    Thus much of thee can still restore,
And sorrow unobserved may pour
    The plaint she dare not speak before.

Oh, pardon that in crowds awhile
    I waste one thought I owe to thee,
And self-condemn'd, appear to smile,
    Unfaithful to thy memory:
Nor deem that memory less dear,
    That then I seem not to repine;
I would not fools should overhear
    One sigh that should be wholly *thine*.

If not the goblet pass unquaff'd,
    It is not drain'd to banish care;
The cup must hold a deadlier draught,
    That brings a Lethe for despair.

And could Oblivion set my soul
    From all her troubled visions free,
I'd dash to earth the sweetest bowl
    That drown'd a single thought of thee.

For wert thou vanish'd from my mind,
    Where could my vacant bosom turn?
And who could then remain behind
    To honour thine abandon'd Urn?
No, no—it is my sorrow's pride
    That last dear duty to fulfil:
Though all the world forget beside,
    'Tis meet that I remember still.

For well I know, that such had been
    Thy gentle care for him, who now
Unmourn'd shall quit this mortal scene,
    Where none regarded him, but thou:
And, oh! I feel in *that* was given
    A blessing never meant for me;
Thou wert too like a dream of Heaven
    For earthly Love to merit thee.

[In 1824 in Greece where he had gone to join the fight for Greek independence, Byron fell in love with the fifteen-year-old son of a Greek widow. Byron took the young man, Lukas Chalandritsanos, into his employ as a page. In the year of his death, Byron wrote his last three poems to Lukas.]

## ON THIS DAY I COMPLETE MY THIRTY-SIXTH YEAR (1824)

'Tis time this heart should be unmoved,
    Since others it has ceased to move:
Yet, though I cannot be beloved,
    Still let me love!

My days are in the yellow leaf;
    The flowers and fruits of love are gone;
The worm, the canker, and the grief
    Are mine alone!

The fire that on my bosom preys
    Is lone as some volcanic isle;
No torch is kindled at its blaze—
    A funeral pile.

The hope, the fear, the jealous care,
    The exalted portion of the pain

And power of love, I cannot share,
    But wear the chain.

But 'tis not *thus*—and 'tis not *here*—
    Such thoughts should shake my soul, nor *now*,
Where glory decks the hero's bier,
    Or binds his brow.

The sword, the banner, and the field
    Glory and Greece, around me see!
The Spartan, borne upon his shield,
    Was not more free.

Awake! (not Greece—she is awake!)
    Awake, my spirit! Think through *whom*
Thy life-blood tracks its parent lake,
    And then strike home!

Tread those reviving passions down,
    Unworthy manhood!—unto thee
Indifferent should the smile or frown
    Of beauty be.

If thou regrett'st thy youth, *why live?*
    The land of honourable death
Is here:—Up to the field, and give
    Away thy breath!

Seek out—less often sought than found—
    A soldier's grave, for thee the best;
Then look around, and choose thy ground,
    And take thy rest.

## LOVE AND DEATH (1824)

I watched thee when the foe was at our side,
    Ready to strike at him—or thee and me,
Were safety hopeless—rather than divide
    Aught with one loved, save love and liberty.

I watched thee on the breakers, when the rock
    Received our prow, and all was storm and fear,
And bade thee cling to me through every shock;
    This arm would be thy bark, or breast thy bier.

I watched thee when the fever glazed thine eyes,
    Yielding my couch, and stretched me on the ground

When overworn with watching, ne'er to rise
　　From thence, if thou an early grave hadst found.

The earthquake came, and rocked the quivering
　　And men and nature reeled as if with wine.
Whom did I seek around the tottering hall?
　　For *thee*. Whose safety first provide for? Thine.

And when convulsive throes denied my breath
　　The faultest utterance to my fading thought,
To thee—to thee—e'en in the gasp of death
　　My spirit turned, oh! oftener than it ought.

Thus much and more; and yet thou lov'st me not,
　　And never wilt! Love dwells not in our will.
　　Nor can I blame thee, though it be my lot
To strongly, wrongly, vainly love thee still.


LAST WORDS ON GREECE (1824)

What are to me those honours or renown
　　Past or to come, a new born people's cry?
Albeit for such I could despise a crown
　　Of aught save laurel, or for such could die.
I am a fool of passion, and a frown
　　Of thine to me is an adder's eye
To the poor bird whose pinion fluttering down
　　Wafts unto death the breast it bore so high;
Such is this maddening fascination grown,
　　So strong thy magic or so weak am I.


## Anonymous

### FROM *DON LEON* (1833)

In 1833 an anonymous poem called *Don Leon*, alleged to be by Lord Byron, advocated the decriminalization of sodomitical acts. Its composition seems to have been prompted in part by the trial and execution for sodomy of a Captain Henry Nicholls, a man of good family and impeccable military background. The author argues that Nicholls's execution is an example of egregious injustice against sodomites. The poem identifies and condemns a combination of religious, moral, legal, and social structures, all of which, the *Don Leon* poet asserts, are founded upon an irrational hatred of and ignorance about sodomy. In effect, the poet has identified what we now call *homophobia* as the cause that leads to the unjust persecution of sodomites. He argues that sodomites, far from being isolated and individual sinners, are an identifiable and persecuted minority bound together by a temperament—what he calls a " predilection"—and possibly by a sensibility, that is intimately founded in and perhaps even defined by their sexual desire. He insists, repeatedly, that the sexual desire of the male sodomite for other males is as natural to him as is the desire of the male non-sodomite for women. The poet frames this argument within a first person autobiographical account that purports to detail the secret homoerotic life of Lord Byron and further describes what we would now call Byron's "coming out." The text demonstrates, moreover, what we might now also describe as an "activist" advocacy of homosexual sex and of a homosexual "lifestyle." Finally, the poem asserts that the emotional and literary manifestations of such desire are worthy of praise and argues for the positive value of homosexual desire in human affairs.

Don Leon is the first imaginative "literary" text in English in modern times, possibly written by one who may well have been what we now call "homosexual," that advocates rather than attacks, and valorizes rather than satirizes or demonizes, male-male sexual desire and sex. It is the first text in modern English poetry to intervene into the largely uncontested site of homophobia. The intent of the Don Leon poet is nothing less than to redefine sodomy, not as sin, crime, or social scourge, but as a legitimate sexual identity worthy of acceptance and undeserving of censure. In addition, as a purported first person autobiographical account of the growth of a homoerotic sensibility, Don Leon is also the first of a genre, introducing into literature the homosexual confessional or "coming out" story.

### [lines 1–40]

Thou ermined judge, pull off that sable cap!
What! Cans't thou lie, and take thy morning nap?
Peep thro' the casement; see the gallows there:
Thy work hangs on it; could not mercy spare?
What had he done? Ask crippled Talleyrand,
Ask Beckford, Courtenay,[2] all the motley band
Of priest and laymen, who have shared his guilt
(If guilt it be) then slumber if thou wilt;
What bonds had he of social safety broke?
Found'st thou the dagger hid beneath his cloak?
He stopped no lonely traveller on the road;
He burst no lock, he plundered no abode;
He never wrong'd the orphan of his own;
He stifled not the ravish'd maiden's groan.
His secret haunts were hid from every soul,
Till thou did'st send thy myrmidons to prowl,
And watch the prickings of his morbid lust,
To wring his neck and call thy doings just.
And shall the Muse, whilst pen and paper lie
Upon the table, hear the victim's cry.
Nor boldly lay her cauterising hand
Upon a wound that cankers half the land?
No! were the bays that flourish round my head
Destined to wither, when these lines are read:

2. Beckford and Courtenay were lovers.

Could all the scourges canting priest invent
To prop their legendary lies, torment
My soul in death or rack my body here,
My voice I'd raise insensible to fear.
. . .


[lines 125–48]

The tree we plant will, when its boughs are grown,
Produce no other blossoms than its own;
And thus in man some inborn passions reign
Which, spite of careful pruning, sprout again.
Then, say, was I or nature in the wrong,
If, yet a boy, one inclination, strong
In wayward fancies, domineered my soul,
And bade complete defiance to control?
What, though my youthful instincts, forced to brood
Within my bosom seemed awhile subdued?
What, though, by early education taught,
The charms of women first my homage caught?
What, though my verse in Mary's praises flowed?
And flowers poetic round her footsteps strewed,
Yet, when her ears would list not to my strain,
And every sigh was answered with disdain,
Pride turned, not stopped, the course of my desires,
Extinguished these, and lighted other fires.
And as the pimple which cosmetic art
Repels from one, invades another part,
My bubbling passions found another vent,
The object changed, but not the sentiment.
And, e'er my years could task my reason why,
Sex[3] caused no qualms where beauty lured the eye.


[lines 165–330]

Among the yeomen's sons on my estate
A gentle boy would at my mansion wait:
And now that time has almost blanched my hair,
And with the past the present I compare,
Full well I know, though decency forbad
The same caresses to a rustic lad;
Love, love it was, that made my eyes delight
To have his person ever in my sight.
Yes, Rushton, though to unobserving eyes,

---

3. That is, the sex of the erotic object was of no concern to him.

My favours but as lordly gifts were prized;
Yet something then would inwardly presage
The predilections of my riper age.
Why did I give the gauds to deck thy form?
Why for a menial did my entrails warm?
Why? but from secret longings to pursue
Those inspirations, which, if books speak true,
Have led e'en priest and sages to embrace
Those charms, which female blandishments efface.[4]
Thus passed my boyhood: and though proofs were none
What path my future course of life would run
Like sympathetic ink, if then unclear,
The test applied soon made the trace appear.
I bade adieu to school and tyro's sports,
And Cam received me in his gothic courts.
Freed from the pedagogue's tyrannic sway,
In mirth and revels I consumed the day.
No more my truant muse her vigils kept;
No more she soothed my slumbers as I slept;
But, idling now, she oft recalled the time
When to her reed I tuned my feeble rhyme.
She knew how those 'midst song and mirth grow dull
Whose tender bosoms soft emotions lull.
As manhood came, my feelings, more intense,
Sighed for some kindred mind, where confidence,
Tuned in just unison, might meet return,
And whilst it warmed my breast, in his might burn.
Oft, when the evening bell to vespers rung,
When the full choir the solemn anthem sung,
And lips, o'er which no youthful down had grown,
Hymned their soft praises to Jehovah's throne,
The pathos of the strain would soothe my soul,
And call me willing from the drunkard's bowl.
Who, that has heard the chapel's evening song,
When peals divine the lengthened note prolong,
But must have felt religious thoughts arise,
And speed their way melodious to the skies.
Among the choir a youth my notice won,
Of pleasing lineaments named Eddleston.
With gifts well suited to a stripling's mood,
His friendship and his tenderness I wooed.
Oh! how I loved to press his cheek to mine;
How fondly would my arms his waist entwine!
Another feeling borrowed friendship's name,

4. That is, these charms efface female blandishments.

And took its mantle to conceal my shame.
Another feeling! Oh 'tis hard to trace
The line where love usurps tame friendship's place.
Friendship's the chrysalis, which seems to die,
But throws its coil to give love wing to fly.
Both are the same, but in another state;
This formed to soar, and that to vegetate.
Of humble birth was he—patrician I.
And yet this youth was my idolatry.
Strong was my passion past all inward cure
And could it be so violent, yet pure?
'Twas like a philter poured into my veins—
And as the chemist, when some vase contains
An unknown mixture, each component tries
With proper tests, the draught to analyze;
So questioned I myself: What lights this fire?
Maids and not boys are wont to move desire;
Else 'twere illicit love. Oh! sad mishap!
But what prompts nature then to set the trap?
Why night and day does his sweet image float
Before my eyes? or wherefore do I doat
On that dear face with ardour so intense?
Why truckles reason to concupiscence?
Though law cries "hold!" yet passion onward draws;
But nature gave us passions, man gave laws,
Whence spring these inclinations, rank and strong?
And harming no one, wherefore call them wrong?
What's virtue's touchstone? Unto others do,
As you would wish that others did to you.
Then tell me not of sex, if to one key
The chords, when struck, vibrate in harmony.
No virgin I deflower, nor, lurking, creep,
With steps adult'rous, on a husband's sleep.
I plough no field in other men's domain;
And where I delve no seed shall spring again.
Thus with myself I reasoned; then I read,
And counsel asked from volumes of the dead.
Oh! flowery path, thus hand in hand to walk
With Plato and enjoy his honeyed talk.
Beneath umbrageous planes to sit at ease,
And drink from wisdom's cup with Socrates.
Now stray with Bion through the shady grove;
Midst deeds of glory, now with Plutarch rove
And oft I turned me to the Mantuan's page,
To hold discourse with shepherds of his age;
Or mixed with Horace in the gay delights

Of courtly revels, theatres, and sights;
And thou, whose soft seductive lines comprise
The code of love, thou hadst my sympathies;
But still, where'er I turned, in verse or prose,
Whate'er I read, some fresh dilemma rose,
And reason, that should pilot me along,
Belied her name, or else she led me wrong.
I love a youth; but Horace did the same;
If he's absolv'd, say, why am I to blame?
When young Alexis claimed a Virgil's sigh,
He told the world his choice; and may not I?
Shall every schoolman's pen his verse extol,
And, sin in me, in him a weakness call?
Then why was Socrates surnamed the sage,
Not only in his own, but every age,
If lips, whose accents strewed the path of truth,
Could print their kisses on some favoured youth?
Or why should Plato, in his Commonwealth
Score tenets up which I must note by stealth?
Say, why, when great Epaminondas died,
Was Cephidorus buried by his side?
Or why should Plutarch with eulogiums cite
That chieftain's love for his young catamite,
And we be forced his doctrine to decry,
Or drink the bitter cup of infamy?
   But these, thought I, are samples musty grown;
Turn we from early ages to our own.
No heathen's lust is matter of surprise;
He only aped his Pagan deities;
But when a Saviour had redeemed the world,
And all false idols from Olympus hurled,
A purer code the Christian law revealed,
And what was venial once as guilt was sealed.
With zeal unwearied I resumed again
My search, and read whate'er the layman's pen
In annals grave or chronicles had writ;
But can I own with any benefit?
'Tis true, mankind had cast the pagan skin,
But all the carnal part remained within
Unchang'd, and nature, breaking through the fence,
Still vindicated her omnipotence.
   Look, how infected with this rank disease
Were those, who held St. Peter's holy keys,
And pious men to whom the people bowed,
And kings, who churches to the saints endowed;
All these were Christians of the highest stamp—

How many scholars, wasting o'er their lamp,
How many jurists, versed in legal rules,
How many poets, honoured in the schools,
How many captains, famed for deeds of arms,
Have found their solace in a minion's arms!
Nay e'en our bard, Dame Nature's darling child,
Felt the strange impulse, and his hours beguiled
In penning sonnets to a stripling's praise,
Such as would damn a poet now-a-days.
  To this conclusion we must come at last:
Wise men have lived in generations past,
Whose deeds and sayings history records,
To whom the palm of virtue she awards,
Who, tempted, ate of that forbidden tree,
Which prejudice denies to you and me.
Then be consistent, and, at once confess;
If man's pursuit through life is happiness,
The great, the wise, the pious, and the good,
Have what they sought not rightly understood;
Or deem not else that aberration crime,
Which reigns in every caste and every clime.


[lines 390–500]

Thus feverish fancies floated in my brain.
Longing, yet forced my purpose to restrain,
Upon the brink of infamy I staid,
Now half resolved to plunge, now half afraid.
But fate, that turns the eddy of our lives,
And, at its will, like straws our fortune drives,
Saved me, ere yet the desperate chance was run;
For death deprived me of my Eddleston.
  I pass the useless hours in college spent—
The morning's lounge, the evening's merriment,
The tutor's lecture flippantly disdained,
The bottle emptied and the punchbowl drained,
The restless slumber and the spewy bed,
And all the horrors of an aching head;
Some of our proud aristocratic joys;
Youth's vision that reality destroys;
The course pursued to people, church, and state.
And rear up senators for grave debate.
These classic pastimes had no charms for me;
They filled my breast with languor and ennui.
The daily round of dull scholastic rules
Amused me not. — "I'll quit these wordy fools,"

Cried I, "who pass unprofitable days
"To square a circle or collate a phrase.
"Be mine a wider field to till the mind,
"I'll ramble, and investigate mankind."
    Launched on the main to distant climes I sailed,
And mental freedom's pure Aurora hailed
With all the glow that ardent youth inspires,
Borne on the tempest of its own desires,
What splendid cities and what navied ports,
What feasts, what revels, and what princely courts
I saw, were matter foreign to my theme:
Love, love, clandestine love, was still my dream.
Methought there must be yet some people found,
Where Cupid's wings were free, his hands unbound
Where law had no erotic statutes framed,
Nor gibbets stood to fright the unreclaimed.
I'll seek the Turk—there undisputed reigns
The little god,[5] and still his rights maintains.
There none can trespass on forbidden ground:
There venal youths in every stew are found
And with their blandishments inveigle man,
As does in Christian lands the courtezan.
    Lo! to the winds the sail its bosom heaves,
Bland zephyrs waft us and the port receives,
Where sable Euxine past is seen to glide,
To join his waters with a fairer bride.
'Tis there Byzantium's minarets arise
Tipt with their golden crescents to the skies:
And trees and palaces from height to height
With vivid hues enrich the novel sight.
    Here much I saw—and much I mused to see
The loosened garb of Eastern luxury.
I sought the brothel, where, in maiden guise,
The black-eyed boy his trade unblushing plies;
Where in lewd dance he acts the scenic show—
His supple haunches wriggling to and fro:
With looks voluptuous the thought excites,
Whilst gazing sit the hoary sybarites:
Whilst gentle lute and drowsy tambourine
Add to the langour of the monstrous scene.
Yes, call it monstrous! but not monstrous, where
Close latticed harems hide the timid fair:
With mien gallant where paederasty smirks,
And whoredom, felon like, in covert lurks.

5. Eros, who presides over homosexual love.

All this I saw—but saw it not alone—
A friend was with me; and I dared not own
How much the sight had touched some inward sense,
Too much for e'en the closest confidence.
Deep in the dark recesses of my mind
I hid my thoughts, nor told what they designed.
Quit we (I cried) these prostituted walls
A second Sodom here my heart appals.
Spare us good Lord! like patriarchial Lot!
If fire and brimstone falls, oh, burn us not!
This mask of horror served my purpose well—
Resolved to do what yet I feared to tell.
I found no kind leaning in the breast
Of those around me, and I felt opprest.
We bent again our topsails to the breeze,
And reached unharmed those smooth cerulean seas,
Whose surface, studded with a hundred isles,
Heaves like the nurse that hugs her babes, and smiles.
"Shipmates, farewell! and thou, John Cam, adieu!"
The nimble sailors up the mainsail clew:
"Starboard the helm"—the topsails fall aback,
And the ship's course seems suddenly to slack.
Down from the davits swiftly glides the boat—
The boatswain whistles, and away we float,
"Now pull together, lads!" We reach the land,
And Zea's rock receives me on the strand.
Hail, freedom, hail! For though the soil I trod,
Still groaning lay beneath the Moslem's rod,
Here first to me her benisons were known,
For mental freedom is to think alone.
Ah! little wots[6] the friend I quitted here,
What strange adventures marked the coming year.
He sought his native shores; and ever brave
In danger's hour the freeman's rights to save,
Stood in the senate by a people's choice,
And, not unheeded, raised his patriot voice.
I, wicked Childe, pursued a different course:
A demon urged, and with Satanic force
Still goaded on. Retrieve the moment lost,
(He whispered)—Haste, and pleasure's cup exhaust.
Go, lay thee down beneath the shady plain,
Where Phaedrus heard grave Plato's voice complain.
Another Phaedrus may perchance go by,
And thy fond dreams become reality.

6. I.e., knows.

[He goes to Greece.]

[lines 555–621]

Chance led me once, when idling through the street,
Beneath a porch my listless limbs to seat
Close to the spot a Grecian dwelling reared
Its modest roof. A courteous man appeared;
And, bowing low, with invitation pressed
To enter in, and on his sofa rest.
I crossed the threshold of the courteous man,
And smoked and chatted. Close by the divan
His son, as Eastern usages demand,
In modest attitude was seen to stand.
And smiling watched the signals of my will,
To pour sherbet, or the long *chibook* fill.
Grace marked his actions, symmetry his form;
His eyes had made an anchorite grow warm,
His long attire, his silken *anteri*,
Gave pleasing doubts of what his sex might be;
And who that saw him would perplexed have been,
For beauty marked his gender epicene.
Day after day my visits I renewed,
His love with presents like a mistress wooed;
Until his sire with dreams of greatness won,
To be my page made offer of his son.
I took him in my train, with culture stored
His mind, and in it choice instruction poured;
Till like the maiden, who some budding rose
Waters with care and watches till it blows,
Then plucks and places it upon her breast,
I too this blossom to my bosom pressed.
    All ye who know what pleasure 'tis to heave
A lover's sigh, the warm caress receive
Of some fond mistress, and with anxious care
Watch each caprice, and every ailment share.
Ye only know how hard it is to cure
The burning fever of love's calenture.
Come, crabbed philosophers, and tell us why
Should men to harsh ungrateful studies fly
In search of bliss, when e'en a single day
Of dalliance can an age of love outweigh!
How many hours I've sat in pensive guise,
To watch the mild expression of his eyes!
Or when asleep at noon, and from his mouth
His breath came sweet like odours from the south,

How long I've hung in rapture as he lay,
And silent chased the insect tribe away.
How oft at morn, when troubled by the heat,
The covering fell disordered at his feet,
I've gazed unsated at his naked charms,
And clasped him waking to my longing arms.
How oft in winter, when the sky o'ercast
Capped the bleak mountains, and the ruthless blast
Moaned through the trees, or lashed the surfy strand,
I've drawn myself the glove upon his hand,
Thrown o'er his tender limbs the rough capote,
Or tied the kerchief round his snowy throat.
How oft, when summer saw me fearless brave
With manly breast the blue transparent wave,
Another Dedalus I taught him how
With spreading arms the liquid waste to plough.
Then brought him gently to the sunny beach,
And wiped the briny moisture from his breech.
    Oh! how the happy moments seemed to fly,
Spent half in love and half in poetry!
The muse each morn I wooed, each eve the boy,
And tasted sweets that never seemed to cloy.


[lines 676–97]

Women as women, me had never charmed,
And shafts that others felt left me unharmed.
But thou, Giraud, whose beauty would unlock
The gates of prejudice, and bid me mock
The sober fears that timid minds endure,
Whose ardent passions women only cure,[7]
Receive this faithful tribute to thy charms,
Not vowed alone, but paid too in thy arms.
For here the wish, long cherished, long denied,
Within that monkish cell was gratified.
And as the sage, who dwelt on Leman's lake,
Nobly his inmost meditations spake,
Then dared the man, who would like him confess
His secret thoughts, to say his own were less;
So boldly I set calumny at naught,
And fearless utter what I fearless wrought.
For who that's shrived can say he never slipped?
Had conscience tongues what back would go unwhipped?

7. That is, timid minds are beset by fears of sexual unorthodoxy and thus turn to women, whose passions are the only "cure" they allow themselves.

Is there an idiosyncracy prevails
In those whose predilection is for males?
And like the satirist, who gravely said,
"When wives are tiresome take a boy to bed."

[lines 710–40]

Sometimes I sauntered from my lone abode
Down to the palace of the town waiwode.
Methinks I see him on his rich divan,
In crimson clad, a proud and lordly man.
An amber-headed pipe of costly wood
Adorned his hand: around kawasses stood.
A sable beard his gravity bespoke,
His measured words the silence rarely broke.
Beside him sat a boy of gentle mien,
In rich attire, in age about fifteen.
His red tarbush o'ertopped his jet black hair,
His cheeks were comely and his skin was fair.
His faultless form, in Grecian garments cloaked,
Thoughts more than mere benevolence provoked.
Not Ganymede, whose all bewitching shape,
Could in Olympus sanctify a rape.
Not Ali, long the Moslem prophet's joy,
Bloomed with such graces as this Grecian boy.
Waiwode, this stripling was thy catamite,
And if by grave examples men do right
To mould their lives, say, Was my conduct weak?
Was it a crime to imitate him? Speak.
Full well I know the answer; thou would'st cry
Shun, shun the monster, from his presence fly.
Alas, my friend, and whither should I go?
The self same usage reigns with high and low.

[lines 1032–39]

Statesmen, in your exalted station know
Sins of omission for commission go;
Since ships as often founder on the main
From leaks unstopped as from the hurricane.
Shore up your house; it totters to the base;
A mouldering rot corrodes it; and the trace
Of every crime you punish I descry:
The least of all perhaps is sodomy.

# 12. Children of Sodom

## Eighteenth-Century French Literature

Uncertainty and anxiety concerning sodomy mark the literature of the eighteenth century. The 1798 anonymous pamphlet *Les Enfans de Sodome* seems to offer a mixed message concerning sodomites, on the one hand satirizing them, on the other expressing sympathy, while the Marquis de Sade's "Manners" from *La Philosophie dans le boudoir* (1795) passionately defends individual sexual freedom and attacks anti-sodomitical hypocrisy. Most of Sade's writing was done during his confinement following his conviction for sodomy in 1772. While his writings, which include *Justine* (1791) and *La Philosophie dans le boudoir*, display and celebrate every kind of sexual experience, Dolmance, who is the chief narrator of *La Philosophie*, is a confirmed sodomite who may well speak for Sade himself.

### Donatien Alphonse François Sade, Comte de Sade (Marquis de Sade) (1740–1814)

"MANNERS" (FROM *LA PHILOSOPHIE DANS LE BOUDOIR*, 1795)
*Translated by Austryn Wainhouse and Richard Seaver*

But sodomy, that alleged crime which will draw the fire of heaven upon cities addicted to it, is sodomy not a monstrous deviation whose punishment could not be severe enough? Ah, sorrowful it is to have to reproach our ancestors for the judiciary murders in which, upon this head, they dared indulge themselves. We wonder that savagery could ever reach the point where you condemn to death an unhappy person all of whose crime amounts to not sharing your tastes. One shudders to think that scarce forty years ago the legislators' absurd thinking had not evolved beyond this point. Console yourselves, citizens; such absurdities are to cease: the intelligence of your lawmakers will answer for it. Thoroughly enlightened upon this weakness occurring in a few men, people deeply sense today that such error cannot be criminal, and that Nature, who places such slight importance upon the essence that flows in our loins, can scarcely be vexed by our choice when we are pleased to vent it into this or that avenue.

What single crime can exist here? For no one will wish to maintain that all the parts of the body do not resemble each other, that there are some which are pure, and others defiled; but, as it is unthinkable such nonsense be advanced seriously, the only possible crime would consist in the waste of semen. Well, is it likely that this semen is so precious to Nature that its loss is necessarily criminal? Were that so, would she every day institute those losses? and is it not to authorize them to permit them in dreams, to permit them in the act of taking one's pleasure with a pregnant woman? Is it possible to imagine Nature having allowed us the possibility of committing a crime that would outrage her? Is it possible that she consent to the destruction by man of her own pleasures, and to his thereby becoming stronger than she? It is unheard of—into what an abyss of folly one is hurled when, in reasoning, one abandons the aid of reason's torch! Let us abide in our unshakable assurance that it is as easy to enjoy a woman in one manner as in another, that it makes absolutely no difference whether one enjoys a girl or a boy, and as soon as it is clearly understood that no inclinations or tastes can exist in us save the ones we have from Nature, that she is too wise and too consistent to have given us any which could ever offend her.

The penchant for sodomy is the result of physical formation, to which we contribute nothing and which we cannot alter. At the most tender age, some children reveal that penchant, and it is never corrected in them. Sometimes it is the fruit of satiety; but even in this case, is it less Nature's doing? Regardless of how it is viewed, it is her work, and, in every instance, what she inspires must be respected by men. If, were one to take an exact inventory, it should come out that this taste is infinitely more affecting than the other, that the pleasures resulting from it are far more lively, and that for this reason its exponents are a thousand times more numerous than its enemies, would it not then be possible to conclude that, far from affronting Nature, this vice serves her intentions, and that she is less delighted by our procreation than we so foolishly believe? Why, as we travel about the world, how many peoples do we not see holding women in contempt? Many are the men who strictly avoid employing them for anything but the having of the child necessary to replace them. The communal aspect of life in republics always renders this vice more frequent in that form of society; but it is not dangerous. Would the Greek legislators have introduced it into their republics had they thought it so? Quite the contrary; they deemed it necessary to a warlike race. Plutarch speaks with enthusiasm of the battalion of lovers: for many a year they alone defended Greece's freedom. The vice reigned amongst comrades-in-arms, and cemented their unity. The greatest of men lean toward sodomy. At the time it was discovered, the whole of America was found inhabited by people of this taste. In Louisiana, amongst the Illinois, Indians in feminine garb prostituted themselves as courtesans. The blacks of Benguela publicly keep men; nearly all the seraglios of Algiers are today exclusively filled with young boys. Not content to tolerate love for young boys, the Thebans made it mandatory; the philosopher of Chaeronea prescribed sodomy as the surest way to a youth's affection.

We know to what extent it prevailed in Rome, where they had public places in which young boys, costumed as girls, and girls as boys, prostituted themselves. In their letters, Martial, Catullus, Tibullus, Horace, and Virgil wrote to men as though to their mistresses; and we read in Plutarch that women must in no way figure in men's love. The Amasians of Crete used to abduct boys, and their initiation was distinguished by the most singular ceremonies. When they were taken with love for one, they notified the parents upon what day the ravisher wished to carry him off; the youth put up some resistance if his lover failed to please him; in the contrary case, they went off together, and the seducer restored him to his family as soon as he had made use of him; for in this passion as in that for women, one always has too much when one has had enough. Strabo informs us that on this very island, seraglios were peopled with boys only; they were prostituted openly.

Is one more authority required to prove how useful this vice is in a republic? Let us lend an ear to Jerome the Peripatetic: "The love of youths," says he, "spread throughout all of Greece, for it instilled in us strength and courage, and thus stood us in good stead when we drove the tyrants out; conspiracies were formed amongst lovers, and they were readier to endure torture than denounce their accomplices; such patriots sacrificed everything to the State's prosperity; it was beheld as a certain thing, that these attachments steadied the republic, women were declaimed against, and to entertain connections with such creatures was a frailty reserved to despots." Pederasty has always been the vice of warrior races. From Caesar we learn that the Gauls were to an extraordinary degree given to it. The wars fought to sustain the republic brought about the separation of the two sexes, and hence the propagation of the vice, and when its consequences, so useful to the State, were recognized, religion speedily blessed it. That the Romans sanctified the amours of Jupiter and Ganymede is well known. Sextus Empiricus assures us that this caprice was compulsory amongst the Persians. At last, the women, jealous and contemned, offered to render their husbands the same service they received from young boys; some few men made the experiment, and returned to their former habits, finding the illusion impossible. The Turks, greatly inclined toward this depravity Mohammed consecrated in the Koran, were nevertheless convinced that a very young virgin could well enough be substituted for a youth, and rarely did they grow to womanhood without having passed through the experience. Sextus Quintus and Sanchez allowed this debauch; the latter even undertook to show it was of use to procreation, and that a child created after this preliminary exercise was infinitely better constituted thanks to it. Finally, women found restitution by turning to each other. This latter fantasy doubtless has no more disadvantages than the other, since nothing comes of the refusal to reproduce, and since the means of those who have a bent for reproduction are powerful enough for reproduction's adversaries never to be able to harm population. Amongst the Greeks, this female perversion was also supported by policy: the result of it was that, finding each other sufficient, women sought less communication with men and their detrimental influence in the republic's affairs was thus held to a minimum. Lucian informs us of what progress this license promoted, and it is not without interest we see it exemplified in Sappho.

In fine, these are perfectly inoffensive manias; were women to carry them even further, were they to go to the point of caressing monsters and animals, as the example of every race teaches us, no ill could possibly result therefrom, because corruption of manners, often of prime utility to a government, cannot in any sense harm it, and we must demand enough wisdom and enough prudence of our legislators to be entirely sure that no law will emanate from them that would repress perversions which, being determined by constitution and being inseparable from physical structure, cannot render the person in whom they are present any more guilty than the person Nature created deformed.

## Anonymous

Sodom (from *Les Enfans de Sodome à l'Assemblée Nationale*, 1798)

*Translated by Gina Fisch-Freedman*

Little is known about the author of this pamphlet that argues for the rights of sodomites by appealing to revolutionary principles of the rights of man. Both serious and witty, intense and pornographic, the pamphlet urges that many great men have been "anti-physicians." The word is derived from *phusis*, the Greek word for nature. Thus anti-physicians are against nature, or sodomitical.

## THE CHILDREN OF SODOM TO THE NATIONAL ASSEMBLY, OR, DELEGATION OF THE ORDER OF THE RUFFLE TO THE REPRESENTATIVES OF THE STATE, SELECTED WITHIN THE 60 DISTRICTS OF PARIS AND OF VERSAILLES INCLUDED

> All tastes are in nature;
> Each man's taste is the best.
> —Chevalier de Florian

The Children of Sodom to the National Assembly. As soon as the question of assembling the General Estates was raised for the first time after two centuries, it became the signal for a general meeting throughout the territories of the French empire. In reassembling, the French followed the Greeks and Romans for whom the mere names of Fatherland and Liberty were rallying cries. Each estate (the Nobility, the Clergy, and the Commons) got together separately to elect their representatives to the Estates General. One heard only of the words *voters* and *elected candidates*. As the monkey eagerly imitates all human gestures, so at the crossroads, on the piers (in a word, everywhere), one saw Assemblies and one heard only motions. The tailor-boys took over the lawn of the Louvre and the servants deserted the wine cellar and also the antechamber in order to declaim windy discourses.

In the midst of this stormy Assembly, the famous Estate of the Ruffle had been inactive up to now (although they did assemble, from time to time, in the garden of the Tuilleries, in the back alleys of the Soupirs, and in the Cloister of the Chartreux, and at the Abbé Viennet, the most zealous partisan of buggery). However, it was not to pass motions on the events of the day that they assembled, but rather to work jointly by banging asses to create the great Parisian fire after the fashion of the Sodomites, who caused their city to burn because of the same maneuver. But now as the Supreme Being had become less rigid about such trifles, and no longer took pleasure in setting fire to cities on account of such trivial matters, he sent the following wholesome philosophy to combat prejudices, and the Buggers immediately adopted as their motto that of the knight Florian, and they said:

> All tastes are in nature;
> Each man's taste is the best.

From that time forward, anyone could see Monvel on the Champs-Elysées, treacherously deflowering some schoolboys. Forced by circumstances, he went to Bavaria to give public lessons in Anti-Physics, the philosophy of buggery.

Or one could see the Marquis of La Villette turning Voltaire's relative, a modern Venus, into a young and handsome Ganymede. . . . One could also see Marcantin, the notary, the scoundrel of high society, sending off Maradans doll, in order to discover more queens and queers and to recruit on the Quais des Augustins, the booksellers of his society, amongst whom one could recognize

Letellier, Volland, and so on. . . . One could say of this splendid Adonis, what the Romans used to say about Caesar: "He is the husband of all wives, and the wife of all husbands."

But in these gatherings . . . one could not prevent oneself from speaking about politics; and it was decided by the Order of the Ruffle that since many of their novices and members were also members of the National Assembly, Sodomy and Buggery had to be invigorated and had to recapture a major consistency, and that the freedom of its practice must absolutely become one of the constitutional articles of the State.

In order to accomplish that, the Order convened a General Assembly under the chestnut trees of the Tuilleries, and it was declared that no propositions, no unveiling of asses would be made before a decision had been taken regarding the delegation to be sent to the National Assembly and which would ask for the right to speak and the right to have the articles of the Order approved.

Then the debate proceeded on in what manner to vote, and it raised violent discussions: the stupidest ones pretended that vote by head was appropriate, but the most experienced and truthful to the principles of the Order passed the motion that it had to be vote by ass, and La Tour du Pin Montauban, archbishop of Ausch, was the first one to show the way. Then it was decided that the order had to choose a president: M. the bishop Viennet, according to the new method of voting, won the greatest number of asses. And yes who but this famous apostle of Sodomy could claim this important place! But the fatigues of a laborious career prevented him from accepting this mark of distinction. . . . [T]he Assembly decided that he would become an honorary president, but they had to name a deputy. M. the duc de Noailles won and gave a speech which showed why he got all the votes:

Sirs,
Anti-physics, which its opponents denounce derogatorily as Buggery, and which for centuries ignorance has made us believe it a lewd and illicit game, and which jurists call "bestiality," from now on will become a science for the future, known and taught in all classes of society.

Because the enlightenment has brought forward the new philosophy, times have changed, and we will not be ashamed to see It walk alone gloriously to the perfection of this science: Because nature gave us all of the necessary knowledge to make known the first and principal elements, it is left to us to use the most thoughtful and wise means to hasten its progress in the country we live in; and to be able to get to it, Sirs, the most important order of business is to kill any remains of prejudices which for all time has tried to destroy us and has made martyrs from our order whose loss we mourn deeply.

The barbarity of the criminal laws took thousands from us; jealousy scattered us many times. Liberty has reunited us—let us use it nobly. Let us instruct the world, that most great men have been anti-physicians, and that this famous and illustrious order can, by virtue of its number and quality, be on the same footing with Malta and Saint-Esprit. Therefore let us teach the coming centuries to revere the souls of the unfortunates who have succumbed under the efforts of female tyranny, and from now on to see in their tragic end only an assassination.

For me, sirs, I will swear without vanity that I always show myself to be the most zealous partisan of the pleasures of the Order. Armed religion and its political whip has vainly expected to punish us, to have penetrated the sweetest mysteries of the Order: the legislator himself, animated by the most exquisite penchant for his little cousin, did he not lead us all, such as we are, in the path of enlightenment? and did he not indicate to us the first elements of that taste, that the fools treat as monstrous and bizarre, but by which we have recognized the divine essence?

Do not accuse me of boasting, sirs, if I retrace here that which I have been able to do for the order, and how many creatures I have recruited for it. Yes, I declare myself the indefatigable precursor of the rebels of our institution's sentimental laws everywhere. I won my uniform and its accouterments; I buggered my vassals when I could; I sodomized my wife, my niece, and I introduced the anvil to the very depths of my grooms; finally, I made as many buggers, fags, queers, and queens, from all who surrounded me. These are my qualifications.

I add this to prove that concubinage is not more natural than antiphysics, and that since a free man, by definition should be able to do what he wants, he ought to be free to more or less get to the bottom of the matter. I don't doubt, sirs, that the members of this august assembly be perfectly in accord with all the points and principles I have just established; but, following my feeling it only remains for us to erect them into law, to make them known and respected in the land of the Franks, and to have the National Assembly, among which we have many followers, annex our constitution to the one they are trying to draw.

# 13. Uranian Renaissance

## German Literature (1820–1869)

Europe in the late eighteenth and early nineteenth centuries saw the appearance of a new homoerotic aestheticism as well as an attempt to construct theories about homosexuality. In Johann Wincklemann's studies of Greek art—studies that Walter Pater would later identify as being in part informed by a sensitivity to the beauty of young men—and in poems by Friedrich Holderlin and Karl August von Platen, they and other German writers conflated classicism with friendship and homoerotic desire. Theoretical discussions by Heinrich Zschokke and Heinrich Hoessli were as determined as those by English theorists like John Addington Symonds and Edward Carpenter to redefine pejorative constructions of sexual difference. Zschokke's *Der Eros* (1821), Hoessli's *Der Eros* (1836), and Karl Heinrich Ulrichs's *Riddle of the Love Between Men* are early attempts to defend homosexuality within a "scientific" context. Hoessli views homosexual literature as not only a valuable record of desire but as the archive of a separate species. In 1869 Karoly Maria Benkert invented the term that would eventually be adopted by science, by the public, and by the new "homosexuals" themselves.

### Heinrich Zschokke (1771–1848)

From *Der Eros* [Eros; or, On Love] (1821)

*Translated by Carl Skoggaard*

Though unknown now, Heinrich Zschokke was one of the most popular writers of the Enlightenment, and his tolerance and liberal views were at one with Enlightenment principles. *Der Eros* is one of the earliest substantive printed discussions in Europe of erotic relations between the ancient Greeks. However, he is not content with exploring the subject as a curiosity of history but rather employs it to highlight and attack the homophobia of his own times. To do so, Zschokke creates the character of the elder Holmar, a judge who, in discussing the execution of one Lukasson for the murder of his "friend" Walter, advocates the decriminalization of homosexual love. The portion of the piece excerpted here is in the form of a dialogue between Holmar, Beda (the narrator), and Gerold, the "religious adviser" to the king. Though Holmar's argument at first seems to be a defense of homosexuality, Zschokke was not able to accept the consequences of total advocacy. He has Holmar—at the end, in a section not included below—make a sudden about-face and admit that Lukasson deserved to be punished for the murder and for sodomy. However, the piece concludes with Holmar equivocally asserting that "the book of nature contains many obscure passages and we should not be surprised when its interpreters differ."

#### 5. Eros

"We know [Holmar tells Beda and Gerold] that the Greeks were familiar with another love besides love between youths and maidens, a love by its nature far from all sensuality and low desire, having nothing in common with the sexual drive; a love that did not render the disposition overly soft and unmanly, but instead elevated and fortified it, making it more godlike. This was soul-love, and its god was called Eros. Sexual love was less esteemed and was called 'common' love—not that it was despised! How could a Greek have despised wife or mother? Could a Greek have lacked feeling for woman's beauty as immortalized by Praxiteles? Didn't the entire youth of Greece lie at the feet of Aspara [Aspasia?] or the enchanting Lais of Corinth?

"Still, the final aim of common love was and remained only to fulfill nature's powerful commandment to preserve the human race. The aim of soul-love, on the contrary, was a mutual delight in friendship, mutual ennoblement through exemplary demonstration of virtues, a glorious emulation. This higher, tenderer, uplifting friendship was found only between men; indeed, it was unthinkable between persons of the opposite sex in view of its purity, nature, and purpose. Soul-love developed between youths and would then endure, with a strength, passionateness, and faithfulness almost inconceivable to us now, into old age.

"What sort of love could it be that has become alien to us, its very name almost forgotten? Where did it come from, whither vanish? The question is: how could soul-love enter into the history of humanity, from time immemorial playing a brilliant role, if it was not deeply embedded in human nature, at least in masculine nature? And if it belonged to human nature, how could it disappear so completely that even the name has vanished? Or do we differ by nature from mortals of remote Antiquity?

"This wonderful, intimate, virtuous love, possessing all the seriousness of heroic masculine friendship; this heroic friendship with all the passionateness and romantic tenderness that rules love between youth and maid—I am not able to refer to it by the name of either friendship or love, for with such words we now associate entirely different concepts. Instead, allow me to follow the Greeks and call it 'Eros'—this affection between men, so full of passionate tenderness.

"The earliest period of Antiquity records manifestations of Eros. It is not confined to a brief era but is found throughout the lengthy course of centuries. Revered as a sanctified and honorable impulse, it was treated with deference by lawgivers, nobly cultivated by the wisest of the nation, and praised by the poets. Its heavenly power found expression not only under a single sky, but in all parts of the world, and would always assume its purest form where peoples remained in intimate contact with nature and had not become artificial through luxury and moral decay. Not only among the ancient Germans do we discover traces of Eros, through which heroic friends were bound by lifelong ties; it is also seen in the stories of American tribes, where youths who loved one another entered into an inviolable warrior-bond, sharing weal and woe together, daring every danger together, the one reconciling himself to the other's death by devoting his every remaining breath to revenge.

"Nevertheless, the manifestations of Eros are most easily traced in the history of the Greek tribes because they were the first to possess an intellectual culture, poets, and chroniclers of their destiny. Who does not know of the friendship between Achilles and his Patroclus from the Homeric sagas of the Trojan War? Who does not remember how Achilles avenged Patroclus' death? Or recall the intimate bond uniting the hearts of Orestes and Pylades? The tales of their friendship still resound among us, as do those about Damon and Pythias or Theseus and Pirithous.

"Even in the days of decadent morality among the Greeks and with loss of their freedom, the right and honor of Eros was preserved, some contemptible instances of defilement notwithstanding. Eros bound Socrates to Alcibiades still unblemished, youthful heart, and divine Plato loved the heart of Dion. Plutarch, who lived in the first century of the Christian era, even he, zealot against sensuality and impurity, still recognizes Eros as the best means of nurturing a manly disposition capable of every virtue.

"The classical writers, too, are God's mouthpiece! Let us honor their understanding of the divine and the holy! Only spiritually deformed ages to come, barbaric, morally abandoned, and degenerate, would misinterpret a Xenophon, a Lycurgus, an apostle of love such as Plato, and would view their approval of Eros, in words animated by the purest virtue, as the hellish fruit of a revolting unnaturalness. But came the days of Rome's infamous laxity, and Eros, too, was dragged into the mire and grew brutal through the vices of the chief city of the world. A sinister, centuries-long night of barbarism fell that threatened to extinguish even the holy light of nascent Christianity. In those days, a grim excess of piety found something shameful even in the love between young men and women; trampling of the laws of nature was seen as saintly work, and the unmarried state was held in higher esteem than wedlock. It was a matter of course then that Eros, the virtuous communion of manly hearts, should appear even more worthy of condemnation than these. Eventually it was inextricably associated with the vice-pit of Rome. In a time when terror ruled through princely whim or ecclesiastical ban, when the virtues of a Socrates or a Cato were regarded as Satan-worship, the study of nature as mere magic, Justinian inscribed Eros in the criminal code. Now, persecuted by church and state alike, punished by fire and the executioner's axe, the soul-ennobling disposition that once had been the salvation of Greece found itself freighted with the whole burden of scorn, mockery, and dishonor. Divine love wandered over the earth enchained in the gloomy procession of crimes. The greatest men of earlier times, ornaments of humanity, would have been disgraced and cursed by us, or sent to the gallows. With what scorn and shudders of horror would they turn their god-consecrated gaze from our monstrous thoughts and deeds!

"The immoral Herder, speaking of Pompeii and Herculaneum, refers to Wincklemann as a divine interpreter of those objects of Antiquity which so repay our study. And to be sure, the genius of humanity hovers over and bestows its blessings on those who employ a self-sacrificing zeal to retrieve from the earth the remains of mankind's greatest flowering. These are indeed venerable, hallowed fragments that still speak to us of the purity of nature, of the true, good, and beautiful, exhaling the vital breath of a more human humanity. Yet they are mere fragments! Oh, bury the fragments, and from out of the graves of bygone days let us instead summon to living warmth the beautiful, purely human outlook of Antiquity!"

Here Holmar fell silent in order to recuperate. He seemed exhausted from the effort of speaking and from his emotion. We who were listening did not interrupt the silence; our thoughts were far too stirred for that. As so often happens with me, I found myself so intent on Holmar's words that I no longer saw with my own eyes but only through his. And I saw more clearly a side of Antiquity that had remained obscure to me. I, too, had long allowed my judgment of the love between Greek heroes to become trammeled in that prejudice which persecutes such love with curses. I shrank from the blindness that had caused me up to now to inflict injury on the shades of those who are still the eternal ornaments of mankind. Soaring above the world of today, I returned in my imagination to the residence of the gods, to eternal Athens, its temples, theaters, gymnasia, athletic games, and orators' platforms. What heroic figures these! What divinely inspired sages, what power of truth, beauty, and greatness emerging with the most vital phase of a noble people, a people endowed with natural gifts of unfathomable abundance! I saw the power of consecrated Eros, of a now stigmatized love. And the world of today seemed maimed to me, the victim of a thousand-year-old delusion, its holy shrines betrayed at a stroke through an annihilating blow of barbarism.

Gerold composed himself sooner than I. "Holmar," said he, "never have I heard you speak with such eloquence and warmth, and over what is certainly an odd chapter in the history of mankind. I confess that up to now I had paid scant attention to this Eros of the Greeks, and had scarcely formed any conception of its nature. In any event, I had imagined it to be the result of prevailing national custom. In the land of the Hellenes, as in Eastern countries today, lifelong friendships with other men were more esteemed than friendship with women. The latter, shut away singly or in harems, occupied a social position beneath that of men, if above slaves; compared to the women of our time, they received less intellectual training and had less right, less ability, to enter the public sphere."

To which Holmar replied, "Your opinion echoes the great multitude of the learned who have gone before you. Such men, lacking a knowledge of nature, believed that they knew the Greeks and wrote thick volumes on love (like Ramdohr), without an inkling of the nature of Eros, marveling that Xenophon and Plato could treat the matter so solemnly! In truth, the Hellenes regarded the tender soul-bond between men as being on equal footing with the tender love between youths and girls and that of spouses. . . . Yet the Greeks knew another love besides love for women, one grown alien to us. In keeping with its nature and origins, their love for women was sensuous, while the latter love, in accordance with its nature, was more spiritual, or if you will, purely a matter of feeling. The one was nature's way of perpetuating the human race, the other her way to perpetuate nobility of mind."

## 6. The Beginnings and the End of Eros

Holmar's last remarks astonished me more than anything he had said before. I supposed that I had misunderstood him, and was about to ask him for a clearer explanation. However, Gerold anticipated me with a different query. "You have entertained us long enough," cried he, "with Eros of the Greeks, and most attractively, I admit, but Holmar, what has this Eros to do with Lukasson who was executed? Do you perhaps mean that Eros made him into the murderer of his friend?"

"Indeed," answered Holmar. "Or say rather it was the unnaturalness and perverseness of our age which entered into the man, bringing him into cruel contradiction with himself, and which then drove him to despair, insanity, self-hatred, and hatred of all humanity."

"Frankly, Holmar," I said, "you are becoming more obscure than you already were moments ago. It almost seems as though you hold soul-love between Greek men for a natural urge, like the mutual affection between the two sexes, or the instinct of mother and infant."

"Well, Beda, don't you?" said Holmar after regarding me with surprise for a while.

"No, I do not," I replied. "Hitherto I've not found anything to prove this, either though reasoning or from anything in the world's history. Even in the history of the Greeks! But let us hear your evidence, and if it should convince me, I'll regard you as one of the greatest discoverers, a Columbus afloat the dark ocean of human nature."

"Hear me, then!" he countered. . . . "The soul is the seat of sensual appetite, of happiness and pain, of longing and loathing. From the mysterious affinity and attraction between souls springs love. . . . Plants attract each other though sexual, souls by sexless means; this is the difference between Eros and seaborn Aphrodite, for once upon a time the earth and what it bears arose from the sea. That is why the Hellenes referred to the love between the sexes as 'common' love, while soul-love, being unconcerned with sex, was the higher type; higher to the same extent that the psyche or soul is raised above the vegetative level, and more closely related to the intellect. Just as in animals the need for vegetative propagation is raised to conscious feeling, so in humans soul-love is ennobled through the efforts of the intellect to achieve perfection.

"Wherever the artificialities of church and state have had the least distorting effect on man—and provided he has risen above a vile animality and developed his threefold being in obedience to nature—there each of his tendencies and urges will reveal itself in all its strength and splendor. That is why we find the soul-love of heroes and sages among the indigenous American warriors and other unspoiled people who lived in freedom; why it existed even among the armed brotherhoods of the free knights of the Middle Ages, though here in disguised Christian form. But the noblest and most open expression of soul-love occurred among the ancient Greeks, precisely because theirs was one of the most developed of human cultures.

"It was and is not caprice that governs love, whether sexless or sexual; rather it is the law and firm hand of nature. Both loves did and do express the workings of our natures; both were and remain equally worthy, and both can be equally tumultuous and passionate, for the one has its origins directly in the soul while the other stirs the wild impulses of the soul's power."

. . . .

"Now," Holmar continued, "just as the soul of the mother is compelled to love, so the souls of adults love each other, instinctively and without regard for sex. The inclination of souls toward one another is Eros. . . . This Eros has ruled since the beginnings of mankind, and rules still, but it is not recognized for what it is. Indeed, through a confusion with bestial and unnatural behavior alien to Eros itself, it has been branded a crime worthy of death. By misunderstanding human nature, we mutilate ourselves, and this mutilation is the source of incalculable secret misery. Among the Greeks, with the fresh and free unfolding of their full and complete natures, Eros was the source of all things great and splendid, revered by their wise men, acknowledged and hallowed in their laws. Eros came to be despised as an unnatural thing when the nations, becoming ever more perverse, at length fell away from nature. Every man and boy who feels this impulse of the soul within him must shudder in horror. Since his whole understanding will have become completely perverse as a result of the world's madness, he will be forced to think himself crazy and unnatural; and should he ever be seized by an unforeseen, irresistible passion for another man, he will actually believe that he is mad. He will not be able to recognize the origins of this holy feeling. Instead he will accept, on the world's authority, that his affection is criminal, even though he himself will not really feel it to be so. What is actually a command of his soul-nature will fill him with superstitious horror, appearing to him as something monstrously and heinously unnatural. So he battles against the impulse and thus changes the first . . . feeling of soullove into an all-destroying passion. Raw contradiction between his inner being will disturb him to his innermost depths. He will despise himself and his nature, and on this account the world also, with whose ways he is in irreconcilable conflict.

"How then will this suffocated, humiliated, lamed, misled, and despised soul, this heart so filled with all the terror of ruination, calmly observe its duties towards society? The man senses that inside himself the mainspring is broken; where is he to find the strength? That sole passion alone swallows his whole existence—tears him, I should say, from himself and hurls him into the abyss; like a fire it issues from the wound of his misused nature, it alone consuming him, making him heedless of the incentives of reputation, money, authority, love of women, heedless of everything that is capable of occupying others. Upon what is he to base his worthless existence? What will lend it some kind of meaning? There is only one thing his sick soul loves, and his understanding of this one thing is not better than his understanding of himself. He loves, and curses his love, which is at the same time the object of his hatred, and this despairing hatred becomes hatred of mankind and of life. Ever desiring the good and the true, he must turn to the bad and the false. The right of his nature in this world is outside the law, and so for him the world has no law. He would be happy if the earth disintegrated before his eyes. And all of this is the raging, the shrieking, the tumult of one condemned by himself and condemning himself, one whose true, unalterable, ineradicable (though putrescent) nature cannot die, yet is not allowed to live."

Holmar fell silent. His words had left us deeply shaken. There was something terrible in the old man's fire. "You talk," I said to him, "as one who laments his own terrible misery. Holmar, have you been, or are you still one of these unfortunates?"

"No," he replied, "I never was. Yet from my childhood I felt driven by an infinite longing to find a friend to be my soul-mate. Who does not know youth's violent yearning for a lifelong Pylades or Pythias? Friends I found, and a wife after my own heart, but never the soul-friend. Still, this has not made me unhappy, for the vague longing, because of its vagueness, could not grow into an enormous passion. I would have become unhappy, perhaps, had I found the friend I sought. Now you will all understand me when I tell you that Lukasson was such as unfortunate! In Greece he might have become one of the great artists, philosophers, or national heroes, through soul-friendship. Among us the same thing made him into a murderer, and the law delivered him to the executioner. All is explained by the unacknowledged claims of his soul: an entire life of contradiction and confusion; his readiness to sacrifice all for the beloved and his never-ending efforts to make the beloved into the most perfect, virtuous, and noble of men; his struggle with himself and a passion that made him appear crazy to himself; his attempts at distraction, the deliberate striving to stupefy himself with spirits; his repeated resolve to take his own life; and finally, the murder of his friend. . . ."

"I am dumbstruck," cried Gerold. "I am afraid to question you, or to reply. Holmar, you are talking to me as though from another world, an exotic region of palms, enormous snakes, and orchids of which I am ignorant. I am familiar only with the firs and oaks of our native landscape. I have a mind to reread Plato's *Symposium*, and Xenophon's, in which Socrates and his friends treat of soul-love. Previously, I took these works more as oratorical exercises on a custom of Greek life, rather than as something deeply serious."

"Do by all means read them!" answered Holmar. "Don't imagine that the ancients would have trifled with matters they regarded as holy. Today we admire the prosperity, strength, and greatness of that former world, whose splendor we have not yet equaled, and which we won't equal unless we return to nature, following the path of truth, goodness, and beauty. Let us seek out the naturalness of nature and the humanity of human beings! Ah, our state machinery, our systems of theology and philosophy often seem to me like the bed of Procrustes. Whoever wants to take his rest on it and is too short is stretched and yanked until he is fully long enough, even though he lose his life in the process, while those too long are truncated. That is the reason for so many kinds of maiming—social, ethical, religious, and intellectual—in a Europe that prides itself on its refinement. The lawmaker wants to fashion people to fit his idea and outlook, not make the law fit the people. But a person must become all or nothing through the nature that he already has, and not through another's. . . .

"The fact that Eros, the soul-love which in ancient times went about nobly and freely, from man to man, has scarcely been nameable for nearly two thousand years, and therefore is still scarcely mentioned—shall we take this as evidence that Eros itself does not exist and is unknown? And consider the reverse: how many are the things that were known of and mentioned for centuries that in fact never did exist, such as manifestations of spirits or the powers of witches. And yet, how many thousands of innocents were slaughtered on behalf of this delusion, in keeping with church ordinances and penitential books! However, the indestructible natural impulse of which we are speaking, Eros, cannot be eradicated, even though at the same time it may be despised and condemned as unnatural and injurious to one's honor and modesty. Eros is always making itself conspicuous, manifesting itself as a dark tendency in the annals of mankind. But it is the hostile madness directed against Eros that perpetually causes misery. . . ."

## Heinrich Hoessli (1784–1864)

### From Eros: *Die Mannerliebe der Griechen* [The Manly Love of the Greeks] (1836)

*Translated by Carl Skoggaard*

Hoessli, at whose insistence Zschokke wrote his *Der Eros*, eventually wrote his own study of homosexuality. While it is not clear whether Zschokke felt emotionally and personally impelled to write, Hoessli certainly did. His immense two-volume work—the first dealing with modern homosexuality, the second with historic and literary manifestations of it— reveals his own personal commitment on every page. His celebration of homosexual love (what he calls Eros), his attack on homophobia, and his attempt to explore the psycho- logical aspects of homosexual love is certainly one of the most powerful, if not the first, attempt to do so in any European language. Hoessli's book was banned after it was issued, and it is now almost impossible to find.

## FROM VOLUME 2 (1838)

Now let us set forth and examine some of the things that up to now have been taught, published, and disseminated about Eros, the lies told about it, the ways these ideas have been put to practical use. I aim to show that there actually have been attempts to interpret, understand, and explain Eros; and, as the present essay is supposed to make clear, it is precisely our contradictions that will reveal the nature and characteristics of Eros to calm reflection all the more convincingly and distinctly.

[Hoessli discusses several propositions, with reference to the Greeks and to his own time, that he argues have been adduced to discredit same-sex love.]

### [1] That Eros was merely a sensitivity to beauty

It was [for the Greeks] a matter of individual sensitivity to beauty, based on sexual- ity. Such sensitivity reveals and must, as it were, betray and lay bare whether a sex- ual love is present in a person, and which kind of sexual love; and this sensitivity is obliged to give outward expression to what is within. It is, moreover, precisely through this sensitivity to beauty that a person is anchored by means of a personal band to Nature, to one's own nature. A person is what he is because of his nature and the sensitivity to beauty that is rooted unconditionally in his nature. Precisely the sensitivity to beauty based on sexuality offers the individual and those who are to mold him a guide, sanctified by Nature—insofar as they themselves, teachers and student, have not been led away from her through lies. Nothing other than sen- sitivity to beauty based on sexuality permits the researcher who is not blind to dis- cover outer and inner sexual individuality. . . .

   Where love or sexual feeling and experience are concerned, the notion of fem- inine or masculine beauty is merely relative; for every human being, the sex he finds more beautiful and to whose attractions he is more susceptible is the sex which he loves, that sex for whom a sex-sympathy within him speaks. Psychosexually the choice is beyond influence, unalterably determined and decided in and for the individual, inaccessible to every act of will and every teach- ing. . . .

### [2] Love between men was soul-love

Had Eros been merely soul-love or friendship [that is, nonsexual love], then it could and would still have to be soul-love now, again, and forever! The only prob- lem is that among us it is not soul-love, precisely because it never was. And if it ever was soul-love, then what are all our unending reproaches of the immortal Greeks about? Soul-love (friendship) is never subject to legislation [as Eros was]. If it had been merely soul-love, it would only have gone from one soul to another, would have received only through the soul (the soul! always the soul!). And then what do we make of all the bodily, sexual, purely sensuous aspects of all the evidence of Eros that has come down to us, and how are we to explain and interpret the hundreds of references in the sources to charm and beauty, the granting of lovers' wishes, to physical possession and enjoyment of the body, to the sufferings and raptures, the torments and bliss of love? Wherever we find such things, they are always in connection with a particular age and a specific sex; never in connection with childhood or old age; no, they are connected with the ripeness of manhood, the time of life when sexual love is strongest. Never do we find in one and the same breast such feelings and also love for a girl, certainly in none of the descriptions provided by the divine Plato. . . .

Let us say for sake of argument that this affection was a sexless soul-love (friendship), or merely an intellectual appreciation, in the man's mind, of the youth's beauty: surely, then, along with this disposition, this sexless affection of the mind and the soul, there would also have been a manifestation of the usual sexual love [for women] and the physical nature of the man, what with its power and dominion over every creature. . . . There is not now and nor will there ever be on earth a friendship that has extinguished the sexual inclination and awareness that is already present, the physical element, in favor of the friendship. . . .

Love, friendship, sexual love: these are three things of which only the last is rooted in the physical and the absolute and not in choice, accident, and condition. The plan of Creation could and would not leave these roots, whose unfolding is to lead to the highest humanity, to chance; this is why they are sunk in the flesh, the reason they are where they are, and belong to the inmost nature and creation, to the original and instinctive existence of mankind, and why they shall always remain there, though with our lies and blindness we make futile attempts to pretend they have no connection with the flesh.

### [3] The masculine love of the Greeks—the love about which Plato wrote, hence platonic love—is a degeneration

Suppose it were, or that they were, and that all these thousands upon thousands of human lives, these individual beings, these psyches with their own organization are a degeneration! If this really is so, then even in this case the Greeks treated such persons in a godlike manner, and we are being satanic—for even degenerate beings are natural beings. If they are degenerate beings, then what the Greeks made out of such persons and degenerates represents the greatest achievement by a nation in history, the greatest which the sun shall ever shine upon. Out of our nonhumans they made superhumans, and what are we making out of millions of true human natures? Cripples in body and soul! Socrates loved the masculine nature; he himself demonstrated and acknowledged as much, as did Euripides and Plato. Degenerates of this sort we cannot point to among us; yet almighty God, how great is our need of them! . . . If such human beings are natural degenerates and are shunned by Nature herself; are rejected by God and belong to no visible or invisible natural order; live and yet are without rights or an original humanity; if they are dehumanized beings as a result of God's plan; if it is His will, if this is what they are, then the Greeks in their day ceased to be merely human, and towered above such a faithless natural order, and above God himself, for they knew to give such persons understanding and honor, justice and a fatherland, education and a way of life, out their abundant divinity. . . .

If, however, they are not unnatural beings (degenerates), if they have their place within the whole of God's plan as part of the human race, if these human beings have their own role to play within humanity (as the Greeks taught, believed, and demonstrated, and as I shall show subsequently), what are we to make of our venomous professors, raging laws, the priests who hurl damnation, and the people who set themselves wildly against this part of God's plan?. . . .

But indeed, this portion of humanity is not a degeneration; no! our God does not trifle with men in this fashion. It would be the idea and the act of a Satan, not God: to create human beings, and then forge their lives—all the deepest springs of their existence, their whole spiritual and intellectual nature, their love with all its mighty stirrings, by means of the iron bands of all the drives, all the senses, and every emotion, by means of all the tremendous power of the lower and higher strivings of the psyche, from the earthly roots of the flesh to the highest enthusiasms and remotest spheres of the human spirit—to ignominy and to crimes worthy of death, and to proclaim in such letters of flame their irretrievable ruin and descent into the fathomless inner dungeons of the human spirit!

### [4] Greek love . . . is a matter of choice, or self-will

According to this delusion he who loves men has renounced his original, primal nature and now inhabits a nature other than his own; his countenance burns with the passion of this arbitrarily chosen love, and it is while inhabiting this other nature that his soul yearns for union, his heart is inflamed, his eyes swim with tears, his breast heaves, and his spirit is radiant with joy. . . . All this is not his nature— supposedly he has set aside that nature, willfully exchanged it, and his true is no longer there. He chooses to change natures even though this other nature, this non-nature, should bring about his complete ruin and even his death.

Let us suppose for the sake of argument that . . . a man could truly and in actual fact trade his nature, his primal sexual inclination for another one, willfully extinguishing the one that was in him, suppressing it, rooting it out, and in its place accepting another, calling forth another, putting it into practice in his life. Is it conceivable that in this case a human being—a man—would give up an inborn love with which he would be able to enjoy undisturbed his existence—enjoy every aspect of his human condition as man, human being, husband, and citizen, behaving and acting and living in honor, creating the basis for a life of happiness, all under the protection of the law and with its acknowledgment, secure in all his outer and inner human rights, esteemed by his family and the whole of society, with the blessings of the established religion, and with public approval contested by none—would trade it for a nature forbidden, of evil repute, dishonoring, scorned, everywhere persecuted, everywhere condemned? That he would make a mockery of his original nature and oppose all the holy impulses in the depths of his innermost humanity so that he could be ostracized, exposed to danger everywhere, scorned, shamed, made to suffer uncertainty and persecution, be without possessions, see his outer and inner well-being undermined and irretrievably destroyed? And wouldn't his primal nature all the while, being itself indestructible, constantly hinder him? . . .

Reader, which sex do you love? Which love is part of your nature? What is it that automatically by itself touches all the strings of your sexual being, of your deepest, innermost human nature, whether you will or not? With such questions we do not address human will, but rather individual nature, the very depths and essential nature of the [individual] psyche, its most intimate and unchanging nature and essence. It is only when our delusion, masquerading as law, religion, or custom — ignorance in any case — forces a person to painful lies, shameful deception, or silence, that Nature will all but perish and remain dumb and commit an outrage against herself — and, undeterred, exact a fearsome vengeance both in hidden ways and outwardly on a depraved people! They are all lost to us, the beings we have tormented, put to death, and dismissed as worthless under the influence of this delusion! . . .

No love is in and of itself a virtue or a vice, any more than it is the product of the will or self-willing. Indeed, these few, simple truths both show the erroneousness of our belief and our ignorance, our injustice and our shamefulness — and prove beyond a doubt that at this very moment we are sunk in the pitch-black darkness of the dehumanizing age of witchcraft and heretics, if only because of our sinister defamation [of Eros]; that in the name of a ghastly false idol we are still murdering no small or unimportant portion of our degraded race. Delusion wears a hood over his eyes to murder, and does not recognize his victims; he is the idol of superstitious, ignorant, blind peoples and ages. . . .

So as to justify the atrocities that our species has perpetrated against itself in the centuries of decay, it has found a way to disguise each of them. Thus our age still says and teaches with regard to this topic [Eros], which is found among us and is a universal phenomenon:

[6] "This unrestrained immorality of the Greeks was abnormal and is found far less, if at all, among us"

. . . . That this love which never inspires a passion for a member of the opposite sex, but for a member of one's own sex instead — Greek love, in short — no longer exists or is now rare: against this greatest of all printed lies I shall raise my voice as loud as I can to proclaim the opposite: it does still exist, and for the most elementary reason, namely, because it is part of nature, as it once was, and therefore cannot cease to exist so long as the human race continues to exist. At this very moment there is not one individual more or less of the masculine sex [with an Eros nature] in the whole world than there was in the age of the Greeks. . . .

Of course! Eros must have existed, and in the very foundations of human nature, even before the immortal ancients gave it a secure place in their science and laws, their art and customs, their sacred ideas. Ask, if you will, where this love of the Greeks is to be found nowadays, or what form it takes, and I shall be glad to answer you: the answer is only too easy. It creeps as a vice under the weight of a general condemnation, a ruin which brings more ruin, sickly, denied encouragement and activity, full of guilt and torment, beyond the pale of human dignity and acknowledgment; most often it has a repulsive appearance, not a Grecian one, and in our very midst creates its own distinctive set of social conditions . . . its own moral degradation, vice, sin, and depravity—whose origins we do not seek. It is an abundant wellspring of poison all its own, of human degradation and misery, sparing not a single area of our domestic and public life. Misunderstood, it destroys a whole world of goodness and humanity. Neglected, it darkens into a terrifying riddle which, depraved and thoroughly confused about itself, hangs over countless innocent families. Ostracized, it howls in a thousand prison cells the world over, cursing itself and the hour of its birth. A monster of incessant contradiction it is now, shrouded in night and obscurity, a monster who each day renews himself and consumes himself, and in this condition provides work and bread for dungeon masters and executioners, or occasionally here and there loosens the shackles of earthly shame, of a life of condemnation, putting an end to the riddle of such an existence through suicides we cannot explain. . . .

### [7] "This love is a vice and a crime like all other vices and crimes"

Love . . . is neither a vice nor a virtue, though it can lead to both; love may exist, as unconditioned nature, between the two, but is always nature, never a matter of individual choice. Love can take a noble or ignoble direction, a pleasant and cheerful path or a wild and savage one; love takes action, but is not the deed itself [for which a person has moral responsibility]. Greece could not have installed a vice as a nonvice in the midst of its great [moral] life any more than it could have relegated a virtue to the vices or have proclaimed something a virtue or a vice that was neither one nor the other. . . .

The lawgiver must be aware of each real, actually existing nature that could do harm to society; he must keep an eye on it, grasp its inner workings, and provide for it under the law. But a law is not supposed to cancel a human being, is not supposed to lie and may not proclaim a natural phenomenon as a non-nature, the better to persecute it. The individual should be magnified by the law, not diminished. . . .

Is the law entitled to lay claim to a person's love? Is an individual entitled to mortgage it to the law, or offer it up? Can the law itself be a sin against the nature of an individual? Under what circumstances can it claim the most sacred part of a person? . . . I may under no circumstances impose conditions on someone's nature that I would not impose on my own, and under no circumstances am I to pawn another's nature in order to guarantee or favor my own. . . . [T]here are no limits to our persecution of the Eros-nature, partly because we do not acknowledge the presence of a nature when Eros appears, and also because this nature does not concern those in authority. They have no direct contact with it, and their lives are not darkened or gladdened by it; they are neither oppressed nor exalted by it. There is no limit to how horrifying our laws for Eros can be, since we are not obliged to submit our own nature to their authority, as we do with all other laws. . . .

Eros elevated an existing type of human nature, redeeming it through a human idea. This type of human nature really is present, and was and is capable of great and powerful effects through the idea [of Eros] as Plato shows it. . . . Eros, then, must have helped to awaken that influence [Greek culture], so clear and many-sided, which promises us countless blessings in the near and more distant future; but those who are bent on destroying true human knowledge and art find none of this in Eros, because they are not looking for it. They would rather prove the opposite, even though it would mean the ruin of the whole human race. . . .

The . . . masculine love of the Greeks—a type of human nature—has even been numbered among the habitual vices! . . . [I]s it possible that such activities are peculiar to certain individuals? That they are rooted in the blameless, unchangeable innermost self of such a person, and thus work their influence, rule over him, and decide his fate? Do these things belong to his original, guiltless, untouched psyche, and are they already present in the womb? Do they fulfill his human existence, do they transfigure his soul, make its nature clear, enlarge its scope, lend it wings? Do they belong among a person's highest endowments and spiritual aspirations? Are they necessary for his full humanity? Do they lead where love leads when it is humanely comprehended? Serve to develop, condition, and create those things within him that love does in following its lifelong path? And in the absence of these activities is a person maimed and stunted, as he is when he lacks love? . . .

## Karl Heinrich Ulrichs (1825–1895)

From *Forschungen über das Rätsel der mannmännlichen Liebe* [Researches into the Riddle of Love Between Men] (1864–1880)

*Translated by Michael A. Lombardi-Nash*

Karl Ulrichs, theorist of homosexual law and advocate of social rights for homosexuals, developed the third-sex theory of homosexuality, the concept that a homosexual was a female soul trapped in the male body. Ulrichs expounded this theory and argued for the decriminalization of homosexuality in a series of booklets written between 1864 and 1879 under the pseudonym Numa Numantius. He collected them into a single volume where he coined the word *Urning*—in English *Uranian*—to denote homosexuals and in an attempt to cancel the negative imputations associated with *sodomite*. His third-sex theory had considerable influence on European and English writers. It was the work of Ulrichs that prompted John Addington Symonds to write his own theoretical text, "A Problem in Modern Ethics." In this excerpt I have heavily edited Ulrichs' rather repetitive comments and for the sake of space have restructured his single-sentence paragraphs.

### From Book One: Vindex: Social and Legal Studies on Man-Manly Love (1864)

#### The Actual Dissemination of Man-Manly Love

1. It is a fact that there are individuals among us whose body is built like a male, and, at the same time, whose sexual drive is directed toward men, who are sexually not aroused by women (i.e., are horrified by any sexual contact with women).

2. I have termed these individuals *Urnings*, while I have used the term *Dionings* for those individuals whom one usually terms "men" (i.e., those whose sexual drive is toward women, feeling horrified by any sexual contact with men). I have termed

the love of Urnings *Uranian love* or *man-manly*; of Dionings, *Dionian*. I believe I had to create a new expression because the word *Knabenliebe* [literally, "boy love"], which has been widely used, leads to the misinterpretation that Urnings are really attracted to boys, when actually they are attracted to young men (*puberes*). Even in ancient Greece, Urnings did not fall in love with boys. *Pais* meant "young man" as well as "boy." My terminology is derived from the names of the gods Uranus and Dione. A poetical piece of fiction by Plato traced the origins of man-manly love to Uranus, the love for women to Dione. . . .

### The Inborn Nature of Man-manly Love

6. Dionings [heterosexuals] unceremoniously start from the hypothesis that in our species no class of born Urnings exists or could exist; in other words: no class of individuals exists or could exist that is born with the sexual drive of women and has the body of a male . . . that all individuals who are male are born with the sexual drive of males. . . .

7. This hypothesis is completely incorrect. There is a class of born Urnings, a class of individuals who are born with the sexual drive of women and who have male bodies. They are a variety of men whose Uranian love is congenital. . . .

9. The inheritance of man-manly love is such that the individual who is affected, the Urning, is not a complete man but rather should be called a "would-be man" [Quasi-Mann], or "half-man." The Urning is not a man, but rather a kind of feminine being when it concerns not only his entire organism but also his sexual feelings of love, his entire natural temperament, and his talents. The dominant characteristics are of femininity both in his behavior and in his body movements. These are the obvious manifestations of the feminine element that resides in him.

10. We Urnings, who are a special sexual species, are similar to hermaphrodites. As a third sex, we are on the same level as the male or female sex, but we are independent of the male or female sex, fully separate from both. We are not fully men or women, but by nature we are different. Yet it is true that we are similar to men because we assume the masculine role in society and because our capacity for work is the same.

11. The hitherto existing ignorance of the presence of Urnings must no longer be tolerated. The question of the Urning's right to life demands a solution, indeed, one that is conciliatory. This demand is not to be made in favor of any one individual but rather in the interest of the general welfare. The Uranian class must now surely be powerful enough to demand equal rights. The process obviously demands some intelligence. Demanding equality in this matter means having the courage to overcoming hitherto existing hesitation and coming bravely forward. I believe I have herewith broken the ice!

### Natural and Unnatural

12. When I love the person I am naturally attracted to, I am not acting contrary to nature. When I, as an Urning, fall in love with a mature and handsome young man, I am not behaving contrary to nature. You [the "heterosexual" Ulrichs is rhetorically addressing] could consider the Urning, who loves a man, as behaving unnaturally only if you start from the wrong assumption: All individuals built as

males, as he is, are born with the love for women and a horror for men; therefore, he, too, is born with the nature of the Dioning. The Urning, who is born to love men and horrified by women, consequently is acting naturally when he, following his natural inclinations, flees from sexual contact with women and satisfies his sexual drive in the embrace and in sexual contact with some young man. . . .

Considering the question what is natural and what is unnatural, one would not apply a standard that is not in conformity with one's own nature. All people must act according to their own nature and their sexual orientation (i.e., their own nature and the nature of their own kind), no matter if one be a Dioning, a woman, or an Urning. When it is a question of their sexuality, all persons are to be judged solely according to their nature and the nature of their own kind.

Likewise, in this matter, you have to judge us Urnings solely by our own standards, not by those of Dionings, whose sexual desires are for women. . . . We completely fulfill our obligations when we follow, not resist, our orientation, which was planted in our hearts by a higher being, be it God or nature. We have no other obligations. If you are unsatisfied with the fruitlessness of our sexual acts, and if you want to know where the responsibility lies, then demand this of that higher being, not of us.

Sexual contact with the body of blossoming young men is our natural desire. For that reason, these, our acts of love, are natural, in spite of their absolute inability to procreate. That which is natural is not made unnatural by infertility.

18. For us Urnings, our nature alone is the standard, not yours. And now we desire to be judged only by standards that apply to us. We protest against every attempt forcefully to apply rules that are formulated as consequences of your nature to love women.

The practice of inborn man-manly love is neither criminal nor immoral; therefore, it is cruel, unjust, and senseless to prosecute. . . .

19. Today, an Urning who follows his inborn sexual orientation by pursuing physical contact with a beloved blossoming young man to satisfy his natural sexual drive is prosecuted regardless of moral or legal considerations, namely, as a disgraceful criminal by the laws instituted in every German state. . . . Prosecution occurs because he satisfies his sexual desires in a different fashion than Dionings. It occurs because the majority, which is composed of Dionings, does not judge him according to his own nature but to theirs, because the majority, like Procrustes, forces him into a Dionian bed that is foreign to his nature.

20. The infamy of the prosecution of Urnings is cruel, unjust, and senseless. And if it were in his power, it would be just as senseless for some Urning to punish Dionings because they find sexual satisfaction in the embrace of young women. This persecution is as senseless as—if you will allow the comparison—punishing hens for laying eggs instead of chicks, or cows for bearing calves instead of laying eggs. The present-day persecution of man-manly love is just as foolish as the persecution of heresy and witchcraft. It, too, was unsuccessful. . . .

21. Man-manly love is a riddle of nature. Any unprejudiced person would recognize it as such after giving it some thought. However, riddles of nature can be solved by, if anything, science. Not by blindly declaring something infamous or by blindly taking up the so-called sword of justice, which has all too often been shown as the sword of injustice to heretics, Jews, and witches.

22. To be sure, it is probably difficult for science to solve the following riddle of man-manly love: How does nature awaken the love for men in individuals whose sexual organs are developed in the womb to form a male and not a female? On the other hand, it is probably not as difficult for science, after a thorough investigation, to yield the following: that nature awakens the love for men in a certain class of these individuals. . . .

23. We Urnings form a small minority. But, by God, we have the same rights as you, who are a powerful majority. You have no authority to take away or encroach upon our equal rights.

24. Who, I ask, gave you the right to force us into your mode of satisfying the sexual drive, of gratification in the embrace of a woman, that is in direct opposition to our sexual orientation; a mode we deplore, one that does not allow us to find satisfaction filled with magnetic force (i.e., one of true gratification of our sexual desires), in short, one which is unnatural to us—namely, to label us infamous and criminal when we practice our natural tendencies which clearly distinguish us— i.e., finding satisfaction in making physical contact with a blossoming and beloved man. Who, I ask, gave you the right to prohibit us for the rest of our lives from participating in our natural tendencies and unceremoniously to scorn that which nature delegated to us and to leave us no other choice than a satisfaction unsuited to our nature, one we utterly deplore?

25. Each act of love performed outside marriage, particularly our own, is considered more often than not as lewdness. This viewpoint of extramarital relationships is thoroughly uncalled-for. . . . Truly, they may be lewd, but then they may also be nothing more than the satisfaction of the sex drive. Finally, they may be just as fulfilling as marital sex. Your viewpoint of lewdness is, therefore, placed in opposition to the viewpoint of the satisfaction of natural behavior.

26. Our sexual drive is one that demands periodical satisfaction, be it complete, be it incomplete. The latter consists of petting and absorbing that magnetic current that flows from the body of a young man, which is transmitted to us through physical contact with him.

27. The legal institution of marriage is not the institution for us. There is no priest or justice of the peace who would bind in marriage one of us and our beloved. Therefore, the natural state of the species exists for us, as it does for the birds in the sky and the animals in the field (i.e., marriage cannot be the prerequisite of a moral license for gratification in any relationship, at least as long as priests and justices of the peace are lacking).

28. We are not eunuchs. Nature gave us, like you, a sexual drive, which needs to be gratified. Also, we have taken no vows of chastity. Who, I ask, gave you the right to order us not to love or to live the rest of our lives as eunuchs or take a vow of chastity? What would you say if some reigning tyrannical Urning were to order the same for you as a reprisal for the treatment you have given us, namely, either to love men or to spend the rest of your lives as eunuchs?

29. We, too, have a right to enjoy the pleasures of love; we, too, have the right to satisfy our sexual drives; we, too, have the right to do this in the manner that is natural for us, not in any other way.

30. In short, we protest against the abuse that has been heaped upon us by the Dionian majority. This majority has poisoned the happiness of many by countless

acts of abuse and persecution and by its lack of respect. It has trod upon the beds of roses where we might have found happiness.

31. From your point of view, which is based on a scientific error and which is a subjective one, you believe the majority has acted justly and in the only way it knows how. The majority is caught up in the error that we are men as Dionians are men and therefore have the same drives that Dionians have. But, taken objectively, you can see the gross error of the viewpoint of the majority. . . .

34. Only after making a comprehensive and unbiased study of man-manly love, a study which is truly taken seriously, which is devoted only to the facts, will the irrational persecution of this kind of love cease in the courts, in the police stations, and in society. . . . The last two centuries saw efforts to abolish the persecution of heresy and witchcraft. In our century, indeed, in our decade, efforts will be made to abolish the persecution of man-manly love. . . . The battle in which I am a warrior is a battle for the freedom of expression.

## K. M. Kertbeny [K. M. Benkert]

"HOMOSEXUALITY" (1869)

*Translated by Michael Lombardi-Nash*

The German-Hungarian writer Karoly Maria Kertbeny invented the word *homosexual* [in German, *homosexualitat*], including it in a letter written to Ulrichs on May 6, 1868. In 1869 "homosexualitat" appeared in print for the first time in Kertbeny's anonymous pamphlet, *The Social Harm Caused by Paragraph 143 of the Prussian Legal Code*, the paragraph that criminalized homosexual acts.

. . . . [I]n the face of a society such as ours is today . . . do [governments] still want to maintain the medieval views concerning sexual excesses, do they want to allow the same acts of the great majority of opposite-sexual natures to go totally unpunished, however, to punish the relationships of the very small minority of homosexual natures as true hardened and brutal criminals and even to declare them as dishonorable? This is not only unjust, it is an unpardonable absurdity of our present standpoint on the view of the world. . . . Such a revolting injustice, which is an absurdity at the same time, cannot be allowed to go unchallenged in our day. . . .

[I]n both of the German great powers, in Prussia and Austria . . . they prosecute most severely "unnatural fornication between people and animals," as well as between persons of the male sex with six months to four years imprisonment with easy labor, as well as the loss of civil rights at the same time. . . . How did this so-so legislation ever come into being except as a consequence of the overuse of morality by men who, moreover, as the stronger sex, domineer over and make unreasonable demands on other men, because this act is dictated to be especially "degenerate" and "degrading" only between one man and another, not also between a man and a woman or two women?

. . . . Because the word *degenerate* no doubt referred to those individuals who are affected by such homosexual passions and sought to satisfy them actively with other people; on the other hand, in the case of passive persons, it is presupposed that they, for their own part, find absolutely no satisfaction by this. [They] abandon themselves to the most despicable interests . . . in such a revolting . . . manner most dangerous to one's health [that] it unconditionally deserves to be called the "degradation of the person." This is not the place here to cram in the scientific details of the study of sexuality. Its conclusions are, in short, [that] besides the normal-sexual drives of all humanity and of animals, nature, in its sovereign frame of mind, appears to have also given a homosexual drive to certain male and female individuals at birth, to have bestowed upon them a sexual constraint which has a physical and mental effect, [despite] the best intentions to have a normal-sexual erection. This presupposes a direct horror for the opposite sex; and it also makes those who are constrained by this passion incapable of withdrawing from the influence which particular individuals of the same sex have over them. . . . Now, it is obvious to thinkers educated in anthropology that those who are constrained by such drives either meet with individuals of their own nature—and, therefore, there is absolutely nothing at all to justify objecting to such reciprocal inclinations because both are lacking normal-sexuality by nature, and, consequently, it would be asking too much of them to live their whole life long in absolute chastity, and to submit their existence to a penalty because, through no fault of their own, nature organized them with this very constraint or else homosexualists must turn their inclinations to normal-sexuals, and, if the modern constitutional state makes a concession to the latter, [then] in principle, in all cases in which [the] rights of others are [not] injured by it, they [ought to be] allowed to do with their bodies as they please. Hence it will not be necessary to differentiate between acts, whether…natural or…unnatural, [whether] they are practiced by the opposite sex or the same sex….

[Kertbeny concludes his argument for equal rights for homosexuals with eighteen points of summary of his remarks. Among these the following suggest his essential position: the law has no place in the regulation of sex and homosexuality since homosexual desire is congenital, and that it is up to society, not the homosexual, to change.]

1. The modern constitutional state, which has only to protect rights (otherwise having no other secondary tasks, for that is what other organizations in society exist for and are called upon to perform), has no reason to become involved with the question of sex where the rights of others are not injured.

4. . . . because history has taught us that homosexualism is and always has been present alongside normal-sexualism among all races and in all climates, and thus cannot be suppressed even by the most brutal persecutions.

5. Furthermore, for this reason as well as for the essence of this drive (its inclinations as well as its antipathies), it is evident that it is rooted in a changeable riddle of nature; thus, it is not voluntary or simple refinement, but rather can only be an inborn drive and therefore cannot be suppressed.

6. This hypothesis is supported by the historical fact that so many important and noble characters of our history in general are either suspected of being or are known for sure to be of this partial drive, which, were it not an inborn one—and consequently one that could be suppressed—would not occur among such important men with their intellectual understanding and physical capabilities, nor among wealthy and powerful people, whose free choice of pleasure is unlimited.

7. In the face of this undeniable fact, we either have to call our ideas of culture into question (that we should consider these same historical people, whose intellect we esteem and honor to such a degree, as fit for imprisonment for their dishonorable acts) or we must find two kinds of law, one for the intellectual and socially powerful, and another for the rest of humanity.

# Part Five
Heirs of Eros

*English Literature (1850–1969)*

# 14. Romantic Friendship and Homosexuality in Nineteenth-Century English Poetry (1850–1900)

## Inventing a Language

### INTRODUCTION: THE LAW

In 1861 England abolished the death penalty for the act of buggery, but public sodomitical offenses were still punishable by ten years, or in some instances, even by life imprisonment. Of all the countries in Europe, England retained the most stringent laws against sodomy and continued the strict prosecutions of those apprehended in sodomitical acts as well as to raid known homosexual gathering places. The criminalization of *all* sodomitical acts, both in public and in private, was accomplished when the "Labouchere Amendment" of the 1885 Criminal Law Amendment Act was passed. The law made illegal "any act of gross indecency" between two males. Despite or perhaps because of this, a literature began to appear that publicly defined and even advocated sexual difference.

### TERMINOLOGY

When Lord Alfred Douglas asserted in 1894 that homosexuality was the love that dared not speak its name, he was writing a homosexual version of the legal formula that defined homosexuality as the vice not to be named among Christians. By 1894 homosexuals probably had more epithets applied to them—opprobrious generally, scientific and definitive occasionally, sympathetic and tolerant rarely—than any other minority. As John Addington Symonds wrote in 1891 in "A Problem in Modern Ethics," "the accomplished languages of Europe in the nineteenth century supply no terms for this persistent feature of human psychology, without importing some implication of disgust, disgrace, vituperation." "Sodomite" and "buggerer" were still primary terms, used early on and continued in law. Euphemistic epithets derived from biblical and classical sources described homosexuals as "men who lie with men," "monsters in human shape," "catamites," "boy lovers," or as practitioners of "abomination," "unnatural filthiness," "foul sin," or "debauchery." By the early nineteenth century, "sodomy" and "pederasty" were joined by such terms as "degradation," "perversion," and "depravity," while popular slang added other terms of effeminization to the very early "queen" and "molly," among them "madge-cull," "marianne," "mollycoddle," and "hermaphrodite." Medical studies added "invert," and of course "homosexual" itself. Homosexual apologists, seeking less inflammatory or less clinical terms, invented "intersexual," "similisexual," "third sex," "androgyne," and "Uranian," derived by Karl Heinrich Ulrichs from Plato's *Symposium*.

### FOUNDING A LITERATURE

If homosexuality had found names in Victorian England, it had also begun to create an imaginative literature that defined a homosexual sensibility. Homosexual writers linked a version of nineteenth-century aestheticism to the specifically homosexual, transforming homosexuality into a special kind of aesthetic experience, and employed a homoeroticized aesthetic language to describe homosexual desire. They were aware that their lifestyle demanded secrecy and evasion; what they wrote was not only forbidden but quite possibly dangerous. Their works were passed from hand to hand among friends, or appeared in private or limited editions and in certain publications devoted to this special subject matter. These included the Oxford magazine *The Spirit Lamp*, which made a brief appearance edited by Alfred Douglas, the even more short-lived *The Chameleon*, and *The Artist and Journal of Home Culture*, in which between 1888 and 1894 the editor Charles Kains Jackson unobtrusively inserted, amidst the articles on modern art, poems and fiction dealing with homoerotic themes. To disguise the intent of a text, writers sometimes couched their works in evasive or coded language in order to allow the knowledgeable to participate in a special confraternity of knowing readers. Produced and disseminated under a cloud of prohibition, these English texts represent one of the most significant bodies of literature concerned with homosexuality published in any language up to that time.

Indeed homosexuality seems to have become for a time *the* subject that engrossed writers. A bibliography of texts dealing with homosexual subjects written by both homosexual and nonhomosexual authors in England and on the continent number not only the major writers of these countries but many of the major literary productions of the time. A list of writers both in England and in Europe who wrote on homosexual themes includes Byron, Goethe, Karl August von Platen, Aleksandr Pushkin, Théophile Gautier, Honoré de Balzac, Charles-Pierre Baudelaire, Arthur Rimbaud, Paul Verlaine, Joris-Karl Huysmans, Gerard Manley Hopkins, John Addington Symonds, Walter Pater, Algernon Swinburne, Edward Carpenter, Oscar Wilde, A. E. Housman, E. M. Forster, and Havelock Ellis, to name only the most well known. By 1895 in both England and Europe, homosexuality had not only found a name but had founded a literature. These texts signaled that the rakish and indiscriminate sodomite, concerned only with the gratification of desire and unaware that there might be social, aesthetic, or political implications or consequences bound up with this gratification, had disappeared. In his place there appeared a new man, willing despite prohibition to love men and often eager to identify himself as a member of a special group.

The impetus for much of this ferment began in the 1860s. The decade of the sixties has special resonance in a history of the growth of a homosexual discourse for it saw the publication in America of Whitman's homoerotic "Calamus" poems (1860 in America, 1868 in England). In 1866 appeared the earliest printed survival of *Don Leon* in a limited edition published by William Dugdale, a publisher of curiosa and erotica. In the 1860s a few writers began to produce texts with titles that hinted (at least to the initiate, through their use of classical allusion, foreign language title, or sensual phrase) at what they were about: In 1866 Swinburne published *Poems and Ballads* in which two of the poems, "Fragoletta" and "Hermaphroditus," dealt with implied homosexuality as did John Addington Symonds's "Eudiades" (1868) and Roden Noel's "Ganymede" (1868). Walter Pater's essay "Wincklemann" (1867) offered the proposition that the homosexual German aesthete's "affinity with Hellenism was not merely intellectual" but that the "subtler threads of temperament" interwoven in it were derived from "his romantic, fervid friendships with young men." This essay marks sexual difference as a component of an "aesthetic" sensibility. In 1865 John Addington Symonds discovered Whitman's poetry and was galvanized by his reading into a kind of intellectual and spiritual coming out. By the time a selection of Whitman's poems appeared in Dante Gabriel Rossetti's 1868 edition, to be read in 1869 by the homosexual apologist-to-be Edward Carpenter, several of the key events that can be described as substantially contributing to definitions of homosexual identity and to the formation of a definitive homosexual literature had occurred. It seems eminently appropriate, then, that Karoly Maria Benkert, the German homosexual apologist, should coin the word *homosexual* at the end of the decade in 1869.

The 1870s brought book titles like Edward Carpenter's *Narcissus and Other Poems* (1873) and Symonds's *Lyra Viginti Cordarum* (c. 1875), in which classical allusions to Hylas, Ganymede, and "Uranian Love" left small doubt as to what context the poet intended for the youth whose "naked form supine" Symonds described as "very white smooth and fine." Poems like Gerard Manley Hopkins's "The Buglers First Communion"(1879), which celebrated a "limber liquid youth" breathing "bloom of chastity in mansex fine" might alert certain readers to a subtext that the religious primary text might conceal from the less discerning. By the 1880s Edward Cracroft Lefroy's "Echoes from Theocritus" (1883) firmly exploited the homoerotic-classical connection, and Mark André Raffalovich expressed the anxious emotional crossroads at which guilt and a desire for free expression intersected when he anatomized homosexuality in "The World Well Lost XVIII" (1886) as "the passion purest of all out of Heaven,/The love in Hell least easily forgiven." But by the end of the decade and into the early years of the twentieth century, even despite the notoriety of the Wilde trial in 1895, numbers of books indicated that homosexuality had fully discovered a voice: Sir Richard Burton's "Terminal Essay" (1885), appended to his translation of the *Arabian Nights*, was a history of homosexuality and the first essay on the subject to be published in English. Oscar Wilde's story "The Portrait of Mr. W. H." (1889–1895), a speculation on the homoerotic relationship between Shakespeare and the Mr. W. H. of the sonnets, was the first story in English written and published in a venue for the general public that invoked romantic homoeroticism. Symonds's essays exploring homosexuality in ancient Greece and modern Europe—"A Problem in Greek Ethics" (1883) and "A Problem in Modern Ethics" (1891)—had both been circulated privately, but the latter was published in Havelock Ellis and Symonds's *Sexual Inversion* (1897). Edward Carpenter's essay "Homogenic Love," far from being hidden by private publication, was delivered as a public lecture in Manchester in 1894. So specific now was the voice of a homoerotic discourse that Theodore Wratislaw's poem "To a Sicilian Boy" (1893), in which he rejects the "dull ennui of a woman's kiss" for a moment in the arms of the boy, could now be published openly—albeit to considerable controversy. Controversial too was Lord Alfred Douglas's publication in the magazine *The Chameleon* (1894) of two poems. The first was "Two Loves," a personification of both heterosexual and homosexual love. It is in this poem that homosexual love famously responds: "I am the Love that dare not speak its name."

Homosexual writers in the nineteenth century turned standard genres like the short story and the novel to homoerotic purposes in stories like John Francis Bloxam's "The Priest and the Acolyte" (1894), which told of the doomed love between a priest and his altar boy, or in the pederastic atmosphere of Frederick Rolfe's "Stories Toto Told Me" (1896). In the novel, "school stories"—like Howard Sturgis's *Tim* (1891)—depicted homoerotic attachments in the all-male public schools while similar homoerotic relationships taking place in classical times were described in Pater's *Marius the Epicurean* (1885). Pornographic novels like *Teleny* (1890) and *The Sins of the Cities of the Plain* (1890s), both anonymously written, provided detailed pictures of homosexual life and sexual practice. Indeed *Teleny* was the first novel in English to concern itself "with homosexuality at its fullest extent" (Reade 1970:49). It was embellished by a full quotient of the same intense fantasy that marks much of the verse of the period while *Cities of the Plain* (here Sodom, one of the "cities of the plain" in the Bible) alleges to be a factual presentation of the world of the London male prostitute.

Oscar Wilde, whose life became a symbol of sodomitical vice, contributed to the formation of homosexual identities. In *The Picture of Dorian Gray* (1891) both Basil Hallward and Lord Henry are aesthetes whose exclusively all-male milieu and intense fascination with Dorian are described in a language that is redolent with all the nuances that aesthetic texts provided to hint at sexual difference. In 1895 Wilde's contest with the Marquis of Queensberry, father of Lord Alfred Douglas, ended in Wilde's conviction and imprisonment as a branded homosexual.

A. E. Housman's proper if suggestive *A Shropshire Lad* (1896) sharply contrasts with Aleister Crowley's *White Stains* (1898), in which one poem that concludes "Ah! you come—you kill me!/Christ! God! Bite! Bite! Ah Bite! Love's fountains fill me!" explosively and explicitly brings the century to a close.

## Further Reading

Louis Crompton, *Byron and Greek Love: Homophobia in Nineteenth-Century England* (Berkeley: University of California Press, 1985); Richard Dellamora, *Masculine Desire: The Sexual Politics of Victorian Aestheticism* (Chapel Hill: University of North Carolina Press, 1990); Byrne R. S. Fone, *A Road To Stonewall: Homosexuality and Homophobia in English and American Literature, 1750–1969* (New York: Macmillan/Twayne, 1995); Brian Reade, *Sexual Heretics: Male Homosexuality in English Literature from 1850 to 1900* (New York: Howard McCann, 1970); Timothy d'Arch Smith, *Love in Earnest: Some Notes on the Lives and Writings of English Uranian Poets from 1889 to 1930* (London: Routledge and Kegan Paul, 1970); Jeffrey Weeks, *Coming Out: Homosexual Politics in Britain from the Nineteenth Century to the Present* (London: Quartet Books, 1977).

## The Law (1861)

24 AND 25 VICTORIA, C. 100

*Sec. 61:* Whosoever shall be convicted of the abominable crime of buggery, committed either with mankind or with any animal, shall be liable, at the discretion of the Court, to be kept in penal servitude for life, or for any term not less than ten years.

*Sec. 62:* Whosoever shall attempt to commit the said abominable crime, or shall be guilty of any assault with intent to commit the same, or of any indecent assault upon any male person, shall be guilty of a misdemeanor, and being convicted thereof shall be liable, at the discretion of the Court, to be kept in penal servitude for any term not exceeding ten years and not less than three years, or to be imprisoned for any term not exceeding two years with or without hard labour.

## Alfred, Lord Tennyson (1809–1892)

Alfred Tennyson's memorial tribute to his friend Arthur Henry Hallam, *In Memoriam* (1850), is a text that provided relevant "undertones to the condition of certain readers"

(Reade 1970:10). By "condition," of course, is meant homosexuality, though there is no evidence that either Tennyson or Hallam were consciously aware of homosexual inclinations. However, Tennyson's poem effects the homoeroticizing of platonic friendship. In it Tennyson explores his feelings resulting from the death of Hallam and creates a relationship in which he describes himself as both bride and widower and hints at the eroticized nature of his affection. But he also places the site of their greatest bliss within the boundary of a Greek—indeed of an Arcadian—realm. There he recalls wandering with Hallam in a spiritual state in which "not a leaf was dumb;/But all the lavish hills would hum/The murmur of a happy Pan." There the two of them experienced a soul's communion: "And many an old philosophy/On Argive heights divinely sang,/And round us all the thicket rang/To many a flute of Arcady."

## FROM *IN MEMORIAM A. H. H.* (1850)

### I

I held it truth, with him who sings
   To one clear harp in divers tones,
   That men may rise on stepping-stones
Of their dead selves to higher things.

But who shall so forecast the years
   And find in loss a gain to match?
   Or reach a hand thro' time to catch
The far-off interest of tears?

Let Love clasp Grief lest both be drown'd,
   Let darkness keep her raven gloss:
   Ah, sweeter to be drunk with loss,
To dance with death, to beat the ground,

Than that the victor Hours should scorn
   The long result of love, and boast,
   "Behold the man that loved and lost,
But all he was is overworn."

### V

I sometimes hold it half a sin
   To put in words the grief I feel;
   For words, like Nature, half reveal
And half conceal the Soul within.

But, for the unquiet heart and brain,
   A use in measured language lies;
   The sad mechanic exercise,
Like dull narcotics, numbing pain.

In words, like weeds, I'll wrap me o'er,
    Like coarsest clothes against the cold:
    But that large grief which these enfold
Is given in outline and no more.

### IX

Fair ship, that from the Italian shore
    Sailest the placid ocean-plains
    With my lost Arthur's loved remains,
Spread thy full wings, and waft him o'er.

So draw him home to those that mourn
    In vain; a favourable speed
    Ruffle thy mirror'd mast, and lead
Thro' prosperous floods his holy urn.

All night no ruder air perplex
    Thy sliding keel, till Phosphor, bright
    As our pure love, thro' early light
Shall glimmer on the dewy decks.

Sphere all your lights around, above;
    Sleep, gentle heavens, before the prow;
    Sleep, gentle winds, as he sleeps now,
My friend, the brother of my love;

My Arthur, whom I shall not see
    Till all my widow'd race be run;
    Dear as the mother to the son,
More than my brothers are to me.

### XIII

Tears of the widower, when he sees
    A late-lost form that sleep reveals,
    And moves his doubtful arms, and feels
Her place is empty, fall like these;

Which weep a loss for ever new,
    A void where heart on heart reposed;
    And, where warm hands have prest and closed,
Silence, till I be silent too.

Which weep the comrade of my choice,
    An awful thought, a life removed,

The human-hearted man I loved,
A Spirit, not a breathing voice.


### XXII

The path by which we twain did go,
    Which led by tracts that pleased us well,
    Thro' four sweet years arose and fell,
From flower to flower, from snow to snow:

And we with singing cheer'd the way,
    And, crown'd with all the season lent,
    From April on to April went,
And glad at heart from May to May:

But where the path we walk'd began
    To slant the fifth autumnal slope,
    As we descended following Hope,
There sat the Shadow fear'd of man;

Who broke our fair companionship,
    And spread his mantle dark and cold,
    And wrapt thee formless in the fold,
And dull'd the murmur on thy lip,

And bore thee where I could not see
    Nor follow, tho' I walk in haste,
    And think, that somewhere in the waste
The Shadow sits and waits for me.


### XXIII

Now, sometimes in my sorrow shut,
    Or breaking into song by fits,
    Alone, alone, to where he sits,
The Shadow cloak'd from head to foot,

Who keeps the keys of all the creeds,
    I wander, often falling lame,
    And looking back to whence I came,
Or on to where the pathway leads:

And crying, How changed from where it ran
    Thro' lands where not a leaf was dumb;
    But all the lavish hills would hum
The murmur of a happy Pan:

When each by turns was guide to each,
    And Fancy light from Fancy caught,
    And Thought leapt out to wed with Thought
Ere Thought could wed itself with Speech;

And all we met was fair and good,
    And all was good that Time could bring,
    And all the secret of the Spring
Moved in the chambers of the blood;

And many an old philosophy
    On Argive heights divinely sang,
    And round us all the thicket rang
To many a flute of Arcady.


### XXV

I know that this was Life, the track
    Whereon with equal feet we fared;
    And then, as now, the day prepared
The daily burden for the back.

But this it was that made me move
    As light as carrier-birds in air;
    I loved the weight I had to bear,
Because it needed help of Love:

Nor could I weary, heart or limb,
    When mighty Love would cleave in twain
    The lading of a single pain,
And part it, giving half to him.


### XXVII

I envy not in any moods
    The captive void of noble rage,
    The linnet born within the cage,
That never knew the summer woods:

I envy not the beast that takes
    His license in the field of time,
    Unfetter'd by the sense of crime,
To whom a conscience never wakes:

Nor, what may count itself as blest,
    The heart that never plighted troth

But stagnates in the weeds of sloth;
Nor any want-begotten rest.

I hold it true, whate'er befall;
    I feel it, when I sorrow most;
      'Tis better to have loved and lost
Than never to have loved at all.


### XLI

Thy spirit ere our fatal loss
    Did ever rise from high to higher;
      As mounts the heavenward altar-fire,
As flies the lighter thro' the gross.

But thou art turn'd to something strange,
    And I have lost the links that bound
      Thy changes; here upon the ground,
No more partaker of thy change.

Deep folly! yet that this could be—
    That I could wing my will with might
      To leap the grades of life and light,
And flash at once, my friend, to thee.

For tho' my nature rarely yields
    To that vague fear implied in death;
      Nor shudders at the gulfs beneath,
The howlings from forgotten fields;

Yet oft when sundown skirts the moor
    An inner trouble I behold,
      A spectral doubt which makes me cold,
That I shall be thy mate no more.


### CXXVI

Love is and was my Lord and King,
    And in his presence I attend
      To hear the tidings of my friend,
Which every hour his couriers bring.

Love is and was my King and Lord,
    And will be, tho' as yet I keep
      Within his court on earth, and sleep
Encompass'd by his faithful guard,

And hear at times a sentinel
   Who moves about from place to place,
   And whispers to the worlds of space,
In the deep night, that all is well.

### CXXIX

Dear friend, far off, my lost desire,
   So far, so near in woe and weal;
   O loved the most, when most I feel
There is a lower and a higher;

Known and unknown; human, divine;
   Sweet human hand and lips and eye;
   Dear heavenly friend that canst not die,
Mine, mine, for ever, ever mine;

Strange friend, past, present, and to be;
   Loved deeplier, darklier understood;
   Behold, I dream a dream of good,
And mingle all the world with thee.

### CXXX

Thy voice is on the rolling air;
   I hear thee where the waters run;
   Thou standest in the rising sun,
And in the setting thou art fair.

What art thou then? I cannot guess;
   But tho' I seem in star and flower
   To feel thee some diffusive power,
I do not therefore love thee less:

My love involves the love before;
   My love is vaster passion now;
   Tho' mix'd with God and Nature thou,
I seem to love thee more and more.

Far off thou art, but ever nigh;
   I have thee still, and I rejoice;
   I prosper, circled with thy voice;
I shall not lose thee tho' I die.

## William Johnson Cory (1823–1892)

In 1858, William Johnson, later to take the name of William Cory after his dismissal from
his teaching post at Eton in 1872 because of the suspicion of too intimate relations with

his pupils, published a small book of poems classically titled *Ionica*. Interspersed among lyrics dealing with such conventional subjects as tributes to Queen Victoria and to Tennyson, and lyrics extolling poetry, childhood, bravery, and the beauty of young women, are poems that deal in one way or another with relationships between the speaker and persons whose names and gender is kept unclear, though the title of the book was enough to signal that the perceived link between classicism and homosexuality might be employed in the text.

## FROM *IONICA* (1858)

### Desiderato

Oh, lost and unforgotten friend,
    Whose presence change and chance deny;
    If angels turn your soft proud eye
To lines your cynic playmate penned,

Look on them, as you looked on me,
    When both were young; when, as we went
    Through crowds or forest ferns, you leant
On him who loved your staff to be;

And slouch your lazy length again
    On cushions fit for aching brow
    (Yours always ached, you know), and now
As dainty languishing as then,

Give them but one fastidious look,
    And if you see a trace of him
    Who humoured you in every whim,
Seek for his heart within his book:

For though there be enough to mark
    The man's divergence from the boy,
    Yet shines my faith without alloy
For him who led me through that park;

And though a stranger throw aside
    Such grains of common sentiment,
    Yet let your haughty head be bent
To take the jetsom of the tide;

Because this brackish turbid sea
    Throws toward thee things that pleased of yon
    And though it wash thy feet no more,
Its murmurs mean: "I yearn for thee."

*Deteriora*

One year I lived in high romance,
　　A soul ennobled by the grace
Of one whose very frowns enhance
　　The regal lustre of the face,
And in the magic of a smile
I dwelt as in Calypso's isle.

One year, a narrow line of blue,
　　With clouds both ways awhile held back:
And dull the vault that line goes through,
　　And frequent now the crossing rack;
And who shall pierce the upper sky,
And count the spheres? Not I, not I!

Sweet year, it was not hope you brought,
　　Nor after toil and storm repose,
But a fresh growth of tender thought,
　　And all of love my spirit knows.
You let my lifetime pause, and bade
The noontide dial cast no shade.

If fate and nature screen from me
　　The sovran front I bowed before,
And set the glorious creature free,
　　Whom I would clasp, detain, adore;
If I forego that strange delight,
Must all be lost? Not quite, not quite.

Die, little Love, without complaint,
　　Whom Honour standeth by to shrive:
Assoiled from all selfish taint,
　　Die, Love, whom Friendship will survive.
Nor heat nor folly gave thee birth;
And briefness does but raise thy worth.

Let the grey hermit Friendship hoard
　　Whatever sainted Love bequeathed,
And in some hidden scroll record
　　The vows in pious moments breathed.
Vex not the lost with idle-suit,
Oh lonely heart, be mute, be mute.

*Parting*

As when a traveller, forced to journey back,
　　Takes coin by coin, and gravely counts them o'er,

Grudging each payment, fearing lest he lack,
    Before he can regain the friendly shore;
So reckoned I your sojurn, day by day,
So grudged I every week that dropt away.

And as a prisoner, doomed and bound, upstarts
    From shattered dreams of wedlock and repose,
As sudden rumblings of the market-carts,
    Which bring to town the strawberry and the rose,
And wakes to meet sure death; so shuddered I,
To hear you meditate your gay Good-bye.

But why not gay? For, if there's aught you lose,
    It is but drawing off a wrinkled glove
To turn the keys of treasuries, free to choose
    Throughout the hundred-chambered house of love,
This pathos draws from you, though true and kind,
Only bland pity for the left-behind.

We part; you comfort one bereaved, unmanned;
    You calmly chide the silence and the grief;
You touch me once with light and courteous hand,
    And with a sense of something like relief
You turn away from what may seem to be
Too hard a trial of your charity.

So closes in the life of life; so ends
    The soaring of the spirit. What remains?
To take whate'er the Muse's mother lends,
    One sweet sad thought in many soft refrains
And half-reveal in Coan gauze of rhyme
A cherished image of your joyous prime.

## John Addington Symonds (1840–1893)

Symonds was one of the most eminent men of letters of his time, author of several volumes of poetry, criticism, and literary history. His attention to the question of homosexuality would be reflected in his essays "A Problem in Greek Ethics" and "A Problem in Modern Ethics," the first dealing with ancient Greek homosexuality, the latter homosexuality in his own time. His early poetry reflects Symonds's own uncomfortable situation in society as a homosexual before he experienced the revelation of Plato, Whitman, and of sex itself. But even those epiphanies did not entirely erase his sense of alienation as Symonds's own case history, anonymously presented in Ellis and Symonds's *Sexual Inversion*, so eloquently testifies: "He has suffered extremely throughout life owing to his sense of the difference between himself and normal human beings. No pleasure he has enjoyed . . . can equal a thousandth part of the pain caused by the internal consciousness of Pariahdom."

"What Cannot Be" (1861) describes how the speaker in a fit of self-incrimination and dissatisfaction with life "nursed rebellious scorn" and rebels against "high heaven," which stands for the sexual conventions of society, and against the "doom" he feels that is inevitable for himself as a homosexual in a homophobic world. A young man passes the speaker's house and with a glance seems to invite him to a life of erotic bliss, a life of love and "the brotherhood of strength" that seems to be "of all convention free." But the speaker is too fearful of the consequences of flouting convention and ends the poem alone, wracked by "sharp self-disdain" and fearful that the apples of love might hide "dust within." The text recognizes that the chance to achieve happiness in a homosexual relationship is blighted by the speaker's own doubts and fears, the self-disdain that is fed by his inability to ignore homophobic conventions.

"Eudiades," set in Greece, is an erotic tale in which an older man, Melanthias, falls in love with the young Eudiades. They become lovers and eventually die together. While the poem alleges a "pure"—that is sex-free—relationship in the best tradition of a reserved and chaste classicism, the subtext of the poem constantly hints at the consummation of a sexual union. The passionate language—that "strange sweet thirst" that they have "slaked at will"—leaves no doubt as to what he hopes might be imagined by a reader already devoted to Grecian fantasy. Perhaps only a few readers then would have found Eudiades' willingness to allow Melanthias to slake his "thirsty lips" at Eudiades' fountains a hint at fellatio. However, many knowing readers might recognize the "mark of shame" that Eudiades is willing to bear as a code, one that was coming to employ the word *shame* to indicate homosexual love. The Greece of Symonds's homoerotic imagination is not the cool habitation of nonsexual philosophy, but a site in which the hot flames of the sacrifice reflect the heat of homosexual passion itself.

In "Love and Death: A Symphony" Symonds envisions a world in which comrades are "strewn thick as flowers," echoing Whitman's own vision of cities of lovers and recalling earlier classical legends. Death is as potent an image for him as is love, and Symonds rather spectacularly employs the linguistic markers of homosexuality, especially the suggestion of a strange and forbidden world, in his "Midnight at Baiae" (1875), a fevered depiction of the discovery by the speaker of a dead young man who has apparently been killed in an orgy of sadomasochistic homosexuality. For additional discussion of Symonds, see sec. 15.

## "What Cannot Be" (1861)

1

Oh! what a pain is here! All through the night
I yearned for power, and nursed rebellious scorn,
Striving against high heaven in hot despite
Of feeble nerves and will by passion torn.
I dreamed; and on the curtain of the gloom
False memory drew an idyll of old hope,
Singing a lullaby to mock my doom
With love far off and joy beyond my scope.
I woke; the present seemed more sad than hell;
On daily tasks my sullen soul I cast;
But, as I worked, a deeper sorrow fell

Like thunder on my spirit, for he passed
Before the house with wondering wide blue eye
That said "I wait: why will you not reply?"


2

My heart was hot and answered "What might be!
Love, peace, content, the brotherhood of strength;
He offers it of all convention free:
Wilt thou not take and eat and rest at length?
His brow is framed of beauty, and his soul
Sits throned within his eyelids orbed in light;
And from his parted lips harmonious roll
Full floods of music, rivers of delight!"
Oh, heart! false heart! why tear'st thou me again?
"To touch, to handle, stretching forth thy palm;
To sleep forgetful of sharp self-disdain:
It were so easy, and so sweet the calm!"
Calm as the dead salt sea; easy as sin;
Sweet as love-apples hiding dust within.


## FROM "EUDIADES" (1868)

. . . In years of old
There lived the boy whom this tale is told,
Fair-haired Eudiades, upon the hill
Which bears the sacred name of Athens still.
Nurtured he was in all the ancient ways
Of nobleness which brought his fathers praise,
What time at Marathon they stained the sea
And broad corn-land with Persian butchery.
He from his couch at earliest break of day
Arising, prayer and orison would pay
To Phoebus and to Hermes, and with pure
Cold baths would brace his beauty to endure
Rough winds and scorching suns, and on his bloom
Flung the broad chlamys: then he left his room,
And with grave earnest eyes and glistening face
Joined his school-fellows in the open place.
. . . . . . . . . . . . . . . . . . . . . . . . . . . .


Then while yet the maiden morn
Shook dewdrops from her tresses, that bright band
Of playfellows, the fairest in the land,
Ran to the wrestling-ground; and off they threw
Their mantles, and their white flesh in the new

Light of the morning shone like ivory,
Which the skilled workman hath wrought daintily
With rosy hues or golden; and their hair
Floating upon their shoulders, like the rare
Curls of the crested hyacinth, made sport
For winds, that wandering through porch and court
Spread summer coolness.
   Now the games began:
Here through the long straight course their races ran
Phaedrus and Phaedon and Agathocles;
Here, rubbed with oil and sand, Eudiades
Wrestled with sturdy Pheidias. Long they strove
In the dry dust beneath the olive grove,
And from the farthest peristyles a throng
Of athletes, like young gods, stately and strong,
Gazed on the goodly pair matched equally
With even issue struggling, arm and knee
Close locked; until Eudiades, by sleight
Of cunning and quick nimbleness, like light
Flickering on vexed waves, while stout Pheidias bowed
His knitted thews in vain, thrice from the crowd
Won swift applause; then panting stood and took
The firm hand of his conquered friend, and shook
The fine dust from his limbs; and laughing they
Inarmed went slowly to the bath away.
Nor, though the eyes of many lovers burned
Upon them, from their forward course they turned:
But modestly, with calm clear brows, whereon
The light of innocence and honour shone,
Sunbright, they passed; then in the water wan
From their pure stainless forms the trace of toil
Purging, they rubbed their breasts with fragrant oil,
And on their forehead wreathed the flowering rush,
Sweet to the scent, whose faint fair petals blush
Like bloom of maidens.

. . . . . . . . . . . . . . . . . . . . . . . . . . . .

Leave we awhile of these fair friends to tell,
And turn to one on whom the miracle
Of boyhood in Eudiades had brought
The wonder of a swift change passion-wrought
From loveless life to love's uncertain good.
For while the striplings strove, Melanthias stood—
Himself of athletes mightiest—and saw,
With unaccustomed eyes and wildering awe,
The form of Beauty, visible and bright,

An effluence of ineffable sunlight,
In the boy's flawless lineaments. The sweat
Rose on his brow, his knees quaked, and his great
Man's bosom throbbed with heart-aches, and his eyes
Swam in a sudden painful sweet surprise.
Nor could he rest from thought; but in the boy
His soul lay sphered; nor was there any joy
Prized hitherto wherein he had delight.
But through the day he pined; and when the night
Came with her dew-drops and live stars and smell
Of strengthened flowers, on the thin grass he fell
Limb-length, where he had seen Eudiades
Lie at noontide beneath the sacred trees.
For there, so fancy feigned or dreamed the man,
Some trace still lingered on crushed herbs and wan
Leaves of pressed asphodel, of each dear limb
Which with its radiance had enraptured him.
The broken flowers he kissed, the grass, the boughs
Brushed by the passing boy, and on his brows,
Hot with quick thoughts, he bound those cool bruised leaves,
And in the twilight that the full moon weaves
Of olive branches, lay drinking the bowl
Of new-born longing, till his languid soul
Sank drowsed with sweetness, and beneath the tree
Endymion-like he slumbered tranquilly.

Fair and full-formed he was, like Hermes, in
The first free dawn of manhood; for his chin
Was woolly as the peach, and bright as bloom
Of hillset galingale, whose pure perfume
Scarce matched his breath. Above his level brow,
Wherein great deep blue eyes were set, the snow
Was overshadowed by crisp curls of brown,
Brightening to golden; and the wavy down
That on his smooth white thighs and perfect breast
Lay soft as sleep was coloured like the west
At sunset, when the silver star shines through
Pale amber spaces spread beneath the blue.
Sweet as spring flowers and blossoming with the fresh
Hues of young health unsullied was his flesh:
Wide shoulders, knitted arms, and narrow waist
Between the broad reins and the massive chest;
Firm feet, and ankles like the winged heels
Of Jove's own messenger, who lightly steals
From cloud to cloud, from mountain peak to peak

On the king's errand. Slow he was to speak,
Yet swift to do; nor of his words had lack
If aught of speech were needed, nor was slack
In jest or song, or when the cups were filled
For merry-making guests; but nothing skilled
In grave discourse or staid philosophy,
Of sage and priest he lived unheedingly.
Such was the youth, Melanthias, the first
Of Attic athletes, on whose soul had burst
The sunrise of Eudiades, the spring
Of sudden love's unlooked-for blossoming.
. . . . . . . . . . . . . . . . . . . . . . . . . . . . .

[Melanthias comes at night to serenade Eudiades. The next day Eudiades speaks with his friend Chariton about love and Chariton advises him to seek it. That night in his father's house a guest sings songs of Hylas and Hercules. Despite his father's warning not to be overcome by a foolish love, Eudiades is inflamed by the poet's songs. Melanthias comes again to sing to him. Eudiades is overwhelmed by the song. The next day he encounters Melanthias, and they make vows of love. Melanthias departs but promises to return that night. Eudiades is at once eager for and fearful of the coming tryst].

This passion was so new, so terrible;
He tried, but tried in vain the strife to quell
Of his o'erburdened bosom. The good thing
Which he had longed for with such sorrowing,
How all untried, immeasurable, full
It was of wild pain and joy wonderful!
Nor could he guess why love like flame could dart
Through the man's marble limbs, or why his heart
Throbbed with the ravening furnace-breath of fire,
His flesh quaked with the fierce tongues of desire.
It was enough for him, the boy, to dream
Of coming days, in fancy down the stream
Of life to glide or rest among its flowers
And rushes on the bank through slumbrous hours
With that unrealized and vague delight
He called his lover. Then the thought of night
Oppressed him, and he cried:
    "What shall be done?
I have heard strange tales told! 'Twere well to shun
The sweetness that brings shame!"
    And yet again
Thrilled in his soul that swift delicious pain
Of love's anticipation.
    Thus all day
He parleyed with his spirit, till the grey
Shadows of evening fell, and on his bed,

Tired out with tears and smiles, he laid his head,
And slumbered. It was scarce the noon of night
When to his window in the pale starlight
Melanthias came, and pushed aside the boughs
Of blossoming rose, and, careful not to rouse
The sleeping boy, doffed cloak and shoes, and hid
His light of limbs beneath the coverlid.
Then the boy stirring in his dream was ware
Of that loved presence, feeling round his bare
Smooth ivory breast the warm arms laid; yet he
Feigned in his guile and wise simplicity
To sleep, and watched with fear what should befall.
But nought befell; nor was he moved at all
Save with new longing, for the lover kissed
His forehead with pure lips and gently pressed
The little swelling softness of his breast.
Then turned Eudiades, and laughed, and cried:
"Didst think me sleeping?" and to the man's side
Nestled, and lay there dreaming, half awake,
While wakeful birds of June sweet sounds did make
Among the cypresses. But at daybreak
Uprose Melanthias, and the boy could see
His beauty naked in the mystery
Of morning; and thenceforth, I ween, no dread
Stayed in his soul where love was harboured:
But day by day living with him he learned
New sweetness, and the fire divine that burned
In the man's heart was mirrored in the boy's,
So that he thirsted for the self same joys,
And knew what passion was, nor could abide
To be one moment severed from the side
Of him in whom whatever maketh sweet
The life of man was centred and complete.
Yea, but the joy that grew between them wove
Their very bodies in a web of love,
So that they seemed to breathe one air and drew
The same delights dropping like honeydew
From all glad things—from scent of summer skies,
From sleep and toil and whispered melodies
Of music.

[Time passes and their love begins to change and Melanthias desires more. Eudiades
offers to make the supreme erotic sacrifice.]

It was in still September nights that this
Shadow of change o'erlaid their happiness:

For when Eudiades had learned to long,
When in his soul the fire of amorous song
Quivered with swift unrest, and love began
To mould the calm boy to a passionate man;
Then by his side, Melanthias, grown bold
Through weeks of joy, mourned that their love was cold,
Nursing the fever of a hidden want,
Till in his wish he waxed extravagant—
Why from the fruits should they their hands withold
Which strewed the paths of loving men with gold?
Nor spake thereof, but often sighed and turned
Wrestling with thoughts that in his bosom burned,
And from his side sometimes the sleeping boy was spurned.
But he, with young desire intoxicate,
Deeming no gift, no sacrifice, too great
For him he worshipped; yea, much pondering
To prove his service by some painful thing,
Offered the pleasure none may touch and live
Thenceforth unshamed:
            "Lo, lover, I will give,"
Said he, "joy is mine. Nay, take
And drink my soul! from my life's fountain slake
Thy thirsty lips! fear not to shed my blood;
For I will die to do thee any good,
Or in my body bear thy mark of shame
To all men visible, cherish the blame
That falls on me for blessings! Only say
That I have gladdened thee! this word will pay
For grief or anguish in all years to come."

So spake he; and the mighty man was dumb,
Marvelling at innocence wherein the fire
Flamed of immaculate white-winged desire,
Till love became a momentary bliss
Of tears and rapture and forgetfulness.
Then from the still depths of his soul there soared
A mist most wonderful, and spread, and poured
Her passion of pure raindrops through his eyes:
And, as before the painful sweet surprise
Of sudden beauty's vision had o'erborne
All thoughts within his soul, so now a scorn
Of baseness, god-begotten, bright with awe,
Subdued his spirit to the perfect law.
Once more he sank and trembled, and the sweat
Rose on his forehead—yea, once more his great
Man's bosom throbbed with heartaches. Then he stood

Self-conquered, slave thenceforth to only good,
In the wide eyes of young Eudiades
Threefold transfigured.
   Lo! if men like these
Peopled this world with selfless deeds and gave
Their longings for a sacrifice to save
Bright honour, we should little need to dream
Of fabled heaven, but earth herself would gleam
With all that souls of mortal man can guess
Of love divine and God's great blessedness.


## FROM "LOVE AND DEATH: A SYMPHONY" (C. 1871)

"To the prophet poet of Democracy, Religion, Love, this verse, a feeble
imitation of his song, is dedicated."

Thou dost establish — and our hearts receive —
New laws of Love to link and intertwine
Majestic peoples; Love to weld and weave
Comrade to comrade, man to bearded man,
Whereby indissoluble hosts shall cleave
Unto the primal truths republican.
. . . . . . . . . . . . . . . . . . . . . . . . . . . .

Friend, Brother, Comrade, Lover! last and best!
That from this dull diurnal strife dost raise
My panting soul to thy celestial rest!
How holy are the heavens when thou art near!
I soar, I float, I rock me on thy breast;
The music of thy melodies I hear;
I see thee aureoled with living light
Lean from the lustrous rondure of thy sphere,
Ethereal, disembodied; whom the blight
Of warping passion hath no power to tame;
Who fearest not with eye serenely bright
To gaze on death and sorrow and mortal shame —
For who art Thou to tremble or turn pale,
Whose life is Love eternally the same?

How shall I praise Thee? with what voice prevail
O'er legioned heretics, that, madly blind,
Imagining a vain thing, rise and rail
Against thy sanctity of godhood shrined
In beauty of white light they may not bear?
Lo! Thou, even Thou, in thine own time shalt bind
And break their kings and captains! from thin air

Forth flashing fiery-browed and unsubdued,
Thine athletes shall consume them unaware!
Yea, even now, like Northern streamers hued
With radiant roses of the ascendant morn,
I see thy fierce unfaltering multitude
Of lovers and of friends in tranquil scorn
Arise, o'erspread the dusky skies, and drown
In seas of flame the pallid stars forlorn.

There shall be comrades thick as flowers that crown
Valdarno's gardens in the morn of May;
On every upland and in every town
Their dauntless and imperturbable array,
Serried like links of living adamant
By the sole law of lover their wills obey,
Shall make the world one fellowship, and plant
New Paradise for nations yet to be.
O nobler peerage than that ancient vaunt
Of Arthur or of Roland! Chivalry
Long sought, last found! Knights of the Holy Ghost!
Phalanx Immortal! True Freemasonry,
Building your temples on no earthly coast,
But with star-fire on souls and hearts of man!
Stirred from their graves to greet your Sacred Host
The Theban lovers, rising very wan,
By death made holy, wave dim palms, and cry:
"Hail, Brothers! who achieve what we began!"

"MIDNIGHT AT BAIAE" (1875)

From "Three Visions of Imperial Rome" in *Lyra Viginti Chordarum* (c. 1875)

It is a night of summer: overhead
Pale stars are slumbering in a liquid sky;
And from the journeying moon blue splendours spread
O'er breathing earth and sea's serenity.
I hear a kissing ripple on some shore
Unseen, not far below me: thick and high
Shoot laurel boughs above: the marble floor,
Laid smooth and cool beneath, like frozen snow,
Gives back no sound; as from the gilded door
Furtive I steal, and with hushed footsteps slow
Glide through the palace between painted wall
And pillared aisle and flowering shrubs arow.
Where am I? Thwart my path dim glimmerings fall

From one tall narrow portal: onward still
It lures me breathless through a silent hall:
Still onward: sense and thought and shrinking will
Are drawn by irresistible control
Unto that core of light that sharp and chill
Shines like the loadstar of my shuddering soul.
Yet would I fain draw back: all is so dark,
So ominously tranquil; and the goal
To which I tend is but one tiny spark
Cleaving the dreamy twilight terrible.
What sound? Nay, quiver not! The watch dogs bark
Far off in farm-yards where men slumber well.
Here stillness broods; save when a cricket chirrs,
Or wheeling on slant wing the black bat shrill
Utters her thin sharp scream. No night wind stirs
The sleeping foliage of the stately bays.
Forward I venture. On warm silky furs
My feet fall muffled now; and now I raise
The latchet of the door that stands ajar.
I enter: with a fixed and frozen gaze
What is within I reckon: —near and far,
Things small and great, sights terrible and strange,
Alike in equal vision, on that bar
Of blackness standing, with firm eyes I range.
It is a narrow room: walls high and straight
Enclose it: here the lights that counterchange
Pale midnight shadows, scarce can penetrate
The fretwork of far rafters rough with gold.
The lamps are silver—Cupids love-elate
Upraising cressets: phallic horns that hold
Pure essences and oils. From gloom profound
Shine shapes of mural gods and heroes old,
Gleaming with hues auroral on the ground
Of ebon blackness: Hylas, Hyacinth,
And heaven-rapt Ganymede: —I know them. Crowned
With lilies dew-bedrenched upon a plinth
Of jasper stands Uranian Love, a god
Carved out of marble for some labyrinth
Of Academic grove where sages trod: —
Here, breathless, in his beauty-bloom, he smiled,
Making more grim the ghastly solitude.
Amid the chamber was a table piled
With fruits and flowers. Thereon there blazed a cup,
Sculptured of sardonyx, where Maenads wild
With wine and laughter, shrieking, seemed to sup

The blood of mangled Pentheus: it was full
Of dark Falernian; the draught bubbling up
From blackness into crimson, rich and cool,
Glowed in the bowl untasted. Wreathes of rose,
Such as the shepherd lads of Paestum pull,
Circled two smaller murrhine cups: but these
Were empty, and no hand the flowers had shed.
Then was I ware how neath the gleaming rows
Of cressets a fair ivory couch was spread:
Rich Tyrian silks and gauzes hyaline
Were bound with jewelled buckles to the bed:
Thereon I saw a naked form supine.
It was a youth from foot to forehead laid
In slumber. Very white and smooth and fine
Were all his limbs; and on his breast there played
The lambent smiles of lamplight. But a pool
Of blood beneath upon the pavement stayed.
There, where blue cups of lotos-lilies cool
With reeds into mosaic-wreathes were blent,
The black blood grew and curdled; and the wool
Whereon his cloudy curls were pillowed, sent
Thick drops slow-soaking down o'er gold and gem.
Yet was the raiment ruffled not nor rent.
Spell-bound I crept, and closer gazed at him:
And lo! from side to side his throat was gashed
With some keen blade; and every goodly limb,
With marks of crisped fingers marred and lashed,
Told the fierce strain of tyrannous lust that here
Life's crystal vase of youth divine had dashed.
It is enough. Those glazed eyes, wide and clear;
Those lips by frantic kisses bruised; that cheek
Whereon foul teeth-dints blackened; the tense fear
Of that white innocent forehead; —vain and weak
Are words, unutterably weak and vain,
To paint how madly eloquent, how meek,
Were those mute signs of dire soul-shattering pain!

## Gerard Manley Hopkins (1844–1889)

The primary athletic image that Victorian homoerotic poetry liked to employ was that of
the naked youth ready to plunge into the sea. Gerard Manley Hopkins wrote perhaps the
best example of the genre in "Epithalamion" (1888). In this poem, a "listless stranger"
comes upon a "bevy" of boys with "downdolphinry and bellbright bodies." He watches
them from a distance as they swim and then "he hies to a pool neighboring" and strips.
This pool is the "sweetest, freshest, shadowiest;/Fairyland." In short, it is Arcadia. The boys
swim in their pool and he in his, but the real though separate communion transforms him

and "we leave him, froliclavish, while he looks about him, laughs, swims," his listlessness gone forever. What the listlessness is Hopkins soon discloses, for this text is "sacred matter" and the twin pools symbolize "Wedlock" and the water and the swimming "Spousal love." The stranger has now been joined to the young men by this ritual act, a special kind of homoerotic baptism that has washed away listlessness, the fear of homosexual encounter.

## Epithalamion (1888)

Hark, hearer, hear what I do; lend a thought now, make believe
We are leafwhelmed somewhere with the hood
Of some branchy bunchy bushybowered wood,
Southern dene or Lancashire clough or Devon cleave,
That leans along the loins of hills, where a candycoloured,
    where a gluegold-brown
Marbled river, boisterously beautiful, between
Roots and rocks is danced and dandled, all in froth and
    water-blowballs, down.
We are there, when we hear a shout
That the hanging honeysuck, the dogeared hazels in the cover
Makes dither, makes hover
And the riot of a rout
Of, it must be, boys from the town
Bathing: it is summer's sovereign good.

By there comes a listless stranger: beckoned by the noise
He drops towards the river: unseen
Sees the bevy of them, how the boys
With dare and with downdolphinry and bellbright bodies
    huddling out,
Are earthworld, airworld, waterworld thorough hurled, all by
    turn and turn about.

This garland of their gambols flashes in his breast
Into such a sudden zest
Of summertime joys
That he hies to a pool neighbouring; sees it is the best
There; sweetest, freshest, shadowiest;
Fairyland; silk-beech, scrolled ash, packed sycamore, wild
    wychelm, hornbeam fretty overstood
By. Rafts and rafts of flake-leaves light, dealt so, painted on
    the air,
Hang as still as hawk or hawkmoth, as the stars or as the angels
    there,
Like the thing that never knew the earth, never off roots
Rose. Here he feasts: lovely all is! No more: offwith—down he
    dings

His bleached both and woolwoven wear:
Careless these in coloured wisp
All lie tumbled-to; then with loop-locks
Forward falling, forehead frowning, lips crisp
Over finger-teasing task, his twiny boots
Fast he opens, last he offwrings
Till walk the world he can with bare his feet
And come where lies a coffer, burly all of blocks
Built of chancequarried, selfquained rocks
And the water warbles over into, filleted with glassy grassy
    quicksilvery shives and shoots
And with heavenfallen freshness down from moorland still
    brims,
Dark or daylight on and on. Here he will then, here he will the
    fleet
Flinty kindcold element let break across his limbs
Long. Where we leave him, froliclavish, while he looks about him, laughs,
    swims.
Enough now; since the sacred matter that I mean
I should be wronging longer leaving it to float
Upon this only gambolling and echoing-of-earth note—
What is . . . the delightful dene?
Wedlock. What is water? Spousal love . . .
Father, mother, brothers sisters, friends
Into fairy trees, wild flowers, wood ferns
Ranked round the bower. . . .

## Edward Carpenter (1844–1929)

(For a discussion of Carpenter, see sec. 15.)

FROM *TOWARDS DEMOCRACY* (1881–1902)

*Through the Long Night*

You, proud curve-lipped youth, with brown sensitive face,
    Why, suddenly, as you sat there on the grass, did you
turn full upon me those twin black eyes of yours,
    With gaze so absorbing so intense, I a strong man
trembled and was faint?
    Why in a moment between me and you in the full
summer afternoon did Love sweep-leading after it in procession across the lawn and the flowers and under the waving
trees huge dusky shadows of Death and the other world?

    I know not.
    Solemn and dewy-passionate, yet burning clear and sted-
fast at the last,

Through the long night those eyes of yours, dear,
remain to me—
    And I remain gazing into them.


## To a Stranger

O faithful eyes, day after day as I see and know
    you—unswerving faithful and beautiful—going about
your ordinary work unnoticed,
    I have noticed—I do not forget you.
    I know the truth the tenderness the courage, I know
the longings hidden quiet there.
    Go right on. Have good faith yet—keep that your
unseen treasure untainted.
    Many shall bless you. To many yet, though no word
be spoken, your face shall shine as a lamp.
    It shall be remembered, and that which you have
desired—in silence—shall come abundantly to you.


## Summer Heat

Sun burning down on back and loins, penetrating the
    skin, bathing their flanks in sweat,
Where they lie naked on the warm ground, and the
    ferns arch over them,
Out in the woods, and the sweet scent of fir-needles
Blends with the fragrant nearness of their bodies;

In-armed together, murmuring, talking,
Drunk with wine of Eros' lips,
Hourlong, while the great wind rushes in the branches,
And the blue above lies deep beyond the fern-fronds
    and fir-tips;

Till, with the midday sun, fierce scorching, smiting,
Up from their woodland lair they leap, and smite,
And strike with wands, and wrestle, and bruise each other,
In savage play and amorous despite.


## Edward Cracroft Lefroy (1855–1891)

Deployment of the manly/unmanly dichotomy is subtly done in Edward Cracroft Lefroy's
"A Palaestral Study," which appears in *Echoes from Theocritus and Other Sonnets* (1885).
The title invokes a classical reference, but the poem is an erotic meditation on the desire
provoked by the intersection of the passive/effeminate with the active/masculine. Under

discussion is male beauty. The language oscillates between images of passive and active sexuality under the guise of a reference to wrestling wherein one set of "quivering limbs" are held by another set of "strong muscles." Here the image of homoerotic struggle is employed. The conclusion that "man's loveliest works are cut with pain" connects pain with homosexual love. Lefroy observes that great art effects us because we recognize the "strain" that is "intense." This intense strain is created at once by sexual intensity and sexual doubt and alarm since the wrestling match has provoked not only an aesthetic response but forbidden homosexual desire. Thus, without mentioning a sexual subject or dealing explicitly with homoeroticism, Lefroy nevertheless creates a powerfully homoerotic text.

## A Palaestral Study

The curves of beauty are not softly wrought;
These quivering limbs by strong muscles held
In attitudes of wonder, and compelled
Through shapes more sinuous than a sculptor's thought,
Tell of dull matter splendidly distraught,
Whisper of mutinies divinely quelled—
Weak indolence of flesh, that long rebelled,
The spirit's domination bravely taught.
And all man's loveliest works are cut with pain.
Beneath the perfect art we know the strain,
Intense, defined, how deep so'er it lies.
From each high master-piece our souls refrain,
Nor tired of gazing, but with stretched eyes
Made hot by radiant flames of sacrifice.

## An Idler Listening to Socrates Discussing Philosophy with His Boy-Friends

The old man babbles on! Ye gods, I swear
My soul is sick of these philosophers!
In truth I marvel that young blood should care
To hear such vapid stuff; yet no one stirs.

Who's for a breath of unpolluted air?
See yonder brown-eyed nursling of the Muse,—
I'll pluck his robe and ask him; if he choose,
We two can steal away and none be ware.

What joy to find a woodland rill and wade
Knee-deep through pebbly shallows; then to lie
With glistening limbs along the open glade
And let the soft-lipped sunbeams kiss them dry;
Or, wandering in the grove's remoter shade,
To sport and jest and talk—Philosophy?

## Marc André Raffalovich (1864–1934)

Never entirely comfortable with homosexuality yet unwilling to hide it, Mark André Raffalovich lived for a good part of his life in a relationship with the handsome John Gray, reputed to be the model for Wilde's Dorian Gray. The problem of being homosexual in a heterosexual world is the subject of two poems entitled "The World Well Lost IV and "The World Well Lost XVIII" (1886). There Raffalovich indicates the difficulty that attends upon daily confrontation with that homophobic society he so tellingly nominates as "They." His poems not only anatomize the price of difference in a world where sexual conformity is prized but also details a particular kind of homosexual identity as well, one in which the effete homosexual style is highly developed. The homosexual who appears here is the precise opposite of the Whitmanian comrade. He is a sexual and somewhat effeminate dandy who will dominate discourses that define homosexual identity well into the mid-twentieth century, finally giving way to (though not disappearing before) the onslaught of the macho-men of the American sixties. This fabulous creature, who drifts on the surface of a world of elegance, costly objects, and witty badinage, has invented himself. His manner—his "tuned" speech and "schooled" glance—is a defense against the social disapprobation that the forbiddingly capitalized "They" represent. But the text also highlights another price elicited by the collision of the aesthetic/erotic pose with homophobia: the need for a constant masquerade that conceals the real beneath an invented identity so that his life, like the gardenia that he wears in his buttonhole, is a careful contrivance supported against collapse by a hidden wire. The damaging effects of homophobia inflict the same wounding self-disdain that Symonds mentions, leading the speaker to doubt that there can ever be the possibility of "friendship, passion, love." But even though the text paints a grim picture of an outsider world encompassed with numerous signs of social difference that are all predicated upon sexual difference—"our" world as opposed to the one "They" inhabit—the title of the sonnet nevertheless suggests that the world of sexual conformity is one well worth losing.

FROM *In Fancy Dress* (1886)

*Rose Leaves When the Rose Is Dead*

Young but not youthful he thou lovest not
Will cease to love thee if thou love not soon:
But he would never weary of thy thought
Did thy hand yield to his this very noon.
His love is pure as thy own life is pure,
And passionate as thy dreams are passionate,
And there is none thou canst so much allure,
And none thou couldst so little satiate.
So much beloved, love who loves thee so,
Glad to be chosen to do love's commands,
Beloved be loving also, straightway go
With graceful footsteps and with gracious hands,
   And pale with pleasure or the sense of doom,
   Knock loudly once and enter thy friend's room.

*The World Well Lost IV*

Because our world has music, and we dance;
Because our world has colour, and They gaze;
Because our speech is tuned, and schooled our glance,
And we have roseleaf nights and roseleaf days,
And we have leisure, work to do, and rest;
Because They see us laughing when we meet,
And hear our words and voices, see us dressed
With skill, and pass us and our flowers smell sweet:
They think that we know friendship, passion, love!
Our peacock Pride! And Art our nightingale!
And Pleasure's hand upon our dogskin glove!
And if They see our faces burn or pale,
    It is the sunlight, think They, or the gas,
    —Our lives are wired like our gardenias.

*The World Well Lost XVIII*

You are to me the secret of my soul
And I to you what no man yet has been.
I, your Prometheus, fire from Heaven stole
And for my theft the world's revenge is keen.
What I have done for you no man has done;
I have nor begged nor bought a common bliss,
But what you are to me you were to none.
And I will suffer this, and more than this,
And much beyond that more, a martyrdom
Without the crown of a celestial birth,
Or any hope of any world to come
Exalting most what lowest was on Earth,
    The passion purest of all out of Heaven,
    The love in Hell least easily forgiven.

FROM *IT IS THYSELF* (1889)

*Sonnet CXX*

Put on that languor which the world frowns on,
That blamed misleading strangeness of attire,
And let them see that see us we have done
With their false worldliness and look up higher.
Because the world has treated us so ill
And brought suspicion near our happiness,
Let men that like to slander as they will;

It shall not be my fault if we love less.
Because we two who never did them harm,
And never dreamt of harm ourselves, find men
So eager to perplex us and alarm
And scare from us our dove-like thoughts, well then
  Since 'twixt the world and truth must be our choice,
  Let us seem vile, not be so, and rejoice.

## Lord Alfred Douglas (1870–1945)

Douglas, of course, was the lover of Oscar Wilde, for whom Wilde sacrificed everything and from whom Wilde received far less. When Alfred Douglas's poem "Two Loves" appeared in the little undergraduate magazine called *The Chameleon* in December 1894, the response from one of the guardians of respectable culture, Jerome K. Jerome, writing in his own newspaper *To-Day*, was immediate and damning: "The publication appears to be nothing more nor less than an advocacy for indulgence in the cravings of an unnatural disease. . . . It can serve no purpose but that of evil. It can please no man or woman with a single grain of self-respect left in their souls. Let us have liberty; but this is unbridled licence. Let all things grow in literature which spring from the seeds of human nature. This is garbage and offal" (quoted in Smith 1970:58). The poem would be read at Wilde's trial and would elicit from Wilde a passionate speech defending homosexual love (see Wilde below, in sec. 15). Douglas's famous phrase ("I am the Love that dare not speak its name") would enter history as *the* defining epithet of nineteenth-century homosexuality—despite the fact that homosexuality spoke its name more loudly and more often than it had at any time before.

*Two Loves (1894)*
I dreamed I stood upon a little hill,
And at my feet there lay a ground, that seemed
Like a waste garden, flowering at its will
With buds and blossoms. There were pools that dreamed
Black and unruffled; there were white lilies
A few, and crocuses, and violets
Purple or pale, snake-like fritillaries
Scarce seen for the rank grass, and through green nets
Blue eyes of shy pervenche winked in the sun.
And there were curious flowers, before unknown,
Flowers that were stained with moonlight, or with shades
Of Nature's wilful moods; and here a one
That had drunk in the transitory tone
Of one brief moment in a sunset; blades
Of grass that in an hundred springs had been
Slowly but exquisitely nurtured by the stars,
And watered with the scented dew long cupped
In lilies, that for rays of sun had seen
Only God's glory, for never a sunrise mars

The luminous air of Heaven. Beyond, abrupt,
A grey stone wall, o'ergrown with velvet moss
Uprose; and gazing I stood long, all mazed
To see a place so strange, so sweet, so fair.
And as I stood and marvelled, lo! across
The garden came a youth; one hand he raised
To shield him from the sun, his wind-tossed hair
Was twined with flowers, and in his hand he bore
A purple bunch of bursting grapes, his eyes
Were clear as crystal, naked all was he,
White as the snow on pathless mountains frore,
Red were his lips as red wine-spilth that dyes
A marble floor, his brow chalcedony.
And he came near me, with his lips uncurled
And kind, and caught my hand and kissed my mouth,
And gave me grapes to eat, and said, "Sweet friend,
Come I will show thee shadows of the world
And images of life. See from the South
Comes the pale pageant that hath never an end."
And lo! within the garden of my dream
I saw two walking on a shining plain
Of golden light. The one did joyous seem
And fair and blooming, and a sweet refrain
Came from his lips; he sang of pretty maids
And joyous love of comely girl and boy,
His eyes were bright, and 'mid the dancing blades
Of golden grass his feet did trip for joy;
And in his hand he held an ivory lute
With strings of gold that were as maidens' hair,
And sang with voice as tuneful as a flute,
And round his neck three chains of roses were.
But he that was his comrade walked aside;
He was full sad and sweet, and his large eyes
Were strange with wondrous brightness, staring wide
With gazing; and he sighed with many sighs
That moved me, and his cheeks were wan and white
Like pallid lilies, and his lips were red
Like poppies, and his hands he clenched tight,
And yet again unclenched, and his head
Was wreathed with moon-flowers pale as lips of death.
A purple robe he wore, o'erwrought in gold
With the device of a great snake, whose breath
Was fiery flame: which when I did behold
I fell a-weeping, and I cried, "Sweet youth,
Tell me why, sad and sighing, thou dost rove
These pleasant realms? I pray thee speak me sooth

What is thy name?" He said, "My name is Love."
Then straight the first did turn himself to me
And cried, "He lieth, for his name is Shame,
But I am Love, and I was wont to be
Alone in this fair garden, till he came
Unasked by night; I am true Love, I fill
The hearts of boy and girl with mutual flame."
Then sighing, said the other, "Have thy will,
I am the Love that dare not speak its name."

## George Ives (1867–1950)

The criminologist George Cecil Ives founded the first reform society in Britain dedicated to alleviating the persecution of homosexuals. Ives described his project as a mission "to set all loves free" (quoted in Weeks 1977:119). His greatest service to what he called the "war of Liberation" was his founding of the Order of Chaeronea sometime in the mid-1890s. Though he saw the project as a cause, he was very much aware that the social climate demanded secrecy in pursuit of the goals of the cause; thus the society was a secret one, with strict vows of confidentiality. Named after the Theban Sacred Band of lovers, the order described itself as "A Religion, A Theory of Life, An Ideal of Duty"; it sought to "demand justice for all manner of people who are wronged and oppressed by individuals or multitudes or laws" (quoted in Weeks, 123).

FROM *A BOOK OF CHAINS* (1897)

*With Whom, then, should I Sleep?*

With whom, then, should I sleep? perhaps with thee,
And gaze into those eyes, those deep sad eyes,
Feeling the drowsy touch of thy vast wings.

Thy brother Sleep I know, with him have lain
Many a night, forgetting all the day
And every pain in that sweet comradeship.

Ah, he is younger, gay, capricious oft,
Dwelling with some for hours, or else away,
As with my friend, for lonely days and nights.

But thou, angel of night, youth of the silent glance,
All sleep with thee, but yet how diversely,
And but the very few hail thee with gladness.

Say would there be a telling of our tryst,
A wild Greek meeting with my spirit free,
Or would it be but rest, a heavy sleeping?

I fancy I could echo sighs with thee,
Picturing all the sights that thou hast seen,
And flying in my thought where thou hast flown.

## Aleister Crowley (1875–1947)

Obsessed by the occult, Aleister Crowley consorted with demons as well as his own
guardian angel, who dictated books to him. Like William Blake, he believed that wisdom
is obtained by the exploration of excess and asserted that there is no law other than that of
desire. He experimented with mind-altering drugs, magic, and with bisexuality. His
poems in *White Stains* reflect his sexual experimentation, though his assertion that he
approved of Plato (who he says recommended sodomy to youths) may also suggest the real
direction of his own desires.

### FROM *WHITE STAINS* (1898)

*Dedicace*

You crown me king and queen. There is a name
    For whose soft sound I would abandon all
    This pomp. I liefer would have had you call
Some soft sweet title of beloved shame.
Gold coronets be seemly, but bright flame
    I choose for diadem; I would let fall
    All crowns, all kingdoms, for one rhythmical
Caress of thine, one kiss my soul to tame.

You crown me king and queen: I crown thee lover!
    I bid thee hasten, nay, I plead with thee,
    Come in the thick dear darkness to my bed.
Heed not my sighs, but eagerly uncover,
    As our mouths mingle, my sweet infamy,
    And rob thy lover of his maidenhead.

Lie close; no pity, but a little love.
    Kiss me but once and all my pain is paid.
Hurt me or soothe, stretch out one limb above
    Like a strong man who would constrain a maid.
Touch me; I shudder and my lips turn back
    Over my shoulder if so be that thus
My mouth may find thy mouth, if aught there lack
    To thy desire, till love is one with us.

God! I shall faint with pain, I hide my face
    For shame. I am disturbed, I cannot rise,
I breathe hard with thy breath; thy quick embrace

Crushes; thy teeth are agony—pain dies
In deadly passion. Ah! you come-you kill me!
Christ! God! Bite! Bite! Ah Bite! Love's fountains fill me.


*A Ballad of Passive Paederasty*

Of man's delight and man's desire
 In one thing is no weariness—
To feel the fury of the fire,
  And writhe within the close caress
  Of fierce embrace, and wanton kiss,
And final nuptial done aright,
  How sweet a passion, shame, is this,
A strong man's love is my delight!

Free women cast a lustful eye
 On my gigantic charms, and seek
By word and touch with me to lie,
  And vainly proffer cunt and cheek;
  Then, angry, they miscall me weak,
Till one, divining me aright,
  Points to her buttocks, whispers "Greek!"
A strong man's love is my delight!

Boys tempt my lips to wanton use,
 And show their tongues, and smile awry,
And wonder why I should refuse
  To feel their buttocks on the sly,
  And kiss their genitals, and cry:
"Ah! Ganymede, grant me one night!"
  This is the one sweet mystery:
A strong man's love is my delight!

To feel him clamber on me, laid
 Prone on the couch of lust and shame,
To feel him force me like a maid
  And his great sword within me flame,
  His breath as hot and quick as fame;
To kiss him and to clasp him tight;
  This is my joy without a name,
A strong man's love is my delight.

To feel again his love grow grand
 Touched by the languor of my kiss;
To suck the hot blood from my gland
  Mingled with fierce spunk that doth hiss,

And boils in sudden spurted bliss;
Ah! God! the long-drawn lusty fight!
    Grant me eternity of this!
A strong man's love is my delight!

    ENVOI
Husband, come early to my bed,
    And stay beyond the dawn of light
In mighty deeds of lustihead.
    A strong man's love is my delight!


*Go into the Highways and Hedges, And Compel Them to Come In*

Let my fond lips but drink thy golden wine,
    My bright-eyed Arab, only let me eat
    The rich brown globes of sacramental meat
Steaming and firm, hot from their home divine,
And let me linger with thy hands in mine,
    And lick the sweat from dainty dirty feet
    Fresh with the loose aroma of the street,
And then anon I'll glue my mouth to thine.

This is the height of joy, to lie and feel
    Thy spiced spittle trickle down my throat;
This is more pleasant than at dawn to steal
    Toward lawns and sunny brooklets, and to gloat
    Over earth's peace, and hear in ether float
Songs of soft spirits into rapture peal.


*Rondels*

1

Maid of dark eyes, that glow with shy sweet fire,
    Song lingers on thy beauty till it dies
In awe and longing on the smitten lyre:
    Maid of dark eyes.

Grant me thy love, earth's last surpassing prize,
    Me, cast upon the faggots of love's pyre
For love of the white bosom that underlies

The subtle passion of thy snowy attire,
    The shadowy secret of thine amorous thighs,
The inmost shrine of my supreme desire,
    Maid of dark eyes!

2

Boy of red lips, pale face, and golden hair,
    Of dreamy eyes of love, and finger-tips
Rosy with youth, too fervid and too fair,
    Boy of red lips.

How the fond ruby rapier glides and slips
    'Twixt the white hills thou spreadest for me there;
How my red mouth immortal honey sips

From thy ripe kisses, and sucks nectar rare
    When each the shrine of God Priapus clips
In hot mouth passionate more than man may bear,
    Boy of red lips!

# 15. Inventing Themselves

## Imagining "Homosexuals" in English Fiction and Theory (1890–1895)

### John Addington Symonds

Eminent Victorian as he was, John Addington Symonds, the primary English theorist of homosexuality in the nineteenth century, tried to reconcile, in both life and work, his desire for homosexual fulfillment with his position as a prolific and respected man of letters. Among the many topics he addressed, homosexuality was the one to which he devoted his most intense energies. Symonds was aware that the extent of homosexual literature was unknown to most readers. In discussions of the ancient Greek poets, Italian and English Renaissance literature, and certain writers in whom he detected an aura of his favorite subject (such as Cellini, Michelangelo, Sir Phillip Sidney, Walt Whitman), he contributed to the formation of a canonical view of the history of homoerotic literature.

Inspired by his reading of Whitman, Symonds printed "A Problem in Greek Ethics" in 1883 in ten privately circulated copies. This is Symonds's first sustained attempt to reclaim Greece as the lost fatherland of homosexuals and to chronicle Greek history as a chapter in homosexual history. In doing so he invented the concept of homosexual history itself. He cites the Greeks as an example for the modern age of a tolerant, unprejudiced society that valued rather than condemned homosexual desire and argues that the "genius" for their unparalleled achievement lay precisely in the passion that his own age abhorred.

The work Symonds began in "A Problem in Greek Ethics" he continued in "A Problem in Modern Ethics." Impelled to write by his serious reservations about nineteenth-century "scientific" investigations into the causes and nature of homosexuality, he began an inquiry into homosexuality in order to correct "vulgar errors," comment on what he felt were inaccurate or intolerant studies and, in the process, to disseminate his own theories. Symonds realized that the ideas of Karl Heinrich Ulrichs, whose "third-sex" theory of homosexuality and arguments for its decriminalization was available only in German, might be a potent weapon to level against intolerance.

"Modern Ethics" offers a historicized argument for decriminalization and for a change in social attitudes toward homosexuality. The text also attempts to rescue the study of homosexuality and homosexuals from the historians of sin and crime and from the investigators of pathology and disease—from the priests, the state, and the doctors—and to return it to those to whom Symonds argues it rightfully belongs, homosexuals themselves. To do this, he advances the project he first began in "Greek Ethics"—a study of history as homosexual history—with a call for a new kind of scholarship that will provide access to the "complete history of inverted sexuality." Symonds's project not only delineated the concept of homophobia (though he had no word for it); he urged the recognition of the contribution made by homosexuality to western European societies, making the significant assertion that these contributions derived from homosexuality itself. He sought to explain what he certainly saw as a homosexual identity uniquely possessed by an unjustly oppressed minority, and he founded that identity on a concept of sexual difference.

## From "A Problem in Modern Ethics" (1891)

### Introduction

There is a passion, or a perversion of appetite, which, like all human passions, has played a considerable part in the world's history for good or evil; but which has hardly yet received the philosophical attention and the scientific investigation it deserves. The reason of this may be that in all Christian societies the passion under consideration has been condemned to pariahdom; consequently, philosophy and science have not deigned to make it the subject of special enquiry. Only one great race in past ages, the Greek race, to whom we owe the inheritance of our ideas, succeeded in raising it to the level of chivalrous enthusiasm. Nevertheless, we find it present everywhere and in all periods of history. We cannot take up the religious books, the legal codes, the annals, the descriptions of the manners of any nation, whether large or small, powerful or feeble, civilised or savage, without meeting with this passion in one form or other. Sometimes it assumes the calm and digni-fied attitude of conscious merit, as in Sparta, Athens, Thebes. Sometimes it skulks in holes and corners, hiding an abashed head and shrinking from the light of day, as in the capitals of modern Europe. It confronts us on the steppes of Asia, where hordes of nomads drink the milk of mares; in the bivouac of Keltish warriors, lying wrapped in wolves' skins round their camp-fires; upon the sands of Arabia, where the Bedaween [Bedouin] raise desert dust in flying squadrons. We discern it among the palm-groves of the South Sea Islands, in the card-houses and temple-gardens of Japan, under Esquimaux [Eskimo] snow-huts, beneath the sultry vegetation of Peru, beside the streams of Shiraz and the waters of the Ganges, in the cold clear air of Scandinavian winters. It throbs in our huge cities. The pulse of it can be felt in London, Paris, Berlin, Vienna, no less than in Constantinople, Naples, Teheran, and Moscow. It finds a home in Alpine valleys, Albanian ravines, Californian canyons, and gorges of Caucasian mountains. It once sat, clothed in Imperial pur-ple, on the throne of the Roman Caesars, crowned with the tiara on the chair of St. Peter. It has flaunted, emblazoned with the heraldries of France and England, in coronation ceremonies at Rheims and Westminster. The royal palaces of Madrid and Aranjuez tell their tales of it. So do the ruined courtyards of Granada and the castle-keep of Avignon. It shone with clear radiance in the gymnasium of Hellas, and nerved the dying heroes of Greek freedom for their last forlorn hope upon the plains of Chaeronea. Endowed with inextinguishable life, in spite of all that has been done to suppress it, this passion survives at large in modern states and towns, penetrates society, makes itself felt in every quarter of the globe where men are brought into communion with men.

Yet no one dares to speak of it; or if they do, they bate their breath, and preface their remarks with maledictions.

Those who read these lines will hardly doubt what passion it is that I am hinting at . . . surely it deserves a name. Yet I can hardly find a name which will not seem to soil this paper. The accomplished languages of Europe in the nineteenth century supply no term for this persistent feature of human psychology, without importing some implication of disgust, disgrace, vituperation. Science, however, has recently—within the last twenty years in fact—invented a convenient phrase, which does not prejudice the matter under consideration. She speaks of the "inverted sexual instinct"; and with this neutral nomenclature the investigator has good reason to be satisfied.

Inverted sexuality, the sexual instinct diverted from its normal channel, directed (in the case of males) to males, forms the topic of the following discourse. The study will be confined to modern times, and to those nations which regard the phenomenon with religious detestation. This renders the enquiry peculiarly difficult, and exposes the enquirer, unless he be a professed expert in diseases of the mind and nervous centres, to almost certain misconstruction. Still, there is no valid reason why the task of statement and analysis should not be undertaken. Indeed, one might rather wonder why candid and curious observers of humanity have not attempted to fathom a problem which faces them at every turn in their historical researches and in daily life. Doubtless their neglect is due to natural or acquired repugnance, to feelings of disgust and hatred, derived from immemorial tradition, and destructive of the sympathies which animate a really zealous pioneer. Nevertheless, what is human is alien to no human being. What the law punishes, but what, in spite of law, persists and energises, ought to arrest attention. We are all of us responsible to some extent for the maintenance and enforcement of our laws. We are all of us, as evolutionary science surely teaches, interested in the facts of anthropology, however repellent some of these may be to our own feelings. We cannot evade the conditions of *atavism* and *heredity*. Every family runs the risk of producing a boy or a girl whose life will be embittered by inverted sexuality, but who in all other respects will be no worse or better than the normal members of the home. Surely, then, it is our duty and our interest to learn what we can about its nature, and to arrive through comprehension at some rational method of dealing with it.

## II

### Vulgar Errors

Gibbon's remarks upon the legislation of Constantine, Theodosius, and Justinian supply a fair example of the way in which men of learning and open mind have hitherto regarded what, after all, is a phenomenon worthy of cold and calm consideration. "I touch," he says, "with reluctance, and despatch with impatience, a more odious vice, of which modesty rejects the name, and nature abominates the idea." After briefly alluding to the morals of Etruria, Greece, and Rome, he proceeds to the enactments of Constantine: "Adultery was first declared to be a capital offence. . . . [T]he same penalties were inflicted on the passive and active guilt of paederasty; and all criminals, of free or servile condition, were either drowned, or beheaded, or cast alive into the avenging flames." Then, without further comment, he observes: "The adulterers were spared by the common sympathy of

mankind; but the lovers of their own sex were pursued by general and pious indignation. Justinian relaxed the punishment at least of female infidelity: the guilty
spouse was only condemned to solitude and penance, and at the end of two years
she might be recalled to the arms of a forgiving husband. But the same Emperor
declared himself the implacable enemy of unmanly lust, and the cruelty of his persecution can scarcely be excused by the purity of his motives. In defiance of every
principle of justice he stretched to past as well as future offences the operations of
his edicts, with the previous allowance of a short respite for confession and pardon.
A painful death was inflicted by the amputation of the sinful instrument, or the
insertion of sharp reeds into the pores and tubes of most exiquisite sensibility." One
consequence of such legislation may be easily foreseen. "A sentence of death and
infamy was often founded on the slight and suspicious evidence of a child or a servant: the guilt of the green faction, of the rich, and of the enemies of Theodora, was
presumed by the judges, and paederasty became the crime of those to whom no
crime could be imputed."

This state of things has prevailed wherever the edicts of Justinian have been
adopted into the laws of nations. The Cathari, the Paterini, the heretics of
Provence, the Templars, the Fraticelli, were all accused of unnatural crimes, tortured into confession, and put to death. Where nothing else could be adduced
against an unpopular sect, a political antagonist, a wealthy corporation, a rival in
literature, a powerful party-leader, unnatural crime was insinuated, and a cry of
"Down with the pests of society" prepared the populace for a crusade.

It is the common belief that all subjects of sexual inversion have originally loved
women, but that, through monstrous debauchery and superfluity of naughtiness,
tiring of normal pleasure, they have wilfully turned their appetites into other channels. This is true about a certain number. But . . . it does not meet by far the larger
proportion of cases, in whom such instincts are inborn, and a considerable percentage in whom they are also incontrovertible. Medical jurists and physicians
have recently agreed to accept this as a fact.

It is the common belief that a male who loves his own sex must be despicable,
degraded, depraved, vicious, and incapable of humane or generous sentiments. If
Greek history did not contradict this supposition, a little patient enquiry into contemporary manners would suffice to remove it. But people will not take this trouble about a matter, which, like Gibbon, they "touch with reluctance and despatch
with impatience." Those who are obliged to do so find to their surprise that "among
the men who are subject to this deplorable vice there are even quite intelligent, talented, and highly-placed persons, of excellent and even noble character."

The vulgar expect to discover the objects of their outraged animosity in the
scum of humanity. But these may be met with every day in drawing-rooms, law-
courts, banks, universities, mess-rooms; on the bench, the throne, the chair of the
professor; under the pelouse of the workman, the cassock of the priest, the
epaulettes of the officer, the smock-frock of the ploughman, the wig of the barrister, the mantle of the peer, the costume of the actor, the tights of the athlete, the
gown of the academician.

It is the common belief that one, and only one, unmentionable act is what the
lovers seek as the source of their unnatural gratification, and that this produces
spinal disease, epilepsy, consumption, dropsy, and the like. Nothing can be more

mistaken, as the scientifically reported cases of avowed and adult sinners amply demonstrate. Neither do they invariably or even usually prefer the *aversa Venus*; nor, when this happens, do they exhibit peculiar signs of suffering in health. Excess in any venereal pleasure will produce diseases of nervous exhaustion and imperfect nutrition. But the indulgence of inverted sexual instincts within due limits cannot be proved to be especially pernicious. Were it so, the Dorians and Athenians, including Sophocles, Pindar, Aeschines, Epaminondas, all the Spartan kings and generals, the Theban legion, Pheidias, Plato, would have been one nation of rickety, phthisical, dropsical paralytics. The grain of truth contained in this vulgar error is that, under the prevalent laws and hostilities of modern society, the inverted passion has to be indulged furtively, spasmodically, hysterically; that the repression of it through fear and shame frequently leads to habits of self-abuse; and that its unconquerable solicitations sometimes convert it from a healthy outlet of the sexual nature into a morbid monomania. . . .

It is the common belief that boys under age are specially liable to corruption. This error need not be confuted here. Anyone who chooses to read the cases recorded by Casper-Liman, Casper in his *Novellen*, Krafft-Ebing, and Ulrichs, or to follow the developments of the present treatise, or to watch the manners of London after dark, will be convicted of its absurdity. Young boys are less exposed to dangers from abnormal than young girls from normal voluptuaries.

It is the common belief that all subjects from inverted instinct carry their lusts written in their faces; that they are pale, languid, scented, effeminate, painted, timid, oblique in expression. This vulgar error rests upon imperfect observation. A certain class of such people are undoubtedly feminine. From their earliest youth they have shown marked inclination for the habits and the dress of women; and when they are adult, they do everything in their power to obliterate their manhood. It is equally true that such unsexed males possess a strong attraction for some abnormal individuals. But it is a gross mistake to suppose that all the tribe betray these attributes. The majority differ in no detail of their outward appearance, their physique, or their dress from normal men. They are athletic, masculine in habits, frank in manner, passing through society year after year without arousing a suspicion of their inner temperament. Were it not so, society would long ago have had its eyes opened to the amount of perverted sexuality it harbours.

The upshot of this discourse on vulgar errors is that popular opinion is made up of a number of contradictory misconceptions and confusions. Moreover, it has been taken for granted that "to investigate the depraved instincts of humanity is unprofitable and disgusting." Consequently the subject has been imperfectly studied; and individuals belonging to radically different species are confounded in one vague sentiment of reprobation. Assuming that they are all abominable, society is content to punish them indiscriminately. The depraved debauchee who abuses boys receives the same treatment as the young man who loves a comrade. The male prostitute who earns his money by extortion is scarcely more contemned than a man of birth and breeding who has been seen walking with soldiers.

[Near the end of the essay, Symonds summarizes the views of Karl Heinrich Ulrichs, whose essays on homosexuality provided the name "Urning" for those devoted to

"Uranian" love. Symonds couches his discussion as a debate between a homophobic "objector" and a defender of Uranian love who is as much Symonds as Ulrichs.]

"But, after all," continues the objector, "you cannot show that inverted sexuality is capable of any moral elevation." Without appealing to antiquity, the records of which confute this objection overwhelmingly, one might refer to the numerous passages in Ulrichs's writings where he relates the fidelity, loyalty, self-sacrifice, and romantic enthusiasm which frequently accompany such loves, and raises them above baseness. But, since . . . he may be considered a suspicious witness [because of his partisanship], it will suffice [to offer] . . . a brief passage from Krafft-Ebing. "The Urning loves, idolizes his friend, quite as much as the normal man loves and idolizes his girl. He is capable of making for him the greatest sacrifices. He suffers the pangs of unhappy, often unreturned, affection; feels jealousy, mourns under the fear of his friend's infidelity." . . . [A] kind of love, however spontaneous and powerful, which is scouted, despised, tabooed, banned, punished, relegated to holes and corners, cannot be expected to show its best side to the world. The sense of sin and crime and danger, the humiliation and repression and distress to which the unfortunate pariahs of inverted sexuality are daily and hourly exposed must inevitably deteriorate the nobler elements in their emotion. Give abnormal love the same chance as normal love, subject it to the wholesome control of public opinion. allow it to be self-respecting, draw it from dark slums into the light of day, strike off its chains and set it free—and I am confident, says Ulrichs, that it will exhibit analogous virtues, checkered, of course, by analogous vices, to those with which you are familiar in the mutual love of male and female. The slave has of necessity a slavish soul. The way to elevate is to emancipate him.

"All that may be true," replies the objector: "it is even possible that society will take the hard case of your Urnings into consideration, and listen to their bitter cry. But, in the meanwhile, supposing these inverted instincts to be inborn, supposing them to be irrepressible and inconvertible, supposing them to be less dirty and nasty than they are commonly considered, is it not the plain duty of the individual to suppress them, so long as the law of his country condemns them?" No, rejoins Ulrichs, a thousand times no! It is only the ignorant antipathy of the majority which renders such law as you speak of possible. Go to the best books of medical jurisprudence, go to the best authorities on psychical deviations from the normal type. You will find that these support me in my main contention. These, though hostile in their sentiments and chilled by natural repugnance, have a respect for science, and they agree with me in saying that the Urning came into this world an Urning, and must remain till the end of his life an Urning still. To deal with him according to your code is no less monstrous than if you were to punish the colour-blind, or the deaf and dumb, or albinoes, or crooked-back cripples. "Very well," answers the objector: "But I will quote the words of an eloquent living writer, and appeal to your generous instincts and your patriotism. Professor Dowden observes that 'self-surrender is at times sternly enjoined, and if the egoistic desires are brought into conflict with social duties, the individual life and joy within us, at whatever cost of personal suffering, must be sacrificed to the just claims of our fellows.' What have you to say to that?" In the first place, replies Ulrichs, I demur in this case to the

phrases *egoistic desires, social duties, just claims of our fellows*. I maintain that in trying to rehabilitate men of my own stamp and to justify their natural right to toleration I am not egoistic. It is begging the question to stigmatise their inborn desire as
selfish. The social duties of which you speak are not duties, but compliances to law
framed in blindness and prejudice. The claims of our fellows, to which you appeal,
are not just, but cruelly inequitous. My insurgence against all these things makes
me act indeed as an innovator; and I may be condemned, as a consequence of my
rashness, to persecution, exile, defamation, proscription. But let me remind you
that Christ was crucified, and that he is now regarded as a benefactor. "Stop,"
breaks in the objector: "We need not bring most sacred names into this discussion.
I admit that innovators have done the greatest service to society. But you have not
proved that you are working for the salvation of humanity at large. Would it not be
better to remain quiet, and to sacrifice your life and joy, the life and joy of an
avowed minority, for the sake of the immense majority who cannot tolerate you,
and who dread your innovation? The Catholic priesthood is vowed to celibacy; and
unquestionably there are some adult men in that order who have trampled out the
imperious appetite of the male for the female. What they do for the sake of their
vow will not you accomplish, when you have so much of good to gain, of evil to
escape?" What good, what evil? rejoins Ulrichs. You are again begging the question; and now you are making appeals to my selfishness, my personal desire for tranquillity, my wish to avoid persecution and shame. I have taken no vow of celibacy.
If I have taken any vow at all, it is to fight for the rights of an innocent, harmless,
downtrodden group of outraged personalities. The cross of a Crusade is sewn upon
the sleeve of my right arm. To expect from me and from my fellows the renounce-
ment voluntarily undertaken by a Catholic priest is an absurdity, when we join no
order, have no faith to uphold, no ecclesiastical system to support. We maintain
that we have the right to exist after the fashion in which nature made us. And if we
cannot alter your laws, we shall go on breaking them. You may condemn us to
infamy, exile, prison—as you formerly burned witches. You may degrade our emotional instincts and drive us into vice and misery. But you will not eradicate
inverted sexuality.

## Edward Carpenter (1844–1929)

The work of Edward Carpenter enlarged upon and advanced Symonds's project and
added to it by markedly insisting that homosexuals were involved, like women and the
working classes, in a struggle for individual rights. Carpenter argued that these rights
would be granted and acceptance achieved if society could be educated about homosexuality. In the process he codified and even invented some of the valorizing myths that
define homosexual identities in the twentieth century.

In his autobiography *My Days and Dreams*, Carpenter suggests that it was after his discovery of Whitman (with whom, like Symonds, he corresponded, and about whom, like
Symonds, he was to write a book) that he began in earnest to address as a public problem
the homosexuality with which he had been so long personally familiar. It was from this
moment that his awareness of even wider social issues—the political and sexual rights of
women, and the political influence of socialism—also dated. He began to express some of
his views in a long prose poem modeled on Whitman called *Towards Democracy*, the first

version of which appeared in 1883, and which he would eventually publish in four parts over the next few years. *Towards Democracy* is an extended versification of Carpenter's advanced views on the need for working-class egalitarianism, the sexual and political rights of women, and the special place of homosexuals in society. But it was soon clear that poetry was not enough, and that a powerful polemic was needed to address all of these topics and especially the one that was closest to him, what he perceived as the oppressed condition of homosexuals and the oppressive attitudes toward sexual love. For him the relations between society and those whom he called the "intermediate sex" had become a subject that "is pressing upon us from all sides."

To this end in 1895 he published an essay in pamphlet form that he called "Homogenic Love." Carpenter expanded much of what Symonds proposed and over the next ten years continued to write, collecting his essays in a single volume, *The Intermediate Sex*, published in 1908. The Wilde trial in 1895 nearly overwhelmed Carpenter's objective advocacy of homosexual rights beneath the hysterical outcry of the press and public for the blood of Wilde and for the virtual extirpation of homosexuals. But Carpenter was not deterred, though he too was attacked in the press, and he continued his work by publishing *Iolaus: An Anthology of Friendship*, the first anthology in English devoted to collecting homosexual texts that Carpenter deemed representative and positive approaches to homosexual love in literature across time. This anthology did much to contribute to a construction of homosexuality as transhistorical and essential, a message that had also been an occasional subtext of Symonds's historical studies. Carpenter continued to write about homosexuality well into the early years of the twentieth century, producing *Intermediate Types Among Primitive Folk* (1914), several essays on Whitman, including *Days with Walt Whitman* (1906), and "Some Friends of Walt Whitman: A Study in Sex Psychology" in 1924.

## From "Homogenic Love" (1894)

[*Carpenter's note*: "Homosexual," generally used in scientific works, is of course a bastard word. "Homegenic" has been suggested, as being from two roots, both Greek i.e., *homos* "same, " and *genos* "sex."]

Of all the many forms that Love delights to take, perhaps none is more interesting (for the very reason that it has been so inadequately considered) than that special attachment which is sometimes denoted by the word Comradeship. In general we may say that the passion of love provides us with at once the deepest problems and the highest manifestations of life, and that to its different workings can be traced the farthest-reaching threads of human endeavor. In one guise, as the mere semi-conscious Sex-love, which runs through creation and is common to man and the lowest animals and plants, it affords a kind of organic basis for the unity of all creatures; in another, as for instance the love of the Mother for her offspring (also to be termed a passion) it seems to pledge itself to the care and guardianship of the growing race; then again in the Marriage of man and woman it becomes a thing of mystic and eternal import, and one of the corner-stones of human society; while in the form of the Comrade-love with which this paper is concerned, it has uses and functions which we trust will clearly appear as we proceed.

To some perhaps it may appear a little strained to place this last mentioned form of attachment on a level of importance with the others, and such persons may be inclined to deny to the homogenic or homosexual love (as it has been called) that intense, that penetrating, and at times overmastering character which would entitle it to rank as a great human passion. But in truth this view, when entertained, arises from a want of acquaintance with the actual facts; and it may not be amiss here, in the briefest possible way, to indicate what the world's History, Literature and Art has to say to us on the whole subject, before we go on to any further considerations of our own. Certainly, if the confronting of danger and the endurance of pain and distress for the sake of the loved one, if sacrifice, unswerving devotion and life-long union, constitute proofs of the reality and intensity (and let us say healthiness) of an affection, then these proofs have been given in numberless cases of such attachment, not only as existing between men, but as between women, since the world began. The records of chivalric love, the feats of enamored knights for their ladies' sakes, the stories of Hero and Leander, etc., are easily paralleled, if not surpassed, by the stories of the Greek comrades-in-arms. . . .

In the first place we may say that to all love and indeed to all human feeling there must necessarily be a physical side. The most delicate emotion which plays through the mind has, we cannot but perceive, its corresponding subtle change in the body, and the great passions are accompanied by wide-reaching disturbances and transformations of corporeal tissue and fluid. . . .

But if this is true of love in general it must be true of the Homogenic Love; and we must not be surprised to find that in all times this attachment has had some degree of physical expression. The question however as to what degree of physical intimacy may be termed in such a case fitting and natural—though a question which is sure to arise—is one not easy to answer: more especially as in the common mind any intimacy of a bodily nature between two persons of the same sex is so often (in the case of males) set down as a sexual act of the crudest and grossest kind. Indeed the difficulty here is that the majority of people, being incapable perhaps of understanding the inner feelings of the homogenic attachment, find it hard to imagine that the intimacy has any other object than the particular form of sensuality . . . (i.e. the Venus aversa, which appears, be it said, to be rare in all the northern countries), or that people can be held together by any tie except the most sheerly material one—a view which of course turns the whole subject upside down, and gives rise to violent and no doubt very natural disapprobation; and to endless recriminations and confusion. . . .

While it is not my object in this paper to condemn special acts or familiarities between lovers (since these things must no doubt be largely left to individual judgement, aided by whatever light Science or Physiology may in the future be able to throw upon the subject)—still I am anxious that it should be clearly understood that the glow of a really human and natural love between two persons of the same sex may be, and often is, felt without implying (as is so often assumed) mere depravity of character or conduct . . . [and] it would be monstrous to suppose that these men, and others, because they were capable of this kind of feeling and willing to confess its sensuous side, were therefore particularly licentious. . . .

That passionate attachment between two persons of the same sex is . . . a phenomenon widespread through the human race, and enduring in history, has been always more or less recognized; and once at least in history—in the Greek age—

the passion rose into distinct consciousness, and justified, or even it might be said glorified, itself; but in later times — especially perhaps during the last century or two of European life — it has generally been treated by the accredited thinkers and writers as a thing to be passed over in silence, as associated with mere grossness and mental aberration, or as unworthy of serious attention.

In latest times however — that is, during the last thirty years or so — a group of scientific and capable men in Germany, France, and Italy . . . have made a special and more or less impartial study of this subject: with the result that a quite altered complexion has been given to it; it being indeed especially noticeable that the change of view among the scientists has gone on step by step with the accumulation of reliable information. . . .

It is not possible here to go into anything like a detailed account of the works of these various authors, their theories, and the immense number of interesting cases and observations which they have contributed; but some of the general conclusions which flow from their researches may be pointed out. In the first place their labours have established the fact, known hitherto only to individuals, that sexual inversion — that is, the leaning of sexual desire to one of the same sex — is in a vast number of cases quite instinctive and congenital, mentally and physically, and therefore twined in the very roots of individual life and practically ineradicable. To Men or Women thus affected with an innate homosexual bias, Ulrichs gave the name of Urning, since pretty widely accepted by scientists. Too much emphasis cannot be laid on the distinction between these born lovers of their own sex, and that class of persons, with whom they are so often confused, who out of mere carnal curiosity or extravagance of desire, or from the dearth of opportunities for a more normal satisfaction (as in schools, barracks, etc.) adopt some homosexual practices. In the case of these latter the attraction towards their own sex is merely superficial and temptational, so to speak, and is generally felt by those concerned to be in some degree morbid. In the case of the former it is, as said, so deeply rooted and twined with the mental and emotional life that the person concerned has difficulty in imagining himself affected otherwise than he is; and to him at least the homogenic love appears healthy and natural, and indeed necessary to the concretion of his individuality.

In the second place it has become clear that the number of individuals affected with "sexual inversion" in some degree or other is very great — much greater than is generally supposed to be the case. It is however very difficult or perhaps impossible to arrive at satisfactory figures on the subject, for the simple reasons that the proportions vary so greatly among different peoples and even in different sections of society and in different localities, and because of course there are all possible grades of sexual inversion to deal with, from that in which the instinct is quite exclusively directed towards the same sex, to the other extreme in which it is normally towards the opposite sex but capable occasionally and under exceptional attractions, of inversion towards its own — this last condition being probably among some peoples very widespread, if not universal.

In the third place, by the tabulation and comparison of a great number of cases and "confessions," it has become pretty well established that the individuals affected with inversion in marked degree do not after all differ from the rest of mankind, or womankind, in any other physical or mental particular which can be distinctly indicated. No congenital association with any particular physical conformation or malformation has yet been discovered; nor with any distinct disease of body or mind. Nor does it appear that persons of this class are usually of a gross or specially low type, but if anything rather the opposite—being often of refined sensitive nature. . . .

We have now I think said enough to show . . . that the homogenic passion is capable of splendid developments; and that a love and capacity of love of so intimate, penetrating and inspiring a kind—and which has played so important a part in the life-histories of some of the greatest races and individuals—is well worthy of respectful and thoughtful consideration. And I think it has become obvious that to cast a slur upon this kind of love because it may in cases lead to aberrations and extravagances would be a most irrational thing to do—since exactly the same charges, of possible aberration and extravagance, might be brought, and the same conclusion enforced, against the ordinary sex-love. . . .

And in truth it seems the most natural thing in the world that just as the ordinary sex-love has a special function in the propagation of the race, so the other love should have its special function in social and heroic work, and in the generation— not of bodily children—but of those children of the mind, the philosophical conceptions and ideals which transform our lives and those of society. . . . But as all love is also essentially creative, we naturally look for the creative activities of different kinds of love in different directions—and seem to find them so.

If there is any truth—even only a grain or two—in these speculations, it is easy to see that the love with which we are specially dealing is a very important factor in society, and that its neglect, or its repression, or its vulgar misapprehension, may be matters of considerable danger or damage to the common-weal. It is easy to see that while on the one hand the ordinary marriage is of indispensable importance to the State as providing the workshop as it were for the breeding and rearing of children, another form of union is almost equally indispensable to supply the basis for social activities of other kinds. Every one is conscious that without a close affectional tie of some kind his life is not complete, his powers are crippled, and his energies are inadequately spent. . . . If—to refer once more to classic story—the love of Harmodius had been for a wife and children at home, he would probably not have cared, and it would hardly have been his business, to slay the tyrant. And unless on the other hand each of the friends had had the love of his comrade to support him, the two could hardly have nerved themselves to this audacious and ever-memorable exploit. So it is difficult to believe that anything except that kind of comrade-union which satisfies and invigorates the two lovers and yet leaves them free from the responsibilities and impedimenta of family life can supply the force and liberate the energies required for social and mental activities of the most necessary kind.

For if the slaughter of tyrants is not the chief social duty nowadays, we have with us hydra-headed monsters at least as numerous as the tyrants of old, and more difficult to deal with, and requiring no little courage to encounter. And beyond the extirpation of evils we have solid work waiting to be done in the patient and life-long building up of new forms of society, new orders of thought, and new institutions of human solidarity—all of which in their genesis will meet with opposition, ridicule, hatred, and even violence. Such campaigns as these—though different in kind from those of the Dorian mountaineers described above—will call for equal hardihood and courage and will stand in need of a comradeship as true and valiant. It may indeed be doubted whether the higher heroic and spiritual life of a nation is ever quite possible without the sanction of this attachment in its institutions; and it is not unlikely that the markedly materialistic and commercial character of the last age of European civilized life is largely to be connected with the fact that the only form of love and love-union that it has recognized has been one founded on the quite necessary but comparatively materialistic basis of matrimonial sex-intercourse and child-breeding. . . .

To those who have dived at all below the surface in this direction it will be familiar enough that the homogenic passion ramifies widely through all modern society, and that among the masses of the people as among the classes, below the stolid surface and reserve of British manners, letters pass and enduring attachments are formed, differing in no very obvious respect from those correspondences which persons of opposite sexes knit with each other under similar circumstances; but that hitherto while this passion has occasionally come into public notice through the police reports, etc., in its grosser and cruder forms, its more sane and spiritual manifestations—though really a moving force in the body politic—have remained unrecognized.

It is hardly needful in these days when social questions loom so large upon us to emphasize the importance of a bond which by the most passionate and lasting compulsion may draw members of the different classes together, and (as it often seems to do) none the less strongly because they are members of different classes. A moment's consideration must convince us that such a comradeship may, as Whitman says, have "deepest relations to general politics." It is noticeable, too, in this deepest relation to politics, that the movement among women towards their own liberation and emancipation which is taking place all over the civilized world has been accompanied by a marked development of the homogenic passion among the female sex. It may be said that a certain strain in the relations between the opposite sexes which has come about owing to a growing consciousness among women that they have been oppressed and unfairly treated by men, and a growing unwillingness to ally themselves unequally in marriage—that this strain has caused the womankind to draw more closely together and to cement alliances of their own. But whatever the cause may be it is pretty certain that such comrade-alliances—and of a quite passionate kind—are becoming increasingly common, and especially perhaps among the more cultured classes of women, who are working out the great cause of their sex's liberation; nor is it difficult to see the importance of such alliances in such a campaign. In the United States where the battle of women's independence has been fought more vehemently perhaps than here, the tendency mentioned is even more strongly marked.

In conclusion there are a few words to be said about the legal aspect of this important question. It has to be remarked that the present state of the Law—arising as it does partly out of some of the misapprehensions above alluded to, and partly out of the sheer unwillingness of legislators to discuss the question—is really quite impracticable and unjustifiable, and will no doubt have to be altered.

The Law, of course, can only deal, and can only be expected to deal, with the outward and visible. It cannot control feeling; but it tries—in those cases where it is concerned—to control the expression of feeling. It has been insisted on in this essay that the Homogenic Love is a valuable social force, and, in cases, an indispensable factor of the noblest human character; also that it has a necessary root in the physical and sexual organism. This last is the point where the Law steps in. "We know nothing"—it says—"of what may be valuable social forces or factors of character, or of what may be the relation of physical things to things spiritual; but when you speak of a sexual element being present in this kind of love, we can quite understand that; and that is just what we mean to suppress. That sexual element is nothing but gross indecency, any form of which by our Act of 1885 we make criminal."

Whatever substantial ground the Law may have had for previous statutes on this subject—dealing with a specific act (sodomy)—it has surely quite lost it in passing so wide-sweeping a condemnation on all relations between male persons. It has undertaken a censorship over private morals (entirely apart from social results) which is beyond its province, and which—even if it were its province—it could not possibly fulfil; it has opened wider than ever before the door to a real social evil and crime—that of blackmailing; and it has thrown a shadow over even the simplest and most natural expressions of an attachment which may, as we have seen, be of the greatest value in national life.

That the homosexual passion may be improperly indulged in, that it may lead, like the heterosexual, to public abuses of liberty and decency we of course do not deny; but as, in the case of persons of opposite sex, the law limits itself on the whole to the maintenance of public order, the protection of the weak from violence and insult and, of the young from their inexperience: so it should be here. Whatever teaching may be thought desirable on the general principles of morality concerned must be given—as it can only be given—by the spread of proper education and ideas, and not by the clumsy bludgeon of the statute-book.

We have shown the special functions and really indispensable import of the homogenic or comrade love, in some form, in national life, and it is high time now that the modern states should recognize this in their institutions—instead of (as is also done in schools and places of education) by repression and disallowance perverting the passion into its least satisfactory channels. If the dedication of lover were a matter of mere choice or whim, it still would not be the business of the State to compel that choice; but since no amount of compulsion can ever change the homogenic instinct in a person, where it is innate, the State in trying to effect such a change is only kicking vainly against the pricks of its own advantage—and trying, in view perhaps of the conduct of a licentious few, to cripple and damage a respectable and valuable class of its own citizens.

## Teleny (1893)

### Attributed to Oscar Wilde and Others

Perhaps the most remarkable work of English homoerotic fiction of the nineteenth century, and a work that illuminates other homoerotic texts that were less explicit, is *Teleny;*

*Or, The Reverse of the Medal,* published anonymously in 1893 and attributed to Oscar Wilde. The authorship of *Teleny* has never been decided, though some profess to find stylistic similarities between it and Wilde's work. It is the story of a young Frenchman who, upon falling in love with the handsome pianist Teleny, finds himself caught up in the homosexual subculture of Paris. Camille des Grieux—whose name of course recalls not only the exotic Bohemian world but its most scandalous text, *Camille,* and is also a happy (even camp) elision of the masculine Des Grieux with the Lady of the Camellias herself—is a privileged member of the educated and moneyed class, but a sexual innocent; though aware of being attracted to men, he has not dared to act upon his desires. In Teleny's arms he discovers not only personal freedom but recognizes the falsehood of the proscription of homosexual love as a crime against nature: "I yielded to my destiny, and encompassed my joy."

*Teleny* is full of imaginative and often eloquent depictions of all sorts of sexual connections. But it is more than that. It is also a serious representation of the destructive, indeed mortal, effect of homophobia on a positively presented relationship between two men. The text affirms the newly developing sense of homosexual identity and the value of that identity. It sites this affirmation within the traditional environment of homosexuality presented as a sexual perversion only. *Teleny* juxtaposes a sexual text that reflects traditional expectations concerning the sexual perversion and promiscuity of sodomites against a tale of fidelity and high romantic love between two men. By valorizing the sex itself as a function of high romance and fidelity instead of a sign of depravity, the text strikes powerfully against the received opinion that homosexuals were monsters of perversion whose sole passion was lust and who were dead to "higher"—and presumably heterosexual—emotions and loyalties. What *Teleny* achieves is to offer not only a full-scale, sentimental, and triumphantly homosexual love affair but to employ the prime convention of the sentimental heterosexual love plot—salvation by love—as the central metaphor of the text. In the following selection from *Teleny* the narrator, Des Grieux, tells the story of his doomed love affair with Teleny to an unnamed listener, who occasionally interrupts to make a comment or ask a question.

## FROM *TELENY* (1893)

[After hearing Teleny play at a concert and being struck by the sexual energy of the event, Des Grieux meets Teleny after the concert and they are instantly attracted. Des Grieux is obsessed by Teleny. Meeting again, Des Grieux finds Teleny "in the clutches" of the foppish Briancourt. He follows Teleny and Briancourt into the erotically charged streets of Paris.]

"As soon as Teleny saw me, he at once broke loose from Briancourt's clutches, and came up to me. Jealousy maddened me. I gave him the stiffest and most distant of bows and passed on, utterly disregarding his out-stretched hands.

"I heard a slight murmur amongst the bystanders, and as I walked away I saw with the corner of my eye his hurt look, his blushes that came and went, and his expression of wounded pride. Though hot-tempered, he bowed resignedly, as if to say: 'Be it as you will,' and he went back to Briancourt, whose face was beaming with satisfaction.

"Briancourt said, 'He has always been a cad, a tradesman, a proud *parvenu!*' just loud enough for the words to reach my ear. 'Do not mind him.'

" 'No,' added Teleny, musingly, 'it is I who am to blame, not he.'

"Little did he understand with what a bleeding heart I walked out of the room, yearning at every step to turn back, and to throw my arms around his neck before everybody, and beg his forgiveness.

"I wavered for a moment, whether to go and offer him my hand or not. Alas! do we often yield to the warm impulse of the heart? Are we not, instead, always guided by the advice of the calculating, conscience-muddled, clay-cold brain?

"It was early, yet I waited for some time in the street, watching for Teleny to come out. I had made up my mind that if he was alone, I would go and beg his pardon for my rudeness.

"After a short time, I saw him appear at the door with Briancourt.

"My jealousy was at once rekindled. I turned on my heels and walked off. I did not want to see him again. On the morrow I would take the first train and go—anywhere, out of the world if I could.

"This state of feeling did not last long; and my rage being somewhat subdued, love and curiosity prompted me again to stop. I did so. I looked round; they were nowhere to be seen; still I had wended my steps towards Teleny's house.

"I walked back. I glanced down the neighbouring streets; they had quite disappeared.

"Now that he was lost to sight, my eagerness to find him increased. They had, perhaps, gone to Briancourt's. I hurried on in the direction of his house.

"All at once, I thought I saw two figures like them at a distance. I hastened on like a madman. I lifted up the collar of my coat, I pulled my soft felt hat over my ears, so as not to be recognized, and followed them on the opposite side-walk.

"I was not mistaken. Then they branched off; I after them. Whither were they going in these lonely parts?

"So as not to attract their attention I stopped where I saw an advertisement. I slackened, and then quickened my pace. Several times I saw their heads come in close contact, and then Briancourt's arm encircled Teleny's waist.

"All this was far worse than gall and wormwood to me. Still, in my misery, I had one consolation; this was to see that, apparently, Teleny was yielding to Briancourt's attentions instead of seeking them.

"At last they reached the Quai de, so busy in the daytime, so lonely at night. There they seemed to be looking for somebody, for they either turned around, scanned the persons they met, or stared at men seated on the benches that are along the quay. I continued following them.

"As my thoughts were entirely absorbed, it was some time before I noticed that a man, who had sprung up from somewhere, was walking by my side. I grew nervous; for I fancied that he not only tried to keep pace with me but also to catch my attention, for he hummed and whistled snatches of songs, coughed, cleared his throat, and scraped his feet.

"All these sounds fell upon my dreamy ears, but failed to arouse my attention. All my senses were fixed on the two figures in front of me. He therefore walked on, then turned round on his heels, and stared at me. My eyes saw all this without heeding him in the least.

"He lingered once more, let me pass, walked on at a brisker pace, and was again beside me. Finally, I looked at him. Though it was cold, he was but slightly dressed.

He wore a short, black velvet jacket and a pair of light grey, closely-fitting trousers marking the shape of the thighs and buttocks like tights.

"I looked at him; he stared at me again, then smiled with that vacant, vapid, idiotic, facial contraction of a *raccrocheuse*. Then, always looking at me with an inviting leer, he directed his steps towards a neighbouring *Vespasienne*.

" 'What is there so peculiar about me,' I mused, 'that the fellow is ogling me in that way?'

"Without turning round, however, or noticing him any further, I walked on, my eyes fixed on Teleny.

"As I passed by another bench, some one again scraped his feet and cleared his throat, evidently bent on making me turn my head. I did so. There was nothing more remarkable about him than there is in the first man you meet. Seeing me look at him, he either unbuttoned or buttoned up his trousers.

"After a while I again heard steps coming from behind; the person was close up to me. I smelt a strong scent—if the noxious odour of musk or of patchouli can be called a scent.

"The person touched me slightly as he passed by. He begged my pardon; it was the man of the velvet jacket, or his Dromio. I looked at him as he again stared at me and grinned. His eyes were painted with kohl, his cheeks were dabbed with rouge. He was quite beardless. For a moment, I doubted whether he was a man or a woman; but when he stopped again before the column I was fully persuaded of his sex.

"Someone else came with mincing steps, and shaking his buttocks, from behind one of these *pissoirs*. He was an old, wiry, simpering man, as shrivelled as a frostbitten pippin. His cheeks were very hollow, and his projecting cheek bones very red; his face was shaven and shorn, and he wore a wig with long, fair, flaxen locks.

"He walked in the posture of the Venus de Medici; that is, with one hand on his middle parts, and the other on his breast. His looks were not only very demure, but there was an almost maidenly coyness about the old man that gave him the appearance of a virgin-pimp.

"He did not stare, but cast a side-long glance at me as he went by. He was met by a workman—a strong and sturdy fellow, either a butcher or a smith by trade. The old man would evidently have slunk by unperceived, but the workman stopped him. I could not hear what they said, for though they were but a few steps away, they spoke in that hushed tone peculiar to lovers; but I seemed to be the object of their talk, for the workman turned and stared at me as I passed. They parted.

"The workman walked on for twenty steps, then he turned on his heel and walked back exactly on a line with me, seemingly bent on meeting me face to face.

"I looked at him. He was a brawny man, with massive features; clearly, a fine specimen of a male. As he passed by me he clenched his powerful fist, doubled his muscular arm at the elbow, and then moved it vertically hither and thither a few times, like a pistonrod in action, as it slipped in and out of the cylinder.

"Some signs are so evidently clear and full of meaning that no initiation is needed to understand them. This workman's sign was one of them.

"Now I knew who all these nightwalkers were. Why they so persistently stared at me, and the meaning of all their little tricks to catch my attention. Was I dreaming? I looked around. The workman had stopped, and he repeated his request in a different way. He shut his left fist, then thrust the forefinger of his right hand in the hole made by the palm and fingers, and moved it in and out. He was bluntly explicit. I was not mistaken. I hastened on, musing whether the cities of the plain had been destroyed by fire and brimstone.

"As I learnt later in life, every large city has its particular haunts—its square, its garden for such recreation. And the police? Well, it winks at it, until some crying offence is committed; for it is not safe to stop the mouths of craters. Brothels of men-whores not being allowed, such trysting-places must be tolerated, or the whole is a modern Sodom or Gomorrah."

"What? there are such cities now-a-days?"

"Aye! For Jehovah has acquired experience with age; so He has got to understand His children a little better than He did of yore, for He has either come to a righter sense of toleration, or, like Pilate, He has washed His hands, and has quite discarded them.

"At first I felt a deep sense of disgust at seeing the old catamite pass by me again, and lift, with utmost modesty, his arm from his breast, thrust his bony finger between his lips, and move it in the same fashion as the workman had done his arm, but trying to give all his movements a maidenly coyness. He was—as I learnt later—a *pompeur de dard*, or as I might call him, a 'sperm- sucker'; this was his speciality. He did the work for the love of the thing, and an experience of many years had made him a master of his trade. He, it appears, lived in every other respect like a hermit, and only indulged himself in one thing—fine lawn handkerchief, either with lace or embroidery, to wipe the amateur's instrument when he had done with it.

"The old man went down towards the river's edge, apparently inviting me for a midnight stroll in the mist, under the arches of the bridge, or in some out-of-the-way nook or other corner.

"Another man came up from there; this one was adjusting his dress, and scratching his hind part like an ape. Notwithstanding the creepy feeling these men gave me, the scene was so entirely new that I must say it rather interested me."

"And Teleny?"

"I had been so taken up with all these midnight wanderers that I lost sight both of him and of Briancourt, when all at once I saw them re-appear.

"With them there was a young Zouave sub-lieutenant and a dapper and dashing fellow, and a slim and swarthy youth, apparently an Arab.

"The meeting did not seem to have been a carnal one. Anyhow, the soldier was entertaining his friends with his lively talk, and by the few words which my ear caught I understood that the topic was an interesting one. Moreover, as they passed by each bench, the couples seated thereon nudged each other as if they were acquainted with them.

"As I passed them I shrugged up my shoulders, and buried my head in my collar. I even put up my handkerchief to my face. Still, notwithstanding all my precautions, Teleny seemed to have recognized me, although I had walked on without taking the slightest notice of him.

"I heard their merry laugh as I passed; an echo of loathsome words was still ringing in my ears; sickening faces of effete, womanish men traversed the street, trying to beguile me by all that is nauseous.

"I hurried on, sick at heart, disappointed, hating myself and my fellow-creatures, musing whether I was any better than all these worshippers of Priapus who were inured to vice. I was pining for the love of one man who did not care more for me than for any of these sodomites.

"It was late at night, and I walked on without exactly knowing where my steps were taking me to. I had not to cross the water on my way home, what then made me do so? Anyhow, all at once I found myself standing in the very middle of the bridge, staring vacantly at the open space in front of me.

"The river like a silvery thoroughfare, parted the town in two. On either side huge shadowy houses rose out of the mist; blurred domes, dim towers, vaporous and gigantic spires soared, quivering, up to the clouds, and faded away in the fog.

"Underneath I could perceive the sheen of the cold, bleak, and bickering river, flowing faster and faster, as if fretful at not being able to outdo itself in its own speed, chafing against the arches that stopped it, curling in tiny breakers, and whirling away in angry eddies, whilst the dark pillars shed patches of ink-black shade on the glittering and shivering stream.

"As I looked upon these dancing, restless shadows, I saw a myriad of fiery, snake-like elves gliding to and fro through them, winking and beckoning to me as they twirled and they rolled, luring me down to rest in those Lethean waters.

"They were right. Rest must be found below those dark arches, on the soft, slushy sand of that swirling river.

"How deep and fathomless those waters seemed! Veiled as they were by the mist, they had all the attraction of the abyss. Why should I not seek there that balm of forgetfulness which alone could ease my aching head, could calm my burning breast?

"Was it because the Almighty had fixed His canon against selfslaughter?"

"How, when, and where?"

"With His fiery finger, when He made that *coup de theatre* on Mount Sinai?

"If so, why was He tempting me beyond my strength?

"Would any father induce a beloved child to disobey him, simply to have the pleasure of chastising him afterwards? Would any man deflower his own daughter, not out of lust, but only to taunt her with her incontinence? Surely, if such a man ever lived, he was after Jehovah's own image.

"No, life is only worth living as long as it is pleasant. To me, just then, it was a burden. The passion I had tried to stifle, and which was merely smouldering, had burst out with renewed strength, entirely mastering me. That crime could there-fore only be overcome by another. In my case suicide was not only allowable, but laudable—nay, heroic.

"What did the Gospel say? 'If thine eye . . .' and so forth.

"All these thoughts whirled through my mind like little fiery snakes. Before me in the mist, Teleny—like a vaporous angel of light—seemed to be quietly gazing at me with his deep, sad, and thoughtful eyes; below, the rushing waters had for me a syren's sweet, enticing voice.

"I felt my brain reeling. I was losing my senses. I cursed this beautiful world of ours—this paradise, that man has turned into hell. I cursed this narrow-minded society of ours, that only thrives upon hypocrisy. I cursed our blighting religion, that lays its veto upon all the pleasures of the senses.

"I was already climbing on the parapet, decided to seek forgetfulness in those Stygian waters, when two strong arms clasped me tightly and held me fast."

"It was Teleny?"

"It was.

" 'Camille, my love, my soul, are you mad?' said he, in a stifled, panting voice.

"Was I dreaming—was it he? Teleny? Was he my guardian angel or a tempting demon? Had I gone quite mad?

"All these thoughts chased one another, and left me bewildered. Still, after a moment, I understood that I was neither mad nor dreaming. It was Teleny in flesh and blood, for I felt him against me as we were closely clasped in each other's arms. I had wakened to life from a horrible nightmare.

"The strain my nerves had undergone, and the utter faintness that followed, together with his powerful embrace, made me feel as if our two bodies clinging closely together had amalgamated or melted into a single one.

"A most peculiar sensation came over me at this moment. As my hands wandered over his head, his neck, his shoulders, his arms, I could not feel him at all; in fact, it seemed to me as if I were touching my own body. Our burning foreheads were pressed against each other, and his swollen and throbbing veins seemed my own fluttering pulses.

"Instinctively, and without seeking each other, our mouths united by a common consent. We did not kiss, but our breath gave life to our two beings.

"I remained vaguely unconscious for some time, feeling my strength ebb slowly away, leaving but vitality enough to know that I was yet alive.

"All at once I felt a mighty shock from head to foot; there was a reflex from the heart to the brain. Every nerve in my body was tingling; all my skin seemed pricked with the points of sharp needles. Our mouths which had withdrawn now clung again to each other with newly-awakened lust. Our lips—clearly seeking to engraft themselves together—pressed and rubbed with such passionate strength that the blood began to ooze from them—nay, it seemed as if this fluid, rushing up from our two hearts, was bent upon mingling together to celebrate in that auspicious moment the old hymeneal rites of nations—the marriage of two bodies, not by the communion of emblematic wine but of blood itself.

"We thus remained for some time in a state of overpowering delirium, feeling every instant, a more rapturous, maddening pleasure in each other's kisses, which kept goading us on to madness by increasing that heat which they could not allay, and by stimulating that hunger they could not appease.

"The very quintessence of love was in these kisses. All that was excellent in us— the essential part of our beings—kept rising and evaporating from our lips like the fumes of an ethereal, intoxicating, ambrosial fluid.

"Nature, hushed and silent, seemed to hold her breath to look upon us, for such ecstacy of bliss had seldom, if ever, been felt here below. I was subdued, prostrated, shattered. The earth was spinning round me, sinking under my feet. I had no longer strength enough to stand. I felt sick and faint. Was I dying? If so, death must be the happiest moment of our life, for such rapturous joy could never be felt again.

"How long did I remain senseless? I cannot tell. All I know is that I awoke in the midst of a whirlwind, hearing the rushing of waters around me. Little by little I came back to consciousness. I tried to free myself from his grasp.

" 'Leave me! Leave me alone! Why did you not let me die? This world is hateful to me, why should I drag on a life I loathe?'

" 'Why? For my sake.' Thereupon, he whispered softly, in that unknown tongue of his, some magic words which seemed to sink into my soul. Then he added, 'Nature has formed us for each other; why withstand her? I can only find happiness in your love, and in your's alone; it is not only part of my heart but my soul that panteth for your's.'

"With an effort of my whole being I pushed him away from me, and staggered back.

" 'No, no!' I cried, 'do not tempt me beyond my strength; let me rather die.'

" 'Thy will be done, but we shall die together, so that at least in death we may not be parted. There is an after-life, we may then, at least, cleave to one another like Dante's Francesca and her lover Paulo. Here,' said he, unwinding a silken scarf that he wore round his waist, 'let us bind ourselves closely together, and leap into the flood.'

"I looked at him, and shuddered. So young, so beautiful, and I was thus to murder him! The vision of Antinous as I had seen it the first time he played appeared before me.

"He had tied the scarf tightly round his waist, and he was about to pass it around me.

" 'Come.'

"The die was cast. I had not the right to accept such a sacrifice from him.

" 'No,' quoth I, 'let us live.'

" 'Live,' added he, 'and then?'

"He did not speak for some moments, as if waiting for a reply to that question which had not been framed in words. In answer to his mute appeal I stretched out my hands towards him. He—as if frightened that I should escape him—hugged me tightly with all the strength of irrepressible desire.

" 'I love you!' he whispered, 'I love you madly! I cannot live without you any longer.'

" 'Nor can I,' said I, faintly; 'I have struggled against my passion in vain, and now I yield to it, not tamely, but eagerly, gladly. I am your's, Teleny! Happy to be your's, your's forever and your's alone!'

"For all auswer there was a stifled hoarse cry from his innermost breast; his eyes were lighted up with a flash of fire; his craving amounted to rage; it was that of the wild beast seizing his prey; that of the lonely male finding at last a mate. Still his intense eagerness was more than that; it was also a soul issuing forth to meet another soul. It was a longing of the senses, and a mad intoxication of the brain.

"Could this burning, unquenchable fire that consumed our bodies be called lust? We clung as hungrily to one another as the famished animal does when it fastens on the food it devours; and as we kissed each other with ever-increasing greed, my fingers were feeling his curly hair, or paddling the soft skin of his neck. Our legs being clasped together, his phallus, in strong erection, was rubbing against mine no less stiff and stark. We were, however, always shifting our position, so as to get every part of our bodies in as close a contact as possible; and thus feeling, clasping, hugging, kissing, and biting each other, we must have looked, on that bridge amidst the thickening fog, like two damned souls suffering eternal torment.

"On the morrow the events of the night before seemed like a rapturous dream. . . .

"I felt the 'clear keen joyance' of the lark that loves, but 'ne'er knew love's sad satiety.' Hitherto, the pleasure that women had given me had always jarred upon my nerves. It was, in fact, 'a thing wherein we feel there is some hidden want.' Lust was now the overflowing of the heart and of the mind—the pleasurable harmony of all the senses.

"The world that had hitherto seemed to me so bleak, so cold, so desolate, was now a perfect paradise; the air, although the barometer had fallen considerably, was crisp, light, and balmy; the sun—a round, furbished, copper disc, and more like a red Indian's backside than fair Apollo's effulgent face—was shining gloriously for me; the murky fog itself, that brought on dark night at three o'clock in the afternoon, was only a hazy mist that veiled all that was ungainly, and rendered Nature fantastic, and home so snug and cosy. Such is the power of imagination.

"You laugh! Alas! Don Quixote was not the only man who took windmills for giants, or barmaids for princesses. If your sluggishbrained, thick-pated costermonger never falls into such a trance as to mistake apples for potatoes; if your grocer never turns hell into heaven, or heaven into hell—well, they are sane people who weight everything in the well-poised scale of reason. Try and shut them up in nutshells, and you will see if they would deem themselves monarchs of the world. They, unlike Hamlet, always see things as they really are. I never did. But then, you know, my father died mad.

"Anyhow, that overpowering weariness, that loathsomeness of life, had now quite passed away. I was blithe, merry, happy. Teleny was my lover; I was his.

"Far from being ashamed of my crime, I felt that I should like to proclaim it to the world. For the first time in my life I understood that lovers could be so foolish as to entwine their initials together. I felt like carving his name on the bark of trees, that the birds seeing it might twitter it from morn till eventide; that the breeze might lisp it to the rustling leaves of the forest. I wished to write it on the shingle of the beach, that the ocean itself might know of my love for him, and murmur it everlastingly."

"Still I had thought that on the morrow—the intoxication passed—you would have shuddered at the thought of having a man for a lover?"

"Why? Had I committed a crime against nature when my own nature found peace and happiness thereby? If I was thus, surely it was the fault of my blood, not myself. Who had planted nettles in my garden? Not I. They had grown there unawares, from my very childhood. I began to feel their carnal stings long before I could understand what conclusion they imported. When I had tried to bridle my lust, was it my fault if the scale of reason was far too light to balance that of sensuality? Was I to blame if I could not argue down my raging motion? Fate, Iago-like, had clearly shewed me that if I would damn myself, I could do so in a more delicate way than drowning. I yielded to my destiny, and encompassed my joy.

## John Francis Bloxam (1873–1928)

### From "The Priest and the Acolyte" (1894)

In John Francis Bloxam's "The Priest and the Acolyte," the acolyte is the ideal friend that Ronald Heatherington, the priest of the title, has long sought. But finding him, he is now accused by his rector of improper affection for the boy. The rector asks for an explanation, and Heatherington's reply effectively sums up not only the need for an ideal friend but also encapsulates other themes: the process of self-definition and self-discovery, the attraction of the eroticized aesthetic ideal, the need to revolt against homophobic convention, and the radicalizing effect on an individual conscience that confrontation with homophobia can ignite. Heatherington's remarkable statement is not only an apologia for same-sex love and a condemnation of homophobia, but it also recognizes that the irreversible fact of sexual difference has potentially irreversible consequences, and that these consequences are both social and political. To characterize Heatherington's transformation from a love-sick priest into what sounds familiarly like a modern homosexual rights activist may be anachronistic, but there can be no doubt that he sees his love as having far more than personal significance as he asserts that what originated as passion has now become a "struggle" against the destructive effects of a blind adherence to homophobic social conventions. Certainly Heatherington's response to the homophobic attack of his superior, and his description of his early life, is one of the most specific "coming out" scenes in English literature of the period.

## From Part Two

The world is very stern with those that thwart her. She lays down her precepts, and woe to those who dare to think for themselves, who venture to exercise their own discretion as to whether they shall allow their individuality and natural characteristics to be stamped out, to be obliterated under the leaden fingers of convention.

Truly, convention is the stone that has become head of the corner in the jerry-built temple of our superficial, self-assertive civilization.

> "And whosoever shall fall on this stone shall be broken: but on whomsoever it shall fall, it will grind him to powder."

If the world sees anything she cannot understand, she assigns the basest motives to all concerned, supposing the presence of some secret shame, the idea of which, at least, her narrow-minded intelligence is able to grasp.

The people no longer regarded their priest as a saint, and his acolyte as an angel. They still spoke of them with bated breath and with their fingers on their lips; they still drew back out of the way when they met either of them; but now they gathered together in groups of twos and threes and shook their heads.

The priest and his acolyte heeded not; they never even noticed the suspicious glances and half-suppressed murmurs. Each had found in the other perfect sympathy and perfect love: what could the outside world matter to them now? Each was to the other the perfect fulfillment of a scarcely preconceived ideal; neither heaven nor hell could offer more. But the stone of convention had been undermined; the time could not be far distant when it must fall.

The moonlight was very clear and very beautiful; the cool night air was heavy with the perfume of the old-fashioned flowers that bloomed so profusely in the little garden. But in the priest's little room the closely drawn curtains shut out all the beauty of the night. Entirely forgetful of all the world, absolutely oblivious of everything but one another, wrapped in the beautiful visions of a love that far outshone all the splendour of the summer night, the priest and the little acolyte were together.

The little lad sat on his knees with his arms closely pressed round his neck and his golden curls laid against the priest's close-cut hair; his white night-shirt contrasting strangely and beautifully with the dull black of the other's long cassock.

There was a step on the road outside—a step drawing nearer and nearer; a knock at the door. They heard it not; completely absorbed in each other, intoxicated with the sweetly poisonous draught that is the gift of love, they sat in silence. But the end had come: the blow had fallen at last. The door opened, and there before them in the doorway stood the tall figure of the rector.

Neither said anything; only the little boy clung closer to his beloved, and his eyes grew large with fear. Then the young priest rose slowly to his feet and put the lad from him.

"You had better go, Wilfred," was all he said.

The two priests stood in silence watching the child as he slipped through the window, stole across the grass, and vanished into the opposite cottage.

Then the two turned and faced each other.

The young priest sank into his chair and clasped his hands, waiting for the other to speak.

"So it has come to this!" he said: "the people were only too right in what they told me! Ah, God! that such a thing should have happened here! that it has fallen on me to expose your shame—our shame! That it is I who must give you up to justice, and see that you suffer the full penalty of your sin! Have you nothing to say?"

"Nothing—nothing," he replied softly. "I cannot ask for pity: I cannot explain: you would never understand. I do not ask you anything for myself, I do not ask you to spare me; but think of the terrible scandal to our dear Church."

"It is better to expose these terrible scandals and see that they are cured. It is folly to conceal a sore: better show all our shame than let it fester."

"Think of the child."

"That was for you to do: you should have thought of him before. What has his shame to do with me? it was your business. Besides, I would not spare him if I could: what pity can I feel for such as he?"

But the young man had risen, pale to the lips.

"Hush!" he said in a low voice; "I forbid you to speak of him before me with anything but respect"; then softly to himself, "with anything but reverence; with anything but devotion."

The other was silent, awed for the moment. Then his anger rose.

"Dare you speak openly like that? Where is your penitence, your shame? have you no sense of the horror of your sin?"

"There is no sin for which I should feel shame," he answered very quietly. "God gave me my love for him, and He gave him also his love for me. Who is there that shall withstand God and the love that is His gift?"

"Dare you profane the name by calling such a passion as this 'love'?"

"It was love, perfect love: it is perfect love."

"I can say no more now; tomorrow all shall be known. Thank God, you shall pay dearly for all this disgrace," he added, in a sudden out-burst of wrath.

"I am sorry you have no mercy; —not that I fear exposure and punishment for myself. But mercy can seldom be found from a Christian," he added, as one that speaks from without.

The rector turned towards him suddenly, and stretched out his hands.

"Heaven forgive me my hardness of heart," he said. "I have been cruel; I have spoken cruelly in my distress. Ah, can you say nothing to defend your crime?"

"No: I do not think I can do any good by that. If I attempted to deny all guilt, you would only think I lied: though I should prove my innocence, yet my reputation, my career, my whole future, are ruined for ever. But will you listen to me for a little? I will tell you a little about myself."

The rector sat down while his curate told him the story of his life, sitting by the empty grate with his chin resting on his clasped hands.

"I was at a big public school, as you know. I was always different from other boys. I never cared much for games. I took little interest in those things for which boys usually care so much. I was not very happy in my boyhood, I think. My one ambition was to find the ideal for which I longed. It has always been thus: I have always had an indefinite longing for something, a vague something that never quite took shape, that I could never quite understand. My great desire has always been to find something that would satisfy me. I was attracted at once by sin: my whole early life is stained and polluted with the taint of sin. Sometimes even now I think that there are sins more beautiful than anything else in the world. There are vices that are bound to attract almost irresistibly anyone who loves beauty above everything. I have always sought for love: again and again I have been the victim of fits of passionate affection: time after time I have seemed to have found my ideal at last: the whole object of my life has been, times without number, to gain the love of some particular person. Several times my efforts were successful; each time I woke to find that the success I had obtained was worthless after all. As I grasped the prize, it lost all its attraction—I no longer cared for what I had once desired with my whole heart. In vain I endeavoured to drown the yearnings of my heart with the ordinary pleasures and vices that usually attract the young. I had to choose a profession. I became a priest. The whole aesthetic tendency of my soul was intensely attracted by the wonderful mysteries of Christianity, the artistic beauty of our services. Ever since my ordination I have been striving to cheat myself into the belief that peace had come at last—at last my yearning was satisfied: but all in vain. Unceasingly I have struggled with the old cravings for excitement, and, above all, the weary, incessant thirst for a perfect love. I have found, and still find, an exquisite delight in religion: not in the regular duties of a religious life, not in the ordinary round of parish organizations; —against these I chafe incessantly; —no, my delight is in the aesthetic beauty of the services, the ecstasy of devotion, the passionate fervour that comes with long fasting and meditation."

"Have you found no comfort in prayer?" asked the rector.

"Comfort? —no. But I have found in prayer pleasure, excitement, almost a fierce delight of sin."

"You should have married. I think that would have saved you."

Ronald Heatherington rose to his feet and laid his hand on his rector's arm.

"You do not understand me; I have never been attracted by a woman in my life. Can you not see that people are different, totally different, from one another? To think that we are all the same is impossible; our natures, our temperaments, are utterly unlike. But this is what people will never see; they found all their opinions on a wrong basis. How can their deductions be just if their premises are wrong?

One law laid down by the majority, who happen to be of one disposition, is only binding on the minority legally, not morally. What right have you, or anyone, to tell me that such and such a thing is sinful for me? Oh, why can I not explain to you and force you to see?" and his grasp tightened on the other's arm. Then he continued, speaking fast and earnestly:

"For me, with my nature, to have married would have been sinful: it would have been a crime, a gross immorality, and my conscience would have revolted." Then he added, bitterly: "Conscience should be that divine instinct which bids us seek after that our natural disposition needs—we have forgotten that; to most of us, to the world, nay, even to Christians in general, conscience is merely another name for the cowardice that dreads to offend against convention. Ah, what a cursed thing convention is! I have committed no moral offense in this matter; in the sight of God my soul is blameless; but to you and to the world I am guilty of an abominable crime—abominable, because it is a sin against convention, forsooth! I met this boy: I loved him as I had never loved anyone or anything before: I had no need to labour to win his affection—he was mine by right: he loved me, even as I loved him, from the first: he was the necessary complement to my soul. How dare the world presume to judge us? What is convention to us? Nevertheless, although I really knew that such a love was beautiful and blameless, although from the bottom of my heart I despised the narrow judgement of the world, yet for his sake and for the sake of our Church, I tried at first to resist. I struggled against the fascination he possessed for me. I would never have gone to him and asked his love; I would have struggled on till the end: but what could I do? It was he that came to me, and offered me the wealth of love his beautiful soul possessed. How could I tell to such a nature as his the hideous picture the world would paint? Even as you saw him this evening, he has come to me night by night, —how dare I disturb the sweet purity of his soul by hinting at the horrible suspicions his presence might arouse? I knew what I was doing.

"I have faced the world and set myself up against it. I have openly scoffed at its dictates. I do not ask you to sympathize with me, nor do I pray you to stay your hand. Your eyes are blinded with a mental cataract. You are bound, bound with those miserable ties that have held you body and soul from the cradle. You must do what you believe to be your duty, In God's eyes we are martyrs, and we shall not shrink even from death in this struggle against the idolatrous worship of convention."

Ronald Heatherington sank into a chair, hiding his face in his hands, and the rector left the room in silence.

For some minutes the young priest sat with his face buried in his hands. Then with a sigh he rose and crept across the garden till he stood beneath the open window of his darling.

"Wilfred," he called very softly.

The beautiful face, pale and wet with tears, appeared at the window.

"I want you, my darling; will you come?" he whispered.

"Yes, father," the boy softly answered.

The priest led him back to his room; then, taking him very gently in his arms, he tried to warm the cold little feet with his hands.

"My darling, it is all over." And he told him as gently as he could all that lay before them.

The boy hid his face on his shoulder, crying softly.

"Can I do nothing for you, dear father?"

He was silent for a moment. "Yes, you can die for me; you can die with me."

The loving arms were about his neck once more, and the warm, loving lips were kissing his own. "I will do anything for you. O father, let us die together!"

"Yes, my darling, it is best: we will."

Then very quietly and very tenderly he prepared the little fellow for his death; he heard his last confession and gave him his last absolution. Then they knelt together, hand in hand, before the crucifix.

"Pray for me, my darling."

Then together their prayers silently ascended that the dear Lord would have pity on the priest who had fallen in the terrible battle of life. There they knelt till midnight, when Ronald took the lad in his arms and carried him to the little chapel.

"I will say Mass for the repose of our souls," he said.

Over his night-shirt the child arrayed himself in his little scarlet cassock and tiny lace cotta. He covered his naked feet with the scarlet sanctuary shoes; he lighted the tapers and reverently helped the priest to vest. Then before they left the vestry the priest took him in his arms and held him pressed closely to his breast; he stroked the soft hair and whispered cheeringly to him. The child was weeping quietly, his slender frame trembling with the sobs he could scarcely suppress. After a moment the tender embrace soothed him, and he raised his beautiful mouth to the priest's. Their lips were pressed together, and their arms wrapped one another closely.

"Oh, my darling, my own sweet darling!" the priest whispered tenderly.

"We shall be together for ever soon; nothing shall separate us now," the child said.

"Yes, it is far better so; far better to be together in death than apart in life."

They knelt before the altar in the silent night, the glimmer of the tapers lighting up the features of the crucifix with strange distinctness. Never had the priest's voice trembled with such wonderful earnestness, never had the acolyte responded with such devotion, as at this midnight Mass for the peace of their own departing souls.

Just before the consecration the priest took a tiny phial from the pocket of his cassock, blessed it, and poured the contents into the chalice.

When the time came for him to receive from the chalice, he raised it to his lips, but did not taste of it.

He administered the sacred wafer to the child, and then he took the beautiful gold chalice, set with precious stones, in his hand; he turned towards him; but when he saw the light in the beautiful face he turned again to the crucifix with a low moan. For one instant his courage failed him; then he turned to the little fellow again, and held the chalice to his lips:

"The Blood of our Lord Jesus Christ, which was shed for thee, preserve thy body and soul unto everlasting life."

Never had the priest beheld such perfect love, such perfect trust, in those dear eyes as shone from them now; now, as with face raised upwards he received his death from the loving hands of him that he loved best in the whole world.

The instant he had received, Ronald fell on his knees beside him and drained the chalice to the last drop. He set it down and threw his arms round the beautiful figure of his dearly loved acolyte. Their lips met in one last kiss of perfect love, and all was over.

When the sun was rising in the heavens it cast one broad ray upon the altar of the little chapel. The tapers were burning still, scarcely half-burnt through. The sad-faced figure of the crucifix hung there in its majestic calm. On the steps of the altar was stretched the long, ascetic frame of the young priest, robed in the sacred vestments; close beside him, with his curly head pillowed on the gorgeous embroideries that covered his breast, lay the beautiful boy in scarlet and lace. Their arms were round each other; a strange hush lay like a shroud over all.

"And whosoever shall fall on this stone shall be broken: but on whomsoever it shall fall, it will grind him to powder."

## Havelock Ellis and John Addington Symonds

FROM *SEXUAL INVERSION* (1897)

When John Addington Symonds sent his essay "A Problem in Modern Ethics" to fifty select friends, many responded with biographical reminiscences of their own homosexual lives. Some of these biographies were published in Havelock Ellis and John Addington Symonds's *Sexual Inversion*, the eventual first volume of Ellis's *Studies in the Psychology of Sex*. What Ellis called case histories in fact contribute as much as any imaginative literature to the formation of homosexual identities at the end of the century. Many of them confessed to being dreamy or indolent in youth, and these dreams became rich fantasy lives inhabited by handsome, available, and muscular young men—roughs, shepherds, working men, soldiers, and sailors—or by more passive and effeminate youths. In life as well as fantasy they ardently pursued friendship, love, and sex, some of them sharing quite incredibly active and adventurous sexual experiences. They responded to women as social, but rarely as sexual, beings, expressing often a positive abhorrence of the notion of heterosexual union and an equally positive conviction that homosexual love was nobler, more passionate, and more profound than heterosexual love. Almost none of them expressed any desire to be anything other than what they were, even though many of them keenly felt that they were outcasts or pariahs in a world that condemned what to them seemed natural and imperative emotions. With remarkable unanimity they celebrated homosexuality and considered it natural, elevating, and the source of creative power. Many of them suspected that they were a discrete and physiologically unique species.

### FROM HISTORY IV

Of sexual inversion in the abstract he says he has no views, but he thus sums up his moral attitude: "I presume that, if it is there, it is there for use or abuse, as men please. I condemn gratification of bodily desire at the expense of others, in whatever form it may take. I condemn it no more in its inverted form than in the ordinary. I believe that affection between persons of the same sex, even when it includes the sexual passion and its indulgence, may lead to results as splendid as human nature can ever attain to. In short, I place it on an absolute equality with love as ordinarily understood."

## HISTORY VI (1897)

[This history was given to Ellis and Symonds by Edward Carpenter.]

My parentage is very sound and healthy. Both my parents (who belong to the professional middle class) have good general health; nor can I trace any marked abnormal or diseased tendency, of mind or body, in any records of the family.

Though of a strongly nervous temperament myself, and sensitive, my health is good. I am not aware of any tendency to physical disease. In early manhood, however, owing, I believe, to the great emotional tension under which I lived, my nervous system was a good deal shattered and exhausted. Mentally and morally my nature is pretty well balanced, and I have never had any serious perturbations in these departments.

At the age of 8 or 9, and long before distinct sexual feelings declared themselves, I felt a friendly attraction toward my own sex, and this developed after the age of puberty into a passionate sense of love, which, however, never found any expression for itself till I was fully 20 years of age. I was a day-boarder at school and heard little of schooltalk on sex subjects, was very reserved and modest besides; no elder person or parent ever spoke to me on such matters; and the passion for my own sex developed gradually, utterly uninfluenced from the outside. I never even, during all this period, and till a good deal later, learned the practice of masturbation. My own sexual nature was a mystery to me. I found myself cut off from the understanding of others, felt myself an outcast, and, with a highly loving and clinging temperament, was intensely miserable. I thought about my male friends—sometimes boys of my own age, sometimes elder boys, and once even a master—during the day and dreamed about them at night, but was too convinced that I was a hopeless monstrosity ever to make any effectual advances. Later on it was much the same, but gradually, though slowly, I came to find that there were others like myself. I made a few special friends, and at last it came to me occasionally to sleep with them and to satisfy my imperious need by mutual embraces and emissions. Before this happened, however, I was once or twice on the brink of despair and madness with repressed passion and torment.

Meanwhile, from the first, my feeling, physically, toward the female sex was one of indifference, and later on, with the more special development of sex desires, one of positive repulsion. Though having several female friends, whose society I like and to whom I am sincerely attached, the thought of marriage or cohabitation with any such has always been odious to me.

As a boy I was attracted in general by boys rather older than myself; after leaving school I still fell in love, in a romantic vein, with comrades of my own standing. Now,—at the age of 37,—my ideal of love is a powerful, strongly built man, of my own age or rather younger—preferably of the working class. Though having solid sense and character, he need not be specially intellectual. If endowed in the latter way, he must not be too glib or refined. Anything effeminate in a man, or anything of the cheap intellectual style, repels me very decisively.

I have never had to do with actual pederasty, so called. My chief desire in love is bodily nearness or contact, as to sleep naked with a naked friend; the specially sexual, though urgent enough, seems a secondary matter. Pederasty, either active or passive, might seem in place to me with one I loved very devotedly and who also loved me to that degree; but I think not otherwise. I am an artist by temperament and choice, fond of all beautiful things, especially the male human form; of active, slight, muscular build; and sympathetic, but somewhat indecisive character, though possessing self-control.

I cannot regard my sexual feelings as unnatural or abnormal, since they have disclosed themselves so perfectly naturally and spontaneously within me. All that I have read in books or heard spoken about the ordinary sexual love, its intensity and passion, lifelong devotion, love at first sight, etc., seems to me to be easily matched by my own experiences in the homosexual form; and, with regard to the morality of this complex subject, my feeling is that it is the same as should prevail in love between man and woman, namely: that no bodily satisfaction should be sought at the cost of another person's distress or degradation. I am sure that this kind of love is, notwithstanding the physical difficulties that attend it, as deeply stirring and ennobling as the other kind, if not more so; and I think that for a perfect relationship the actual sex gratifications (whatever they may be) probably hold a less important place in this love than in the other.

## From History VII

You will rightly infer that it is difficult for me to say exactly how I regard (morally) the homosexual tendency. Of this much, however, I am certain, even if it were possible, I would not exchange my inverted nature for a normal one. I suspect that the sexual emotions and even inverted ones have a more subtle significance than is generally attributed to them; but modern moralists either fight shy of transcendental interpretations or see none, and I am ignorant and unable to solve the mystery these feelings seem to imply.

. . . I have absolutely no words to tell you how powerfully such beauty affects me. Moral and intellectual worth is, I know, of greater value, but physical beauty I *see* more clearly, and it appears to me the most *vivid* (if not the most perfect) manifestation of the divine. A little incident may, perhaps, reveal to you my feelings more completely. Not long ago I happened to see an unusually well-formed young fellow enter a house of assignation with a common woman of the streets. The sight filled me with the keenest anguish, and the thought that his beauty would soon be at the disposal of a prostitute made me feel as if I were a powerless and unhappy witness to a sacrilege. It may be that my rage for male loveliness is only another outbreaking of the old Platonic mania, for as time goes on I find that I long less for the actual youth before me, and more and more for some ideal perfect being whose bodily splendor and loving heart are the realities whose reflections only we see in this cave of shadows.

## History XIII

Age 25; is employed in an ordinary workshop, and lives in the back alley of a large town in which he was born and bred. Fair, slight, and refined in appearance. The sexual organs are normal and well developed, and the sexual passions strong. His mother is a big masculine woman, and he is much attached to her. Father is slight and weakly. He has seven brothers and one sister. Homosexual desires began at an early age, though he does not seem to have come under any perverse influences.

He is not inclined to masturbation. Erotic dreams are always of males. He declares he never cared for any woman except his mother and that he could not endure to sleep with a woman.

He says he generally falls in love with a man at first sight—as a rule, some one older than himself and of higher class—and longs to sleep and be with him. In one case he fell in love with a man twice his own age, and would not rest until he had won his affection. He does not much care what form the sexual relation takes. He is sensitive and feminine by nature, gentle, and affectionate. He is neat and orderly in his habits, and fond of housework; helps his mother in washing, etc. He appears to think that male attachments are perfectly natural.

## HISTORY XVII

[This is John Addington Symonds's own history of his erotic life.]

Englishman, of independent means, aged 49.

Sexual consciousness awoke before the age of 8 . . .

About the same time he became subject to curious half-waking dreams. In these he imagined himself the servant of several adult naked sailors; he crouched between their thighs and called himself their dirty pig, and by their orders he performed services for their genitals and buttocks, which he contemplated and handled with relish. At about the same period, when these visions began to come to him, he casually heard that a man used to come and expose his person before the window of a room where the maids sat; this troubled him vaguely. Between the age of 8 and 11 he twice took the penis of a cousin into his mouth, after they had slept together; the feeling of the penis pleased him. When sleeping with another cousin, they used to lie with hands outstretched to cover each other's penis or nates. He preferred the nates, but his cousin the penis. Neither of these cousins was homosexual, and there was no attempt at mutual masturbation. He was in the habit of playing with five male cousins. One of these boys was unpopular with the others, and they invented a method of punishing him for supposed offenses. They sat around the room on chairs, each with his penis exposed, and the boy to be punished went around the room on his knees and took each penis into his mouth in turn. This was supposed to humiliate him. It did not lead to masturbation. On one occasion the child accidentally observed a boy who sat next to him in school playing with his penis and caressing it. This gave him a powerful, uneasy sensation. With regard to all these points the subject observes that none of the boys with whom he was connected at this period, and who were exposed to precisely the same influences, became homosexual.

He was himself, from the first, indifferent to the opposite sex. In early childhood, and up to the age of 13, he had frequent opportunities of closely inspecting the sexual organs of girls, his playfellows. These roused no sexual excitement. On the contrary, the smell of the female parts affected him disagreeably. When he once saw a schoolfellow copulating with a little girl, it gave him a sense of mystical horror. Nor did the sight of the male organs arouse any particular sensations. He is, however, of opinion that, living with his sisters in childhood, he felt more curious about his own sex as being more remote from him. He showed no effeminacy in his preferences for games or work.

He went to a public school. Here he was provoked by boy friends to masturbate, but, though he often saw the act in process, it only inspired him with a sense of indecency. In his fifteenth year puberty commenced with nocturnal emissions, and, at the same time, he began to masturbate, and continued to do so about once a week, or once a fortnight, during a period of eight months; always with a feeling that that was a poor satisfaction and repulsive. His thoughts were not directed either to males or females while masturbating. He spoke to his father about these signs of puberty, and by his father's advice he entirely abandoned onanism; he only resumed the practice, to some extent, after the age of 30, when he was without male comradeship.

The nocturnal emissions, after he had abandoned self-abuse, became very frequent and exhausting. They were medically treated by tonics such as quinine and strychnine. He thinks this treatment exaggerated his neurosis.

All this time, no kind of sexual feeling for girls made itself felt. He could not understand what his schoolfellows found in women, or the stories they told about wantonness and delight of coitus.

His old dreams about the sailors had disappeared. But now he enjoyed visions of beautiful young men and exquisite statues; he often shed tears when he thought of them. These dreams persisted for years. But another kind gradually usurped their place to some extent. These second visions took the form of the large, erect organs of naked young grooms or peasants. These gross visions offended his taste and hurt him, though, at the same time, they evoked a strong, active desire for possession; he took a strange, poetic pleasure in the ideal form. But the seminal losses which accompanied both kinds of dreams were a perpetual source of misery to him.

There is no doubt that at this time—that is, between the fifteenth and seventeenth years—a homosexual diathesis had become established. He never frequented loose women, though he sometimes thought that would be the best way of combating his growing inclination for males. And he thinks that he might have brought himself to indulge freely in purely sexual pleasure with women if he made their first acquaintance in a male costume. . . .

His ideal of morality and fear of venereal infection, more than physical incapacity, kept him what is called chaste. He never dreamed of women, never sought their society, never felt the slightest sexual excitement in their presence, never idealized them. Esthetically, he thought them far less beautiful than men. Statues and pictures of naked women had no attraction for him, while all objects of art which represented handsome males deeply stirred him.

It was in his eighteenth year that an event occurred which he regards as decisive in his development. He read Plato. A new world opened, and he felt that his own nature had been revealed. Next year he formed a passionate, but pure, friendship with a boy of 15. Personal contact with the boy caused erection, extreme agitation and aching pleasure, but not ejaculation. Through four years he never saw the boy naked or touched him pruriently. Only twice he kissed him. He says that these two kisses were the most perfect joys he ever felt.

His father now became seriously anxious both about his health and his reputation. He warned him of the social and legal dangers attending his temperament. But he did not encourage him to try coitus with women. He himself thinks that his own sense of danger might have made this method successful, or that, at all events, the habit of intercourse with women might have lessened neurosis and diverted his mind to some extent from homosexual thoughts.

A period of great pain and anxiety now opened for him. But his neurasthenia increased; he suffered from insomnia, obscure cerebral discomfort, stammering, chronic conjunctivitis, inability to concentrate his attention, and dejection. Meanwhile his homosexual emotions strengthened, and assumed a more sensual character. He abstained from indulging them, as also from onanism, but he was often forced, with shame and reluctance, to frequent places—baths, urinaries, and so forth—where there were opportunities of seeing naked men.

Having no passion for women, it was easy to avoid them. Yet they inspired him with no exact horror. He used to dream of finding an exit from his painful situation by cohabitation with some coarse, boyish girl of the people; but his dread of syphilis stood in the way. He felt, however, that he must conquer himself by efforts of will, and by a persistent direction of his thoughts to heterosexual images. He sought the society of distinguished women. Once he coaxed up a romantic affection for a young girl of 15, which came to nothing, probably because the girl felt the want of absolute passion in his wooing. She excited his imagination, and he really loved her; but she did not, even in the closest contact, stimulate his sexual appetite. Once, when he kissed her just after she had risen from bed in the morning, a curious physical repugnance came over him, attended with a sad feeling of disappointment.

He was strongly advised to marry by physicians. At last he did so. He found that he was potent, and begot several children, but he also found, to his disappointment, that the tyranny of the male genital organs on his fancy increased. Owing to this cause his physical, mental, and moral discomfort became acute. His health gave way.

At about the age of 30, unable to endure his position any longer. he at last yielded to his sexual inclinations. As he began to do this, ho also began to regain calm and comparative health. He formed a close alliance with a youth of l9. This liaison was largely sentimental, and marked by a kind of etherealized sensuality. It involved no sexual acts beyond kissing, naked contact, and rare involuntary emissions. About the ago of 36 he began freely to follow homosexual inclinations. After this he rapidly recovered his health. The neurotic disturbances subsided.

He has always loved men younger than himself. At about the age of 27, he had begun to admire young soldiers. Since he yielded freely to his inclinations the men he has sought are invariably persons of a lower social rank than his own. He carried on one liaison continuously for twelve years; it began without passion on the friend's side, but gradually grew to nearly equal strength on both sides. He is not attracted by uniforms, but seeks some uncontaminated child of nature.

The methods of satisfaction have varied with the phases of his passion. At first they were romantic and Platonic, when a hand-touch, a rare kiss, or mere presence sufficed. In the second period sleeping side by side, inspection of the naked body of the loved man, embracements, and occasional emissions after prolonged contact. In the third period the gratification became more frankly sensual. It took every shape: mutual masturbation, intercrural coitus, fellatio, irrumatio, and occasionally active pedicatio; always according to the inclination or concession of the beloved male.

He himself always plays the active, masculine part. He never yields himself to the other, and he asserts that he never has the joy of finding himself desired with ardor equal to his own. He does not shrink from passive pedicatio; but it is never demanded of him. Coitus with males, as above described, always seems to him healthy and natural; it leaves a deep sense of well-being, and has cemented durable friendships. He has always sought to form permanent ties with the men whom he has adored so excessively.

He is of medium height, not robust, but with great nervous energy, with strong power of will and self-control, able to resist fatigue and changes of external circumstances.

In boyhood he had no liking for female occupations, or for the society of girls, preferring study and solitude. He avoided games and the noisy occupations of boys, but was only non-masculine in his indifference to sport, was never feminine in dress or habit. He never succeeded in his attempts to whistle. He is a great smoker, and has at times drunk much. He likes riding, skating, and climbing, but is a poor horseman, and is clumsy with his hands. He has no capacity for the fine arts and music, though much interested in them, and is a prolific author.

He has suffered extremely throughout life owing to his sense of the difference between himself and normal human being. No pleasure he has enjoyed, he declares, can equal a thousandth part of the pain caused by the internal consciousness of pariahdom. The utmost he can plead in his own defense, he admits, is irresponsibility, for he acknowledges that his impulse may be morbid. But he feels absolutely certain that in early life his health was ruined and his moral repose destroyed owing to the perpetual conflict with his own inborn nature, and that relief and strength came with indulgence. Although he always has before him the terror of discovery, he is convinced that his sexual dealings with men have been thoroughly wholesome to himself, largely increasing his physical, moral, and intellectual energy, and not injurious to others. He has no sense whatever of moral wrong in his actions, and he regards the attitude of society toward those in his position as utterly unjust and founded on false principles.

# 16. Symbolic Sodomite

## Society, Oscar Wilde, and the Law

The story of Oscar Wilde is so well known that it is enough to say that after a brilliant career as the master practitioner of nineteenth-century aestheticism, as an accomplished poet, controversial novelist, and the most brilliant dramatist of the age, all was shattered by the accusation brought against him by the Marquis of Queensberry, the father of Wilde's lover, Lord Alfred Douglas. Wilde sued for libel, lost, and was in turn sued by Queensberry, with the result that Wilde's involvement with Douglas, his relations with a number of male prostitutes, as well as an interpretation of some of his writing as advocating "perversion" was more than adequate evidence to lead to his conviction for sodomy and his imprisonment for two years at hard labor. Wilde's early poetry reflects some of the coded homoeroticism of aestheticism, and *The Picture of Dorian Gray* presents a full-scale portrait of three men, Basil Hallward, Lord Henry, and Dorian Gray, whose homosexuality would have been clear to any even moderately suspicious reader. His plays, including *The Importance of Being Earnest* (which in effect celebrates the pleasures of a double life), often create an ambiance in which the sexuality of men is dubiously presented, with questions of desire hanging upon the expression of wit and revealed by verbal double meaning. Both his alleged composition of *Teleny* and his actual writing of "The Portrait of Mr. W. H."—an attempt to identify the object of Shakespeare's sonnets—suggest his interest in homosexuality as a subject for texts. At his trial, Wilde passionately defined and defended "the Love that dare not speak its name." In his letters to Douglas—who he called Bosie—he reveals some of the blindness that lead him to his fate, in his *De Profundis*, a long letter to Douglas written from prison, he recognizes what the world has come to believe, that he stood in symbolic relation to his times, indeed a symbolic sodomite.

### The Law

THE CRIMINAL LAW AMENDMENT ACT OF 1885

*48 and 49 Victoria, C. 69 II*: Any male person who, in public or private, commits or is a party to the commission of, or procures or attempts to procure the commission by any male person of, any act of gross indecency with another male person, shall be guilty of a misdemeanor, and being convicted thereof shall be liable at the discretion of the Court to be imprisoned for any term not exceeding two years, with or without hard labour.

### Oscar Wilde (1854–1900)

*Wasted Days* (1877)

A fair slim boy not made for this world's pain,
With hair of gold thick clustering round his ears,

And longing eyes half veil'd by foolish tears
Like bluest water seen through mists of rain;
Pale cheeks whereon no kiss hath left its stain,
 Red under-lip drawn in for fear of Love,
 And white throat whiter than the breast of dove—
Alas! alas! if all should be in vain.
Behind, wide fields, and reapers all a-row
In heat and labour toiling wearily,
To no sweet sound of laughter or of lute.
The sun is shooting wide its crimson glow,
Still the boy dreams: nor knows that night is nigh,
And in the night-time no man gathers fruit.


FROM *ELEUTHERIA*

*Helas!* (1881)

To drift with every passion till my soul
Is a stringed lute on which all winds can play,
Is it for this that I have given away
Mine ancient wisdom, and austere control?
Methinks my life is a twice-written scroll
Scrawled over on some boyish holiday
With idle songs for pipe and virelay,
Which do but mar the secret of the whole.
Surely there was a time I might have trod
The sunlit heights, and from life's dissonance
Struck one clear chord to reach the ears of God:
Is that time dead? Lo! with a little rod
I did but touch the honey of romance—
And must I lose a soul's inheritance?


FROM *ROSA MYSTICA*

*Vita Nuova*

I stood by the unvintageable sea
 Till the wet waves drenched face and hair with spray;
 The long red fires of the dying day
Burned in the west; the wind piped drearily;
And to the land the clamorous gulls did flee:
 "Alas!" I cried, "my life is full of pain,
 And who can garner fruit or golden grain
From these waste fields which travel ceaselessly!"
My nets gaped wide with many a break and flaw,
 Nathless I threw them as my final cast

Into the sea, and waited for the end.
When lo! a sudden glory! and I saw
   The argent splendour of white limbs ascend,
   And in that joy forgot my tortured past.


LETTERS FROM OSCAR WILDE TO LORD ALFRED DOUGLAS (1893–1895)

[January 1893]
My Own Boy, Your sonnet is quite lovely, and it is a marvel that those red rose-leaf lips of yours should have been made no less for music of song than for madness of kisses. Your slim gilt soul walks between passion and poetry. I know Hyacinthus, whom Apollo loved so madly, was you in Greek days.

   Why are you alone in London, and when do you go to Salisbury? Do go there to cool your hands in the grey twilight of Gothic things, and come here whenever you like. It is a lovely place—it only lacks you; but go to Salisbury first. Always, with undying love, yours, Oscar.

[March 1893]
Dearest of all Boys, Your letter was delightfull, red and yellow wine to but I am sad and out of sorts. Bosie, you must not make scenes with me. They kill me, they wreck the loveliness of life. I cannot see you, so Greek and gracious, distorted with passion. I cannot listen to your curved lips saying hideous things to me. I would sooner [be blackmailed by every renter in London] than have you bitter, unjust, hating. I must see you soon. You are the divine thing I want, the thing of grace and beauty; but I don't know how to do it. Shall I come to Salisbury? My bill here is 49 for a week. I have also got a new sitting-room over the Thames. Why are you not here, my dear, my wonderful boy? I fear I must leave; no money, no credit, and a heart of lead.

[July–August 1894]
. . . Your father is on the rampage again—been to Cafe Royal to enquire for us, with threats etc. I think now it would have been better for me to have had him bound over to keep the peace, but what a scandal! Still, it is intolerable to be dogged by a maniac.

   When you come to Worthing, of course all things will be done for your honour and joy, but I fear you may find the meals, etc, tedious. But you will come, won't you? at any rate for a short time—till you are bored.

   Ernesto has written to me begging for money—a very nice letter—but I really have nothing just now.

   What purple valleys of despair one goes through! Fortunately there is one person in the world to love.

[April 5, 1895]
My dear Bosie, I will be at Bow Street Police Station tonight—no bail possible I am told. Will you ask Percy, and George Alexander, and Waller, at the Haymarket, to attend to give bail.

Would you also wire Humphreys to appear at Bow Street for me. Wire to 41 Norfolk Square, W.

Also, come to see me.

Monday Evening [April 29, 1895]

My dearest boy, This is to assure you of my immortal, my eternal love for you. Tomorrow all will be over. If prison and dishonour be my destiny, think that my love for you and this idea, this still more divine belief, that you love me in return will sustain me in my unhappiness and will make me capable, I hope, of bearing my grief most patiently. Since the hope, nay rather the certainty, of meeting you again in some world is the goal and the encouragement of my present life, ah! I must continue to live in this world because of that.

. . . As for you (graceful boy with a Christ-like heart), as for you, I beg you, as soon as you have done all that you can, leave for Italy and regain your calm, and write those lovely poems which you do with such a strange grace. Do not expose yourself to England for any reason whatsoever. If one day, at Corfu or in some enchanted isle, there were a little house where we could live together, oh! life would be sweeter than it has ever been. Your love has broad wings and is strong, your love comes to me through my prison bars and comforts me, your love is the light of all my hours. Those who know not what love is will write, I know, if fate is against us, that I have had a bad influence upon your life. If they do that, you shall write, you shall say in your turn, that it is not so. Our love was always beautifull and noble, and if I have been the butt of a terrible tragedy, it is because the nature of that love has not been understood. In your letter this morning you say something which gives me courage. I must remember it. You write that it is my duty to you and to myself to live in spite of everything. I think that is true. I shall try and I shall do it. . . .

I am so happy that you have gone away! I know what that must have cost you. It would have been agony for me to think that you were in England when your name was mentioned in court. I hope you have copies of all my books. All mine have been sold. I stretch out my hands towards you. Oh! may I live to touch your hair and your hands. I think that your love will watch over my life. If I should die, I want you to live a gentle peaceful existence somewhere, with flowers, pictures, books, and lots of work. Try to let me hear from you soon. I am writing you this letter in the midst of great suffering; this long day in court has exhausted me. Dearest boy, sweetest of all young men, most loved and most lovable. Oh! wait for me! wait for me! I am now, as ever since the day we met, yours devout and with an immortal love

[May 1895]

As for you, you have given me the beauty of life in the past, and in the future if there is any future. That is why I shall be eternally grateful to you for having always inspired me with adoration and love. Those days of pleasure were our dawn. Now, in anguish and pain, in grief and humiliation, I feel that my love for you, your love for me, are the two signs of my life, the divine sentiments which make all bitterness bearable. Never has anyone in my life been dearer than you, never has any love been greater, more sacred, more beautiful. . . .

Dear boy, among pleasures or in prison, you and the thought of you were everything to me. Oh! keep me always in your heart; you are never absent from mine. I think of you much more than of myself, and if, sometimes, the thought of horrible and infamous suffering comes to torture me, the simple thought of you is enough to strengthen me and heal my wounds. Let destiny, Nemesis, or the unjust gods alone receive the blame for everything that has happened.

Every great love has its tragedy, and now ours has too, but to have known and loved you with such profound devotion, to have had you for a part of my life, the only part I now consider beautiful, is enough for me. My passion is at a loss for words, but you can understand me, you alone. Our souls were made for one another, and by knowing yours through love, mine has transcended many evils, understood perfection, and entered into the divine essence of things.

Pain, if it comes, cannot last for ever; surely one day you and I will meet again, and though my face be a mask of grief and my body worn out by solitude, you and you alone will recognize the soul which is more beautiful for having met yours, the soul of the artist who found his ideal in you, of the lover of beauty to whom you appeared as a being flawless and perfect. Now I think of you as a golden-haired boy with Christ's own heart in you. I know now how much greater love is than everything else. You have taught me the divine secret of the world.

## A Defense of Uranian Love

### From the Transcripts of the Second Trial

#### The Second Trial (April 26–30, 1895)

"Was the evidence you gave at the Queensberry trial absolutely and in all respects true?"

"Entirely true evidence."

"Is there any truth in any of the allegations of indecent behaviour made against you in the evidence in the present case?"

"There is no truth whatever in any one of the allegations, no truth whatsoever."

[Charles Gill then rose to cross-examine the witness.]

"You are acquainted with a publication entitled *The Chameleon?*"

"Very well indeed," Wilde answered with a wry smile.

"I believe that Lord Alfred Douglas was a frequent contributor?"

"Hardly that, I think. He wrote some verses occasionally, and indeed for other papers."

"The poems in question were somewhat peculiar, were they not?"

"They certainly were not mere commonplaces, like so much that is labelled poetry."

"The tone of them met with your critical approval?"

"It was not for me to approve or disapprove. I left that to the reviews."

"At the last trial you described them as beautiful poems."

"I said something tantamount to that. The verses were original in theme and construction, and I admired them."

"Listen, Mr. Wilde, I shall not keep you very long in the witness box."

[Counsel then produced a copy of *The Chameleon*, from which he read from "In Praise of Shame."]

Last night unto my bed methought there came
Our lady of strange dreams, and from an urn
She poured live fire, so that mine eyes did burn
At sight of it. Anon the floating flame
Took many shapes, and one cried: "I am
Shame That walks with Love, I am most wise to turn
Cold lips and limbs to fire; therefore discern
And see my loveliness, and praise my name."

And afterwards, in radiant garments dressed
With sound of flutes and laughing of glad lips
A pomp of all the passions passed along
All the night through; till the white phantom ships
Of dawn sailed in. Whereat I said this song,
"Of all sweet passions Shame is loveliest."

"Your view, Mr. Wilde, is that the 'shame' mentioned here is that shame which is a sense of modesty?"

"That was the explanation given to me by the person who wrote it. The sonnet seemed to me obscure."

"During 1893 and 1894 you were a great deal in the company of Lord Alfred Douglas?"

"Oh, yes."

"Did he read that poem to you?"

"Yes."

"You can perhaps understand that such verses as these would not be acceptable to the reader with an ordinary balanced mind?"

"I am not prepared to say. It appears to me to be a question of taste, temperament, and individuality. I should say that one man's poetry is another man's poison!"

"I daresay! The next poem is one described as 'Two Loves.' It contains these lines [*reading*]:

Sweet youth,
Tell me why, sad and sighing, dost thou rove
These pleasant realms? I pray thee tell me sooth,
What is thy name? He said: "My name is Love,"
Then straight the first did turn himself to me,
And cried: "He lieth, for his name is Shame.
But I am Love, and I was wont to be

Alone in this fair garden, till he came
Unasked by night; I am true Love, I fill
The hearts of boy and girl with mutual flame."
Then sighing said the other: "Have thy will;
I am the Love that dare not speak its name."

"Was that poem explained to you?"
"I think that is clear."
"There is no question as to what it means?"
"Most certainly not."
"Is it not clear that the love described relates to natural love and unnatural love?"
"No."
"What is the 'Love that dare not speak its name'?" Gill now asked.
" 'The Love that dare not speak its name' in this century is such a great affection of an elder for a younger man as there was between David and Jonathan, such as Plato made the very basis of his philosophy, and such as you find in the sonnets of Michelangelo and Shakespeare. It is that deep, spiritual affection that is as pure as it is perfect. It dictates and pervades great works of art like those of Shakespeare and Michelangelo, and those two letters of mine, such as they are. It is in this century misunderstood, so much misunderstood that it may be described as the 'Love that dare not speak its name,' and on account of it I am placed where I am now. It is beautiful, it is fine, it is the noblest form of affection. There is nothing unnatural about it. It is intellectual, and it repeatedly exists between an elder and a younger man, where the elder has intellect and the younger man has all the joy, hope, and glamour of life before him. That it should be so, the world does not understand. The world mocks at it and sometimes puts one in the pillory for it."

[*DE PROFUNDIS*]

[Wilde's letter to Douglas begins with an analysis of the events that led to his imprisonment and Douglas's part in them. He continues, as he says, by taking the burden from Douglas and placing it upon himself.]

[January–March 1897]
To Lord Alfred Douglas
H.M. Prison, Reading

EPISTOLA: IN CARCERE ET VINCULIS

I must say to myself that I ruined myself, and that nobody great or small can be ruined except by his own hand. I am quite ready to say so. I am trying to say so, though they may not think it at the present moment. This pitiless indictment I bring without pity against myself. Terrible as was what the world did to me, what I did to myself was far more terrible still.

I was a man who stood in symbolic relations to the art and culture of my age. I had realised this for myself at the very dawn of my manhood, and had forced my age to realise it afterwards. Few men hold such a position in their own lifetime, and have it so acknowledged. It is usually discerned, if discerned at all, by the historian, or the critic, long after both the man and his age have passed away. With me it was different. I felt it myself, and made others feel it. Byron was a symbolic figure, but his relations were to the passion of his age and its weariness of passion. Mine were to something more noble, more permanent, of more vital issue, of larger scope.

The gods had given me almost everything. I had genius, a distinguished name, high social position, brilliancy, intellectual daring; I made art a philosophy and philosophy an art: I altered the minds of men and the colours of things; there was nothing I said or did that did not make people wonder. I took the drama, the most objective form known to art, and made it as personal a mode of expression as the lyric or sonnet; at the same time I widened its range and enriched its characterisation. Drama, novel, poem in prose, poem in rhyme, subtle or fantastic dialogue, whatever I touched, I made beautiful in a new mode of beauty: to truth itself I gave what is false no less than what is true as its rightful province, and showed that the false and the true are merely forms of intellectual existence. I treated art as the supreme reality and life as a mere mode of fiction. I awoke the imagination of my century so that it created myth and legend around me. I summed up all systems in a phrase and all existence in an epigram. Along with these things I had things that were different. But I let myself be lured into long spells of senseless and sensual ease. I amused myself with being a *flaneur*, a dandy, a man of fashion. I surrounded myself with the smaller natures and the meaner minds. I became the spendthrift of my own genius, and to waste an eternal youth gave me a curious joy. Tired of being on the heights, I deliberately went to the depths in the search for new sensation. What the paradox was to me in the sphere of thought, perversity became to me in the sphere of passion. Desire, at the end, was a malady, or a madness, or both. I grew careless of the lives of others. I took pleasure where it pleased me, and passed on. I forgot that every little action of the common day makes or unmakes character, and that therefore what one has done in the secret chamber one has some day to cry aloud on the house-tops. I ceased to be lord over myself. I was no longer the captain of my soul, and did not know it. I allowed pleasure to dominate me. I ended in horrible disgrace. There is only one thing for me now, absolute humility. . . .

Still, in the very fact that people will recognise me wherever I go, and know all about my life, as far as its follies go, I can discern something good for me. It will force on me the necessity of again asserting myself as an artist, and as soon as I possibly can. If I can produce only one beautiful work of art I shall be able to rob malice of its venom, and cowardice of its sneer, and to pluck out the tongue of scorn by the roots.

And if life be, as it surely is, a problem to me, I am no less a problem to life. People must adopt some attitude towards me, and so pass judgment both on themselves and me. I need not say I am not talking of particular individuals. The only people I would care to be with now are artists and people who have suffered: those who know what beauty is, and those who know what sorrow is: nobody else interests me. Nor am I making any demands on life. In all that I have said I am simply concerned with my own mental attitude towards life as a whole; and I feel that not to be ashamed of having been punished is one of the first points I must attain to, for the sake of my own perfection, and because I am so imperfect. . . .

I don't regret for a single moment having lived for pleasure. I did it to the full, as one should do everything that one does. There was no pleasure I did not experience. I threw the pearl of my soul into a cup of wine. I went down the primrose path to the sound of flutes. I lived on honeycomb. But to have continued the same life would have been wrong because it would have been limiting. I had to pass on. The other half of the garden had its secrets for me also. . . . It could not have been otherwise. At every single moment of one's life one is what one is going to be no less than what one has been. Art is a symbol, because man is a symbol. . . .

People used to say of me that I was too individualistic. I must be far more of an individualist than ever I was. I must get far more out of myself than ever I got, and ask for less of the world than ever I asked. Indeed, my ruin came not from too great individualism of life, but from too little. The one disgraceful, unpardonable, and to all time contemptible action of my life was to allow myself to appeal to Society for help and protection. To have made such an appeal would have been from the individualist point of view bad enough, but what excuse can there ever be put forward for having made it? Of course once I had put into motion the forces of Society, Society turned on me and said, "Have you been living all this time in defiance of my laws, and do you now appeal to those laws for protection? You shall have those laws exercised to the full. You shall abide by what you have appealed to." The result is I am in gaol. Certainly no man ever fell so ignobly, and by such ignoble instruments, as I did. I say in *Dorian Gray* somewhere that "A man cannot be too careful in the choice of his enemies." I little thought that it was by a pariah I was to be made a pariah myself.

The Philistine element in life is not the failure to understand art. Charming people, such as fishermen, shepherds, ploughboys, peasants and the like, know nothing about art, and are the very salt of the earth. He is the Philistine who upholds and aids the heavy, cumbrous, blind, mechanical forces of Society, and who does not recognise dynamic force when he meets it either in a man or a movement. People thought it dreadful of me to have entertained at dinner the evil things of life, and to have found pleasure in their company. But then, from the point of view through which I, as an artist in life, approach them they were delightfully suggestive and stimulating. It was like feasting with panthers; the danger was half the excitement. I used to feel as a snake-charmer must feel when he lures the cobra to stir from the painted cloth or reed basket that holds it and makes it spread its hood at his bidding and sway to and fro in the air as a plant sways restfully in a stream. They were to me the brightest of gilded snakes, their poison was part of their perfection. I did not know that when they were to strike at me it was to be at another's piping and at another's pay. I don't feel at all ashamed at having known them, they were intensely interesting; what I do feel ashamed of is the horrible Philistine atmosphere into which I was brought. My business as an artist was with Ariel, I set myself to wrestle with Caliban. . . .

All trials are trials for one's life, just as all sentences are sentences of death; and three times have I been tried. The first time I left the box to be arrested, the second time to be led back to the house of detention, the third time to pass into a prison for two years. Society, as we have constituted it, will have no place for me, has none to offer; but Nature, whose sweet rains fall on unjust and just alike, will have clefts in the rocks where I may hide, and secret valleys in whose silence I may weep undisturbed. She will hang the night with stars so that I may walk abroad in the darkness without stumbling, and send the wind over my footprints so that none may track me to my hurt: she will cleanse me in great waters, and with bitter herbs make me whole. . . .

What lies before me is my past. I have got to make myself look on that with different eyes, to make the world look on it with different eyes, to make God look on it with different eyes. This I cannot do by ignoring it, or slighting it, or praising it, or denying it. It is only to be done fully by accepting it as an inevitable part of the evolution of my life and character: by bowing my head to everything that I have suffered. How far I am away from the true temper of soul, this letter in its changing uncertain moods, its scorn and bitterness, its aspirations and its failures to realise those aspirations, shows you quite clearly. But do not forget in what a terrible school I am sitting at my task. And incomplete, imperfect, as I am, yet from me you may have still much to gain. You came to me to learn the pleasure of life and the pleasure of art. Perhaps I am chosen to teach you something much more wonderful—the meaning of sorrow and its beauty.

Your affectionate friend,

Oscar

# 17. Athletic Love

## English Literature (1896–1969)

The sentencing of Wilde in 1895 cast a shadow across the lives of most of those who might have wanted to reveal their homosexuality or write about it. The major works resisting homophobic law and public opinion—those of Carpenter and of Symonds and Ellis—were subjected to suppression and censorship. Symonds and Ellis's *Sexual Inversion* was effectively banned from publication, Symonds's family insisted that his name be removed from it, and Carpenter's *Love's Coming of Age*, containing his essay on "The Intermediate Sex," was refused publication by his publisher (though later published by the more radical Labour Press). Most writers now preferred to retire from the spotlight generated by Wilde's misfortunes.

When Forster wrote *Maurice* in 1913, the literary energy released by the Uranian poets of the 1880s and 1890s was still to be found in some works published after 1900 by writers like A. E. Housman, E. E. Bradford, John Leslie Barford, and Ralph Chubb, the last of the Uranians whose poems were published up until his death in 1960. However, in 1913 homosexual acts whether in public or in private between adults were still criminal. There were no public organizations in England advocating homosexual reform, and it was rarely spoken of in public or in the press. It is therefore not strange that few of the major homosexual writers of the twentieth century were willing to publicly admit their homosexuality. Most were unwilling to allow what they did write that dealt with homosexuality to be published during their lifetime, and if they were published and were subject to homosexual interpretation, that interpretation was often rejected and denied by the authors themselves. It has to be said that the influence of twentieth-century English homosexual texts on the twentieth-century construction of homosexual identities and on the liberation of homosexuals from the oppression of homophobia cannot be described as either so potent or so profound as is the contribution to American texts written before Stonewall to the rise of an American gay literature. English texts written after 1969 owe much to the American invention of ideals of homosexual liberation. In England, what had to be done had been done in the nineteenth century. The Wilde trial let it be known that to do more could lead to imprisonment, a threat often made and just as often carried out, since large numbers of homosexual men, as well as some homosexual writers, were indeed entrapped, prosecuted, convicted, and imprisoned during the years between 1895 and the passage of a law in 1967 decriminalizing homosexual acts between consenting a adults.

Indeed the British government took strong action against texts that depicted "perversion." In 1918 an attempt was made by the government to suppress a novel by "A. T. Fitzroy" called *Despised and Rejected*. The book is one of the first novels published in England with an openly homosexual theme. The British Museum Library kept its copy locked in the "private case" and did not include its title in the general catalogue. In 1928 Radclyffe Hall's *The Well of Loneliness*, the first novel about a lesbian relationship, was declared by the British courts to be an "obscene libel," and copies of the book were ordered destroyed. Forster's decision not to publish *Maurice* was made against this background of repressive censorship which, he felt, and probably rightly, would have led to the suppression and possible prosecution of his book. British laws against sexually explicit material, or material dealing with homosexuality, remained—and still remain—rigidly homophobic.

Nevertheless, British authors did begin to publish books with oblique homosexual themes. None of them can be said to be so forward-looking as *Maurice*, and between 1918 and the beginning of the 1970s the British gay novel remained a minor, restrained, even respectable, part of British literature, sometimes becoming campily adventurous in the works of Ronald Firbank, or exploring homosexuality in often positive but not especially confrontational fashion, in such books as Angus Wilson's *Hemlock and After*, or Mary Renault's *The Charioteer*, or Julian Mitchell's *Imaginary Toys*, in which homosexuality is presented without moralizing commentary and the homosexual character is accepted by his nonhomosexual friends. British writers seemed willing to keep their books about homosexuals set in the drawing rooms or schools that had traditionally been the site of homosexual encounters in the past, and to avoid, well into the late sixties, the realism and the portrayal of explicit homosexuality that had already entered into American novels.

Nevertheless, writers did not stop writing. In works of A. E. Housman, D. H. Lawrence, T. E. Laurence, W. H. Auden, J. R. Ackerley, Christopher Isherwood, Lytton Strachey, Saki, Siegfried Sassoon, Somerset Maugham, Norman Douglas, Harold Nicholson, E. F. Benson, Stephen Spender, Cyril Connolly, Evelyn Waugh, Noel Coward, and others, strategies were employed in which the love that dared not speak its name suggested itself in a thousand other indirect ways. Homosexuality was the secret that everyone knew, everyone alluded to, and in which it sometimes seemed everyone discreetly participated, yet in self-righteous England homosexuality remained under ban until the sixth decade of the century when, responding at last to the Wolfenden Report of 1953, homosexuality and homosexual acts were finally decriminalized in 1967.

## A. E. Housman (1859–1936)

### POEMS (1896–1936)

During his lifetime, Alfred Edward Housman confided the secret of his homosexuality only to the austere confessional page of poetry. As a scholar of classical Latin, he was famous throughout England and Europe in academic circles. Upon the publication of his first volume of poetry Housman became celebrated by a generation of Englishmen who found in his poetry an Arcadian simplicity, manly virtue, and calm stoicism in the face of adversity that they liked to believe marked Englishmen off from other men. If the atmosphere of controlled despair, the hint of rebellion against society, and even of a bleak atheism was ignored by most of his readers, even more so was an ambiance that spoke passionately of manly love. Housman allowed only some of what he wrote to be published during his life: *A Shropshire Lad* (1896) and *Last Poems* (1922). These poems were selected with an eye to maintaining a secret that only death and posthumous publication would reveal. When read in light of the posthumous poems—*More Poems* (1936) and *Additional Poems* (1939), which were edited by Housman's brother Laurence after Housman's death—his poetry can be seen as a thoughtful and committed, if anguished, exploration of the plight of a homosexual in the twentieth century. Though none of the poetry he published during his lifetime is explicitly homosexual nor even especially homoerotic, those that he did not publish reveal distinctive themes that portray an acute sensibility to love and difference. Difference is a curse, the result of being unwillingly but irrevocably subject to "the foreign laws of God and man" that mark the poet as other and as an outcast.

Difference is also "an ancient evil," an "ill not for mending," the "sickness" of a soul. Yet in (number) XII of *Last Poems*, Housman resoundingly rejects any allegiance to the laws of both God and man. His unrequited but lifelong passion for the handsome and heterosexual Moses Jackson, to whom he confessed that it was Jackson who was responsible for his writing poetry, is present in most of the poems Housman wrote. In nos. XXX and XXXI of *More Poems*, and no. VII of *Additional Poems*, Housman wrote some of the most moving and concisely expressed lyrics in English written by one man to another.

## FROM *A SHROPSHIRE LAD* (1896)

### XV  *Look not in my eyes*

Look not in my eyes, for fear
    They mirror true the sight I see,
And there you find your face too clear
    And love it and be lost like me.
One the long nights through must lie
    Spent in star-defeated sighs,
But why should you as well as I
    Perish? gaze not in my eyes.

A Grecian lad, as I hear tell,
    One that many loved in vain,
Looked into a forest well
    And never looked away again.
There, when the turf in springtime flowers,
    With downward eye and gazes sad,
Stands amid the glancing showers
    A jonquil, not a Grecian lad.

### XXXIII  *If truth in hearts that perish*

If truth in hearts that perish
    Could move the powers on high,
I think the love I bear you
    Should make you not to die.

Sure, sure, if stedfast meaning,
    If single thought could save,
The world might end to-morrow,
    You should not see the grave.

This long and sure-set liking,
    This boundless will to please,
—Oh, you should live for ever
    If there were help in these.

But now, since all is idle,
    To this lost heart be kind,
Ere to a town you journey
    Where friends are ill to find.


XLIV  *Shot? So quick*

Shot? so quick, so clean an ending?
    Oh that was right, lad, that was brave:
Yours was not an ill for mending,
    'Twas best to take it to the grave.

Oh you had forethought, you could reason,
    And saw your road and where it led,
And early wise and brave in season
    Put the pistol to your head.

Oh soon, and better so than later
    After long disgrace and scorn,
You shot dead the household traitor,
    The soul that should not have been born.

Right you guessed the rising morrow
    And scorned to tread the mire you must:
Dust's your wages, son of sorrow,
    But men may come to worse than dust.

Souls undone, undoing others,—
    Long time since the tale began.
You would not live to wrong your brothers:
    Oh lad, you died as fits a man.

Now to your grave shall friend and stranger
    With ruth and some with envy come:
Undishonoured, clear of danger,
    Clean of guilt, pass hence and home.

Turn safe to rest, no dreams, no waking;
    And here, man, here's the wreath I've made:
'Tis not a gift that's worth the taking,
    But wear it and it will not fade.


FROM *LAST POEMS* (1922)

XII  The laws of God
The laws of God, the laws of man,

He may keep that will and can;
Not I: let God and man decree
Laws for themselves and not for me;
And if my ways are not as theirs
Let them mind their own affairs.
Their deeds I judge and much condemn,
Yet when did I make laws for them?
Please yourselves, say I, and they
Need only look the other way.
But no, they will not; they must still
Wrest their neighbour to their will,
And make me dance as they desire
With jail and gallows and hell-fire.
And how am I to face the odds
Of man's bedevilment and God's?
I, a stranger and afraid
In a world I never made.
They will be master, right or wrong;
Though both are foolish, both are strong.
And since, my soul, we cannot fly
To Saturn nor to Mercury,
Keep we must, if keep we can,
These foreign laws of God and man.

FROM *MORE POEMS* (1936, POSTHUMOUS)

*XXX  Shake hands, we never shall be friends*

Shake hands, we shall never be friends, all's over,
      I only vex you the more I try;
All's wrong that ever I've done or said,
And naught to help it in this dull head;
      Shake hands, here's luck, good-bye.

But if you come to a road where danger
      Or guilt or anguish or shame's to share
Be good to the lad that loves you true
And the soul that was born to die for you,
      And whistle and I'll be there.

*XXXI  Because I liked you better*

Because I liked you better
      Than suits a man to say,
It irked you, and I promised
      To throw the thought away.

To put the world between us
   We parted, stiff and dry;
"Good-bye," said you, "forget me."
   "I will, no fear," said I.

If here, where clover whitens
   The dead man's knoll, you pass,
And no tall flower to meet you
   Starts in the trefoiled grass,

Halt by the headstone naming
   The heart no longer stirred,
And say the lad that loved you
   Was one that kept his word.

## FROM *ADDITIONAL POEMS* (INCLUDED IN *COLLECTED POEMS*, 1940)

### VII *He would not stay for me*

He would not stay for me; and who can wonder?
   He would not stay for me to stand and gaze.
I shook his hand and tore my heart in sunder
   And went with half my life about my ways.

### XVIII *Oh who is that young sinner*

Oh who is that young sinner with the handcuffs on his wrist?
And what has he been after that they groan and shake their fists?
And wherefore is he wearing such a conscience-stricken air?
Oh they're taking him to prison for the colour of his hair.

'Tis a shame to human nature, such a head of hair as his;
In the good old time 'twas hanging for the colour that it is;
Though hanging isn't bad enough and flaying would be fair
For the nameless and abominable colour of his hair.

Oh a deal of pains he's taken and a pretty price he's paid
To hide his poll or dye it of a mentionable shade;
But they've pulled the beggar's hat off for the world to see and stare,
And they're haling him to justice for the colour of his hair.

## E. M. Forster (1879–1970)

### FROM *MAURICE* (1913)

Forster claimed that *Maurice* was directly inspired by a visit to Edward Carpenter and Carpenter's lover George Merrill. Carpenter was, Forster recalls, "a rebel appropriate to his age." He was not only a socialist and a poet but "a believer in the Love of Comrades whom he sometimes called Uranians. It was this last aspect of him that attracted me in my loneliness. For a short time he seemed to hold the key to every trouble. I approached him . . . as one approaches a saviour." After his visit, during which, Forster also recalls, George Merrill "touched my backside," thereby uniting Carpenter's idealistic homoerotic theory with direct homosexual sensation, Forster "immediately began to write *Maurice*." The result was a book like no other that had ever been written in England, a story in which a respected and solid member of the upper-middle-class establishment becomes a rebel against birth and class, and enters into a love affair with a social inferior. As Forster puts it: "A happy ending was imperative. I shouldn't have bothered to write otherwise. I determined that in fiction anyway two men should fall in love and remain in it for the forever and ever that fiction allows."

Maurice, the inhabitant of English middle-class suburbia who falls in love with Alec the "lower-class" gamekeeper, is in every way the solid representative of English probity. But into his psychology Forster "dropped an ingredient that puzzles him, and wakes him up, and torments him, and finally saves him." This ingredient is Maurice's love for men. Because of his torment, Maurice becomes exasperated by the "very normality" of his life and his respectability. His comfortable job, his comfortable home, "gradually turn out to be Hell." Maurice realizes, in what his age had come to firmly believe was the crucial and central arena of sexuality, that he is a rebel. There is no alternative for him, Forster argues, but to rebel against society itself and against the "comfortable" symbols of sexual and class repression, and "he must either smash them or be smashed." This revolutionary advocacy is embodied not only in Maurice's love for Alec the gamekeeper, and their subsequent rejection of society, but in Maurice's confrontation with Clive, once his platonic lover at Cambridge who, after a trip to Greece, loses his desire for men and, having become attracted to women, can no longer care for Maurice. Certainly at the end of the book, in order to take his place "in society," Clive rejects homosexual desire and sacrifices his love for Maurice. In the last pages Maurice tells the complacent Clive, now married to a woman who is equally a symbol of middle-class sexual repression, that he has shared everything with Alec, including his body, and that their first nearly sacramental consummation took place in the bedroom of Clive's family home, a bastion of the very society that Forster urges Maurice to smash.

*Maurice* is the first modern homosexual novel, and Alec and Maurice are the first modern homosexual characters in the twentieth-century English novel. *Maurice* predicts what the best homoerotic novels of the twentieth century written before Stonewall would ultimately achieve: confrontation with the intention of changing society, and the construction of a positive identity for homosexual readers that rewrote social myths of sickness, insanity, perversion, and universal effeminacy. Forster's book may well be the first homoerotic text that directly advocates a kind of revolutionary action against what Christopher Isherwood would eventually call the "heterosexual dictatorship" in order to eradicate sexual and social oppression.

## FROM CHAPTERS 43, 44, 46

[In chapter 43, Maurice meets Alec in the British Museum, to which Alec has summoned him with hints of blackmail. In chapter 44 they spend the night together. In these, the climactic moments of the book, Forster creates a tense confrontation that addresses one of the central facts of English homosexual life, the attraction between men of different classes. Instead of the traditional resolution wherein the upper-class male introduces his young man for a time to the fringes of his society and then usually rejects him, Forster reverses the pattern by having Maurice, the upper-middle-class Englishman, reject the values of his class, realizing that he must do so, first in bed with Alec in chapter 44, and then in chapter 46 on the playing fields, as it were, of his own world, when he reveals everything to Clive in an act of defiant coming out.]

## Chapter 43

The rain was coming down in its old fashion, tapping on a million roofs and occasionally effecting an entry. It beat down the smoke, and caused the fumes of petrol and the smell of wet clothes to linger mixed on the streets of London. In the great forecourt of the Museum it could fall uninterruptedly, plumb onto the draggled doves and the helmets of the police. So dark was the afternoon that some of the lights had been turned on inside, and the great building suggested a tomb, miraculously illuminated by spirits of the dead.

Alec arrived first, dressed no longer in corduroys but in a new blue suit and bowler hat—part of his outfit for the Argentine. He sprang, as he had boasted, of a respectable family—publicans, small tradesmen—and it was only by accident that he had appeared as an untamed son of the woods. Indeed, he liked the woods and the fresh air and water, he liked them better than anything and he liked to protect or destroy life, but woods contain no "openings," and young men who want to get on must leave them. He was determined in a blind way to get on now. Fate had placed a snare in his hands, and he meant to set it. He tramped over the courtyard, then took the steps in a series of springs; having won the shelter of the portico he stood motionless, except for the flicker of his eyes. These sudden changes of pace were typical of the man, who always advanced as a skirmisher, was always "on the spot" as Clive had phrased it in the written testimonial; "during the five months A. Scudder was in my service I found him prompt and assiduous": qualities that he proposed to display now. When the victim drove up he became half cruel, half frightened. Gentlemen he knew, mates he knew; what class of creature was Mr Hall who said, "Call me Maurice"? Narrowing his eyes to slits, he stood as though waiting for orders outside the front porch at Penge.

Maurice approached the most dangerous day of his life without any plan at all, yet something kept rippling in his mind like muscles beneath a healthy skin. He was not supported by pride but he did feel fit, anxious to play the game, and, as an Englishman should, hoped that his opponent felt fit too. He wanted to be decent, he wasn't afraid. When he saw Alec's face glowing through the dirty air his own tingled slightly, and he determined not to strike until he was struck.

"Here you are," he said, raising a pair of gloves to his hat. "This rain's the limit. Let's have a talk inside."

"Where you wish."

Maurice looked at him with some friendliness, and they entered the building. As they did so, Alec raised his head and sneezed like a lion.

"Got a chill? It's the weather."

"What's all this place?" he asked.

"Old things belonging to the nation." They paused in the corridor of Roman emperors.

"Yes, it's bad weather. There've only been two fine days. And one fine night," he added mischievously, surprising himself.

But Alec didn't catch on. It wasn't the opening he wanted. He was waiting for signs of fear, that the menial in him might strike. He pretended not to understand the allusion, and sneezed again. The roar echoed down vestibules, and his face, convulsed and distorted, took a sudden appearance of hunger.

"I'm glad you wrote to me the second time. I liked both your letters. I'm not offended—you've never done anything wrong. It's all your mistake about cricket and the rest. I'll tell you straight out I enjoyed being with you, if that's the trouble. Is it? I want you to tell me. I just don't know."

"What's here? *That's* no mistake." He touched his breast pocket, meaningly. "Your writing. And you and the squire—*that's* no mistake—some may wish as it was one."

"Don't drag in that," said Maurice, but without indignation, and it struck him as odd that he had none, and that even the Clive of Cambridge had lost sanctity.

"Mr Hall—you reckernize it wouldn't very well suit you if certain things came out, I suppose."

Maurice found himself trying to get underneath the words.

He continued, feeling his way to a grip. "What's more, I've always been a respectable young fellow until you called me into your room to amuse yourself. It don't hardly seem fair that a gentleman should drag you down. At least that's how my brother sees it." He faltered as he spoke these last words. "My brother's waiting outside now as a matter of fact. He wanted to come and speak to you hisself, he's been scolding me shocking, but I said, 'No Fred no, Mr Hall's a gentleman and can be trusted to behave like one, so you leave 'im to me,' I said, 'and Mr Durham, he's a gentleman too, always was and always will be.' "

"With regard to Mr Durham," said Maurice, feeling inclined to speak on this point: "It's quite correct that I cared for him and he for me once, but he changed, and now he doesn't care any more for me nor I for him. It's the end."

"End o' what?"

"Of our friendship."

"Mr Hall, have you heard what I was saying?"

"I hear everything you say," said Maurice thoughtfully, and continued in exactly the same tone: "Scudder, why do you think it's 'natural' to care both for women and men? You wrote so in your letter. It isn't natural for me. I have really got to think that 'natural' only means oneself."

The man seemed interested. "Couldn't you get a kid of your own, then?" he asked, roughening.

"I've been to two doctors about it. Neither were any good."

"So you can't?"

"No, I can't."

"Want one?" he asked, as if hostile.

"It's not much use wanting."

"I could marry tomorrow if I like," he bragged. While speaking, he caught sight of a winged Assyrian bull, and his expression altered into naive wonder. "He's big enough, isn't he," he remarked. "They must have owned wonderful machinery to make a thing like that."

"I expect so," said Maurice, also impressed by the bull. "I couldn't tell you. Here seems to be another one."

"A pair, so to speak. Would these have been ornaments?"

"This one has five legs."

"So's mine. A curious idea." Standing each by his monster, they looked at each other, and smiled. Then his face hardened again and he said, "Won't do, Mr Hall. I see your game, but you don't fool me twice, and you'll do better to have a friendly talk with me rather than wait for Fred, I can tell you. You've had your fun and you've got to pay up." He looked handsome as he threatened—including the pupils of his eyes, which were evil. Maurice gazed into them gently but keenly. And nothing resulted from the outburst at all. It fell away like a flake of mud. Murmuring something about "leaving you to think this over," he sat down on a bench. Maurice joined him there shortly. And it was thus for nearly twenty minutes: they kept wandering from room to room as if in search of something. They would peer at a goddess or vase, then move at a single impulse, and their unison was the stranger because on the surface they were at war. Alec recommenced his hints—horrible, reptilian—but somehow they did not pollute the intervening silences, and Maurice failed to get afraid or angry, and only regretted that any human being should have got into such a mess. When he chose to reply their eyes met, and his smile was sometimes reflected on the lips of his foe. The belief grew that the actual situation was a blind—a practical joke almost—and concealed something real, that either desired. Serious and good-tempered, he continued to hold his own, and if he made no offensive it was because his blood wasn't warm. To set it moving, a shock from without was required, and chance administered this.

He was bending over a model of the Acropolis with his forehead a little wrinkled and his lips murmuring, "I see, I see, I see." A gentleman near overheard him, started, peered through strong spectacles, and said "Surely! I may forget faces but never a voice. Surely! You are one of our old boys." It was Mr Ducie.

Maurice did not reply. Alec sidled up closer to participate.

"Surely you were at Mr Abrahams's school. Now wait! Wait! Don't tell me your name. I want to remember it. I will remember it. You're not Sanday, you're not Gibbs. I know. I know. It's Wimbleby."

How like Mr Ducie to get the facts just wrong! To his own name Maurice would have responded, but he now had the inclination to lie; he was tired of their endless inaccuracy, he had suffered too much from it. He replied, "No, my name's Scudder."

The correction flew out as the first that occurred to him. It lay ripe to be used, and as he uttered it he knew why. But at the instant of enlightenment Alec himself spoke. "It isn't," he said to Mr Ducie, "and I've a serious charge to bring against this gentleman."

"Yes, awfully serious," remarked Maurice, and rested his hand on Alec's shoulder, so that the fingers touched the back of the neck, doing this merely because he wished to do it, not for another reason.

Mr Ducie did not take notice. An unsuspicious man, he assumed some uncouth joke. The dark gentlemanly fellow couldn't be Wimbleby if he said he wasn't. He said, "I'm extremely sorry, sir, it's so seldom I make a mistake," and then, determined to show he was not an old fool, he addressed the silent pair on the subject of the British Museum—not merely a collection of relics but a place round which one could take—er—the less fortunate, quite so—a stimulating place—it raised questions even in the minds of boys—which one answered—no doubt inadequately; until a patient voice said, "Ben, we are waiting," and Mr Ducie rejoined his wife. As he did so Alec jerked away and muttered, "That's all right. . . . I won't trouble you now."

"Where are you going with your serious charge?" said Maurice, suddenly formidable.

"Couldn't say." He looked back, his colouring stood out against the heroes, perfect but bloodless, who had never known bewilderment or infamy. "Don't you worry—I'll never harm you now, you've got too much pluck."

"Pluck be damned," said Maurice, with a plunge into anger.

"It'll all go no further—" He struck his own mouth. "I don't know what came over me, Mr Hall; I don't want to harm you, I never did."

"You blackmailed me."

"No, sir, no . . ."

"You did."

"Maurice, listen, I only . . ."

"Maurice am I?'"

"You called me Alec. . . . I'm as good as you."

"I don't find you are!" There was a pause; before the storm; then he burst out: "By God, if you'd split on me to Mr Ducie, I'd have broken you. It might have cost me hundreds, but I've got them, and the police always back my sort against yours. You don't know. We'd have got you into quod, for blackmail, after which—I'd have blown out my brains."

"Killed yourself? Death?"

"I should have known by that time that I loved you. Too late . . . everything's always too late." The rows of old statues tottered, and he heard himself add, "I don't mean anything, but come outside, we can't talk here." They left the enormous and overheated building, they passed the library, supposed catholic, seeking darkness and rain. On the portico Maurice stopped and said bitterly, "I forgot. Your brother?"

"He's down at father's—doesn't know a word—I was but threatening—"

"—for blackmail."

"Could you but understand . . ." He pulled out Maurice's note. "Take it if you like. . . . I don't want it . . . never did. . . . I suppose this is the end."

Assuredly it wasn't that. Unable to part yet ignorant of what could next come, they strode raging through the last glimmering of the sordid day; night, ever one in her quality, came finally, and Maurice recovered his self-control and could look at the new material that passion had gained for him. In a deserted square, against railings that encircled some trees, they came to a halt, and he began to discuss their crisis.

But as he grew calm the other grew fierce. It was as if Mr Ducie had established some infuriating inequality between them, so that one struck as soon as his fellow tired of striking. Alec said savagely, "It rained harder than this in the boathouse, it was yet colder. Why did you not come?"

"Muddle."

"I beg your pardon?"

"You've to learn I'm always in a muddle. I didn't come or write because I wanted to get away from you without wanting. You won't understand. You kept dragging me back and I got awfully frightened. I felt you when I tried to get some sleep at the doctor's. You came hard at me. I knew something was evil but couldn't tell what, so kept pretending it was you."

"What was it?'"

"The—situation."

"I don't follow this. Why did you not come to the boathouse?"

"My fear—and your trouble has been fear too. Ever since the cricket match you've let yourself get afraid of me. That's why we've been trying to down one another so and are still."

"I wouldn't take a penny from you, I wouldn't hurt your little finger," he growled, and rattled the bars that kept him from the trees.

"But you're still trying hard to hurt me in my mind."

"Why do you go and say you love me?"

"Why do you call me Maurice?"

"Oh let's give over talking. Here—" and he held out his hand. Maurice took it, and they knew at that moment the greatest triumph ordinary man can win. Physical love means reaction, being panic in essence, and Maurice saw now how natural it was that their primitive abandonment at Penge should have led to peril. They knew too little about each other—and too much. Hence fear. Hence cruelty. And he rejoiced because he had understood Alec's infamy through his own—glimpsing, not for the first time, the genius who hides in man's tormented soul. Not as a hero, but as a comrade, had he stood up to the bluster, and found childishness behind it, and behind that something else.

Presently the other spoke. Spasms of remorse and apology broke him; he was as one who throws off a poison. Then, gathering health, he began to tell his friend everything, no longer ashamed. He spoke of his relations. . . . He too was embedded in class. No one knew he was in London—Penge thought he was at his father's, his father at Penge—it had been difficult, very. Now he ought to go home—see his brother with whom he returned to the Argentine: his brother connected with trade, and his brother's wife; and he mingled some brag, as those whose education is not literary must. He came of a respectable family, he repeated, he bowed down to no man, not he, he was as good as any gentleman. But while be bragged his arm was gaining Maurice's. They deserved such a caress—the feeling was strange. Words died away, abruptly to recommence. It was Alec who ventured them.

"Stop with me."

Maurice swerved and their muscles clipped. By now they were in love with one another consciously.

"Sleep the night with me. I know a place."

"I can't, I've an engagement," said Maurice, his heart beating violently. A formal dinner party awaited him of the sort that brought work to his firm and that he couldn't possibly cut. He had almost forgotten its existence. "I have to leave you now and get changed. But look here: Alec, be reasonable. Meet me another evening instead—any day."

"Can't come to London again—father or Mr Ayres will be passing remarks."

"What does it matter if they do?"

"What's your engagement matter?"

They were silent again. Then Maurice said in affectionate yet dejected tones, "All right. To Hell with it," and they passed on together in the rain.

Chapter 44

"Alec, wake up." An arm twitched.

"Time we talked plans."

He snuggled closer, more awake than he pretended, warm, sinewy, happy. Happiness overwhelmed Maurice too. He moved, felt the answering grip, and forgot what he wanted to say. Light drifted in upon them from the outside world where it was still raining. A strange hotel, a casual refuge protected them from their enemies a little longer.

"Time to get up, boy. It's morning."

"Git up then."

"How can I the way you hold me!"

"Aren't yer a fidget, I'll learn you to fidget." He wasn't deferential any more. The British Museum had cured that. This was 'oliday, London with Maurice, all troubles over, and he wanted to drowse and waste time, and tease and make love.

Maurice wanted the same, what's pleasanter, but the oncoming future distracted him, the gathering light made cosiness unreal. Something had to be said and settled. O for the night that was ending, for the sleep and the wakefulness, the toughness and tenderness mixed, the sweet temper, the safety in darkness. Would such a night ever return?

"You all right, Maurice?"—for he had sighed. "You comfortable? Rest your head on me more, the way you like more . . . that's it more, and Don't You Worry. You're With Me. Don't Worry."

Yes, he was in luck, no doubt of it. Scudder had proved honest and kind. He was lovely to be with, a treasure, a charmer, a find in a thousand, the longed-for dream. But was he brave?

"Nice you and me like this . . ." the lips so close now that it was scarcely speech. "Who'd have thought. . . . First time I ever seed you I thought, 'Wish I and that one . . .' just like that . . . 'wouldn't I and him . . .' and it is so."

"Yes, and that's why we've got to fight."

"Who wants to fight?" He sounded annoyed. "There's bin enough fighting."

"All the world's against us. We've got to pull ourselves together and make plans, while we can."

"What d'you want to go and say a thing like that for, and spoil it all?"

"Because it has to be said. We can't allow things to go wrong and hurt us again the way they did down at Penge."

Alec suddenly scrubbed at him with the sun-roughened back of a hand and said, "That hurt, didn't it, or oughter. That's how I fight." It did hurt a little, and stealing into the foolery was a sort of resentment. "Don't talk to me about Penge," he went on. "Oo! Mah! Penge where I was always a servant and Scudder do this and

Scudder do that and the old lady, what do you think she once said? She said, 'Oh would you most kindly of your goodness post this letter for me, what's your name?' What's yer name! Every day for six months I come up to Clive's bloody front porch door for orders, and his mother don't know my name. She's a bitch. I said to 'er, 'What's yer name? Fuck yer name.' I nearly did too. Wish I 'ad too. Maurice, you wouldn't believe how servants get spoken to. It's too shocking for words. That Archie London you're so set on is just as bad, and so are you, so are you. 'Haw my man' and all that. You've no idea how you nearly missed getting me. Near as nothing I never climbed that ladder when you called, he don't want me really, and I went flaming mad when you didn't turn up at the boathouse as I ordered. Too grand! We'll see. Boathouse was a place I always fancied. I'd go down for a smoke before I'd ever heard of you, unlock it easy, got the key on me still as a matter of fact . . . boathouse, looking over the pond from the boathouse, very quiet, now and then a fish jump and cushions the way I arrange them."

He was silent, having chattered himself out. He had begun rough and gay and somehow factitious, then his voice had died away into sadness as though truth had risen to the surface of the water and was unbearable.

"We'll meet in your boathouse yet," Maurice said.

"No, we won't." He pushed him away, then heaved, pulled him close, put forth violence, and embraced as if the world was ending. "You'll remember that anyway." He got out and looked down out of the grayness, his arms hanging empty. It was as if he wished to be remembered thus. "I could easy have killed you."

"Or I you."

"Where's my clothes and that gone?" He seemed dazed. "It's so late. I h'aint got a razor even, I didn't reckon staying the night. . . . I ought—I got to catch a train at once or Fred'll be thinking things."

"Let him."

"My goodness if Fred seed you and me just now."

"Well, he didn't."

"Well, he might have—what I mean is, tomorrow's Thursday isn't it, Friday's the packing, Saturday the *Normannia* sails from Southampton, so it's goodbye to Old England."

"You mean that you and I shan't meet again after now."

"That's right. You've got it quite correct."

And if it wasn't still raining! Wet morning after yesterday's downpour, wet on the roofs and the Museum, at home and on the greenwood. Controlling himself and choosing his words very carefully, Maurice said, "This is just what I want to talk about. Why don't we arrange so as we do meet again?"

"How do you mean?'"

"Why don't you stay on in England?"

Alec whizzed round, terrified. Half naked, he seemed also half human. "Stay?" he snarled. "Miss my boat, are you daft? Of all the bloody rubbish I ever heard. Ordering me about again, eh, you would."

"It's a chance in a thousand we've met, we'll never have the chance again and you know it. Stay with me. We love each other."

"I dessay, but that's no excuse to act silly. Stay with you and how and where? What'd your Ma say if she saw me all rough and ugly the way I am?"

"She never will see you. I shan't live at my home."

"Where will you live?"

"With you."

"Oh, will you? No thank you. My people wouldn't take to you one bit and I don't blame them. And how'd you run your job, I'd like to know?"

"I shall chuck it."

"Your job in the city what gives you your money and position? You can't chuck a job."

"You can when you mean to," said Maurice gently. "You can do anything once you know what it is." He gazed at the grayish light that was becoming yellowish. Nothing surprised him in this talk. What he could not conjecture was its outcome. "I shall get work with you," he brought out: the moment to announce this had now come.

"What work?"

"We'll find out."

"Find out and starve out."

"No. There'll be enough money to keep us while we have a look round. I'm not a fool, nor are you. We won't be starving. I've thought out that much, while I was awake in the night and you weren't."

There was a pause. Alec went on more politely: "Wouldn't work, Maurice. Ruin of us both, can't you see, you same as myself."

"I don't know. Might be. Mightn't. 'Class.' I don't know. I know what we do today. We clear out of here and get a decent breakfast and we go down to Penge or whatever you want and see that Fred of yours. You tell him you've changed your mind about emigrating and are taking a job with Mr Hall instead. I'll come with you. I don't care. I'll see anyone, face anything. If they want to guess, let them. I'm fed up. Tell Fred to cancel your ticket, I'll repay for it and that's our start of getting free. Then we'll do the next thing. It's a risk, so's everything else, and we'll only live once."

Alec laughed cynically and continued to dress. His manner resembled yesterday's, though he didn't blackmail. "Yours is the talk of someone who's never had to earn his living," he said. "You sort of trap me with I love you or whatever it is and then offer to spoil my career. Do you realize I've got a definite job awaiting me in the Argentine? Same as you've got here. Pity the *Normannia*'s leaving Saturday, still facts is facts isn't it, all my kit bought as well as my ticket and Fred and wife expecting me."

Maurice saw through the brassiness to the misery behind it, but this time what was the use of insight? No amount of insight would prevent the *Normannia* from sailing. He had lost. Suffering was certain for him, though it might soon end for Alec; when he got out to his new life he would forget his escapade with a gentleman and in time he would marry. Shrewd working-class youngster who knew where his interests lay, he had already crammed his graceful body into his hideous blue suit. His face stuck out of it red, his hands brown. He plastered his hair flat. "Well, I'm off," he said, and as if that wasn't enough said, "Pity we ever met really if you come to think of it."

"That's all right too," said Maurice, looking away from him as he unbolted the door.

"You paid for this room in advance, didn't you, so they won't stop me down-stairs? I don't want no unpleasantness to finish with."

"That's all right too." He heard the door shut and he was alone. He waited for the beloved to return. Inevitable that wait. Then his eyes began to smart, and he knew from experience what was coming. Presently he could control himself. He got up and went out, did some telephoning and explanations, placated his mother, apologized to his host, got himself shaved and trimmed up, and attended the office as usual. Masses of work awaited him. Nothing had changed in his life. Nothing remained in it. He was back with his loneliness as it had been before Clive, as it was after Clive, and would now be for ever. He had failed, and that wasn't the sad-dest: he had seen Alec fail. In a way they were one person. Love had failed. Love was an emotion through which you occasionally enjoyed yourself. It could not do things.

## Chapter 46

Dissatisfied with his printed appeal to the electors—it struck him as too patron-izing for these times—Clive was trying to alter the proofs when Simcox announced, "Mr Hall." The hour was extremely late, and the night dark; all traces of a magnificent sunset had disappeared from the sky. He could see nothing from the porch though he heard abundant noises; his friend, who had refused to come in, was kicking up the gravel, and throwing pebbles against the shrubs and walls.

"Hullo Maurice, come in. Why this thusness?" He asked, a little annoyed, and not troubling to smile since his face was in shadow. "Good to see you back, hope you're better. Unluckily I'm a bit occupied, but the Russet Room's not. Come in and sleep here as before. So glad to see you."

"I've only a few minutes, Clive."

"Look here man, that's fantastic." He advanced into the darkness hospitably, still holding his proof sheets. "Anne'll be furious with me if you don't stay. It's awfully nice you turning up like this. Excuse me if I work at unimportancies for a bit now." Then he detected a core of blackness in the surrounding gloom, and, suddenly uneasy, exclaimed, "I hope nothing's wrong.

"Pretty well everything . . . what you'd call."

Now Clive put politics aside, for he knew that it must be the love affair, and he prepared to sympathize, though he wished the appeal had come when he was less busy. His sense of proportion supported him. He led the way to the deserted alley behind the laurels, where evening primroses gleamed, and embossed with faint yel-low the walls of night. Here they would be most solitary. Feeling for a bench, he reclined full length on it, put his hands behind his head, and said, "I'm at your ser-vice, but my advice is sleep the night here, and consult Anne in the morning."

"I don't want your advice."

"Well, as you like of course there, but you've been so friendly in telling us about your hopes, and where a woman is in question I would always consult another woman, particularly where she has Anne's almost uncanny insight."

The blossoms opposite disappeared and reappeared, and again Clive felt that his friend, swaying to and fro in front of them, was essential night. A voice said, "It's miles worse for you than that; I'm in love with your gamekeeper"—a remark so unexpected and meaningless to him that he said "Mrs Ayres?" and sat up stupidly.

"No. Scudder."

"Look out," cried Clive, with a glance at darkness. Reassured, he said stiffly, "What a grotesque announcement."

"Most grotesque," the voice echoed, "but I felt after all I owe you I ought to come and tell you about Alec."

Clive had only grasped the minimum. He supposed "Scudder" was a *façon de parler*, as one might say "Ganymede," for intimacy with any social inferior was unthinkable to him. As it was, he felt depressed, and offended, for he had assumed Maurice was normal during the last fortnight, and so encouraged Anne's intimacy. "We did anything we could," he said, "and if you want to repay what you 'owe' us, as you call it, you won't dally with morbid thoughts. I'm so disappointed to hear you talk of yourself like that. You gave me to understand that the land through the look-ing-glass was behind you at last, when we thrashed out the subject that night in the Russet Room."

"When you brought yourself to kiss my hand," added Maurice, with deliberate bitterness.

"Don't allude to that," he flashed, not for the first and last time, and for a moment causing the outlaw to love him. Then he relapsed into intellectualism. "Maurice—oh, I'm more sorry for you than I can possibly say, and I do, do beg you to resist the return of this obsession. It'll leave you for good if you do. Occupation, fresh air, your friends. . . ."

"As I said before, I'm not here to get advice, nor to talk about thoughts and ideas either. I'm flesh and blood, if you'll condescend to such low things—"

"Yes, quite right; I'm such a theorist, I know."

"—and'll mention Alec by his name."

It recalled to both of them the situation of a year back, but it was Clive who winced at the example now. "If Alec is Scudder, he is in point of fact no longer in my service or even in England. He sailed for Buenos Aires this very day. Go on though. I'm reconciled to reopening the subject if I can be of the least help."

Maurice blew out his cheeks, and began picking the flowerets off a tall stalk. They vanished one after another, like candles that the night has extinguished. "I have shared with Alec," he said after deep thought.

"Shared what?"

"All I have. Which includes my body."

Clive sprang up with a whimper of disgust. He wanted to smite the monster, and flee, but he was civilized, and wanted it feebly. After all, they were Cambridge men . . . pillars of society both; he must not show violence. And he did not; he remained quiet and helpful to the very end. But his thin, sour disapproval, his dogmatism, the stupidity of his heart, revolted Maurice, who could only have respected hatred.

"I put it offensively," he went on, "but I must make sure you understand. Alec slept with me in the Russet Room that night when you and Anne were away."

"Maurice—oh, good God!"

"Also in town. Also—" here he stopped.

Even in his nausea Clive turned to a generalization—it was part of the mental vagueness induced by his marriage. "But surely—the sole excuse for any relation-ship between men is that it remain purely platonic."

"I don't know. I've come to tell you what I did." Yes, that was the reason of his visit. It was the closing of a book that would never be read again, and better close such a book than leave it lying about to get dirtied. The volume of their past must be restored to its shelf, and here, here was the place, amid darkness and perishing flowers. He owed it to Alec also. He could suffer no mixing of the old in the new. All compromise was perilous, because furtive, and, having finished his confession, he must disappear from the world that had brought him up. "I must tell you too what he did," he went on, trying to keep down his joy. "He's sacrificed his career for my sake . . . without a guarantee I'll give up anything for him . . . and I should-n't have earlier. . . . I'm always slow at seeing. I don't know whether that's platonic of him or not, but it's what he did."

"How sacrifice?"

"I've just been to see him off—he wasn't there—"

"Scudder missed his boat?" cried the squire with indignation. "These people are impossible." Then he stopped, faced by the future. "Maurice, Maurice," he said with some tenderness. "Maurice, quo vadis? You're going mad. You've lost all sense of—May I ask whether you intend—"

"No, you may not ask," interrupted the other. "You belong to the past. I'll tell you everything up to this moment—not a word beyond."

"Maurice, Maurice, I care a little bit for you, you know, or I wouldn't stand what you have told me."

Maurice opened his hand. Luminous petals appeared in it. "You care for me a little bit, I do think," he admitted, "but I can't hang all my life on a little bit. You don't. You hang yours on Anne. You don't worry whether your relation with her is platonic or not, you only know it's big enough to hang a life on. I can't hang mine on to the five minutes you spare me from her and politics. You'll do anything for me except see me. That's been it for this whole year of Hell. You'll make me free of the house, and take endless bother to marry me off, because that puts me off your hands. You do care a little for me, I know"—for Clive had protested—"but nothing to speak of, and you don't love me. I was yours once till death if you'd cared to keep me, but I'm someone else's now—I can't hang about whining for ever—and he's mine in a way that shocks you, but why don't you stop being shocked, and attend to your own happiness?"

"Who taught you to talk like this?" Clive gasped.

"You, if anyone."

"I? It's appalling you should attribute such thoughts to me," pursued Clive. Had he corrupted an inferior's intellect? He could not realize that he and Maurice were alike descended from the Clive of two years ago, the one by respectability, the other by rebellion, nor that they must differentiate further. It was a cesspool, and one breath from it at the election would ruin him. But he must not shrink from his duty. He must rescue his old friend. A feeling of heroism stole over him; and he began to wonder how Scudder could be silenced and whether he would prove extortion-ate. It was too late to discuss ways and means now, so he invited Maurice to dine with him the following week in his club up in town.

A laugh answered. He had always liked his friend's laugh, and at such a moment the soft rumble of it reassured him; it suggested happiness and security. "That's right," he said, and went so far as to stretch his hand into a bush of laurels. "That's better than making me a long set speech, which convinces neither yourself nor me." His last words were "Next Wednesday, say at 7.45. Dinner—jacket's enough, as you know."

They were his last words, because Maurice had disappeared thereabouts, leaving no trace of his presence except a little pile of the petals of evening primrose, which mourned from the ground like an expiring fire. To the end of his life Clive was not sure of the exact moment of departure, and with the approach of old age he grew uncertain whether the moment had yet occurred. The Blue Room would glimmer, ferns undulate. Out of some external Cambridge his friend began beckoning to him, clothed in the sun, and shaking out the scents and sounds of the May term.

But at the time he was merely offended at a discourtesy, and compared it with similar lapses in the past. He did not realize that this was the end, without twilight or compromise, that he should never cross Maurice's track again, nor speak to those who had seen him. He waited for a little in the alley, then returned to the house, to correct his proofs and to devise some method of concealing the truth from Anne.

## From Forster's "Terminal Note" to *Maurice* (1960)

In its original form, which it still almost retains, *Maurice* dates from 1913. It was the direct result of a visit to Edward Carpenter at Milthorpe. Carpenter had a prestige which cannot be understood today. He was a rebel appropriate to his age. He was sentimental and a little sacramental, for he had begun life as a clergyman. He was a socialist who ignored industrialism and a simple-lifer with an independent income and a Whitmannic poet whose nobility exceeded his strength and, finally, he was a believer in the Love of Comrades, whom he sometimes called Uranians. It was this last aspect of him that attracted me in my loneliness. For a short time he seemed to hold the key to every trouble. I approached him through Lowes Dickinson, and as one approaches a saviour.

It must have been on my second or third visit to the shrine that the spark was kindled and he and his comrade George Merrill combined to make a profound impression on me and to touch a creative spring. George Merrill also touched my backside—gently and just above the buttocks. I believe he touched most people's. The sensation was unusual and I still remember it, as I remember the position of a long vanished tooth. It was as much psychological as physical. It seemed to go straight through the small of my back into my ideas, without involving my thoughts. If it really did this, it would have acted in strict accordance with Carpenter's yogified mysticism, and would prove that at that precise moment I had conceived.

I then returned to Harrogate, where my mother was taking a cure, and immediately began to write *Maurice*. No other of my books has started off in this way. The general plan, the three characters, the happy ending for two of them, all rushed into my pen. And the whole thing went through without a hitch. It was finished in 1914. The friends, men and women, to whom I showed it liked it. But they were carefully picked. It has not so far had to face the critics or the public, and I have myself been too much involved in it, and for too long, to judge.

A happy ending was imperative. I shouldn't have bothered to write otherwise. I was determined that in fiction anyway two men should fall in love and remain in it for the ever and ever that fiction allows, and in this sense Maurice and Alec still roam the greenwood. I dedicated it "To a Happier Year" and not altogether vainly. Happiness is its keynote—which by the way has had an unexpected result: it has made the book more difficult to publish. Unless the Wolfenden Report becomes law, it will probably have to remain in manuscript. If it ended unhappily, with a lad dangling from a noose or with a suicide pact, all would be well, for there is no pornography or seduction of minors. But the lovers get away unpunished and consequently recommend crime. Mr Borenius is too incompetent to catch them, and the only penalty society exacts is an exile they gladly embrace. . . .

## HOMOSEXUALITY

Note in conclusion on a word hitherto unmentioned. Since *Maurice* was written there has been a change in the public attitude here: the change from ignorance and terror to familiarity and contempt. It is not the change towards which Edward Carpenter had worked. He had hoped for the generous recognition of an emotion and for the reintegration of something primitive into the common stock. And I, though less optimistic, had supposed that knowledge would bring understanding. We had not realized that what the public really loathes in homosexuality is not the thing itself but having to think about it. If it could be slipped into our midst unnoticed, or legalized overnight by a decree in small print, there would be few protests. Unfortunately it can only be legalized by Parliament, and Members of Parliament are obliged to think or to appear to think. Consequently the Wolfenden recommendations will be indefinitely rejected, police prosecutions will continue and Clive on the bench will continue to sentence Alec in the dock. Maurice may get off.

*September 1960*

## Wilfrid Owen (1893–1918)

Five poems only were published during Owen's brief lifetime. His friendship with the homosexual poet Sigfried Sassoon, the counsel Sassoon gave him in the craft of verse, and his introduction by Sassoon into the circle surrounding Edward Carpenter may have allowed Owen to come to terms with a homosexuality that has never been proven and upon which he may never have acted, but which informs his poetry which, like Housman's, is rich with an all-male ambiance and filled with description, praise, and half-concealed longing for the beauty of doomed young men even while describing the terrors and tragic loss of the battlefield. Owen was killed in France in World War I.

*To Eros*

In that I loved you, Love, I worshipped you,
In that I worshipped well, I sacrificed

All of most worth. I bound and burnt and slew
Old peaceful lives; frail flowers; firm friends; and Christ.

I slew all falser loves; I slew all true,
That I might nothing love but your truth, Boy.
Fair fame I cast away as bridegrooms do
Their wedding garments in their haste of joy.

But when I fell upon your sandalled feet,
You laughed; you loosed away my lips; you rose.
I heard the singing of your wing's retreat;
Far-flown, I watched you flush the Olympian snows
Beyond my hoping. Starkly I returned
To stare upon the ash of all I burned.

*Music (1916–17)*

I have been urged by earnest violins
And drunk their mellow sorrows to the slake
Of all my sorrows and my thirsting sins.
My heart has beaten for a brave drum's sake.
Huge chords have wrought me mighty: I have hurled
Thuds of God's thunder. And with old winds pondered
Over the curse of this chaotic world,
With low lost winds that maundered as they wandered.

I have been gay with trivial fifes that laugh;
And songs more sweet than possible things are sweet;
And gongs, and oboes. Yet I guessed not half
Life's sympathy till I had made hearts beat,
And touched Love's body into trembling cries,
And blown my love's lips into laughs and sighs.

*Anthem for a Doomed Youth*

What passing-bells for these who die as cattle?
Only the monstrous anger of the guns.
    Only the stuttering rifles' rapid rattle
Can patter out their hasty orisons.
No mockeries for them from prayers or bells,
    Nor any voice of mourning save the choirs,—
The shrill, demented choirs of wailing shells;
    And bugles calling for them from sad shires.

What candles may be held to speed them all?
    Not in the hands of boys, but in their eyes

Shall shine the holy glimmers of good-byes.
　　The pallor of girls' brows shall be their pall;
Their flowers the tenderness of silent minds,
And each slow dusk a drawing-down of blinds.


*To My Friend (With an Identity Disc)*

If ever I had dreamed of my dead name
High in the heart of London, unsurpassed
By Time for ever, and the Fugitive, Fame,
There seeking a long sanctuary at last,—

Or if I onetime hoped to hide its shame,
Shame of success, and sorrow of defeats,—
Under those holy cypresses, the same
That shade always the quiet place of Keats,

Now rather thank I God there is no risk
Of gravers scoring it with florid screed.
Let my inscription be this soldier's disc. . . .
Wear it, sweet friend, inscribe no date nor deed.
But may thy heart-beat kiss it, night and day,
Until the name grow blurred and fade away.


# D. H. Lawrence (1885–1930)

### PROLOGUE TO *WOMEN IN LOVE* (1921)

The acquaintance between the two men was slight and insignificant. Yet there was a subtle bond that connected them.

They had met four years ago, brought together by a common friend, Hosken, a naval man. The three, Rupert Birkin, William Hosken, and Gerald Crich had then spent a week in the Tyrol together, mountain-climbing.

Birkin and Gerald Crich felt take place between them, the moment they saw each other, that sudden connection which sometimes springs up between men who are very different in temper. There had been a subterranean kindling in each man. Each looked towards the other, and knew the trembling nearness.

Yet they had maintained complete reserve, their relations had been, to all knowledge, entirely casual and trivial. Because of the inward kindled connection, they were even more distant and slight than men usually are, one towards the other.

There was, however, a certain tenderness in their politeness, an almost uncomfortable understanding lurked under their formal, reserved behaviour. They were vividly aware of each other's presence, and each was just as vividly aware of himself, in presence of the other.

The week of mountain-climbing passed like an intense brief lifetime. The three men were very close together, and lifted into an abstract isolation, among the upper rocks and the snow. The world that lay below, the whole field of human activity, was sunk and subordinated, they had trespassed into the upper silence and loneliness. The three of them had reached another state of being, they were enkindled in the upper silences into a rare, unspoken intimacy, an intimacy that took no expression, but which was between them like a transfiguration. As if thrown into the strange fire of abstraction, up in the mountains, they knew and were known to each other. It was another world, another life, transfigured, and yet most vividly corporeal, the senses all raised till each felt his own body, and the presence of his companions, like an essential flame, they radiated to one enkindled, transcendent fire, in the upper world.

Then had come the sudden falling down to earth, the sudden extinction. At Innsbruck they had parted, Birkin to go to Munich, Gerald Crich and Hosken to take the train for Paris and London. On the station they shook hands, and went asunder, having spoken no word and given no sign of the transcendent intimacy which had roused them beyond the everyday life. They shook hands and took leave casually, as mere acquaintances going their separate ways. Yet there remained always, for Birkin and for Gerald Crich, the absolute recognition that had passed between them then, the knowledge that was in their eyes as they met at the moment of parting. They knew they loved each other, that each would die for the other.

Yet all this knowledge was kept submerged in the soul of the two men. Outwardly they would have none of it. Outwardly they only stiffened themselves away from it. They took leave from each other even more coldly and casually than is usual.

And for a year they had seen nothing of each other, neither had they exchanged any word. They passed away from each other, and, superficially, forgot.

But when they met again, in a country house in Derbyshire, the enkindled sensitiveness sprang up again like a strange, embarrassing fire. They scarcely knew each other, yet here was this strange, unacknowledged, inflammable intimacy between them. It made them uneasy.

Rupert Birkin, however, strongly centred in himself, never gave way in his soul, to anyone. He remained in the last issue detached, self-responsible, having no communion with any other soul. Therefore Gerald Crich remained intact in his own form.

The two men were very different. Gerald Crich was the fair, keen-eyed Englishman of medium stature, hard in his muscles and full of energy as a machine. He was a hunter, a traveller, a soldier, always active, always moving vigorously, and giving orders to some subordinate.

Birkin on the other hand was quiet and unobtrusive. In stature he was long and very thin, and yet not bony, close-knit, flexible, and full of repose, like a steel wire. His energy was not evident, he seemed almost weak, passive, insignificant. He was delicate in health. His face was pale and rather ugly, his hair dun-coloured, his eyes were of a yellowish-grey, full of life and warmth. They were the only noticeable thing about him, to the ordinary observer, being very warm and sudden and attractive, alive like fires. But this chief attraction of Birkin's was a false one. Those that knew him best knew that his lovable eyes were, in the last issue, estranged and unsoftening like the eyes of a wolf. In the last issue he was callous, and without feeling, confident, just as Gerald Crich in the last issue was wavering and lost.

The two men were staying in the house of Sir Charles Roddice, Gerald Crich as friend of the host, Rupert Birkin as friend of his host's daughter, Hermione[1] Roddice. Sir Charles would have been glad for Gerald Crich to marry the daughter of the house, because this young man was a well-set young Englishman of strong conservative temperament, and heir to considerable wealth. But Gerald Crich did not care for Hermione Roddice, and Hermione Roddice disliked Gerald Crich.

She was a rather beautiful woman of twenty-five, fair, tall, slender, graceful, and of some learning. She had known Rupert Birkin in Oxford. He was a year her senior. He was a fellow of Magdalen College, and had been, at twenty-one, one of the young lights of the place, a coming somebody. His essays on Education were brilliant, and he became an inspector of schools.

Hermione Roddice loved him. When she had listened to his passionate declamations, in his rooms in the Blackhorse Road, and when she had heard the respect with which he was spoken of, five years ago, she being a girl of twenty, reading political economy, and he a youth of twenty-one, holding forth against Nietzsche, then she devoted herself to his name and fame. She added herself to his mental and spiritual flame.

Sir Charles thought they would marry. He considered that Birkin, hanging on year after year, was spoiling all his daughter's chances, and without pledging himself in the least. It irked the soldierly knight considerably. But he was somewhat afraid of the quiet, always-civil Birkin. And Hermione, when Sir Charles mentioned that he thought of speaking to the young man, in order to know his intentions, fell into such a white and overweening, contemptuous passion, that her father was nonplussed and reduced to irritated silence.

"How vulgar you are!" cried the young woman. "You are not to dare to say a word to him. It is a friendship, and it is not to be broken-in upon in this fashion. Why should you want to rush me into marriage? I am more than happy as I am."

Her liquid grey eyes swam dark with fury and pain and resentment, her beautiful face was convulsed. She seemed like a prophetess violated. Her father withdrew, cold and huffed.

So the relationship between the young woman and Birkin continued. He was an inspector of schools, she studied Education. He wrote also harsh, jarring poetry, very real and painful, under which she suffered; and sometimes, shallower, gentle lyrics, which she treasured as drops of manna. Like a priestess she kept his records and his oracles, he was like a god who would be nothing if his worship were neglected.

Hermione could not understand the affection between the two men. They would sit together in the hall, at evening, and talk without any depth. What did Rupert find to take him up, in Gerald Crich's conversation? She, Hermione, was only rather bored, and puzzled. Yet the two men seemed happy, holding their commonplace discussion. Hermione was impatient. She knew that Birkin was, as usual,

---

1. Lawrence substituted the name *Hermione* in place of the name *Ethel*.

belittling his own mind and talent, for the sake of something that she felt unworthy. Some common correspondence which she knew demeaned and belied him. Why would he always come down so eagerly to the level of common people, why was he always so anxious to vulgarize and betray himself? She bit her lip in torment. It was as if he were anxious to deny all that was fine and rare in himself.

Birkin knew what she was feeling and thinking. Yet he continued almost spitefully against her. He *did* want to betray the heights and depths of nearly religious intercourse which he had with her. He, the God, turned round upon his priestess, and became the common vulgar man who turned her to scorn. He performed some strange metamorphosis of soul, and from being a pure, incandescent spirit burning intense with the presence of God, he became a lustful, shallow, insignificant fellow running in all the common ruts. Even there was some vindictiveness in him now, something jeering and spiteful and low, unendurable. It drove her mad. She had given him all her trembling, naked soul, and now he turned mongrel, and triumphed in his own degeneration. It was his deep desire, to be common, vulgar, a little gross. She could not bear the look of almost sordid jeering with which he turned on her, when she reached out her hand, imploring. It was as if some rat bit her, she felt she was going insane. And he jeered at her, at the spiritual woman who waited at the tomb, in her sandals and her mourning robes. He jeered at her horribly, knowing her secrets. And she was insane, she knew she was going mad.

But he plunged on triumphant into intimacy with Gerald Crich, excluding the woman, tormenting her. He knew how to pitch himself into tune with another person. He could adjust his mind, his consciousness, almost perfectly to that of Gerald Crich, lighting up the edge of the other man's limitation with a glimmering light that was the essence of exquisite adventure and liberation to the confined intelligence. The two men talked together for hours, Birkin watching the hard limbs and the rather stiff face of the traveller in unknown countries, Gerald Crich catching the pale, luminous face opposite him, lit up over the edge of the unknown regions of the soul, trembling into new being, quivering with new intelligence.

To Hermione, it was insupportable degradation that Rupert Birkin should maintain this correspondence, prostituting his mind and his understanding to the coarser stupidity of the other man. She felt confusion gathering upon her, she was unanchored on the edge of madness. Why did he do it? Why was he, whom she knew as her leader, star-like and pure, why was he the lowest betrayer and the ugliest of blasphemers? She held her temples, feeling herself reel towards the bottomless pit.

For Birkin did get a greater satisfaction, at least for the time being, from his intercourse with the other man, than from his spiritual relation with her. It satisfied him to have to do with Gerald Crich, it fulfilled him to have this other man, this hard-limbed traveller and sportsman, followimg implicitly, held as it were consummated within the spell of a more powerful understanding. Birkin felt a passion of desire for Gerald Crich, for the clumsier, cruder intelligence and the limited soul, and for the striving, unlightened body of his friend. And Gerald Crich, not understanding, was transfused with pleasure. He did not even know he loved Birkin. He thought him marvellous in understanding, almost unnatural, and on the other hand pitiful and delicate in body. He felt a great tenderness towards him, of superior physical strength, and at the same time some reverence for his delicacy and fineness of being.

All the same, there was no profession of friendship, no open mark of intimacy. They remained to all intents and purposes distant, mere acquaintances. It was in the other world of the subconsciousness that the interplay took place, the interchange of spiritual and physical richness, the relieving of physical and spiritual poverty, without any intrinsic change of state in either man.

Hermione could not understand it at all. She was mortified and in despair. In his lapses, she despised and revolted from Birkin. Her mistrust of him pierced to the quick of her soul. If his intense and pure flame of spirituality only sank to this guttering prostration, a low, degraded heat, servile to a clumsy Gerald Crich, fawning on a coarse, unsusceptible being, such as was Gerald Crich and all the multitudes of Gerald Criches of this world, then nothing was anything. The transcendent star of one evening was the putrescent phosphorescence of the next, and glory and corruptibility were interchangeable. Her soul was convulsed with cynicism. She despised her God and her angel. Yet she could not do without him. She believed in herself as a priestess, and that was all. Though there were no God to serve, still she was a priestess. Yet having no altar to kindle, no sacrifice to burn, she would be barren and useless. So she adhered to her God in him, which she claimed almost violently, whilst her soul turned in bitter cynicism from the prostitute man in him. She did not believe in him, she only believed in that which she could gather from him, as one gathers silk from the corrupt worm. She was the maker of gods.

So, after a few days, Gerald Crich went away and Birkin was left to Hermione Roddice. It is true, Crich said to Birkin: "Come and see us, if ever you are near enough, will you?," and Birkin had said yes. But for some reason, it was concluded beforehand that this visit would never be made, deliberately.

Sick, helpless, Birkin swung back to Hermione. In the garden, at evening, looking over the silvery hills, he sat near to her, or lay with his head on her bosom, while the moonlight came gently upon the trees, and they talked, quietly, gently as dew distilling, their two disembodied voices distilled in the silvery air, two voices moving and ceasing like ghosts, like spirits. And they talked of life, and of death, but chiefly of death, his words turning strange and phosphorescent, like dark water suddenly shaken alight, whilst she held his head against her breast, infinitely satisfied and completed by its weight upon her, and her hand travelled gently, finely, oh, with such exquisite quivering adjustment, over his hair. The pain of tenderness he felt for her was almost unendurable, as her hand fluttered and came near, scarcely touching him, so light and sensitive it was, as it passed over his hair, rhythmically. And still his voice moved and thrilled through her like the keenest pangs of embrace, she remained possessed by him, possessed by the spirit. And the sense of beauty and perfect, blade-keen ecstasy was balanced to perfection, she passed away, was transported.

After these nights of superfine ecstasy of beauty, after all was consumed in the silver fire of moonlight, all the soul caught up in the universal chill-blazing bonfire of the moonlit night, there came the morning, and the ash, when his body was grey and consumed, and his soul ill. Why should the sun shine, and hot gay flowers

.come out, when the kingdom of reality was the silver-cold night of death, lovely and perfect.

She, like a priestess, was fulfilled and rich. But he became more hollow and ghastly to look at. There was no escape, they penetrated further and further into the regions of death, and soon the connection with life would be broken.

Then came his revulsion against her. After he loved her with a tenderness that was anguish, a love that was all pain, or else transcendent white ecstasy, he turned upon her savagely, like a maddened dog. And like a priestess who is rended for sacrifice, she submitted and endured. She would serve the God she possessed, even though he should turn periodically into a fierce dog, to rend her.

So he went away, to his duties, and his work. He had made a passionate study of education, only to come, gradually, to the knowledge that education is nothing but the process of building up, gradually, a complete unit of consciousness. And each unit of consciousness is the living unit of that great social, religious, philosophic idea towards which mankind, like an organism seeking its final form, is laboriously growing. But if there *be* no great philosophic idea, if, for the time being, mankind, instead of going through a period of growth, is going through a corresponding process of decay and decomposition from some old, fulfilled, obsolete idea, then what is the good of educating? Decay and decomposition will take their own way. It is impossible to educate for this end, impossible to teach the world how to die away from its achieved nullified form. The autumn must take place in every individual soul, as well as in all the people, all must die, individually and socially. But education is a process of striving to a new, unanimous being, a whole organic form. But when winter has set in, when the frosts are strangling the leaves off the trees and the birds are silent knots of darkness, how can there be a unanimous movement towards a whole summer of florescence? There can be none of this, only submission to the death of this nature, in the winter that has come upon mankind, and a cherishing of the unknown that is unknown for many a day yet, buds that may not open till a far off season comes, when the season of death has passed away.

And Birkin was just coming to a knowledge of the essential futility of all attempt at social unanimity in constructiveness. In the winter, there can only be unanimity of disintegration, the leaves fall unanimously, the plants die down, each creature is a soft-slumbering grave, as the adder and the dormouse in winter are the soft tombs of the adder and the dormouse, which slip about like rays of brindled darkness, in summer.

How to get away from this process of reduction, how escape this phosphorescent passage into the tomb, which was universal though unacknowledged, this was the unconscious problem which tortured Birkin day and night. He came to Hermione, and found with her the pure, translucent regions of death itse]f, of ecstasy. In the world the autumn was setting in. What should a man add himself on to?—to science, to social reform, to aestheticism, to sensationalism? The whole world's constructive activity was a fiction, a lie, to hide the great process of decomposition, which had set in. What then to adhere to?

He ran about from death to death. Work was terrible, horrible because he did not believe in it. It was almost a horror to him, to think of going from school to school making reports and giving suggestions, when the whole process to his soul was pure futility, a process of mechanical activity entirely purposeless, sham growth which was entirely rootless. Nowhere more than in education did a man feel the horror of false, rootless, spasmodic activity more acutely. The whole business was like dementia. It created in him a feeling of nausea and horror. He recoiled from it. And yet, where should a man repair, what should he do?

In his private life the same horror of futility and wrongness dogged him. Leaving alone all ideas, religious or philosophic, all of which are mere sounds, old repetitions, or else novel, dexterous, sham permutations and combinations of old repetitions, leaving alone all the things of the mind and the consciousness, what remained in a man's life? There is his emotional and his sensuous activity, is not this enough?

Birkin started with madness from this question, for it touched the quick of torture. There was his love for Hermione, a love based entirely on ecstasy and on pain, and ultimate death. He *knew* he did not love her with any living, creative love. He did not even desire her: he had no passion for her, there was no hot impulse of growth between them, only this terrible reducing activity of phosphorescent consciousness, the consciousness ever liberated more and more into the void, at the expense of the flesh, which was burnt down like dead grey ash.

He did not call this love. Yet he was bound to her, and it was agony to leave her. And he did not love anyone else. He did not love any woman. He *wanted* to love. But between wanting to love, and loving, is the whole difference between life and death.

The incapacity to love, the incapacity to desire any woman, positively, with body and soul, this was a real torture, a deep torture indeed. Never to be able to love spontaneously, never to be moved by a power greater than oneself, but always to be within one's own control, deliberate, having the choice, this was horrifying, more deadly than death. Yet how was one to escape? How could a man escape from being deliberate and unloving except a greater power, an impersonal, imperative love should take hold of him? And if the greater power should not take hold of him, what could he do but continue in his deliberateness, without any fundamental spontaneity?

He did not love Hermione, he did not desire her. But he wanted to force himself to love her and to desire her. He was consumed by sexual desire, and he wanted to be fulfilled. Yet he did not desire Hermione. She repelled him rather. Yet he *would* have this physical fulfilment, he would have the sexual activity. So he forced himself towards her.

She was hopeless from the start. Yet she resigned herself to him. In her soul, she knew this was not the way. And yet even she was ashamed, as of some physical deficiency. She did not want him either. But with all her soul, she *wanted* to want him. She would do anything to give him what he wanted, that which he was raging for, this physical fulfilment he insisted on. She was wise; she thought for the best. She prepared herself like a perfect sacrifice to him. She offered herself gladly to him, gave herself into his will.

And oh, it was all such a cruel failure, just a failure. This last act of love which he had demanded of her was the keenest grief of all, it was so insignificant, so null. He had no pleasure of her, only some mortification. And her heart almost broke with grief.

She wanted him to take her. She wanted him to take her, to break her with his passion, to destroy her with his desire, so long as he got satisfaction. She looked forward, tremulous, to a kind of death at his hands, she gave herself up. She would be broken and dying, destroyed, if only he would rise fulfilled.

But he was not capable of it, he failed. He could not take her and destroy her. He could not forget her. They had too rare a spiritual intimacy, he could not now tear himself away from all this, and come like a brute to take its satisfaction. He was too much aware of her, and of her fear, and of her writhing torment, as she lay in sacrifice. He had too much deference for her feeling. He could not, as she madly wanted, destroy her, trample her, and crush a satisfaction from her. He was not experienced enough, not hardened enough. He was always aware of *her* feelings, so that he had none of his own. Which made this last love-making between them an ignominious failure, very, very cruel to bear.

And it was this failure which broke the love between them. He hated her, for her incapacity in love, for her lack of desire for him, her complete and almost perfect lack of any physical desire towards him. Her desire was all spiritual, all in the consciousness. She wanted him all, all through the consciousness, never through the senses.

And she hated him, and despised him, for his incapacity to wreak his desire upon her, his lack of strength to crush his satisfaction from her. If only he could have taken her, destroyed her, used her all up, and been satisfied, she would be at last free. She might be killed, but it would be the death which gave her consummation.

It was a failure, a bitter, final failure. He could not take from her what he wanted, because he could not, bare-handed, destroy her. And she despised him that he could not destroy her.

Still, though they had failed, finally, they did not go apart. Their relation was too deep-established. He was by this time twenty-eight years old, and she twenty-seven. Still, for his spiritual delight, for a companion in his conscious life, for someone to share and heighten his joy in thinking, or in reading, or in feeling beautiful things, or in knowing landscape intimately and poignantly, he turned to her. For all these things, she was still with him, she made up the greater part of his life. And he, she knew to her anguish and mortification, he was still the master-key to almost all life, for her. She wanted it not to be so, she wanted to be free of him, of the strange, terrible bondage of his domination. But as yet, she could not free herself from him.

He went to other women, to women of purely sensual, sensational attraction, he prostituted his spirit with them. And he got *some* satisfaction. She watched him go, sadly, and yet not without a measure of relief. For he would torment her less, now.

She knew he would come back to her. She knew, inevitably as the dawn would rise, he would come back to her, half-exultant and triumphant over her, half-bitter against her for letting him go and wanting her now, wanting the communion with her. It was as if he went to the other, the dark, sensual, almost bestial woman thoroughly and fully to degrade himself. He despised himself, essentially, in his attempts at sensuality, she knew that. So she let him be. It was only his rather vulgar arrogance of a sinner that she found hard to bear. For before her, he wore his sins with braggadocio, flaunted them a little in front of her. And this alone drove her to exasperation to the point of uttering her contempt for his childishness and his instability.

But as yet, she forbore, because of the deference he still felt towards her. Intrinsically in his spirit, he still served her. And this service she cherished.

But he was becoming gnawed and bitter, a little mad. His whole system was inflamed to a pitch of mad irritability, he became blind, unconscious to the greater half of life, only a few things he saw with feverish acuteness. And she, she kept the key to him, all the while.

The only thing she dreaded was his making up his mind. She dreaded his way of seeing some particular things vividly and feverishly, and of his acting upon this special sight. For once he decided a thing, it became a reigning universal truth to him, and he was completely inhuman.

He was, in his own way, quite honest with himself. But every man has his own truths, and is honest with himself according to them. The terrible thing about Birkin, for Hermoine, was that when once he decided upon a truth, he acted upon it, cost what it might. If he decided that his eye did really offend him, he would in truth pluck it out. And this seemed to her so inhuman, so abstract, that it chilled her to the depths of her soul, and made him seem to her inhuman, something between a monster and a complete fool. For might not she herself easily be found to be this eye which much needs be plucked out?

He had stuck fast over this question of love and of physical fulfilment in love, till it had become like a monomania. All his thought turned upon it. For he wanted to keep his integrity of being, he would not consent to sacrifice one half of himself to the other. He would not sacrifice the sensual to the spiritual half of himself, and he could not sacrifice the spiritual to the sensual half. Neither could he obtain fulfilment in both, the two halves always reacted from each other. To be spiritual, he must have a Hermione, completely without desire: to be sensual, he must have a slightly bestial woman, the very scent of whose skin soon disgusted him, whose manners nauseated him beyond bearing, so that Hermione, always chaste and always stretching out her hands for beauty, seemed to him the purest and most desirable thing on earth.

He knew he obtained no real fulfilment in sensuality, he became disgusted and despised the whole process as if it were dirty. And he knew that he had no real fulfilment in his spiritual and aesthetic intercourse with Hermione. That process he also despised, with considerable cynicism.

And he recognized that he was on the point either of breaking, becoming a thing, losing his integral being, or else of becoming insane. He was now nothing but a series of reactions from dark to light, from light to dark, almost mechanical, without unity or meaning.

This was the most insufferable bondage, the most tormenting affliction, that he could not save himself from these extreme reactions, the vibration between two poles, one of which was Hermione, the centre of social virtue, the other of which was a prostitute, anti-social, almost criminal. He knew that in the end, subject to this extreme vibration, he would be shattered, would die, or else, worse still, would become a mere disordered set of processes, without purpose or integral being. He knew this, and dreaded it. Yet he could not save himself.

To save himself, he must unite the two halves of himself, spiritual and sensual. And this is what no man can do at once, deliberately. It must happen to him. Birkin willed to be sensual, as well as spiritual, with Hermione. He might will it, he might act according to his will, but he did not bring to pass that which he willed. A man cannot create desire in himself, nor cease at will from desiring. Desire, in any shape or form, is primal, whereas the will is secondary, derived. The will can destroy, but it cannot create.

So the more he tried with his will, to force his senses towards Hermione, the greater misery he produced. On the other hand his pride never ceased to contemn his profligate intercourse elsewhere. After all, it was not that which he wanted. He did not want libertine pleasures, not fundamentally. His fundamental desire was, to be able to love completely, in one and the same act: both body and soul at once, struck into a complete oneness in contact with a complete woman.

And he failed in this desire. It was always a case of one or the other, of spirit or of senses, and each, alone, was deadly. All history, almost an art, seemed the story of this deadly half-love: either passion, like Cleopatra, or else spirit, like Mary of Bethany or Vittoria Colonna.

He pondered on the subject endlessly, and knew himself in his reactions. But self-knowledge is not everything. No man, by taking thought, can add one cubit to his stature. He can but know his own height and limitation.

He knew that he loved no woman, that in nothing was he really complete, really himself. In his most passionate moments of spiritual enlightenment, when like a saviour of mankind he would pour out his soul for the world, there was in him a capacity to jeer at all his own righteousness and spirituality, justly and sincerely to make a mock of it all. And the mockery was so true, it bit to the very core of his righteousness, and showed it rotten, shining with phosphorescence. But at the same time, whilst quivering in the climax-thrill of sensual pangs, some cold voice could say in him: "You are not really moved; you could rise up and go away from this pleasure quite coldly and calmly; it is not radical, your enjoyment."

He knew he had not loved, could not love. The only thing then was to make the best of it, have the two things separate, and over them all, a calm detached mind. But to this he would not acquiesce. "I should be like a Neckan," he said to himself, "like a sea-water being, I should have no soul." And he pondered the stories of the wistful, limpid creatures who watched ceaselessly, hoping to gain a soul.

So the trouble went on, he became more hollow and deathly, more like a spectre with hollow bones. He knew that he was not very far from dissolution.

All the time, he recognized that, although he was always drawn to women, feeling more at home with a woman than with a man, yet it was for men that he felt the hot, flushing, roused attraction which a man is supposed to feel for the other sex. Although nearly all his living interchange went on with one woman or another, although he was always terribly intimate with at least one woman, and practically never intimate with a man, yet the male physique had a fascination for him, and for the female physique he felt only a fondness, a sort of sacred love, as for a sister.

In the street, it was the men who roused him by their flesh and their manly, vigorous movement, quite apart from all the individual character, whilst he studied the women as sisters, knowing their meaning and their intents. It was the men's physique which held the passion and the mystery to him. The women he seemed to be kin to, he looked for the soul in them. The soul of a woman and the physique of a man, these were the two things he watched for, in the street.

And this was a new torture to him. Why did not the face of a woman move him in the same manner, with the same sense of handsome desirability, as the face of a man? Why was a man's beauty, the beauté mâle, so vivid and intoxicating a thing to him, whilst female beauty was something quite unsubstantial, consisting all of look and gesture and revelation of intuitive intelligence? He thought women beautiful purely because of their expression. But it was plastic form that fascinated him in men, the contour and movement of the flesh itself.

He wanted all the time to love women. He wanted all the while to feel this kindled, loving attraction towards a beautiful woman, that he would often feel towards a handsome man. But he could not. Whenever it was a case of a woman, there entered in too much spiritual, sisterly love; or else, in reaction, there was only a brutal, callous sort of lust.

This was an entanglement from which there seemed no escape. How can a man *create* his own feelings? He cannot. It is only in his power to suppress them, to bind them in the chain of the will. And what is suppression but a mere negation of life, and of living.

He had several friendships wherein this passion entered, friendships with men of no very great intelligence, but of pleasant appearance: ruddy, well-nourished fellows, good-natured and easy, who protected him in his delicate health more gently than a woman would protect him. He loved his friend, the beauty of whose manly limbs made him tremble with pleasure. He wanted to caress him.

But reserve, which was as strong as a chain of iron in him, kept him from any demonstration. And if he were away for any length of time from the man he loved so hotly, then he forgot him, the flame which invested the beloved like a transfiguration passed away, and Birkin remembered his friend as tedious. He could not go back to him, to talk as tediously as he would have to talk, to take such a level of intelligence as he would have to take. He forgot his men friends completely, as one forgets the candle one has blown out. They remained as quite extraneous and uninteresting persons living their life in their own sphere, and having not the slightest relation to himself, even though they themselves maintained a real warmth of affection, almost of love for him. He paid not the slightest heed to this love which was constant to him, he felt it sincerely to be just nothing, valueless.

So he left his old friends completely, even those to whom he had been attached passionately, like David to Jonathan. Men whose presence he had waited for cravingly, the touch of whose shoulder suffused him with a vibration of physical love, became to him mere figures, as nonexistent as is the waiter who sets the table in a restaurant.

He wondered very slightly at this, but dismissed it with hardly a thought. Yet, every now and again, would come over him the same passionate desire to have near him some man he saw, to exchange intimacy, to unburden himself of love of this new beloved.

It might be any man, a policeman who suddenly looked up at him, as he inquired the way, or a soldier who sat next to him in a railway carriage. How vividly, months afterwards, he would recall the soldier who had sat pressed up close to him on a journey from Charing Cross to Westerham; the shapely, motionless body, the large, dumb, coarsely-beautiful hands that rested helpless upon the strong knees, the dark brown eyes, vulnerable in the erect body. Or a young man in flannels on the sands at Margate, flaxen and ruddy, like a Viking of twenty-three, with clean, rounded contours, pure as the contours of snow, playing with some young children, building a castle in sand, intent and abstract, like a seagull or a keen white bear.

In his mind was a small gallery of such men: men whom he had never spoken to, but who had flashed themselves upon his senses unforgettably, men whom he apprehended intoxicatingly in his blood. They divided themselves roughly into two classes: these white-skinned, keen-limbed men with eyes like blue-flashing ice and hair like crystals of winter sunshine, the northmen, inhuman as sharp-crying gulls, distinct like splinters of ice, like crystals, isolated, individual; and then the men with dark eyes that one can enter and plunge into, bathe in, as in a liquid darkness, dark-skinned, supple, night-smelling men, who are the living substance of the viscous, universal heavy darkness.

His senses surged towards these men, towards the perfect and beautiful representatives of these two halves. And he knew them, by seeing them and by apprehending them sensuously, he knew their very blood, its weight and savour; the blood of the northmen sharp and red and light, tending to be keenly acrid, like cranberries, the blood of the dark-limbed men heavy and luscious, and in the end nauseating, revolting.

He asked himself, often, as he grew older, and more unearthly, when he was twenty-eight and twenty-nine years old, would he ever be appeased, would he ever cease to desire these two sorts of men. And a wan kind of hopelessness would come over him, as if he would never escape from this attraction, which was a bondage.

For he would never acquiesce to it. He could never acquiesce to his own feelings, to his own passion. He could never grant that it should be so, that it was well for him to feel this keen desire to have and to possess the bodies of such men, the passion to bathe in the very substance of such men, the substance of living, eternal light, like eternal snow, and the flux of heavy, rank-smelling darkness.

He wanted to cast out these desires, he wanted not to know them. Yet a man can no more slay a living desire in him, than he can prevent his body from feeling heat and cold. He can put himself into bondage, to prevent the fulfilment of the desire, that is all. But the desire is there, as the travelling of the blood itself is there, until it is fulfilled or until the body is dead.

So he went on, month after month, year after year, divided against himself, striving for the day when the beauty of men should not be so acutely attractive to him, when the beauty of woman should move him instead.

But that day came no nearer, rather it went further away. His deep dread was that it would always be so, that he would never be free. His life would have been one long torture of struggle against his own innate desire, his own innate being. But to be so divided against oneself, this is terrible, a nullificatlon of all being.

He went into violent excess with a mistress whom, in a rather anti-social, ashamed spirit, he loved. And so for a long time he forgot about this attraction that men had for him. He forgot about it entirely. And then he grew stronger, surer.

But then, inevitably, it would recur again. There would come into a restaurant a strange Cornish type of man, with dark eyes like holes in his head, or like the eyes of a rat, and with dark, fine, rather stiff hair, and full, heavy, softly-strong limbs. Then again Birkin would feel the desire spring up in him, the desire to know this man, to have him, as it were to eat him, to take the very substance of him. And watching the strange, rather furtive, rabbit-like way in which the strong, softly-built man ate, Birkin would feel the rousedness burning in his own breast, as if this were what he wanted, as if the satisfaction of his desire lay in the body of the young, strong man opposite.

And then in his soul would succeed a sort of despair, because this passion for a man had recurred in him. It was a deep misery to him. And it would seem as if he had always loved men, always and only loved men. And this was the greatest suffering to him.

But it was not so, that he always loved men. For weeks it would be all gone from him, this passionate admiration of the rich body of a man. For weeks he was free, active, and living. But he had such a dread of his own feelings and desires, that when they recurred again, the interval vanished, and it seemed the bondage and the torment had been continuous.

This was the one and only secret he kept to himself, this secret of his passionate and sudden, spasmodic affinity for men he saw. He kept this secret even from himself. He knew what he felt, but he always kept the knowledge at bay. His a priori were: "I *should not* feel like this," and "It is the ultimate mark of my own deficiency, that I feel like this." Therefore, though he admitted everything, he never really faced the question. He never accepted the desire, and received it as part of himself. He always tried to keep it expelled from him.[2]

Gerald Crich was the one towards whom Birkin felt most strongly that immediate, roused attraction which transfigured the person of the attracter with such a glow and such a desirable beauty. The two men had met once or twice, and then Gerald Crich went abroad, to South America. Birkin forgot him, all connection died down. But it was not finally dead. In both men were the seeds of a strong, inflammable afffinity.

Therefore, when Birkin found himself pledged to act as best man at the wedding of Hosken, the friend of the mountain-climbing holiday, and of Laura Crich, sister of Gerald, the old affection sprang awake in a moment. He wondered what Gerald would be like now.

Hermione, knowing of Hosken's request to Birkin, at once secured for herself the position of bridesmaid to Laura Crich. It was inevitable. She and Rupert Birkin were running to the end of their friendship. He was now thirty years of age, and she twenty-nine. His feeling of hostility towards Hermione had grown now to an almost constant dislike. Still she held him in her power. But the hold became weaker and weaker. "If he breaks loose," she said, "he will fall into the abyss."

Nevertheless he was bound to break loose, because his reaction against Hermione was the strongest movement in his life, now. He was thrusting her off,

---

2. At one time the Prologue chapter ended here, for the next page of the manuscript is headed *Chapter* 11 *The Wedding.* This heading is cancelled and the direction "Run on" is twice inserted.

fighting her off all the while, thrusting himself clear, although he had no other foothold, although he was breaking away from her, his one rock, to fall into a bottomless sea.

## J. R. Ackerley (1896–1967)

FROM *MY FATHER AND MYSELF* (1968)

Joseph Randolph Ackerley's memoir *My Father and Myself* is one of the frankest accounts of the life of a homosexual man in twentieth-century English literature. No closeted Housman, no reticent Forster—who was one of his closest friends—Ackerley pursued sex in life and homosexuality in literature with remarkable and eager enthusiasm. His memoir *Hindoo Holiday: An Indian Journal* (1932) is an account of his sojourn in India as secretary to a homosexual maharaja. His play *The Prisoners of War* (1925), which reflects his own experiences in a German prisoner of war camp, employs homosexuality to motivate the characters in perhaps the first twentieth-century play to do so openly. Some of his poetry, collected in *Micheldelver and Other Poems* (1972), reflects autobiographical and homoerotic experience. But his memoir of his father's life and apparent homosexual relationship with a count of the Holy Roman Empire allowed Ackerley to describe in detail his own homosexuality and meditate upon some of the considerations that attended upon being homosexual in the early years of this century in England. Ackerley's quest is ever for the ideal friend, the chimerical vision of much of nineteenth-century homosexual literature, and Ackerley looks for this friend in the homosexual gathering places of London, among soldiers, sailors, and working-class men. Unlike many homosexual men of time, he wanted to live in no concealed closet nor pretend to be anything but what he was. Though the actual record of his sexual life is in fact marked by more inhibition and frustration than the ideal picture he sometimes seems to want to paint in *My Father and Myself*, yet he asserts that he is proud of his place on the homosexual map—"surrounded," as he said, and "supported by the famous homosexuals of history."

Chapter 12

To psychologists, my love-life, into which I must now again go before continuing with my father's, may appear somewhat unsatisfactory; in retrospect it does not look perfectly satisfactory to me, indeed I regard it with some astonishment. It may be said to have begun with a golliwog and ended with an Alsatian bitch; in between there passed several hundred young men, mostly of the lower orders and often clad in uniforms of one sort or another. . . .

Instinctively evading older men who seemed to desire me, I could not approach the younger ones whom I desired. . . . The working classes also, of course, now took my eye. Many a handsome farm- or tradesboy was to be found in the ranks of one's command, and to a number of beautiful but untouchable NCOs and privates did I allot an early sentimental or heroic death in my nauseous verse. My personal runners and servants were usually chosen for their looks; indeed this tendency in war to have the prettiest soldiers about one was observable in many other officers; whether they took more advantage than I dared of this close, homogenous, almost paternal relationship I do not know. Then came capture and imprisonment. In the hospital in Hanover, to which I was taken with my splintered pelvis, I became enamoured of a Russian medical orderly, a prisoner like myself, named Lovkin; he was gentle and kind, with a broad Slav face, but apparently without personal feelings; we had no common language, but liking to be in his arms I wanted no one else to carry me to and from the operating theatre and to dress my wound, which suppurated for weeks until all the little fragments of bone had been extracted. My memory of the rest of my imprisonment in Germany is emotionally featureless; there were two or three middle-aged officers, among the various lagers I was sent to, with whom I formed friendships and whose feelings I believe I aroused and frustrated, but I remember them only as shadows.

. . .

However, my knowledge of life now began to increase. I met in Switzerland a mocking and amusing fellow with whom I became very thick. He was the second forceful intellectual under whose dominance I fell. His name was Arnold Lunn, and with his energetic, derisive, iconoclastic mind and rasping demonic laugh he was both the vitality and the terror of the community. Almost the first mischievous question he shot at me was "Are you homo or hetero?" I had never heard either term before; they were explained and there seemed only one answer. He himself, like Mais, was hetero; so far as I recall I never met a recognisable or self-confessed adult homosexual (except an ancient master at school, called "the Nag," who was mysteriously sacked) until after the war; the Army with its male relationships was simply an extension of my public school. Lunn lent or recommended me books to read, Otto Weininger, Edward Carpenter, Plutarch, and thus and with his malicious, debunking thought opened my mind. . . .

I was now on the sexual map and proud of my place on it. I did not care for the word "homosexual" or any label, but I stood among the men, not among the women. Girls I despised; vain, silly creatures, how could their smooth, soft, bulbous bodies compare in attraction with the muscular beauty of men? Their place was the harem, from which they should never have been released; true love, equal and understanding love, occurred only between men. I saw myself therefore in the tradition of the Classic Greeks, surrounded and supported by all the famous homosexuals of history—one soon sorted them out—and in time I became something of a publicist for the rights of that love that dare not speak its name. Unfortunately in my own private life also it seemed to have some impediment in its speech; love and sex, come together as I believed they should, failed to meet, and I got along at Cambridge no better than anywhere else. In varying degrees and at various times I was attracted to a number of other undergraduates; I had sexual contact with none of them. So far as I know, all but one were normal boys, and the normal, manly boy always drew me most. Certainly effeminacy in men repelled me almost as much as women themselves did. But although I felt that, had I tried to kiss these normal, friendly boys who came so often to my rooms, my advances would not have been rebuffed, I could not take that step. It seemed that I needed a degree of certainty so great that only unambiguous advances from the other side would have suited me; these I never got, and even had I got them I might not, for another reason, have been able to cope. To one boy I was so attracted that I bought him an expensive pair of gold and platinum cuff-links at Asprey's which linked our engraved

Christian names together. My homosexual undergraduate friend thought him a horrid little boy and I did see that he was perfectly brainless, but he had the kind of dewy prettiness I liked, the innocent look of Snook and "Grayle"—and innocence was difficult to tamper with. Him I managed to kiss, but went no further; the distance between the mouth and the crotch seemed too great. Yet I believe that he himself wished it to be spanned, for our last meeting took place in my Richmond home, to which he had been invited for a dance-party and to stay the night, and having spent a chaste one there he remarked ruefully the following morning, "Every time one meets you, one has to start all over again." Another boy provided a similar but plainer and therefore sadder lesson. He was a Persian and, I thought, the most ravishingly pretty boy I'd ever seen. I knew him only by sight and would trail about Cambridge after him whenever I spied him in the street, wondering how to get into conversation. Once, I followed him to the station and he got into a London train. I got in too, though I had not the least intention or wish to visit London. Not daring to sit beside him I eyed him covertly across the carriage. Whenever he looked at me I looked away. At Liverpool Street he entered a taxi and I returned to Cambridge by the next available train. Some ten years later, when I was well into my sexual stride, I ran into him at Marble Arch and managed to recognise him, though the bloom and the charm had vanished, the wonderful astrakhan hair receded. More surprisingly, he recognised me. I told him of my admiration for him in Cambridge; he said with a laugh that he had been well aware of it, what a pity I had not spoken, he had always hoped I would speak, and how about returning with him to his flat now? It was just round the corner. He was no longer attractive to me, but the glamorous memory remained and I went. Our deferred pleasures were, to me, closer to pain; to him a fiasco. He smelt rather nice of some musky perfume with which he and his flat were drenched, but my apparently artless ideas of love had no place in his highly sophisticated repertoire. He disliked being kissed, and the attentions and even acrobatics he required to stimulate his jaded sex were not merely disagreeable to me but actually uncomfortable. Within limits I attempted to oblige him, but he said scathingly at last, "The trouble with you is you're innocent." It was a wounding word, but kinder than the right one.

It was in my Cambridge years that I began to meet and mix with other acknowledged homosexuals. The emotional feelings and desires we shared, which, at any rate in their satisfaction, made us outcasts and criminals in the sight of the impertinent English laws, naturally drove us into each other's company and the society of those who, though not homosexual themselves, or not exclusively homosexual, were our intelligent, enlightened friends. In such company one was able to enjoy perfect freedom of speech. To understand and explain oneself, which I am trying to do, is very difficult, so I don't know whether to attribute to mere bad luck or to the inscrutable perversities of my nature the fact that neither in Cambridge nor afterwards did I ever meet a homosexual with whom I wanted to set up house. The simplest answers to our dilemmas are not always the ones we desire. Many of my friends brought off enduring "marriages" with men of their own class and kind, others with men of their own kind though of a different class, and I myself have had some short episodes with homosexuals who came attractively in my way; but for some reason I never established myself with any of them. Certain, perhaps relevant, notes about my Cambridge character, as I try to discern it, may be put down. I saw myself, in affairs of the heart, in the masculine role, the active agent; the undergraduates who seemed to me attractive were always younger than I. I myself was attractive, but I did not like to be thought so and pursued by others to whom I was not attracted, as sometimes happened. I avoided or repelled undesirable intimacies. I remember that a middle-aged homosexual novelist, whom I had met only twice and whose name I have now forgotten, said to me, "May I call you Joe?" I said, "No." I was not out to give pleasure but to get it. It was particularly embarrassing when my homosexual friends seemed to fall for me if they themselves had no physical appeal. I dodged and frustrated them and hurt their feelings. In later life, when I tried to improve a character which I saw to be ungenerous, I found that, try as I did, I could not produce the smallest physical response to the passions of those who loved me and of whom indeed I was fond, though not in a physical way. Thus did I hurt their feelings again. It is easier to mend one's manners than one's psychology, and it has sometimes seemed to me that, in my case, the feelings of the heart and the desires of the flesh have lain in separate compartments.

. . .

However, if I was cheerless then, life brightened for me after I came down. I met socially more and more homosexuals and their boy friends and had an affair with a good-natured normal Richmond tradesboy who delivered groceries to my parents' house but, through some kind of physical apathy, delivered nothing material to me. By the time I reached, with my father, the dog's turd in the Bois de Boulogne I was well into my predatory stride. I had just come up from Ragusa, where I had been idling about with a lisping little artist whose girlishness had ended by sickening me; my homosexual Cambridge friend was now living in Paris and we were exploring the queer bars and Turkish baths where one was able to select one's masseur from photographs displayed by the proprietor; I was busy making assignations with a Corsican waiter in the Cafe de la Paix under my parents' noses. Later on, when my play was in production in London, actors were added to my social list; I do not like to boast, but Ivor Novello took me twice into his bed. Though I can't remember my state of mind at this period, I expect that much of all this seemed fun. It certainly afforded pleasure and amusement, it was physically exciting, and in England it had the additional thrill of risk. A single instance of this mixture of fun and risk may be described. Early in the decade I travelled up to Liverpool with my father to visit his sisters. In the restaurant car where we were having lunch a good-looking young waiter was instantly recognised by me as a "queer." While my father studied the menu I exchanged smiles and winks with this youth. Towards the end of the meal, when the business of serving it was over, he passed me with a meaning look and backward glance and disappeared down the corridor. Excusing myself to my father for a natural need, I followed him. He was waiting for me by the door of the toilet. We entered together, quickly unbuttoned, and pleasured each other. Then I returned to finish my coffee. I had scribbled down my address for this amusing youth, but never heard from him again.

Yet in spite of such adventures, if anyone had asked me what I was doing I doubt if I should have replied that I was diverting myself. I think I should have said that I was looking for the Ideal Friend. If I had not said that in the beginning I would certainly have said it later. Though two or three hundred young men were to pass through my hands in the course of years, I did not consider myself promiscuous but monogamous, it was all a run of bad luck, and I became ever more serious over this as time went on. Perhaps as a reaction to my school, Army, and Cambridge difficulties, the anxiety, nervousness, guilt that had dogged me all along the line (though I did not think of it then as guilt, if indeed it was), I was developing theories of life to suit myself: sex was delightful and of prime importance; the distance between the mouth and the crotch must be bridged at once, clothes must come off as soon as possible, no courtship, no nonsense, no beating, so to speak, about the bush; the quickest, perhaps the only, way to get to know anyone thoroughly was to lie naked in bed with him—both were at once disarmed of all disguise and pretence, all cards were on the table, and one could tell whether he was the Ideal Friend. What I meant by the Ideal Friend I doubt if I ever formulated, but now, looking back over the years, I think I can put him together in a partly negative way by listing some of his many disqualifications. He should not be effeminate, indeed preferably normal; I did not exclude education but did not want it, I could supply all that myself and in the loved one it had always seemed to get in the way; he should admit me but no one else; he should be physically attractive to me and younger than myself—the younger the better, as closer to innocence; finally he should be on the small side, lusty, circumcised, physically healthy and clean: no phimosis, halitosis, bromidrosis. It may be thought that I had set myself a task so difficult of accomplishment as almost to put success purposely beyond my reach; it may be thought too that the reason why this search was taking me out of my own class into the working class, yet still towards that innocence which in my class I had been unable to touch, was that guilt in sex obliged me to work it off on my social inferiors. This occurred to me only as a latter-day question and the answer may be true, I cannot tell; if asked then I would probably have said that working-class boys were more unreserved and understanding, and that friendship with them opened up interesting areas of life, hitherto unknown.

Difficult of discovery though my Ideal Friend might seem, I found him, as I thought, quite soon. He was a sailor, an able-bodied seaman, a simple, normal, inarticulate, working-class boy whom I met by introduction. I already knew some of his family. Small in stature and a lightweight boxer quite famous in the Navy, his silken-skinned, muscular, perfect body was a delight to behold, like the Ephebe of Kritios. His browneyed, slightly simian face, with its flattened nose and full thick lips, attracted me at once. If he smelt of anything it was the salt of the sea. He had had no sexual experience with anyone before, but wanted it and instantly welcomed it with me. In fact he satisfied all my undefined specifications, and if men could marry, I would have proposed to him. He might even, in the first delight, have accepted me, for he never manifested the slightest interest in girls (he did not marry until well into his forties), was proud of me and my friendship and excited by all it had to offer—my flat, which became his second home, my car, which I taught him to drive, and the admiration which provided him with such presents as a smart civilian suit.

This boy engrossed my heart and thought for four years, but in a way I had not foreseen he was not Ideal: being a sailor he was too seldom available. Had he been more available, perhaps the affair would not have lasted so long. He was stationed in Portsmouth, free only at weekends, if then. Sometimes he went off for a long cruise on his ship. Whenever he had leave he came to stay with me; but because of his sporadic appearances, his conventional background, his unsophistication, and the "manly respectability" of our relationship (the Greek view of life), all my anxieties found their fullest play. I was not faithful to him (not that he demanded faithfulness), he was too much away, but concealed from him my nature and the kind of life I led (not that he ever exhibited the least curiosity about it). I did not want him to think me "queer" and himself a part of homosexuality, a term I disliked since it included prostitutes, pansies, pouffs, and queans. Though he met some of my homosexual friends, I was always on edge in case they talked in front of him the loose homosexual chatter we talked among ourselves. My sailor was a sacred cow and must be protected against all contamination.

The setting of the nuptial scene whenever he was due to arrive was fraught with anxieties. Idle callers of a "contaminating" kind, of whom I had too many, had to be warned off or turned away from the door; my boiling incontinence had some-how to be concealed; I would have liked instantly to undo his silks and ribbons, but the conventions by which he lived required, I supposed, the delays of conversation, drinks, supper: sex should be postponed to its proper respectable time, bedtime; the Red Lavender lozenges had to be handy, a towel also, though hidden from him, to obviate the embarrassment of turning out naked in search of one to dry us down, and to prevent, if possible, stains on the sheets as a speculation for my char. He liked dancing with me to the gramophone, readily accepting the female role, and often when I had ascertained that he too was in a state of erection we would strip and dance naked, so unbearably exciting that I could not for long endure the pres-sure of his body against mine. Our pleasures were, I suppose, fairly simple; kisses, caresses, manipulations, intercrural massage; he got his own satisfaction quite soon, though not as soon as I; whether we ever repeated these pleasures during the night (we slept in one bed) I don't recall; I doubt it; since he was an athlete, always boxing or training for it, I expect it was tacitly understood that he should conserve his strength. I am quite sure that if further turnings towards each other occurred, it was never he who turned. There seemed, indeed, always something to worry about—as there had been throughout my sexual life; and when a friend once asked me whether I ever "lost myself" in sex, the answer had to be no.

Careful though I seemed to myself to be with my sailor, my desire for him out-ran prudence, he began to feel an unwelcome emotional pressure, there were failed appointments when I waited for him in vain, and I started to lose my head. Advice came from a close friend [E. M. Forster] of mine:

> "I'm sure that if one tries to live only for love one cannot be happy, but perhaps happiness is not your deepest need. . . . The standards which are so obvious to you are very remote to him and his class, and he was bound to relapse from them sooner or later. And by standards I mean not only con-ventions but methods of feeling. He can quite well be deeply attached to you and yet suddenly find the journey up too much of a fag. It is difficult for us, with our middle-class training, to realise this, but it is so. Also if you want a permanent relationship with him or anyone, you must give up the idea of ownership, and even the idea of being owned. Relationships based on own-

ership may be the best (I have never known or tried to know them), but I'm certain they never last. Not being you and not knowing him I can't say any more, except to beg you to write nothing to him beyond brief notes of affection until you meet again. Don't rebuke, don't argify, don't apologise. . . ."

How much of this excellent advice I took, or was constitutionally able to take, I don't remember; very little, I imagine, for later on I went so far as to rent a flat in Portsmouth for the sailor and myself in order to see more of him than I was seeing in London. There, like any possessive housewife, I catered and cooked for him while he was at work, impatiently awaiting the moment of his return. One evening he said irritably, "What, chicken again!" It is the only speech he ever made that has stuck in my mind. The end was clearly in view, but it came, strangely and sadly enough, not through anything I put into his mouth, but through something I took into my own. I did to him the very thing that had so revolted me in Cambridge in the revelations of my homosexual friend's love-life. This was a thing I had never done before, reluctantly since and out of politeness if requested. It is a form of pleasure I myself have seldom enjoyed, passively or actively, preferring the kiss upon the lips, nor have I ever been good at it. Some technical skill seems required and a retraction of the teeth, which, perhaps because mine are too large or unsuitably arranged, seem always to get in the way. Squeamishness with comparative strangers over dirt or even disease disturbs me, and I have noticed that those normal young men who request for themselves this form of amusement never offer it in return. It is also, in my experience, a stimulation usually desired by a somewhat exhausted sex; it may produce quicker results for them than masturbation, but they are not quick, and to be practically choked for ten minutes or so after one's own orgasm has passed is something I have never enjoyed.

I suppose I acted towards my sailor thus because his body was so beautiful and desirable that I simply wanted to eat it. It was a fatal mistake. He cut future appointments, plunging me in despair. When, at length, I saw him again I asked if I had displeased him in any way. Roughly he replied, "You know what you did! You disgusted me!" After that he deserted me entirely for a year and a half, while I pined for him in the darkest dejection of spirit and lost much weight. Then, through the mediation of one of his brothers (a homosexual, oddly enough, and of a far more affectionate character, but unfortunately too effeminate to attract me), he wrote to apologise ("I behaved rottenly to you and you didn't deserve it") and called. He had a new gentleman friend now, I had learned from his brother, who took him for holidays to Nice and Cannes and had doubtless completed his education in matters of sex, thereby arousing his conscience over me; yet I think he would have resumed sex with me too, if only I had been able to control the emotion in my voice and the trembling of the arm I put around his shoulders. He did not want emotion, only fun. He then disappeared out of my life.

The Ideal Friend was never so nearly found again, though, as I interpret my life now, I devoted most of my leisure in the succeeding fifteen years to the search for him, picking up and discarding innumerable candidates. . . . The Ideal Friend was always somewhere else and might have been found if only I had turned a different way. The buses that passed my own bus seemed always to contain those charming boys who were absent from mine; the ascending escalators in the tubes fiendishly carried them past me as I sank helplessly into hell. Unless I had some actual business or social engagement (often maddening, for then, when punctuality or responsibility was unavoidable and I was walking with my host or guest, the Ideal Friend would be sure to appear and look deep into my eyes as he passed) I seldom reached my destination, but was forever darting off my buses, occupied always, it seemed, by women or Old Age Pensioners, because on the pavements below, which I was constantly scanning, some attractive boy had been observed. Yet one of my old anxieties, now in public form, persisted: I had to feel an absolute degree of confidence. Industrious predator though I was, I was not a bold or reckless one. . . . I did not want rebuffs or cuffs, nor did I want the police summoned. I had to feel reasonably safe and developed furtive techniques to aid me. I did not like boys to think I was pursuing them, they might turn nasty; the safest thing was the quick "open" exchange of understanding looks or smiles. For this it was necessary to meet people face to face, a problem if the particular boy was moving in the same direction. In such a case I would hasten after him, pass him without a glance (in the hope of not being noticed), and when I had reached what I considered to be an invisible distance ahead, turn about to retrace my steps for a head-on collision. If then I got a responsive look, a smile, a backward glance, if he then stopped to stare after me or to study the goods in the nearest shop-window (the more incongruous they were the safer I felt) I judged I might act, though still with caution in case he was luring me into some violent trap. The elaborateness of this manoeuvre often lost me the boy, he had gone into a house or disappeared up some side turning behind my back — and therefore remained in my chagrined thought as the Ideal Friend.

## Christopher Isherwood (1904–1986)

From *Christopher and His Kind* (1980)

When Isherwood left England for Germany, he went there because, as he says in *Christopher and His Kind*, Berlin for Christopher meant boys. Isherwood would eventually become one of the great apostles of homosexual freedom and rights and an elder statesman in America of gay liberation. Most of his life was spent away from England, for though boys may have been available there, the sexual freedom that having them implied was far more evident in Germany and on the Continent. Thus Isherwood, if not precisely an exile, chose to exile himself from an England that for him stood for everything repressive, inhibited, and hypocritical in middle-class morality. In Germany, where he stayed for three years from 1930 to 1933, he gathered material for a number of stories and novels, among them the famous *Berlin Stories* (written in the thirties and collected in 1954), which depict a number of homosexual characters including the amazing Mr. Norris. *All the Conspirators* (1928) and *The Memorial* (1932) also offer portraits of homosexual life. In 1939, along with his closest friend W. H. Auden, he emigrated to America. By this time Isherwood was beginning to develop the activist vision of homosexual life and politics that would eventually become so important in his life. In *The World in the Evening* (1954) he looks at homosexuality in terms of its minority status and argues for the need for liberation. *A Single Man* (1964), perhaps his greatest novel, presents a middle-aged homosexual, left alone after the death of his lover. The protagonist, George, whose recovery of life parallels his awakening into what can be described as a full-fledged gay consciousness, is one of the most profoundly drawn characters in Isherwood's contribution to what should be called Anglo-American gay literature.

The selection below from the autobiography *Christopher and his Kind* locates Isherwood in London when for the first time he meets E. M. Forster, and when, in a sense, Forster passed a torch to Isherwood, silently inspiring him to say in public what Forster had until then only dared to say in the privacy of an unpublished book.

### From Chapter 6 [London 1932]

Yesterday evening, [William] Plomer and I visited an opium den. Today he is taking me to see E. M. Forster. I shall spend the entire morning making-up.

I have only the dimmest memory of the alleged opium den. I think it was a pub somewhere in the dockland area, frequented by local Chinese and visiting Asian seamen. Plomer liked to keep the outskirts of his life hidden in an intriguing fog of mystery; now and then he would guide you through the fog to one of his haunts, with the casualness of a habitue. No doubt, opium was obtainable there, but I am sure that he and Christopher didn't smoke any. . . . By "making-up" I suppose Christopher merely meant that he would try in every way to look and be at his best for this tremendous encounter.

It was tremendous for Christopher. Forster was the only living writer whom he would have described as his master. In other people's books he found examples of style which he wanted to imitate and learn from. In Forster he found a key to the whole art of writing. The Zen masters of archery—of whom, in those days, Christopher had never heard—start by teaching you the mental attitude with which you must pick up the bow. A Forster novel taught Christopher the mental attitude with which he must pick up the pen.

Plomer had been able to arrange this meeting because Forster had read *The Memorial*—at his suggestion, probably—and had liked it, at least well enough to be curious about its author. (Thenceforward, Christopher was fond of saying, "My literary career is over—I don't give a damn for the Nobel Prize or the Order of Merit—I've been praised by Forster!" Nevertheless, Christopher's confidence in his own talent easily survived the several later occasions when Forster definitely didn't like one of his other books or when he praised books by writers whom Christopher found worthless.)

Forster must have been favorably impressed by Christopher; otherwise, he wouldn't have gone on seeing him. And Christopher made a good disciple; like most arrogant people, he loved to bow down unconditionally from time to time. No doubt he gazed at Forster with devoted eyes and set himself to entertain him with tales of Berlin and the boy world, judiciously spiced with expressions of social concern—for he must have been aware from the start that he had to deal with a moralist.

Forster never changed much in appearance until he became stooped and feeble in his late eighties. He was then fifty-three but he always looked younger than his age. And he never ceased to be babylike. His light blue eyes behind his spectacles were like those of a baby who remembers his previous incarnation and is more amused than dismayed to find himself reborn in new surroundings. He had a baby's vulnerability, which is also the invulnerability of a creature whom one dare not harm. He seemed to be swaddled, babylike, in his ill-fitting suit rather than wearing it. A baby with a mustache? Well, if a baby could have a mustache, it would surely be like his was, wispy and soft. . . . Nevertheless, behind that charming, unalarming exterior, was the moralist; and those baby eyes looked very deep into you. When they disapproved, they could be stern. They made Christopher feel false and tricky and embarrassed. He reacted to his embarrassment by trying to keep Forster amused. Thirty-eight years later, a friend who was present at the last meeting between them made the comment: "Mr. Forster laughs at you as if you were the village idiot."

I suppose that this first meeting took place in Forster's flat, and that, on the wall of its living room, there hung Eric Kennington's pastel portrait of T. E. Lawrence's bodyguard, quarrelsome little Mahmas, with his fierce eyes and naked dagger. This was the original of one of the illustrations to the privately printed edition of *Seven Pillars of Wisdom*. Lawrence had given copies of the book away to his friends, including Forster. Christopher left the flat clasping this magic volume, which Forster had lent him.

On April 5, Christopher went to London, taking with him books, papers, and other belongings which he wanted to store in Kathleen's house before he left Germany for good.

. . .

It was at this time that Forster showed Christopher the typescript of *Maurice*. Christopher felt greatly honored, of course, by being allowed to read it. Its antique locutions bothered him, here and there. When Alec speaks of sex with Maurice as "sharing," he grimaced and wriggled his toes with embarrassment. And yet the wonder of the novel was that it had been written when it had been written; the wonder was Forster himself, imprisoned within the jungle of pre-war prejudice, putting these unthinkable thoughts into words. Perhaps listening from time to time, to give himself courage, to the faraway chop-chop of those pioneer heroes, Edward Carpenter and George Merrill, boldly enlarging their clearing in the jungle. Carpenter and Merrill had been *Maurice*'s godparents. Merrill, as Forster was later to disclose, had psychophysically inspired him to write it by touching him gently just above the buttocks. (Forster—how characteristically!—comments, "I believe he touched most people's.")

Did Christopher think *Maurice* as good as Forster's other novels? He would have said—and I still agree with him—that it was both inferior and superior to them: inferior as an artwork, superior because of its purer passion, its franker declaration of its author's faith. This moved Christopher tremendously on that first reading.

At their meeting in 1932, the Master had praised the Pupil. This time, the Pupil was being asked by the Master, quite humbly, how *Maurice* appeared to a member of the thirties generation. "Does it date?" Forster was asking. To which Christopher, I am proud to say, replied, "Why shouldn't it date?" This was wise and true as well as encouraging, and it cheered Forster greatly. He told Christopher so in a subsequent letter.

My memory sees them sitting together, facing each other. Christopher sits gazing at this master of their art, this great prophet of their tribe, who declares that there can be real love, love without limits or excuse, between two men. Here he is, humble in his greatness, unsure of his own genius. Christopher stammers some words of praise and devotion, his eyes brimming with tears. And Forster—amused and touched, but more touched than amused—leans forward and kisses him on the cheek. (Nevertheless, he continued to call Christopher "Isherwood" for two more years.)

Almost every time they met, after this, they discussed the problem: how should *Maurice* end? That the ending should be a happy one was taken for granted; Forster had written the novel in order to affirm that such an ending is possible for homosexuals. But the choice of a final scene remained open. Should it be a glimpse of Maurice and Alec enjoying a life of freedom, outside the bounds of society? Should it be Maurice's good-humored parting from his faithless former lover, Clive: "Why don't you stop being shocked and attend to your own happiness?" Christopher wasn't satisfied with either ending. (The second was the one finally adopted.) He made his own suggestions—as did several of Forster's other friends. He loved this continuing discussion, simply as a game.

## Stephen Spender (1909–1995)

One of a circle at Oxford University that included Isherwood and Auden, Spender, like them, became fascinated by Germany and, like Isherwood, spent time there before the beginning of World War II. In his autobiography *World Within World* (1951), he candidly mentions his attractions to other men and from time to time comments on homosexual life in the 1930s. A novel, *The Temple*, written in 1929 but not published until 1988, is a fictionalized autobiography. There he employs material from his German experiences in the thirties and portrays not only his own social and sexual awakening but includes fictionalized portraits of Auden and Isherwood. Spender was reluctant to dwell on homosexual themes to any great extent, and they do not figure largely in his poetry. When he did address such subjects he preferred to emphasize the possibilities of bisexuality rather than exclusive homosexuality in human relationships. Indeed, he seemed to distance himself from the social and political aspects of the homosexual rights movement, maintaining that such a focus limits rather than inspirits a writer. In the autobiography, he made a point of noting that homosexual writers of his time were limited by social and legal condemnation of homosexuality, leaving them the choice of rebellion or sexual exile.

*Abrupt and charming mover*

Abrupt and charming mover,
Your pointed eyes under lit leaves,
Your light hair, your smile,
I watch burn in a foreign land
Bright through my dark night
And sheltered by my hand.

My ribs are like a Jonah's whale
In which I dream you: from day

I have recalled your play
Disturbing as birds flying
And with the Spring's infection
And denial of satisfaction.

You dance, forgetting all: in joy
Sustaining that instant of the eye
Which like a Catherine wheel spins free.
Your games of cards, hockey with toughs,
Winking at girls, shoes cribbed from toffs.
Like the encircling summer dew
Glaze me from head to toe.

By night I hold you, and by day
I watch you weave the silk cocoon
Of a son's or a skater's play.
We have no meeting place
Beneath the brilliantine-bright surface.
The outward figure of delight
Creates your image that's no image
Dark in my dark language.

*To T.A.R.H.*

Even whilst I watch him I am remembering
The quick laugh of the wasp-gold eyes.
The column turning from the staring window
Even while I see I remember, for love
Dips what it sees into a flood of memory
Vaster than itself, and makes the seen
Be drowned in all that past and future seeing
Of the once seen. Thus what I wore I wear
And shall wear always—the glint of the quick lids
And the body's axle turning: these shall be
What they are now within the might of Ever.
Night when my life lies with no past or future
But only endless space. It wakes and watches
Hope and despair and the small vivid longings
Gnaw the flesh, like minnows. Where it drank love
It breathes in sameness. Here are
The signs indelible. The wiry copper hair,
And the notched mothlike lips, and that after all human
Glance, which makes all else forgiven.

## Ralph Nicholas Chubb (1892–1960)

Prophet and visionary of androgyny, Chubb remains one of the least known and most curious—and sometimes most original—poets of twentieth-century homosexual literature. His poetry preaches the virtues of highly sexualized encounters between men and men and boys that will in turn become the scenes of spiritual, social, and political revelation. His books are as interesting for the history of book production as they are for that of poetry. He produced his books himself, in some reproducing his own complex and florid calligraphy, in others creating lithographed texts on handmade paper, complete with his own drawings, and in large folio size in very limited editions. His books are now extremely rare, and it is difficult to cull out of the tangled thicket of fairy stories, fables, mystical meditation, and sexual fantasies about the love of boys, poems that adequately reflect what he wrote and that also suggest the true originality of his talent. In style his poetry recalls that of Blake, and the occult homosexual mythology Chubb creates is equally complex. In no fewer than sixteen volumes with titles like *The Sacrifice of Youth, The Child of Dawn,* and *Flames of Sunrise: A Book of the Man Child concerning the Redemption of Albion,* he creates a mythology in which both in text and in illustration boys—whose images range from androgynous youths to muscular and erotic young men—are elevated to divine status and sex to the realm of ecstasy. The best essay on Chubb appears in Timothy d'Arch Smith's *Love in Earnest: Some Notes on the Lives and Writings of English Uranian Poets from 1889 to 1930.*

FROM *SONGS OF MANKIND* (1930)

*Song of My Soul*

The form of youth without blemish, is not such the form divine?
Children of love, today I will sing my song to you!

Under the sky in the hot noon-beam, in the water-meadow,
The sound of the rushing fall;
We two alone together screen'd by the trees and the thicket;
Naked the lecherous urchin, the slim beautiful boy,
Naked myself, dark, muscled like a god, the hardy enduring man;
He a fully form'd human being in his way,
Myself a fully form'd human being in my way;
No patronage between us, mutual respect, two equal persons;
He knowing the universe, I knowing the universe, equal together;
I having every whit as much to learn from him as he from me;
From him to me, from me to him, reciprocal sexual spiritual love.

No word needed, scarce ev'n a glance, mystically
Limbs interlace, bodies interpenetrate,
Spirits coalesce.
(He scarce needs to be there, 'tis in Imagination's realm true lovers meet.)
O burning tongue and hot lips of me exploring my love!

Lave his throat with the bubbling fountain of my verse!
Drench him! Slake his loins with it, most eloquent!
Leave no part, no crevice unexplored; delve deep, my minstrel tongue!
Let our juices flood and mingle! Let the prophetic lava flow!
Drink deep of love, the pair of us, O sacramental communion,
As our souls meet and melt!
The sweat of our armpits runneth down upon our breasts.
Be our bodies sealed together, part they with a smack!
I will be father and mother at once to thee, my son, thou shalt feed from my
    bosom.
And you shall be mother and father to me, and give me to suck my honey'd inspi-
    ration from your right nipple and from your left.
You shall leave no portion of me untasted, I will become fluid for your sake.
I will feed you spiritually with a stuff that shall make a man of you,
With the milk of divine manhood will I satisfy your soul.
Quick, your lips under my poetic dug,
My own soul's calf, pull, pull. Well out the manly hymns!
For I am he that shall fill your young veins with the seeds of all futurity.


FROM *THE HEAVENLY CUPID* (1934)

*Transfiguration*

Once as abroad I stray'd
In the soft evening gleam,
I saw by shadow'd stream
Two naked figures bright,
Shameless and unafraid,
Dancing in sheer delight,
As might two graceful girls.
Amid the willows cool
I saw their flesh as pearls
Shine by the shadowy pool
All opalescent white!
Crown'd by their misty curls!
So lovely delicate
It soothes me to relate!

My spirit was entranc'd
To see such artless grace.
On tip-toe I advanced.
O, 'twas a holy place!
And when I peep'd, behold!
Each bather was in truth
No girl, but a ripe youth
Seventeen summers old.

Their skin was smooth & fair,
And one had raven hair,
The other amber red,
That toss'd upon his head.

Lads of the common flock,
Their day spent at the desk,
At eve the mortal stock
Put off as fauns to frisk.
And pure as ivory
Transfigured each appears
As in a summer's dream,
Mysterious and agleam,
To visionary eye.
O! how the sight endears!
My bosom melted quite!
So holy was the sight!
Holy the ground I trod,
Where I saw mortal sprite
At play like stripling god!

Yet may I live to prove
The Grecian lover's dream
When naked youth and love
Caress 'neath sunlight's beam,
And love is freed from blame
And beauty knows no shame,
And boyish lovers meet
In soft endearments sweet,
And the boyish form divine
Is worship'd in nature's shrine,
And many a holy place
Sanctifies boyish grace;
And strip'd of mortal guise
Naked before my eyes
Spiritual bodies seen
of pretty mate with mate
Shall wanton, amorous clean,
In man's essential state.
Such was the sight sublime.

## W. H. Auden (1907–1973)

When Auden and Isherwood emigrated to America in 1939 they were both committed to attacking the hypocritical smugness of English sexual inhibitions. Yet Auden did not carry to America, as Isherwood did, a willingness to express a growing awareness of the political potential of homosexual identity or a concern to employ his talent to further such a sexual politics. Auden long insisted that the life of the artist was not always relevant to the work, and homosexuality in fact plays little obvious role in the larger body of his poetry, though it was central to his life, during which he never denied his orientation or concealed his long relationship with Chester Kallman. Nevertheless, the history of his life with Kallman, of his sexual adventures with numbers of young men (among them those he occasionally paid for sex), and the general homoerotic ambiance of his life with Isherwood and in the homosexual circles of Germany, England, and America can sometimes be discerned in his texts. If love is often his theme, the source of desire and the object of love more often than not is homosexual. If he explores politics and questions concerning human freedom, the text of personal freedom always writes a subtext in which sexual freedom, however obliquely indicated, plays an important role. Like Spender, Auden avoided overt expressions of homosexuality. But he did allow a piece of erotica, "The Platonic Blow," to be published in 1965, and he let stand in the collected works some poems that suggest homosexual desire.

*Legend (1931)*

Enter with him
These legends, Love;
For him assume
Each diverse form,
To legend native,
As legend queer;
That he may do
What these require,
Be, Love, like him
To legend true.

When he to ease
His heart's disease
Must cross in sorrow
Corrosive seas,
As dolphin go;
As cunning fox
Guide through the rocks
Tell in his ear
The common phrase
Required to please
The guardians there;
And when across
The livid marsh
Big birds pursue,
Again be true,
Between his thighs
As pony rise,

And swift as wind
Bear him away
Till cries and they
Are left behind.

But when at last,
These dangers passed,
His grown desire
Of legend tire,
Then, Love, standing
At legend's ending,
Claim your reward;
Submit your neck
To the ungrateful stroke
Of his reluctant sword,
That, starting back,
His eyes may look
Amazed on you,
Find what he wanted
Is faithful too
But disenchanted,
Love as love.

*Song IX [Funeral Blues] (1936)*

Stop all the clocks, cut off the telephone,
Prevent the dog from barking with a juicy bone,
Silence the pianos and with muffled drum
Bring out the coffin, let the mourners come.

Let aeroplanes circle moaning overhead
Scribbling on the sky the message He Is Dead,
Put crepe bows round the white necks of the public doves,
Let the traffic policemen wear black cotton gloves.

He was my North, my South, my East and West,
My working week and my Sunday rest,
My noon, my midnight, my talk, my song;
I thought that love would last for ever: I was wrong.

The stars are not wanted now: put out every one;
Pack up the moon and dismantle the sun;
Pour away the ocean and sweep up the wood;
For nothing now can ever come to any good.

## THREE POSTHUMOUS POEMS (1964–1967)

*I. Glad*

Hugerl, for a decade now
My bed-visitor,
An unexpected blessing
In a lucky life,
For how much and how often
You have made me glad.

Glad that I know we enjoy
Mutual pleasure:
Women may cog their lovers
With a feigned passion,
But males are so constructed
We cannot deceive.

Glad our worldss of enchantment
Are so several
Neither is tempted to broach:
I cannot tell a
Jaguar from a Bentley,
And you never read.

Glad for that while when you stole
(You burgled me too),
And were caught and put inside:
Both learned a lesson,
But for which we well might still
Be *Strich* and *Freier*.

Glad, though, we began that way,
That our life-paths crossed,
Like characters in Hardy,
At a moment when
You were in need of money
And I wanted sex.
How is it now between us?
Love? Love is far too
Tattered a word. A romance
In full fig it ain't,
Nor a naked letch either:
Let me say we fadge,

And how much I like Christa
Who loves you but knows,

Good girl, when not to be there.
I can't imagine
A kinder set-up: if mims
Mump, *es ist mir Wurscht*.


## II. *Aubade*

At break of dawn
he takes a street-car, happy
after a night of love.

Happy,
but sleepily wondering
how many away is the night

when an ecto-endomorph
cock-sucker must put on
The Widow's Cap.


## III. *Minnelied*

When one is lonely (and You,
My Dearest, know why,
as I know why it must be),
steps can be taken, even
a call-boy can help.
To-night, for instance, now that
Bert has been here, I
listen to the piercing screams
of palliardising cats
without self-pity.

# Part Six
Modern Love

*European Writers from 1870*

# 18. Inventing Homosexuals

## European Writing (1870–1969)

Nineteenth-century writers defined homosexuals in any number of configurations: the lone seeker after multiple sexual sensations or the chaste admirer of male beauty, a woman in the body of a man or a super-virile manly male. Usually the homosexual was pictured as one whose talents and sensibilities made him a species unique in nature. Relationships were portrayed as unions of valiant comrades, romantic lovers, chaste friends, or supportive relationships between man and youth. In general, most written creations of homosexual identity prior to the twentieth century challenged popular conceptions of homosexuals as sinful and criminal, as pathologically unmanly and afflicted members of a despised species. In the twentieth century, however, many of the weapons employed to demonize homosexuals were seized by homosexual writers themselves, and literature employed criminality, transvestism, effeminacy, and promiscuity not as definitions to destroy or deride but as weapons against oppression, bigotry, and hypocrisy, using the very terms and roles invented by social opprobrium to goad the oppressor and celebrate the variety of modern homosexual identities.

European inventions of modern homosexuality were products of a world between wars, of a Europe in which the vision of emancipation from the homophobia of ancien régimes was soon to be one more casualty of antidemocratic and totalitarian regimes. The increased oppression of homosexuals by totalitarian governments in Germany, Italy, and Spain, and the continued homophobia of British law did not provide a fertile ground in which literature with a new vision of homosexual relationships or a movement for liberation could flourish. Some European writers were willing to recognize and celebrate the role of the homosexual as rebel and revolutionary—Gide, Genet, Cernuda come to mind as the most outspoken. Yet certain popular conceptions about homosexuality remained strong: it was exclusively a relationship between men and youths, it was an illness and an abnormality; homosexuals were effeminate or deliberately adopted a pose of languid effeteness as a mark of homosexuality. All these views survived from the nineteenth century and remained central to the portrayal of homosexuals in Europe and Latin America. It would be several years after World War II before any country in Europe was able to support, in the way that they had done in the years before World War I, the creation of new ways of looking at homosexuality and to entertain the possibility that homosexuals might become a political force. Europe would require a vision and voice from the New World for such a thing. When American gay people marched on Stonewall in 1969, such a vision was at hand. The selections below include some of the central and seminal European texts that contributed to a written creation of homosexual identities before the appearance of the various liberationist movements that flowered in Europe and America in the late 1960s.

# 19. Les Monstres Sacrés

## France (1870–1945)

In England and Germany after 1850, writers were creating a literary and political dialogue advocating the decriminalization of homosexual acts and a radical reevaluation of social attitudes toward homosexuality. In France where homosexual acts had not been criminal since 1791 and where Englishmen like Oscar Wilde sought the sexual freedom their country denied them, there was little place, perhaps even little apparent need, for such an effort. Homosexuality of course was hardly unknown in nineteenth-century texts. In *Illusions perdues* and in *Splendeurs et misères des courtisanes* (1844–1846), Balzac includes a number of characters who appear to be touched by what the French still called the sin of Sodom. Balzac also treated of androgyny in *Seraphita* and lesbianism in *La fille aux yeux d'or*. The stormy love affair between Arthur Rimbaud and Paul Verlaine allowed Verlaine to confront and explicitly employ male homosexuality in poetry. Encouraged perhaps by Verlaine's daring, literary productions of the *fin de siècle*, that complex of attitudes and literary experimentation that marked what the French called "decadence," explored the spectrum of eroticism and sensuality, emphasizing often the appeal of androgyny and the sensuality of lesbianism, the latter made especially resonant in Pierre Louÿs's *Chanson de Bilitis* (1894). In 1884, Joris-Karl Huysmans's novel *Á rebours* offers tantalizing hints about male homosexuality interwoven within the lush and hothouse atmosphere that Huysmans creates for his bachelor sensualist.

It would not be, however, until after World War I that male homosexuality as a theme would achieve an importance in French literature that would allow it to enter the discourse of French intellectual society where such topics could flourish, be discussed and dissected, and finally, leaving the intimacy of the salon, enter into the table talk of a generally conservative, usually misapprehending, and almost always disapproving French public. Marcel Proust and André Gide began the process that would bring public attention to homosexuality—Proust in *Remembrance of Things Past* and Gide in his collection of four essays, *Corydon*. But writing about homosexuality remained if not under ban at least under strong disapproval—and occasionally under legal constraint, as is evidenced by the fate of the homosexual journal *Inversions*, which was banned from publication in 1925.

Some Americans came to France between the wars to seek the freer shores that France legendarily promised, among them Gertrude Stein, Natalie Barney, Robert McAlmon, and Charles Henri Ford. They created a homosexual presence, at least among the younger members of the literary elite of Paris, that allowed the beginning of a transatlantic dialogue that would have some effect on the parallel but more vigorous debate about homosexuality then being engaged in by American writers during the twenties and thirties. In 1929 Jean Cocteau's *Le Livre blanc*, which presented homosexuality autobiographically, did so anonymously. Though homosexuality was a topic openly discussed, to be openly homosexual was still problematic and the openly homosexual René Crevel was shunned by those communists and surrealists with whom intellectually, politically, and artistically he had the closest connections, leading him to commit suicide in 1935.

Defining homosexuality and siting it, perhaps dangerously, within the mise en scène of French culture is the mission that Proust and Gide undertook to perform during the years between the publication of *Corydon* and the occupation of France by Germany. In 1942 the Vichy government, under the German occupation, re-criminalized homosexual acts. Though again under prohibition, homosexuality was nevertheless the subject of Roger Peyrfittes' *Les amities particulières* (1943), portraying the yearning love of adolescents. Once mentioned, however, homosexuality could not be silenced, and in the work of Jean Genet, France produced its greatest homosexual writer. After the war, though the Gaullist regime was hostile to homosexuality, Genet continued to write, and the magazine *Arcadie*, the first homosexual journal in French, published articles about gay causes. The task of gay liberation in France was profoundly influenced by the gay liberation movement in America, and in France it was furthered after 1969 in works by Michel Foucault, Roland Barthes, and Guy Hocquenghem, whose *Homosexual Desire* (1972) is a modern French manifesto of gay liberation. French homosexuals began then to create a gay subculture and a political dialogue that attempted to continue the definition of homosexuality and to educate a conservative French public about a presence that had always been among them.

## Further Reading

Rommel Mendes-Leite and Pierre-Olivier de Busscher, eds., *Gay Studies from the French Cultures* (New York: Harrington Park Press,1993); George Stambolian and Elaine Marks, eds., *Homosexualties and French Literature* (Ithaca, N.Y.: Cornell University Press, 1979).

## Arthur Rimbaud (1854–1891)

The sometimes public and certainly tempestuous love affair between Arthur Rimbaud and Paul Verlaine impelled both poets to some of their best work, though in Rimbaud's symbolist text homosexuality is not so prominent as it is in Verlaine's poems. Rimbaud's poetry was almost all written during the years of his involvement with Verlaine, between 1871 and 1873 when they quarreled, after which Rimbaud wrote *Une saison en enfer*, describing what he called the season in hell he had endured with Verlaine. After Rimbaud's death Verlaine continued his explorations of homosexuality in life and in literature, celebrating it and defining it in a number of poems, including poems in *Hombres* and in *Parrallèlement*. No French poet of stature before Verlaine had been so willing to utilize explicit homosexuality in poems, and by doing so he made a homoerotic language available for all of French literature, a language not unlike that which Genet would later employ.

FROM *LES STUPRA*

*Translated by Paul Schmidt*

*Our Assholes Are Different*
*[Nos fesses ne sont pas les leurs (1872–73)]*

Our assholes are different from theirs. I used to watch
Young men let down their pants behind some tree,
And in those happy floods that youth set free
I watched the architecture of our crotch.

Quite firm, in many cases pale, it owes
Its form to muscles, and a wickerwork
Of hairs; for girls, the most enchanting lurk
In a dark crack where tufted satin grows.

The touching and wonderful innocence
Of painted cherubs on a Baroque shrine
Is recalled in that cheek a dimple indents . . .

Oh! If only we were naked now, and free
To watch our protruding parts align;
To whisper—both of us—in ecstasy!

## Paul Verlaine (1844–1896)

*Sonnet to the Asshole*

*Translated by Alan Stone*

*[Le sonnet du trou du cul (1872–73)]*

[The octet was written by Verlaine; the sestet by Rimbaud.]

Like a mauve carnation puckered up and dim
it breathes, meekly nestled amid the foam,
damp, too, from caresses tracing the smooth dome
of creamy buttocks up to the innermost rim.

Filaments oozing like drops of milk, driven
by the pitiless south wind, are blown
back across the russet marl's small stones
to vanish where the white slope sucks them in.

My mouth mates often with this air hole.
Jealous of this carnal union, my soul
fashions its nest of musky tears and sobs.

It's the drunken olive, the cajoling flute,
the heavenly praline's earthward chute,
feminine Canaan mid come bursting in gobs.

FROM *HOMBRES* (1891)

*Translated by Alan Stone*

*Balanide II*

Glans, high point of the soul
    of my lord,
of my beloved boy,
by you my happy asshole
    is bored

with a mixture of dread and joy.
(Anus drilled so long
    as some wrong
swells, straightens, and, full of pride
over brave, manly deeds
    parts cheeks
and savagely thrusts inside.)

Salter of red, meaty cunt,
    eternal font
my lips juicily lick,
glans, gross dainty
    no modesty
can spoil—now, you prick,

delicious glans, come, lift
    your shaft
of hot caressing mauve silk
rigged out by my hand
    in one grand
flourish with opal and milk.

It's just to milk my prick
    real quick
that I summon you today.
What's this! Your heat sizzles,
    I fizzle!
Goodbye to curds and whey!

Your whims none may foretell:
    Again you swell
mouth and anus wanting more;
now here they are all set,
    in a sweat
for you, unvanquished lord.

Glans, nectar made to console
    my soul,
go back in your foreskin, slow
like a god into his cloud.
    I'm bowed
before you, reverent, as you go.


*Mille e tre*

My lovers aren't members of the gentry,
they're common laborers from suburbs or farms,

fifteen to twentyish, no frills, but with plenty
of brute vigor and rough, cocky charms.

Virile in dungarees and coats—their work clothes—
it's not perfume but health they ooze, pure and simple;
their gait, though rather lumbering, goes
in a poised, springy fashion, young and nimble.

With friendly mischief their cunning eyes twinkle
while their wet lips, full of robust kisses,
mouth slyly naive sweet nothings sprinkled
for good measure with a few "shits" and "pisses."

Their long strong guns and nice hot buns
delight my dork and asshole every night.
By dawnlight or lamplight their gleeful guns
set my sagging, unconquered passions aright.

Thighs, souls, hands, my topsy-turvy brain,
feet, hearts, backs, ears, noses, traces
of nights, guts—all howl a refrain
and tread a wild jig in those boys' mad embraces.

Wild jig, mad refrain, more heaven's gift
than hell's, more infernal than sublime
—dizzied by this dancing I drift
in their rivulets of sweat, on their breath I climb.

My two Charleses—one a frisky tiger, eyes of a cat,
altar boy of sorts turning into an old blade;
the other a fine fellow, an impudent brat,
you only get randy when I go for your blade.

Odilon, street kid who's hung like a man,
your feet worship mine which burn even more
for your toes, still more for your can,
good and husky, but O those perfect feet I adore!

Fine, caressing phalanxes, satin-smooth
beneath the soles, around the ankles, branching where
arches flow with veins, and those strange, soothing
kisses of four feet having one soul, I swear!

Anthony, legendary in phallic size,
my triumphant king, god whom I revere
piercing my heart with your big blue eyes,
piercing my ass with your iron-tipped hunting spear.

Paul, blond athlete, pectorals resplendent
on a creamy chest whose hard tits I suck
same as your spout; Francis, sheafs of wheat bending
are your dancer's legs as shapely as your cock!

Augustus (a killer when we were just scratching
our first pubes) grows manlier with each new day;
Jules, your pale beauty makes you a bit bitchy;
Henry, stunning recruit who's off, drats! to the fray.

And all you lovers, whether had in a throng,
one by one, or alone—clear vision of the past,
present lusts, future stretching long,
no end to you sweethearts, yet never enough ass!

## Marcel Proust (1871–1922)

FROM *À LA RECHERCHE DU TEMPS PERDU* (1913–1927)

[*REMEMBRANCE OF THINGS PAST*]

Proust's monumental confrontation of the subject of homosexuality in *Remembrance of Things Past* allowed readers to suspect that homosexuality might well be more than just the act of a lustful sodomite or the single-minded obsession of effete men bereft of and denying manhood. Instead Proust's novel showed that homosexuality is a complex and multilayered subject that, if examined closely, defeated stereotypes. Proust's own accommodation with homosexuality was complex. Obsessed by it, half convinced of its degeneracy as he was half convinced that society was wrong in persecuting it, he introduced many homosexual characters into his works. He began his examination of the topic in *Contre Sainte-Beuve*, a volume of essays written between 1908 and 1910 in which the chapter "A Race Accursed" contains material he would later use in *Sodome et Gomorrhe* (*Cities of the Plain*) and *Le temps retrouvé* (*Time Regained*), where he devotes a lengthy section to a male brothel. In this selection, Proust portrays the effete Baron Charlus as one of the children of Sodom as he engages in a mannered seduction of the tailor Jupien. Proust employs the occasion to write one of the great twentieth-century meditations on homosexuality and its place in French society of his time.

FROM *SODOME ET GOMORRHE I* (1921)

*Translated by C. K. Scott Moncrieff and Terence Kilmartin*

[Proust describes the meeting between Baron Charlus and the effeminate Jupien. This meeting provokes a meditation upon those who Proust describes as a "race upon which a curse is laid."]

## [A RACE ACCURSED]

I now understood . . . why . . . I had managed to arrive at the conclusion that M. de Charlus looked like a woman: he was one! He belonged to that race of beings, less paradoxical than they appear, whose ideal is manly precisely because their temperament is feminine, and who in ordinary life resemble other men in appearance only; there where each of us carries, inscribed in those eyes through which he beholds everything in the universe, a human form engraved on the surface of the pupil, for them it is not that of a nymph but that of an ephebe. A race upon which a curse is laid and which must live in falsehood and perjury because it knows that its desire, that which constitutes life's dearest pleasure, is held to be punishable, shameful, an inadmissible thing; which must deny its God, since its members, even when Christians, when at the bar of justice they appear and are arraigned, must before Christ and in his name refute as a calumny what is their very life; sons without a mother, to whom they are obliged to lie all her life long and even in the hour when they close her dying eyes; friends without friendships, despite all those which their frequently acknowledged charm inspires and their often generous hearts would gladly feel—but can we describe as friendships those relationships which flourish only by virtue of a lie and from which the first impulse of trust and sincerity to which they might be tempted to yield would cause them to be rejected with disgust, unless they are dealing with an impartial or perhaps even sympathetic spirit, who however in that case, misled with regard to them by a conventional psychology, will attribute to the vice confessed the very affection that is most alien to it, just as certain judges assume and are more inclined to pardon murder in inverts and treason in Jews for reasons derived from original sin and racial predestination? And lastly—according at least to the first theory which I sketched in outline at the time, which we shall see subjected to some modification in the sequel, and in which this would have angered them above all else had not the paradox been hidden from their eyes by the very illusion that made them see and live—lovers who are almost precluded from the possibility of that love the hope of which gives them the strength to endure so many risks and so much loneliness, since they are enamoured of precisely the type of man who has nothing feminine about him, who is not an invert and consequently cannot love them in return; with the result that their desire would be for ever unappeased did not their money procure for them real men, and their imagination end by making them take for real men the inverts to whom they have prostituted themselves. Their honour precarious, their liberty provisional, lasting only until the discovery of their crime; their position unstable, like that of the poet one day feted in every drawingroom and applauded in every theatre in London, and the next driven from every lodging, unable to find a pillow upon which to lay his head, turning the mill like Samson and saying like him: "The two sexes shall die, each in a place apart!" excluded even, save on the days of general misfortune when the majority rally round the victim as the Jews rallied round Dreyfus, from the sympathy—at times from the society—of their fellows, in whom they inspire only disgust at seeing themselves as they are, portrayed in a mirror which, ceasing to flatter them, accentuates every blemish that they have refused to observe in themselves, and makes them understand that what they have been calling their love (and to which, playing upon the word, they have by association annexed all that poetry, painting, music, chivalry, asceticism have contrived to add to love) springs not from an ideal of beauty which they have chosen but from an incurable disease; like the Jews again (save some who will associate only with those

of their race and have always on their lips the ritual words and the accepted pleas-
antries), shunning one another, seeking out those who are most directly their opposite, who do not want their company, forgiving their rebuffs, enraptured by their
condescensions; but also brought into the company of their own kind by the
ostracism to which they are subjected, the opprobrium into which they have fallen,
having finally been invested, by a persecution similar to that of Israel, with the
physical and moral characteristics of a race, sometimes beautiful, often hideous,
finding (in spite of all the mockery with which one who, more closely integrated
with, better assimilated to the opposing race, is in appearance relatively less
inverted, heaps upon one who has remained more so) a relief in frequenting the
society of their kind, and even some support in their existence, so much so that,
while steadfastly denying that they are a race (the name of which is the vilest of
insults), they readily unmask those who succeed in concealing the fact that they
belong to it, with a view less to injuring them, though they have no scruple about
that, than to excusing themselves, and seeking out (as a doctor seeks out cases of
appendicitis) cases of inversion in history, taking pleasure in recalling that Socrates
was one of themselves, as the Jews claim that Jesus was one of them, without reflecting that there were no abnormal people when homosexuality was the norm, no
anti-Christians before Christ, that the opprobrium alone makes the crime because
it has allowed to survive only those who remained obdurate to every warning, to
every example, to every punishment, by virtue of an innate disposition so peculiar
that it is more repugnant to other men (even though it may be accompanied by
high moral qualities) than certain other vices which exclude those qualities, such
as theft, cruelty, breach of faith, vices better understood and so more readily
excused by the generality of men; forming a freemasonry far more extensive, more
effective and less suspected than that of the Lodges, for it rests upon an identity of
tastes, needs, habits, dangers, apprenticeship, knowledge, traffic, vocabulary, and
one in which even members who do not wish to know one another recognise one
another immediately by natural or conventional, involuntary or deliberate signs
which indicate one of his kind to the beggar in the person of the nobleman whose
carriage door he is shutting, to the father in the person of his daughter's suitor, to
the man who has sought healing, absolution or legal defence in the doctor, the
priest or the barrister to whom he has had recourse; all of them obliged to protect
their own secret but sharing with the others a secret which the rest of humanity
does not suspect and which means that to them the most wildly improbable tales
of adventure seem true, for in this life of anachronistic fiction the ambassador is a
bosom friend of the felon, the prince, with a certain insolent aplomb born of his
aristocratic breeding which the timorous bourgeois lacks, on leaving the duchess's
party goes off to confer in private with the ruffian; a reprobate section of the human
collectivity, but an important one, suspected where it does not exist, flaunting
itself, insolent and immune, where its existence is never guessed; numbering its
adherents everywhere, among the people, in the army, in the church, in prison, on
the throne; living, in short, at least to a great extent, in an affectionate and perilous
intimacy with the men of the other race, provoking them, playing with them by
speaking of its vice as of something alien to it—a game that is rendered easy by the
blindness or duplicity of the others, a game that may be kept up for years until the

day of the scandal when these lion-tamers are devoured; obliged until then to make a secret of their lives, to avert their eyes from the direction in which they would wish to stray, to fasten them on what they would naturally turn away from, to change the gender of many of the adjectives in their vocabulary, a social constraint that is slight in comparison with the inward constraint imposed upon them by their vice, or what is improperly so called, not so much in relation to others as to themselves, and in such a way that to themselves it does not appear a vice. But certain among them, more practical, busier men who have not the time to go and drive their bargains, or to dispense with the simplification of life and the saving of time which may result from co-operation, have formed two societies of which the second is composed exclusively of persons similar to themselves. . . .

It is true that inverts, in their search for a male, often content themselves with other inverts as effeminate as themselves. But it is enough that they do not belong to the female sex, of which they have in them an embryo which they can put to no useful purpose, as happens with so many hermaphrodite flowers, and even with certain hermaphrodite animals, such as the snail, which cannot be fertilised by themselves, but can by other hermaphrodites. In this respect the race of inverts, who readily link themselves with the ancient East or the golden age of Greece, might be traced back further still, to those experimental epochs in which there existed neither dioecious plants nor monosexual animals, to that initial hermaphroditism of which certain rudiments of male organs in the anatomy of women and of female organs in that of men seem still to preserve the trace.

. . . Admittedly, every man of M. de Charlus's kind is an extraordinary creature since, if he does not make concessions to the possibilities of life, he seeks out essentially the love of a man of the other race, that is to say a man who is a lover of women (and incapable consequently of loving him); contrary to what I had imagined in the courtyard, where I had seen Jupien hovering round M. de Charlus like the orchid making overtures to the bumble-bee, these exceptional creatures with whom we commiserate are a vast crowd, as we shall see in the course of this book, for a reason which will be disclosed only at the end of it, and commiserate with themselves for being too many rather than too few. For the two angels who were posted at the gates of Sodom to learn whether its inhabitants (according to Genesis) had indeed done all the things the report of which had ascended to the Eternal Throne must have been, and of this one can only be glad, exceedingly ill chosen by the Lord, who ought to have entrusted the task to a Sodomite. Such a one would never have been persuaded by such excuses as "I'm the father of six and I've two mistresses," to lower his flaming sword benevolently and mitigate the punishment. He would have answered: "Yes, and your wife lives in a torment of jealousy. But even when these women have not been chosen by you from Gomorrah, you spend your nights with a watcher of flocks upon Hebron." And he would at once have made him retrace his steps to the city which the rain of fire and brimstone was to destroy. On the contrary, they allowed all the shameless Sodomites to escape, even if these, on catching sight of a boy, turned their heads like Lot's wife, though without being on that account changed like her into pillars of salt. With the result that they engendered a numerous progeny with whom this gesture has remained habitual, like that of the dissolute women who, while apparently studying a row of shoes displayed in a shop window, turn their heads to keep track of a passing student. These descendants of the Sodomites, so numerous that we may apply to them that other verse of Genesis: "If a man can number the dust of the earth, then shall thy seed also be numbered," have established themselves throughout the entire world; they have had access to every profession and are so readily admitted into the most exclusive clubs that, whenever a Sodomite fails to secure election, the black balls are for the most part cast by other Sodomites, who make a point of condemning sodomy, having inherited the mendacity that enabled their ancestors to escape from the accursed city. It is possible that they may return there one day. Certainly they form in every land an oriental colony, cultured, musical, malicious, which has charming qualities and intolerable defects. We shall study them with greater thoroughness in the course of the following pages; but I have thought it as well to utter here a provisional warning against the lamentable error of proposing (just as people have encouraged a Zionist movement) to create a Sodomist movement and to rebuild Sodom. For, no sooner had they arrived there than the Sodomites would leave the town so as not to have the appearance of belonging to it, would take wives, keep mistresses in other cities where they would find, incidentally, every diversion that appealed to them. They would repair to Sodom only on days of supreme necessity, when their own town was empty, at those seasons when hunger drives the wolf from the woods. In other words, everything would go on very much as it does today in London, Berlin, Rome, Petrograd or Paris.

## André Gide (1869–1951)

Gide may have been prompted to embrace the aesthetic doctrine that the life of the senses should be explored in every aspect when he met Oscar Wilde in 1891. Certainly this is the message of much of his writing, including the early *The Fruits of the Earth* (1897) and *The Immoralist* (1902). In 1907 Gide began and in a private edition in 1911 published a short version of what would become four essays entitled *Corydon*, taking the name from the love-sick young man mad for Alexis in Virgil's Second Eclogue. He did not sign his name to the original publication but did so in the longer version published in 1924. It may be that Gide was emboldened to publish by the appearance of Marcel Proust's *Sodome et Gomorrhe* in 1921. Both texts stirred debate about homosexuality, opening the modern exploration of the subject in French literature. Gide also was responding to the public fascination with and condemnation of homosexual scandals surrounding the court of the German Kaiser Wilhelm II, whose favorite, Philip Furst zu Eulenberg, had been exposed as a homosexual in the public press. In addition, the topic that Gide uses to open the essays, a debate over Walt Whitman's homosexuality, had brought to the fore the old stereotypes about the presumed unnaturalness and unmanliness of homosexuals. The reversal of stereotypes was what interested Gide, and he argued that homosexuality is natural in human beings, and throughout the essay implies that homosexuals are not only a sexual but a political minority whose situation in society needed to be the subject of radical reevaluation. He further asserted that homosexuality makes important contributions to society, and that definitions that depict homosexuals as effeminate, as inverts, or as degenerate do not recognize the complexity of homosexuality. In the four dialogues (of which the first is reprinted below), Corydon answers the objection of the homophobic narrator, but it is Gide himself who is the spokesman for a positive advocacy of homosexuality.

FROM *CORYDON* (1907; 1924)

*Translated by Richard Howard*

FROM THE FIRST DIALOGUE

In the year 190—, a scandalous trial raised once again the irritating question of uranism. For eight days, in the salons as in the cafés, nothing else was mentioned. Impatient with theories and exclamations offered on all sides by the ignorant, the bigoted, and the stupid, I wanted to know my own mind; realizing that reason rather than just temperament was alone qualified to condemn or condone, I decided to go and discuss the subject with Corydon. He, I had been told, made no objection to certain unnatural tendencies attributed to him; my conscience would not be clear until I had learned what he had to say in their behalf.

It was ten years since I had last seen Corydon. At that time he was a high-spirited boy, as gentle as he was proud, generous, and obliging, whose very glance compelled respect. He had been a brilliant medical student, and his early work gained him much professional approval. After leaving the Lycée where we had been students together, we remained fairly close friends for a long time. Then several years of travel separated us, and when I returned to Paris to live, the deplorable reputation his behavior was acquiring kept me from seeking him out.

On entering his apartment, I admit I received none of the unfortunate impressions I had feared. Nor did Corydon afford any such impression by the way he dressed, which was quite conventional, even a touch austere perhaps. I glanced around the room in vain for signs of that effeminacy which experts manage to discover in everything connected with inverts and by which they claim they are never deceived. However, I did notice, over his mahogany desk, a huge photographic reproduction of Michelangelo's "Creation of Man," showing Adam naked on the primeval slime, reaching up to the divine Hand and turning toward God a dazzled look of gratitude. Corydon's vaunted love of art would have accounted for any surprise I might have shown at the choice of this particular subject. On the desk, the portrait of an old man with a long white beard, whom I immediately recognized as the American poet Walt Whitman, since it appears as the frontispiece of Leon Bazalgette's recent translation of his works. Bazalgette had also just published a voluminous biography of the poet which I had recently come across and which now served as a pretext for opening the conversation.

"After reading Bazalgette's book," I began, "I don't see much reason for this portrait to be on display here."

My remark was impertinent; Corydon pretended not to understand. I insisted.

"First of all," he answered, "Whitman's work remains just as admirable as it ever was, regardless of the interpretation each reader chooses to give his behavior . . ."

"Still, you have to admit that your admiration has diminished somewhat, now that Bazalgette has proved that Whitman didn't behave as you so eagerly assumed he did."

"Your friend Bazalgette has proved nothing whatever; his entire argument depends on a syllogism that can just as easily be reversed. Homosexuality, he postulates, is an unnatural tendency . . . Now, Whitman was in perfect health; you might say he was the best representative literature has ever provided of the natural man . . ."

"*Therefore* Whitman wasn't a pederast. I don't see how you can get around that."

"But the work is there, and no matter how often Bazalgette translates the word 'love' as 'affection' or 'friendship,' and the word 'sweet' as 'pure,' whenever Whitman addresses his 'comrade,' the fact remains that all the fervent, tender, sensual, impassioned poems in the book are of the same order—that order you call *contra naturam*.

"I don't call it an order at all . . . But how would you reverse his syllogism?"

"Like this: Whitman can be taken as the typical normal man. Yet Whitman was a pederast . . ."

"*Therefore* pederasty is normal . . . Bravo! Now all you have to prove is that Whitman was a pederast. As far as begging the question goes, I prefer Bazalgette's syllogism to yours—it doesn't go so much against common sense."

"It's not common sense but the truth we should avoid going against. I'm writing an article about Whitman—an answer to Bazalgette's argument."

"These questions of behavior are of great interest to you ?"

"I should say so. In fact, I'm writing a long study of the subject."

"Aren't the works of Moll and Krafft-Ebing and Raffalovich enough for you?"

"Not enough to satisfy me. I'd like to deal with the subject in a different way."

"I've always thought it was best to speak of such things as little as possible—often they exist at all only because some blunderer runs on about them. Aside from the fact that they are anything but elegant in expression, there will always be some imbecile to model himself on just what one was claiming to condemn."

"I'm not claiming to condemn anything."

"I've heard that you call yourself tolerant."

"You don't understand what I'm saying. I see I'll have to tell you the title of what I'm writing."

"By all means."

"What I'm writing is a *Defense of Pederasty*."

"Why not a Eulogy, while you're at it?"

"A title like that would distort my ideas; even with a word like 'Defense,' I'm afraid some readers will take it as a kind of provocation."

"And you'll actually publish such a thing?"

"Actually," he answered more seriously, "I won't."

"You know, you're all alike," I continued, after a moment's silence; "you swagger around in private and among yourselves, but out in the open and in front of the public your courage evaporates. In your heart of hearts you know perfectly well that the censure heaped on you is entirely deserved; you protest so eloquently in whispers, but when it comes to speaking up, you give in."

"It's true that the cause lacks martyrs."

"Let's not use such high-sounding words."

"I'm using the words that are needed. We've had Wilde and Krupp and Eulenberg and Macdonald . . ."

"And they're not enough for you?"

"Oh, victims! As many victims as you like—but not martyrs. They all denied—they always will deny."

"Well of course, facing public opinion, the newspapers, or the courts, each one is ashamed and retracts."

"Or commits suicide, unfortunately! Yes, you're right, it's a surrender to public opinion to establish one's innocence by disavowing one's life. Strange! we have the courage of our opinions, but never of our behavior. We're quite willing to suffer, but not to be disgraced."

"Aren't you just like the rest, in avoiding publication of your book?"

He hesitated a moment, and then: "Maybe I won't avoid it."

"All the same, once you were dragged into court by a Queensberry or a Harden, you can anticipate what your attitude would be."

"I'm afraid I can. I would probably lose courage and deny everything, just like my predecessors. We're never so alone in life that the mud thrown at us fails to dirty someone we care for. A scandal would upset my mother terribly, and I'd never forgive myself. My younger sister lives with her and isn't married yet—it might not be so easy to find someone who would accept me as his brother-in-law."

"Well, I certainly see what you mean; so you admit that such behavior dishonors even the man who merely tolerates it."

"That's not an admission, it's an observation of the facts. Which is why I'm looking for martyrs to the cause."

"What do you mean by such a word?"

"Someone who would forestall any attack—who without bragging or showing off would bear the disapproval, the insults; or better still, who would be of such acknowledged merit—such integrity and uprightness—that disapproval would hesitate from the start . . ."

"You'll never find such a man."

"Let me hope he'll appear."

"Listen, just between ourselves: do you really think it would do much good? How much of a change in public opinion can you expect? I grant that you're a little . . . constrained. If you were a little more so, it would be all the better for you, believe me. Such wretched behavior would come to a stop quite naturally, just by not having to put itself on show." I noticed that he shrugged his shoulders, which didn't keep me from insisting: "Don't you suppose there are enough turpitudes on display as it is?" And I permitted myself to remark that homosexuals find any number of facilities in one place or another. "Let them be content with the ones that are concealed, and with the complicity of their kind; don't try to win the approval or even the indulgence of respectable people on their behalf."

"But it's the esteem of just such people I cannot do without."

"If you can't do without it, then change your behavior."

"I can't do that. It can't be 'changed'—that's the dilemma for which Krupp and Macdonald and the rest saw no other solution than a bullet."

"Luckily you're less tragic."

"I wouldn't swear to it. But I would like to finish my book."

"Admit that there's more than a little pride in your case.

"None whatever."

"You cultivate your strangeness, and then in order not to be ashamed of it you congratulate yourself on not feeling like all the rest."

He shrugged again and walked up and down the room without a word; then, having apparently overcome the impatience my last remarks aroused:

ii

"Not so long ago, you used to be my friend," he said, sitting down again beside me. "I remember that we could understand each other. Is it really necessary for you to make such a show of sarcasm each time I say a word? Of course I'm not asking for your approval, but can't you even listen to me in good faith—the same good faith in which I'm talking to you . . . at least, the way I *would* talk if I felt you were listening . . ."

"Forgive me," I said, disarmed by the tone of his words. "It's true that I've lost touch with you. Yes, we were once quite close, in the days when your behavior still held out against your inclinations."

"And then you stopped seeing me; to be frank about it, you broke off relations."

"Let's not argue about that; but suppose we talked the way we used to," I went on, holding out my hand. "I have time to listen to anything you have to say. When we used to see each other, you were still a student. Did you already have such a clear notion of yourself back then? Tell me—I want to know the truth."

He turned toward me with a new expression of confidence, and began:

"During my years as an intern in the hospital, the awareness I came to of my . . . anomaly plunged me into a state of mortal distress. It's absurd to maintain, as some people still do, that you only come to pederasty because you're seduced into it, that it's the result of nothing but being dissipated or blasé. And I couldn't see myself as either degenerate or sick. Hard-working and extremely chaste, I was living with the firm intention, once my internship was over, of marrying a girl who has since then died, and whom I used to love above anything else in the world.

"I loved her too much to realize clearly that I didn't desire her at all. I know that some people are reluctant to admit that the one can exist without the other; I was entirely unaware of it myself. Yet no other woman ever haunted my dreams, or wakened any desire in me whatever. Still less was I tempted by the prostitutes I saw almost all my friends chasing. But since at the time I hardly suspected I might actually desire others altogether, I convinced myself that my abstinence was a virtue, gloried in the notion of remaining a virgin until marriage, and prided myself on a purity I could not suppose was a delusion. Only gradually did I manage to understand what I was; finally I had to admit that these notorious allurements which I prided myself on resisting actually had no attraction for me whatever.

"What I had regarded as virtue was in fact nothing but indifference. This was an appalling humiliation—how could it be anything else?—to a rather high-minded young spirit. Only work managed to overcome the melancholy which darkened and diminished my life; I soon persuaded myself I was unsuited for marriage and, being able to acknowledge none of the reasons for my depression to my fiancée, my behavior toward her became increasingly evasive and embarrassed. Yet the few experiments I then attempted in a brothel certainly proved to me that I wasn't impotent; but at the same time they afforded convincing proof . . ."

"Proof of what?"

"My case seemed to me altogether exceptional (for how could I suspect at the time that it was common?). I saw that I was capable of pleasure; I supposed myself incapable, strictly speaking, of desire. Both my parents were healthy, I myself was robust and energetic; my appearance revealed nothing of my wretchedness; none of my friends suspected what was wrong; nothing could have persuaded me to speak a word to a soul. Yet the farce of good humor and risqué allusions which I felt obliged to act out in order to avoid all suspicion became intolerable. As soon as I was alone I slipped into despondency."

The seriousness and the conviction in his voice compelled my interest. "You were letting your imagination run away with you!" I said gently. "The fact is, you were in love, and therefore full of doubts. As soon as you were married, love would have developed quite naturally into desire."

"I know that's what people say . . . How right I was to be skeptical!"

"You don't seem to have hypochondriacal tendencies now. How did you cure yourself of this disease of yours?"

"At the time, I did a great deal of reading. And one day I came across a sentence which gave me some sound advice. It was from the Abbé Galiani: 'The important thing,' he wrote to Mme d'Epinay, 'the important thing is not to be cured but to be able to live with one's disease.' "

"Why don't you tell that to your patients?"

"I do, to the incurable ones. No doubt those words seem all too simple to you, but I drew my whole philosophy from them. It only remained for me to realize that I was not a freak, a unique case, in order to recover my self-confidence and escape my self-hatred."

"You've told me how you came to realize your lack of interest in women, but not how you discovered your tendency . . ."

"It's quite a painful story, and I don't like telling it. But you seem to be listening to me carefully—maybe my account will help you speak of these matters less frivolously."

I assured him, if not of my sympathy, at least of my respectful attention.

"You already know," he began, "that I was engaged; I loved the girl who was to become my wife tenderly but with an almost mystical emotion, and of course with my lack of experience I scarcely imagined that there could be any other real way of loving. My fiancée had a brother, a few years younger than she, whom I often saw and who felt the deepest friendship for me."

"Aha!" I exclaimed involuntarily.

Corydon glanced at me severely. "No: nothing improper took place between us; his sister was my fiancée."

"Excuse me."

"But you can imagine my confusion, my consternation when, one evening of heart-to-heart exchanges, I had to acknowledge that this boy wanted not only my friendship but was soliciting my caresses as well."

"Your tenderness, you mean. Like many children, after all! It's our responsibility, as their elders, to respect such needs."

"I did respect them, I promise you that. But Alexis was no longer a child; he was a charming and perceptive adolescent. The avowals he made to me then were all the more upsetting because in every revelation he made, all described with precocious exactitude, I seemed to be hearing my own confession. Nothing, however, could possibly justify the severity of my reaction."

"Severity ?"

"Yes: I was scared out of my wits. I spoke severely, almost harshly, and what was worse, I spoke with extreme contempt for what I called effeminacy, which was only the natural expression of his feelings."

"It's hard to know how to deal with such cases."

"I dealt with this one so badly that the poor child—yes, he was still a child—took my scolding quite tragically. For three days he tried with all the sweetness in his power to overcome what he took to be my anger; and meanwhile I kept exaggerating my coldness no matter what he said, until it happened . . ."

"What happened?"

"Then you didn't know that Alexis B. committed suicide?"

"But you wouldn't go so far as to suggest that . . ."

"No, I'm not suggesting anything at all. At first it was said to be an accident. We were in the country at the time: the body was found at the foot of a cliff . . . An accident? I suppose I could make myself believe anything. But here's the letter I found next to my bed."

He opened a drawer, took out a sheet of paper with a shaking hand, glanced at it, and then said:

"No, I'm not going to read you this letter; you would misjudge the child. The substance of it—and written in the most moving way—was the agony our last conversation had caused him . . . especially certain remarks I had made. 'To spare yourself this physical torment,' I had shouted in a fit of hypocritical rage against the inclinations he was confessing to me, 'the best thing you could do would be to fall in love.' '*Unfortunately*,' he wrote me, '*I have fallen in love, but with you, my friend. You haven't understood me and you feel contempt for me. I see that I am becoming an object of disgust to you—as I am for myself for that very reason. If I can't change my awful nature, at least I can get rid of it . . .*' Four more pages of that slightly pompous pathos characteristic of that stage of life, the kind of thing it becomes so easy for us to call declamation."

This story had made me more than a little uncomfortable . . . "Of course," I said at last, "such a declaration, and made to you specifically, was a nasty trick of fate; I can understand that the episode must have affected you."

"To the point that I immediately gave up all thoughts of marrying my friend's sister."

"But," I went on with my train of thought, "I'm more or less convinced that each of us gets the disasters he deserves. You must admit that if this boy hadn't sensed in you some possible response to his own guilty passion, that passion . . ."

"Maybe some obscure instinct could have made him aware of it, as you say; but in that case, what a crying shame that same instinct couldn't make me aware of it too.

"What if you had been aware—what would you have done?"

"I think I could have cured that child."

"You were just saying that these were incurable cases; didn't you just quote the Abbé's words—'the important thing is not to be cured . . .'"

"All right, enough of that! I could have cured him the same way I've cured myself."

"And that is . . ."

"By convincing him he wasn't sick."

"Why don't you just come right out and say that the perversion of his instinct was natural!"

"By convincing him that the deviation of his instinct was quite natural."

"And if you had it all to do over again, you would have yielded to him, *naturally*."

"Oh, that's another question altogether. When the physiological problem is solved, the moral problem begins. No doubt my feelings for his sister would have led me to try to argue him out of this passion, in the same way that I would no doubt have tried to argue myself out of my own; but at least this passion itself would have lost that monstrous character it had assumed in his eyes.—This drama, by opening my own eyes to my own nature, showing me the real nature of my feelings for this child, this drama I've thought about so long has finally determined my attitude toward . . . the particular thing you find so despicable; in memory of this victim, I want to cure other victims suffering from the same misunderstanding: to cure them in the way I just told you."

iii

"I think you understand now why I want to write this book. The only serious books I know on this subject are certain medical works which reek of the clinic from the very first pages."

"So you don't plan on writing as a doctor?"

"As a doctor, a naturalist, a moralist, a sociologist, a historian . . ."

"I didn't know you were so protean."

"I mean I'm making no claims to speak about my subject as a specialist—only as a man. The doctors who usually write about the subject treat only uranists who are ashamed of themselves—pathetic inverts, sick men. They're the only ones who consult doctors. As a doctor myself, those are the ones who come to me for treatment too; but as a man, I come across others, who are neither pathetic nor sickly—those are the ones I want to deal with."

"Yes, with the normal pederasts!"

"Precisely. You understand that in homosexuality, just as in heterosexuality, there are all shades and degrees, from Platonic love to lust, from self-denial to sadism, from radiant health to sullen sickliness, from simple expansiveness to all the refinements of vice. Inversion is only one expression. Besides, between exclusive homosexuality and exclusive heterosexuality there is every intermediate shading. But most people simply draw the line between normal love and a love alleged to be *contra naturam*—and for convenience's sake, all the happiness, all the noble or tragic passions, all the beauty of action and thought are put on one side, and to the other are relegated all the filthy dregs of love . . ."

"Don't get carried away. Sapphism actually enjoys a certain favor among us nowadays."

He was so worked up that he completely ignored my remark and continued his argument.

"Nothing could be more grotesque than the spectacle, whenever there's a morals case in the courts, of the righteous indignation of the newspapers at the 'virile' attitude of the accused. No doubt the public expected to see them in skirts. Look: I cut this out of the *Journal* during the Harden trial . . ."

He searched among various papers and handed me a sheet on which the following was underlined:

> *Graf von Hohenau, tall in his tight-fitting frock coat, dignified and even stately, gives no impression of being an effeminate man. He is the perfect type of the Guards officer, entirely committed to his profession. And yet this man of martial and noble bearing is charged with the gravest offense. Graf von Lynar, a man of prepossessing appearance as well . . . etc.*[1]

"In the same way," he went on, "MacDonald and Eulenberg seemed, even to the most prejudiced observers, intelligent, handsome, dignified . . ."

"In short, desirable from every point of view."

He said nothing for a moment, and I saw a look of scorn flash across his face; but recovering himself, he continued as if he had not caught my meaning.

"One is justified in expecting the object of desire to have some beauty, but not necessarily the subject of it. I am not concerned with the beauty of these men. If I made a point, just now, of their physical appearance, it is because it matters to me that they be healthy and virile. And I am not claiming that every uranist is any such thing; homosexuality, just like heterosexuality, has its degenerates, its vicious and sick practitioners; as a doctor, I have come across as many painful, distressing, or dubious cases as the rest of my colleagues. I shall spare my readers that experience; as I've already said, my book will deal with healthy uranism or, as you just put it yourself, with *normal pederasty*."

"Didn't you understand I was using the phrase derisively? It would be all too easy for you if I conceded this first point."

"I shall never ask you to concede anything just to please me. I prefer you to be obliged to do so."

"Now it's your turn to be joking."

"Not in the least. I'm willing to bet that in twenty years it will be impossible to take words like 'unnatural' and 'perverted' seriously. The only thing in the world I concede as not natural is a work of art. Everything else, like it or not, belongs to the natural order, and once we no longer consider it as a moralist, we had better do so as a naturalist."

"The words you indict have their uses—at least they reinforce our decency. Where would we be, once you had suppressed them?"

"We wouldn't be any more demoralized than we are; and I'm making a con-

---

1. Graf von Hohenau was one among several German officers who were exposed in homosexual scandals shortly before Gide wrote *Corydon*. In 1906, Prince Philip zu Eulenberg, a German diplomat and close friend of Kaiser Wilhem II was also a member of a group of homosexual men who occupied positions of influence in the German government. The discovery of the group resulted in a sensational scandal in which the press alleged that the government was riddled with "homosexuality." The use of the word by the press contributed to the popularization of the term. Sir Hector MacDonald, a British general and much admired war hero, was revealed in 1902 to be homosexual. When the story appeared in the press, MacDonald committed suicide.

scious effort not to add: 'On the contrary!' . . . What frauds you heterosexuals are—
to hear some of you tell it, it's enough for sexual relations to be between different
sexes to be permissible; at least, to be 'normal.' "

"It's enough for them to be so potentially. Homosexuals are depraved by nature
necessarily."

"Do you really suppose that self-denial, self-control, and chastity are entirely
unknown to them?"

"No doubt it's a good thing that laws and human respect occasionally have some
hold over them."

"Whereas you think it's a 'good thing' that Laws and conventions have so little
hold over you?"

"I'm coming to the end of my patience with you! Look, on our side we have marriage, honest marriage, which I don't imagine is to be found on yours. You make
me feel like one of those moralists who regard all extramarital pleasures of the flesh
as sin and who condemn all relationships that are not legally sanctioned."

"Oh, I'm more than a match for them there, and if you were to encourage me,
I could turn out to be even more intransigent than they are. Of all the conjugal
beds I've been called upon to examine as a physician, I assure you that very few
were made with clean linen, and I wouldn't like to wager that more ingenuity,
more perversity, if you prefer, is always to be found among prostitutes than in certain 'honest' households."

"You're disgusting."

"But if the bed is a conjugal one, then whatever vice is there is immediately
laundered."

"Surely married couples can do whatever they like; that's their privilege. And
besides, it's none of your business."

" 'Privilege'—yes, I like that word much better than 'normal.' "

"I had been warned that the moral sense was strangely warped among your kind.
But I'm amazed to discover to what a degree. You seem to have completely lost
sight of this natural act of procreation—an act which marriage sanctifies and which
perpetuates the great mystery of life."

"And once performed, the act of love is at liberty to run wild no more than a gratuitous fantasy, a game. No, I'm not losing sight of that; in fact, it's on that finality
that I want to construct my own ethics. Apart from procreation, nothing remains
but the persuasions of pleasure. But think it over for a minute—the act of procreation need not be frequent: once every ten months is sufficient."

"That's rather seldom."

"Very seldom; especially since nature suggests an infinitely greater expenditure;
and . . . I hardly dare finish my sentence."

"Go on—you've already said so much."

"All right, then: I maintain that far from being the only 'natural' one, the act of
procreation, in nature, for all its disconcerting profusion is usually nothing but a
fluke."

"You'd better explain that one!"

"I'll be glad to, but it brings us to natural history; that's where my book begins and how I approach my subject. If you have a little patience, I'll tell you what I mean to say. Come back tomorrow. By then I'll have put my papers into something like order."

FROM THE *JOURNALS* (1889–1949)

*Translated by Justin O'Brien*

## 1918

Had Socrates and Plato not loved young men, what a pity for Greece, what a pity for the whole world!

Had Socrates and Plato not loved young men and aimed to please them, each one of us would be a little less sensible.

If only, instead of getting angry, people tried to find out what is being discussed. Before discussing, one ought always to define. Most quarrels amplify a misunderstanding.

I call a pederast the man who, as the word indicates, falls in love with young boys. I call a sodomite ("The word is sodomite, sir," said Verlaine to the judge who asked him if it were true that he was a sodomist) the man whose desire is addressed to mature men.

I call an invert the man who, in the comedy of love, assumes the role of a woman and desires to be possessed.

These three types of homosexuals are not always clearly distinct; there are possible transferences from one to another; but most often the difference between them is such that they experience a profound disgust for one another, a disgust accompanied by a reprobation that in no way yields to that which you (heterosexuals) fiercely show toward all three.

The pederasts, of whom I am one (why cannot I say this quite simply, without your immediately claiming to see a brag in my confession?), are much rarer, and the sodomites much more numerous, than I first thought. I speak of this on the basis of the confidences I have received, and am willing to believe that in another time and in another country it would not have been the same. As to the inverts, whom I have hardly frequented at all, it has always seemed to me that they alone deserved the reproach of moral or intellectual deformation and were subject to some of the accusations that are commonly addressed to all homosexuals.

I add this, which may seem specious but which I believe altogether exact: that many heterosexuals, either through diffidence or through semi-impotence, behave in relation to the other sex like women and, in an apparently "normal" pair, play the role of true inverts. One is tempted to call them male Lesbians. Dare I say that I believe them to be very numerous?

It is the same as with religion. The kindest thing those who have it can do for those who don't is to pity them.

"But we are not to be pitied. We are not unhappy."

"All the more unhappy since you don't know that you are. We shall cease to pity you, then. We shall detest you."

We are accepted if we are plaintive; but if we cease to be pitiable we are at once accused of arrogance. No, not at all, I assure you. We are merely what we are; we simply admit what we are, without priding ourselves on it, but without grieving about it either.

That such loves can spring up, that such relationships can be formed, it is not enough for me to say that this is natural; I maintain that it is good; each of the two finds exaltation, protection, a challenge in them; and I wonder whether it is for the youth or the elder man that they are more profitable.

## 1942, 19 OCTOBER [CORYDON]

*Corydon* remains in my opinion the most important of my books; but it is also the one with which I find the most fault. The least well done is the one it was most important to do well. I was probably ill-advised to treat ironically such serious questions, which are generally handled as a subject of reprobation or of joking. If I went back to them, people would not fail to think I am obsessed by them. People prefer to envelop them in silence as if they played but a negligible role in society and as if the number of individuals tormented by such questions were negligible in society. And yet when I began to write my book, I thought that number to be much smaller than it eventually appeared to be and than it is in reality; smaller, however, in France than in many other countries I came to know later, for probably in no other country (with the exception of Spain) do the cult of Woman, the religion of Love, and a certain tradition of amorous intercourse so much dominate manners or so servilely influence the way of life. I am obviously not speaking here of the cult of woman in its profoundly respectable aspect, nor of noble love, but of debasing love that sacrifices the best in man to skirts and the alcove. The very ones who shrug their shoulders when faced with such questions are those who proclaim that Love is the most important thing in life and consider it natural that a man should subordinate his career to it. They are naturally thinking of love as desire and of sensual pleasure; and in their eyes desire is king. But, in their opinion, that desire loses all value and does not deserve to be taken into consideration the moment it ceases to be in harmony with, and similar to, theirs. They are very sure of themselves, having Opinion on their side.

Yet I believe I said in that book just about everything I had to say on this most important subject that had not been said before me, but I reproach myself with not having said it as I should have. None the less, certain attentive minds will manage to discover it there later on.

## René Crevel (1900–1935)

*Translated by Michael Taylor*

René Crevel, open and self-proclaimed homosexual and surrealist poet, was rejected by the surrealists, who professed to despise homosexuality, and by the communists, who rejected both homosexuality and the leftist Trotskyite views that Crevel professed. Driven to despair by multiple rejections and an inability to capture either love or fame, Crevel committed suicide in 1935.

*Nighttime (1924?)*

Softly
so as to sleep in the black shadow of oblivion
tonight
I will kill the prowlers
the silent dancers
of the night
whose black velvet feet
torment my naked flesh
as gently as the wing of a bat
and so subtly they send
fright into the folds where skin quails, moved to
fiercer love and fear
at another body and the cold.
But what river for escape oh my mind this evening?
It is the hour of nightwalkers
and delinquents.
Two wide shadowy eves in the dark
could be so sweet, so sweet to me.
I, the prisoner of mournful seasons,
am alone
a perfect crime for him.
Lurking over there on the horizon
a viper perhaps cold from not loving.
But where
where does the
river flow for my mind
to run away on?
Along the banks the girls go
with weary eyes and glistening hair.
I am wordless before these girls
whose apaches
whose proud pimps
are on the prowl.
I am alone a perfect crime for him.
Two great shadowy eyes in the dark
would be so sweet, so sweet to me.
It is the hour of nightwalkers.

## Jean Cocteau (1889–1963)

The immense and flamboyant genius of Jean Cocteau—he wrote plays, novels, poetry, made films, acted, and was an artist of brilliance—is perhaps a testimony to the battered cliché about homosexual genius. His drawings often revel in homoerotic subjects, and the sensibility he displays in many works, including an adaptation for the stage of Wilde's *The Picture of Dorian Gray*, is everywhere infused with homoeroticism. However, despite this,

*Le Livre blanc*, which he published anonymously in 1928, is the only text from him in his lifetime that directly deals with homosexuality. Cocteau was always unwilling to publicly admit his homosexuality, but this reluctance prevented few from suspecting and probably had only the slightest tangential connection with the honors rightfully heaped upon him, including his election to the French Academy, in recognition of a body of work of unparalleled originality. Yet even though the love that dare not speak its name is nominally silent in his work, it speaks on every page.

## FROM *LE LIVRE BLANC* (1928)

*Translated by Margaret Crosland*

I had to return to Toulon. It would be tedious to describe that delightful Sodom where the fire of heaven falls without danger, striking by means of caressing sunshine. Before dusk an even softer atmosphere floods the town and as in Naples, as in Venice, a fairground crowd moves through the squares ornamented with fountains, noisy shops, waffle-stalls and street hawkers. Men in love with masculine beauty come from all corners of the globe to admire the sailors who walk about idly, alone or in groups, respond to glances with a smile and never refuse an offer of love. Some nocturnal salt transforms the most brutal jailbird, the roughest Breton, the most savage Corsican, into those tall, flower-decked girls with low décolletes and loose limbs who like dancing and lead their partners, without the slightest embarrassment, into the shady hotels by the port.

One of the cafés with a dance-floor was kept by a former café-concert singer who had a woman's voice and used to exhibit himself in women's clothes. Now he sported a pullover and rings. He was flanked by colossal men wearing caps with red pompoms; they worshipped him and he ill-treated them; his wife called out lists of drinks in a harsh, naive voice, and he noted them down in large, childish handwriting, with his tongue hanging out.

One evening when I opened the door to the place kept by this astonishing creature, surrounded by the respectful attentions of his wife and his men, I remained rooted to the spot. I had just caught sight of the ghost of Dargelos, a man I could see from the side leaning against the pianola. Dargelos in sailor's uniform.

This double possessed in particular the arrogance, the insolent and absent-minded air of Dargelos. On his cap, which was tilted forward over his left eyebrow, could be read in gold letters Tapageuse, he wore a tight black scarf around his neck and those trousers with tabs which in the past allowed sailors to roll them up to their thighs and are today forbidden by regulations on the pretext that they are worn by pimps.

In any other place I would never have dared stand in the orbit of that arrogant gaze. But Toulon is Toulon; dancing avoids the awkwardness of introductions, it throws strangers into each other's arms and forms a prelude to love.

To music full of ringlets and kiss-curls we danced a waltz. The backward-leaning bodies were linked together at the groin, profiles were grave and eyes lowered, faces moved round more slowly than the feet which wove in and out and sometimes came down like horses' hooves. The free hands assumed the graceful pose affected by the working class when they drink a glass of wine and when they piss it away. A springtime ecstasy excited those bodies. Branches grew in them, hardness crushed hardness, sweat mingled together and the couples would leave for the bedrooms with clock-case lampshades and eiderdowns.

Stripped of the accessories which intimidate a civilian, those which are affected by sailors to give themselves confidence, Tapageuse became a timid animal. He had had his nose broken by a wine carafe during a fight. A straight nose might have made him colourless. The carafe had added the final thumbstroke to the masterpiece.

This boy, who for me represented good luck, bore on his chest the words PAS DE CHANCE tattooed in blue capital letters. He told me his story. It was short. He had just come out of a naval prison. After the mutiny on the *Ernest Renan* he had been mistaken for a colleague; this is why he had a crew-cut, which he hated and which suited him wonderfully well.

"I'm unlucky," he repeated, shaking his little bald head, like some antique bust, "and I always will be."

I put my gold chain round his neck. "I'm not giving it to you," I told him, "that wouldn't protect either of us, but keep it for this evening."

Next, with my fountain-pen I crossed out the ominous tattooing. Beneath it I drew a star and a heart. He smiled. He understood, more with his skin than with anything else, that he was safe, that our encounter was not like those he was used to: brief moments of self-gratification.

PAS DE CHANCE! Was it possible? With that mouth, those teeth, those eyes, that belly, those shoulders, those iron muscles, those legs? PAS DE CHANCE, with that fabulous little underwater plant, lying dead and crumpled on the moss, which unfolded, grew bigger, reared up and threw its seed far away as soon as it found the element of love. I couldn't get over it; and in order to resolve this problem I sank into a feigned sleep.

PAS DE CHANCE remained motionless beside me. Gradually I felt that he was embarking on a delicate maneuver in order to free his arm on which my elbow was resting. Not for a second did it enter my head that he was contemplating some sly trick. This would have meant disregarding naval ceremonial. "Honesty, good behaviour" illuminate the vocabulary of sailors.

I watched him through barely closed eyelids. First he weighed the chain in his hands several times, kissed it and rubbed it on his tattoo. Then, with the terrible slowness of a player who is cheating, he tested my sleep, coughed, touched me, listened to my breathing, brought his face close to my right hand which lay wide open near my face and gently leaned his cheek against it.

I was the indiscreet witness of this attempt by an unlucky boy who could feel a lifebelt coming close to him on the open sea, and I had to restrain myself from losing my head, pretending to wake up and ruining my life.

At dawn I left him. My eyes avoided his, which were full of all the hope which he felt but could not express. He returned the chain to me. I embraced him, tucked him in bed and put out the light.

I had to return to my hotel and write down on a slate in the hall the time (five o'clock) when sailors wake, beneath countless other requests of the same kind. Just as I picked up the chalk I noticed that I had forgotten my gloves. I went back upstairs. Light shone through the glass over the door. Someone must have switched the lamp on again. I couldn't resist putting my eye to the keyhole; it made a bizarre frame for a small shaven head. PAS DE CHANCE had buried his face in my gloves and was weeping bitterly.

I hesitated outside that door for ten minutes. I was about to open it when the face of Alfred superimposed itself with great precision on that of PAS DE CHANCE. I went downstairs on tiptoe, asked for the door to be unlocked and banged it behind me. Outside, a fountain was conducting a grave monologue over the empty square.

No, I thought, we don't belong to the same order. He's already beautiful enough to move a flower, a tree or an animal. Impossible to live with.

Day was breaking. Cocks were crowing over the sea. A dark coolness gave away its presence. A man emerged from a street carrying a shotgun. I went back to the hotel weighed down with a heavy burden.

## Jean Genet (1910–1986)

Genet's vision of homosexuality is set in a world where power and sex define the parameters of love, and where relations between men, usually conducted in the closed and brutal world of the prison, simultaneously engage dark sadomasochism and lyric if explicit sexual fantasy. In Genet homosexuality is a sign of defiant difference and a symbol of revolt against every respectable bourgeois prohibition, a rebellion in which the criminal and the homosexual are conflated and in which effeminacy and transvestism are celebrated. Genet's works contribute not only to a mythology of homosexuality but are in a sense part of the tradition of rigorous verbal analysis that marks the French intellectual position in which literature is seen to be as much a ground upon which the deconstruction of a topic or a text may take place as it is a site for the celebration or the elaboration of it.

THE MAN CONDEMNED TO DEATH (1942)

[LE CONDAMNÉ À MORT]

Translated by David Fisher and Guy Wernham

The wind that rolls a heart on the pavement of courtyards,
An angel who sobs enhooked in a tree,
The column of azure that enwraps the marble
Make open in my night the gates of rescue.

A poor bird who dies and the taste of ashes,
The memory of an eye asleep on the wall,
And this dolorous fist that threatens the azure
Make in the hollow of my hand your face descend.

This face more hard and light than a mask
Is heavier to my hand than to the fence's fingers

The jewel that he pockets; it is drowned with tears.
It is sombre and fierce, a green bouquet casques it.

Your face is stern: it is that of a Greek shepherd's.
It rests shuddering in the hollows of my closed hands.
Your mouth is of a dead woman where your eyes are roses,
And your nose of an archangel is perhaps the beak.

The sparkling rime of a wicked chastity
That would powder your hair with bright steel stars,
That would crown your forehead with thorns of the rose-bush
What high evil has melted it if your visage sing?

Tell me what mad misfortune makes your eye blaze
With a despair so high that the wild pain,
Maddened, in person, ornaments your round mouth
Despite your frozen tears, with a smile of mourning?

Don't sing tonight the "Bullies of the Moon."
Urchin of gold be rather princess of a tower
Dreaming melancholic of our poor love;
Or be the blond cabin-boy who watches from the maintop.

He descends toward evening to sing on the bridge
Among the bare-headed kneeling sailors
The "Ave Maria stella." Each sailor holds ready
His rod which leaps in his rascal's hand.

And it is to haft you, pretty cabin-boy of adventure,
That they stiffen beneath their pants the muscled sailors.
My love, my love, will you steal the keys
Which will open for me the heaven where the rigging trembles

Whence you sow, royally, the white enchantments,
These snows on my page, in my mute prison:
Terror, the corpses in violet flowers
Death with his cockerels! His phantoms of lovers!

On his velvet feet a prowling jailer passes.
Sleep in my hollow eyes the memory of you.
It may be that one might escape by passing over the roof.
They say that Guyana is a hot country.

O the sweetness of the far and impossible gaol!
O the heaven of the Beautiful, o the sea and the palms,
The transparent mornings, the mad evenings, the calm nights,
O the crew-cut hair and the Skins-of-Satin.

Let us dream together, Love, of some tough lover
Big as the Universe but the body blemished with shadows.
He will buckle us naked in these gloomy taverns,
Between his gold thighs, on his smoking belly,

A dazzling punk carved into an archangel
Stiffening on bouquets of carnations and jasmine
That your luminous hands will bear trembling
Upon his august flank which your kiss deranges.

Sadness in my mouth! Bitterness swelling
Swelling my poor heart! My perfumed loves
Farewell will depart! Farewell beloved balls!
O on my strangled voice farewell insolent prick!

Street-child, do not sing, put aside your apache air!
Be the young girl with the pure radiant throat,
Or if you have no fear the melodious child
Dead in me well before the axe chops me off.

Child of honour so beautiful crowned with lilacs!
Lean over my bed, let my mounting prick
Strike your gilded cheek. Listen, he is telling you,
Your lover the assassin his geste in a thousand flashes.

He sings that he once had your body and your face,
Your heart that the spurs of a massive horseman
Will never open. To have your round knees!
Your fresh neck, your sweet hand, o child to have your age!

To fly, to fly your sky spattered with blood
And make a single master-piece with the deaths gathered
Here and there in the meadows, the hedgerows, the deaths dazzled
With preparing his death, his adolescent heaven . . .

The solemn mornings, the rum, the cigarette
The shadows of tobacco, of jail and sailors
Visit my cell where rolls and clasps me tightly
The spectre of a killer with a heavy fly.

The song that traverses a tenebrous world
It's the cry of a hoodlum carried away by your music,
It's the song of a hanged man stiff as a cudgel.
It's the enchanted call of an amorous thief

A sleeper of sixteen years calls for life-buoys
Which no sailor throws to the crazed sleeper.

A child rests upright, glued to the wall.
Another sleeps buckled within his knotted legs.

I have killed for the blue eyes of an indifferent beauty
Who never understood my love restrained,
In her black gondola an unknown lover,
Beautiful as a ship and dead while adoring me.

You when you will be ready, armed for the crime,
Masked with cruelty, casqued with blond hair,
To the mad and brief cadence of violins
Slit the throat of a woman of means in love with your line.

There will appear on earth an iron knight
Impassible and cruel, visible despite the hour
In the imprecise gesture of a weeping old woman.
Above all do not tremble before his clear glance.

This apparition comes from the redoubtable sky
Of love crimes. Child of depths
There will be born from his body astonishing splendours,
From the perfumed fucking of his adorable cock.

Rock of black granite on the wool rug
A hand on his hip, listen to him walk.
March toward the sun of his body without sin
And stretch yourself out peacefully at the brim of his fountain.

Each feast of blood assigns a beautiful boy
To sustain the child in his first trial.
Pacify your fear and your new anguish.
Suck my hard member as one sucks an icicle.

Nibble tenderly the slap that smacks your cheek,
Kiss my swollen prick, cram into your neck
The bundle of my cock swallowed all at once.
Strangle yourself with love, puke, and make your grimace!

Adore upon both knees, as a sacred pole,
My tattooed torso, adore unto tears
My sex that erupts, which strikes you better than a weapon,
Adore my staff which is going to penetrate you.

It leaps beneath your eyes; it pierces your soul,
Lean your head over a little and watch it stand up.
Perceiving it so noble and so ready for kissing
You bow very low while calling it: "Madame!"

Madame listen to me! Madame one dies here!
The manor is haunted! The prison flies and trembles!
To the rescue, we are stirring! Carry us off together,
Into your room in the sky, Lady of mercy!

Call the sun, that he may come and console me.
Strangle all these roosters! Put the executioner to sleep!
The day smiles wretched behind my window-pane.
The prison is a pointless school for dying.

Upon my neck without armour and without hate, my neck
That my hand more light and solemn than a widow
Presses lightly under my collar, without your heart stirring,
Let your teeth take on their wolf-smile.

O come my beautiful sun, o come my night of Spain,
Arrive in my eyes which will be dead tomorrow.
Arrive, open my door, bring me your hand,
Lead me far from here to scour the battleground.

Heaven may awaken, the stars may blossom,
Nor flowers sigh, and from the meadows the black grass
Gather the dew where morning is about to drink,
The bell may ring: I alone am about to die.

O come my heaven of rose, o my blond basket!
Visit in his night your condemned-to-death.
Tear away your own flesh, kill, climb, bite,
But come! Place your cheek against my round head.

We had not finished speaking to each other of love.
We had not finished smoking our *gitanes*.
Well we might ask why the Courts condemn
A murderer so beautiful he makes the day to pale.

Love come to my mouth! Love open your doors!
Run through the hallways, come down, step lightly,
Fly down the stairs more supple than a shepherd,
More borne up by the air than a flight of dead leaves.

O cross the walls; so it must be walk on the brink
Of roofs, of oceans; cover yourself with light,
Use menace, use prayer,
But come, o my frigate, an hour before my death.

The murderers of the wall drape themselves with dawn
In my cell open to the song of tall fir-trees,

That cradles it, hooked up by slender cordages
Knotted by sailors whom the clear morning gilds.

Who etched in the plaster a Rose of the Winds?
Who dreams of my house, from the depth of his Hungary?
What child has rolled on my rotted straw
At the moment of the awakening of friends remembering?

Wander my Madness, beget for my joy
A consoling hell peopled with beautiful soldiers,
Naked to the waist, and from pale green frocks
Extract these heavy flowers whose odor thunderstrikes me.

Scare up from who knows where the maddest gestures.
Steal children, invent tortures,
Mutilate beauty, work the shapes,
And give Guyana to the guys for a meeting-place.

O my old Maroni, o Cayenne the sweet!
I see the leaning bodies of fifteen or twenty faggots
About the blond punk who is smoking butts
Spat out by the keepers into the flowers and the moss.

A soggy footstep suffices to desolate us all.
Erected alone above the rigid ferns
The youngest is posed upon his wanton hips
Immobile, waiting to be the sacred spouse.

And the ancient murderers hastening for the rite
Crouched in the evening draw from a dry stick
A little fire which the little punk, active, steals
More moving and pure than a moving prick.

The toughest bandit, in his polished muscles
Bows with respect before this frail gamin.
Climbs the moon to the sky. Slakes itself a quarrel.
Stir themselves the mysterious folds of the black flag.

They enwrap you so finely, your gestures of lace!
One shoulder leaning against a palm, blushing
You smoke. The smoke descends in your throat
While the convicts, in solemn dance,

Grave, silent, by turns, childlike,
Are going to take from your mouth a fragrant drop,
One drop, not two, of the round smoke
That your tongue rolls to them. O triumphant brother,

Terrible divinity, invisible and evil,
You remain impassive, sharp, of bright metal,
Attentive to yourself, fatal distributor
Carried away on the cord of your hammock which sings.

Your delicate soul is beyond the mountains
Accompanying still the enchanted flight
Of an escaped convict, in the hollow of a valley
Dead, without thought of you, from a ball in the lungs.

Raise yourself in the air of the moon o my ball.
Come pour in my mouth one little heavy sperm
That flows from your throat to my teeth, my Love,
To make fecund at last our adorable nuptials.

Fasten your ravished body against mine which dies
From fucking the tenderest and sweetest of rogues.
As I weigh in my hand delighted your round blond balls
My black marble prick pierces you to the heart.

O aim at it upstarted in its setting that burns
And will consume me! It won't take me long,
If you dare, come, leave your pools,
Your swamps, your mire where you make bubbles

Souls of my victims! Kill me! Burn me!
Worn-out Michelangelo, I have carved in life
Only beauty Lord, always I have served
My belly, my knees, my hands red with emotion.

The chickenhouse cocks, the gallic lark,
The dairyman's milkcans, a bell in the air,
A step on the gravel, my white and shining window,
It's the joyful shining upon the prison of slate.

Gentlemen, I am not afraid! If my head rolled
In the sound of the basket with your white head,
Mine happily upon your slender hip
Or for greater beauty, on your neck my chicken . . .

Watch out! Tragic king with parted lips
I have access to your gardens of desolate sands,
Where you harden, clotted alone, with two fingers upraised,
From a veil of blue linen your covered head.

Through an idiot delirium I see your double purely!
Love! Song! My queen! Is it a male spectre

Glimpsed at the time of play in your pale pupil
That examines me thus on the plaster of the wall?

Do not be stern, let matins be sung
To your bohemian heart; accord me one single kiss . . .
My God I'll croak without being able to hug you
In my life one time on my heart and my prick!

Forgive me Lord for I have sinned!
The tears of my voice, my fever, my agony,
The evil of sending me from the beautiful Country of France,
Is this not enough Lord for me to go lie down
    Stumbling with hope

In your fragrant arms, within your snowy castles!
Lord of dark places, I still know how to pray.
It is I my father, one day, who cried out:
Glory to the highest of heaven to the god who protects me
    Hermes of the tender foot!

I ask from death peace, long slumbers,
The song of seraphim, their perfumes, their garlands,
The cherubs of wool in warm greatcoats,
And I hope for nights without moons or suns
    On motionless moors.

It is not this morning that I am to be guillotined.
I may sleep peacefully. On the upper storey
My little lazy one, my pearl, my Jesus
Wakens. He is about to kick with his hard boot
    My shaven head.

It seems that next door lives an epileptic.
The prison sleeps erect in the darkness of a death song
So some sailors on the water see the ports advance.
My sleepers are about to flee towards another America.

*I have dedicated this poem to the memory of my friend
Maurice Pilorge whose body and radiant face haunt my sleepless nights. In spirit I relive with him the forty last days he
spent, manacles on his feet and sometimes on his wrists, in
the death-cell of the prison of Saint-Brieuc. The newspapers
lack relevance. They contrived idiotic articles to explain his
death which coincided with the entry into office of the executioner Desfourneaux. Commenting on Maurice's attitude
before death, the paper l'Oeuvre stated: "How worthy that
child would have been of another fate."*

*In short they misrepresented him. As for me, who knew*
*him and loved him, I desire here, as gently as possible, ten-*
*derly, to affirm that he was worthy, by the double and*
*unique splendour of his soul and of his body, to have the*
*blessing of such a death. Each morning, when I would go,*
*thanks to the complicity of a jailer enchanted by his beauty,*
*his youth and his agony of Apollo, from my cell to his, to*
*take him a few cigarettes, awakened early he was humming*
*a tune and would greet me thus, smiling: "Greetings, Little-*
*Jean-of-the-morning!"*

*A native of Puy-de-Dome, he had a trace of the accent*
*of Auvergne. The jury, offended by so much charm, stupid*
*but nevertheless prestigious in their role as Fates, sentenced*
*him to twenty years hard labor for burglary of coast-town*
*villas, and next day, because he had killed his lover Escudero*
*in order to steal from him less than a thousand francs, that*
*same criminal court sentenced my friend Maurice Pilorge*
*to have his head cut off. He was executed March 17, 1939*
*at Saint-Brieuc.*

## FROM OUR LADY OF THE FLOWERS (1941–42; 1943)

### [NOTRE-DAME DES FLEURS]

*Translated by Bernard Frechtman*

Divine appeared in Paris to lead her public life about twenty years before her death. She was then thin and vivacious and will remain so until the end of her life, though growing angular. At about two A.M. she entered Graff's Café in Montmartre. The customers were a muddy, still shapeless clay. Divine was limpid water. In the big café with the closed windows and the curtains drawn on their hollow rods, over-crowded and foundering in smoke, she wafted the coolness of scandal, which is the coolness of a morning breeze, the astonishing sweetness of a breath of scandal on the stone of the temple, and just as the wind turns leaves, so she turned heads, heads which all at once became light (giddy heads), heads of bankers, shopkeep-ers, gigolos for ladies, waiters, managers, colonels, scarecrows.

She sat down alone at a table and asked for tea.

"Specially fine China tea, my good man," she said to the waiter.

With a smile. For the customers she had an irritatingly jaunty smile. Hence, the "you-know-what" in the wagging of the heads. For the poet and the reader, her smile will be enigmatic.

That evening she was wearing a champagne silk short-sleeved blouse, a pair of blue trousers stolen from a sailor, and leather sandals. On one of her fingers, though preferably on the pinkie, an ulcer-like stone gangrened her. When the tea was brought, she drank it as if she were at home, in tiny little sips (a pigeon), putting down and lifting the cup with her pinkie in the air. Here is a portrait of her: her hair is brown and curly; with the curls spilling over her eyes and down her cheeks, she looks as if she were wearing a cat-o'-nine-tails on her head. Her forehead is somewhat round and smooth. Her eyes sing, despite their despair, and their melody moves from her eyes to her teeth, to which she gives life, and from her teeth to all her movements, to her slightest acts, and this charm, which emerges from her eyes, unfurls in wave upon wave, down to her bare feet. Her body is fine as amber. Her limbs can be agile when she flees from ghosts. At her heels, the wings of terror bear her along. She is quick, for in order to elude the ghosts, to throw them off her track, she must speed ahead faster than her thought thinks. She drank her tea before thirty pairs of eyes which belied what the contemptuous, spiteful, sorrowful, wilting mouths were saying.

Divine was full of grace, and yet was like all those prowlers at country fairs on the lookout for rare sights and artistic visions, good sports who trail behind them all the inevitable hodge-podge of side shows. At the slightest movement—if they knot their tie, if they flick the ash off their cigarette—they set slot machines in motion. Divine knotted, garroted arteries. Her seductiveness will be implacable. If it were only up to me, I would make her the kind of fatal hero I like. Fatal, that is, determining the fate of those who gaze at them, spellbound. I would make her with hips of stone, flat and polished cheeks, heavy eyelids, pagan knees so lovely that they reflected the desperate intelligence of the faces of mystics. I would strip her of all sentimental trappings. Let her consent to be the frozen statue. But I know that the poor Demiurge is forced to make his creature in his own image and that he did not invent Lucifer. In my cell, little by little, I shall have to give my thrills to the granite. I shall remain alone with it for a long time, and I shall make it live with my breath and the smell of my farts, both the solemn and the mild ones. It will take me an entire book to draw her from her petrifaction and gradually impart my suffering to her, gradually deliver her from evil, and, holding her by the hand, lead her to saintliness.

The waiter who served her felt very much like snickering, but out of decency he did not dare in front of her. As for the manager, he approached her table and decided that as soon as she finished her tea, he would ask her to leave, to make sure she would not turn up again some other evening.

Finally, she patted her snowy forehead with a flowered handkerchief. Then she crossed her legs; on her ankle could be seen a chain fastened by a locket which we know contained a few hairs. She smiled all around, and each one answered only by turning away, but that was a way of answering. The whole café thought that the smile of (for the colonel: the invert; for the shopkeepers: the fairy; for the banker and the waiters: the fag; for the gigolos: "*that* one"; etc.) was despicable. Divine did not press the point. From a tiny black satin purse she took a few coins which she laid noiselessly on the marble table. The café disappeared, and Divine was metamorphosed into one of those monsters that are painted on walls—chimeras or griffins—for a customer, in spite of himself, murmured a magic word as he thought of her:

"Homoseckshual."

That evening, her first in Montmartre, she was cruising. But she got nowhere. She came upon us without warning. The habitués of the café had neither the time nor, above all, the composure to handle properly their reputations or their females. Having drunk her tea, Divine, with indifference (so it appeared, seeing her), wriggling in a spray of flowers and strewing swishes and spangles with an invisible furbelow, made off. So here she is, having decided to return, lifted by a column of smoke, to her garret, on the door of which is nailed a huge discolored muslin rose. Her perfume is violent and vulgar. From it we can already tell that she is fond of vulgarity. Divine has sure taste, good taste, and it is most upsetting that life always puts someone so delicate into vulgar positions, into contact with all kinds of filth. She cherishes vulgarity because her greatest love was for a dark-skinned gypsy. On him, under him, when, with his mouth pressed to hers, he sang to her gypsy songs that pierced her body, she learned to submit to the charm of such vulgar cloths as silk and gold braid, which are becoming to immodest persons. Montmartre was aflame. Divine passed through its multi-colored fires, then, intact, entered the darkness of the promenade of the Boulevard de Clichy, a darkness that preserves old and ugly faces. It was three A.M. She walked for a while toward Pigalle. She smiled and stared at every man who strolled by alone. They didn't dare, or else it was that she still knew nothing about the customary routine: the client's qualms, his hesitations, his lack of assurance as soon as he approaches the coveted youngster. She was weary; she sat down on a bench and, despite her fatigue, was conquered, transported by the warmth of the night; she let herself go for the length of a heartbeat and expressed her excitement as follows: "The nights are mad about me! Oh the sultanas! My God, they're making eyes at me! Ah, they're curling my hair around their fingers (the fingers of the nights, men's cocks!). They're patting my cheek, stroking my butt." That was what she thought, though without rising to, or sinking into, a poetry cut off from the terrestrial world. Poetic expression will never change her state of mind. She will always be the tart concerned with gain.

There are mornings when all men experience with fatigue a flush of tenderness that makes them horny. One day at dawn I found myself placing my lips lovingly, though for no reason at all, on the icy banister of the Rue Berthe; another time, kissing my hand; still another time, bursting with emotion, I wanted to swallow myself by opening my mouth very wide and turning it over my head so that it would take in my whole body, and then the Universe, until all that would remain of me would be a ball of eaten thing which little by little would be annihilated: that is how I see the end of the world. Divine offered herself to the night in order to be devoured by it tenderly and never again spewed forth. She is hungry. And there is nothing around. The pissoirs are empty; the promenade is just about deserted. Merely some bands of young workmen—whose whole disorderly adolescence is manifest in their carelessly tied shoelaces which hop about on their insteps—returning home in forced marches from an evening of pleasure. Their tight-fitting jackets are like fragile breastplates or shells protecting the naïveté of their bodies. But by the grace of their virility, which is still as light as a hope, they are inviolable by Divine.

She will do nothing tonight. The possible customers were so taken by surprise that they were unable to collect their wits. She will have to go back to her attic with hunger in her belly and her heart. She stood up to go. A man came staggering toward her. He bumped her with his elbow.

"Oh! sorry," he said, "terribly sorry!"

His breath reeked of wine.

"Quite all right," said the queen.

It was Darling Daintyfoot going by.

Description of Darling: height, 5 ft. 9 in., weight 165 Ibs., oval face, blond hair, blue-green eyes, mat complexion, perfect teeth, straight nose.

He was young too, almost as young as Divine, and I would like him to remain so to the end of the book. Every day the guards open my door so I can leave my cell and go out into the yard for some fresh air. For a few seconds, in the corridors and on the stairs, I pass thieves and hoodlums whose faces enter my face and whose bodies, from afar, hurl mine to the ground. I long to have them within reach. Yet not one of them makes me evoke Darling Daintyfoot.

When I met Divine in Fresnes Prison, she spoke to me about him a great deal, seeking his memory and the traces of his steps throughout the prison, but I never quite knew his face, and this is a tempting opportunity for me to blend him in my mind with the face and physique of Roger.

Very little of this Corsican remains in my memory: a hand with too massive a thumb that plays with a tiny hollow key, and the faint image of a blond boy walking up La Canebiére in Marseilles, with a small chain, probably gold, stretched across his fly, which it seems to be buckling. He belongs to a group of males who are advancing upon me with the pitiless gravity of forests on the march. That was the starting point of the daydream in which I imagined myself calling him Roger, a "little boy's" name, though firm and upright. Roger was upright. I had just got out of the Chave prison, and I was amazed not to have met him there. What could I commit to be worthy of his beauty? I needed boldness in order to admire him. For lack of money, I slept at night in the shadowy corners of coal piles, on the docks, and every evening I carried him off with me. The memory of his memory made way for other men. For the past two days, in my daydreams, I have again been mingling his (made-up) life with mine. I wanted him to love me, and of course he did, with the candor that required only perversity for him to be able to love me. For two successive days I have fed with his image a dream which is usually sated after four or five hours when I have given it a boy to feed upon, however handsome he may be. Now I am exhausted with inventing circumstances in which he loves me more and more. I am worn out with the invented trips, thefts, rapes, burglaries, imprisonments, and treachery in which we were involved, each acting by and for the other and never by or for himself, in which the adventure was ourselves and only ourselves. I am exhausted; I have a cramp in my wrist. The pleasure of the last drops is dry. For a period of two days, between my four bare walls, I experienced with him and through him every possibility of an existence that had to be repeated twenty times and got so mixed up it became more real than a real one. I have given up the daydream. I was loved. I have quit, the way a contestant in a six-day bicycle race quits; yet the memory of his eyes and their fatigue, which I have to cull from the face of another youngster whom I saw coming out of a brothel, a boy with firm legs and ruthless cock, so solid that I might almost say it was knotted, and his face (it alone, seen without its veil), which asks for shelter like a knight-errant—this memory refuses to disappear as the memory of my dream-friends usually does. It floats about. It is less sharp than when the adventures were taking place, but it lives in me nevertheless. Certain details persist more obstinately in remaining: the little hollow key with which, if he wants to, he can whistle; his thumb; his sweater; his blue eyes. . . . If I continue, he will rise up, become erect, and penetrate me so deeply that I shall be marked with stigmata. I can't bear it any longer. I am turning him into a character whom I shall be able to torment in my own way, namely, Darling Daintyfoot. He will still be twenty, although his destiny is to become the father and lover of Our Lady of the Flowers.

. . . .

Here is how our Great Divine died.

Having looked for her little gold watch, she found it between her thighs and, with her fist closed over it, handed it to Ernestine, who was sitting at her bedside. Their two hands met in the form of a shell with the watch in the middle. A vast physical peace relaxed Divine. Filth, an almost liquid shit, spread out beneath her like a warm little lake, into which she gently, very gently—as the vessel of a hopeless emperor sinks, still warm, into the waters of Lake Nemi—was engulfed, and with this relief she heaved another sigh, which rose to her mouth with blood, then another sigh, the last.

Thus did she pass away, one might also say drowned.

Ernestine was waiting. Suddenly, by some miracle, she realized that the throbbing of their joined hands was the ticking of the watch.

Because she lived among omens and signs, she was not superstitious. She therefore laid out the corpse all by herself and dressed Divine in a very modest blue cheviot suit of English cut.

So here she is dead. The Quite-Dead. Her body is caught in the sheets. It is, from head to foot, forever a ship in the breaking-up of ice-floes, motionless and rigid, drifting toward infinity: you, Jean, dear heart, motionless and rigid, as I have already said, drifting on my bed to a happy Eternity.

And with Divine dead, what is left for me to do? To say?

This evening, the poplars, of which I see only the tops, are being cruelly dashed together by an angry wind. My cell, lulled by that kindly death, is so sweet today!

What if I were free tomorrow?

(Tomorrow is the day of the hearing.)

Free, in other words, exiled among the living. I have made myself a soul to fit my dwelling. My cell is so sweet. Free: to drink wine, to smoke, to see ordinary people. And tomorrow, what will the jury be like? I have anticipated the stiffest possible sentence it can inflict. I have prepared myself for it with great care, for I have chosen my horoscope (according to what I can read of it from past events) as a figure of fatality. Now that I can obey it, my grief is less great. It is annihilated in the face of the irremediable. It is my hopelessness, and what will be, will be. I have given up my desires. I too am "already far beyond that" (Weidmann). Let me therefore live between these walls for a man's lifetime. Who will be judged tomorrow? Some stranger bearing a name that was once my name. I can continue to die, until my death, amidst all these widowers. Lamp, washbasin, regulations, broom. And the straw mattress, my spouse.

I do not feel like going to sleep. Tomorrow's hearing is a solemnity that requires a vigil. It is this evening that I should like to weep—as one who stays behind—for my farewells. But my lucidity is like a nakedness. The wind outside is getting wilder and wilder and is being joined by the rain. The elements are thus a prelude to tomorrow's ceremonies. Today is the 12th, isn't it? What shall I decide? Warnings are said to come from God. They don't interest me. I already feel that I no longer belong to the prison. Broken is the exhausting fraternity that bound me to the men of the tomb. Perhaps I shall live. . . .

At times I am shaken with a burst of brutal and unaccountable laughter. It resounds within me like a joyous cry in the fog, which it seems to be trying to dissipate, but it leaves no trace other than a wistful longing for sun and gaiety.

What if I am condemned? I shall don homespun again, and this rust-colored garment will immediately entail the monastic gesture: hiding my hands in my sleeves; and the equivalent attitude of mind will follow: I shall feel myself becoming humble and glorious; then, snug under my blankets—it is in *Don Juan* that the characters come back to life on the stage and kiss each other—I shall, for the enchantment of my cell, refashion lovely new lives for Darling, Divine, Our Lady and Gabriel.

I have read moving letters, full of wonderful touches, of despair, of hopes, of songs; and others more severe. I am choosing from among them one which will be the letter Darling wrote to Divine from prison:

"Dearest,

I'm writing a few lines to give you the news, which isn't good. I've been arrested for stealing. So try to get a lawyer to handle my case. Arrange to pay him. And also arrange to send me a money order, because you know how lousy things are here. Also try to get permission to come and see me and bring me some linens. Put in the blue and white silk pajamas. And some undershirts. Dearest, I'm awfully sorry about what's happened to me. Let's face it, I'm plain unlucky. So I'm counting on you to help me out. I only wish I could have you in my arms so I could hold you and squeeze you tight. Remember the things we used to do together. Try to recognize the dotted lines. And kiss it. A thousand big kisses, sweetheart, from

Your Darling."

The dotted line that Darling refers to is the outline of his prick. I once saw a pimp who had a hard-on while writing to his girl place his heavy cock on the paper and trace its contours. I would like that line to portray Darling.

# 20. Vaterlandslosen

## Germany (1899–1939)

In 1871 when Germany was unified under Prussian leadership, Paragraph 175, which criminalized homosexual acts, was written into the new German penal code. This led to the growth of a German homosexual rights movement that flourished until its suppression by the Nazis in the 1930s. The movement was institutionalized in the Scientific Humanitarian Committee founded in 1897 by Magnus Hirschfeld, a sexologist. Hirschfeld, in his book *Sappho und Sokretes* (1896), had argued that homosexuality was a natural form of human sexuality and urged that it should be objectively studied, not persecuted or criminalized. In 1899 Hirschfeld and the committee founded the *Jarbuch für sexuelle Zwischenstufen*, a journal devoted to the scholarly study of homosexuality. Hirschfeld's own vision of homosexuality was based on Ulrichs's "third sex" model. Hirschfeld had some success in attracting support from famous people though he was opposed by those who rejected the effeminization implicit in his views in favor of a construction of homosexuality that defined it as a manifestation of virility masculinized though romantic friendships between men, or, after the Greek model, between older and younger men in which sexual activity could also play a legitimate part. One of those opposing Hirschfeld was publisher Adolf Brand, who in 1896 founded a homosexual journal, *Der Eigene*, from which the selections below are taken and which had more of a literary and polemical thrust than Hirschfeld's *Jahrbuch*. Brand published Benedict Friedlander, Elisar von Kupffer, and the pseudonymous Gotamo, most of whom supported his views advocating notions of homosexual superiority (but which were also often racist, usually antifeminist, and mixed with an extreme German nationalism). To help propagate these views, Brand and Benedict Friedlander (who also led a movement to secede from Hirschfeld's committee) founded their own organization, the Gemeinschaft der Eigenen.

Hirschfeld represented a science that sought to explain homosexuality in terms of medical and physiological models which asserted that homosexuality was biological, innate, and differed from the constitution of what they called "normal" men; therefore, homosexuals as a sexual minority deserved no persecution and indeed should be liberated from the stigma and oppression of society. Brand and his followers were less interested in science and more keen to pursue an ideal construction of history derived from a German tradition of romantic friendship between men that also resonated with echoes of classical Greece. However, neither Hirschfeld's science nor Brand's nationalist views prevented their movements from being suppressed by the Nazis. The Institute for Sexual Science, which was the site of Hirschfeld's work and the repository of his voluminous research, was destroyed and its books burned by the Nazis in 1933. Hirschfeld, who was Jewish, died in exile in France in 1935. Brand's writings were banned in Germany as was his organization. However, Brand (who was married) did not feel impelled to flee Germany. He and his wife were killed by American bombs in 1945.

Further Reading

Harry Oosterhuis and Hubert Kennedy, eds., *Homosexuality and Male Bonding in Pre-Nazi Germany: Original Transcripts from "Der Eigene," the First Gay Journal in the World* (New York and London: Haworth Press, 1991); Thomas Waugh, *Hard to Imagine: Gay Male Eroticism in Photography and Film from Their Beginnings to Stonewall* (New York: Columbia University Press, 1996).

## Elisar von Kupffer (1872–1942)

Elisar von Kupffer was a painter, writer, and aesthete who, in response to the growing homosexual rights movement in Germany and the Wilde trial in England, in 1899 edited an anthology of homoerotic literature entitled *Lieblingminne und Freundesliebe in der Weltliteratur.* The book is the first such anthology, and in it von Kupffer selected texts from periods in literary history during which homoeroticism was most pronounced. He sought to demonstrate that friendship between men and homosexual love were closely allied and that homosexuality was significant to culture and literature during these times. The book was nearly banned, but influential friends allowed it to see one edition (a second edition was confiscated). Von Kupffer and his friend Eduard von Mayer eventually left Germany because of the outbreak of World War I, and he continued his work in Switzerland, founding the Sanctuarium Artis Elisarion in 1927, in which the homoerotic arts were pursued, and which was decorated with frescoes by von Kupffer depicting androgynous youths and allegories of male friendship. The introduction to his anthology, excerpted below, suggests some of the ideals advocated by von Kupffer and other homosexual emancipationists, ideals in which a masculinized anti-effeminate homosexuality was celebrated and *lieblingminne*—love between lovers or comrades—was seen to be the intimate form of *freunddesliebe*, love between friends.

FROM "THE ETHICAL-POLITICAL SIGNIFICANCE OF LIEBLINGMINNE" (1899)

["DIE ETHISCH-POLITISCHE BEDEUTUNG DER LIEBLINGMINNE," FROM *DER EIGENE* (1899), NOS. 6–7)]

*Translated by Hubert Kennedy*

It has now become the fashion in humane-scientific and, on the other hand, closely concerned circles to speak of a "third" sex, whose spirit and body are said not to agree with one another. The Hannoverian jurist K. H. Ulrichs, to be sure a brave and honorable character, but not exactly a circumspect person, even found a designation for this third sex, to which he counted himself; this word "Urning" (from Venus Urania), along with the adjective "urnisch" (uranian), has spread like a generalized epidemic. . . .

It has by now become a moral duty, in all that confused talk of sickness and that mire of lies and filthiness, to let fall a ray of sunshine from the reality of our historical development. It is a thankless task, to be sure, if one is conscious of how much ignorance, malice, and cowardice he has to fight in doing so. It is much easier to let things go on as they have been going, and to live one's inclinations undisturbed in quiet. But, as I said, when it is a question of the common good, of the healthy development of culture, and of personal freedom, then the manly sense demands that we act and speak without cowardly concern.

What do I understand by culture? The possibility of living out our drives and strengths, but without acts of force. Nothing lies further from me than to preach deliverance through an excess of sensual pleasure; no, precisely in the repeated, voluntary limitation and restraint of one's self does one become master; but I would also like to repeat the words of the Greek sage: "It shows manliness to rule over sensual pleasure, without being subservient to it, but not to abstain from it."

We live—as always—in a world of slogans, and little thought is given to them. We hear of decadence and decay and name things thus without seriously asking about the meaning of the words. What then does decadence mean? The dying out of the life force, the inability to carry on the struggle with life, the longing for dissolution, disintegration. Only where that is found may we speak of decadence. And now certain people—to name no names here—come and say: Lieblingminne [a coined word, from *Liebling* (favorite) and *Minne* (chivalric love)] is a symptom of decadence. . . . And now some dare to twist and turn facts and even falsify them, while others anxiously look for a sign of the third sex, for a purely female spirit in the poor male shell. Here a god could become impatient! What is the purpose of all this?! Whoever does not see and perceive the richness of nature with open eyes, no glasses will help him. . . .

If in fact it were to a certain extent the case that Lieblingminne (and love of friends) could be more harmful to the state, to health, to morality than the usual Frauenminne (chivalric love of women), if neither were cultivated excessively, then I would be among the first to call for its limitation. Certainly the state is there for the sake of people, not the other way around; but we need the state, for in spite of all humaneness. . . one person is in a struggle with the other, and there's nothing to complain about, that's the way nature is. For this reason the state and its healthy prosperity is to be judged a natural necessity. Therefore we want to promote only that which helps and makes healthy and strong. And precisely for this reason and only because I hold the close relationship of man to man, of man to youth, of youth to youth to be a strong element of the state and of culture, have I undertaken this difficult task in the interest of the common good and free personal development.

Every rational and reflective person must ask himself: Can it be chance that so many outstanding representatives of our cultural history have cultivated that inclination and those love relationships or, where they were themselves still caught up in the madness of their times, were ruled by that inclination? If we declare it to be abominable, then we must rationally turn away from them in abomination and also rob our culture for the future of elements that are noble and full of life's force. But what is the good of declaring so many bearers of our culture to be half-crazy? What have we won thereby, if a great part of our culture is an institution of lunatics? . . .

Now to the meaning of Lieblingminne. I point out that this word is a new coinage of mine; I had to find a word that—until now—had not been dirtied in the mouths of people. I selected a double title so as to indicate by Freundesliebe (love of friends) that in this collection is much that is less consciously characteristic of Minne (chivalric love), much in which this feeling perhaps unconsciously pulses under the surface. Every expression of life that is suppressed grows secretly into an ugly shadow-plant. It is, therefore, the task of a rational state to draw into the sun of public life whatever is not an act of force against the state and the common good, such as murder, robbery, theft, etc.; so too the intimate relationship of man to man. A first condition for this, of course, is that the penal code contain no dirtying paragraph against it, except against an act of force. That is indeed the basis for a healthy development, but it is not sufficient: we see that in practice in today's France and Italy, where Lieblingminne enjoys legal freedom and yet has attained to no cultural bloom, consequently has not become useful to public life. It is not a question of closing one's eyes to a vice or tolerating an insanity. That is a fruitless half-measure. It is much more a question of drawing an advantage from a phenomenon of life. It is not my purpose here to make propaganda for the governing legislature to take pity on certain of life's "disinherited," who have been neglected by nature; no, it is my purpose to point out that we are passing up a source of strength.

Yes, a source of strength: these relationships can be such. If we leaf through the pages of history with open eyes, we will also find proof of this. In the first place stands ancient Greece—not to speak foolishly of antiquity, for the Romans and the Greeks resembled one another as much as the French and the Germans. The Greeks were certainly not an unblemished ideal people. Where was there ever such! But whoever supposes that this love was to blame for the fact that they failed politically only shows how little he knows history or is willing to know it. It would be just as foolish as to suppose that Christ was to blame for the horrors of Christianity. . . . Precisely in the time of decline did the Lieblingminne disappear in Hellas as an honorable factor of the state, at the same time as the crumbling of all the great old institutions. . . .

Youth must enjoy youth in an open joining with one another. In joining to another a person forgets to think only of himself; in the love and concern and teaching, which the lad experiences from his lover, he learns to know from his youth on the blessing of giving of himself; in the love that he demonstrates, in the small and large offerings of an intimate relationship, he becomes accustomed to the giving of himself to another. Thus indeed is the young man educated to be a member of the community, a useful member, who does not always and only have himself in mind. How much closer the individual grows to the individual here, so that the whole in fact feels itself as a whole. . . .

The close relationship of men has the further effect that one instinctively and not without reason joins with the other; therefore if the one is respectable and honorable, then it is up to him not to let the other bring shame to him. Thus there arises a band of moral responsibility regarding excellence. And what can better promote public life than that the individual members feel themselves responsible for one another? It is just this which makes up the national consciousness, the strength of a people: that it is a whole in itself, where one feels in himself an attack on another. Such connections can be of the highest social value, as the family is. Precisely in the hour of danger is the effect of this togetherness proved, for where the one stands or falls with the other, where self-sacrifice, schooled in small things, has become at the same time a warm-hearted instinct, then there is a force of incalculable importance, a force that only madness could little respect.

## "Gotamo"

"Gotamo" is the pseudonym of an author who still remains unknown. He theorized that homosexual relationships between adult males derives from psychological and physiological predisposition, while love between men and boys, as in the Greek model (which implied both bisexuality and a component of erotic pedagogy), was a superior form of homosexuality because it included an aesthetic and moral element while the other was based on mere sexual desire.

## "Into the Future!" (1903)

### ["In die Zukunft!" *Der Eigene*, 1903]

*Translated by Hubert Kennedy*

As an introduction to his collection *Lieblingminne*, Elisar von Kupffer wrote an essay on the ethical-political significance of the love of a man for a man. It is difficult, after that really excellent presentation, to say anything further essentially new. And yet, allow me here to return once again to that theme and also discuss a few points of that essay more closely.

Doubtless we find ourselves in a decidedly transitional period. The whole civilization of western Europe is based on Christianity. But this foundation has been badly shaken by the Enlightenment of the eighteenth century and in the nineteenth has received so many terrible blows, through the enormous progress that science has made in all fields in a truly dizzying pace, that it will hardly recover. Let us not deceive ourselves about it! Let the Christian churches build ever so many more "God's" houses, seek to shore up the shaky faith by suggestive means in thousands of prayer services, and with an expenditure of enormous amounts of money convert yearly a couple of thousand heathen souls: these external manifestations cannot cover up in the long run its inner apostasy and disintegration! In the colossal development of power, especially in the Catholic Church, we meet with a sign quite similar to what characterized the last varnishing of the Roman political *weltanschauung*. There too, with a completely neurasthenic overrefinement, they madly built temple after temple and invented new forms of worship and new gods. And the masses cheered them on and did not feel how the storm winds of Christianity were already rumbling, which were to overpower the beautifully decorated but rotten and empty edifice. Today the representatives of Christianity know, to be sure, that the struggle for life and death is unavoidable and they are arming themselves for it! And thus we are experiencing the curiously splendid drama that the beginning of the twentieth century shows a high point of priestly power such as it hardly had before, whereas a century ago one could have held Christianity to be nearly conquered. All its forces are being united for the final battle, and a fine tragedy could result if the modern world were not to act so sober, so businesslike. There is also a change in the *weltanschauung* of whole peoples. Everything is in a ferment. From the slight doubts of the schoolboy, who is told that God created the world in seven days, to the mountain-moving exultation of Nietzsche's Zarathustra over the death of God is only a step. And yet, all nuances of the transition have been retained. One doubts, one still seeks to persuade himself that he believes, or one is honest with himself and only lies to the others. One learns to lie so well! Then one day someone comes and coins the expression of the conventional lie. People read it and find it so true that they say it is really nothing new, but then they shrug their shoulders and continue to lie. And the great number of those who also think Nietzsche correct help in the lying. Everyone must lie; all instinctively feel that the shaky edifice of social order is built on lies and fear the truth more than pestilence and death. And yet there are so many who would gladly have the truth, and all of them consciously feel the longing, the great longing for a new civilization. (Kupffer: "Civilization is the possibility of fully living out our drives and strengths.")

We have to lie somewhat more than the others, we, in whom the elements were so mixed that our eyes perceive above all the beauty of those of our own sex, that the seething passion of our senses show where to seek our complement, the primal wonder, the mystic, and thousandfold mysterious love. They let us wander a couple of years in darkness by an artificial concealment and by making open expression impossible. And when we then discovered ourselves and have found the way, we see with horror that it leads over centuries-old fossilized prejudices, which glare at us threateningly. No matter, we must go through! *Anagke*, the force of necessity! And here each must help himself as best he can. But the world, the wide world, in which the received morality is carefully protected, is astonished that homosexuals are so eccentric, so bizarre, so unprincipled, so given to lying when it occasionally stumbles upon one who through years-long playacting has ruined his moral foundation even more fundamentally than his "normal" fellow human beings, whom these characteristics do not hinder from belonging to the exclusive "pillars of throne and altar."

We may safely grant that homosexual society, at least as it presents itself in Berlin, stands on no higher civilized standpoint than the other, rather the opposite. The mystic twilight of being unknown, of the hidden, and of the forbidden, with which this society forms a state within the state, is not suited to bringing the better characteristics of its more or less effeminate members to development. Therefore there are in fact many to whom those bad characteristics may correctly be attributed. They are just women and can become hysterical like the true ones. On the other hand, one finds among the male prostitutes exactly the same smut and the same ethical inferiority that, according to all reports, distinguishes their female colleagues.

It is wrong, however, to generalize these reproaches.

Precisely the noblest, the most distinguished, and the most masculine of those who are devoted to this eros come to light the least and are observed the least. For them, however, there lies in their being forced to hide a slander and an insult that often enough does not allow the most splendid dispositions to develop and which leads to an embittered isolation from human society. And human beings need other human beings so much!

Thus we see that a numerous class of people, through the prejudices of the crowd, has gotten into a truly piteous position, from which few are able to raise themselves with their own strength. The majority will not even feel how shameful their continuing hypocrisy is. One is weakened, goes recklessly on, and seeks forgetfulness in a frantic intoxication of the senses, in ever new refinements of pleasure. And indeed in the large cities, in the very large cities, it is so easy to accomplish that. One goes to Friedrichstrasse and fetches himself a boy. Nothing simpler! The story repeats itself and people gradually become incapable of a greater, more beautiful love! And if his drunkenness once carries someone away and his mouth overflows with him who fills his heart, then the whole honorable society of the guardians of Zion cry bloody murder and all the well-intentioned people excommunicate the imprudent man like a mangy dog. The more strict call for the penitentiary and corporal punishment, the mild shake their heads and are of the opinion that if one is like that then he should at least just keep silent and not give public offense! Then they speak a few interesting words about sexual psychopathology and decadence, and afterwards—keep silent. Behind them, however, hobbles the state's attorney, who drags out some mummified paragraph or other so as to teach morality with the power of the law to the all-too-daring man who worships the god in his heart with praise and sacrifice instead of denying him. Truly, it is a poisonous sump into which they have forced us. We must get out, cost what it will!

Let us make use of the opportunity. Everything is pressing toward a new civilization. Here we must also raise our voices and engage our strengths so that what is to come will be more beautiful and higher than before. Through our own lives we must demonstrate to those who have learned to see at all that this prohibited love, to which Elisar von Kupffer gave the lovely name *Lieblingminne*, in fact represents a quiet, powerful fountain of strength and that it is a sin against the holy spirit of creation if one seeks to dam up this fountain or to poison it. Let us, each in his own sphere, let it spring up and become a mighty stream, and then shall the enemies see how that stream fertilizes its banks!

But first, people must learn to see! They must know what it is that is being discussed. Here the book of Kupffer was indeed a stroke of ethical culture. But it is not the concern of all people to work their way through a literary collection, and then—as incredible as it may seem—there are still enough people who, after their reading, quite simply explain: Yes, if it is so, then all those great men are to be viewed as pathological; there is degeneration everywhere! And occasionally there comes someone who swears by Lombroso and finds here material suitable to support the hypothesis of the connection between genius and insanity. All these will only believe that we are healthy if either they are able to observe us themselves or if science points it out to them. Therefore we should gratefully accept the help that this has provided us in recent times. On this point I do not agree with Kupffer. I too am no friend of those dissecting investigations and psychological doings that have here and there been the consequence, perhaps even the prerequisite of that strange, late-born science of "psychopathia sexualis." But in fact the writings of Krafft-Ebing, Moll, and Hirschfeld have had an uncommonly informative and instructional effect in wide circles. Above all, they bring to the eyes of the lawgivers the necessary "scientific assumptions" to alter the legal code. Already, at least in the large cities, almost all educated people are convinced that a change must take place here, whereas twenty years ago such a proposal still would simply have been ridiculed. If these men, and with them as many others as possible, do not cease to announce their *ceterum censeo paragraphum esse tollendum* [i.e., but I am of the opinion that the paragraph should be removed], then after a couple of decades our present legal code will appear completely medieval. And on this we are probably all united, that the first outward success that we are aiming at must be the removal of that disastrous paragraph which has crept into the laws of almost every state. That this is not enough, however, has also been emphasized by Elisar von Kupffer with reference to conditions in France and Italy. But the repeal of this law is the necessary starting point for all further development. This law will not run away without a violent struggle, certainly. All the better! For that gives us the possibility of fighting with a goal before our eyes and will assure us the collaboration of all enlightened people. This fight will then force public opinion to occupy itself with us. And when the paragraph falls, which must happen sooner or later, then in the eyes of many that will mean a greater success, the longer and more desperately we have had to struggle for it. This success will equally mean for them the recognition of *Lieblingminne*. This fight must be carried out, therefore, with all our strength, and we should welcome all our fellow citizens who wish to stand on our side.

But when we have attained that goal, oh then, upwards! upwards! A new day draws us to new shores! Unimaginable, immeasurable cultural perspectives open up to us and we already see the clear, sunny civilization of ancient Hellas renew itself. But we will not even content ourselves with that. Our civilization is to become even higher and more splendid.

When finally the justification of our love is granted, then must we above all come out in public and prove by deeds not merely that we have earned tolerance, but rather that *Lieblingminne* is in ethical significance, in strength and beauty, equal to the formerly only justified *Frauenminne* [love of women]. Then we will also attain the goal of being allowed to publicly court a return of love and friendship, and fathers will no longer shortsightedly warn and restrain their sons from relations with friends. On the contrary, they will be happy when a competent man courts the favor of their sons and a smart youth will find in his attachment to his lover many things that will have a valuable meaning for his whole life, which the school and often even his parent's home are unable to offer him. . . .

It is surely no accident that the majority of Hellenes felt themselves drawn above all to the youthful representatives of their own sex. The opposite probably also existed, but the number of persons completely "inverted" in their sex drive was, relative to the entire population, only small, exactly like today. Therefore attention was not very much directed toward them. We can only explain the extraordinary extent of Socratic love in Hellas through the doctrine of bisexuality, and through it every apparent puzzle is solved by itself. Dr. Hirschfeld has shown that in the case of an innate "contrary sexual feeling" it is a question of intermediate stages, transitional types from the complete man to the complete woman. Along the way all nuances are found, and psychosexual hermaphroditism, bisexuality, is discovered to be the transition from normality to homosexuality. The history of antiquity teaches us that numerous outstanding men found pleasure in the mature form of woman and then again in the blooming beauty of youths, and we absolutely cannot assume that all of them did so from vice, craving for pleasure, satiety, or because it was the general custom. Poets such as Anacreon and Horace celebrate their lovers of both sexes with the same ardor. In those Greek states where the Socratic love enjoyed special recognition or was even protected and regulated by the state, such as Athens and Crete, the whole culture, as far as it is connected in any way with sexual life, appears to be based on a bisexual foundation. The homosexual part of the sex drive of the bisexual was directed above all toward youthful individuals who were to some extent related to the feminine type, and the whole Greek cultural history is the most telling proof of the splendid, moral heights to which this drive can be advanced.

The opponents of the repeal of 175 have also already based their standpoint on the indication that, after the repeal, the number of homosexuals would increase. They are not entirely incorrect. To be sure, the repeal in and of itself would not change the situation very much. But when "public opinion" recognizes our love as having equal rights, when an arising new culture has again established the basis of aesthetic feeling, when also, perhaps, an urgently necessary transformation of our male clothing again allows the recognition of the splendid lines and proportions of well-formed bodies, then surely thousands will reflect on themselves and also bring to development their homosexual drive, which in addition to the "normal" one was asleep in them and which our contemporary culture has suppressed and destroyed with a hundred thousand influences. But a bisexuality on such a basis appears no danger to us. When thus the possibility of living out our tendency is offered, then must the level of civilization be raised and then too will a noble form be found for all. Our athletic fields will play a role similar to the Gymnasia of Athens. And then we will regain for youth its lost adolescence!

How one can see in such efforts a danger to society is incomprehensible. As a rule they finally take shelter behind the fear that an eventual "sexual intercourse" could harm the boy in body and soul. First, however, this "intercourse" is just not the most important thing, and many will in the future also endure life quite well without it. On the other hand, solitary masturbation, which is carried out by at least four-fifths of our youth—which only a ridiculous hypocrisy and prudery dares to deny—is certainly more harmful by far to virtue and health. Boys just satisfy their drive in one way or another, whether through masturbation, that "sad caricature" of normal satisfaction, or with the help of prostitutes, by which they acquire the seeds of the degeneration of their whole families, not to speak of the moral damage.

Others have feared that women could again fall into a degrading position similar to that in Greece. I hold this danger to be very slight; women are already defending themselves today. Elisar von Kupffer is quite right when he speaks of the necessity of the emancipation of men and compares our efforts with the well-known women's movement. One does not know, of course, to what extent women will achieve their demands—at any rate, precisely to the extent they deserve. And if their sex then stands opposite the male sex in a greater independence, that is still a long way from meaning the battle of the two parties. Women can only gain if men cease to view them as the exclusive object of courting. The relation of the two sexes will be freer on both sides, therefore nobler and happier.

One may hold all this to be utopian. But we see that something new must take shape and thus may we picture the surging chaos developed. Truly, in spite of all difficulties, it is a splendid time in which to live! We may fight in the conviction that we are laying the foundation for a new civilization.

And thus we look confidently into the future.

## John Henry Mackay (1864–1933)

*Selections Translated by Hubert Kennedy*

Mackay was born in Scotland of a German mother who returned to Germany upon the death of her husband. Mackay began writing in the 1880s and by 1911 had published eight volumes of poems, novels, and pamphlets. His homosexuality was turned to literary use when he began writing homoerotic poetry addressed to boys, one of which, "Morgen," so pleased Richard Strauss that he set it to music as one of the Four Last Songs. Mackay was soon fired to more revolutionary writing by the homosexual emancipation movement and under the name of Sagitta he wrote pieces defending what he called "the nameless love." In his novel *Fenny Skeller* (1905), Mackay propagandized for the kind of man-boy love so favored by one wing of the German rights movement. In 1913 he gathered some of his writings on homosexual rights together in volumes called *The Books of Nameless Love*, of which "The Nameless Love: A Creed" was the first book. His writings were condemned as immoral in Imperial Germany, but in 1924, again writing as Sagitta, he published a novel, this no propaganda but a highly competent and surely deeply felt book called *The Hustler*, which examines the underworld of Berlin gay bars and the love between Hermann and a young hustler named Gunther. *The Hustler* was privately printed and was not a success, but together with Mackay's other writings, after the triumph of Hitler, it was entered into the Nazi list of impure and forbidden books.

*The Nameless Love (1905)*
*[Die namenlose Liebe]*
Because still on the youthful wing
    The scent of innocent beauty lies
    That touched by a stranger scatters and dies—

Yet since you think it a dirty thing
    Have dragged it through mud and infamy
    And kept under lock and key—

To love persecuted my song I bring
    And to the outcasts of our time
    Since happy or not this love is mine–
This love dare I loudly sing

*Tomorrow*
*[Morgen]*
Tomorrow again will shine the sun
and on my sunlit path of earth,

unite us again, as it has done,
and give our bliss another birth.
    The spacious beach under wave-blue skies
we'll reach by descending soft and slow,
    and mutely gaze in each other's eyes,
and over us rapture's great hush will flow.


## THE NAMELESS LOVE: A CREED (1906)

Once, more than two thousand years ago, it was one of the roots from which the in so many ways unrivalled culture of a people, the most thirsty for beauty and drunk on beauty that the world has ever known, drew its best nourishment. Health, strength, and greatness blossomed for the Greeks from the love of a man for a youth, of a youth for a man, a love prized by its thinkers and sung by its poets. A brightness was over it—the brightness of understanding and freedom.

Then came the night, and it came with Christianity and its monstrous falsification of all our natural feeling of optimism and joy in life. For centuries this love, which the Greeks set in its beauty and nobility in the bright sunshine and before the eyes of the world, was buried: its name was debased and outlawed, it was itself dishonored, persecuted and despised, so much so that it, which lived because it was imperishable and therefore could not die, hid and concealed itself from the world and from itself, and its martyred cries died away without echo in the silence of fear and terror for dark centuries.

We the living, the blessed-accursed children of the nineteenth century, which laid the foundation of all future freedom of the human race, we were the first to again dare to acknowledge it. But instead of finally raising it up from under the dirt and dust covering it and setting it in the triumph of its untouched beauty in the place it deserves, crowning its white brow with fresh roses and celebrating the festival of life at its feet, they dragged what had been dishonored at the judge's bench and the priest's pulpit onto the dissecting table of the doctor, gave it a place between the two sexes, and in their own opinion they were as mild as they were correct, those who decided: it does not belong here, but rather in the insane asylums.

This love, which lived in spite of all the chains and tortures, this healthy love was to be "healed" by the hypnotic treatments of quacks and the straitjackets of force. Having branded it as a crime against nature until then, they began to do something worse—to kindly excuse it as an aberration of nature.

Then it finally raised its beautiful head and—smiled! It smiled again for the first time since the days when it saw a happier and therefore more beautiful race. Nature! She who created us all, not as we wanted, but as she must, she alone knows why she created us as we are. We are all her children. And she is the mother of us all. Everything in her is natural, for everything is in her and there is no crime against her that does not bring about its own downfall by itself. Our life is carried out in the never-ending struggle for self-preservation. Every being has to fight for its place on her life-giving breast. We too, so long disowned, let us struggle finally for our place and not miserably hunger longer for it, just because her apparently privileged children shove us away from her. . . .

We? But then who are this "we"?

Every single one of us who has suffered undeserved and unsought loneliness has imagined that he is all alone. Despised in people's circles, shoved away from the table of life, he fought with the drives of his own nature as with a spiteful enemy, every day anew, today conquering and tomorrow beaten down, already feeling himself a criminal with every glance, every handshake, every kiss of his persecuted love, until the day he dares to open his eyes and recognize that there are others like him all around, alike and yet different.

And if his view widens and goes deeper, a new understanding must join his understanding of this difference: the understanding, as the most mature carried over from the century just past, that the welfare of the future lies in the liberation of the individual, of each individual, in his development, hindered in no way by social and group pressure, into himself as the highest happiness of his life, its meaning and its goal.

One day, when in this freedom the development of a person to be different takes new, not yet imagined paths, then will this love also show itself in its true form. No longer for sale because of need or calculation, no longer shamelessly placed under the eyes and the permission of others, the free gift of one heart to another, and the most precious, will be this creating and sustaining love and, even if not everywhere equally to both, it will be given and taken—without worry or concern for hate and misunderstanding.

Then we shall see who we are and how many. For who today can even guess how many we are, when in fear and disgrace in the face of savage prejudices and laws that are themselves crimes we kill the most tender inclinations of our heart and hoist a screen between them and us, so as not to see and not to be seen! . . .

But how shall I name you, my life's love?!

Each name that has named you until now has become a term of abuse in the dirty mouth of the vulgar, a misunderstanding in dull minds, which is worse than all insults; and none names you correctly.

You still have no name.

So let me call you—nameless! . . .

Nameless love—when will the future finally call you by your true name?

I will keep silent no longer.

I speak late. My fearful, oppressed breast choked off the cry of my youth; eternal disappointment murdered its longing; restless thinking early destroyed its freshness.

Thus the last hope of my life broke through to the recognition of a monstrous and unexampled injustice, and its highest wish now became this, to serve this understanding with my last strength.

If it is no longer a cry, then it will still be a call; and what it has lost in strength, it must have won in depth.

And I feel that it will fall on the ears of those who, in the terrible silence around them, still listen as if for an answer to the puzzling question of their lives—will fall like a word of comfort, a message of new courage.

I have lived in night.

Now I will loudly greet the dawning day, and cool my burning eyes, weary with lonely tears, in its young light.

Courage and comfort are necessary for us all today.

My late work shall yet give courage and comfort to me. And, if it is possible, also to others who in lonely fear despair, who silently hunger for love, who search for themselves in vain, unable to find themselves in confusion and distress—each alone and all undeserving of their fate!

Courage and comfort—for them and for me!

## Benedict Friedlander (1866–1908)

Friedlander's vision of homosexuality sharply differed from the third-sex theory postulated by Ulrichs and adopted by numerous medical theorists including Magnus Hirschfeld, whose Scientific Humanitarian Committee was the most influential group working for homosexual emancipation in Germany. In *Die Renaissance der Eros Uranios* (1904), Friedlander urged his ideal of a masculinized homosexuality and of the social value of male bonding and sex between men. Freidlander argued for a renaissance of Uranian love on the model of the Greeks. In 1907 he attempted to secede from Hirschfeld's committee. The excerpt below explains why and outlines his position on homosexual relations.

FROM "MEMOIR FOR THE FRIENDS AND CONTRIBUTORS OF THE
SCIENTIFIC HUMANITARIAN COMMITTEE IN THE NAME OF THE SECESSION
OF THE SCIENTIFIC HUMANITARIAN COMMITTEE" (1907)

[DENKSCHRIFT FÜR DIE FREUNDE UND FONDSZEICHNER DES
WISSENSCHAFTLICH-HUMANITÄREN KOMITEES].

*Translated by Hubert Kennedy*

### I. SCIENTIFIC POINTS OF DIFFERENCE

. . . . The importance of our separation for the whole emancipation movement . . . lies chiefly in the area of theory: The path is open for a less dogmatic, more impartial, and more correct evaluation of same-sex love. Let it be sharply emphasized here that we lay far less weight on a scientific theory than Herr Hirschfeld and see the question much more from the standpoint of natural rights as one of personal freedom. . . .

Now, just what is the science of the Scientific Committee?

Not only Hirschfeld but the medical writers all together have spread about, with small divergences and insignificant additions, the contents of the twelve brochures of the jurist K. H. Ulrichs. Ulrichs was a sincere, courageous, and original man. With his appearance, which for that time was truly pioneering, he had seemingly little success. A generation later, when the question was no longer so undiscussable, there came eager medical doctors, armored with their authority, who believed that they had tracked down a new field of activity for theory and practice. . . .

In truth the medical writers on homosexuality presented to the public, partly in thick volumes, partly in tract format, everything that . . . [Ulrichs] had brought into the world, supplied with the stamp of medical authority almost without any criticism, partly translated into the jargon of medical quackery, and decorated with so-called "case histories."

For the knowledgeable, these latecomers betray themselves as such principally through the fact that they even copy the errors and tastelessness of the original. . . . Thus the dependence of the medical literature on the truths and errors of Ulrichs is seen externally by the fact that the silly, ungrammatical, and tasteless word "Urning," invented by Ulrichs in an evil hour, has by now, along with its derivations, come into circulation with the serious aspect of a "scientific" technical term. . . . Ulrichs is the inventor of the theory, celebrated in propaganda and subsidized by thousands, of the "sexual intermediate," the theory of the poor female soul that languishes in a male body, and of the "third sex."

Certainly there are "sexual intermediates." Earlier they were called hermaphrodites. They are the rare malformations, which may be estimated to make up—at most—a small fraction per thousand. Of those who are aware of their same-sex feelings . . . [but] a glance at the non- and pre-Christian cultures is sufficient to prove the complete untenability of the theory. In ancient Hellas in particular most of the generals, artists, and thinkers would have to have been hermaphrodites. Every people from whose initiative in all higher human endeavors every later European culture fed must have consisted in great part of sick, hybrid individuals, and indeed especially before and at their golden age. . . . That custom was indeed much, much too universal to have been able to be borne by the assumed 1.5 percent of "homosexuals"! Rather, it was obvious that that state of affairs rested predominantly on the very much larger number of so-called "bisexuals" and the idea at least suggested itself that a certain degree of "bisexuality" was still more widespread than the modern statistic shows. . . .

[This] was discussed in detail by me three years ago in my *Renaissance der Eros Uranios*. Until then there was little talk of bisexuals in the Urning camp, since it was unsuited to theory and agitation, and it was only my writing and also, perhaps, the results of statistics that forced the champions of the theory of intermediates to concern themselves a bit more with bisexuality. . . .

Recently the most productive of the medical doctors who have been writing about things sexual have wanted to separate Hellenic paederasty, sanctified by national custom, as a "pseudo-homosexuality" connected with bisexuality, from "genuine" homosexuality. That this national custom was based in a much higher degree on bisexuality than on pure homosexuality is correct of course, as has been said, and this was long ago emphasized by us and others. But since it is still a matter of true love among those truly of the same sex, it is simply incomprehensible what should be "pseudo" about it. . . .

In spite of its lack of originality the medical literature has doubtless been extremely useful. The medical authority that spoke of "observations of illness" was allowed expressions otherwise made difficult by the touch-me-not stamp of prudery and suppressive laws. Only through the intercession of several doctors, no matter whether through selflessness or self-interest, could wider circles be educated about the mere presence of same-sex love and the fact be made the object of universal knowledge, that there is really a large number of purely "homosexually" inclined men—something asserted till now by only a few and doubted by others. And only thereby has that movement come about that is constantly drawing in wider circles and can surely no longer be stopped by any power. Far be it from us to underestimate the significance of the medical agitation.

Through its undivided dominance, however, the movement has fallen into a fateful one-sidedness that, if allowed to continue undisturbed, must in the end do more damage than the whole medical propaganda has otherwise done good. For one would finally get rid of [Paragraph] 175 on the basis of purely juridical considerations, just as the analogous penal clauses in other countries have passed away without medical help.

The mere circumstance that the larger public always sees only doctors at the head of the movement must further the error that it is a question of a sickness or at least a pathology. With sicknesses one can have pity, of course, and act "humanely" toward the sick, and even seek to "cure" them; the equal rights of those alleged to be physically inferior will never be recognized.

Now, it is true that the more progressive among the medical men have expressly dropped the doctrine of the sickness of same-sex love: they also had to do it, for otherwise their clients would have run away from them.

But a remainder of the error is left and can only disappear along with the false "intermediate stage" theory. An admixture of feminine characteristics . . . such as the Ulrichs theory teaches as an explanation of same-sex love, must of course always give the appearance that all men who have complete or partial same-sex feelings are to be considered to be not quite whole and afflicted with an incompleteness. As long as the love for a male being is presented as a specific and exclusively feminine characteristic . . . it will not help to deny sickness: there remains an unavoidable image of a partial hermaphrodite, that is, a kind of psychic malformation. Here too one cannot claim respect, but only at most beg for pity and at best tolerance. . . .

Thus the tabu of same-sex love among men contributes very essentially to the improper absolute rule of woman-love, to the suppression of male friendship, and thereby to a feminization of the whole culture. A comparison of the appreciation which that friendship enjoyed in classic antiquity—without regard for the foolish and indiscreet question of whether it came to "sexual" acts or not!—with our condition makes that all too clear. At that time there was still no one who seriously talked that nonsense about the equal intellect and equal rights of women. In the case of the whole white race it has come to a fateful exaggeration of the family principle—that most primitive form of socialization, which human beings share even with the beasts of prey—which breaks up states and eats away the national unity. The other, world-enriching love, which is reserved to the social species, which Walt Whitman called "love of comrades," and which is most closely connected with so-called homosexuality, has on the contrary withdrawn entirely into the background.

Poor Whitman! What hope you had for the love of comrades for your United States! And you forgot that over there by you the prevailing "lady-economy" will never allow the love of comrades, which reaches beyond feminine show and family life. . . .

The public is even less ready for the last and highest branch of the homosexual question than it is for the physical foundation; it was perhaps an indeed regrettable, but necessary precept of wisdom to keep silent about it in the agitation in the beginning. But it certainly should have been exceptionally emphasized that man-man love is capable of the same spiritualization and emotional depth as man-woman love. . . . But what is one to say when the principal spokesman, Herr Hirschfeld himself, in a half-literary, half-popular scientific form talks about "Berlin's third sex" and leads the reader into a sort of "thieves' den" milieu, as if that belonged to the essence of the matter! In my *Renaissance* I rather warned against forming a judgment in the matter from the doings of this "third sex" in the well-known bars, since one gets to see there only some of the symptoms of degeneration caused by the pressure of modern morality.

Through such presentations the cause advocated will, without need and against the truth, be degraded and harmed. . . . There are really enough bright sides to the love of friends! Let us just not hide the fact that really intimate and passionate young friendships, even those that predominantly incline toward women, are permeated by the spirit of Eros Uranios—no matter whether it thereby comes to sexual trifles or not! Let us just understand that no one can be a good educator who does not love his pupils! And let us not lie to ourselves that in love the so-called "spiritual" element can ever be completely detached from its physiological foundation. It is an eternal verity. . . .

## II. OUR PROGRAM

. . . . From a scientific view, regarding the theoretical judgment of same-sex love, we reject the Ulrichs-theory of intermediates for the reasons set forth above. Thus we all not speak of "Urnings," nor of the "third sex," nor yet of "sexual intermediates." We are further of the opinion that through the exclusively medical treatment of a general human matter a basic error has been made. The object of the doctor is sicknesses; therefore he is inclined, because of his profession, to classify everything possible under the concept of sickness or pathology. . . . We are of the view that the scientist who does not have a one-sided medical training, the physiologist and anthropologist, is by profession at least as competent an expert to scientifically judge the question of same-sex love as the medical man, whose general scientific education is mostly poorly cultivated. We are of this opinion for the reason that . . . . most cases of same-sex love are not in the least pathological, but are rather completely normal. . . .

We are rather of the opinion that the last word on the nature, significance, and goal of same-sex love either has not yet been spoken at all, or that it will last a long time before in fact a definite conception will have banished all competing conceptions from the field by the inner force of its truth. . . . Sufficient for us is the fact of the presence and frequency of same-sex love, in connection with the axiomatic principle of the demand for personal freedom in all cases where no rights are injured.

We likewise believe that comparative cultural history must be called upon for a judgment in the question. In particular, we place value on the proof that male friendship and every more intimate relationship among men, in short all men's unions in the ethnological sense, is affected and made difficult by the excessive tabu of sexual forms of male friendship. This especially holds true of the pedagogically quite irreplaceable deep personal relationship between mature men and youths.

As for . . . [Paragraph] 175, we shall fight it from purely juridical and moral viewpoints. For whereas the medical theory is controversial and in part really quite vacuous, the juridical and moral consideration is clear, simple, and convincing:

Two responsible people, freely consenting and without harm to a third or even merely to themselves, produce for each other a pleasant feeling. Then comes the state — if by exception it once learns of it — and locks up the culprits, as if they had done something wrong!

On the basis of 175, every year 500–600 men who have made no one suffer in the least, nor have done harm to anyone, are "sentenced" to prison, exactly as if they had swindled or stolen!

That is as absurd as any tabu of wild primitive peoples. . . . 175 is only a partial symptom of a wider superstition and fraud. We mean the ascetic madness spread by the Christian priests of the early Middle Ages, according to which everything sexual was suspicious, and a feeling of lust — without regard to the question of harming a third — was posed as sinful in itself. That was partly superstition and partly fraud. Just as doctors live from healing sicknesses, those medieval priests lived from the forgiveness of sins. Thus, just as the doctor is dependent on the presence of the real or imagined sick person, so too the medieval priest was dependent on the presence of people who held themselves, with or without reason, to be "sinners." Now, the amount of genuine wrong, that is, the sum of all unjust harm between one person and another, did not suffice for the needs of the all too massive and pretentious budding priesthood of the Middle Ages; it therefore made the attempt to produce in all people, even the best, a sort of hypochondriac madness of sinfulness — and that succeeded most surely by pretending that something was sinful which every healthy man has need of from time to time or at least bears an intensive desire for. Hence the propagation of the ascetic spirit. . . . Man-woman love could not entirely be made tabu; the priests had to be satisfied with making its admissibility dependent on their sanction. Same-sex love, however, whose necessity [is] not so obvious as man-woman love, could be posed absolutely as sinful. . . . Thus we shall fight against 175, as far as we treat it at all, as a juridical and moral monstrosity and emphasize its origin from ascetic fraud overcome by the modern weltanschauung.

It is precisely this sincerer, stronger, and more manly change in direction that the representatives of the Urning theory have made an accusation and pose as dubious; they fear it will heighten the resistance and animosity of the opponents. We reply, first, that our view obviously has truth on its side and, further, that the opposition in the two orthodox camps can probably not become stronger than it already is; further, that it is our change in direction that makes the so-called homosexual movement recognizable at all as a part of the modern freedom movement and therefore must awake sympathy in all liberally thinking people.

# 21. Erotic Revolutionaries

## Russian Literature (1836–1922)

Though early Russian literature shows some evidence of same-sex love (for example, in the religious *Legend of Boris and Gelb* from the eleventh century), there is little evidence for a homosexual literary presence until the nineteenth century. A few stories by Konstantine Leontyev (1831–1891), such as "Khamid and Manoli," describes a tragic love affair between two men; or one finds a few poems in the tradition of the Greek anthology by Aleksandr Pushkin (1799–1837) who, though not homosexual, seems to have been aware and tolerant of homosexuality among his friends. Nikolay Gogol (1809–1852), as Simon Karlinsky argues, was an anguished and guilt-ridden homosexual who sublimated his desire in his opaque and fantastic texts. In general though, homosexuality appears in Russian literature some time after it had already become a topic in literature in most of the countries of Europe, an effect caused no doubt by the legal and religious prohibitions against it in Russia. In the early twentieth century, Russian writers Mikhail Kuzmin, Nikolay Klyuev, and Sergei Esenin began to employ homosexual themes in their work, most of which they accomplished during the period of relative liberalism that encompassed the Revolution of 1905, the October Revolution of 1917 when Lenin and Trotsky took power, and the final solidification of that power in the early 1920s. After that time homosexuality effectively disappears from Russian literature as the Russian government became increasingly hostile to it. Under Stalin sexual acts with minors were outlawed in 1922 and homosexual relations between men were proscribed in 1934. The official doctrine of the Communist state was that homosexuality was a capitalist phenomenon that could not exist in a socialist country and that those who might be guilty of it were in fact counterrevolutionaries. In the 1970s Russian gay writers, touched perhaps by the gay rights movement in the United States and its echoes in Europe, began to publish their work privately, though secretly, mindful perhaps of the fate of Gennedy Trifonov, who was sentenced to four years at hard labor for privately circulating gay poetry, or of Evgeny Popov, whose application for entry into the official Writers' Union was indefinitely denied because of his short story "The Reservoir."

Further Reading

Simon Karlinsky, "Russia's Gay History and Literature," in Winston Leyland, ed., *Gay Roots: Twenty Years of Gay Sunshine*, vol. 1 (San Francisco: Gay Sunshine Press, 1991), 81–104.

## Aleksandr Sergeyevich Pushkin (1799–1837)

There is little evidence that Pushkin was homosexual though, as Michael Green says in an essay on the poet, "his attitude toward the physical expression of desire between men seems to have been one of cheerful and benign acceptance." His imitation of an Arabic poem, and his quatrain inspired by a statue of a Russian peasant youth playing the game *svaika*, whom he sees as a fit companion for the Greek youth portrayed in the classical statue Discobulous, suggest his tolerance.

TWO POEMS

*Translated by Michael Green*

*Imitation of the Arabic (1835)*

Sweet lad, tender lad,
Have no shame, you're mine for good;
We share a sole insurgent fire,
We live in boundless brotherhood.

I do not fear the gibes of men;
One being split in two we dwell,
The kernel of a double nut
Embedded in a single shell.

*On the Statue of a Player at Svaika (1836)*

Full of beauty, full of tension, to effort a stranger, a stripling,
    Slender, sinewy, light as air—is reveling in the nimble sport!
Here's a fitting companion for you, O Discobulous! Worthy by my oath,
    When sportings done with to rest beside you, locked in amicable embrace.

## Nikolay Klyuev (1887–1937)

The poems of Klyuev, influenced by the symbolist movement as well as by an intense nationalism and devotion to Russian folklore, also reflect a strong awareness of sexual difference. He had become something of a celebrity when he met Sergei Esenin in 1915. The two men lived together in St. Petersburg and devoted themselves to writing poetry, but after two years Esenin left Klyuev. Increasingly Klyuev advocated the free expression of homosexual desire, and when Lenin came to power he believed that the new regime would support such freedom. He soon became convinced of his error, and in "The Fourth Rome" (1922), dedicated to his lover Nikolay Arkhipov, he made his homosexuality clear and in his writings proclaimed his opposition to the government. He was arrested in 1933, sentenced to four years hard labor, and died in 1937.

THE FOURTH ROME (1922)

*Translated by Simon Karlinsky*

*To Nikolay Ilyich Arkhipov*

*And now I go about in a top hat*
*And in patent leather shoes . . .*
—Sergei Esenin

I do not want to be a famous poet
In a top hat and patent leather shoes.

I'll confront the world clad in my song
With the ursine sun in the depths of my eyes,
With pine-needle darkness in my shaggy beard,
Where a wood goblin, copulating with a lynx, growls!
Out of words I wove a bast shoe, vast as the sunset,
A cradle for my child—the roar of centuries.
In that enchanted cradle are gray-haired fears,
Drowsy sorceries, hunchbacked non-existence . . .
My face is like a child on an executioner's block,
Like a prelate visiting a cannibal witch,
And my heart is a hut, its logs like paws,
Where the inner chamber is a feast of angels,
Where Rublyov's colors ooze from the icons,
The milk of prayers and the cheese of infatuation.
There is a larder of mysteries, a bench for dreams and thoughts,
But the chamber of my heart is no match for your crotch:
Oh, that land of golden hay-mowings and threshing floors!
Oh, that weaver's shop of rainbows, the ballgame of spring!
It is toward it that treasure seekers hasten
My fingers, five fellows both reckless and wild,
And in red-haired woodland, near waterfall veins,
They drill the strata to reach the diamond wellsprings.
My soul, a star-feathered rooster on his perch,
Is lost is listening to the furious smacks of the drill.
    My poems are bonfires for my lovely bride,
Whose balls are two wild boars, two fierce eagles.

I do not want to hide under a top hat
My forest demon's horns.
The shores of my seas and rivers
Are for hoary sperm whales, for wolf-fish and otters.
There is the shore of nipples, the torrid island of buttocks,
The valley of the groin, the plateau of knees;
Song-filled pebbles and colored seashells
Lure whole gangs of sirens to come swimming this way.
But the sea of witching flesh may become overcast
And bury passion's ships in its waves.
To a triton's flute music, in the swamp of tile haunches,
A wood goblin and earth's spirits shallowly splash.
O flesh! Those blue lindens on the hillside,
Where bumblebees pierce the lips of blossoms!
Your falling leaves are raked in by Arkhipov
With the rake of his kisses into bagfuls of verse.
These bagfuls of verse are filled with linden honey,
With horseshoes of rainbows, with forest halloos . . .
My beloved shall be beloved by my people
Because he comforted my least little tear.

My beloved is a stone with a thousand facets
In whose depth a daredevil sturgeon lurks.
In a snakeskin headband, astride a gray boar,
Lechery observes the abode of our sleep.
My beloved is the harvest of northern fields,
Where the least storm cloud is an infant in a funereal wreath,
The migratory crane-like sadness of Russia's spaces
Which pleat together, criss-cross, grasses and stars.

I do not want the top hat and shoes
To cover up the torpedo gash in the barge of my soul.
I blossom forth, as a meadow blossoms with peasant huts' gables,
With smiles of lakes in a song-ringing stillness.
And I am loyal to my sad and humble cradle,
To my mother's dear grave, to the threshing floor's face.
This is why seraphs converge like baby goldfinches
On my feeder, where I offer love and springtime.

## Sergei Esenin (1895–1925)

For a time Esenin, who was bisexual, was the lover of Klyuev. Though he later married
(among his wives were the actress Isadora Duncan and the granddaughter of Tolstoy), he
still had affairs with men and used most of his these to advance his own literary fortunes.
With Klyuev, Esenin at first embraced the revolution but soon recognized its authoritar-
ian direction and left Russia for America. He returned to the Soviet Union in 1925 but,
convinced of his own failure and feeling outcast from the new Russian society, he hanged
himself later that same year.

THREE POEMS

*Translated by Simon Karlinsky*

*[Yesterday's rain . . .] (1916)*

Yesterday's rain is still on the ground,
Green water in the grass . . .
Abandoned plowed fields are full of yearning
And goosefoot-plants are wilting.

I wander through the streets and puddles.
The autumnal day is wary and wild.
In every man I encounter I want to discern your beloved face.

Ever more enigmatic, ever more handsome,
You behold some obscure realms . . .
Oh, only for you is our happiness,
Only for you my loyal friendship.

And should death, by God's will,
Close your eyes with its hand,
I swear that like a shadow in an open field
I shall follow death and you.


From *Prayers for the Dead* (1918)

The horn of doom is blaring!
What is to become of us now
On the threadbare legs of highways?

Hey, you, who like picking fleas off songs,
How would you like to suck off a gelding?

Wipe those meek expressions from your lazy mugs
Whether you like it or not—you'll have to take it.
Ah, it's good when the twilight mocks us
And shoves up our fat asses
The bloodstained broom of sunset.

Soon the hoarfrost will whitewash
That village and those meadows.
There's nowhere you can hide from your doom,
No way of escaping the enemy.
There he is, with his iron belly
Reaching for your throat with the valleys of his fingers.

The old windmill cocked its ear
Sniffing with its flour-grinding nose.
And the silent monk of the barnyard, the bull
Who spilled all his brains on the heifers
Wiping his tongue on the fencepost
Sensed misfortune descending on the fields.


[*Esenin's Suicide Note*] (1925)

Goodbye, my friend, goodbye.
My dear fellow, I hold you in my heart.
This foreordained separation
Is a token of our future reunion.

Goodbye, my friend, without a handshake, without a word.
Do not grieve, don't knit your eyebrows.
There's nothing new about dying in this world,
But to go on living isn't exactly newer.

## Mikhail Alekseevich Kuzmin (1872–1936)

When Kuzmin traveled to Egypt in 1895, he found the inspiration for a group of poems that he called *Alexandrian Songs*, which explicitly deal with homosexuality. Returning to Russia and St. Petersburg, Kuzmin became fascinated by the aestheticism of the circle he discovered there, which included Sergei Diaghilev, then editor of an arts journal called *The World of Art*. The Revolution of 1905 had caused a relaxation of strict censorship, and in this atmosphere he began writing seriously, producing poetry and works for the theater, in several of which he portrayed homosexual relationships between men. One play called *The Perilous Precaution* was deemed immoral by the authorities, who confiscated the published text. In 1906 he wrote a novel, *Wings*, in which a young man discovers his homosexuality. The book caused a scandal and a sensation and was reprinted several times. His first collection of poetry, *Nets*, appeared in 1908, followed by a number of other collections, among them *Clay Doves* (c. 1915) and his last and greatest work, *The Trout Breaks the Ice* (1929). However, Kuzmin's homosexuality and his unwillingness to conceal it in his work led to a campaign against him, and *The Trout Breaks the Ice* was allowed to appear in only a few copies to the universal condemnation of state-appointed critics. Kuzmin was forbidden to publish and he died in oblivion, his name erased by the Soviet state from the annals of Russian literature.

FROM *ALEXANDRIAN SONGS* (1897; 1906)

*Translated by Michael Green*

1

When it was I first encountered you
poor memory cannot tell me:
was it morning, or in the afternoon,
evening, perhaps, or late at night?
I remember only the wan cheeks,
the gray eyes beneath dark brows
and the deep-blue collar at the swarthy throat,
and all this seems to come to me from childhood,
although I am older than you, older by many years.

2

Were you apprenticed to a fortune teller? —
My heart lies open to you,
you can divine my every thought,
my deepest meditations are not hidden from you;
but knowing this, you know but little,
few words are needed for the telling of it,
no crystal ball or glowing brazier: my heart,
my thoughts, my deepest meditations
are filled with voices endlessly repeating:
"I love you, and my love shall have no ending!"

## 3

At noon I must have been conceived,
at noon I must have come into the world,
and from my childhood I have loved
the beaming radiance of the sun
One day I looked upon your eyes
and I became indifferent to the sun:
why should I adore a single sun
now that two of them are mine?

## 4

People see gardens and houses
and the sea crimson with the sunset,
people see gulls skimming the waves,
and women on flat roofs,
people see warriors in armor
and pie-sellers in the town square,
people see sun and stars,
brooks and bright rivers, but I see only
gray eyes beneath dark brows,
the touch of pallor in the swarthy cheeks,
the form of matchless grace —
thus do the eyes of lovers see
no more than the wise heart wills.

## 5

Leaving my house in the morning,
I look up at the sun and think:
"How like my love when he bathes in the river,
or gazes at the distant vegetable plots!"
And when in the heat of noon I gaze
at the same burning sun,
again you come into my mind, my dearest one:
"How like my love
when he rides through the crowded streets!"
And when I look upon soft sunsets,
it is to you that memory returns,
drowsing, wan from our caresses,
your drooping eyelids shadowed deep.

## 6

Not for nothing did we read the theologians
and studied the rhetoricians not in vain,

for every word we have a definition
and can interpret all things seven different ways.
In your body I can locate the four virtues,
and, needless to say, the seven sins;
nor am I backward in tasting these delights;
but of all words one is changeless:
when, gazing deep into your gray eyes,
I say, "I love you"—the cleverest rhetorician
will understand only, "I love you"—nothing more.

7

Were I a general of olden times,
I would subdue the Ethiops and the Persians,
I would dethrone Pharaoh,
I would build myself a pyramid
higher than Cheops'
and I would become
more glorious than any man in Egypt.

Were I a nimble thief,
I would rob the tomb of Menkaure,
I would sell the gems to the Jews of Alexandria,
I would buy up land and mills,
and I would become
richer than any man in Egypt.

Were I a second Antinous,
he who drowned in the sacred Nile—
I would drive all men mad with my beauty,
temples would be raised to me while I yet lived
and I would become
more powerful than any man in Egypt.

Were I a sage steeped in wisdom,
I would squander all my wealth,
I would shun office and occupation,
I would guard other men's orchards,
and I would become
freer than any man in Egypt.

Were I your lowliest slave,
I would sit in a dungeon
and once a year or once in two years
I would glimpse the golden tracery of your sandals
when you chanced to walk by the prison house,

and I would become
happier than any man in Egypt.


*[Antinous]*

Three times I saw him face to face.
The first time was in the gardens—
I had been sent to fetch food for my comrades
and to make the journey shorter
I took the path by the palace wing;
suddenly I caught the tremor of strings,
and, being tall of stature,
I peered through the broad window and saw
him:
he was sitting alone and sad,
his slender fingers idly plucking the strings of a lyre;
a white dog
lay silent at his feet,
and only the fountain's plashing
mingled with the music.
Sensing my gaze,
he put down his lyre
and lifted his lowered face.
Magic to me his beauty
and his silence in the empty room,
in the noontide stillness.
Crossing myself, I ran away in fear,
away from the window . . .
Later, on guard duty at Lochias,
I was standing in the passage
leading to the quarters of the imperial astrologer.
The moon cast a bright square on the floor,
and the copper buckles of my sandals
glinted
as I trod the patch of brightness.
Hearing footsteps,
I halted.
From the inner chamber,
a slave bearing a torch before them,
three men came forth
he being one.
He was pale,
but it seemed to me
that the room was lit
not by the torch, but by his countenance.
As he passed, he glanced at me

and said, "I've seen you before, my friend,"
and withdrew to the astrologer's quarters.
Long after his white robes were lost to view
and the torch had been swallowed in darkness,
I stood there, not moving, not breathing,
and afterwards in the barracks,
feeling Martius, who slept next to me,
touch my hand in his usual way,
I pretended to be asleep.
And then one evening
we met again.
We were bathing
near the tents of Caesar's camp,
when suddenly a cry went up.
We ran, but it was too late.
Dragged from the water, the body
lay on the sand,
and that same unearthly face,
the face of a magician,
stared with wide-open eyes.
Still far off, the Emperor was hurrying toward us,
shaken by the grievous tidings;
but I stood seeing nothing,
not feeling tears unknown to me since childhood
running down my cheeks.
All night I whispered prayers,
raving of my native Asia, of Nicomedia,
and angel voices sang:
"Hosannah!
A new god
is given unto men!"


FROM *NETS* (1908)

*Translated by Simon Karlinsky*

*Ah, those lips, kissed by so many,*

Ah, those lips, kissed by so many,
By so many other lips,
You pierce me with bitter arrows,
With hundreds of bitter arrows.

You blossom with boisterous smiles
Like radiant springtime shrubs,
Like caresses of light fingers,
Of light, beloved fingers.

Whether a pilgrim or an insolent brigand—
Everyone reaches you with his kiss.
Whether he's Antinous or a disgusting Thersites—
Everyone finds his happiness.

Every kiss that touches you
Is imprinted like a firm seal.
Whoever partakes of your beloved lips
Is united to all those in your past.

An imploring gaze that touches the icon
Is left there like a heavy chain.
The ancient image, glorified in prayer,
Unites all supplicants with that chain.

Thus you pass through slippery places,
Through slippery, sacred places.
Ah, those lips, kissed by so many,
By so many other lips.


*At the Party*

You and I and a fat lady,
Having softly closed the door
Withdrew from the general din.

I played for you my "Chimes of Love,"
There was a constant creak of the door
Fashion plates and dandies walked by.

I understood the hint in your eyes
And together we went through the door
And everyone else became at once remote.

The fat lady remained at the piano
The dandies crowded in a herd at the door
The skinny fashion plate shrilly laughed.

We went up the poorly lit staircase,
Opened my familiar door,
Your smile became even more languid.

Our eyes became veiled with love
And now we locked still another door.
If only such nights would occur more often!

FROM *CLAY DOVES* (C. 1915)

*Translated by Simon Karlinsky*

*Nine delightful birthmarks*

Nine delightful birthmarks
I count with my kisses
And as I count them, I read
A mystery, sweeter than heavenly mysteries.
On your cheeks, on your dear neck,
On your chest, where your heart is beating.
That which is darker than musk
Will not be erased by kisses.
Thus, over the heavenly staircase,
As I tell the beads of caresses,
I shall reach the gates of paradise
Of your miraculous beauty.
Now, that eighth birthmark
Is the most precious one in the world
Sweeter than the shade in sultry summer
And lovelier than the breeze in May.
And when I reach the ninth one
I no longer bother counting,
I simply melt, I melt, I melt
Enveloped in a tender flame.

# 22. Eros in Egypt

## Alexandrian Songs

**Constantine Cavafy (1863–1933)**

*Translated by Edmund Keeley and Philip Sherrard*

In about 150 lyrics, Cavafy invoked classical history, pondered philosophical questions, and created concise anatomies of homosexual desire. The homoerotic poems—about a third of the total work—are mostly set in the streets of modern Alexandria where he constructs a passionately homoerotic milieu in which the experiences of homosexual life are played out. In a language that is spare and modernist, Cavafy looks at male beauty and desires it, reflects on the ironies of desire, and regrets the lost possibilities of love. An intensely private person, Cavafy lived most of his life in Alexandria, writing his poems in modern Greek. None of the poetry was published during his lifetime.

*At the Cafe Door (1915)*

Something they said beside me
made me look toward the cafe door,
and I saw that lovely body which seemed
as though Eros in his mastery had fashioned it,
joyfully shaping his well-formed limbs,
molding its tall build,
shaping its face tenderly,
and leaving, with a touch of the fingers,
a particular impression on the brow, the eyes, the lips.

*One Night (1915)*

The room was cheap and sordid,
hidden above the suspect taverna.
From the window you could see the alley,
dirty and narrow. From below
came the voices of workmen
playing cards, enjoying themselves.

And there on that ordinary, plain bed
I had love's body, knew those intoxicating lips,
red and sensual,
red lips so intoxicating
that now as I write, after so many years,
in my lonely house, I'm drunk with passion again.

*When They Come Alive (1916)*

Try to keep them, poet,
those erotic visions of yours,
however few of them there are that can be stilled.
Put them, half-hidden, in your lines.
Try to hold them, poet,
when they come alive in your mind
at night or in the noonday brightness.

*In the Street (1916)*

His attractive face a bit pale,
his brown eyes looking tired, dazed,
twenty-five years old but could be taken for twenty,
with something of the artist in the way he dresses
—the color of his tie, shape of his collar—
he drifts aimlessly down the street,
as though still hypnotized by the illicit pleasure,
the very illicit pleasure he's just experienced.

*Passing Through (1917)*

The things he timidly imagined as a schoolboy
are openly revealed to him now. And he walks the streets,
stays out all night, gets involved. And as is right (for our kind of art)
his blood—fresh and hot—
offers itself to pleasure. His body is overcome
by forbidden erotic ecstasy; and his young limbs
give in to it completely.
     In this way a simple boy
becomes something worth our looking at, for a moment
he too passes through the exalted World of poetry,
the young sensualist with blood fresh and hot.

*Comes to Rest (1919)*

It must have been one o'clock at night
or half past one.
     A corner in a taverna,
behind the wooden partition:
except for the two of us the place completely empty.
A lamp barely gave it light.
The waiter was sleeping by the door.

No one could see us.
But anyway, we were already so worked up
we'd become incapable of caution.

Our clothes half opened—we weren't wearing much:
it was a beautiful hot July.

Delight of flesh between
half-opened clothes;
quick baring of flesh—a vision
that has crossed twenty-six years
and now comes to rest in this poetry.

*Their Beginning (1921)*

Their illicit pleasure has been fulfilled.
They get up and dress quickly, without a word.
They come out of the house separately, furtively;
and as they move off down the street a bit unsettled,
it seems they sense that something about them betrays
what kind of bed they've just been lying on.

But what profit for the life of the artist:
tomorrow, the day after, or years later, he'll give voice
to the strong lines that had their beginning here.

*In Despair (1923)*

He's lost him completely. And he now tries to find
his lips in the lips of each new lover,
he tries in the embrace of each new lover
to convince himself that it's the same young man,
that it's to him he gives himself.

He's lost him completely, as though he never existed.
He wanted, his lover said, to save himself
from the tainted, sick form of sexual pleasure,
the tainted, shameful form of sexual pleasure.
There was still time, he said, to save himself.

He's lost him completely, as though he never existed.
Through fantasy, through hallucination,
he tries to find his lips in the lips of other young men,
he longs to feel his kind of love once more.

# 23. Southern Dawn

## Italian Literature in the Twentieth Century

Like many Latin and Catholic countries in which homosexuality is officially decriminalized, Italy still stigmatizes homosexuality socially while officially ignoring it. Homosexuality is seen as a phase through which young men may pass without scandal on their way to "normal" heterosexual life. The view that reads homosexuality as a temporary sexual relation between an older man and a youth, or that sees the confirmed homosexual as a woman trapped in the body of a man, is still part of the popular sexual mythology.

The censorship and repression of the war years did not allow a true Italian homosexual literature to develop until after World War II. The poet Umberto Saba's "secret book" *Ernesto*, written in 1953 and published in 1975, was an early and seminal text in modern Italian homoerotic letters. It tells a story of adolescent homosexual awakening, a tale rewritten in the streetwise fantasies and recollections of the poetry of Sandro Penna. Influenced by the American gay rights movement, recent Italian writing about homosexuality has experienced a considerable renaissance, and with the writing of Aldo Busi, Pervittorio Tondelli, and Stefano Moretti, the voice of Italian gay literature has come of age.

### Sandro Penna (1906–1977)

Penna published several volumes of poems, beginning in 1938 until his death in 1977. His subject is the love of boys, and his form is the epigrammatic vignette, in which he captures his boys in a variety of erotic poses and movement. His collected poems, *Poesie*, won the Viareggio Prize in 1956, which he shared with Pasolini.

Seven Poems

*Translated by John McRae*

1

Found—my little angel,
at a dirty picture show.
He was smoking a cigarette
and his eyes had a lustrous glow . . .

2

Life . . . is remembering waking up
sad in a train at dawn: having seen
outside the uncertain light: having felt
the virgin and bitter melancholy
of the biting air in the weary body.

But remembering the unexpected
liberation is sweeter: beside me
a young sailor: the blue
and white of his uniform, and outside
a sea all awash with colour.

## 3

A pitiless war of love I fought,
boys the enemy once.
The battle now is against myself,
No arms left, but I fight it so well.

## 4

Shadowless sun on male bodies
abandoned. All virtue silent.

The soul slowly submerges—with the sea—
into a light-filled dream. Suddenly
the senses—tiny young islands—skip.

But sin exists no longer.

## 5

When I don't feel well, I wander among
the suburban crowd. But the grey
winter damp makes me solitary and sad.
Puffs of hot stale air rise to the street
from basement gym
where naked young animals attack
imaginary enemies, down there fitfully
puffing.
    An old beggar watches the scene,
with me without nostalgia.

## 6

Always boys in my poems!
But I can't talk of anything else.
Other things bore me.
Don't ask me to sing you Holy Works.

## 7

My poetry will not be
a frivolous game

made out of delicate words
and sickly
(clear sun of March
on shivering leaves
of plane trees to brightly green).
My poetry will fling its force
till it is lost in infinity
(games of a beautiful athlete
in a long summer eventide).

# 24. Amor Oscuro

## Spanish Literature

Though homoerotic literature in Spain can be found in both Islamic and Hebrew texts written in that part of Spain that Muslim writers called al-Andalus, in medieval and Renaissance Christian Spain homosexuality was severely punished, perhaps more severely than in any place in Europe. In the sixteenth century a literature of male friendship sometimes hints at but generally avoids intimations that might be thought sodomitical. Classical homoeroticsm is obliquely alluded to in the seventeenth century in Luis de Góngora y Argote's *Solitudes*, which presents a protagonist who is described as being more beautiful than Ganymede and in Pedro Soto de Rojas' long poem on Adonis, but in general, the repressive religious and political climate of Spain prevented writers from dealing with a subject that was the object of social, religious, and legal suspicion. In the nineteenth century Spain began to have some contact with the homosexual emancipation movements developing in Germany and in England and with the Hellenistic studies that informed these movements, though it was still nearly impossible to deal with homosexuality directly in literature.

Homosexuality finally began to enter Spanish texts through the efforts of writers from other Spanish-speaking countries, among them Augusto d'Halmar, from Chile, who in *La pasión y muerte del cura Deusto* (1924) tells the story of the love between a Basque priest, Father Deusto, and the gypsy boy Pedro Miguel. The commemoration of the tercentenary of Góngora in 1927 became the occasion for a number of writers, who sought to liberate themselves from what they believed to be the oppression of a Spanish culture dominated by the Roman Catholic church, to celebrate the influence of Andalusian literature on their work. Among this group who thought of themselves as the generation of 1927 were Federico García Lorca and Luis Cernuda. The availability in Spanish of works by Wilde, Proust, and Gide, especially his *Corydon*, added further to the climate that encouraged experimentation in literature. The advent of the republic in 1931 further liberalized Spain. When Luis Cernuda published *The Forbidden Pleasures* in 1931, and Lorca, after a visit to the United States, published his "Ode to Walt Whitman" in Mexico in 1933, homosexuality in Spanish literature made its first tentative appearance (though Lorca's work was privately published). However, the civil war, the fall of the republic, and the advent of the Franco regime (which opposed homosexuality as vehemently as it did democracy) returned Spain to an oppressive atmosphere in which advocacy of homosexuality in literature was considered a criminal offense. Near the end of the Franco regime—and now with the restoration of the monarchy—Spain's gay rights movement has begun to grow, influenced by the birth of the gay rights movement in the United States. Spanish writers concerned with homosexuality—among them Juan Goytisolo, Manuel Gamez Quintana, and Agustin Gomez-Arcos—are producing a significant literature that deserves its own anthology.

Further Reading

"Spain" by Daniel Eisenberg, in Wayne R. Dynes et. al., eds., *The Encyclopedia of Homosexuality* (New York: Garland, 1990), vol. 2, p. 1236.

## Luis Cernuda (1902–1963)

Cernuda was the first Spanish poet to write openly about homosexual subjects. He was not only open about his homosexuality but believed that repressive Spanish attitudes toward homosexuality should be changed. Cernuda began writing homosexual love poetry in the 1920s, influenced by Andalusian poetry of Moorish Spain and by the generation of 1927. He based his poetry on his own experience and became part of a circle of writers who were probably homosexual, among whom was Lorca, with whom he developed an intimate friendship. Cernuda published his first book of distinctly homoerotic pieces, *The Forbidden Pleasures*, in 1931. He actively supported the Spanish Republic, and at the outbreak of civil war, both because of his politics and his open homosexuality, he was forced to leave Spain. He spent his life teaching in England, the United States, and in Mexico, where he died in 1963.

NINE POEMS

*Translated by Rick Lipinski*

From *The Young Sailor and Other Poems* (and later reprinted in *The Forbidden Pleasures*, 1931)

*I'll Tell You How You Were Born*

I'll tell you how you were born, forbidden pleasures,
As a desire is born over towers of fear,
Threatening battens, discolored ice,
Night petrified by the power of fists,
Before all, including the most rebellious,
Fitting only in a life without walls.

Impenetrable, coats of mail, lances or daggers,
Everything's good if it deforms a body;
Your desire is to drink those lascivious leaves
Or to sleep in that caressing water.
It doesn't matter;
They already declared your spirit impure.

Purity doesn't matter, the gifts that a destiny
Raised up to the birds with never-ending hands;
Youth, a dream, isn't more important than man,
The so noble smile, silk beach beneath the storm
Of a fallen regime.

Forbidden pleasure, earthly planets,
Marble extremities with summer's taste,
Juice of sponges abandoned by the sea,
Iron flowers, resonant like a man's chest.

Lofty solitudes, fallen crowns,
Memorable freedoms, youths' aegis;
Whosoever insults those fruits, darkness on their tongue,
Is vile like a king, like a king's shadow
Dragging behind footsteps on the ground
To get a piece of life.

They don't know the limits imposed,
Limits of metal or paper,
Since chance made them open their eyes beneath a light so high,
Where empty realities,
Stinking laws, codes, and rats of ruined landscapes
Don't come.

Extending your hand then
Is finding a mountain that forbids,
An impenetrable forest that denies,
A sea that swallows rebellious adolescents.

But if anger, outrage, shame, and death,
Eager teeth still without flesh,
Threaten to open their torrents,
You, on the other side, forbidden pleasures,
Proud bronze, blasphemy that brings about nothing,
Hold out the mystery, a taste that no bitterness corrupts,
In a hand,
Skies, lightning skies that annihilate.

Below, anonymous statues,
Shadows of shadows, misery, precepts of fog;
A spark of those pleasures
Shines at the hour of revenge.
Its brightness could destroy your world.


From *The Young Sailor and Other Poems* (and later reprinted in *Living Without Being Alive* (1944–1949)

*The Shadow*

Awaking from a dream, you look for
Your youth, as if it were the body

Of the comrade who slept
By your side and whom you can't find at dawn.

Familiar absence, always new,
That bothers you. And though perhaps
Today you're more than was the youth
Who left, still

You mutely call him, how many times;
Forgetting that by his youth was fed
That sharp pain, the awareness
Of your life some time ago. Now,

Gone also, it's only
A vague bad feeling, an unconsciousness
Quieting the past, leaving the other that you are
Indifferent, without pain, without comfort.

## FROM *THE CHIMERA'S WASTELAND* (1956–1962)

### For Two Voices

"Your eyes are the eyes of a man in love;
Your lips are the lips of a man who doesn't believe
in love." "Then, tell me the remedy, friend,
If reality and desire are in discord."

### That Which Is Enough for Love

Once again love has hold
Of you. In spite of yourself
Not even age exempts you
From serving him.

You were free, without love,
When your eyes beheld
The new boy
Who awakened desire.

Your eyes still feed on
That enchantment of the soul
And you want nothing else.
Is contemplating enough?

Is that enough for you? And how,
Seeing him, everything has purpose;

Not seeing him,
And nothing has purpose.

Gazing upon what you love.
If that enchantment were enough,
Nothing more; if only this looking
Upon what you love were enough.

In love's first phase
You go slowly
Without approaching the body
Whose existence you adore.


FROM *POEMS FOR A BODY* (LATER INCLUDED IN *WITH
COUNTED HOURS*, 1950)

*The Lover Digresses*

Perhaps in hell time has
The fiction of measurement we give it
Here, or perhaps it has the abundance
Of life's precious moments.
I don't know. Beyond, they say, time
Goes backwards, so we go on unliving ourselves.

So, this our story, mine and yours
(Probably better to say mine only,
Though yours are the motive and opportunity,
Which isn't a little), we will live again
You and I (or, I alone will live),
From its end to the beginning.

Strange it will be then
To pass from the beginnings of oblivion
To that illusive fervor, when all
Was animated by you, because you lived,
And from there to no knowing
You, before finding each other.

But in hells, by that reckoning,
I would stop believing, and at the same time
I might reject the idea of paradises;
Hell and paradise,
Aren't they probably our own doing, of this
Earthly life we're made for and isn't it enough?

With our own acts
We create hell and paradise here,
Where love and hate blossom together,
Animating life. And I don't want
Life where you no longer have a part:
Forgetful, yes, but not never knowing you.

The road that goes up
And the road that goes down
Are one and the same; and my desire
Is that, at the end of the one and the other,
With hate or with love, with oblivion or memory,
Your existence is there, my hell and my paradise.

FOUR POEMS FROM *WHERE OBLIVION DWELLS* (1932–33)

## VIII

Nocturnal, you sword-fight
Deafly profound hours;
The light of self-absorbed eyes
Shines at these hours.

Beneath the iron sky
Bitterness strikes its blade,
Slowly among the chains
That sustain life.

Made vibrant fire
Or an unextinguishable edge,
The bodies of the condemned
Twist in their shadows.

No longer is life or death
The nameless torment,
A fallen world is,
Hissing with rage.

It's a delirious sea,
A clamor rising everywhere,
A voice that from its very being raises
The wings of a posthumous god.

## XI

I don't want to return a sad spirit
Across the places of my weeping,

A secret throbbing among the living bodies
I once was.

I don't want to remember
A happy instant among the torments;
Pleasure or pain, it's the same,
Returning all is sad.

That childhood destiny
Still goes with me, a distant light,
Those sweet juvenile eyes,
That old wound.

No, I don't want to return,
But to die even more,
To squeeze out a shade,
To forget something forgotten.


## XIV

*To Concha Méndez*
*and Manuel Altoaguirre*

You were a tender desire, an insinuating cloud,
You lived with the air among friendly bodies,
You breathed without form, you smiled without voice,
An inspired aftertaste of an invisible spirit.

Our impotence, a slow thorn
Perhaps in you it could've been an adolescent force;
Neither insignificant pain nor selfish pleasure
Neither life's dream nor triumphant evil.

As a felicitous cloud passes by without rain,
As a bird forgets the branch of its birth,
You possessed death and life at the same time
Without having died, without having lived.

Among the so sad smoke, the narrow streets
Of land measured out by old hatreds,
You haven't thus discovered, turned against your bliss,
Power with its swampy hands,
An abject god disposing destinies,
Lying and its round tail erect over the world,
Weaponless love crying among the tombs.

Your light absence, echo without pitch, time without history
Passing like a wing,
Leaves a transparent truth;
Truth that knew and didn't feel,
Truth that saw and didn't love.

## XV

The invisible wall
Among all arms,
Among all bodies,
Islands of laughable evil.

There are no kisses, only flagstones;
There is no love, only flagstones
Measured so many times by the feverish
Pacing of a prisoner.

Perhaps the outside air
Dreams, singing the hymn
Of faithful happiness to the world;
Perhaps radiant wings,
Glories gone by, pass overhead.

An immense desire,
The urge of a truth,
Beats against walls,
Beats against flesh
Like a sea in irons.

For a moment
Avid eyes look up
Towards the daylight,
Victorious copper lightning
With its sword so high.

Truth breathes
Among shadowy rocks,
Rocks of anger, of weeping, of oblivion.

Prison,
The living prison.

## Federico García Lorca (1898–1936)

Lorca, the greatest Spanish writer of the twentieth century, was most certainly homosexual, though homoeroticism and homosexuality appear only obliquely in his work. In 1929

Lorca visited New York—it is alleged in order to recover from the breakup of a love affair with the sculptor Emilio Aladren. There he discovered a vibrant American homosexual life. He also read Whitman's *Leaves of Grass* and met the American poet Hart Crane. When he returned to Spain he began to write a number of poems with opaque homosexual undertones. In 1933 he wrote "Ode To Walt Whitman," which he privately published in Mexico. He was also working on a cycle of poems that would become *The Poet in New York (Poeta en Nueva York)*. At about the same time his play *El publico* (The audience), which also deals with homosexuality, was completed. In addition to other plays—*Blood Wedding, Yerma,* and *The House of Bernarda Alba*—he was also writing a group of sonnets, left unfinished at his death—the *Sonetos del amor oscuro* (Sonnets of dark love), perhaps inspired by an affair with Rodriguez Rapun, a member of a Madrid theater group that Lorca directed. Because of his leftist sympathies and probably because of his homosexuality—which is still denied by many in Spain—Lorca was murdered by the Fascists in 1936.

"Ode to Walt Whitman" was included in *The Poet in New York,* published in 1940. His *Sonetos del amor oscuro* were withheld from publication by his family, and finally published in 1984.[2] The versions here have been translated for this anthology.

## From *Sonetos del amor oscuro* (1935–36)

### [Sonnets of dark love]

*Translated by David William Foster*

#### Night of Sleepless Love

The night on high the two of us in full moon, I began to cry and you were laughing.
Your disdain was a god, my complaints moments and doves strung together.

Night down below the two of us. Crystal of pain, you were crying aer profound distances. My suffering was a knot of agonies upon your weak heart of sand.

Dawn joined us on the bed, our mouths placed on the freezing jet of an endless spurting blood.

And the sun entered through the shuttered balcony and the coral of life opened its fan over my shrouded heart.

#### Sonnet of Sweet Weeping

I am afraid of losing the marvel of your eyes of a statue, and the accent the solitary rose of your breath lays on my cheek at night.

It makes me suffer to be a trunk without branches on that shore, and what makes me most sorry is to be without the flower, the pulp or the clay for the worm of my suffering.

If you are my hidden treasure, if you are my cross and my wet suffering, if I am the dog of your domain,

---

2. Federico García Lorca, *Sonetos del amor oscuro,* 1935–1936. Originally published in an edition organized by Marta Teresa Casteros. Buenos Aires: Instituto de Estudios de Literatura Latinoamericana, 1984.

do not let me lose what I have won and decorate the waters of your river with leaves from my estranged autumn.

### The Poet Asks His Love to Write to Him

Love of my heart, living death, I await in vain your written word and I think with the dying flower, that if I live without myself I want to lose you.

The air is immortal. The inert stone neither knows the shade nor avoids it. The inner heart has no need for the freezing honey that the moon spills forth.

But I suffered you. I tore at my veins, tiger and dove, above your waist, in a duel of bitings and lilies.

Fill, then, my madness with words or let me live in my serene night of the soul forever dark.

### The Poet Speaks with Love by Telephone

Your voice watered the doubt of my breast in the sweet wooden booth. At the south of my feet it was spring, and at the north of my forehead a fern blossomed.

A pine of light in the narrow space sang without dawn and without sowing and my tears enflamed crowns of hope on the ceiling for the first time.

Sweet and distant voice spilled forth for me, sweet and distant voice enjoyed by me, sweet and distant voice that swooned away.

Distant like a dark and wounded doe, sweet like a sobbing in the snow. Distant and sweet from deep within my marrow!

### The Poet Asks His Love About the Enchanted City of Cuenca

Did you like the city the water wrought drop by drop in the center of the pines? Did you see dreams and faces and roads and air-whipped walls of suffering?

Did you see the blue crack of broken moon the Jucar dampens with warbling crystal? Have the thorns that crown with love the remote stone kissed your fingers?

Did you remember me when you climbed up to the silence the serpent suffers, a prisoner of shackles and shadows?

Did you not see in the transparent air a dahlia of sorrows and joys my heated heart sent to you?

### Untitled ["Ah secret voice of dark love!"]

Ah secret voice of dark love! Ah bleating without wool! Ah wound! Ah prick of gall, sunken camellia! Ah torrent without sea, city without wall!

Ah immense night of firm profile, celestial mountain of erect anguish! Ah dog in the heart, persecuted voice, silence without confines, mature lily!

Flee from my heated voice of ice, refuse to lose me in the thicket where flesh and heaven moan without fruit.

Leave the hard ivory of my head. Have mercy on me, break my mourning, for I am love, for I am nature!

*The Poet Speaks the Truth*

I want to cry my pain and I am telling you so you will love me and cry for me in a nightfall of nightingales with a dagger, with kisses and with you.

I want to kill the only witness to the assassination of my flowers and change my weeping and my sweating into an eternal mound of hard wheat.

May there never be an end to the skein of I love you you love me always burning with day, scream, salt and old moon, may you give it to me and I not beg it from you it will remain for the death that casts not even a shadow for the shivering flesh.

# 25. Latin American and Cuban Literature

## Paradiso

Though representing a great variety of cultures and a diversity of populations, Cuba and most Latin American societies (to make a very broad generalization) have tended to enforce the gender-bound dichotomy between the active male and the passive female, and to carry this concept over into the definition and the practice of homosexual relations. Latino males tend to perceive homosexuality as weakness, passivity, and effeminacy—so much so that only those men who passively accept homosexual sex are deemed to be, strictly speaking, *homosexuales*. Hence, in addition to the pederastic model of man-boy relationships significant in many European and European-inspired literatures, the woman-identified man, the transvestite, and the drag queen play significant roles in Cuban and Latin American literature, and the relationship between *hombres machos* and effeminate *homosexuales*—or *maricones* or *locas*—is the subject of a number of texts. The most striking example of this latter situation in modern Latin American literature is probably Manuel Puig's *Kiss of the Spider Woman*, published in Spain in 1976.

Given the rigid social construction of the nature of homosexual relationships as well as the influence of the Roman Catholic church in maintaining a pejoratively dogmatic interpretation of homosexuality, or as in Cuba, a socialist government that maintains the same kind of dogmatic prohibition, it is not surprising that Cuban and Latin American society and governments have not been hospitable to manifestations of homosexuality in literature. Nevertheless, in the nineteenth and twentieth centuries Cuban and Latin American literatures produced a body of work in which homosexuality had a presence. The first such literary work written in a Latin American country was written in Portuguese in 1895 by the Brazilian novelist Adolfo Caminha. His novel *O Bom-Crioulu* tells the story of an interracial love affair between a sailor and a cabin boy. Caminha's novel seems to create sexual identities and conflate questions of race with questions about social attitudes toward reviled sexual activities, allowing his characters to confront opprobrium and rejection by an act of social rebellion. The Colombian poet Porfirio Barba-Jacob and the Cuban writer Julian del Casal both treat of homosexual themes in early works as does the Chilean writer Augusto d'Halmer in *La pasíon y muerte del cura Deusto* in 1924 and Xavier Villaurrutia in Mexico. More recently, Manuel Puig in Argentina, Luis Zapata in Mexico, Darcy Penteado and Caio Abreu in Brazil, and Cuba's Reinaldo Arenas and José Lezama Lima (whose *Paradiso* is a masterpiece in any language) are a few of the many writers in the 1970s, 1980s, and 1990s—in part influenced by the American gay rights movement—who have produced a substantial body of Cuban and Latin American gay texts of unparalleled originality and scope, only a sampling of which is possible here.

Further Reading:

David Wayne Foster, *Gay and Lesbian Themes in Latin American Literature* (Austin: University of Texas Press, 1991); Winston Leyland, ed., *My Deep Dark Pain Is Love: A*

*Collection of Latin American Gay Fiction* (San Francisco: Gay Sunshine Press, 1983); Winston Leyland, ed., *Now the Volcano: An Anthology of Latin American Gay Literature* (San Francisco: Gay Sunshine Press, 1979); and the essay by E. A. Lacey, plus selections from various texts, in Winston Leyland, ed., *Gay Roots*, 2 vols. (San Francisco: Gay Sunshine Press, 1991, 1993).

# Brazil

## Adolfo Caminha (1867–1897)

FROM *O BOM-CRIOULO* (1895)

*Translated by Arthur Hughes*

CHAPTER II

The victory of abolition was still far away, very distant, when Bom-Crioulo, then simply known as Amaro, arrived from God knows where, wrapped in cotton clothes, his clothing in a container over his shoulder, a big straw hat on his head and rawhide shoes. Young (about some eighteen years of age), and ignorant of the difficulties which every black has to undergo in a slave-owning society as profoundly superficial as that of the Court, he fled without stopping to think of the consequences of his flight, in all his naiveté and resoluteness.

In that period the "runaway slave" terrorized the population in an incredible manner. Slaves were hunted down with spurs and rifles like animals, through the forest, over precipices, across rivers, and over mountains. After the fact was denounced—*This belongs to the King!*—, the forests filled with men in a mad rush, couriers went through the backlands in a strange clamor, following trails, tracking with dogs, destroying coffee plantations. Even the doors of houses were locked at night out of fear. . . . The newspapers published a picture of a fugitive runaway on the third page, a bag of clothes on his shoulder and below, the words, almost always in big letters, detailed, explicit, including all the information, such as height, age, distinguishing features, vices and other characteristics of the fugitive. Apart from this, the "owner" promised to generously recompense whoever captured the slave.

Despite all this, he managed to escape the vigilance of his persecutors, and after spending a whole night, the most bitter of his life, in a kind of cage with bars of iron Amaro, whose only fear was of returning to the plantation, of going back to the bosom of slavery, trembled at the sight of a very wide and tranquil river, where boats navigated in all directions, some by sail and others by steam; at the banks of the water, a pointed peak, of a height that he had never before seen, pierced the clouds.

Later he was ordered to take off his clothes (he felt very embarrassed), they examined his back, his chest, his groin, and then he was given a sailor's blue shirt.

That same day he went to the fort and as soon as the craft left the pier with a strong surge, the new seadog felt his whole being vibrate in an extraordinary manner for the first time, as if the delicious freshness of a mysterious fluid had been injected into his African blood. Freedom entered him through the eyes, the ears, the nasal cavities, through all his pores, like the very essence of light, of sound, of smell and of all ethereal things. Everything that surrounded him: the great stretch of water that sang on the prow of the boat, the immaculate blue of the sky, the distant profile of the mountains, the ships balancing themselves between the islands, the immobile mansion of the city that was left behind—even the companions, rowing at the same rhythm as if they were a single arm—and above all, Holy cow!, the luminous amplitude of the bay, most of all; in fact, the entire countryside in its totality communicated so powerful a sensation of freedom and life, that he even felt like crying, to the extent of weeping frankly and openly in the presence of the others, as if he were going mad. That magnificent scenery would remain engraved on his retina for the whole of his life: never again would he forget it, no, never again. He, the slave, the "runaway slave," felt himself a real man, the equal of other men and happy to be one; big as nature itself in all the virile thrust of his youth, he felt pain, a lot of pain for those who remained behind on the hacienda working, without earning money, from early dawn until . . . God knows when!

In the beginning, before embarking, he found it difficult to forget the past, to forget "Mother Sabina," the customs that he had learned in the coffee plantations. . . . Very often he felt a vague desire to embrace his former colleagues, with whom he had worked on the farms, but soon that memory began to disappear like the distant and wispy smoke of burnings, and he returned to reality, opening his eyes, with an infinite pleasure, toward the sea covered with ships.

With all its excesses, military discipline was nothing in comparison with the painful work of the hacienda, with its terrible regime of the whip and the pillory. There was a vast difference. There in the fort, at least he had his hammock, his pillow, his clean clothes, he ate good food, sometimes he felt too full, just like any other person: stewed meat one day; another, a succulent feijoada; and on Fridays, a delicious codfish with peppers and "blood of Christ." How could life be better? Besides, freedom, the mere fact of being free compensated for everything! There nobody noticed either the race or color of the sailor: everyone was equal, had the same rights, the same treatment, the same diversions, the same days of rest. "And when one works to obtain the esteem of one's superiors, when one has no enemies, then life is a blessing: one does not think of tomorrow."

Amaro was able to gain the affection of the officers. In the beginning they could not help laughing at the novice, new to military practices. Ungainly in his savage ways, every step he took caused irrepressible outbursts of mirth due to the ingenuous manners of the novice; but after a couple of months, everyone agreed that "the Negro could be converted into a human being." Amaro already knew how to handle a musket according to the rules of the profession, and no fool in matters of artillery, he soon began to acquire the reputation of a good sailor.

During that first year of apprenticeship he never committed errors that merited disciplinary punishment; his nature was so affable that the officers began to call him Bom-Crioulo. However, his greatest desire, his greatest preoccupation was to embark on any sailing vessel, to live on the sea, get to know the customs on board ship while he was still young, know the practice of securing the foreleech to the yard, taking in a reef, and boxing the compass. He hoped to be promoted soon, and he envied those who went on the high seas, far from land, wandering in liberty through those wonderful places. How nice it would be for the soul and the body to breathe the fresh free air over there, on the seas!

He amused himself building wooden sailing vessels on a small scale: warships with a pennant at the top of the masthead and gunlocks, miniature ocean liners, small yachts, all with the aid of a penknife and the tenacious patience of an architect.

But he was never able to get a definite position. He went aboard at times on practices, rowing in the boat, but he always returned quickly in the company of the other apprentices, sad at not having gained a permanent place, dreaming up stories of journeys, things that he would be able to see for the first time when he finally left the fort.

That day finally arrived: Bom-Crioulo had been chosen to embark on an old transport ship that was heading south.

"At last!" he said, raising his arms in a gesture of overflowing joy. "Thank God they finally remembered Bom-Crioulo!"

He went to meet his companions, very pleased, all excited, to announce to them his destination: Did they want something from the south? Some small souvenir from Rio Grande? Nothing?

"Bring me a Paraguayan woman, Bom-Crioulo," one of them joked.

"Listen, I would settle for a dozen eggs, from Santa Catarina. . . ."

Others asked for impossible things: a piece of roasted "gringo," a measure of Spanish blood, the ear of a "green belly" . . .

All the people in the ranch laughed, and everybody hoped that Amaro would be happy with his first journey, that he would return big and strong "to kill Gallegos" on the pier of Los Mineros.

Some praised the commander of the ship, the old Novais, a good man, who did not like punishment and was also a friend of the sailors.

And the second officer?

Well, the second officer was a man named Pontes, with sideburns, who had been shipwrecked on the corvette *Isabel*, a very nice person although very ugly; he did nobody any harm, on the contrary: the sailor who got on well with him was treated like the best of port wine.

Bom-Crioulo was in seventh heaven!

He had to be on board ship in the afternoon, shortly before the "striking of the flag."

He was prepared and this was apparent in the way he looked, in his way of speech, his gestures, the enormous happiness that invaded his heart. It was a strange kind of happiness, a well-being never experienced, somewhat like the beginning of an inoffensive and serene madness, which made him twenty times a man, made him stronger and more disposed to face the world. A soft drunkenness of the senses, one derived from a great joy or an infinite sadness. . . . Bom-Crioulo had only experienced a similar pleasure when he was recruited into the army, obliging him to know freedom. This freedom now was extended before his eyes, growing wildly in his imagination, provoking shocks of a hallucinatory nature, opening up in his soul horizons of a pink color, broad and unknown.

He did not leave a single enemy in the fort, not even a rival. He left at peace with everyone, selfish in his happiness, but with the irresistible nostalgia of those who leave on a journey.

When the boat that was taking him distanced itself from the bridge, where his companions were waving enthusiastically with their caps, he felt moved and felt the warmth of a fugitive tear running down his face; to conceal it he got to his feet and began to make signs, watching the outlines of the island and the good-byes of his companions disappear slowly in the fog of the dusk.

It seemed to him he could still hear, standing at the prow of the boat, like in the last remains of a dream, the voice of his companions embracing him:

"Good-bye, Bom-Crioulo, be happy!"

He did not sleep the whole night. On his back, lying on the floor, as if he was on a soft, wide bed, he saw the stars disappear one by one in the twilight that precedes the dawn. The day dawned gloriously, with the sun bathing the mountains of Los Organos; it painted the buildings gold, singing the triumphal hymn of resurrection.

Shortly after, the splendid scenery of the bay was transformed into a vast deserted and resplendent ocean, which extended itself in an immense circle of water, where not a single oasis of greenery showed. The enormity of the sea filled him with a Spartan valor. Around him could be found the sublime expression of an infinite freedom and of absolute sovereignty, things which his instinct perceived only vaguely through the mist of ignorance.

The days went by and then more days. On board ship everyone appreciated him like in the fort, and the first day they saw him naked, a beautiful morning, after the swilling, larking around in a salty bath, there were exclamations of admiration. There were no bones in that gigantic body: his chest was wide and robust, his arms, stomach, muscles, and legs formed a respectable union of muscles, which gave the impression of superhuman physical strength, which amazed greatly the sailors, hugely amused at the sight of the Negro. From that time Bom-Crioulo came to be considered a "dangerous man." This produced a decisive influence on the spirit of the crew, imposing himself unconditionally and absolutely as the strongest arm, the most valiant breast. It was he who lifted the most weighty things; in all situations the iron strength of Bom-Crioulo could be found, showing how to raise the shroud, how to lower sails in a tempest, how to work with pleasure with all his eighty-kilo mass.

Meanwhile he began to acquire a reputation on all the ships: "One hell of a brute, that Bom-Crioulo" said the sailors. "No, a complete animal."

He still had a great desire: he longed to embark on a certain ship whose commander, a nobleman, was said to be a friend of all robust sailors; he was also considered an excellent educator of young men, a perfect gentleman in his manners and strict.

Bom-Crioulo only knew him by sight, but he had immediately felt a great empathy with him. Besides, Commander Albuquerque remunerated the services of his people, he did not object to promoting his favorites. Those rumors that he preferred one sex to another in his amorous relations could be slander like many others that floated around. Bom-Crioulo did not mind in the least. That was a separate issue. What the hell! Nobody is free of vices.

But the journey of the corvette was announced and Bom-Crioulo had to leave the warship to go on his new destination.

In that period he was around thirty years of age and had obtained his title of second mate. Left to himself alone he would no longer leave the fort: in ten years he had traveled all round the world, risking his life fifty times, sacrificing himself in vain: "One gets bored after a while. A poor sailor works like an animal, from sunrise to sunset, spends whole nights awake, has to suffer the caprices of everybody, without the least benefit. The best thing would be to lead a peaceful life."

On that journey, Bom-Crioulo was no happier than the others. Appointed topman of the bows, a kind of inspector of the fore and top sails, he had initially fulfilled his duties in an impeccable manner; you could see the cleanliness and order there, from the topmast board to the bottom, the metal hoops and the belaying pins. It was a pleasure to watch the skill with which the maneuvers were carried out. Jobs were always completed in the most precise manner, free of accidents, as if the entire mast were one great machine moved by steam, challenging the people of the other masts.

Now however, on the return journey, things had changed. The foresail was one of the last to be ready; there was always some obstacle, a difficulty: a rope that "got stuck," a lifeline that was frayed or something else that was missing . . .

"Hurry up with that!" shouted an officer of the watch, already impatient.

And only after a considerable lapse of time did Bom-Crioulo announce, from the top of the mast, in a hoarse voice:

"Ready!"

Some said that the rum was weakening the Negro. But others insinuated that Bom-Crioulo had always been like this, forgetful and indifferent, since he "had become embroiled" with Aleixo, the cabin boy, the beautiful sailor with blue eyes who had enlisted in the south of the country. That devil of a black man was really becoming shameless! And it served no purpose giving him advice or scolding him: he was a real man, capable of fighting it out with anyone.

Even the Captain had become aware of his scandalous friendship with the boy. He feigned indifference, as if he was not aware of what was happening, but a certain warning glitter could be seen in his eyes, as if he wanted to catch them himself in the act.

The officers gossiped about the affair under their breath, and frequently they laughed maliciously, between sips of lemonade, in the weapons room.

But they could only base their knowledge on suspicion, and as far as Bom-Crioulo was concerned, brutal in appearance, the left eye permanently injected with blood, the broad face and jutting jaw, the opinion of other people left him singularly indifferent; at least so long as they made no mention of the matter to his face, because if they did, they would be punished. The switch was created for the sailor, and he would bear it until he died, like a stubborn animal, but he would show them what it meant to be a man!

His friendship with the ship boy had been born, as happens in the case of all great emotions, unexpectedly, without antecedents of any kind, in the fatal moment in which his eyes became aware of him for the first time. That indefinable movement that assaults two natures of the opposite sex at the same time, determining the physiological desire of mutual possession; that animal attraction that makes the man the slave of the woman and which in all species moves the male toward the female, thus felt Bom-Crioulo irresistibly on crossing gazes for the first time with the young ship boy. He had never felt such a thing, never had any man or woman produced such a strange impression on him in all his life. Meanwhile, the truth of the matter was that the young man, a boy of fifteen years, made his whole soul tremble, dominating it, captivating it immediately, with the attractive force of a magnet.

He called him, with a voice filled with tenderness, and wanted to know what his name was.

"My name is Aleixo" said the ship boy lowering his eyes, very timidly.

"Poor boy, his name is Aleixo" replied Bom-Crioulo.

And without taking his eyes off the adolescent, he said with the same soft and tender voice:

"Well listen: my name is Bom-Crioulo, don't forget it. When someone provokes you, or does anything, I am here to defend you, understood?"

"Yes sir" replied the sailor, raising his eyes with an expression of gratitude.

"Don't be embarrassed, eh? Bom-Crioulo, topman of the bows. All you need to do is call me."

"Yes sir . . ."

"Another thing" said the black man, taking firmly the hand of the adolescent, "be inconspicuous in your place so that you are not punished, eh?"

Aleixo did nothing but respond timidly "Yes sir," with his ingenuous appearance of an obedient boy, his very clear eyes a greenish blue color, and the full lips, extremely reddish.

He was the son of a poor family of fishermen who had made him enlist in Santa Catarina, and he was just growing into a young man. His work on board consisted of coiling up the cables and sanding the metals, when he was not on nightwatch duty.

Bom-Crioulo frightened him in the beginning, and he had almost made him cry at one time, because he had caught him smoking secretly with the chief of the prow on the deck. The black man had stared at him with such a look! . . . Fortunately nothing happened. But from that time on, without realizing it, Aleixo began to get used to that overindulgence, a generous concern that did not stop at sacrifices, nor was stingy with money, and, soon, there already was in him a pronounced rapport with Bom-Crioulo, the visible beginning of a recognized and sincere affection.

That was when the Negro, jealous of his new friendship, wanted to show the ship boy his great power over the others and the extent to which his fervor went, a passionate egotism, when he beat up implacably a second mate who had maltreated Aleixo.

The idea that Bom-Crioulo had suffered for his sake penetrated the spirit of the boy to such an extent that he considered him an altruistic protector, a friend of the weak.

When he returned from that long journey to the south, Amaro was even stronger than before, more vigorous. He was a brute mass of muscles at the service of a magnificent human structure. With respect to discipline, he had also changed somewhat: now nobody saw in him those scruples of obedience and seriousness; he had even lost that attitude, that respectful conduct which made him esteemed by the officials in the Villegaignon fort, which distinguished him from the indolent and rebellious sailors. He had abandoned the docile and tolerant behavior on the high seas or the lands he had traveled. Now he treated superiors with disdain, taking advantage of the concessions they made him, cursing them in their absence, considering them bad and unfair. However, one thing he had conserved: the physical force, with which he imposed his will more often on the other sailors who did not dare to attack him not even in jest. His reputation as a violent man had spread so far that even in the province people spoke prudently of Bom-Crioulo. Who had not heard of him, for goodness sake? What was more, he had been a slave and the damned Negro was not ugly either. . . .

From the ship on which he had made his first journey he went on to serve aboard a cruiser recently arrived from Europe. There, his life was not very peaceful. The Captain, a man named Varela, a superior marine officer, strict and inflexible like no other officer of that period, a man who never laughed, called him one day to take him to account, and almost left him without speech, simply because Bom-Crioulo had hit another sailor on the head with an oar over a question of work. That was his first punishment in four years of service. Profoundly humiliated, he retired to reappear later, lazy and insubordinate, full of resentment, ignoring his obligations, working "for the good name of the company," without inconveniences nor sacrifices: "Only a stupid person would kill himself over work." He would receive his salary whether he worked or not. The damned son of a bitch!

So he slowly became less and less trustworthy, looking out only for his own interests, spending one month in hospital and the other on board or ashore with permission.

## Chapter III

The equatorial calm of the previous night had been followed by a brisk and refreshing breeze that roiled the vast surface of water, filling out the sails and giving all the structures an appearance of good cheer and joviality.

The sky had a pale blue color, clear of clouds, high and immense in the eternal glory of light. . . . A few white-necked little birds that accompanied the corvette landed playfully on the water, harbingers of good luck, mixing their noisome happiness with the mute uproar of the waves, rapidly flapping their wings.

This time, everybody was pleased with the thought of arriving soon, safe and sound, to the Bay of Guanabara, where there was repose and abundance, and life went by softly and full of tranquillity, because one was near one's family, close to the city, without the worry of those who sail on the high seas. . . . And what was more, it was high time! Twenty days tacking stupidly, with not a piece of land in sight, not even an island, living a dog's life. It was about time. . . .

Only one person wished that the journey be prolonged indefinitely, that the corvette never come to port, and that the volume of the sea would suddenly increase, submerging islands and continents in a tremendous flooding; that only the old ship, like something fantastic, would survive the cataclysm, gracious and indestructible, stay up floating, floating for all eternity. It was Bom-Crioulo, the Negro Amaro, whose soul struggled, like a bird in agony, over this one thought: the ship boy Aleixo, who no longer allowed him to think of anything else, who tortured him deliciously. Cursed the day that the young man set foot on board! Until then his life transpired in the most normal manner, more or less peacefully, without too many preoccupations, sometimes sad, others happy, truth to say, because nothing was forever fixed in this world, but, anyway, one went on living. . . . And now? Now . . . well . . . now there was no remedy: what had to happen would inevitably happen.

And the thought of the little boy with his blue eyes, blond hair and rounded form, flashed through his mind, totally provocative.

Whether it was during rest hours or time of service, whether it was raining or fire was pouring in flames from the sky, nothing could make him forget the ship boy: it was a constant persecution, a fixed and stubborn idea, the relaxation of a will irresistibly dominated by the desire to fuse with the sailor as if he was of the opposite sex, to possess him, to have him close to him, to love him, to enjoy him.

At the thought of this, Bom-Crioulo became transformed in an incredible manner; he felt his flesh traversed by that vehement desire, like the tip of a sting, the spines of the wild nettle; a tantalizing thirst for forbidden pleasure, which seemed to burn the inside of his entrails and his nerves.

He did not remember having ever loved anyone, not even having risked one of those adventures with easy women so common in adolescence; on the contrary he had always been indifferent to certain things, preferring the binges on board ship, among the boys, far from the intrigues and deceptions of women. His memory only recorded two incidents which went against the almost virginal purity of his habits, and really had been products of an exceptional eventuality: at twenty years of age, and without thinking too much of it, he had found himself obliged to sleep with a woman in Angra dos Reis, near the waterfalls, and truth to tell, he had given a very poor impression of himself as a man; on the second occasion, totally drunk, he had knocked on the door of the house of a Frenchwoman in Rocio plaza, from where he had left completely ashamed, swearing that he would never more involve himself with "those things."

But now, why was it that he did not have the strength to resist the impulses transmitted by his blood? How could one explain the love, the desire for animal possession between two people of the same sex, between two men?

All this confused his spirit, his ideas became all mixed up, he felt repulsion for his own feelings, in a revival of certain scruples. It was true that he would not be the first to set that example, assuming that the young man was of the same mind. But—whether from instinct or because of a lack of practice—something inside him rebelled against such an immorality that others of a higher category practiced almost every night right there on the floor. Had he not lived very well without that? To hell with it, then! It was not worth sacrificing the ship boy, a child. There was at his disposal when he felt "the need," an abundance of women of all nations: French, English, Spanish . . .

He came back to himself, repentant and cold, doubting everything, trying to set standards of behavior, filling himself with a tenderness that was at times languid and compassionate, his gaze wandering through the seamless blue sky.

The punishment he suffered for Aleixo's sake had brought with it another disadvantage: that same day, he left the post of topman of the bows, which in the long run was a relief, for this way he would work less. Everything they did to him seemed fine to him, as long as they left him in his corner, in his routine: he had never asked anyone for favors.

"Listen" he advised the ship boy with some irony in his voice, "don't get into trouble with the officers. They are good people, very friendly, as long as they need us, only when they need us, but after that, So long! They kick us in the face."

Aleixo, loved, esteemed by all, though envied by some, was more than satisfied with the life he lived on the open sky of the corvette. He did not lack for anything, absolutely nothing. He was even a sort of princeling among his companions, the "handsome boy" of the officers, who called him "boy." Rapidly becoming used to this easy form of life, he began to lose his brusqueness, his former timidity; everyone who saw him now, agile and spirited, always well dressed at maneuvers, with clean clothes, his cap to one side, a slightly open shirt that left exposed the neck cavity, ended up liking him, holding him in esteem. This rapid metamorphosis without a perceptible transition was due to Bom-Crioulo, whose advice triumphed unrestrictedly in the spirit of the ship boy, opening in the child's naive soul the desire to conquer sympathies, to attract to his person the attention of all.

Bom-Crioulo, boasting of knowing "the world," thought first of all of praising Aleixo's vanity by making him the gift of a cheap little mirror that he had bought in Rio de Janeiro "so he would see how handsome he was."

"Don't talk to me about handsome! I look like a mutilated animal!" he exclaimed, but he did not abandon the utensil; on the contrary, he guarded it jealously at the bottom of his hammock, like one guards a precious object, a rare gem. He went every day to look at himself, and he stuck out his tongue, he examined himself carefully, after having washed his face.

Bom-Crioulo realized the effect of the experiment and tried to complete the "education" of the sailor. He showed him how to knot his kerchief ("not tie" he told him; "this is not called a tie, it's called a kerchief"); he advised him never to put on his cap on the right side, in the middle of his head:

"A sailor should put his cap on to one side, with a sort of panache . . ."

And the shirt? Ah, the shirt had to be left slightly open, to show what was under, the undergarment. The cowl makes the monk, eh?

The cabin boy accepted everything with a filial attitude, without seeking a reason for his taking so much trouble. He saw filthy sailors, badly dressed, who smelt of their own sweat, but they were few in number. There were those who even used perfumes in their kerchiefs and pomade in their hair.

After a few days Aleixo was transformed, and Bom-Crioulo contemplated him with the pride of a master who observes the advances of his disciple.

One fine Sunday in which everyone had to appear in white uniform, according to the order of the day, the ship boy was the last to arrive on deck for the inspection. He was impeccably dressed in his uniform, the blue ruff stiff with starch, bell-bottomed trousers, cap to one side, shiny buskins.

Bom-Crioulo, who had already gone up on deck, was amazed at seeing him so elegant, and was on the point of doing something silly. His desire was to embrace the little boy, there, in the presence of the crew, devour him with kisses, consume him with caresses. Yes, indeed! He looked like a girl in that attire. He really looked marvelous. The little mirror seemed to have been of some use, eh?

With a rapid gesture, nervous, disguising his concupiscence, he said to him: "Beautiful boy!"

The little lad, far from getting angry at the compliment, looked at himself from top to bottom, excited, proffered a "bah!" with some coquettishness, and made his way toward the line without saying a word.

Later, after the reading of the Rules, with the inspection over, Bom-Crioulo called him over to the bows and they engaged in a long conversation, delightful to the Negro, to judge from the increasingly brilliant expression of his physiognomy.

The sea was relatively tranquil, hardly moved by a soft breeze that caressed the hot days. The clouds were gathering toward the south, growing into fierce-looking black clouds, as if they had been pushed by a great force, still distant, almost joined to the horizon. Up, at the top of the great hemisphere burned by the midday sun, the sky, always a light blue color, an immaculate blue, transparent and soft, infinite and mysterious. . . . It looked like land was very close by, because through the same horizon of the corvette one could see a small triangular sail of a raft, microscopic and fugitive. On the starboard wing one could also see the somber figure of a big steamship with two stacks.

Bom-Crioulo and Aleixo conversed in the shade of the bowsprit, close to each other, indifferent to the happiness of the other sailors, whose attention was now centered on the ocean liner. Everyone else, with the exception of the two, wanted to know what the nationality of the "monster" was. Some affirmed that it was English, due to its size; others saw in the two colors of the chimneys the emblem of Messageries Marifimes: it must have been the *Equateur* or the *Gironde*—either of the two. Bets were made while the monster silently approached and the raft slowly disappeared.

"Now look, don't try to provoke other people" said Bom-Crioulo. "Rio de Janeiro is the land of the devil. If I ever catch you with anyone, you know . . . The little lad distractedly bit the tip of the dark blue calico kerchief decorated with white spots. He listened to the other's promises, dreaming of a rose-colored life, there, in that Rio de Janeiro of such fame, where there was a big mountain called Sugarloaf and where the emperor had his palace, a beautiful mansion with walls of gold . . .

Everything was growing immeasurably in his imagination, a sailor who was traveling for the first time. Bom-Crioulo had promised to take him to the theaters, to the Corcovado (another mountain from which the whole city and the sea could be observed), to Tijuca, to Passeiro Publico, and all the important places. They would live together, in a room on Rua da Misericordia, in an apartment of fifteen thousand reis in which two metal beds, or even only one, which, spacious . . . He, Bom-

Crioulo, would pay for everything with his salary. They could live a peaceful life. If they continued on the same ship, even better! If, on the other hand, luck separated them, they would somehow find a way. Nothing was impossible under the sun.

"And you don't have to say any of this to anyone" concluded the Negro. Not a word: leave all the arrangements to me.

At that moment, the ocean liner which was in front of the corvette hoisted astern the English flag, an enormous red material, and saluted the warship, whose flag (green and gold) also floated astern, with three thunderous whistles.

A great number of people were moving in the bows of the English boat, without doubt Italian immigrants who were arriving in Brazil. It was easy to make out the Captain, in white uniform, with a hat of cork, walking the passageway with a telescope in hand. They made signals with flags to the corvette, which was being left behind, all sails set, slow and dignified.

The ocean liner disappeared like a shadow, and the corvette continued on its route, alone in the middle of the sea, desolated and lugubrious. The sailors had distributed themselves all over the deck, occupied with their jobs, waiting for the four o'clock meal.

The mountain of clouds that only a short while ago raised itself fantastically in the distance, in a southerly direction, now extended itself to the sky, getting progressively closer, a leaden color, tempestuous, spreading itself out in outlines of a charming figure, like an enormous obstacle that suddenly lifted itself up between the corvette and the horizon. Already covered up, the sun filtered its sad light through the clouds, producing a multicolor and brilliant band that irradiated from them, a kind of aureole, which descended to the ocean.

The storm was imminent.

"Control the top gallant sails and the masts!" shouted the officer of the guard.

At this order, there was a general movement. Whistles sounded immediately, and the deck was filled with sailors and officers, who came up the hatchways running, bumping into one another confusedly. The figure of the guard Agostinho stood out on the bows, calm and solemn, observing the masts.

"Down sails, steer!"

Again, the whistles sounded with the desperation of hurried maneuvers; waves of sailors launched themselves from one end to another in races of savage hordes, lowering cables, running into one another, while the pulleys shrilled like a cart pulled by oxen during field labors.

"Steady at the wheel!" shouted the officer, wrapped in an impermeable oilskin.

The day had gone completely dark, and the wild wind, freshening, whistled in the masts with a sinister sound, with the extraordinary force of invisible titans. The sea and the sky became confused in the dark, forming a single black shape over and surrounding the corvette; it was as if everything that was inside was going to disappear under the waters and the clouds. Roaring under the keel, high haughty waves danced a terrible and vertiginous dance in the bows, each time that the belly of the ship went under water at the risk of breaking up in the middle. The interminable rain filled the deck floor, obliging the sailors to roll up their sleeves, soaking the piles of cables, in a general and unexpected swilling.

The corvette had been left with only the topsails and the mizzenmasts, and it floated now over the sea as if it were a simple small pleasure craft, light, its sails bloated by the wind, galloping over the waves, with the rails almost at the level of the water.

What an honor for the officer of the guard! How well he felt at this moment, covered in his impermeable oilskins, soaked to the toes, all eyes so that the ship would not stray from its path. He felt filled with responsibility, calm in his post, while the others rested in the weapons room. From time to time he glanced at the bows and saw, with great joy in his heart, the wide streak of foam that the corvette left in its wake. He felt strong, he felt masculine! "Without doubt, a sailor's life is the best test of valor, he thought."

The storm lasted an hour and a half, a closed and persistent rain, oblique, that seemed to be interminable. The sky suddenly opened, clear and blue; light began to illuminate the horizon once again, and slowly the last vestiges of the "joke," in the words of Lieutenant Sousa, later, began to disappear. Earlier he had been furious at the calm and now he was to take his turn at the watch.

The wind, however, continued to lash the cables, punishing the surface of the water, moaning sadly like a fantastic cello, in bursts that made the whole ship tremble.

The little craft reached ten miles, ten miles an hour.

"Careful with the steer!"

The sailors swept the deck floor, while the others spent the time passing the swab over spots that no longer had any water. Up, on the deck, the voice of the officers could be heard conversing in the gunlock, seated in a grotesque disorder, smoking and laughing. . . . The Commissar, a thin man with big sideburns, was practicing the clarinet below, in the weapons room, keeping his balance with admirable patience. The rain had reanimated all of the them, officers and sailors, making their bodies more agile.

Tired after work, Bom-Crioulo went below deck and conversed with Aleixo, from whom he had been separated only during the time of duty.

The humidity, the cold that entered through the hatchways, that glacial temperature, filled him with a mad desire for physical love, an irresistible effeminacy. Joined to the ship boy in what was almost an embrace, his hand on the shoulder of Aleixo who, in the face of that contact, experienced the vague sensation of a caress, the Negro forgot completely his companions, all that surrounded him, and could only think of the ship boy, of his "beautiful boy" and of the future of that inexplicable friendship.

"Were you very frightened?"

"Of what?"

"Of the weather . . ."

"No, not in the least."

And Aleixo took advantage of the opportunity to talk of the case of the "southwest" in Santa Catarina: he and his father had gone out in a fishing canoe, around midday. Suddenly, the sea began to get choppy, the wind began to make itself felt. . . . And then? They were completely alone, close to the island of Ratones, in a canoe that looked like the shell of a nut. The old man did not hesitate for one

moment, no sir! He took the oar—"Hold on tight, my son"—with the wind growing stronger each moment, buzzing in the ears like the very devil. At that moment
a burst of wind suddenly blew, a terrible gust, and when he, Aleixo, wanted to hold
on to his father, it was already too late: the canoe had capsized.

Bom-Crioulo feigned great surprise:

"It capsized?"

"Yes, it did, don't you believe me? I know that I went down to the bottom and
came back to the surface. Then I became unconscious. When I recovered, I was
on the shore, safe and sound, thank God!"

"Well, you were lucky" said the Negro with feeling. "You could have died of
drowning."

Bom-Crioulo also wanted to tell his story, and the conversation was prolonged
until nightfall, when all of them went up on deck for the distribution of jobs.

Instead of diminishing, the southwest blew even stronger, hard and tenacious,
threatening to blow away all the cables and sails. The corvette, the "old skiff," as
they called her, sailed across those dizzy seas, pitching softly, oscillating sometimes
when the waves were immense, with its two colored lamps—red on the starboard
and green on the port side—and the little lantern of the foremast, pale and microscopic at the top of the bowsprit.

Even with only topsail and mizzenmast, with the wind behind, large and
somber in the clear night, spectral and silent, the corvette sailed desperately on its
way to its home port.

Rising very slowly, the moon, a fire color at the beginning that later became
slowly cold and opal, a mixture of fog and light, the soul of solitude, turned the
extensive scenery of the waves melancholic, pouring over the sea that caressing
light, an ideal light that penetrated the heart of the sailor communicating to him
the infinite nostalgia of those who ride the waves.

Meanwhile the wind would not calm down!

At that speed they would soon land. It was a question of perhaps a day more . . .

While the sad hour of official silence drew near, the hour of sleep, which would
be prolonged until the beginning of the dawn, the sailors enjoyed themselves in the
bows, singing to the sound of a wailing guitar a country tune, laughing, tapping
their heels, trying to see who improvised the best songs with badly made verses,
"songs of the jungle." They would not miss a moon like that one. They had worked
a lot: it was also important to have fun. Sprawled on the floor, some on their backs,
others face down, with the chin resting on their palms. One was seated quietly,
another smoking with his legs crossed, all of them in total freedom, they formed a
choir up there in the castle, while it was still very early.

The officer of the guard, striding unceasingly, listened to them with tenderness,
full of consideration for those poor people, homeless and without families, who
would die singing, far from all love, sometimes far away from their native land,
wherever destiny would send them. Those clumsy songs, improvised, almost without rhyme or rhythm, had, however, the penetrating taste of the native fruits and
the mysterious charm of ingenuous confessions. . . . It made one feel good to hear
them: the heart seemed to dilate in a hypertrophy of tender and consoling nostalgia.

Let them sing, the poor sailors; let them forget the unstable life that they live, leave them alone. . . .

The guitar moans; a soul sobs in each refrain; songs that defy the infinite silence of the clear night sound . . .

Time flies, nobody is aware of how the hours go by; nobody remembers to sleep, to close the eyes to the cold and translucent scenery, bathed in the tropical moon and swept by the south wind. Mysterious instrument that guitar, that made one forget all the unpleasantness of life, intoxicating the soul, tonifying the spirit!

Bom-Crioulo did not participate in the merrymaking. He was tired of hearing songs: the time had passed when he too had had fun dancing the baiao, making the group laugh.

When the bow bell rang nine, they saw him retire felinely, carrying his hammock. He left in a hurry, running away from the sight of the others, dumb, impenetrable, somber. . . .

He entered the hatchway in a state of agitation, down the stairs, and disappeared into the corvette.

What was he going to do? Commit some crime? Some kind of betrayal? Nothing of that sort: Bom-Crioulo only wanted to go to bed, like any other mortal, in the most comfortable place possible. Up on the deck the air was freezing cold; below deck was always a bit more warm. He who takes precautions lives a long life!

He opened the hammock, tied it up over the deck floor carefully, with feminine hands, examined the sheet, and, taking off his blue flannel shirt, he lay down with a great sigh of relief. Ah, finally he felt the way he wanted! Good night! No voice broke the reglamentary silence, except that of the officer, each hour:

"Guard!"

The wind still blew strongly.

The deck presented the appearance of a nomadic camping. The crew, debilitated by work, had fallen in a profound somnolence, scattered around, in a general disorder of gypsies who do not choose the place where they may find repose. They cared little for the damp floor, the drafts of air, the cold, beriberi. Down below, the discomfort was even greater. The canvas hammocks slung from metal bars, piled together, dirty like kitchen rags, oscillated to the moribund and wan light of the lamps. Imagine the hold of a merchant ship filled with misery. In the space between the rooms, in the semi-penumbra of the cave-like rooms almost naked bodies, indistinct, were in motion. The nauseous smell of prison filled the air, a bitter smell of human sweat diluted with urine and tar. Some Negroes snored profoundly with their mouths open, wallowing in the unconsciousness of sleep. Naked torsos could be seen embracing the floor, indecorous postures that the light showed up cruelly. From time to time a voice murmured unintelligible words in its sleep. A sailor woke up among the others, completely naked, with eyes wide open in terror, screaming that they wanted to kill him. It turned out that the poor devil was suffering from the effects of a nightmare, nothing more. Everything became silent again.

Up above, in the passageway, the officer of the guard, vigilant and imperturbable, shouted every hour:

"Guard!"

There was a light agitation; the guard whistled waking up the people on duty:

"Wake up, wake up! Its your turn to take the watch!"

And the hours continued passing by in this way, monotonously.

Bom-Crioulo was taking his break. His spirit had not been calm during the whole evening, ruminating strategies with which to confront decisively the ship boy, to come to a solution once and for all, his strong manly desire tortured by Grecian carnality.

On occasions he had wanted to test the mood of the ship boy, trying to convince him, stimulating his organism; but the little youth did not seem to rise to the bait, rejecting softly some of the caresses of the Negro with gestures of one in love.

"Stop that, Bom-Crioulo, be more serious!"

That day, Priapus swore to take the battle to its ultimate consequences. Vanquish or die! The little one had to make up his mind or they would break the relationship. It was vital to resolve "the issue."

"What issue?" asked the young man with great surprise.

"Nothing; but I don't want you to get angry with me."

And in a rush he asked him:

"Where are you going to sleep tonight?"

"There in the bows, below deck, because of the cold."

"Good, we have to talk."

At nine o'clock, when Bom-Crioulo became aware that Aleixo was going down, he took his hammock and ran to catch up with him. It was just then that they saw him pass with the bulk beneath his arm, slinking away felinely.

When he came near the ship boy, feeling the heat of his well-filled body, the bland warmth of that desired flesh, free as yet from impure contact, a savage appetite left the Negro speechless. The light was not enough to illuminate the hiding place where they had taken refuge. They could not see each other: they felt each other, guessing beneath the bedclothes.

After a cautious and quick silence, Bom-Crioulo, approaching the ship boy, spoke in his ear. Aleixo became immobile, left breathless. Timidly, his eyelids closing instinctively from sleep, he heard the blows of the waves on the bow, with his ears stuck to the floor, without the desire to murmur a word. As in a dream, he saw visions of the thousand and one promises of Bom-Crioulo: the little room on the Rua da Misericordia in Rio de Janeiro, the theaters, the promenades. . . . He remembered the punishment the Negro had suffered for his sake; but he did not say a word. A sensation of total happiness traversed his whole body. He began to feel in his own blood impulses he had never experienced before, a kind of innate desire to give in to the caprices of the Negro, to abandon himself to him for whatever he wanted, a vague distention of the nerves, an eagerness for passivity. . . . "Alright" he murmured urgently, turning himself around. And the crime against nature was consummated.

# Colombia

## Porfirio Barba-Jacob (1883–1942)

[Pseudonym of Miguel Angel Osorio Benitez]

From *Song of an Impossible Blue*

*Translated by Jeff Bingham and Juan Antonio Serna Servin*

Song of the Fleeting Day

(In the court of Nicomedes of Bitthynia)

As in Sodom one day, our day
is for sterile joy;
and you have, oh Iamma!, oh my flesh!
all the melody of the moment
in the blue whiteness of your countenance.

Let me garland
your brow with my kisses.
For who knows what destinies of the depths,
or possibly for what divine inspiration,
when the larks sang to pure Eve
I heard the song and confused the trills.
And the day for me was like a garrulous young man
of intimate whiteness, and blue-eyed, and warm,
and the wind was mine
and the ambiguous sea . . .

The love in my blood was made into flames.
I saw my temples of showered effulgence.
In my garden the pomegranates hastened their sweetness.
The lights burned, the fairies flocked,
and I longed to fly toward pinnacles never tread upon.

But the burning inside me was melancholy.
All human impulse is circumscribed by the day
—the minuscule circle of the day—
bubble of illusion, vain bubble
on which you flow, oh Iamma!, oh my flesh!
and that which is now and will not be tomorrow.

I remember briefly, evoking as in dreams
an ancient reverie,
under the wing of light of the pure dawn
that announces the mystic birth of the day,
your blue hand, of virile formation,
guided the vehicle in the mature extent
of the valley, that October loosened.

A zephyr, a zephyr wounded the shafts of wheat,
and the rumor of the ages in the wind

behind the wind I rushed to attain it.
With its ancient gold, ducal lichens
depicted the knots of the poplar
and there was an assembly of thrushes
among the chaste and naked branches.

A zephyr, a zephyr wounded the shafts of wheat,
and the rumor of the ages in the wind, behind the wind,
was like a lament and a failure.

We saw clinging the bride of the peasant,
fertile and matinal, clinging to the bars of her window:
he kisses her and then makes her color
with the blush of love, oh pommace of life!
And you sing, oh Iamma! And the sound of the shafts of wheat,
the aeolian wave, the melodic flow,
It sounds to me like something untold and yet something given.

Suspended in the moment of love,
your first, original and beautiful deed,
damp with blue milk of day,
still trembling in the morning mists,
I longed to be eternal in its wonder,
with its flow,
with its undulation,
among the rustle
of the shafts of wheat,
in the sweetness
of life.

Where is my vision: the mystic birth,
the gold of October, the chariot, the day,
your open voice, your joyful gesture;
in short, the entire and perfect reality
of that hour of the world,
with its flow
with its undulation,
among the rustle of the shafts of wheat,
in the sweetness
of life?

As the tone of the sea takes form in the pearl,
may that rustling take form in this song:
and may the sweet day of your love be a lament
that travels in the wind
through my trembling and my pain!

Day! Day! Its nimble tunic,
embellished by a rainbow of bubbles,
with only sad cinders wafting in its wake.
Love, Pain, Daydream . . . The Soul
was big and the day was minuscule!

But as in Sodom one day, our day
is for sterile joy;
and you have, oh Iamma!, oh my flesh!
all the melody of the instant
in the blue whiteness of your countenance.

Toward the lighted garden of illusion,
amid the mist of ages,
I let my heart fly.
Consumed by passion
I long to return to my infancy.

Unencumbered, harsh, sad heart,
intoxicated by the bitter wine of ages,
shrouded in black flames of passion:
You must return to your infancy,
broken, weary, ancient heart.

Oh, yes! To return to infancy,
toward the blue garden of illusion . . .
How does one travel amid the mist of ages,
having already lost the simplicity of the heart?

## Mexico

### Xavier Villaurrutia (1903–1950)

Two Poems

*Translated by Fanny Arango-Ramos and William Keeth*

*They and I*

They know how to live
and I do not,
I have forgotten how if I ever knew,
or maybe I never began . . .
They know how to kiss,
and I do not even know what it is.
I am afraid to try
to know . . .

They know how to laugh
My God, I do not . . .
And to have to go on
like this . . . !
They know how to do
a thousand more things
than I will ever
accomplish . . .

They know how to live
and laugh
and kiss
I only know how to cry . . .


*Nocturnal Sea*

[To Salvador Novo]

Neither your hard crystal silence of solid rock,
nor the coldness of the hand that you extend to me,
neither your frozen words, timeless, colorless,
nor my name, not even my name
that you pronounce like a naked figure of meaning;

neither the deep wound, nor the blood
that flows trembling from his lips,
nor the distance that each time grows colder
snowy sheet of winter hospital
spread out between both of us like doubt;

nothing, nothing can ever be more bitter
than the sea I have inside, alone and blind,
the ancient Oedipus sea that flows over me blindly
from all the centuries
when my blood was not yet my blood,
when my skin grew in the skin of another body,
when someone was breathing for me as I was not yet born.

The sea that rises mute to my lips,
the sea that saturates itself
with the lethal poison that does not kill
as it prolongs life and it hurts more than pain.
The sea that slowly and slowly works
forging in the cavity of my chest
the furious fist of my heart.

Sea with neither wind nor sky,
without waves, desolate,
nocturnal sea without foam in its lips,
nocturnal sea without rage, satisfied
with the licking of the walls that keep it imprisoned
enslaved unable to break its banks
and blind unable to seek the light that they have stolen
a lover that only wants indifference.

The sea that drags away silent remains
forgotten oblivions and wishes,
syllables of memories and resentments,
drowned dreams of newborns,
mutilated profiles and perfumes,
fibers of light and shipwrecked hair.

Bitter nocturnal sea
that circulates in narrow corridors
of coral arteries and roots
and veins and capillary jellyfishes.

Sea that knits in the shadow its floating tissue,
with blue threaded needles
with nerve strands and tense cords.

Bitter nocturnal sea
that moistens my tongue with its slow saliva,
that makes my nails grow with the force
of its dark tie.

My ear follows its secret murmur,
I hear its rocks and its growing plants
which extend more and more its fingers, lips.

I carry it inside me like a regret,
another's sin and mysterious dream,
and I lull it to sleep
and I hide it and I care for it and I keep the secret.

# Argentina

### Eduardo Gudino Keifer (1935–)

FROM *A SINNER'S GUIDEBOOK* (1972)

[*GUIA DE PECADORES*]

*Translated by Ronald Christ and Gregory Kolovakos*

She knows it, she knows she's the One and Only of Buenos Aires, *rara avis in terris*, she knows there's no other who can do what she does with the skill she does it; she knows she's the Phoenix, the Chosen One, the Incomparable, the heroic Joan of Arc, but no virgin, thank God;

she knows others exist, sure, she knows it because she herself belongs to that garrulous and multicolor fauna, because secret tropisms pushed her toward closed lodges, mysterious clans, guilds whose passwords are smirks, gasps, and sashaying;

she knows others exist but few of them dare to wear the bracelets, necklaces, beads, plumes, high heels, and fake eyelashes except in clandestine mystical phallic ceremonies while she, the One and Only, can strut all that in public, in front of rows and rows of seats packed with hot bodies with lascivious or jeering eyes; the All Defiant, the All Enlightened and not because of some miraculous Celestial Charity but because of Violet Spots describing a centerstage halo at the Orleans; guided not by Voices but by the Sublime Electronic Music;

and she also knows she has almost or completely magical powers; she knows how that audience shouts obscenities at Leila (Rita Fuad in real life) while she takes off her veils to the tune of "In a Persian Market"; they stamp and whistle while Yoko (Yolanda Cardoza in real life) takes off her kimono to "Poor Butterfly"; they get worked up to fever pitch while Marilyn (Rosita Kluczinsky in real life) takes off her tight-fitting black dress to "Blues in the Night"; but they grow quiet, surprised at first, and then absolutely fascinated, stupefied, bewitched, wrapping her in an almost frightening silence when the esoteric violet aura is switched on and the choral prelude "Jesu, Joy of Man's Desiring" starts up unexpectedly, solemnly, strangely, anagogically;

that's when she comes out of the shadows to station herself under the lights, in her snow-white, floor-length tunic and her jewels like scapulars, like medallions? and her fluttering false silky eyelashes and her ceremonial high heels and the languid wig; she comes forward and hardly begins to move to the contemplative phrasing of the chords;

first raise the right arm then the left in immolation and holocaust let the hair fall forward covering the face bending the head slowly push out the hip advance the leg letting the taut muscle be seen through the furtive slit; oh anointed priestess in the androlatrous ritual of her own adoration, first take off the earrings then the necklaces then the bracelets then one shoe then the other to the beat of the holy sacrifice, and the crowd's silence getting denser moment by moment and the music more overwhelming moment by moment essentially more and more Bach moment by moment interpreted by Walter Carlos on the Moog neosynthesizer and toward the end of the two minutes and fifty-seven seconds which is exactly how long the number lasts let the white tunic drop dramatically turn away from the audience unsnap the bra turn around again facing the thousand-headed monster silenced transported hypnotized modestly covering the breasts with both arms and now without uncovering it with one arm lower the other slllooowllly slloowlly until loosening the small rose on the panties and then with a properly miraculous precision "Jesu, Joy of Man's Desiring" ends and the spots go off and the violet halo is extinguished and the darkness covers her total nudity with mourning clothes and crepe and she runs off between the teasers and quickly puts on the raincoat she left hanging there on a nail just for that purpose;

she also knows that during those two seconds after the lights go out, those two clocked seconds, silence will reign over the orchestra of the Orleans like smoke from the cigarettes, like the echo of that already faded music; and then someone will clap and applause from those who have realized for the very first time that strip tease can be something like a solemn mass, a votive mass, a mass of purification with the body present; she also knows (although she'd like to forget it) that the applause would roar out of a maddened beast if the light didn't go out at exactly the right moment and if the public discovered the truth, that deceitful truth or, better said, that painful reality she feels between her legs while walking toward the dressing room, oh God, dear God of my soul how mean you were to me when you put this right here, what do I want with something so lovely on men so useless on me, why do you make me feel more of a woman than any woman and you stuck a prick where I'd like to have something else, warm and loving;

sure, the applause would roar out and she would die, crushed by the cheated furious irate iconoclastic crowd and maybe it would be beautiful to die like that with all those sweaty drunken ferocious men on top, stepping on her, spitting on her, and tearing at her;

but the lights always go out on time and she goes to the dressing room (the girls, her associates, say "changing room," but she prefers to say dressing room, it's so much more elegant, so much more aristocratic, dressing room instead of changing room, maybe Sarah Bernhardt had a changing room, no, surely she had a dressing room, maybe Maria Callas has a changing room, but enough of that);

and in the dressing room the noisy chatterboxes talking complaining it's disgraceful three thousand pesos a day and on my last tour of Central America I was earning a thousand dollars a month; shut up what're you talking about Central America for if you never made it past Berazategui; it's easy to see you're blabbing out of jealousy, what's happening is if you keep getting fatter you're not going to be able to strip any more, who's going to pay to see cellulitis, and the laughing and the nasty cracks and did'ja get a load of that and, but what a thing to say;

and when she enters and sits down in front of the mirror and begins to take off her makeup with Aqualane even though Aqualane is used for other necessities, there's a very short silence having nothing to do with the great majestic silence in the theater; a short silence caused by the fact that the others, even doing what she is doing, would love to feel as feminine as she does;

and while she makes the blush and rouge and shadow disappear with a slow and circular massaging of her fingertips on her forehead, on her cheeks, on her neck, the others watch waiting for that ridiculous and sublime moment that is repeated like a sacrament every night;

that moment she waits for too, a martyr facing the lions, a sacrificial victim; that moment which should also have some background music because it is the moment of true nudity, awesome solemn Wagnerian music that would make the last interior masks fall away:

THE MOMENT OF TAKING OFF THE WIG

now,

like this;

and what is it as if they don't know by heart, as if I haven't repeated it every night these last three years;

take it off suddenly, with a quick jerk, in a defiant gesture that exposes her skull where two or three stray hairs do not cover the miserable premature baldness, sign of a masculinity unchosen but inevitable;

that moment;

she with the wig in her hand looking at the others with a blank stare, the others lowering their eyes as if ashamed suddenly breaking the silence with small talk, something about the weather or about the fat man in the front row, anything;

and little by little the return to normality, she taking off the false eyelashes now with Johnson's Baby Oil, as good for her very delicate eyelids as for very delicate babies' rear ends; the others beginning to ask her things and she replying as if she were the lonely-hearts column, answering Yoko (Yolanda Cardoza in real life) who consults her about whether it's worthwhile to give up the Orleans and devote herself to studying anthropology, or listening to the moaning of Leila (Rita Fuad in real life) who complains that men are all the same or ducking the innuendoes of Marilyn (Rosita Kluczinsky in real life) who attacks her because she's envious, of course;

but the one sure thing is that when all is said and done they all depend on her, all revolve around her, the One and Only of Buenos Aires, *rara avis in terris*, Phoenix, Joan of Arc;

the One and Only capable of imagining that it's possible to strip to Bach put to electronic music;

the One and Only capable of dominating that dragon audience;

the One and Only whose sex is a false sex and yet more genuine than the female bearers of a genuine sex;

the only One and Only;

Corybant at the mad feast of Cybele, druid in the forest of skyscrapers, hierophant officiating at secret ceremonies;

Pope Joan on a canopied throne but on the pyre every day as well, on the sacrificial altar ready to receive a dagger in the center of her breast;

the only One and Only;

who's now entirely clean of makeup, entirely divested of wig, high heels, and false eyelashes, who now stands up, letting the raincoat slip off, who with perfect naturalness walks naked in front of the others who don't even look at her because they're so used to her by now, who walks trying to move her skimpy buns as if they were the mighty buttocks of the others, showing off what she doesn't have and embarrassing herself with what she does have, oh God my God how mean you were to me;

heading toward the locker where the striped pants pink shirt sandals are that she'll wear on the street because obviously, on the street you can't dress like a woman even if you'd like to;

listening to the little cries of the others the goodbyes of the others who and, dressed now, watching them with her head thrown back and the right eyebrow disdainfully raised like Maria Felix as an Aztec deity, sweeping them with a circular gaze, a fiery gaze that could incinerate these other poor women for no more than being just that: women;

and flinging a half languid, half scornful ciao that drops in the midst of Leila, Yoko, and Marilyn like a wilted carnation that tears out the other carnations, other flowers other ciao sweetheart see you tomorrow, good luck, hope something turns up, hope everything goes well, see ya', good night;

and going out on to the street and crossing over to the bar to dial a number on the payphone;

beep beep beep beep busy;

then sitting down at the usual table asking Mario for the usual Mario coffee please

Mario attentive bringing her the coffee asking how're you how're things going;

sweetheart, things are always pretty good, justa little tired, you know, when a lady's an artist;

a startled customer who turns around hearing the hoarse voice refer to herself in the feminine gender, when the voice as well as the appearance indicate the masculine;

she winking an accomplice eye at Mario and another devilish eye at the customer and the customer turning red up to here and burying himself in the pages of *La Razón* and Mario's accomplice smile;

the hot coffee does her good, stimulates her stomach, awakens the gratifying memory of her strip tease, the only number of the One and Only, others would've liked to have had the idea, but what were they going to do, so few like classical music, so few who'd think of using Bach for the art of stripping in public;

ten minutes and to the telephone again, once again to dial the number engraved in her memory and now, yes, ringing, one, two, three, then the click and his sleepy voice:

hello who's it;

and she the only One and Only suddenly quaking shivering timid trembling Joan of Arc defeated, handed over letting herself be condemned, yearning for the burning flames, pronouncing just one word:

love;

oh, it's you;

love, tell me that you love me;

shit, you want to be flattered at this hour;

I'm done now, I'm coming out there, I want to see you, please let me in don't be mean;

look, you nut, I'm really tired;

please, sweetheart;

go fuck yourself;

oh cruel stab, oh another click from him when he hangs up, oh injustice, oh pain, oh broken heart;

suddenly wilted, humiliated, repentant, hurt alone

paying for the coffee while Mario looks on sympathetically

going out on to the street alone

walking to the bus stop alone

getting on the bus alone riding alone

getting off the bus alone

entering her two-room apartment in the Abasto, right there

on Gardel Street alone;

looking at the photo of Manfredi under the glass on the bedside table alone;
getting ready for bed alone;
looking at herself in the mirror, seeing herself alone;
alone alone so alone,
and to top it off bald.


# Cuba

### Julian del Casal (1863–1893)

*El amante de las torturas* (1893)

[The torture lover]

*Translated by David William Foster*

"Is the owner in?" I asked the clerk in the bookstore who, looking back over his shoulder, fixed me with his startled gaze from the top steps of a ladder.

"Please take a seat," he replied, "he'll be here in a moment."

While I waited for him, I began distracted to leaf through the pages of a book of poetry, lined in mauve silk and with a purple title, lying on top of a stack of similar volumes. But then a subtle perfume, half like something from a church and half like something from a boudoir, made me raise my head and look around.

The slightest movement of my head was enough to find myself face to face with a young man tall in stature and dressed extremely elegantly who was moving with indifference among the shelves of books like a bored prince strolling in the slave market without paying any heed to any of them.

He seemed to be one of the regulars, because it was enough for him to glance at the bookshelves to determine that they contained nothing but the same titles as before. When he discerned some unfamiliar book lying on the floor, he would bend down to pick it up, only to cast it aside with visible distaste, unconcerned as to where it fell. To judge by the disdainful curl of his lips, you would think he had cut into a fruit filled with worms or that he had touched the viscous skin of a reptile's underbelly. He strode around in this manner for a few moments from one end of the bookstore to the other, leaving in his wake the aroma of an unusual perfume that seem mixed with grains of incense and mignonette, when I saw him stop before a pile of yellow volumes. His nostrils flared and he turned livid with emotion. He opened wide his glowing pupils and extended his hand, like a marble claw, and picked up one of the volumes which were stacked horizontally at his feet.

Since the owner had returned, he sat down next to me, his catch in his hand, which gave me the opportunity to get a better look at him. Despite his youth—he seemed to be thirty at the most—his person bore such signs of boredom, exhaustion, and even decrepitude that his person produced a certain uneasiness. He gave the impression of a convalescent who had risen from his bed after a long and painful sickness. It was enough to examine his head along the sides, with their irregular patches of baldness, or the glassy color of his pupils, which would dart out a few seconds, in the sharpness of his nose, which betrayed his labored breathing, in the almost diaphanous pallor of his face, the skin stretched taut over the bones, in the violaceous arch of his bloodless lips, and in the nervous jolts of his body, which betrayed the physical suffering that required him to shift his position frequently to understand that his organism had been harboring absolute decay for a long time and that the strength of his youth and strict adherence to medical knowledge were powerless to stop it.

His head was resting on his chest like the blossom of a flower droops against its stem, as he examined the shiny pages of the volume he held propped up on his knees, lost in the ecstasy of some and turning rapidly others. Then when the book-seller arrived, he went over to talk to him and, with the book under his arm, he left without a word.

"Who is that young man?" I asked the owner of the store who, stroking his chin, smiled malignly.

"He's an old client of mine, someone you've probably seen a lot here. I don't know him well, and I don't think anyone can claim to know him, but I can tell you he's one of the strangest, somberest and most curious of persons you'll ever find. Every morning, as long as it's not cloudy, because then he stays at home, afraid of the damp air which somehow makes him sick, you'll find him making the rounds of the bookstores. He's a man who's always looking for books, but not the sort of books everybody else likes, but certain kinds of books that I've only seen him buy. Every week he brings me a list of works that he orders from abroad from his own house, books that always leave me totally stupefied. They all have strange titles like 'Night Chimes,' by someone named Rette, or 'Imitation of our Lady of the Moon,' by Jules Laforgue, who he was told was a reader of the Empress Augusta. He does-n't always receive what he orders, because his contact informs me that almost everything is out of print. But then, somehow, I don't exactly how, he's able to get a hold of them."

"And what book did he buy today?"

"A sort of history of the martyrdoms that occurred among Catholic missionaries in barbarian territories. His library contains a lot of books like that. He snaps up anything along that line as soon as its written. I assure you that there's no one else in the whole world like him. He likes anything having to do with what is deformed, monstrous, bloody, anything to do with torture and suffering. He's a man who mar-tyrs himself to get rid of his spleen. Haven't you noticed how he often slips his hand into the top of his pants and that right after that he begins to walk in a contorted sort of way? Well, it's because he wears a hair shirt around his waist and every time it comes loose, he draws it tight around his skin. What is more, he always wears a strange kind of perfume, something that smells like a temple, but also like a whore-house, a perfume that permeates every corner of his house."

"Have you ever been there?"

"Yes, I was there once, but I don't plan on ever going back."

"Did something happen?"

"Nothing happened to me, but I couldn't sleep for a week after that. Just imag-ine, he lives in an outlying quarter of the city, almost on the outskirts of the city, out where the only people you find are types who are sick, sinister, and spectral. Seen from the outside, there's nothing strange about his house, except for the fact it's falling down, which would scare the devil out of anyone who had to walk beneath its balconies. But once you cross the threshold, where there's a lame old man with green glasses and a white beard that covers his whole chest, you begin to feel a certain oppressiveness, a certain unexplained trembling, a certain uneasiness like what you feel when you enter a cemetery. You feel like you want to run away, just like you do when you first open your eyes after a nightmare, but at the same time you feel like you're under the sway of a mysterious force that freezes your movements. There are mornings when he turns up I feel like asking him about his life, but he is so cold, so closed-mouth, so disdainful that I can never bring myself to satisfy my curiosity."

"But, what was it you saw in that house?"

"After the man at the door had a child, as blond as an angel and as beautiful as an ephebe, announce my visit, I was told to proceed upstairs. I was led into a severely furnished study, but there was nothing that bothered me about its strangeness. I began to attribute the uneasiness I felt to the perfume you mentioned before. The only thing that upset me was how long it took the man to appear. Since there was nothing better for me to do, the silence in the room allowed me to discern a swishing sound, followed by sobs, as though someone in the house were being whipped, someone nevertheless who was not allowed to cry out in pain. At the same time, the perfume became more intense while at the same time it seemed to me that a puff of smoke came through the keyhole of the door into the next room. I was just about to go downstairs when I saw a Sister of Charity slip down an adjacent hallway, adjusting her habit. She held a golden censer in her right hand and a cloak of Our Lady of Sorrow made out of black velvet with stars under her arm. She was followed by another nun, pale and breathing heavily, who was folding a blue wool tunic of the sort enfolding the body of the Magdalenes in ancient Italian paintings. And, finally, trailing the two, I could see the upper portion of a huge cross made of black wood which a flushed halfbreed dressed like an executioner was carrying with difficulty."

"Could they have been practicing some scene from the Passion?"

"I don't know. But I already had my hat in my hand when I saw that man, almost transparent he was so pale and thin to the point of being cadaverous. He was motioning to me through a cloud of smoke from the adjoining room, telling me I could come in.

"I had gone to take him some books he had ordered and that had arrived during one of the periods in which he would disappear. While he occupied himself with examining them, I began to scrutinize the room with care. We were in a vast hall, almost square, covered by a flaming red carpet, decorated with mandrakes of euphorbia and hellebores and all kinds of lethal plants. The table at which he wrote, made entirely of ebony with marble inlays, was covered with the usual instruments, but from the inkwell down to the penknife they were all in the shape of instruments of torture. There was a gold bracelet lying next to a pen, covered in black lacquer and blood-red rubies, and it looked like it had that very moment come off of someone's arm. Hairy spiders crawled up the lace curtains that fluttered outside the balconies, and their topaz-colored glass let in a candle-colored light, a funereal light that filled the entire room with a melancholy atmosphere. The pictures hanging on the way, framed with a dark green paper and festooned with autumn leaves, also represented scenes of torture, scenes of blood, scenes of cruelty, scenes of desolation."

When his account was over, the old bookseller wiped his forehead that was pearled in sweat, and he turned to take up his place behind his desk full of books, periodicals, and letters.

I shook his hand without saying a word and picked up my hat, taking refuge in my solitude, where I have spent much time thinking about that strange youth who has turned suffering into voluptuousness in order to rid himself of his spleen.

*La Habana Elegante, February 26, 1893*

## Emilio Ballagas (1908–1954)

Two Poems

*Translated by Fanny Arango-Ramos and William Keeth*

*Nocturne and Elegy*

If he asks about me, trace on the ground
a cross of silence and ashes
over the impure name that afflicts me.
If he asks about me, say that I have died
and that I am decaying beneath the ants.
Tell him that I am a branch of an orange tree,
the simple weather vane of a tower.

Do not tell him that I still cry
embracing the hollow of his absence
where his blind statue stood imprinted.
always waiting for the body to return.
The flesh is a laurel that sings and suffers
and I waited in vain beneath his shadow.
It is already late. I am a deaf minnow.

If he asks about me, give him these eyes,
these grey words, these fingers:
and the drop of blood in the handkerchief.
Tell him that I have lost myself, that I have become
a dark partridge, a false ring
or a bank of forgotten camel grass:
tell him that I fade from saffron to iris.

Tell him that I wanted to prolong his lips,
live within the palace of his forehead.
Navigate one night in his hair.
Learn the color of his pupils

and smother myself slowly in his chest,
submerged nightly, listless
in the murmur of veins and mute.

Now I cannot even see although I implore
the body that I dressed with love,
I remain steadfast, broken, detached.
And if you all doubt me, believe the wind,
look north, ask the sky.
And they will tell you if I still wait or if I am becoming night.

Oh! If he asks tell him what you know.
One day the olive tree will speak of me
when I am the moon's eye,
an oddity on the face of night,
reading the sand's shells,
a nightingale suspended from an evening star
and the hypnotic charm of the tides.

It is true that I am sad, but I have
planted a smile in thyme,
hid another smile on Saturn
and have lost another, I'm not sure where.
It's better that I wait until midnight,
for the distant odor of the jasmines,
and the cold eve canopy.

Don't remind me of his sacrificed blood
nor that I left spines and worms
to gnaw on his friendship of cloud and breeze.
I am not the ogre that spit in his water
nor the one that a tired love pays in change.
I am not the one that frequents that house
presided over by a leech!

(There one goes with a bouquet of lilies
so that an angel with dark wings can bruise him.)
I'm not the one that betrays doves,
children, the stars . . .
I am a green homeless voice
that his innocence looks for and asks for
with the sweet whistle of an injured pastor.

I am a tree, the head of a needle,
a tall equestrian gesture in equilibrium:
the cross of a swallow, the startle of a groundhog.

I am everything, except for that which draws
an index finger with mire on the walls
of the brothels and the cemeteries.

Everything, except what hides itself
beneath the dry mask of esparto.
Everything, except for the flesh that yields
voluptuous rings of serpents
constricting in slow and vicious spiral.
I am that which you compel me to be, that which you invent
in order to bury my sorrow in the mist.

If he asks about me, tell him that I live
in the leaf of the acanto and in the acacia.
Or tell him, if you prefer, that I have died.
Give him this my sigh, my handkerchief;
my illusion in the vessel of the mirror.
Perhaps he will cry for me in the laurel or search for
my memory in the shape of a star.


*Of Another Fashion*

If instead of being this way,
if the things behind us (certain for centuries)
would turn around face front
and the things in front (unchangeable)
would turn their backs,
and the right would become sinister
and the left right . . .
I do not know how to say it!

Dream it
with a dream that lies beyond dream
a dream not even dreamt,
where one would have to go,
where one has to go,
(I do not know how to say it!)
like pulling down a thousand veils of fog
and at last the same dream would be fog.

Anyhow, dream it
in that world, or in this one that encloses us and silences us
where things are as they are, or how they say they are
or how you say they should be . . .
We would come singing along the same path
and I would open my arms

and you would open your arms
and we would take hold of each other.
Our united voices would roll
forming one echo.

To see us happy
all the stars would come out
The rainbow would want to meet us
touching us with all his colors
and the roses would rise
in order to bathe themselves with a little of our fortune.
(If it could be like this,
or like it's not . . . Not different at all!)

But never,
never.
Do you know the size of this word:
Never?
Do you know the grey deafness of this stone:
Never?
And the noise it makes
falling forever in the void:
Never?

Do not pronounce it, leave it to me.
(When I am alone I will say it silently
softly sobbing, like this:
                    Never . . .)

## José Lezama Lima (1910–1976)

FROM *PARADISO* (1966)

*Translated by Gregory Rabassa*

José Lezama Lima was a major Cuban novelist whose *Paradiso* was one of the most controversial novels of the 1960s. Poetic and autobiographical, *Paradiso* confronts both the persecution of homosexuals in Cuba and the author's own complex understanding of the development of human sexuality.

Foción lived alone in a spacious house in Miramar. He took leave of the group, promising to appear promptly the next morning. The house had an imposing front, and, without being palatial, was ample enough for a rich bourgeois family. Between the house and the surrounding iron grillwork and walls, the garden felt the anchor of the cold moon on its thorns and leaves and the metallic silence of the guava trees. A cricket stepped out into the center of a corolla; then a hand seemed to pull him toward the earth that had been tamped down by the lunar gravity.

The key passed smoothly into the lock and as he pushed open the gate he glanced toward the end of the street. The street light flickered and blurred the image, and Foción had to squint: sitting on the curb was the redhaired youth who had run off with the Chinese toothbrush. The street light emphasized the extreme whiteness of the hand on his cheek, his hair standing out in the light, with the two flames fusing in a single sheet of metal, the highlights of which twisted inward. His anguished repose was evident, a night after a very fatiguing day of wine and strange incitements. The night gave him a momentary nobility, like an adolescent who has been imprisoned and, on regaining his freedom, feels that life has been changed into a crossroads. His vitality collapses and he is forced to choose a road. Motionless, he isn't aware of the revealing expression on his face, the swaying of the bird trapped in the glowing circle of the street light.

Foción locked the gate again and walked towards the redhaired youth. The carved bone handle of the Chinese toothbrush poked out of his pocket like a comb. Foción's feet walked on rocky sand; he was a fish wrapped in sandpaper; he felt a squeaking, a harshness, the sound of footlight projectors, the demand of the cigarette end that begins to burn the flesh; and suddenly he was inside a circle bristling with well-scrubbed light, inside a circle that was aflame, with the redhaired youth.

"Will you sell me that Chinese brush? I need it," Foción said to him.

The redhead, master of the flaming circle, didn't answer. The street light, with a fatal jump, hands pointed down, seized Foción's words and transferred them to the youth's freshly whitewashed back.

"Aren't you cold? It's late, you don't have any protection with that open shirt, you're going to freeze."

The youth didn't even try to pretend he wasn't interested in those questions. He refused to admit that there was someone else within the Luciferine circle; his was a hieratic indifference; he didn't hear or see the one who had burst into the light cast by the street lamp.

"Perhaps the cold has made you mute," Foción suggested, "like those polar explorers who think they've lost their voices and have to decipher the steam that comes out of their mouths to understand one another. But you wouldn't even let a person try to read the steam that might come out of your mouth." Foción tried to give what he was saying the tone of a weird joke, feeling his way in the dark, but what he provoked was a look of pent-up hatred that raked the path of the lamp light. The body had not moved but the hatred had turned his eyes' green into the topaz of a coyote prowling in the electrified night.

That was when—Foción already felt defeated in his quest—he staked everything on one card.

"I live near here, if you want to come along we can uncork a Felipe II, which will provide the timely service of thawing the night out."

After proffering that invitation Foción made a half turn and headed home. Not too surprised, he knew instantly that his daring play had won. The redhaired youth was getting up and following him, hardly with the joy of a dog playing with his own shadow, but rather, silent as a cat.

On one side of Foción's house there was a drive leading to a two-story wing; the car was kept on the ground floor, and above it Foción had set up his study, where he slept when he got home late and didn't want to awaken his parents, or when his family was on a trip, so as not to feel the coldness of the empty house, the echoes of the absent ones, or when he wanted to talk to someone without being disturbed.

He climbed the iron stairway to the second floor, which had only one large room, with full bookshelves on three of its walls. On his desk he kept a small bronze statue of Narcissus, a Greek vase with a naked ephebe practicing some tunes on the flute; and there was the wise old child Lao-tse, who had written his book on the dictates of the silent heaven, and was riding a buffalo toward the west, laughing like a creature being reborn in his reclamation of the mist. When anyone visited, as if to display his character in the animism of the objects that surrounded him, Foción would point to the Narcissus and say, "The image of the image, nothingness." He would point to the apprenticeship of the Greek adolescent and say, "The desire that knows, knowledge through the continuous thread of the sound of hell." Then he would give a small pat to the rump of Lao-tse's buffalo, and say, "The egg hatches in empty space." Foción performed like that on days when he felt like teasing, providing a little scenery for those friends who, as he liked to say, needed a first act with a lot of people bumping into one another.

Foción turned on the cold light and the room filled with a fragmented opalescence. He asked the redhaired youth to sit down while he poured drinks. He moved off a few paces, turning his back on the little devil. He crossed the room again and stared at the malignant one. Putting a hand on his hair, which seemed to be almost blue-black, with the color of honey spreading, the yellow of a resting hawk. He kept looking at him, but the strange visitor lowered his head and in that cold eternity their look never met, the tempting shadow and the caressing shadow cast onto a circular course.

As Foción poured the cognac, he looked at the wall. He saw a strange animal. The redhead had raised his hand with a knife; on the wall, its shadow left the finality of death with a plaster arm; the uplifted knife penetrated it like a wedge, shattering it while the silence remained intact, and the knife began to feed on the whitewash.

"I already knew," Foción heard, "that today I was going to have to kill someone. It was very clear to me. Ever since the day my mother stopped caressing my forehead, because I ran away from home, I've seen nothing but perverts and miserable people. Starting with the swine who came to my town to organize baseball teams, the one who brought me to Havana, he didn't waste any time showing me his filthy intentions, in spite of constantly repeating that he was my friend and wanted to help me. Then I slept in parks, on the Malecón wall, I sold newspapers, and always those evil ones coming up from behind you, telling you how much they want to help you; after a while I wouldn't answer them any more and I'd just stare at them, but no matter, the invitation always came, always to do the same thing, 'spend a little time together.' And the one you saw me with in the café, with his suitcase full of ancient coins and medals, he was really an idiot, but a pervert nonetheless. He called me Arcangeli, after somebody, according to him, who once killed a German savant. I felt like killing him, but I just grabbed the Chinese brush and ran out so as not to kill him. But I knew this day wouldn't end without my killing someone. Why don't they go out after women, these vampires, perverts, degenerates? And then you, under the lamppost, starting up a conversation so you could begin the same story I already know by heart. Posing as good people."

While Foción listened to the redhaired youth, he was taking off his undershirt, and as he lifted it to pull it over his head he thought that this might be the chance for the knife to strike him, but that dark moment passed without incident. "What do you care," the voice went on, "if I'm cold, if I'm hungry, since all of you have got one devouring fixed idea that makes you more ravenous than wolves? You hunger for a food you don't know, but one that you need more than bread."

Foción turned his glance on the redhead's eyes. "Take a good look at me," Foción said and pointed with his forefinger at the black circle he had drawn around his left breast. The redhaired youth was forced to listen, knife raised, to what Foción was slowly telling him.

"You say that today is the day you chose to kill someone, and by chance today is the day I chose to kill myself. You can see I've got this black circle drawn so that I wouldn't miss the target. So the two of us coincided. I don't know how my parents will be, friendship is beginning not to matter a damn to me, I have to spend most of the day with a bunch of idiots just to have a few pesetas in my pocket. The sum of days is becoming unbearable for me, my will is no longer prepared to pursue any goal, and my energy, if I have any and if it can be called energy, gets all wound up in itself inextricably, it can barely get beyond my skin. The only joy you've given me in this long night is that now I know there is someone who can satisfy me, that you are ready to kill me." Foción finished proffering his invitation and began to advance toward the redhaired youth. The fragment of skin inside the black circle bulged whitely. "Kill me," he urged, "put your arm in the place of my own, do me that favor, don't let it be me who has to kill myself."

The youth was slowly lowering his knife. Foción turned to fetch the glasses of cognac. Turning back, he saw that the malignant one was getting undressed and was putting the knife under the two pillows. In two gulps he extinguished the heat of the cognac through the narrow mouth of the balloon. The glass in his hands was as somber as the knife. The youth turned his back. Foción didn't put out the lamp on the night table but instead dragged the table over to the foot of the bed and bent the lampshade away to avoid the light's excessive curiosity.

At six o'clock in the morning Foción was up, quietly shutting his two suitcases. In his stocking feet he crept step by step down the stairs, sitting on the last one to put on his shoes. He made for the street corner; now the lamp light, diluted in the broad clearness of dawn, had lost its presage of vultures. Its useless brilliance had something of a playing card with a bent corner, its play between the two serpents intertwined by the tail was now an overturned glass of water.

The sudden squeal of the brakes sent flying the morning-water-straightened hair of those in the car coming to fetch Foción, who, on the corner waiting very anxiously, ran to keep the car from stopping, so that the noise of the engine starting again would not wake up the sleeping redhaired youth. All that could be heard was the sound of the door, among the heads of hair straightened by the orderly comb before the morning mirror, excepting Foción's, whose comb had failed to distribute what the withdrawal of the knife had failed to unify.

The redhead rolled over to free himself from the sheet, his eyes growing larger as Foción's absence became clear. He gave a jump to get out of bed and another into his shirt and pants. The leap caused the Chinese brush to fall. He stamped on it over and over and bit his lips at the same time. Then he went to the shoe rack, which held three or four old pairs of shoes, began to spit on them, then pulled back his foreskin and with his whole glans exposed urinated into the old shoes. They were the shoes Foción wore to work in the garden. The hide, irrigated by the urine's ammonium carbamate, cracked, breaking the small earthen agglomerations and giving back the cold and unused seed it received.

Then he went to the writing table. One of his hands moved toward the Narcissus to grab it. The other sank into the neck of the vase with the apprentice flautist. He kicked the lamp on the night table without putting it out. In fury he went down the iron staircase, then he gave a long look to the two floors, moving his head up and down with disdain. He hurled the Narcissus to the top of the stairs, causing it to roll down the expanse of the steps. It came to rest in the cat's plate, licked in the succulence of some recent ganoid repast, the cheap enamel shine reflecting the image of the one who wanted to be the other at the same time. The Greek musician remained intact on his own shard while his flute broke off. His Orphism polished the surface of the branches and multiplied their pairs of leaves.

"Who's there?" shouted the early-rising old man next door. Dogs could be heard, barking and howling. The redhaired youth stooped in his retreat to hide his body behind the wall's vines. Inside Foción's room, the buffalo, ridden by the master of the void and the silent heaven, once more perceived himself lord of the mountain and the lake and the west, goaded on by the sound of dangling plates of jade, the sonorous stone.

# Part Seven
Masculine Landscapes

*American Literature 1840 to 1933*

# 26. "Serene Friendship Land"

## American Homoerotic Texts (1840–1908)

### LOVING COMRADES

In the 1840s America could claim only a small number of texts that even vaguely suggested anything about male-male love: guarded hints in Emerson's or Thoreau's unpublished journals and in one or two of Thoreau's poems, some intimations of same-sex desire (manifest in his admiration of handsome sailors) in Melville's early novels, a few poems by Bayard Taylor. In 1855 Whitman's *Leaves of Grass* opened infinite possibilities—though few other writers were willing to explore this territory, being content to hint at sexual dubiety in novels like Theodore Winthrop's *John Brent* and *Cecil Dreeme* from the 1860s, or in the allusively homoerotic subtext of Taylor's novel *Joseph and His Friend*, or in the south sea island exoticism and largely all-male eroticism of Charles Warren Stoddard's *South Sea Idyls* and his *The Island of Tranquil Delights* from the 1870s. In 1889 appeared *A Marriage Below Zero* by "Alan Dale," in which a young woman must contend with another man for the love of her husband. The book is resolutely homophobic and introduces the homosexual villain into American fiction. The end of the century saw Whitman's vision of a city of lovers clouded by the growth of homophobia fostered by the legal and medical construction of homosexuality as a criminal practice, a psychological abnormality, and as a danger to society. However, at the same time, the influence of sympathetic European discussions of homosexuality led "Professor X" to send a powerful manifesto defending homosexuality to Ellis and Symonds in England. In 1906 Edward Prime-Stevenson, writing under the pseudonym of "Xavier Mayne," produced *Imre*, the first openly homosexual American novel, and in 1908 Mayne published *The Intersexes*, the first American exploration of homosexuality in history, literature, and social life.

Further Reading

Roger Austen, *Playing the Game: The Homosexual Novel in America* (New York: Bobbs-Merrill, 1977); Walt Whitman, *Leaves of Grass*, ed. Sculley Bradley and Harold W. Blodgett (New York: Norton, 1973); Byrne R. S. Fone, *Masculine Landscapes: Walt Whitman and the Homoerotic Text* (Carbondale: Southern Illinois University Press, 1992); Byrne R. S. Fone, *A Road To Stonewall: Homosexuality and Homophobia in English and American Literature, 1750–1969* (New York: Macmillan/Twayne, 1995); Jonathan Ned Katz, *Gay American History* (New York: Thomas Y. Crowell, 1976), and *Gay/Lesbian Almanac* (New York: Harper and Row, 1983); James Levin, *The Gay Novel in America* (New York: Garland, 1991); Robert K. Martin, *The Homosexual Tradition in American Poetry* (Austin and London: University of Texas Press, 1979); Michael Moon, *Disseminating Whitman: Revision and Corporeality in "Leaves of Grass"* (Cambridge and London: Harvard University Press, 1991); Walt Whitman, *Daybooks and Notebooks*, ed. William White (New York: New York University Press, 1978), 3 vols. (hereafter, *DBN*); Gregory Woods, *Articulate Flesh: Male Homoeroticism in Modern Poetry* (New Haven and

London: Yale University Press, 1987); Thomas Yingling, *Hart Crane and the Homosexual Text* (Chicago and London: University of Chicago Press, 1990).

## Henry David Thoreau (1817–1862)

In 1838 Thoreau defined friendship erotically in a poem called "Friendship," in which lovers who are intended "to be mates" are like "two sturdy oaks" whose "roots are intertwined insep'rably." He argues in a witty association of love with the known homoeroticism of Greece that "love cannot speak . . . without the help of Greek,/or any other tongue." In a journal entry in January 1840 he explores the associations of Greece with homoeroticism: "History tells us of Orestes and Pylades, Damon and Pythias, but why should not we put to shame those old reserved worthies by a community of such." His community of "such" lovers—forecasting Whitman's cities of lovers—flourishes in an erotic Arcadia: "Constantly, as it were through a remote skylight, I have glimpses of a serene friendship land," a land where "I would live henceforth with some gentle soul such a life as may be conceived, double for variety, single for harmony,—two, only that we might admire at our oneness,—one, because indivisible. Such a community to be a pledge of holy living. How could aught unworthy be admitted into our society?"

Thoreau was not willing to reveal his desire in any place but his private journals where the secret of his friendship can be safely inscribed. Whether Thoreau's yearning sexual mythmaking reveals any more than desire can not be certainly ascertained. It was written in private and in isolation, in what may well have been, in part at least, a self-imposed sexual exile. Thoreau sought finally, instead of caresses, the chaste solitude of Walden. Before that, however, in "Sympathy," he described a relationship with a " gentle boy" that suggests an intimacy located in deep emotion.

*Sympathy (1839)*

Lately, alas, I knew a gentle boy,
    Whose features all were cast in Virtue's mould,
As one she had designed for Beauty's toy,
    But after manned him for her own strong-hold.

On every side he open was as day,
    That you might see no lack of strength within,
For walls and ports do only serve alway
    For a pretence to feebleness and sin.

Say not that Caesar was victorious,
    With toil and strife who stormed the House of Fame,
In other sense this youth was glorious,
    Himself a kingdom wheresoe'er he came.

No strength went out to get him victory,
    When all was income of its own accord;
For where he went none other was to see,
    But all were parcel of their noble lord.

He forayed like the subtile haze of summer,
    That stilly shows fresh landscapes to our eyes,
And revolutions works without a murmur,
    Or rustling of a leaf beneath the skies.

So was I taken unawares by this,
    I quite forgot my homage to confess;
Yet now am forced to know, though hard it is,
    I might have loved him had I loved him less.

Each moment as we nearer drew to each
    A stern respect withheld us farther yet,
So that we seemed beyond each other's reach,
    And less acquainted than when first we met.

We two were one while we did sympathize,
    So could we not the simplest bargain drive—
And what avails it now that we are wise,
    If absence doth this doubleness contrive?

Eternity may not the chance repeat,
    But I must tread my single way alone,
In sad remembrance that we once did meet
    And know that bliss irrevocably gone.

The spheres henceforth my elegy shall sing,
    For elegy has other subject none
Each strain of music in my ears shall ring
    Knell of departure from that other one.

Make haste and celebrate my tragedy;
    With fitting strain resound ye woods and fields;
Sorrow is dearer in such case to me
    Than all the joys other occasion yields.

Is't then too late the damage to repair?
    Distance, forsooth, from my weak grasp hath reft
The empty husk, and clutched the useless tare,
    But in my hands the wheat and kernel left.

If I but love that virtue which he is,
    Though it be scented in the morning air,
Still shall we be truest acquaintances
    Nor mortals know a sympathy more rare.

## Ralph Waldo Emerson (1803–1882)

In a journal written in 1834, Ralph Waldo Emerson, that essential American philosopher, wondered about "the disturbance, the self-discord which young men feel" and concluded that it "is a most important crisis" (Katz 1976:461). In the same journal he speculates about a similar feeling he intuits in Shakespeare's sonnets, speculating on Shakespeare's "unknown self." He observes "how remarkable in every way are Shakespeare's sonnets. Those addressed to a beautiful young man seem to show some singular friendship amounting to a passion." Perhaps his curiosity about "singular friendship" led him to write in 1841 a poem and an essay both called "Friendship" in which he provided America with a New World version of an ancient genre, defining friendship in masculine terms for a nation that celebrated manhood and eroticizing it: friendship is a "delicious torment," for "we seek our friend . . . with an adulterous passion which would appropriate him to ourselves." Emerson will not "treat friendship daintily, but with roughest courage." Like Whitman, Emerson prefers "the company of ploughboys and tin-peddlers to . . . silken and perfumed amity" and attempts to separate friendship from any imputation of effeminacy. Through friendship course "the fountains of my hidden life." If Emerson gave America a basic text that defined friendship, he revealed no more about his personal involvement with the eroticism that he seemed to find in there, but he did give his disciple Walt Whitman an authoritative text on which to base his grand and all-encompassing construction of erotic comradeship.

*Friendship* (1841)

A ruddy drop of manly blood
The surging sea outweighs,
The world uncertain comes and goes;
The lover rooted stays.
I fancied he was fled, —
And, after many a year,
Glowed unexhausted kindliness,
Like daily sunrise there.
My careful heart was free again,
O friend, my bosom said,
Through thee alone the sky is arched,
Through thee the rose is red;
All things through thee take nobler form,
And look beyond the earth,
The mill-round of our fate appears
A sun-path in thy worth.
Me too thy nobleness has taught
To master my despair;
The fountains of my hidden life
Are through thy friendship fair.

FROM "FRIENDSHIP" (1841)

We have a great deal more kindness than is ever spoken. Maugre all the selfishness that chills like east winds the world, the whole human family is bathed with an element of love like a fine ether. How many persons we meet in houses, —whom we scarcely speak to, whom yet we honor, and who honor us! How many we see in the street, or sit with in church, whom, though silently, we warmly rejoice to be with! Read the language of these wandering eye-beams. The heart knoweth.

The effect of the indulgence of this human affection is a certain cordial exhilaration. In poetry and in common speech the emotions of benevolence and complacency which are felt towards others are likened to the material effects of fire; so swift, or much more swift, more active, more cheering, are these fine inward irradiations. From the highest degree of passionate love to the lowest degree of goodwill, they make the sweetness of life. . . .

What is so pleasant as these jets of affection which make a young world for me again? What so delicious as a just and firm encounter of two, in a thought, in a feeling? How beautiful, on their approach to this beating heart, the steps and forms of the gifted and the true! The moment we indulge our affections, the earth is metamorphosed; there is no winter and no night; all tragedies, all ennuis vanish —all duties even; nothing fills the proceeding eternity but the forms all radiant of beloved persons. Let the soul be assured that somewhere in the universe it should rejoin its friend, and it would be content and cheerful alone for a thousand years. . . .

I confess to an extreme tenderness of nature on this point. It is almost dangerous to me to "crush the sweet poison of misused wine" of the affections. A new person is to me a great event and hinders me from sleep. I have often had fine fancies about persons which have given me delicious hours; but the joy ends in the day; it yields no fruit. Thought is not born of it; my action is very little modified. I must feel pride in my friend's accomplishments as if they were mine, and a property in his virtues. I feel as warmly when he is praised, as the lover when he hears applause of his engaged maiden. We over-estimate the conscience of our friend. His goodness seems better than our goodness, his nature finer, his temptations less. Every thing that is his—his name, his form, his dress, books and instruments—fancy enhances. Our own thought sounds new and larger from his mouth. . . .

Is it not that the soul puts forth friends as the tree puts forth leaves and presently, by the germination of new buds, extrudes the old leaf? The law of nature is alternation for evermore. Each electrical state superinduces the opposite. The soul environs itself with friends that it may enter into grander self-acquaintance or solitude; and it goes alone for a season that it may exalt its conversation or society. This method betrays itself along the whole history of our personal relations. The instinct of affection revives the hope of union with our mates, and the returning sense of insulation recalls us from the chase. Thus every man passes his life in the search after friendship, and if should record his true sentiment, he might write a letter like this to each new candidate for his love:

Dear Friend,
   If I was sure of thee, sure of thy capacity, sure to match my mood with thine, I should never think again of trifles in relation to thy comings and goings. I not very wise; my moods are quite attainable, and I respect thy

genius; it is me as yet unfathomed; yet dare I not presume in thee a perfect intelligence of me, and so thou art to me a delicious torment. Thine ever, or never.

.... I do not wish to treat friendships daintily, but with roughest courage. When they are real, they are not glass threads or frostwork, but the solidest thing we know. For now, after so many ages of experience, what do we know of nature or of ourselves? Not one step has man taken toward the solution of the problem of his destiny. In one condemnation of folly stand the whole universe of men. But the sweet sincerity of joy and peace which I draw from this alliance with my brother's soul is the nut itself whereof all nature and all thought is but the husk and shell. ...

There are two elements that go to the composition of friendship, each so sovereign that I can detect no superiority in either, no reason why either should be first named. One is truth. A friend is a person with whom I may be sincere. Before him I may think aloud. I am arrived at last in the presence of a man so real and equal that I may drop even those undermost garments of dissimulation, courtesy, and second thought, which men never put off, and may deal with him with the simplicity and wholeness with which one chemical atom meets another. Sincerity is the luxury allowed, like diadems and authority, only to the highest ranks; that being permitted to speak truth, as having none above it to court or conform unto. Every man alone is sincere. At the entrance of a second person, hypocrisy begins. We parry and fend the approach of our fellow-man by compliments, by gossip, by amusements, by affairs. We cover up our thought from him under a hundred folds. ... Almost every man we meet requires some civility—requires to be humored; he has some fame, some talent, some whim of religion or philanthropy in his head that is not to be questioned, and which spoils all conversation with him. But a friend is a sane man who exercises not my ingenuity, but me. My friend gives me entertainment without requiring any stipulation on my part. A friend therefore is a sort of paradox in nature. I who alone am, I who see nothing in nature whose existence I can affirm with equal evidence to my own, behold now the semblance of my being, in all its height, variety and curiosity, reiterated in a foreign form; so that a friend may well be reckoned the masterpiece of nature.

The other element of friendship is tenderness. We are holden to men by every sort of tie, by blood, by pride, by fear, by hope, by lucre, by lust, by hate, by admiration, by every circumstance and badge and trifle—but we can scarce believe that so much character can subsist in another as to draw us by love. Can another be so blessed and we so pure that we can offer him tenderness? When a man becomes dear to me I have touched the goal of fortune. ... I hate the prostitution of the name of friendship to signify modish and worldly alliances. I much prefer the company of ploughboys and tin-peddlers to the silken and perfumed amity which celebrates its days of encounter by a frivolous display, by rides in a curricle and dinners at the best taverns. ...

Friendship requires that rare mean betwixt likeness and unlikeness that piques each with the presence of power and of consent in the other party. Let me be alone to the end of the world, rather than that my friend should over step, by a word or a look, his real sympathy. I am equally balked by antagonism and by compliance. Let him not cease an instant to be himself. The only joy I have in his being mine, is that the not mine is mine. I hate, where I looked for a manly furtherance or at least a manly resistance, to find a mush of concession. Better be a nettle in the side of your friend than his echo. The condition which high friendship demands is ability to do without it. . . .

Friendship demands a religious treatment. We talk of choosing our friends, but friends are self-selected. Reverence is a great part of it. Treat your friend as a spectacle. Of course he has merits that are not yours, and that you cannot honor if you must needs hold him close to your person. Stand aside; give those merits room; let them mount and expand. Are you the friend of your friend's buttons, or of his thought? To a great heart he will be a stranger in a thousand particulars, that he may come near in the holiest ground. Leave it to girls and boys to regard a friend as property, and to suck a short and all-confounding pleasure, instead of the noblest benefit.

. . . . Why should we desecrate noble and beautiful souls by intruding on them? Why insist on rash personal relations with your friend? Why go to his house, or know his mother and brother and sisters? Why be visited by him at your own? Are these things material to our covenant? Leave this touching and clawing. Let him be to me a spirit. A message, a thought, a sincerity, a glance from him, I want, but not news, nor pottage. I can get politics and chat and neighborly conveniences from cheaper companions. Should not the society of my friend be to me poetic, pure, universal and great as nature itself?

## Walt Whitman (1819–1892)

Whitman called *Leaves of Grass* a "language experiment." His experiment included an attempt to create a language that would adequately express his feelings about comradeship and manly love and define its place in the new American literature. In a journal Whitman was writing before he published *Leaves of Grass* in 1855, he speculated upon the relationship between language and manly friendship: "the young men of these states, with a . . . a passionate fondness for their friends . . . have remarkably few words . . . for the friendly sentiments." He defines masculine words as "all words that have arisen out of the qualities of mastership . . . words to identify . . . an erect, sweet lusty, body, without taint" (*DBN* 3:739–40). These words, he is confident, will one day appear: "Men like me . . . will gradually get to be more and more numerous . . . then the words will follow" (*DBN* 3:745).

In a "Letter to Ralph Waldo Emerson" in 1856 Whitman prophesied that if masculine words can be found, they will form a language that will make American texts "strong, limber . . . full of ease, of passionate friendliness" (Bradley, 741). The texts he intends to displace are "without manhood or power" in which only "geldings" are depicted. In these flaccid texts weak words are like the unaroused penis, "its flesh is soft; it shows less and less of the indefinable hard something that is Nature." The literature he deplores is created and read by "helpless dandies" who "can neither fight, work, shoot, ride, run, command" but who are instead "devout, some quite insane, castrated," who can be seen "smirking and skipping along . . . no one behaving . . . out of any natural and manly tastes of his own." These dandies produce literature in which the "lives of men and women . . . appear to have been . . . of the neuter gender . . . if the dresses were changed the men might easily pass for women, and the women for men." This literature makes "unmentionable" the "manhood of a man . . . sex, womanhood, maternity, desires, lusty animations, organs, acts" (Bradley, 736–39). This attack against literary dandyism and prudery is infused with the same clichés that were developing as definitions of the effeminate homosexual. His use of "insane" and "castrated" predicts medical perceptions of homosexuals, while "smirking and skipping" reflect homophobic clichés of effeminacy. But Whitman is not devaluing homosexuality, only effeminacy. Indeed he is employing the very terms that demonize same-sex love in order to redefine the literary basis he feels is necessary to valorize it. In an oblique reference to same-sex affection he insists that there must be a language which can apply to "men not fond of women, women not fond of men" (*DBN* 3:746). Whitman's opposition to effeminacy in literature is an attempt to recover for American literature a masculine, antiaristocratic, democratic style that he sites within a homoerotic aesthetic. As he observed in another notebook, "what is lacking in literature can . . . only be generated from the seminal freshness and propulsion of new masculine persons" (*DBN* 1:223).

In 1856 Whitman argued that literature should repeal the "filthy law" that enforces silence about sex. Such open texts will allow the expression of free sexuality among both women and men. If sex is admitted to literature women will "approach the day of organic equality with men" (Bradley 739). By "organic" he means quite simply an equality in the use of the genital organs. The greatest triumph of organic equality will be that men will be able to celebrate their own "organic" liberation, for without organic equality between men and women "men cannot have organic equality among themselves." Whitman knew that the construction of sexualities depends as much on language as on sexual acts, and so because there is no eroticized and defining language there is no literature to express the reality of manly friendship. What is "important in poems" is to name "in specific words" the "main matter" that "is so far quite unexpressed in poems; but . . . the body is to be expressed and sex is." Sex, "avowed, empowered, unabashed" is that on which "all existence, all souls, all realization, all decency, all health, all that is worth being here for, all of women and of men, all beauty, all purity, all sweetness, all friendship, all strength, all life, all immortality depend" (Bradley 739–40). In that rush of language the subtle inclusion of "friendship" nestled tellingly between sweetness and strength should be noted, for like all the other terms of his list friendship also depends on sex.

The following selections from Whitman's poetry and prose include a selection from "Song of Myself" (1855) that focuses on the question of sexual awakening, and a larger selection of Calamus poems than is generally published in anthologies. Among these are the twelve "Live-Oak with Moss" poems from the 1860 Calamus poems, which are anthologized here for the first time in the order in which he wrote them. All the selections attempt to suggest his growing awareness that homosexuality—what he called the love of comrades—was not only a vital aspect of his own sexuality but the informing if not the central text of his art and the message of his role as a "teacher of athletes."

## Fierce Wrestler

### An Early Draft of "Song of Myself" (Sec. 28) (c. 1847[?])

Whitman kept notebooks in which he was constantly entering notes, memoranda, portions of poems that came to him, records of events, and lists of young men he encountered on the streets. In a notebook written perhaps as early as 1847, he entered an extensive draft of what would become section 28 of "Song of Myself." In this entry, far more explicit in fact than that which eventually derives from it in "Song of Myself" (1855, 1881), the imagery is violent and physically homoerotic, and the satisfactions of sexual reciprocity and the processes of sexual and aesthetic rejuvenation are the primary subjects. Whitman implies that the ultimate power of sexuality—and here, clearly, homosexuality—is as an instrument of spiritual power, an avenue through mystical ecstasy to a new life. Here he introduces the "Fierce Wrestler," a figure of raw phallic power and untamed original energy.

From *Notebook* ("albot Wilson")

One touch of a tug of me has unhaltered all my senses but
    feeling
That pleases the rest so, they have given up to it in
    submission
They are all emulous to swap themselves off for what it can
    do to them,
Every one must be a touch.—
Or else she will abdicate and nibble only at the edges of
    feeling .
They move caressingly up and down my body

[80] They leave themselves and come with bribes to
    whatever part of me touches.—
To my lips, to the palms of my hands, and whatever my
    hands hold.
Each brings the best she has,
For each is in love with touch.

[85; 81–84 cut out]

I do not wonder that one feeling now,
    does so much for me,
He is free of all the rest,—and swiftly begets offspring of
    them, better than dams.

A touch now reads me a library of knowledge in an instant,
    It smells for me the fragrance of wine and lemon-blows,
It tastes for me ripe strawberries and melons.

[86] It talks for me with a tongue of its own,
    It finds an ear wherever it rests or taps,
It brings the rest around it, and enjoy them[?] meanwhile
    and then they all stand on a headland and mock me
        The sentries have deserted every other part of me
They have all come to the headland to witness and assist
    against me.—
    They have left me helpless to the torrent of touch

[87] I am given up by traitors,
  I talk wildly I [?] am surely out of my head,
  I am myself the greatest traitor
  I went myself first to the headland

Unloose me touch you are taking the breath from my throat
Unbar your gates—you are too much for me.—

[88] Fierce Wrestler! do you keep your heaviest grip for the
      last?
Will you sting me most even at parting?
Will you struggle even at the threshold with spasms more
      delicious than all before?
Does it make you ache so to leave me?
Do you wish to show me that even what you did before was
      nothing to what you can do
Or have you and all the rest combined to see how much I
      can endure

[89] Pass as you will; take drops of my life if that is what
      you are after
Only pass to someone else, for I can contain you no longer.
  I held more than I thought
  I did not think I was big enough for so much exstasy
Or that touch could take it all out of me.

## LEAVES OF GRASS (1855)

When Walt Whitman's *Leaves of Grass* appeared in America in 1855, some moralists attacked his poems as sexually aberrant. A review by Rufus Griswold began with a general diatribe against writers who disregard "all the politeness and decencies of life," and inveighed against "the tendency of thought in these later years" that allows in texts "a degrading, beastly sensuality that is fast rotting the healthy core of all the social virtues." He continues: "In our allusion to this book, we have found it impossible to convey any, even the most faint idea of its style and contents, and of our disgust and detestation of them, without employing language that cannot be pleasing to ears polite; but it does seem that some one should, under circumstances like these, undertake a most disagreeable, yet stern duty. The records of crime show that many monsters have gone on in impunity, because the exposure of their vileness was attended with too great indelicacy. *Peccatum illud horribile, inter Christianos non nominandum.*" There can be no doubt about what he sees Whitman's poems to be and what he thinks it advocates when he employs the Latin legal description of sodomy—"the sin not to be named among Christians—" in his assessment of Whitman's work.

  Whitman published the first edition of *Leaves of Grass* in July 1855. The book contained a long prose preface and twelve untitled poems, the first of which would in later editions be titled "Song of Myself." In "Song of Myself" Whitman becomes "undisguised

and naked" in order to allow himself free space to confront and change the "forms of custom and the engrossing anxieties" of American sexual life, and to confront his own homosexual desire. The selections from "Song of Myself" below reprint the text of the first
(1855) edition and highlight that confrontation.

*From [Song of Myself] (1855)*

[1]
I celebrate myself,
And what I assume you shall assume,
For every atom belonging to me as good belongs to you.

I loafe and invite my soul,
I lean and loafe at my ease . . . . observing a spear of
    summer grass.

[2]
Houses and rooms are full of perfumes . . . . the shelves
    are crowded with perfumes,
I breathe the fragrance myself, and know it and like it,
The distillation would intoxicate me also, but I shall not let it.

The atmosphere is not a perfume . . . . it has no taste of
    the distillation . . . . it is odorless,
It is for my mouth forever . . . . I am in love with it,
I will go to the bank by the wood and become undisguised
    and naked,
I am mad for it to be in contact with me.

The smoke of my own breath,
Echoes, ripples, and buzzed whispers . . . . loveroot,
    silkthread, crotch and vine,
My respiration and inspiration . . . . the beating of my heart
    . . . . the passing of blood and air through my lungs,
The sniff of green leaves and dry leaves, and of the shore
    and darkcolored sea-rocks, and of hay in the barn,
The sound of the belched words of my voice . . . . words
    loosed to the eddies of the wind,
A few light kisses . . . . a few embraces . . . . a reaching
    around of arms,
The play of shine and shade on the trees as the supple
    boughs wag,
The delight alone or in the rush of the streets, or along the
    fields and hillsides,
The feeling of health . . . . the full-noon trill . . . . the
    song of me rising from bed and meeting the sun.

Have you reckoned a thousand acres much? Have you
    reckoned the earth much?
Have you practiced so long to learn to read?
Have you felt so proud to get at the meaning of poems?

Stop this day and night with me and you shall possess the
    origin of all poems,
You shall possess the good of the earth and sun . . . . there
    are millions of suns left,
You shall no longer take things at second or third hand
    . . . . nor look through the eyes of the dead . . . .
    nor feed on the spectres in books,
You shall not look through my eyes either, nor take things
    from me,
You shall listen to all sides and filter them from yourself.

[3]
I have heard what the talkers were talking . . . . the talk of
    the beginning and the end,
But I do not talk of the beginning or the end.

There was never any more inception than there is now,
Nor any more youth or age than there is now;
And will never be any more perfection than there is now,
Nor any more heaven or hell than there is now.

Urge and urge and urge,
Always the procreant urge of the world.

Out of the dimness opposite equals advance . . . . Always
    substance and increase,
Always a knit of identity . . . . always distinction . . . .
    always a breed of life.

To elaborate is no avail . . . . Learned and unlearned feel
    that it is so.

Sure as the most certain sure . . . . plumb in the uprights,
    well entretied, braced in the beams,
Stout as a horse, affectionate, haughty, electrical,
I and this mystery here we stand.

Clear and sweet is my soul . . . . and clear and sweet is all
    that is not my soul.

Lack one lacks both . . . . and the unseen is proved by the seen,
Till that becomes unseen and receives proof in its turn.

Showing the best and dividing it from the worst, age vexes
    age,
Knowing the perfect fitness and equanimity of things, while
    they discuss I am silent, and go bathe and admire myself.

Welcome is every organ and attribute of me, and of any man
    hearty and clean,
Not an inch nor a particle of an inch is vile, and none shall
    be less familiar than the rest.
I am satisfied . . . . I see, dance, laugh, sing;
As God comes a loving bedfellow and sleeps at my side all
    night and close on the peep of the day,
And leaves for me baskets covered with white towels bulging
    the house with their plenty,
Shall I postpone my acceptation and realization and scream
    at my eyes,
That they turn from gazing after and down the road,
And forthwith cipher and show me to a cent,
Exactly the contents of one, and exactly the contents of two,
    and which is ahead?

[4]
Trippers and askers surround me,
People I meet . . . . the effect upon me of my early life
    . . . . of the ward and city I live in . . . . of the nation,
The latest news . . . . discoveries, inventions, societies
    . . . . authors old and new,
My dinner, dress, associates, looks, business, compliments,
    dues,
The real or fancied indifference of some man or woman I
    love,
The sickness of one of my folks—or of myself . . . . or ill-
    doing . . . . or loss or lack of money . . . . or
    depressions or exaltations,
They come to me days and nights and go from me again,
But they are not the Me myself.

Apart from the pulling and hauling stands what I am,
Stands amused, complacent, compassionating, idle, unitary,
Looks down, is erect, bends an arm on an impalpable certain
    rest,
Looks with its sidecurved head curious what will come next,
Both in and out of the game, and watching and wondering at it.

Backward I see in my own days where I sweated through fog
    with linguists and contenders,
I have no mockings or arguments . . . . I witness and wait.

[5]
I believe in you my soul . . . . the other I am must not abase
    itself to you,
And you must not be abased to the other.

Loafe with me on the grass . . . . loose the stop from your
    throat,
Not words, not music or rhyme I want . . . . not custom or
    lecture, not even the best,
Only the lull I like, the hum of your valved voice.

I mind how we lay in June, such a transparent summer
    morning;
You settled your head athwart my hips and gently turned
    over upon me
And parted the shirt from my bosom-bone, and plunged your
    tongue to my barestript heart,
And reached till you felt my beard, and reached till you held
    my feet.

Swiftly arose and spread around me the peace and joy and
    knowledge that pass all the art and argument of the
    earth;
And I know that the hand of God is the elderhand of my
    own,
And I know that the spirit of God is the eldest brother of my
    own,
And that all the men ever born are also my brothers . . . .
    and the women my sisters and lovers,
And that a kelson of the creation is love;
And limitless are leaves stiff or drooping in the fields,
And brown ants in the little wells beneath them,
And mossy scabs of the wormfence, and heaped stones, and
    elder and mullen and pokeweed.
. . . . . . . . . . . . . . . . . . . . . . . . . . . . .

[11]
Twenty-eight young men bathe by the shore,
Twenty-eight young men, and all so friendly,
Twenty-eight years of womanly life, and all so lonesome.

She owns the fine house by the rise of the bank,
She hides handsome and richly drest aft the blinds of the
    window.

Which of the young men does she like the best?
Ah the homeliest of them is beautiful to her.

Where are you off to, lady? for I see you,
You splash in the water there, yet stay stock still in your room.

Dancing and laughing along the beach came the twenty-
   ninth bather,
The rest did not see her, but she saw them and loved them.

The beards of the young men glistened with wet, it ran from
   their long hair,
Little streams passed all over their bodies.

An unseen hand also passed over their bodies,
It descended tremblingly from their temples and ribs.

The young men float on their backs, their white bellies
   swell to the sun . . . . they do not ask who seizes fast to them,
They do not know who puffs and declines with pendant and
   bending arch,
They do not think whom they souse with spray.

. . . . . . . . . . . . . . . . . . . . . . . . . . . . .

[19]
This is the meal pleasantly set . . . . this is the meat and
   drink for natural hunger,
It is for the wicked just the same as the righteous . . . . I
   make appointments with all,
I will not have a single person slighted or left away,
The keptwoman and sponger and thief are hereby invited
   . . . . the heavy-lipped slave is invited . . . . the
   venerealee is invited,
There shall be no difference between them and the rest.

This is the press of a bashful hand . . . . this is the float
   and odor of hair,
This is the touch of my lips to yours . . . . this is the
   murmur of yearning,
This is the far-off depth and height reflecting my own face,
This is the thoughtful merge of myself and the outlet again.

Do you guess I have some intricate purpose?
Well I have . . . . for the April rain has, and the mica on
   the side of a rock has.

Do you take it I would astonish?
Does the daylight astonish? or the early redstart twittering
   through the woods?
Do I astonish more than they?

This hour I tell things in confidence,
I might not tell everybody but I will tell you.

[20]
Who goes there! hankering, gross, mystical, nude?
How is it I extract strength from the beef I eat?

What is a man anyhow? What am I? and what are you?
All I mark as my own you shall offset it with your own,
Else it were time lost listening to me.

I do not snivel that snivel the world over,
That months are vacuums and the ground but wallow
      and filth,
That life is a suck and a sell, and nothing remains at the end
      but threadbare crape and tears.

Whimpering and truckling fold with powders for invalids
      . . . . conformity goes to the fourth-removed,
I cock my hat as I please indoors or out.

Shall I pray? Shall I venerate and be ceremonious?

I have pried through the strata and analyzed to a hair,
And counselled with doctors and calculated close and found
      no sweeter fat than sticks to my own bones.

In all people I see myself, none more and not one a
      barleycorn less,
And the good or bad I say of myself I say of them.

And I know I am solid and sound,
To me the converging objects of the universe perpetually flow,
All are written to me, and I must get what the writing means.

And I know I am deathless,
I know this orbit of mine cannot be swept by a carpenter's
      compass,
I know I shall not pass like a child's carlacue cut with a
      burnt stick at night.

I know I am august,
I do not trouble my spirit to vindicate itself or be understood,
I see that the elementary laws never apologize,
I reckon I behave no prouder than the level I plant my
      house by after all.

I exist as I am, that is enough,
If no other in the world be aware I sit content,
And if each and all be aware I sit content.

One world is aware, and by far the largest to me, and that is
    myself,
And whether I come to my own today or in ten thousand or
    ten million years,
I can cheerfully take it now, or with equal cheerfulness I
    can wait.

My foothold is tenoned and mortised in granite,
I laugh at what you call dissolution,
And I know the amplitude of time.

[21]
I am the poet of the body,
And I am the poet of the soul.

The pleasures of heaven are with me, and the pains of hell
    are with me,
The first I graft and increase upon myself . . . . the latter I
    translate into a new tongue.

I am the poet of the woman the same as the man,
And I say it is as great to be a woman as to be a man,
And I say there is nothing greater than the mother of men.

I chant a new chant of dilation or pride,
We have had ducking and deprecating about enough,
I show that size is only development.

Have you outstript the rest? Are you the President?
It is a trifle . . . . they will more than arrive there every
    one, and still pass on.

I am he that walks with the tender and growing night;
I call to the earth and sea half-held by the night.

Press close barebosomed night! Press close magnetic
    nourishing night!
Night of south winds! Night of the large few stars!
Still nodding night! Mad naked summer night!

Smile O voluptuous coolbreathed earth!
Earth of the slumbering and liquid trees!

Earth of departed sunset! Earth of the mountains misty-topt!
Earth of the vitreous pour of the full moon just tinged
    with blue!
Earth of shine and dark mottling the tide of the river!
Earth of the limpid gray of clouds brighter and clearer for
    my sake!
Far-swooping elbowed earth! Rich apple-blossomed earth!
Smile, for your lover comes!

Prodigal! you have given me love! . . . . therefore I to you
    give love!
O unspeakable passionate love!

Thruster holding me tight and that I hold tight!
We hurt each other as the bridegroom and the bride hurt
    each other.

[22]
You sea! I resign myself to you also . . . . I guess what
    you mean,
I behold from the beach your crooked inviting fingers,
I believe you refuse to go back without feeling of me;
We must have a turn together . . . . I undress . . . . hurry
    me out of sight of the land,
Cushion me soft . . . . rock me in billowy drowse,
Dash me with amorous wet . . . . I can repay you.

Sea of stretched ground-swells!
Sea breathing broad and convulsive breaths!
Sea of the brine of life! Sea of unshovelled and always-ready
    graves!
Howler and scooper of storms! Capricious and dainty sea!
I am integral with you . . . . I too am of one phase and of
    all phases.

Partaker of influx and efflux . . . . extoller of hate and
    conciliation,
Extoller of amies and those that sleep in each others' arms.

I am he attesting sympathy;
Shall I make my list of things in the house and skip the
    house that supports them?

I am the poet of commonsense and of the demonstrable and
    of immortality;
And am not the poet of goodness only . . . . I do not
    decline to be the poet of wickedness also.

Washes and razors for foofoos . . . . for me freckles and a
    bristling beard.
What blurt is it about virtue and about vice?
Evil propels me, and reform of evil propels me . . . . I stand
    indifferent,
My gait is no faultfinder's or rejecter's gait,
I moisten the roots of all that has grown.

. . . . . . . . . . . . . . . . . . . . . . . . . . . . . .

[24]
Walt Whitman, an American, one of the roughs, a kosmos,
Disorderly fleshy and sensual . . . . eating drinking and
    breeding,
No sentimentalist . . . . no stander above men and women or
    apart from them . . . . no more modest than immodest.

Unscrew the locks from the doors!
Unscrew the doors themselves from their jambs!

Whoever degrades another degrades me and whatever
    is done or said returns at last to me,
And whatever I do or say I also return.

Through me the afflatus surging and surging . . . . through
    me the current and index.

I speak the password primeval . . . . I give the sign of
    democracy;
By God! I will accept nothing which all cannot have their
    counterpart of on the same terms.

Through me many long dumb voices,
Voices of the interminable generations of slaves,
Voices of prostitutes and of deformed persons,
Voices of the diseased and despairing, and of thieves and
    dwarfs,
Voices of cycles of preparation and accretion,
And of the threads that connect the stars—and of wombs,
    and of the fatherstuff,
And of the rights of them the others are down upon,
Of the trivial and flat and foolish and despised,
Of fog in the ail and beetles rolling balls of dung.

Through me forbidden voices,
Voices of sexes and lusts . . . . voices veiled, and I remove
    the veil,
Voices indecent by me clarified and transfigured.

I do not press my finger across my mouth,
I keep as delicate around the bowels as around the head and    heart,
Copulation is no more rank to me than death is.


I believe in the flesh and the appetites,
Seeing hearing and feeling are miracles, and each part and
    tag of me is a miracle.


Divine am I inside and out, and I make holy whatever I
    touch or am touched from;
The scent of these arm-pits is aroma finer than prayer,
This head is more than churches or bibles or creeds.


If I worship any particular thing it shall be some of the
    spread of my body;
Translucent mould of me it shall be you,
Shaded ledges and rests, firm masculine coulter, it shall be you,
Whatever goes to the tilth of me it shall be you,
You my rich blood, your milky stream pale strippings of my life;
Breast that presses against other breasts it shall be you,
My brain it shall be your occult convolutions,
Root of washed sweet-flag, timorous pond-snipe, nest of
    guarded duplicate eggs, it shall be you,
Mixed tussled hay of head and beard and brawn it shall be you,
Trickling sap of maple, fibre of manly wheat, it shall be you;
Sun so generous it shall be you,
Vapors lighting and shading my face it shall be you,
You sweaty brooks and dews it shall be you,
Winds whose soft-tickling genitals rub against me it shall
    be you,
Broad muscular fields, branches of liveoak, loving lounger
    in my winding paths, it shall be you,
Hands I have taken, face I have kissed, mortal I have ever
    touched, it shall be you.


I dote on myself . . . . there is that lot of me, and all so
    luscious,
Each moment and whatever happens thrills me with joy.


I cannot tell how my ankles bend . . . . nor whence the cause of my faintest wish,
Nor the cause of the friendship I emit . . . . nor the cause
    of the friendship I take again.


To walk up my stoop is unaccountable . . . . I pause to
    consider if it really be,
That I eat and drink is spectacle enough for the great
    authors and schools,

A morning-glory at my window satisfies me more than the
    metaphysics of books.

To behold the daybreak!
The little light fades the immense and diaphanous shadows,
The air tastes good to my palate.

Hefts of the moving world at innocent gambols, silently
    rising, freshly exuding,
Scooting obliquely high and low.

Something I cannot see puts upward libidinous prongs,
Seas of bright juice suffuse heaven.

The earth by the sky staid with . . . . the daily close of
    their junction,
The heaved challenge from the east that moment over my
    head,
The mocking taunt, See then whether you shall be master!
. . . . . . . . . . . . . . . . . . . . . . . . . . . . .

[27]
To be in any form, what is that?
If nothing lay more developed the quahaug and its callous
    shell were enough.

Mine is no callous shell,
I have instant conductors all over me whether I pass or stop,
They seize every object and lead it harmlessly through me.

I merely stir, press, feel with my fingers, and am happy,
To touch my person to some one else's is about as much as I
    can stand.

[28]
Is this then a touch? . . . . quivering me to a new identity,
Flames and ether making a rush for my veins,
Treacherous tip of me reaching and crowding to help them,
My flesh and blood playing out lightning, to strike what is
    hardly different from myself,
On all sides prurient provokers stiffening my limbs,
Straining the udder of my heart for its withheld drip,
Behaving licentious toward me, taking no denial,
Depriving me of my best as for a purpose,
Unbuttoning my clothes and holding me by the bare waist,
Deluding my confusion with the calm of the sunlight and
    pasture fields,

Immodestly sliding the fellow-senses away,
They bribed to swap off with touch, and go and graze at the
    edges of me,
No consideration, no regard for my draining strength or my
    anger,
Fetching the rest of the herd around to enjoy them awhile,
Then all uniting to stand on a headland and worry me.

The sentries desert every other part of me,
They have left me helpless to a red marauder,
They all come to the headland to witness and assist against me.

I am given up by traitors;
I talk wildly . . . . I have lost my wits . . . . I and nobody
    else am the greatest traitor,
I went myself first to the headland . . . . my own hands
    carried me there.

You villain touch! what are you doing? . . . . my breath
    is tight in its throat;
Unclench your floodgates! you are too much for me.

[29]
Blind loving wrestling touch! Sheathed hooded sharptoothed
    touch!
Did it make you ache so leaving me?

Parting tracked by arriving . . . . perpetual payment of the
    perpetual loan,
Rich showering rain, and recompense richer afterward.

Sprouts take and accumulate . . . . stand by the curb
    prolific and vital,
Landscapes projected masculine full-sized and golden.
. . . . . . . . . . . . . . . . . . . . . . . . . . . .

[46]
I know I have the best of time and space—and that I was
    never measured, and never will be measured.

I tramp a perpetual journey,
My signs are a rain-proof coat and good shoes and a staff
    cut from the woods;
No friend of mine takes his ease in my chair,
I have no chair, nor church nor philosophy;
I lead no man to a dinner-table or library or exchange,
But each man and each woman of you I lead upon a knoll,

My left hand hooks you round the waist,
My right hand points to landscapes of continents, and a
    plain public road.

Not I, not any one else can travel that road for you,
You must travel it for yourself.

It is not far . . . . it is within reach,
Perhaps you have been on it since you were born, and did
    not know,
Perhaps it is every where on water and on land.

Shoulder your duds, and I will mine, and let us hasten forth;
Wonderful cities and free nations we shall fetch as we go.

If you tire, give me both burdens, and rest the chuff of your
    hand on my hip,
And in due time you shall repay the same service to me;
For after we start we never lie by again.

This day before dawn I ascended a hill and looked at the
    crowded heaven,
And I said to my spirit, When we become the enfolders of
    those orbs and the pleasure and knowledge of every
    thing in them, shall we be filled and satisfied then?
And my spirit said No, we level that lift to pass and
    continue beyond.

You are also asking me questions, and I hear you;
I answer that I cannot answer . . . . you must find out for
    yourself.

Sit awhile wayfarer,
Here are biscuits to eat and here is milk to drink,
But as soon as you sleep and renew yourself in sweet clothes
    I will certainly kiss you with my goodbye kiss and open
    the gate for your egress hence.

Long enough have you dreamed contemptible dreams,
Now I wash the gum from your eyes,
You must habit yourself to the dazzle of the light and of
    every moment of your life.
Long have you timidly waded, holding a plank by the shore,
Now I will you to be a bold swimmer,
To jump off in the midst of the sea, and rise again and nod
    to me and shout, and laughingly dash with your hair.

[47]
I am the teacher of athletes,
He that by me spreads a wider breast than my own proves
    the width of my own,
He most honors my style who learns under it to destroy the
    teacher.

The boy I love, the same becomes a man not through derived
    power but in his own right,
Wicked, rather than virtuous out of conformity or fear,
Fond of his sweetheart, relishing well his steak,
Unrequited love or a slight cutting him worse than a wound
    cuts,
First rate to ride, to fight, to hit the bull's eye, to sail a skiff,
    to sing a song or play on the banjo,
Preferring scars and faces pitted with smallpox over all
    latherers and those that keep out of the sun.

I teach straying from me, yet who can stray from me?
I follow you whoever you are from the present hour;
My words itch at your ears till you understand them.

I do not say these things for a dollar, or to fill up the time
    while I wait for a boat;
It is you talking just as much as myself . . . . I act as the
    tongue of you,
It was tied in your mouth . . . . in mine it begins to be loosened.
. . . . . . . . . . . . . . . . . . . . . . . . . . . .

[50]
There is that in me . . . . I do not know what it is . . . .
    but I know it is in me.

Wrenched and sweaty . . . calm and cool then my body
    becomes;
I sleep . . . . I sleep long.

I do not know it . . . . it is without name . . . . it is a
    word unsaid,
It is not in any dictionary or utterance or symbol.

Something it swings on more than the earth I swing on,
To it the creation is the friend whose embracing awakes me.

Perhaps I might tell more . . . . Outlines! I plead for my
    brothers and sisters.

Do you see O my brothers and sisters?
It is not chaos or death . . . . it is form and union and plan
 . . . . it is eternal life . . . . it is happiness.

[51]
The past and present wilt . . . . I have filled them and
 emptied them,
And proceed to fill my next fold of the future.

Listener up there! Here you . . . . what have you to confide
 to me?
Look in my face while I snuff the sidle of evening,
Talk honestly, for no one else hears you, and I stay only a
 minute longer.

Do I contradict myself?
Very well then . . . . I contradict myself;
I am large . . . . I contain multitudes.

I concentrate toward them that are nigh . . . . I wait on
 the door-slab.

Who has done his day's work and will soonest be through
 with his supper?
Who wishes to walk with me?

Will you speak before I am gone? Will you prove already
 too late?

[52]
The spotted hawk swoops by and accuses me . . . . he
 complains of my gab and my loitering.

I too am not a bit tamed . . . . I too am untranslatable,
I sound my barbaric yawp over the roofs of the world.

The last scud of day holds back for me,
It flings my likeness after the rest and true as any on the
 shadowed wilds,
It coaxes me to the vapor and the dusk.

I depart as air . . . . I shake my white locks at the runaway
 sun,
I effuse my flesh in eddies and drift it in lacy jags.

I bequeath myself to the dirt to grow from the grass I love,

If you want me again look for me under your bootsoles.

You will hardly know who I am or what I mean,
But I shall be good health to you nevertheless,
And filter and fibre your blood.

Failing to fetch me at first keep encouraged,
Missing me one place search another,
I stop some where waiting for you

## NOTEBOOKS: "ADHESIVENESS"

In a notebook of 1855–56 Whitman wrote a note that he would later incorporate into *Leaves of Grass* (1856). In that notebook and later in a poem called "Poem of the Road "in 1856 and "Song of the Open Road" thereafter, he first mentions the new word he has chosen to mean manly love: *adhesiveness*. Whitman's deletions are in brackets.

### From *Notebook* (c. 1855–56)

Why be there men I meet, and [many] others I know, that while they are with me, the sunlight of Paradise [warms] expands my blood—that [if] I walk with an arm of theirs around my neck, my soul leaps and laughs . . . that when they leave me the pennants of my joy sink flat and lank in the deadest calm? . . . Some fisherman . . . . some carpenter . . . some driver . . . men, rough, not handsome, not accomplished, why do I know that the subtle chloroform of our spirits is affecting each other, and though we may [never meet] encounter not again, [we know feel that] we two have [pass] exchanged the right [mysterious] [unspoken] password [of the night], and [have] are thence free [entrance] comers to [each] the guarded tents of each other's [love] most interior love? (What is the [cause] meaning, any how, of my [love attachment] adhesiveness for toward others?—

What is the cause of theirs [love for] toward [for] me?)—(Am I loved by them boundlessly because my love for them is more boundless? (*DBN* 3:764–65)

## LEAVES OF GRASS (1856)

### "Organic Equality": From a letter from Whitman to Emerson (August 1856)

In a letter to Ralph Waldo Emerson that was included in the 1856 edition as a kind of preface, Whitman expatiated on the subject of sexual freedom in general, on the need for women to have "organic equality" with men—that is, to be sexually equal in their deployment of sexuality and sex organs—and daringly urged that men also need to have "organic equality among themselves," by which he meant a right to share sexuality and the use of the sex organs between men as well as between men and women. Finally he laments the absence of "manly friendship" in American literature.

A word remains to be said, as of one ever present, not yet permitted to be acknowledged, discarded or made dumb by literature, and the results apparent. To the lack of an avowed, empowered, unabashed development of sex, (the only salvation for the same,) and to the fact of speakers and writers fraudulently assuming as always dead what every one knows to be always alive, is attributable the remarkable non-personality and indistinctness of modern productions in books, art, talk; also that in the scanned lives of men and women most of them appear to have been for some time past of the neuter gender; and also the stinging fact that in orthodox society today, if the dresses were changed, the men might easily pass for women and the women for men.

Infidelism usurps most with foetid polite face; among the rest infidelism about sex. By silence or obedience the pens of savans, poets, historians, biographers, and the rest, have long connived at the filthy law, and books enslaved to it, that what makes the manhood of a man, that sex, womanhood, maternity, desires, lust, animations, organs, acts, are unmentionable and to be ashamed of, to be driven to skulk out of literature with whatever belongs to them. This filthy law has to be repealed—it stands in the way of great reforms. Of women just as much as men, it is the interest that there should not be infidelism about sex, but perfect faith. Women in These States approach the day of that organic equality with men without which, I see, men cannot have organic equality among themselves. This empty dish, gallantry, will then be filled with something. This tepid wash, this diluted deferential love, as in songs, fictions, and so forth, is enough to make a man vomit; as to manly friendship, everywhere observed in The States, there is not the first breath to be observed in print. I say that the body of a man or woman, the main matter, is so far quite unexpressed in poems, but that the body is to be expressed, and sex is.

## From "Poem of the Road" (1856; later, "Song of the Open Road")

In "Song of Myself" Whitman implicitly defined the word *adhesiveness* to express manly friendship: "the unfolding word of the ages . . . a word of the modern . . . a word en masse . . . a word of faith that never balks." This word is a "password primeval" and it allows him to speak in "forbidden voices," voices expressing sexual power that strip away veils and transgress the established boundaries of traditional power. In 1856 he announces the word in "Poem of the Road": "Here is adhesiveness, it is not previously fashioned, it is apropos" (LG Var1:230, l.91).[1] *Adhesiveness* was a term used in phrenology to imply nonsexual friendship. Whitman uses it differently. His use is not a borrowing for he insists it is "not previously fashion'd." It is a new word with a new meaning that signifies manly love. The word "is apropos" for it suggests daily experience and the unspoken sexual signs exchanged between strangers: "Do you know what it is, as you pass, to be loved by strangers?/Do you know the talk of those turning eye-balls?" This "talk" is the language of adhesiveness and only men like him are fluent in it.

Here is adhesiveness—it is not previously fashion'd
    —it is apropos;
Do you know what it is, as you pass, to be loved by
    strangers?

---

1. See Sculley Bradley, Harold W. Blodgett, Arthur Golden, and William White, eds., *Leaves of Grass: A Textual Variorum of the Printed Poems*, vol. 1, p. 230, line 91, in *The Collected Writings of Walt Whitman* (New York: New York University Press, 1980).

Do you know the talk of those turning eye-balls?

Here is the efflux of the Soul,
The efflux of the soul comes through beautiful gates of laws, provoking questions;
These yearnings, why are they? these thoughts in the darkness, why are they?
Why are there men and women that while they are nigh me, the sunlight
    expands my blood?
Why when they leave me do my pennants of joy sink flat and lank?
Why are there trees I never walk under but large and melodious thoughts
    descend upon me?
(I think they hang there winter and summer on those trees and always drop
    fruit as I pass;)
What is it I interchange so suddenly with strangers?
What with some driver, as I ride on the seat by his side?
What with some fisherman drawing his seine by the shore, as I walk by and pause?

### NOTEBOOKS: "LIVE-OAK WITH MOSS" (1859)

The "Calamus" sequence that appeared in the 1860 edition of *Leaves of Grass* consisted of forty-five numbered poems. Whitman's manuscripts for many of the Calamus selections have been preserved. The story of these manuscripts, together with a physical description of them, is thoroughly and fascinatingly told by Fredson Bowers in *Whitman's Manuscripts: "Leaves of Grass" (1860)* (Chicago: University of Chicago Press, 1955). Bowers discovered that twelve of the poems that would later appear in Calamus in 1860 were written earlier and included in a manuscript, each poem indicated by a Roman numeral, that Whitman titled "Live-Oak with Moss," and later "Calamus Leaves." These poems, slightly revised but radically reordered, were included among the forty-five in the Calamus section of the 1860 edition. Over the years Whitman revised the Calamus section and excluded V and VIII of the "Live-Oak" series from the final edition of his poems. The Calamus poems rarely appear in anthologies, and if they do then only those that tend to be innocent of homoerotic content are included (though complete texts of Calamus are of course available in collected editions of Whitman's poetry).

The "Live-Oak with Moss" sequence seems to tell a story of love found, love lost, and of loss accepted. To better follow this story, the sequence is printed below in the order and with the Roman numeral numbering of the poems as they appear in the manuscript "Live-Oak with Moss." When Whitman included them in the 1860 edition, he slightly revised them and distributed them out of sequence throughout the Calamus section. To identify the poems in later editions, both the number of the poem in the 1860 edition and the title Whitman gave to it in subsequent editions are affixed. The text is that of Whitman's pre-1860 manuscript, perhaps less finished, perhaps more personal, than the revised version of 1860 that Whitman wanted the world to read. Though the difference between the two texts is sometimes minor, yet the revisions are also sometimes telling, and a glance at a modern edition of Whitman's poems will show the nature of his revisions. For example, in number I the phrase "to seek my life long lover" was deleted in 1860, and in number III the phrase "the friend I love lay sleeping by my side" of the manuscript appears in 1860 as the more intimate if somewhat more anonymous revision "the one I love most lay sleeping by me under the same cover." The poems appear here in their original order for the first time in an anthology.

I [Calamus 14: *Not Heat Flames up and Consumes*]

Not the heat flames up and consumes,
Not the sea-waves hurry in and out,
Not the air, delicious and dry, the air of ripe summer,
    bears lightly along white down-balls of myriads of seeds,
    wafted, sailing gracefully, to drop where they may,
Not these—O none of these, more than the flames
    of me, consuming, burning for his love whom I love!
    O none, more than I, hurrying in and out;
Does the tide hurry, seeking something, and never
    give up?—O I, the same, to seek my life long lover;
O nor down balls, nor perfumes, nor the high
    rain-emitting clouds, are borne through the open
    air,
    more than my copious soul is borne through open
    air,
Wafted in all directions, for friendship, for love.—


II [Calamus 20: *I Saw in Louisiana a Live-Oak Growing*]

I saw in Louisiana a live-oak growing,
All alone stood it, and the moss hung down from the
    branches,
Without any companion it grew there glistening out joyous
    leaves of dark green,
And its look, rude, unbending, lusty, made me think
    of myself;
But I wondered how it could utter joyous leaves,
    standing alone there without its friend, its lover—
For I knew I could not,
And I plucked a twig with a certain number of
    leaves upon it, and twined around it a little moss,
And brought it away–and I have placed it in sight
    in my room,
It is not needed to remind me as of my
    friends,
(For I believe lately I think of little else than of
    them,)
Yet it remains to me a curious token, it makes me
    think of manly love;
For all that, and though the live-oak glistens there in
    Louisiana, solitary in a wide flat space,
Uttering joyous leaves all its life without a friend, a
    lover, near,
I know very well I could not.

### III [Calamus 11: When I Heard at the Close of the Day]

When I heard at the close of the day how I had
    been praised in the Capitol, still it was not
    a happy night for me that followed,
And else when I caroused—nor when my favorite plans were
    accomplished—was I really happy,
But the day when I rose at dawn from the bed of perfect
    health, electric, inhaling sweet breath
When I saw the full moon in the west grow pale and
    disappear in the morning light,
When I wandered alone over the beach, and undressing, bathed,
    laughing with the waters, and saw the sun rise,
And when I thought how my friend, my lover, was on
    his way coming, then O I was happy,
Each breath tasted sweeter—and all that day my food
    nourished me more—and the beautiful day passed well,
And the next came with equal joy—and with the next,
    at evening, came my friend,
And that night while all was still I heard the waters roll
    slowly continually up the shores,
I heard the hissing rustle of the liquid and sands, as directed
    to me, whispering to congratulate me,
For the friend I love lay sleeping by my side,[2]
In the stillness his face was inclined toward me, while the
 moon's clear beans shone
And his arm lay lightly over my breast—and that night I was happy.

### IV [Calamus 23: This Moment Yearning and Thoughtful]

This moment as I sit alone, yearning and pensive, it seems to me
    there are other men, in other lands, yearning and pensive.
It seems to me I can look over and behold them, in Germany, Italy,
    France, Spain—Or far away in China, India, or Russia—
    talking other dialects;
And it seems to me if I could know those men I should
    love them as I love men in my own lands,
It seems to me they are as wise, beautiful, benevolent, as any in my
    own lands;

2. An earlier version of these lines read
And that night O you happy
    waters, I heard you beating
the shores—But my heart
    beat happier than you—for
he I love is returned
    and sleeping by my side. . . .

O I think we should be brethren—
I think I should be happy with them.[3]


## V [Calamus 8: Long I Thought That Knowledge Alone Would Suffice]

Long I thought that knowledge alone would suffice me—O if I could
    but obtain knowledge!
Then the land of the Prairies engrossed me—
    the southern savannas, engrossed me—For them I would live-
    I would be their orator;
Then I met the examples of old and new heroes—I heard of warriors,
    sailors, and all dauntless persons—And it seemed to me I too
    had it in me to be as dauntless as any, and would be so;
And then to finish it all, it came to me to strike up the songs of the
    New World—And then I believed my life must be spent in singing;
But now take notice, Land of the prairies, Land of the south savannas,
    Ohio's land,
Take notice, you Kanuck woods—and you, Lake Huron—and all that
    with you roll toward Niagara—and you Niagara also,
And you, Californian mountains—That you each and all find some-
    body else that he be your singer of songs,
For I can be your singer of songs no longer—I have ceased to enjoy them.
    I have found him who loves me, as I him in perfect love,[4]
With the rest I dispense—I sever from all that I thought would suffice
    me, for it does not—it is now empty and tasteless to me,
I heed knowledge, and the grandeur of The States, and the example
    of heroes, no more,
I am indifferent to my own songs—I am to go with him I love,
    and he is to go with me,
It is to be enough for each of us that we are together—We never separate
    again .


## VI [Calamus 32: What Think You I Take My Pen in Hand?]

What think you I have taken my pen to record?
Not the battle-ship, perfect-model'd, majestic, that I saw today arrive in the offing
    under full sail,
Nor the splendors of the past day—nor the splendors of the night
    that envelops me—

3. In 1860 these lines became
O I know we should be brethren and lovers
O I know I should be happy with them.

4. In 1860 this line was revised to read
One who loves me is jealous of me,
and withdraws me from all but love.

Nor the glory and growth of the great city spread around me,
But the two men I saw to-day, on the pier,
    parting the parting of dear friends,
The one to remain hung on the other's neck and passionately kissed
    him—
While the one to depart, tightly prest the one to remain in his arms.


## VII [Calamus 10: Recorders Ages Hence]

You bards of ages hence! when you refer to me, mind not so much my
    poems,
Nor speak of me that I prophesied of The States, and led them the way
    of their glories;
But come, I will inform you who I was underneath that impassive exterior—I
    will tell you what to say of me:
Publish my name and hang up my picture as that of the tenderest lover,
The friend, the lover's portrait, of whom his friend, his lover, was
    fondest,
Who was not proud of his songs, but of the measureless ocean of love
    within him—and freely poured it forth,
Who often walked lonesome walks, thinking of his dearest friends, his
    lovers,
Who pensive, away from one he loved, often lay sleepless and dissatisfied
    at night,
Who, dreading lest the one he loved might after all be indifferent to him,
    felt the sick feeling—O sick! Sick![5]
Whose happiest days were those, far away, through fields, in woods, on hills,
    he and another, wandering hand in hand, they twain, apart from
    other men,
Who ever, as he sauntered the streets, curved with his arm the manly shoulder of
    his friend—while the curving arm of his friend rested upon him also.


## VIII [Calamus 9: Hours Continuing Long][6]

Hours continuing long, sore and heavy-hearted,
Hours of the dusk, when I withdraw to a lonesome and unfrequented spot, seat-
    ing myself, leaning my face in my hands;
Hours sleepless, deep in the night, when I go forth, speeding swiftly the country
    roads, or through the city streets, or pacing miles and miles, stifling plaintive
    cries;

5. In 1860 Whitman revised this line to read: "Who knew too well the sick, sick dread lest the
one he loved might secretly be indifferent to him." The last line, in 1860, was revised to the
more innocent "curved with his arm the shoulder of his friend—while the arm of his friend
rested upon him also."

6. This intense and revealing poem was published only in the 1860 edition and rejected from
all later editions.

Hours discouraged, distracted,—For he, the one I cannot content myself without—soon I saw him content himself without me;

Hours when I am forgotten—(O weeks and months are passing, but I
believe I am never to forget!)

Sullen and suffering hours—(I am ashamed—but it is useless—I am
what I am;)

Hours of torment—I wonder if other men ever have the like, out
of the like feelings?

Is there even one other like me—distracted—his friend, his lover, lost
to him?

Is he too as I am now? Does he still rise in the morning, dejected,
thinking who is lost to him? and at night, awaking, think who is lost?

Does he too harbor his friendship silent and endless? Harbor his anguish
and passion?

Does some stray reminder, or the casual mention of a name, bring the
fit back upon him, taciturn and deprest?

Does he see himself reflected in me? In these hours, does he see the face
of his hours reflected?

### IX [Calamus 34: I Dreamed in a Dream]

I dreamed in a dream of a city where all men were like brothers,

O I saw them tenderly love each other—I often saw them , in numbers, walking
hand in hand;

I dreamed that was the city of robust friends—Nothing was greater there than
manly love—it led the rest,

It was seen in every hour in the actions of the men of that city , and in all their
looks and words.—7

### X [Calamus 43: O You Whom I Often and Silently Come]

O you whom I often and silently come where you are, that I may be
with you,

As I walk by your side, or sit near, or remain in the same room with you,

Little you know the subtle electric fire that for your sake is
playing within me.

7. Whitman substantially rewrote this poem for the 1860 edition:

I dreamed in dream I saw a city invincible to the attacks of the whole
of the rest of the earth,

I dreamed that was the new City of Friends,

Nothing was greater there than the quality of robust love—it led the
rest,

It was seen every hour in the actions of the men of that city,

And in all their looks and words.

## XI [*Calamus 36: Earth My Likeness*]

Earth!
Though you look so impassive, ample and spheric there,
I now suspect that is not all;
I now suspect there is something terrible in you, ready to break forth;
For an athlete loves me—and I him—
But toward him, there is something fierce and terrible in me,
I dare not tell it in words—not even in these songs.

## XII [*Calamus 42: To A Western Boy*]

To the young man, many things to absorb, to engraft, to develop,
    I teach, that he be my eleve [student],
But if through him speed not the blood of friendship,
    hot and red—
If he be not silently selected by lovers, and do not silently select lovers
Of what use were it for him to seek to become eleve of mine?

## LEAVES OF GRASS (1860)

In the late 1850s Whitman was busy writing poems for a third edition of *Leaves of Grass*.
He had written a manuscript version of a long poem entitled "Premonition" that would
appear in the 1860 edition as "Proto-Leaf" and in later editions as "Starting from
Paumonok." The poem is a lengthy chant that intends to create a program for a new
America. In "Proto-Leaf," which introduced the third edition, he sings a "song of companionship . . . a new ideal of manly friendship" to be enunciated in the "new evangel-
poem of lovers and comrades" (Bowers 1955:13). Here "adhesiveness" is described, to a
comrade, "as a "pensive aching to be together" (Bowers, 34–35). "Adhesiveness" becomes
now the "word to clear one's path ahead endlessly."

From "Proto-Leaf"

21

. . . . I will put in my poems, that with you is heroism,
    upon land and sea—And I will report all heroism from an Ameri-
    can point of view;
And sexual organs and acts! do you concentrate in me—For I am de-
    termined to tell you with courageous clear voice, to prove you
    illustrious.

22

I will sing the song of companionship,
    I will show what alone must compact These,
I believe These are to found their own ideal of manly love, indicating
    it in me;

I will therefore let flame from me the burning fires that were threaten-
ing to consume me,
I will lift what has too long kept down those smouldering fires,
I will give them complete abandonment,
I will write the evangel-poem of comrades and of love,
(For who but I should understand love, with all its sorrow and joy?
And who but I should be the poet of comrades?)

64

O my comrade!
O you and me at last—and us two only;
O power, liberty, eternity at last!
O to be relieved of distinctions! to make as much of vices as virtues!
O to level occupations and the sexes! O to bring all to common
ground! O adhesiveness!
O the pensive aching to be together—you know not why, and I know
not why.

65

o a word to clear one's path ahead endlessly!
O something extatic and undemonstrable! O music wild!
O now I triumph—and you shall also;
O hand in hand—O wholesome pleasure—O one more desirer and
lover,
O haste, firm holding—haste, haste on, with me.

## From CALAMUS (1860)

The first Calamus poem, "In Paths Untrodden," was in fact one of the last to be written. Whitman completed it shortly before he took the 1860 edition to the publisher. This poem sums up the results of his investigations of homosexual desire. After the publication of the Calamus poems, Whitman would never again produce so extensive a collection of homoerotic texts.

In a twentieth-century phrase this poem records what we now call "coming out." Whitman rejects the exhibited life that he sees as being opposed to the hidden life in which he finds the love of comrades. The exhibited life has long-established "standards" (laws and prohibitions) as well as "pleasures" (accepted forms of sexual desire) and, most of all, "conformities" (a code of majority social and sexual conduct) that he has for too long unquestioningly followed. He is aware of the impelling need to seek a new world and a new life where the new standards will be founded upon the love of comrades. He is aware that the desires and the standards he wishes to publish cannot yet safely be announced. Thus he has journeyed to the hidden pond where his doctrine can be fully be expressed "by myself, away from the clank of the world." Society not only forbids his acts but even his words, and so he has sought a "secluded spot" where "I can respond as I would not dare elsewhere." This is the most profound of Whitman's definitions of homosexuality, for in it he invokes one of the dominant themes of homoerotic literature, namely, that homosexual desire is not merely a sexual component of the individual but a profound psychic and spiritual situation that defines and controls the entire self.

In the Calamus poems Whitman now has found the strength to "unbare my breast," "sound myself and love," and "utter the cry of friends" (Calamus 2). In the course of the poems he asks numbers of important questions about himself and homosexuality: "I wonder if other men ever have the like, out of the like feelings?" "Is there even one other like me?" He wonders too if there are "other men in other lands, yearning and thoughtful." He alludes to a sexual community wherein he can catch the "frequent and swift flash of eyes offering me love" (Calamus 18). He intimates in Calamus 41 that there is a spiritual and mystical bond between men like himself: "I perceive one picking me out by secret and divine signs." In 1876 Whitman argued that the importance of the Calamus sequence "resides in its Political significance," for it is by the "fervent, accepted development of Comradeship, the beautiful and sane affection of man for man, latent in all young fellows . . . and what goes indirectly and directly along with it, that the United States of the future, (I cannot too often repeat,) are to be most effectually welded together, intercalated, anneal'd into a Living Union" (Bradley, 753). The "sane" affection of man for man and what goes directly or indirectly along with it is the cure for the "insane" and castrated effeminacy of texts and society, and what "goes directly and indirectly along with it" is the sexual expression of affection. The text is that of Whitman's authorized version of 1891–92.

## [CALAMUS 1]

In paths untrodden,
In the growth by the margin of pond waters,
Escaped from the life that exhibits itself,
From all the standards hitherto publish'd—
    from the pleasures, profits, conformities,
Which too long I was offering to feed my Soul;
Clear to me now standards not yet publish'd—
    clear to me that my Soul,
That the Soul of the man I speak for
    rejoices in comrades;
Here, by myself, away from the clank of the world,
Tallying and talked to here by tongues aromatic,
No longer abash'd—for in this secluded spot I can
    respond as I would not dare elsewhere,
Strong upon me the life that does not exhibit itself,
    yet contains all the rest,
Resolved to sing no songs to-day but those of manly
    attachment,
Projecting them along that substantial life,
Bequeathing, hence, types of athletic love,
Afternoon, this delicious Ninth Month, in my forty-
    first year,[8]

8. This would have been September 1859.

I proceed, for all who are, or have been young
    men,
To tell the secret of my nights and days,
To celebrate the need of comrades.


## [CALAMUS 3]

*Whoever You are Holding Me Now in Hand*

Whoever you are holding me now in hand,
Without one thing all will be useless,
I give you fair warning before you attempt me further,
I am not what you supposed, but far different.

Who is he that would become my follower?
Who would sign himself a candidate for my affections?

The way is suspicious, the result uncertain, perhaps destructive,
You would have to give up all else, I alone would expect to be your sole and
    exclusive standard,
Your novitiate would even then be long and exhausting,
The whole past theory of your life and all conformity to the lives around you
    would have to be abandon'd,
Therefore release me now before troubling yourself any further, let go your
    hand from my shoulders,
Put me down and depart on your way.

Or else by stealth in some wood for trial,
Or back of a rock in the open air,
(For in any roof'd room of a house I emerge not, nor in company,
And in libraries I lie as one dumb, a gawk, or unborn, or dead,)
But just possibly with you on a high hill, first watching lest any person for
    miles around approach unawares,
Or possibly with you sailing at sea, or on the beach of the sea or some quiet
    island,
Here to put your lips upon mine I permit you,
With the comrade's long-dwelling kiss or the new husband's kiss,
For I am the new husband and I am the comrade.

Or if you will, thrusting me beneath your clothing,
Where I may feel the throbs of your heart or rest upon your hip,
Carry me when you go forth over land or sea;
For thus merely touching you is enough, is best,
And thus touching you would I silently sleep and be carried eternally.

But these leaves conning you con at peril,
For these leaves and me you will not understand,

They will elude you at first and still more afterward, I will certainly elude you,
Even while you should think you had unquestionably caught me, behold!
Already you see I have escaped from you.

For it is not for what I have put into it that I have written this book,
Nor is it by reading it you will acquire it,
Nor do those know me best who admire me and vauntingly praise me,
Nor will the candidates for my love (unless at most a very few) prove
    victorious,
Nor will my poems do good only, they will do just as much evil, perhaps more,
For all is useless without that which you may guess at many times and not hit,
    that which I hinted at;
Therefore release me and depart on your way.


## [CALAMUS 6]

*Not Heaving from My Ribb'd Breast Only*

Not heaving from my ribb'd breast only,
Not in sighs at night in rage dissatisfied with myself,
Not in those long-drawn, ill-supprest sighs,
Not in many an oath and promise broken,
Not in my wilful and savage soul's volition,
Not in the subtle nourishment of the air,
Not in this beating and pounding at my temples and wrists,
Not in the curious systole and diastole within which will one day cease,
Not in many a hungry wish told to the skies only,
Not in cries, laughter, defiances, thrown from me when alone far in the wilds,
Not in husky pantings through clinch'd teeth,
Not in sounded and resounded words, chattering words, echoes, dead words,
Not in the murmurs of my dreams while I sleep,
Nor the other murmurs of these incredible dreams of every day,
Nor in the limbs and senses of my body that take you and dismiss you continually—
not there,
Not in any or all of them O adhesiveness! O pulse of my life!
Need I that you exist and show yourself any more than in these songs.


## [CALAMUS 7]

*Of the Terrible Doubt of Appearances*

Of the terrible doubt of appearances,
Of the uncertainty after all, that we may be deluded,
That may-be reliance and hope are but speculations after all,
That may-be identity beyond the grave is a beautiful fable only,
May-be the things I perceive, the animals, plants, men, hills, shining and
    flowing waters,

The skies of day and night, colors, densities, forms, may-be these are (as doubtless they are) only apparitions, and the real something has yet to be
  known,
(How often they dart out of themselves as if to confound me and mock me!
How often I think neither I know, nor any man knows, aught of them,)
May-be seeming to me what they are (as doubtless they indeed but seem) as
  from my present point of view, and might prove (as of course they
  would) nought of what they appear, or nought anyhow, from entirely
  changed points of view;
To me these and the like of these are curiously answer'd by my lovers, my
  dear friends,
When he whom I love travels with me or sits a long while holding me by
  the hand,
When the subtle air, the impalpable, the sense that words and reason hold
  not, surround us and pervade us,
Then I am charged with untold and untellable wisdom, I am silent, I require
  nothing further,
I cannot answer the question of appearances or that of identity beyond the
  grave,
But I walk or sit indifferent, I am satisfied,
He ahold of my hand has completely satisfied me.

## [CALAMUS 18]

*City of Orgies*

City of orgies, walks and joys,
City whom that I have lived and sung in your midst will one day make you
  illustrious,
Not the pageants of you, not your shifting tableaus, your spectacles, repay me
  Not the interminable rows of your houses, nor the ships at the wharves,
Nor the processions in the streets, nor the bright windows with goods in them,
Nor to converse with learn'd persons, or bear my share in the soiree or feast;
Not those, but as I pass O Manhattan, your frequent and swift flash of eyes
  offering me love,
Offering response to my own—these repay me,
Lovers, continual lovers, only repay me.

## [CALAMUS 24]

*I Hear It Was Charged against Me*

I hear it was charged against me that I sought to destroy institutions,
But really I am neither for nor against institutions,
(What indeed have I in common with them? or what with the destruction
  of them?)
Only I will establish in the Mannahatta and in every city of these States inland
  and seaboard,

And in the fields and woods, and above every keel little or large that dents
    the water,
Without edifices or rules or trustees or any argument,
The institution of the dear love of comrades.

## [CALAMUS 41]

*Among the Multitude*

Among the men and women the multitude,
I perceive one picking me out by secret and divine signs,
Acknowledging none else, not parent, wife, husband, brother, child, any
nearer than I am,
Some are baffled, but that one is not—that one knows me.

Ah lover and perfect equal,
I meant that you should discover me so by faint indirections,
And I when I meet you mean to discover you by the like in you.

## [CALAMUS 44]

*Here the Frailest Leaves of Me*[9]

Here the frailest leaves of me, and yet my strongest lasting,
Here I shade, and hide my thoughts, I myself do not expose them,
And yet they expose me more than all my other poems.

### LEAVES OF GRASS (1866)

Though he was never again to write poems of such unabashed homoeroticism as
Calamus, his civil war sequence *Drum-Taps* expresses not only his tender love for young
men but his compassionate view of the toll that the war had taken on America. In one of
these poems, "Vigil Strange . . ." Whitman wrote the finest brief elegy in American poetry.

From *Drum-Taps*

*Vigil Strange I Kept on the Field One Night*

Vigil strange I kept on the field one night;
When you my son and my comrade dropt at my side that day,
One look I but gave which your dear eyes return'd with a
    look I shall never forget,
One touch of your hand to mine O boy, reach'd up as you
    lay on the ground,
Then onward I sped in the battle, the even-contested battle,
Till late in the night reliev'd to the place at last again I made
    my way,
Found you in death so cold dear comrade, found your body

9. This poem was next to last in the 1860 (first) publication of *Calamus* and had a different first
line ("Here my last words, the most baffling,"].

son of responding kisses, (never again on earth
   responding,)
Bared your face in the starlight, curious the scene, cool blew
   the moderate night-wind
Long there and then in vigil I stood, dimly around me the
   battle-field spreading,
Vigil wondrous and vigil sweet there in the fragrant silent
   night,
But not a tear fell, not even a long-drawn sigh, long, long I
   gazed,
Then on the earth partially reclining sat by your side leaning
   my chin in my hands,
Passing sweet hours, immortal and mystic hours with you
   dearest comrade—not a tear, not a word,
Vigil of silence, love and death, vigil for you my son and my
   soldier,
As onward silently stars aloft, eastward new ones upward stole,
Vigil final for you brave boy, (I could not save you, swift
   was your death,
I faithfully loved you and cared for you living, I think we
   shall surely meet again,)
Till at latest lingering of the night, indeed just as the dawn
   appear'd,
My comrade I wrapt in his blanket, envelop'd well his form,
Folded the blanket well, tucking it carefully over head and
   carefully under feet,
And there and then and bathed by the rising sun, my son in
   his grave, in his rude-dug grave I deposited,
Ending my vigil strange with that, vigil of night and battle-
   field dim,
Vigil for boy of responding kisses, (never again on earth
   responding,)
Vigil for comrade swiftly slain, vigil I never forget, how as
   day brighten'd,
I rose from the chill ground and folded my soldier well in
   his blanket,
And buried him where he fell.


*O Tan-Faced Prairie Boy*

O tan-faced prairie-boy,
Before you came to camp came many a welcome gift,
Praises and presents came and nourishing food, till at last
   among the recruits,
You came, taciturn, with nothing to give—we but look'd on each other,
When lo! more than all the gifts of the world you gave me.

## As I Lay With My Head in Your Lap Camerado

As I lay with my head in your lap camerado,
The confession I made I resume, what I said to you and the
    open air I resume,
I know I am restless and make others so,
I know my words are weapons full of danger, full of death,
For I confront peace, security, and all the settled laws, to
    unsettle them,
I am more resolute because all have denied me than I could
    ever have been had all accepted me,
I heed not and have never heeded either experience,
    cautions, majorities, nor ridicule,
And the threat of what is call'd hell is little or nothing to
    me,
And the lure of what is call'd heaven is little or nothing to
    me;
Dear camerado! I confess I have urged you onward with me,
    and still urge you, without the least idea what is our
    destination,
Or whether we shall be victorious, or utterly quell'd and
    defeated.


## LEAVES OF GRASS (1867)

To the 1867 (second) edition of *Calamus* Walt Whitman added the following poem.


## [CALAMUS 5]

### [Come, I will make the continent indissoluble]

Come, I will make the continent indissoluble,
I will make the most splendid race the sun ever shone upon,
I will make divine magnetic lands,
    With the love of comrades,
    With the life-long love of comrades.

I will plant companionship thick as trees along all the rivers of America, and
    along the shores of the great lakes, and all over the prairies,
    I will make inseparable cities with their arms about each other's necks,
    By the love of comrades,
    By the manly love of comrades.

For you these from me, O Democracy, to serve you ma femme!
For you, for you I am trilling these songs.

## From "Democratic Vistas" (1870)

It may be that out of the Civil War came Whitman's final and political interpretation of the significance of homosexual desire to the nation. His vision appears as a footnote to "Democratic Vistas," and again as a brief but telling comment in the Centenial Edition (1876) of *Leaves of Grass*.

It is to the development, identification, and general prevalence of that fervid comradeship, (the adhesive love, at least rivaling the amative love hitherto possessing imaginative literature, if not going beyond it,) that I look for the counterbalance and offset of our materialistic and vulgar American democracy, and for the spiritualization thereof. . . . I confidently expect a time when there will be seen running, like a half-hid warp through all the myriad audible and visible worldly interests of America, threads of manly friendship, fond and loving, pure and sweet, strong and life-long, carried to degrees hitherto unknown—not only giving tone to individual character, and making it unprecedentedly emotional, muscular, heroic, and refined, but having the deepest relation to general politics. I say democracy infers such loving comradeship, as its most inevitable twin or counterpart, without which it would be incomplete, in vain, and incapable of perpetuating itself. (*PW* 2:414–15)[10]

## From Preface to *Leaves of Grass* (1876)

Whitman again notes, as he did in "Democratic Vistas," that the health of American Democracy depends on the "sane affection" of man for man, but stresses also that "what goes directly and indirectly with it"—by which he means sexual experience—must be accepted also.

Besides, important as they are in my purpose as emotional expressions for humanity, the special meaning of the Calamus cluster of LEAVES OF GRASS, (and more or less running through that book, and cropping out in Drum-Taps,) mainly resides in its Political significance. In my opinion it is by a fervent, accepted , development of Comradeship, the beautiful and sane affection of man for man, latent in all the young fellows, North and South, East and West—it is by this, I say, and by what goes directly and indirectly along with it, that the United States of the future, (I cannot too often repeat,) are to be most effectually welded together, intercalated, anneal'd into a Living Union.

Then, for enclosing clue of all, it is imperatively and ever to be borne in mind that LEAVES OF GRASS entire is not to be construed as an intellectual or scholastic effort or Poem mainly, but more as a radical utterance out of the abysms of the Soul, the Emotions and the Physique—an utterance adjusted to, perhaps born of, Democracy and Modern Science, and in its very nature regardless of the old conventions, and, under the great Laws, following only its own impulses.

10. Walt Whitman, *Prose Works*, ed. Floyd Stovall. 2 vols. New York: New York University Press, 1964.

## Bayard Taylor (1825–1878)

In a letter to Walt Whitman in 1866, the American poet and novelist Bayard Taylor said that he found in *Leaves of Grass* what he "finds nowhere else in literature," that is, "that tender and noble love of man for man which once certainly existed but now almost seems to have gone out of the experience of the race." Long before that, however, Taylor was fascinated by this noble love. In "Hylas" (1850), he seems to be quite sure in what direction desire lies. When the water nymphs, taken by his beauty, pull Hylas into their sacred pond, Hercules, mad with grief, leaves the Argonauts to search for him, repeatedly calling his name in vain. Theocritus had told the story, and Taylor uses it as a literary exercise in homoerotic poetry. "Hylas" glows with an aura of intense eroticism, and as Taylor describes his slow disrobing, the florid diction does not conceal the erotic nature of the portrait. It is daring, desirous, and specifically sexual. No euphemism is present when Taylor looks hard at that intimated point where "downward the supple lines have less of softness." Taylor's gaze is as obsessively fixed upon Hylas' loins and thighs and upon the rising "pulse of power" that awakens to "springy fulness" and soon becomes "outswerving," dropping breathtakingly to Hylas' knee. To Whitman he would speak of "the awe and wonder and reverence and beauty of Life, as expressed in the human body, with the physical attraction and delight of mere contact which it inspires."

In his *Poems of the Orient* (1855) Taylor writes about similar if veiled desire. There Taylor constructs Greece as an erotic site. In "A Paean to the Dawn" he praises Greece as a place where "love was free, and free as air/The utterance of Passion." In Greece Taylor imagines an ideal figure that possessed a "perfect limb and perfect face" that "surpassed our best ideal . . . the Beautiful was real." The association of beauty, physical perfection, and Greece with the "true expression" of love in texts conflates homosexual passion with aesthetic principles. Indeed, Taylor insists that in Greece "men acknowledged true desires." In "To a Persian Boy" Taylor hints at some of the possibilities connected with an unshackled life, and he concludes his oriental poems with a final intriguing comment. In the East, he says, "I found, among those Children of the sun,/The cipher of my nature,—the release/Of baffled powers, which else had never won/That free fulfillment." His references to "nature" and "baffled powers" in the context of sexual freedom perhaps suggests that for Taylor, access to homoerotic passion also allowed access to inspiration.

In his next book, *The Poet's Journal* (1862), in a poem called "On The Headland," Taylor expressed fascination with and eroticizes a sunburnt sailor, lamenting: "I have a mouth for kisses, . . . O warmth of love that is wasted! . . . I could take the sunburnt sailor,/Like a brother, to my breast." In 1870 Taylor's novel of friendship, *Joseph and His Friend*, finds such a brother and translates his exotic and erotic locales into the very heartland of America. He creates in prose two American comrades whose search for the happy valley unites them with all the lovers in homoerotic texts who looked longingly toward Arcadia.

From "Hylas" (1850)

*Hylas*

Storm-wearied Argo slept upon the water.
No cloud was seen; on blue and craggy Ida;
The hot noon lay, and on the plain's enamel
Cool, in his bed alone, the swift Scamander.

"Why should I haste?" said young and rosy Hylas:
"The seas were rough, and long the way from Colchis."
Beneath the snow-white awning slumbers Jason
Pillowed upon his tame Thessalian panther;
The shields are piled, the listless oars suspended
On the black thwarts, and all the hairy bondsmen
Doze on the benches. They may wait for water,
Till I have bathed in mountain-born Scamander."
So said, unfilleting his purple chlamys,
And putting down his urn, he stood a moment,
Beathing the faint, warm odor of the blossoms
That spangled thick the lovely Dardan meadows,
Then, stooping lightly, loosened he his buskins
And felt with shrinking feet the crispy verdure
Naked, save one light robe that from his shoulder
Hung to his knee, the youthful flush revealing
Of warm, white limbs, half-nerved with coming manhood
Yet fair and smooth with tenderness of beauty.
Now to the river's sandy marge advancing,
He dropped the robe, and raised his head exalting
In the clear sunshine, that with beam embracing
Held him against Apollo's glowing bosom.
For sacred to Latona's son is Beauty
Sacred is Youth, the joy of youthful feeling.
A joy indeed, a living joy, was Hylas,
Whence Jove-begotten Heracles, the mighty,
To men though terrible, to him was gentle
Smoothing his rugged nature into laughter
When the boy stole his club, or from his shoulders
Dragged the huge paws of the Nemaean lion.
The thick, brown locks, tossed backward from his forehead
Fell soft about his temples; manhood's blossom
Not yet had sprouted on his chin, but freshly
Curved the fair cheek, and full the red lips, parting
Like a loose bow, that just has launched its arrow.
His large blue eyes, with joy dilate and beamy,
Were clear as the unshadowed Grecian heaven;
Dewy and sleek his dimpled shoulders rounded
To the white arms and whiter breast between them
Downward, the supple lines had less of softness:
His back was like a god's; his loins were moulded
As if some pulse of power began to waken;
The springy fulness of his thighs, outswerving,
Sloped to his knee, and, lightly dropping downward
Drew the curved lines that breathe, rest, of motion.
He saw his glorious limbs reversely mirrored

In the still wave, and stretched his foot to press it
On the smooth sole that answered at the surface
Alas! the shape dissolved in glimmering fragments.
Then, timidly at first, he dipped, and catching
Quick breath, with tingling shudder, as the waters
Swirled round his thighs, and deeper, slowly deeper,
Till on his breast the River's cheek was pillowed,
And deeper still, till every shoreward ripple
Talked in his ear, and like a cygnet's bosom
His white, round shoulder shed the dripping crystal.
There, as he floated, with a rapturous motion
The lucid coolness folding close around him.

[The poem then describes the death of Hylas.]


FROM *POEMS OF THE ORIENT* (1855)

A *Paean to the Dawn*

The dusky sky fades into blue
    And blue waters bind us
The stars are glimmering faint and few,
    The night is left behind us!
Turn not where sinks the sullen dark
    Before the signs of warning,
But crowd the canvas on our bark
    And sail to meet the morning.
Rejoice! rejoice! the hues that fill
    The orient, flush and lighten
And over the blue Ionian hill
    The Dawn begins to brighten!

We leave the Night, that weighed so long
    Upon the soul's endeavor,
For Morning, on these hills of Song,
    Has made her home forever.
Hark to the sound of trump and lyre,
    In the olive groves before us,
And the rhythmic beat, the pulse of fire
    Throbs in the full-voice chorus!
More than Memnonian grandeur speaks
    In the triumph of the paean
And all the glory of the Greeks
    Breaths o'er the old Aegean.

Here shall the ancient Dawn return
    That lit the earliest poet

Whose very ashes in his urn
    Would radiate glory through it,—
The Dawn of Life, when Life was Song,
    And Song the life of Nature,
And the Singer stood amidst the throng,—
    A God in every feature!
When Love was free, as free as air
    The utterance of Passion
And the heart in every fold lay bare,
    Nor shamed its true expression.

Then perfect limb and perfect face
    Surpassed our best ideal;
Unconscious Nature's law was grace,—
    The Beautiful was real.
For men acknowledged true desires,
    And lights as garlands wore them;
They were begot by vigorus sires
    And noble mothers bore them.
Oh, when the shapes of Art they planned
    Were living forms of passion,
Impulse and Deed went hand in hand,
    And life was more than fashion.

The seeds of Song they scattered first
    Flower in all later pages;
Their forms have woke the Artist's thirst
    Through all succeeding ages;
But I will seek the fountain head
And lead the unshackled life they led,
    Accordant with Creation,
The World's false life, that follows still,

    Has ceased its chain to tighten,
And over the blue Ionian hill
    I see the sunrise brighten.

*To a Persian Boy in the Bazaar at Smyrna*

The gorgeous blossoms of that magic tree
Beneath whose shade I sat a thousand nights,
Breathed from their opening petals all delights
Embalmed in spice of Orient Poesy
When first, young Persian, I beheld thine eyes,
And felt the wonder of thy beauty grow
Within my brain, as some fair planet's glow

Deepens, and fills the summer evening skies.
From under thy dark lashes shone on me
The rich, voluptuous soul of Eastern land,
Impassioned, tender, calm, serenely sad,—
Such as immortal Hafiz felt when he
Sang by the mountain-streams of Rocamabad
Or in the bowers of blissfull Samarcand.

FROM *THE POET'S JOURNAL* (1862)

*On the Headland*

I sit on the lonely headland,
Where the sea-gulls come and go:
The sky is gray above me,
And the sea is gray below.

There is no fisherman's pinnace
Homeward or outward bound;
I see no living creature
In the world's deserted round.

I pine for something human,
Man, woman, young or old,—
Something to meet and welcome,
Something to clasp and hold.

I have a mouth for kisses,
But there's no one to give or take,
I have a heart in my bosom
Beating for nobody's sake.

O warmth of love that is wasted!
Is there no one to stretch a hand?
No other heart that hungers
In all the living land?

I could fondle the fisherman's baby,
And rock it into rest;
I could take the sunburnt sailor,
Like a brother, to my breast.

I could clasp the hand of any
Outcast of land or sea,
If the guilty palm but answered
The tenderness in me!

The sea might rise and drown me,—
Cliffs fall and crush my head,—
Were there one to love me, living,
Or weep to see me dead!


*Love Returned*

He was a boy when first we met
   His eyes were mixed of dew and fire
And on his candid brow was set
   The sweetness of a chaste desire.
But in his Veins the pulses beat
   Of passion waiting, for its wing,
As ardent veins of summer heat
   Throb through the innocence of spring.

As manhood came, his stature grew,
   And fiercer burned his restless eyes
Until I trembled, as he drew
   From wedded hearts their young disguise.
Like wind-fed flame his ardor rose
   And brought, like flame, a stormy rain:
In tumult, sweeter than repose
   He tossed the souls of joy and pain.

So many years of absence change!
   I knew him not when he returned:
His step was slow, his brow was strange,
   His quiet eye no longer burned.
When at my heart I heard his knock,
   No voice within his right confessed:
I could not venture to unlock
   Its chambers to an alien guest.

Then, at the threshold, spent and worn
   With fruitless travel, down he lay:
And I beheld the gleams of morn
   On his reviving beauty play.
I knelt, and kissed his holy lips,
   I washed his feet with pious eare;
And from my life the long eclipse
   Drew off, and left his sunshine there.

He burns no more with youthful fire;
   He melts no more in foolish tears;
Serene and sweet, his eyes inspire

The steady faith of balanced years.
His folded wings no longer thrill,
    But in some peaceful flight of prayer:
He nestles in my heart so still,
    I scarcely feel his presence there.


O Love, that stern probation o'er,
    Thy calmer blessing is secure!
Thy beauteous feet shall stray no more,
    Thy peace and patience shall endure!
The lightest wind deflowers the rose,
    The rainbow with the sun departs,
But thou art entered in repose,
    And rooted in my heart of hearts!


## Correspondence Between Taylor and Walt Whitman

### Taylor to Whitman (December 2, 1866)

My dear Whitman: I find your book and cordial letter, on returning home from a lecturing tour in New York, and heartily thank you for both. I have had the first edition of your *Leaves of Grass* among my books, since its first appearance, and have read it many times. I may say, frankly, that there are two things in it which I find nowhere else in literature, though I find them in my own nature. I mean the awe and wonder and reverence and beauty of Life, as expressed in the human body, with the physical attraction and delight of mere contact which it inspires, and that tender and noble love of man for man which once certainly existed, but now almost seems to have gone out of the experience of the race. I think there is nothing in your volume which I do not fully comprehend in the sense in which you wrote; I always try to judge an author from his own standpoint rather than mine, but in this case the two nearly coincide. We should differ rather in regard to form than substance, I suspect. There is not one word of your large and beautiful sympathy for men, which I cannot take into my own heart, nor one of those subtle and wonderful physical affinities you describe which I cannot comprehend. I say these things, not in the way of praise, but because I know from my own experience that correct appreciation of an author is less frequent than it should be. It is welcome to me, and may be so to you.

I did not mean to write so much when I commenced, and will only say that I shall be in Washington on the 27th—only for that night—and would be very glad if we can come together for awhile after my lecture is over. I am afraid I shall not arrive in time to call at the Dep't before the lecture, but if I can I will. If not, will you either come to Willard's or tell me where to find you, and oblige

Your friend,
Bayard Taylor

FROM *JOSEPH AND HIS FRIEND* (1870)

> The better angel is a man right fair;
> The worser spirit a woman colored ill.
>
> —Shakespeare, *Sonnets*

## CHAPTER IX

### Joseph and His Friend

The train moved slowly along through the straggling and shabby suburbs, increasing its speed as the city melted gradually into the country; and Joseph, after a vain attempt to fix his mind upon one of the volumes he had procured for his slender library at home, leaned back in his seat and took note of his fellow-travellers. Since he began to approach the usual destiny of men, they had a new interest for him. Hitherto he had looked upon strange faces very much as on a strange language, without a thought of interpreting them but now their hieroglyphics seemed to suggest a meaning. The figures around him were so many sitting, silent histories, so many locked-up records of struggle, loss, gain, and all the other forces which give shape and color to human life. Most of them were strangers to each other, and as reticent (in their railway conventionality) as himself; yet, he reflected, the whole range of passion, pleasure, and suffering was probably illustrated in that collection of existences. His own troublesome individuality grew fainter, so much of it seemed to be merged in the common experience of men.

There was the portly gentleman of fifty, still ruddy and full of unwasted force. The keenness and coolness of his eyes, the few firmly marked lines on his face, and the color and hardness of his lips, proclaimed to everybody: "I am bold, shrewd, successful in business, scrupulous in the performance of my religious duties (on the Sabbath), voting with my party, and not likely to be fooled by any kind of sentimental nonsense." The thin, not very well-dressed man beside him, with the irregular features and uncertain expression, announced as clearly, to any who could read: "I am weak, like others, but I never consciously did any harm. I just manage to get along in the world, but if I only had a chance, I might make something better of myself." The fresh, healthy fellow, in whose lap a child was sleeping, while his wife nursed a younger one,—the man with ample mouth, large nostrils, and the hands of a mechanic,—also told his story: "On the whole, I find life a comfortable thing. I don't know much about it, but I take it as it comes, and never worry over what I can't understand."

The faces of the younger men, however, were not so easy to decipher. On them life was only beginning its plastic task, and it required an older eye to detect the delicate touches of awakening passions and hopes. But Joseph consoled himself with the thought that his own secret was as little to be discovered as any they might have. If they were still ignorant of the sweet experience of love, he was already their superior; if they were sharers in it, though strangers, they were near to him. Had he not left the foot of the class, after all?

All at once his eye was attracted by a new face, three or four seats from his own. The stranger had shifted his position, so that he was no longer seen in profile. He was apparently a few years older than Joseph, but still bright with all the charm of early manhood. His fair complexion was bronzed from exposure, and his hands, graceful without being effeminate, were not those of the idle gentleman. His hair, golden in tint, thrust its short locks as it pleased about a smooth, frank forehead; the eyes were dark gray, and the mouth, partly hidden by a mustache, at once firm and full. He was moderately handsome, yet it was not of that which Joseph thought; he felt that there was more of developed character and a richer past history expressed in those features than in any other face there. He felt sure—and smiled at himself, notwithstanding, for the impression—that at least some of his own doubts and difficulties had found their solution in the stranger's nature. The more he studied the face, the more he was conscious of its attraction, and his instinct of reliance, though utterly without grounds, justified itself to his mind in some mysterious way.

It was not long before the unknown felt his gaze, and, turning slowly in his seat, answered it. Joseph dropped his eyes in some confusion, but not until he had caught the full, warm, intense expression of those that met them. He fancied that he read in them, in that momentary flash, what he had never before found in the eyes of strangers,—a simple human interest, above curiosity and above mistrust. The usual reply to such a gaze is an unconscious defiance: the unknown nature is on its guard: but the look which seems to answer, "We are men, let us know each other!" is—alas!—too rare in this world.

While Joseph was fighting the irresistible temptation to look again, there was a sudden thud of the car-wheels. Many of the passengers started from their seats, only to be thrown into them again by a quick succession of violent jolts. Joseph saw the stranger springing towards the bell-rope; then he and all others seemed to be whirling over each other; there was a crash, a horrible grinding and splintering sound, and the end of all was a shock, in which his consciousness left him before he could guess its violence.

After a while, out of some blank, haunted by a single lost, wandering sense of existence, he began to awaken slowly to life. Flames were still dancing in his eye-balls and waters and whirlwinds roaring in his ears; but it was only a passive sensation, without the will to know more. Then he felt himself partly lifted and his head supported; and presently a soft warmth fell upon the region of his heart. There were noises all about him, but he did not listen to them; his effort to regain his consciousness fixed itself on that point alone, and grew stronger as the warmth calmed the confusion of his nerves.

"Dip this in water!" said a voice, and the hand (as he now knew it to be) was removed from his heart.

Something cold came over his forehead, and at the same time warm drops fell upon his cheek.

"Look out for yourself: your head is cut!" exclaimed another voice.

"Only a scratch. Take the handkerchief out of my pocket and tie it up; but first ask yon gentleman for his flask!"

Joseph opened his eyes, knew the face that bent over his, and then closed them again. Gentle and strong hands raised him, a flask was set to his lips, and he drank mechanically, but a full sense of life followed the draught. He looked wistfully in the stranger's face.

"Wait a moment," said the latter; "I must feel your bones before you try to move. Arms and legs all right,—impossible to tell about the ribs. There! now put your arm around my neck and lean on me as much as you like while I lift you."

Joseph did as he was bidden, but he was still weak and giddy, and after a few steps, they both sat down together upon a bank. The splintered car lay near them upside-down; the passengers had been extricated from it, and were now busy in aiding the few who were injured. The train had stopped and was waiting on the track above. Some were very pale and grave, feeling that Death had touched without taking them; but the greater part were concerned only about the delay to the train.

"How did it happen?" asked Joseph: "where was I? how did you find me?"

"The usual story,—a broken rail," said the stranger. "I had just caught the rope when the car went over, and was swung off my feet so luckily that I somehow escaped the hardest shock. I don't think I lost my senses for a moment. When we came to the bottom you were lying just before me; I thought you dead until I felt your heart. It is a severe shock, but I hope nothing more."

"But you,—are you not badly hurt?"

The stranger pushed up the handkerchief which was tied around his head, felt his temple, and said: "It must have been one of the splinters; I know nothing about it. But there is no harm in a little blood-letting except"—he added smiling—"except the spots on your face."

By this time the other injured passengers had been conveyed to the train; the whistle sounded a warning of departure.

"I think we can get up the embankment now," said the stranger. "You must let me take care of you still: I am travelling alone."

When they were seated side by side, and Joseph leaned his head back on the supporting arm, while the train moved away with them, he felt that a new power, a new support, had come to his life. The face upon which he looked was no longer strange; the hand which had rested on his heart was warm with kindred blood. Involuntarily he extended his own; it was taken and held, and the dark-gray, courageous eyes turned to him with a silent assurance which he felt needed no words.

"It is a rough introduction," he then said: "my name is Philip Held. I was on my way to Oakland Station; but if yon are going farther—"

"Why, that is my station also!" Joseph exclaimed, giving his name in return.

"Then we should have probably met, sooner or later, in any case. I am bound for the forge and furnace at Coventry, which is for sale. If the company who employ me decide to buy it,—according to the report I shall make—the works will be placed in my charge."

"It is but six miles from my farm," said Joseph, "and the road up the valley is the most beautiful in our neighborhood. I hope you can make a favorable report."

"It is only too much to my own interest to do so. I have been mining, and geologizing in Nevada and the Rocky Mountains for three or four years, and long for a quiet, ordered life. It is a good omen that I have found a neighbor in advance of my settlement. I have often ridden fifty miles to meet a friend who cared for something else than horse-racing or monte; and your six miles,—it is but a step!"

"How much you have seen!" said Joseph. "I know very little of the world. It must he easy for you to take your own place in life."

A shade passed over Philip Held's face. "It is only easy to a certain class of men," he replied,—"a class to which I should not care to belong. I begin to think that nothing is very valuable, the right to which a man don't earn,—except human love, and that seems to come by the grace of God."

"I am younger than you are, not yet twenty-three," Joseph remarked. "You will find that I am very ignorant."

"And I am twenty-eight, and just beginning to get my eyes open, like a nine-days' kitten. If I had been frank enough to confess my ignorance, five years ago, as you do now, it would have been better for me. But don't let us measure ourselves or our experience against each other. That is one good thing we learn in Rocky Mountain life; there is no high or low, knowledge or ignorance, except what applies to the needs of men who come together. So there are needs which most men have, and go all their lives hungering for, because they expect them to be supplied in a particular form. There is something," Philip concluded, "deeper than that in human nature."

Joseph longed to open his heart to this man, every one of whose words struck home to something in himself. But the lassitude which the shock left behind gradually overcame him. He suffered his head to be drawn upon Philip Held's shoulder, and slept until the train reached Oakland Station. When the two got upon the platform, they found Dennis waiting for Joseph, with a light country vehicle. The news of the accident had reached the station, and his dismay was great when he saw the two bloody faces. A physician had already been summoned from the neighboring village, but they had little need of his services. A prescription of quiet and sedatives for Joseph, and a strip of plaster for his companion, were speedily furnished, and they set out together for the Asten place.

It is unnecessary to describe Rachel Miller's agitation when the party arrived; or the parting of the two men who had been so swiftly brought near to each other; or Philip Held's farther journey to the forge that evening. He resisted all entreaty to remain at the farm until morning, on the ground of an appointment made with the present proprietor of the forge. After his departure Joseph was sent to bed, where he remained for a day or two, very sore and a little feverish. He had plenty of time for thought,—not precisely of the kind which his aunt suspected, for out of pure, honest interest in his welfare, she took a step which proved to be of doubtful benefit. If he had not been so innocent,—if he had not been quite as unconscious of his inner nature as he was over-conscious of his external self,—he would have perceived that his thoughts dwelt much more on Philip Held than on Julia Blessing. His mind seemed to run through a swift, involuntary chain of reasoning, to account to himself for his feeling towards her, and her inevitable share in his future; but towards Philip his heart sprang with an instinct beyond his control. It was impossible to imagine that the latter also would not be shot, like a bright thread, through the web of his coming days.

[Joseph decides to marry Julia and loses no time in writing to Philip Held, announcing his approaching marriage and begging him—with many apologies for asking such a mark of confidence on so short an acquaintance—to act the part of nearest friend, if there are no other private reasons to prevent him doing so.]

Four or five days later the following answer arrived:—

My Dear Asten, Do you remember that curious whirling, falling sensation, when the car pitched over the edge of the embankment? I felt a return of it on reading your letter; for you have surprised me beyond measure. Not by your request, for that is just what I should have expected of you; and as well now, as if we had known each other for twenty years; so the apology is the only thing objectionable—But I am tangling my sentences; I want to say how heartily I return the feeling which prompted you to ask me, and yet how embarrassed I am that I cannot unconditionally say, "Yes, with all my heart!" My great, astounding surprise is, to find you about to be married to Miss Julia Blessing,—a young lady whom I once knew. And the embarrassment is this: I knew her under circumstances (in which she was not personally concerned, however) which might possibly render my presence now, as your groomsman, unwelcome to the family: at least, it is my duty—and yours, if you still desire me to stand beside you—to let Miss Blessing and her family decide the question. The circumstances to which I refer concern them rather than myself. I think your be plan will be simply to inform them of your request and my reply, and add that I am entirely ready to accept whatever course they may prefer.

Pray don't consider that I have treated your first letter to me ungraciously. I am more grieved than you can imagine that it happens so. You will probably come to the city before the wedding, and I insist that you shall share my bachelor quarters, in any case.

Always your friend,
Philip Held

This letter threw Joseph into a new perplexity. Philip a former acquaintance of the Blessings! Formerly, but not now; and what could those mysterious "circumstances" have been, which had so seriously interrupted their intercourse? It was quite useless to conjecture; but he could not resist the feeling that another shadow hung over the aspects of his future. Perhaps he had exaggerated Elwood's unaccountable dislike of Julia, which had only been implied, not spoken; but here was a positive estrangement on the part of the man who was so suddenly near and dear to him. He never thought of suspecting Philip of blame; the candor and cheery warmth of the letter rejoiced his heart. There was evidently nothing better to do than to follow the advice contained in it, and leave the question to the decision of Julia and her parents.

[Julia answers and, while casting doubt on Philip's character, yet leaves the choice finally to Joseph. The time arrives for the wedding and Joseph goes to the city, accepting Philip's invitation to stay with him.]

Philip met him on his arrival in the city, and after taking him to his pleasant quarters, in a house looking on one of the leafy squares, good-naturedly sent him to the Blessing mansion, with a warning to return before the evening was quite spent. The family was in a flutter of preparation and though he was cordially welcomed, he felt that, to all except Julia, he was subordinate in interest to the men who came every quarter of an hour, bringing bouquets, and silver spoons with cards attached, and pasteboard boxes containing frosted cakes. Even Julia's society he was only allowed to enjoy by scanty instalments; she was perpetually summoned by her mother or Clementina, to consult about some indescribable figment of dress. Mr. Blessing was occupied in the basement, with the inspection of various hampers. He came to the drawing-room to greet Joseph, whom he shook by both hands, with such incoherent phrases that Julia presently interposed. "You must not forget, pa," she said, "that the man is waiting: Joseph will excuse you, I know." She followed him to the basement, and he returned no more.

Joseph left early in the evening, cheered by Julia's words: "We can't complain of all this confusion when it's for our sakes; but we'll be happier when it's over, won't we?"

He gave her an affirmative kiss and returned to Philip's room. That gentleman was comfortably disposed in a chair, with a book and a cigar. "Ah!" he exclaimed, "you find that a house is more agreeable any evening than that before the wedding?"

"There is one compensation," said Joseph; "it gives me two or three hours with you."

"Then take that other arm-chair, and tell me how this came to pass. You see I have the curiosity of a neighbor already."

He listened earnestly while Joseph related the story of his love, occasionally asking a question or making a suggestive remark, but so gently that it seemed to come as an assistance. When all had been told, he rose and commenced walking slowly up and down the room. Joseph longed to ask, in turn, for an explanation of the circumstances mentioned in Philip's letter; but a doubt checked his tongue.

As if in response to his thought, Philip stopped before him and said: "I owe you my story, and you shall have it after a while, when I can tell you more. I was a young fellow of twenty when I knew the Blessings, and I don't attach the slightest importance, now, to anything that happened. Even if I did, Miss Julia had no share in it. I remember distinctly; she was then about my age, or a year or two older; but hers is a face that would not change in a long while."

Joseph stared at his friend in silence. He recalled the latter's age, and was startled by the involuntary arithmetic which revealed Julia's to him. It was unexpected, unwelcome, yet inevitable.

"Her father had been lucky in some of his 'operations,'" Philip continued, "but I don't think he kept it long.

"I hardly wonder that she should come to prefer a quiet country life to such ups and downs as the family has known. Generally, a woman don't adapt herself so readily to a change of surroundings as a man: where there is love, however, everything is possible."

"There is! there is!" Joseph exclaimed, certifying the fact to himself as much as to his friend. He rose and stood beside him.

Philip looked at him with grave, tender eyes.

"What can I do?" he said.

"What should you do?" Joseph asked.

"This!" Philip exclaimed, laying his hands on Joseph's shoulders, — "this, Joseph! I can be nearer than a brother. I know that I am in your heart as you are in mine. There is no faith between us that need be limited, there is no truth too secret to be veiled. A man's perfect friendship is rarer than a woman's love, and most hearts are content with one or the other: not so with yours and mine! I read it in your eyes, when you opened them on my knee: I see it in your face now. Don't speak: let us clasp hands."

But Joseph could not speak.

[After the marriage it becomes clear that Julia Blessing is not as perfect as Joseph had imagined her, as he discovers her to be scheming, bitter, and duplicitous. Her father, who has borrowed a large sum from Joseph, also is not to be trusted. The friendship between Philip and Joseph deepens and a new character — Philip's twin sister, Madelaine Held — is introduced into the story; she is as upright as her brother. After receiving more disturbing financial news from Mr. Blessing and unwisely giving him power of attorney over some of his holdings, Joseph then learns more distressing information about his wife. In chapter 20 Joseph seeks out Philip.]

## Chapter XX

### A Crisis

He retraced his steps, took the road up the valley, and walked rapidly towards the Forge. The tumult in his blood gradually expended its force, but it had carried him along more swiftly than he was aware. When he reached the point where, looking across the valley, now narrowed to a glen, he could see the smoke of the Forge near at hand, and even catch a glimpse of the cottage on the knoll, he stopped. Up to this moment he had felt, not reflected; and a secret instinct told him that he should not submit his trouble to Philip's riper manhood until it was made clear and coherent in his own mind. He must keep Philip's love, at all hazards; and to keep it he must not seem simply a creature of moods and sentiments, whom his friend might pity, but could not respect.

He left the road, crossed a sloping field on the left, and presently found himself on a bank overhanging the stream. Under the wood of oaks and hemlocks the laurel grew in rich, shining clumps; the current, at this point deep, full and silent, glimmered through the leaves, twenty feet below; the opposite shore was level, and green with an herbage which no summer could wither. He leaned against a hemlock bole, and tried to think, but it was not easy to review the past while his future life overhung him like a descending burden which he had not the strength to lift. Love betrayed, trust violated, aspiration misinterpreted, were the spiritual aspects; a divided household, entangling obligations, a probability of serious loss were the material evils which accompanied them. He was so unprepared for the change that he could only rebel, not measure, analyze, and cast about for ways of relief.

It was a miserable strait in which he found himself; and the more he thought—
or, rather, seemed to think—the less was he able to foresee any other than an unfortunate solution. What were his better impulses, if men persisted in finding them
evil? What was life, yoked to such treachery and selfishness? Life had been to him
a hope, an inspiration, a sound, enduring joy; now it might never be so again! Then
what a release were death!

He walked forward to the edge of the rock. A few pebbles, dislodged by his feet,
slid from the brink, and plunged with a bubble and a musical tinkle into the dark,
sliding waters. One more step, and the release which seemed so fair might be
attained. He felt a morbid sense of delight in playing with the thought. Gathering
a handful of broken stones, he let them fall one by one, thinking, "So I hold my
fate in my hand." He leaned over and saw a shifting, quivering image of himself
projected against the reflected sky, and a fancy, almost as clear as a voice, said:
"This is your present self: what will you do with it beyond the gulf, where only the
soul superior to circumstances here receives a nobler destiny ?"

He was still gazing down at the flickering figure, when a step came upon the
dead leaves. He turned and saw Philip, moving stealthily towards him, pale, with
outstretched hand. They looked at each other for a moment without speaking.

"I guess your thought, Philip," Joseph then said. "But the things easiest to do are
sometimes the most impossible."

"The bravest man may allow a fancy to pass through his mind, Joseph, which
only the coward will carry into effect."

"I am not a coward!" Joseph exclaimed.

Philip took his hand, drew him nearer, and flinging his arms around him, held
him to his heart.

Then they sat down, side by side.

"I was up the stream, on the other side, trolling for trout," said Philip, "when I
saw you in the road. I was welcoming your coming, in my heart: then you stopped,,
stood still, and at last turned away. Something in your movements gave me a sudden, terrible feeling of anxiety: I threw down my rod, came around by the bridge at
the Forge, and followed you here. Do not blame me for my foolish dread."

"Dear, dear, friend," Joseph cried, "I did not mean to come to you until I
seemed stronger and more rational in my own eyes. If that were a vanity, it is gone
now: I confess my weakness and ignorance. Tell me, if you can, why this has come
upon me? Tell me why nothing that I have been taught, why no atom of the faith
which I still must cling to, explains, consoles, or remedies any wrong of my life!"

"Faiths, I suspect," Philip answered, "are, like laws, adapted to the average character of the human race. You, in the confiding purity of your nature, are not an
average man: you are very much above the class, and if virtue were its own reward,
you would be most exceptionally happy. Then the puzzle is, what's the particular
use of virtue?"

"I don't know, Philip, but I don't like to hear you ask the question. I find myself
so often on the point of doubting all that was my Truth a little while ago; and yet,
why should my misfortunes, as an individual, make the truth a lie? I am only one
man among millions who must have faith in the efficacy of virtue. Philip, if I
believed the faith to be false, I think I should still say, 'Let it be preached!' "

Joseph related to Philip the whole of his miserable story, not sparing himself, nor concealing the weakness which allowed him to be entangled to such an extent. Philip's brow grew dark as he listened, but at the close of the recital his face was calm, though stern. . . .

"Is there no way out of this labyrinth of wrong?" Philip exclaimed. "Two natures, as far apart as Truth and Falsehood, monstrously held together in the most intimate, the holiest of bonds,—two natures destined for each other monstrously kept apart by the same bonds! Is life to be so sacrificed to habit and prejudice? I said that Faith, like Law, was fashioned for the average man: then there must be a loftier faith, a juster law, for the men—and the women—who cannot shape themselves according to the common-place pattern of society,—who were born with instincts, needs, knowledge, and rights—ay, rights—of their own!"

"We know this, Joseph,—and who can know it and be patient ?—that the power which controls our lives is pitiless, unrelenting! There is the same punishment for an innocent mistake as for a conscious crime. A certain Nemesis follows ignorance, regardless how good and pure may be the individual nature. Had you even guessed your wife's true character just before marriage, your very integrity, your conscience, and the conscience of the world, would have compelled the union, and Nature would not have mitigated her selfishness to reward you with a tolerable life. O no! You would still have suffered as now. Shall a man with a heart feel this horrible injustice, and not rebel? Grant that I am rightly punished for my impatience, my pride, my jealousy, how have you been rewarded for your stainless youth, your innocent trust, your almost miraculous goodness? Had you known the world better, even though a part of your knowledge might have been evil, you would have escaped this fatal marriage. Nothing can be more certain; and will simply groan and bear? What compensating fortune have you, or can you ever expect to find?"

Joseph was silent at first; but Philip could see, from the trembling of his hands, and his quick breathing, that he was profoundly agitated. "There is something within me," he said, at last, "which accepts everything you say; and yet, it alarms me. I feel a mighty temptation in your words: they could lead me to snap my chains, break violently away from my past and present life, and surrender myself to will and appetite. O Philip, if we could make our lives wholly our own! If we could find a spot—"

"I know such a spot!" Philip cried, interrupting him,—"a great valley, bounded by a hundred miles of snowy peaks; lakes in its bed; enormous hillsides, dotted with groves of ilex and pine; orchards of orange and olive; a perfect climate, where it is bliss enough just to breathe, and freedom from the distorted laws of men, for none are near enough to enforce them! If there is no legal way of escape for you, here, at least, there is no force which can drag you back, once you are there: I will go with you, and perhaps—perhaps—"

Philip's face glowed, and the vague alarm in Joseph's heart took a definite form. He guessed what words had been left unspoken.

"If we could be sure!" he said.

"Sure of what? Have I exaggerated the wrong in your case? Say we should be outlaws there, in our freedom!—here we are fettered outlaws."

"I have been trying, Philip, to discover a law superior to that under which we suffer, and I think I have found it. If it be true that ignorance is equally punished with guilt; if causes and consequences, in which there is neither pity nor justice, govern our lives,—then what keeps our souls from despair but the infinite pity and perfect justice of God? Yes, here is the difference between human and divine law! This makes obedience safer than rebellion. If you and I, Philip, stand above the level of common natures, feeling higher needs and claiming other rights, let us shape them according to the law which is above, not that which is below us!"

Philip grew pale. "Then you mean to endure in patience, and expect me to do the same?" he asked.

"If I can. The old foundations upon which my life rested are broken up, and I am too bewildered to venture random path. Give me time; nay, let us both strive to wait a little. I see nothing clearly but this: there Divine government, on which I lean now as never before. Yes, I say again, the very wrong that has come upon us makes God necessary!"

It was Philip's turn to be agitated. There was a solemn conviction in Joseph's voice which struck to his heart. He had spoken from the heat of his passion, it is true, but he had the courage to disregard the judgment of men, and make his protest a reality. Both natures shared the desire and were enticed by the daring of his dream; but out of Joseph's deeper conscience came a whisper, against which the cry of passion was powerless.

"Yes, we will wait," said Philip, after a long pause. "You came to me, Joseph, as you said, in weakness and confusion: I have been talking of your innocence and ignorance. Let us not measure ourselves in this way. It is experience alone which creates manhood. What will come of us I cannot tell, but I will not, I dare not, say you are wrong!"

They took each others hands. The day was fading, landscape was silent, and only the twitter of nesting birds was heard in the boughs above them. Each gave way to the impulse of his manly love, rarer, alas! but as tender and true as the love of woman, and they drew nearer and kissed each other. As they walked back and parted on the highway, each felt that life was not wholly unkind, and that happiness was not yet impossible.

[More examples of Julia's duplicity are revealed and more financial catastrophes occur, until Joseph confesses that he no longer loves Julia, that instead he hates her. Hearing this, Julia loses her mind and takes poison. By desperate labor Joseph extricates himself from his financial difficulties and his friendship with Philip deepens, as does that with Madelaine Held. At the end, Joseph, not so willing as Philip to cast aside the constructing laws of society, sees in Madelaine, Philip's twin, the wife he needs, recognizing, perhaps, that this union is all that he can do to obtain Philip within the bounds of social conformity.]

## Charles Warren Stoddard (1843–1909)

The homophobia that Whitman had experienced firsthand (see p. 534, this volume) may have influenced his response to a letter from another enthusiastic young writer whose tales were also drenched in homoeroticism. This writer was Charles Warren Stoddard, who invoked Whitman "In the name of CALAMUS" as he was about to set sail for his own happy valley. Stoddard recorded his sojourn there in his *South Sea Idyls* (1873), which Whitman had read, describing the book as "beautiful and soothing." Whitman warns Stoddard about the dangers of American homophobia, warnings which may reflect Whitman's disillusionment with the possibility that the free love of comrades might be realized and fear and disappointment that the homoerotic aesthetic he had tried to construct had not only been misunderstood but labeled perversion. Stoddard, however, continued his own explorations of American homosexuality. The hero of *For the Pleasure of His Company* (1903) lives in San Francisco, and when he can no longer confront American homophobia leaves the country to live in the South Seas. *The Island Of Tranquil Delights* (1904) is another version of the South Sea idyll.

## Correspondence Between Stoddard and Walt Whitman

### Stoddard to Whitman (March 2, 1869)

[Stoddard had written to WW asking for an autograph, and in his next letter, from Honolulu, gave WW a description of his life there.]

The native villagers gather about me, for strangers are not common in these parts. I observe them closely. Superb looking, many of them. Fine heads . . . Proud, defiant lips, a matchless physique, grace and freedom in every motion. I mark one, a lad of eighteen or twenty years who is regarding me. I call him to me, ask his name, giving mine in return. He speaks it over and over, manipulating my body unconsciously, as it were, with bountiful and unconstrained love. I go to his grass-house, eat with him his simple food. Sleep with him upon his mats, and at night sometimes waken to find him watching me with earnest, patient looks, his arm over my breast and around me.

### Whitman to Stoddard (June 12, 1869)

Your letters have reached me. I cordially accept your appreciation, & reciprocate your friendship. I do not write many letters, but like to meet people. Those tender & primitive personal relations away off there in the Pacific Islands, as described by you, touched me deeply.

In answer to your request, I send you my picture—it was taken three months since. I also send a newspaper.

Farewell, my friend. I sincerely thank you, & hope some day to meet you.

### Stoddard to Whitman (April 2, 1870)

To Walt Whitman. In the name of CALAMUS listen to me! before me hangs your beautiful photograph, twice precious, since it is your gift to me. Near at hand lies your beloved volume and with it the Notes of Mr. Burroughs.

May I not thank you for your picture and your letter? May I not tell you over and over that where I go you go with me, in poem and picture and the little volume of notes also, for I read and reread trying to see you in the flesh as I so long to see you!

I wrote you last from the Sandwich Islands. I shall before long be even further from you than ever, for I think of sailing towards Tahiti in about five weeks. I know there is but one hope for me. I must get in amongst people who are not afraid of instincts and who scorn hypocrisy. I am numbed with the frigid manners of the Christians; barbarism has given me the fullest joy of my life and I long to return to it and be satisfied. May I not send you a prose idyl wherein I confess how dear it is to me? There is much truth in it and I am praying that you may like it a little. If I could only know that it has pleased you I should bless my stars fervently.

I have been in vain trying to buy from our Library a copy of your *Leaves*, edition of 1855. I think it your first and I have somewhere read that you set the type for it yourself. Is it true? Do you think I could obtain a copy of it by addressing some Eastern publisher or bookseller?

You say you "don't write many letters." O, if you would only reply to this within the month! I could then go into the South Seas feeling sure of your friendship and I should try to live the real life there for your sake as well as for my own. Forgive me if I have worried you: I will be silent and thoughtful in future, but in any case know, dear friend, that I am grateful for your indulgence.

Affectionately yours,

## WHITMAN TO STODDARD (APRIL 23, 1870)

Dear Charles Stoddard,

I received some days since your affectionate letter, & presently came your beautiful & soothing South Sea Idyll which I read at once.

Now, as I write, I sit by a large open window, looking south & west down the Potomac & across to the Virginia heights. It is a bright, warm spring-like afternoon. I have just re-read the sweet story all over, & find it indeed soothing & nourishing after its kind, like the atmosphere. As to you, I do not of course object to your emotional & adhesive nature, & the outlet thereof, but warmly approve them—but do you know (perhaps you do,) how the hard, pungent, gritty, worldly experiences & qualities in American practical life, also serve? how they prevent extravagant sentimentalism? & how they are not without their own great value & even joy?

It arises in my mind, as I write, to say something of that kind to you—

I am not a little comforted when I learn that the young men dwell in thought upon me & my utterances—as you do—& I frankly send you my love—& I hope we shall one day meet—I wish to hear from you always,

## FROM *SOUTH SEA IDYLS* (1873)

### PART I

### CHUMMING WITH A SAVAGE

#### Kana-Ana

Well! here, as I was looking about at the singular loveliness of the place—you know this was my first glimpse of its abrupt walls, hung with tapestries of fern and clambering convolvulus; at one end two exquisite waterfalls, rivalling one another in whiteness and airiness, at the other the sea, the real South Sea, breaking and foaming over a genuine reef, and even rippling the placid current of the river that slipped quietly down to its embracing tide from the deep basins at these water-falls—right in the midst of all this, before I had been ten minutes in the valley, I saw a straw hat, bound with wreaths of fern and maile; under it a snow-white garment, rather short all around, low in the neck, and with no sleeves whatever.

There was no sex to that garment; it was the spontaneous offspring of a scant material and a large necessity. I'd seen plenty of that sort of thing, but never upon a model like this, so entirely tropical—almost Oriental. As this singular phenomenon made directly for me, and, having come within reach, there stopped and stayed, I asked its name, using one of my seven stock phrases for the purpose; I found it was called Kana-ana. Down it went into my note-book; for I knew I was to have an experience with this young scion of a race of chiefs. Sure enough, I have had it. He continued to regard me steadily, without embarrassment. He seated himself before me; I felt myself at the mercy of one whose calm analysis was questioning every motive of my soul. This sage inquirer was, perhaps, sixteen years of age. His eye was so earnest and so honest, I could return his look. I saw a round, full, rather girlish face; lips ripe and expressive, not quite so sensual as those of most of his race; not a bad nose, by any means; eyes perfectly glorious—regular almonds—with the mythical lashes "that sweep," etc., etc. The smile which presently transfigured his face was of the nature that flatters you into submission against your will.

Having weighed me in his balance—and you may be sure his instincts didn't cheat him; they don't do that sort of thing—he placed his two hands on my two knees, and declared, "I was his best friend, as he was mine; I must come at once to his house, and there live always with him." What could I do but go? He pointed me to his lodge across the river, saying, "There was his home and mine."

## PART II

### How I Converted My Cannibal

When people began asking me queer questions about my chum Kana-ana, some of them even hinting that "he might possibly have been a girl all the time," I resolved to send down for him, and settle the matter at once. I knew he was not a girl, and I thought I should like to show him some American hospitality, and perhaps convert him before I sent him back again.

I could teach him to dress, you know; to say a very good thing to your face, and a very bad one at your back; to sleep well in church, and rejoice duly when the preacher had got at last to the "Amen." I might do all this for his soul's sake; but I wanted more to see how the little fellow was getting on. I missed him so terribly—his honest way of showing likes and dislikes; his confidence in his intuitions and fidelity to his friends; and those quaint manners of his, so different from anything in vogue this side of the waters.

That is what I remarked when I got home again, and found myself growing as practical and prosy as ever. I awoke no kindred chord in the family bosom. On the contrary, they all said, "It was no use to think of it: no good could come out of Nazareth." The idea of a heathen and his abominable idolatry being countenanced in the sanctity of a Christian home was too dreadful for anything. But I believed some good might come out of Nazareth, and I believed that, when it did come, it was the genuine article, worth hunting for, surely. I thought it all over soberly, finally resolving to do a little missionary work on my own account. So I wrote to the Colonel of the Royal Guards, who knows everybody and has immense influence everywhere, begging him to catch Kana-ana, when his folks weren't looking, and send him to my address, marked C.O.D., for I was just dying to see him. That was how I trapped my little heathen and began to be a missionary, all by myself.

I informed the Colonel it was a case of life and death, and he seemed to realize it, for he managed to get Kana-ana away from his distressed relatives (their name is legion, and they live all over the island), fit him out in real clothing—the poor little wretch had to be dressed, you know; we all do it in this country—then he packed him up and shipped him, care of the captain of the bark S— —. When he arrived I took him right to my room and began my missionary work. I tried to make all the people love him, but I'm afraid they found it hard work. He wasn't half so interesting, up here anyhow. I seemed to have been regarding him through chromatic glasses, which glasses being suddenly removed, I found a little dark-skinned savage, whose clothes fitted him horribly and appeared to have no business there. Boots about twice too long, the toes being heavily charged with wadding; in fact, he looked perfectly miserable, and I've no doubt he felt so. How he had been studying English on the voyage up! He wanted to be a great linguist, and had begun in good earnest. He said "good morning" as boldly as possible about seven P.M., and invariably spoke of the women of America as "him." He had an insane desire to spell, and started spelling-matches with everybody, at the most inappropriate hours and inconvenient places. He invariably spelled God, d-o-g; when duly corrected— thus, G-o-d, he would triumphantly shout, dog. He jumped at these irreverent conclusions about twenty times a day.

What an experience I had, educating my little savage! Walking him in the street by the hour; answering questions on all possible topics; spelling up and down the blocks; spelling from the centre of the city to the suburbs and back again, and around it; spelling one another at spelling—two latter-day peripatetics on dress parade, passing to and fro in high and serene strata of philosophy, alike unconscious of the rudely gazing and insolent citizens, or the tedious calls of labor. A spell was over us; we ran into all sorts of people, and trod on many a corn, loafing about in this way. Some of the victims objected in harsh and sinful language. I found Kana-ana had so far advanced in the acquirement of our mellifluous tongue as to be very successful in returning their salutes. I had the greatest difficulty in convincing him of the enormity of his error. The little convert thought it was our mode of greeting strangers, equivalent to their more graceful and poetic password, Aloha, "Love to you."

My little cannibal wasn't easily accustomed to his new restraints, such as clothes, manners, and forbidden water privileges. He several times started on his daily pilgrimage without his hat; once or twice, to save time, put his coat on next his skin; and though I finally so far conquered him as to be sure that his shirt would be worn on the inside instead of the outside of his trousers (this he considered a great waste of material), I was in constant terror of his suddenly disrobing in the street and plunging into the first water we came to—which barbarous act would have insured his immediate arrest, perhaps confinement; and that would have been the next thing to death in his case.

So we perambulated the streets and the suburbs, daily growing into each other's grace; and I was thinking of the propriety of instituting a series of more extended excursions, when I began to realize that my guest was losing interest in our wonderful city and the possible magnitude of her future.

He grew silent and melancholy; he quit spelling entirely, or only indulged in rare and fitful (I am pained to add, fruitless) attempts at spelling God in the orthodox fashion. It seemed almost as though I had missed my calling; certainly, I was hardly successful as a missionary.

The circus failed to revive him; the beauty of our young women he regarded without interest. He was less devout than at first, when he used to insist upon entering every church we came to and sitting a few moments, though frequently we were the sole occupants of the building. He would steal away into remote corners of the house, and be gone for hours. Twice or three times I discovered him in a dark closet, in puris naturalibus, toying with a singular shell strung upon a feather chain. The feathers of the chain I recognized as those of a strange bird held as sacred among his people. I began to suspect the occasion of his malady: he believed himself bewitched or accursed of some one—a common superstition with the dark races. This revelation filled me with alarm; for he would think nothing of lying down to die under the impression that it was his fate, and no medicine under the heaven could touch him further.

I began telling him of my discovery, begging his secret from him. In vain I besought him. "It was his trouble; he must go back!" I told him he should go back as soon as possible; that we would look for ourselves, and see when a vessel was to sail again. I took him among the wharves, visiting, in turn, nearly all the shipping moored there. How he lingered about them, letting his eyes wander over the still bay into the mellow hazes that sometimes visit our brown and dusty hills!

His nature seemed to find an affinity in the tranquil tides, the far-sweeping distances, the alluring outlines of the coast, where it was blended with the sea-line in the ever-mysterious horizon. After these visitations he seemed loath to return again among houses and people; they oppressed and suffocated him.

One day, as we were wending our way to the city front, we passed a specimen of grotesque carving, in front of a tobacconist's establishment. Kana-ana stood eying the painted model for a moment, and then, to the amazement and amusement of the tobacconist and one or two bystanders, fell upon his knees before it, and was for a few moments lost in prayer: It seemed to do him a deal of good, as he was more cheerful after his invocation—for that day, at least; and we could never start upon any subsequent excursion without at first visiting this wooden Indian, which he evidently mistook for a god.

He began presently to bring tributes, in the shape of small cobble- stones, which he surreptitiously deposited at the feet of his new-found deity, and passed on, rejoicing. His small altar grew from day to day, and his spirits were lighter as he beheld it unmolested, thanks to the indifference of the tobacconist and the street contractors.

His greatest trials were within the confines of the bath-tub. He who had been born to the Pacific, and reared among its foam and breakers, now doomed to a seven-by-three zinc box and ten inches of water! He would splash about like a trout in a saucer, bemoaning his fate. Pilgrimages to the beach were his greatest delight; divings into the sea, so far from town that no one could possibly be shocked, even with the assistance of an opera-glass. He used to implore a daily repetition of these cautious and inoffensive recreations, though, once in the chilly current, he soon came out of it, shivering and miserable. Where were his warm sea-waves, and the shining beach, with the cocoa-palms quivering in the intense fires of the tropical day? How he missed them and mourned for them, crooning a little chant in their praises, much to the disparagement of our dry hills, cold water; and careful people!

In one of our singular walks, when he had been unusually silent, and I had sought in vain to lift away the gloom that darkened his soul, I was startled by a quick cry of joy from the lips of the young exile—a cry that was soon turned into a sharp, prolonged, and pitiful wail of sorrow and despair. We had unconsciously approached an art-gallery, the deep windows of which were beautified with a few choice landscapes in oil. Kana-ana's restless and searching eye, doubtless attracted by the brilliant coloring of one of the pictures, seemed in a moment to comprehend and assume the rich and fervent spirit with which the artist had so successfully imbued his canvas.

It was the subject which had at first delighted Kana-ana—the splendid charm of its manipulation which so affected him, holding him there wailing in the bitterness of a natural and uncontrollable sorrow. The painting was illuminated with the mellowness of a tropical sunset. A transparent light seemed to transfigure the sea and sky. The artist wrought a miracle in his inspiration. It was a warm, hazy, silent sunset forever. The outline of a high, projecting cliff was barely visible in the flood of misty glory that spread over the face of it—a cliff whose delicate tints of green and crimson pictured in the mind a pyramid of leaves and flowers. A valley opened its shadowy depths through the sparkling atmosphere, and in the centre of this veiled chasm the pale threads of two waterfalls seemed to appear and disappear, so exquisitely was the distance imitated. Gilded breakers reeled upon a palm-fringed shore; and the whole was hallowed by the perpetual peace of an unbroken solitude.

I at once detected the occasion of Kana-ana's agitation. Here was the valley of his birth—the cliff, the waterfall, the sea, copied faithfully, at that crowning hour when they are indeed supernaturally lovely. At that moment, the promise to him of a return would have been mockery. He was there in spirit, pacing the beach, and greeting his companions with that liberal exchange of love peculiar to them. Again he sought our old haunt by the river, watching the sun go down. Again he waited listlessly the coming of night.

It was a wonder that the police did not march us both off to the station-house; for the little refugee was howling at the top of his lungs, while I endeavored to quiet him by bursting a sort of vocal tornado about his ears. I then saw my error. I said to myself, "I have transplanted a flower from the hot sand of the Orient to the hard clay of our more material world—a flower too fragile to be handled, if never so kindly. Day after day it has been fed, watered, and nourished by nature. Every element of life has ministered to its development in the most natural way. Its attributes are God's and Nature's own. I bring it hither, set it in our tough soil, and endeavor to train its sensitive tendrils in one direction. There is no room for spreading them here, where we are overcrowded already. It finds no succulence in its cramped bed, no warmth in our practical and selfish atmosphere. It withers from the root upward; its blossoms are falling; it will die!" I resolved it should not die. Unfortunately, there was no bark announced to sail for his island home within several weeks. I could only devote my energies to keeping life in that famishing soul until it had found rest in the luxurious clime of its nativity.

At last the bark arrived. We went at once to see her; and I could hardly persuade the little homesick soul to come back with me at night. He who was the fire of hospitality and obliging to the uttermost, at home, came very near to mutiny just then.

It was this civilization that had wounded him, till the thought of his easy and pleasurable life among the barbarians stung him to madness. Should he ever see them again, his lovers? ever climb with the goat-hunters among the clouds yonder? or bathe, ride, sport, as he used to, till the day was spent and the night come?

Those little booths near the wharves, where shells, corals, and gold-fish are on sale, were Kana-ana's favorite haunts during the last few days he spent here. I would leave him seated on a box or barrel by one of those epitomes of Oceanica, and return two hours later, to find him seated as I had left him, and singing some weird melody—some legend of his home. These musical diversions were a part of his nature, and a very grave and sweet part of it, too. A few words, chanted on a low note, began the song, when the voice would suddenly soar upward with a single syllable of exceeding sweetness, and there hang trembling in bird-like melody till it died away with the breath of the singer.

Poor, longing soul! I would you had never left the life best suited to you—that liberty which alone could give expression to your wonderful capacities. Not many are so rich in instincts to read Nature, to translate her revelations, to speak of her as an orator endowed with her surpassing eloquence.

It will always be a sad effort, thinking of that last night together. There are hours when the experiences of a lifetime seem compressed and crowded together. One grows a head taller in his soul at such times, and perhaps gets suddenly gray, as with a fright, also.

Kana-ana talked and talked in his pretty, broken English, telling me of a thousand charming secrets; expressing all the natural graces that at first attracted me to him, and imploring me over and over to return with him and dwell in the antipodes. How near I came to resolving, then and there, that I would go, and take the consequences—how very near I came to it! He passed the night in coaxing, promising, entreating; and was never more interesting or lovable. It took just about all the moral courage allotted me to keep on this side of barbarism on that eventful occasion; and in the morning Kana-ana sailed, with a face all over tears, and agony, and dust.

I begged him to select something for a remembrancer; and of all that ingenuity can invent and art achieve he chose a metallic chain for his neck—chose it, probably, because it glittered superbly, and was good to string charms upon. He gave me the greater part of his wardrobe, though it can never be of any earthly use to me, save as a memorial of a passing joy in a life where joys seem to have little else to do than be brief and palatable.

He said he "should never want them again"; and he said it as one might say something of the same sort in putting by some instrument of degradation—conscious of renewed manhood, but remembering his late humiliation, and bowing to that remembrance.

So Kana-ana, and the bark, and all that I ever knew of genuine, spontaneous, and unfettered love sailed into the west, and went down with the sun in a glory of air, sea, and sky, trebly glorious that evening. I shall never meet the sea when it is bluest without thinking of one who is its child and master. I shall never see mangoes and bananas without thinking of him who is their brother born and brought up with them. I shall never smell cassia, or clove, or jessamine, but a thought of Kana-ana will be borne upon their breath. A flying skiff, land in the far distance rising slowly, drifting sea-grasses, a clear voice burdened with melody, all belong to him, and are a part of him.

I resign my office. I think that, perhaps, instead of my having converted the little cannibal, he may have converted me. I am sure, at least, that if we two should begin a missionary work upon one another, I should be the first to experience the great change. I sent my convert home, feeling he wasn't quite so good as when I first got him; and I truly wish him as he was.

I can see you, my beloved, sleeping, naked, in the twilight of the west. The winds kiss you with pure and fragrant lips. The sensuous waves invite you to their embrace. Earth again offers you her varied store. Partake of her offering, and be satisfied. Return, O troubled soul! to your first and natural joys; they were given you by the Divine hand that can do no ill. In the smoke of the sacrifice ascends the prayer of your race. As the incense fadeth and is scattered upon the winds of heaven, so shall your people separate, nevermore to assemble among the nations. So perish your superstitions, your necromancies, your ancient arts of war, and the unwritten epics of your kings.

Alas, Kana-ana! As the foam of the sea you love, as the fragrance of the flower you worship, shall your precious body be wasted, and your untrammelled soul pass to the realms of your fathers!

Our day of communion is over. Behold how Night extends her wings to cover you from my sight! She may, indeed, hide your presence; she may withhold from me the mystery of your future; but she cannot take from me that which I have; she cannot rob me of the rich influences of your past.

Dear comrade, pardon and absolve your spiritual adviser, for seeking to remould so delicate and original a soul as yours; and, though neither prophet nor priest, I yet give you the kiss of peace at parting, and the benediction of unceasing love.

[In part III he returns to search for Kana-ana, only to find that he has died from grief at the loss of his friend.]

## "Professor X" [James Mills Peirce]

At the end of the century the pseudonymous "Professor X," in a letter that had appeared in the first edition of Havelock Ellis and John Addington Symonds's *Sexual Inversion* (1897), forecast the resistance to homophobia that would be the significant in twentieth-century texts. Ellis and Symonds described him as "an American of eminence who holds a scientific professorship in one of the first universities of the world." His letter, they observe, is "the furthest extent to which the defense of sexual inversion has gone, or, indeed, could go, unless anyone were bold enough to assert that homosexuality is the only normal impulse, and heterosexual love a perversion" (Ellis 1897:275). Professor X, who may have been James Mills Peirce, confronts not only moral and religious stigmatizations but the substantial body of scientific speculation about the normality of homosexuality. He posits a modern theory of sexual orientation rather than sexual preference, shifting desire from the object to the subject. Rather than being defined as a sickness or as a forgivable aberration from the heterosexual norm, Peirce argues that either homosexuality should be recognized as a normal sexual response or that the very notion of the norm itself should be abandoned.

## From "A Letter to Havelock Ellis" (1897)

I have considered and enquired into this question for many years; and it has long been my settled conviction that no breach of morality is involved in homosexual love; that, like every other passion, it tends, when duly understood and controlled by spiritual feeling, to the physical and moral health of the individual and the race, and that it is only its brutal perversions which are immoral. I have known many persons more or less the subjects of this passion, and I have found them a particularly high-minded, upright, refined, and (I must add) pureminded class of men. In view of what everybody knows of the vile influence on society of the intersexual passion, as it actually exists in the world, making men and women sensual, low-minded, false, every way unprincipled and grossly selfish, and this especially in those nations which self-righteously reject homosexual love, it seems a travesty of morality to invest the one with divine attributes and denounce the other as infamous and unnatural.

There is an error in the view that feminine love is that which is directed to a man, and masculine love that which is directed to a woman. That doctrine involves a begging of the whole question. It is a fatal concession to vulgar prejudice, and a contradiction to all you have so firmly adduced from Greek manners, and, indeed, I may say, to all the natural evolution of our race. Passion is in itself a blind thing. It is a furious pushing out, not with calculation or comprehension of its object, but to anything which strikes the imagination as fitted to its need. It is not characterised or differentiated by the nature of its object, but by its own nature. Its instinct is to a certain form of action or submission. But how that instinct is determined is largely accidental. Sensual passion is drawn by certain qualities which appeal to it. It may see them, or think that it sees them, in a man or a woman. But it is in either case the same person. The controlling influence is a certain spiritual attraction, and that may lie in either. The two directions are equally natural to unperverted man, and the abnormal form of love is that which has lost the power of excitability in either the one or the other of these directions. It is unisexual love (a love for one sexuality) which is a perversion. The normal men love both.

It is true enough that in primitive society all passion must have been wholly or mainly animal, and spiritual progress must have been conditioned on subduing it. But there is no reason why this subjugation should have consisted in extirpating, or trying to extirpate, one of the two main forms of sexual passion, and cultivating the other. The actual reasons were, I take it, two: (1) to reserve all sexual energy for the increase of the race; (2) to get the utmost merely fleshly pleasure out of the exercise of passion. Whether either of these reasons adds to the spiritual elevation of love may be doubted. Certainly not the second, which is now the moving influence in the matter. It is true enough that all passion needs to be unceasingly watched, because the worst evils for mankind lie hidden in its undisciplined indulgence. But this is quite as true of intersexual as of homosexual love. I clearly believe that the Greek morality on this subject was far higher than ours, and truer to the spiritual nature of man; that our civilisation suffers for want of the pure and noble sentiment which they thought so useful to the state; and that we ought to think and speak of homosexual love, not as "inverted" or "abnormal," as a sort of colour-blindness of the genital sense, as a lamentable mark of inferior development, or as an unhappy fault, a "masculine body with a feminine soul," but as being in itself a natural, pure and sound passion, as worthy of the reverence of all fine natures as the honourable devotion of husband and wife, or the ardour of bride and groom.

## Xavier Mayne [Edward Prime-Stevenson] (1868–1942)

In 1906 Edward Prime-Stevenson, writing as "Xavier Mayne," published privately and in Italy the first American openly homosexual novel called *Imre*. Two years later, also in Italy, he published a monumental study, *The Intersexes*, the first survey by an American of the subject of homosexuality. Stevenson was an aesthete and a professional writer, a considerable traveler, and a man of voracious curiosity. He was born in 1868 and died in Switzerland in 1942. Though he trained for the law, his writer's avocation became a vocation and he published his first book in 1887 under his own name, a boys' book called *The White Cockade*. Astute readers of homoerotic texts will find hints of Stevenson's interests there and a later book, *Left to Themselves; Being the Ordeal of Philip and Gerald*, further substantiates what *The White Cockade* implied. "Xavier Mayne," equally obscure, deserves a special place in the study of gay history.

*Imre* is the first homosexual novel to be written by an American in which there is no dissembling, no coded discourse, no pretense that friendship is platonic or that desire is allegorical. Instead it is a romantic, even florid text, breathless in its passionate account of a male homosexual love affair and equally passionate in its defense of homosexual life, love, and sex. The story—not set in America but in exotic Hungary—is about a man who falls in love with a handsome Hungarian officer, and after some agony, reveals his secret to him and happily finds that the officer reciprocates. At the end they determine to live together for life.

The pederastic yearnings discovered in nineteenth-century English texts, and the man-boy flavor so prominent in them, or the aesthetic flamboyance that markedly displays homoeroticism in other English texts of the same period, is not a feature of *Imre*. *Imre* in this sense stands very much in the tradition of nineteenth-century American homoerotic idealism that combines romance with masculine desire. *Imre* represents a pivotal moment when American homoerotic fiction, as it were, comes out. It gathers together many of the myths and inventions of the nineteenth century concerning homosexuality—whether homophobic or homophilic—and weaves them into a story that appropriates for itself the special ending that heretofore had been thought appropriate only to heterosexual romance: "and they lived happily ever after."

## From *Imre* (1906)

In Part I—"Masks"—Oswald, the "past thirty" narrator, tells of meeting the handsome, twenty-five-year-old Lieutenant Imre von N— in the Hungarian city of Szent-Istvanhely. Oswald becomes fascinated by Imre, but Imre, even though seeming to welcome Oswald's friendship, keeps a distance and, Oswald observes, is remarkably undemonstrative. Oswald speculates about Imre and (clearly having read Ulrichs and Krafft-Ebing) wonders of he is "an Uranian, or a sexually normal Dionian." One night, during a walk, they encounter a fellow officer who has been suspended from service because of a homosexual affair. Crossing the Lanczhid bridge, their talk turns to the subject. Oswald several times is on the verge of revealing himself to Imre, but does not, and Imre seems, finally, after some curious allusions, to be firmly opposed to homosexuality. In the next section things go further. Oswald has been called to London, and Imre to his army unit. They walk in silence until Oswald determines to speak to Imre about Imre's seeming refusal to pursue his profession, a topic that leads to one much closer to Oswald's heart.

## From Part II

### Masks and—a Face

"From the time when I was a lad, Imre, I felt myself unlike other boys in one element of my nature. That one matter was my special sense, my passion, for the beauty, the dignity, the charm . . . the, what shall I say? . . . the lovableness of my own sex. I hid it, at least so far as, little by little, I came to realize its force. For, I soon perceived that most other lads had no such passionate sentiments, in any important measure of their natures, even when they were finestrung, impressionable youths. There was nothing unmanly about me; nothing unlike the rest of my friends in school, or in townlife. Though I was not a strong-built, or rough-spirited lad, I had plenty of pluck and muscle, and was as lively on the playground, and fully as indefatigable, as my chums. I had a good many friends; close ones, who liked me well. But I felt sure, more and more, from one year to another even of that boyhood time, that no lad of them all ever could or would care for me as much as I could and did care for one or another of them! Two or three episodes made that clear to me. These incidents made me, too, shyer and shyer of showing how my whole young nature, soul and body together, Imre—could be stirred with a veritable adoration for some boy-friend that I elected . . . an adoration with a physical yearning in it—how intense was the appeal of bodily beauty, in a lad, or in a man of mature years.

"And yet, with that beauty, I looked for manliness, poise, will-power, dignity and strength in him. For, somehow I demanded those traits, always and clearly, whatever else I sought along with them. I say 'sought'; I can say, too, won—won often to nearness. But this other, more romantic, emotion in me . . . so strongly physical, sexual, as well as spiritual . . . it met with a really like and equal and full response once only. Just as my school-life was closing, with my sixteenth year (nearly my seventeenth) came a friendship with a newcomer into my classes, a lad of a year older than myself, of striking beauty of physique, and uncommon strength of character. This early relation embodied the same precocious, absolutely vehement passion (I can call it nothing else) on both sides. I had found my ideal! I had realized for the

first time, completely, a type; a type which had haunted me from first consciousness of my mortal existence, Imre; one that is to haunt me till my last moment of
it. All my immature but intensely ardent regard was returned. And then, after a few
passionate months together, my love, my schoolmate, all at once, became ill during an epidemic in the town, was taken to his home, and died. I never saw him after
he left me. . . .

"I grew older, I entered my professional studies, and I was very diligent with
them. I lived in a great capital, I moved much in general society. I had a large and
lively group of friends. But always, over and over, I realized that, in the kernel, at
the very root and fibre of myself, there was the throb and glow, the ebb and the
surge, the seeking as in a vain dream to realize again that passion of friendship
which could so far transcend the cold modern idea of the tie; the Over-Friendship,
the Love-Friendship of Hellas—which meant that between man and man could
exist, the sexual psychic love. That was still possible! I knew that now! I had read it
in the verses or the prose of the Greek or Latin and Oriental authors who have written out every shade of its beauty or unloveliness, its worth or debasements—from
Theokritos to Martial, or Abu-Nuwas, to Platen, Michel Angelo, Shakespeare. I
had learned it from the statues of sculptors, with those lines so often vivid with a
merely physical male beauty—works which beget, which sprang from, the sense of
it in a race; I had half-divined it in the music of a Beethoven and a Tschaikovsky
before knowing facts in the life-stories of either of them—or of an hundred other
tone-autobiographists.

"And I had recognized what it all meant to most people today!—From the disgust, scorn and laughter of my fellow men when such an emotion was hinted at! I
understood perfectly that a man must wear the Mask, if he, poor wretch, could neither abide at the bound of ordinary warmth of feeling for some friend of friends,
that drew on his innermost nature; or if he were not content because the other
stayed within that bound. Love between two men, however absorbing, however
passionate, must not be—so one was assured—solemnly or in disgusted
incredulity—as sexual love, a physical impulse and bond. That was now as ever, a
nameless horror—a thing against all civilization, sanity, sex, Nature, God!
Therefore, I was, of course . . . what then was I? Oh, I perceived it! I was that
anachronism from old—that incomprehensible incident in God's human creation
. . . the man-loving man! The man-loving man! whose whole heart can be given
only to another man, and who when his spirit is passing into his beloved friend's
keeping would demand, would surrender, the body with it. The man-loving man!
He who seeks not merely a spiritual unity with him whom he loves, but seeks the
embrace that joins two male human beings in a fusion that no woman's arms, no
woman's kisses can ever realize. No woman's embrace? No, no! . . . for instead of
that, either he cares not a whit for it, is indifferent to it, is smilingly scornful of it;
or else he tolerates it, even in the wife he has married (not to speak of any less honourable ties) as an artifice; a mere quietus to that undeceived sexual passion burning in his nature; wasting his really unmated individuality, years-long. Or else he
surrenders himself to some woman who bears his name, loves him—to her who
perhaps in innocence and ignorance believes that she dominates every instinct of
his sex!—making her a wife that she may bear to him children; or thinking that

marriage may screen him, or even (vain hope!) 'cure' him! But oftenest, he flies from any woman, as her sexual self; wholly shrinks from her as from nothing else created; avoids the very touch of a woman's hand in his own, any physical contact with woman, save in a calm cordiality, in a sexless and fraternal reserve, a passionless if yet warm . . . friendship! Not seldom he shudders (he may not know why) in something akin to dread and to loathing, though he may succeed in hiding it from wife or mistress, at any near approach of his strong male body to a woman's feminine one, however far, however harmonious in lines! Yes, even were she Aphrodite herself!

"And yet, Imre, thousands, thousands, hundreds of thousands, of such human creatures as I am, have not in body, in mind, nor in all the sum of our virility, in all the detail of our outward selves, any openly womanish trait! Not one! It is only the ignorant and the vulgar who nowadays think or talk of the homosexual as if he were an—hermaphrodite! In every feature and line and sinew and muscle, in every movement and accent and capability, we walk the world's way as men. We hew our ways through it as men, with vigour, success, honour . . . one master-instinct unsuspected by society for, it may be, our lives long! We plough the globe's roughest seas as men, we rule its States as men, we direct its finance and commerce as men, we forge its steel as men, we grapple with all its sciences, we triumph in all its arts as men, we fill its gravest professions as men, we fight in the bravest ranks of its armies as men, or we plan out its fiercest and most triumphant battles as men . . . in all this, in so much more, we are men! Why, (in a bitter paradox!) one can say that we always have been, we always are, always will be, too much men! So supermale, so utterly unreceptive of what is not manly, so aloof from any feminine essences, that we cannot tolerate woman at all as a sexual factor! Are we not the extreme of the male? Its supreme phase, its outermost phalanx?—Its climax of the aristocratic, the All-Man? And yet, if love is to be only what the narrow, modern Jewish-Christian ethics of today declare it, if what they insist be the only natural and pure expression of 'the will to possess, the wish to surrender..' . oh, then is the flouting world quite right! For then we were indeed not men! But if not so, what are we? Answer that, who can?

"The more perplexed I became in all this wretchedness (for it had grown to that by the time I had reached my majority) . . . the more perplexed I became because so often in books, old ones or new, nay, in the very chronicles of the criminal-courts, I came face to face with the fact that though tens of thousands of men, in all epochs, of noblest natures, of most brilliant minds and gifts, of intensest energies . . . scores of pure spirits, deep philosophers, bravest soldiers, highest poets and artists, had been such as myself in this mystic sex-disorganization . . . that nevertheless of this same Race, the Race-Homosexual, had been also, and apparently ever would be, countless ignoble, trivial, loathe-some, feeble-souled and feeble-bodied creatures! . . . the very weaklings and rubbish of humanity!

"Those, those, terrified me, Imre! To think of them shamed me; those types of man-loving-men who, by thousands, live incapable of any noble ideals or lives. Ah, those patently depraved, noxious, flaccid, gross, womanish beings! Perverted and imperfect in moral nature and even in bodily tissues! Those homosexual legions that are the straw-chaff of society; good for nothing, except the fire that purges the world of garbage and rubbish! A Heliogabalus, a Gilles de Rais, a Henri Trois, a Marquis de Sade; the painted male-prostitutes of the boulevards and twilight-glooming squares! The effeminate artists, the sugary and fibreless musicians! The Lady Nancyish, rich young men of higher or lower society; twaddling aesthetic sophistries; stinking with perfume like cocottes! The second-rate poets and the neuesthenic, precieux poetasters who rhyme forth their forged literary passports out of their mere human decadence; out of their marrowless shams of all that is man's fancy, a man's heart, a man's love-life! The cynical debauchers of little boys; the pederastic perverters of clean-minded lads in their teens; the white haired satyrs of clubs and latrines.

What a contrast are these to the great Oriental princes and the heroes and heroic intellects of Greece and Rome! To a Themistocles, an Agesilaus, an Aristides and a Kleomenes; to Socrates and Plato, and Saint Augustine, to Servetus and Beza; to Alexander, Julius Caesar, Augustus, and Hadrian; to Prince Eugene of Savoy, to Sweden's Charles the Twelfth, to Frederic the Great, to indomitable Tilly, to the fiery Skobeleff, the austere Gordon, the ill-starred Macdonald; to the brightest lyricists and dramatists of old Hellas and Italia; to Shakespeare, (to Marlowe also, we can well believe), Platen, Grillparzer, Holderlin, Byron, Whitman; to an Isaac Newton, a Justus von Liebig—to Michel Angelo and Sodoma; to the masterly Jerome Duquesnoy, the classic-souled Winckel-mann; to Mirabeau, Beethoven, Bavaria's unhappy King Ludwig;—to an endless procession of exceptional men, from epoch to epoch! Yet as to these and innumerable others, facts of their hidden, inner lives have proved without shadow of doubt (however rigidly suppressed as 'popular information') or inferences vivid enough to silence scornful denial, have pointed out that they belonged to Us.

"Nevertheless, did not the widest overlook of the record of Uranianism, the average facts about one, suggest that the most part of homosexual humanity has always belonged, always would belong, to the worthless or the wicked? Was our Race gold or excrement?—as rubies or as carrion? If that last were one's final idea, why then all those other men, the Normalists, aye, our severest judges, those others whether good or bad, whether vessels of honour or dishonour, who are not in their love-instincts as are we . . . the millions against our tens of thousands, even if some of us are to be respected . . . why they do right to cast us out of society; for after all, we must be a vitiated breed! . . . We must be judged by our commoner mass.

"And yet, the rest of us! The Rest, over and over! Men so high-minded, often of such deserved honour from all that world which has either known nothing of their sexual lives, or else has perceived vaguely, and with a tacit, a reluctant pardon! Could one really believe in God as making man to live at all, and to love at all, and yet at the same time believe that this love is not created, too, by God? is not of God's own divinest nature, rightfully, eternally—in millions of hearts? . . . Could one believe that the eternal human essence is in its texture today so different from itself of immemorial time before now, whether Greek, Latin, Persian, or English? . . . ."

I paused. Doing so, I heard from Imre, who had not spoken so much as a word—was it a sigh? Or a broken murmur of something coming to his lips. Was it—no, impossible! . . . was it a sort of sob, strangled in his throat! The evening had grown so dark that I could not have seen his face, even had I wished to look into it.

However . . . absorbed now in my own tenebrous retrospect, almost forgetting that anyone was there, at my side, I went on:

"You must not think that I had not had friendships of much depth, Imre, which were not, first and last, quite free from this other accent in them. Yes, I had had such; and I have many such now; comradeships with men younger, men of my own age, men older, for whom I feel warm affection and admiration, whose company was and is a true happiness for me. But somehow they were not and, no matter what they are they still are not, of the Type; of that eternal, mysteriously-disturbing cruel Type which so vibrates sexually against my hidden Self.

"How I dreaded, yet sought that Type! . . . how soon was I relieved, or dull of heart, when I knew that this or that friend was not enough dear to me, however dear he was, to give me that hated sexual stir and sympathy, an inner, involuntary thrill! Yet I sought it ever, right and left, since none embodied it for me; while I always feared that some one might embody it! There were approaches to it. Then, then, I suffered or throbbed with a wordless pain or joy of life, at one and the same time! But fortunately these encounters failed of full realization. Or what might have been my fate passed me by on the other side. But I learned from them how I could feel toward the man who could be in his mind and body my ideal; my supremest Friend. Would I ever meet him? . . . meet him again? . . . I could say to myself— remembering the episode of my schooldays. Or would I never meet him! For to be all my life alone, year after year, striving to be content with a pleasant shadow instead of glowing verity! . . ."

[Oswald falls in love with a heterosexual man. At the same time, he takes the advice of a doctor who urges him to marry as a "cure" for his torment. He becomes engaged to a woman. He has doubts.]

"I knew that no marriage, of any kind yet tolerated in our era, would 'cure' me of my 'illusion', my 'nervous disease', could banish this 'mere psychic disturbance', the result of 'too much introspection.' I had no disease! No . . . I was simply what I was born!—a complete human being, of firm, perfect physical and mental health; outwardly in full key with all the man's world: but, in spite of that, a being who from birth was of a vague, special sex; a member of the sex within the most obvious sexes; or apart from them. I was created as a man perfectly male, save in the one thing which keeps such a 'man' back from possibility of ever becoming integrally male— his terrible, instinctive demand for a psychic and a physical union with a man— not with a woman.

"Presently, during the same winter, accident opened my eyes wider to myself. From then, I have needed no further knowledge from the Tree of Good and Evil. I met with a mass of studies . . . on the similisexual topic. . . . I learned of the much-discussed theories of 'secondary sexes' and 'intersexes.' I learned of the theories and facts of homosexualism, of the Uranian love, of the Uranian Race, of 'the sex within a sex.' . . .

"I came to know of their enormous distribution over the world today. . . . I could pursue intelligently the growing efforts to set right the public mind as to so inerad-icable and misunderstood a phase of humanity. I realized that I had always been a member of that hidden brotherhood and Sub-Sex, or Super-Sex. In wonder, too, I informed myself of its deep instinctive freemasonries—even to organized ones—in every social class, every land, every civilization of the signs and symbols and safeguards of concealment. . . . 'Cure?' By marriage? By marriage when my blood ran cold at the thought! . . . The idea was madness. In a double sense. Better a pistol shot to my heart!

[Oswald breaks the engagement. He devotes himself to his heterosexual friend and decides to tell him all.]

" So—I yielded! Lately, the maddening wish to tell him all at any risk, the pressure of passion and its concealment . . . they had never so fiercely attacked me! In a kind of exalted shame, but in absolute sincerity, I told him all! I asked for nothing from him, except his sympathy, his belief in whatever was my higher and manlier nature . . . as the world judges any man . . . and the toleration of our friendship on the lines of its past. Nothing more: not a handclasp, not a look, not a thought more; the mere continued sufferance of my regard. Never again need pass between us so much as a syllable to remind him of this pitiable confession from me, to betray again the mysterious fire that burned in me underneath our intimacy. He had not suspected anything of it before. It could be forgotten by him from now onward.

"Did I ask too much? By the God that made mankind, Imre—that made it not only male or female but also as We are. . . . I do not think I did!

"But he, he thought otherwise. He heard my confession through with ever more hostile eyes, with an astonished unsympathy . . . disgust . . . curling his lips. Then he spoke slowly—pitilessly: 'I have heard that such creatures as you describe yourself are to be found among mankind. I do not know, nor do I care to know, whether they are a sex by themselves, a justified, because helpless, play of Nature; or even a kind of logically essential link, a between-step . . . as you seem to have persuaded yourself. Let all that be as it may be. I am not a man of science nor keen to such new notions! From this moment, you and I are strangers! I took you for my friend because I believed you to be a . . . man. You chose me for your friend because you believed me . . . stay, I will not say that! . . . because you wished me to be . . . a something else, a something more or less like to yourself, whatever you are! I loathe you! . . . I loathe you! When I think that I have touched your hand, have sat in the same room with you, have respected you! . . . Farewell! . . . If I served you as a man should serve such beings as you, this town should know your story tomorrow! Society needs more policemen than it has, to protect itself from such lepers as you! I will keep your hideous secret. Only remember never to speak to me! . . . never to look my way again! Never! From henceforward I have never known you and never will think of you!—if I can forget anything so monstrous in this world!'

"So passed he out of my life, Imre. Forever! Over the rupture of our friendship not much was said, nevertheless. For he was called to London a few days after that last interview; and he was obliged to remain in the capital for months. Meantime I had changed my life to meet its new conditions; to avoid gossip. I had removed my lodgings to a suburb. I had taken up a new course in professional work. It needed all my time. Then, a few months later, I started quietly on a long travel-route on the Continent, under excuse of ill-health. I was far from being a stranger to life in at least half a dozen countries of Europe, east or west. But now, now, I knew what it was to be a refugee, an exile! . . .

"But one thing I have, Imre; and I have kept my word! That so surely as ever again I may find myself even half-way drawn to a man by the inner passion of an Uranian love—not by mere friendship of a colder psychic complexion—if that man really shows me that he cares for me with respect, with intimate affection, with trust . . . then he shall know absolutely what manner of man I am! . . . I must be taken as I am, pardoned for what I am, or neither pardoned nor taken. I have learned my lesson well. But the need of my maintaining such painful honesty has come seldom. I have been growing into expecting no more of life, no realizing whatever of the Type that had been my undoing, that must mean always my peace or my deepest unrest . . . till I met you, Imre! Till I met you! . . .

"I cannot tell thee, Imre, . . . oh, I have no need now to try! What thou hast become for me. My Search ended when thou and I met. Never has my dream given me what is this reality of thyself. I love this world now only because thou art in it. I respect thee wholly—I respect myself—certain, too, of that coming time, however far away now, when no man shall ever meet many intelligent civilization's disrespect simply because he is a similisexual, Uranian! But—oh, Imre, Imre!—I love thee, as men can only love. Once more helpless, and therewith hopeless! But this time no longer silent, before the Friendship which is Love, the Love which is Friendship.

"Speak my sentence. I make no plea. I have kept my pledge to confess myself tonight. But I would have fulfilled it only a little later, were I not going away from thee tomorrow. I ask nothing, except what I asked long ago of that other, of whom I have told thee! Endure my memory, as thy friend! Friend? That at least! For, I would say farewell, believing that I shall still have the right to call thee 'friend'—even—O God!—when I remember tonight. But whether that right is to be mine, or not, is for thee to say. Tell me!"

I stopped.

Full darkness was now about us. Stillness had so deepened that the ceasing of my own low voice made it the more suspenseful. The sweep of the night-wind rose among the acacias. The birds of shadow flitted about us. The gloom seemed to have entered my soul—as Death into Life. Would Imre ever speak?

His voice came at last. Never had I heard it so moved, so melancholy. A profound tenderness was in every syllable.

"If I could . . . my God! If I only could! . . . say to thee what I cannot. Perhaps . . . some time . . . Forgive me, but thou breakest my heart! . . . Not because I care less for thee as my friend . . . no, above all else, not that reason! We stay together, Oswald! . . . We shall always be what we have become to each other! Oh, we cannot change, not through all our lives! Not in death, not in anything! Oh, Oswald! that thou couldst think, for an instant, that I—I—would dream of turning away from thee . . . suffer a break for us two . . . because thou art made in thy nature as God makes mankind—as each and all, or not as each and all! We are what we are! . . . Forever! Forever, Oswald! . . . Here, take my hand! As long as I live . . . and beyond then!" cried Imre. "Yes, my God above us, my God in us! . . . Only, only, for the sake of the bond between us from this night, promise me that thou wilt never speak again of what thou hast told me of thyself—never, unless I break the silence. Nevermore a word of—of thy—thy—feeling for me. There are other things for us to talk of, are there not, my dear brother? Thou wilt promise?"

With his hand in mine, my heart so lightened that I was as a new creature, forgetting even the separation before me, we promised secrecy to one another. Gladly, too. For, instead of loss, with this parting, what gain was mine! Imre knew me now as myself!—he really knew me: and yet was now rather the more my friend than less, so I could believe, after this tale of mine had been told him . . ! It seemed to me that I had everything that my heart had ever sought of him, or would seek! I made the promise too, gladly with all my soul.

[It is then Imre's turn to reveal himself to Oswald. He tells his story of the concealment of his desires, and the two men realize that they have been chosen by fate for one another.]

## FROM THE INTERSEXES (1908)

*The Intersexes: A History of Similisexualism as a Problem in Social Life* (New York: Napler, 1908) is the first book written by an American that attempted to present a history of homosexuality and therefore is the first American text to theorize homosexuality in a historical rather than in a moralistic or medical context. Unlike European medical texts that preceded it, *The Intersexes* does not construct homosexuality as an anomaly or as a medical, legal, or social "problem" which must be dealt with by some form of social engineering, punishment, or treatment that will change the homosexual. Instead, Mayne argues that it is not the homosexual but the nonhomosexual who must change to accommodate what he insists is a natural manifestation of human affection.

*The Intersexes* is the first nonfiction book by an American to be written from a positive homosexual point of view by an author who leaves little doubt that he is himself homosexual even though pseudonymous. In a text of over six hundred pages, Mayne discusses homosexuality in both women and men. He argues that sex is not determined by physical characteristics—that is, that biology is not destiny. He rejected any formula that stigmatized homosexuals as mentally or physiologically aberrant. Instead, in his view homosexuals combine attributes of both sexes to form separate but biologically equal sexual structures, each one being sited equidistantly on a scale of sexuality. He advocates that these two separate sexes (homosexual men, homosexual women) are "indisputably entitled to recognition as to [their] individual rights." Mayne's achievement is not so much to construct a theory of homosexual etiology as to construct an argument against oppression: "We find them victims of sexual repression, seekers after a sexual expression they cannot obtain without disgraces, dangers, crimes. Not less . . . are they petitioners for a . . . consideration and tolerance, social and legal: fugitives from miseries and injuries." Difference, he insists, is a prime cause of homosexual oppression: "It is true that they present . . . many traits, claims, theories, impulses, practices, deviations from the more or less normally human. . . . They have sex idioms that repel and terrify us." Here he recognizes the existence of a homosexual style or sensibility, and he theorizes its categories as being far broader than mere sexual acts. He also defines homophobia as a negative reaction to this style, one that is fueled by fear and ignorance. This is probably the most succinct (and perhaps the earliest) definition of homophobia in any American text. He also recognizes the effect homophobia can have on society as a whole: "the fact remains that a great proportion of Intersexual lives are led . . . under a sexual, social, and moral ban that blots our human civilization" (Mayne 1908:18–20).

He concludes with a defiant peroration in which he insists that homosexuals, no matter what their position in society, necessarily become resistant adversaries to social orthodoxies: "Each day proves how powerless are legal provisions to lessen the similisexual impulse in humanity the world over: how vain are ethical or religious positions to pit it out of the heart and the life impulses of mankind in each class. Similisexual love flourishes today in every phase of finer or deteriorated character and expression, from binding the master-bond of high souls to being the living of the sordid male prostitutes of a boulevard. It defies clandestinely all penalties, and all social intolerances" (Mayne, 71). It is impossible to do justice to all that Mayne discusses in *The Intersexes*, all the unknown texts he lists and translates (many for the first and only time), or to his intriguing speculations on homoerotic textuality. If canons are sought, Mayne provides a foundation for them. He should also be recognized as the founder of modern American gay studies, and in his tightly packed pages a thousand doctoral dissertations lie waiting to be realized. Though *Imre* is very much a nineteenth-century novel, in which friendship rather than homosexuality is the dominant metaphor, and though *The Intersexes* is a response to nineteenth-century constructions of homophobia and of homosexuality, yet Mayne must be read as a pivotal writer standing on the edge of two sensibilities. He looks back to the nineteenth century, subjecting its texts to a radical critique, yet informed by its vision of manly friendship. But he also writes in the first decade of the twentieth century, and from that vantage he seems to forecast both the increasingly intense resistance to homophobia as well as the authoritative rewriting of homosexual and gender identities that the twentieth century will set in train.

## FROM CHAPTER II

### THE THEORY OF INTERSEXES

Nature has always maintained in the human species a series of graduated and necessary Intersexes, between the two great major sexes that we recognize as distinctively "man" and "woman" i.e. as the extreme masculine and the extreme feminine. These Intersexes are not physically obvious in the frank degree that we have foolishly expected such natural differences would be expressed. The average eye and mind have never learned even how to look for them, though they are around us daily in their positive attributes. They are the less perceived because their physical differences. . .are not necessarily visible. . . . Especially are these Intersexes established, determined, and excused by the one supremely natural factor in them—the sexual instinct. . . . Their existence is as irrefutable as it is immemorial. For centuries, the world has narrowed-down mankind into two sexes. There are at least two more than our traditional anthropological spectrum has perceived and recognized; each of primary importance always. . . .

Taking this series of conclusions as our guidance let us re-distribute the human race sexually. To the one extreme and perfect masculine sex, a man, and in the other extreme and perfect female sex, a woman, we will add at least two Intersexes. These Intersexes partake of the natures and temperaments and physiques of both the male and the female, now to one extent, now to another. Departing from the first sex a man, we establish a second and "intersexual" sex, known to European medicopsychologic literature as the Urning or Uranian sex. The name is derived from the classic fable of the "Venus Urania" and from the Platonic discussions concerning a mystic "nobler Venus" the divine patroness of similisexual, passional loves, especially between males re-affirming the theory of there having been created only one single human sex of old; that only later came to subsist two types with their separate sexual instincts in mankind, each by divine insinuation. We next establish or proceed to re-establish, a third sex, or intersex, called the Uraniad which refers to the feminine, but the feminine sexually masculinized of which sex many "women-seeming" women are members. Last, we place the perfectly feminine sex, its extreme, the woman as we have long recognized her. The arrangement of these four sexes the sorting of the two "intersexes" thus, has been questioned. There are subtle and interesting arguments for putting the Uranian, or masculine intersex, absolutely as the first and completest of the sexes known, not simply as an intersex: at the same time relegating the man-type as commonly met, to the merely intersexual degree. There is also a considerable line of finer intersexual distinctions and types, adjusted by various psychiaters which makes the list of intersexes exceed the four here established. But for all ordinary purposes the reduction to four, and the foregoing adjustments are sufficient.

These two Intersexes named here as the Uranian and the Uraniad, the one partaking most of the outwardly and inwardly masculine yet not fully a man, the other leaning toward the typic feminine yet not fully woman, are each indisputably a blend of the two extreme sexes. Each is more or less indisputably entitled to recognition as to its individual rights; each exists now as ever in a most important proportion to the rest of mankind. These Intersexes are constantly working-out about us, with or without social recognition and sanction, their own sexual instincts. Too often such types are not only unknown to their fellow-men for what they are, but also too often not known to—themselves. Especially do we find them the victims of sexual repression, seekers after a sexual expression that they cannot obtain without disgraces, dangers, and crimes. Not less especially are they petitioners for at least a tentative, a cautious consideration and tolerance, social and legal: fugitives from miseries and injustices which an unreasoning and ill-informed world, with its tendency to generalize, has far too little suspected. It is true that they present inevitably and often painfully, whether taken as individuals or as classes, many traits, claims, theories, impulses, practices, deviations from the more or less normally human, which cannot be tolerated in ethics and social life by even philosophic justice however dispassionate. They have sex-idioms that repel and terrify us, no matter how elastic is our human sympathy. But admitting all which will deepen around them this undeniable shadow, the fact remains that a great proportion of Intersexual lives are led and probably for a long time to come must be led, under a sexual, social and moral ban that blots our human civilization. Day by day is continued about us, no matter with what outward serenity a chronicle of undeserved martyrdom that can be dramatic beyond any description in its emotional currents; demanding relief by a psychiatric enlightenment not yet more than begun.

## From Chapter III

## Similisexual Friendships

If friendship be free from real love-emotion, then friendship will be found to reach its truest expression between individuals of the same sex. It represents thus what we will call "similisexual friendship." I am not disparaging here warm and dispassionate friendships between the opposite sexes, constantly met, and so-called (by a term long mis-used) "Platonic" in their nature. In place of that phrase we will call these "heterosexual friendships." But, no matter how firm and deep are countless instances of heterosexual friendships between persons of the opposite sexes, they do not compare favourably with similisexual friendships. Too frequently they attack elementary purity of the sentiment. Frequently also are they more or less sustained with self-deceptions: no matter what arguments and examples may bring against such a charge. We shall find it needful presently to question nicely the nature of many heterosexual friendships.

We shall be obliged also to question, even more sharply in the close study of the Uranian and Uraniad life, the character of many similisexual ties, whether between men and men, or women and women; and our conventional ideas of them are likely to be changed before the analysis of this study will be finished. The whole theory of so-called Platonic friendships, of psychic ties of heterosexual kind, is ill-sustained by realities in human-nature and social history. The finest, most unalloyed friendship must be similisexual: even if we admit presently, in a sort of paradox that many relationships seeming precisely friendship are not so: many that seem not so being precisely such.

There is no grossening of human-nature, no injustice to the finer psychic qualities in us, when we accept the idea that love from one human being toward another must include the wish to possess physically, and the yearning to give oneself, physically. Even if such a rule seems to accentuate the merely animal-nature in men, we cannot get far away from the conclusion. If we are honest with ourselves and humanity we ought not to try to get away from it. Love must contain the sexual desire, the wish for physical possession of beauty. . . .

The instant that the physical desire with or without a concurrent spiritual desire, springs up in us, stirred to life by a quickening sense of physical beauty in the object of our interest, then there cannot be a logical question of our sentiment being more than mere strong friendship, or more than a minor "natural affection." We are in the presence of passional sexual love; of such love in its lighter or more vehement character perhaps, but of erotic love. It is love, no matter what are the real or supposed sexes of the persons concerned. The instant that even vaguely we want to possess, and even vaguely feel that we would be willing to surrender ourselves along with the possession, then no matter how "impossible," how terrifying, how bewildering such an impulse be to us we love sexually. From friendship, we are already far afield.

But, with this logical and inevitable conclusion, we come face to face with a convention long-sustained in generally intelligent circles of human thought, with which we are put into startling and bewildered warfare. During a long succession of centuries, including especially those influenced by Jewish and Christian theological systems of morals and law, has been affirmed and re-affirmed, has been asserted in public literature and in private conversation, has been held as a basal truth, that a man should love, should be sexually drawn to, a woman only: never to another man. In like manner, that a woman should love, be attracted sexually, only to a man: never to another woman.

We have been assured, peremptorily, argumentatively, for at least a couple of thousand years, that if a man do not feel his sexual nature going out toward a woman, then something is distinctly minus in his body or in his temperament. But if he goes a step farther, and not only feels no sexual attraction to women, but by some mysterious psychologic processes finds himself sexually attracted toward men, feels an admiring physical desire for them and their beauty, feels concurrent yearning to surrender himself physically to a man, youthful or elder, then he is a diseased abnormality, a shocking degenerate from manhood, a monster or a maniac. During long centuries the statute-books of the majority of European nations have expressly recognized such a man only as a monster and anomaly: and in respect of his working-out his sexual impulses of the kind, he ranks legally as a felon, in even many countries to-day. . . .

Such is a brief statement of similisexual love, and of its positive distinctions from friendships: whether heterosexual or similisexual. We are all of us familiar, from youth up, with the attitude of the world, intolerant, horrified, arbitrary, toward any mature phases of it. We have heard it mocked in our boyish school-days, often with boyish hypocrisy. We have grown to manhood and to womanhood, accepting it as a vice and perversion, rightfully opposed by law, by all sound social morality. . . . That such similisexual love, is now as ever, capable of agreement with the finest and purest social and moral civilization, the most distinct ascetic superiority, with the strongest religious quality of the race or the individual—these ideas will not be endured for a moment by the average Anglo-Saxon. He regards them as out of discussion. He has not even found it worth while, as a special and ethical problem, to think twice about them seriously, in his life. . . .

If one argue with them against classifying all homosexual impulses with barbarism, pointing out that precisely this instinct of similisexual love between man and man has always existed, side by side, with the finest social life, with the most virile militarism, with the highest moral and aesthetic civilizations of the past, even to being recognized as a great factor for social good, the argument is not accepted for a moment.

For one is assured that no ancient civilizations obeyed the Christian Dispensation, or compare well with it: that Christian morals as the basis of all sound social and moral law, abhor the homosexual impulse: that the Christian Scriptures have placed it in the category of gravest sins and felonies: and that homosexualism entered into the decadence of races and nations, as an essential factor. We are also informed that similisexual love "has relatively disappeared": is more and more forgotten, has become vagabond a moral perversion from humanity to-day, in all "high civilizations" and all "superior moral life." We are assured that human nature has emphatically "changed," in this respect as in others thanks to especially the powerful influence of the contemporary Judaic-Christian basis of social ethics. . . .

Meantime, however displeasing to the reader, let it be affirmed that all real friendships between men have a sexual germ. Also can one declare it as a perfectly assured fact, in hundreds of instances of noble and honoured "friendships," those suggesting the "model," the "ideal" sort, between men, that the concrete sexual tie and its satisfaction, have been of the first importance in the relation. That has been originally its master-factor. That has rendered such so-called "friendships" the most concentrated and absorbing of similisexual loves. No matter what have been the biographic glosses and subterfuges, no matter what have been the amiable fictions, no matter how indignant have been the denials, the real bond was welded by a profound, mysterious, noble, passionate sexualism. Such too, are examples that every day could disclose about us, right and left. Everywhere are the ties absolutely embodying the antique, eternal sentiment: yet trembling at revelation of it to the outside world. The link is a marriage of the body as well as of the soul. It is a love: not a friendship. It is the supremely virile love, expressing itself as human nature, naturally and inevitably, ever has expressed itself in a vast proportion of all races and grades of mankind. But such physical erotism in multitudinous instances has not a jot impaired the high spiritual quality of the relation. It has often enriched it. The psychic and the physical have been blent in it, in an harmonious chemistry, too subtle and natural for vulgar analysis. The bodily and the spiritual passion have been each the complement of the other, by Nature's initiative, and by Divine impulse.

### From Chapter IV

#### Similisexual Love in Ancient Civilizations and Religions

Naturally one is told . . . that the "earlier," "ante-Mosaic," civilization opposed similisexual love: punished mercilessly sexual intercourse of the kind. So we have been informed, when especially the story of Lot and his mysterious guests in Sodom is cited. But such objectors will do well to understand once and for all (likely for the first time) that the entire episode of Lot and the wicked men of Sodom does not afford any grounds for arguing that Sodom was destroyed on account of its similisexual tastes and practices, or that Sodom was really given to such. Further, we have no proof that homosexual intercourse was ever special to Sodom, ever was or is an offense to God, even in a Jehovistic concept of God; nor that what the world's statute-books, and pulpit-parlance, especially, have so long termed "sodomy" should ever have such a meaning. The incident of Lot and his guests, and of the mob that attacked Lot's house in Sodom with the clamorous "Bring out the men, that we may know them!" correctly read, is simply a common civic episode of the suspicious Oriental town. A mob-element being excited, feared some political treachery: and violated the hospitality that Lot had offered to two strangers, supposed to be spies or what else, by the unfriendly crowd. There is no textual or other reason to give the verb "know" a sexual value, no warrant for sexual colouring of the affair. Almost exactly the same incident occurs in another defense of guests: set forth in Judges XIX, v. 16–27 (retold in Chap. XX.13) in the night attack of the curious and alarmed townsmen of the city of Gibeah. There, too, a stranger, a Levite, had been taken into a house, with the same Eastern hospitality, and saved his life by allowing his concubine to be the victim of the mob, precisely as Lot offered his virgin daughters. Both episodes are plainly tales of violated hospitality. The same devices to appease the citizens are mentioned: but there is no evidence even in this last detail of sexual insults to the guest. In the story of the Levite, we distinctly read that the object of the attack was because "they thought to have slain" him: and Sodom's mob included both "young and old, all the people from every quarter." The two stories are absolutely of Oriental "guest and host" duties and claims.

The Mosaic charge to Israel that similisexual love was an abomination in the sight of the Jewish Jehovah, a particular moral enormity meriting death, had no basis in any moral "revelation to Moses," any more than had other wise provisions of the Mosaic Code. The warning, the death-penalty, were inserted for directly practical motives, not theological nor ethical objections. (The very words that are used of similisexual relations as a sin, refer to many other matters often: to what we consider quite minor offenses.) Let us note, for other example, the story of Onan. There is absolutely no ground in the incident of Onan and the spilled seed, for regarding masturbation as a moral obliquity. Onan was not punished for what was a moral sexual dereliction per se: but for unwillingness to marry his brother's widow, and to raise up a family for his brother's name: a breach of religion, of Oriental civil-custom, in Onan's early day. Onan, like many men, has his name used as a reproach against sin and his posterity, by an injustice to the man and the action. We can admit that the Mosaic Code put similisexual passion and its gratifi-cation in line with grave moral, social, religious offenses, with rape, murder, idola-try, bestiality. But such a juxtaposition and the death-penalty for homosexual rela-tions should never have been taken by later and non-Israelitish peoples as referring to such sexual intercourse, between men and men, or women and women, to the unnatural, or to the ethically vicious.

## From Chapter V

### The Uranian; His General Physical and Psychical Diagnosis

When we examine the intellectual, moral, temperamental, nervous traits of the Uranian, we have further indices. No class of humanity makes a finer intellectual showing, example by example, of one grade or of another. But we detect a defi-ciency in robustly originative intellectualism, where the mind must deal with the abstract and practical, rather than with the more concrete, or with the aesthetic and emotional. Many exceptions point out the rule. The Uranian is less likely to be suc-cessful in philosophy, in mathematics, abstract mechanics, and so on, than in let-ters, arts, and lighter applications of science. He is often highly appreciative of what goes on in these fields, yet not productive in them. But in the more aesthetic pro-fessions his work has been the wonder of the world since it began. The practicing physician, consulted by similisexual clients, hoping to understand their own abnor-malisms better, or to be treated for them as for a disease, is continually meeting the man of letters, the artist, the sculptor, the musician, the architect, the actor and singer, or instrumentalist. Numberless are homosexuals whose gifts, business or professions keep them busy in occupations where they deal with practical aesthetics, or with distinctly aesthetic results; not the sterner mind-work. The intellectuality of the uranistic type is brilliant. It has dazzled the world forever with its genius. But it often wants elasticity, and brunt-force in initial conceptions and in hard applications of reason and analysis.

The ethical nature of the Uranian varies greatly. It ranges from the finest moral and spiritual feelings and practices to the feeblest sense of morals of any kind: much as is the case with the Dionian man. There is no truth in the idea that the similisexual is necessarily morally bad, or feels even the least indifference toward religions. Too many lofty types of all philosophies, all creeds, too many respected officials and model private citizens have lived and died uranistic, for this error to stand. But the fact is proved every day in society, that the more sensuous the Uranian and the more circumscribed his mental horizon, just so weakened or debased is his moral sense. His distinctively similisexual instincts, when his general equipment otherwise is sound, seem to have uncertain bearings on his conduct: while the converse is true of the less fortunate and respectable Uranian. Socrates was similisexual. Not readily can we dismiss the idea that Christ was such—and saints many have been Uranians. But so were Philippe of Orleans, Caligula, de Sade: so is the blackmailing catamite that prostitutes himself for a shilling, incidentally to rob, to murder, to ruin socially some unlucky victim. The reader has seen that he must throw away the unscientific idea that the homosexual, in loving the male with his sexual love, in seeking to satisfy his passion physically, necessarily is committing offense against Nature or an individual morality. He acts absolutely according to Nature, simply working out his fixed, legitimate, sexual sentiment and necessity, exactly as the dionistic man seeks female society to the same end. In the most conclusively Uranian-type homosexuality is inborn: with its concurrent utter sexual indifference to women. Frequently there is an utter horror of such intercourse, a distressing nervous inability toward it. Uranianism has its own excuses for existing, the general ethical furnishment of the man often is analyzable much or wholly apart.

But it is in the nervous fabric of the Uranian that we find more striking data. The uranistic nature, as a German writer has admirably pointed out, is the most sensitive fine-strung, exquisitely emotional one yet known. We find the homosexual turning emphatically to the aesthetic professions, with alert senses to all that is beautiful. His vivid impressionability, his creative powers are so supreme that one may say that the world of poetry, the graphic and plastic arts, most especially music (that most neurotic of all arts) and belles-lettres of all sorts are richest by the distinctively similisexual genius. Here he is ever inventive, originative. History, biography, every psychiatric physician, can confirm this. Its chief contrast may be thought, by some, to occur with the fact that the soldier is so notably similisexual: that so many great military men have been Uranians. But the military profession is really one that is highly aesthetic and nervous, as well as one that throws the Uranian into intimate, exclusive, and admiring relations with men. It fosters philarrenism, frequently dignifying it. Aesthetics are to the Uranian the breath of life. No wonder that we find them as author, painter, sculptor, composer, singer, actor: whatever demands nerves and concentrated idealism, pouring forth his genius from one epoch of the world to the next. Genius and madness are old allies. We need not be surprised to find that the Uranian often confirms that painful mystery. . . .

But, alas! between conditions kindly or adverse that meet the normal man in love and which the Uranian encounters, exists one terribly significant difference: tyrannic during modern eras of faiths, morals and laws. It may be called the curse upon the Uranian. For, the "normal" man can speak without shame of his passion to the woman who inspires it. Even if she reject it, she is not insulted by it, if it be worthy: spiritual enough and sincere in her eyes. The woman-lover can demand the sympathy of his confidential friend, he can receive such sympathy if he will. He can be the object of sympathy to even the outside world: for his secret can be guessed by it without disgrace on any ground of "unnatural" emotion. But the Uranian must often "go through" the most overwhelming, soul-prostrating of loves, finding his nerves and mind and body beaten down under the passion, his days and nights vivified or poisoned by it, all without his doing anything so persistently as to hide his sentiment forever from the object of it! To hide from his closest friends, from suspicion by the world! Hide it he must. Accounted a diseased human thing, an outcast from men, a beast, if his secret be probed: hopeless often of its toleration for an instant by the being that often under the name of friendship, he loves with all the fire of intersex: fighting the emotion in himself in bewilderment or shame: perhaps living, side by side with some stranger that is more than any mere friend to him, playing his part like a man, frequently without one human confidant in the wide world, so can pass his social life. Ever the Mask, the shuddering concealment, the anguish of hidden passion that burns his life away! Not always: for sometimes, as if by a Divine grace, the Uranistic love is accepted: or at least its physical side is pardoned and tolerated by the man to whom it goes out. But this pre-supposes either a peculiarly deep regard and broad-minded nature in the dionian object—if he be decidedly dionistic, as is likely to be the case in the finer grades of uranian loves: or else he is (most luckily for the Uranian) imbued with an uranistic element himself. Fortunate then is the Uranian, or half-fortunate! He can at least be honest. For he can at least receive sympathy and brotherly pity, human respect and regard. Perhaps he wins more, and so becomes unspeakably blessed. But often he is hopeless as he is helpless, and wears his mask with the smiling hypocrisy of anxious self-protection. He sits in his club and hears similisexualism, not merely in gross and unworthy forms but in manly ideals, mocked as infamy. He listens to the coarsest jests, at the expense of the Uranian nature, when some accident brings his "case" to public notice. He must deny his ability to understand how a man can fall in love with another man. Particularly, as one invaluable sham, must he take pains to appear sexually interested in women, to be intimate with women, to seem to relish open, and frequently obscene sexual talk about women. This last is much in his programme for hiding sexual indifference or downright physical aversion to women. The Mask, ever the Mask! It becomes like the natural face of the wearer.

# 27. Camp Sites: Armies of Androgynes

## American Literature (1918–1933)

### SEXUALITY AND HOMOSEXUALITY (1880–1900)

After about 1880, American medical texts seemed to be increasingly obsessed with the topic of sexual inversion, and the American public began to notice this obsession. Conceptions of homosexuality as a medical "problem" found their way from the circumspect pages of professional journals into the popular press, though the words to describe this new sexual species were as elusive as they had been to Whitman forty years earlier.

However, in 1892 the word did appear—imported from Europe. "Homosexual" was employed by Dr. James Kiernan in an American medical journal when he defined the "pure homosexual" as one whose "general mental state is that of the opposite sex" (Katz 1983:232). Kiernan's "homosexual" is the familiar unmanly and effeminate male who imitates a woman. Definitions of sexuality inevitably relied on the presumption that certain characteristics of "masculinity" and "femininity" were a fixed and irreducible component of every sexual subject: The "true woman" was submissive socially and sexually, the manager of domestic life, and pious as well as morally pure. Men were socially and sexually assertive, benign and somewhat aloof rulers of the patriarchal family, and the active providers of material goods. Victorian theorists argued that these roles were dictated by nature and biology and that their qualities were "naturally" associated with the biological sex. Males and females "naturally" engaged in sex as the respectively active and passive partners. The binary opposition of active and passive seemed, so they believed, almost to be written into the structure of sex itself.

The new "sexuality" was seen to be all-encompassing and mysterious, the dominating and defining principle that explained and underlay all human actions. As Dr. William Howard explained it in 1904, summing up the speculations of half a century of scientific discourse: "Every physician should understand the sexual side of life, for it is sexual activity that governs life, permits the continuation of the species and promotes crime and its causes. It is the basis of all society" (quoted in Katz 1983:312).

### CONSTRUCTING HOMOPHOBIA (1885–1900)

By the end of the century the image of the homosexual was that of an effeminate weakling, morbid, morose, melancholy by nature, abnormally sexed and physically deficient, whose perverse desires and abnormal acts could lead to violence, insanity, and suicide. A lecture by Dr. G. Frank Lydston in 1889 raises the specter of numerous and well-organized colonies of homosexuals. "There is" he says, "in every community of any size a colony of male sexual perverts; they are usually known to each other, and are likely to congregate together. At times they operate in accordance with some definite and concerted plan in quest of subjects wherewith to gratify their abnormal sexual impulses" (quoted in Katz 1983:213). Lydston contributed to the formation of a myth of a "homosexual conspiracy" that at mid-point in the twentieth century would have disastrous and even tragic consequences for many gay people.

Such medicalized demonization of homosexuals led to medicalized attempts at social control. In 1898 a Dr. Anthony saw the control of sexual perverts as a kind of crusade to be undertaken by doctors: "It may fall to the lot of one of you to be the active means of destroying such a school of vice and perversion. Nay, more than that, it may be your son or the son of your intimate friend whom you are called upon to rescue. If it comes in the line of duty to take a hand in the overthrow of such a circle, I beg of you to let no dread of notoriety, no consideration of position, . . . come between you and the fulfillment of such a duty. Exercise all due charity, have the suspected and accused submitted to a most thorough examination to determine his responsibility, and then have him removed from the community to his proper place, be it asylum or be it prison" (quoted in Katz 1983:294).

All this served only to fan homophobic flames and also enforced for homosexuals themselves a self-image that accepted rather than questioned the definitions society and medicine imposed upon them. Medical definition created for homosexuals a negative identity that, as Katz says, "served to induce the invert to accept an anti-invert morality" and caused them to respond to the "social production of shame and guilt" (Katz 1983:156). But while some accepted guilt and suffered under intolerance, others resisted it and responded in ways that perhaps those who deployed the homophobic tools of control had not anticipated.

## AMERICAN HOMOSEXUAL FICTION (1900–1933)

Fiction produced between 1900 and after the end of World War I addressed the "riddle" of homosexuality. Charles Warren Stoddard's novel *For the Pleasure of His Company* (1903) is set in San Francisco, and the hero, as in Stoddard's other books, eventually seeks happiness in the South Seas. In Henry Fuller's *Bertram Cope's Year* (1919), the scene is America and a thoroughly modern young American man goes off with his boyfriend at the end and rejects the heterosexual arrangements that have been laid to entrap him. Sherwood Anderson's "Hands," also written in 1919, confronts what one anonymous Boston writer called the "deep-rooted prejudice" of "Anglo-American hypocrisy." Rather than imagining separate cities of lovers or recalling the classical past, writers after 1900 put their characters, often flamboyantly, on the streets of New York, Boston, and Chicago. Novelists no longer lamented that their love could not speak its name; instead they spoke it openly and confronted homophobia where they saw it, advocating active resistance to what they viewed as social, medical, and political oppression.

Much of the homosexual fiction of the period between 1900 and the 1930s addresses the proposition that homosexual identities can no longer be founded on ancient models and that justification for homosexuality can no longer be derived exclusively from the past. In 1925 Robert McAlmon wrote a group of stories included in a collection called *Distinguished Air*, one of which, "Miss Knight," is a remarkable picture of an American drag queen. In 1926 the openly homosexual writer Bruce Nugent, under the pseudonym of "Richard Bruce," published a short story, "Smoke, Lilies and Jade," which is the first story in American fiction to explore both gay and African-American identity. In 1933 *A Scarlet Pansy*, by the possibly pseudonymous "Robert Scully," as well as Charles Henri Ford and Parker Tyler's *The Young and The Evil* (1933), are outrageous and too little known masterpieces of American homoerotic writing. The principle argument of this literature was that homosexuals, though certainly different, and very much outcasts (and perhaps even a separate species), should confront rather than retire from society, achieving power through this confrontation.

## Further Reading

Roger Austen, *Playing the Game: The Homosexual Novel in America* (New York: Bobbs-Merrill, 1977); George Chauncey, *Gay New York: Gender, Urban Culture, and the Making of the Gay Male World, 1890–1940* (New York: Basic Books, 1994); Byrne R. S. Fone, *A Road To Stonewall: Homosexuality and Homophobia in English and American Literature 1750–1969* (New York: Macmillan/Twayne, 1995); Jonathan Ned Katz, *Gay American History* (New York: Thomas Y. Crowell, 1976), and *Gay/Lesbian Almanac* (New York: Harper and Row, 1983); James Levin, *The Gay Novel in America* (New York: Garland, 1991).

## Earl Lind ("Ralph Werther"/"Jennie June") (b. 1874)

Earl Lind, a homosexual author nervy enough to send one of his books to Anthony Comstock—whose business as head and founder of the New York Society for the Suppression of Vice (1873) was "hunting down inverts and hauling them off to prison"—was told that his book ought to be destroyed. Comstock's opinions, expressed in 1900, are not tempered with the pretense to reasoned discourse that medical texts of the time assumed, and so what he says may suggest what the popular voice was beginning to say: "These inverts are not fit to live with the rest of mankind. They ought to have branded in their foreheads the word 'Unclean,' . . . Instead of the law making twenty years' imprisonment the penalty for their crime, it ought to be imprisonment for life. . . . They are willfully bad, and glory and gloat in their perversion. Their habit is acquired and not inborn. Why propose to have the law against them now on the statute books repealed? If this happened, there would be no way of getting at them. It would be wrong to make life more tolerable for them. Their lives ought to be made so intolerable as to drive them to abandon their vices" (as quoted in Lind, *Autobiography of an Androgyne* [New York: Medico-Legal Journal, 1918], 24–25). Undeterred by such homophobic hysteria, Lind went on to publish the remarkable volumes that together comprise the most candid autobiographical memoir of a homosexual life as well as the most detailed account of homosexual life between 1895 and the mid-twenties to have been written in America.

Lind published his first book of reminiscences of a life spent in the homosexual underworld of New York in *Autobiography of an Androgyne* (1918), which surveys his homosexual life—especially that portion of it as an active "androgyne" in the city between 1895 and about 1905. The second book, *The Female Impersonators*, details more of that life while also offering speculations on the history and causes of homosexuality as well as providing some case histories of fellow androgynes, along with excerpts from news accounts of crimes committed against them and a sampling of medical opinion about them. For the latter volume Lind wrote under the pseudonym of "Ralph Werther" and cruised the New York streets using the name of "Jennie June," dressing appropriately to lend verisimilitude to this pseudonym.

That these were pseudonyms to disguise the writer Earl Lind does not entirely decide the question as to whether "Earl Lind" is not also a pseudonym as well. Though written under so many pseudonymous layers, Lind's books purport to be true relations of a promiscuous homosexual life and the autobiography of what even then were called "fairies," what Lind calls androgynes, and what we would call drag queens. They are also first-rate erotic fantasy, and as "Jennie June" (the name he emphatically prefers), he becomes a character as fabulous as any in fiction, a true fairy godmother to those later activist androgynes who threw the first stones at Stonewall.

## From *Autobiography of an Androgyne* (1918)

Lind believed himself to be a woman trapped in the body of a man—thus his choice of "androgyne" to describe himself, and his rather one-sided vision of homosexuals as imprisoned feminine spirits. Lind's mind is an overdecorated room, filled with specific and graphic scenes of sexual experiment, perhaps real, perhaps fantasized, usually rendered in part in Latin and embellished with some of the furniture of nineteenth-century morality, religiosity, and sentimentality. Yet the primary motif of this decor is curiously modern: liberation, freedom, sexual emancipation, tolerance for sexual difference. When Lind appears as "Jennie June," he is a creature of both fact and fiction. His life—he would prefer "her" Life—has a baroque and epicene splendor, a profusion of finely observed sensual detail. If June is a creature of fiction, then Lind is also a master of the art of the erotic confessional tale as well as of what might be called high operatic pornography: suspenseful, titillating, even indeed arousing if one knows a little Latin, which he often uses to detail his explicit sexual adventures (though not much Latin is required to guess just what is being done, with what, how, and to whom). The tale is told in a breathless confidential style that lures the reader eagerly and helplessly into a sexual adventure and leaves him fascinated, amused, and perhaps even envious as Jennie June, in one or another of her various disguises, disappears into rooms or back alleys with handsome young men who throw themselves at Jennie's feet—or, in more violent moments, throw her at theirs. We follow his transformation from a "low class fairie" cruising Stuyvesant Park to a high-class drag queen looking for men on the "gay Rialto" (Fourteenth Street). We watch with incredulity Lind's—now June's—seduction of a squad—a company, a battalion—of U.S. Army men, and watch with fascination his deeply felt masquerade as the coquettish Baby June.

Lind confronts with incredible bravery the cruelty and the often violent response of society to his person, his appearance, and his sexuality. He hides nothing, and he makes it clear that the men he entertains are avid seekers as eager for sexual sensation as he. Few men, in his account at least, reject him, though many after using him attempt to kill him, and many, again he claims, make the first advances. Lind has no erotic interest in his sexual confreres; he does not seek out liaisons with other homosexuals, though they thickly populate his book. But Lind does have another kind of interest in those homosexuals who share his world. With a very modern pride and in very eloquent voice he argues for, indeed, demands, that society recognize not only the sexual but the social and political rights of those "fairies" and "androgynes" who, even then, may have been called gay people. Though stricken with guilt over what he calls his cravings, he nevertheless finally decides that he must "follow Nature's behest" and live "according to the dictates of my peculiar instincts." This revelation leads him to become a sexual suffragette, marching for the rights of those whom he clearly sees as his people. After detailing his highly sexed childhood, he describes his life in New York in 1892, where he was studying at the university.

During this winter of '91–'92, paroxysms of melancholia occasionally came upon me at night. When I felt their approach, I could not stand it to remain in my room, where I must be noiseless, but went out to a deserted spot in a large park near which I lived, where I would shriek repeatedly. All my muscles seemed to be rigid, and my fists were clinched. I would dig my finger-nails into my palms, and wave my arms wildly. Within a few minutes, my strength would be completely gone. I looked upon these paroxysms as fits of insanity, and feared I would become permanently and violently insane. I now attribute these attacks largely to unsatisfied, involuntary yearnings for the mate which Nature had designed me to have. If society had permitted me one, and I had been taught that it was right for me to have one, I would have been saved an enormous amount of suffering, as well as perhaps my subsequent career as a fairie. . . .

During these terrible days, I felt that a crisis in my life was at hand. I felt that I stood at the dividing of the ways, one leading to honor and self-approbation, the other to ignominy and the blasting of all my legitimate ambitions. As each month of my first year in the university went by, the struggle against sensuality had been growing harder and harder.

Finally, on an evening in early June, I arose from my studies and prepared for my first nocturnal ramble. I put on a cast-off suit which I kept for wear only in my room, placed some coin in a pocket and several bills in a shoe, stuffed a few matches in one pocket and in another a wet sponge, wrapped in paper so as not to dry out, and then carefully went through my clothing a second time to make sure that I had not by oversight left on me some clue to my identity.

On account of my shabby clothing, precaution was necessary to leave my place of residence—a high-class boarding-house—without being seen. I crept stealthily out of my room, closing the door softly so as not to attract attention. After listening to make sure that no one was about to ascend the outside steps leading to the street, I opened the outer door and glided out bare-headed, a cast-off soft cap crumpled up in my hand because I was ashamed to be seen wearing it by any one who knew me. Hurriedly crossing to the opposite side of the street, I put on the cap, pulling the tip down over my eyes. Walking a few blocks to a park, I took my house key from my pocket and hid it in the grass, so that it could not be stolen and I was thereby rendered unable to let myself in on my return.

The reader now beholds me for the first time transformed into a sort of secondary personality inhabiting the same corpus as my proper self, to which personality I soon gave the name of " Jennie June," and which personality was to become far more widely known in the immediately following dozen years than the other side of my dual nature, the unremitting student and scholar, was ever to be known. The feminine side of my dual nature, for many years, as a matter of conscience, repressed, was now to find full expression in " Jennie June." For it was not alone fellatio that I craved, but also to be looked upon and treated as a member of the gentler sex. Nothing would have pleased me more than to adopt feminine attire on this and my multitudinous subsequent female-impersonation sprees, as some other ordinarily respectable androgynes are in the habit of doing when going out on similar promenades, but my position in the social organism was much higher than theirs, and the adoption of female apparel would in my case have been attended with too great risk. The mere wearing of it on the street by an adult male would render him liable to imprisonment.

I made my way to the quarter of the city bordering the Hudson River that is given over largely to factories and freight yards and is known as "Hell's Kitchen" because of the many steam vents. In this lonely and at night little frequented neighborhood, perhaps the most advantageous in the city for highway robbery, where nothing else than burning passion could have induced me to go at night, I ran across a stalwart adolescent of about my own age seated alone on a beer keg in front of a bar room. By a great effort of the will I accosted him. My voice trembled and my whole body shook as if I had the ague.

I had anticipated little difficulty in securing a companion, but events showed it to be otherwise. For years subsequently I associated intimately with hundreds of unmarried toughs of the slums from seventeen to twenty-four years of age, and so I know their nature. Approximately one-third have a distaste for coitus with an invert. The other two-thirds would accommodate him provided their sexual needs were not fully met by normal intercourse—which is generally the case. Moreover, there is a difference between their attitude toward a perfect stranger who accosts them, and an invert with whom they have become somewhat acquainted. The impulse to rob a perfect stranger tends to drown out all the movings of carnality. In addition, the feeling that he is a stranger and an outlaw—the latter fact being almost universally known—prompts them to assault him.

Along with an outline of what happened on this my first nocturnal ramble, I describe below my general method of approaching strangers in the poor quarters of the city. Of course I cannot recall the exact dialogue in a particular case, but all the sample conversations given in this autobiography are woven from actual remarks passed at different times. I have taken part in hundreds of dialogues of the kind sampled here and there in this book, and the reader can be assured of obtaining a truthful impression of the words exchanged by me—an androgyne—with my youthful virile associates. On the present occasion, after a few commonplace remarks, the conversation was of the following character:

"What big, big strong hands you have! I bet you are a good fighter." My aim was to talk rather babyishly so as gradually to betray my nature.

"There's a few as kin lick me but not many."

"I love fighters. If you and I had a fight, who do you think would win?"

"I could lick a dozen like yer together."

"I know you could. I am only a baby."

"Hah hah! A baby!"

"Say, you have a handsome face."

"Me hansome! Stop your kiddin."

"Really you are handsome. I am going to tell you a secret. I am a woman-hater. I am really a girl in a fellow's clothes. I would like to get some fellow to marry me. You look beautiful to me. Would you be willing to?"

"How much does it cost yer to git married? Give me a V"—meaning five dollars—"and I'll be yourn, or else git out of here."

My statement that I had not that amount with me brought the threat of a pummeling. I was beginning to wish I was far away, but concealed my uneasiness as best I could. After a few minutes more of conversation, several pals happened to come along. He called out, "I've got a fairie here!" and clutching my shoulder with one hand, he clinched his other fist, shook it threateningly in my face, and demanded: "Hand out your money! Hand out your money!"

Frightened to death, I handed him all the coin I had, amounting to a little more than a dollar. I protested I had no more, and after they had searched my pockets and felt my clothing all over for concealed bills, one of them gave me a blow in the face. With that wonderful agility which supposedly grave danger to one's life can arouse, I sprinted away, one of the ruffians pursuing a few steps and giving me several blows in the back. But I was so terrified that I did not halt until I had run several blocks. Panting and exhausted, I seated myself on a door-step and felt that I was forever cured of seeking a paramour. I called to mind the biblical text, "The way of the transgressor is hard," and I felt glad that it was hard so as to help me never to transgress again.

But after I had rested, my intense desire for fellatio induced me to make an endeavor in another poor neighborhood. I passed many groups of ruffians congregated in front of bar-rooms, but must find some solitary adolescent. At last I ran across one standing in front of a factory, evidently, as I later concluded, its watchman. I walked past him several times, unable to pluck up courage to speak. But he called out angrily: "Who are you looking at?"

"Pardon me for my rudeness, but I was wishing I could get acquainted with you. I am a baby, and I want a big, strong, brave fellow like you to pet me. I'll give you a dollar if you'll pet me for a few minutes, and let me sit on your lap."

Much to my surprise and disappointment, he sent me away with a curse. Twice repulsed, I decided to try again in a part of the city where the immigrant element predominates. Both the neighborhoods tried were quasi-American. I strolled down the Bowery, staring longingly and beseechingly into the eyes of the adolescents I passed, but too timid to accost any. Those who had known me all my life, had they met me now, would have wondered what could have brought into the then theatre and red-light district of the foreign laboring classes of the city, at an hour approaching midnight, a timid youth, hitherto called an "innocent," naturally pious, and generally esteemed for his intellectual tastes. My friends would never have dreamed that I would frequent that red-light district near midnight, and would never have believed it if any one told them that I was there for no good purpose...

While I have thus in my more mature judgment considered myself practically irresponsible for the conduct just described, in that early stage of my career, I was not so sure, and during the day following this first nocturnal ramble, was overwhelmed with a sense of shame and guilt. When night came on, I made my way to a solitary spot in a large park, where I threw myself on the ground to weep and shriek and pray. The burden of my prayer was that God would change my nature that very moment and give me the mind and powers of a man. I soon heard footsteps approaching, arose instantly, and walked from the spot. The men said they were looking for an owl which they had heard hooting. It was probably only my peculiar insane, half-suppressed shrieks they had heard.

[1892]

If the reader had been on Mulberry Street between Grand and Broome on an evening in November of 1892, he would have seen meandering slowly along from one side of the street to the other with a mincing gait, a haggard, tired-looking, short and slender youth between eighteen and nineteen, clad in shabby clothes, and with a skull cap on his head. As he walks along, whenever he meets any robust, well-built young man of about his own age, who is alone, he is seen to stop and address to him a few words. If we had been able to follow this queer acting individual for the previous hour before he passed us on Mulberry Street, we would have seen him roaming about through all the streets of the then dark and criminal 4th Ward, occasionally halting near the groups of ruffians congregated in front of the bar-rooms, and then failing of courage to speak, pass along.

Finally on the corner of Broome and Mulberry Streets, he addresses a tall, muscular, splendid specimen of the adolescent (subsequently a member of the New York police force) who continues in conversation with him, and walks along by his side. The little adolescent takes the arm of the big one into his own, and presses as closely as possible against him. The spirits of the little one are visibly heightened, he appears more lively and animated, and walks along with a quicker but extremely nervous step. He is soon seized with a sort of ague—due to sexual excitement—which causes his whole body to shake, and hardly permits him to speak. If we watched closely whenever the pair passed under a shadow, we would have seen the little one throw his arms rapturously around the neck of his big companion, and kiss him passionately. They finally pass out of sight down one of the dark covered alleys leading to tenements in the rear.

When after an interval the pair again emerge, the smaller is clinging tighter than ever to his big companion, as if afraid he might escape. They walk a block together, and then the big fellow tries to get rid of the little one, much against the latter's wishes. He tells the little fellow to go on his way, but adds, "Come round again, do yer hear?"

"I don't know whether I shall or not. I am afraid we shall never meet again. How it pains me to part from you!"

"What do yer call yourself, and where do yer hang out?"

"I call myself Jennie, and I work in a restaurant up on Third Avenue. What's your name, and where could I find you again?"

"You kin find me round on this block any time. Just ask any one fur Red Mike."

"Well, good-by. The Lord bless you. I never expect to see you again, although I love you with all my heart, and would like to live with you and be your slave."

The two start out in opposite directions. The little fellow walks rapidly, turns the first corner, sprints, turns another corner and sprints, and repeats this maneuver several times, as if bent on giving the slip to any possible follower. He finally reaches the Bowery and takes a train uptown from the Grand Street station.

## 1893—Fairie Apprenticeship Begins

Over five months after my previous visit, I again found myself on Mulberry Street, corner of Grand. I have always suspected that I was incited to this particular quest by an aphrodisiac. On or about that day, my physician administered a new drug. He probably hoped it would incite me to seek normal relations, but it acted along the line of my peculiar instincts.

Walking northward on the west side of the street, I encountered a mixed group of Italian and Irish "sports" of foreign parentage between sixteen and twenty-one years of age seated or standing around the portal of a warehouse. I timidly addressed them: "I am looking for a friend named Red Mike. Do any of you know him?"

One of them replied that he had just seen him up the street. Proceeding in that direction, I stopped occasionally to make the same inquiry of other adolescents. After walking several blocks in vain, I returned to the "gang" at the warehouse's portal, and asked: "Do you mind if I sit down to rest here? I am tired and lonesome. I have not been in the city long and don't know any one."

"Where did yez come from?"

"Philadelphia. I couldn't get any work there, so I came here."

It was not long before Red Mike happened to stroll by and recognized me even before I did him. An hour now passed, while they smoked and drank, hiding the beer-pail whenever a policeman went by. I had no desire to join in the drinking and smoking, and indeed up to my middle forties, when this autobiography goes to press, have never had any desire to learn to smoke, although having a few times put the lighted cigarette of a paramour in my mouth. I have always considered myself too feminine to smoke. Moreover, all my life I have been practically a total abstainer from alcoholic beverages.

But I reclined in the arms of one after another, covering face, neck, hands, arms, and clothing with kisses, while they caressed me and called me pet-names. I was supremely happy. For the first time in my life I learned about the fairie inmates of the lowest dives. They proposed to install me in one. I told them the story of my own life, only with such variations from the truth as were necessary for my own protection. We sang plantation songs, "Old Black Joe," "Uncle Ned," etc. These they had learned from Bixby's " Home Songs," published in that very neighborhood by the well-known shoe-blacking firm as an advertisement. I sang with them in the mock soprano or falsetto that fairies employ, trying to imitate the voice of a woman. Singing in this voice was not a novelty to me, as I had previously at times aped the warbling of a woman instinctively.

At the end of an hour, we adjourned down an alley, where the drinking and love-making continued even more intensely. After I had refused their repeated solicitations, one of them grasped my throat tightly to prevent any outcry and threw me down, while another removed part of my clothing, appropriating whatever of value he found in my pockets. With my face in the dust, and half suffocated by the one ruffian's tight grip on my throat, I moaned and struggled with all my might, because of the excruciating pain. But in their single thought to experience an animal pleasure, they did not heed my moans and broken entreaties to spare me the suffering they were inflicting. For two months afterward I suffered pain at every step because of fissures and lacerations about the anus.

When finally released, terror-stricken and with only half my clothing, I rushed out through the alley and down Mulberry Street, and did not halt until I reached what I considered a safe refuge on brightly lighted Grand Street. Breathless and exhausted, I seated myself on the curb. "I am cured of my slumming," I said to myself. "God's will be done. It is His hand which has brought this about, in order to drive me back to the path of virtue. Truly the Lord ruleth in all things."

Because of my exhausted condition, I remained seated for several minutes. In the meantime, two of my assailants had followed me up, and expressed their regret that one of their number had stolen my cap and coat, promising to get them back, and assuring me of their friendly feelings. "You are only a baby," they said, "and so we will fight for you and protect you."

I was so touched by their gallantry, so enamoured of them, and so sure that the assault was not committed through malevolence, that I accompanied them back to our first meeting place on the warehouse steps. I still had great fear of violence at their hands—rape, not a beating—but I was powerfully drawn toward them. Fellatio was welcome; paedicatio, horrible to my moral sense, and physically, accompanied by excruciating pain. The "gang" received me kindly, petted and soothed me as one would a peevish baby, which I resembled in my actions, fretting and sobbing in happiness as I rested my head against their bodies. To lie in the bosom of these sturdy young manual laborers, all of whom were good-looking and approximately my own age, was the highest earthly happiness I had yet tasted. With all my money gone, and cap and coat stolen besides, I finally had to walk home, a distance of several miles. Obtaining my keys in their hiding place, I succeeded in reaching my room without attracting attention.

The next day I wrote in my journal: "What a strange thing is life! Mephistopheles last night carried me through one of the experiences through which he carried Faust. . . . My carnal nature was aroused as never before. I groaned in despair. Never before in all my experience have I seen such a conflict between the flesh and the spirit. . . . How like an animal is man! Thus God has seen fit to make him."

A few days later I again wrote: " My present psychical state is most strange. I cannot yet repent of my conduct last Friday night, yet on the Sunday following I had one of the happiest experiences of nearness to God that I ever had. That afternoon I presented the Gospel in love for my Savior and for perishing souls. I have in my heart an intense desire to save from their lives of sin those in whose company I was Friday night, especially my Bill, so young, and yet so deep in sin. I want to rescue him, and make of him a strong educated champion for Christ. My heart yearns to carry blessings and peace to all those who are suffering in the slums of New York."
. . .

[1897]

This autobiography has now reached my twenty-third year. I had received my baccalaureate degree with honors, and was in my second year of graduate study. I had not really degenerated morally or religiously. For the entire year ending at the date at which I had now arrived, the aggregate time devoted to female impersonation and coquetry was approximately one hundred hours, as compared with about twenty-one hundred devoted to my studies and two hundred and fifty to the worship of my Creator and religious culture. Surely I was not to be tabooed as a moral leper. While the average church member, through lack of understanding of the conditions surrounding my life, would have branded me as a hypocrite, I sincerely believed and lived up to the fundamental truths of the Christian religion.

I still enjoyed an unblemished reputation. I associated with all my beaux, including my soldier friend, incognito. Always on returning home after an evening passed as "Jennie June," I took precautions that I was not followed.

The wreck of my happy and highly successful student career was now brought about by a physician whom I had consulted in hope of a cure for my inversion, but not one of the two gentlemen already named. He happened to number the president of the university among his friends, and whispered to him that I ought not to be continued as a student. I was immediately expelled.

I earned my living in a minor capacity in the university, and expulsion also meant that my income was cut off. The shock of expulsion rendered me a mental wreck. But I did not have the courage to return to my village home. Nor could I even apply to my father for money. Since soon after my arrest two years prior to the present date, he had, as already described, displayed a pronounced antipathy for me, rendering my visits home almost intolerable. In addition, because of the double life my nature forced me to lead, I decided I must remain in New York.

I removed to a part of the city where I would not be likely to encounter any of my college acquaintances, and began to look around for means of support. I spent several hours every day in answering advertisements. I would have been only too glad to accept such a position as shoveling coal into a furnace, but at the end of a month, had found nothing. In applying for positions, I was abashed in the consciousness that I was ranked as a degenerate and an outcast from society. I could not name as reference any member of the university or let it become known that I had been a student there. After my expulsion I called on the two professors with whom I was most intimate, and asked if I could refer to them. One replied: "Knowing your nature, I could not recommend you for any position, however menial. You cannot be trusted." (And yet shortly afterward I was for thirty months in the employ of a millionaire in the most confidential capacity, and was surpassed in faithfulness by no employee.) The other: "You must realize that you are an outcast from society."

All hope for the future and all courage for battling with the world were gone, and every day on my return from several hours' fruitless search, I would throw myself on the bed and give vent to my feelings in a violent fit of weeping. While walking the street, I would weep aloud and be on the borderline of hysterical screaming. I repeatedly entertained thoughts of suicide.

In a few weeks I was penniless and a shelterless wanderer on the streets in midwinter. I was driven for shelter to the Bowery, because there alone lodging could be obtained for fifteen cents, and a big meal of coarse and even disgusting food for ten cents. Thus I was compelled to live for nine weeks before a way was opened to something better.

During the nine weeks I was of the opinion that I must pass the rest of my days as an outcast from society, while of course living out the "Jennie-June" life to which I was apparently predestined. I was grateful to Providence that it was I and not one of my sisters who was predetermined to the life of a fille de joie and an outcast. In suffering such a fate, I believed that I was paying the penalty to God for the sin of some progenitor. I believed myself appointed by the God who visits the iniquities of the fathers upon the children to live out the rest of my life in mourning and paroxysms of grief, such as then visited me every day. . . .

Living as I was now compelled to live and necessarily mingling daily with men of loose morals, the charm of masculine beauty proved more powerful than ever before. Furthermore, it is not surprising that a person, deprived of even what are regarded as the necessities of a decent existence, should indulge immoderately in the single one of life's pleasures of which there was an abundant supply. In the environment in which forces outside of my control placed me, there was in me a practically irresistible impulse to adopt the manner of life I did. I would never have made the profession of the fairie the main business of life if it had not been for the peculiar concurrence of circumstances, expulsion from college, inability to find respectable employment, etc. That I now led the life I did was perhaps more the fault of Christian society than my own. While the world condemned, I have always believed that the Omniscient Judge pardoned because I was the victim of circumstances and of innate psychical forces.

The fact that I could now satisfy every day my instinctive yearnings to pass for a female and spend six evenings a week in the company of adolescent ruffians went far towards counterbalancing the many tears I had to shed when there was nothing to divert my thoughts from my condition of an outcast and an outlaw. I never coquetted on Sunday evenings, which I devoted to worship of my Creator at some mission. I no longer experienced any shame at displaying my feminine mentality everywhere outside of the missions, as no one knew who I was. In many neighborhoods I was hailed as "Jennie June."

[Lind/June's account takes his life to 1919, his forty-fifth year. In 1922 he published *The Female Impersonators*, in which he describes the homosexual underworld of New York from the 1890s to 1920s.]

From *The Female Impersonators* (1922)

In his next book, *The Female Impersonators*, Lind details his career as a "high class fairie." Here the complex choreography of demimonde homosexual life is extensively revealed: names, gathering places, cruising sites, sexual practices, even fragments of camp conversation. We meet other androgynes: Frank-Eunice, Angelo-Phyllis, Prince Pansy, Manon Lescaut. For entertainment they frequented Paresis Hall, the Hotel Comfort, or a bar called The Pugilist's Haven. They meet men in Stuyvesant Square, doing then and there what is still done today, and cruised Fourteenth Street that in "the last decade of the 19th century" Lind describes as being "as gay as any European bright light district I was fated to explore." Lind's description of life on this gay Rialto is filled with subcultural details that fascinate: homosexual men wore red ties to distinguish themselves so that if they were not in drag they would be known to the apparently vast numbers of nonhomosexual men, so Lind asserts, who were looking for androgyne love. Men carried their female-impersonating lovers to sumptuous drag fetes with names like the Philhedonic Ball. We know that Lind joined the Cercle Hermaphroditos, a club formed to "unite for defense against the world's bitter persecution" of homosexuals. He opines at one point in *The Female Impersonators* that "the emergence of androgynism is a sign of national health." That opinion alone strikes at the heart of centuries of homophobia and qualifies Lind to be a founding member of that academy that is even now constructing theory out of homosexual life. At the end of that book he lets us know why he is to be valued: "My own . . . is a Herculean task: to be an intellectual iconoclast. To break down the last remnant of cultured man's savage, criminal instincts and mores." "Surely," he continues, "we androgynes who for two thousand years have been despised, hunted down, and crushed under the heel of normal men . . . have no reason to be ashamed of our heritage."

## FROM *PART ONE: THE THIRD SEX*

### Chapter IV. Man Is a Passional, Rather Than a Rational, Being

My own is . . . a Herculean task: To be an intellectual iconoclast. To break down the last remnant of cultured man's savage, criminal instincts and mores. But, like Roger Bacon, I may comfort myself with the thought that my views are centuries in advance of my time; but, like him, I am therefore bitterly persecuted. . . .

"Away with any one who attempts to bring out the truth about sex!" cry the conservatives. "Crucify him! Crucify him! Sex is a theme too disgusting for discussion!"

In the twentieth century, leaders of thought have evolved from the belief in witchcraft. They must look elsewhere than to semi-bearded hags for their sacrificial victims on whom to load the sins of mankind, and the blame for the decline and fall of nations. Since, next to hags, they consider sexual cripples as the most loathsome of humans, they make the latter the scape-goats of present-day society. While they no longer burn them at the stake or bury them alive (as provided in old European law), they are permitted by twentieth-century statutes to imprison inoffensive androgynes for twenty years. And these archaic statutes are still frequently enforced. . . .

Why are androgynes so hated? Primarily because the leaders of thought have always identified them with the men of ancient Sodom (mistakenly, because the Sodomites were full-fledged males) and historians have mistakenly (because they never met androgynes personally and were taught in their boyhood to hate them with all their heart, soul, mind, and strength) laid upon them all the blame for the decline and fall of nations, and declared that therefore effeminacy or androgynism is a type of moral depravity to be crushed mercilessly. Better that some thousands of androgynes be deprived of life, liberty, and the pursuit of happiness than that the general welfare of the nation be imperilled! Androgynes—they argue—are unavoidably the scape-goats of the race. . . .

It is not necessary to crush androgynes in order to guard against the spread of effeminacy. Effeminacy, in the sense of androgynism, does not spread by example. It is entirely congenital. Only a physical male born with quasi-feminine predilections would adopt the role of a female after becoming adult. An androgyne's predilections and practices are regarded with such repugnance by all full-fledged males that none would stoop to them unless constrained by instinct.

Why imprison and murder the androgyne any more than the deaf-mute? The former is no more abnormal than the latter; no more degenerate; no more depraved. It is unfortunate that the human race is handicapped with either of these defective classes. But the androgyne deserves only pity, the same as the deaf-mute.
. . .

It is more likely that the emergence of androgynism is a sign of national health. The ultra-brilliant Age of Pericles surpassed all other periods in the recognition and influence of androgynism, which promotes art and general culture. The androg-yne, being a combination of man and woman in a single individual, has a wider view of life than the full-fledged man or woman. He possesses, in a measure, the mental qualities peculiar to each sex. That is why the Shakespeare-Author knew both the masculine and the feminine mind better than any other writer. Such dual-ity is the reason artistic genius crops out far more frequently among androgynes than among the sexually full-fledged. The amalgamated man-woman nature gets nearest to sentiment and emotion — to the soul of art.

Why do cultured androgynes carefully conceal their quasi-feminine sexual predilections? Why did [Michel] Angelo not publish any of his homosexual son-nets? Why did Raphael not proclaim on the housetops the happenings in his house at night? Androgynes hide their sexual predilections and practices, not because of consciousness of personal degeneracy, but because grossly misunderstood by the sexually full-fledged. By exception, Oscar Wilde was open and above board, and was therefore shut up in prison.

## From *Part Three: The Faerie Boy*

### Chapter V. Evenings at Paresis Hall [1895]

During the last decade of the nineteenth century, the headquarters for avocational female-impersonators of the upper and middle classes was "Paresis Hall," on Fourth Avenue several blocks south of Fourteenth Street. In front was a modest bar-room; behind, a small beer-garden. The two floors above were divided into small rooms for rent. In 1921 I visited the site, as well as that of the "Hotel" Comfort (the two Rialto resorts with which I was most intimately identified), in order to take pho-tographs for publication in this book, but found both structures supplanted.

Paresis Hall bore almost the worst reputation of any resort of New York's Underworld. Preachers in New York pulpits of the decade would thunder Philippics against the "Hall," referring to it in bated breath as "Sodom!" They were laboring under a fundamental misapprehension. But even while I was an habitue, the church and the press carried on such a war against the resort that the "not-care-a-damn" politicians who ruled little old New York had finally to stage a spectacu-lar raid. After this, the resort, though continuing in business (because of political influence), turned the cold shoulder on androgynes and tolerated the presence of none in feminine garb.

But there existed little justification for the police's "jumping on" the "Hall" as a sop to puritan sentiment. Culturally and ethically, its distinctive clientele ranked high. Their only offence — but such a grave one as to cause sexually full-fledged Pharisees to lift up their own rotten hands in holy horror — was, as indicated, female-impersonation during their evenings at the resort. A psychological and not an ethical phenomenon! For ethically the "Hall's" distinctive clientele were con-genital goody-goodies, incapable (by disposition) of ever inflicting the least detri-ment on a single soul. . . . The "Hall's" distinctive clientele were bitterly hated, and finally scattered by the police, merely because of their congenital bisexuality. The sexually full-fledged were crying for blood . . . as did the "good" in the days of witch-burning. Bisexuals must be crushed — right or wrong! The subject does not permit investigation! The fact that it is race suicide justifies the denial of all mercy! Let Juggernaut's car crush out their lives! . . .

Paresis Hall was as innocuous as any sex resort. Its existence really brought not the least detriment to any one or to the social body as a whole. More than that: It was a necessary safety-valve to the social body. It is not in the power of every adult to settle down for life in the monogamous and monandrous love-nest ordained for all by our leaders of thought. . . .

While in this book I use the resort's popular name, androgyne habitues always abhorred it, saying simply "the Hall." The full nickname arose in part because the numerous full-fledged male visitors—it was one of the "sights" for out-of-towners who hired a guide to take them through New York's Underworld—thought the bisexuals, who were its main feature, must be insane in stooping to female-impersonation. They understood "paresis" to be the general medical term for "insanity." The name also in part arose because in those days even the medical profession were obsessed with the superstition that a virile man's association with an androgyne induced paresis in the former, it not yet having been discovered that this type of insanity is a rare aftermath of syphilis. . . .

Paresis Hall was never my own headquarters. I visited it only now and then. I had too early become wedded to the "Hotel" Comfort. Moreover, I wandered more widely, and in some respects flaunted my androgynism to a greater extent, than any other female impersonator of my day. I took greater chances than any other, except in the appearing in public places in feminine apparel, but was never arrested in the Rialto because always careful never to render myself liable. Never for a moment did I forget the possibility of being arrested. I was even hypersensitive in this matter. A common dream was that of being arrested. But this hypersensitiveness probably saved me, since others of my type were continuously being arrested and sent to the penitentiary. But the cultured androgyne is almost never caught by the police. Only those of poor mentality.

On one of my earliest visits to Paresis Hall—about January, 1895—I seated myself alone at one of the tables. I had only recently learned that it was the androgyne headquarters—or "fairie" as it was called at the time. Since Nature had consigned me to that class, I was anxious to meet as many examples as possible. As I took my seat, I did not recognize a single acquaintance among the several score young bloods, soubrettes, and androgynes chatting and drinking in the beer-garden.

In a few minutes, three short, smooth-faced young men approached and introduced themselves as Roland Reeves, Manon Lescaut, and Prince Pansy—aliases, because few refined androgynes would be so rash as to betray their legal name in the Underworld. Not alone from their names, but also from their loud apparel, the timbre of their voices, their frail physiques, and their feminesque mannerisms, I discerned they were androgynes. Indeed effeminacy stuck out all over Prince Pansy. Manon Lescaut's only conspicuous anatomical feminesqueness was extraordinary breadth of hips. While Reeves' trunk and legs were not so feminine, he excelled in womanly features, with such marine-blue eyes and pink-peony cheeks as any beholder regretted should be wasted on a member (?) of the sterner sex. Moreover, Reeves alone, of the two score ultra-androgynes that I at different times met at Paresis Hall, was naturally beardless.

While Roland, Manon, and the "Prince" looked to be between twenty and twenty-five, I later ascertained the first mentioned was thirty-seven. As already observed, perennial youth is an earmark of ultra-androgynism.

Roland was chief speaker. The essence of his remarks was something like the following:

"Mr. Werther—or Jennie June, as doubtless you prefer to be addressed—I have seen you at the Hotel Comfort, but you were always engaged. A score of us have formed a little club, the CERCLE HERMAPHRODITOS. For we need to unite for defense against the world's bitter persecution of bisexuals. We care to admit only extreme types—such as like to doll themselves up in feminine finery. We sympathize with, but do not care to be intimate with, the mild types, some of whom you see here to-night even wearing a disgusting beard! Of course they do not wear it out of liking. They merely consider it a lesser evil than the horrible razor or excruciating wax-mask.

"We ourselves are in the detested trousers because having only just arrived. We keep our feminine wardrobe in lockers upstairs so that our every-day circles can not suspect us of female-impersonation. For they have such an irrational horror of it!"

On the basis of different visits to an upper room permanently rented by the CERCLE HERMAPHRODITOS, I am going to build up a typical hour's conversation in order to disclose into what channels the thoughts of ultra-androgynes run when half-a-score find themselves together. The reason for its unnatural ring is that I omit the nine-tenths that were prattle, retaining only the cream that I consider of scientific value.

It was about eight o'clock on an evening of April, 1895. Some of the hermaphroditoi were still in male apparel; some changing to feminine evening dress and busy with padding and the powder-puff; some in their completed evening toilette ready to descend to the beer-garden below to await a young-blood friend.

"Hello, Mith Nighty!" several called as one of the tallest, oldest, and most brunette of the hermaphroditoi entered the Cercle's dressing-room. The androgyne who had adopted the name of a romantic woman had, during his twenties, before becoming thick-set, been a female-impersonator on the vaudeville stage.

"Mith Nighty!" one of the youngest hermaphroditoi shouted in a falsetto. "Queenie and I want you to coach us in female-impersonation. Next Friday at the Masked Ball we make our debut as public female impersonators."

A senior: "The world would call our hobby insanity. But the explanation is that we were created psychic females, who yearn for the dress and role of that sex—to feel skirts flapping about our ankles—and nevertheless Nature has been so cruel as to incarnate our woman-souls in the abhorred male body."

Another: "But other than in us women-men, the male figure is infinitely more artistic than the female. The only disgusting thing in man is the beardal growth. I can tolerate in a beau a small moustache only, but prefer him clean-shaven. But feminine breasts are the very badge of beastliness! You, of course, excepted, Ralph-Jennie. The short, fat, knock-kneed feminine legs are monstrosities! If you'll pardon me for saying it, Phyllis. On the other hand, the muscles of an athlete compel the attention."

Later it chanced that Roland Reeves and myself entered into a soft-spoken dialogue: "Ralph, do you know any woman-man whom we ought to get into the Cercle?"

"Four! But they do not realize anybody is wise outside the young athlete each has selected as chum. No one but another woman-man, or a full-fledged man who had read Krafft-Ebing, would ever suspect them. Their public conduct is always the height of propriety. One of them even makes it a practice to boast of excesses cum femina—to ward off suspicion, for he has always shunned females as one would the plague. But on the basis of self-knowledge, we women-men easily recognize our own kind. I need only hear the voice and glimpse the features and figure.

"But none of the four ever visits the Underworld. They do not feel the need. Their being so fortunate as to have secured soul-mates among their every-day circle has proved their safety-valve. You, Roland, and I have simply been denied by Providence a hero-confidant from among our every-day circle. Moreover, we have been unwilling to risk betrayal to that circle. We are not hunting for high-figured blackmail and possibly years in prison.

"One is a university student. The college body refers to his ultra-virile roommate and himself as "X and wife." But no user of the phrase ever dreams of its real significance, not knowing of the existence of intermediates. Of course they have heard of homosexuality, but think only the scum of mankind could be guilty. Impossible in the case of a high-minded intellectual!

"Here's Plum. Plumkin, you look as if you had lost your last friend!"

The 23-year Mollie Coddle sobbed: "Everything looks dark. Two days ago I was fired. I have hardly slept a wink since. I have hope for the future only in the grave. Some bigot denounced me to the boss. He called me into his private office. As this had never happened before, I guessed the reason."

Plum outlined his conference. I have listened to several similar confessions. The following is a composite.

Plum: "I confess to being a woman-man and throw myself upon your mercy."

Fairsea: "That confession is sufficient, and proves you an undesirable person to have around!"

Plum: "It will be hard to find a new job, since I have been with you for five years and must depend on your recommendation."

Fairsea: "Knowing your nature, Plum, I could not recommend you even to shovel coal into a furnace!"

Plum: "But you have steadily advanced me for five years! Why should to-day's discovery make any difference in your opinion of my business ability?"

Fairsea with a sneer: "An invert ought to leave brain work for others! He ought to exhaust himself on a farm from sunrise to sunset so that the psychic movings would be next to non-existent. He should pass his life in the back woods; not in a city. He has no right in the front ranks of civilization where his abnormality is so out of place!"

Plum: "You mean that he should commit intellectual and social suicide in obedience to the aesthetic sense of Pharisees?"

Fairsea: "Certainly! The innate feelings and the conscience, as well as the Bible, teach that the invert has no rights! I myself have only deep-rooted contempt for him! Every fibre in my body, every cell in my tissues, cries out in loud protest against him! He is the lowest of the low! I dare say that at the bottom of your heart, Plum, you are thoroughly ashamed of the confession you made a moment ago?"

Plum: "By no means. I have learned to look upon bisexuality as a scientist and a philosopher. But you have just shown yourself to be still groping in the Dark Ages.

"No, Mr. Fairsea, I can hardly bring myself to be ashamed of the handiwork of God. A bisexual has no more reason than a full-fledged man or woman to be ashamed of his God-given sexuality.

"You appear, Mr. Fairsea, to be unable to get my point of view. All in my anatomy and psyche that you gloat in calling depraved and contemptible I have been used to since my early teens. If your views have any justification in science or ethics, I am unable to see it. Although it almost breaks my heart to be made an outcast and penniless by yourself, I prefer that lot, knowing I am in the right, than to be in the wrong even if sitting, as yourself, in the chair of president of the X Company.

"How do you define 'depraved', Mr. Fairsea? If in such a way as to exclude Socrates, Plato, Michael Angelo, and Raphael, then you exclude me also."

Fairsea: "But the phenomenon works against the multiplication of the human race. Nature, with this in view, instilled in all but the scum of mankind this utter disgust for the invert. To the end of the continued existence of the race, he must be condemned to a life of unsatisfied longing. For this reason he should be imprisoned for life, not for only ten or twenty years as the statutes now provide!

"We strictly segregate diphtheria and scarlet fever, Plum. Why should we not similarly quarantine against inversion?"

Plum: "Because there is a vast difference. Contagious disease, if not strictly segregated, would occasion death and acute suffering to many additional persons. Whereas the bisexuals' being at liberty occasions not the least detriment to any individual, nor to the race as a whole.

"A second reason: The quarantining of contagious disease is only a matter of shutting up a few persons for a few weeks in their own homes. It causes no serious privation or suffering. Whereas the segregation of bisexuals would affect for a lifetime tens of thousands of our most useful members of society. It would occasion, among these already accursed by Nature, additional intense mental suffering, despair, and suicide.

"Any one who can suggest the latter segregation is unable to see farther away than the end of his nose.

"And as to race suicide, Mr. Fairsea. You should be the very last to lecture anybody on that subject! You are the father of only two children and have put three wives under the sod through your beastly, excessive demands!

"Can it be that you shut your eyes to all evidence? Do ocular proofs count for nothing? Hasn't the human race survived the best decades of classic Greece? While the Greeks are acknowledged by all modern historians to have attained the highest development of mind and body ever known, they at the same time gave to the women-men who happened to be born among them—as among all races of all ages—an honorable place. And by far more place, both in their personal and social life, than in the case of any other nation of the ancient or modern world."

Fairsea: "But I had hoped that the human race had evolved above this phenomenon! I hate to believe it of the human race! Because the phenomenon lowers humanity down to the lowest levels of animal life!"

Plum: "So does eating!"

Fairsea: "I detest it! My disgust is innermost and deepseated! To begin now to show any mercy to the invert, after having for two thousand years confined him in dungeons, burned him at the stake, and buried him alive, would be a backward step in the evolution of the race!

"Plum, the invert is not fit to live with the rest of mankind! He should be shunned as the lepers of biblical times! If generously allowed outside prison walls, the law should at least ordain that the word 'UNCLEAN' be branded in his forehead, and should compel him to cry: 'UNCLEAN! UNCLEAN!' as he walks the streets, lest his very brushing against decent people contaminate them!"

Plum: "All that is only bigotry and bias! Nearly every man's conduct is still governed by bias!"

Fairsea: "I even acknowledge that it is bias! For bias is justifiable in matters of sex! . . . You say that medical writers have declared inverts irresponsible! That declaration proves that they know nothing about them! You say inverts are assaulted and blackmailed! They deserve to be! It would be wrong for any one at all to show any leniency! Their existence ought to be made so intolerable as to drive them to lead their sexual life along the lines followed by all other men! Your case, Plum, fills me with such disgust that I could not rest knowing you were around the office!"

## Robert McAlmon (1896–1956)

Set in Europe but populated by Americans is a book by Robert McAlmon, one of the best writers of the period and one of the first to represent openly homosexual characters. A collection of stories, Distinguished Air: Grim Fairy Tales was published in a limited edition by McAlmon's own Contact Editions Press in Paris in 1925 and includes the title story and "Miss Knight," a full-length and even sympathetic portrait of a drag queen from Illinois who confesses: "Whoops dearie! What us bitches will do when we draw the veil. Just lift up our skirts and scream." Miss Knight, near relative to Jennie June (though without June's real intelligence, her "refined" and "elegant" pretentious, or social perspicuity), represents the outlandish and exotic picture of homosexuals that the few novels of the twenties that bothered to present them had begun to draw.

The witty, bitchy repartee in "Miss Knight" provides for homosexuals in American fiction what Ronald Firbank had done in England: establish a tradition of arch and self-conscious linguistic pyrotechnics that defines the male homosexual as much by the way he speaks as by the way he acts or dresses and one that places him in a scene where the amusing repartee mirrors an equally amusing and irresponsible life. McAlmon's use of "camp" in the story identifies a significant marker of homosexual verbal style. And while the picture of gay life and identity constructed by "Miss Knight" may show only a narrow aspect of what gay life of the period actually may have been about, it does construct a viable reality—as well as a fictional mythology—to which both novelist and reader might begin to subscribe. "Miss Knight" pinpoints one vital identity recognized by homosexual and nonhomosexual alike. Homosexuals in fiction or out of it were now "queers" whose behavior when not blatantly crossing gender roles was seen to be almost constantly suggestive of difference. Miss Knight continually seeks out what she calls "rough trade," thus siting another bit of homosexual argot firmly at an early point in the century. Indeed the use of "cruising" and "queer," the repeated litany of "Mary" and "drag" (and even "gay") in a vaguely suggestive sexual context hint at their currency at this early date. Miss Knight, reminiscent of the street exploits of Jennie June, picks up soldiers, sailors, and assorted other uniformed professionals, wittily gloating as she sits with her hand in their pocket, "My god, Mary, I've got my hand on a real piece of meat at last, oh Mary." Indeed, Miss Knight is so far "out" that she creates a new kind of masquerade, the woman within worn flamboyantly on the body of the man without.

## MISS KNIGHT (1925)

With her it was "now I'm tellin' you, Mary," or "now when these bitches get elegant I lay 'em out stinkin'," many times a day, if her mood was a vital one. Apparently he to the outside world of acute observation, she would hastily apologize had she used the Mary phrase on a man who did not know her well, or who might resent queerness and undue familiarity. "Just a way I talk, yuh know," she would explain in a conciliatory tone. But in a group of sister bitches she had few thoughts but to see that none of them rose above the proper clan manner in elegance without being "raised proper."

"I am so glad I'm a real man," she shrieked across the room or cafe every now and then to relieve the tension of ennui that might, and does, settle upon all atmospheres at times. Properly she believed herself appointed as a camping comedian, ready to earn a right to her presence by keeping undue seriousness from making dullness exist through an overlong period.

If a man in uniform, a policeman, soldier, or young cadet, passed her gaze she would call out to or after him unless the uniformed man's face was an austere one: "Come, get your supper, dearie, now come on," she'd comment, while jerking her head coquettishly.

"I was talkin' to a guy—one of these here highbrows, you get me, just scientifically interested and all that, you know—and he sez to me, 'did you get queer in the army?' and I sez to him, 'my god Mary, I've been queer since before you wore diddies.' I wuz on to that guy too; trying to pass off as a real man. He's one of them kind that tell you they're real men until they get into bed with you, and then they sez, 'Oh dearie, I forgot, I'm queer.' Whoops dearie! What us bitches will do when we draw the veil. Just lift up our skirts and scream."

Miss Knight was holding forth when an American brother in sisterhood came into the Berlin bitchery that many travelers slummed in through the two years after the great war. Miss Knight had already given the newcomer a careless onceover, and then recognition dawned upon her face and she whooped out, "Well, lookie who's here. If it ain't Miss Collins. And her and me used to be together in the chorus in the 'Red Pirates.' Now I'm asking you, Mary, wasn't that a grand show? Don't I wish Miss Jenkins would drift in too, and she's up to it. Why she'd just take one step and be down the aisle leapin'; and if she was skatin'—you know, coke, I mean, and they sells it in this burg by the bowlfuls. . . . Oh Miss Collins, don't you want some powder for yer nose too? They sell it for ten marks a deck here; serve it by the barrel if you give them the sign."

The next ten minutes were spent by the two in reminiscing about chorus days in the "Red Pirates." "My god Mary, I'd bead my eyelashes out six inches, and one night—yuh remember—we all came out done up stinkin' with pretty pink cheeks, supposed to look like honest to gawd rough pirates you know, and the director took one look at us and sez, 'For christ's sake, yer supposed to be men, not bitches, when yer on the stage at least. Tomorrow night you come out with real makeups on or we'll import a new load of fairies to take your places. This show ain't to be used for cruising your trade while you're on the stage at least.' " Miss Knight babbled on, and after a breath continued, "and in the dressing room after the show you couldn't see a one of us for the powder in the air. We spent more time makin' up to go out on the street cruisin' than we did in makin' up for the show. I'm tellin' you, Mary, you shudda seen us when we stepped out of the stagedoor. Miss Jenkins got picked up by a cop one day—in plain clothes—and he told her if she was caught out again with that calcimine makeup he'd put her in the jug . . . But, my god Mary, these Berlin cops is different. Please, Mister officer, won't you arrest me? . . . I'm tellin' you, Mary, if I sticks around Berlin much longer they'll take me home in a little wooden box."

Miss Knight was so built that she could have passed as a real man; even her voice didn't generally give her away. It was not bass, but it functioned in the lower registers. She swore that she had passed herself off as rough trade upon occasions, but her instincts were all womanly and housewifely. She liked to cook and sew, and she liked men, real men.

The life of Miss Knight had started some thirty years before in a little Illinois village, but her career proper had started when at about seventeen she went into a roadshow chorus. She didn't visit home often after that, though her family moved to Chicago two years after she left them. Speaking of one of her rare visits home she related:

"I hadn't seen the old woman for five years, so I sez to myself I'd drop in on her some afternoon, because I wuz playing that summer in a show in Chicago. I'd just had my hair hennaed and it was shinin' goldbrick. I wuz just sittin' myself easy in the parlor talkin' to my mother and sister when in comes my brother. Him and me never did like each other. He just took one look at me and walked out and a little later as I wuz going out he stopped me in the hall and sez, 'For christ's sake, yer a disgrace to the family.' I'm tellin' you, Mary, I didn't stick around home much. My brother ain't queer. He used to follow me when I went out cruising down State Street, and one night he wuz watching me from the other side and saw me pick up a soldier. That night when I went to visit the old lady just as I came into the house bang!—he soaked me just once on the jaw. I'm tellin' you Mary, I snuk out of that house and didn't say nothing not at all."

How long Miss Knight had sniffed cocaine she herself could not have said, because she didn't remember dates or think ideas, only the idea of the emotion at the moment. For ten years perhaps. At least she said her nose was paralyzed by now. "One night in Madrid—me an' my lover wuz puttin' on a show there—and I'm tellin' you I had some grand wardrobe then—gowns with beads all over them and gowns with silver and gold strings, with earrings that would knock you cold—I woke up one night shivering all over. I'm tellin' you, I thought I wuz going home in a crate the next day and I just grabs the pitcher of water from the washstand and drank six gallons right down at a gulp," he related one day, while recalling a dream of the night before that had nearly knocked him cold with despairing fright.

Miss Knight's chief complex was against elegance. The one thing she could not stand was to have some stuckup bitch she'd known in the chorus get to acting elegant. For all her conversation about laying them out stinkin' when they got upstage however, she actually drew into herself, or went away to unbosom herself with hurt to some more sympathetic being. Often she would herself in a moment of decision and ambition declare: "I'm tellin' you, Mary, I'm going to be elegant myself for a spell. Been as common as horseshit all my life, I have."

Miss Knight drifted into a Berlin cafe one night, looking to strangers much like a heavy-set, be-barbered traveling salesman from Holland or America. Soon she was at a table with other Americans, one only of whom had known her before, and it was from this one that she wished to learn where some of these queer cafes that she'd heard were all over Berlin were located. She informed the party that she'd just come from Italy, where she had been doing a female impersonation act. Before that she had been in Paris where she had performed other acts, it could be surmised.

Miss Knight felt a trifle ill at ease in the party she was with as none of the strangers were recognizable types to her. In her perplexity she was afraid that some of the members were upstage and elegant, and she couldn't judge whether they were queer or not so that she could lay them out cold. A cautious reserve was forced upon her, and that was uncomfortable to so relaxed a disposition as hers. However, during the course of the conversation it was revealed to her that all of the party were quite aware of her biologic type, and were also ready to laugh at her rough comedy, without disapproving of her presence. Still her reserve kept her from revealing too much of herself by talkativeness. She listened. The conversation was a manufactured one, a bored one. Apparently before Miss Knight's entrance a discussion on European against American culture had been going on. One young man stated, with pompous pedantry, that, "A cultured man is one who enjoys to the fullest all of his appetites and senses."

Another man, irritated by the atmosphere evidently, responded curtly: "You're talking plain balls Foster," he said, "culture is nothing but a matter of perception, plain intelligence, ability to observe things and conditions for what they are. Then maybe the senses can judge."

As Miss Knight listened, and became aware that she need not feel ill at ease with these people, she also became uncomfortable at having the conversation so beyond her depths. So when the man who had first spoken said with an injured, over-refined air, as of one whose finer sensibilities are revolted: "Well really, Jerome, we could have a gentlemanly discussion . . ." Miss Knight felt called upon to relieve the situation. So she spoke:

"Now listen here, Mary excuse me, just my way of talkin' you know—but are youse guys trying to get elegant? Don't do it, I'm askin' you. I'm common as dirt myself. Lay off this elegant stuff. An Mizz Astor, won't you have another cup of tea—having a lovely time, so distinguished. Just grand, Mizz Astor. So glad you ast me over. What's yer name? Send me a postcard. I had a lovely time," Miss Knight chattered, having had four cognacs, so that her first caution and reserve was gone, as it easily did go in so impulsive a nature.

After these words Miss Knight went skating to the lavatory, and a few minutes later leaped back, with her eyes more concentrated into black pupils.

"I'm snowbound now, Mary," she confided to inform the others that she had just sniffed cocaine. "Just coked to the eyeballs, you know, an' I'm lookin' for a bigger skating rink." Seating herself, she leaned back her head with a gesture meant to express hauteur, narrowed her eyes into a squint, and began at once to camp an imitation of "Miss Gwendolyn Rollins," who had been in the chorus with her, who had been with the Shuberts for twenty years without losing a spangle off her dress, and who had used to declare that when she played Romeo and Juliet there wasn't a dry seat in the house.

Though Miss Knight talked largely of an engagement she was to have at the Winter Garden, several weeks passed with no sign of her appearance. The night after the one which she had said she was to appear she was still about, doing what the nightlife and her finances permitted her. She was black with gloom except at moments when she was completely done up with cocaine, and she was completely without money so that unless someone invited her to drink she had not that release. However, she was not altogether unhappy because a number of Americans were about who laughed at her jokes, bought her drinks, lent her money, and liked her professional gaiety as a relief from after-war Berlin atmosphere. Some of them experimented with her cocaine, and always when there was a party or a collection of them her presence was permitted as a relief from pretentious intellectuality, personal antagonisms, and the morbid personalities of escaped Americans who were trying to make nihilism a cover for their ineffectuality. It seldom happened that some collection of Americans, or English, had not gathered by nine o'clock somewhere, any night. However, some of the people who were ready to encounter her in cafes which they had visited "to see Berlin nightlife," said it was a bore to have her greet them so familiarly in more respectable gathering places: the Adlon Hotel lobby, or semifashionable dance rendezvous.

Thanksgiving Day approached, and for days before Miss Knight talked of the magnificent dinner she would cook for everybody she knew in Berlin. She had a bare but large apartment which she had rented upon first arriving, and had paid three months in advance for while she still had money. Nostalgia, sentimentality about a real Thanksgiving dinner, and a wish to have some real American cooking, swelled her guest list to some twenty people, all of whom contributed money with which she might purchase a turkey, champagne, and other essentials for a real feed. Several of the guests assured her they would bring bottles of liquor with them.

After two days' preparation on Miss Knight's part, Thanksgiving Day came around, and her dinner party was scheduled for eight o'clock. As all her guests were aware of her eccentricity, she laid aside her men's clothing for the evening, and arrayed herself in a glittering garment made by herself. Upon her head she wore a bright red wig, and about her head she fashioned an imitation but entirely gorgeous aigrette. Two German guests arrived: Miss Knight spoke German poorly, and hardly knew how to entertain these first arrivals, and also she was in a fever about her dinner party. All the guests were at the moment a half-hour late. She felt tragic. At nine to nine-thirty other guests began to arrive, all of them semi- or completely intoxicated, in black moods, and fightingly antagonistic towards some other of the guests.

Kate Matthews came in, demanding immediately, "jes' one more cocktail to set me up, you know, Charlie, jes' one cognac to set . . . uh hic . . . to set me up." With Kate came Anne Simpson, a lumberjack-looking Lesbian. Anne's latest love—an elaborately double-lived person—had left the day before to meet the man she was to marry in Paris, and in consequence Anne had taken six decks of cocaine and uncounted cognacs—which she declared was the only safe drink to take when breathing snow. Foster Morris came in soddenly drunk, bringing with him a new soldier lover that he had picked up on the street in the afternoon. He was violently despondent and reckless because he had just discovered that a blond German boy he'd been keeping, and who had left him two days before, had taken with him Foster's evening suit, his diamond cuff links, and a watch that was an old family heirloom. At a low moment he mumbled, however, soft with a readiness to forgive anybody anything, "perhaps he needed them worse than I do, though."

Miss Knight began to serve the dinner, and what other guests he had invited came in gradually, till there were eighteen in the party. With housewifely pride he brought in a great roasted turkey to display to his besotted and gloomy guests between whom only counter-currents of irritation were running. In displaying the platter he spilled gravy on his glittering gown. Foster Morris, who had been drinking steadily since his arrival, insisted upon carving and serving the turkey, and Miss Knight, who knew the grief of having lost a lover, permitted it. Turkey flesh, legs and wings splattered about the room, to be rescued by the other guests and eaten. The lovely mashed potatoes, ornamentally placed upon a borrowed giltedged platter, went clattering to the floor from the hands of Kate Simpson. At ten-thirty the German man and wife departed, because, they explained later, though they did conduct a cafe for queer men, they did not like seeing Foster Morris being unduly familiar with his soldier lover in front of them.

Soon after, the other guests departed, a good deal drunker than when they had come and still morose, though drunkenness had robbed their antagonisms of violence. The next day or so some of them explained to Miss Knight that it had been a wonderful party, but that something had just happened to get them all in the wrong mood. Miss Knight felt crushed for a time, but took more cocaine and on the third day, having discovered a beautiful blond policeman who was real rough trade, so he said, was quite convalesced. He would sit with his right hand in the left pocket of his policeman when they were in queer cafes, and would babble, "My god, Mary, I've got my hand on a real piece of meat at last, oh Mary." He was additionally happy because Kate Matthews assured him that she, who could spot a queer man a mile off, knew that the policeman was just a war-made queer one, because he had tried to hold her hand.

One night there was to be a grand ball and the word passed around that all queer people could go the limit with costumes and there would be no police interference. Miss Knight arrived as Madame Recamier, supposedly, but the neck of her gown was much less in evidence than in the well-known Madame Recamier portrait, for Miss Knight's bulky shoulders showed like the white flesh of a newly bathed coal-heaver above all the glitter of her gown. Later she was elated with vanity and delight because of getting the first prize for costume display; until yet later she noticed that her policeman lover was getting amorous with Kate Matthews. It was Foster Morris who called her attention to the fact.

"My god, Kate thinks she's had a real man fall for her at last, and even if she doesn't want to break up your family she's excited, and she's so drunk she'll be careless. She hadn't ought to do it," Foster told Miss Knight.

Miss Knight was all wrought up. She went out into the hallway to take a sniff of coke behind the door. She was stricken with grief, anger and desolation. Everything was turning bad on her. No money; no luck with her lovers; no friends, only people who thought she was a clown, but didn't want her around at decent places with them. After another breath of snow, however, she became understanding. She wasn't afraid really that Kate would attract her policeman. But she didn't trust Foster. Going back into the main ballroom she encountered Foster again, and remarked forgivingly of her policeman: "After all, though, what they want is a woman, you know. They're real men. They ain't queer bitches like you and me." Her voice sounded like that of a mother of the world understanding all things.

Within ten minutes, however, Kate's momentary happiness was broken in upon by her superstition. She knew things couldn't really happen well to her. She was sure that she had seen two plain clothes men watching her in the offing. It was her intuition, she declared, that let her smell a raid a mile off, and she wasn't going to be arrested in Berlin with her passport in the shape it was in. Kate, a harmless soul, driven to drink and dope for company, expression, and to escape eternal depression, seemed to invite arrest. Already she'd been arrested in most of the world's great cities—New York, Chicago, London, and once already in Berlin. A born defect in her gait made her look suspicious. Always she had been released and apologized to, but she was getting leery, and was particularly so this night, when she was drunk, and at no one could say what kind of a ball. Miss Knight, too, joined in Kate's warning. "I'm tellin' yuh, Mary, I've been in so many raids that I get a hunch of one a month ahead, and I sez to all of you, and you can tell them elegant bitches that try to pretend they ain't to me—Mizz Astor an' Mizz Vanderbilt I mean—that I'm drifting right now."

A half hour later a party of Americans were installed at a secluded midnight place that earlier in the evening was too frightfully vicious to enter. They had dubbed it Murder Cave because from four in the afternoon till ten at night its habitues were all degradedly vicious types; off the streets, complete dope fiends; down and out whores grown too aged for street trade; cocaine merchants; and altogether cutthroat-looking types. By ten, however, the patron cleared most of these types out, or they themselves departed on errands surely not innocent.

At this hour, past twelve o'clock midnight, the place was supposed to be closed, but the patron of the place let the party in when he saw who they were. They were the only people in the place then, and the patron assured them that they could stay and as late as they wished. The atmosphere was confined and secretive. Most of the party spoke in whispers until Miss Knight, again happy as her policeman sat next to her, began to converse in monologue, although eternally playing to an audience:

"Did'ja ever hear of the Portland-Oregon scandal? I wuz in it. I wuz at the Y.M.C.A.—in drag you know —some outfit I had too, stars and spangles and jewels all over me, Mary. Whoops my dear, you must come over, ah come on, come over an' call on me some afternoon. I never have nuthin' on afternoons. Just a lovely time you know. I'd just come from the theatre—had shown my act there you know, and then the cops came in and pinched us, and them Y.M.C.A. boys was scared stiff. They let me go because one of the plain clothes guys had seen my act at the theatre and I sez to him that I didn't know nuthin' about what kind of a party it wuz, and had come there as a paid entertainer.

"But Mary, did I ever tell about the time in Rockyford, New York. I'd been to a drag dance with earrings on and wuz at the theatre when a man came up to me and held out his hand. He had my earrings which I hadn't noticed I lost. He sez, 'Are these yours?' and I sez, 'Yes,' and he sez: 'You'd better come with me to the police station.' My god, Mary, I wuz knocked cold, but I sez to him kinda nervous like: 'Wait a minute. You ain't in a hurry, are you? I gotta get my wardrobe into a trunk because we got to go on to another town to show our show tomorrow.' He waited for me and after I collected what little I got I ast him if they wasn't some way we could fix it up, and he sez he'd have to call up the chief, so I did, and talked real refined and elegant over the phone. I'm tellin' you Mary, I can act like a real lady when I needs to, but that night I talked like rough trade real manly tones—and I sez to the chief that I was sorry all this had happened and that it wouldn't happen again, and I had to be out of town tonight to play the next night with the show, and we wuz only stagin' a little act, and the chief talked it over with me for a while and finally sez, 'All right, but the next time *Mis*ter Knight'—and god Mary, you should of heard him dwell on that Mizz—'the next time you'd better not drop your earrings around so conspicuous.' My god Mary, when I wuz out of that I breathed better than coke's ever made me.

"And another time Miss Brachman—you know Miss Brachman, Carmen the second, sure you know her, a real grand bitch she is—you know her sure, that one that pencils her eyebrows so fine and uses a calcimine makeup—she was giving a real swell party at her apartment and all the rich bitches were there—a canvas out before her place like for a wedding or a funeral—and limousines and all sorts of private cars—and you shudda seen some of the drag costumes them bitches wore—cost five thousand dollars a costume some of them did, and honest to god jewelry. Well, the party was jest gettin' real gay when along comes a knock on the door and Miss Brachman shrieked out, 'the dicks,' and lifted up her skirts and ran down a sidestairs weepin', and I ran around like blind and finally got into the bathroom and back the bath tub, and there wuz one of them real ladylike bitches and he kept on sayin', 'Oh if I'm caught I'll take poison; I can't stand the scandal,' and I sez to her, 'Close up, do you want to call in them dicks on us,' and she whimpered and shut her gab, and I sneaked out and locked the door, and when someone knocked, 'who's in there?' I heard a voice saying, thats the bathroom, and no one's in there,' and I don't know why but the dicks didn't say the door had to be opened. Oh Mary, I'm tellin' you I've been in some raids, and you bet on a bitch's hunch, me and Kate both smelled a raid back there tonight. I bet that place back there now is being taken away in wagonloads of bitches in little black wagons."

Though Miss Knight's days in Berlin had not been joyful ones it was just after this period that she began really to taste misery. Her repertoire of humor was exhausted so that people avoided her, and, themselves weary of Berlin, departed, or came no more to the places where they had been accustomed to assemble. Miss Knight found it difficult to locate people from whom she could borrow money to go on living.

At one of her darkest moments she had one flickering gleam of gleeful hope. Seated one night in a queer cafe she noted the entrance of a party of English swells: three men in evening clothes with two women, actresses or demi-mondaines. A few minutes later after their entrance a note was handed to Miss Knight from a man in the party. A few minutes later she was babbling about it.

"My god Mary, he's fallen for me at sight," she exclaimed excitedly, "an' Mizz Foster tells me he's a real Austrian duke. I'll be riding in a limousine next, with a grand elegant apartment all my own, next thing you know. Won't I be the upstage bitch then!"

Two nights later, however, Miss Knight was more than usually disconsolate, and afraid that nobody liked her. She asked one man if they were all off her. "I'm a common piece of turd, but I ain't never pretended I wasn't. Whatcha all got against me just now because I'm hard up?" she queried, and a few minutes later, after being assured that she was not being turned against, confided: "My god, these Berlin bitches! Do you know that Austrian duke guy—well I kept the appointment he asked for in his note and he went to my room with me, and he sez to me just as I was slipping pretty into my gorgeous lavender kimona, 'Before we go any further I want you to understand that this will cost you a good sum of money. You Americans have plenty,' and I gasped and caught my breath, and got it quick, and I sez to him, 'Lookie here, Annie, you aristocratic bitch, just you put on your coat and run right along. Now run along, Annie.'

"I'm sayin' right now I ain't paying to sleep with no man. I get paid myself if there's any paying done. But I ain't having no luck at all these days. Losing my figure, I guess, or gettin' old, or those German bitches are too thick around, and they can live on nothin.'" Miss Knight looked around her with a secretive air, lowered her voice a little, and confided on. "I suppose you'll be shocked and hold it against me if I tell you something—"

Upon being assured that nothing she could reveal would shock her listener, Miss Knight went on:

"You know just before I came to Berlin, and I was lined with money them days, you remember. Well, what do you think? You know I got stranded in Paris, and a guy took me to a house where there were only men, and you know, right away the Madam running the place offered me a job, and I was hard up, and I stuck in that place for months . . . Now you are shocked, aren't you? Ain't I always told you I wuz nothin' . . . But Paris wasn't nothin' like I'm gettin' it in Berlin, and I couldn't even get a job in a house here. And do you know, last night I picked up a cop. How that guy had the nerve to go home with anybody I don't get. You know I hate well, you know—blind meat—you know what I mean." Miss Knight chattered, sure of the queer erudition of whoever happened to be her listener, however bewildered and curious his or her expression might be.

Having spontaneously confided all of his life that occurred to his mind at the moment, Miss Knight, recklessly feeling the need for uplift, glided out to the water-closet to take a deck of cocaine. Within three minutes she glided back in the room, and out of a now gayer mood and of an habitual bitchy gaiety, shouted across the aisle to a Germany boy she knew, "Oh you Suzie stoopantakit, I got your number. It's—69—ain't it? You know dearie, I think yer queer. Honest to god." Then, with a condorlike twist of her neck and head, with eyes narrowed to "look 'em over haughty like," he declared to the whole room, "Whoops, I'm so glad I'm a real man."

Such were the depressing circumstances of Miss Knight's life at the moment, however, that gaiety did not linger long, and he relapsed into moody confidences. "Oh Mary, did I tell you about the dream I had last night? I wuz paralyzed from my nose to the top of my head with coke. Kinda blue, you maybe noticed I wuz last night, so I took more'n usual. And I thought I wuz in a raid and couldn't move, and then I woke up and drank six bucketsfull of water like I always do, and I shivered inside and out. I'm tellin' you I'll be taken out of Berlin all done up like a mummy and stiff, if I ain't floating down the river. And there ain't goin' to be nobody to send me flowers either."

Again Miss Knight arose to retire. "I'm going to fly my tin hip out just to powder my nose a little . . . who's that yer looking at, Mr. Policeman—? No, sir, yer wrong, I ain't queer. I'm a real man. What'd you say yer name wuz? Send me a postcard. I had a lovely time."

Two days later Miss Knight had disappeared, black with gloom. She had been reproached by Foster Morris for having said that he was a coke fiend. Miss Knight denied having remarked this, but was later confronted by the person she had made the remark to. Looking utterly beaten, Miss Knight went out the back door of the cafe and was not seen again by any of the people he knew in Berlin. Those used to seeing him about, and knowing that he had not a cent money to get out of Berlin with, wondered as to his whereabouts. It was generally concluded that he was "floating down the river," into which despondency and pennilessness had caused him to throw himself. Kate Matthews, however, believed otherwise.

"No sir, believe me, you can trust the bitches to take care of themselves. He's probably alive and eating better than any of us by now. Luck changes quick for them.

Six weeks passed, and Miss Knight had been well nigh forgotten, and when mentioned was only laughed at as one of the world's exaggerated types until one day Kate Matthews was showing about a letter which she had received from New York.

It read:

Dear Kate,—Well, old dear, how are you? I am back in U.S.A. How are all the others? Will be back in Paris February 1st, 1922. I am sending you twenty-five dollars for the marks you laid out for me, and hope that you will always be my friend, as I love you and hope that you are well—I am, yours, Charlie Knight

"How in the devil did he get back to New York and send back a letter to you in six weeks?" Foster Morris marveled. "He had not one sou on him when he went out the back door because I called him down."

"Didn't I tell you the bitches could look out for themselves?" Kate Matthews responded. "That one! If she was run over by a truck or a steam roller she'd turn up, about to appear in Paris, or London, or Madrid, or Singapore. She's just that international."

## Bruce Nugent (b. 1906)

Nugent's "Smoke, Lilies and Jade" is believed to be the first fictional portrait of African-American gay male life written in the United States. It was published under the pseudonym "Richard Bruce" in the Harlem magazine, *Fire!!* (1926), edited by the writer Wallace Thurman. Nugent was openly homosexual and one of the leading figures in the social and intellectual ferment of the Harlem Renaissance. A painter, poet, and dancer, Nugent's story of a Harlem homosexual who falls in love with a handsome Latino is as notable for its experimental style as it was, at the time, for its daring content.

### SMOKE, LILIES AND JADE (1926)

He wanted to do something . . . to write or draw . . . or something . . . but it was so comfortable just to lay there on the bed . . . his shoes off . . . and think . . . think of everything . . . short disconnected thoughts—to wonder . . . to remember . . . to think and smoke . . . why wasn't he worried that he had no money . . . he had had five cents . . . but he had been hungry . . . he was hungry and still . . . all he wanted to do was . . . lay there comfortably smoking . . . think . . . wishing he were writing . . . or drawing . . . or something . . . something about the things he felt and thought . . . but what did he think . . . he remembered how his mother had awakened him one night . . . ages ago . . . six years ago . . . Alex . . . he had always wondered at the strangeness of it . . . she had seemed so . . . so . . . so just the same . . . Alex . . . I think your father is dead . . . and it hadn't seemed so strange . . . yet . . . one's mother didn't say that . . . didn't wake one at midnight every night to say . . . feel him . . . put your hand on his head . . . then whisper with a catch in her voice . . . I'm afraid . . . sh don't wake Lam . . . yet it hadn't seemed as it should have seemed . . . even when he had felt his father's cool wet forehead . . . it hadn't been tragic . . . the light had been turned very low . . . and flickered . . . yet it hadn't been tragic . . . or weird . . . not at all as one should feel when one's father died . . . even his reply of . . . yes he is dead . . . had been commonplace . . . hadn't been dramatic . . . there had been no tears . . . no sobs . . . not even a sorrow . . . and yet he must have realized that one's father couldn't smile . . . or sing any more . . . after he had died . . . every one remembered his father's voice . . . it had been a lush voice . . . a promise . . . then that dressing together . . . his mother and himself . . . in the bathroom . . . why was the bathroom always the warmest room in the winter . . . . as they had put on their

clothes . . . his mother had been telling him what he must do . . . and cried softly .
. . and that had made him cry too but you mustn't cry Alex . . . remember you have
to be a little man now . . . and that was all . . . didn't other wives and sons cry more
for their dead than that . . . anyway people never cried for beautiful sunsets . . . or
music . . . and those were the things that hurt . . . the things to sympathize with . .
. then out into the snow and dark of the morning . . . first to the undertaker's . . . no
first to Uncle Frank's . . . why did Aunt Lula have to act like that . . . to ask again
and again . . . but when did he die . . . when did he die . . . I just can't believe it . .
. poor Minerva . . . then out into the snow and dark again . . . how had his mother
expected him to know where to find the night bell at the undertaker's . . . he was
the most sensible of them all tho . . . all he had said was . . . what . . . Harry Francis
. . . too bad . . . tell mamma I'll be there first thing in the morning . . . then down
the deserted streets again . . . to grandmother's . . . it was growing light now . . . it
must be terrible to die in daylight . . . grandpa had been sweeping the snow off the
yard . . . he had been glad of that because . . . well he could tell him better than
grandma . .. grandpa .. . father's dead . . . and he hadn't acted strange either . . .
books lied . . . he had just looked at Alex a moment then continued sweeping . . .
all he said was . . . what time did he die . . . she'll want to know . . . then passing
thru the lonesome street toward home . . . Mrs. Mamie Grant was closing a window and spied him . . . hallow Alex . . . an' how's your father this mornin' . . . dead
. . . get out . . . tch tch tch an' I was just around there with a cup a' custard yesterday . . . Alex puffed contentedly on his cigarette . . . he was hungry and comfortable
. . . and he had an ivory holder inlaid with red jade and green . . . funny how the
smoke seemed to climb up that ray of sunlight . . . went up the slant just like imagination . . . was imagination blue . . . or was it because he had spent his last five
cents and couldn't worry . . . anyway it was nice to lay there and wonder . . . and
remember. . . why was he so different from other people . . . the only things he
remembered of his father's funeral were the crowded church and the ride in the
hack . . . so many people there in the church . . . and ladies with tears in their eyes
. . . and on their cheeks . . . and some men too . . . why did people cry . . . vanity
that was all . . . yet they weren't exactly hypocrites . . . but why . . . it had made him
furious . . . all these people crying . . . it wasn't *their* father . . . and he wasn't crying
. . . couldn't cry for sorrow altho he had loved his father more than . . . than . . . it
had made him so angry that tears had come to his eyes . . . and he had been
ashamed of his mother . . . crying into a handkerchief . . . so ashamed that tears had
run down his cheeks and he had frowned . . . and some one . . . a woman . . . had
said . . . look at that poor little dear . . . Alex is just like his father . . . and the tears
had run fast . . . because he *wasn't* like his father . . . he couldn't sing . . . he didn't
want to sing . . . he didn't want to sing . . . Alex blew a cloud of smoke . . . blue
smoke . . . when they had taken his father from the vault three weeks later . . . he
had grown beautiful . . . his nose had become perfect and clear . . . his hair had
turned jet black and glossy and silky . . . and his skin was a transparent green . . .
like the sea only not so deep . . . and where it was drawn over the cheek bones a
pale beautiful red appeared . . . like a blush . . . why hadn't his father looked like
that always . . . but no . . . to have sung would have broken the wondrous repose of
his lips and maybe that was his beauty . . . maybe it was wrong to think thoughts

like these . . . but they were nice and pleasant and comfortable . . . when one was smoking a cigarette thru an ivory holder . . . inlaid with red jade and green . . . .

he wondered why he couldn't find work . . . a job . . . when he had first come to New York he had . . . and he had only been fourteen then was it because he was nineteen now that he felt so idle . . . and contented . . . or because he was an artist . . . but was he an artist . . . was one an artist until one became known . . . of course he was an artist . . . and strangely enough so were all his friends . . . he should be ashamed that he didn't work . . . but . . . was it five years in New York . . . or the fact that he was an artist . . . when his mother said she couldn't understand him . . . why did he vaguely pity her instead of being ashamed . . . he should be . . . his mother and all his relatives said so . . . his brother was three years younger than he and yet he had already been away from home a year . . . on the stage . . . making thirty-five dollars a week . . . had three suits and many clothes and was going to help his mother . . . while he . . . Alex . . . was content to lay and smoke and meet friends at night . . . to argue and read Wilde . . . Freud . . . Boccaccio and Schnitzler . . . to attend Gurdjieff meetings and know things . . . Why did they scoff at him for knowing such people as Carl . . . Mencken . . . Toomer . . . Hughes . . . Cullen . . . Wood . . . Cabell . . . oh the whole lot of them . . was it because it seemed incongruous that he . . . who was so little known . . . should call by first names people they would like to know . . . were they jealous . . . no mothers aren't jealous of their sons . . . they are proud of them . . . why then . . . when these friends accepted and liked him . . . no matter how he dressed . . . why did mother ask . . . and you went looking like that . . . Langston was a fine fellow . . . he knew there was something in Alex . . . and so did Rene and Borgia . . . and Zora and Clement and Miguel . . . and . . . and . . . and all of them . . . if he went to see mother she would ask . . . how do you feel Alex with nothing in your pockets . . . I don't see how you can be satisfied . . . Really you're a mystery to me . . . and who you take after . . . I'm sure I don't know . . . none of my brothers were lazy and shiftless . . . I can never remember the time when they weren't sending money home and your father was your age he was supporting a family . . . where you get your nerve I don't know . . . just because you've tried to write one or two little poems and stories that no one understands . . . you seem to think the world owes you a living . . . you should see by now how much is thought of them . . . you can't sell anything . . . and you won't do anything to make money . . . wake up Alex . . . I don't know what will become of you . . .

it was hard to believe in one's self after that . . . did Wilde's parents or Shelly's or Goya's talk to them like that . . . but it was depressing to think in that vein . . . Alex stretched and yawned . . . Max had died . . . Margaret had died . . . so had Sonia . . . Cynthia . . . Juan-Jose and Harry . . . all people he had loved . . . loved one by one and together . . . and all had died . . . he never loved a person long before they died . . . in truth he was tragic . . . that was a lovely appellation . . . The Tragic Genius . . . think . . . to go thru life known as The Tragic Genius . . . romantic . . . but it was more or less true . . . Alex turned over and blew another cloud of smoke . . . was all life like that . . . smoke . . . blue smoke from an ivory holder . . . he wished he were in New Bedford . . . New Bedford was a nice place . . . snug little houses set complacently behind protecting lawns . . . half open windows showing prim interiors from behind waving cool curtains . . . inviting . . . like precise courtesans winking

from behind lace fans . . . and trees . . . many trees . . . casting lacey patterns of shade
on the sun dipped sidewalks . . . small stores . . . naively proud of their pseudo
grandeur . . . banks . . . called institutions for saving . . . all naive . . . that was it . . .
New Bedford was naive . . . after the sophistication of New York it would fan one
like a refreshing breeze . . . and yet he had returned to New York . . . and sophistication . . . was he sophisticated . . . no because he was seldom bored . . . seldom
bored by anything . . . and weren't the sophisticated continually suffering from
ennui . . . on the contrary . . . he was amused . . . amused by the artificiality of
naivety and sophistication alike . . . but may be that in itself was the essence of
sophistication or . . . was it cynicism . . . or were the two identical . . . he blew a
cloud of smoke . . . it was growing dark now . . . and the smoke no longer had a ladder to climb . . . but soon the moon would rise and then he would clothe the silver
moon in blue smoke garments . . . truly smoke was like imagination . . . . .

Alex sat up . . . pulled on his shoes and went out . . . it was a beautiful night . . .
and so large . . . the dusky blue hung like a curtain in an immense arched doorway
. . . fastened with silver tacks . . . to wander in the night was wonderful . . . myriads
of inquisitive lights . . . curiously prying into the dark . . . and fading unsatisfied . .
. he passed a woman . . . she was not beautiful . . . and he was sad because she did
not weep that she would never be beautiful . . . was it Wilde who had said . . . a cigarette is the most perfect pleasure because it leaves one unsatisfied . . . the breeze
gave to him a perfume stolen from some wandering lady of the evening . . . . it
pleased him . . . why was it that men wouldn't use perfumes . . . they should . . .
each and every one of them liked perfumes . . . the man who denied that was a liar
. . . or a coward . . . but if ever he were to voice that thought . . . express it . . . he
would be misunderstood . . . a fine feeling that . . . to be misunderstood . . . it made
him feel tragic and great . . . but may be it would be nicer to be understood . . . but
no . . . no great artist is . . . then again neither were fools . . . they were strangely
akin these two . . . Alex thought of a sketch he would make . . . a personality sketch
of Fania . . . straight classic features tinted proud purple . . . sensuous fine lips . . .
gilded for truth . . . eyes . . . half opened and lids colored mysterious green . . . hair
black and straight . . . drawn sternly mocking back from the false puritanical forehead . . . maybe he would make Edith too . . . skin a blue . . . infinite like night . .
. and eyes . . . slant and grey . . . very complacent like a cat's . . . Mona Lisa lips . .
. red and seductive as . . . as pomegranate juice . . . in truth it was fine to be young
and hungry and an artist . . . to blow blue smoke from an ivory holder . . . .

here was the cafeteria . . . it was almost as tho it had journeyed to meet him . . .
the night was so blue . . . how does blue feel . . . or red or gold or any other color .
. . if colors could be heard he could paint most wondrous tunes . . . symphonious .
. . think . . . the dulcet clear tone of a blue like night . . . of a red like pomegranate
juice . . . like Edith's lips . . . of the fairy tones to be heard in a sunset . . . like rubies
shaken in a crystal cup . . . of the symphony of Fania . . . and silver . . . and gold . .
. he had heard the sound of gold . . . but they weren't the sounds he wanted to catch
. . . no . . . they must be liquid . . . not so staccato but flowing variations of the same
caliber . . . there was no one in the cafe as yet . . . he sat and waited . . . that was a
clever idea he had had about color music . . . but after all he was a monstrous clever
fellow . . . Jurgen had said that . . . how does one go about getting an introduction

to a fiction character . . . go up to the brown cover of the book and knock gently . . . and say hello . . . then timidly . . . is Duke Jurgen there . . . or . . . no because if entered the book in the beginning Jurgen would only be a pawn broker . . . and one didn't enter a book in the center . . . but what foolishness . . . Alex lit a cigarette . . . but Cabell was a master to have written Jurgen . . . and an artist . . . and a poet . . . Alex blew a cloud of smoke . . . a few lines of one of Langston's poems came to describe Jurgen . . . . .

Somewhat like Ariel
Somewhat like Puck
Somewhat like a gutter boy
Who loves to play in muck.
Somewhat like Bacchus
Somewhat like Pan
And a way with women
Like a sailor man . . .

Langston must have known Jurgen . . . suppose Jurgen had met Tonio Kroeger . . . what a vagrant thought . . . Kroeger . . . Kroeger . . . Kroeger . . . why here was Rene . . . Alex had almost gone to sleep . . . Alex blew a cone of smoke as he took Rene's hand . . . it was nice to have friends like Rene . . . so comfortable . . . Rene was speaking . . . Borgia joined them . . . and de Diego Padro . . . their talk veered to . . . James Branch Cabell . . . beautiful . . . marvelous . . . Rene had an enchanting accent . . . said sank for thank and souse for south . . . but they couldn't know Cabell's greatness . . . Alex searched the smoke for expression . . . he . . . he . . . well he has created a phantasy mire . .. that's it . .. from clear rich imagery . . . life and silver sands . . . that's nice . . . and silver sands . . . imagine lilies growing in such a mire . . . when they close at night their gilded underside would protect . . . but that's not it at all . . . his thoughts just carried and mingled like . .. like odors . . . suggested but never definite . . . Rene was leaving . . . they all were leaving .. . Alex sauntered slowly back . .. the houses all looked sleepy . . . funny . . . made him feel like writing poetry . . . and about death too . . . an elevated crashed by overhead scattering all his thoughts with its noise . . . making them spread . . . in circles . . . then larger circles . . . just like a splash in a calm pool . . . what had he been thinking . . . of . . . a poem about death . . . but he no longer felt that urge . . . just walk and think and wonder . . . think and remember and smoke . . . blow smoke that mixed with his thoughts and the night . . . he would like to live in a large white palace . . . to wear a long black cape . . . very full and lined with vermillion . . . to have many cushions and to lie there among them . . . talking to his friends . . . lie there in a yellow silk shirt and black velvet trousers . . . like music-review artists talking and pouring strange liquors from curiously beautiful bottles . .. bottles with long slender necks . .. he climbed the noisy stair of the odorous tenement . . . smelled of fish . . . of stale fried fish and dirty milk bottles . . . he rather liked it . . . he liked the acrid smell of horse manure too . . . strong . . . thoughts . . . yes to lie back among strangely fashioned cushions and sip eastern wines and talk . .. Alex threw himself on the bed . . . removed his shoes . . . stretched and relaxed . . . yes and have music waft softly into the darkened and incensed room . . . he blew a cloud of smoke . . . oh the joy of being an artist and of blowing blue smoke thru an ivory holder inlaid with red jade and green . . . .

the street was so long and narrow . . . so long and narrow . . . and blue . . . in the distance it reached the stars . . . and if he walked long enough . . . far enough . . . he could reach the stars too . . . the narrow blue was so empty . . . quiet . . . Alex walked music . . . it was nice to walk in the blue after a party . . . Zora had shone again . . . her stories . . . she always shone . . . and Monty was glad . . . every one was glad when Zora shone . . . he was glad he had gone to Monty's party . . . Monty had a nice place in the Village . . . nice lights . . . and friends and wine . . . mother would be scandalized that he could think of going to a party . . . without a copper to his name . . . but then mother had never been to Monty's . . . and mother had never seen the street seem long and narrow and blue . . . Alex walked music . . . the click of his heels kept time with a tune in his mind . . . he glanced into a lighted cafe window . . . inside were people sipping coffee . . . men . . . why did they sit there in the loud light . . . didn't they know that outside the street . . . the narrow blue street met the stars . . . that if they walked long enough . . . far enough . . . Alex walked and the click of his heels sounded . . . and had an echo . . . sound being tossed back and forth . . . back and forth . . . some one was approaching . . . and their echoes mingled . . . and gave the sound of castanets . . . Alex liked the sound of the approaching man's footsteps . . . he walked music also . . . he knew the beauty of the narrow blue . . . Alex knew that by the way their echoes mingled . . . he wished he would speak . . . but strangers don't speak at four o'clock in the morning . . . at least if they did he couldn't imagine what would be said . . . maybe . . . pardon me but are you walking toward the stars . . . yes, sir, and if you walk long enough . . . then may I walk with you I want to reach the stars too . . . perdone me senor tiene una fosforo . . . Alex was glad he had been addressed in Spanish . . . to have been asked for a match in English . . . or to have been addressed in English at all . . . would have been blasphemy just then . . . Alex handed him a match . . . he glanced at his companion apprehensively in the match glow . . . he was afraid that his appearance would shatter the blue thoughts . . . and stars . . . ah . . . his face was a perfect compliment to his voice . . . and the echo of their steps mingled . . . they walked in silence . . . the castanets of their heels clicking accompaniment . . . the stranger inhaled deeply and with a nod of contentment and a smile . . . blew a cloud of smoke . . . Alex felt like singing . . . the stranger knew the magic of blue smoke also . . . they continued in silence . . . the castanets of their heels clicking rhythmically . . . Alex turned in his doorway . . . up the stairs and the stranger waited for him to light the room . . . no need for words . . . they had always known each other . . . as they undressed by the blue dawn . . . Alex knew he had never seen a more perfect being . . . his body was all symmetry and music . . . and Alex called him Beauty . . . long they lay . . . blowing smoke and exchanging thoughts . . . and Alex swallowed with difficulty . . . he felt a glow of tremor . . . and they talked and . . . slept . . . .

Alex wondered more and more why he liked Adrian so . . . he liked many people . . . Wallie . . . Zora . . . Clement . . . Gloria . . . Langston . . . John . . . Gwenny . . . oh many people . . . and they were friends . . . but Beauty . . . it was different .

. . once Alex had admired Beauty's strength . . . and Beauty's eyes had grown soft and he had said . . . I like you more than any one Dulce . . . Adrian always called him Dulce . . . and Alex had become confused . . . was it that he was so susceptible to beauty that Alex liked Adrian so much . . . but no . . . he knew other people who were beautiful . . . Fania and Gloria . . . Monty and Bunny . . . but he was never confused before them . . . while Beauty . . . Beauty could make him believe in Buddha . . . or imps . . . and no one else could do that . . . that is no one but Melva . . . but then he was in love with Melva . . . and that explained that . . . he would like Beauty to know Melva . . . they were both so perfect . . . such compliments . . . yes he would like Beauty to know Melva because he loved them both . . . there . . . he had thought it . . . actually dared to think it . . . but Beauty must never know . . . Beauty couldn't understand . . . indeed Alex couldn't understand . . . and it pained him . . . almost physically . . . and tired his mind . . . Beauty . . . Beauty was in the air . . . the smoke . . . Beauty . . . Melva . . . Beauty . . . Melva . . . Alex slept . . and dreamed . . . .

he was in a field . . . a field of blue smoke and black poppies and red calla lilies . . . he was searching . . . on his hands and knees . . . searching . . . among black poppies and red calla lilies . . . he was searching pushed aside poppy stems . . . and saw two strong white legs . . . dancer's legs . . . the contours pleased him . .. his eyes wandered . . . on past the muscular hocks to the firm white thighs . . . the rounded buttocks . . . then the lithe narrow waist . . . strong torso and broad deep chest . . . the heavy shoulders . . . the graceful muscled neck . . . squared chin and quizzical lips . . . grecian nose with its temperamental nostrils . . . the brown eyes looking at him . . . like . . . Monty looked at Zora . . . his hair curly and black and all tousled . . . and it was Beauty . . . and Beauty smiled and looked at him and smiled . . . said . . . I'll wait Alex . . . and Alex became confused and continued his search . . . on his hands and knees . . . pushing aside poppy stems and lily stems . . . a poppy . . . a black poppy . . . a lily . . . a red lily . . . and when he looked back he could no longer see Beauty . . . Alex continued his search . . . thru poppies . . . lilies . . . poppies and red calla lilies . . . and suddenly he saw . . . two small feet olive- ivory . . . two well turned legs curving gracefully from slender ankles . . . and the contours soothed him . . . he followed them . . . past the narrow rounded hips to the tiny waist . . . the fragile firm breasts . . . the graceful slender throat . . . the soft rounded chin . . . slightly parting lips and straight little nose with its slightly flaring nostrils . . . the black eyes with lights in them . . . looking at him . . . the forehead and straight cut black hair . . . and it was Melva . . . and she looked at him and smiled and said . . . I'll wait Alex . . . and Alex became confused and kissed her . . . became confused and continued his search . . . on his hands and knees . . . pushed aside a poppy stem . . . a black-poppy stem . . . pushed aside a lily stem . . . a red-lily stem . . . a poppy . . . a poppy . . . a lily . . . and suddenly he stood erect . . . exultant . . . and in his hand he held . . . an ivory holder . . . inlaid with red jade . . . and green . . . .

and Alex awoke . . . Beauty's hair ticked his nose . . . Beauty was smiling in his sleep . . . half his face stained flush color by the sun . . . the other half in shadow . . . blue shadow . . . his eye lashes casting cobwebby blue shadows on his cheek . . . his lips were so beautiful . . . quizzical . . . Alex wondered why he always thought of that passage from Wilde's *Salome* . . . when he looked at Beauty's lips . . . I would kiss your lips . . . he *would* like to kiss Beauty's lips . . . Alex flushed warm . . . with shame . . . or was it shame . . . he reached across Beauty for a cigarette . . . Beauty's cheek felt cool to his arm . . . his hair felt soft .. . Alex lay smoking . . . such a dream . . . red calla lilies . . . red calla lilies . . . and . . . what could it all mean . . . did dreams have meanings . . . Fania said . . . and black poppies . . . thousands . . . millions . . . Beauty stirred . . . Alex put out his cigarette . ... closed his eyes . . . he mustn't see Beauty yet . . . speak to him . . . his lips were too hot . . . dry . . . the palms of his hands too cool and moist . . . thru his half closed eyes he could see Beauty . . . propped . . . cheek in hand . . . on one elbow . . . looking at him . . . lips smiling quizzically . . . he wished Beauty wouldn't look so hard . . . Alex was finding it difficult to breathe . . . breathe normally . . . why *must* Beauty look so long . . . and smile *that* way . . . his face seemed nearer . . . it was . . . Alex could feel Beauty's hair on his forehead . . . breathe normally . . . breathe normally . . . could feel Beauty's breath on his nostrils and lips . . . and it was clean and faintly colored with tobacco . . . breathe normally Alex . . . Beauty's lips were nearer . . . Alex closed his eyes . . . how did one act . . . his pulse was hammering . . . from wrists to finger tip . . . wrist to finger tip . . . Beauty's lips touched his . . . his temples throbbed . . . throbbed . . . his pulse hammered from wrist to finger tip . . . Beauty's breath came short now . . . softly staccato . . . breathe normally Alex . . . you are asleep . . . Beauty's lips touched his . . . breathe normally . . . and pressed . . . pressed hard .. . cool . . . his body trembled . . . breathe normally Alex . . . Beauty's lips pressed cool . . . cool and hard . . . how much pressure does it take to waken one . . . Alex sighed . . . moved softly . . . how does one act . . . Beauty's hair barely touched him now . .. his breath was faint on . . . Alex's nostrils . . . and lips . . . Alex stretched and opened his eyes . . . Beauty was looking at him . . . propped on one elbow . . . cheek in his palm . . . Beauty spoke . . .

scratch my head please Dulce . . . Alex was breathing normally now . . . propped against the bed head . . . Beauty's head in his lap . . . Beauty spoke . . . I wonder why I like to look at some things Dulce . . . things like smoke and cats . . . and you . . . Alex's pulse no longer hammered from . . . wrist to finger tip . . . wrist to finger tip . . . the rose dusk had become blue night . . . and soon . . . soon they would go out into the blue . . . .

the little church was crowded . . . warm . . . the rows of benches were brown and sticky . . . Harold was there . . . and Constance and Langston and Bruce and John . . . there was Mr. Robeson . . . how are you Paul . . . a young man was singing . . . Caver . . . Caver was a very self assured young man . . . such a dream . . . poppies . . . black poppies . ... they were applauding . . . Constance and John were exchanging notes . . . the benches were sticky . . . a young lady was playing the piano . . . fair . . . and red calla lilies . . . who had ever heard of red calla lilies . . . they were applauding . . . a young man was playing the viola . . . what could it all mean . . . so many poppies . . . and Beauty looking at him like . . . like Monty looked at Zora . . . another young man was playing a violin . . . he was the first real artist to perform . . . he had a touch of soul . . . or was it only feeling . . . they were hard to differentiate on the violin . . . and Melva standing in the poppies and lilies . . . Mr. Phillips was singing . . . Mr. Phillips was billed as a basso . . . and he had kissed her

. . . they were applauding . . . the first young man was singing again . . . Langston's
spiritual . . . Fy-ah-fy-ah-Lawd . . . fy-ah's gonna burn ma soul . . . Beauty's hair was
so black and curly . . . they were applauding . . . encore . . . Fy-ah Lawd had been
a success . . . Langston bowed . . . Langston had written the words . . . Hall bowed
. . . Hall had written the music . . . the young man was singing it again . . . Beauty's
lips had pressed hard . . . cool . . . cool . . . fy-ah Lawd . . . his breath had trembled
. . . fy-ah's gonna burn ma soul . . . they were all leaving . . . first to the roof dance
. . . fy-ah Lawd . . . there was Catherine . . . she was beautiful tonight . . . she always
was at night . . . Beauty's lips . . . fy-ah Lawd . . . hello Dot . . . why don't you take
a boat that sails . . . when are you leaving again . . . and there's Estelle . . . every one
was there . . . fy-ah Lawd . . . Beauty's body had pressed close . . . close . . . fy-ah's
gonna burn my soul . . . let's leave . . . have to meet some people at the New World
. . . then to Augusta's party . . . Harold . . . John . . . Bruce . . . Connie . . . Langston
. . . ready . . . down one hundred thirty-fifth street . . . fy-ah . . . meet these people
and leave . . . fy-ah Lawd . . . now to Augusta's party . . . fy-ahs gonna burn ma soul
. . . they were at Augusta's . . . Alex half lay . . . half sat on the floor . . . sipping a
cocktail . . . such a dream . . . red calla lilies . . . Alex left . . . down the narrow streets
. . . fy-ah . . . up the long noisy stairs . . . fy-ahs gonna burn ma soul . . . his head felt
swollen . . . expanding . . . contracting . . . expanding . . . contracting . . . he had
never been like this before . . . expanding . . . contracting . . . it was that . . . fy-ah .
. . fy-ah Lawd . . . and the cocktails . . . and Beauty . . . he felt two cool strong hands
on his shoulders . . . it was Beauty . . . lie down Dulce . . . Alex lay down . . . Beauty
. . . Alex stopped . . . no no . . . don't say it . . . Beauty mustn't know . . . Beauty could-
n't understand . . . are you going to lie down too Beauty . . . the light went out
expanding . . . contracting . . . he felt the bed sink as Beauty lay beside him . . . his
lips were dry . . . hot . . . the palms of his hands so moist and cool . . . Alex partly
closed his eyes . . . from beneath his lashes he could see Beauty's face over his . . .
nearer . . . nearer . . . Beauty's hair touched his forehead now . . . he could feel his
breath on his nostrils and lips . . . Beauty's breath came short . . . breathe normally
Beauty . . . breathe normally . . . Beauty's lips touched his . . . pressed hard . . . cool
. . . opened slightly . . . Alex opened his eyes . . . into Beauty's . . . parted his lips . .
. Dulce . . . Beauty's breath was hot and short . . . Alex ran his hand through Beauty's
hair . . . Beauty's lips pressed hard against his teeth . . . Alex trembled . . . could feel
Beauty's body . . . close against his . . . hot . . . tense . . . white . . . and soft . . . soft .
. . soft . . . .

they were at Forno's . . . every one came to Forno's once maybe only once . . . but
they came . . . see that big fat woman Beauty . . . Alex pointed to an overly stout and
bejeweled lady making her way thru the maze . . . that's Maria Guerrero . . . Beauty
looked to see a lady guiding almost the whole opera company to an immense table
. . . really Dulce . . . for one who appreciates beauty you do use the most abominable English . . . Alex lit a cigarette . . . and that florid man with white hair . . .
that's Carl . . . Beauty smiled . . . The blind bow boy . . . he asked . . . Alex wondered . . . everything seemed to . . . so just the same . . . here they were laughing
and joking about people . . . there's Rene . . . Rene this is my friend Adrian . . . after
that night . . . and he felt so unembarrassed . . . Rene and Adrian were talking . . .

there was Lucricia Bori . . . she was bowing at their table . . . oh her cousin was with them . . . and Peggy Joyce . . . every one came to Forno's . . . Alex looked toward the door . . . there was Melva . . . Alex beckoned . . . Melva this is Adrian . . . Beauty held her hand . . . they talked . . . smoked . . . Alex loved Melva . . . in Forno's . . . every one came there sooner or later . . . maybe once . . . but

. . . up . . . up . . . slow . . . jerk up . . . up . . . not fast . . . not glorious . . . but slow . . . up . . . up into the sun . . . slow . . . sure like fate . . . poise on the brim . . . the brim of life . . . two shining rails straight down . . . Melva's head was on his shoulder . . . his arm was around her . . . poise . . . the down . . . gasping . . . straight down . . . straight like sin . . . down . . . the curving shiny rail rushed up to meet them . . . hit the bottom then . . . shoot up . . . fast . . . glorious . . . up into the sun . . . Melva gasped . . . Alex's arm tightened . . . all goes up . . . then down . . . straight like hell . . . all breath squeezed out of them . . . Melva's head on his shoulder . . . up . . . up . . . Alex kissed her . . . down . . . they stepped out of the car . . . walking music . . . now over to the Ferris Wheel . . . out and up . . . Melva's hand was soft in his . . . out and up . . . over mortals . . . mortals drinking nectar . . . five cents a glass . . . her cheek was soft on his . . . up . . . up . . . till the world seemed small . . . tiny . . . the ocean seemed tiny and blue . . . up . . . up and out . . . over the sun . . . the tiny red sun . . . Alex kissed her . . . up . . . up . . . their tongues touched . . . up . . . seventh heaven . . . the sea had swallowed the sun . . . up and out . . . her breath was perfumed . . . Alex kissed her . . . drift down . . . soft . . . soft . . . the sun had left the sky flushed . . . drift down . . . soft down . . . back to earth . . . visit the mortals sipping nectar at five cents a glass . . . Melva's lips brushed his . . . then out among the mortals . . . and the sun had left a flush on Melva's cheeks . . . they walked hand in hand . . . and the moon came out . . . they walked in silence on the silver strip . . . and the sea sang for them . . . they walked toward the moon . . . we'll hang our hats on the crook of the moon Melva . . . softly on the silver strip . . . his hands molded her features and her cheeks were soft and warm to his touch . . . where is Adrian . . . Alex . . . Melva trod silver . . . Alex trod sand . . . Alex trod sand . . . the sea *sang* for her . . . Beauty . . . her hand felt cold in his . . . Beauty . . . the sea *dinned* . . . Beauty . . . he led the way to the train . . . and the train dinned . . . Beauty . . . dinned . . . dinned . . . her cheek *had* been soft . . . Beauty . . . Beauty . . . her breath *had* been perfumed . . . Beauty . . . Beauty . . . the sands *had* been silver . . . Beauty . . . Beauty . . . they left the train . . . Melva walked music . . . Melva said . . . don't make me blush again . . . and kissed him . . . Alex stood on the steps after she left him and the night was black . . . down long streets to . . . Alex lit a cigarette . . . and his heels clicked . . . Beauty . . . Melva . . . Beauty . . . Melva . . . and the smoke made the night blue . . . .

Melva had said . . . don't make me blush again . . . and kissed him . . . and the street had been blue . . . one *can* love two at the same time . . . Melva had kissed him . . . one *can* . . . and the street had been blue . . . one *can* . . . and the room was clouded with blue smoke . . . drifting vapors of smoke and thoughts . . . Beauty's hair was so black . . . and soft . . . blue smoke from an ivory holder . . . was that why he loved Beauty . . . one *can* . . . or because his body was beautiful . . . and white and warm . . . or because his eyes . . . one *can* love . . . .

## Robert Scully

FROM *A SCARLET PANSY* (1933)

*A Scarlet Pansy* is the earliest novel to portray an American homosexual whose drag serves an even more radical and original purpose than that of Jennie June's daring masquerade and who is even more flamboyant than Miss Knight. Indeed, *A Scarlet Pansy* seems almost to translate Jennie June's facts into fiction, and Jennie's sometimes morose seriousness into wicked high camp.

Fay Etrange—in whimsical French "strange fairy"—inhabits a sexually dubious world in which sex is the constant subtextual secret and in which gender is the constantly deconstructed and destabilized concept. The narrator's firmly tongue-in-cheek discourse needs little decoding to understand that stereotypes are being broken on every side and that sex, sexuality, and gender roles are the target. Making nearly every description and event a double-entendre, the narrator carries Fay through a dizzying series of eroticized adventures in which gender becomes a trope to be deconstructed and language is a vehicle to deceive. For example, in one early chapter Fay finds herself in New York where "she lived a life of actualities and a dream life. In this dream life she was successful, financially at ease, the center of a deferential admiring circle of people. Curiously she never pictured any real women in this circle. The avenue seemed full of gay people those days, persons as happy as she." The "real women" absent from her dreams of course define the truth of her reality, and that delicious misdirection—"persons as happy as she"—allows "gay people" to enter the language of American fiction here perhaps for the first time if, as may be possible, the book was written not in the 1930s but shortly after World War I as its mise-en-scène and somewhat stylized language might suggest.

Fay's interest throughout the book as she moves from a small town in Pennsylvania to the more alluring locales of Baltimore, Chicago, New York, Washington, San Francisco, and eventually Paris and Berlin—America and Europe's acknowledged and flourishing homoerotic sites according to Mayne—is to find real men—"rough trade" as she calls them. To find them she frequents the streets as we have seen, goes to "fairy bars," dresses in "drag," and "cruises." In the process she encounters "pansies," "fairies," and "queens." She "camps" and "dishes" with her "sisters," comments on those who are "too obvious" and those who have just been "brought out." Like Whitman and Jennie June, Fay finds firemen, Irish cops, and street car conductors especially accommodating.

*A Scarlet Pansy* is radical, for it breaks gender boundaries but does not reinforce gender stereotypes. It does not insist that Fay is a woman trapped in the body of a man who succumbs passively to male conquest or victimization. Fay has no imprisoning restraints. She cheerfully employs the most fluid enactment of homosexuality as a gender-breaking weapon to mount a deliberately destructive attack on social bastions. In this book every policemen is ready for a fling with Fay, every soldier succumbs, and sailors beg to be admitted to her company. But unlike Jennie June, who allows herself to be victimized by them, Fay makes these real men her passive toys, and in a sense erases their stereotyped masculinity by conquering it, bringing them to their knees before her triumphant otherness. Jennie June believes herself to be a woman. Fay knows precisely what she is and does not hesitate to use her remarkable intelligence and the spectacle of her consummate masquerade to seduce "real men" into situations so eroticized and emptied of sexual restraint and moral content that "real men" no longer care that she too is as much a "real" man as they. They are all powerless against her and indeed they seem eager to give up their "masculine" roles. She seduces doctors, lawyers, bankers, and even ministers, not only insinuating herself into the privileged sanctuary of the masculine American establishment but luring these totemic figures of masculine and national virtue into her own transgressive world by so addicting them to her sexual power that she erases their restraint and identity. When she conquers an American cowboy, masculine symbol of the American dream, it is clear that Fay's dreams have become synonymous with the nation's.

Fay is no good-hearted and charmingly illiterate Miss Knight, no mincing homosexual or pouting baby June. Not only can she can shovel coal and plow fields, she is a financial and intellectual genius who creates a fortune for herself, takes several advanced degrees including a medical degree, becomes a doctor, masters several languages, and independently travels through America and the world, advocating freedom for her sex (whichever one it may be), very much like the independent "New Woman" who even then was striking fear into the conservative hearts of real men. She ends up very rich and, near the novel's conclusion, arrives in Paris on the eve of World War I. There she becomes a war hero(ine), a trangressive Florence Nightingale. She meets an American soldier, an incredibly handsome, football-playing, good, decent All-American boy, notably and extensively successful with women, who in the frenzy of wartime and in liberated Paris, becomes her lover. Patriotically unable to remain in Paris while American boys are fighting at the front, including her own lover, she joins him there. In a moment of hysterically poignant high camp melodrama, having taken the bullet meant for him, she dies in the arms of her Lieutenant Frank. Like the best characters in American myth, she dies for love and country.

## CHAPTER 19

Fay was very busy for months, working hard during the day and attending classes evenings and at odd hours. Once a week, when Saturday came, she permitted herself relaxation. Almost as regularly she brought to a conclusion some flirtation started during the week. Since she did not drink or smoke to any extent, she found that about the only exhausting experience was loss of sleep. So she formed the habit, advised by Henri, of "flopping" at five of a Saturday, sleeping till either eight or nine, relying on food later in the night to make up for the lost dinner. She tried out various types of men. But more and more she found herself drawn toward the athletic type. She told Henri—"They are amenable, these athletes—very!"

Also Fay attended many boxing bouts and thus became acquainted with delightful young pugs from all walks of life. Too, she became acquainted with many college men, sometimes by introduction, quite as often by the simple ruse of asking the direction to some nearby place. As the spring advanced she attended the Saturday afternoon baseball games. Quite often, learning at which hotels the players were stopping, she would dine there with some of her friends. In a city like New York a professional outdoor athlete can be recognized almost invariably. The baseball players in particular have a very tanned skin, unusually clear bright eyes, very erect carriage, expensive clothing, and a short snappy jerky gait which betrays their quickness of action. All of their movements are swift. Fay tried turning her head with the same speed with which the ball players move. The jerk which resulted made her dizzy and gave her a headache.

Fay's earliest experience had been with men of the intellectual type, muscularly soft; of too soft speech. Now she began to judge her men by two outstanding characteristics; the tones of their voices and the cleanliness of their teeth. With the years, Fay acquired greater charm. She spoke little, only sufficient to keep a man talking about himself, his favorite pursuits, his hopes and ambitions. Her wide knowledge of business, her keen appreciation of the true values of life (outside of her questionable love game), her college experiences, all made her desired and respected by these men. They were proud to be loved by her. They would end their description of Fay, "She's been brought out—good and proper—but she's worth knowing."[11]

In summer many of Fay's conquests were made at the bathing beaches. In a swimming suit her own remarkably symmetrical build was shown to perfection. Her muscles of steel, beneath skin of velvet, showed to their fullest advantage. Like all of her kind, she looked younger than her years—innocently young; one of her ruses on the beach was to get in the way of a ball, be struck and then, "poor kid," be properly pitied.

Frequently she would swim out to the life savers, look at them and smile. Often as not a life saver is a young Greek god taking this means to save up money to attend college in the fall. They do not make overmuch. An invitation to dine and go to a show after the day's work means just so much more ahead. They start out meaning to be companionable; they end by becoming violent lovers, temporarily, at least. Fay found that the more virile the man, the more readily he succumbed to her open advances.

Sometimes Fay would cross a street where a lovely young policeman was stationed. A simple query as to the location of some nearby place would be the entering wedge. Then she would ask "By-the-way, what do you smoke? I'll bring you a cigar on my way back." The fictitious errand accomplished, she would return. The next day, or a few days later, she would again pass his way; this time she would have the cigar ready. They were now old friends. Each day would make them better acquainted. By the end of a week, a trip to a theatre, or to some summer resort would be arranged. In telling one of her boon companions of some of her adventures, the less practiced one remarked, "But I should be so afraid of policemen. How do you broach the subject to them?"

"I don't," answered Fay, "they broach it to me."

"And I suppose you use the language of flowers?"

"Yes, dearie, scarlet pansies!"

Fay Etrange had become a oncer—that is, she was through with a man after one experience.

One Sunday, having spent the afternoon beaches with Henri, he suggested that she accompany him to a restaurant in what was beginning to be popularly called "Greenwich Village." Fay had never heard of the eating place before. He described it as "an Italian dump where not the foods but the people, are what you go to enjoy," and added provokingly, "Wait till you see for yourself."

First they stopped in the basement of the old Brevoort, where at that time one of the gayest and most interesting crowds gathered nightly. From there they went to Tenth Street and west almost to noisy Sixth Avenue. They descended into a base-

11. In gay parlance of the twenties and thirties, rather than "coming out" people were "brought out."

ment on the south side of the street, passed through the kitchen and emerged into what had been a backyard but had been converted into a galleried garden. They chose seats on the balcony, close to the railing, where they could both see and, if desired, also be seen. Fay remarked—"It seems very ordinary."

"Wait till they drink some Italian red," said Henri, "then you'll get more than an earful. No one has come here yet and gone away saying that he did not get more than his money's worth."

A fat, pudgy, old, grey, grinning man raised his glass to drink to Fay. She smiled over the brim of her own glass, "Just to keep in practice of being naughty," she informed Henri. Then the old man motioned for them to join his table. Fay shook her head no. A friend of the old man called out to him—"Oh, behave, Jack, be yourself. Can't you see it's fish?"

Billy Pickup entered. Fay went below to have a word with him. As she passed a table at the foot of the stairs, one of the two sitting there nudged the other and spoke audibly, indicating Fay—"Ain't it grand?"

"Grand?" said the other, "It's most marvellously gorgeous. I'd like to make it." She feigned not to hear.

Fay had recently finished a course in abnormal psychology. In this restaurant she saw, with the exception of the actually psychotic, practically every type she had studied about. There were bulldikers with their sweeties; fairies with their sailors or marines or rough trade; tante's (aunties) with their good looking clerks or chorus molls, and all singing, gesticulating, calling back and forth, in a medley of artificial forced gaiety. An effeminate young man shrieked in an assumed falsetto—"I see a mouse let me get up on a chair. Protect me, protect me. I demand! I must have protection."

"Ah, sit down, yer rockin' the boat. You've mixed your drinks!" a young sailor cautioned.

Another, when opportunity came as the racket subsided temporarily, minced: "Gawd knows my name is pure. Your calumnies are unwarranted. You are slanderous. Don't you insinuate anything about me. I don't have to be insinuated about. My life is an open book. I'm a broad-minded woman. The world sees me as I am. Whoops! I should worry!"

Evidently some sailor had befouled a reputation, for Fay heard someone shriek in falsetto—"Sailor boy, if you don't take back those indecent words, I'll bring my long shoreman over here and he'll almost choke you to death. He's big enough. He's done it to me several times. At first I thought I'd never get over it."

The bulldikers, with few exceptions, were more quiet. But there was one blonde, "Dolly" they called her, not more than seventeen, pink cheeked, exquisite, extremely neat in collar and tie, a mannish coat, and a short tight skirt. As she removed a boy's hat she revealed beautiful hair combed straight back like a college man's. Fay was attracted to this miss. The blonde was sufficiently inebriated to be talkative. She walked up to Fay and began, "Listen, dearie, this is no place for you. Go back where you belong. I know high grade people when I see them. Used to be one of them too. You don't belong here. This life has got me; don't let it get you!"

Here sailors came with their "boy friends" hoping they would meet some unattached girl and run away with her, meantime having their food and drink and not paying for it. There was a continual din, a coming and going, a visiting back and forth between tables which would not be permitted in an uptown place. There was the most open lovemaking between people who should not have given themselves away in public.

Acquaintances met, rushed madly up to each other, embraced, kissed. One gushed, "Sweetheart," another, "Dearie." A verbose queenly one burst forth to her sister, "You're looking most marvellously grand. I declare the way you keep your youth and beauty is a source of wonder all along Broadway. You must give me the secret too. Of all things, I must be young."

A marine, overhearing the last sentence called out, "Young, I don't want 'em young, I want 'em experienced." "And with money too, don't forget the price," suggested the boy friend who was with the marine.

An absurd old man went to the piano and begged someone to play his accompaniment. The sole song in his repertory was "When You and I Were Young, Maggie." His appearance was greeted with hoots and screams of "Maggie! Maggie! Maggie!" some in hoarse male voices, some in truly feminine voice, but by far the most in shrieking falsetto. He sang and at the end of the lines where "Maggie" occurs, there were bellows and screams as everyone "Maggied." He finished with éclat; the applause was thunderous. Then that part of his exhibition complex satisfied he quietly went over into a corner to get drunk. "He works in a livery stable," a queen volunteered.

After a lull, with time between for drinks, a fat Jewish boy, with a high-pitched voice, delivered a patter song, with exaggerated rolling of eyes, shimmying movement of shoulders, swaying of hips, wriggling and overdone femininity, as he sang, "I cannot make my eyes behave, nor my lips either."

Here one heard fruit, banana, meat, fish, tomato, cream, dozens of everyday words used with double meaning. With their voices pitched high and in imitation of the effusive type of woman, the guests declaimed with the utmost exaggeration possible, what they had to say, each and all trying at the same time to be the centre of interest. They burlesqued all life. This they designated "camping," and to "camp" brilliantly fixed one's social status.

## Charles Henri Ford (b. 1913) and Parker Tyler (1907–1974)

### From *The Young and the Evil* (1933)

Charles Henri Ford and Parker Tyler's *The Young and the Evil* was published in Paris in 1933. The book is set in the bohemian purlieus of Greenwich Village. The protagonists, Karel and Julian, are Village homosexuals and thinly disguised versions of Ford and Tyler themselves. Together with their friends and occasional lovers Louis and Gabriel, they inhabit a world of drugs and parties, gay bars, drag queens, fairies, rough trade, and copious amounts of sex. The plot is of less consequence than the style—both the style of the prose and the style of the men who speak it—for it is here that the full-blown high camp homosexual style of "Miss Knight" and *A Scarlet Pansy* achieves its most outrageous, complex, and, indeed, profound form.

*The Young and the Evil* is a book that seriously employs the erotic surreal—both in scene and in prose style—to magnify, satirize, and define that combination of the melodramatically trivial, the obsessively sexual, and the intense attention to the nuance and double meanings of language that typifies the high homosexual style of the thirties, a style that will dominate the image of the homosexual until the eve of Stonewall. The most experimental of the homosexual novels—and surely the best of those written in the thirties—it is as indebted to the prose of Gertrude Stein as it is reminiscent of Joyce. Neither Julian nor Karel nor any of the characters take part in the kind of everyday transvestism that marks Jennie June, Miss Knight, or the engaging and omnisexual protagonist of *A Scarlet Pansy*, Fay Etrange. But their mannered deconstruction of American manhood marks them as the first modern homosexuals, bending gender and its rules for fun and for the purposes of transgression against the rule makers. While many other books of the thirties (such as Blair Nile's *Strange Brother* or André Tellier's *Twilight Men*, which dealt, often pejoratively, with homosexuality) ruled that homosexuals should lead melancholy and tragic lives, *The Young and the Evil* triumphantly derides that convention. In so doing, it marks the most comprehensive and complex act of literary resistance to homophobia of the early part of the century.

## CHAPTER 13: I DON'T WANT TO BE A DOLL

It was a long ride on the subway to 155th Street but they hadn't the money for a taxi. Frederick was not in drag nor was Julian who wore striped pants with a coat that didn't match, his black shirt with an orange tie and a slouch cap. Frederick was not made up more than usual except his eyebrows were plucked thinner but Julian had on his face the darkest powder he could borrow, blue eyeshadow and several applications of black mascara; on his lips was orange-red rouge and a brown pencil had been on his eyebrows showing them longer. He wanted to be considered in costume and so get in for a dollar less. When they arrived at the Casino Palace policemen and others were about the entrance. They passed under the canopy and went in.

I hope we don't get arrested tonight Julian said. Your judgement of my trousers is true but your moral wrong he thought, getting his ticket cheaper than Frederick who said I wonder if money will ever be as unimportant as I think it.

They had to wind up a long gold-banistered staircase above which a terrible racket was taking serene form.

There is only one sex—the female said Frederick.

Now they are doing without beauty said Julian when he saw the first creation. It was all black lace but only stockings and step-ins and brassiere and gloves. Fanny Ward is supposed to come.

Yes my dear Frederick said. She's so young she has to learn to play the piano all over again!

The ball was too large to be rushed at without being swallowed. The negro orchestra on the stage at one end was heard at the other end with the aid of a reproducer. On both sides of the wall a balcony spread laden with people in boxes at tables. Underneath were more tables and more people. The dancefloor was a scene whose celestial flavor and cerulean coloring no angelic painter or nectarish poet has ever conceived.

This place is neither cozy nor safe Frederick said. It's lit up like high mass.

One was with blonde hair and a brown face and yellow feathers and another was with black hair and a tan face and white feathers. Some had on tango things and some blue feathers. One wore pink organdie and a black picture hat. There were many colors including a beard in a red ballet skirt and number 9 shoes and some others who, conjuring with their golden-tipped wands against the voices of their mutually male consciences, yet remained more serious than powdered—they seemed to be always on their way to far off mistresses.

They found Tony and Vincent at a table with K-Y and Woodward. Vincent spoke with the most wonderful whisky voice Frederick! Julian! Tony was South American. He had on a black satin that Vincent had made him, fitted to the knee and then flaring, long pearls and pearl drops.

Tony dear aren't you overdressed! asked Frederick.

I suppose you would say overdressed Tony answered but I'm not Sheba surrounded by food and Mary what you look like in that outfit he said to Julian. Look at her!

Vincent had on a white satin blouse and black breeches. Dear I'm master of ceremonies tonight and you should have come in drag you'd have gotten a prize. He had large eyes with a sex-life all their own and claimed to be the hardest boiled queen on Broadway. Frederick he said you look like something Lindbergh dropped on the way across. Dry yourself Bella!

When are you going to remove your mask and reveal a row of chamber pots Frederick replied in his resonant voice which could also be nasal at the wrong time.

The music was playing wavy and sad and so true.

Let's dance Julian said to K-Y and they went on the floor.

You've mastered the art of makeup she said. I must have he said when I did things that were pleasant surprises, not wicked because they were unusual and necessary.

Dancing drew the blood faster through their bodies. Drink drusic drowned them. A lush annamaywong lavender-skinned negro gazed at him.

They are looking this way so hard said Julian their eyes go through us and *button* in the back.

A boy with an innocent exterior said to him over his shoulder how is your dog bite?

My dog bite Julian said sweetly. Your mouth hasn't been that close to my leg all evening.

This is dreadfully amusing said K-Y.

One may divide people into thrills and frills I think Julian said. What he was really thinking was that it must be the white-pink flesh like some Italians with the lippink scarlet as heliotrope and the black of hair and the eyebrows with the miraculous slant bespeaking benevolence. He knew the precise youth of it there and the vulgarity raw enough to be exhilarating. He saw another as they danced by a table and the sharkmouth of a hope tore his womb, carrying a piece of it away.

Someone shouted Bessie if you don't believe Heliogabalus died by having his head stuck in a toilet bowl you NEEDN'T COME AROUND any more.

They all ought to be in a scrap-book Julian said. Would blood, paste and print make them stick together?

No said K-Y. There is no holding people back. It will go on until it stops and
then there will be something else.

shut your hole watching
    them for a moment but when she opened her
upstairs cunt and started to belch the greetings of
the season I retired in a flurry her boyfriend with
the imperfect lacework in the front of his mouth
    was a thunderclap could indeed would have been
    gentler Fairydale Bedagrace a prize bull in the
2000 pound class and his proud owner is Harry A.
    Koch there's my Uncle looking for
    me Beulah calm your bowels two o'clock
    and not a towel wet that
    would be both justice and
    amusement Jim! I told you to stay home and
mind the babies wished for nothing better well
who could? than a man lover and a woman lover
in the same
    bed ladies and gentlemen I was born in Sydney
Australia twenty-two years
    ago everything nowadays to invent something
right things have been wrong so
    long has wanted to break away but couldn't
find me anywhere else so he changed his
    mind come on Margie come on Helen the
usher on the right side said to sit on the left side
the usher on the left side said to sit on the right
side so we'll sit in the *mid*dle Who pushed
    me aw look what your old man got for
    pushing I may be wrong but I think he's
    wonderful kiss it you bastard listen
    Kate whoops Mr. Cunningham! there's
Mr. Cunningham I said feel it not play with it thank
    YOU wouldn't that jar your mother's
    preserves the
    French are so easy to enrage poor dears close
the coffin lid the
    STEnch dont think about it analysis will kill
    it I'm ever so much obliged shit
    mother my feet
    stink the pantry is full and the toilet articles
burst with expectation all that's needed is
    love aren't you the one I'd
    hate to go beyond it unless taken by a
    guide

what would I find a fatuous madness that I've
found
    get a load of her skin like the bark of a
    canteloupe he's a
    quEry goody goody
    goody for our side we've won the chocolate
    cake madam I haven't said a word I haven't
    spOken dearie it wouldn't take much coaching
to make you lisp into the
    grave did you see that
    basket your opinions don't change your appear-
ance I thought they wOuld she
    peddles her can
    with her one avoids far worse
    things I'd rather be Spanish than
    mannish he eats
    it some things aRe like a fall down
    stairs so few people know anything at all about
the general subject of
    grace beautiful can come out of him because
he's just clean
    clay I came home Flora and found her in one
bed drunk with her eyes made up
    and I want to have the texture of
    it look you Up and dowN one
    meets no end of celebrities all having nothing
to do with
    sex it's a false landscape only art giving it full
    colors
    picked me up on Eighth Street and did me for
trade in Christopher Street some
    books aren't even read things
    about the Village because they are bound to be
ninety percent
    lies there a new place called Belle's Jeans it
must be horribly vulgar if
    I had your money
    baby think that liking is
    knowing of Laura with wistfulness the hard
poor girl no Miss Suckoffski smelt the
worst Miss Johnnie didn't smell she just lay
    there I closed her door after two pages had
slipped in my esophagus I've been getting up with
a cold ever since all they omitted was the
    diaper laid out every last corpse though it took
us till

dawn the kind of wit servants could be tipped
with if they could use it had
    trembled so he said my but you're
    sensitive that old auntie please! once
    confessed his love for a man so I didn't stand
up and wave the flag I just sat there you know me
Mabel and
    smiled Mr. Schubert get OFF my face I can't
see the CONtract the wine came up and he looked
at my intellect so often got
    out of the way of a big truck and put my hand
over my cunt like
    this just too bad isn't it buttercup scalps
    of her victims of which she must have cabinets
    full says he wears a flower in his buttonhole
because it simply Wont stay in his
    hair! memories are
    best couldn't stomach his crotch once so he
would be spiteful a kiss is a
    promise she looks like death's daughter brought
in backwards and went
    up bold as you please dropped my lilac
    robe could hardly get two articulate sentences
out on the subject of homosexuality before
someone interrupted us Phoebe-Phobia in person
not a college pennant she had one in her hand
though that bore a distinct
    resemblance ninety-five percent of the world
is just naturally queer and are really according to
the degree of
    resistance I don't say I do and I don't say I don't
but if the fur coat had fit me he would have had a
DIFferent answer people
    do better than you think they
    do in these days men will be great if they have
to walk out as
    skeletons living I learned from the inside with
a big old Queen Kitty I laid her to
    filth likes to abhor people and it's all liking
the end I
    suppose strangely mature like the
    continent very
    sensual and sees a reason for discipling appa-
rently because she can't live without
    comfort suddenly as suddenly always
    is lit up like a country

church empty couch took it out of me rather
didn't take it out of
    me divine not at all only human ever
    saying life words can
    always afford to be tolerant of that which we
    misunderstand likes the brave dear that one
best
    some Lesbians make me think of alligators I
saw a little girl holding up one in the movies and
the angles seemed so
    characteristic fancy work done at
    home and if I look real a definition of love isn't
    needed seven yards of lace
    curtain six of the finest rats jumped
    out spoke to me said it was a good racket I
should keep it up I was good at it he held my arm
my dear as we walked back after I had petrified
four or five males who walked into the tea-room
two standing before the urinal dying to and yet
so embarrassed waiting for my permission to
pull their things out and another said standing still
on entering my leg being strung across the wash
    basin blind as a bat screaming for the
    daylight excuse me for putting this bromide
in pink curlpapers take them off in the
    morning did not shit Miss Bitch though she's
here according to farts deprived
    of house and home if
    one does needlework one has to talk too such
genteel innocent malice is almost more than
human flesh can bear I mean the tongue gets
mixed up with the needle your mouth is
    bleeding Belle I but the clock doesn't stop when
somebody is
    hit seems to have adopted the habits of a
gentleman in every particular which naturally
includes the payment of paramours if only in
bohemian
    dinners Becky could you spare it?
    the macabre is not omitted from any universe
why not find it in his
    bread-box she's a flag that's never been taken
    down I'm sure he draws lewd pictures in spare
moments and tears them up in tears and speaking
of tears could you ever be drowned in
    them makes me think of a Christmas tree been

standing all
   year has a fish
   hooves? looks at one through oceans of lemonade
slightly sweet slightly
   sour empty as paper
   bags can't you tell by his manner that he lives
on an
   hallucination she's a whole egg upheld by the
shimmering sea of
   humanity what's the use of knowing people if
not to attack their souls or what they consider
   inviolable? the universal stillbirth or homicide
in the womb you
   were made to walk along with me and speak
to me like
   that the first thing I knew she was groping me
like
   mad thinks she has the only bedroom back at
the
   ball does he rent his brains my
   dear just dirt you
   silly! loose as a cut
   jockstrap
   still dead as far as my mouth
   goes a
   big chisler while he was here feature it
   adores me to stick it in his and flew into a
temper last night when after the regular party my
poor thing wouldn't get a hard on enough to go in
and STAY in but I promised to do my husbandly
duty next
   time orgasm right in his
   pants it may have been the first intimate introduction to Miss 69 in
   *person* is to be a comfort standing in a tall
scooped out penislike
   niche squiffy on
   weed observe my dear the bloated lemons
waiting to be
   selected the first Bess ever to conceive a hopeless
romantic affection for
   me thrill market the
   haughty after breakfast hour grime
   in the creases parting his hair has given him a
new better
   flavor discovered a brazen speakeasy with

awfully good stuff
   cheap mentioned something about a hashish
   party please
   noticing my excellent features and asking why
I didn't have a screen test taken until a professional
routine came into his
   compliments flew down on special
   wheels couldn't say no to the sensations he gives
   me gayest thing on two
   feet harlot making theatrical costumes like one
demented and renting the
   bed them to come down here and fight like
mEn startling
   expert symmetry she wanted to make
   her have a cuter sissylip
   one never say anus you mUst have been stunned
into
   chillness said why and I said I wanted to see
whether he would 69 and he said of course he
didn't and I said but he
   did may look Chinese but she's American can
   you imagine he wanted to brown I mean bugger
   me woman quite mad so cunty in her dark land
so idiosyncratic and blind so obvious so abnormal
only
   fairy voice about 20 made me really
   pretty oh you twisted piece of
   lilac the curtain's going
   up
   looks like the wrath of
God aroma one of Harvard and autumn leaves
the Russian ballet hanging on the wall of his
   heart dished as though
   drunken showing
   everything mattress on the
   floor Byzantine
   baggage grand cocksucker
   fascinated by fairies of the Better
   Class chronic
   liar fairy
   herself sexual
   estimate crooning I'M A CAMPfire girl
   gratuitous sexually meaning
   both my thighs are so much
   stouter tongue's hanging
   out sprawled in

bed lower than my
navel tie beginning between his
breasts nest of
Lesbians eyebrows so perfect what it is to
blossom before his style started going uphill
on one-ballbearing rollerskates and the curious
pain
began Norma Shearer hairbob the wild evening
one and they turned the spot on me with applause
hisses pennies tenderness in sex you know I hate
nothing God has bursting breakfast for two Daisy
he's the type that's aged by its prospects taken
for 18 tonight by a broker make this another leaf
in your hair my dear stunning seaman dreadful
bugger sort of jaw coming from the sort of neck
with an open collar that flattens wombs huge
meat that's why no matter how many publishers'
offices she unpacked her undies in she couldn't
give old man Criticism a hard on sped on his
way cradle days! crushed her like I always do asks
to be insulted and you know my rule Anna
said have you seen Pauline's novel I said intimat-
ing that it's good? said it's an act of God! said
I have no doubt there are so many objects for
criticism they Must come from a source so
abundant never cease shocking with his diseases
hide it in your vagina and carry on do you have
to go into a song and dance about a face artist
turn over kid I want to use you. . . .

At Sixth Avenue and Eighth Street he got out. It was scarcely dawn.

A doll does not believe in itself he thought it believes only in its dollness I have
the will to doll which is a special way of willing to live my poetry may merely be a
way of dolling up and then it may be the beginning of ego I think I would be practically nothing without my poetry unless a DOLL my homosexuality is just a habit
to which I'm somehow bound which is little more than a habit in that it's not love
or romance but a dim hard fetich I worship in my waking dreams it's more a symbol of power than a symbol of pleasure not a symbol inducing pleasure but exem-
plifying it not a specific symbol no I am not a fairy doll.

On Third Street he used his key for the door. There was Karel in bed with one
hand behind his neck. He seemed to be sleeping with his eyes open.

Where is Louis? Julian asked though not caring particularly to know.

Love? said Karel without changing his eyes and speaking softly. Horror! Has that
word escaped my lips again? O divine power. O hymn of praise. I am too weak to
hear it. I cannot lift my voice.

Do you love him desperately? Asked Julian.

If I could only go over America painlessly from now on said Karel give me the needle doctor. Imagine the state of the poor girl sent to the hospital continually I mean America by Mr. Wriggle. She lived next door to him in Baltimore and spread her big brown bossy buttocks for him on the Montana plains but in New York she's homeless and the Round Table isn't exactly the place is it? She came in carpet slippers hanging on to Mr. Wriggle's arm like she wanted to be back home or at least on the prairie where there was room and I'm telling you when Mr. Wriggle brought his thing out and tried to put it in her it was time for somebody to laugh. And so Harold laughed you should have seen the poor thing's eyes roll feeling Mr. Wriggle's thing inside her and moving around the edges. I didn't know whether to laugh or sob or To Help but I felt like saying stop Eli she'll only carry the memory of you to her grave to bury it because it's a shame to her. Karel was wiping the tears away.

What's the matter with you? Julian said.

She never lies down or even sits Karel laughed through his tears she's older than the headless horseman and even more eternal.

O dove's puff! Julian said beginning to undress.

I sometimes think of poor little Miss Rector Karel continued who tried so much to crawl away from her skin but succeeded only in coming out with a hard on and then skidding right back again. Do you know I don't think I ever told you Julian two days later he called me over the phone and said that he had to have five dollars so next morning I met him. I met him on the street having just cashed a check from the Sun. I took it out and handed it to him and wanted to know how he felt about homosexuality and he told me.

You must have paid for the information Julian said.

How far away and insignificant it is and yet not insignificant.

Julian was removing his makeup over the sink. I suppose you used to paint his arm muscles lilac with your tongue he said.

Lilac or blackberrywaste I don't remember which Karel said.

I think he must have been influenced by Louis said Julian. Did he fancy himself as your intellectual mentor and physical disciple?

Yes Karel said but he was detestable later developing a manner socially and artistically repellent to the last degree. Megalomania with particularly bad blood into the bargain. Oh God, how can I live another life? Will it begin all over again? Oh God, this vessel is frail.

Julian emerged in his pajamas. Are you going to sleep anymore or haven't you slept? Karel didn't move. What could be bitterer than love or stink worse on a cold day he asked.

Mrs. Dodge of course said Julian. Let me get in with you. He got in.

Karel's speech came to life and he said what is one to do on this planet tied to George Bernard Shaw, Gandhi and other weekend guests.

Gandhi is this century's answer to Christ Julian said.

Karel covered his eyes with a hand. Have you seen John Wannamaker's windows dear? Not even father Alive and Breathing by the fireside could be more elegiac. The only horror left would be resurrection.

Brains will fall out especially from corpses Julian said. He wasn't sleepy but he felt so bad he had to dredge the spontaneous. Have you any ideas about happiness Karel?

Not really said Karel. Even when ideas about happiness amount to common morality they are no less important than mine but I'm talking morality anyway and morality is rotten.

Why?

Because it's a stage of rot. It's the skin beginning to fall off.

Yes but about happiness can't we argue ourselves somehow into it?

Happiness is Being not Knowing and let it go but I say Knowing is not quite but almost happiness. Being can go where it pleases said Karel.

Let it go Julian said. One begins to have ideas about happiness as soon as one sees that happiness is impossible.

If I went down entirely I could be happy, knowing nothing, but his mouth drew away and I'm still here Karel said. Here, Mr. Policeman, here do what you will with me.

And speaking of deceptive appearances I think of all the live people wearing death so impassively Julian said.

My YES would have to be beaten up with the white of an egg and set to chill on his body. Karel laughed as though he were still weeping.

The point is Julian said sleepily that the amount of stupidity is never equaled by the amount of elimination by the individual intellect.

Karel said some of them not only wear death they wear it out and then lie in coffins as though it were new, in fact all dead people look as though life were still fresh in their minds but that's as far as it all goes: they can't wholly disappear.

It's the handsome ones I pity most said Julian.

Pity is love after a while. My chest hurts said Karel.

You mean love becomes pitylove and finally pity. Love of all kinds does. I love you.

You don't know what love is said Karel turning his cheek over. You've never wanted me so that every line of me made you ache.

What does my love mean then?

It may be some minor pathology. Whether it is or not I love it.

You love my love for you.

Yes. It is a little curious and a little strange. Believe that I am perfectly truthful now.

But isn't love want?

But what want? What form is this want? Is it affection or something mystic? Where is the line between the strange and the common?

Perhaps love is loneliness Julian said. Simple, honest loneliness.

But that would be common.

My love isn't wholly common.

Julian you know how little I feel for people, how little anyone has now to give me even of naivete or resistance. I mean pure pleasure except in physical beauty is almost out of the question. I like seeing Louis and Gabriel act but there is nothing between them and me now: nothing but disgusting trivial acts.

What do you mean? I'll tell you. You're very selfish is what I've noticed about you; unwilling that is to forget yourself and certain definite preconceived ideas or plans. Maybe I am one of these plans.

And you don't love me.

I do love you but only because you do not disturb me, you face the way I do and you are moving in that direction, and so turn to me with sweet words in your throat that are altogether for me, addressed to no one else. Maybe that is the way you feel about me.

But such an explanation is too cold.

Perhaps it is because it is all necessary, perhaps that is why it is at all.

It is too sterile said Julian.

That is always the artist's plaint Karel said. I feel around me a great coarse essentially foreign world in which only the objets d'art seem friendly, seem able to walk and talk with me.

When you think of the number of superfluous but exact people.

Let me go on, life. How many understand cadence Karel said.

Do you?

One can't do anything about medieval statues can one the same of Eliot. That sentence is a study in cadence.

You are always untrue if you go far enough said Julian.

The experience of space Karel went on is the elimination of dirt and that is outer. The experience of time is the growth of everything in the body to the very pores and that is inner.

I suppose the end comes said Julian when the pores can't blow out any more.

Both are divine Karel said accident and inevitability.

No! said Julian.

Accident is that for which we are insufficiently prepared and inevitability is that for which we are even more insufficiently prepared. Louis has left me.

Birds of plumage screamed through the room.

What do you mean, he's left you Julian said getting more and more sleepy.

I mean he's gone.

He'll come back murmured Julian. He'll come back like a door closing on your littlest finger.

No he won't come back said Karel. He's with Gabriel for good this time and when he left he took your typewriter and a suitcase of my manuscripts. I yelled for the police but none came and then I cried.

There was a lovely dead silence with a white, white face who opened its lips and said what difference does it make what difference does it make to me and then went to sleep.

# Part Eight

Deconstructing "Manhood"

*American Literature 1916 to 1969*

# 28. Out of the Shadow World

## Inventing and Enforcing Modern Homophobia (1933–1969)

If the early twentieth century imagined the homosexual as a medical abnormality and a sexual deviant whose perverted practices threatened both moral and social health, the thirties read homosexuality as an offense against the trinity of American virtue: God, Country, and Family. Diatribes against homosexuality appealed to patriotic ideals; sexual difference was pictured as un-American and homosexuals as a danger to those pioneer traditions that, as was usually said, had made America great, and as they didn't say but implied, exclusively heterosexual.

In 1933 advertisements for a popular book by Dr. La Forest Potter called *Strange Loves: A Study in Sexual Abnormalities* luridly warned: "Do you know what really goes on among the men and women of the Shadow World? Do you know that their number is constantly increasing? The strange power they wield over normal people is almost unbelievable." At one point in the book Potter looked back on the impeccable sexual climate of pre-Great War America and nostalgically recalled: "Before the war we used to consider homosexuality as a more or less foreign importation. We regarded ourselves as the true exponents of the sane and uncompromising traditions of our pioneer ancestors." Potter goes on to say that "all those foreigners who were fortunate to have been permitted entrance to our shores, so we thought, were leavened by our practical matter-of-factness. The dross of abnormal desire—assuming that they may have been thus infected when they landed in this country—was burned away in the melting pot of our staunch masculine or commendably feminine characteristics." A Dr. James Segall added to the climate of apprehension when he warned in 1934 that not only are there "ten million male and female 'queers' in this country" but there is "something terribly sinister in this decadence—in this repulsive suggestion of senility and impotence. It is so out of keeping with the lusty traditions, the he-man virility of our country" (Austen 1977:57). Potter and Segall's concern that homosexuality was undermining basic American virtues often found its way into the pages of the popular press and eventually peaked with the political hysteria of the 1950s. This notion also began to appear in the smaller (though equally combative and influential) intellectual arena of American literary criticism, where homophobia masqueraded as judgment on the part of a number of American critics who argued that homosexuality, because of its triviality and sterility, could have no place in an American literary tradition.

But even earlier, in 1925, a Dr. Robinson had affirmed what perhaps everyone wanted to believe: "I cannot help regarding homosexuals as abnormal. . . . I insist, the homosexuals are mentally, morally, and physically different from normally sexed men and women" (Katz 1976:425). With this assertion of absolute abnormality went the corollary presumption that homosexuals, perversely, did not *want* to be "cured." Thus the abnormal homosexual was set against the normal heterosexual, an exemplary creature that the determined homosexual could—should he wish to—become. But because of the willful homosexual's refusal to embrace what was becoming compulsory heterosexuality, then, as one doctor warned, "if the pervert homosexual insists on not following advice, he knows society's attitude and must bear the responsibility for his conduct."

The threat implicit in these comments and attitudes of the twenties and thirties acknowledges the appearance of officially sanctioned homophobia and increased violence against homosexuals. The United States Army had by this time been routinely investigating homosexuals since at least the end of World War I, and a New York police raid on a gay bathhouse in April 1929 was only one of many such official actions against homosexual gathering places. In 1936 the New York Times reported the existence of a group calling themselves the White Legion, which had participated in the beating of a suspected homosexual. By 1937 the FBI began to collect its own private files on known or suspected homosexuals in public life — including information which implied that the master collector, J. Edgar Hoover, was himself homosexual.

In 1948 the so-called Kinsey Report appeared and stunned the nation with its finding that one in six American men were exclusively homosexual and that even more had had at least one homosexual experience: with these shocking statistics homosexuality forever entered into the mainstream of American consciousness. A 1948 issue of Parents magazine insisted that "homosexuals are not born — they are made." "Homosexuality," the magazine reported, "is not a reflection on sex but only a sign that it has been diverted into the wrong channels, according to our social and cultural standards." These standards "are the monogamous ones of marriage and the establishment of a family." Parents called for pity not punishment, since homosexuals "through no fault of their own have been unable to fall in love with a person of the opposite sex" even though they "would like to if they could." Homosexuality "is not wicked or unfortunate since it is often sterile instead of creative." That homosexuals are presumably unable to have "meaningful" adult heterosexual relationships is seen to be a symptom of their emotional sterility and arrested development.

Between 1950 and 1955, suspicion of homosexuality ignited one of the most appalling public episodes of homophobic panic ever to have been seen in America. The government of the United States investigated its own employees, members of the armed forces, and many outside the government in an attempt to link their political beliefs with suspicions of homosexuality. Communism and/or homosexuality, whether known, suspected, or alleged, made these people dangerous security risks, it was claimed. By the time this hysterical witch-hunt was finished, to all the other imputations of social undesirability already entrenched had been added the image of the homosexual as a danger to the state, disloyal to the nation, a political as well as a sexual menace to society.

In 1950 a New York Times article signaled the beginning of the story when it indicated that inquiries were under way to establish just what percentage of government personnel had resigned because of the real or possible threat of being investigated as security risks. The article reported that many who had resigned "were homosexuals." A few weeks later, Sen. Joseph McCarthy (R–Wis.) alleged in the Senate that the State Department contained a "flagrantly homosexual" employee who was at risk because of the possibility of blackmail. In April 1950 the Times reported that the Republican National Chairman asserted that "sexual perverts who have infiltrated our government in recent years" were "perhaps as dangerous as the actual communists" (Katz 1976:92). In May a private study by two Republican senators from Nebraska and Alabama alleged that, according to the Washington vice squad, over 3,500 "perverts" were employed by the government. By December 1950 the federal government issued a document on the "Employment of Homosexuals and Other Sex Perverts in Government." The Times reported the committee as saying that "the lack of emotional stability which is found in most sex perverts and the weakness of their moral fibre makes them susceptible to the blandishments of foreign espionage agents" and "easy prey to blackmailers." By January 1955 more than eight thousand people had been separated from their government jobs as security risks, of which more than six hundred were described as being involved in "sex perversion."

In 1969, on the eve of Stonewall, Sara Harris published a book called *The Puritan Jungle: America's Sexual Underground*. Harris interviewed a cross section of "lesbians, homosexuals, hustlers, vice cops, alcoholics, sadists, masochists, transvestites, wife swappers, and the wives they swap." In one interview, she asked John Sorenson, "a Baptist Church deacon, and former head of the Miami vice squad," about his feelings concerning homosexuality. Sorenson replied: "I would rather see any of my children dead than homosexual. . . . I feel there is no cure . . . because of the complete degeneracy of these people. They appear on the surface to be respectable, but they're the lowest forms of people." Homosexuals should be regulated, because no matter what they do in private, Sorenson asserts, sooner or later "they have to come out of that room and they may be school teachers. . . . They are mentally ill . . . and their philosophies and morals spill over." Harris asked if the law should include the death penalty for homosexuality. " 'If homosexuality could be a reason for the death penalty, you would see almost a stop to the whole thing,' Mr. Sorenson said with conviction" (Katz 1976:123–24).

## HOMOSEXUALITY IN AMERICAN LITERATURE (1933–1969)

In the thirty years before Stonewall, homosexuality was becoming almost a national obsession. Few thought of homophobia as a prejudice and even fewer condemned it—but homosexuality was a subject everyone seemed eager to talk about. Homosexual writers, too, were more willing to address the issue. Homosexuality increasingly appeared as the subject of novels; it was hinted at, reticently, in plays; and some poets boldly took it as their central subject.

### Homosexuality and American Poetry

In 1924 a book called *Men and Boys* was made available "for sale only to mature and discreet persons." These persons were those who wanted to read "an anthology of verses and poems on the charm of boyhood and young manhood." The book is the first anthology of homoerotic verse published in America and only the second such anthology published in English (Edward Carpenter's *Iolaus*, an anthology of both verse and prose, having preceded *Men and Boys* in 1902). American poetry was again ready for homosexuality to find a place in its texts, and Hart Crane, Robert Duncan, Frank O'Hara, and Allen Ginsberg were ready to revivify Whitman's mandate to introduce manly love into poetry.

### Homosexuality in the American Theater

In 1927 Mae West's *The Drag*, which William Hoffman in *Gay Plays* (New York: Avon, 1979) calls "the first modern gay play," opened in Bridgeport, Connecticut, and was promptly closed. Shortly thereafter, the New York State legislature banned 'sexual perversion' as a theme on the state's stages, a law that remained on the books until 1967. Homosexuality in drama was there largely by innuendo, and rarely welcomed. As an example, when *The Green Bay Tree* by Mordaunt Shairp opened in New York in 1933 the *New York Times* reviewer described it as the story of "a relationship between Mr. Dulcimer, a rich hot-house sybarite and Julian Dulcimer, whom he adopted at a tender age and has reared in emasculating luxury. The relationship is abnormal, since Mr. Dulcimer with all his petty sensuousness is an abnormal person. But there is nothing in the play to indicate that the relationship is more than passively degenerate" (Katz 1983:488). The language of this review invokes nearly every cliché associated with homosexuality, from imputations of excessive and possibly depraved sensuality ("hot-house sybarite") to the suggestion of child molestation ("at a tender age") to unmanly weakness ("petty sensuousness and emasculating luxury") and a depraved but nevertheless inadequate and sterile sexuality ("passively degenerate"). Though Tennessee Williams allowed the spectral off-stage presence of a dead homosexual to inform the ambiance and the essence of *A Streetcar Named Desire* (1947), yet it is not homosexuals about whom Williams wrote—nor are his female characters homosexuals in disguise, as is often suggested. If his plays encapsulate both homosexual and heterosexual myths— Brick in *Cat on a Hot Tin Roof*, Sebastian in *Suddenly Last Summer*, Kilroy in *Camino Real*, and Val Xavier in *Orpheus Descending* are all doomed, unobtainable to the women who love them (and sometimes actually homosexual)—they also seem to suggest that love is itself doomed though eternally desirous. In Williams's plays, love is always looking for the sensitive damaged youth to heal, for the unquestionably masculine hero to rescue or subvert, for the unseen difference sometimes concealed beneath a veneer of irreproachable heterosexuality.

In 1953 Robert Anderson's *Tea and Sympathy* gave homosexuals a high camp line to use at parties ("In years to come when you talk about me, and you will, be kind"), but it did not give anything more—for the sensitive young man accused of being homosexual by a schoolmaster (who is probably homosexual himself) finds heterosexual salvation in the arms of an older woman. In several plays written in the fifties, homosexuality is vaguely suggested though never outwardly stated; for example, the plays of William Inge (e.g., *Picnic*) are populated with handsome young men whose ultra-virility and tight jeans are often equally admired by both men and women, and whose sexuality is curiously and sometimes ambiguously presented.

However, the 1960s did see an increasing number of homosexuals portrayed on stage. Edward Albee's *Zoo Story* has, though Albee has denied it, a strong homosexual subtext that conflates homosexuality, violence, and death, just as does Leroi Jones's *The Toilet* (1964), where a violent encounter between a black and a white youth ends in an evocative moment of homoerotic tenderness. By the mid-sixties, the American theater was beginning to consider the possibility that homosexuality might be portrayed on stage sympathetically if not daringly or originally. However, since the commercial Broadway stage was not yet ready for any full-scale sympathetic portrayal, it was left to Off-Broadway and small experimental theaters to produce plays like Lanford Wilson's *The Madness of Lady Bright* and Robert Patrick's *The Haunted Host* (1964), which were among the first to present homosexual characters that broke out of stereotypical molds.

However, in large part stereotypes were what the theater most effectively employed, and in 1968 Mart Crowley's controversial landmark play, *The Boys in the Band*, gathered together in one setting every stereotypical version of mid-twentieth-century gay identity. *The Boys in the Band* allowed straight America to imagine that what it had always suspected was indeed true—that homosexuals were self-hating, pitiable and pitiful, though incredibly funny, promiscuous, alcoholic, drug-taking, and ultimately trivial denizens of a minority culture, some of whom, the play shows, attempt to "pass" as straight, while others allow themselves to become freaks, while still others more properly see the true nature of their sickness but are unable because of their disability to find a "cure" for it anywhere save in drugs, alcohol, or "mindless" promiscuity. The play was, for its time, just sad enough, funny enough, and daring enough, and it had a societally appropriate moral conclusion in which the young men, each more or less damaged but none destroyed, disappear into the morning light to live another day, while Michael's grim admonition ("You show me a happy homosexual and I'll show you a gay corpse") is left to echo in the ears of the audience. Nevertheless, this allowed straight America to see, as the *Times* reviewer said, that "the 'boys' in Mart Crowley's band are human beings" who just "happen to be deviates."

The play had perhaps a rather different effect on the gay community, for *The Boys in the Band* bore witness to what gay America not only enacted and invented but also what it both loved and embraced, hated and rejected, for Crowley's version of gay life was far too precisely on target to be only a fiction, and far too accurately reflective of a certain kind of urban gay sensibility to be dismissed as a mere sensational exposé. More than any other play, indeed probably more than any other work of literature in the twentieth century to that time, *The Boys in The Band* publicized for both straight and gay alike a fully formed catalogue of gay identity. Produced on the eve of Stonewall, *The Boys in the Band* opened the closet door and allowed homosexuality to come out into the mainstream of heterosexual American life.

### Homophobic Novels

Many novels of the late thirties and forties were gratuitous contributions as much to homophobic as to homosexual mythology. Often the homophobia engaged in by nonhomosexual writers is interpreted by them and by critics and readers as being a "sensitive" portrayal of what they often call a " difficult" or a "delicate" subject, as if sensitivity or delicacy could blunt the edge of bias or bigotry. Much American fiction has read homosexual lives as being inevitably tragic and inevitably confined to a closet of furtive isolation. Written by both straight and gay writers, these novels declared the inadequacy or even the impossibility of homosexual love, portrayed homosexual life as invariably deviant, and assumed that the necessary and even appropriate end of homosexuality would be isolation or death.

In 1949 James Baldwin, in a provocative and prophetic essay entitled "Preservation of Innocence: Studies for the New Morality," argued that both the source and the curse of American constructions of manhood are to be discovered in the American male's obsession with a masculinity that is founded "in the most infantile and elemental externals" which in turn cause his attitude toward women to be a "wedding of the most abysmal romanticism and the most implacable distrust." Baldwin further argued that the American hatred of the homosexual and "our present debasement of and our obsession with him corresponds to the debasement of the relations between the sexes; and that his ambiguous and terrible position in our society reflects the ambiguities and terrors which time has deposited on that relationship." In the American novel, especially the novel by or about homosexuals Baldwin asserted, brutality "rages unchecked" and the death visited upon so many homosexual characters is not only a function of some novelistic bias but a mirror of American homophobia itself which is "compelled by a panic which is close to madness. These novels are not concerned with homosexuality but with the ever-present danger of sexual activity between men" (Katz 1983:647–50). Writing in 1949, Baldwin was able to look back not only on a significant number of gay novels but also on the treatment of gay people in " mainstream" novels by writers who were not—and often assertively claimed that they were not—homosexual. In Hemingway's novels and short stories, from his 1938 short story "The Mother of a Queen" to the homosexuals in *The Sun Also Rises*, gay people are pansies and effeminate. In the works of Thomas Wolfe, and F. Scott Fitzgerald, homosexuals pass through on the edges of life, mysterious, always effeminate, distanced from the reality of the heterosexual characters. John Dos Passos in *U.S.A.* creates a considerable gallery of gay characters, almost none sympathetic, while in James Cain's "tough guy" thrillers there was often a fairy to beat up, or put down.

This punitive and heterosexually oriented fiction—in short, a homophobic gay fiction in Baldwin's terms—is forecast by Sherwood Anderson's "Hands" and realized by Mrs. Blair Niles in *Strange Brother* (1931). This book is the first of a series of books written between 1930 and the later fifties that demonize homosexuality under the guise of "sympathy" and "compassion" and that purport to confront homosexuality as a "problem." In regard to what a *New York Times* reviewer in the fifties disdainfully called the "groaning shelf" of homosexual fiction published after 1930, books of this kind represent the largest numbers. Their titles—*Twilight Men, Butterfly Man, Shadows Flying, The Divided Path, The Dark Tunnel, Dark Desires*—indicate the melodramas of sexual anxiety and homophobia played out in their pages, and also imply the psychoanalytic theories that inform many of them, since most were written during the thirties, forties, and early fifties when psychiatric and psychoanalytic theory dominated the medical construction of "the homosexual" identity. In these books the "causes" of homosexuality were often laid to the absence of the father and/or a domineering or effeminizing mother. Homosexual men, as a presumed consequence, were therefore thought to be usually effeminate or at best "sensitive," and if not that then outright villains and sexual predators. They were all lonely, self-absorbed, isolated, and incapable of love. They frequented a gay underworld that was often luridly and, more often than not, stereotypically described, and their usual end was suicide or death by violence. If they are left alive they are promised nothing but isolated celibacy, which was, many of these books insisted, the only real "cure" for homosexuality, which was usually diagnosed as a social and personal illness that damaged creativity and emotional growth and reflected a seriously arrested development.

### Resisting Homophobia: American Fiction (1933–1969)

After 1933, even though homosexual liberation itself was still a fledgling and uncertain movement, the homosexual as a character and homosexuality as a theme began to appear as one of the great if still very controversial subjects in the American novel. In addition to *Imre* (1906), *Bertram Cope's Year* (1919), McAlmon's "Miss Knight" (1925), Ford and Tyler's *The Young and the Evil* (1933), and Robert Scully's *A Scarlet Pansy* (1933) already mentioned, Bruce Kenilworth's *Goldie* (1933) and Richard Meeker's *Better Angel* (1933) dealt with homosexual themes. Between 1934 and 1945 over a dozen novels appeared, including some of the vaguely homoerotic novels of Frederic Prokosch and Djuna Barnes's superb *Nightwood* (1936). Beginning in the mid-forties, and between 1940 and 1950, nearly two dozen novels with homosexual themes appeared, including Christopher Isherwood's *Berlin Stories* (1946), John Horne Burns's *The Gallery* (1947), Gore Vidal's *The City and the Pillar* (1948), Tennessee Williams's homoerotic stories in his collection *One Arm* (1948), Burns's second novel *Lucifer with a Book* (1949), and Truman Capote's *Other Voices, Other Rooms* (1948).

After 1950 nearly one hundred homosexual novels of varying kinds and quality were published, including James Barr's *Quatrefoil* (1950), one of a number of novels set in the military that seemed to resist the idea that homosexuality was incompatible with military service, Fritz Peters's *Finistere* (1951), as well as Williams's second collection of stories *Hard Candy* (1954). In James Baldwin's *Giovanni's Room* (1956), perhaps the most famous of all American gay novels, Baldwin presents a love story, set in Paris, between two men, one an American. The book suggests that unless America rejects its puritanical homophobia, homosexual love can never flourish on American soil; at the end, both men, the American David and his lover Giovanni, are driven to different kinds of desperation, Giovanni to murder and David to what Baldwin hints will be a lonely and futile life of sexual searching and unhappiness. However, Baldwin's *Another Country* (1962) not only presents homosexuality positively as an ethically superior kind of love, describing its rituals and love-making in some of the finest lyric prose yet written about male-male love in the twentieth century, but defined effectively, for the first time in American fiction, its troubled affiliation with race. Unlike *Giovanni's Room*, *Another Country* did not avoid the problematical nexus of race and homosexuality. Instead Baldwin weaves a drama in which homophobia and racism are conflated and in which homosexual love becomes the potential instrument that might destroy racial barriers.

The late fifties and early sixties saw several novels presenting widely contrasting versions of homosexual life. William Burroughs's *Naked Lunch* (1959), John Rechy's *City Of Night* (1963), and Hubert Selby's *Last Exit to Brooklyn* (1964) resist homophobia by the shock tactics of confirming the worst fears of all homophobes, portraying American homosexuality in its grittiest and most spectacularly audacious sexual style. Isherwood's *A Single Man* (1964) and Sanford Friedman's *Totempole* (1965) look at the lives of ordinary gay men and present positive portrayals of homosexual lives. Isherwood's book offers a finely drawn picture of what was and would continue to be an unusual character in a gay fiction often devoted to young men, a middle-aged gay male. Isherwood neither apologizes for nor explains the homosexuality of his hero; homosexuality is a given that neither inhibits nor especially enhances life. In 1966 a work of homosexual pornography, Richard Armory's *The Song of the Loon*, became not only a best-selling underground book (now, as a consequence, a rare item for gay bibliophiles), it also returned to

American fiction some of the exotic, sexually charged, and satiric euphoria that had entered the mainstream of fiction with *A Scarlet Pansy* and *The Young and the Evil*. The book, however, that recalled American gay fiction to its great project was Gore Vidal's *Myra Breckinridge* (1968). which, on the eve of Stonewall, was one of the most remarkable, funniest, and transgressive novels of the decade.

Further Reading

Roger Austen, *Playing the Game: The Homosexual Novel in America* (New York: Bobbs-Merrill, 1977); David Bergman, *Gaiety Transfigured: Gay Self-Representation in American Literature* (Madison: University of Wisconsin Press, 1991); George Chauncey, *Gay New York: Gender, Urban Culture, and the Making of the Gay Male World, 1890–1940* (New York: Basic Books, 1994); Byrne R. S. Fone, *A Road To Stonewall: Homosexuality and Homophobia in English and American Literature, 1750–1969* (New York: Macmillan/Twayne, 1995); Jonathan Ned Katz, *Gay American History* (New York: Thomas Y. Crowell, 1976), and *Gay/Lesbian Almanac* (New York: Harper and Row, 1983); James Levin, *The Gay Novel in America* (New York: Garland, 1991); Robert K. Martin, *The Homosexual Tradition in American Poetry* (Austin and London: University of Texas Press, 1979); Gregory Woods, *Articulate Flesh: Male Homoeroticism in Modern Poetry* (New Haven and London: Yale University Press, 1987); Thomas Yingling, *Hart Crane and the Homosexual Text* (Chicago and London: University of Chicago Press, 1990).

# Lighting the Shadow World

FROM *MEN AND BOYS: AN ANTHOLOGY OF POETRY* (1924)

In this anthology are to be found poems by men whose sense of their own identity is as certain as *Imre*'s Oswald or Earl Lind's "Jennie June." The book offers not only a selection of "present day poets" but anthologizes homoerotic poetry from the earliest times to the twentieth century. Among those "present day poets" presumably living at that time, *Men and Boys* included writers whose work is now forgotten and whose names remain unidentified, in most instances deservedly so. Among the known (though distinctly minor) American poets found in this collection are Robert Hillyer, Charles Hanson Towne, Burges Johnson, Donald Malloch, Willard Austin Wattles, and James Fenimore Cooper Jr., grandson of the novelist. The book was edited (and some of the poems even rewritten!) by the compiler of the anthology, who was the poet "Edwin Edwinson" but who almost certainly was Edward Mark Slocum, by profession a chemist.

More tantalizing are the unidentified poets, among them the pseudonymous "Clement Andrews," the mysterious "Fidian," and the unknown Sydney Wilmer, especially since these writers' works are among the best in the book. Of these, Wilmer's poem "The Mess Boy"—the most arresting in the book—engages a more "modern" style, and in doing so encapsulates in a few lines a very contemporary homosexual sensibility that confronts and conquers homophobia rather than being debased by it. The mess boy of the title (whose function seems to be both servant and sexual object for sailors) is, despite the willing prostitution of his body, clearly intellectually and spiritually superior to those he services and so remains immune to their homophobic insults. Indeed, his Pan-like kisses translate him near to divinity and mark his crucial difference. The last poem of the book, "Manly Love" by Donald Malloch, moves the focus of the collection away from poems

celebrating "boyhood" and into the erotic arena of "young manhood,"onto a "trail" leading into a homoerotic vision of the American West.

## "Clement Andrews"

*Morn's Recompense*

I woke at dawn—and you were lying there
Close to my side, yet turned away from me.
So when sleep caught us, you lay wearily
Within my arms; the fragrance of your hair
Like a narcotic drugged me into rest;
Though I would fain have foresworn sleep for joy,—
That you, quintessent Youth, my darling Boy,
Should lie abandoned on my throbbing breast.
So as I yearned above you, the first ray
Of the glad morning quickened through the gloom,
You felt my eager kisses on your face,
Opened your eyes and smiled—And it was day!
The sun burst forth and flooded all the room
With radiance as you turned to my embrace.

## Sydney Wilmer

*The Mess Boy*

He had contempt that was divine
    For every sailor that he fed,
For while they talked of "Fun" and "Wine"
    He read.

He washed their dishes, made their bed,
And gave their bodies joy with grace;
Nor could their insults on his head
    Erase

That fine immobile pride of his,
    In the embraces of each man
He was as different as a kiss
From Pan!

## Giles de Gillies

*De Puerorum osculis*

Red mouths of lads for love God made:
    God mindeth ever poor wights' ease;—
Yet men His kindly Will gainsayed!

In seemly innocence arrayed
    To be in sooth, a grace to please,—
Red lips of lads for love God made.

He weened that Love might there be stayed
    That steals into the blood to tease;—
Yet men His kindly Will gainsayed.

Ah, pretty kisses they had prayed
    Did not cold Pride their duty seize:—
Red mouths of lads for Love God made;
    Yet men His kindly Will gainsayed!

## Donald Malloch (1877–1938)

*Manly Love*

Deep in your heart understand
    the love of a man for a man;
He'll go with you over the trail,
    the trail that is lonesome and long;
His hith will not falter nor fail,
    nor falter the lilt of his song.
He knows both your soul and your sins,
    and does not too carefully scan,—
The Highway to Heaven begins
    with the love of a man for a man.

## Hart Crane (1899–1932)

Hart Crane, our greatest homosexual poet after Whitman, published his first poem in 1916 and titled it "C33," the number of Oscar Wilde's cell in Reading Gaol. In another early poem, "Modern Craft," he explores questions about the nature of love and the nature of poetry, especially when its muse is constructed to be female rather than male. He ends the poem with the admission that: "My modern love were/Charred at a stake in younger times than ours." Both of these references—the one to Wilde's imprisonment and the other to the burning of sodomites situate homosexuality as a subtext in his poetry.

Crane was an obsessive collector of the past, a reader in all eras of poetry, and no where did he find a more congenial master than in Walt Whitman, and a more suggestive example of how homosexuality could be written into texts. In "Voyage IV," for example, Crane describes a moment of sad revelation between the two men: "Knowing I cannot touch your hand . . ./In all the argosy of your bright hair I dreamed/Nothing so flagless as this piracy." Even in a moment of homoerotic tenderness, Crane feels constrained because the prohibitions of heterosexuality decree that "I cannot touch your hand." The "piracy" exercised by the exclusive heterosexualizing of desire and the exclusion of homosexual desire from legitimate paradigms of love creates a sense of loss and hopelessness. In "Episode of Hands," Crane speaks directly to the secrecy and signs of homosexual passion. Here there is quiet triumph, and the signs of conforming masculinized worlds disappear ("factory sounds and factory thoughts"), banished by the touch of the factory owner's son whose hands partake not only of conventional images of manhood—iron, leather—but when they touch the worker's hands, create images implying difference—wings of butterflies. At the end, the factory owner's son and the factory worker are translated out of the ordinary world defined by conventional male relationships.

Crane's short life—he committed suicide in 1932 at the age of thirty-two—has been unsparingly documented. His presumed alcoholism and his known homosexuality have not been ignored by recent critics, though the admission of homosexuality has usually been accompanied with some such assertion as that of Wallace Fowlie in 1965 who argues that "sexual aberration and drunkenness were the pitfalls in which his spirit wrestled with a kind of desperation" (quoted in Woods 1987:140). Crane's poems are famously recognized as some of the most difficult texts in early twentieth-century American poetry. Indeed the complexity of his poems has been attributed by some critics to a desire to inscribe within his texts, yet not admit, his homosexuality. That same complexity has also been described as a kind of poetic failure and laid at the door of his homosexuality by critics who urge that the emotional limitation ascribed to homosexuality is mirrored in a consequent emotional limitation in the art. As Thomas Yingling points out in his study of Crane, *Hart Crane and the Homosexual Text* (1990), Crane presents the dilemma of the American homosexual poet: of being unable to clearly express what he felt impelled and yet forbidden to say.

## C33 (1916)

He has woven rose-vines
About the empty heart of night,
And vented his long mellowed wines
Of dreaming on the desert white
With searing sophistry.
And he tented with far truths he would form
The transient bosoms from the thorny tree.
O Materna! to enrich thy gold head
And wavering shoulders with a new light shed

From penitence, must needs bring pain,
And with it song of minor, broken strain.
But you who hear the lamp whisper through night
Can trace paths tear-wet, and forget all blight.

## Modern Craft (1917)

Though I have touched her flesh of moons,
Still she sits gestureless and mute,
Drowning cool pearls in alcohol.
O blameless shyness;—innocence dissolute!
She hazards jet; wears tiger-lilies;—
And bolts herself within a jewelled belt.

Too many palms have grazed her shoulders:
Surely she must have felt.

Ophelia had such eyes; but she
Even, sank in love and choked with flowers.
This burns and is not burnt .... My modern love were
Charred at a stake in younger times than ours.

*Episode of Hands (1920)*

The unexpected interest made him flush.
Suddenly he seemed to forget the pain, —
Consented, — and held out
one finger from the others.

The gash was bleeding, and a shaft of sun
That glittered in and out among the wheels,
Fell lightly, warmly, down into the wound.

And as the fingers of the factory owner's son,
That knew a grip for books and tennis
As well as one for iron and leather, —
As his taut, spare fingers wound the gauze
Around the thick bed of the wound,
His own hands seemed to him
Like wings of butterflies
Flickering in sunlight over summer fields.

The knots and notches, — many in the wide
Deep hand that lay in his, — seemed beautiful.
They were like the marks of wild ponies' play, —
Bunches of new green breaking a hard turf.

And factory sounds and factory thoughts
Were banished from him by that larger, quieter hand
That lay in his with the sun upon it.
And as the bandage knot was tightened
The two men smiled into each other's eyes.

*Voyages (1921–1926)*

I

Above the fresh ruffles of the surf
Bright striped urchins flay each other with sand.
They have contrived a conquest for shell shucks,

And their fingers crumble fragments of baked weed
Gaily digging and scattering.

And in answer to their treble interjections
The sun beats lightning on the waves,
The waves fold thunder on the sand;
And could they hear me I would tell them:

O brilliant kids, frisk with your dog,
Fondle your shells and sticks, bleached
By time and the elements; but there is a line
You must not cross nor ever trust beyond it
Spry cordage of your bodies to caresses
Too lichen-faithful from too wide a breast.
The bottom of the sea is cruel.

## II

—And yet this great wink of eternity,
Of rimless floods, unfettered leewardings,
Samite sheeted and processioned where
Her undinal vast belly moonward bends,
Laughing the wrapt inflections of our love;

Take this Sea, whose diapason knells
On scrolls of silver snowy sentences,
The sceptred terror of whose sessions rends
As her demeanors motion well or ill,
All but the pieties of lovers' hands.

And onward, as bells off San Salvador
Salute the crocus lustres of the stars,
In these poinsettia meadows of her tides,—
Adagios of islands, O my Prodigal,
Complete the dark confessions her veins spell.

Mark how her turning shoulders wind the hours,
And hasten while her penniless rich palms
Pass superscription of bent foam and wave,—
Hasten, while they are true,—sleep, death, desire,
Close round one instant in one floating flower.

Bind us in time, O Seasons clear, and awe.
O minstrel galleons of Carib fire,
Bequeath us to no earthly shore until
Is answered in the vortex of our grave
The seal's wide spindrift gaze toward paradise.

### III

Infinite consanguinity it bears—
This tendered theme of you that light
Retrieves from sea plains where the sky
Resigns a breast that every wave enthrones;
While ribboned water lanes I wind
Are laved and scattered with no stroke
Wide from your side, whereto this hour
The sea lifts, also, reliquary hands.

And so, admitted through black swollen gates
That must arrest all distance otherwise,—
Past whirling pillars and lithe pediments,
Light wrestling there incessantly with light,
Star kissing star through wave on wave unto
Your body rocking!
    And where death, if shed,
Presumes no carnage, but this single change,—
Upon the steep floor flung from dawn to dawn
The silken skilled transmemberment of song;

Permit me voyage, love, into your hands . . .

### IV

Whose counted smile of hours and days, suppose
I know as spectrum of the sea and pledge
Vastly now parting gulf on gulf of wings
Whose circles bridge, I know, (from palms to the severe
Chilled albatross's white immutability)
No stream of greater love advancing now
Than, singing, this mortality alone
Through clay aflow immortally to you.

All fragrance irrefragably, and claim
Madly meeting logically in this hour
And region that is ours to wreathe again,
Portending eyes and lips and making told
The chancel port and portion of our June—

Shall they not stem and close in our own steps
Bright staves of flowers and quills today as I
Must first be lost in fatal tides to tell?
In signature of the incarnate word
The harbor shoulders to resign in mingling

Mutual blood, transpiring as foreknown
And widening noon within your breast for gathering
All bright insinuations that my years have caught
For islands where must lead inviolably
Blue latitudes and levels of your eyes,—

In this expectant, still exclaim receive
The secret oar and petals of all love.

V

Meticulous, past midnight in clear rime,
Infrangible and lonely, smooth as though cast
Together in one merciless white blade—
The bay estuaries fleck the hard sky limits.

—As if too brittle or too clear to touch!
The cables of our sleep so swiftly filed,
Already hang, shred ends from remembered stars.
One frozen trackless smile . . . What words
Can strangle this deaf moonlight? For we

Are overtaken. Now no cry, no sword
Can fasten or deflect this tidal wedge,
Slow tyranny of moonlight, moonlight loved
And changed . . . "There's

Nothing like this in the world," you say,
Knowing I cannot touch your hand and look
Too, into that godless cleft of sky
Where nothing turns but dead sands flashing.

"—And never to quite understand!" No,
In all the argosy of your bright hair I dreamed
Nothing so flagless as this piracy.

But now

Draw in your head, alone and too tall here.
Your eyes already in the slant of drifting foam;
Your breath sealed by the ghosts I do not know:
Draw in your head and sleep the long way home.

VI

Where icy and bright dungeons lift
Of swimmers their lost morning eyes,

And ocean rivers, churning, shift
Green borders under stranger skies,

Steadily as a shell secretes
Its beating leagues of monotone,
Or as many waters trough the sun's
Red kelson past the cape's wet stone;

O rivers mingling toward the sky
And harbor of the phoenix' breast—
My eyes pressed black against the prow,
—Thy derelict and blinded guest

Waiting, afire, what name, unspoke,
I cannot claim: let thy waves rear
More savage than the death of kings,
Some splintered garland for the seer.

Beyond siroccos harvesting
The solstice thunders, crept away,
Like a cliff swinging or a sail
Flung into April's inmost day—

Creation's blithe and petalled word
To the lounged goddess when she rose
Conceding dialogue with eyes
That smile unsearchable repose—

Still fervid covenant, Belle Isle,
—Unfolded floating dais before
Which rainbows twine continual hair—
Belle Isle, white echo of the oar!

The imaged Word, it is, that holds
Hushed willows anchored in its glow
It is the unbetrayable reply
Whose accent no farewell can know.

The matrix of the heart, lift down the eye
That shrines the quiet lake and swells a tower . . .
The commodious, tall decorum of that sky
Unseals her earth, and lifts love in its shower.

## Robert Duncan (1919–1988)

Robert Duncan announced his own homosexuality in 1944 in an essay about Hart Crane.
Duncan felt that what he called the "cult of the homosexual," the assumption of a con-

scious superiority to heterosexuals and the claim to possess a special knowledge, was a pernicious deployment of difference. In his essay "The Homosexual in Society," he argued
that it was not difference but human community that the homosexual poet ought to
emphasize. Duncan called for a rejection of the ghettoized locales often found in homosexual novels and the separatist condescension often to be found in urban homosexual
enclaves.

The problem for homosexuals, Duncan said, was that "there is in the modern scene
no homosexual who has been willing to take in his own persecution a battlefront toward
freedom. Almost co-incident with the first declarations for homosexual rights was the
growth of a cult of homosexual superiority to the human race; the cultivation of a secret
language, the camp, a tone and vocabulary that is loaded with contempt for the human. .
. . In what one would believe the most radical, the most enlightened 'queer circles.' . . [are
instead] filled with unwavering hostility and fear, gathering an incredible force of exclusion and blindness" (Katz 1983:592). Duncan argued that the solution for homosexuals
was to "face in their own lives both the hostility of society in that they are queer and the
hostility of the homosexual cult of superiority." If this were to be done, then the homosexual, both as artist and citizen, must assert "that only one devotion can be held by a
human being" who seeks "creative life and expression, and that is a devotion to human
freedom, toward the liberation of human love, human conflicts, human aspirations. To do
this one must disown all special groups . . . that would claim allegiance" (Katz 1983:593).

Duncan's words prophesy attempts by some homosexuals in the fifties and sixties who
wanted to assimilate with heterosexual society, arguing that the basic humanity of homosexuals ought to be recognized and their human rights granted because they were no different from "normal" Americans. But Duncan's indictment of difference goes against the
American homosexual grain, for difference is the essence of homosexual culture as well
as the message of the best American homosexual texts.

In his poem "The Torso" (1968), Duncan describes a sexual epiphany that defines one
pathway of homoerotic difference. In his collected poems in 1966, Duncan seems to have
come to believe that difference and resistance after all may be the motive force in his texts
when he says in describing his first homosexual love and its effect on his poetry: "there had
been an awakening of rhythm, the imprint of a cadence at once physical and physiological, that could contain and project the components of an emerging homosexuality. . . .
Perhaps the sexual irregularity underlay and led to the poetic; neither as homosexual nor
as poet could one take over readily the accepted paradigms and conventions of the
Protestant ethic" (quoted in Martin 1979:174). His polite term for homophobia ("the conventions of the Protestant ethic") echoes interestingly against another kind of religious
ethic he identifies in a *Gay Sunshine* interview where he suggests approvingly in 1978–79
that "there is a kind of homosexual religion. . . . There is a level in which I think we can
identify a kind of religion of the homosexual and also the homoerotic."[1] Duncan's new
cult of the homosexual, a post-Stonewall cult, suggests just how far homosexual constructions of difference as a positive rather than negative element had come. Duncan observed
that "we have yet to begin to create the psychological and mythological tradition to build
the gay culture and gay arts movement that would be needed." To do that he suggests that
in America "we have never treated sexuality as language."

Perhaps he is suggesting that culture—in part homosexual style—and a language of
sexuality will produce the kind of homosexual religion he envisions. In "Night Scene"

---

1. Winston Leyland, ed., *Gay Sunshine Interviews* 2:93 (San Francisco: Gay Sunshine Press,
1982).

(1964), Duncan engages a highly eroticized language in which sexuality is firmly inscribed within a poetics of homoeroticism.

## FROM *EARLY POEMS* (1939–1946)

*I Am a Most Fleshly Man*

I am a most fleshly man, and see
in your body what stirs my spirit.
And my spirit is intimate of my hand,
intimate of my breast and heart,
intimate of my parted lips
that would seek their solace
in your lips.

Receive me; worn and warm body I am.
I am a most fleshly fire, and yearn
for your body to replenish my flame.
I would embrace you and name myself
anew in your flesh.

The green of eucalyptus boughs
hung in the distances of the air.
*Les terraces au clair de la lune*
playd in the orb of the afternoon, blue
and sunlit area where
we moved.
The *japonaiserie* of bay
and islands in the smoky haze
seemd to bear the fine imprint,
distinct and lonely, of the mind's design,
and beckoning intimation of a love
in which the days like swallows flew,
one by one, from the heart's dim grove
to trace in their flight the lineaments of truth.
I spoke to you and tried to say
I seek the body's rest in grace.

O I should have knelt upon the floor
and wept.
I should have surrenderd to the body's faith
and knelt,
suppliant to the hour's god that came
and went,
a luminous shadow in the blood.

I have made my vow in Hesh, and see
in you the body's golden covenant.
And the spirit is intimate of your hand,
intimate of your breast and lips.
I woo that carnal sacrament of you,
the lover's testament of faith
in which in body we release
the spirit's immortality.

Come unto me, questioning dark spirit.
You dwell upon the threshold of my mind.
his yearning is a vast eternity
that waste about us questioning lies,
and we, in the limbo of disembodied love,
stare upon the bodies we deny.

I am a most fleshly fire.
I would embrace you in that flame,
and we should lie brought then to rest
and gaze, gaze upon each other in that hour
when newly created each in the other
we hang like smoky music in the air.


FROM *THE OPENING OF THE FIELD* (1960)

**This Place Rumord To have Been Sodom**
    might have been.
Certainly these ashes might have been pleasures.
Pilgrims on their way to the Holy Places remark
this place. Isn't it plain to all
that these mounds were palaces? This was once
a city among men, a gathering together of spirit.
It was measured by the Lord and found wanting.

It was measured by the Lord and found wanting,
destroyd by the angels that inhabit longing.
Surely this is Great Sodom where such cries
as if men were birds flying up from the swamp
ring in our ears, where such fears that were once
desires walk, almost spectacular,
stalking the desolate circles, red eyed.

This place rumord to have been a City surely was,
separated from us by the hand of the Lord.
The devout have laid out gardens in the desert,

drawn water from springs where the light was blighted.
How tenderly they must attend these friendships
or all is lost. All is lost.
Only the faithful hold this place green.

Only the faithful hold this place green
where the crown of fiery thorns descends.
Men that once lusted grow listless. A spirit
wrappd in a cloud, ashes more than ashes,
fire more than fire, ascends.
Only these new friends gather joyous here,
where the world like Great Sodom lies under fear.

The world like Great Sodom lies under Love
and knows not the hand of the Lord that moves.
This the friends teach where such cries
as if men were birds fly up from the crowds
gatherd and howling in the heat of the sun.
In the Lord Whom the friends have named at last Love
the images and loves of the friends never die.
This place rumord to have been Sodom is blessd
in the Lord's eyes.


From *Bending the Bow* (1968)

*The Torso*                                    *Passages 18*

Most beautiful!      the red-flowering eucalyptus,
    the madrone, the yew

Is he . . .

*So thou wouldst smile, and take me in thine arms*
*The sight of London to my exiled eyes*
*Is as Elysium to a new-come soul*

If he be Truth
I would dwell in the illusion of him

His hands unlocking from chambers of my male body

such an idea in man's image

rising tides that sweep me towards him

. . . *homosexual?*

and at the treasure of his mouth

pour forth my soul

his soul        commingling

I thought a Being more than vast, His body leading
into Paradise,      his eyes

quickening a fire in me, a trembling

hieroglyph:      At the root of the neck

*the clavicle,* for the neck is the stem of the great artery
upward into his head that is beautiful

At the rise of the pectoral muscle,

*the nipples,* for the breasts are like sleeping fountains
of feeling in man, waiting above the beat of his heart,
shielding the rise and fall of his breath, to be
awakend

At the axis of his mid hriff

*the navel,* for in the pit of his stomach the chord from
which first he was fed has its temple

At the root of the groin

*the pubic hair,* for the torso is the stem in which the man
flowers forth and leads to the stamen of flesh in which
his seed rises

a wave of need and desire over        taking me

cried out my name

(This was long ago. It was another life)

and said,

What do you want of me?

I do not know, I said.      I have fallen in love.      He
has brought me into heights and depths my heart

               would fear       without him.       His look

    pierces my side  •  fire eyes  •

I have been waiting for you, he said:
               I know what you desire

     you do not yet know     but through me  •

And I am with you everywhere.     In your falling

I have fallen from a high place.     I have raised myself

     from darkness in your     rising

          wherever you are

   my hand in your hand     seeking     the locks, the keys

I am there.    Gathering me, you gather

    your Self  •

For my Other is not a woman but a man

*the King upon whose bosom let me lie.*

## Gore Vidal (b. 1925)

Gore Vidal's novel *The City and the Pillar* asserts that gay men are not women in disguise nor, indeed, even very special and sets out to prove that effeminacy and homosexuality do not need to occupy the same conceptual space in novels. As Vidal explained, "I decided to examine the homosexual underworld . . . and in the process show the 'naturalness' of homosexual relations. . . . In 1946 . . . it was part of the American folklore that homosexuality was a form of mental disease, confined for the most part to interior decorators and ballet dancers. Knowing this to be untrue, I set out to shatter the stereotype by taking as my protagonist a completely ordinary boy of the middle class and through his eyes observing the various strata of the underworld" (quoted in Austen 1977:119). Vidal's book carried the normalizing of homosexuality into respectable fiction and would in turn be the model for much of the normalizing fiction to follow, including James Barr's *Quatrefoil* (1950) in which two gay men, both in the Navy, both irreproachably "straight"-appearing, become lovers. However, despite his desire to shatter stereotypes, Vidal still ended his book with a murder when his ordinary American boy, Jim, kills the thing he loves, Bob, the man with whom Jim had had his first homosexual experience, not with a kiss but by strangling him. This is the ending of the 1948 version of the book as published. Vidal had originally ended the book with violence, but with retributive violence against straight stereotypes—for when Jim meets Bob again after many years and tries to make love to him again, Bob in a fit of homosexual panic and disgust rejects Jim. Jim then rapes Bob. Vidal's publisher changed the ending to the even more violent one. However, Vidal restored the original intended ending in his revision of the book in 1965.

If *The City and The Pillar* could present homosexual love in a vein of high seriousness while claiming that homosexual men were ordinary middle-class boys, in 1956 Vidal wrote a wicked parody of the effete homosexual that his characters in *The City and The Pillar* would never be. Vidal's story "Pages from an Abandoned Journal," published in a collection of his short stories called *A Thirsty Evil*, chronicles the transformation — a camp coming out — of a half-hearted academic posing as an equally half-hearted heterosexual into a brilliant member of an international gay society in which everyone is either an interior decorator, an antique dealer, or in the arts and all are wildly camp and bitchily witty. Vidal's story perfectly captures the intonations and pretentions of that pre-Stonewall time.

## PAGES FROM AN ABANDONED JOURNAL (1956)

APRIL 30, 1948

After last night, I was sure they wouldn't want to see me again but evidently I was wrong because this morning I had a call from Steven . . . he spells it with a "v" . . . asking me if I would like to come to a party at Elliott Magren's apartment in the *Rue du Bac*. I should have said no but I didn't. It's funny: when I make up my mind *not* to do something I always end up by doing it, like meeting Magren, like seeing any of these people again, especially after last night. Well, I guess it's experience. What was it Pascal wrote? I don't remember what Pascal wrote . . . another sign of weakness: I should look it up when I don't remember . . . the book is right here on the table but the thought of leafing through all those pages is discouraging so I pass on.

Anyway, now that I'm in Paris I've got to learn to be more adaptable and I do think, all in all, I've handled myself pretty well . . . until last night in the bar when I told everybody off. I certainly never thought I'd see Steven again . . . that's why I was so surprised to get his call this morning. Is he still hopeful after what I said? I can't see how. I was *ruthlessly* honest. I said I wasn't interested, that I didn't mind what other people did, etc., just as long as they left me alone, that I was getting married in the fall when I got back to the States (WRITE HELEN) and that I don't go in for any of that, never did and never will. I also told him in no uncertain terms that it's very embarrassing for a grown man to be treated like some idiot girl surrounded by a bunch of seedy, middle-aged Don Juans trying to get their hooks into her . . . him. Anyway, I really let him have it before I left. Later, I felt silly but I was glad to go on record like that once and for all: now we know where we stand and if they're willing to accept me on my terms, the way I am, then there's no reason why I can't see them sometimes. That's really why I agreed to meet Magren who sounds very interesting from what everybody says, and everybody talks a lot about him, at least in those circles which must be the largest and busiest circles in Paris this spring. Well, I shouldn't complain: this is the Bohemian life I wanted to see. It's just that there aren't many girls around, for fairly obvious reasons. In fact, except for running into Hilda Devendorf at American Express yesterday, I haven't seen an American girl to talk to in the three weeks I've been here.

My day: after the phone call from Steven, I worked for two and a half hours on Nero and the Civil Wars . . . I wish sometimes I'd picked a smaller subject for a doctorate, not that I don't like the period but having to learn German to read a lot of books all based on sources available to anybody is depressing: I could do the whole thing from Tacitus but that would be cheating, no bibliography, no footnotes, no scholastic quarrels to record and judge between. Then, though the day was cloudy, I took a long walk across the river to the Tuileries where the gardens looked fine. Just as I was turning home into the *rue de l'Universite* it started to rain and I got wet. At the desk Madame Revenel told me Hilda had called. I called her back and she said she was going to Deauville on Friday to visit some people who own a hotel and why didn't I go too? I said I might and wrote down her address. She's a nice girl. We were in high school together back in Toledo; I lost track of her when I went to Columbia.

Had dinner here in the dining room (veal, french fried potatoes, salad and something like a pie but very good . . . I like the way Madame Revenel cooks). She talked to me all through dinner, very fast, which is good because the faster she goes the less chance you have to translate in your head. The only other people in the dining room were the Harvard professor and his wife. They both read while they ate. He's supposed to be somebody important in the English Department but I've never heard of him . . . Paris is like that: everyone's supposed to be somebody important only you've never heard of them. The Harvard professor was reading a mystery story and his wife was reading a life of Alexander Pope. . . .

I got to the *Rue du Bac* around ten-thirty. Steven opened the door, yelling: "The beautiful Peter!" This was about what I expected. Anyway, I got into the room quickly . . . if they're drunk they're apt to try to kiss you and there was no point in getting off on the wrong foot again . . . but luckily he didn't try. He showed me through the apartment, four big rooms one opening off another . . . here and there an old chair was propped against a wall and that was all the furniture there was till we got to the last room where, on a big bed with a torn canopy, Elliott Magren lay, fully dressed, propped up by pillows. All the lamps had red shades. Over the bed was a painting of a nude man, the work of a famous painter I'd never heard of (read Berenson!).

There were about a dozen men in the room, most of them middle-aged and wearing expensive narrow suits. I recognized one or two of them from last night. They nodded to me but made no fuss. Steven introduced me to Elliott who didn't move from the bed when he shook hands; instead, he pulled me down beside him. He had a surprisingly powerful grip, considering how pale and slender he is. He told Steven to make me a drink. Then he gave me a long serious look and asked me if I wanted a pipe of opium. I said I didn't take drugs and he said nothing which was unusual: as a rule they give you a speech about how good it is for you or else they start defending themselves against what they feel is moral censure. Personally, I don't mind what other people do. As a matter of fact, I think all this is very interesting and I sometimes wonder what the gang back in Toledo would think if they could've seen me in a Left-Bank Paris apartment with a male prostitute who takes drugs. I thought of those college boys who sent T. S. Eliot the record "You've Come a Long Way From St. Louis."

Before I describe what happened, I'd better write down what I've heard about Magren since he is already a legend in Europe, at least in these circles. First of all, he is not very handsome. I don't know what I'd expected but something glamorous, like a movie star. He is about five foot ten and weighs about a hundred sixty pounds. He has dark straight hair that falls over his forehead; his eyes are black. The two sides of his face don't match, like Oscar Wilde's, though the effect is not as disagreeable as Wilde's face must've been from the photographs. Because of drugs, he is unnaturally pale. His voice is deep and his accent is still Southern; he hasn't picked up that phony English accent so many Americans do after five minutes over here. He was born in Galveston, Texas about thirty-six years ago. When he was sixteen he was picked up on the beach by a German baron who took him to Berlin with him. (I always wonder about details in a story like this: what did his parents say about a stranger walking off with their son? was there a scene? did they know what was going on?) Elliott then spent several years in Berlin during the twenties which were the great days, or what these people recall now as the great days . . . I gather the German boys were affectionate: It all sounds pretty disgusting. Then Elliott had a fight with the Baron and he walked, with no money, nothing but the clothes he was wearing, from Berlin to Munich. On the outskirts of Munich, a big car stopped and the chauffeur said that the owner of the car would like to give him a lift. The owner turned out to be a millionaire ship-owner from Egypt, very fat and old. He was intrigued with Elliott and he took him on a yachting tour of the Mediterranean. But Elliott couldn't stand him and when the ship got to Naples, Elliott and a Greek sailor skipped ship together after first stealing two thousand dollars from the Egyptian's stateroom. They went to Capri where they moved into the most expensive hotel and had a wonderful time until the money ran out and the sailor deserted Elliott for a rich American woman. Elliott was about to be taken off to jail for not paying his bill when Lord Glenellen, who was just checking in the hotel, saw him and told the police to let him go, that *he* would pay his bill . . . here again: how would Glenellen know that it would be worth his while to help this stranger? I mean you can't tell by looking at him that Elliott is queer. Suppose he hadn't been? Well, maybe that soldier I met on Okinawa the night of the hurricane was right: they can always tell about each other, like Masons. Glenellen kept Elliott for a number of years. They went to England together and Elliott rose higher and higher in aristocratic circles until he met the late King Basil who was then a Prince. Basil fell in love with him and Elliott went to live with him until Basil became king. They didn't see much of each other after that because the war started and Elliott went to California to live. Basil died during the war, leaving Elliott a small trust fund which is what he lives on now. In California, Elliott got interested in Vedanta and tried to stop taking drugs and lead a quiet . . . if not a normal . . . life. People say he was all right for several years but when the war ended he couldn't resist going back to Europe. Now he does nothing but smoke opium, his courtesan life pretty much over. This has been a long account but I'm glad I got it all down because the story is an interesting one and I've heard so many bits and pieces of it since I got here that it helps clarify many things just writing this down in my journal. . . . It is now past four o'clock and I've got a hangover already from the party but I'm going to finish, just as discipline. I never seem to finish anything which is a bad sign, God knows.

While I was sitting with Elliott on the bed, Steven brought him his opium pipe, a long painted wooden affair with a metal chimney. Elliott inhaled deeply, holding the smoke in his lungs as long as he could; then he exhaled the pale medicinal-scented smoke, and started to talk. I can't remember a word he said. I was aware, though, that this was probably the most brilliant conversation I'd ever heard. It might have been the setting which was certainly provocative or maybe I'd inhaled some of the opium which put me in a receptive mood but, no matter the cause, I sat listening to him, fascinated, not wanting him to stop. As he talked, he kept his eyes shut and I suddenly realized why the lamp shades were red: the eyes of drug addicts are hypersensitive to light; whenever he opened his eyes he would blink painfully and the tears would streak his face, glistening like small watery rubies in the red light. He told me about himself, pretending to be a modern Candide, simple and bewildered but actually he must have been quite different, more calculating, more resourceful. Then he asked me about myself and I couldn't tell if he was really interested or not because his eyes were shut and it's odd talking to someone who won't look at you. I told him about Ohio and high school and the University and now Columbia and the doctorate I'm trying to get in History and the fact I want to teach, to marry Helen . . . but as I talked I couldn't help but think how dull my life must sound to Elliott. I cut it short. I couldn't compete with him . . . and didn't want to. Then he asked me if I'd see him some evening, alone, and I said I would like to but . . . and this was completely spur of the moment . . . I said I was going down to Deauville the next day, with a girl. I wasn't sure he'd heard any of this because at that moment Steven pulled me off the bed and tried to make me dance with him which I wouldn't do, to the amusement of the others. Then Elliott went to sleep so I sat and talked for a while with an interior decorator from New York and, as usual, I was floored by the amount these people know: painting, music, literature, architecture . . . where do they learn it all? I sit like a complete idiot, supposedly educated, almost a Ph.D. while they talk circles around me: Fragonard, Boucher, Leonore Fini, Gropius, Sacheverell Sitwell, Ronald Firbank, Jean Genet, Jean Giono, Jean Cocteau, John Brown's body lies a'mouldering in Robert Graves. God damn them all. I have the worst headache and outside it's dawn. Remember to write Helen, call Hilda about Deauville, study German two hours tomorrow instead of one, start boning up on Latin again, read Berenson, get a book on modern art (what book?), read Firbank. . . .

## II

May 21, 1948

Another fight with Hilda. This time about religion. She's a Christian Scientist. It all started when she saw me taking two aspirins this morning because of last night's hangover. She gave me a lecture on Christ-Scientist and we had a long fight about God on the beach (which was wonderful today, not too many people, not too hot).

Hilda looked more than ever like a great golden seal. She is a nice girl but like so many who go to Bennington feels she must continually be alert to the life about her. I think tonight we'll go to bed together. Remember to get suntan oil, change money at hotel, finish Berenson, study German grammar! See if there's a Firbank in a paper edition.

May 22, 1948

It wasn't very successful last night. Hilda kept talking all the time which slows me down, also she is a good deal softer than she looks and it was like sinking into a feather mattress. I don't think she has bones, only elastic webbing. Well, maybe it'll be better tonight. She seemed pleased but then I think she likes the idea better than the actual thing. She told me she had her first affair at fourteen. We had another argument about God. I told her the evidence was slight, etc. but she said evidence had nothing to do with faith. She told me a long story about how her mother had cancer last year but wouldn't see a doctor and the cancer went away. I didn't have the heart to tell her that Mother's days are unpleasantly numbered. We had a wonderful dinner at that place on the sea, lobster, *moules*. Write Helen.

May 24, 1948

A fight with Hilda, this time about Helen whom she hardly knows. She felt that Helen was pretentious. I said who isn't? She said many people weren't. I said name me one. She said *she* wasn't pretentious. I then told her all the pretentious things she'd said in the past week starting with that discussion about the importance of an aristocracy and ending with atonalism. She then told me all the pretentious things I'd said, things I either didn't remember saying or she had twisted around. I got so angry I stalked out of her room and didn't go back: just as well. Having sex with her is about the dullest past-time I can think of. I went to my room and read Tacitus in Latin,, for practice.

My sunburn is better but I think I've picked up some kind of liver trouble. Hope it's not jaundice: a burning feeling right where the liver is. Wrote a long letter to Helen, studied Latin grammar. . . . I'm more afraid of my Latin than of anything else in either the written or the orals: can't seem to concentrate, can't retain all those irregular verbs. Well, I've come this far. I'll probably get through all right.

May 28, 1948

This morning I knocked on Elliott's door around eleven o'clock. He'd asked me to pick him up on my way to the beach. When he shouted come in! I did and found both Elliott and the boy on the floor together, stark naked, putting together a Meccano set. Both were intent on building an intricate affair with wheels and pulleys, a blueprint between them. I excused myself hurriedly but Elliott told me to stay . . . they'd be finished in a moment. The boy who was the color of a terra-cotta pot gave me a wicked grin. Then Elliott, completely unself-conscious, jumped to his feet and pulled on a pair of trunks and a shirt. The boy dressed, too, and we went out on the beach where the kid left us. I was blunt. I asked Elliott if this sort of thing wasn't very dangerous and he said yes it probably was but life was short and he was afraid of nothing, except drugs. He told me then that he had had an electrical shock treatment at a clinic shortly before I'd first met him. Now, at last, he was off opium and he hoped it was a permanent cure. He described the shock treatment, which sounded terrible. Part of his memory was gone: he could recall almost nothing of his childhood . . . yet he was blithe even about this: after all, he believed only in the present. . . . Then when I asked him if he always went in for young boys he said yes and he made a joke about how, having lost all memory of his own childhood, he would have to live out a new one with some boy.

May 29, 1948

I had a strange conversation with Elliott last night. Andre went home to his family at six and Elliott and I had an early dinner on the terrace. A beautiful evening: the sea green in the last light . . . a new moon. Eating fresh sole from the Channel, I told Elliott all about Jimmy, told him things I myself had nearly forgotten, had wanted to forget. I told him how it had started at twelve and gone on, without plan or thought or even acknowledgment until, at seventeen, I went to the army and he to the Marines and a quick death. After the army, I met Helen and forgot him completely; his death, like Elliott's shock treatment, took with it all memory, a thousand summer days abandoned on a coral island. I can't think now why on earth I told Elliott about Jimmy, not that I'm ashamed but it was, after all, something intimate, something nearly forgotten . . . anyway, when I finished, I sat there in the dark, not daring to look at Elliott, shivering as all in a rush the warmth left the sand about us and I had that terrible feeling I always have when I realize too late I've said too much. Finally, Elliott spoke. He gave me a strange disjointed speech about life and duty to oneself and how the moment is all one has and how it is dishonorable to cheat oneself of that. . . . I'm not sure that he said anything very useful or very original but sitting there in the dark, listening, his words had a peculiar urgency for me and I felt, in a way, that I was listening to an oracle. . . .

June 1, 1948

Shortly before lunch, the police came and arrested Elliott. Luckily, I was down on the beach and missed the whole thing. . . . The hotel's in an uproar and the manager's behaving like a mad man. It seems Andre stole Elliott's camera. His parents found it and asked him where he got it. He wouldn't tell. When they threatened him, he said Elliott gave him the camera and then, to make this story credible, he told them that Elliott had tried to seduce him. . . . The whole sordid business then proceeded logically: parents to police . . . police to Elliott . . . arrest. I sat down shakily on the terrace and wondered what to do. I was . . . I am frightened. While I was sitting there, a gendarme came out on the terrace and told me Elliott wanted to see me, in prison. Meanwhile, the gendarme wanted to know what I knew about Mr. Magren. It was only too apparent what his opinion of me was: another *pederast americain.* My voice shook and my throat dried up as I told him I hardly knew Elliott . . . I'd only just met him . . . I knew nothing about his private life. The gendarme sighed and closed his note book: the charges against Elliott were tres grave, tres grave, but I would be allowed to see him tomorrow morning. Then, realizing I was both nervous and uncooperative, the gendarme gave me the address of the jail and left. I went straight to my room and packed. I didn't think twice. All I wanted was to get away from Deauville, from Elliott, from the crime . . . and it *was* a crime, I'm sure of that. I was back in Paris in time for supper at the hotel.

June 4, 1948

Ran into Steven at the Cafe Flore and I asked him if there'd been any news of Elliott. Steven took the whole thing as a joke: yes, Elliott had called a mutual friend who was a lawyer and everything was all right. Money was spent; the charges were dropped and Elliott was staying on in Deauville for another week . . . doubtless to be near Andre. I was shocked but relieved to hear this. I'm not proud of my cowardice but I didn't want to be drawn into something I hardly understood.

Caught a glimpse of Hilda with some college boy, laughing and chattering as they left the brasserie across the street. I stepped behind a kiosk, not wanting Hilda to see me. Write Helen. See the doctor about wax in ears, also liver. Get tickets for Roland Petit ballet.

### III

December 26, 1953

The most hideous hangover! How I hate Christmas, especially this one. Started out last night at the *Caprice* where the management gave a party, absolutely packed. The new room is quite stunning, to my surprise: black walls, white driftwood but not artsy-craftsy, a starlight effect for the ceiling . . . only the upholstery is really *mauvais gout*: tufted velveteen in SAFFRON! . . . but then Piggy has no sense of color and why somebody didn't stop him I'll never know. All the tired old faces were there. Everyone was going to the ballet except me and there was all the usual talk about who was sleeping with whom, such a bore . . . I mean who cares who . . . whom dancers sleep with? Though somebody did say that Niellsen was having an affair with DR Bruckner which is something of a surprise considering what a mess there was at Fire Island last summer over just that. Anyway, I drank too many vodka martinis arid, incidentally, met Robert Gammadge the English playwright who isn't at all attractive though he made the biggest play for me. He's supposed to be quite dreary but makes tons of money. He was with that awful Dickie Mallory whose whole life is devoted to meeting celebrities, even the wrong ones. Needless to say, he was in seventh heaven with his playwright in tow. I can't understand people like Dickie: what fun do they get out of always being second fiddle? After the *Caprice* I went over to Steven's new apartment on the river; it's in a remodeled tenement house and I must say it's fun and the Queen Anne desk I sold him looks perfect heaven in his living room. I'll say one thing for him: Steven is one of the few people who has the good sense simply to let a fine piece go in a room. There were quite a few people there and we had New York champagne which is drinkable when you're already full of vodka. Needless to say, Steven pulled me off to one corner to ask about Bob. I wish people wouldn't be so sympathetic not that they really are of course but they feel they must *pretend* to be: actually, they're only curious. I said Bob *seemed* all right when I saw him last month. I didn't go into any details though Steven did his best to worm the whole story out of me. Fortunately, I have a good grip on myself nowadays and I am able to talk about the break-up quite calmly. I always tell everybody I hope Bob will do well in his new business and that

I like Sydney very much . . . actually, I hear things are going badly, that the shop is doing *no* business and that Bob is drinking again which means he's busy cruising the streets and getting into trouble. Well, I'm out of it and any day now I'll meet somebody . . . though it's funny how seldom you see anyone who's really attractive. There was a nice young Swede at Steven's but I never did get his name and anyway he is being kept by that ribbon clerk from the Madison Avenue Store. After Steven's I went to a real brawl in the Village: a studio apartment, packed with people, dozens of new faces, too. I wish now I hadn't got so drunk because there were some really attractive people there. I was all set, I thought, to go home with one but the friend intervened at the last moment and it looked for a moment like there was going to be real trouble before our host separated us . . . I never did get the host's name, I think he's in advertising. So I ended up alone. Must call doctor about hepatitis pills, write Leonore Fini, check last month's invoices (re. missing Sheraton receipt), call Mrs. Blaine-Smith about sofa.

December 27, 1953

I finally had tea with Mrs. Blaine-Smith today . . . one of the most beautiful women I've ever met, so truly chic and well-dressed. . . . I'm hopelessly indebted to Steven for bringing us together: she practically keeps the shop going. She had only six or seven people for tea, very much *en famille*, and I couldn't've been more surprised and pleased when she asked me to stay on. (I expect she knows what a discount I gave her on that Heppelwhite sofa.) Anyway, one of her guests was an Italian Count who was terribly nice though unattractive. We sat next to each other on that delicious ottoman in the library and chatted about Europe after the war: what a time that was! I told him I hadn't been back since 1948 but even so we knew quite a few people in common. Then, as always, the name Elliott Magren was mentioned. He's practically a codeword . . . if you know Elliott, well, you're on the inside and of course the Count (as I'd expected all along) knew Elliott and we exchanged bits of information about him, skirting carefully drugs and small boys because Mrs. Blaine-Smith though she knows everyone (and everything) *never* alludes to that sort of thing in any way, such a relief after so many of the queen bees you run into. Hilda, for instance, who married the maddest designer in Los Angeles and gives, I am told, the crudest parties with everyone drunk from morning till night. (Must stop drinking so much: nothing *after* dinner, that's the secret . . . especially with my liver.) We were discussing Elliott's apartment in the *Rue du Bac* and that marvelous Tchelichew that hangs over his bed when a little Englishman whose name I never did get, turned and said: did you know that Elliott Magren died last week? I must say it was stunning news, sitting in Mrs. Blaine-Smith's library so far, far away. . . . The Count was even more upset than I (could he have been one of Elliott's numerous admirers?) I couldn't help recalling then that terrible time at Deauville when Elliott was arrested and I had had to put up bail for him and hire a lawyer, all in French! Suddenly everything came back to me in a flood: that summer, the affair with Hilda . . . and Helen (incidentally, just this morning got a Christmas card from Helen, the first word in years: a photograph of her husband and three ghastly children, all living in Toledo: well, I suppose she's happy). But what an important summer that was, the chrysalis burst at last which, I think, prepared me for all the bad luck later when I failed my doctorate and had to go to work in Steven's office. . . . And now Elliott's dead. Hard to believe someone you once knew is actually dead, not like the war where sudden absences in the roster were taken for granted. The Englishman told us the whole story. It seems Elliott was rounded up in a police raid on dope addicts in which a number of very famous people were caught, too. He was told to leave the country; so he piled everything into two taxicabs and drove to the Gare St. Lazare where he took a train for Rome. He settled down in a small apartment off the Via Veneto. Last fall he underwent another series of shock treatment, administered by a quack doctor who cured him of drugs but lost his memory for him in the process. Aside from this, he was in good health and looked as young as ever except that for some reason he dyed his hair red . . . too mad! Then, last week, he made a date to go to the opera with a friend. The friend arrived . . . the door was open but, inside, there was no Elliott. The friend was particularly annoyed because Elliott often would not show up at all if, enroute to an appointment, he happened to see someone desirable in the street. I remember Elliott telling me once that his greatest pleasure was to follow a handsome stranger for hours on end through the streets of a city. It was not so much the chase which interested him as the identification he had with the boy he followed: he would become the other, imitating his gestures, his gait, becoming himself young, absorbed in a boy's life. But Elliott had followed no one that day. The friend finally found him face down in the bathroom, dead. When the autopsy was performed, it was discovered that Elliott had had a malformed heart, an extremely rare case, and he might have died as suddenly at any moment in his life . . . the drugs, the shock treatments and so on had contributed nothing to his death. He was buried Christmas day in the Protestant cemetery close to Shelley, in good company to the end. I must say I can't imagine him with red hair. . . . The Count asked me to have dinner with him tomorrow at the Colony!) and I said I'd be delighted. Then Mrs. Blaine-Smith told the most devastating story about the Duchess of Windsor in Palm Beach.

Find out about Helen Gleason's sphinxes. Call Bob about the keys to the back closet. Return Steven's copy of "Valmouth." *Find out the Count's name before dinner tomorrow.*

## "Donald Webster Cory" [Pseudonym of Edward Sagarin] (1913–1986)

The first book published in a national milieu to address the question of homosexual rights was *The Homosexual in America* (1951), written under the pseudonym of Donald Webster Cory. Cory's book was the first extensive and careful examination of the current state of knowledge about homosexuality to be written by an American since Mayne's *The Intersexes* (1908), which remained almost totally unknown.

Cory's account of the oppression and repression of homosexuals in America made a strong case for the recognition of homosexuals as a minority group whose concerns were similar to those of other oppressed American minorities. He argued that homosexuality is not a vice or an illness and raised the issue of civil liberties and human rights. He pointed out that "there is no homosexual problem except that created by heterosexual society," a society that founds its homophobia in a general fear of sexuality. He discussed theoretical concepts of a "gay culture" and enunciated a liberationist and even revolutionary view of the task that lay ahead for gay people as he saw it in 1951. If homophobia is a creation of heterosexuality—a position to be taken forty years later by gay theorists—then the only possible action for the homosexual, Cory argued was "to take the initiative in bringing about change" since the "homosexual problem" is "a majority problem, but only the minority is interested in solving it." Therefore, "the homosexual is thus locked in his present position. If he does not rise up and demand his rights, he will never get them, but until he gets those rights, he cannot be expected to expose himself to the martyrdom that would come should he rise up and demand them" (Cory 1951:228–35).

## From *The Homosexual in America* (1951)

### The Society We Envisage

What does the homosexual want? He cries out against the injustice of society, yet offers no alternative. He finds the discrimination and the calumnies a manifestation of the grossest intolerance, but he fails to offer the world at large a pattern for a better social organization in which he could be integrated.

This is not at all surprising, for the development of such a plan would, by its very nature, imply freedom of discussion. It is only from the exchange of opinion in a free press and by all other methods of communication that a subject of this type, wrought with so many unknowns and paradoxes, can reach adequate solution.

What does the homosexual want? The question cannot be answered because each person can speak only for himself, and his reply will be prejudiced by his religious and ethical background, by his philosophy of life, and by the degree of happiness he has been able to achieve. The actress whose predilections are almost public knowledge and are no impediment to her stardom and public acceptance is hardly likely to feel the same need for social reorganization as the lonely, the wretched, and the frustrated. A deeply religious Roman Catholic invert who professes that there is no justification for any sexual pleasure outside of the sacrament of marriage can hardly share aspirations for social change with two men who are living together in a happy physical and spiritual union.

The homosexual society, such as it is and to the extent that it exists at all, reflects differences of opinion on the social solution of this question just as does any other group of people on any problem confronting them. There is no single, quasi-official, universally accepted version of the social organization envisaged by homosexuals, any more than there could be a single opinion of college professors on loyalty oaths, of university students on the accomplishments of education, of physicians on socialized medicine.

But the homosexual viewpoint is less well developed than that of other groups on other questions because of the virtual impossibility of having an exchange of opinion through the usual channels of thought expression. First, the facts themselves on which an opinion must be based are difficult to obtain and, once found, are difficult to communicate to others. There are very few reliable statistics, and even the words of experts are usually based on the most atypical homosexuals, namely those who fall into the hands of the law or who are seeking help from a psychiatrist.

Even were the facts more readily available, an expression of opinion requires a free and open debate, and American society is hardly more advanced in this respect than the totalitarian lands. There is, of course, no interference with the effort to discuss the subject by word of mouth, provided the discussion remains within the homosexual group. It is almost impossible to have, except in a few and rare circles, a full interchange of opinion between people of all sexual temperaments in which each viewpoint is defended ably and each argument refuted honestly.

Homosexuals have had little opportunity for the development of a well-defined outlook. Within the homosexual group, there is little uniformity of opinion, and perhaps even less so than would be found in another minority group. . . .

There is probably only one thing on which homosexuals would in general agree with regard to the attitude of society, and that is that the present situation is unjust and that change is necessary. The injustice is not so much before the bar, nor in the effort to obtain employment, but is found above all in the general social attitude of the heterosexual society. No one can prevent an individual from expressing hostility toward another, provided he stays within the law and neither libels nor physically harms his enemy, but when this hostile attitude is officially sponsored by all possible means among the population, it is no longer the private affair of a single person.

The homosexual, first and foremost, wants recognition of the fact that he is doing no one any harm. He wants to live and let live, to punish and be punished when there are transgressions, and to go about the ordinary and everyday pursuits of life, unhindered either by law or by an unwritten hostility which is even more effectual than the written law.

This is a far-reaching program, requiring the modification of attitudes over a period of generations, and it is only natural that it must fall upon those most concerned with this problem—the inverts—to take the initiative in remolding public opinion.

However, the invert is not alone in feeling that the present situation is unsatisfactory. The dominant group in our society tacitly understands and is ready to concede that it has no proposal for bettering a situation which is obviously unjust. It would like—in a manner similar to the attitude of many white persons on the color question—to "wish" the problem out of existence. It dreams of a world in which the problem does not exist, hopes that the problem will not touch the lives of individuals personally related to oneself, and just does not think, talk, or write about it. But its dreams are in vain.

The dominant society cannot offer a cure for homosexuality. It urges in a weak, ineffectual, and ignorant manner that willpower be exerted, but willpower solves nothing. It talks of suppression and sublimation, while its own scientists scoff at such a proposal. It damns in the harshest of terms in the hope that damnation will be a deterrent, but again there is failure. It passes laws that make felons of homosexuals, but ignores its own laws and admits that it cannot put homosexuals behind bars. It concedes that homosexuals must earn a living, and banishes them from employment. And, as society always does when it is in a blind alley, tied by tradition and folkways to a system which is unreasonable and which does not answer the needs of the people, it uses silence as the answer. It hides its head in the sand, pretends that the problem does not exist, and forbids discussion, save in professional circles.

But the problem does exist, and it will be discussed. Furthermore, it is not a problem created by the homosexuals. A sociologist writing on racial minorities—and again the parallel is inescapable—has stated that there are no minority problems. There are only majority problems. There is no Negro problem except that created by whites; no Jewish problem except that created by Gentiles. To which I add: and no homosexual problem except that created by the heterosexual society.

There would be no economic dilemma for the invert were he not excluded from practically all jobs unless he hides his identity. There would be no blackmail problem for the homosexual except that he cannot live happily after exposure, because the world which has learned of his temperament will inflict severe sanctions. There would be no ethical problem of being a lawbreaker except that the laws have been codified in such manner that he cannot be a homosexual without at least aspiring to break them. And thus the problems of the homosexual could be enumerated, and it could be seen that they are majority problems—not minority ones!

Even the psychological aspects of the homosexual's dilemma primarily involve adjustment to a hostile world. There would be no need for the invert to feel guilty, to suffer remorse, to be forced to express hatred toward his love-object, if society did not condemn it so bitterly. He would not be faced with the paradoxical problem of attempting on the one hand to be proud of himself and on the other to deny his temperament, if it were not so difficult to live in a world that demanded such denial.

It is a majority problem, but only the minority is interested in solving it. The fundamental dilemma is that it must rest primarily upon the homosexuals, being the most interested party, to take the initiative in bringing about change, but until such change is effected, anyone taking such initiative is open to pillory and contumelious scorn.

The homosexual is thus locked in his present position. If he does not rise up and demand his rights, he will never get them, but until he gets those rights, he cannot be expected to expose himself to the martyrdom that would come if he should rise up and demand them. It is a vicious circle, and what the homosexual is seeking, first and foremost, is an answer to this dilemma.

It is an answer that I contend can be found and one which happens, by the most fortunate of coincidences, to be identical with the needs of society at large and with the historic task of the democratic forces of our generation. The answer is to be found in the liberalization of our newspapers, radio, and theater, so that homosexuality can be discussed as freely as any other subject and within the confines that circumscribe any other type of discussion. Already a beginning has been made in the very large interest shown in the subject by novelists, and in the occasional portrayal of homosexuality on the stage. A few popular magazines in the United States have at least mentioned it. . . .

This discussion may prove to be an opening wedge. There will be more articles, books, and further utilization of other means of thought communication, and out of this will come the interchange of opinion, the conflict and the controversy, which alone can establish truth.

And all of this is good for society, good particularly in this era, when no greater threat to the democratic way of life and to everything that has evolved in modern civilization, both Western and Eastern, appears than the suppression of all differences of opinion, the repression of all controversy. . . . Thus, as the first answer to the society we homosexuals envisage, we seek freedom of thought and expression on this question. This involves not only the right to publish books and magazines without interference from the police, but the right to employ the main channels of communication, the leading newspapers, magazines, and the air for the expression of a viewpoint in the spirit and traditions of American freedoms. . . .

If the day of free and open discussion arrives, and if, during the course of such discussion, the struggle for it, and as a consequence of it, the social stigma attached to being a homosexual begins to be lifted, there will automatically come about a happier milieu in which the individual can live, love, thrive, and work. Part of that happier relationship will be found in the dropping of the disguise.

Many homosexuals consider that their greatest fortune, their one saving grace, has been the invisibility of the cross which they have had to bear. The ease with which they were able to hide their temperaments from the closest friends and business associates, from their parents, wives, and children, made it possible to partake of the full benefits and material and spiritual advantages life offers to the heterosexual. Many such people—and I include myself—have constantly striven to perfect their technique of concealment.

Actually, the inherent tragedy—not the saving grace—of homosexuality is found in the ease of concealment. If the homosexual were as readily recognizable as are members of certain other minority groups, the social condemnation could not possibly exist. Stereotype thinking on the part of the majority would, in the first instance, collapse of its own absurdity if all of us who are gay were known for what we are. Secondly, our achievements in society and our contributions to all phases of culture and social advancement would become well-known, and not merely the arsenal of argument in the knowledge of a few. The laws against homosexuality could not be sustained if it were flagrantly apparent that millions of human beings in all walks of life were affected. Blackmail, naturally enough, would be non-existent as a problem facing the invert.

It is a chimera, but worthy of speculation. If only all of the inverts, the millions in all lands, could simultaneously rise up in our full strength! For the fact is that we homosexuals are defeated by the self-perpetuation of the folkways which inflict severe punishment on those who protest against these folkways. Again, the circle is vicious. We need freedom of expression to achieve freedom of inversion, but only the free invert is in a position to demand and to further freedom of expression. . . .

What the homosexual wants is freedom—not only freedom of expression, but also sexual freedom. By sexual freedom is meant the right of any person to gratify his urges when and how he sees fit, without fear of social consequences, so long as he does not use the force of either violence, threat, or superior age; so long as he does not inflict bodily harm or disease upon another person; so long as the other person is of sound mind and agrees to the activity. This means that both on the statute books and in the realm of public opinion all sexual activity is accepted as equally correct, right, and proper so long as it is entered into voluntarily by the parties involved, they are perfectly sane and above a reasonable age of consent, free of communicable disease, and no duress or misrepresentation is employed. . . .

The homosexual often feels that the source of his difficulty lies in the fact that he is born into a hostile world, and this hostility is inherent, he believes, in that he lives in a heterosexual society. He is, in my opinion, entirely wrong in this concept. The root of the homosexual difficulty is that he lives, not in a heterosexual world, but in an anti-sexual world. . . .

The homosexual, thus, has two historic missions to perform. Whether he is a democrat or a totalitarian by political conviction, he is historically forced to enter the struggle for the widening of freedom of expression. . . . He is historically compelled to enlist in the legions fighting for liberalization of the sexual mores of modern civilization. . . .

In [the] totalitarian state, there [is] no room for a group of people who, by their very sexual temperaments, could never be assimilated, must always remain apart with their own ways of life, their own outlooks, their own philosophies.

And it is this inherent lack of assimilability that is the greatest historic value of homosexuality. Any minority which does not commit anti-social acts, which is not destructive of the life, property, or culture of the majority or of other minority groups, is a pillar of democratic strength. So long as there are such minorities in our culture, whether of a sexual or religious or ethnic character, there will be many broths in the melting pot, many and variegated waves in the seas. . . .

Thus on three scores, homosexuality—fortunately but unwittingly—must inevitably play a progressive role in the scheme of things. It will broaden the base for freedom of thought and communication. It will be a banner-bearer in the struggle for liberalization of our sexual conventions, and will be a pillar of strength in the defense of our threatened democracy.

## Frank O'Hara (1926–1966)

Openly gay in the fifties, Frank O'Hara anatomized homosexuality—his own and the idea of it—in "Homosexuality," in which he described as the motive power of his poetry "the law of my own voice," a law derived from desire for homosexual love. In the context of cruising the subways men's rooms and parks of New York, O'Hara sees homosexuals as remarkable creatures whose "delicate feet" may never "touch the earth again," as they— he among them—utter a cry "to confuse the brave": "Its a summer day,/and I want to be wanted more than anything else in the/world." O'Hara, like Robert Duncan, explores sexuality as language, and both assert that difference is the marker that makes that language comprehensible.

*Lebanon (1953)*

Perhaps he will press his warm lips
to mine in a phrase exceptionally historic,
which seemed to have lived on lips
in Galilee now that I have already felt

its sting. The sweet fetid dust
of his breath will linger upon my lips

as if my understanding were affected and a soul
of passion and arrogant surmise had my lips

for a moment and then passed through my lips
into the rendering azure of the temple.
It was coolly dawning and his lips
opened, "I'll go with you to the other country,

no matter that my all is here,
my childhood on the plains' grapelike lips,
my father's handkerchief, my mother's tomb,
my memory of games; they go up like lips

in a stadium; all that comes from my white lips
and shall ease you on the unnecessary journey."
And thus the day did blanch upon his lips
despite the dirty windowpanes and cold air.

He did go to the mountains and perhaps I
shall be daily upon those wooded sloping lips,
so that as he is fleetly hunting goats
my breath will find its altar in those lips.

my will relaxes with the fresh green reeds
which spring arrogantly though they're not sown.
Indeed, they want no wind. They are a lake,
and bend when they wish and do not invite
the sun. They flay the air and do not break;
indifferently they disappear at night,
     and just as calmly earth's of them bereft.
     They found earth mute and passionless, and left.


*Homosexuality (1954)*

So we are taking off our masks, are we, and keeping
our mouths shut, as if we'd been pierced by a glance!

The song of an old cow is not more full of judgment
than the vapors which escape one's soul when one is sick;

so I pull the shadows around me like a puff
and crinkle my eyes as if at the most exquisite moment

of a very long opera, and then we are off!
without reproach and without hope that our delicate feet

will touch the earth again, let alone "very soon."
It is the law of my own voice I shall investigate.

I start like ice, my finger to my ear, my ear
to my heart, that proud cur at the garbage can

in the rain. It's wonderful to admire oneself
with complete candor, tallying up the merits of each

of the latrines. 14th Street is drunken and credulous,
53rd tries to tremble but is too at rest. The good

love a park and the inept a railway station,
and there are the divine ones who drag themselves up

and down the lengthening shadow of an Abyssinian head
in the dust, trailing their long elegant heels of hot air

crying to confuse the brave "It's a summer day,
and I want to be wanted more than anything else in the
world."

## Allen Ginsberg (1926–1997)

It almost seemed, Robert Martin said, that "in the 1950s . . . the only openly gay poet was Allen Ginsberg" (Martin 1979:165). It was indeed Allen Ginsberg whose poetry, more than that of any American homosexual poet since Whitman, was to take to heart Whitman's injunction not only to celebrate the love of comrades but to write about "the midnight orgies of young men." Ginsberg became, in the fifties, the essential homosexual poet, the heir of Whitman and American celebrant of difference and unabashedly textualized homosexual desire. His poem "Howl" (1956) asserted that the only way to confront homophobia was to deliberately affront the sensibility that supported it. In a moment Ginsberg banished the simpering pose of the homosexual cult so despised by Duncan. He also left no dogmatic ground for novels like Vidal's *The City and the Pillar*, or for the philosophy of some of the ameliorating homosexual rights activists who tried to reconstruct homosexuality into a version of heterosexuality.

In "Howl" Ginsberg's fairies are as joyful in their sexual experiments as Whitman's twenty-eight bathers or as Whitman in the embrace of his fierce wrestler. In "Howl" they are "fucked in the ass by saintly motorcyclists and screamed with joy." Not since Whitman had an American homosexual poet dared to intimate, let alone announce, that joy not pain was the result of homosexual rape and to suggest that sex not philosophy might be the most powerful weapon against oppression. Sex becomes for Ginsberg not a furtive or perhaps even anticlimactic conclusion to a prelude of highly romanticized desire, but the eucharistic point at which all literary constructions of desire are obliterated in a moment that liberates sex from any intellectualization of desire. In "Howl," and later in "Please Master" (a poem which has been much anthologized but which is nevertheless of great importance as the text that introduced sado-masochism and leathermen, if not to the

American scene at least to American poetry), written the year before Stonewall, Ginsberg's constructions of homosexual identities inscribe homosexual desire most powerfully in scenes of ecstatic homosexual rape and the passive surrender of all remaining emotionally held myths about American manhood to that demanding penetration. In "A Supermarket in California" (1955), Ginsberg testifies to Whitman's influence when he describes him as "dear father, graybeard, lonely old courage-teacher." Ginsberg, inheritor, son of the courage-teacher, found an America in the 1950s that was ripe for the redemption of Whitman's pledge to "sing no songs today but those of manly attachment."

## A Supermarket in California (1955)

What thoughts I have of you tonight, Walt Whitman,
for I walked down the sidestreets under the trees with a headache
self-conscious looking at the full moon.
   In my hungry fatigue, and shopping for images, I went
into the neon fruit supermarket, dreaming of your enumerations!
   What peaches and what penumbras! Whole families
shopping at night! Aisles full of husbands! Wives in the
avocados, babies in the tomatoes!—and you, García Lorca,
what were you doing down by the watermelons?

   I saw you, Walt Whitman, childless, lonely old grubber,
poking among the meats in the refrigerator and eyeing the
grocery boys.
   I heard you asking questions of each: Who killed the
pork chops? What price bananas? Are you my Angel?
   I wandered in and out of the brilliant stacks of cans
following you, and followed in my imagination by the store
detective.
   We strode down the open corridors together in our
solitary fancy tasting artichokes, possessing every frozen
delicacy, and never passing the cashier.

   Where are we going, Walt Whitman? The doors close in
an hour. Which way does your beard point tonight?
   (I touch your book and dream of our odyssey in the
supermarket and feel absurd.)
   Will we walk all night through solitary streets? The trees
add shade to shade, lights out in the houses, we'll both be
lonely.
   Will we stroll dreaming of the lost America of love past
blue automobiles in driveways, home to our silent cottage?
   Ah, dear father, graybeard, lonely old courage-teacher,
what America did you have when Charon quit poling his ferry
and you got out on a smoking bank and stood watching the
boat disappear on the black waters of Lethe?

*Chances "R" (1966)*

Nymph and shepherd raise electric tridents
       glowing red against the plaster wall,
The jukebox beating out magic syllables,
A line of painted boys snapping fingers
        & shaking thin Italian trouserlegs
            or rough dungarees on big asses
                bumping and dipping
ritually, with no religion but the
           old one of cocksuckers
naturally, in Kansas center of America
      the farmboys in Diabolic bar light
        alone stiff necked or lined up
        dancing row on row like Afric husbands
& the music's sad here, whereas Sunset Trip or
Jukebox Corner it's ecstatic pinball machines—
Religiously, with concentration and free
           prayer; fairy boys of the plains
           and their gay sisters of the city
step together to the center of the floor
        illumined by machine eyes, screaming drumbeats,
          passionate voices of Oklahoma City
            chanting No Satisfaction
Suspended from Heaven the Chances R
      Club floats rayed by stars
         along a Wichita tree avenue
       traversed with streetlights on the plain.


*Please Master (1968)*

Please master can I touch your cheek
please master can I kneel at your feet
please master can I loosen your blue pants
please master can I gaze at your golden haired belly
please master can I gently take down your shorts
please master can I have your thighs bare to my eyes
please master can I take off my clothes below your chair
please master can I kiss your ankles and soul
please master can I touch lips to your hard muscle hairless thigh
please master can I lay my ear pressed to your stomach
please master can I wrap my arms around your white ass
please master can I lick your groin curled with blond soft fur
please master can I touch my tongue to your rosy asshole
please master may I pass my face to your balls,
please master, please look into my eyes,
please master order me down on the floor

please master tell me to lick your thick shaft
please master put your rough hands on my bald hairy skull
please master press my mouth to your prick-heart
please master press my face into your belly, pull me slowly strong thumbed
till your dumb hardness fills my throat to the base
till I swallow & taste your delicate flesh-hot prick barrel veined Please
Master push my shoulders away and stare in my eye, & make me bend over
the table
please master grab my thighs and lift my ass to your waist
please master your hand's rough stroke on my neck your palm down my
backside
please master push me up, my feet on chairs, till my hole feels the breath
of your spit and your thumb stroke
please master make me say Please Master Fuck me now Please
Master grease my balls and hairmouth with sweet vaselines
please master stroke your shaft with white creams
please master touch your cock head to my wrinkled self-hole
please master push it in gently, your elbows enwrapped round my breast
your arms passing down to my belly, my penis you touch w/ your fingers
please master shove it in me a little, a little, a little,
please master sink your droor thing down my behind
& please master make me wiggle my rear to eat up the prick trunk
till my asshalfs cuddle your thighs, my back bent over,
till I'm alone sticking out, your sword stuck throbbing in me
please master pull out and slowly roll into the bottom
please master lunge it again, and withdraw to the tip
please please master fuck me again with your self, please fuck me Please
Master drive down till it hurts me the softness the
Softness please master make love to my ass, give body to center, & fuck
me for good like a girl,
tenderly clasp me please master I take me to thee,
& drive in my belly your selfsame sweet heat-rood
you fingered in solitude Denver or Brooklyn or fucked in a maiden in
Paris carlots
please master drive me thy vehicle, body of love drops, sweat fuck
body of tenderness, Give me your dog fuck faster
please master make me go moan on the table
Go moan O please master do fuck me like that
in your rhythm thrill-plunge & pull-back-bounce & push down
till I loosen my asshole a dog on the table yelping with terror delight to be
loved
Please master call me a dog, an ass beast, a wet asshole,
& fuck me more violent, my eyes hid with your palms round my skull
& plunge down in a brutal hard lash thru soft drip-flesh
& throb thru five seconds to spurt out your semen heat
over & over, bamming it in while I cry out your name I do love you
please Master.

## John Wieners (b. 1934)

*A Poem for Cocksuckers* (1958)

Well we can go
in the queer bars w/
our long hair reaching
down to the ground and
we can sing our songs
of love like the black mama
on the juke box, after all
what have we got left.

   On our right the fairies
giggle in their lacquered
voices & blow
smoke in your eyes let them
it's a nigger's world
and we retain strength.
The gifts do not desert us,
fountains do not dry
up there are rivers running,
there are mountains
swelling for spring to cascade.

   It is all here between
the powdered legs &
painted eyes of the fairy
friends who do not fail us
    in our hour of
    despair. Take not
away from me the small fires
I burn in the memory of love.

## William Burroughs (1914–1997)

FROM *NAKED LUNCH* (1959)

*Naked Lunch* represented for its time the most daring (if unsatisfying) experiment with homoerotic sexual and sadistic fantasy yet attempted in the American novel. Burroughs employs a strategy initiated by *A Scarlet Pansy* and *The Young and the Evil*: he writes into American fiction the worst fears of American heterosexuals concerning homosexuals. In Burroughs's books—and in works soon to follow like *Last Exit to Brooklyn* and *City of Night*—the nightmares America dreamed about transvestite homosexuals, sexual predators, and insatiable seducers of boys are offered as a version of homosexual reality, but without apology and, sometimes, without explanation.

## "Hassans Rumpus Room"

Gilt and red plush. Rococo bar backed by pink shell. The air is cloyed with a sweet evil substance like decayed honey. Men and women in evening dress sip pousse-cafés through alabaster tubes. Near East Mugwump sits naked on a bar stool covered in pink silk. He licks warm honey from a crystal goblet with a long black tongue. His genitals are perfectly formed—circumcised cock, black shiny pubic hairs. His lips are thin and purple-blue like the lips of a penis, his eyes blank with insect calm. The Mugwump has no liver, maintaining himself exclusive on sweets. Mugwump push a slender blond youth to a couch and strip him expertly.

"Stand up and turn around," he orders in telepathic pictographs. He ties the boy's hands behind him with a red silk cord. "Tonight we make it all the way."

"No, no!" screams the boy.

"Yes. Yes."

Cocks ejaculate in silent "yes." Mugwump part silk curtains, reveal a teak wood gallows against lighted screen of red flint. Gallows is on a dais of Aztec mosaics.

The boy crumples to his knees with a long "OOOOOOOOH," shitting and pissing in terror. He feels the shit warm between his thighs. A great wave of hot blood swells his lips and throat. His body contracts into a foetal position and sperm spurts hot into his face. The Mugwump dips hot perfumed water from alabaster bowl, pensively washes the boy's ass and cock, drying him with a soft blue towel. A warm wind plays over the boys body and the hairs float free. The Mugwump puts a hand under the boy's chest and pulls him to his feet. Holding him by both pinioned elbows, propels him up the steps and under the noose. He stands in front of the boy holding the noose in both hands.

The boy looks into Mugwump eyes blank as obsidian mirrors, pools of black blood, glory holes in a toilet wall closing on the Last Erection.

An old garbage collector, face fine and yellow as Chinese ivory, blows The Blast on his dented brass horn, wakes the Spanish pimp with a hard-on. Whore staggers out through dust and shit and litter of dead kittens, carrying bales of aborted foetuses, broken condoms, bloody Kotex, shit wrapped in bright color comics.

A vast still harbor of iridescent water. Deserted gas well flares on the smoky horizon. Stink of oil and sewage. Sick sharks swim through the black water, belch sulphur from rotting livers, ignore a bloody, broken Icarus. Naked Mr. America, burning frantic with self bone love, screams out: "My asshole confounds the Louvre! I fart ambrosia and shit pure gold turds! My cock spurts soft diamonds in the morning sunlight!" He plummets from the eyeless lighthouse, kissing and jacking off in face of the black mirror, glides oblique down with cryptic condoms and mosaic of a thousand newspapers through a drowned city of red brick to settle in black mud with tin cans and beer bottles, gangsters in concrete, pistols pounded flat and meaningless to avoid short-arm inspection of prurient ballistic experts. He waits the slow striptease of erosion with fossil loins.

The Mugwump slips the noose over the boy's head and tightens the knot caressingly behind the left ear. The boy's penis is retracted, his balls tight. He looks straight ahead breathing deeply. The Mugwump sidles around the boy goosing him and caressing his genitals in hieroglyphs of mockery. He moves in behind the boy with a series of bumps and shoves his cock up the boy's ass. He stands there moving in circular gyrations.

The guests shush each other, nudge and giggle.

Suddenly the Mugwump pushes the boy forward into space, free of his cock. He steadies the boy with hands on the hip bones, reaches up with his stylized hieroglyph hands and snaps the boy's neck. A shudder passes through the boy's body. His penis rises in three great surges pulling his pelvis up, ejaculates immediately.

Green sparks explode behind his eyes. A sweet toothache pain shoots through his neck down the spine to the groin, contracting the body in spasms of delight. His whole body squeezes out through his cock. A final spasm throws a great spurt of sperm across the red screen like a shooting star.

The boy falls with soft gutty suction through a maze of penny arcades and dirty pictures.

A sharp turd shoots clean out his ass. Farts shake his slender body. Skyrockets burst in green clusters across a great river. He hears the faint put-put of a motor boat in jungle twilight. . . . Under silent wings of the anopheles mosquito.

The Mugwump pulls the boy back onto his cock. The boy squirms, impaled like a speared fish. The Mugwump swings on the boy's back, his body contracting in fluid waves. Blood flows down the boy's chin from his mouth, half-open, sweet, and sulky in death. The Mugwump falls with a fluid, sated plop.

Windowless cubicle with blue walls. Dirty pink curtain cover the door. Red bugs crawl on the wall, cluster in corners. Naked boy in the middle of the room twang a two-string ouad, trace an arabesque on the floor. Another boy lean back on the bed smoking keif and blow smoke over his erect cock. They play game with tarot cards on the bed to see who fuck who. Cheat. Fight. Roll on the floor snarling and spitting like young animals. The loser sit on the floor chin on knees, licks a broken tooth. The winner curls up on the bed pretending to sleep. Whenever the other boy come near kick at him. Ali seize him by one ankle, tuck the ankle under his arm pit, lock his arm around the calf. The boy kick desperately at Ali's face. Other ankle pinioned. Ali tilt the boy back on his shoulders. The boy's cock extends along his stomach, float free pulsing. Ali put his hands over his head. Spit on his cock. The other sighs deeply as Ali slides his cock in. The mouths grind together smearing blood. Sharp musty odor of penetrated rectum. Nimun drive in like a wedge, force jism out the other cock in long hot spurts. (The author has observed that Arab cocks tend to be wide and wedge shaped.)

Satyr and naked Greek lad in aqualungs trace a ballet of pursuit in a monster vase of transparent alabaster. The Satyr catches the boy from in front and whirls him around. They move in fish jerks. The boy releases a silver stream of bubbles from his mouth. White sperm ejaculates into the green water and floats lazily around the twisting bodies.

Negro gently lifts exquisite Chinese boy into a hammock. He pushes the boy's legs up over his head and straddles the hammock. He slides his cock up the boy's slender tight ass. He rocks the hammock gently back and forth. The boy screams, a weird high wail of unendurable delight.

A Javanese dancer in ornate teak swivel chair, set in a socket of limestone buttocks, pulls an American boy—red hair, bright green eyes—down onto his cock with ritual motions. The boy sits impaled facing the dancer who propels himself in circular gyrations, lending fluid substance to the chair. "Weeeeeeeeeee!" scream the boy as his sperm spurt up over the dancer's lean brown chest. One gob hit the corner of the dancer's mouth. The boy push it in with his finger and laugh: "Man, that's what I call suction!"

Two Arab women with bestial faces have pulled the shorts off a little blond French boy. They are screwing him with red rubber cocks. The boy snarls, bites, kicks, collapses in tears as his cock rises and ejaculates.

Hassan's face swells, tumescent with blood. His lips turn purple. He strip off his suit of banknotes and throw it into an open vault that closes soundless.

"Freedom Hall here, folks!" he screams in his phoney Texas accent. Ten-gallon hat and cowboy boots still on, he dances the Liquefactionist Jig, ending with a grotesque can-can to the tune of She Started a Heat Wave.

"Let it be! And no holes barred!!!"

Couples attached to baroque harnesses with artificial wings copulate in the air, screaming like magpies.

Aerialists ejaculate each other in space with one sure touch.

Equilibrists suck each other off deftly, balanced on perilous poles and chairs tilted over the void. A warm wind brings the smell of rivers and jungle from misty depths.

Boys by the hundred plummet through the roof, quivering and kicking at the end of ropes. The boys hang at different levels, some near the ceiling and others a few inches off the floor. Exquisite Balinese and Malays, Mexican Indians with fierce innocent faces and bright red gums. Negroes (teeth, fingers, toe nails and pubic hair gilded), Japanese boys smooth and white as China, Titian-haired Venetian lads, Americans with blond or black curls falling across the forehead (the guests tenderly shove it back), sulky blond Pollacks with animal brown eyes, Arab and Spanish street boys, Austrian boys pink and delicate with a faint shadow of blond pubic hair, sneering German youths with bright blue eyes scream "Heil Hitler!" as the trap falls under them. Sollubis shit and whimper.

Mr. Rich-and-Vulgar chews his Havana lewd and nasty, sprawled on a Florida beach surrounded by simpering blond catamites:

"This citizen have a Latah he import from IndoChina. He figure to hang the Latah and send a Xmas TV short to his friends. So he fix up two ropes—one gimmicked to stretch, the other the real McCoy. But that Latah get up in feud state and put on his Santa Claus suit and make with the switcheroo. Come the dawning. The citizen put one rope on and the Latah, going along the way Latahs will, put on the other. When the traps are down the citizen hang for real and the Latah stand with the carny-rubber stretch rope. Well, the Latah imitate every twitch and spasm. Come three times.

"Smart young Latah keep his eye on the ball. I got him working in one of my plants as an expeditor."

Aztec priests strip blue feather robe from the Naked Youth. They bend him back over a limestone altar, fit a crystal skull over his head, securing the two hemispheres back and front with crystal screws. A waterfall pour over the skull snapping the boy's neck. He ejaculate in a rainbow against the rising sun.

Sharp protein odor of semen fills the air. The guests run hands over twitching boys, suck their cocks, hang on their backs like vampires.

Naked lifeguards carry in iron-lungs full of paralyzed youths.

Blind boys grope out of huge pies, deteriorated schizophrenics pop from a rubber cunt, boys with horrible skin diseases rise from a black pond (sluggish fish nibble yellow turds on the surface).

A man with white tie and dress shirt, naked from the waist down except for black garters, talks to the Queen Bee in elegant tones. (Queen Bees are old women who surround themselves with fairies to form a "swarm." It is a sinister Mexican practice.)

"But where is the statuary?" He talks out of one side of his face, the other is twisted by the Torture of a Million Mirrors. He masturbates wildly. The Queen Bee continues the conversation, notices nothing.

Couches, chairs, the whole floor begins to vibrate, shaking the guests to blurred grey ghosts shrieking in cock-bound agony.

Two boys jacking off under railroad bridge. The train shakes through their bodies, ejaculate them, fades with distant whistle. Frogs croak. The boys wash semen off lean brown stomachs.

Train compartment: two sick young junkies on their way to Lexington tear their pants down in convulsions of lust. One of them soaps his cock and works it up the other's ass with a corkscrew motion. "Jeeeeeeeeeeeeeeesus!" Both ejaculate at once standing up. They move away from each other and pull up their pants.

"Old croaker in Marshall writes for tincture and sweet oil."

"The piles of an aged mother shriek out raw and bleeding for the Black Shit. . . . Doc, suppose it was your mother, rimmed by resident leaches, squirming around so nasty. . . . De-active that pelvis, mom, you disgust me already"

"Let's stop over and make him for an RX."

The train tears on through the smoky, neon-lighted June night.

Pictures of men and women, boys and girls, animals, fish, birds, the copulating rhythm of the universe flows through the room, a great blue tide of life. Vibrating, soundless hum of deep forest—sudden quiet of cities when the junky copes. A moment of stillness and wonder. Even the Commuter buzzes clogged lines of cholesterol for contact.

Hassan shrieks out: "This is your doing; A.J.! You poopa my party!"

A.J. looks at him, face remote as limestone: "Uppa your ass, you liquefying gook."

A horde of lust-mad American women rush in. Dripping cunts, from farm and dude ranch, factory, brothel, country club, penthouse and suburb, motel and yacht and cocktail bar, strip off riding clothes, ski togs, evening dresses, levis, tea gowns, print dresses, slacks, bathing suits and kimonos. They scream and yipe and howl, leap on the guests like bitch dogs in heat with rabies. They claw at the hanged boys shrieking: "You fairy! You bastard! Fuck me! Fuck me! Fuck me!" The guests flee screaming, dodge among the hanged boys, overturn iron lungs.

A.J.: "Call out my Sweitzers, God damn it! Guard me from these she-foxes!"

Mr. Hyslop, A.J.'s secretary, looks up from his comic book: "The Sweitzers liquefy already."

(Liquefaction involves protein cleavage and reduction to liquid which is absorbed into someone else's protoplasmic being. Hassan, a notorious liquefactionist, is probably the beneficiary in this case.)

A.J.: "Gold-bricking cocksuckers! Where's a man without his Sweitzers? Our backs are to the wall, gentlemen. Our very cocks at stake. Stand by to resist boarders, Mr. Hyslop, and issue short arms to the men."

A.J. whips out a cutlass and begins decapitating the American Girls. He sings lustily:

Fifteen men on the dead man's chest Yo Ho Ho and a bottle of rum. Drink and the devil had done for the rest Yo Ho Ho and a bottle of rum.

Mr. Hyslop, bored and resigned: "Oh Gawd! He's at it again." He waves the Jolly Roger listlessly.

A.J., surrounded and fighting against overwhelming odds, throws back his head and makes with the hogcall. Immediately a thousand rutting Eskimos pour in grunting and squealing, faces tumescent, eyes hot and red, lips purple, fall on the American women.

(Eskimos have a rutting season when the tribes meet in short Summer to disport themselves in orgies. Their faces swell and lips turn purple.)

A House Dick with cigar two feet long sticks his head in through the wall: "Have you got a menagerie in here?"

Hassan wrings his hands: "A shambles! A filthy shambles! By Allah I never see anything so downright nasty!"

He whirls on A.J. who is sitting on a sea chest, parrot on shoulder, patch over one eye, drinking rum from a tankard. He scans the horizon with a huge brass telescope.

Hassan: "You cheap Factualist bitch! Go and never darken my rumpus room again!"

## John Rechy (b. 1934)

### FROM CITY OF NIGHT (1963)

In John Rechy's *City of Night* (1963) the social transgression signaled by the giddy drag and masquerade of *A Scarlet Pansy* is transformed into a new American homosexual transgressive genre — the super-sexual masquerade of the super-stud macho gay male, whose clones would dominate seventies' style. Because of its daring and often nearly lyric evocation of sex, no matter how lurid or tawdry it may have seemed to more orthodox reviewers, *City of Night* possesses an original and influential place in the inventive and transgressive tradition of American gay confrontational fiction. In *City of Night* the political and cultural differences between the straight world and the gay are subsumed in the highly charged atmosphere of sexual difference and homosexual desire, for though the hustlers who populate the book nearly all swear allegiance to the peculiar masculinized construction of American heterosexual values, their every act is informed by a politics of power, of dominance and subordination, that is entirely defined in homosexual terms.

FROM PART ONE

## CITY OF NIGHT

From the thundering underground—the maze of the New York subways—the world pours into Times Square. Like lost souls emerging from the purgatory of the trains (dark rattling tunnels, smelly pornographic toilets, newsstands futilely splashing the subterranean graydepths with unreal magazine colors), the newyork faces push into the air: spilling into 42nd Street and Broadway—a scattered defeated army. And the world of that street bursts like a rocket into a shattered phosphorescent world. Giant signs—Bigger! Than! Life!—blink off and on. And a great hungry sign groping luridly at the darkness screams:

F*A*S*C*I*N*A*T*I*O*N

I had been in the islandcity several weeks now, and already I had had two jobs, briefly: each time thinking now I would put down Times Square. But like a possessive lover—or like a powerful drug—it lured me. FASCINATION! I stopped working. . . . And I returned, dazzled, to this street. The giant sign winked its welcome: FASCINATION!

I surrendered to the world of Times Square, and like a hype who needs more and more junk to keep going, I haunted that world not only at night now but in the mornings, the afternoons. . . .

That world of Times Square that I inhabited extends from 42nd Street to about 45th Street, from grimy Eighth Avenue to Bryant Park—where, nightly, shadows cling to the ledges: malehungry looks hidden by the darkness of the night, and occasionally, shadowy figures, first speaking briefly, disappear in pairs behind the statue with its back to the library and come out after a few frantic moments, from opposite directions: intimate nameless strangers joined for one gasping brief space of time. Periodically the newyork cop comes by meanly swinging his stick superiorly, sometimes flashing his light toward the bushes—and the shadows scatter from the ledges, the benches, the trees—walking away aimlessly.

But that world exists not only along the streets; it extends into the movie theaters. And the moviehouse toilets on 42nd Street and the toilets in the subways—with the pleading scrawled messages—form the boiling subterranean world of Times Square. Steps lead down from the moviehouse lobbies as if into a dungeon—and in the toilet, the purpose may be realized, and you walk up the steps—aware of the danger after the danger is over—you and he complete strangers again after the cold intimacy. You may move from the dungeon into the cavern of the moviebalconies and try to score again: swallowed instantly by that giant wolfmouth of dark at the opening of which the dreamworld of a certain movie is being projected: the actors like ghosts from an altogether Different world. . . .

By now winter was approaching in New York. Hurricanes and threats of hurricanes had stopped, and the air was clear. Daily the leaves turned browner, the orange disappeared. Along the walks in the parks, leaves fell like rejected brown stars.

As the weather had changed, from hurricane warnings to cool, I had stood along 42nd Street and Bryant Park waiting to be picked up, and with the changing season

I felt a change within me too: a frantic lonesomeness that sometimes took me, para-doxically, to the height of elation, then flung me into depression. The figure of my Mother standing by the kitchen door crying, watching me leave, hovered ghostlike over me, but in the absence of that overwhelming tearing love—away from it if only physically—I felt a violent craving for something indefinable.

Throughout those weeks, on 42nd Street, the park, the moviehouses, I had learned to sift the different types that haunted those places: The queens swished by in superficial gayety—giggling males acting like teenage girls; eyeing the young-men coquettishly: but seldom offering more than a place to stay for the night. And I could spot the scores easily—the men who paid other men sexmoney, anywhere from $5.00—usually more—but sometimes even less (for some meals and drinks and a place to stay); the amount determined by the time of the day, the day of the week, the place of execution of the sexscene (their apartment, a rented room, a public toilet); their franticness, your franticness; their manner of dress, indicating affluence or otherwise; the competition on the street—the other youngmen sta-tioned along the block like tattered guards for that defeated army which, Somehow, life had spewed out, Rejected.

I found that you cant always tell a score by his age or appearance: There are the young and the goodlooking ones—the ones about whom you wonder why they pre-fer to pay someone (who will most likely at least not indicate desiring them back) when there exists—much, much vaster than the hustling world—the world of unpaid, mutually desiring males —the easy pickups. . . . But often the scores are near-middleaged or older men. And they are mostly uneffeminate. And so you learn to identify them by their method of approaching you (a means of identifica-tion which becomes instinctively surer and easier as you hang around longer). They will make one of the standard oriented remarks; they will offer a cigarette, a cup of coffee, a drink in a bar: anything to give them time in which to decide whether to trust you during those interludes in which there is always a suggestion of violence (although, for some, I would learn later, this is one of the proclaimed appeals—that steady hint of violence); time in which to find out if you'll fit their particular sexfantasy.

I learned that there are a variety of roles to play if you're hustling: young-manoutofajob butlooking; dontgiveadamnyoungman drifting; perrenialhustler easytomakeout; youngmanlostinthebigcity pleasehelpmesir. There was, too, the pose learned quickly from the others along the street: the stance, the jivetalk—a mixture of jazz, joint, junk sounds—the almost-disdainful, disinterested, but, at the same time, inviting look; the casual way of dress.

And I learned too that to hustle the streets you had to play it almost-illiterate.

The merchant marine at the Y had been the first to tell me that. With Mr. King I had merely acted instinctively. But I was to learn it graphically from a man I had met on Times Square. As he sat in his apartment studying me, I leafed through a novel by Colette. The man rose, visibly angered. "Do you read books?" he asked me sharply. "Yes," I answered. "Then Im sorry, I dont want you anymore," he said; "really masculine men dont read!" Hurriedly, his sexfantasy evaporated, he gave me a few bucks. Minutes later I saw him again on Times Square talking to another youngman. . . .

And so I determined that from now on I would play it dumb. And I would discover that to many of the street people a hustler became more attractive in direct relation to his seeming insensitivity—his "toughness." I would wear that mask.

By now, of course, I have met several of the shadows along Times Square.

There was Carlo, an actor, whom I met coming out of the subway head, who took me home and for a week came on strong—"helping me out": How sad that I should hang around the streets. If I move in with him, he'll give me Everything I Need. And when I was almost conned, he got a job in Hollywood, and, with apologies, split, giving me $5.00 that night—and a smiling! triumphant! goodbye! . . .

And Raub—a bastard—whose frog-shape and inclinations make me remember him as a "fraggot"—the fraggot with the enormous black-velvetdraped bed on Park Avenue: I was swiftly succeeded by, as I had very briefly succeeded, a string of others. . . . And there was Lenny from New Jersey, whom I saw twice a week, until one night he didn't show; and I learned later he'd been arrested for selling pornographic pictures.

There was, too, Im perversely glad to tell you, a cop met in an extension of the same world of 42nd Street. After midnight walking from the west to the east side, I crossed Central Park, and he was out rousting the bums sleeping in the park—the wagon parked a distance away. When he stopped me, I came on I was square: Just Now Came To The Big City. And he goes through the identification scene. Well, you havent really seen New York then," he said. "Maybe I can meet you somewhere on my day off and I'll show you around." I saw him a couple of times, but My Pride won out: To be with a cop—even for scoring—humiliated me, and that stopped.

## FROM PART THREE

### FROM NEIL: MASQUERADE

When the inevitable happened (which had lurked in my mind, and which at the same time—I am now sure, looking back on it—I had thought to thwart through that very contact with Neil: although I was becoming aware of perhaps the most elaborate of seductions—or, rather, I would become aware of it in retrospect: a seduction, through ego and vanity, of the very soul), when that inevitable happened, it happened swiftly like this:

I found Neil at home one late afternoon watching television: a western; the box set completely out of place in that bedroom suffused with the atmosphere of some dim past. I could tell that watching that program was such a ritual with him that I sat alone in the other room. Through the door, I could see him. He was dressed in full cowboy costume, replete with holster, gun. . . . As the sharp bang-bang! of the television villain's gun burst from the screen, Neil drew his own and made a motion of firing back.

When the program was over, we sat in the bedroom (he pushed the television set out of sight), drinking tea. . . . The manikins stared menacingly. Today, one was a military policeman; the other, whose costume I couldn't make out, was somberly dressed in black.

"We have a fine relationship, dont we?" Neil said.

The statement surprised me. The several times I had been with him since that afternoon with Carl—only briefly for lunch or dinner—I had felt an even greater tension and self-consciousness than before—especially since lately he had begun to talk to me in almost fatherly tones.

"Except," he went on, "that you hold back. Why? I *know* youre intrigued by Violence. I could sense your excitement when I presented you to the mirror. You saw yourself, Then, as you should be—as you would *like* to be!—as you *could* be! Out of my clothes, you know, youre very ordinary—like hundreds and hundreds of others. (Youre really not my cup of tea)," he added cuttingly. "But I can transform you—if you Let Yourself Go!" he exhorted me forcefully. "Let me!—and I'll open the door—Wide!—for you. Youll exist in My Eyes! I'll be a mirror! . . . Why should we fight our natures, which are meant to be violent?" he went on in the strangely gentle tones. "The past—with its grandeur, its nobility—yes, its purifying Violence—that was the time! It wasnt the 'compassionate' hypocrisy of our feeble day! he sneered. He rose to add a thicker belt to the dummy in black. (Almost every inch of the dummies is covered, except for the faces.)

He goes on, now speaking about the weak and the strong, how the former are to be used by the latter, extolling violence, drawing pictures of what his world would be like. "Power," he was saying. "Contempt!" he shouted. "Contempt for the weakness of compassion," he derides. . . .

Tense, cold in the warm afternoon, I found myself—although I didnt realize it until he said what he did next—automatically twisting the ring on my finger.

"Who gave you that ring?" he asked abruptly.

I hesitated to answer. Finally I said: "My father—a long time ago." Even to mention my father—to recall the memories of that ring—in the presence of this man suddenly seemed blasphemous.

Neil made a face of supreme disgust, and I felt anger mushrooming inside of me. "Things like that—which people cling to as memories," he said, "it's those things that keep men from realizing their True Nature. My movement will be an upheaval: Nothing is sacred, except Violence and Power. Sentimentality—false memories of tenderness— . . . Fathers, mothers!" he said contemptuously. "That ring you wear as a symbol of—whatever!" he spat.

My anger became hatred for him.

And did he sense this? And had he been counting on this? I didnt have time to consider that, because the scenes that follow will come suddenly like a movie in fast motion.

Suddenly Neil is crouching before me where I am sitting on the bed. He is sliding a pair of thick-soled, high-length studded boots onto my feet. I stare motionless at him as he winds a thick belt about my waist. (*I remember that other man in San Francisco: "You will eventually . . . if not with me, with someone else."*) This time, sensing my immediate mood—the mood he has cunningly put me into and will use—he will not even take the time to "dress me up" completely.

Swiftly he has flung himself on the floor, his head rubbing over the surface of the boots—the tongue licking them. He rolls on his back. His face looks up pleadingly at me.

Automatically responding (the anger, the hatred like a live gnawing thing inside

me)—feeling myself suddenly exploding with that all-enveloping hatred for him
(*has he counted on this? does he always?*) and also for what I know I will do at last
(senses magnetized on pinpoint), and, too, feeling a tidal-sweeping excitement at
the reflections from the mirror which he has carefully moved before the bed so that
it records from various angles the multiplied adoration of his face (an adoration
augmented shrewdly by the remembered hint, the challenge, of its possible withdrawal: "Out of my costumes you're very ordinary . . .)—his eyes as if about to burst
into flame, his tongue like an animal desperate to escape its bondage—I stand over
him as he reaches up grasping, urgently opening the fly of my pants.

"Please— . . . On me— . . . Please do it!" he pleaded.

And as the meaning of the tea looms in my mind, I realize suddenly what he
wants me to do. But I cant execute the humiliation he now craves. He rushed into
the bathroom, turned the water faucets on fullblast. "Do it," he pleads. . . .

The sound of the water, splashing. . . .

The scene reels in all the incomprehensible, impossible images that follow.

A gurgling in his throat—and he rises on his knees, face pressed against the wide
belt, which he unbuckled urgently with his teeth. Like a dog retrieving a stick and
bringing it back to its master, with his teeth clutching the buckle, he slid the belt
out of the pants straps—and he crouched on all fours brandishing the belt before
me, dangling it from his mouth extended beggingly toward me. "Use it, use it!" he
insisted.

Something inside me had been set aflame, a fire impossible to quench until it
has consumed all that it can burn: something aflame with the anger he had
counted on. I acted inevitably and as he had wanted all along: I pulled on the belt,
which he clung to with his teeth, so that, released, it snapped in a lashing sound
against his cheek, leaving its burning imprint. . . . He knelt there, eyes closed,
expectantly. . . .

I dropped the belt, which fell coiled beside him, the gleaming studs like staring
blind eyes on the floor. . . . He gnaws ravenously on the straps inside the tops of the
boots, falls back in one swift movement lying again on the floor as he reaches for
my legs with his hands, looping his fingers into the inside straps, bringing one studded boot pushed into his groin. He makes a sound of excruciating pain. Even then,
his hands will not release my foot, crushing it into his groin with more pressure.
"Harder!" he begs. "Please! *Do It Harder!!!*"

Rocked by currents inside me which sealed off this experience from anything
that had ever happened previously to me—aware all the time that it was I who was
being seduced by him—seduced into violence: that using the sensed narcissism in
me—and purposely germinating that hatred toward him—he had played with all
my hungry needs (magnified by the hint of the withdrawing of attention), had
twisted them in order to use them for his purposes, by unfettering the submerged
cravings carried to that inevitable extreme—and disassociating myself from all feelings of pity and compassion, to which—despite the compulsive determination to
stamp out all innocence within me and thereby to meet the world in its own savage terms; to leave behind that lulling, esoteric, life-shuttering childhood, that
once-cherished place by the window—to which, despite all those things, I had, I
know, still clung: to compassion, to pity—and knowing only that this was the

moment when I could crush symbolically (as in a dream once in which I had stamped out all the hatred in the world) whatever of innocence still remained in me (crush that and something else—something else surely lurking—but what?—what!!)—that at this moment I could prove irrevocably to the hatefully initiating world that I could join its rot, its cruelty—I saw my foot rise over him, then grind violently down as if of its own kinetic volition into that now pleading, most vulnerable part of that man's body. . . .

He let out a howl.

A dreadful sound hurled inhumanly like a bolt out of his throat—a plunging bolt which buried itself instantly within my mind. His face turned to one side as if he would bite the floor in pain. Tears came from his eyes in a sudden deluge which joined the perspiration and turned his face into a gleaming mask of pain. And he sobbed:

"Why . . . hurt? . . . Why . . . do you . . .? I . . . did . . . for you— . . . did everything! . . . Wanted— . . . want— . . . Why? . . . hurt . . . why? . . . Wanted lo— . . ."

Clenched teeth choked the word he had been about to utter.

The scene exploded in my mind. I was seized by the greatest revulsion of my whole life—a roiling, then a quick flooding invading my whole being like electricity; a maelstrom of revulsion—for myself, for him, loathing for him, for what he wanted done—loathing for what I was doing.

And hearing the racked baleful sobs which continue ("Why . . . hurt? . . ." And again the unfinished word: "Wanted—want lo— . . .")—seeing that writhing pitiful body, the boot pinioning him to the floor (like a worm! like a helpless worm! like a helpless worm tortured by children!)—seeing that face gleaming with tears and sweat—and feeling, myself, as if the world will now burst in a bright crashing light which will consume us both in judgment—I bent down over him, extending my hand to him—my foot removed from his scorched groin: extending my hand to him, to help him up—to help him!—as if he were the whole howling painracked ugly crushed mutilated, sad sad crying world, and I could now, at last, in that moment, by merely extending my hand to him in pity, help him—and It. Compassion flooded me as turbulently as, only seconds before, the seducing savagery had rocked me to my violated soul.

And as the man sobbing on the floor in the disheveled wet costume saw my hand extended to him in pity, the howling stopped instantly as if a switch had been turned off within him, and his look changed to one of ferocious anger.

And he shouted fiercely:

*"No, no! Youre not supposed to care!"*

# John Giorno (b. 1936)

*Pornographic Poem (1967)*

Seven Cuban
army officers
in exile
were at me
all night.

Tall,
sleek,
slender
Hispanic types
with smooth dark
muscular bodies
and hair
like wet coal
on their heads
and between their legs.
I lost count
of the times
I was fucked
by them
in every conceivable
position.
At one point
they stood
around me
in a circle
and I had
to crawl
from one crotch
to another
sucking
on each cock
until it was hard.
When I got all
seven up
I shivered
looking up
at those erect pricks
all different lengths
and widths
and knowing
that each one
was going up
my ass hole.
Everyone
came
at least twice
and some three times.
Once they put me
on the bed
kneeling,
one fucked me

in the behind,
another face fucked
my mouth
while I jacked off
one
with each hand
and two others
rubbed
their dicks
on my bare feet
waiting
their turns
to get
in my butt.
Just when I thought
they were all spent
two of them
got together
and fucked me
at once.
The positions
we were in
were crazy
but with two
big fat
Cuban cocks
up my ass
at one time
I was
in paradise.

## James Purdy (b. 1923)

James Purdy writes both with and against the grain of American homosexual life. In
*Malcolm* (1959) and *Eustace Chisolm and the Works* (1969) he created novels in which
homosexuality—if darkly, even dubiously perceived—was a constant obligato, though
rarely spoken. His poetry, not so well known as his novels, more directly addresses the
specifics of American homosexual life.

*Faint Honey*

Solitary hotel, I know you!
You have a ballroom
where boys of 15
dance under yellow globes
with men of 45.

None of the dancers are allowed to kiss
but close pressure slips by unnoticed.
When the dance hall closes
the boys depart with escorts,
and the 40-year old men,
exhausted, footsore
slump down at tables where
coffee is served
by 25-year old waiters
who were themselves once ballrooms boys.
Drinking cup after cup of cappuccino
the men catch again whiffs of
the shampooed scalps and
woodsy armpits
of the dancing boys.


## Do You Wonder Why I Am Sleepy

Last night it was already half past eleven
the doorbell rang.
Paul a young hustler barely 19
but with
body and face of a 14-year old
stood on my threshold.
Yes, I let him in
though I know he is
a profiteer.
Our relation is tense and tentative.
I never was one of his clients.
I know I should have sent him away,
but he went on sitting on the edge of the bed.
As I lay trying to sleep
he caressed and stroked my legs and feet.
I smiled and closed my eyes.
There followed a deep all-encompassing silence.
Suddenly without warning he flew away
like a little bird.
He was afraid
because I asked nothing of him.


## From rivers, and from the earth itself

From rivers, and from the earth itself
clouds and steam arise
like the breath of the lovers.

Sounds pass through walls
and spread through closed mansions.
Stiff cold penetrates to the bone.
Rising on his elbow, the younger boy
rolls back his foreskin
as he would his eyelid,
revealing the corona glandis
to his rapt companion.
The moon is after all a nocturnal sun.

# Part Nine
Out There

*American Literature from 1969*

# 29. Becoming Gay

## Out There: Gay American Literature

Much literature concerned with homosexuality from the late 1860s to the beginning of the Second World War accepted the dominant social, legal, and medical formulations of homosexuality as in some way a "condition," an anomaly, or a deviation. These writings accepted as just—or at least as inevitable—the repugnance that society generally and often vocally exhibited against homosexuality. A few writers were willing to recognize that sexual difference need not be a curse and could be a cause for celebration and indeed for the confrontation of what they were beginning to formulate as homophobia. But even these confrontations were often accomplished in books published in limited and/or privately printed editions. After the Wilde trial, some writers, even if advocating that homosexuality ought not to be criminalized or medically or morally stigmatized, still argued that, as a condition, it was something to be borne bravely without undue publicity. Others more cautiously urged quiet accommodation with homophobia or simply chose silence. Some others, perhaps despairingly dubious about the chance for an equal accommodation of homosexuality within a homophobic society, favored separatist fantasies, looking for the creation of an arcadian homosexual utopia. Some argued for the superiority—cultural, emotional, physical, and sexual—of homosexuality and urged its beneficial and even necessary place in modern life.

In the twentieth century, a handful of writers, insouciantly embracing theories about a third sex, chose to exaggerate rather than silence difference by creating outrageous camp masquerades, elaborating effeminacy in life and in literature as a transgressive and deconstructive style that questioned every received propriety that had heretofore defined sexual roles and identities. If definitions of manhood were in question, then other aspects of manhood—an exaggerated masculinity that opposed images of effeminacy, the sexually predatory or even criminal tendencies that were supposed to define "real" men—were chosen by some writers as those elements most to be celebrated, thus exhibiting in texts the very horrors that society fearfully imagined most attended upon homosexuality in life—promiscuity, terrible sexual perversions, criminality. Just prior to Stonewall some writers attempted to normalize homosexuals, turning them into images conforming to heterosexual norms so that they looked and acted like, indeed were, indistinguishable from other men—except that it was other men they desired.

Since Stonewall, American gay writers have inaugurated a debate that explores the personal and the social but especially the political implications of "coming out." Coming out in pre-Stonewall literature was only occasionally political—the important exceptions being *Don Leon's* anonymous author, Walt Whitman, John Addington Symonds, and Edward Carpenter—and even then the political element was subject to the imperatives and dangers attendant upon public exposure. Thus coming out in pre-Stonewall texts more often tended to be an essentially personal, private, and often anonymous enterprise. Even Whitman, who in "Calamus" clearly announced the necessary association between the political and the personal revelation of desire, was at first able to do so only by indirection and under the safe anonymity of the 1855 edition of *Leaves of Grass*.

Post-Stonewall writers, however, have moved coming out away from being a question of private recognition and acceptance and translated it into the realm of public political action, arguing that coming out is a necessary political act and the primary political weapon in the battle against homophobia. If gay literature after Stonewall celebrated the immediate intoxication of gay liberation, it soon turned to portraying the dizzying sexual and social choreography of the late 1970s and early 1980s: gay life—and what had come to be called a gay lifestyle—had suddenly become rich with the multiple possibilities of desire, a desire reflected in life in the ultra-masculine, outfront "clone"-style fashions of the seventies and eighties, which resolutely repudiated the more uptight elegance of the straight world's jacket and tie as well as the nelly effeminacy that characterized the pre-Stonewall gay's self-image. Some of the literature of the period in turn tended to reflect the dictates of gay fashion and sexual style in works that were themselves revelatory and promiscuous, exuberant and hiding nothing—and, some critics said, that also documented glamorous but empty lives that had only style and little meaning.

By the early to mid-eighties though, fashion and decor, all-night dancing and seemingly unlimited quantities of sex—but not the urgent need for liberation, self-identification, or the unmasking of homophobia—gave way to a dawning horror: the tragic reality of what eventually came to be known as Acquired Immune Deficiency Syndrome. To the devastation of AIDS gay writers responded with grief and rage, with renewed activism, and with writing that sought to find triumph or at least hope even in tragedy. After the mid-eighties—that is, after the initial fear and panic in the homosexual community occasioned by AIDS—writers shifted their focus from gay life as a fabulous fantasy of high style, mannered excess, and indiscriminate sensual/sexual fulfillment to one that at its most radical questioned the concept of gay identity itself. Some writers explored the mediation of inner and even spiritual life in connection with the demands of sexual identities and the immutable fact of AIDS. Others initiated wishful domestic fantasies and family fictions—their own brand of arcadian romance—in an attempt to remodel images of gay life. For if gay life was once imagined to be all glitter, style, and excessive flamboyance, with uninhibited rituals enacted in discos, backrooms, and dinner parties from San Francisco to Manhattan to Fire Island, some new gay books now abandoned all that luminosity to reveal smaller and sometimes darker human dramas taking place in gritty and often anonymous neighborhoods or in the living rooms and around the kitchen tables of middle and ethnic America. Now, on the tense ground where race and homosexual identity converged, literature by African-American writers questioned the relationship and the priorities of being gay *and* black.

These writings are especially poignant and seminal in a world that had been largely the uncontested province of white gay men. Some gay writers have preferred to avoid or ignore the term *gay* entirely in their work, showing little interest in the ideal of Stonewall, or of gay pride and coming out, or in exploring gay culture, choosing instead to practice in their craft what some critics described as a more universal vision but which more activist critics denounced as simply another closet. From academia some writers engaged in worrisome and theorized clashes over the indeterminacies of gender. This last project also influenced gay literary writing, and for certain writers "gay" became "queer," while for others *queer* remained a term poisoned by memories that no co-option could erase.

## AMERICAN LITERATURE AFTER STONEWALL

In the early seventies much gay literature was self-published or gathered in poetry anthologies like Ian Young's *The Male Muse* (1973) or the groundbreaking collections published by Winston Leyland's Gay Sunshine Press or by Felice Picano's Seahorse Press or in the pages of *Fag-Rag* or *Christopher Street* or books published by Alyson Press. Later, in anthologies of gay fiction like the multivolumed Men on Men series (New York: New American Library, 1986–), edited by George Stambolian and more recently by David Bergman, gay literature moved from the margins into the mainstream when prominent publishing houses began to publish gay books. Edmund White, Felice Picano, Andrew Holleran, Michael Grumley, Robert Ferro, Christopher Cox, George Whitmore—the members of the Violet Quill, gay literature's most famous and seminal East Coast writing group—defined a direction for gay fiction in the eighties. In poetry, Walta Borawski, Alfred Corn, Edward Field, Essex Hemphill, Jim Everhard, Daryl Hine, Michael Lassell, Carl Morse, and Assotto Saint all appeared in Carl Morse and Joan Larkin's pathbreaking anthology *Gay and Lesbian Poetry in Our Time* (1988), while Hemphill, Michael Smith, Joseph Beam, and Assoto Saint each made major contributions in their own writing or in anthologies which they edited, publishing among others Melvin Dixon, Donald Woods, and Samuel R. Delaney—thus documenting the contribution of people of color to gay writing. The poetry of Morse, Picano, Perry Brass, and, especially, the remarkable life work of Thom Gunn joins that of Allen Ginsberg as important contributions to the history of all American poetry.

In the eighties, too, the plays of Robert Patrick, Richard Hall, Harvey Fierstein, William Hoffman, Lanford Wilson, Terence McNally, Larry Kramer, and Doric Wilson opened the American theater to gay drama and prepared the way for Tony Kushner's Pulitzer Prize and Tony Award-winning "gay fantasia," *Angels in America*. In fiction the work of Armistead Maupin, Christopher Coe, Dale Peck, Richard Hall, Ethan Mordden, Brad Gooch, Jaime Manrique, and David Leavitt have fulfilled the mandate of writers like Edmund White and Felice Picano, which insisted that gay writing must leap beyond the self-imposed limitations of a merely sexual identity and explore the wider aspects of gay sensibility and political engagement—and which also directed that gay writing must *always* be among the best writing that America produced.

In its recent and triumphant incursion into the mainstream of American literature, not to mention the economic mainstream of American publishing, modern gay literature has come to occupy an increasingly central place and indeed a cautionary one in American and in world letters. American gay literature has been seminal and influential in world literatures, for just as gay liberation after Stonewall was the source for the vocabulary of gay liberationist movements throughout the world, so American gay literature has provided similar inspiration to writers in other national literatures to challenge their own forms of national and literary homophobia. Further, though more addressed to academe than to the greater public, gay studies centering on the recovery of gay male literature and history have also entered the list of combatants against homophobia and, in a sometimes uneasy though fertile dialogue with feminism and lesbian studies, has initiated a major reevaluative project that ambitiously aims to critique and if need be alter or deconstruct all previous interpretations of homosexualities in all academic disciplines (often enrolling this project within the confrontational discipline of queer studies). In America, gay literature is a mirror that reflects not only the lives, actions, and attitudes of gay people but of nongay people as well, and the true reflection of America seen there, while not always kind, is often profound and sometimes unnerving. In gay texts America's greatest fear and deepest terror—difference—is constantly reevaluated, anatomized, not infrequently satirized, and indeed often uncomfortably and even corrosively portrayed. Gay literature has become a standard against which the unexamined certainties of all American nonhomosexual literature must now be measured.

It is clear that no anthology—let alone a section of a larger one—can reprint even a fraction of the list of contemporary gay writers, nor can a brief historical commentary adequately explore it. I have therefore decided to let the following texts speak for themselves as commentaries on the times. The selection is more emblematic than inclusive, a snapshot rather than a full-scale portrait of the decades since Stonewall as seen in some of the texts of those times. No survey of gay literature since 1969 can do justice to the diversity, the multicultural breadth, the imaginative originality of the work of all those participating in a literary project that has attempted to do no less than rewrite in modern terms the definition of love between men and to confront with the potency of the word a millennium of homophobia.

## Further Reading

Roger Austen, *Playing the Game: The Homosexual Novel in America* (New York: Bobbs-Merrill, 1977); Adam Barry, *The Rise of a Gay and Lesbian Movement* (Boston: Twayne, 1987); David Bergman, *Gaiety Transfigured: Gay Self-Representation in American Literature* (Madison: University of Wisconsin Press, 1991); George Chauncey, *Gay New York: Gender, Urban Culture, and the Making of the Gay Male World, 1890–1940* (New York: Basic Books, 1994); Martin Duberman, *Stonewall* (New York: Dutton, 1993); Byrne R. S. Fone, *A Road To Stonewall: Homosexuality and Homophobia in English and American Literature, 1750–1969* (New York: Macmillan/Twayne, 1995); Jonathan Ned Katz, *Gay American History* (New York: Thomas Y. Crowell, 1976), and *Gay/Lesbian Almanac* (New York: Harper and Row, 1983); James Levin, *The Gay Novel in America* (New York: Garland, 1991); Robert K. Martin, *The Homosexual Tradition in American Poetry* (Austin and London: University of Texas Press, 1979).

## Questions

### Ralph Pomeroy (b. 1926)

*Gay Love and the Movies (1969)*

Watching love stories on TV,
watching a movie,
I wonder where we are.
I've wondered for a long time.
I've never seen any of us there,
straight on, like nouvelle vague lovers,
like psychedelic dancers.
I've never seen us, arms akimbo,

standing in the morning, waiting,
lying around in grassy meadows,
reeling in the pounding surf in a
burst of sunshine—
pale colors out of focus
or in focus, bright colors,
black and whites . . .

Where have we been all this time?
Where are we now, the right now which
we're living?—Dark boy and blond boy
up there no different than any two people together.

I've wondered sometimes if that's what
it feels like to be black—
looking on all the time at exquisite or
banal white rituals:—
the car racing along the curves of the Riviera,
Miss Crawford striding despairingly in full
sequins into suicidal waters—
but have been caught up short wondering
if a black would be offended by such a comparison.

So where do we go to see what we know exists?
Other than some campy enclave—the "in" resort
or "special" bar?
How feel or develop good longings,
good works, good words,
to make into poems or plays or novels
or songs or movies
that will celebrate our realities?

And where can we go to see,
like everybody else, those untrue-true,
crescendo-ridden technicolor fables
which begin by accident,
as do all true love stories,
and end in death,
as do all men's affairs?

# Answers

## William Barber (b. 1947)

*The Gay Poet* (1971)

I have broken the sound barrier of morality

with one crunchy bite on the phallic biscuit.
In my boyish womanhood, with my soul in drag,
I have been personal concubine to hundreds
of queens and princes, mistress of many
hedonists, lover of all.

I have pricked, prodded, pampered and pumped,
held my knees to my ears in the amyl twilight
and gone totally and obtusely mad, because
one halfway beautiful man weighed
a thousand tons on my fragile psyche.
My anima is stripped by the sight of my
wrinkled ego hanging out his back pocket
always two steps ahead of me.

I will go on, unknown lovers in my future,
I will be there, waiting with my mouth in my hand
to show you the ways into my body/being,
curling my wits to help you laugh out your orgasms,
but I am totally insane
because one of you, one too many of you
walked out that morning with all my reason
crumpled inside your tawny levis.


*Explanation*

I am not gay by your definition.
I will not stand in the drab beige men's room
like a fern watered with urine,
and wait for penises. I'm sorry.
Morality will just have to change.

I speak directly to the sons of
your officials, under the moon,
with the professors listening.
We have burned the closet door in effigy.
There will be no more watching for the feet
of policemen under the partitions.

          Nor
the mediocrity of masses of shuffling gays
in the dark bars, ghettoed and ethnic.

I love men. I tell them so directly.
Wherever we encounter, there are no categories.

## Perry Brass (b. 1947)

*Only Silly Faggots Know (1973)*

—Only Silly Faggots Know only faggots know
only silly faggots know
pain, nights and nights of dark
streets, rain, raining alone
and parks full of crocodiles
Men who beat up faggots know crocodiles
eat men slowly, little by little bit by bit
and shit them out into the dark sewage water
of jungles without flowers—but
only silly faggots know and know and know
and see and see and see cha-cha down the streets of tinsel
and dinosaur rhinestone teeth and know and know and know
what only silly faggots know and drugs don't know
and Men who beat up faggots don't know
and faggots from the Stock Exchange don't know
and faggots from Abercrombie and Fitch don't know
and faggots from the Metropolitan Opera don't know

but the subways at three o'clock in the morning know
and Christopher Street at 4 a.m. knows
and the baths too exhausted to care
and too exalted to give up know
and split the sides with tell-it-all
tell-it-all tell-it-all tell-it-all
because that's what we're here for
and that's why I love you
because you do know
where I have been and you have walked with me
through the mined crocodile fields
and passed the straight apes on the street corners
and gone through the morning hours with me, afraid
oh, sooooo afraid,
but not turned-off, not to turn back
but to reach for me
to reach out for me sitting here
when I needed you
because only you know.

*I Have This Vision of Madness (1972)*

I have this vision of madness:
dear gay brothers,

please get out of the trucks,
the sun is rising,
before it is too late.
Make lines, hold hands
and form a procession out to the sea;
when the sun rises
turn around and face each other
ask where the day goes
and
what have you done with the time?
Some of you will answer,
"but what about astrology,
where is the moon, now
that the sun has risen?"
"And what about my hair. Is it too long?
Should I have it cut?"
"What about my clothes,
are they the right style,
does my ass show to its best advantage?"
but
the moon will cover your body,
the sun, the sun will linger
and dwindle . . . until all becomes
endless words only meant
to cover your nakedness.
Strike out and go mad.
Frozen with fear, eyes blinding mad
detest everything that holds you apart from me:
an end to fantasy
an end to innocence
an end to everything that
is not pure and fantastic.
The poignant hour of the day has come
when evening tells its own story
when you go out of your house
to find your true love
in the banana forests
in the rain gardens of Central Park
in the steaming beaches of baths and bars
when the heat of desire has frozen
your lust, has bent your heart
into a thousand masturbatory images
that cannot be fulfilled
and only some urgent insanity
some call to reach and touch and reach back
will find me waiting in the lobby of your heart

all the time hoping that
you will come, full of rage
and crazy kindness.

## Harold Norse (b. 1916)

*I'm Not a Man (1972)*

I'm not a man. I can't earn a living, buy new things for my
family. I have acne and a small peter.

I'm not a man. I don't like football, boxing and cars.
I like to express my feelings. I even like to put an arm
around my friend's shoulder.

I'm not a man. I won't play the role assigned to me—the role
created by Madison Avenue, Playboy, Hollywood and Oliver
Cromwell. Television does not dictate my behavior. I am under
5 foot 4.

I'm not a man. Once when I shot a squirrel I swore that I would
never kill again. I gave up meat. The sight of blood makes me
sick. I like flowers.

I'm not a man. I went to prison resisting the draft. I do not
fight back when real men beat me up and call me queer. I dislike
violence.

I'm not a man. I have never raped a woman. I don't hate blacks.
I do not get emotional when the flag is waved. I do not think
I should love America or leave it. I think I should laugh at it.

I'm not a man. I have never had the clap.

I'm not a man. Playboy is not my favorite magazine.

I'm not a man. I cry when I'm unhappy.

I'm not a man. I do not feel superior to women.

I'm not a man. I don't wear a jockstrap.

I'm not a man. I write poetry.

I'm not a man. I meditate on peace and love.

I'm not a man. I don't want to destroy you.

## Edward Field (b. 1924)

*Street Instructions at the Crotch (1975)*

> It is not against the law to grope yourself
>     D.D.T.

> Remember yourself
>     —Gurdjieff

While walking toward housewife wheeling baby
reach down and squeeze your cock,
looking at her casually.
Adjust cock from left side to right
causing half hard-on,
then shift it back.

Wear balls on one side, cock on other.

Tug at crotch of pants as if to free genitals
tangled in underwear.
Give it a good tugging.
Go out without underwear.

Make small tear in bulge of basket
exposing skin.
Sew patch on crudely.

Wear pants of some material
flimsy as the law allows.

Go out with fly unzipped.
Go out with fly half unbuttoned.
Break zipper and fasten with safety pin.
Rip crotch and sew with large jagged stitches.

While talking with friends
unzip fly, lower pants, and arrange shirt tails.

Ask policeman for directions
and while he's telling you
give yourself a feel.

Walk loosely
to give yourself as much stimulation as you can.
Let it all move.
Be there.

## Kenneth Pitchford (b. 1931)

*Surgery (1973)*

So now, just suppose that someone wanted to know
if faggots are men—a fair question.
Would I then trot out all the masculinists I have known
who are homosexual
and show how they did and do and will oppress women and
are certainly male supremacist, no less than I,
or should that be no more?—which is not even to speak
of hideous straight men with their most of the most.
And then should I apologize
about how long we've existed and haven't had any
consciousness to speak of
but have allowed them to kill Oscar Wilde with that longdrawnout
    torture
from which he died
and have allowed them to keep on using J. Edgar Hoover against us
without anyone's avenging that suffering life from
the death-brain they clamped over him as a child,
not to speak of Hart Crane, and here fill in your long
list of faggots murdered by the hatred of straight men,
and how Andy Warhol can make millions only by
showing how disgusting faggots are.
If he showed anything else—how beautiful, how usual, how human—
no dough.
No, faggots aren't not men. It's just that they
tried to cut something out of us very early on,
and sometimes succeeded, sometimes failed,
and they have counted ever since on the quarrel that got set up
between those they damaged and those who escaped what they meant
to do (whatever other damages got done escaping that one).
And I care so much about the part of me they wanted to kill
that I will risk any death to continue cherishing that part—
listen how it sings along in forbidden music and poetry,
listen how it sings inside a man when, stroking another man's brow,
he even experiments with meaning it for a full minute.
When they came with their knife, I lied as sincerely as I knew how,
saying Oh yes, I do hate girls and dolls and singing and picking
flowers and drawings and dancing,
and they went away and didn't cut that out of me,
although they beat me up every time
they caught it ulping out of me afterwards.
I don't really want this body or any other,
I don't know who I might hope could hold my hand and
walk half a block with me without needing to say anything.

But if it isn't you, my fellow faggot hearing or reading this, then
I'm in a bad way, because faggots are men, or else they'd have killed
and who else am I to share that knowledge with
if not you? Learning to love
in each other The Other no other way.
And I want to have that taste in my mouth before they catch me
and lock me
away (sanatorium/crematorium): my own warm
blood welling up arrogant and fanatic from having told
the last unutterable truth about how I know they've already failed
and are going to die and how all that will be left afterwards
will be wild gigantic whorls of purple-green fingerpaint colors
dancing as though to an effeminist etude,
my very atoms indestructibly subversive
of everything they did to me.
The only way they might have succeeded is if
they could have cut out of my body
the whole universe infolded there under amnion like
a bud or a tumor.
No wonder they failed.
They wouldn't even know what the universe looks like, much
less how to spell it.

## Joseph Cady (b. 1938)

*After Hearing Heterosexual Poets in October 1974: What It Seems Like To Write a Male Homosexual Love Poem Now (1974)*

*for Joseph Chaikin*
It is to be without the staple references
    of male heterosexual poets.

It is to be without a wife whose beauty and faithfulness
    can be mentioned convivially to audiences at readings.
It is to be without a son whose discovery of the world
    can be turned into a parable of the loss of innocence
    that demonstrates our wonder and sorrow
It is to be without an exhaustive history of mistresses,
    whose delicious parts can be listed as marks of our lustiness
    or whose riddle can be claimed as the source of our pain.

It is to cut the ties of such familiar images,
to start again at the first cries of speech,
over and over, inventing our voices,
until our unheard-of testimony
transforms the understanding of reality irrevocably.

New language
in amazement
from this plain statement:
I am a man; you are a man; I love you.

## Joe Brainard (b. 1942)

*I Remember (1975)*

I remember when, in high school if you wore green and yellow on Thursday it meant that you were queer.

I remember when, in high school I used to stuff a sock in my underwear.

I remember "queers can't whistle."

I remember the skinny guy who gets sand kicked in his face in body-building ads.

I remember how much I used to stutter.

I remember how little your dick is getting out of a wet bathing suit.

I remember daydreams of a doctor who (on the sly) was experimenting with a drug that would turn you into a real stud. All very "hush-hush." (As it was illegal.) There was a slight chance that something might go wrong and that I'd end up with a really giant cock, but I was willing to take that chance.

I remember my first sexual experience in a subway. Some guy (I was afraid to look at him) got a hardon and was rubbing it back and forth against my arm. I got very excited and when my stop came I hurried out and home where I tried to do an oil painting using my dick as a brush.

I remember when I had a job cleaning out an old man's apartment who had died. Among his belongings was a very old photograph of a naked young boy pinned to an old pair of young boy's underwear. For many years he was the choir director at church. He had no family or relatives.

I remember how many other magazines I had to buy in order to buy one physique magazine.

I remember jerking off to sexual fantasies of Troy Donahue

with a dark tan in a white bathing suit down by the ocean. (From a movie with Sandra Dee)

I remember sexual fantasies of seducing young country boys. (But old enough) Pale and blond and eager.

I remember the way John Kerr was always flexing his jaw muscles in "South Pacific."

I remember that Rock Hudson and Charlie Chaplin and Lyndon Johnson have "giant cocks."

I remember magazine pictures of very handsome male models with perfect faces and, with an almost physical pang, wondering what it would be to look like that. (Heaven)

I remember those sexy little ads in the back of Esquire magazine of skimpy bathing suits and underwear with enormous baskets.

I remember the first time I met Frank O'Hara. He was walking down Second Avenue. It was a cool early Spring evening but he was wearing only a white shirt with the sleeves rolled up to his elbows. And blue jeans. And moccasins. I remember that he seemed very sissy to me. Very theatrical. Decadent. I remember that I liked him instantly.

I remember Frank O'Hara's walk. Light and sassy. With a slight bounce and a slight twist. It was a beautiful walk. Confident. "I don't care." And sometimes "I know you are looking."

I remember seeing Frank O'Hara write a poem once. We were watching a western on TV and he got up as tho to fix a drink or answer the telephone but instead he went over to the typewriter, leaned over it a bit, and typed for 4 or 5 minutes standing up. Then he pulled the piece of paper out of the typewriter and handed it to me and then lay back down to watch more TV. (The TV was in the bedroom) I don't remember the poem except that it had some cowboy dialect in it.

I remember not liking myself for not picking up boys I probably could pick up because of the possibility of being rejected.

I remember deciding at a certain point that I would cut through all the bull shit and just go up to boys I liked and say "Do you want to go home with me?" and so I tried it. But it didn't work. Except once, and he was drunk. The next morning he left a card behind with a picture of Jesus on it signed "with love, Jesus" on the back. He said he was a friend of Allen Ginsberg.

I remember tight white pants. Certain ways of standing. Blond heads of hair. And spotted bleached blue jeans.

I remember pretty faces that don't move.

I remember (recently) getting blown while trying to carry on a normal conversation on the telephone, which, I must admit, was a big turn-on somehow.

I remember fantasizing about being a super-stud and being able to shoot enormous loads. And (would you believe it?) (yes, you'll believe it) I still do.

# Celebrations

### Adrian Brooks (b. 1947)

*[Here is the queen . . . ] (1975?)*

Here is the queen
getting ready for a party.
He stands in the bathroom
pinning a flower in his hair.
It is a silk rose.
He touches his collarbone—
ascertains its definition:
He will wear something
with a low front.
At the mirror
he powders his face.
He surveys it like virgin land
ready for development.
He pencils thin brows
and views his progress.
There's a lot to do.
Our queen must leave in five minutes.
He adds green to the eyelids
finds the rouge and colors
the white base.
The queen stands back:
He darkens the lips.

He decides the rose is too much
and adds rhinestone clips.
It's starting to work.
The eyes darken—
lines are extended.
Quick dabs of sandalwood
at the wrist, elbow and neck—
It's getting *hot*.
A vamp replaces the country lass
(not for the first or last time).
One minute to touch down
the queen slips into a white satin dress
and brushes his hair
away from his face.
Transformation is complete.
A creature of the night
ready to enter the neon arena
picks up the raincoat
throws it over the satin dress
and trips out the door
on his way toward the glory of sidewalks
and the light of passing cars.
Out on the street
the queen moves between lamplight
and shadows
as if drawn to a magnet
invisible to the naked eye.
If you listen carefully
you can hear the rustle of a gown
on castle stairs—
the wheels of imaginary carriages
rattling along cobblestone streets
toward a fatal rendez-vous.
The queen cruises past the donut shop.
His legs—inside the satin gown—
are coming alive.
His body is electric again
he is living cinema—
only distantly related
to this century.

## Michael Rumaker (b. 1932)

*The Fairies Are Dancing All Over the World (1975)*

The fairies are dancing all over the world
    In the dreams of the President

they are dancing
   although he dares not mention this at cabinet meetings
In the baby blood of the brandnew
    they are dancing O most rapturously
and over the graves of the fathers and mothers
    who are dead
and around the heads of the mothers and fathers who are not dead
  in celebration of the sons and daughters
    they've given the earth
The fairies are dancing in the paws and muzzles
  of dogs larking in the broad field next to the church
The fairies have always danced in the blood of the untamed
    in the muscular horned goat
    and the shining snake
  in the blood of Henry Thoreau
    and most certainly Emily Dickinson
And they skip in the blood of the marine recruit
  in his barracks at night
    his bones aching with fatigue and loneliness
   and pure dreams of women
      and his goodbuddy in the next bunk
They are most lovely in the eyes of the black kid
    trucking in front of the jukebox
      at the local pizzeria,
more timorous in the eyes of his white friend
    whose hips are a bit more calcified
with hereditary denunciation of the fairies
    May the fairies swivel his hips
On sap green evenings in early summer
     the fairies danced under the moon in country places
    danced among native american teepees
and hung in the rough hair of buffalos racing across the prairies
     and are dancing still
       most hidden
     and everywhere
In some, only in the eyes
  in others a reach of the arm
    a sudden yelp of joy
 reveals their presence
The fairies are dancing from coast to coast
  all over deadmiddle America
     they're bumping and grinding on the Kremlin walls
   the tap of their feet is eroding all the walls
    all over the world as they dance
In the way of the western world
    the fairies' dance has become small

a bleating, crabbed jerkiness
but there for all that,
   a bit of healthy green in the dead wood
       that spreads an invisible green fire
  around and around the globe
encircling it in its dance
   of intimacy with the secret of all living things
The fairies are dancing even in the Pope's nose
    and in the heart of the most stubborn macho
  who will not and will not
    and the fairies will
      most insistently
   because he will not
In the Pentagon the fairies are dancing
    under the scrambled egg hats
   of those who see no reason why youths should live to old age
The fairies bide their time and wait
   They dance in invisible circlets of joy
    around and around and over the planet
They are the green rings unseen by spaceships
    their breath is the earth of the first spring evening
They explode in the black buds of deadwood winter
      Welcome them with open arms
    They are allies courting in the bloodstream
    welcome them and dance with them

## Alfred Corn (b. 1943)

*Billie's Blues (1977)*

Their red lamps make a childlike stab
At decadence. Now and again a hoot
That pretends to know too much. And all
Of us jammed tight together in
The clubbiness of drinking. Gauged pressures
Of a hip, an elbow, mean whatever—
Nothing, or the first step toward
A glance, an appraisal, a mirrored
Interest. Also, a mirror reflects
Shiny bottles and the company behind
One's back: studied nonchalance, arched
Or puzzled brows, tight jackets, scratching
Of a beard. Cliches from the juke box
Suddenly ring true; so that I leave
The bar—and none too steady—for
A corner table a mosquito candle
Beacons me to. There. A relief

To have stopped being after anything.
Who needs it? Besides, one cruises
Mainly to cruise, navigating from island
To island, not counting on landfalls—
Though in fact I met you in a place
Much like this. You. So often
I've thought the word in that upper case
We use for what is one of a kind.
Thought, and sometimes written; wondering
Whether dispensing with names,
An apparent gender, showed, oh,
Cowardice, betrayal; or good sense.
I always wrote to You, supposing
The alert would catch on anyway.
And not wanting to seem a special case
Myself–though who isn't one? Holiday,
For example; with her ambiguous first name.
Nothing vague about the voice, certainly.
Listen: love mixed with a little hate for
Him. Sounds universal to me.

*To Hermes*

Lord Quicksilver, god of erections, come down
in your winged Nikes, your hard-hat brilliant
as an oiled mirror, and lend some assistance.
I have a young partner, handsome and eager,
whose love I want, whose pleasure pleases me.
When a smile as mischievous as his seems to ask
for a second round or a third, naturally
every spurred nerve aches to pump up the tempo,
like a dark horse the last heat of the day,
sweatsoaked and burning to win. My age, though,
men are long past the satyrs we once were,
flesh quickens or not after its own will or whim.
Now, I have no use for clever devices; so take
your wand (its twin snakes intertwined like vines),
touch my equipment, and work your famous magic.
If you do this, I will free two doves in your name
to fly beside you on your early morning errands.
Divine messenger boy, send me like a letter,
a fox to its burrow, a hand in its silk-lined glove.
Let me keep unwavering purpose—to embody feeling
till all the senses answer, blazing the path to our own
Olympus, no medal like the light in each other's eye.

## John Iozia

*Fag Art (1976)*

Fag art sucks.
Fag art takes it up the ass.

Fag art will make you go
To the Eagle's Nest Saturday nights,
Put five dollars in the jukebox
And sniff poppers while
Cruising Jack Brusca.

Fag Art will make you
Change your clothes a lot
At Fire Island.

Gay Art will make you play
Inez Foxx 45s at 33rpm
And make you think it's a man
Singing about another man.

Fag Art will make you squander
Your most profound insights
On Vince Aletti's sex life.

Fag Art will drive you to writing
Manifestoes in subway tea rooms.

Fag Art is not only queer at night,
It's queer during the day
When you don't want to think about it.

Fag Art is a wet dream
You'll never be able to explain
If you've got a dick in your mouth.


*Last Night at the Flamingo (1978)*

There were two thousand queens last night at the Flamingo.
Before the sun came up they dropped a thousand dollars
in drugs on the dance floor.

Eighteen superb mixes got sixty thousand oohs and
Forty thousand aahs last night at the Flamingo.

Two queens got six replays on a pinball machine

As I stared at the Rockola jukebox next to them
Last night at the Flamingo.

Two hundred and twenty-eight egos were destroyed
Last night at the Flamingo.

Forty thousand cigarettes were smoked
Last night at the Flamingo.
Thirty five thousand of them were menthol.
The rest were Mafia.

Seven queens forgot where they were
At least half the evening
Last night at the Flamingo.

Ten thousand plastic cups
Were flung to the floor

As six thousand cups of coffee disappeared
Last night at the Flamingo.

Four thousand sleeping pills were swallowed
In a masturbatory rush of self-administration
Last night at the Flamingo.

Seventeen hysterectomies were performed
Last night at the Flamingo.

I saw one queen checking hemlines
Behind a banquet
Last night at the Flamingo.

Twenty people fell out of the booth
Last night at the Flamingo.

Eight thousand questions were asked
And nine thousand answered
Last night at the Flamingo.

A thousand conversations
Drowned in music
Last night at the Flamingo.

Thirty-seven queens changed their clothes
At least twice last night at the Flamingo.

Five hundred phone numbers

And seven hundred promises
Changed partners
Last night at the Flamingo.

Eight hot records, so new
They're not even on the radio yet
Produced a thousand yawns
Last night at the Flamingo.

Two people fell in love
with each other
Last night at the Flamingo.

The seeds of eight thousand orgasms
In three downtown bath houses
Were planted last night at the Flamingo.

Three hundred-fifty bottles of Ethyl Chloride
Were consumed by six hundred white goddesses
On a honky-tonk safari
Last night at the Flamingo.

At least one person passed out
Last night at the Flamingo.
Unfortunately, I was dancing with him
And didn't get to see who it was.

Fluctuations in the price of life
Caught my eye last night at the Flamingo
And several bids couldn't survive introductions.

On my way home I spotted two queens
Licking the pavement outside the door
Last night at the Flamingo.

When I brought my white pants to the cleaner today,
He asked me if I'd been rolling around with the pigs.
"No," I said, "Last night I was at the Flamingo."

## Andrew Holleran (b. 1943?)

FROM *DANCER FROM THE DANCE* (1978)

The chapters selected depict the drop-dead gorgeous Malone as he dances through Manhattan and Fire Island gay life and look at the end and aftermath of his idyllic affair with the equally drop-dead handsome Frankie. In chapter four Malone encounters Sutherland, a Very Grand Queen. The story—perhaps the most lyric and pointed description of late 1970s gay life—is told by a narrator who is nearly as grand and surely as royal as Sutherland. *Dancer from the Dance* appeared in the same year as Larry Kramer's *Faggots* and Edmund White's *Nocturnes for the King of Naples*. Instead of being published by small gay presses, all three books were published by large "trade" houses, marking a commercial breakthrough for gay novels. All three detail a white and urban gay community and all three construct a cosmopolitan picture of sexually uninhibited gay life that would provide both legend and historical reality in the creation of gay men's images of themselves and their lives in the seventies and pre-AIDS eighties. Of the three, it may be *Dancer* that best captures the almost mythic quality of that period ten years after Stonewall that now appears to be at once the most intense and perhaps the final chapter in the heady intoxication of post-Stonewall gay life.

## CHAPTER 1

He was just a face I saw in a discotheque one winter, but it was I who ended up going back to Fire Island to pick up his things. Now my father used to say, and I agree: There is nothing so unhappy as going through the clothes of a friend who has died, to see what may be used and what should be given to charity.

But Malone was hardly even a friend, something much more, and much less, perhaps—and so it felt odd to be traveling out there yesterday afternoon. It was a fine autumn day, the last week of October, and as the taxi drove from the train station in Sayville to the docks, that village had never looked more attractive. There was an unspoken celebration in the very silence, of the end of that long summer season, when a hundred taxis a day like ours crisscrossed the streets between the train station and the docks, taking the inhabitants of Manhattan across that shallow bay to their revelries on the beach of Fire Island. It was a journey between islands, after all: from Manhattan, to Long Island, to Fire Island, and the last island of the three was nothing but a sandbar, as slim as a parenthesis, enclosing the Atlantic, the very last fringe of soil on which a man might put up his house, and leave behind him all—absolutely all—of that huge continent to the west. There are New Yorkers who boast they've never been west of the Hudson, but the exhausted souls who went each weekend of summer to their houses on that long sandbar known among certain crowds as the Dangerous Island (dangerous because you could lose your heart, your reputation, your contact lenses), they put an even more disdainful distance between themselves and America: free, free at last.

Well, now the village of Sayville had been left in perfect peace. The strenuous season was behind, and as the taxi drove, more slowly, through the puddles of sunlight and crimson leaves, we passed one tableau after another of small-town life. Kids were playing football in the town park, and another football game swept across the high school field, and boys on bicycles were drawing lazy circles in the supermarket parking lot, and families were out in their backyards raking leaves. It was the sort of scene Malone turned sentimental over. He always passed through Sayville with a lingering regret for its big white houses and friendly front yards with picket fences and climbing roses. He always looked back as he went through, saying this might be the perfect town he was always searching for, where elms and lawns would be combined with the people he loved. But those summer taxis drove inevitably through it, like vans bearing prisoners who are being transferred from one prison to another—from Manhattan to Fire Island—when all we dreamed of, really, in our deepest dreams, was just such a town as this, quiet, green, untroubled by the snobberies and ambition of the larger world; the world we could not quit.

"Isn't this beautiful?" Malone would exclaim as we drove past the girl doing handstands on the lawn, a young woman walking a flock of children down a dappled sidewalk. "Why don't we take a house here next summer instead?" But he knew we wouldn't, and we knew he wouldn't, for even now the drums were in our blood, we sat forward almost hearing them across the bay, and the van raced on through the streets so that the driver could hustle back for another load of pleasure-seekers, so bent on pleasure they were driving right through Happiness, it seemed, a quieter brand of existence that flourished under these green elms. We kept driving right through all the dappled domesticity, like prisoners, indeed, being moved from jail to jail imprisoned in our own sophistication. The truth was the town reminded Malone of his days at boarding school in Vermont; the sight of a football arcing across a green wall of woods made him sigh with a passionate regret. He always looked like a student who has just come in off the playing fields, eyes glowing from an afternoon of soccer. He always looked like that, even in the depths of a subway station, on the dingiest street in Manhattan.

"People are fools to go back after Labor Day," Malone murmured that sunny afternoon. "We should come out after Labor Day," he said; but then he was always trying to refine his pleasures. He loved the shore in autumn when the crowds had vanished, and in the winter he used to go out dancing at five in the morning, and why? Because then the crowd had gone, the discaire was no longer playing for them, but for his friends, and that was the best dancing. And that was why he wanted all his friends to be with him in the country and watch the seasons change in a rustic valley he never found.

The nasal voice that crackled on the taxi's radio in summer was silent now, as silent as the still air, except for a single burst of static requesting the driver to pick up Mrs. Truscott, who wanted to go shopping, at 353 Elm Street. The driver said he would pick the lady up in five minutes—news that must have gladdened her heart, for in the summer Mrs. Truscott had to wait for the minions of advertising agencies, the doctors, designers, models, and producers to get to their houses on the beach.

As we waited at that streetcorner in the vivid, fiery air of late October, we stared dumbly through the windows at the autumn we'd forgotten, living in the city, the autumn blazing out here in the villages along the bay. The van went down one last dappled street and then rounded a bend to present us with a sight that never failed to make our hearts beat faster: the marshy inlets where the trees stopped and the masts of ships rose instead into the air.

The ferries had stopped running a month ago, however, and as we waited for the motorboat we'd hired to take us across, the only sound in all that crisp, clean air was the sound of hammers clattering around us as men in woolen caps repaired their boats in dry dock. Malone had said one day: "I am not spending next summer here. I'll go out west, I'll live in a tent in Africa, I'll do anything but waste another summer on the Island."

"Waste?" said Sutherland, turning his head slightly as if he had heard a bird chirp behind him in the bushes. "Who can waste a summer on the Island? Why, it's the only antidote to death we have. Besides," he said, blowing out a stream of smoke, "you know very well that if you did go to Africa, you would be lying in your tent among the gazelles and lions, and you would not even pull back the flap to look at them, because you will be wondering only who is dancing with Frank Post and whether Luis is playing 'Law of the Land.' Don't be a fool," he said. "Don't think for a moment of escaping. You can't!"

There was nothing very sinister about the place that Malone had protested hopelessly against that day when our motorboat puttered into the harbor across the bay. The Island lay bathed in the same autumn light falling on Sayville. Only one big white boat was still moored there, sharing the inlet with a family of migratory geese, and as we floated past, a big woman in a cerise caftan sat playing cards on the afterdeck with a young man in a hooded sweat shirt. They waved to us, improbable couple, and we waved back. The awnings had been taken down from the Botel, the sliding glass doors were boarded up with sheets of plywood, pasted with the dead leaves an earlier rainstorm had blown against them. It had never looked so bare. There wasn't a soul in sight when we got off.

It was easy to see how thieves from the villages of Long Island crossed over in the winter and looted houses. We passed one big, forlorn place after another, houses with turrets and skylights, houses with pennants drooping in the windless air, houses like castles, houses like cottages, houses hiding in the woods, and houses on display. The sagging electrical lines glistened in the clear October light. Leaves had accumulated under the holly trees, and portions of the shrubbery had turned a dull maroon. Above, the thinnest skein of clouds served only to emphasize the aching blue. We walked to a high point and saw, stretching down the beach, in the nooks of houses, a string of bright turquoise swimming pools, absurdly full. When we got to Malone's we stopped at the pool and stared at it—the pool that all the Puerto Rican boys used to dive into from the balcony, the roof, in the exhilaration of drugs—and then we walked around the deck and looked for a moment at the listless sea. It was the green of an empty Coke bottle. It was very still. But it had been very stormy, for the beach bore no resemblance at all to the one we had sprawled on all summer long—it had been completely washed away, and with it the summer itself: the music, clothes, dances, lovers. The sea had gouged out a new beach, with new coves and hillocks. I turned back to the house—famous for its electricity bills (three thousand a month), for the parties, for the people who had come here and their amusements. In an airy bedroom on the second floor, overlooking the pool and the ocean, we opened the closets and the drawers and began sorting Malone's clothes.

The clothes! The Ralph Lauren polo shirts, the Halston suits, the Ultrasuede jackets, T-shirts of every hue, bleached fatigues and painter's jeans, plaid shirts, transparent plastic belts, denim jackets and bomber jackets, combat fatigues and old corduroys, hooded sweat shirts, baseball caps, and shoes lined up under a forest of shoe trees on the floor; someone had once left the house and all he could tell his friends was that Malone had forty-four shoe trees in his closet. There were drawers and drawers of jump suits, shirts by Ronald Kolodzie, Estée Lauder lotions and astringents, and drawers and drawers of bathing suits, of which he had twenty-eight, in racing and boxer styles. And then there were the drawers of the clothes Malone really wore: the old clothes he had kept since his days at boarding school in Vermont—old khaki pants, button-down shirts with small collars (for someone who ran around with the trendiest designers, he loathed changes in style), a pair of rotten tennis sneakers, an old tweed jacket. There was one drawer filled with nothing but thirty-seven T-shirts in different colors, colors he had bleached them or dyed them, soft plum and faded shrimp and celery green and all shades of yellow, his best color. He had scoured the army-navy surplus stores in lower Manhattan looking for T-shirts, for underwear, plaid shirts, and old, faded jeans. There was a closet hung with thirty-two plaid shirts, and a bureau filled entirely with jeans faded to various shades of blue.

I finally stood up, depressed at all these things—for what were they but emblems of Malone's innocent heart, his inexhaustible desire to be liked?

There are boys in New York whose lovers die of drugs, and who give the dead lover's clothes to their new lover without a second thought; but a dead man's clothes have always seemed ghoulish to me, and so I gave up sorting the clothes, and left it all to my friend and began wandering through the rest of the house.

The house, with all its redundant pavilions, had been taken by an Italian princess, who had remained in Manhattan all summer in her air-conditioned rooms above Central Park eating hot dogs—and who wanted the place there in case she should want, some summer day, to go to the beach. She had taken it and Sutherland—with his peculiar talent for producing these bizarre benefactor—had used it the latter half of the summer for himself and Malone.

But the house was silent now, and as I turned and walked back through the empty rooms, they were devoid of the spirits who had once wasted all that electricity, both human and inhuman, humming through the rooms. A succession of houseboys had passed through the place and they had been replaced as casually as fuses. One of them, a dancer from Iowa, had been discovered renting rooms to strangers for fifty dollars a day during the week. He later had his head blown off on St. Marks Place by a Mafia hit man when he started a new career as a drug dealer; his funeral had been more glittering than any party of the winter. Well, these personalities had vanished and now the house was empty. And as I wandered through I felt a guilty pleasure I have always known in places the crowd has departed—a dormitory room on graduation day, a church after mass, bungalows by the sea when the season is past. There was something mute yet eloquent about such places, as if they were speaking a very old tale of loss, futility, and peace. Post offices in small towns, late at night . . .

October on Fire Island was lovely partly because it had been abandoned by the crowd. And wasn't that the whole allure of love, and why Malone had been such a genius at it: our struggle, always, to isolate from the mob the single individual, having whom society meant nothing? There were lovers whose affair was purely public, whose union consisted of other people's considering them lovers, but the reason I loved the beach in autumn (besides the elegance of the weather, the enameled light that layered everything from carpenters to butterflies to the tips of the dune grass) was that now the false social organism had vanished and left it what Malone had always wished it to be: a fishing village, in which, presumably, no one lied to one another.

A sudden wish to feast on the past made me sit down on the steps leading to the beach for a moment, the steps where in the hot August sunlight we had rested our feet from the burning sand and shaded our eyes to look out at the figures in the dazzling light. There had been a dwarf that summer, a squat hydrocephalic woman who wandered up and down the beach among those handsome young men like a figure in an allegory. And there had been the Viet Nam veteran who had lost a leg, and walked along the water's edge in a leather jacket in the hottest weather, hobbling with a cane. He had drowned that Sunday so many swimmers had drowned. Not twenty feet from the steps on which I sat now, a corpse had lain all afternoon beneath a sheet because the police were too busy to remove it, and five feet away from the corpse, people lay taking the sun and admiring a man who had just given the kiss of life to a young boy. Death and desire, death and desire.

The whole long, mad summer came back in the warmth of that pale, distant sun burning high above the deserted sea. The summer gym shorts had become fashionable as bathing suits, the summer Frank Post (who each spring contemplated suicide because he could not rise to the occasion again—of being the most voluptuous, beautiful man on the Island, the homosexual myth everyone adored—but managed to go to the gym, take his pills, and master yet another season) shaved his body and wore jockstraps to Tea Dance, and his lover died of an overdose of Angel Dust and Quaaludes. The summer "I'll Always Love My Mama" lasted all season and we never grew tired of it. The summer that began with the Leo Party and ended with the Pink and Green Party (which Sutherland had given, and from which Malone had vanished). The summer nude sunbathing began, the summer Todd Keller, from Laguna Beach, was the "hot number" and Angel Dust the favorite drug. The summer Kenny Lamar was arrested in the bar for sniffing a popper, the summer certain people got into piss, the summer his guests threw a birthday cake into Edwin Giglio's face, they all loathed him so, the summer Lyman Quinn's deck collapsed at the Heat Wave Party, with two thousand people on it; the summer a whale beached itself near Water Island in July, and a reindeer appeared swimming offshore in August. The summer Louis Deron dressed in gas masks, the summer Vuitton became pretentious, along with Cartier tank watches, and Lacostes were out. The summer the backpacking look began, the summer the grocery store changed hands, and people began to worry about the garbage floating three miles out in the Atlantic Ocean, the summer George Renfrew took the Kane House and built a new pool for the Esther Williams Party, the summer the new policeman drove everyone crazy, and Horst Jellaby began flying the flag of the country of his lover for one week: One only had to see the flag of Argentina to know he had snared the gorgeous physician visiting from Buenos Aires, or the flag of Colombia to know the coach of the national soccer team was in his bed at that moment. The summer the models moved to Water Island to get away from the mobs who had started to come to this place in greater numbers each summer. The summer two Cessnas collided in midair and the sky rained bodies into a grove of trees where everyone was in the middle of having afternoon sex. The summer some nameless ribbon clerk died trying to sniff a popper at the bottom of a pool . . . it was a blur, all of it, of faces, and parties, and weekends and storms; it vanished, as did all weeks, months, years in New York in one indistinguishable blur, life speeded up, life so crowded that nothing stood out in relief, and people waited, as they had one autumn weekend here, for a hurricane to provide some kind of sublime climax that never came . . .

A single figure was walking along the ravaged beach frowning at the sand and then looking out to sea: alone with the late October sky, the coming storm. As we had watched so many figures approach, and pass, and disappear those furious summers given over to nothing more than watching figures like this one come near, and then finding them flawed or flawless, this late-autumn visitor assumed a face and body—and I recognized one of Malone's first lovers: a Hungarian nuclear physicist we had all adored one summer. This place, the city, was full of Malone's former lovers. He compared them once to the garbage of New York accumulating in a giant floating island off the coast of this very beach, floating nearer each year, as if accumulated loves, like waste, could choke us. The physicist passed by brooding over private sorrows. We had all of us wanted him with scant success. Which recalled a rule of Malone's, with which he used to comfort those who despaired of ever wedding their dreams, spoken with a rueful regret that it was true (for, if true lovers are either chaste or promiscuous, Malone belonged, in the end, to the first school): "Over a long enough period of time, everyone goes to bed with everyone else." And cheap as it was, that was the truth.

They had taken no notice of his disappearance, these people: no funeral pennants on the turrets of their houses, no black sash across the swimming pool. The Island waited now in bleak desuetude for next season; the very beach of that particular summer had been mercifully obliterated by autumn storms so that next summer's strand might assume its shape; and it was right. One came here for very selfish reasons; after all, it was a purely pagan place. Malone would be memorialized in gossip. He would be remembered at a dozen dinner parties next summer, or in those casual conversations after sex in which two strangers discover they know exactly the same people and live exactly the same lives. One would expect as much sentiment for the departure of an Island beauty as one would for the patron of a gambling casino who walks away from the roulette wheel. For such a private place, it was very public: Anyone could come here, and anyone did. If not this gypsy throng, who would mourn Malone? He lived perhaps in my memory: I would always think of this place, this sea, this sky, his face together, and wonder if he had wasted his life.

Can one waste a life? Especially now? "Well," Malone would say when some conceited beauty refused to even meet his eyes, "we're all part of the nitrogen cycle." Oh, yes, and the butterflies rising in golden clouds from the dunes on their way to Mexico, the deer lifting its head on a bluff to gaze down the beach, the silver fish suffocating in the back of the trucks, the very sky would not be subject to anything more. But in that narrower, human sense, of course it can. Malone worried that he had wasted his; and many felt he had. Those smug people who had bought their own houses out here and arrived by seaplane with their Vuitton. Malone only wanted to be liked. Malone wanted life to be beautiful and Malone believed quite literally in happiness—in short, he was the most romantic creature of a community whose citizens are more romantic, perhaps, than any other on earth, and in the end—he learned—more philistine.

He wanted to be liked, and so he ran away to New York—away from his own family—and he vanished on Manhattan, which is a lot easier than vanishing in the jungles of Sumatra. And what did he do? Instead of becoming the success they expected him to be, instead of becoming a corporate lawyer, he went after, like hounds to the fox, the cheapest things in life: beauty, glamour . . . all the reasons this beach had once thrilled us to death. But the parties, the drugs, the T-shirts, the music were as capable of giving him his happiness as this sea I sat beside now was of stinging beneath the whips that Xerxes had his servants turn on the waves for swallowing up his ships.

The rain began to fall as the clouds eclipsed the sun and I got up and went back to the intersection where the suitcases of Malone's T-shirts and Lacostes sat as forlorn as the houses in the sparkling rain, and began dragging them down the boardwalk. The wind came up, the rain thickened, now that the first cloud was over this improbable sandbar—and figures appeared from the dense shrubbery hurrying toward the harbor with their own mementos. "Indian summer is like a woman!" someone yelled to his companion as they scurried. "Ripe, hotly passionate, but fickle!" It was the opening line of Peyton Place, the favorite mockery of an aspiring novelist. Witty people came out in autumn; beauties in July.

Our little boat was covered with a tarpaulin when we came to the harbor, with its countless wagons rusting in the rain—a heap of abandoned souls, lying there in the rain till the bodies attached to them came back—and the owner sat in the shelter of the grocery store porch. We dragged our luggage up the stairs of the Sandpiper, and to our surprise found the back door flapping open in the wind. We went inside and shut it behind us, and heard the ghostly murmur of a couple who had already sat down in a far alcove, just where they sat on those blistering, crowded nights to watch the dancers. The room was plunged into a gray-and-silvery gloom, the mirrors and chrome gleaming in an eerie light. We shook ourselves like dogs, and sat down at a table and looked at the empty dance floor where we had spent so many sweaty, ecstatic nights in the past. That blond rectangle of polished wood that had seemed to be at one point the aesthetic center of the universe. It was here I had first seen Rick Hafner glistening with sweat like an idol around which people knelt in a drugged confusion, unconsciously adoring his beauty, assuming the pose of supplicants at some shrine. It was here Stanley Farnsworth would stop dancing with the boy he was seducing that night (for they all ended up with Stanley Farnsworth) in the middle of a song to embrace and kiss him with long, deep, searching kisses that gradually immobilized his prey, like the poison sea corals inject into fish, while everyone whirled like dervishes around them, and the air grew stale with the odor of used poppers, and we danced in our bare feet on their broken cylinders, as ladies had once danced on rose petals in silver slippers at Tea Dance years ago. It was here lovers had come with hollow-eyed, glum faces the first night after breaking up, and here they had desired each other, eyes floating above the crowd, mournful, romantic. It was here Lavalava used to come in sequined helmets and dance with Spanish Lily in a swirl of veils, it was here Malone had been arrested by the police.

"Tell me," I said to a friend who had come into the room and its ghostly light, "where did you first see Anthony Malone?"

"At the Twelfth Floor," he said. "Six years ago this fall."

"Me, too," I said. "I thought Malone was the handsomest man I'd ever seen. But then I was in love with half those people, and I never said hello or good-bye to any of them."

## From Chapter Four

And then someone caught his eye: a wigged duchess emerging from the back door of a warehouse in which the Magic, Fantasy, and Dreams Ball was just breaking up. "Help me," said Malone. "My dear," said Sutherland after taking one look at his terrified face, "the house of Guiche shall never refuse the protection of its manor to the poorest of its subjects," and he assisted Malone into a cab pulled up at the curb. They rode in silence for some time as Malone panted beside Sutherland, his legs vibrating like windshield wipers. Neither spoke. Sutherland offered Malone a cigarette, Malone shook his head, and Sutherland smoked in silence, glancing at Malone from time to time in the light of passing streets as they floated north. Time had passed since he had stood outside the bookstore in Georgetown, peering in at volumes on the French cathedrals, and Malone no longer looked as if he were a young man peering into a bookstore in Georgetown on a summer night; he looked more like the fellow who had just run in off the playing fields in New Hampshire, his eyes brilliant—a rather exhausted soccer player now, his face scratched from the fray—the earring hidden behind a cluster of golden curls. Malone would always have that ambiguous look, half-fine, half-rough, and it so intrigued Sutherland that when the taxi slowed at his block of Madison Avenue, he turned to Malone and said: "Forgive me for inquiring, but— are you for rent?"

And Malone, as polite as this stranger who sat smoking a Gauloise beside him under a white wig of the seventeenth century, in brocade and rhinestones, smiled weakly and said: "Thank you, no." For he was so softhearted he hated refusing anyone. Rejecting another person upset him far more than being refused himself— and he was one of the few homosexuals in New York who went home with people because he did not wish to hurt their feelings. "I'm recovering from a lovers' brawl," he added. "Unlucky in love."

"Then come to the Carlyle," said Sutherland, extending his arm, "and let's have a drink. I always go to the Carlyle to rub an ice cube, bathed in Pernod, on my bruises. And then go dancing at the Twelfth Floor."

After the Carlyle they went to Sutherland's room above a little gallery on upper Madison Avenue, since one could not arrive at the Twelfth Floor before two A.M. and it was just past one. Sutherland pushed off his bed the manuscript on the history of religion that he had been writing the past five years, and lay Malone down, to wash his bruises—and it was this, years later, he never forgot, as Christ's definition of charity is the simplest and truest: You took me in when I was wounded. He made Malone tell his story again, as he washed his face with Germaine Monteil astringents, gasping at different parts and saying, his eyes very bright, "Ah!" For Sutherland, like the emperor with Scheherazade, could listen for hours to love stories. He knew perfectly well what Malone had run from. "Of course he beat you up," said Sutherland, dabbing with a cotton swab at Malone's lavender temple. "Latins are the last egocentrics on earth! Enslaved as you are to dark beauties, I see only dolors ahead for you—heartbreak dead ahead," he said. "Couldn't you, wouldn't you, love someone like me instead?"

But this very question was rhetorical, an invitation that Sutherland himself no longer believed in. He looked at Malone even now and said: "God! There are so many people I'm going to have to introduce you to!"

And then, as if preserving in wrapping paper a fine piece of bric-a-brac he had found on the street, he covered Malone in a blanket and said, "Of course he beat you. Let it be a lesson. This ethnic gene pool in which we sit, like children in their own shit."

He poured Malone a glass of Perrier, "The mineral water of aware French women everywhere," he mumbled.

"God knows I looked for it," he resumed when he had sipped his own glass, sighed, and handed Malone a Cuban cigar. "Uptown, downtown. I used to even go out to the boroughs on Saturday nights because there were so many dark-eyed beauties out there. For a while I was commuting to Philadelphia. To Rhode Island. But let's be honest. As divine as they are in bed, a guinea hasn't got a heart! They are ruined by their women from the crib, adored, coddled, assumed to be gods. Sad they happen to be so handsome. The real lovers, alas, are Wasps like you and me, even though we're supposed to be the ones who are emotionally stunted—well, of course, we are cold as fish in one sense. In another, we are the only true lovers. Let the Italians and the Jews wave their arms about and claim to be passionate, but they understand nothing, but nothing about love! They are show girls, my friend, and don't forget it! It takes a northern European to really suffer the pangs of heartache." And here he blew out a stream of smoke and stared at Malone; for he was looking at himself ten, even fifteen years before, as he saw Malone sitting there with his bruised ribs and blotchy face in the lamplight on that latesummer evening in Sutherland's room on Madison Avenue. He was Sutherland those many years ago, his visage still capable of registering that romantic hopefulness with which so many came to this city; and Sutherland took pleasure in the spectacle. "My God," he murmured again, in a low voice, "there are so many people I have to introduce you to." Malone sat there amused and fascinated by this strange wisdom pouring from this man and conscious that he had no other place to go. It was half-past midnight and he knew no one in the city but the lover he had just fled.

"We live, after all, in perilous times," Sutherland went on, lighting another cigar, "of complete philosophic sterility, we live in a rude and dangerous time in which there are no values to speak to and one can cling to only concrete things— such as cock," he sighed, tapping his ashes into a bowl of faded marigolds. He stood up and walked over to a closet and opened the door to reveal, like the Count of Monte Cristo his fabulous treasure, the accumulated wardrobe of fifteen seasons on the circuit. They stared silently for a moment at the stacks of jungle fatigues, and plain fatigues, bleached fatigues and painter's jeans, jeans with zippers and jeans with buttons, tank tops and undershirts, web belts, plaid shirts, and dozens of T-shirts in every color; nylon bomber jackets hanging beside leather bomber jackets, brown and black; and, on the floor in rows, work boots, engineer boots, cowboy boots, work shoes, hiking shoes, baseball caps, coal miner's caps, and, in one wicker basket, coiled like snakes, the transparent plastic belts that Sutherland found one day in a store on Canal Street and that he had introduced to gay New York, which meant, eventually, the nation, several seasons ago. Whistles, tambourines, knit caps, aviator glasses, aluminum inhalers, double-tipped dark glasses in both Orphan Annie and aviator styles, and huge mother-of-pearl fans occupied another basket that testified to the various accouterments Sutherland had considered necessary when he went dancing in winters past.

"But after a while you realize," sighed Sutherland, in a dejected mood because he had been rejected that evening at the party by someone he had been waiting to talk to for two years, "that there is nothing but these," he said, picking up a pale orange-and-red plaid shirt from Bloomingdale's and letting it dangle onto a pile of pastel-colored T-shirts from an army-navy surplus store on Canal Street and the basket filled with transparent plastic belts. He put a baseball cap on and left the closet. "Is there anything here you'd like to put on?" he asked. "You must get out of those tennis sneakers."

He tossed Malone a pair of Herman Chemi-Gums from Hudson's on Thirteenth Street. "They're far more sturdy. So what remains for us?" he said, as he sat down beside Malone and lifted his glass of Pernod to his lips. "What, we may well ask, is there left to live for? Why get out of bed? For this dreary round of amusing insincerity? This filthy bourgeois society that the Aristotelians have foisted upon us? No, we may still choose to live like gods, like poets. Which brings us down to dancing. Yes," he said, turning to Malone, "that is all that's left when love has gone. Dancing," he said, indicating with a wave of his hand the stacks of tapes and records in another corner of the room. "There is no love in this city," he said, looking down at Malone with a cool expression, "only discotheques—and they too are going fast, under the relentless pressure of capitalist exploitation . . ." He looked at Malone a moment more and then said quietly: "And what more appropriate way to begin your education than to take you to the Twelfth Floor?"

Malone slept instead that evening, and slept a lot more those first weeks of autumn—for when we have nothing in our lives, we simply stay in bed—and he would hear, vaguely, through his sleep, or see, through half-opened eyes, the tangle of eyelashes, strange figures slipping in and out of the room, doing their best to keep the silence: It was Sutherland (and friends he brought by to simply look at Malone, sleeping like a Norman prince on a stone tomb) in huge constructions of papier-mache—monstrous heads, birds of paradise, courtiers of France and Padua, figures from Fellini films—going to the costume parties of that season. Malone missed, that year, the Fellini Ball in the Rainbow Room, the Leo Party at the Armory, the Illusions and Nightmares affair in the Automat on Forty-second Street, while he lay in bed, hearing, as at the bottom of the sea, the distant, reverberating echo of taxicabs honking in the street—a sound that came up to him from the depths as a memory of childhood, when he had come through New York on his vacations from school. Sutherland had fallen in love with the city in the same way—if New York was to Malone that distant quaver of a taxi horn, deep in the chasms of mid-Manhattan, it was to Sutherland the curious taste of an egg-salad sandwich sold in hotel coffee shops, where he'd sat wide-eyed and wondering as he waited for the bellhops to bring down his mother's luggage before they got a taxi for Pier Forty-seven, where a stateroom on the S.S. Rotterdam waited to take them to Europe. He had fallen in love with New York City passing through it as a child, and the distinct smell of its damp, vivid air, the sea gulls circling the masts of his ship as it pushed up the Hudson River to its berth. He had fallen in love with the city then, and even though it was now a different city, this residue of affection remained, overlaid by the loves of his adolescence and manhood. At five o'clock now, the hour at which he had wandered down into the streets with his mother to visit a museum, a department store, a restaurant, and the theater, he awoke from the party of the previous night, doused his face, and rushed downstairs to meet the handsome men coming home from work, and have, if not sex, at least cocktails.

Sometimes Malone would awaken and find Sutherland in the uniform of Clara Barton, washing his face with a bottle of Ernst Lazslo and saying: "You must get well, dear, there are so many people who can't wait to talk to you! I've had to turn down so many invitations, from the Vicomtesse de Ribes, Babe Paley, that dance maven on Second Avenue with the Art Deco bathroom, you know," he said, putting the cotton swab drenched in cleanser to his neck before returning it to Malone's forehead. He awoke at other hours to find Sutherland trying to perfect his quiche, or sitting in a pinstripe suit beside a lamp reading aloud Ortega y Gasset on love.

Malone lay on the sofa like a convalescent, listening to the words as he watched the lamp's shadows on the ceiling. As for Sutherland, he could not have been happier having a new charge both handsome and willing to listen. It was always a joy to sponsor a new face in the crowd he ran with—among the most bored and frenetic on earth—and it was moving to see someone as charmingly lost as Malone.

Still there were enormous differences between them and as Malone watched Sutherland move through his mottled days he found much that appalled. Why then did he stay? Years later he would wonder why he remained with Sutherland that evening, and the next seven years. He never knew. As he listened to Sutherland's tales, as he spent the afternoons reading the volumes of Santayana, Plato, and Ortega y Gasset with which Sutherland left him alone, he began to think that the city is the greatest university of all, the real one, and all his education until now had been a mime. He who had spent hours poring over the history of the Supreme Court, the rise of the Protestant Ethic, the religious credo of Herman Melville, lay there now through the first crisp days of autumn as immobile on his sofa as a man recovering from some radical operation. And then one day he got up and went downtown in the early afternoon, when he knew Frankie was at work, to get his things; and he walked into their old factory building to find their home stripped bare . . . only a small pile of jeans huddled in one corner, and his journal, open still to the very page on which Frankie had read of his adulteries, on the mattress. Malone went to the window and looked down on the sparkling blue harbor and remembered how they had stood there in the hot breezes of July, embracing; he looked at the refrigerator, where Frankie seemed to be always standing with a tray of ice cubes; at the mattress, now dusty in a shaft of sunlight—and he suddenly bolted from the room. It was all over: dead. He had no idea where Frankie had gone.

But what was worse, he was everywhere: Going back uptown to Sutherland's room, Malone saw, in the subway, on the streets, half a dozen boys whose grave expressions and dark eyes invited him to turn back, his heart racing. This was his first taste of despair. He got to Sutherland's and closed the door behind him like a man fleeing the police.

And so Malone was grateful to remain behind, shut away from the city, on the most splendid afternoons of autumn when Sutherland would spend the day in the men's rooms of subways, or the rush hour at Grand Central Station, catching the explosive desires of insurance brokers trapped between a day at the office and an evening at home with the wife. Malone read and sighed and reflected, but he seldom spent the day alone; for people were constantly running up the stairs to Sutherland's room.

"How do you live?" Malone asked Sutherland one day, and he replied: "Hand to mouth." The usual exigencies didn't seem to apply in his case; people sent him plane tickets, and the latter half of October Sutherland spent in Cartagena playing bridge. Malone lay there and watched a whole race of handsome men come through the apartment, men he had never seen before. They were the faces that helped sell cereal and gin to the masses, and they came by at all hours of the day and night until finally Sutherland, on his return from Colombia, established "office hours" and sat at his desk in a big black picture hat with painted nails and a gardenia on the lapel of his Chanel suit, ringing up sales on an office calculator. "Ignore them, darling," he breathed to Malone. "They are simply people who will take anything in pill form. Does the sight of a syringe bother you?" he asked in a solicitous voice. "If so, we can go downstairs . . ."

It was a rainstorm rather that drove Malone downstairs; a storm that drifted down from Boston and stayed for two ways in late October made Malone put on a pair of tennis sneakers, take an umbrella, and flee the apartment. Lovers were everywhere: waiting for each other outside grocery stores with lost, annoyed expressions till the mate emerged with a sack of groceries, and hand in hand, they walked off together to cook dinner. Bearded students and their girl friends standing in the subway close together mesmerized Malone, staring at the man's white, veined hand resting lightly on the girl's neck. He tramped around the streets for hours and ended up lost in the Chambers Street station at three in the morning, all alone in the damp, chill, fluorescent light, thinking as he waited for the uptown train that he had first seen Frankie walking down one of these tracks with a lantern in his hand at about this hour one night long ago. Later he found himself walking home on Madison Avenue, having massacred, walked to death, the night whose gentle rain undid him. He saw a man he'd seen earlier lurch into a doorway for protection from the storm walking unsteadily toward him now. The man suddenly stopped on the sidewalk, in the slanting clouds of rain, looked at Malone, his face etched in the garish glow of the streetlight, and said: "Take me home with you. Please." Malone said nothing and walked on, just as he had learned to walk by lunatics giving speeches and beggars asking for money, horrified.

He went home to Ohio at Thanksgiving on the train along the Susquehanna, in the early darkness filled with snowflakes at bends in the dark woods. He took the slowest way home, like a diver who must allow himself time coming up from the depths in order to avoid poisoning. He was so sad he felt ill. He sat beside an anxious college student whose problems were maintaining an academic average good enough to secure him a place in medical school; Malone listened to him talk about his fears with a certain relief. He watched this fellow being greeted by his parents on the train platform, and felt suddenly that he could not face his own family. But when he arrived at his sister's house, the slamming of car doors, the screams of nephews and nieces flocking around him in the thickening snow flurry with the new puppies the family had acquired, the terror he had felt evaporated. "When are you going to get married?" chirped his youngest niece as she leaned against him at the Thanksgiving table. "Why don't you have a car?" These were the two things in her five-year-old mind that constituted—and was she wrong?—adulthood in America. He made some excuse as his parents, who had returned to Ohio that fall, hung on every word; even though they, out of that austere respect for one another's privacy peculiar to his family, had never asked the question themselves. They thought he was writing a book on jurisprudence. Later in the evening, dozing beneath a coverlet of newspapers in the den, the fire crackling beside him, the house filled with the faraway shouts of children playing in rooms upstairs, of adults playing cards in the dining room, he looked up once at the dog—and the dog looked up, inquiring, at him. "I'm gay," he whispered to the dog. The snow was falling lightly through the delicate branches of the fir trees pressed against the windowpanes, and he thought of it falling on all the shopping centers in the hills around that town, filled with families just like this one, and he heard the hiss of station wagons passing on the road outside, filled with children in Eskimo hoods, dozing in each other's laps. He smiled at the quirk of fate that kept him from it all like a prisoner being escorted down the corridor of a hospital in handcuffs, past the other patients, and then he fell asleep. When he awoke, much later in the night, the fire embers, the house suddenly chill and silent, his lips were damp with spittle and he thought, I was dreaming of Frankie, and he had, for an instant, a desire to rush down to the airport on some pretext and fly back to New York because he could not bear to be without what now seemed the source of his being: those dark-eyed, grave young men passing in the light of liquor stores on dingy streets, their eyes wide and beautiful, in the early winter darkness of that hard, unreal city.

When he did return to New York a week later laden with good wishes and fudge, he found Sutherland standing in the middle of the room with a mudpack on his face, round earrings; and a red dress pulled down to his waist—all that remained of the costume in which he had gone to a dinner dance as La Lupe—and the twenty-five-foot telephone cord wrapped around his body. He squirmed, like Laocoön trapped by snakes, and made an anguished face at Malone. "I simply must get off," he said into the phone, "the bank beneath us is on fire and we're being evacuated." He hung the telephone up and said, as he shook Malone's hand gravely: "My sister, in Boston. Our brother just cut off three toes in the lawn mower, after defaulting on a bank loan, our other sister has hepatitis and will have to finish school in Richmond, Mother is drinking, Father refuses to see anyone, and the woman across the street went into her garage yesterday and turned on the automobile and asphyxiated herself. What is wrong with this country, for God's sake?" he said, pulling off the red clip earrings. "Americans, for my money, are just too damned sophisticated!" He waved his arms in the air. "But, darling, how was the Heartland? So good to go home," he said. "So good to be with the family after a divorce. Who else will comfort?" But when he handed Malone a glass of Pernod, he saw his melancholy face and said: "I told you, dear, you shouldn't go."

They sat down and Sutherland began removing his facial with a warm washcloth, and Malone, feeling more depressed than ever, could not refrain from asking: "Do you sometimes not loathe being—gay?"

"My dear, you play the hand you're dealt," said Sutherland as he examined his face in the mirror. "Which reminds me, I'm due for bridge at Helen Auchincloss.'"

"What do you mean?" said Malone anxiously.

"I mean," said Sutherland, who turned frosty at the slightest sign of complaint, self-pity, or sentimentality on this or any subject (for beneath his frivolity, he was hard as English pewter), "that if Helen Keller could get through life, we certainly can."

"Oh," said Malone weakly, leaning back in his chair.

"You, however, may be a homosexual manqué," said Sutherland, turning back to the mirror. "Oh God," he said, "I'm late again."

"Where are you going?" said Malone sadly.

"I'm supposed to be at the opening of Teddy Ransome's gallery on Seventy-eighth Street, I'm supposed to be playing bridge with Helen Auchincloss, I'm supposed to be reading to the blind, and going out to East Hampton at eight, but you see I'm stuck right here," he said, sitting down with a sigh and the bright eyes of a koala bear, "because the exterminator is coming."

"The exterminator?" said Malone.

"Yes," he said. "He exterminates the roaches with his insecticide, then exterminates me by tugging at his crotch to adjust his scrotum. He is the most divine Puerto Rican you've ever seen. The most beautiful Puerto Rican in New York—and God assigned him to this building," he said, spilling some wine on the rug as a libation. "Now that's an accolade!" he said, picking up the phone to dial his regrets to four different people and cancel his dates because of the imminent arrival of this exotic visitor. "Don't you love these winter nights," he said, turning to Malone as he dialed a number, "and the possibility of so much dick?"

All winter long Malone declined the many invitations to parties and dinners that Sutherland gave him; till one crisp February night he met Sutherland in the Oak Room, where Sutherland often went after an hour or two in the men's room at Grand Central, and had drinks while he read the notes he and strange men had passed to one another from stall to stall on segments of toilet paper. "The trouble with this one was," said Sutherland in a cloud of cigarette smoke as he raised his martini to sip, "his shoes. Cheap shoes, you see. American men will not spend money on their footwear, whereas in Europe it is crucial. "I found his notes quite dreamy," he said, expelling another stream of smoke, "but the shoes were out of the question. Don't look now," he murmured, lowering his eyes demurely, "but the most handsome man in Brookfield, Connecticut, has just walked in the room. He's married now and has two kids, but we were once very much in love. Like a young Scott Fitzgerald, don't you think? Almost a Gibson boy, no, don't look yet, I'll tell you when," he said to Malone, who could feel someone sitting down behind him. "I must only add as a brief footnote that besides the hyacinth hair, the classic teeth, he sports one of the greatest schlongs in the Northeast Corridor. Try catching him on the shuttle to Washington sometime," he said, and finished off his drink. "We were deeply in love."

When they finally left, the twilight was filled with men hurrying on errands, handsome, dark-eyed messenger boys disappearing into the vaulted, steel-gray lobbies of tall office buildings; businessmen hurrying to catch a taxi to the airport; pale proofreaders going on the night shift at law firms on Park Avenue; waiters going to the Brasserie; students returning to the boroughs; and Malone began to feel the promise of the city once again. He did not go off like Sutherland with cashew nuts and dried apricots in his pockets to spend the day in the men's rooms of the BMT and IRT, but he began to meet him more often in the evenings, to linger on the boulevards and watch the throngs of people rushing past: a messenger boy from Twentieth Century Fox, a researcher at Sloan-Kettering, a public relations man hurrying about the business of Pan American Airways. "He lives with his parents in Forest Hills, he subscribes to the Atlantic Monthly and After Dark, his bedroom is all wicker, he falls in love with boys on the tennis courts," Sutherland would say. "Have you met him?" asked Malone. "No," said Sutherland as they watched the handsome figure disappear into Rizzoli's. "That would be quite superfluous." They strolled on, peering, like cupids, not at the Beatific Vision, but the windows of Bendel's.

And then out of the evening would materialize a pair of eyes that would lock with Malone's eyes with the intensity of two men who have reduced one another to immobility as wrestlers. It happened one evening entering a church on Fifth Avenue to hear a concert—a young man handing out programs, a dealer named Rafael who had come in fact to deliver cocaine to a priest. It was with a heavy heart that Malone whispered to Sutherland as they paused to anoint themselves with holy water after the concert, staring even then at Rafael's dark eyes with the dumb helplessness of an animal poisoned by a scorpion: "Can I call you later at the apartment?"

"The heart is a lonely hunter," sighed Sutherland, who understood perfectly that either one of them could disappear at any moment, alone in the end, to pursue the superior call of love . . .

And Malone would go off to the Upper West Side with Rafael, or Jesus, or Luis, and lie in a room, a prisoner of a pair of eyes, a smooth chest, enveloping limbs. But love was like drinking seawater, Malone discovered. The more he made love the more he desired the replicas of his current lover he inevitably found on every corner. Malone was love-sick, he was feverish, and it glowed in his eyes so that other people only had to look at him to realize instantly he was theirs. Yet each time he looked at someone tenderly, he felt he was seeing a double exposure in which the face behind the one in front of him bore the outlines of Frankie—and the half an inch between his lips and these others was a crevasse he could not cross. Then

Malone would walk back across the park with a miserable heart to find Sutherland hanging out his window in an orange wig, frilly peasant blouse, and gas-blue beads, screaming in Italian to the people passing on the street below to come up and suck his twat. The mask of comedy was sometimes difficult to put on; and Malone might linger in the doorway of the Whitney Museum for an hour or so, watching Sutherland finger the avocados in his blouse, throw out his arms, pat his hair, finger his beads, wave coquettishly like a marionette. before he felt himself able finally to cross the street. Sutherland was happy without love. So could he be. He waited till this lady who had just put out her wash, chattering happily as she drank in the life of the street and waited for Mario to come home, spotted him and then he went upstairs, with the melancholy heart of a sailor who is returning from an unsuccessful voyage. "Darling!" Sutherland gasped, at the sight of Malone coming into his room after so long an absence. "Is he playing poker? Did he give you the afternoon off?"

And Sutherland gave him the elaborate parody of a cocktail kiss, which he was fond of: missing, by a foot, at least, both cheeks.

"Entre nous," Malone said, "it's over."

"Ahhhhh," said Sutherland in a melancholy tone, fingering his beads, "l'amore non fa niente." He collapsed on the sofa in a cloud of perfumed powder. "There have been so many parties while you were away," he sighed. "There have just been too many to respond to. Does love mean never having to say you're sorry," he said, dabbing his upper chest with a bit of perfume, "or too sore to get fucked again?" He threw more cologne on the inside of his thighs. "I've been sitting home all afternoon hoping to receive the stigmata," he said, closing the autobiography of Saint Theresa, which he had been reading when he began his impersonation of a Neapolitan whore, "but all I got were invitations to brunch this weekend. No more quiches, please! One could die of quiches!"

He looked at Malone, tender and serious for a moment. "It's not like Plato, is it?" he said, taking down a volume of the Symposium from his bookshelf. "It's not like Ortega y Gasset, or even Proust, is it?" he said. "Or, for that matter, Stendhal. It's so hopelessly ordinary—I don't even think people have souls anymore. And not having souls, they cannot be expected to have love affairs . . ."

He removed the avocados from his blouse and mixed daiquiris for himself and Malone. The telephone rang and Sutherland picked it up and said: "I'm sorry, I have to keep this line open for sex." He hung up, for he was, once again, waiting for a boy he had met in the street the previous night to call. "Oh, God," he sighed to Malone as he regarded his gleaming refrigerator—which contained a kind of emblem of life on the circuit: a leftover salmon mousse and a box of poppers—"the young ones are so cruel. Such oblivious assassins! He was so wonderful, such huge dark eyes, such a long-limbed body, such good sex, and this morning he can't even remember my name." He went to the window and said: "He's out there somewhere, that perfect beauty!" He turned, handed Malone his daiquiri and plate of salmon mousse and said: "The cruelty of people is beyond measure. Well," he sighed, "though it is very soon after the divorce, could we twist your arm to go dancing tonight? After, of course, we take a beauty nap. One can't go out dancing anymore before four. And hope to make an entrance, I mean."

And he sighed and grew drowsy as the light turned blue in the street, and murmuring a request to Malone to pass the vial of Vitamin E to him, Sutherland applied the oil to the area beneath his eyes—with the gentle, upward strokes of the weakest finger of his hand, the fourth—and then fell into a deep sleep. His body began discharging whatever drug he had taken that morning, and refreshed itself for the next endeavor. He would awaken at three and take another drug and begin to dress for the evening at the Twelfth Floor. Malone, who could not sleep, left a note that said he would meet Sutherland there, and went downtown. A sliver of a moon floated in the sky above the West Side Highway. He alone walked down the cobblestoned street to the old factory building where he and Frankie had lived that summer. He walked up the riverside till he came to that forlorn neighborhood whose awningcovered sidewalks, and meat-packing plants, and air of rural desertion he loved. He saw the dark figures crossing the piazzas far ahead of him; he paused to see the carcasses of pigs, blue-white and bright red, slide on steel wire from the trucks into the refrigerated depths of the butcher's, while at his back homosexual young men trod that Via Dolorosa searching in a dozen bars, a string of parked trucks, abandoned piers, empty lots, for the magician of love. Malone paused beneath the pale, chaste moon and watched the dark figures vanish and appear again; he drew in the silvery air with one hand the Sign of the Cross and then he went dancing.

He danced till seven that morning, and he danced for three winters after that. He was a terrible dancer at first: stiff and unhappy. I used to see him standing on the floor with a detached look of composure on his face while Sutherland danced brilliantly around him. Sutherland danced with a cigarette in one hand, hardly moving at all, as he turned slowly around and surveyed the other dancers for all the world like someone at a cocktail party perusing the other guests. He always danced with a cigarette, with very subtle movements, loose, relaxed, of the shoulders and hips; except when a song came on he loved from the old days—for Sutherland had been dancing long before any of us—such as "Looking for My Baby," and then he would cut away and leave Malone standing self-consciously on the floor while Sutherland cut back and forth across the room in a choreography only a natural dancer can improvise. Then he would calm down again and stand there with his cigarette, barely moving to the music. I was once in a place with Sutherland when, over the din of the music, I became aware of a single high note being sustained, and, deciding it was in the record, thought no more until I heard it again in another song and realized finally it was Sutherland, singing a piercing, high E-flat as he danced to Barrabas.

The two of them began to dance the winter the Twelfth Floor opened, the year we returned from Fire Island in September distressed because—what with the demise of Sanctuary—there was as yet no place to dance. Such was our distress at that time: We would not stop dancing. We moved with the regularity of the Pope from the city to Fire Island in the summer, where we danced till the fall, and then, with the geese flying south, the butterflies dying in the dunes, we found some new place in Manhattan and danced all winter there. The composition of our band of dancers changed, but it usually included one doctor, one hustler, one designer, one discaire, one dealer, and the assorted souls who had no idea what they were doing on earth and moved from disguise to disguise (decorator, haircutter, bank teller, magazine salesman, stockbroker) with a crazy look in their eyes because their real happiness was only in music and sex.

We danced the fall of 1971 in a dive off Times Square, living on rumors that the Twelfth Floor would open soon after Thanksgiving; and that is when we first saw Malone with Sutherland. Sutherland we all knew, or knew of: even among us, he was thought to come from another planet. Now of all the bonds between homosexual friends, none was greater than that between the friends who danced together. The friend you danced with, when you had no lover, was the most important person in your life; and for people who went without lovers for years, that was all they had. It was a continuing bond and that is what Malone and Sutherland were for years, starting that fall: two friends who danced with one another.

The bar we saw them in that first season was frequented by a mean crowd, messengers and shop-girls and dealers by day, conceited beauties by night. The first evening we stood behind Malone waiting to go in, and heard the Mafia bouncer ask him twice (for Malone hadn't heard the first time) if there were a "gun, knife, or bottle" in the bag he was carrying, Malone bent forward politely, and when he finally understood, said, "Ah! No," and then was ushered into paradise. It was extraordinary, the emotions in those rooms: At the beach, the music floated out of open windows, wandered over the bay, lost itself in the starry night, just as sexual desire on summer evenings in the city rose into the sky with the pigeons and the heat itself. But in winter, in those rooms in the city, with the music and the men, everything was trapped, and nature being banished, everyone was reduced to an ecstatic gloom. How serious it was, how dark, how deep—how aching, how desperate. We lived on certain chords in a song, and the proximity of another individual dancing beside you, taking communion from the same hand, soaked with sweat, stroked by the same tambourines.

Malone was appalled the first night he went to that particular bar, by the music (the likes of which he had never heard before, and hadn't the ears to hear at first) and the rudeness of the crowd, while Sutherland loved the very sordidness. Later that night, a queen spun around and embraced Malone at the waist and threw her head back and began dancing to him as if to some idol in the jungle—pulled him out onto the floor, where he tried to dance because even then he could not bear to reject anyone. He was wise to do so. Egos were huge and tempers quick in that place; the slightest insult could set off a fight with hidden knives. The queen spun around Malone, some Rita Hayworth in a movie that was never made, until the song ended and then Malone smiled, murmured something, and drifted unobtrusively back to Sutherland, who was shaking with laughter. Malone still had only one set of manners, for all people, and they were somewhat too polite for this place. In fact he was abducted many times that way until he began standing in the corners, behind several lines of people, for he was shy and did not want to be out there on the floor. Furthermore, he was not a good dancer. They were all good dancers in that place. It was a serious crowd—the kind of crowd who one night burned down a discotheque in the Bronx because the music had been bad. As Sutherland murmured one night when he began to look around for an emergency exit (we all would have been snuffed out in a minute had that place caught on fire, as was the case with nearly every place we went, from baths to bars to discotheques): "If there were a fire in this place, darling, no one would be a hero." We stayed until closing anyway, because the music was superb, dancing beside those messenger boys so drugged they danced by themselves in front of mirrors (with their eyes closed), and when we finally emerged, it was in time to see the sun come up on the empty sidewalks of Times Square, which at that hour was as empty, as clean, as ghostly as the oceans of the moon.

We had all seen Malone, yet going home on the subway no one spoke of him, even though each one of us was thinking of that handsome man—and he had seen us. What must he have thought of us at that time. What queens we were! We had been crazed for several years already when we danced at the Bearded Lady that winter. We lived only to dance. What was the true characteristic of a queen, I wondered later on; and you could argue that forever. "What do we all have in common in this group?" I once asked a friend seriously, when it occurred to me how slender, how immaterial, how ephemeral the bond was that joined us: and he responded "We all have lips." Perhaps that is what we all had in common: No one was allowed to be serious, except about the importance of music, the glory of faces seen in the crowd. We had our songs, we had our faces! We had our web belts and painter's jeans, our dyed tank tops and haircuts, the plaid shirts, bomber jackets, jungle fatigues, the all-important shoes.

What queens we were! With piercing shrieks we met each other on the sidewalk, the piercing shriek that sometimes, walking down a perfectly deserted block of lower Broadway, rose from my throat to the sky because I had just seen one of God's angels, some languorous, soft-eyed face lounging in a doorway, or when I was on my way to dance, so happy and alive you could only scream. I was a queen ("Life in a palace changes one," said another), my soul cries out to Thee. The moon, which already floated in the sky when we awoke, above the deserted buildings on the Bowery was more beautiful to me than any summer moon that I had seen hanging over the golden walls of the city of Toledo. Some strange energy was in the very air, the pigeons fluttering to rest in the gutters of the tenement behind the fire escape. In the perfect silence the telephone would ring, thrilling, joyous, and we would slip into the stream of gossip as we would slip into a bath, to dissect, judge, memorialize the previous night and forecast the one to come.

The queen throws on her clothes, discarding at least ten shirts, five pairs of pants, innumerable belts before she settles on her costume, while the couple next door throws things at each other. She has her solitary meal, as spartan as an athlete's before a race (some say to avoid occlusion of the drugs she plans to take), as they scream drunkenly. And then, just as the Polish barbers who stand all evening by the stoop are turning back to go upstairs to bed, she slips out of her hovel—for the queen lives among ruins; she lives only to dance—and is astride the night, on the street, that ecstatic river that flows through New York City as definitely as the Adriatic washes through Venice, down into the dim, hot subway, where she checks the men's room. An old man sits morosely on the toilet above a puddle of soggy toilet paper, looking up as she peeks in, waiting himself for love. The subway comes; she hurries to the room in which she has agreed to dance this night. Some of the dancers are on drugs and enter the discotheque with the radiant faces of the Magi coming to the Christ Child; others, who are not, enter with a bored expression, as

if this is the last thing they want to do tonight. In half an hour they are indistinguishable, sweat-stained, ecstatic, lost. For the fact was drugs were not necessary to
most of us, because the music, youth, sweaty bodies were enough. And if it was too
hot, too humid to sleep the next day, and we awoke bathed in sweat, it did not matter: We remained in a state of animated suspension the whole hot day. We lived for
music, we lived for Beauty, and we were poor. But we didn't care where we were
living, or what we had to do during the day to make it possible; eventually, if you
waited long enough, you were finally standing before the mirror in that cheap
room, looking at your face one last time, like an actor going onstage, before rushing out to walk in the door of that discotheque and see some one like Malone.
Through those summers, at the beach, and those winters, in the city, we seldom
lost him for very long. He was at the huge parties in the Pines, one of which
Sutherland arrived at by helicopter, lowered on a huge bunch of polyethylene
bananas, dressed as Carmen Miranda, and he was at the most obscure bars in
Hackensack where we sometimes went because we heard a certain discaire was
playing. In fact, as it all became a business and the public began to dance, we had
to abandon places when they became too professional, too knowing, too slick.
Places we had loved—such as the dive off Times Square we often saw Malone in—
were written about now in New York magazine, Newsweek, and GQ, and then, the
final stage of death, we would pass their doors one evening and see, where we had
once thronged to begin those ecstatic rites of Dionysius, a mob of teen-agers and
couples from Queens whose place it was now. And so we would go out to New
Jersey on those perfumed Saturday nights of summer, against the river of young
Puerto Ricans in flowered shirts and thin leather jackets, taking their girls into the
city to dance, crowds of people drenched in sweet cologne. But every time we got
to this obscure bar in Queens or Jersey City, who was there already? Sutherland
(and Malone), for Sutherland, as far as being jaded was concerned, was way ahead
of any of us; Sutherland had danced at Sanctuary, the Alibi, the Blue Bunny, for
that matter, when places never lasted more than a month and gay life was a floating crap game that moved about the city as nomads pitch and strike their tents,
before we had even come to this city. So we traveled in parallel careers, and
Malone eventually became a very good dancer, and it was wonderful to dance
beside him, on Fire Island, in Jersey City, in those hot, hot rooms, or at the beach,
his shirt off, his chest silver with sweat, his face as serious as ours, enveloped in the
same music.

  We danced near one another for several years and never said a word; even at the
very end of an evening, when everyone converged at an after-hours club on
Houston Street where the people who could not stop went, who artificially
extended the night by remaining in rooms whose windows were painted with black
paint, where the dregs of night, the bartenders, the discaires themselves, all tum-
bled down into one room in which pretensions were impossible. The bathroom
was jammed with people sharing drugs, drag queens danced with designers, hustlers played pool, sharing another kind of communion, till, hours later, I would
look up to see Malone standing with a drink on the edge of the crowd, and above
him the light glowing in the ribs of the ventilating fan over the door—which gave
away the whole fiction, the pretense that it was still night, and proved not only that

day had come, but it was maturing rapidly—and I would wonder in the sudden stillness why I did not speak to him. It was not simply his beauty—having danced with these people as long as we had, that was no bar to introducing oneself; it was the expression on his face. It was deeply serious, and more, it seemed to promise love. But how could that be? We were too smart to believe in that. We wished to keep him at a distance, as a kind of untried resource, a reward we should have in our secret hearts. We wanted to be loved by Malone, with this egotistic detail: that it would be an exclusive love. At first we thought he was a medical student; then we heard he worked on Seventh Avenue for Clovis Ruffin; besides that, he was dying of an incurable bone disease. Then someone said he didn't work at all and was being kept by an Episcopalian bishop; and so Malone went through as many guises as the discotheques we danced at. But that look never vanished from his eyes. Sutherland—who looked like a lumberjack one night, a Gucci queen the next, a prep school swim star, or an East Village dropout—dressed Malone like a doll each night and ushered him out into the city to be a fantasy for someone. How much was Malone aware of what he was doing? At that time he didn't know he was the object of so many eyes; he didn't care that we possessed each other through the medium of gossip.

And then Malone would vanish for a while, in love with one of the young Latin beauties who made up half our crowd (the other half being the doctors, designers, white boys who loved to dance), and of whom Frankie had been the first. But there were so many Frankies—that was the horror—and eventually Malone would return to find Sutherland hanging out the window of his apartment, swinging his gas-blue beads and talking in Italian to the passersby. Sutherland would see Malone, clutch the avocados in his blouse, and scream, "My son! He is back from that bitch he married!" and Malone would walk into the apartment with a rueful smile and sit down and tell Sutherland what had gone wrong with his latest marriage. Then they would go out dancing. Seeing Malone, we would realize how much we had missed him.

One night he ran into the real Frankie in a bar in Hackensack where Luis Sanchez was playing (our favorite discaire who eventually went off to Paris to play for a count and who seemed to take the best music with him). Frankie was, after all, Malone's first love. Malone was a sentimental soul and when he asked to meet him the next afternoon to talk, Malone agreed. They met in Central Park. Frankie had since been promoted at work and was even wearing glasses to appear more intellectual (though his vision was perfect, and the glass clear), and as they sat by the pond near Seventy-second Street, the conversation was polite. Then Frankie began to query Malone on the crowd into which he had disappeared as totally as a mermaid returning to the sea who leaves her human lover staring blankly at the waves, and of which Frankie disapproved utterly. Frankie was a Latin, Catholic, a conservative soul who hated queens. He had no use for them. He had one dream in life: a home, a wife, a family, and if Nature had made a joke of this, he was not about to smile with her; he would have it anyway, with Malone, in a room somewhere. For such a handsome boy, his soul was a dead weight; the very seriousness Malone had loved at first now seemed to Malone lugubrious, and in fact, as they continued sitting there, Frankie began to cry. Then he lost his temper. He hit

Malone twice in the face and stopped only when a policeman came up, at which point Malone fled without a word.

He ran all the way back to Sutherland's apartment, where he found Sutherland in a black Norell standing beside the baby grand piano and singing in a velvet voice: "This time we almost made the pieces fit, didn't we?" He held out his long-gloved arm to Malone and said: "Were you a model of propriety? Did you conduct yourself with dignity?" And then, seeing Malone was distraught, he took off his long gloves, made him a cup of tea, and sat with him on the sofa and listened to his tale of regret and loss until it was time to go to the White Party.

The next afternoon when they awoke with the empty heads of angels being born, pushed their costumes off their limbs, and walked to the window to see if it was day or night, Malone saw Frankie on the corner opposite. Malone drew back; he was convinced, once again, that Frankie was mad. "To take love so seriously!" said Sutherland in a thrilled voice as he came to the window. "Only Latins take love seriously, and he is so beautiful. We northern Europeans are cold as fish," he smiled, and wrapped his robe around him as he sat down with a bottle of Perrier. But then Malone looked out at him and felt a vague melancholy: He was crazy, but at least he valued love more than anything, and had adored him. And his very seriousness, his very earnest fury, as he stood there on the corner looking across the street at Sutherland's windows, took Malone's breath away. He knew nothing of discotheques and gossip, body-building and baseball caps, bleached fatigues and plaid shirts, the whole milieu of trends on which the city, and the society that revolved around the Twelfth Floor, thrived, even originated. He stood there in his jeans (the wrong kind, cheap knock-offs from a discount house in Jersey City) and windbreaker (shapeless and green), frowning at Sutherland's window, his dark eyes cloudy as the sky filled that afternoon with an impending thunderstorm, and dark hair blowing about his ears, a creature from a different planet, unfashionable, unself-conscious, unknowing. Yet vain in his own way, Malone reminded himself as he put down the binoculars and turned from the window with a feeling of sadness.

"I don't know if he's waiting to take me to lunch," Malone said, "or stick a knife in my ribs."

"I ask myself the same question every time I go over to Ceil Tyson's for dinner," said Sutherland, peering out the window. "Perhaps you should go to Rome until we clear this up."

"But I can't leave the city," said Malone miserably, "as long as he's in it."

"Poor baby," said Sutherland, withdrawing from the window. "Then what do you plan to do?"

It began to rain and Frankie stepped under the portico of the museum as Malone said: "I want to disappear. Can I leave Manhattan without leaving Manhattan? I'd just better vanish in the metropolitan equivalent of one of those holes scientists have discovered in the universe."

"Well," said Sutherland, putting a finger to his lips judiciously, "you could move to Harlem. One hundred thirtieth Street? But then, northern blacks are so rude. No, I think you should go in the other direction," he said. "I think you should go to the Lower East Side."

That day friends found for Malone—who had little money now—a small apartment on St. Marks Place in which to hide till Frankie went home himself. "They forget me," said Sutherland enviously, "within five minutes after leaving the apartment. But then I have such a tiny wink," he sighed.

And so late one night a caravan of taxicabs rolled down Second Avenue south of Fourteenth Street—where Sutherland had once lived as part of Warhol's stable—down the sordid streets of the East Village, bathed in the orange glare of the latest streetlights designed to prevent street crime, and which made each street into a Gaza Strip lacking only barbed wire to prevent the pedestrians on one block from migrating to the one opposite. The whores watched them rumble past; the bums were already sprawled in the doorway of the Ottendorf Library, and the bag ladies were asleep on the sidewalk beside baby carriages heaped with trash. "So much local color!" said Sutherland as the three yellow cabs rolled down the bricks of Second Avenue. "So much raw life. Very Hogarth. Very pretty!" he said, as a man stood shaking his penis against the windshield of a car stopped for a red light, whose driver, a young woman, stared bravely off into the distance, ignoring its presence. "Do you know who used to live along Second Avenue in all these buildings in the twenties?" he said, leaning forward on the seat to look up at the big stone apartment houses in which lighted windows glowed. "Jewish gangsters! Yes!" he said excitedly. "The famous Rosy Segal lived here, and Bugsy Levine and all the boys who used to hang around the Cafe Metropole. They kept mistresses in these buildings, just like me," he said, for he still got occasional checks from his Brazilian neurosurgeon and his Parisian art dealer. "The biggest Jewish gangsters of the twenties, this was their block," he said, as the pale cornices went by beneath the radiance of a yellow summer moon. "They are huge apartments," said one of the friends who were accompanying them downtown, an urban planner from Boston, "as big as the ones on the Upper West Side."

"And who lives in them now?" Sutherland said. But before the friend could answer, Sutherland replied himself. "Faggots!" he said. 'Faggots where the Jewish gangsters used to keep their mistresses! Ah, this avenue has never been anything but declasse, it is the perfect place in which to disappear," he said, turning back to Malone. "The perfect place for social oblivion. Not only will nobody know where you are, but when they do find out, they won't visit you after four o'clock in the afternoon!" he said, as they got out of the cab and stepped over the supine body of a man sleeping in the gutter. "Mira!" he said, pointing to a young Puerto Rican man bent at the waist, as he reached for something on the sidewalk at his feet—but as they gazed at him, he remained in that impossible pose, immobilized by a drug he had taken earlier that evening. "I believe," said Sutherland breathlessly, "I believe he is trying to pick up his comb!" "Welcome," he said, turning to Malone. "Welcome to Forgetfulness."

## Melvin Dixon (1950–1992)

*Getting Your Rocks Off (1978)*

Reading clouds beyond the road
I calculate our distance, survey

the space between our clothes
where rising curves and mountain
tug for air, touch release?

You drive to the hairpin slope,
hesitate, turn up and in. We ride
on every naked fear you have
and discover that men like us
are not all granite, shale,
deceptive quartz, or
glittering layers of mica.

From here you see the whole world
differently: brownskin,
tufts of black grass.
And many times I have given myself
to summits like these.
Ride in, ride high.
Ride until the clouds break.

You will learn to read rain. You will
follow the white gravel it leaves.

## Walter Holland (b. 1953)

*Christopher Street 1979*

Storm, park, and restless,
one preservation on the Hudson docks for
homosexuals hand in hand,
cornering the bar with leathered glances—
we are the boys who love.

Where are my lovers?
Penis and limp flesh,
city doves and pale sheets,
the shedding of denim and cotton briefs

The Village Cigar store at two a.m.
Light drooling on the street
and the alabaster adonis alone.

How warm is your sperm
like milk and beer and morning
beside your hardness.

Heaven sucks the angels
and our groans fill the street with desolation—

so we are fallen creatures
children of the wasted seed.

## Politics

### Walta Borawski (1947–1994)

*Power of One (1980?)*

I am the sole homosexual
in Wilton, New Hampshire, & I

was imported only this afternoon.
Rafts of whirligigs scatter

as I approach by canoe; cut-
worms devour potatoes,

raccoons split wood houses,
scoop, eat, birds inside,

are hunted & shot in turn
by black dogs, & hunters.

Mining insects leave striations
'cross leaves of water lilies,
beavers topple trees, water
rises, raises mosquitoes, fleas.

Grey, white, black, yellow
birches dwarf blueberries:

no safe spot, no domain. Hurricane David yanks branches

from fruit trees. Japanese
beetles make lettuce artless lace,

porcupines pierce the tongues
of hunters' dogs—all because
there's a faggot in New Hampshire.


*Some of Us Wear Pink Triangles (1980)*

*(for Rudy Kikel)*
At the Lesbian & Gay Pride March we
strode through main streets shouting

"Two/four/six/eight: Gay is just
as good as straight." Their hundreds
looked at our thousands. Some threw
insults, some supported. Most were
silent. We were noisy inside the
shelter of numbers. Balloons flew
into the face of the sky, forcing
all to see: we are everywhere.

At a dinner party in Somerville,
eight of us sit talking about music,
gay politics, gay literature, gay
love. In the conversation's first
lull we hear it: First come wolf
whistles, then: "Hey! Why don't
you guys look out? Lots of beautiful
guys on the sidewalk down here. You
talking about Anita Bryant up there?
You drinking any orange juice? Hey—
play us some more Beethoven." We
look at each other, trying to find
words. Rudy talks of gays beat up
after trying to throw a gay-straight
party. Kenny's been hit by a beer
bottle the night before. He'd had
his arm about a man. We all have
our stories. Then: THUD!—
Patrick hears it, I hear it, something's
been thrown against the house. Twice
more it happens, & laughter, & whistles,

& then: "Goodnight, guys. See ya
tomorrow." Already we've been moving
from windows, & changing
the subject. But there's no room
for music now, & literature seems

removed. No matter how real Henry James
can make a character, we have to deal with
characters in the street, we have to
get from here to there & worry about
survival between Ball & Harvard squares.

Once Bruce told me he'd try gay sex, only
he'd never want to be branded homosexual.
I used to laugh.

# Edmund White (b. 1940)

## THE POLITICAL VOCABULARY OF HOMOSEXUALITY (1980)

Gay liberation is a new phenomenon, yet it has already transformed attitudes among homosexuals and modified the ways in which they speak. In June 1969, a group of lesbians and gay men resisted a routine police raid on the Stonewall, a popular dance bar in Greenwich Village. Opposition to police harassment was unusual enough to signal a quickening sense of solidarity. Soon after the Stonewall Resistance gay organizations and publications were springing up across the country and, by now, gay liberation has become both a national and an international movement.

I was present at that original event and can recall how the participants cast about for political and linguistic models. Black power, feminism, resistance to the war in Vietnam and the New Left were all available, and each contributed to the emerging gay style and vocabulary. Discussing the beginning of the movement in this way, however, makes it sound too solemn and deliberate. Our recognition that we formed an oppressed minority struck us as *humorous* at first; only later did we come to take ourselves seriously.

I can remember that after the cops cleared us out of the bar we clustered in Christopher Street around the entrance to the Stonewall. The customers were not being arrested, but a paddy wagon had already hauled off several of the bartenders. Two or three policemen stayed behind, locked inside with the remaining members of staff, waiting for the return of the paddy wagon. During that interval someone in the defiant crowd outside called out 'Gay Power', which caused us all to laugh. The notion that gays might become militant after the manner of blacks seemed amusing for two reasons—first because we gay men were used to thinking of ourselves as too effeminate to protest anything, and second because most of us did not consider ourselves to be a legitimate minority.

At that time we perceived ourselves as separate individuals at odds with society because we were "sick" (the medical model), "sinful" (the religious model), "deviant" (the sociological model) or "criminal" (the legal model). Some of these words we might have said lightly, satirically, but no amount of wit could convince us that our grievances should be remedied or our status defended. We might ask for compassion but we could not demand justice. Many gays either were in therapy or felt they should be, and the words *gay liberation* would have seemed as preposterous to us as *neurotic liberation* (now, of course, Thomas S. Szasz in the United States, R. D. Laing in Britain and Felix Guattari on the Continent have, in their different ways, made even that phrase plausible enough).

What I want to stress is that before 1969 only a small (though courageous and articulate) number of gays had much pride in their homosexuality or a conviction that their predilections were legitimate. The rest of us defined our homosexuality in negative terms, and those terms isolated us from one another. We might claim Plato and Michelangelo as homosexuals and revere them for their supposed affinities with us, but we could just as readily dismiss, even despise, a living thinker or artist for being gay. Rich gays may have derived pleasure from their wealth, educated gays from their knowledge, talented gays from their gifts, but few felt anything but regret about their homosexuality as such. To be sure, particular sexual encounters, and especially particular love relationships, were gratifying then as now, but they were explained as happy accidents rather than as expected results.

Moreover, the very idea that sexual identity might demarcate a political entity was still fairly novel. Minority status seemed to be vouchsafed by birth, to be involuntary. One was born into a race or religion or nationality or social class—that was the way to become a member of a real minority. One could also be born a woman, though the large claims advanced by feminists still struck many people then as preposterous. Women, after all, formed a majority and they scarcely seemed to have much in common. Did an upper-class WASP woman from Boston share a perspective with a poor Chicano Catholic woman from Waco? The question could be asked about gays: what was our common bond? This "category confusion" assailed us and may have been one source of our laughter upon hearing the phrase gay power.

Then there was the problem about how people become gay. If they're born that way, they may represent, depending on the point of view, a genetic mistake or an evolutionary advance or a normal variation. If, on the other hand, they choose to be gay, then their rights seem less defensible; what has been chosen can be rejected. A third possibility is that the environment makes people gay against their will—but this etiology, because of conventional associations if not logical arguments, again smacks of pathology and suggests gays should seek to be "cured."

I raise these issues not because I propose answers (the whole discussion strikes me as politically retrograde, since at this point any etiology would disguise a program for prevention). I bring up the matter only because I want to demonstrate what a strange sort of "minority" homosexuals belong to and why we were reluctant to embrace the political vocabulary (and stance) that had been useful in securing the civil rights of other groups.

Nevertheless, because the black movement was highly vocal and visible at the time of Stonewall, slogans such as "black is beautiful" were easily translated into "gay is good" and "black power" became "gay power." Some of the resistants even dubbed themselves "pink panthers," but that name did not catch on. These derivations, I should hasten to point out, were not approved of by black militants who, like most young white leftists, regarded homosexuality as "decadent" and "bourgeois." In 1971, I believe, H. Rap Brown did propose a coalition between blacks and gays, but that suggestion was not very popular among his constituents.

A less obvious imitation of the black movement by gays was the elevation of the word gay itself. Just as Negro had been rejected as something contaminated because it had been used by (supposedly hypocritical) liberals and the seemingly more neutral black was brought into currency, in the same way homosexual, with its medical textbook ring, was dismissed in favor of the more informal and seemingly more innocuous gay (I say "seemingly" because these words, black and gay, do have complex etymologies).

No one I know has any real information about the origins of the word gay; the research all remains to be done. Those who dislike the word assume that it is synonymous with happy or lighthearted and that its use implies that homosexuals regard heterosexuals, by contrast, as "grim." But gay has had many meanings, including "loose" and "immoral," especially in reference to a prostitute (a whore-house was once called a "gay house"). In the past one asked if a woman was "gay," much as today one might ask if she "swings." The identification of gay with "immoral" is further strengthened by the fact that *queen* (a male homosexual) is almost certainly derived from *quean* (the Elizabethan word for prostitute).

In American slang at the turn of the century, a "gay cat" was a younger, less experienced man who attached himself to an older, more seasoned vagrant or hobo; implicit in the relationship between gay cat and hobo was a sexual liaison. Yet another slang meaning of gay is "fresh," "impertinent," "saucy" (not so very distant from "immoral"). In French *gai* can mean "spicy" or "ribald." My hunch (and it's only a hunch) is that the word may turn out to be very old, to have originated in France, worked its way to England in the eighteenth century and thence to the colonies in America. It has died out in Europe and Britain and is now being re-introduced as a new word from the United States. But this is only speculation.

If the exact etymology is vague, no wonder; the word served for years as a shibboleth, and the function of a shibboleth is to exclude outsiders. Undoubtedly it has had until recently its greatest vogue among Americans. In England, the standard slang word has been *queer*. In Bloomsbury *bugger* was the preferred term, presumably because it was salty and vulgar enough to send those rarefied souls into convulsions of laughter. One pictures Virginia Woolf discussing "buggery" with Lytton Strachey; how they must have relished the word's public school, criminal and eighteenth-century connotations.

Today heterosexuals commonly object to *gay* on the grounds that it has ruined for them the ordinary festive sense of the word; one can no longer say, "How gay I feel!" It seems frivolous, however, to discuss this semantic loss beside the political gain the word represents for American homosexuals. An English novelist visiting the States, after boring everyone by saying she felt gay life was actually sad (an observation she presented as though it were original), proceeded to call gay men "queer," which I presume is less offensive in Britain than in America (a few older Americans use the word).

Many homosexuals object to *gay* on other grounds, arguing that it's too silly to designate a lifestyle, a minority or political movement. But, as the critic Seymour Kleinberg has mentioned in his introduction to *The Other Persuasion: Short Fiction about Gay Men and Women*, "For all its limitations, 'gay' is the only unpompous, unpsychological term acceptable to most men and women, one already widely used and available to heterosexuals without suggesting something pejorative." Gay is, moreover, one of the few words that does not refer explicitly to sexual activity. One of the problems that has beleaguered gays is that their identity has always been linked to sexual activity rather than to affectional preference. The word *gay* (whatever its etymology) at least does not sound sexual.

In any event, *gay* is so workable a word that in the last ten years it has shifted from being just an adjective to being both an adjective and a noun. One now says, "Several gays were present," though such a construction sounds awkward to older American homosexuals. Just as Fowler in A *Dictionary of Modern English Usage* objects to *human* as a noun and prefers *human being*, so many homosexuals still prefer *gay person* to *gay man*.

The connection between feminism and gay liberation has been strong for a decade, though now it has broken down. Because of this break, the word gay now generally refers to homosexual men alone. Homosexual women prefer to be called *lesbians*, pure and simple. Most lesbian radicals feel they have more in common with the feminist movement than with gay liberation. Since political lesbians tend to resent a male spokesman, I have confined most of my remarks in this essay to the gay male experience which, in any event, is more within my range of competence and understanding.

This fairly recent rupture, however, should not obscure the debt that gay liberation owes to feminism. The members of both movements, for instance, regard their inner experiences as political, and for both gays and feminists the function of consciousness-raising sessions has been to trace the exact contours of their oppression. Women and gay men, as the argument goes, have been socialized into adopting restricting roles that are viewed with contempt by heterosexual men (despite the fact that these very roles reinforce the values of a virilist society). Accordingly, at least one aim of feminism and gay liberation has been to end the tyranny of stereotyped behavior. Much of this stereotyping, of course, is perpetuated by the victimized themselves. Many women have a low opinion of other women, and many gays are quick to ridicule other gays.

For example, political gays have fought the use of the feminine gender when employed by one homosexual man of another. In the past a regular feature of gay male speech was the production of such sentences as: 'Oh *her!* She'd do anything to catch a husband . . ." in which the "she" is Bob or Jim. This routine gender substitution is rapidly dying out, and many gay men under twenty-five fail to practice it or even to understand it. This linguistic game has been attacked for two reasons: first, because it supposedly perpetuates female role-playing among some gay men; and second, because it is regarded in some quarters as hostile to women. Since one man generally calls another "she" in an (at least mildly) insulting context, the inference is that the underlying attitude must be sexist: to be a woman is to be inferior.

Following the same line, a large segment of the lesbian and gay male population frowns on drag queens, who are seen as mocking women, all the more so because they get themselves up in the most *retardataire* female guises (show girls, prostitutes, sex kittens, Hollywood starlets).

This rejection of transvestites has been harsh and perhaps not well thought out. As long ago as 1970 Kate Millett in *Sexual Politics* saw the drag queen in quite another light—as a useful subversive:

> As she minces along the street in the Village, the storm of outrage an insouciant queen in drag may call down is due to the fact that she is both masculine and feminine at once—or male, but feminine. She has made gender identity more than frighteningly easy to lose, she has questioned its reality at a time when it has attained the status of a moral absolute and a social imperative. She has defied it and actually suggested its negation. She has dared obloquy, and in doing so has challenged more than the taboo on homosexuality, she has uncovered what the source of this contempt implies—the fact that sex role is sex rank.

Anyone familiar with drag knows that it is an art of impersonation, not an act of deception, still less of ridicule. The drag queen performing in a night club, for instance, is often careful to reveal his true masculinity (deep voice, flat chest, short hair) at some point in his performance; such a revelation underscores the achievements of artifice. Since, in addition, most gay transvestites are from the working class and many are either black or Puerto Rican, discrimination against them may be both snobbish and racist. The greatest irony is that the Stonewall Resistance itself and many other gay "street actions" were led by transvestites.

As to why drag queens have singled out prostitutes and show girls to imitate, the explanation may be at least partially historical. In Jonathan Katz's *Gay American History*, one discovers a clue. Testimony given to the New York police in 1899 has this to say of male prostitutes: "These men that conduct themselves there well, they act effeminately; most of them are painted and powdered; they are called Princess this and Lady So and So and the Duchess of Marlboro, and get up and sing as women, and dance; ape the female character; call each other sisters and take people out for immoral purposes."

Obviously, then, many of the early drag queens actually were prostitutes. Others may have found that the world of the theater and prostitution was the only one where overt homosexuals were welcome. Or perhaps the assertive make-believe of such women, purveyors of sex and fantasy, seemed naturally related to the forbidden pleasures of gay men. Or perhaps the assault on convention staged by prostitutes and performers appealed to gay men because it was a gaudy if ambiguous expression of anger. In any event, this legacy can still be faintly heard in gay speech today, though less and less often ("Don't be such a cunt," "Look, bitch, don't cross me," "Go, girl, shake that money-maker," and in a vagueness about proper names and the substitution of the generic *darling* or *Mary*). Much more hardy is a small but essential vocabulary derived from prostitute's slang, including: *trick* (a casual sex partner as a noun, to have quickie sex as a verb); *box* (the crotch); *trade* (one-sided sex); *number* (a sex partner); *john* (a paying customer); *to hustle* (to sell sex); *to score* or *to make out* (to find sex) and so on. Few young gays, however, know the origins of these words, and certain locutions borrowed from prostitutes have been modified in order to obscure their mercenary connotations. For instance, few homosexuals still say, "I'd like to turn that trick." Instead, they say, "I'd like to trick with him." That homosexual slang should be patterned after the slang of prostitutes suggests that in the past the only homosexual men who dared talk about their sexual tastes and practices either were prostitutes themselves or lived in that milieu. Curiously, that vocabulary has flourished among gay men who have never dreamed of selling sex.

In the past, feminization, at least to a small and symbolic degree, seemed a necessary initiation into gay life; we all thought we have to be a bit *nelly* (effeminate) in order to be truly gay. Today almost the opposite seems to be true. In any crowd it is the homosexual men who are wearing beards, army fatigues, checked lumberjack shirts, work boots and T-shirts and whose bodies are conspicuously built up. Ironically, at a time when many young heterosexual men are exploring their androgyny by living with women in platonic amicability and by stripping away their masculine stoicism and toughness, young gays are busy arraying themselves in these cast-offs and becoming cowboys, truckers, telephone linemen, football players (in appearance and sometimes also in reality).

This masculinization of gay life is now nearly universal. Flamboyance has been traded in for a sober, restrained manner. Voices are lowered, jewelry is shed, cologne is banished and, in the decor of houses, velvet and chandeliers have been exchanged for functional carpets and industrial lights. The campy queen who screams in falsetto, *dishes* (playfully insults) her friends, swishes by in drag is an anachronism; in her place is an updated Paul Bunyan.

Personal advertisements for lovers or sex partners in gay publications call for men who are "macho," "butch," "masculine" or who have a "straight appearance." The advertisements insist that "no femmes need apply." So extreme is this masculinization that it has been termed "macho Fascism" by its critics. They point out that the true social mission of liberated homosexuals should be to break down, not reinforce, role-playing stereotypes. Gay men should exemplify the dizzying rewards of living beyond gender. But they have betrayed this promise and ended up by aping the lost banal images of conventionally "rugged" men—or so the antimacho line would have it.

In the heady early days of gay liberation, certainly, apologists foresaw the speedy arrival of a unisex paradise in which gay angels, dressed in flowing garments and glorying in shoulderlength, silken hair, would instruct heterosexual men in how to discard their cumbersome masculinity and ascend to the heights of androgyny. Paradoxically, today it is the young straights who wear their hair long and style it daily, who deck themselves out in luxurious fabrics and gold filaments, who cover their bodies in unguents, dive into a padded conversation pit and squirm about in "group gropes" (in which, mind you, lesbianism may be encouraged for its entertainment value to male spectators but never the swains shall meet). Simultaneously but elsewhere, crew-cut gays garbed in denim and rawhide are manfully swilling beer at a Country and Western bar and, each alone in the crowd, tapping a scuffed boot to Johnny Cash's latest.

Another objection to the masculinization of gay life is that it has changed a motley crew of eccentrics into a highly conformist army of clones. Whereas gays in the past could be slobs or bohemians or Beau Brummels or aesthetes striking "stained-glass attitudes" or tightly closeted businessmen in gray flannel suits, today this range of possibility has been narrowed to a uniform look and manner that is uninspiredly butch. The flamboyance and seediness and troubling variety of gay life (a variety that once embraced all the outcasts of society, including those who were not gay) have given way to a militant sameness.

This argument, I think, ignores our historical moment. In the past gay men embraced the bias of the oppressor that identified homosexuality with effeminacy, degeneracy, failure. To have discovered that this link is not necessary has released many homosexuals into a forceful assertion of their masculinity, normality, success—an inevitable and perhaps salutary response. Moreover, the conformism of gay life, I suspect, is more on the level of appearance than reality. The butch look is such a successful get-up for cruising that some sort of "natural selection" in mating has made it prevail over all other costumes. But this look does not preclude the expression of individuality, of tenderness and zaniness, in conversation and private behavior.

Yet another thought occurs to me. In the past many homosexuals despised each other and yearned for even the most fleeting and unsatisfactory sexual (or even social) contact with straight men. Some gays considered sex with other homosexuals pointless and pitiable, a poor second best, and thirsted for the font of all value and authenticity, a "real" (i.e., straight) man. Today, fortified by gay liberation, homosexuals have become those very men they once envied and admired from afar.

The apotheosis of the adult macho man has meant that the current heart throb in gay pornography—and in actual gay cruising situations—is no longer the lithe youth of nineteen but rather the prepossessing stud of thirty-five. The ephebe with hyacinthine curls has given way to the bald marine drill sergeant, and Donatello's *David* demurs to Bernini's.

The change has affected the language of approbation. In the past one admired a "boy" who was "beautiful" or "pretty" or "cute." Now one admires a man who is "tough" or "virile" or "hot." Perhaps no other word so aptly signals the new gay attitudes as *hot*; whereas *beautiful* in gay parlance characterizes the face first and the body only secondarily, *hot* describes the whole man, but especially his physique. One may have a lantern jaw or an asymmetrical nose or pockmarked skin and still be hot, whereas the signs of the beautiful face are regular features, smooth skin, suave coloring—and youth. The hot man may even fail to have an attractive body; his appeal may lie instead in his wardrobe, his manner, his style. In this way "hotness" is roughly equivalent to "presence" with an accent on the sexy rather than magisterial sense of that word. In addition, hot can, like the Italian *simpatico*, modify everything from people to discos, from cars to clothing. Gay-chartered cruises promise a hot vacation and designers strive after a hot look. If an attractive man strolls by, someone will murmur, "That's hot." The "that" in place of "he" may be an acknowledgment that the person is as much a package as a human being, though more likely the impersonal pronoun is a last echo of the old practice (now virtually abandoned) of referring to a one-time-only sex partner as an "it" (as in, "The trick was fine in bed, but I had to throw it out this morning shut up").

Gay male culture, as though in flight from its effeminate past, is more and more gravitating towards the trappings of sado-masochism. The big-city gay man of today no longer clusters with friends around a piano at a bar to sing songs from musicals; now he goes to a leather and Western bar to play pool and swill beer. Gay men belong to motorcycle clubs or engage in anonymous sex in back rooms, those dimly lit penetralia behind the normally sociable bar.

Sado-masochistic sex has introduced new words into the gay vocabulary . . . and interestingly, gay men, usually so fastidious about staying *au courant*, are willing to utter outmoded hippie words from the drug culture of the 1960s such as *scene, trip* and *into* if those words enable paraphrases that stand in for the still more ludicrous vocabulary of classical sadism.

I have tried to point out that gay male culture and language have registered a shift in taste away from effeminacy to masculinity and from youth to maturity. But now a larger question might be posed: has the status of—and the need for—a private language itself become less important to homosexuals?

I think it has. In the past homosexuality was regarded with such opprobrium and homosexuals remained so inconspicuous that we faced some difficulty in detecting one another. A familiar game was to introduce into an otherwise normal conversation a single word that might seem innocent enough except to the initiated ("I went to a very lively and gay party last night"). If that risk was greeted with words from the same vocabulary ("I'm afraid the party I went to was a real drag; everyone acted like royalty," i.e., "queens"), a contact was established. Two businessmen could thus identify themselves to one another in the midst of a heterosexual gathering.

But the value of a private language was not merely practical. It also allowed gays to name everything anew, to appropriate experience in terms that made sense only to the few. Sailors became "sea food," "chicken" (always singular) were teenage boys and so on—there is a whole book, *The Queen's Vernacular*, that lists these words. Equally amusing and subversive was the pleasure of referring to a revered public leader as "Miss Eisenhower," or to oneself (as Auden does at the end of an otherwise serious poem) as "Miss Me." When gay frustration had no outlet in action, it could find expression only in language. But even in language the impulse had become sour and self-destructive through long suppression; its target was more often other gays than straights or in the fiction that respectable straights were actually outrageous queens. In self-satire lies the reflexive power of thwarted anger. Gay identity, now rehearsed nightly in thronged discos and in a myriad of gay bars, was once much more tenuous. It was an illegitimate existence that took refuge in language, the one system that could swiftly, magically, topple values and convert a golf-playing general into a co-conspirator in a gingham frock and turn a timid waiter into a drag queen for a night—or at least into the Duchess of Marlboro.

Now that homosexuals have no need for indirection, now that their suffering has been eased and their place in society adumbrated if not secured, the suggestion has been made that they will no longer produce great art. There will be no liberated Prousts, the argument goes, an idea demonstrated by pointing to the failure of *Maurice* in contrast to Forster's heterosexual novels. A review of my novel *Nocturnes for the King of Naples* claimed that it was not as strong as my earlier, "straight" *Forgetting Elena* precisely because I no longer needed to resort to the pretense of heterosexuality.

This position strikes me as strange and unexamined. Proust, of course, *did* write at length about homosexual characters—in fact, one of the complaints against his novel is that so many characters implausibly turn out to be homosexual. *Maurice*, I suspect, is a failure not because it is homosexual but because it is a rather exalted, sentimentalized masturbation fantasy. When he wrote *Maurice* Forster had even less knowledge of the homosexual than of the heterosexual world, and he was forced back on his daydreams rather than on his observations from life. It is not for me to judge the merits of my own books, but what strikes me as most "homosexual" about *Nocturnes* is not the content so much as the technique, one that uses endless dissolves of time and geography, as though the same party were being reassembled over decades and on different continents, something like that "marvellous party" in the Noel Coward song. Anyone who has experienced the enduring and international links of gay life will recognize how the technique is a formal equivalent to the experience.

Unless one accepts the dreary (and unproved) Freudian notion that art is a product of sublimated neuroses, one would not predict that gay liberation would bring an end to the valuable art made by homosexuals. On the contrary, liberation should free gays from tediously repetitive works that end in madness or suicide,

that dwell on the "etiology" of the characters' homosexuality (shadowy Dad, suffocating Mum, beloved, doomed, effeminate Cousin Bill) and that feature long, static scenes in which Roger gently weeps over Hank's mislaid hiking boot. Now a
new range of subject matter has opened up to gays, much of it comic; Feydeau,
after all, would have loved gay life, since every character can cheat with every other
and the mathematical possibilities of who may be hiding under the bed (if not in
the closet) have been raised geometrically. Still more importantly, gay liberation
means that not so many talentless souls need to continue lingering about in the
sacred precincts (i.e., the gay ghetto) of high culture. Finally they are free to pursue all those other occupations they once feared to enter—electrical engineering,
riding the range, plumbing. The association between homosexuals and the arts, I
suspect, suited some of us but not most; the great majority of gays are as reassur-
ingly philistine as the bulk of straights.

## Carl Morse (b. 1934)

*Dream of the Artfairy (1982)*

One day over the course of a week or so,
all the art ever made by fairies
became invisible to straights,
starting with the Sistine Chapel.
It was mid-July, and thousands of riled-up visitors
demanded an apocalypse or their money back,
although it was noticed certain persons
continued to point and giggle at the ceiling
—for the fairies could still see perfectly well.

Then the Last Supper went.
And some noted art historians tried to get back their vision
by clumsily attempting a gross indecency or two,
and traffic in forged fairy papers became a nightmare.
But nothing worked
—including the ethically dubious practice
of tempting real fairies to simulate
the shapes of the Elgin marbles.

And then to indelible effect
a Tchaikovsky symphony disappeared
in the middle of Avery Fisher Hall,
but for a piping fairy here and there
who could still read the music on the page
and one panicky but determined violin.

And the bins of Sam Goody bulged
with the unsold silent discs of Broadway hits,

and hum-along fairies ruled the Met,
and Take-a-fairy-to-Tanglewood clubs were formed,
in case any Brahms or Ravel was played,
and the first Easter passed without even one *Messiah*.

And then in the classroom of our days
the fairy voices died in mid-pronunciation. So:

—I taste a liquor never brewed
    from tankards _____ ____ _____,
—The mass of men lead lives ____ _____

    _____,
—A rose is a rose ___ __ _____,
—They told me to take a streetcar _____ _____,
—Out of the cradle _____ _____,
—Call me _____,
—Oh, Mama, just look at me one minute as though you really saw
    me . . . Mama! Fourteen years have gone by! —I'm dead!
    —You're a grandmother, Mama— . . . I married George
    Gibbs, Mama! —Wally's dead, too. —Mama! His appendix
    burst on a camping trip to Crawford Notch. We felt just terrible
    about it, don't you remember?— . . . But, just for a moment
    now we're all together —Mama, just for a moment let's all be
    happy— . . . Let's _____ _____ _____ _____! *

And the publishers failed when so many books
went blank in mid-fulfillment,
and no-one but fairies passed their bar exams.

At last only Clifton Webb kept making love
to the hole where Garbo used to be,
and a touchdown pass in the closing game
never reached its tight end on the screen,
and all hell really broke loose in the land.

And the Good Fairy saw that it was bad,
or at least not so hot,
and that a sense of justice can go a long way.
So she kicked the transmitter
and the straights woke up restored.
And the earthfairies didn't mind so much,
since they had more time to draw
—and interpreting isn't the best of jobs,
no matter how you get paid.

*If you filled in any of the above, even in your head, you may be a gifted fairy. [See top of
opposite page for correct responses—ED.]

*Scooped in pearl (Emily Dickinson)*
*of quiet desperation (Henry David Thoreau)*
*is a rose (Gertrude Stein)*
*named Desire (Tennessee Williams)*
*endlessly rocking (Walt Whitman)*
*Ishmael (Herman Melville)*
*look at one another (Thornton Wilder)*

## Jim Everhard (b. 1946)

*Curing Homosexuality* (1982)

> for three incurables, Frank, Stu and Richard

"There are no homosexuals, only fallen heterosexuals."
—DR. REUBEN SEBASTIAN WILDCHILD

Of the many known and proven
cures for homosexuality,
the most familiar, perhaps,
is the Catholic Church's version of
"Confession-is-good-for-the-soul."
According to this ritual, every time
you feel an unclean urge to touch yourself, you stop your hand with the
mental image of the Pope staring you
in the face and these words: "if-I-do-this-
I-have-to-tell-the-priest-again."
Then, when you go to confession you
enumerate and fully describe every such
forbidden act leaving out not the
slightest detail and the priest,
who lives anonymously in a dark box,
tells you what you must do to redeem your lost
soul. This usually amounts to kneeling
before a statue of this virgin
who has never allowed the sinful hands
of any man to ever infest her body
with the puerile desires of the flesh and
mutter a prayer that
you won't touch other men hail Mary as you,
in a religious rapture,
fondle your beads.
     If this doesn't work,
and one wonders about these

good men whose career it is to sit in the dark
and listen to the pornography of everybody
else's life, the next step is psychoanalysis.
The doctor sits solemnly in the dark
behind you, his hands suspiciously folded
in his lap, and doesn't say a word
while you lie down on a long, lumpy sofa
and tell him about your childhood
and how much you hate yourself
for thinking the things you think
so uncontrollably
and you wish your tongue would fall out
and it almost does as you go on and on
wondering what the hell this fellow
is listening for as you start inventing
stories about Uncle's anus and house pets.
You soon find out he is interpreting
the things you tell him. According to
psychoanalytic theory, everything you say
means something else even more sinister
than what you meant. Your unknown desires
live within you and control your outward behavior. For instance, if you say,
"It's such a beautiful day today
I wanted to leave work early,"
the psychiatrist will interpret this to mean
you are dissatisfied with your job
and this in turn means you are sexually frustrated and this goes back to your miserable
childhood which means he'll probably
respond with, "Do you think that this means
you resented your mother when she
wouldn't let you play with yourself?"
If you say you had a dream about flying
he'll interpret it as a dream of sexual
frustration and penis envy meaning
you are really sick since only women
are supposed to have penis envy. He'll
probably ask you, "How did you feel when
you first saw your father's instrument?
Did you notice if it was bigger than yours?
Did he seem ashamed of his?
Did you want to touch it?"
If you tell him you don't recall
what it looked like he'll tell you
you unconsciously wanted it to fall off

so you could flush it down the toilet.
If you tell him you wanted to kill your father
and rape your mother he'll tell you
you had an Oedipus conflict.
He will listen for key words like
umbrella, closet, brother, rooster, shit, nude —
and Judy Garland, all of which convey
a large surplus of unconscious homosexual material. For instance, never say:
"I put my umbrella in the closet
and found my brother in the backyard
beating the shit out of a rooster
while looking at nude pictures of
Judy Garland." To a psychiatrist this means:
umbrella = phallic symbol = womb = death = fear that it will
    rain at your funeral and no one will come
closet = phallic symbol = womb = mother = castration = desire
    to work for a fast food chain = prostitution = fear of underwear
brother = phallic symbol = sibling rivalry = castration = desire to
    stick your finger up your ass and smell it
rooster = phallic symbol = cock = flying = fear of Karen Black =
    crashing = fear of impotence = hatred of women = fear of
    oxygen
shit = phallic symbol = fear of dirt = work = puritan work ethic
    = father's penis = sexual frustration = deviations = fascination
    with dirt = bad toilet training = sexual hostility toward pilgrims
nude = phallic symbol = opposite sex = original sin = truth =
    fear of gardens = self-deception = poor sanitation habits =
    desire for death and return to Earth Mother = return to disco =
    hatred of mother = love of analyst but always waiting for
    someone to come along and say no = desire to live in a hole in
    the ground
Judy Garland = phallic symbol = fear of tornadoes = love/hate of
    sucking = confusion of identity = desire to have oral relations
    with a lap dog = necrophilia = fear of Easter bonnets = desire
    to be a woman = fear of bad breath = spiritual destitution =
    desire to be Dr. Kinsey = existential malfunction = fear of tubas
    = fear of dude ranches and desire to perform unnatural acts with
    Mickey Rooney = fear of short, pimply people

Like a cancer, one sentence can devour your entire psyche.

If you say you had a hard time coming today
and you don't have anything to say
he'll call that resistance. If you say
it isn't, he'll say that's more resistance.

If you stop resisting, he'll call that
passive-aggressive. If you tell him
you've had it, you're tired of wasting
time and money when you haven't even begun
talking about homosexuality, he'll tell you
your problems run even deeper than he
initially realized and you need hospitalization.

Once you are hospitalized, the doctors
will begin electric shock therapy.
They call it therapy. There is no resistance.
You are not sure who's getting the therapy,
you or the sadistic maniacs who strap you down
and wire you up and turn on the juice
while they flash pictures of naked men
on a screen. The idea is to associate pain
and the fear of death by electrocution
with naked men. Then a comforting female
nurse unstraps you and wheels you, unconscious,
back to your room where she slowly
but surely revives you and stuffs a few pieces of
stale toast and cold eggs down your gullet.
This is supposed to turn you on to women.

          If
none of these cures works
you will probably be thrown out of high school
as a bad influence for all those guys who
make you suck them off in the shower,
then beat you up at the bus stop. If you
still wish to remain homosexual, you will probably be arrested in the public library
for browsing too long in the "Sexuality"
section or during one of the periodic raids
of a local gay bar or face charges for soliciting
a cop who arrested you and forced you
to give him a blow job while he played
with his siren. In prison
you will probably be gang raped by
lusty straight men who are only acting out
their healthy but stifled heterosexual impulses
and if you are lucky one of them may even
win you in a knife fight and protect you
from the gang except when he trades you
out for a night for a pack of cigarettes or
a shot of heroin. Once you are released

you will become an expert in American
legal procedures as you face future charges
of child molestation, murder and attempts
to overthrow the common decency, whatever that is.
When you have had it, and decide to hijack
a jet and escape, you will discover the small
but important fact that no nation under god
or red offers asylum, political or otherwise,
to a plane full of pansies.
Your best bet is to fly over
the Bermuda Triangle and click
your little red pumps together whispering,
"There's no place like home, there's no
place like home."
   In olden days
the main cure for homosexuality (then
often known simply as witchcraft) was
to tie the suspected faggot to a tiny seat
on the end of a long pole suspended
over boiling water. The suspected faggot was then
submerged for half an hour or until
he stopped struggling, whichever happened first.

If he was still alive when they lifted him
from the vat, they spread an oil slick over the water,
resubmerged the suspect and struck a match.
If he went up in smoke,
it meant he was a godless heathen faggot
who deserved to go up in smoke. If a choir
of angels emblazoned the sky and God,
humming the Hallelujah Chorus,
personally pissed out the flames dancing
around the suffocating faggot's body,
he was allowed to return home if he promised
to register four times daily with the local
police and never get his hair cut
in a place called a boutique.

   So, you see,
liberalism has increased the life expectancy
of fairies. That's because we've evolved
into the world's wittiest, best groomed
ballroom dancers. Everyone's into
the Queen's vernacular, pierced ears, disco
and poppers. So long as you seek your partner
after dark in the mountains of Montana

at least one hundred miles distant
from the nearest living heterosexual
and keep your meeting anonymous and
under fifteen minutes with no visible
body contact or non-contacting foreplay,
you could not conceivably, even by the
most homophobic, be considered
or accused homosexual by anyone but the most
adamantine and intolerant straight person.
Thanks to science it is now well known
that homosexuality is not transmitted by
tiny springing bugs or bats. We are not burned
at the stake (except during ceremonial
occasions of state for example only)
in the larger urban centers today
though we may still face a constant barrage
of misdemeanors (nastier than a case of crabs)
such as littering, (i.e.,
don't drop your hanky in a city park),
jaywalking (i.e., no matter how cute the
cop may be, don't wiggle your ass when
you buzz across Connecticut Avenue
during rush hour in the middle of the block
waving you-whoo, you-whoo to your color-
ful friends) and loitering (i.e., situated
under the romantic moon in an open
park after dark behind willowy shade trees
on your knees with a look of ecstasy
on your face as he creams into your eager mouth
is considered loitering among other things).
Simple precautions will save you
from a life of humiliation and
all those long blank spots on your resume
that you have to explain as time
to get your head together or
extended vacation or time spent nursing
your mother back to health
when you were really fired for
turning on a fellow office employee.

In conclusion, there are no known cures
for homosexuality. Faggots have survived
Christianity, psychiatry, social ostracism, jail,
earth, air, wind and fire, as well as the pink
triangle and concentration camps. Nothing
can reckon with you if you can reckon with yourself.

The facts have been available for a long, long time:
where there are human beings, there are faggots.
We were around clubbing each other over the head
just like straight cave men. We were considered magical
by some people. We were considered mysterious.
We were obviously different but not always hated.
Hatred is always self-hatred.
Denial is always fear.
It's easier for THEM when
we hate ourselves,
FEAR OURSELVES.
I don't have to and
I WON'T.
None of us knows how he got here,
for what reason we are here or
why we are who we are.
It is not obvious
and a swish doesn't make me any more obvious
than the lack of one.
I am obvious
because I AM.


## James Baldwin (1924–1987)

*Guilt, Desire and Love (1983?)*

At the dark street corner
where Guilt and Desire
are attempting to stare
each other down
(presently, one of them
will light a cigarette
and glance in the direction
of the abandoned warehouse)
Love came slouching along,
an exploded silence
standing a little apart
but visible anyway
in the yellow, silent, steaming light,
while Guilt and Desire wrangled,
trying not to be overheard
by this trespasser.

Each time Desire looked towards Love,
hoping to find a witness,
Guilt shouted louder
and shook them hips

and the fire of the cigarette
threatened to burn the warehouse down.
Desire actually started across the street,
time after time,
to hear what Love might have to say,
but Guilt flagged down a truckload
of other people
and knelt down in the middle of the street
and, while the truckload of other people
looked away, and swore that they
didn't see nothing
and couldn't testify nohow,
and Love moved out of sight,
Guilt accomplished upon the standing body
of Desire
the momentary, inflammatory soothing
which seals their union
(for ever?)
and creates a mighty traffic problem.

# Grieving

## Thom Gunn (b. 1929)

*Lament (1984)*

   *for Allan Noseworthy, died June 21, 1984*
Your dying was a difficult enterprise.
First, petty things took up your energies,
The small but clustering duties of the sick,
As irritant as the cough's dry rhetoric.
Those hours of waiting for pills, shot, X-ray
Or test (while you read novels two a day)
Already with a kind of clumsy stealth
Distanced you from the habits of your health.
  In hope still, courteous still, but tired and thin,
You tried to stay the man that you had been,
Treating each symptom as a mere mishap
Without import. But then the spinal tap.
It brought a hard headache, and when night came
I heard you wake up from the same bad dream
Every half-hour with the same short cry
Of mild outrage, before immediately
Slipping into the nightmare once again
Empty of content but the drip of pain.
No respite followed: though the nightmare ceased,
Your cough grew thick and rich, its strength increased.
Four nights, and on the fifth we drove you down
To the Emergency Room. That frown, that frown:
I'd never seen such rage in you before
As when they wheeled you through the swinging door.
For you knew, rightly, they conveyed you from
Those normal pleasures of the sun's kingdom
The hedonistic body basks within
And takes for granted—summer on the skin,
Sleep without break, the moderate taste of tea
In a dry mouth. You had gone on from me
As if your body sought out martyrdom
In the far Canada of a hospital room.
Once there, you entered fully the distress
And long pale rigors of the wilderness.
A gust of morphine hid you. Back in sight
You breathed through a segmented tube, fat, white,
Jammed down your throat so that you could not speak.

   How thin the distance made you. In your cheek
One day, appeared the true shape of your bone
No longer padded. Still your mind, alone,
Explored this emptying intermediate
State for what holds and rests were hidden in it.

You wrote us messages on a pad, amused
At one time that you had your nurse confused
Who, seeing you reconciled after four years
With your gray father, both of you in tears,
Asked if this was at last your "special friend"
(The one you waited for until the end).
"She sings," you wrote, "A Philippine folk song
To wake me in the morning . . . It is long,
And very pretty." Grabbing at detail
To furnish this bare ledge toured by the gale,
On which you lay, bed restful as a knife,
You tried, tried hard, to make of it a life
Thick with the complicating circumstance
Your thoughts might fasten on. It had been chance
Always till now that had filled up the moment
With live specifics your hilarious comment
Discovered as it went along; and fed,
Laconic, quick, wherever it was led.
You improvised upon your own delight.
I can remember when one summer night
We talked between our sleeping bags, below
A molten field of stars five years ago:
I was so tickled by your mind's light touch
I couldn't sleep, you made me laugh too much,
Though I was tired and begged you to leave off.

Now you were tired, and yet not tired enough
Still hungry for the great world you were losing
Steadily in no season of your choosing—
And when at last the whole death was assured,
Drugs having failed, and when you had endured
Two weeks of an abominable constraint,
You faced it equably, without complaint,
Unwhimpering, but not at peace with it.
You'd lived as if your time was infinite:
You were not ready and not reconciled,
Feeling as incompleted as a child

Till you had shown the world what you could do
In some ambitious role to be worked through,
A role your need for it had half-defined,
But never wholly, even in your mind.
You lacked the necessary ruthlessness,
The soaring meanness that pinpoints success.
We loved that lack of self-love, and your smile,
Rueful, at your own silliness.
        Meanwhile,
Your lungs collapsed, and the machine, unstrained,

Did all your breathing now. Nothing remained
But death by drowning on an inland sea
Of your own fluids, which it seemed could be
Kindly forestalled by drugs. Both could and would:
Nothing was said, everything understood,
At least by us. Your own concerns were not
Long-term, precisely, when they gave the shot
—You made local arrangements to the bed
And pulled a pillow round beside your head.
    And so you slept, and died, your skin gone gray,
Achieving your completeness, in a way.

Outdoors next day, I was dizzy from a sense
Of being ejected with some violence
From vigil in a white and distant spot
Where I was numb, into this garden plot
Too warm, too close, and not enough like pain.
I was delivered into time again
—The variations that I live among
Where your long body too used to belong
And where the still bush is minutely active.
You never thought your body was attractive,
Though others did, and yet you trusted it
And must have loved its fickleness a bit
Since it was yours and gave you what it could,
Till near the end it let you down for good,
Its blood hospitable to those guests who
Took over by betraying it into
The greatest of its inconsistencies
This difficult, tedious, painful enterprise.


*Terminal (1986)*

    *(J.L., August '86)*


The eight years' difference in age seems now
Disparity so wide between the two
That when I see the man who armoured stood
Resistant to all help however good
Now helped through day itself, eased into chairs,
Or else led step by step down the long stairs
With firm and gentle guidance by his friend,
Who loves him, through each effort to descend,
Each wavering, each attempt made to complete
An arc of movement and bring down the feet
As if with that spare strength he used to enjoy,
I think of Oedipus, old, led by a boy.

*The Missing (1987)*

Now as I watch the progress of the plague,
The friends surrounding me fall sick, grow thin,
And drop away. Bared, is my shape less vague
—Sharply exposed and with a sculpted skin?

I do not like the statue's chill contour,
Not nowadays. The warmth investing me
Led outward through mind, limb, feeling, and more
In an involved increasing family.
Contact of friend led to another friend,
Supple entwinement through the living mass
Which for all that I knew might have no end,
Image of an unlimited embrace.

I did not just feel ease, though comfortable:
Aggressive as in some ideal of sport,
With ceaseless movement thrilling through the whole,
Their push kept me as firm as their support.

But death—Their deaths have left me less defined:
It was their pulsing presence made me clear.
I borrowed from it, I was unconfined,
Who tonight balance unsupported here,

Eyes glaring from raw marble, in a pose
Languorously part-buried in the block,
Shins perfect and no calves, as if I froze
Between potential and a finished work.

—Abandoned incomplete, shape of a shape,
In which exact detail shows the more strange,
Trapped in unwholeness, I find no escape
Back to the play of constant give and change.

*In The Post Office (1991)*

Saw someone yesterday looked like you did,
Being short with long blond hair, a sturdy kid
Ahead of me in line. I gazed and gazed
At his good back, feeling again, amazed,
That almost envious sexual tension which
Rubbing at made the greater, like an itch,
An itch to steal or otherwise possess
The brilliant restive charm, the boyishness

That half aware — and not aware enough —
Of what it did, eluded to hold off
The very push of interest it begot,
As if you'd been a tease, though you were not.
I hadn't felt it roused, to tell the truth,
In several years, that old man's greed for youth,
Like Pelias's that boiled him to a soup,
Not since I'd had the sense to cover up
My own particular seething can of worms,
And settle for a friendship on your terms.

Meanwhile I had to look: his errand done,
Without a glance at me or anyone,
The kid unlocked his bicycle outside,
Shrugging a backpack on. I watched him ride
Down 18th Street, rising above the saddle
For the long plunge he made with every pedal,
Expending far more energy than needed.
If only I could do whatever he did,
With him or as a part of him, if I
Could creep into his armpit like a fly,
Or like a crab cling to his golden crotch,
Instead of having to stand back and watch.
Oh complicated fantasy of intrusion
On that young sweaty body. My confusion
Led me at length to recollections of
Another's envy and his confused love.

That Fall after you died I went again
To where I had visited you in your pain
But this time for your — friend, roommate, or wooer?
I seek a neutral term where I'm unsure.
He lay there now. Figuring she knew best,
I came by at his mother's phoned request
To pick up one of your remembrances,
A piece of stained-glass you had made, now his,
I did not even remember, far less want.
To him I felt, likewise, indifferent.

"You can come in now," said the friend-as-nurse.
I did, and found him altered for the worse.
But when he saw me sitting by his bed,
He would not speak, and turned away his head.
I had not known he hated me until
He hated me this much, hated me still.
I thought that we had shared you more or less,

As if we shared what no one might possess,
Since in a net we sought to hold the wind.
There he lay on the pillow, mortally thinned,
Weaker than water, yet his gesture proving
As steady as an undertow. Unmoving
In the sustained though slight aversion, grim
In wordlessness. Nothing deflected him,
Nothing I did and nothing I could say.
And so I left. I heard he died next day.

I have imagined that he still could taste
That bitterness and anger to the last,
Against the roles he saw me in because
He had to: of victor, as he thought I was,
Of heir, as to the cherished property
His mother—who knows why?—was giving me,
And of survivor, as I am indeed,
Recording so that I may later read
Of what has happened, whether between sheets,
Or in post offices, or on the streets.


## POST SCRIPT: THE PANEL

Reciprocation from the dead. Having finished the postoffice poem, I think I will take a look at the stained-glass panel it refers to, which C made I would say two years before he died. I fish it out from where I have kept it, between a filing cabinet and a small chest of drawers. It has acquired a cobweb, which I brush off before I look at it. In the lower foreground are a face with oriental features and an arm, as of someone lying on his stomach: a mysteriously tiered cone lies behind and above him. What I had forgotten is that the picture is surrounded on all four sides by the following inscription:
The needs of ghosts embarrass the living.
A ghost must eat and shit, must pack his
body someplace. Neither buyer nor bundle,
a ghost has no tally, no readjusting value,
no soul counted at a bank.
Is this an excerpt from some Chinese book of wisdom, or is it C himself speaking? When he made the panel, C may have already suspected he had AIDS, but the prescience of the first sentence astonishes me—as it does also that I remembered nothing of the inscription while writing the poem but looked it up immediately on finishing it.

Yes, the needs of him and his friend to "embarrass" me after their deaths. The dead have no sense of tact, no manners, they enter doors without knocking, but I continue to deal with them, as proved by my writing the poem. They pack their bodies into my dreams, they eat my feelings, and shit in my mind. They are no good to me, of no value to me, but I cannot shake them and do not want to. Their story,

being part of mine, refuses to reach an end. They present me with new problems,
surprise me, contradict me, my dear, my everpresent dead.

August 7, 1991

## Walter Holland

FROM *A JOURNAL OF THE PLAGUE YEARS*

*A Journal of the Plague Years*

I remember dancing in July on the banks of the Hudson in the City,
the way some of us, innocent then, reported the rumors
we had heard I remember you, a doctor, discussing your work
on the wards of San Francisco and the way we worried about
our friends and the way you stood in the elevator
pushing an i.v. stand, not really speaking—the calls
at night and the endless plans to move from the city and the fevers
you had and the pills by your bed and the vigil I kept until
you died. I remember the party for your birthday, the way
you wore a floral-print shirt, an amused smile on your thin
face, the flash of my camera filling the room, sudden,
startling even now. Then Scott fell ill soon after and Raymond
was said to have disappeared, no word of funeral or forwarding
address, just unanswered calls to his mother—the never knowing
if he had died and the way I watched Robert stare at the panel
they'd made for Kyle—the way we stood astonished in a room spread full
of names, the fabric of the quilt unfurled, silk-like, brilliant.

## Michael Lassell (b. 1947)

*How to Watch Your Brother Die (1985)*

When the call comes, be calm.
Say to your wife, "My brother is dying. I have to fly
to California."
Try not to be shocked that he already looks like
a cadaver.
Say to the young man sitting by your brother's side,
"I'm his brother."
Try not to be shocked when the young man says,
"I'm his lover. Thanks for coming."

Listen to the doctor with a steel face on.
Sign the necessary forms.
Tell the doctor you will take care of everything.
Wonder why doctors are so remote.

Watch the lover's eyes as they stare into

your brother's eyes as they stare into
space.
Wonder what they see there.
Remember the time he was jealous and
opened your eyebrow with a sharp stick.
Forgive him out loud
even if he can't understand you.
Realize the scar will be
all that's left of him.

Over coffee in the hospital cafeteria
say to the lover, "You're an extremely good-looking
young man."
Hear him say,
"I never thought I was good enough looking to
deserve your brother."
Watch the tears well up in his eyes. Say,
"I'm sorry. I don't know what it means to be
the lover of another man."
Hear him say,
"It's just like a wife, only the commitment is
deeper because the odds against you are so much
greater."
Say nothing, but
take his hand like a brother's.

Drive to Mexico for unproven drugs that might
help him live longer.
Explain what they are to the border guard.
Fill with rage when he informs you,
"You can't bring those across."
Begin to grow loud.
Feel the lover's hand on your arm,
restraining you. See in the guard's eye
how much a man can hate another man.
Say to the lover, "How can you stand it?"
Hear him say, "You get used to it."
Think of one of your children getting used to
another man's hatred.

Call your wife on the telephone. Tell her,
"He hasn't much time.
I'll be home soon." Before you hang up say,
"How could anyone's commitment be deeper than
a husband and wife?" Hear her say,
"Please, I don't want to know all the details."

When he slips into an irrevocable coma,
hold his lover in your arms while he sobs,
no longer strong. Wonder how much longer
you will be able to be strong.
Feel how it feels to hold a man in your arms
whose arms are used to holding men.
Offer God anything to bring your brother back.
Know you have nothing God could possibly want.
Curse God, but do not
abandon Him.

Stare at the face of the funeral director
when he tells you he will not
embalm the body for fear of
contamination. Let him see in your eyes
how much a man can hate another man.
Stand beside a casket covered in flowers,
white flowers. Say,
"Thank you for coming" to each of several hundred men
who file past in tears, some of them
holding hands. Know that your brother's life
was not what you imagined. Overhear two mourners say,
"I wonder who'll be next."

Arrange to take an early flight home.
His lover will drive you to the airport.
When your flight is announced say,
awkwardly, "If I can do anything, please
let me know." Do not flinch when he says,
"Forgive yourself for not wanting to know him
after he told you. He did."
Stop and let it soak in. Say,
"He forgave me, or he knew himself?"
"Both," the lover will say, not knowing what else
to do. Hold him like a brother while he
kisses you on the cheek. Think that
you haven't been kissed by a man since
your father died. Think,

"This is no moment not to be strong." Fly
first class and drink scotch. Stroke
your split eyebrow with a finger
and think of your brother alive. Smile
at the memory and think
how your children will feel in your arms,
warm and friendly and without challenge.

## Daryl Hine (b. 1936)

*Apart from You*

Apart from you, the
World is as unimportant
   As it never was.

Your body grammar
Spells out a better portent
   Than your language does.

Landscape, you apart,
Looks utterly transparent;
   Still you stay opaque,

Indispensable
To me as air, apparent
   With each breath I take.

No comparison
Seems too hackneyed to explain
   What these portents mean:

Parted lips remain
Apart as flowers or shutters
   Open to the sun;

Compulsive digits
Dial again and again the
   Ghost in your machine.

# Surviving

## Essex Hemphill (b. 1957)

*Better Days (1985)*

In daytime hours
guided by instincts that never sleep,
the faintest signals come to me
over vast spaces
of etiquette and restraint.
Sometimes I give in
to the pressing call of instinct,
knowing the code of my kind
better than I know

the National Anthem
or the Lord's Prayer.
I am so driven by my senses
to abandon restraint,
to seek pure pleasure
through every pore.
I want to smell the air around me
thickly scented
with a playboy's freedom.
I want impractical relationships.
I want buddies and partners,
names I will forget by sunrise.
I don't want to commit my heart.
I only want to feel good.
I only want to freak sometimes.

There are no other considerations.
A false safety
compels me to think
I will never need kindness,
so I don't recognize
that need in someone else.
But it concerns me,
going off to sleep and awakening
throbbing with wants—
that I am being consumed by want.
And I wonder where stamina comes from
to search all night until my footsteps
ring awake the sparrows,
and I go home, ghost walking,
driven indoors to rest
my hunters guise,
to love myself as fiercely
as I have in better days.


*Cordon Negro (1985)*

I drink champagne early in the morning
instead of leaving my house
with an M16 and nowhere to go.

I'm dying twice as fast
as any other American
between eighteen and thirty-five.
This disturbs me,
but I try not to show it in public.

Each morning I open my eyes is a miracle.
The blessing of opening them
is temporary on any given day.
I could be taken out.
I could go off.
I could forget to be careful.
Even my brothers, hunted, hunt me.
I am the only one who values my life
and sometimes I don't give a damn.
My love life can kill me.
I'm faced daily with choosing violence
or a demeanor that saves every other life
but my own.
I won't cross-over.
It's time someone else came to me
not to patronize me physically,
sexually or humorously.
I'm sick of being an endangered species,
sick of being a goddamn statistic.
So what are my choices?
I could leave with no intention
of coming home tonight.
I could go crazy downtown
and raise hell on a rooftop with my rifle.
I could live for a brief moment
on the six o'clock news,
or I can masquerade another day
through the corridors of commerce
and American dreams.

I'm dying twice as fast
as any other American.
So I pour myself a glass of champagne,
I cut it with a drop of orange juice.
After I swallow my liquid valium,
my private celebration
for being alive this morning,
I leave my shelter.
I guard my life with no apologies.
My concerns are small
and personal.

## Walta Borawski (1947–1994)

*Talking to Jim (1988)*
So nothing is left of your agony.
Already your friends remember

your service, splendid occasion.
Your final lover talks only of

you, everyone's pleased he has
a new friend. Your sister's
defying your will, trying to
have you declared insane, adding

you were trying to go straight.
I remember when KS reached the
tip of your nose I'll never be
ready for my close-up now, you
said in the living room. No one
was reaching for the camera.

## Craig Reynolds (b. 1952)

*The worst of it*

Death is not the worst of it
   for I have died before—
   at the hands of gangs who guzzled their courage
   or boy/men who cuddled then cudgeled me to death,
   at the hands of healers who electroshocked my brains
   as if they were frying eggs,
   and at my own hands.
   So death is not the worst of it
   for I have known death—
   gang death on the docks, sudden death in my bedroom,
   slow death in the sanitarium, and chosen death on my chaise.

Because I have known death I have thwarted it.
I learned to avoid deserted streets, to stay in on Halloween,
to ask my sisters how tricky a trick was,
to distrust all psychiatrists, and psychologists, and even M.D.s
who asked too many questions,
and to be my own best friend.
The worst of it is knowing that neither
street queen brazenness, nor middle-class discretion,
nor Wildean wit and hauteur,
neither being active nor passive, neither avoiding doctors nor
visiting them—
nothing I have done before can snatch
me from the oncoming headlight of death.
The worst of it is to stand naked before death's harsh glare
which stuns like the dread paparazzo's flash
once he's breached and betrayed my boudoir
naked before death, the policeman's spotlight

which has caught me in flagrante delicto
naked to be sun-poisoned, naked without radiation shielding.
I am reminded of the worst of it each day;
as if at Hiroshima, I see about me freshly blasted kage
the palest apparitions of former lovers, friends, and desires.
The worst of it is that it poisons not through enemies but through
friends
The worst of it is that there is no catastrophic moment, no zero hour
flash,
but that it lingers, lies, and insinuates itself
worse than the subtlest homophobia.
The worst of it is that I may not have seen the worst of it
that today's horror may be to tomorrow's
as a candle is to the sun, and the sun to a supernova.

But . . . I have survived the worst of it before . . .
the raids, entrapment, and pissy paddy wagons
the bashings, prison rapes, and background checks turned expose.
Each solar flare of hatred and fear
I have survived, then sifted the ashes—a prospector
No fire has destroyed my best and most malleable stuff
each time I have risen a purer gold iridescing lavender.
So, if the worst of it is a supernova, I will remember:
stars burst in death dark new worlds begin
I have risen before; I will rise again . . .
After the worst of it . . . I will rise again.

## Salih Michael Fisher (b. 1956)

*Hometown (1988)*

Long before morning glories perched upon opening day
I left yesterday underneath a worn goose mattress
The cotton tapestry still had creases
from my nocturnal lullabies of dreams long past

Those silent moments twelve years later
youth still worn as a regalia of survival upon my mocha face
flashes of undying love in my eyes of charcoal
the breeze from the Greyhound bus blew through the windows
of paradise in transit and clothed me with a garment of rebirth

Ferment with a seed of nostalgia and love
for roots and family childhood friends
growing inside me
I had to return
I pressed my face upon doors to other dimensions
looking into foreign worlds and sighed in glory

at the spring fields in rapture
the even flow of spriteful corn
again I was born

Upon the ground stationed at home
my feet became a chariot of water
as I sailed through ships of friends and family

Songs of letters and glad to see you back
acknowledgements from aunts uncles momma and poppa
I was no longer a baby boy

Invitations to a dance
plans for romances with women
by other folks kinfolks plain folks
Those who spoke so bluntly about getting miss hitch up
heavenly bliss whom cupid arrow will not miss

How could I tell them my heart belongs to me
That I have been married to seven men since ten years ago
Hadn't anyone told them
Hadn't the nightingale echoed
in sonnets my secret silent song

Hadn't the spirits of night heard my sheets
bleed their passion
Brown hues of a chocolate rainbow
an ebony fan of shades held against daylight's splendor
pink and olive hues

Toes and torsos kissed to fullest
the billowing of sails out to sea
these erotic symphonies of the men once loved

I smiled then laughed and said I'm not getting married
I'm taking a bath so good night to all
And as I stepped upstairs
my name was still heard against the wall

Long before I could mention the hallowed words
they heard and accepted with silent disfigured glances
but I realized I could no longer dance here in my old hometown

## D. Rubin Green

*Names and sorrows (1989)*
I have walked the distance of the earth

since first I saw you
In your carpet of milk,
perpetually shining. Thinking,
revolving beneath streetlamps,
among laundromats and sundials
I have wandered,
troubling myself with questions:

Shall I disfigure chandeliers?
Or shall I with teeth and liver and spine
swallow whole shores of stone and twilight?
Shall I tell you?
Burn down cathedrals?
Shatter the membrane not to enter,
but to exit?
Abandon myself in your wilderness?
Give my mind to the text of flowers?
How simple-minded life is.
How tiresome that we are still
the outlaws of the grain, Luis:
we who are as unbodied snow-fragile,
open and mild.
How strange that we must be so careful,
you and I.
For night cares nothing for we humans;
as neither do pine, nor wave,
nor the lunatic stars
contemplate our names or sorrows.
But here doubt invades us,
and everywhere the cities
drown the dove
in waves of mud and hatred.

But even so—even though
I have wandered in the boulevards,
and the red lakes may grow
tired of our weeping,
even though we are alone,
and the public microphones cry
with the venom of old charlatans—

let me speak openly and say:

I could take up residence in your hair.
I could weep and turn to dust,
or light, or poppies in your arms,

for I have been a ghost,
a shroud of smoke.

I could sing for the bright muscle
of your voice,
your smile of linen,
your oceanic eyes.

I could take up residence in you.

You, who came to me as a garment of flame,
of coal ore,
and luminous rain.

## Donald Woods (1957–1992)

*Prescription (1989)*

no point in crying injustice
shooting off in public places
they are slack-handed and wet-eyed
with sympathy

can confession aid the process
the fellowship of mourners
propping themselves up
on heart-rending commiserations
brave corners bending
blank eyes staring

time waits for no man
it comes for you
alone you spit
yank your flaccid member
cry envious tears for
young folks caressing
at your side

strike back with amorphous ammunition
refuse the paisley-patterned despair
take the violate in hand
massage with the oils of
your heart valve
wash your battered spirit
in the salty extract
of self-pity

shore up the heart for the
thankless task of living
breathe through your nose
taste fruit with your tongue
loiter at crosswalks
while crowds pass by and laugh at the rush
of euphoria when your mother calls you
from a sweaty sleep

yawn loud
make noise
make love to the body you have
now bathe it in african oils
now dress it in royal cloth
now lay it in a single bed and listen for it
digesting raisins and bananas

full of your self get
ready to battle a raging fool
a venom-dripping motherfucker
lurks behind a green door of shame
and pain and guilt and bullshit

fight back with stuff that lasts
the melody in your head that massages your insides
the name jesus in repetition
toenail polish on sandaled feet

fight back with roughage
personal spinach
spiritual broccoli

call on herbs
ginseng for heartache
and seamoss coats the lining
of an empty stomach
hungry for full mouth kisses

medicate the time
the hours
the moments
with a mantra that
grows in your temples
and radiates your fibers
your busy weekdays
and quiet evenings

your own arms
against a sea of trouble
take them
wrap them
round and round
what belongs to you and
hold tight
hold tight
hold tight gently


*Waiting*

my feet mark the passage of time
i leave off where i started
the hospital
fingering my toes

in time i am healthy
robust waiting
for the light
humming waiting

bells toll
in slow solid measures
the bolt that connects my arm whispers
and the way i sweat
in bursts and starts
in increments
i talk in measures
if and when
plan in yardsticks
less than three feet long
i will go to the wedding
the graduation is a wait and see
see and wait
for the light at sixth and somewhere
ten years past the flirting muslims
if i wait my prince will come
it's a promise
the way stars twinkle
the way light bursts against the back of your lids
when pain beats your ass with short stabs
lower pelvic pain
you tell the doctor who has waited all day
for his favorite patient
with my meditation walkman

well, peaceful and happy
i am still hopeful waiting

on the corner of sixth and something
i am breathing deep through my mouth
exhaling through wide nostrils
i am tired of waiting
the passage the ritual the long ride sitting
'cross from someone who never cries
weary of listening to my breathing
when i don't know what to listen for
when am i massaging the feet of death itself
searching with confident fingers for the corollary
between the sole and the soul's song
singing at the bedside of another brother
who will sing for me
who sings for me now
where is that man the muslims promised
the messiah of love
the self-healed herald of our age
always waiting
told bert that and he
remembered recalled it aloud
as i waited for
a train—a bus—a man
he said "i know how you hate to wait"
and smiled at me

breathing measuring sweating
sniffing at the feet of death
my hands anointed by their own work
my prayers and poems a tangled mass
of flashing lights and signals
waiting for themselves to unlock the
lazarus the job the mary virgin mystery
why me they cried and waited
watching my children grow
my waistline shrink
in measures and increments
research on mice and monkeys
lipstick stains a thousand paper cups
the amusement park opens then closes
the season ended
the kids overdressed for school
wait for the crossing guard in her reflector vest
she signals to them and they cross

at sixth and somehow
time stands still for them
i wait for it to resume
the hairs on my neck
the clearing of my throat
helps me to measure
the time that belongs to me
time left over
minutes left out of the scheme
of waiting patient
if i wait here patient it will happen

i will die
crashing noiselessly into my own consciousness
pillows of waiting of sickness of health
featherbed of lingering near the edges
waiting for my change to come
cushions of sorrow and regret
catch my nose dive my dead weight
plummet by here in a minute
you'll see soar past your dead weight fall
pouring my living into a glass of bubbles
their iridescence is reflective
but i can't get caught in the mirror on the way
the way waiting has no end
the way waiting makes you wait
listening makes you listen
and your ideas don't solve the puzzle
your ideas are not in this
it's you and me who hates to wait
it's me and you waiting for this weight i lost
no one understood that
his peeling his bound feet his cranky whining
were mine his limp rag suffering tubes and tracheotomies
boiler plate passages indexed in our
mutual living

burning oxygen together was a pleasure
heaving and spewing stories to pass the time
the time the time the clock
spring forward fall back
lose an hour or what
gain a day by waiting quiet
lose a week by running scared
filling the book with precious appointments
talking in measured tones

lean against the buzzer
lean against the buzzer
and wait for the time to come

## Assotto Saint (1957–1994)

*Heart & Soul (1990)*

*to essex hemphill*


every day
every time i leave my house
everywhere i go
i pin on my knapsack
twin petal-small flags
to which my allegiance is pledged
whole

*these flags are not monkeys on my back*
*i carry them as a coat of arms*
*mantles of double brotherhood*
*they shield like second skin*
*to drape my dreams*

one floats rainbow
the other wings tricolor
both bold with movement
i am not ashamed
of what they stand for
when their meaning is
questioned

*these flags are not chips on my shoulders*
*i carry them as beauty spots*
*markings of double brotherhood*
*they shine like mirror beads*
*to reflect prejudice*

one unfurls the future of the queer nation
the other salutes african ancestors
both wave s.o.s. signals
i am not afraid
to stand my ground
when their beauty is
challenged

*these flags are not crossbones on my life*
*i carry them as amulets*

*emblems of double brotherhood*
*they spellbind like stars*
*to stripe america*

glory
that becomes me in tribal rituals
& battle against bigots
i have honored with my blood
everywhere i go
every time i leave my house
every day

## Perry Brass (b. 1947)

*There Isn't Any Death (1990)*

There isn't any death
but only constant life
lingering in the cells and the marrow
and the eyes of the world,

and how private
is this vision, this spinning
filament of grasses

and gentle seeds that blow,
and birds that fly back
on their way to the sun,

that often we miss the evidence
of turbulence and glow,
of after-peace and still dusks

when the winds seep in
to the joints of rocks and tree trunks,
when the branches

whistle like coyotes
and the clouds skidding through
the distance make remarks

about ages and ages,
and lifetimes that repeat
themselves forever down below.

# Copyright Acknowledgments

## BETWEEN MEN ~ BETWEEN WOMEN
## LESBIAN AND GAY STUDIES

Lillian Faderman and Larry Gross, Editors

Noreen O'Connor and Joanna Ryan, *Wild Desires and Mistaken Identities: Lesbianism and Psychoanalysis*

Don Paulson with Roger Simpson, *An Evening in the Garden of Allah: A Gay Cabaret in Seattle*

Judith Roof, *Come As You Are: Sexuality and Narrative*

Judith Roof, *A Lure of Knowledge: Lesbian Sexuality and Theory*

Claudia Schoppmann, *Days of Masquerade: Life Stories of Lesbians During the Third Reich*

Alan Sinfield, *The Wilde Century: Effeminacy, Oscar Wilde, and the Queer Moment*

Jane McIntosh Snyder, *Lesbian Desire in the Lyrics of Sappho*

Chris Straayer, *Deviant Eyes, Deviant Bodies: Sexual Re-Orientations in Film and Video*

Dwayne C. Turner, *Risky Sex: Gay Men and HIV Prevention*

Ruth Vanita, *Sappho and the Virgin Mary: Same-Sex Love and the English Literary Imagination*

Thomas Waugh, *Hard to Imagine: Gay Male Eroticism in Photography and Film from Their Beginnings to Stonewall*

Kath Weston, *Families We Choose: Lesbians, Gays, Kinship*

Kath Weston, *Render Me, Gender Me: Lesbians Talk Sex, Class, Color, Nation, Studmuffins . . .*

Carter Wilson, *Hidden in the Blood: A Personal Investigation of AIDS in the Yucatán*

Jacquelyn Zita, *Body Talk: Philosophical Reflections on Sex and Gender*